MW01090034

EARLY
CHRISTIAN
MISSION

VOLUME TWO

PAUL & THE EARLY CHURCH

ECKHARD J. SCHNABEL

InterVarsity Press
Downers Grove, Illinois

Apollos
Leicester, England

InterVarsity Press, USA
P.O. Box 1400, Downers Grove, IL 60515-1426, USA
World Wide Web: www.ivpress.com
E-mail: mail@ivpress.com

APOLLOS (an imprint of Inter-Varsity Press, England)
38 De Montfort Street, Leicester LE1 7GP, England
Website: www.ivpbooks.com
E-mail: ivp@uccf.org.uk

English translation ©2004 by Eckhard J. Schnabel. Original German edition published as Urchristliche
Mission *by Eckhard J. Schnabel, ©2002 R. Brockhaus Verlag, Wuppertal.*

All rights reserved. No part of this publication may be reproduced, stored in a retrieval system or transmitted
in any form or by any means, electronic, mechanical, photocopying, recording or otherwise, without the prior
permission of InterVarsity Press.

InterVarsity Press®, U.S.A., is the book-publishing division of InterVarsity Christian Fellowship/USA®, a student
movement active on campus at hundreds of universities, colleges and schools of nursing in the United States
of America, and a member movement of the International Fellowship of Evangelical Students. For
information about local and regional activities, write Public Relations Dept., InterVarsity Christian
Fellowship/USA, 6400 Schroeder Rd., P.O. Box 7895, Madison, WI 53707-7895, or visit the IVCF website at
<www.intervarsity.org>.

Scripture quotations, unless otherwise noted, are from the New Revised Standard Version of the Bible,
copyright 1989 by the Division of Christian Education of the National Council of the Churches of Christ in the
USA. Used by permission. All rights reserved.

Design: Cindy Kiple

Images: Monastery Icons

USA ISBN 0-8308-2792-7
UK ISBN 1-84474-046-3

Printed in the United States of America ∞

Library of Congress Cataloging-in-Publication Data

Schnabel, Eckhard J.
  Early Christian mission/Eckhard J. Schnabel
      p. cm.
  Includes bibliographical references and index.
  ISBN 0-8308-2791-9 (v. 1: hardcover: alk. paper)
  1. Missions—History—Early church, ca. 30-600. I. Title.
  BR165.S3585 2004
  266'.009'015—dc22

                                                        2004017281

British Library Cataloguing in Publication Data

A catalogue record for this book is available from the British Library.

P	18	17	16	15	14	13	12	11	10	9	8	7	6	5	4	3	2	1
Y	18	17	16	15	14	13	12	11	10	09	08	07	06	05	04			

CONTENTS OF VOLUME 2

PART V

PIONEER MISSIONARY WORK

The Mission of the Apostle Paul

24

PAUL FROM TARSUS
AND FROM JERUSALEM

The discussion in Parts I-IV demonstrated that the early Christian mission began with Jesus of Nazareth, and that the Twelve initiated missionary outreach to both Jews and Gentiles after Easter as commissioned by the risen Lord. The available sources did not allow the construction of a detailed description of the missionary work of the Twelve. It became evident, however, that the apostle Paul was not the first missionary who reached non-Jews with the message of Jesus Christ. The view that Paul was the greatest missionary among Gentiles in the first century is a notion based on the fact that writings of Paul survive that allow us to describe his theological convictions, in which the Gentiles and their salvation loom large, and on the fact that Luke devotes the entire second part of his account of the early Christian mission to the work of Paul. Since we have much less information about John and Peter and no information whatsoever about the work of the rest of the Twelve, the view that Paul was the greatest missionary remains true, perhaps, less by comparison and evaluation than by default. The missionary work of Paul is the subject of Part V: his conversion and commissioning to missionary work, his self-understanding as a missionary and his geographical vision (§24), the contacts and conferences with the Jerusalem apostles and the conflicts with Jewish-Christian opponents (§25), the early missionary work in Arabia, Syria and Cilicia (§26), the missionary work and church planting in Asia Minor and Greece and his plans to go to Spain (§27), and his missionary strategy and his methods for preaching the message of Jesus Christ and planting churches (§28).

24.1 The Conversion of the Pharisee and Rabbi Saul

Paul was born in Tarsus into a devout Jewish family belonging to the Pharisaic movement.[1] It is not entirely clear where Paul spent his formative years. The tra-

---

[1]Gal 1:13-14; Phil 3:5-6; 2 Cor 11:22-23; Rom 11:1; Acts 9:11, 30; 21:39; 22:3; on Tarsus see §26.2, and on the Pharisees §8.3. On the "pre-Christian" Paul see Hengel 1990; 1991; Niebuhr 1992; Légasse 1995; Murphy-O'Connor 1996, 32-70; Hengel and Schwemer 1998.

ditional assumption is Tarsus in Cilicia. If Paul grew up in Tarsus, his educational experience may have resembled that of Philo, his contemporary in Alexandria. The sons of Jewish Diaspora families were educated in the following Jewish and Hellenistic institutions: synagogue, elementary school in the synagogue, gymnasiums, ephebeia, public lectures, public library, private philosophical school.[2] The number of years that Paul formally attended school is unknown to us.

The comparison of Paul and Philo is warranted for several reasons. Both grew up as Jews in a large Greek city. Both were politically active: Philo was a member of an Alexandrian embassy to Rome; Paul (before his conversion) took the initiative in curbing the nascent Christian movement in collaboration with the Sanhedrin in Jerusalem, and (after his conversion) he participated in a leading role in conferences with the Jerusalem apostles. Both engaged in literary production. Both had double citizenship, which was very rare for Jews: Philo's family seems to have possessed Alexandrian and Roman citizenships, and Paul's family had Tarsian and Roman citizenships. Philo's family evidently had a high social standing in Alexandria; the prerequisite for Alexandrian citizenship was the qualification as ephebe and thus Hellenistic education.[3]

Paul and his family evidently possessed Tarsian[4] and Roman[5] citizenships.[6] Hellenistic cities made citizenship dependent upon the fulfillment of specific conditions, in many cases financial contributions or involvement in public building projects.[7] Augustus had prohibited Athens from selling citizenship rights, but this does not mean that the practice was abandoned in all cities in Asia Minor. In his letters Paul never comments on his origins in Tarsus. That is why Eduard Lohse remains skeptical, in typical fashion distrusting the information provided by Luke: "But whether Paul indeed grew up in Tarsus must remain uncertain, because he maintains silence about his hometown."[8] Most scholars, however, accept Luke's information that Paul was born in Tar-

---

[2]See Noack 2000, 5.
[3]See Barclay 1996, 65-70; Noack 2000, 5-6 n. 15.
[4]See Doer 1969; Hemer 1989, 122 with n. 59; Hengel 1991, 188-93; Riesner 1994, 130-31 (ET, 148-49). Cautious are Hengel and Schwemer (1998, 32, 250 [ET, 160]). Légasse (1995, 367-68) and Cineira (1999, 349-51) remain skeptical.
[5]See Doer 1969, 69; Lüdemann 1987, 249-50 (ET, 240-41); Tajra 1989, 76-89; Baugh 1990, 165-93; Hengel 1991, 193-208; S. R. Llewelyn, in *New Docs* 6:1992, 152-55; Riesner 1994, 129-39 (ET, 147-56); Légasse 1995, 368-72; Murphy-O'Connor 1996, 39-41; Hengel and Schwemer 1998, 32, 194 (ET, 16, 160). A Lukan construct is assumed by W. Stegemann, "War der Apostel Paulus ein römischer Bürger?" *ZNW* 78 (1987): 200-229; Lentz 1993, 43-56; Cineira 1999, 351-63.
[6]On the Tarsian citizenship see Acts 21:39, and on the Roman citizenship Acts 16:37-38; 22:25-29; 23:27; cf. 25:10-11; 28:19. On the debate concerning skepticism about the Lukan evidence see the literature cited in the preceding note.
[7]Philippe Gauthier, *Les cités grecques et leurs bienfaiteurs (IVe-Ier siècle avant J.-C.)* (Bulletin de correspondance hellénique, Suppl. 12; Paris: Boccard, 1985), 150-51; R. A. Kearsley, ed., *I. GRIAsia,* 156 n. 18; for the comment that follows above, with reference to Dio 54.7.3, see ibid.
[8]Lohse 1996, 19.

sus.[9] As a "Hebrew born of Hebrews" (Phil 3:5), as a full Jew whose family maintained the Jewish customs, his (Hebrew) name was Saul (Heb., *Shaʾul;* Gk., *Saulos*). His Roman (or Greek) name was *Paulos:* this was either (1) the *cognomen,* an official element of the *tria nomina* that his family received after manumission from the Roman owner who had released an ancestor (his father?) from slavery, or (2) the *signum* or *supernomen,* the Roman, Latin-sounding surname that the family used. Many exegetes regard the second option as more likely. They believe it only a remote possibility that a Jewish family that had received Roman citizenship only a generation earlier had the *cognomen* of famous senatorial families of Rome such as the Aemilii Paullii, the Vettenii Paulli or the Sergii Paullii.[10]

Niclas Förster points to a passage in the 121st letter of Jerome in which he gives four examples of unusual and rare words and phrases that indicate that Paul spoke a local Cilician dialect of Koine:[11] in Col 2:18 the term καταβραβεύειν (*katabrabeuein*), in 1 Cor 4:3 the phrase ὑπὸ ἀνθρωπίνης ἡμέρας (*hypo anthrōpinēs hēmeras*), in Rom 6:19 the phrase ἀνθρώπινον λέγω (*anthrōpinon legō*), in 2 Cor 11:9; 12:12, 13, 14 the formulation οὐ κατεναρκησα ὑμᾶς (*ou katenarkēsa hymas*). Jerome comments, "These and many other words the Cilicians use until today. And we should not be surprised that the apostle uses them according to the custom of the language in which he was born and brought up."[12] Förster accepts Jerome's analysis as correct. (1) Jerome would have become familiar with research into local dialects, which was a part of Greek philological studies, in the course of his education. There is evidence that he was interested in linguistic phenomena, including the Celtic language. Jerome would have encountered the Cilician dialect during his journey to Cilicia in A.D. 373. (2) The words and phrases that Jerome cites are indeed terms that are rare in Greek literature: "The few passages in which καταβραβεύειν (*katabrabeuein*) occurs are found, in part, in sources and authors who come from Cilicia or neighboring Syria."[13] Tourists visiting Tarsus are shown "St. Paul's Well," which supposedly stood in the courtyard of the house in which the apostle was born, but there is no evidence whatsoever for this claim. The Christian emperor Mauritius of Constantinople (A.D. 582-602) had a church built in Tarsus in honor of Paul, which later was transformed into a mosque that still stands today.[14]

Roman citizenship (see §18.1) could be obtained through birth by Roman parents, through manumission (Lat., *manumissio*) when the owner of the slave was a Roman citizen, as reward for special services rendered, after twenty-five years of service in the auxiliary troops, or by official decree. To possess Roman citizenship meant to possess privileges in private, criminal and civil law (right to vote,

---

[9]See Bornkamm 1993, 27; Becker 1992, 35 (ET, 34); Niebuhr 1992, 45-8; Murphy-O'Connor 1996, 32.

[10]See Murphy-O'Connor (1996, 42-43), who develops a suggestion made by Sherwin-White 1963, 153.

[11]Niclas Förster, "Sprach Paulus einen kilikischen Koine-Dialekt?" *ZNW* 88 (1997): 316-21.

[12]Jerome, *Epist.* 1.3, 121.10 (CSEL 56.42-43); quoted in Förster, "Paulus," 316-17 n. 4.

[13]Förster, "Paulus," 319 n. 13.

[14]Dassmann 1989, 272.

exemption from certain forms of corporal punishment, the *ius provocationis*),
but it also implied duties in taxation and military service. In 28 B.C., at the time
of Augustus, there were 4,937,000 Roman citizens, and during Claudius's reign
the number had climbed to 5,984,672,[15] most living in Italy or serving as legion-
aries in the army. It is possible that Paul's father received Roman citizenship
through *manumissio*. Several church fathers claim to know that Paul's father had
been sold as a slave as a prisoner of war, originally living in Gischala in Galilee.[16]
Since Pompey had occupied Palestine in 63 B.C., "there were other disturbances
as well during which Galilean Jews might have become Roman slaves."

Some scholars assume that Paul came from Tarsus to Jerusalem even as a
child—that is, that he not only studied in Jerusalem but also spent his childhood
and teenage years in the Jewish capital.

Willem van Unnik defends this view on the basis of the three participles that are used in
Acts 22:3 to describe the outline of Paul's biography. Van Unnik argues that the verbs take
up a literary scheme that traditionally itemizes three stages of development:[17] the birth in
Tarsus in Cilicia (γεγεννημένος, *gegennēmenos*), childhood and education in the parental
home before reaching school age (ἀνατεθραμμένος, *anatethrammenos*), education by
teachers (πεπαιδευμένος, *pepaideumenos*). The reference to "this city" (ἐν τῇ πόλει ταύτῃ,
en tē polei tautē), meaning Jerusalem, is linked with ἀνατεθραμμένος (*anatethrammenos*).
This means that Paul may have moved from Tarsus to Jerusalem at an age at which "he
could not travel alone,"[18] as a child. But as Martin Hengel points out, this assumption cannot be proven; the excellent control that Paul has of the Greek language and his sovereign
use of the Greek translation of the Hebrew Bible indicate that "Tarsus cannot be totally
suppressed, even though it must take second place after Jerusalem in Paul's biography."[19]

The fact that young Saul/Paul came to Jerusalem to study indicates that his parents
were well-to-do.[20] The "high" social status of Paul provides the easiest explanation
for Paul's friendship with the Asiarchs in Ephesus.[21] Paul clearly had access to the
elites in the Greek and Roman cities in which he preached the gospel. His native
language probably was Greek, a result of his early years living in Tarsus. He
would have spoken fluent Aramaic and Hebrew due to his upbringing in a devout
and conservative Jewish family and to his rabbinic studies. And it is possible that
he spoke some Latin, although his status as a Roman citizen does not prove this.[22]

---

[15] *Res Gestae (Monumentum Ancyranum)* 4-5; Tacitus, *Ann.* 11.25.

[16] Jerome, *Comm. Phlm.* 23; *Vir. ill.* 3, 5; Photius, *Quaest. Amphil.* 116 (PG 101:687-690). This
possibility is defended by Zahn (1924, 1:33-35, 47-50); cf. Riesner 1994, 134-35 (ET, 151-53);
the quotation that follows above, ibid., 135 (ET, 152).

[17] Unnik 1952; cf. Haacker 1988a, 63; Barrett, *Acts,* 2:1035; Zmijewski, *Apg,* 783, Fitzmyer, *Acts,*
704; Witherington, *Acts,* 668-69; Jervell, *Apg,* 542; Niebuhr 1992, 44; Légasse 1995, 373.

[18] Burchard 1970, 32; followed by Niebuhr 1992, 44.

[19] Hengel 1991, 238.

[20] See Haacker 1995b, 830.

[21] See Baugh 1990, 153; cf. Riesner 1994, 130-32 (ET, 148-49).

[22] See Hengel and Schwemer 1998, 193 (ET, 119).

Paul became a Pharisee (Acts 23:6; 26:5) probably in connection with his education in Jerusalem rather than in Tarsus (Pharisees have not been documented in Jewish Diaspora communities).[23] We do not know when his father became a Pharisee (Acts 23:6), but probably it was not in Tarsus. Scholars have been unable to determine whether Saul/Paul belonged to the strict school of Rabbi Shammai or to the more "liberal" school of Hillel; passages in Paul's letters that are said to demonstrate that he was a "Shammaite" or a "Hillelite" have been overinterpreted. Karl-Wilhelm Niebuhr concludes a survey of the discussion by pointing out that "the pre-Christian Paul belongs neither to the 'right' nor to the 'left' spectrum of Judaism, but in its center." Paul's letters and the book of Acts indicate that he studied the Torah from a Pharisaic perspective under Rabbi Gamaliel, and that he received a basic (Greek) rhetorical education in a Jewish-Hellenistic school in Jerusalem.[24]

Saul/Paul persecuted the followers of Jesus at least in Jerusalem (Acts 8:3),[25] and he planned to arrest believers in Damascus as well (Acts 9:2-3; 22:5; 26:12). Luke mentions Saul for the first time in connection with the stoning of Stephen. It is unlikely, however, that he worked for the physical destruction of the followers of Jesus, as there was no legal basis on which he could have relied. When Paul says that he wanted to "destroy" the church (Gal 1:13; cf. 1:23), his statement probably reflects that "the controversy concerned the right of the followers of Jesus to exist within the institution of the synagogue. Paul may have attempted to deny this right by all means, whether with the help of learned rabbinic discussion, or by organizing disciplinary measures of the synagogues against the Christians, or by spontaneous eruptions of bodily force."[26] Paul himself later suffered punishments meted out by people from synagogues (2 Cor 11:24-25), and he repeatedly experienced the psychological and physical pressure that local synagogue congregations could bring to bear.

Why did Saul/Paul persecute the followers of Jesus? (1) Some scholars suggest that the reason for the synagogal punishments was connected with the followers of Jesus admitting Gentile Christians without circumcision. This explanation is implausible because uncircumcised Gentiles could attend synagogue services as God-fearers without any problem. (2) Equally implausible is the suggestion that the contacts of Jewish Christians with Gentile Christians provoked the punishment of the "forty minus one" lashes because they broke fundamental *kashrut* rules in their daily routine—for example, by consuming nonkosher food.[27] The question of the requirements of the purity laws or the Torah became

---

[23]See Niebuhr 1992, 44-55; the quotation that follows above, ibid., 57.

[24]Hengel 1991, 240; cf. Niebuhr 1992, 47.

[25]See Niebuhr 1992, 58-60, with cogent arguments against doubts concerning Luke's account voiced by Conzelmann 1969, 65-66 (ET, 80-81); Suhl 1975, 26-27; Dietzfelbinger 1985, 15-16; Bornkamm 1993, 38-39.

[26]Niebuhr 1992, 60-61.

[27]Reinbold 2000, 178-79, 207-8, with regard to Paul.

a problem in the Christians churches only at a later date. (3) Not very plausible is the recent suggestion that Paul persecuted the Christians on account of the potentially disastrous political consequences of their beliefs and public activities, proclaiming—before Gentile audiences!—a Galilean who had been executed as a troublemaker by the Roman authorities as Messiah and Savior who soon would return and establish the promised messianic age by bringing the existing world order to an end, implementing the kingdom of God. The message of the followers of Jesus potentially was politically dangerous indeed. However, since Paul, who proclaimed the same message, later was cleared by the highest Roman officials of the charge of dangerous seditious activities, it is doubtful that he persecuted Christians for political reasons. We have no information about Paul's political convictions before his conversion. Also, it probably is simplistic to assume that the early Christians consistently preached the imminence of Jesus Christ's return ushering in the end of the present world order and the kingdom of God: following Jesus' teaching (Mt 25), they obviously *also* reckoned at an early date with the possibility that the parousia might be delayed. If Jesus' commission to the Twelve to go to the ends of the earth is indeed authentic, then the early Christians could hardly have believed that the end of the world would happen momentarily. (4) More plausible is the suggestion that the pre-Christian Paul regarded the proclamation of a crucified Messiah to be so utterly despicable and erroneous that he became convinced that the adherents of this new movement must not be tolerated and that active measures be taken to stop their activities.[28] Jews who rejected the claims of the (Jewish) Christians evidently were convinced that the belief in Jesus as the Messiah and in the atoning efficacy of his death on the cross put into question "the foundations of Torah obedience as the basis of the Jewish concept of salvation," concerns that surfaced in the attacks made by Jerusalem Jews against Stephen and other Hellenistic Jewish Christians.[29]

Saul's life changed during a journey from Jerusalem to Damascus, the old Syrian capital, where he wanted to arrest believers in Jesus. Paul himself speaks repeatedly about his conversion, and Luke provides further details in the book of Acts.[30] There is no good reason to doubt the reliability of Luke's account.[31]

---

[28]Thus most scholars. The objections by Fredriksen (1991, 551-52) are unconvincing.

[29]Niebuhr 1992, 62-65; quotation, ibid., 66; similarly Dietzfelbinger 1985, 22-42.

[30]Gal 1:11-17; Phil 3:3-17; 1 Tim 1:12-16; Acts 9:1-21; 22:6-21; 26:12-18. On Paul's conversion see, besides the commentaries and monographs on Paul's life, Burchard 1970; S. Kim 1981; Dietzfelbinger 1985; A. F. Segal 1990; Everts 1993b; Longenecker 1997; Howell 1998, 67-70; Hengel and Schwemer 1998, 63-80 (ET, 24-61); Kraus 1999, 82-105.

[31]See Hengel and Schwemer 1998, 63-64 with n. 224 (ET, 38-39, 341 n. 163, expanded in the German version); they ask rhetorically and polemically with regard to explanations by Walter Schmithals and Hans Conzelmann, "Is not the 'formation of legends' more the work of the modern, oh so 'critical' New Testament scholars?"

Paul describes his conversion experiences as "seeing the Lord" (1 Cor 9:1), as an "appearance" of the risen Christ (1 Cor 15:8). Luke describes a "light from heaven" (Acts 9:3; 22:6; 26:13). Paul fell to the ground[32] and was addressed by a voice that identifies itself as belonging to Jesus the Kyrios, who has been exalted at the right hand of God and who turns Paul's current activities and intentions as a persecutor against him as a negative charge. After Paul arrived in Damascus, blinded by the light from heaven, a follower of Jesus living in Damascus, Ananias, conveyed to him in a word of Jesus the commission to proclaim his name to the Gentiles and to the people of Israel. This is the sequence of events according to Luke's first and second accounts of Paul's conversion (Acts 9:15-16; 22:14-15), while the third account, which narrates Paul's speech before Agrippa II and Festus, summarizes the main theological points and reports his commission as missionary to the Gentiles immediately after the self-identification of the risen Lord (Acts 26:26-27).

In the third account of Paul's conversion (Acts 26:4-23) Luke omits the earlier references to Paul's blindness (Acts 9:8-12, 17-18; 22:11, 13). Instead, it is the risen Lord himself who reminds Paul of what he has "seen" (Acts 26:16) and what will enable him to obey the calling that he has received, to "open the eyes" of Israel and of the Gentiles and so that "they may turn from darkness to light and from the power of Satan to God, so that they may receive forgiveness of sins and a place among those who are sanctified by faith in me" (Acts 26:18), in keeping with the prophets and with Moses, who had said that "the Messiah must suffer, and that, by being the first to rise from the dead, he would proclaim light both to our people and to the Gentiles" (Acts 26:23). Thus when Paul describes his conversion in his speech before Agrippa II and Festus, he explains the healing of the blindness that he had suffered as a symbol for the mission of Israel in the last days, as a symbol of the mission of Jesus and as a symbol of his own mission.[33]

Paul describes the "seeing" of the Lord Jesus (1 Cor 9:1) as "a real, 'objective' seeing of a supernatural reality in divine splendor of light, which makes itself known as the 'Lord' and is recognized by him as such."[34] Paul argues in 1 Cor 15:5-8 that he is an apostle because he has seen the Lord as the Twelve have seen him. It is difficult if not impossible to provide a historically cogent answer to the question of how the audiovision given to Paul before Damascus compared with the bodily appearance of the risen Jesus among the disciples after Easter, even though it probably played a role in the later discussions about the apostolic status of Paul.

---

[32]Acts 9:4; 22:7; 26:14. The horse that is sometimes mentioned in this context is a later embellishment, reflected in Christian art and children's Bibles.

[33]See Hamm 1990, with reference to the literary intentions of Luke.

[34]Hengel and Schwemer 1998, 65 (ET, 39); for the remark that follows above see ibid., 67-68 (ET, 40-41).

The psychological considerations of Gerd Lüdemann[35] are entirely speculative and also show a total ignorance of the reality and causes of conversions of people to faith in Jesus Christ. His hypothesis that Paul was working out a guilt complex is indeed the reduction of an extraordinary event to "everyday banality" that completely disregards the available sources. Jerome Murphy-O'Connor is correct when he points out that Paul had not been prepared psychologically or otherwise for his conversion: "It is certain that Paul was in no way disposed to expect anything to happen en route to Damascus."[36] Martin Hengel and Anna Maria Schwemer emphasize that "in strong contrast to the characterization of Cornelius and his pious works in Acts 10:2-4, with Paul everything depends on God's free, unfathomable concern. Here there is no room for a psychological preparation in either Luke's or Paul's accounts. For both, a miracle of God took place that turned the life of the zealous persecutor upside down."

Andreas Lindemann argues that neither 1 Cor 9:1 nor 1 Cor 15:8 constitutes a statement that can be evaluated in terms of providing historical evidence.[37] He suggests that although Paul does not doubt that the resurrection of Jesus Christ from the dead is being proclaimed, he does not think "in terms of a 'historical fact' that was confirmed to him by his vision; rather, Jesus' resurrection by God is a matter of faith for him." He claims that the question of the historical basis for faith in Jesus' resurrection is a "modern" question. Lindemann formulates a helpful critique of Lüdemann's psychological interpretation, but he has not advanced his own position. If the expression ὤφθη (ōphthē, "he appeared") in 1 Cor 15:1-11 (vv. 5, 6, 7, 8) serves only "to legitimize the truth of the proclamation of those to whom Christ appeared," then Lindemann underestimates the dramatic significance of the alternative that Lüdemann consistently and cogently places in the center of the discussion: if Jesus did not rise from the dead after his death on the cross, then there are serious and immediate consequences for the faith and proclamation of the church. For the apostles, who literally risked their lives in the course of their missionary activity, the "truth of the proclamation" indeed depended on the historical factuality of Jesus' resurrection. What is "modern" is not the question of whether the resurrection of Jesus is a historical fact, but rather the evasion of the "modern" scholar at this crucial point and the reference to "faith" that is not much more than a vague theological statement.[38]

Nor are psychological explanations of Paul's conversion in terms of a hallucination convincing. Paul accepted the crucified Jesus as Messiah not because the "pre-Christian self" of Paul had been involved in a (subconscious) conflict with the Mosaic law that caused a hallucination or a vision during his journey to Damascus that helped him to deal with this conflict in an "intra-psychical" manner.[39] There is no evidence whatsoever for such a conflict.

Bruce Malina and Jerome Neyrey suggest in their study of Paul's personality that his turn from persecutor to preacher and missionary was indeed *not* the result of an individual decision resulting from personal self-knowledge, uncertainty, search for answers or some other psychological condition. Rather, the change in Paul's life came "from outside,"

---

[35]Lüdemann 1994, 16-19, 108-12, 126-28; see the critique in Hengel and Schwemer 1998, 68 n. 246 (ET, 40, 342-43 n. 179); the quotation that follows above, ibid.

[36]Murphy-O'Connor 1996, 77. For the quotation that follows above see Hengel and Schwemer 1998, 70 (ET, 41-42).

[37]Lindemann 1998, 29-30; cf. ibid., 35, 36, for the following quotations; see idem *1 Kor,* 201, 334.

[38]See E. J. Schnabel, *JETh* 14 (2000): 217-19 (review of A. Lindemann).

[39]Thus Reichardt (1999; quotation, ibid., 337), who proposes an autobiographical-psychological interpretation of Rom 7:7-25 (cf. ibid., 269-334). Reichardt believes that Luke's accounts of Paul's conversion in the book of Acts are historically worthless (ibid., 220-26).

· from God, who revealed new information to him (Gal 1:15-16), from God's Messiah, Jesus, who directed him to change the direction of his activities in God's service (Acts 22:7-10; 26:14-18). Malina and Neyrey evaluate Paul against the background of a study of ancient "personality" that leads them to conclude that Paul's zeal was constantly diverted to new projects: "Paul is essentially obedient to group norms and group-sanctioned persons. He accepts the directives given to him, and thus manifests himself once more as a group-oriented person, a loyal 'party member.'"[40] This analysis owes more to the heuristic model that Malina and Neyrey use than to hard evidence of the primary sources about the life of Paul. When they state that Paul never was a Jew who thought and acted individualistically or made solitary decisions, they formulate an important insight that "existentialist" or postmodern scholars who operate within the confines of the "First World" cannot afford to ignore. However, the suggestion that Paul did not make decisions of his own, that he was a "loyal party member" who obediently accepted directives, is clearly erroneous, as the available evidence demonstrates for his specific actions: he planned missionary outreach to the provinces of Asia and Bithynia that could not be realized due to a communication from the Spirit but that had indeed been planned by Paul. When Barnabas, who had come from Jerusalem and who brings him to Antioch, wanted to take John Mark along to the new missionary initiative into the province of Asia, Paul decides against John Mark and even against Barnabas, clearly "alone" and without directives from another group. When Paul returned from missionary work in Ephesus via Corinth to Jerusalem, he was warned by Christian prophets that he would be arrested if he traveled to Jerusalem: Paul makes the "solitary" decision to continue his journey. The argument that Paul wanted to be loyal to the Jerusalem apostles is not completely wrong. But his primary loyalty was to the message of Jesus the crucified and risen Lord and to the consequences that ensued from Jesus' redemptive action for the Torah and for the identity of the people of God.

24.2 The Commission to Be an "Apostle to the Nations"

Paul's far-reaching, international missionary work has been explained in terms of diverse trajectories of convictions and traditions: as a result of an alleged dethronement of the Mosaic law that made a ministry to non-Jews possible;[41] as a result of Paul's conviction that Jesus Christ rules as heavenly Kyrios, providing the apostle with a universal vision;[42] as a result of a new interpretation of the Old Testament and Jewish notion of God's impartiality;[43] as the result of a new interpretation of Old Testament and Jewish expectations concerning the conversion of the nations in the messianic era;[44] as the result of a lack of success of missionary work among Jews who refused and continued to refuse the message about Jesus;[45] as a result of his conversion, which took place in connection with a Jewish-Christian community that was actively reaching Gentiles with the gos-

---

[40]Malina and Neyrey 1996, 206.
[41]See W. Davies 1967, 67; Cerfaux 1967, 69.
[42]See Hahn 1963, 84-85 (ET, 74-75); S. Kim 1981, 268, with reference to Ezek 1; Dan 7.
[43]See Bassler 1985, 546-48, 551.
[44] See Hays 1989, 71, 162; Donaldson 1993; 1997b.
[45]See Klausner 1950, 330-32; Munck 1954, 272, 275; 1956, 74-75; Blair 1965, 19-33; F. Watson 1986, 32; J. Sanders 1987; Haenchen, *Apg,* 111-12 (ET, 100-101), and passim.

pel.[46] The following description is based on Paul's letters and on Luke's account in the book of Acts.[47] Both sources report that "Damascus" was the hour in which Paul became a missionary to the Gentiles.[48]

Christoph Burchard maintains that Paul is a product of the Hellenistic Jewish Christians in Jerusalem who influenced him "as a Christian" and "who were already open to share the salvation with non-Jews."[49] There is no evidence for this view in the sources. Scholars who argue that the Gentile mission was the result of the Jews' rejection of the gospel[50] often point to Acts 13:46-47; 18:6; 28:25-28, Luke's narrative of Paul's mission in Antiocheia, Corinth and Rome: "Then both Paul and Barnabas spoke out boldly, saying, 'It was necessary that the word of God should be spoken first to you. Since you reject it and judge yourselves to be unworthy of eternal life, we are now turning to the Gentiles. For so the Lord has commanded us, saying, "I have set you to be a light for the Gentiles, so that you may bring salvation to the ends of the earth" ' " (Acts 13:46-47, quoting Is 49:6). "When they opposed and reviled him, in protest he shook the dust from his clothes and said to them, 'Your blood be on your own heads! I am innocent. From now on I will go to the Gentiles' " (Acts 18:6). "So they disagreed with each other; and as they were leaving, Paul made one further statement: 'The Holy Spirit was right in saying to your ancestors through the prophet Isaiah, "Go to this people and say, You will indeed listen, but never understand, and you will indeed look, but never perceive. For this people's heart has grown dull, and their ears are hard of hearing, and they have shut their eyes; so that they might not look with their eyes, and listen with their ears, and understand with their heart and turn—and I would heal them." Let it be known to you then that this salvation of God has been sent to the Gentiles; they will listen' " (Acts 28:25-28, quoting Is 6:9-10).

These passages do not prove Burchard's theory. (1) Luke continues to describe Paul's missionary outreach among Jews after Acts 13 and Acts 18. Neither Luke nor Paul gives up on the Jews as "hopeless cases." (2) In Acts 13:46-47 Paul argues on three levels: he points to the rejection of the Jews of Antiocheia, to the directive of the Lord, and to a word of God in the Scriptures (Is 49:6). Matthäus Buss observes, "This clarifies the fact that the ultimate reason for the Gentile mission was not the failure of the mission to the Jews but the will of God."[51] (3) None of the three passages speaks of a final rejection of Israel or of the Jews: the apostles never stop being concerned for the salvation of Israel. (4) It is somewhat ironic that Jacob Jervell and Gerhard Lohfink argue for the exact opposite position: Luke maintains in the book of Acts that the Gentile mission originated in the fact that Israel has accepted the gospel:[52] (a) Israel did not totally reject

---

[46]See Räisänen 1983, 251-63.
[47]Gal 1:15-16; 1 Cor 9:1; 15:8; Acts 9:1-19; 22:3-16; 26:9-18.
[48]See Haas 1971, 5-23; Stendahl 1976, 7-23; Polhill 1981; Dunn 1987; Bowers 1993, 612-13; O'Brien 1995, 22-25; Hengel 1996; Hübner 1996, 136-37; Donaldson 1997b; Köstenberger and O'Brien 2001, 161-64.
[49]Burchard 1984, 26.
[50]See Schlier 1942, 94-96; Hahn 1963, 117 (ET, 134); Conzelmann 1962, 135; Wilckens 1974, 96-100. See the critique in Nolland 1998, 76-81.
[51]Buss 1980, 137.
[52]See Jervell 1972; G. Lohfink 1975; for a description of this position see Talbert (1991, 100-101), who seeks to combine both positions in the concept of the plan of God (ibid., 101-5).

the gospel, but was divided—some rejected it,[53] others accepted it.[54] (b) The Jews who repented and came to faith in Jesus as the Messiah constitute for Luke the restored, purified, true Israel, while the unrepentant Jews lost their membership in the people of God (Acts 3:23). (c) The admission of Gentiles into the people of God depends not on Israel's rejection of the gospel but on the fulfillment of the promises for Israel, as Acts 15:15-18, with the quotation of Amos 9:11-12, demonstrates. (5) The early Christian mission originated in Jesus' missionary commission, as I have sought to demonstrate earlier.

Jouette Bassler argues that Paul reflected on the Old Testament and Jewish notion of God's impartiality,[55] which had primarily a legal sense: God rewards the righteous and punishes the guilty, he treats the poor exactly as he treats the rich, and he will treat Israel, if the people persist in sin, as he treats the pagan nations, on whom his judgment will fall. Paul takes up this concept in Rom 1:18—2:29 and applies it in Rom 3:21-31 to the new era of salvation, reinterpreting it: God achieves the impartial treatment of Gentiles and Jews not in punishment and judgment, but in the replacement of the notion of merit (works) by the principle of faith.[56] This interpretation fails to convince, for two reasons: (1) Paul seeks to demonstrate to his Jewish discussion partner in Rom 1—2 not that God is impartial but that Jews are sinners, just like Gentiles, and are in need of God's forgiveness, and that the insistence of salvation-historical privileges such as the Torah and circumcision do not avert God's judgment, as salvation is now possible (only) through Jesus Christ (Rom 3:21-31). (2) For Paul, the theological "justification" of the Gentile mission lies not in the concept of impartiality but in God's new revelation in Jesus the Messiah and in the reality of the messianic era of salvation in which God fulfills his promises and grants salvation to the nations as well.

In Paul's case conversion and call to missionary service coincided, a fact that is more clearly expressed in Paul's statements than in Luke's accounts of Paul's conversion.[57] According to Acts 9:15 and Acts 22:14-15, it was Ananias, a member of the Christian community in Damascus, who communicated to Paul God's election and calling to be his witness. When Paul speaks of his conversion and call, usually in a polemical context, he emphasizes that God himself called and commissioned him directly in the encounter with Jesus Christ.[58]

This emphasis on a direct divine commissioning presents no problem if we take the "epiphany conversation" (*Erscheinungsgespräch* [Pesch]) between Jesus and Ananias seriously. If Paul regarded Ananias's vision as authentic and accepted Jesus' message communicated by Ananias as relevant for himself and as normative for his future, he does not commit a historical error when he emphasizes that his calling was communicated to him in a direct revelation. Howard Marshall interprets the fact that the conversion accounts in Acts 9 and 22 have Ananias communicate Paul's election by God and the calling to be a witness among the nations, whereas this happens in Acts 26 through the heavenly voice

---

[53]See Acts 4:1-3; 5:17, 27-28; 13:45; 14:2, 4-5; 17:5-7; 17:13; 28:24-25.
[54]See Acts 2:41; 4:4; 5:14; 6:1, 7; 12:24; 13:43; 14:1; 17:10-11; 21:20; 28:24-25.
[55]Bassler 1982; cf. idem 1985.
[56]Bassler 1985, 546-48, 551.
[57]Cf. 1 Cor 15:5-8 with Acts 22:4-16; 26:9-18. See Pesch, *Apg,* 1:308. On Paul's conversion in the book of Acts see Burchard 1970, 51-135.
[58]See Pesch, *Apg,* 1:309.

that speaks to Paul directly, in terms of a "telescoping" of the narrative in Acts 26: "Such condensation of a narrative is not unknown elsewhere in the Bible (compare, for example, Mt 9:18 with Mk 5:22-23, 35), and here it serves to concentrate attention on the heavenly command to Paul which had led to the way of life on account of which he now stood on trial. There was no need here to dwell on the part played by Ananias."[59]

The missionary commission given to Paul at the time of his conversion is formulated in diverse ways in the primary sources. We begin with Paul's own testimony, before citing the relevant descriptions from the accounts in the book of Acts.

Gal 1:15-16: "But when God, who had set me apart before I was born and called me through his grace, was pleased [16]to reveal his Son to me [in me], so that [ἵνα] I might proclaim him among the Gentiles [εὐαγγελίζωμαι αὐτὸν ἐν τοῖς ἔθνεσιν] . . ."

Gal 2:7: "On the contrary, when they saw that I had been entrusted with the gospel for the uncircumcised [εὐαγγέλιον τῆς ἀκροβυστίας], just as Peter had been entrusted with the gospel for the circumcised . . ."

1 Cor 9:1-2: "Am I not free? Am I not an apostle? Have I not seen Jesus our Lord? Are you not my work in the Lord [οὐ τὸ ἔργον μου ὑμεῖς ἐστε ἐν κυρίῳ]? [2]If I am not an apostle to others, at least I am to you; for you are the seal of my apostleship in the Lord [ἡ γὰρ σφραγίς μου τῆς ἀποστολῆς ὑμεῖς ἐστε ἐν κυρίῳ]."

2 Cor 10:13-16: "We, however, will not boast beyond limits, but will keep within the field that God has assigned to us [τὸ μέτρον τοῦ κανόνος οὗ ἐμέρισεν ἡμῖν ὁ θεὸς μέτρου], to reach out even as far as you. [14]For we were not overstepping our limits when we reached you; we were the first to come all the way to you with the good news of Christ. [15]We do not boast beyond limits, that is, in the labors of others; but our hope is that, as your faith increases, our sphere of action among you may be greatly enlarged, [16]so that we may proclaim the good news in lands beyond you, without boasting of work already done in someone else's sphere of action."

Acts 9:15: "But the Lord said to him, 'Go, for he is an instrument [σκεῦος] whom I have chosen to bring my name [τοῦ βαστάσαι τὸ ὄνομά μου] before Gentiles and kings and before the people of Israel [ἐνώπιον ἐθνῶν τε καὶ βασιλέων υἱῶν τε Ἰσραήλ].'"

Acts 22:14-15: "Then he said, 'The God of our ancestors has chosen you to know his will [προεχειρίσατό σε γνῶναι τὸ θέλημα αὐτοῦ], to see the Righteous One and to hear his own voice; [15]for you will be his witness to all the world [ἔσῃ μάρτυς αὐτῷ πρὸς πάντας ἀνθρώπους] of what you have seen and heard.'"

Acts 26:16-18: "But get up and stand on your feet; for I have appeared to you for this purpose, to appoint you to serve and testify [προχειρίσασθαί σε ὑπηρέτην καὶ μάρτυρα] to the things in which you have seen me and to those in which I will appear to you. [17]I will rescue you from your people and from the Gentiles—to whom I am sending you [εἰς

---

[59]Marshall, *Acts*, 395; quotation, ibid., 396.

οὓς ἐγὼ ἀποστέλλω σε] [18]to open their eyes so that they may turn from darkness to light and from the power of Satan to God, so that they may receive forgiveness of sins and a place among those who are sanctified by faith in me."

The following discussion provides not an exhaustive interpretation of these passages but a summary of the most important results concerning Paul's self-understanding as a missionary, or an apostle, sent by Jesus Christ.

1. Paul describes in Gal 1:16 his calling at the time of his encounter with Jesus Christ on the road to Damascus as a commission to missionary outreach among Gentiles.[60] It is important to note that the context in Gal 1:11-24 does not suggest the motif of the Gentile mission, which confirms the authenticity of Paul's account. The phrase *en tois ethnesin* in Gal 1:16 can be interpreted in ethnic terms: Paul is commissioned to preach the gospel to *ta ethnē,* to Gentiles. Or it can be understood as reference to the region in which Paul is directed to preach the gospel: outside of Judea, including Jews living in the Greek and Roman Diaspora.[61] Paul's basic statement in Rom 1:14 indicates that Gal 1:16 should be interpreted in ethnic terms: Paul understands himself as directed by the risen Lord to preach the gospel to Gentiles in particular—that is, non-Jews, polytheists, including proselytes and God-fearers whom he would encounter in the Diaspora synagogues.

2. Paul asserts in Gal 2:7 that he received the approval of the Jerusalem apostles for his conviction that the risen Lord called him to preach the gospel to Gentiles, when he discussed his proclamation of Jesus Christ with the apostles in Jerusalem (Gal 2:2).[62] The commission to preach the gospel to "the uncircumcised" that Peter, John and James acknowledged in the Jerusalem conference took place in connection with his conversion to Jesus Christ as reported in Gal 1:16.

3. The series of rhetorical questions in 1 Cor 9:1-2, with which Paul provokes positive answers, constitutes the start of Paul's exposition of his apostolic ministry. Following the second question ("Am I not an apostle?") Paul explains his concept of apostleship: he has seen the Lord, and he has established churches in areas that had not been reached with the message of Jesus Christ. The existence of the church in Corinth is the "seal" of his apostleship; it is the "legal attestation or attesting sign."[63] The fact that Luke designates only the Twelve as apostles in the book of Acts (with the exception of Paul and Barnabas in Acts

---

[60]S. Kim 1981, 56-66; O'Brien 1995, 10-11, 20; Dunn 1998, 178; Reinbold 2000, 167-68; Wisdom 2001, 131. Differently F. Watson (1986), who believes that Paul turned to the Gentiles only after his missionary efforts among Jews failed. Differently also N. Taylor (1992, 62-74), who believes that Gal 1:15-16 is the result of later reflection that Paul read back into his conversion experience.

[61]Thus Schlier, *Gal,* 56; Munck 1954, 101; Beker 1987, 8; J. M. Scott 1995, 121-22.

[62]See, besides the commentaries, O. Betz, *EWNT* 1:132-33 (*EDNT* 1:55).

[63]T. Schramm, *EWNT* 3:759 (*EDNT* 3:317); cf. Lindemann, *1 Kor,* 201.

14:4, 14) probably is to be explained with reference to Jesus' statement in Lk
22:28-30 in which he speaks of the Twelve sitting on thrones from which they
will judge the twelve tribes of Israel, which indicates that for Luke the Twelve
have a special role for Israel, a role that Paul does not possess.[64]

4. Paul's description of his mission in 2 Cor 10:13-16 is part of his defense
against attacks from false "apostles." Paul speaks of "the measure of the sphere
which God apportioned to us as a measure" (2 Cor 10:13 NASB). This "measure"
(μέτρον, metron) includes the city of Corinth as part of the sphere of the mission
field that God had assigned to him (ἐφικέσθαι ἄχρι καὶ ὑμῶν). Paul refers three
times to the "sphere" that God has assigned to him (κανών, kanōn [2 Cor 10:13,
15, 16]).[65] Alexander Sand comments, "God himself has given him the measure,
the direction, according to which he should go to Corinth in fulfillment of the
apostolic authority with which he has been commissioned."[66] Paul's mission
field, whose boundaries and extent include the Roman colony of Corinth, is
God's assignment (τὸ μέτρον, to metron): he has not chosen his mission field;
God has given it to him.[67]

5. In Luke's first account of Paul's conversion the Lord describes Paul as his
"instrument" (Acts 9:15)[68] who has been chosen to carry the "name" of Jesus to
the Gentiles, to kings and to the "sons of Israel." A comparison with the parallel
accounts of Paul's conversion as well as with his own statements helps us to
understand the unusual phrase "carry the name (of Jesus)." The expression "the
name [to onoma] (of Jesus)" stands in the book of Acts for "Jesus" (Acts 3:16;
4:30) or for the proclamation of Jesus (Acts 8:12)[69] and designates the good
news of Jesus the Messiah and Savior. The term "carry" (bastazein) here means
"to confess" and designates more generally missionary service[70] in which the
message of Jesus is carried to people who have not heard it before. The description of Paul's calling in Acts 9:15 shows that his commissioning as a missionary
to Gentiles does not preclude missionary proclamation among Jews: Paul
preaches the gospel to the uncircumcised, but also to the "sons of Israel."

Jürgen Roloff argues that the phrase "to carry the name" never had the meaning "to
preach, to proclaim in a missionary situation" in the early Christian period, but rather it
means "to submit to the name of Jesus Christ by baptism, to confess Christ, to be a Christian publicly."[71] This explanation is anachronistic. More serious attention should be given

---

[64]See I. H. Marshall 1990, 46-47.
[65]The only other occurrence of kanōn in Paul's letters is Gal 6:16.
[66]A. Sand, EWNT 2:614 (EDNT 2:249).
[67]See R. Pesch, EWNT 2:1037 (EDNT 2:421).
[68]Compare the metaphor of the potter in Rom 9:20-21.
[69]L. Hartman, "ὄνομα," EWNT 2:1271-72 (EDNT 2:520-21).
[70]W. Stenger, "βαστάζω," EWNT 1:500 (EDNT 1:208), who follows G. Lohfink, BZ 10 (1966):
108-15; see also Zmijewski, Apg, 382-83; Fitzmyer, Acts, 428-29; Jervell, Apg, 283.
[71]Roloff, Apg, 151; cf. Weiser, Apg, 1:226; Burchard 1970, 100-101.

to the view of Wolfgang Reinbold, who recently argued that Paul never understood himself as a missionary to Jews, but rather as a missionary to Gentiles only:[72] (a) The description of Paul's conversion and call and of his agreement with the Jerusalem apostles in Gal 1:15-16; 2:7-9, and his statements in Rom 15:15-16, speak only of Gentiles. (b) The description of his apostolic task in Rom 11:13-15 explicitly excludes missionary outreach in synagogues: Paul hopes, at the most, that he might succeed in making some of his fellow Jews jealous as Gentiles experience the salvation of the messianic era and that some Jews may be converted to faith in Jesus Christ in this indirect manner. (c) The argument that we know of Jews who were converted as a result of Paul's ministry does not prove that Paul preached the gospel in synagogues: the *archisynagōgos* Crispus is the only Jew we know of who was converted in the context of Paul's missionary work, while "the tradition" knows nothing of missionary sermons that Paul preached in synagogues or of Crispus being converted through such a sermon. Timothy, the "beloved child" of Paul (1 Cor 4:17; cf. Phil 2:2), constitutes no proof to the contrary, as Acts 14:8-20 does not mention missionary preaching in the synagogue. (d) Paul's statements in 1 Cor 9:19-23 do not formulate his missionary program, but merely state that Paul is a Jew who is willing to live like a "Gentile" and behave like a Jew when he has contacts with Jews. (e) The fact that Paul received the synagogue punishment of "forty minus one" lashes (2 Cor 11:24) does not prove that he preached the gospel of Jesus Christ among Jews, but proves only that he visited synagogues.

These arguments are unconvincing. (a) Reinbold is correct when he states that Paul mentions Gentiles rather than Jews when he describes his conversion and call. We must recall, however, that the relevant passages in the letter to the Galatians belong to a historical and theological context in which Paul does not describe his conversion in a "neutral" manner but rather defends his circumcision-free message as a missionary among Gentiles. (b) In Rom 11:13-15 Paul describes not his apostolic ministry as such but his hope that more and more Jews could be converted. I cannot see how this passage excludes the possibility of missionary sermons in synagogues: competent missionaries use different means; they do not rely on a single method. (c) Reinbold's argument that "the tradition" does not mention synagogue sermons through which Crispus, for example, was converted is incomprehensible.[73] His view that Luke's "scheme"—synagogue sermon, success, conflict, expulsion—is stylized, redactional and historically worthless is totally implausible. If Paul did not "give up" on the Jews but hopes that at least some of them might be won for Jesus Christ (granted by Reinbold in his comments on Rom 11:13-15), and if Paul visited the synagogues in the cities in which he does missionary work (granted by Reinbold for, e.g., Corinth and Philippi), then it follows that he preached sermons in synagogue services in which he explained the significance of Jesus of Nazareth. As a rabbi who studied in Jerusalem with the famous Gamaliel, Paul would have been invited to participate in the activities of the synagogue, to preach and to teach. Paul could have avoided appearances in the synagogues only if he decided as a matter of principle not to speak publicly in synagogues—an entirely absurd assumption for an active and dynamic missionary who was willing to sacrifice his own life for the salvation of his fellow Jews. Luke reports missionary sermons in the synagogue in Corinth in Acts

---

[72]Reinbold 2000, 164-82; on the evidence of Acts see ibid., 117-63, 207-10. Similarly E. P. Sanders 1983, 179-90.

[73]Reinbold 2000, 140 n. 96, 175; for comments that follow above see ibid., 130, 132, 148; on contacts with the synagogues in Corinth and Philippi, ibid., 125-26, 136, 186-87; on the conversion of Crispus, ibid., 141.

18:4; whether Crispus was converted later rather than sooner is less important than the fact that he heard Paul preach. Reinbold's theory about the conversion of Crispus shows that he knows very little about missionaries and missionary drive: "Paul moves in the environment of the synagogue, establishes contacts, gets to know people who are interested, invites them to the assemblies of the Ekklesia and wins them [Lydia in Philippi, Titius and Crispus in Corinth] through the authority of his teaching, through the charisma of the ἅγιοι, through the work of the Spirit, through 'conviction' in the Ekklesia (1 Cor 14:24), etc.; finally Crispus decides to be baptized and turns his back to the synagogue." If Paul "moved" in the "environment" of synagogues, he did so as a missionary who used every available opportunity to proclaim the gospel of Jesus Christ. The notion that Paul understood himself as a missionary to Gentiles and abstained for this reason from preaching the gospel to Jews reminds us more of bureaucratic concerns for clearly demarcated areas of responsibility of ecclesiastical officers than of the courageous missionary work of apostles who were willing to die in proclaiming the message of Jesus the crucified and risen Messiah. (d) Reinbold's brief discussion of 1 Cor 9:19-23 is just plain wrong: the verb κερδαίνειν (*kerdainein*, "win") does not mean "to captivate for himself and for the Ekklesia" but rather "to win (for the truth of the gospel)," and in the context of 1 Cor 9:20 "to win Jews for faith in Jesus as Messiah." Some scholars suggest that Paul's hope that he might "by all means save some" (1 Cor 9:22b) means that Paul speaks of his own behavior that leads "indirectly" to the conversion of a small number of Jews. This interpretation misses the point of the text. (*i*) The verb *kerdainein* is transitive, consistently used with an accusative object. Paul wants to "win people" for the salvation that has become possible through God's revelation in Jesus Christ (1 Cor 9:22c); he does not want to "captivate for himself" or "for the Ekklesia." (*ii*) Paul does not state in 1 Cor 9:20 that he wants to attract Jews in some way or other and indirectly: the parallel formulations in 1 Cor 9:20, 21 indicate that Paul's intentions in his contacts with Jews corresponded to the motivation and goals of his missionary work among Gentiles. (*iii*) Some scholars suggest that the "weak" whom Paul seeks to win according to 1 Cor 9:22a are weak Christians;[74] whether this is correct or not, the verb *kerdainein* in 1 Cor 9:20, 21 is related to the missionary "winning" of Gentiles. (*iv*) Paul's reference to the salvation of "some" (τίνες, *tines*) in 1 Cor 9:22b is connected not only with Jews but also with Gentiles: Paul knows that in both cases it is only "some" who are converted to faith in Jesus Christ. (*v*) The passage 1 Cor 9:19-23 is central as far as Reinbold's position is concerned; it is perhaps symptomatic from a methodological point of view that he deals with this text on less than two pages and that he manages to "explain" the verb *kerdainein* with a definition unsubstantiated by evidence and with a short footnote in which he criticizes the generally accepted definition of the term. (e) Reinbold argues that Paul visits synagogues because that is what Jews traditionally do, increasingly as a "symbolical act" to demonstrate the unity of "Israel" consisting of Jews and Gentiles, and because he could meet God-fearers for whom he felt responsible because they were Gentiles. This argument is weak: Luke's narrative in the book of Acts in which he portrays Paul as a missionary who uses every opportunity to preach the gospel of Jesus Christ is historically far more plausible than Reinbold's theories about Paul's motivation to visit synagogues while avoiding speaking about Jesus as the Messiah. It is hard to imagine a more irresponsible rabbi than a Torah scholar educated in Jerusalem who had become convinced

---

[74]Barrett, *1 Cor,* 215; Reinbold 2000, 178 n. 57; cf. Kremer, *1 Kor,* 195; Collins, *1 Cor,* 355l. Interpreting in the contextual meaning of non-Christians are Schrage, *1 Kor,* 2:346; Thiselton, *1 Cor,* 705-6.

that the Messiah had arrived but who would not mention and explain this conviction in his visits to synagogues.

Helga Botermann argues that the reason why the boundaries of the synagogue community were crossed in Philippi (Acts 16:13-40) was not primarily Paul's ministry.[75] Considering the dream-vision in which a "Macedonian man," evidently a Gentile, asks Paul for help (Acts 16:9), which causes Paul and his coworkers to cross the Aegean Sea and travel to Macedonia, this interpretation is implausible. The argument that Paul and Silas are described not as Christians but as Jewish proselytizers is unconvincing simply because there is no evidence for a Jewish (proselyte) mission. It is no contradiction when the Jews and the mob of the city of Thessalonike accuse Paul of causing trouble "all over the world" through his worldwide missionary activity. Botermann's argument that "Paul appeared to his contemporaries either as a Jewish or as a Christian missionary" construes a wrong alternative: the Gentile population would have viewed Paul's message, the "Christian proclamation," simply as the presentation of a (particular) Jewish position. Botermann believes "that Paul moved in the environment of the synagogue and that his mission did not go beyond the boundary of Judaism, including the God-fearers," but at the same time she insists that Paul was the most significant "motor for the formation of an independent Christian identity" on account of his "absolute conviction that the law had been overtaken as path to salvation by the death and the resurrection of Christ."[76] It is difficult to see how both assertions can hold true at the same time. Equally unconvincing is the suggestion that it was "only the baptism of the uncircumcised" that provoked the question "whether the law continues to be a path to salvation or whether it had been surpassed by the gospel of Jesus Christ," and that it was only the recognition that the expected imminent return of Jesus was being delayed that led to the realization that the believers should learn how to live together in a community. A different scenario is historically more likely: the question of whether and in what sense the Mosaic law is still valid seems to have arisen at a very early date in Jerusalem, in the context of the theological reflection of Stephen and his friends and in the context of their proclamation in the synagogues in Jerusalem; and the question of living together in community arose immediately when Jews, proselytes, God-fearers and Gentiles were converted to faith in Jesus the Messiah, as the events in Antioch demonstrate.

Anders Runesson argues that the position of Paul can be described as "closed-ethnic" or "open-ethnic," and that he did not fully move to a "non-ethnic" stance.[77] The "religious system" of Rom 11 indeed includes both Jews and Gentiles, but in such a way that they do possess the same status: according to Rom 4:16, Abraham is the father of the non-Jewish believers in Jesus the Messiah as well! It is true, however, that neither Paul nor other Christians forced the separation from the synagogue during this period, and that it is unwarranted to refer to Paul as "a former Jew," as Jürgen Becker does.[78]

6. According to Luke's account of Paul's conversion in Acts 22:6-16, Paul's

---

[75]Botermann 1993, 78.

[76]Botermann 1993, 81-82. She writes in the last paragraph, "Thus we can say that the 'Gentile apostle' who has dominated the Western tradition represents the interpretation that Luke gave to the activities of Paul. It reflects the historical situation in which a Christian self-consciousness was formed that was independent of Judaism." For the comment that follows above see Botermann 1991, 304.

[77]Runesson 1999, 65-66; for the comments that follow above see ibid., 74 with n. 42.

[78]Becker 1992, 213 (ET, 201); cf. Botermann 1991, 304.

call by God communicated through Ananias implied three tasks:[79] (a) Paul shall know the will of God (Acts 22:14a)—not the will of God as revealed in the Torah, which he studied with Gamaliel, but the new will of God, who offers salvation through Jesus the Messiah. (b) Paul shall "see the Righteous One and hear his own voice" (Acts 22:14b); that is, he knows the will of God if and when he acknowledges Jesus as Messiah—the phrase "the Righteous One" is one of the titles of the expected Davidic ruler (Jer 23:5-6; 33:15)—and accepts his words as authoritative. (c) Paul shall be Jesus' "witness to all the world" of what he has seen and heard (Acts 22:15); that is, he is directed to proclaim Jesus as the risen Lord and the message of Jesus before all people (πρὸς πάντας ἀνθρώπους, *pros pantas anthrōpous*), both Jews and Gentiles.[80] Paul's question on the road to Damascus "What am I to do, Lord?" (Acts 22:10) expresses in a poignant manner the willingness of the Pharisaic rabbi to accept any task that the risen Lord would give to him.[81]

7. Paul's calling is directly linked with the encounter with the risen Jesus on the road to Damascus in the third account of his conversion (Acts 26:9-18). The commission that the Kyrios Jesus communicates to Paul has three parts.[82] (a) The risen Lord says that he chose Paul to appoint him as his "servant and witness" (προχειρίσασθαί σε ὑπηρέτην καὶ μάρτυρα, *procheirisasthai se hypēretēn kai martyra* [Acts 26:16a]). This description characterizes the missionary work of Paul, Jesus' witness, as "service in the sense of a 'duty dependent on a commission' that he cannot and must not shirk." (b) The content of the message that Paul is to convey as Jesus' witness is, first, "the things in which you have seen me" (Acts 26:16b)—that is, the fact, undeniable because of the encounter with Jesus on the road to Damascus, that the crucified Jesus of Nazareth is the risen Lord who sits as Messiah at God's right hand. Second, he is to proclaim what the Lord would let him see of him in the future (Acts 26:16c), perhaps in future visions that Paul recounts later only with hesitation.[83] The future "seeing" that Paul will proclaim as part of his message might also refer to the conversion of the nations.[84] Some scholars suggest that the "appearance of the Lord" is the intellectual understanding of the gospel by Paul that was still in the future at the time of his conversion; it is unlikely, however, that this is what Luke wanted to communicate with his formulation.[85] (c) The commission ends with the promise

---

[79]See Zmijewski, *Apg*, 785.

[80]Barrett, *Acts*, 2:1042; cf. Zmijewski, *Apg*, 785; Fitzmyer, *Acts*, 707.

[81]Barrett, *Acts*, 2:1039.

[82]See Zmijewski, *Apg*, 847; for the quotation that follows above see ibid. (with reference to Stolle 1973, 128).

[83]See 2 Cor 12:1-5; cf. Acts 16:7, 9-10; 18:9-10; 22:17-21; 23:11; 27:23-24. Thus most commentaries; see Pesch, *Apg*, 2:277; Zmijewski, *Apg*, 847; Jervell, *Apg*, 594.

[84]Löning 1973, 142; cf. Zmijewski, *Apg*, 847.

[85]Barrett, *Acts*, 2:1159.

of protection, like the missionary commission of the Twelve in Mt 28:18-20: the risen Lord will rescue Paul from all dangers that he will face from his people and from the Gentiles "to whom I am sending you" (εἰς οὓς ἐγὼ ἀποστέλλω σε, *eis hous egō apostellō se* [Acts 26:17]). Therefore it becomes clear that Paul received a commission to universal missionary ministry: he will be a witness of Jesus before Jews and Gentiles, sent directly by the risen Kyrios himself, whom Paul has seen as the Twelve have seen him after Easter. Luke formulates at the end of this account in a concise manner the purpose of Paul's calling and the basic convictions of the witnesses:[86] the purpose and result of the missionary ministry of the witnesses is the opening of the eyes of Jews and Gentiles (ἀνοῖξαι ὀφθαλμούς, *anoixai ophthalmous* [Acts 26:18a]) so that they see and grasp the truth of God's redemptive revelation in Jesus Christ and "turn from darkness to light" (ἐπιστρέψαι ἀπὸ σκότους εἰς φῶς, *epistrepsai apo skotous eis phōs* [Acts 26:18b])—that is, from the power of Satan to God (ἀπὸ . . . τῆς ἐξουσίας τοῦ Σατανᾶ ἐπὶ τὸν θεόν, *apo tēs exousias tou Satana epi ton theon* [Acts 26:18c]).[87] The result of the opening of the eyes and of the turning to God of Jews and Gentiles is the reception of "forgiveness of sins" (τοῦ λαβεῖν αὐτοὺς ἄφεσιν ἁμαρτιῶν, *tou labein autous aphesin hamartiōn* [Acts 26:18d]) and the reception of "a place among those who are sanctified by faith" (κλῆρον ἐν τοῖς ἡγιασμένοις, *klēron en tois hēgiasmenois* [Acts 26:18e])—that is, "a place of salvation in the community of the people of God"[88] through faith in Jesus as the crucified and risen Messiah, who has been exalted to the right hand of God (πίστει τῇ εἰς ἐμέ, *pistei tē eis eme* [Acts 26:18-19)]. Gustav Stählin comments that the commission ends with the emphasis "that faith in Jesus is *the* way of sanctification (cf. Acts 15:9) and thus of salvation (cf. Acts 13:39; 10:43; 14:9) for all people."[89]

8. Another text needs to be considered that is connected not with Paul's conversion but with his calling to be a witness among Gentiles. Luke tells in Acts 22:17-21 of a vision that Paul had in the temple in Jerusalem, evidently at the time of his first visit to the Jewish capital after his conversion (i.e., in A.D. 33/34).[90]

Acts 22:17-21: "After I had returned to Jerusalem and while I was praying in the temple, I fell into a trance [18]and saw Jesus saying to me, 'Hurry and get out of Jerusalem quickly, because they will not accept your testimony about me.' [19]And I said, 'Lord, they them-

---

[86]Zmijewski, *Apg,* 848.

[87]On the opening of eyes see Is 42:7; on turning from darkness to light, Is 42:16; 1 Thess 5:4; 2 Cor 4:6; Eph 5:8; Col 1:13; 1 Pet 2:9; on turning from Satan to God, 1 Thess 1:9.

[88]Pesch, *Apg,* 2:278; cf. Zmijewski, *Apg,* 848. The suggestion by Zmijewski that this happens "specifically in baptism" (ibid.) is read into the text: in the book of Acts and in Paul's theology baptism follows conversion to faith in Jesus Christ.

[89]Stählin, *Apg,* 309; cf. Zmijewski, *Apg,* 848.

[90]Haenchen, *Apg,* 556-57 (ET, 580-81); Ramsay (1896, 60-64) argues for the second (famine relief) visit.

selves know that in every synagogue I imprisoned and beat those who believed in you. [20]And while the blood of your witness Stephen was shed, I myself was standing by, approving and keeping the coats of those who killed him.' [21]Then he said to me, 'Go, for I will send you far away to the Gentiles [ἐγὼ εἰς ἔθνη μακρὰν ἐξαποστελῶ σε].'"

There is no convincing reason to doubt the historicity of Luke's account of Paul's vision.[91] The formulation of the command in Acts 22:21 does not assert that the task of missionary work among Gentiles was given here for the first time; the short statement makes sense precisely when read in the context of a prior commission to missionary activity among Gentiles. Luke's account is entirely plausible: Paul was called to be a missionary to Gentiles in his conversion experience on the road to Damascus, a calling that was confirmed in a later vision that he received in the temple in Jerusalem. The suggestion that Paul received his missionary commission in the Jerusalem temple rather than on the road to Damascus[92] is unconvincing: (a) The statement in Gal 1:16-17 indicates that Paul links his conversion with his commission as a missionary to the Gentiles. (b) Paul's behavior during the decade after his conversion is no argument against his commission to Gentile mission in his Damascus experience: the time that he spent in Arabia and the forced flight from Damascus are evidence that Paul engaged in missionary work that reached Gentiles immediately after his conversion (see §26.1).

Luke's account of Paul's vision is given in the context of the speech that Paul gave in the Jerusalem temple after he had been rescued by Roman soldiers from people who wanted to lynch him on the temple mount. Paul points out that his sending, or the confirmation of his calling by God, took place in the temple in Jerusalem (Acts 22:17). In other words, Paul interprets his calling "as an event that is relevant for all Israel."[93] The exalted Lord confirmed that he has sent him to the *ethnē* living far away (Acts 22:21). Here the *ethnē* are the non-Jewish nations,[94] or the nations outside of Jerusalem and Palestine where he will proclaim the gospel among Jews and Gentiles.[95] Paul had been informed earlier that his missionary work would take place far from Jerusalem. Saul/Paul, the Jewish student who had moved from the Cilician Diaspora to Jerusalem, is directed not to remain in Jerusalem but to travel to the nations.

The accounts of Paul's conversion and other texts show that Paul understood his missionary work among the nations as a continuation of the ministry of the Servant of God of Isaiah's prophecy.[96] When the Jews of Antiocheia in Pisidia reject the message of Jesus the Messiah, Paul and Barnabas tell them,

"It was necessary that the word of God should be spoken first to you. Since you reject it

---

[91]See Blair 1965.
[92]Thus Blair (1965, 22-26), who dates the vision in the temple to the time of the apostolic council (Acts 15), which he dates before the mission to Cyprus and southern Galatia (Acts 13—14).
[93]Weiser, *Apg,* 2:611.
[94]See Weiser, *Apg,* 2:611; Barrett, *Acts,* 2:1045; Fitzmyer, *Acts,* 708.
[95]See Burchard 1970, 165-66; Stolle 1973, 247-48. The refusal by Jervell (*Apg,* 546) to interpret ἔθνη in the sense of "Gentiles" can only be explained as hermeneutical prejudice.
[96]See Cerfaux 1951.

and judge yourselves to be unworthy of eternal life, we are now turning to the Gentiles. [47]For so the Lord has commanded us, saying, 'I have set you to be a light for the Gentiles, so that you may bring salvation to the ends of the earth'" (Acts 13:46-47).

The missionaries quote Is 49:6, portraying themselves as ambassadors who fulfill the commission of the Servant of God in the book of Isaiah. When Paul preached the gospel in Corinth, the Lord told him in a dream-vision,

"Do not be afraid, but speak and do not be silent; [10]for I am with you, and no one will lay a hand on you to harm you, for there are many in this city who are my people" (Acts 18:9-10).

Cf. Is 41:10: "Do not fear, for I am with you, do not be afraid, for I am your God; I will strengthen you, I will help you, I will uphold you with my victorious right hand."

The allusion to Is 41:10 makes the same assertion: Paul will fulfill in Corinth the task of the Servant because God is with him. In his speech before Festus, Paul describes the commission that he had received from Jesus Christ at the time of his conversion as follows:

"But get up and stand on your feet; for I have appeared to you for this purpose, to appoint you to serve and testify to the things in which you have seen me and to those in which I will appear to you. [17]I will rescue you from your people and from the Gentiles—to whom I am sending you [18]to open their eyes so that they may turn from darkness to light and from the power of Satan to God, so that they may receive forgiveness of sins and a place among those who are sanctified by faith in me" (Acts 26:16-18).

The allusion to Is 42:6-7, 16, another text about the Servant of Yahweh, is unmistakable:

"I am the LORD, I have called you in righteousness, I have taken you by the hand and kept you; I have given you as a covenant to the people, a light to the nations, [7]to open the eyes that are blind, to bring out the prisoners from the dungeon, from the prison those who sit in darkness. . . . [16]I will lead the blind by a road they do not know, by paths they have not known I will guide them. I will turn the darkness before them into light, the rough places into level ground. These are the things I will do, and I will not forsake them" (Is 42:6-7, 16).

This understanding of Paul's role is not simply Luke's interpretation but rather reflects his self-understanding, as 2 Cor 6:1-2 shows:

"As we work together with him, we urge you also not to accept the grace of God in vain. For he says, 'At an acceptable time I have listened to you, and on a day of salvation I have helped you.' See, now is the acceptable time; see, now is the day of salvation!" (2 Cor 6:1-2, quoting Is 49:8).

Paul knows himself to be commissioned by Jesus Christ to carry out the work of the Servant of the Lord as the prophet Isaiah has described it: the light of the gospel will shine among the nations.[97] The goal of Paul's missionary work was "to win obedience from the Gentiles, by word and deed" (εἰς ὑπακοὴν ἐθνῶν, λόγῳ καὶ ἔργῳ [Rom 15:18]).

Jens Schröter points to 2 Cor 6:1-2 as confirmation for his view that Paul believes "that the acceptance of his proclamation *through his person* constitutes the only possibility for the Corinthians to obtain God's grace. . . . They have received the grace of God only if they accept him as the reconciler whom God has sent."[98] According to Schröter, Paul believed that God offers salvation to the Corinthian church "*exclusively* through Paul," as he has integrated his apostleship "consistently into his soteriological conception." In other words, Paul interprets his role in terms of an "exclusive position" as "God's medium" and as greater "mediator of reconciliation" than Moses in the old covenant. This interpretation is a serious misunderstanding that could be labeled "personalized sacramentalism." Schröter's views are negated by Paul's argument in 1 Cor 1:12-13 that the emphasis on, or preferential respect for, individual missionaries or preachers contradicts the essence of the gospel, and by his emphatic point in 1 Cor 1:13-17 that God has not sent him to baptize. The proclamation of the gospel should never create an exclusive link between congregation and apostle. The view that a local congregation "cannot share several apostles"[99] is quite wrong, as the example of the church in Jerusalem demonstrates. The proclamation of the gospel creates a relationship with Jesus Christ that relativizes *coram Deo* all apostles, all missionaries, all coworkers in the church, as Paul emphasizes in 1 Cor 3:7-8: "So neither the one who plants nor the one who waters is anything, but only God who gives the growth. The one who plants and the one who waters have a common purpose, and each will receive wages according to the labor of each."

Oscar Cullmann interprets the phrase "what is now restraining" (τὸ κατέχον, *to katechon*) the lawless one in the apocalyptic drama of the last days before the "appearance"—that is, the return of Jesus Christ (2 Thess 2:6)—in terms of the Gentile mission.[100] He argues that according to Mk 13:10 and Mt 24:14, the gospel will be preached to all nations before the end will come; since 2 Thess 2:7 uses a term in the masculine (ὁ κατέχων, *ho katechōn*) for "the one who restrains," Paul certainly must refer to the entity that has been entrusted with the fulfillment of this task. Thus, according to Cullmann, "the κατέχων is the person whose actions and whose thinking is based consistently on the consciousness of being called to

---

[97]See Cerfaux 1951, 451-52, with further evidence concerning echoes of Isaianic texts describing the ministry of the Servant of the Lord (ibid., 449-51). J. Ross Wagner (2002) does not interpret Paul's understanding of his role in the context of Isaiah's Servant of the Lord; he concludes, more generally, that "Isaiah prefigures the crucial role Paul himself will play in the proclamation of that message to those who have not yet heard" (340; cf. ibid., 359).

[98]Schröter 1993, 195; for the comment that follows above see ibid., 341.

[99]Schröter (1993, 343), who describes the result of his research as *Gesandtentheologie* ("theology of the ambassador").

[100]Cullmann 1936; the quotation that follows above, ibid., 314; followed by Munck 1959, 36-42. On the discussion see the commentaries; for a critique of Cullmann and Munck see Knox 1964, 4-6.

preach to the Gentiles, i.e., *Paul himself.*" This interpretation is untenable for two reasons. (a) Paul reckons with the possibility that he may still be alive at the time of Jesus' return (1 Thess 4:15). (b) Paul never states that his own missionary work has a central significance for God's plan of salvation for the last days and for the return of Jesus. If the notoriously difficult passage 2 Thess 2:6 is indeed connected with the Gentile mission as mentioned in Mt 24:14/Mk 13:10,[101] it qualifies the Gentile mission as an important component of eschatological reality, perhaps even as the singlemost significant aspect of the last days that have begun with Jesus' ministry, death and resurrection, linked, perhaps, with the trials of the eschatological "birth pangs" that are to be expected before the end.

9. Finally, we must ask whether Paul knew Jesus' missionary discourse in Mt 10:1-15/Mk 6:6-13/Lk 9:1-6; 10:1-12. While some scholars reject this possibility,[102] others give a positive answer.[103] Dale Allison demonstrates that Lk 10:1-12 has several parallels to Paul's letters. (a) The sentence "The laborer deserves to be paid" (Lk 10:7b) corresponds to 1 Cor 9:14: "In the same way, the Lord commanded that those who proclaim the gospel should get their living by the gospel."[104] (b) The statement "Remain in the same house, eating and drinking whatever they provide" (Lk 10:7b) can be compared with 1 Cor 9:4, 7, 13: "Do we not have the right to our food and drink? . . . Who plants a vineyard and does not eat any of its fruit? . . . Do you not know that those who are employed in the temple service get their food from the temple, and those who serve at the altar share in what is sacrificed on the altar?" The similar statements in 1 Tim 5:18 and *Did.* 13:1-2 do not prove that Lk 10:7b originally circulated as an isolated saying. (c) The statement "Whenever you enter a town and its people welcome you, eat what is set before you" (Lk 10:8) corresponds to 1 Cor 10:27: "If an unbeliever invites you to a meal and you are disposed to go, eat whatever is set before you without raising any question on the ground of conscience." (d) The statement "Whoever listens to you listens to me, and whoever rejects you rejects me, and whoever rejects me rejects the one who sent me" (Lk 10:16) corresponds to 1 Thess 4:8: "Therefore whoever rejects this rejects not human authority but God, who also gives his Holy Spirit to you." This evidence makes the assumption plausible that Paul was familiar with Jesus' missionary discourse, as least in the version of Lk 10.

24.3 Paul's Self-understanding as a Missionary

Paul describes his self-understanding as a missionary in several significant pas-

---

[101]Marshall, *Thess,* 199-200. See the critique in Wanamaker, *Thess,* 250-51.

[102]See Tuckett 1984.

[103]For the comments that follow above see Allison 1985.

[104]Lindemann (*1 Kor,* 207) merely acknowledges that Paul "uses traditions that speak of the right of missionaries to be supported."

sages: 1 Cor 3:10-15; 9:19-23; 15:1-11; 2 Cor 2:14-16; 4:7-15; Rom 1:14; 10:14-21; 15:15-21; Col 1:24-29. The texts that summarize Paul's missionary preaching will be discussed in §28.3.

1 Cor 3:5-15

This passage in which Paul explains his self-understanding as a pioneer missionary belongs to the first section of 1 Corinthians, which discusses the activities of Christian teachers in the church in Corinth. The problem that Paul discusses concerns Corinthian Christians who believe that human *sophia* ("wisdom") is a decisive reality for the spirituality of Christians and congregations and a fundamental criterion for evaluating the effectiveness of Christian preachers and teachers. This kind of thinking prompted Christians in Corinth to champion different teachers of the church, causing the formation of groups within the church and provoking divisions.

1 Cor 3:5-15: "What then is Apollos? What is Paul? Servants through whom you came to believe, as the Lord assigned to each. [6]I planted, Apollos watered, but God gave the growth. [7]So neither the one who plants nor the one who waters is anything, but only God who gives the growth. [8]The one who plants and the one who waters have a common purpose, and each will receive wages according to the labor of each. [9]For we are God's servants, working together; you are God's field, God's building. [10]According to the grace of God given to me, like a skilled master builder I laid a foundation, and someone else is building on it. Each builder must choose with care how to build on it. [11]For no one can lay any foundation other than the one that has been laid; that foundation is Jesus Christ. [12]Now if anyone builds on the foundation with gold, silver, precious stones, wood, hay, straw—[13]the work of each builder will become visible, for the Day will disclose it, because it will be revealed with fire, and the fire will test what sort of work each has done. [14]If what has been built on the foundation survives, the builder will receive a reward. [15]If the work is burned up, the builder will suffer loss; the builder will be saved, but only as through fire."

Paul describes his role as founder of the church because the activities of the wisdom teachers in the congregation concern the identity of the church. And he describes the role of other teachers and preachers who work in the church that he has founded. Paul's arguments reveal his convictions about his work as a missionary.

1. Paul understands himself as a "servant" (διάκονος, *diakonos* [1 Cor 3:5]). Since Apollos and any other teachers who have been or are active in the church are also *diakonoi,* all high-handedness concerning missionary work and all self-interest concerning successful church work are rendered impossible.[105] Some scholars compare Paul's emphasis to Cynic-Stoic parallels in which the philosophical teacher also understands himself as *diakonos* of the deity, as "the representa-

---

[105]See Schrage, *1 Kor,* 1:290. For the comment that follows above see Lindemann, *1 Kor,* 80.

tive of a god" with a corresponding self-confidence. These parallels do not explain Paul's self-understanding. Paul knows himself to be bound to God and to Jesus Christ, which excludes the possibility that he or anyone else might rule over the church or within the church. Paul's identification of preachers and teachers as "servants" turns the frame of reference of Greco-Roman society and its notion of social prestige upside down. This is a deliberate and consistent emphasis of Paul: all apostles, missionaries and preachers who teach and who are evaluated and appreciated by the Corinthian Christians are simply *diakonoi,* servants, people who get something done at the behest of a superior, assistants who attend to the tasks at hand.[106] Paul uses metaphors from agriculture and house construction to describe the tasks and activities of missionaries, preachers and teachers: they plant, they water, they build—tasks and activities that surely are no cause for boasting! The Greco-Roman elites despised manual labor. Missionaries and church leaders are not respected patrons who disdain people who had to earn their living by manual labor. Rather, they are *diakonoi* whose behavior and intentions are totally focused on serving their superiors, God and the Lord Jesus Christ.

2. God is the "Lord" (κύριος, *kyrios* [1 Cor 3:5]) of missionary work and of church work. He is the "superior" whose "assistants" all missionaries, preachers and teachers are. It was God who assigned to each missionary and preacher "his task" (TNIV) and who gave to each and every one different gifts. Both the task that God has assigned and the gift to carry out this task are God's gracious gifts.[107] Both missionary ministry and church ministry are tasks that God has given, work that God has assigned, commissions that God has granted.

3. The bond that ties preachers and teachers to the Lord not only excludes high-handedness but also establishes the unity of the ministry of all preachers and teachers who serve the church. Friedrich Lang observes, "The preachers are active in the work of the Lord on behalf of God; they work not with their own talents but with gifts that they have received; their ministry is therefore marked by unity."[108] The pioneer missionary who "plants" and the teacher in the church who "waters" are involved in one and the same task, and both are dependent upon the same Lord: they have "a common purpose" (NRSV), they are (literally) "one" (ἕν εἰσιν, *hen eisin* [1 Cor 3:8a]). It is preposterous to argue that Paul felt "superior to the other preachers because he proclaims the risen Christ more clearly and more consistently, drawing the proper theological conclusions from Jesus' death on the cross."[109]

---

[106]Clarke 1993, 119-20; on the *diakonoi* as people who get something done and as assistants see BDAG 230-31. For the observations that follow above see Clarke 1993, 199-20. For a critical discussion of the suggestions of J. N. Collins 1990 on the meaning of διάκονος see Clarke 2000, 234-45.

[107]Schrage, *1 Kor,* 1:288, 291; Thiselton, *1 Cor,* 300-301.

[108]Lang, *Kor,* 49.

[109]Wehr 1996, 74, with reference to Gal 2:11-21; 1 Cor 9; 15:1-11.

4. Paul sees himself as pioneer missionary called by God to "plant" (1 Cor 3:6) and to "lay the foundation" (1 Cor 3:10)—that is, to establish new churches. Apollos and other preachers and teachers "water" (1 Cor 3:6) and "build on the foundation" (1 Cor 3:10); that is, they encourage and promote the further growth of the church, teaching the believers and reaching unbelievers. Paul's statement that the Lord assigned different tasks to "each" (ἕκαστος, *hekastos* [1 Cor 3:5]), emphasizing the diversity of gifts and tasks, must be protected from two possible misunderstandings. Paul does not make an individualistic statement, he does not promote people focusing on their "own" ministry, which could very easily lead to self-promotion. Nor does Paul make a statement of uniformity, implying that all are involved in the same ministry or are able to carry out the same task. Paul criticizes the attitude of the Corinthian Christians who focus on the personality of the preacher and teacher (1 Cor 1:10-17; 3:1-4). This attitude may correspond to the Hellenistic praxis of itinerant philosophers, but it contradicts the character and the nature of the Christian message, whose center is the crucified Messiah (1 Cor 1:13, 17-18; 2:2). Paul sees himself and all other Christian preachers and teachers not as people who are in the foreground or in the center of the action but as people who have important, and at the same time, diverse tasks.[110]

5. Success always comes from God and God alone. This is true both for pioneer missionaries and for preachers and teachers in local congregations: only God gives growth (ὁ θεὸς ηὔξανεν, *ho theos ēuxanen* [1 Cor 3:6b]; ὁ αὐξάνων θεός, *ho auxanōn theos* [1 Cor 3:7b]). The effectiveness of missionary work and of church ministry does not depend on persons or programs, it does not depend on rhetorical techniques or methods of accommodation, but only on God's activity. Preachers are "nothing" (οὔτε . . . οὔτε, *oute . . . oute* [1 Cor 3:7a]), "a nothing from which only a creative act of God can make something. Genuine preachers of the gospel can understand themselves and their work only on the basis of *creatio ex nihilo*."[111] Johann Bengel points, with customary insight, to the contrast between Paul's understanding of ministry and a mechanical model of ministry: if God does not grant organic growth, the seed or the grain of wheat would be "like a pebble right from the beginning of the sowing," whereas the growth of the word of God that God grants leads to faith.[112] A. H. Francke commented on the claims to prestige of the preacher: "The brightest and the most erudite are not always the best in the kingdom of God either, nor do they always bring the richest or the most noble fruit." Paul emphasizes that the nature of the ministry prohibits deference to and exclusivistic respect for individual preachers

---

[110]Clarke 1993, 119; Schrage, *1 Kor,* 1:290-91; Thiselton, *1 Cor,* 301; cf. Young 1989, 76-79.
[111]Schrage, *1 Kor,* 1:292.
[112]Bengel, *Gnomon Novi Testamenti,* 629: "Sine hoc incremento granum a primo sationis momento esset instar lapilli: ex incremento protinus fides germinat." For the quotation of A. H. Franke that follows above see Schrage, *1 Kor,* 1:309.

and teachers: they are all instruments of God on whose work all "success" depends. Apostles and missionaries are just "coworkers," specifically "coworkers of God" (θεοῦ συνεργοί, *theou synergoi* [1 Cor 3:9a; 1 Thess 3:2]): they are all involved in *God's* work, and preachers and teachers are just "God's 'helpers' and 'handymen.'"[113] Every preacher is "a representative of God in the mission 'work' (ἔργον, *ergon* 1 Cor 3:12-14; Phil 2:30) of proclamation."

6. The churches that are established as the fruit of missionary work belong neither to Paul nor to other teachers: the church is "God's field, God's building" (θεοῦ γεώργιον, θεοῦ οἰκοδομή, *theou geōrgion, theou oikodomē* [1 Cor 3:9b]). Since the origin and the growth of the church are the effects of God's own work, the church is neither the work nor the possession of the apostle: it is the work and the possession of God.[114] Missionaries, preachers and teachers work an "alien land," on land that belongs to God. The apostles and teachers belong *together with the church* to the "plantation" that is growing, to the "building" that is being constructed.

7. The responsibility of the missionary to God becomes apparent in the statement that "each will receive wages [τὸν ἴδιον μισθόν, *ton idion misthon*] according to the labor of each [τὸν ἴδιον κόπον, *ton idion kopon* (1 Cor 3:8b)]": God himself is their "employer," and they are all accountable to him. A second thought is implied as well: it is God alone who decides what constitutes success or failure of the work of the preacher and teacher, not the church or coworkers. God knows the value of the work of the missionaries and of the preachers.[115] Paul does not specify the "wages" in 1 Cor 3:8; later he speaks of "the prize" (τὸ βραβεῖον, *to brabeion* [1 Cor 9:24]), of an "imperishable wreath" (ἄφθαρτος στέφανος, *aphtharton stephanos* [1 Cor 9:25]), of "the crown of righteousness" (2 Tim 4:8). The apostle Peter speaks of "the crown of glory that never fades away" (1 Pet 5:4), and James and John speak of "the crown of life" (Jas 1:12; Rev 2:10). Paul seems to indicate in 1 Cor 3:8 that there are different "wages": God rewards according to the "work" of the individual missionary, preacher or teacher "in accordance with the energy displayed and the burdens accepted."[116] Paul does not indicate, however, what the different wages consist of.[117] Adolf Schlatter comments, "The scale [of the reward] does not depend on the degree of the giftedness or on the scope of the success, because it is he who 'gives the growth' who decides the giftedness and the success. The reward is promised only to sacrificial service of the individual: it is with this that Paul linked the expectation of a

---

[113]G. Bertram, *ThWNT* 7:872 (*TDNT* 7:874). For the quotation that follows above see W.-H. Ollrog, *EWNT* 3:727 (*EDNT* 3:304).

[114]Schrage, *1 Kor,* 1:295; for the comment that follows above (with a quotation of V. Mosheim) see ibid.

[115]See Thiselton, *1 Cor,* 304.

[116]Schlatter, *Kor,* 131; the quotation that follows above, ibid.

[117]Kuck 1992, 168.

reward, without any inhibitions (1 Cor 9:17, 18). Human action receives from God's action, human devotion receives God's gifts."

8. The metaphor of the "building" and of the activity of "building" (οἰκοδομή, *oikodomē;* οἰκοδομεῖν, *oikodomein;* ἐποικοδομεῖν, *epoikodomein*) refers, initially, not to the individual believer but to the church as a whole. The primary object of the "building activity" is the church as a whole. Where individuals appear as object of the word group, they do so "exclusively as members who already belong to the church or who are potential members."[118]

9. The description of Paul as "skilled master builder" (σοφὸς ἀρχιτέκτων, *sophos architektōn*) who lays the "foundation" (θεμέλιον ἔθηκα, *themelion ethēka* [1 Cor 3:10a]) describes in concrete terms the specific task that Paul received from God. Paul is a pioneer missionary who travels from city to city and from region to region and proclaims the message of Jesus the Messiah and Savior before audiences who had never heard that message before; he helps them to find faith in the revelation of Israel's God in Jesus Christ, particularly in the death and resurrection of Jesus, and he gathers the new believers into a new community. In antiquity the builder of a new house made a contract with the individual workers, supervised and coordinated by a *tektōn* ("builder, carpenter, artisan") who had superior knowledge and experience and who therefore was the *architektōn,* the "master builder" or "director of works."[119] Such "architects" were very much in demand as specialists, and their prestige far surpassed that of stonemasons, carpenters, mosaic layers or merchants. They had the technical responsibility for planning and constructing public buildings such as temples, council halls, colonnaded halls in the markets and theaters.[120] The *archi-* in *architektōn* expresses here, perhaps, the notion of "first among equals, more probably leading in experience and skill rather than in managerial status." Paul uses the metaphor of the master builder to describe himself as appointed and employed by God, together with a team of coworkers, to proclaim the gospel in pioneer situations, to lead people to faith in Jesus Christ and to establish new communities of believers. This is the "foundation" (a term that includes the foundation walls in antiquity) without which there would be no church in the city of Corinth. Paul is only to lay the foundation; other preachers and teachers whom God has appointed finish the building. The fact that Paul was active in Corinth for over one and a half years (Acts 18:2, 11, 12) clarifies that Paul regarded pioneer missionary work not as evangelistic *Blitz* whose results need to

---

[118]Kitzberger 1986, 282; cf. Klauck 1992a, 55.

[119]LSJ 253. See Thiselton, *1 Cor,* 308; for the metaphor see Shanor 1988; Derrett 1997, 130-33.

[120]Derrett 1997, 130-31; R. A. Tomlinson, *OCD* 147; cf. John J. Coulton, *Greek Architects at Work: Problems of Structure and Design* (London: Elek, 1977); Werner Müller, *Architekten in der Welt der Antike* (Leipzig: Koehler & Amelang, 1989). For the quotation that follows above see Thiselton, *1 Cor,* 308.

be consolidated by other preachers and teachers in "follow-up" work. For Paul, to lay the "foundation" included instructing the new believers in the fundamental content of faith in Jesus Christ and in the basic teachings of Scripture (i.e., the Hebrew Scriptures, the Old Testament). Wolfgang Schrage states that Paul's description of his role as master builder who lays the foundation points to "the temporal and material priority of his apostolic work" and asserts his "authority and special position."[121] This interpretation is correct only if other preachers and teachers likewise have "authority" and a "special position" in the context of the tasks for which God has appointed them. Paul clearly does not seek to emphasize how important he is; the context of 1 Cor 3:10 makes that highly unlikely. Rather, he emphasizes "that he remained faithful to his divine assignment."[122] William MacDonald writes in his introductory study to the architecture of the Roman Empire that "great buildings are the work of great architects."[123] Paul probably would not have applied this dictum to the local congregations that he founded: the credit for the fact that believers in Jesus Christ are "saints" and that the Christian communities are "the body of Christ" goes not to Paul but to God. It is important to note, and this is part of Paul's emphasis, that the foundation that has been laid cannot be altered by those who continue to erect the building: if someone attempts to replace the existing foundation by another foundation, he starts another, "alien" building.[124]

10. The foundation that Paul lays is Jesus Christ himself (1 Cor 3:11), specifically Jesus the crucified Messiah (1 Cor 1:23; 2:2). The crucified and risen Jesus Christ is the content of the missionary proclamation and thus the foundation and the measure of the establishment of the church and of the growth of the church. It is for this very reason that the decisive factor in the mission of the apostles is not the missionary, the preacher or the teacher but the One who is preached and taught—Jesus Christ, who granted salvation to the apostle and who assesses his ministry. Wolfgang Schrage remarks, "There is no mere formal authority for Paul. Only Jesus Christ himself can guarantee the basis and the stability of the church."[125] As a building has only one foundation, there no alternative to Jesus Christ: the existing foundation that Paul had laid in Corinth cannot be changed.

11. Preachers and teachers are responsible for the way they build on the "foundation Jesus Christ" (1 Cor 3:12-15) that Paul or other pioneer missionaries have laid. They have the responsibility for the priorities and for the perspectives, for the motivations and for the methods that are displayed and used in the build-

---

[121]Schrage, *1 Kor,* 1:297.

[122]Lang, *Kor,* 52.

[123]W. MacDonald 1982, 122.

[124]Lindemann, *1 Kor,* 84.

[125]Schrage, *1 Kor,* 1:298. The question of whether God's revelation in the sacred Scriptures and, for Paul and the early Christians, in the Jesus tradition constitutes a "formal" authority would need to be discussed further.

ing up of the church. When an *architektōn* had laid the foundation of a building and left the city or died, catastrophes could happen if the builders who continued to work on the edifice were not careful to follow the measurements that were "given" by the foundation that already existed. An important issue was, for example, the question of how much weight the foundation could carry. When Herod I disregarded existing foundations during his rebuilding and renovation of the Jerusalem temple and sought to build his grandiose new edifice on newly dug foundations, it sank into the ground (Josephus, *A.J.* 15.391)—the nightmare not only of every architect but also of every owner or sponsor of a new building. Any builder who seeks to finish a building that has been started on foundations laid by another architect must adhere carefully to the benchmarks provided by the architect, even if the builder regards the style of the building as antiquated.[126] There is a way of erecting a building that has lasting results, the outcome of faithfulness to the foundations and to the measurements that they provide, and there is a way of erecting a building that is provisional, resulting from new measurements chosen according to new standards. Materials such as gold, silver and precious (marble) stones will survive a fire (fires were a constant problem in the cities of the Mediterranean world): the missionary, preacher and teacher who follows the crucified and risen Jesus Christ as the foundation, ground and measure of his faith and his "strategic" and "tactical" behavior need not fear the fire of the final judgment (1 Cor 3:12-14). Wood, hay and straw burn easily and quickly: preachers and teachers who think that they can leave the message of the crucified and risen Savior behind will "suffer loss" in the final judgment (1 Cor 3:15). They will be saved, barely, but they will experience some "deficit," perhaps the shame of the missionary "who stands before God without fruit after he has lost his work."[127]

Paul also speaks of the responsibility of the individual Christian for his or her moral behavior, for which each will be asked to give account in the judgment (2 Cor 5:10). However, the subject matter of 1 Cor 3:12-15 clearly is not the individual believer but rather preachers who teach in a local congregation, with implications for all preachers who teach, including the pioneer missionary.

All "builders" who are involved in building the church of God are responsible to God for their actions. This is a responsibility that will become evident and will have consequences in the final judgment. Paul implies that missionary work and preaching and teaching ministries exist that will be rejected by God on judgment day because the message of the crucified and risen Jesus Messiah was misconstrued and misrepresented—independently of the question of whether there

---

[126]See Derrett 1997, 132.
[127]Lang, *Kor,* 55. Most modern interpreters correctly observe that this is no reference to "purgatory"; see Schrage, *1 Kor,* 1:303-4, 307-8.

was growth despite these deficiencies, whether people joined the church and whether people received support in their Christian lives. Missionary work and church work will "remain" on judgment day if and when Jesus, the crucified and risen Messiah and Savior, was at the center of the proclamation of the preachers and teachers, if and when Jesus was the criterion and measure of the behavior of the preachers and thus also of the behavior of the believers.

1 Cor 9:19-23

When Paul discusses the question of whether Christians may eat meat sacrificed to idols and whether Christians may participate in communal meals, such as banquets, held in pagan temples, he describes his behavior as a missionary whom God has called to preach to Jews and Gentiles.[128]

1 Cor 9:19-23: "For though I am free with respect to all, I have made myself a slave to all, so that I might win more of them [ἵνα τοὺς πλείονας κερδήσω]. [20]To the Jews I became as a Jew, in order to win Jews. To those under the law I became as one under the law (though I myself am not under the law) so that I might win those under the law. [21]To those outside the law I became as one outside the law (though I am not free from God's law but am under Christ's law) so that I might win those outside the law. [22]To the weak I became weak, so that I might win the weak. I have become all things to all people, that I might by all means save some [τοῖς πᾶσιν γέγονα πάντα, ἵνα πάντως τινὰς σώσω]. [23]I do it all for the sake of the gospel [πάντα δὲ ποιῶ διὰ τὸ εὐαγγέλιον], so that I may share in its blessings."

Paul formulates in this passage the rule of his missionary existence. "This rule follows the gospel, because the manner in which Paul devotes himself in his ministry to people, coming into closest contact with his listeners, sharing their world, speaking their language, corresponds to God's care for people."[129] We note the following fundamental elements of missionary work, as Paul understood and practiced it.

1. The basic rule of missionary existence requires the missionary to take the listener seriously in a fully consistent manner (1 Cor 9:19). The behavior of the preacher is subordinated to the preaching of the gospel. It is appropriate to describe this rule as "solidarity with the listener,"[130] as long as "solidarity" is not simply a term for sentiments that have no consequences for one's behavior. The freedom that faith in Jesus Christ implies and creates is a freedom that obligates one to take action for others. Wolfgang Schrage comments, "The free person remains free only as long as he remains free from his freedom."[131] Paul is prepared

---

[128]See Daube 1948; Bornkamm 1971, and the commentaries. Stephen Barton (1996, 279, 284-85) sets up false alternatives when he disputes that 1 Cor 9:19-23 is relevant for Paul's missionary strategy.

[129]Eichholz 1972, 49, and passim; see also Iovino 1990.

[130]Schrage, *1 Kor,* 2:346, with reference to Eichholz 1972, 49; Hahn 1971a, 65.

[131]Schrage, *1 Kor,* 2:338.

to relinquish his freedom if he can win people for faith in Jesus Christ: "He wants to win people, and he would not win them if he who is free and who does not owe anything to anybody and who is dependent on nobody would interact with them on the basis of his freedom, unwilling to budge from his rights."[132] Paul's willingness to became "all things to all people" (1 Cor 9:22b) corresponds to the subject matter of his proclamation. Georg Eichholz observes, "This is more than tactical behavior. This is the consequence of the gospel."[133] Paul goes to people wherever they are "at home" in terms of space, language or history.

2. Paul the missionary makes himself dependent upon his listeners; he becomes their "slave" (1 Cor 9:19). The audience decides the "form" in which the gospel is proclaimed. Paul's "incarnational" (or, better, "identificatory") maxim of missionary behavior results in the fact that the "language" in which the proclamation proceeds has been decided upon in terms of the situation of the listener. The listener needs to understand the gospel. "Those who proclaim the gospel must not encode it linguistically, since the New Testament witnesses themselves are linguistically on the move towards the listener, challenged to new interpretations of the tradition."[134] In the words of Adolf Schlatter, "He wins people not by separating himself from them, what he could do in virtue of his freedom, but by subordinating himself to them, by belonging to them and by serving them. Their need tells him what to do, and it is their salvation that he desires. He listens to them so that they will listen to him, and because he expects them to do what he demands of them, he does what they ask of him."[135]

The intention of Paul's adaptation or accommodation to Gentile listeners is the reason why it is not entirely useful to make a comparison with Rabbi Hillel, who accepted a Gentile as a proselyte despite that fact that the Gentile rejected the oral Torah. Hillel did not engage in missionary outreach, and he did not abandon oral tradition in his own behavior.[136] Nor does Paul's missionary principle correspond to Hillel's rule: "When you come to a town, behave according to its customs":[137] law and lawlessness describe for a Jew such as Paul "extreme opposites of a religious nature."[138]

3. The audiences of the missionary proclamation must be acknowledged and taken seriously in their diversity. Paul is sent to "all" (1 Cor 9:19), but he differ-

---

[132]Schlatter, *Kor,* 279.

[133]Eichholz 1972, 49, 53, for the comment that follows above see ibid. See also Chadwick 1954-1955.

[134]Eichholz 1972, 49.

[135]Schlatter, *Kor,* 279.

[136]Contra Daube (1948, 336-51, esp. 336), who refers to *b. Šabb.* 31a; *'Abot R. Nat.* 15; *m. 'Abot* 2:5; *t. Ber.* 2:24; similarly Schoeps 1959, 244 (ET, 231). See also the critique in Schrage, *1 Kor,* 2:339 with n. 348.

[137]Cf. *Gen. Rab.* 48 on Gen 18:8; *Exod. Rab.* 47. See Schoeps 1959, 244 (ET, 231).

[138]Bornkamm 1971, 150.

entiates among his listeners. People are not mere objects of the preaching of the gospel: they are different in terms of, for example, their religious heritage, and they need to be addressed differently. Jews live in obedience to the Torah, while Gentiles live without the Torah, obedient to other religious principles and practices. In view of such differences in audiences, Paul has a specialized assignment: God called him to preach primarily among Gentiles. The speeches of Paul that Luke records in the book of Acts demonstrate that Paul indeed adapted his preaching to his audiences in their ethnic or locally conditioned diversity.

4. Paul does not exclude anybody from his preaching. Despite the differentiation of audiences and despite his specialized commission as missionary to Gentiles, Paul understands himself as obligated to the "people under the Torah" (1 Cor 9:20). Paul never excuses himself from preaching the message of Jesus Christ to his Jewish compatriots.[139] His view of the church does not allow such a "separated coexistence" of preaching among Gentiles and preaching among Jews. Alan Segal rightly comments on 1 Cor 9:19-23, "If Paul's call for unity is taken seriously, he did not merely want to be the apostle to the gentiles. He wants to be an apostle of all the church, for his vision was for a new community formed of all gentiles and Jews (1 Cor 9:20-22)."[140] The concern for the unity of the church in the sense of the unity of the people of God who experienced God's salvation does not mean that Paul engaged in missionary work only "inside the synagogue" and that he and his followers remained "within the Jewish community."[141] An "institutional" separation from the synagogue was not among the strategic goals of Paul's missionary work, but neither was it a consequence that ensued at a much later date. Paul and the new believers were forced to leave the local synagogues with tragic regularity because his proclamation of Jesus as the crucified Messiah and Savior was regarded as blasphemous by many Jews, while an increasing number of Gentiles accepted the message that Paul and his coworkers proclaimed (see Acts 18:6-7, 11 for the development in Corinth).

5. Missionary accommodation formulates no limitations in advance: Paul becomes "all things" to "all people" (1 Cor 9:22).[142] Even though Paul is no longer controlled by the stipulations of the Torah that regulate daily life, he does not impede the potential conversion of his Jewish listeners by provocative "lawlessness."[143] He himself is no longer "under Torah," which means that he does not follow all stipulations of the Mosaic law, particularly the laws that distinguish between Jews and Gentiles, such as the food laws and the purity laws. But Paul

---

[139]Eichholz 1972, 51, contra Schmithals 1963, 43-44.
[140]A. Segal 1990, 265; cf. S. Barton 1996, 284-85.
[141]Botermann 1993, 76.
[142]Schrage, *1 Kor,* 2:347.
[143]Eichholz 1972, 52.

emphasizes that his freedom from the law is not lawlessness (antinomianism), that it does not imply the abrogation of the law: as far as the law is the law of God "in Christ," modified by the climax of God's revelation in Jesus the Messiah, it remains valid and he continues to live "in the law" (ἔννομος Χριστοῦ, *ennomos Christou* [1 Cor 9:21]). At the same time Paul maintains the freedom that is given with Jesus Christ in his contacts with Gentiles: he does not require them to keep the stipulations of the Torah; he eats what they eat, even if it includes meat sacrificed to idols. He does not transform them into Jews (which would require circumcision) before they can become full members of the people of God. We should note, however, that Paul never says that he became "a pagan to the pagans" (or an adulterer to the adulterers): the religious relativism and polytheism of Greco-Roman society make it impossible for a missionary to live "as a Gentile" in every respect. However, Paul engages the "weak" polytheists and the timid and superstitious unbelievers in such a way that they are not put off by provocative "freedom," as he wants to win all people for faith in Jesus Christ.[144]

Peter Richardson accuses Paul of not having followed his apostolic principle of accommodation consistently when he confronted Peter in Antioch: as Paul claims that he adapts to specific situations in a flexible manner, he should not have criticized Peter, who adapted his behavior to the demands of Jewish Christians from Jerusalem, having the right to do so as apostle for the Jews. Richardson suggests that the excitement of Paul concerning Peter's behavior becomes understandable only if we are dealing with a breach of the territorial agreement between the apostles (Gal 2:7-9) rather than a breach of the principle of accommodation.[145] This interpretation is unconvincing. (a) Paul engages in "accommodation" with the goal of winning people for faith in Jesus Christ. Peter does not engage in accommodation in *that* sense: he gives in to Jewish Christians from Jerusalem who demand that Jewish Christians and Gentile Christians adhere to the stipulations of the Mosaic law.[146] The issue in Antioch was not the mode of missionary outreach but whether or not to make allowances to the theological position of conservative Jewish Christians. (b) Paul's principle of accommodation does not imply that the content of the gospel is negotiable: he lives "in the law of Christ." For example, Paul insists on the reality of the resurrection of the body precisely in view of difficulties with this teaching (1 Cor 15). If the truth of the gospel, as Paul understands it, is at stake, he is more than willing to sacrifice dialogical contingency to dogmatic necessity. He expects of polytheists who convert to faith in Jesus Christ to change their worldview and many aspects of their behavior in daily life.[147] (c) Paul does not reject the Torah in toto, as he is not "without the law of God" and as he indeed establishes the law with his message (Rom 3:31). (d) Paul's principle of accommodation is not a maxim that champions a laissez-faire attitude but rather is the concrete form of his endeavors to win as many people to Jesus Christ as possible. (e) In Paul's view

---

[144]Schrage, *1 Kor,* 2:346, with reference to Weiss, Bachmann, Hurd, Wolff, Black, Patte for the interpretation of the "weak" in 1 Cor 9:22.
[145]P. Richardson 1979-80. For a critique of Richardson's position see Carson 1986, which I follow. See also Wehr 1996, 60-73.
[146]Wehr 1996, 72.
[147]See Beker 1987, 336; Carson 1986, 11.

there are no "weak" brothers and sisters in Antioch whose presence would have prompted the "application" of the accommodation principle. The Gentile Christians of Antioch did not represent believers for whom he needed to make allowances, as their conscience had not come under pressure (thus the definition of "weak" in 1 Cor 8). Nor did the Jewish Christians of Antioch—or Peter—represent "weak" brothers and sisters, since table fellowship with the Gentile Christians had not been a problem. And the Jewish Christians from Jerusalem were not "weak" believers either who needed to be won for faith in Jesus Christ: their position did not involve neutral modes of behavior that allowed for different decisions; rather, they demanded the adoption and practice of all stipulations of the Torah by the converted Gentiles, including circumcision. This position and these demands did not represent "weakness" that needed to initiate the application of the accommodation principle.[148] (f) Richardson fails to see that Antioch is not "Pauline territory" (in contrast to Jerusalem as "Petrine territory"), that the church in Antioch is not a Gentile-Christian church, and that the agreement in Gal 2:7-9 is not primarily a territorial demarcation of the mission field. Richardson divides the accommodation principle along territorial lines, which cannot be verified by the facts of the early Christian mission: Peter preaches not only to Jews but also to Gentiles, and Paul preaches not only to Gentile audiences but also in synagogues. Paul's principle of accommodation would not be consistent if it did not apply *also* to missionary outreach to Jews. (g) Paul accused Peter of hypocrisy because Peter had understood the theological truth of the new function and significance of the Torah (new since the death and resurrection of Jesus Christ) but then acted in contradiction to his convictions. Peter understands that adherence to the stipulations of the Mosaic food laws and purity laws was no longer binding for believers in Jesus Christ, whether Gentile Christians or Jewish Christians. The gracious gift of justification through faith in Jesus Christ, explained by Paul succinctly and emphatically in this very context (Gal 2:11-21), eliminates the possibility that Jewish Christians *demand* of Gentile Christians obedience to the commandments of the Mosaic law. Paul can be flexible if the behavior of Christians is shaped in diverse ways *in obedience to Jesus Christ* and if it does not jeopardize their being "in the law of Christ." If, on the other hand, Jewish Christians demand, *on the basis of Mosaic law,* that everyone must keep the holiness code, the purity laws, the food laws and the circumcision stipulations of the Torah, then they have abandoned the foundation of God's redemptive revelation in Jesus Christ.

Marcel Dumais suggests that the principle that Paul formulates in 1 Cor 9:19-23 is meant to characterize the life of Christians in diverse cultural settings: "Everyone lives his faith according to his cultures and its customs."[149] It surely is true that the Jewish Christians in Jerusalem lived differently than did the Gentile Christians in Corinth. Paul, however, argued at least since Antioch that if Jewish Christians and Gentile Christians belong to the same local congregation, they should understand themselves as members of one single body and meet not only for worship but also for communal meals. Jewish Christians had to learn to abandon traditional ways of behavior that were sanctioned, even demanded, by the Scriptures, and particularly traditions concerning the selec-

---

[148]Carson 1986, 19-20; for the two points that follow above see ibid., 29-30, 32-33.

[149]Dumais 1981, 77: "Chacun vit sa foi selon sa culture et ses coutumes."

tion and preparation of food. Gentile Christians, at least wealthy Christians in whose houses the local congregation met that included Jewish-Christian members, might have to rethink the interior decoration of their living rooms and dining rooms that displayed mythological motifs and nude gods. The New Testament sources repeatedly refer to discussions about Jewish-Christian sensibilities. Gentile-Christian sensibilities are not discussed: perhaps Gentile Christians were quicker or more radical in their willingness to abandon religious traditions and transform cultural customs. Paul expected that faith in the one and only God and in his Messiah Jesus would transform cultural traditions, which in antiquity were always religious traditions as well. In 1 Cor 9:19-23 Paul describes the principles of his missionary praxis without specifying the limits of accommodation.

6. Paul seeks to win "more" people (τοὺς πλείονας, *tous pleionias* [1 Cor 9:19]). The unusual Greek phrase certainly does not mean "the majority, most,"[150] as Paul knows that most times only a few people come to faith (cf. 1 Cor 9:22). Perhaps Paul wants to say that he would win even fewer people for faith in Christ if he behaved differently—for example, if he always displayed the full scope of his freedom. "If he made it difficult for his listeners to understand the Word by showing them the distance that separates him from them, the number of people whom he might win would be smaller than it is now when he makes himself subject to all."[151]

7. Paul emphasizes that the goal of his missionary work is to "win" people (κερδαίνειν, *kerdainein* [1 Cor 9:19, 20a, 20b, 21, 22]). In extrabiblical Greek the verb *kerdainein* means "to gain, derive profit or advantage, make profit" and is never used in a figurative sense with people as direct object; in the Septuagint the term is not used at all.

David Daube suggests that the term comes from the terminology of the Jewish proselyte mission: the Hebrew verb שָׂכַר (*śakar*), often used in the Niphal נִשְׂכַּר (*niśkar*) or the Hiphil הִשְׂתַּכֵּר (*hiśtakker*), means "to earn, profit." The Greek phrase was used by Symmachus as a translation of *śakar* (Eccl 4:9), which is used in some rabbinic texts in the sense of "winning people," referring to Israelites who had been rejected by God but whom God "wins" again.[152] Daube traces this meaning of the term to Jews or rabbis who "win" proselytes. Many New Testament scholars have adopted this interpretation,[153] even though Daube points out that he did not find passages in the rabbinic texts in which נִשְׂכַּר or הִשְׂתַּכֵּר is used in connection with the conversion of a Gentile. Thus we should not

---

[150]BAA 1382; BDAG 848 ("perhaps"); Schrage, *1 Kor,* 2:333 (translation).

[151]Schlatter, *Kor,* 280; also Kremer, *1 Kor,* 193; Schrage, *1 Kor,* 2:339 (as a possibility). Lindemann (*1 Kor,* 211) interprets Paul's statement as "a sign of realistic thinking."

[152]Daube 1948, 352-61, with reference to *Pesiq. Rab.* 166b; 32b-33a; *b Pesah* 119a.

[153]See H. Schlier, *ThWNT* 3:672 (*TDNT* 3:672-73); G. Schneider, *EWNT* 2:700 (*EDNT* 2:283-84); Schrage, *1 Kor,* 1:339; Thiselton, *1 Cor,* 701; cautious is Luz, *Mt,* 2:43 with n. 30. The interpretation by B. Siede and K. Haacker (*ThBLNT* 2:1337-38) is lackluster.

regard the term *kerdainein* as a technical term of the Jewish proselyte mission, especially since the existence of such a mission has not been confirmed. In Mt 18:15 the verb *kerdainein* describes the "winning" of a church member who has sinned and is to be rescued for the community of Jesus' followers by personal exhortation: the member is not lost, but instead "wins" his or her life back, and the community "profits" from this person's repentance.

Whatever the origins of the meaning of *kerdainein* with the sense of "to win," there is no doubt that this term was highly significant in the early Christian mission (cf. 1 Cor 9:19-21; 1 Pet 3:1). To "win" a person means to "rescue" him or her,[154] as the formulation 1 Cor 9:22 demonstrates: it is the convert who has a "gain." But the apostle "profits" as well: the metaphor of building with durable materials in 1 Cor 3:12-15 emphasizes that Paul, as preacher of the gospel, knows himself responsible to God, who will examine his work for its durability on judgment day.[155] His work as a missionary is durable when Jews and Gentiles are converted to faith in God's revelation in Jesus Christ.

8. The normative center of the accommodating behavior of the missionary is the gospel, not the pragmatic motif of effectivity: "I do it all for the sake of the gospel, so that I may share in its blessings" (1 Cor 9:23). The phrase "for the sake of the gospel" (διὰ τὸ εὐαγγέλιον, *dia to euangelion*) excludes the abandonment of the gospel. Wolfgang Schrage comments, "One surely cannot mention Paul in the same breath with relativism, lack of principles, syncretism, tolerance for anything and everybody. . . . Nor is this about currying favor or about tactical missionary tricks. If this had been Paul's motto, he could have saved himself many struggles, including his letter to the Corinthians, and let the enthusiasts continue to do mischief. There is indeed a boundary."[156] Paul argues not for cultural relativism but for cultural relevance.[157] Henry Chadwick suggests that Paul argues for elasticity and flexibility that allows him to even agree to extreme positions, and that he introduces restrictions only ad hoc, depending on the situation.[158] This view fails to understand the fundamental fact that Paul is not tied to the communicative situation: he is "slave" of his listeners always and only as "slave of Christ."

9. The central content of Paul's missionary proclamation is "the gospel" (1 Cor 9:23). He came to Corinth with "the gospel of Christ" (2 Cor 10:14), which God had entrusted to him (1 Thess 2:4). The "pillar apostles" in Jerusalem recognized and affirmed that God had entrusted him with "the gospel for the uncircumcised" (Gal 2:7). In Troas he preached "the gospel of Christ" (2 Cor 2:12). The Christians in Philippi worked with Paul for "the gospel" (Phil 1:5). Paul de-

---

[154]The explanation of Lindemann (*1 Kor,* 211) that it was clear for Paul that "church work should be as successful as possible" is anachronistic and superficial.

[155]Thiselton, *1 Cor,* 701.

[156]Schrage, *1 Kor,* 2:347; cf. Bornkamm 1971, 151.

[157]Nida 1954, 52.

[158]Chadwick 1954-1955, 261-75; similarly Bennett 1980.

votes himself totally to the task of proclaiming "the gospel of God" among the Gentiles (Rom 15:16), whose servant he has become (Col 1:23).

10. The *cantus firmus* of missionary outreach among the nations is the sacrificial love of the missionary. Paul's missionary rule refers to the "weak" because he discusses the problems in the Corinthian church and the behavior of Christians who are invited to the home of a pagan acquaintance or business partner and face the question of whether they should eat meat sacrificed to idols or not. Paul expects that the strong relinquish "any demonstration of his freedom if the brother could be exposed to danger, even when the strong thinks that the understanding of the brother is limited or when it indeed is limited."[159] The strong person is told to respect the fact that the weak person wants to be obedient in the framework of his or her understanding. "And this intention is the key to the interpretation of the canon of Paul's missionary praxis. It is the intention of love. Love limits freedom—the freedom that I could have if I were alone. But the gospel never allows that it is all about myself." There is always the brother and the sister and the people, Jews and Gentiles, who have not heard or who have not yet accepted the gospel.

1 Cor 15:1-11

A third text in which Paul formulates his missionary self-understanding is 1 Cor 15:1-11, the first section of the apostle's exposition of the resurrection:

1 Cor 15:1-11: "Now I would remind you, brothers and sisters, of the good news that I proclaimed to you, which you in turn received, in which also you stand, [2]through which also you are being saved, if you hold firmly to the message that I proclaimed to you—unless you have come to believe in vain. [3]For I handed on to you as of first importance what I in turn had received: that Christ died for our sins in accordance with the scriptures, [4]and that he was buried, and that he was raised on the third day in accordance with the scriptures, [5]and that he appeared to Cephas, then to the twelve. [6]Then he appeared to more than five hundred brothers and sisters at one time, most of whom are still alive, though some have died. [7]Then he appeared to James, then to all the apostles. [8]Last of all, as to one untimely born, he appeared also to me. [9]For I am the least of the apostles, unfit to be called an apostle, because I persecuted the church of God. [10]But by the grace of God I am what I am, and his grace toward me has not been in vain. On the contrary, I worked harder than any of them—though it was not I, but the grace of God that is with me. [11]Whether then it was I or they, so we proclaim and so you have come to believe."

In his interaction with those who reject the teaching of the resurrection of the body, Paul reminds the Christians in Corinth of the message that he preached as a pioneer missionary in their city. The following points are important for Paul.[160]

---

[159]Eichholz 1972, 55; the quotation that follows above, ibid.
[160]See, besides the commentaries, Lohse 1991.

1. Paul preaches the gospel (τὸ εὐαγγέλιον, *to euangelion*) of Jesus, the cru-cified and risen Messiah, who died for the sins of humankind. The proclamation of this message leads people to faith in Jesus Christ and thus to salvation (σῴζεσθε, *sōzesthe* [1 Cor 15:2]). Since it is faith in Jesus Christ that saves from God's wrath, the gospel is "the power of God for salvation to everyone who has faith" (Rom 1:16).

2. The preacher communicates to the listeners the content of faith. Paul passed on to the citizens of Corinth (παρέδωκα, *paredōka*) what he has received (παρέλαβον, *parelabon* [1 Cor 15:3]). "The Corinthians did not receive the gos-pel's message of salvation 'straight from heaven' or from any Tom, Dick or Harry, but from the apostle . . . whose content has been assigned to him."[161] Paul proclaims not a message that he created or invented but a message whose content has been prescribed. The encounter with the crucified and risen Christ is possible "after the end of the appearances (cf. v. 8) only through the word that effects salvation and leads to faith (vv. 2, 11)."

3. The gospel is communicated through oral proclamation (εὐηγγελισάμην, *euēngelisamēn* [1 Cor 15:1, 2]; κηρύσσομεν, *kēryssomen* [1 Cor 15:11])—that is, in missionary preaching and in the instruction of believers in the church.

4. The proclamation of the gospel employs fixed formulations, traditional wording (1 Cor 15:3b-5) that reaches back to the earliest beginnings of the Christian community and summarizes the essential content of the gospel, which is both fundamental and possesses material priority over all else.[162] Eduard Lohse states, "Christians recognize from the start the unity that links all members of the one people of God as they speak the familiar words of the common con-fession."[163] Paul often varies traditional creedal formulations and adds explana-tory comments and an explanatory conclusion (as here in 1 Cor 15:6-8). The gospel is not preached with stereotypical formulas in perpetual repetition; rather, "it is explained in expository preaching, whose task it is to demonstrate the present validity of the word that has been received." Paul emphasizes at the end of the passage, however, that all missionaries, preachers and teachers pro-claim the same gospel (1 Cor 15:11).

5. Paul the missionary knows that the proclamation of the gospel and the ac-ceptance of the gospel through faith in Jesus Christ represent only the begin-ning: new believers must maintain the "stand" that they have gained in and through the gospel (ἐν ᾧ καὶ ἑστήκατε [1 Cor 15:1]); they must "hold firmly" to the message that has been preached (εἰ κατέχετε [1 Cor 15:2]) so that it will be-

---

[161]Schrage, *1 Kor,* 4:28; the quotation that follows above, ibid. Lindemann (*1 Kor,* 328) argues that Paul only wants to say "that the formula that he will quote has not been created by him-self." This interpretation is too restrictive: in 1 Cor 15:3 Paul is concerned not with creedal formulas as such but with the central content of the early Christian proclamation.

[162]Schrage, *1 Kor,* 4:32; for the discussion of the tradition that Paul quotes see ibid., 18-24.

[163]Lohse 1991, 173; the quotation that follows above, ibid., 174.

come evident that their faith is not an illusion (εἰκῇ [1 Cor 15:2]) but a faith that is sure and firm. And this is the reason why Paul writes his letter to the Corinthian Christians: the truth of the gospel needs to be explained by the missionary and the teachers of the church again and again.

2 Cor 2:14-16

When Paul reviews his relationship with the Corinthian church in his second letter, he formulates his understanding of his missionary work with the metaphor of the Roman triumphal procession.

2 Cor 2:14-16: "But thanks be to God, who in Christ always leads us in triumphal procession [πάντοτε θριαμβεύοντι ἡμᾶς ἐν τῷ Χριστῷ], and through us spreads in every place the fragrance that comes from knowing him [τὴν ὀσμὴν τῆς γνώσεως αὐτοῦ φανεροῦντι]. [15]For we are the aroma of Christ to God among those who are being saved and among those who are perishing; [16]to the one a fragrance from death to death [ὀσμὴ ἐκ θανάτου εἰς θάνατον], to the other a fragrance from life to life [ὀσμὴ ἐκ ζωῆς εἰς ζωήν]."

Paul uses the Roman *pompa triumphalis* to describe his missionary existence. Some scholars dispute this,[164] but most agree that this is the background of Paul's description.[165] Apart from Latin parallels, there is also evidence in Greek for the figurative use of the metaphor of the triumphal procession.[166] The verb *thriambeuein* without accusative object means "to celebrate a prior victory by means of a triumph," with accusative object (as in 2 Cor 2:14) "to celebrate (by means of a triumph) a victory over," and in the passive voice (as in 2 Cor 2:14) "to be displayed (as a prisoner of war) in a triumph." The term regularly refers to military victories that the Romans celebrated with a *pompa triumphalis*.[167]

A triumphal procession, which the senate had to authorize, honored a victorious general who had been granted the *imperium* and who had won a just war (*bellum iustum*) in which at least five thousand enemies had been killed. The triumphant general sat in a carriage drawn by four white horses (since Julius Caesar); he was clothed in a purple toga and his

---

[164]See G. Dautzenberg, "θριαμβεύω," *EWNT* 2:385 (*EDNT* 2:155); Dautzenberg translates with "make known."

[165]G. Delling, "θριαμβεύω," *ThWNT* 3:159-60 (*TDNT* 3:159-60); L. Williamson, "Led in Triumph: Paul's Use of thriambeuō," *Int* 22 (1968) 317-32; P. Marshall, "A Metaphor of Social Shame: ΘΡΙΑΜΒΕΥΕΙΝ in 2 Cor 2:14," *NovT* 25 (1983): 302-17; Hafemann 1986, 43-54; Breytenbach 1990.

[166]For Latin examples see Marshall, "A Metaphor of Social Shame," 304-6; for the reference to Epictetus 3.24.85 see Breytenbach 1990, 264; for the definitions that follow above see ibid., 260, 262, 264-65.

[167]See Helmuth Vretska, *KP* 5:973-75; Ernst Badian, *OCD* 1554; Ernst Künzl, *Der römische Triumph: Siegesfeiern im antiken Rom* (Munich: Beck, 1988); Hendrik S. Versnel, *Triumphus: An Inquiry into the Origin, Development and Meaning of the Roman Triumph* (Leiden: Brill, 1970); Brent R. Kinman, *Jesus' Entry into Jerusalem: In the Context of Lukan Theology and the Politics of His Day* (AGJU 28; Leiden: Brill, 1995), 25-47.

face was painted red. A slave held a laurel wreath above his head to remind him of his mortality. The procession moved from the Campus Martius to the temple of Jupiter Optimus Maximus. At the head of the procession, the victory was portrayed (on paintings) and the booty was displayed, followed by lictors with *fasces* wrapped in laurel, followed by prominent prisoners (who subsequently were executed, generally) and prisoners of war who had been released (clothed as freedmen of the victorious general); then came the carriage of the triumphant general, followed by the troops and the sacrificial animals. The senate and the members of the magistrate were expected to accompany the procession. Musicians and carriers of cinnamon, incense and torches participated as well. Josephus describes in *B.J.* 7.132-157 the Roman triumph over the defeated Jews after the catastrophe of A.D. 70.

When Paul compares his missionary work with a Roman triumph, he expresses the following convictions about his identity as a missionary.[168]

1. Paul understands his missionary outreach as public proclamation of the victory of God, who defeated him who had persecuted the eschatological people of God, on the road to Damascus—a victory that is being celebrated in a continuous triumphal procession in the missionary travels of the apostle (emphasis on the accusative object).[169]

Scott Hafemann suggests a different interpretation: Paul understands himself as prisoner of war, sentenced to death, whom God has defeated, displaying him in his triumphal procession (emphasis on the passive voice). The reference to the "fragrance" (*osmē*) and the "aroma" (*euōdia*) that Paul says he is spreading is connected with Old Testament passages in which these terms relate to the fragrance of sacrifices (e.g., Gen 8:21; Ezek 20:40-41).[170] This interpretation understands Paul as saying that he is marching in Christ's triumphal procession as prisoner of war sentenced to death, a reality that has a revelatory function: the "sacrificial fragrance" of his apostolic sufferings is being made known everywhere through his apostolic ministry. One problem for this interpretation is the fact that not all prisoners of war who were displayed in a triumphal procession were subsequently executed. Another problem is that the terms *osmē* and *euōdia* do not automatically allude to sacrifices, at least not in the context of 2 Cor 2:14-15. We should also note that sacrificial animals were taken along in a Roman triumph: Paul would identify himself with the prisoners of war in a triumph in 2 Cor 2:14a, and with the sacrificial animals in 2 Cor 2:14b, 15. This seems hardly plausible, if the emphasis is less on the (impending) death of the prisoner of war but rather more on the shame to which Paul was exposed. In this case Paul would emphasize the humiliations that he suffers as an apostle.[171] However, the readers of Paul's letter would not understand such a connotation in his reference to the Roman triumphal procession without an explanation.

Paul certainly never forgot that he once persecuted the Christian churches when

---

[168]Paul frequently uses military metaphors when describing his missionary work: 1 Thess 5:8; Rom 6:13; 10:3-4; 13:12; 2 Cor 6:7; 10:3-5; Eph 6:13-18; Philem 2; 1 Tim 6:12; 2 Tim 2:4.

[169]Breytenbach 1990, 268-69; Lambrecht, *2 Cor,* 38-39.

[170]Hafemann 1990, 35-79, for the comment that follows above see ibid., 45-46; see also idem 2000, esp. 174-80.

[171]Thus P. Marshall, "A Metaphor of Social Shame," 302-17. Schröter's critique (1993, 21-23) of Hafemann's position is one-sided; Schröter himself assumes a reference to Paul's conversion and call; see also Hafemann 2000, 175 n. 27.

he was a rabbi in Jerusalem, that he was active as an enemy of God and of Jesus the Messiah, and that God defeated him when Jesus Christ revealed himself to him on the road to Damascus. Paul, the great missionary to the Gentiles, never took his conversion and his faith in Jesus Christ for granted.

2. Paul owes his missionary existence to the irresistible power of God. This point clearly is a main element in Paul's metaphor of the Roman triumphal procession.[172] Paul's status as apostle is not the result of personal achievements; on the contrary, his self-understanding is completely determined by the conviction that God overpowered him on the road to Damascus. The manifestation of God's power in his life and in his mission is inseparably connected with Jesus Christ (ἐν τῷ Χριστῷ [2 Cor 2:14]).

Paul's statement must be understood against the background of his interaction with Christians in the Corinthian church who, furnished with letters of recommendation, claim to be "apostles of Christ" (cf. 2 Cor 11:13), who cast doubts on Paul's apostolic authority and proclamation and who influence people by emphasizing miracles, states of ecstasy, visions and electrifying rhetoric. Paul calls the activity and the message of these Christians a falsification of the word of God (2 Cor 2:17; 4:2), as a "different gospel" inspired by a "different spirit" (2 Cor 11:4) "because they claim for themselves abilities, acts of salvation and glory in such a way that there remains no room for the reality of God's gracious power."[173] These Christian teachers were so much taken with their "perfection enthusiasm" that they despised suffering and regarded the suffering of Paul as proof that the "weak apostle" was no real apostle at all (cf. 2 Cor 4:8-18; 6:3-10; 10:2, 10; 11:21; 13:2). Paul attacks these teachers' position as a one-sided Christology, as a fundamental misunderstanding of the grace and the power of God manifested in the cross (2 Cor 13:4). Horst Baum comments, "What the Corinthians may have regarded as improvement of their Christian life, as intensification of their church experience and as enhancement of their glory and fame, having sympathy for and listening to the opponents, is a lethal danger: the danger of falling from faith in Christ by relying on external, impressive, sarkic advantages (2 Cor 13:4, 5); the delusion of being able to avoid every suffering and cross by a one-sided and utopian *doxa* enthusiasm and to live already 'by sight' rather than 'by faith' (2 Cor 5:7; cf. also Phil 3:12ff.); the danger that people put themselves not theoretically but *factually* in the place of Christ, as they rob the Crucified of his saving power in their egoistic thinking, clamoring for renown and glory."

3. Paul's conversion is "fragrance" (ὀσμή, *osmē*) and "aroma" (εὐωδία, *euōdia*). These terms have been interpreted in various ways.[174] It is unlikely that Paul refers to the incense of the Roman triumphal procession, or to perfume in general, in terms of the presence of God. Most explanations face the problem that the "fragrance" that Paul refers to has a twofold effect, leading both to life and to death. This makes it unlikely that, for example, Paul alludes to the Jewish tradition of divine wisdom, whose "fragrance" gives life and guarantees that people

---

[172]See Thrall, *2 Cor,* 1:195.
[173]H. Baum 1977, 219; the quotation that follows above, ibid.
[174]See Thrall, *2 Cor,* 1:196-207; for the comments that follow above see ibid.

"prosper" (Sir 24:15; 39:13-14). Some scholars point to rabbinic texts that describe the Torah in terms of a medicine that turns out to be either elixir of life (חיים סם, *sam ḥayîm*) or deadly poison (המות סם, *sam ha-māwet*), depending on one's reaction to the commandments of the Torah: the gospel of Jesus Christ that Paul proclaims as God's revelation is either accepted as reality that gives life or is rejected, which leads to death. Some scholars suggest that Old Testament sacrifices provide the background for Paul's description, since the two terms are combined in the Septuagint in the phrase ὀσμὴ εὐωδίας (*osmē euōdias*),[175] and since Paul describes his missionary work as a priestly ministry in other passages (cf. Rom 15:16): the "fragrance" of the proclamation of the gospel originates "from" (ἐκ, *ek*) death, referring to the death of Jesus Christ, and it originates "from" (ἐκ, *ek*) life, meaning the resurrection of Jesus. People who reject the gospel see only Jesus' death and thus are not saved from their own (eternal) death, while people who are saved know and understand Jesus as the risen Kyrios and have accepted him as the source of their (eternal) life. Whatever the background of Paul's metaphor of "fragrance" and "aroma," it remains true that many people have heard the gospel of God's revelation in Jesus Christ as a result of Paul's missionary work, even though not all who have heard believe.[176]

2 Cor 4:7-15

A fifth text that expresses Paul's missionary self-understanding is 2 Cor 4:7-15:[177]

"But we have this treasure in clay jars, so that it may be made clear that this extraordinary power belongs to God and does not come from us. [8]We are afflicted in every way, but not crushed; perplexed, but not driven to despair; [9]persecuted, but not forsaken; struck down, but not destroyed; [10]always carrying in the body the death of Jesus, so that the life of Jesus may also be made visible in our bodies. [11]For while we live, we are always being given up to death for Jesus' sake, so that the life of Jesus may be made visible in our mortal flesh. [12]So death is at work in us, but life in you. [13]But just as we have the same spirit of faith that is in accordance with scripture—'I believed, and so I spoke'—we also believe, and so we speak, [14]because we know that the one who raised the Lord Jesus will raise us also with Jesus, and will bring us with you into his presence. [15]Yes, everything is for your sake, so that grace, as it extends to more and more people, may increase thanksgiving, to the glory of God."

Paul describes in this passage the realities of his missionary work, external realities that do not correspond at all to the divine radiance of the knowledge of God that the gospel of Jesus Christ communicates (2 Cor 4:6). Paul emphasizes the following points.

---

[175]This expression occurs fifty-eight times: e.g., Gen 8:21; Ex 29:18, 25, 41; Lev 1:9, 13, 17; 2:2, 9, 12; 3:5, 11, 16.

[176]Legrand 1989, 310-11.

[177]See, besides the commentaries, Schröter 1993, 142-207. Cartledge (1993) attempts to provide a missiological contextualization of this text.

1. The gospel is a "treasure" (θησαυρός, *thēsauros* [2 Cor 4:7a]), a valuable and desirable reality that guarantees life and makes people truly fulfilled and glad. As a missionary Paul proclaims the good news that everyone who believes in Jesus Christ will own, will participate in, this treasure.

2. This treasure of the gospel is contained in "clay jars" (ὀστράκινα σκεύη, *ostrakina skeuē* [2 Cor 4:7a]): missionaries who proclaim the gospel are, like pottery made of clay, weak, fragile, not very impressive, in themselves quite insignificant.[178] Paul emphasizes that the Corinthians should not take offense if some people regard his person or the rhetoric of his preaching and teaching as unimpressive: clay jars that contain a valuable treasure are *quantité négligeable,* insignificant, undeserving of much attention or excitement.

3. The fact that Paul's missionary proclamation is unimpressive serves to emphasize that the extraordinary power (ἡ ὑπερβολὴ τῆς δυνάμεως, *hē hyperbole tēs dynameōs*) that can be observed in the work of the missionaries is exclusively God's power and not the power of the missionary (μὴ ἐξ ἡμῶν, *mē ex hēmōn* [2 Cor 4:7b]). Friedrich Lang observes, "The fact that God uses weak people as instruments to communicate the message of salvation has a deeper reason and serves a salutary purpose: it clarifies that the power that transcends human possibilities comes from God and not from apostles. The redemptive effect of the proclamation derives not from the dazzling magnetism of the human instrument but from the truth of the word of God and the power of the Spirit."[179]

4. Paul enumerates the difficulties and the suffering that he encountered and continues to experience in his missionary work. He has been "hard pressed on every side" (ἐν παντὶ θλιβόμενοι, *en panti thlibomenoi* [2 Cor 4:8a]): he was repeatedly attacked by unbelievers, both Jews and pagans, but also by Christians, in Jerusalem and also in Corinth, who criticized his theology, ethics and rhetoric. Paul often was "perplexed" (ἀπορούμενοι, *aporoumenoi* [2 Cor 4:8b]): once he despaired of life in an incident that took place in the province of Asia (2 Cor 1:8), perhaps a serious illness or a situation in which he nearly died. Paul was "persecuted" (διωκόμενοι, *diōkomenoi* [2 Cor 4:9a]) and he was "struck down" (καταβαλλόμενοι, *kataballomenoi* [2 Cor 4:9b]): he had powerful enemies who put him under immense pressure. In some situations he was literally struck to the ground—for example, his experience of being stoned by a crowd in Lystra.

5. Paul describes his life as a paradox: he experiences the death of Jesus Christ in his own body (2 Cor 4:10). This means that his suffering represents a public demonstration, a graphic image of the death of Jesus Christ. And the power of God that is displayed in his life and ministry, supporting him in the midst of the trials and the attacks, is evidence for the reality of the resurrection

---

[178]For a discussion of the background of this metaphor see Martin, *2 Cor,* 85; Thrall, *2 Cor,* 1:322-24.

[179]Lang, *Kor,* 280, with reference to 1 Cor 2:4.

of Jesus Christ in the present.[180] The Corinthians, whom Paul challenges to imitate him (1 Cor 11:1), see in Paul "the structure of the gospel that is established on the life of Christ, which in the end is nothing else than the structure of the cross: strength in weakness, life from death."[181] Adolf Schlatter remarks that Paul "reveals that he proclaims the One who did not circumvent the attack of his enemies or his suffering and who not only served God because he gave his life but also glorified him by being killed, since humanity lives under the judgment that procures death. Paul was ready to suffer on account of the connection between his suffering and Jesus' suffering; thus his suffering serves his ministry as a messenger. Paul tells his own passion narrative as Jesus' herald, but he not only tells this story, he also experienced it (Phil 3:10)."

6. Paul never abandons the hope that more people might be converted to faith in the gospel of Jesus Christ: the "thanksgiving" of more and more people (διὰ τῶν πλειόνων τὴν εὐχαριστίαν, *dia tōn pleionōn tēn eucharistian* [2 Cor 4:15]) refers probably to non-Christians who accept the gospel of the grace of God, which thus reaches more and more people.[182] Margaret Thrall notes, "Divine grace increases in influence within a Christian community by means of the growing numbers within whom it becomes operative and finds a genuine response."

2 Cor 5:20

Paul formulates his understanding of himself and his coworkers as messengers of Jesus Christ succinctly in 2 Cor 5:20. This is the first passage in which Paul uses the term πρεσβεύειν (*presbeuein*), which derives from the languages of diplomacy, describing the activity of "envoys" or "ambassadors." Paul uses the verb also in Eph 6:20.[183]

2 Cor 5:20: "So we are ambassadors for Christ [ὑπὲρ Χριστοῦ οὖν πρεσβεύομεν], since God is making his appeal through us [ὡς τοῦ θεοῦ παρακαλοῦντος δι᾽ ἡμῶν]; we entreat you on behalf of Christ, be reconciled to God."

Eph 6:18-20: "Pray in the Spirit at all times in every prayer and supplication. To that end keep alert and always persevere in supplication for all the saints. [19]Pray also for me, so that when I speak, a message may be given to me to make known with boldness the mystery of the gospel, [20]for which I am an ambassador in chains [ὑπὲρ οὗ πρεσβεύω ἐν ἁλύσει]. Pray that I may declare it boldly, as I must speak."

The person of the "envoy" or "ambassador" (πρεσβευτής, *presbeutēs;* Lat., *legatus*) played a very important role in diplomacy in the Hellenistic world.[184] The

---

[180]See Thrall, *2 Cor,* 1:334-35.
[181]Roloff 1993, 135. The quotation that follows above is from Schlatter, *Kor,* 533.
[182]See Martin, *2 Cor,* 90; Thrall, *2 Cor,* 1:344-47; the quotation that follows, ibid., 346-47.
[183]The noun πρεσβεία (*presbeia*) occurs in the New Testament only in Lk 14:32; 19:14.

following characteristics and responsibilities of the Hellenistic "envoy" are important. (1) The sender and the envoy are connected by a specific and unique relationship: the envoy knew the interests of the principal who appointed him, and he normally knew the content of the message that he was to carry and that he might need to explain. The ambassador is the representative of the principal. Ambassadors usually were leading citizens who were wealthy, rhetorically gifted and highly regarded in their city. (2) The principal or patron conveys to the ambassador the authority to speak for him within the framework of the instructions that he has received. The ambassador carries a written or an oral message of his patron to the recipients. (3) An envoy was treated according to the status of his principal: the envoy of an aristocrat had to be treated like an aristocrat and not like a slave (even though the envoy might be a slave). The proper reception of the envoy signals the proper reception of the principal or of his message. (4) The behavior of the envoy had to correspond to the dignity of the principal. Paul uses the metaphor of the ambassador to make the following points.[185]

1. Paul knows Jesus the Messiah, who commissioned him as an ambassador, he shares his interests, and he knows the content of the message that he has been directed to carry to people. He speaks "on behalf of Christ" as Jesus Christ speaks "in him" (cf. 2 Cor 13:3); he communicates "what Christ has accomplished" through him (Rom 15:18). When people hear Paul speaking, they hear Jesus; when they see Paul, they should see Jesus.

2. Paul preaches and teaches in the authority of Jesus Christ: he is Jesus' apostle "by the will of God" (2 Cor 1:1). That is why it would be preposterous if he boasted about his accomplishments to the Corinthians (2 Cor 5:12); he does not need letters of recommendation (2 Cor 3:1), as it is his goal to "please" the Lord (2 Cor 5:9). On the other hand, the fact that he has been sent by Jesus Christ establishes his "high" status: he is the envoy of the Messiah!

Less plausible is the suggestion by Anthony Bash, who maintains that Paul had a "high standing" as a result of his Jewish identity and his Roman citizenship:[186] these biographical details play no role whatsoever in the context of 2 Cor 5:20 or Eph 6:20, and the referent to Paul's travels[187] and to his suffering (2 Cor 6:4-10) is a "boasting" to which the Corinthians have forced Paul, a boasting that Paul gladly would do without (2 Cor 5:13; 12,11). The Corinthians are not to be "proud" of him (cf. 2 Cor 5:12a; 12:11) because he has a "high standing" that justifies his status as Christ's ambassador; rather, they should be "proud" of him because he is their "father" who can expect obedience and who can hope

---

[184]See Bornkamm, *ThWNT* 6:680-82 (*TDNT* 6:681-83); D. Kienast, "Presbeia," PWSup 13 (1973): 499-628; Spicq, *TLNT* 3:172-76; Mosley 1973; Breytenbach 1989, 64-65; M. Mitchell 1992; and especially Bash 1997.

[185]See, besides the commentaries, particularly Bash 1997, 87-116.

[186]Bash 1997, 105-7.

[187]Cf. 2 Cor 1:8 (Asia); 1:16 (Judea); 1:16; 2:13; 7:5 (Macedonia); 1:23 (Corinth); 2:12 (Troas).

that they will imitate his behavior.[188] Bash also argues that Paul's use of the metaphor of the ambassador was regarded by the Corinthians as scandalous: an ambassador appeared as petitioner, and when Paul describes himself as "ambassador of Christ," both Jesus Christ and God appear as petitioners as well, a notion that provoked a robust reaction among the Corinthians that prompted Paul in 2 Cor 10—13 to defend his apostolic authority.[189] This interpretation is unconvincing because the text provides no concession for this reconstruction.

3. As Paul is the ambassador of Jesus Christ, he can expect a reception among the Corinthian Christians that corresponds to this status. He admonishes the believers in the church in Corinth because some reject him: "We have spoken frankly to you Corinthians; our heart is wide open to you. There is no restriction in our affections, but only in yours. In return—I speak as to children—open wide your hearts also" (2 Cor 6:11-13). Paul is received by people who accept the gospel in correspondence with his status as God's messenger: "Though my condition put you to the test, you did not scorn or despise me, but welcomed me as an angel of God [ὡς ἄγγελον θεοῦ], as Christ Jesus" (Gal 4:14).

4. Paul's behavior corresponds to his principal, Jesus Christ. The apostle sometimes describes his connection with Jesus in a rather graphic manner: "I carry the marks of Jesus branded on my body" (Gal 6:17); "for we are the aroma of Christ to God" (2 Cor 2:15); "always carrying in the body the death of Jesus" (2 Cor 4:10).

5. When Paul writes that he is Christ's "ambassador in chains" (Eph 6:20), this is not only an ironic statement but also a contradiction: the reference to the chains contradicts the status, honor and dignity of an ambassador. The imprisonment of an ambassador was regarded as a serious insult not only to the ambassador but also to his principal.[190] The chains are at the same time a symbol for the commission that Paul had been given: his life as ambassador of Christ is totally controlled by God, who demands that he preach the gospel "with boldness" (παρρησιάσωμαι ὡς δεῖ με λαλῆσαι [Eph 6:20; cf. 1 Cor 9:16-17]). This is why he asks the Christians in Ephesus to pray for him "so that when I speak, a message may be given to me to make known with boldness the mystery of the gospel" (ἐν παρρησίᾳ γνωρίσαι τὸ μυστήριον τοῦ εὐαγγελίου [Eph 6:19]). What is important, therefore, is not the well-being of the suffering of the ambassador but the fulfillment of the commission that he has been given. As a prisoner in Caesarea Paul had the opportunity to explain the gospel of Jesus Christ before the Jewish king and the Roman governor, and as a prisoner in Rome he waits

---

[188]See Martin, *2 Cor*, 124, with reference to 1 Cor 4:21; 2 Cor 1:9; 7:15; 10:6; Phil 2:12; Philem 21; as well as 1 Cor 4:16; 10:33—11:1; 1 Thess 1:6; Phil 3:17; 4:9; Gal 4:12.

[189]Bash 1997, 108-16.

[190]Bash 1997, 132: "An embassy by a prisoner . . . is without precedent and contradicts the status, honour and prestige characteristic of ambassadors." Cf. O'Brien, *Eph*, 488-89; for the comments that follow above see ibid.

for a hearing before one of the highest officials of the Roman Empire. If 2 Tim
4:17 refers to this hearing, then the prayer of Paul and of the Ephesian Christians
was answered: "But the Lord stood by me and gave me strength, so that through
me the message might be fully proclaimed and all the Gentiles might hear it
[ἀκούσωσιν πάντα τὰ ἔθνη, *akousōsin panta ta ethnē*]. So I was rescued from the
lion's mouth."

Rom 1:14

Paul briefly explains his self-understanding as a missionary in the introduction
to his letter to the Christians in Rome before he mentions the subject of the letter
in Rom 1:16-17.

Rom 1:14-15: "I am a debtor both to Greeks and to barbarians, both to the wise and to
the foolish—15hence my eagerness to proclaim the gospel to you also who are in Rome."

This basic statement must be understood in the context or Rom 1:16: "For I am
not ashamed of the gospel; it is the power of God for salvation to everyone
who has faith, to the Jew first and also to the Greek." Paul describes himself as
a missionary to people who have not heard the gospel or who have not yet
accepted the gospel. Adolf Schlatter observes that Paul "is the debtor of all people because he has what they lack and what they need. What he has and what
they have a right to receive is the message of God. Jesus' command that he give
his gift to the disciple in order that he may pass it on to others dominates Paul
as well."[191]

Paul states that God has commissioned him to proclaim the gospel to all people without any distinction: to the "Greeks" (*hellēnes*), meaning the elites of the
Greco-Roman world, as well as to the "foreigners" (*barbaroi*), meaning the people who had no Greek culture and whom the elites excluded from all decision-
making processes; to the "wise" (*sophoi*), meaning those who were educated,
probably those who had attended school, and to the "foolish" (*anoētoi*), meaning the uneducated. Paul the missionary deliberately disregards these social and
cultural categories and classifications, which were defined and drawn up by the
elites. Paul sees himself obligated "to exclude neither the Greek because as an
educated person he belongs to the ruling elite, nor the barbarian because he
has no culture and is of no significance (cf. 1 Cor 1:26ff.). The gospel concerns
all people without regard to person, as it makes all people equal *coram deo*."[192]
The language of Paul's preaching "is conditioned neither by the socio-cultural
committedness of people—both Greeks and barbarians are addressed—nor by
the eschatological and final boundary that the past history of salvation and of

---

[191]Schlatter, *Röm,* 31; cf. Minear 1959, 43-44.
[192]Wilckens, *Röm,* 1:81; the quotation that follows above, ibid., 1:92.

judgment has erected between those who have salvation and those who are distant. Faith in Christ as redemptive reliance upon the righteousness of God is open to both Jews and Gentiles. The gospel reaches everyone, as language of saving love, from beyond all these boundaries established by social and religious origins, in a totally unexpected way, and therefore in a manner that cannot be manipulated."

Rom 10:14-21

In Rom 10:14-21 Paul describes the missionary work of the apostles and thus his own missionary work. The quotation from Joel in Rom 10:13 raises the question of whether it is possible, and whether it is happening in the present, that "everyone who calls on the name of the Lord shall be saved."

Rom 10:14-21; 11:11-14: "But how are they to call on one in whom they have not believed? And how are they to believe in one of whom they have never heard? And how are they to hear without someone to proclaim him? [15]And how are they to proclaim him unless they are sent? As it is written, 'How beautiful are the feet of those who bring good news!' [Is 52:7] [16]But not all have obeyed the good news; for Isaiah says, 'Lord, who has believed our message?' [Is 53:1] [17]So faith comes from what is heard, and what is heard comes through the word of Christ. [18]But I ask, have they not heard? Indeed they have; for 'Their voice has gone out to all the earth, and their words to the ends of the world.' [Ps 19:5] [19]Again I ask, did Israel not understand? First Moses says, 'I will make you jealous of those who are not a nation; with a foolish nation I will make you angry.' [Deut 32:21] [20]Then Isaiah is so bold as to say, 'I have been found by those who did not seek me; I have shown myself to those who did not ask for me.' [Is 65:1] [21]But of Israel he says, 'All day long I have held out my hands to a disobedient and contrary people' [Is 65:2]. . . . [11:11]So I ask, have they stumbled so as to fall? By no means! But through their stumbling salvation has come to the Gentiles, so as to make Israel jealous. [12]Now if their stumbling means riches for the world, and if their defeat means riches for Gentiles, how much more will their full inclusion mean! [13]Now I am speaking to you Gentiles. Inasmuch then as I am an apostle to the Gentiles, I glorify my ministry [14]in order to make my own people jealous, and thus save some of them."

Many scholars suggest that Paul discusses in Rom 10:14-18 the mission to Israel—that is, to the Jews.[193] Richard Bell shows, however, that Paul describes the apostolic mission that seeks to reach both Jews and Gentiles.[194] The implied subject of "they are to call on" (ἐπικαλέσωνται, *epikalesōntai*) in Rom 10:14 is the expression "(all) who call on him" (ἐπικαλουμένους, *epikaloumenous*) in Rom 10:12, where Paul asserts that "there is no distinction between Jew and Greek." The universal scope of the proclamation of the gospel is also the subject in Rom 10:18. Paul emphasizes in Rom 10:14-21 the following convictions.

---

[193]See Michel, *Röm,* 332-37; Schlier, *Röm,* 316; Cranfield, *Rom,* 2:533; Munck 1954, 295-96.
[194]Bell 1994, 83-105; cf. Käsemann, *Röm,* 284 (ET, 293-94); Wilckens, *Röm,* 2:228; Dunn, *Rom,* 2:620; Moo, *Rom,* 662-63.

1. The apostolic mission involves the sending of (ἀποσταλῶσιν, *apostalōsin*) and proclamation by (κηρύξωσιν, *kēryxōsin*) preachers (κηρύσσοντος, *kēryssontos*), followed by hearing (ἤκουσαν, *ēkousan*), faith (ἐπίστευσαν, *episteusan*) and calling (ἐπικαλέσωνται, *epikalesōntai*) on the Lord. The sequence of these elements (stated rhetorically in reverse in Rom 10:14-15) is essential, as is demonstrated by Paul's argumentation with four parallel questions that form a logical chain and by the quotation from Is 52:7.

2. The focus is on the necessity of the proclamation of the gospel by messengers who have been sent by the Lord. The scriptural quotation in Rom 10:15 "shows that the sending on which all else depends has taken place and does take place."[195] Apostles and other missionaries do not preach from their own authority, and they do not preach a message that they have created themselves. They are messengers, ambassadors sent by God and empowered by the Spirit, who proclaim the word of God that saves. The sending of the messengers corresponds to the sending of the Son by the Father (Gal 4:4; cf. Mt 10:40; Jn 20:21). Ferdinand Hahn comments, "The essence of mission is implied in and established by Jesus' mission: the powerful, earthly activity for the salvation of all people."[196]

3. The primacy of the proclamation of the word is repeated and thus emphasized again in Rom 10:17: faith comes from the message that is heard (ἡ πίστις ἐξ ἀκοῆς, *hē pistis ex akoēs*) and in which the word of the crucified and risen Jesus Christ is manifested (ἡ δὲ ἀκοὴ διὰ ῥήματος Χριστοῦ, *hē akoē dia rhēmatos Christou*). The genitive construction "word of Christ" is ambiguous, perhaps deliberately so: there is no need to decide between an objective genitive and a genitive of authorship. Paul asserts that Jesus himself speaks and acts in the proclamation of the word of faith in the crucified and risen Christ.[197]

4. The quotation in Rom 10:15 of Is 52:7, a text that Jewish exegetes interpreted as a reference to the messianic period,[198] emphasizes the fulfillment of this promise in the sending of the apostolic messengers and thus highlights the eschatological character of the early Christian mission. Paul changes the singular participle (εὐαγγελιζομένου, *euangelizomenou* [LXX]) into the plural:[199] the proclamation activity of the messengers of the gospel realizes the salvation that God had promised. Paul omits the phrase "on the mountains," which focused the message of the messengers of joy announced by Isaiah on Mount Zion. Paul thus highlights his conviction that the mission of the messengers of the gospel is a

---

[195]Käsemann, *Röm,* 284 (ET, 294); cf. Cranfield, *Rom,* 2:534; Oss 1992, 90-91.
[196]Hahn 1984, 47.
[197]Käsemann, *Röm,* 285 (ET, 295); Wilckens, *Röm,* 2:229.
[198]Str-B 3:282-83; Michel, *Röm,* 333; Käsemann, *Röm,* 284 (ET, 294); Bell 1994, 87; now particularly J. Wagner 2002, 170-86.
[199]Perhaps by combining the quotation from Isaiah with Joel 3:5 LXX; see Stuhlmacher, *Röm,* 144.

universal mission. The "beautiful feet" should be interpreted as "timely feet":[200] the emphasis is on "the moment of the eschatological actualization of the promise" and on the implication that the "lone herald of the LXX" (πόδες εὐαγγελιζομέ-νου, *podes euangelizomenou*) has been transformed "into multiple preachers of the good news" (πόδες τῶν εὐαγγελιζομένων, *podes tōn euangelizomenōn*).

5. The missionaries experience the fact that "only very few" (οὐ πάντες, *ou pantes* [litotes]) became obedient to the gospel: the proclamation of the gospel of Jesus Christ has been largely rejected in Israel (Rom 10:16).[201] The reason for this rejection was not a lack of messengers but rather a lack of faith. Paul supports this assertion with a quotation from Is 53:1: as the message of the prophet encountered rejection, so the proclamation of the gospel is rejected by many Jews, despite the fact that they hear the message of the messengers of joy. Paul states that a word sent by God or a message authorized by God is not always accepted by everyone, not even Israel. In Rom 10:20-21 Paul refers to Isaiah's prophecy (in Is 65:1, 2)[202] and asserts that on the one hand, the Gentiles, who did not seek God, experience and receive God's revelation (Rom 10:20), and on the other hand, the Jews remain disobedient despite the fact that God holds out his hands to Israel every day (Rom 10:21). It is not because of God that the Gentiles receive God's righteousness while Israel does not, but because of Israel itself.[203]

6. The apostolic mission has a universal dimension. Paul uses in Rom 10:18 the language of Ps 19:5 to describe the universal scope of the proclamation of the gospel:[204] The voice of the gospel can be heard in "all the earth" (εἰς πᾶσαν τὴν γῆν, *eis pasan tēn gēn*); the word of the gospel goes out "to the ends of the world" (εἰς τὰ πέρατα τῆς οἰκουμένης, *eis ta perata tēs oikoumenēs*). These formulations very probably do not refer to the geography of the Roman Empire: Paul has not yet been to Spain.[205] Nor does Paul refer to the success of his missionary work in the Jewish communities of the Diaspora,[206] nor does he predict the future "success of Christian preaching" before the imminent return of Christ.[207] Ulrich Wilckens surely is correct when he states that Paul describes the

---

[200]BDAG, s.v. "ὡραῖος," 1103; Käsemann, *Röm*, 284-85 (ET, 294-95); Wilckens, *Röm*, 2:228; Dunn, *Rom*, 2:627-28; Fitzmyer, *Rom*, 597; Moo, *Rom*, 664; contra H. Balz, *EWNT* 3:1215 (*EDNT* 3:508). The quotations that follow above are from Käsemann, *Röm*, 284-85 (ET, 294-95), and J. Wagner 2002, 173, respectively.

[201]For arguments supporting the reference to Israel see Bell 1994, 90-92; see also Käsemann, *Röm*, 285 (ET, 295); Wilckens, *Röm*, 2:229; Moo, *Rom*, 664.

[202]See Oss 1992, 93-95; J. Wagner 2002, 205-17.

[203]Wilckens, *Röm*, 2:231.

[204]Hays 1989, 175; Moo, *Rom*, 667; for the comment that follows above see ibid. See also J. Wagner 2002, 184-86.

[205]See Bell 1994, 94.

[206]See Klausner 1950, 330-31; Munck 1954, 272, 275; 1956, 74-75; Blair 1965, 19-33.

[207]See Käsemann, *Röm*, 286 (ET, 296).

gospel as word of the risen Christ "that speaks from heaven to all nations."[208] Wilckens's comment that Paul speaks of the "eschatological reality of the word" that the human ambassadors simply "realize" is a nice formulation, but it leaves open the question of where this "eschatological reality" should be located between Jerusalem and the ends of the world. Paul either refers to people—Jews and Gentiles—who have heard the gospel, or he uses hyperbolic speech to emphasize that many people in many regions of the world have heard the gospel.[209] In Rom 10:19 Paul states that Israel knew that the gospel would go out both to Gentiles and to Jews: Moses prophesied (in Deut 32:21) that God would provoke Israel to jealous anger through "those who are not a nation" (ἐπ᾽ οὐκ ἔθνει, *ep᾽ ouk ethnei*).[210] The addition of converted Gentiles into the people of God provokes the Jews to a jealous and angry reaction against the messengers of the gospel and their message.[211] Since Israel has rejected the gospel, the Gentiles have received salvation (Rom 11:11): Paul repeatedly concentrates his missionary work on Gentiles after he had been rejected by Jews in whose synagogues he had preached.[212]

7. Paul interprets Israel's "jealousy" in Rom 11:11-14 positively in terms of God's salvation-historical purposes and in terms of his own hopes. Paul hopes and expects that the acceptance of the gospel by the Gentiles and the realization of messianic salvation in the Christian communities, predominantly Gentile outside of Judea, will provoke the unbelieving Jews to "jealousy" so that the Jews who have "stumbled" (Rom 11:11)—that is, rejected Jesus the Messiah and the righteousness of God that he offers—will see the reality of messianic salvation in the Gentile-Christian churches and be prompted to convert to faith in Jesus as well.

The view that this hope is "absurd"[213] certainly is located in the context of churches, such as state churches, in which everyone is baptized regardless, where no distinction is made between believers and unbelievers and where the notion of "conversion" has become difficult. Ernst Käsemann is correct when he states that "this hope can be imagined only if the conversion itself stands beyond any doubt and only if the way to it appears obscure." Paul, of course, speaks of truly converted people. It is important to note that the "obedience of faith" (Rom 1:5) of the converted Jews and Gentiles consists not simply in accepting the message of salvation but in "sanctification in active obedience" (Käsemann) as "subordination to the rule of Jesus."[214] The goal of Paul's missionary work was to help

---

[208]Wilckens, *Röm,* 2:230; for the comment that follows above see ibid.

[209]See Moo, *Rom,* 667.

[210]See Bell 1994, 95-103; Käsemann, *Röm,* 287 (ET, 297); Cranfield, *Rom,* 2:539; on Deut 32:21 and Is 65:1-2 in Rom 10:19-21 see further J. Wagner 2002, 187-217.

[211]See Moo, *Rom,* 668.

[212]Acts 13:44-47; 14:1-3; 18:4-7; 19:8-10; 28:23-29. See Moo, *Rom,* 687.

[213]See Käsemann, *Röm,* 295 (ET, 305); the quotation that follows above, ibid.; on Rom 1:5 see ibid., 12 (ET, 14).

[214]Stuhlmacher, *Röm,* 22; cf. Moo, *Rom,* 52. See Garlington 1991; for the comment that follows above see ibid., 254-55.

people of all nations, Jews and polytheists, to find saving faith in Jesus Christ and become members of the covenant that God has granted to his people. The "new creation" of the messianic era that began with Jesus Christ finds visible expression in the lives of believers and in the church. It is in view of this reality that the Jews should become "jealous" and be prompted to believe in Jesus the Messiah. This train of thought is not "fully apocalyptic" (Käsemann); rather, Paul thinks in terms of missionary strategy, in terms of concrete Christian communities whose members are consistent followers of Jesus whom the Holy Spirit made "alive in the Messiah Jesus" and whom he "set free from the law of sin and of death" (Rom 8:2), who do not live "according to the flesh" but who have "life and peace" through God's Spirit (Rom 8:6-16), and who therefore should be attractive for the Jews, who are still awaiting the arrival of the Messiah.

Paul understands himself as called to be an "apostle to the Gentiles" (εἰμι ἐγὼ ἐθνῶν ἀπόστολος, *eimi egō ethnōn apostolos* [Rom 11:13]). Does this mean that Paul thought of himself as the only missionary to the Gentiles? Does the agreement with Peter described in Gal 2:7-9 mean that Paul believed that he had a unique responsibility with regard to the Gentiles that no other apostle had? Is he the one and only missionary to the Gentiles?[215] Paul never would have asserted that Peter and James are the only missionaries to Jews, which makes it unlikely that he would have doubted that there are other missionaries to Gentiles.[216] The interpretation of Gal 2:7-9 will be discussed below (see §25.1).

Rom 15:15-21

Another text in which Paul describes his missionary self-understanding is Rom 15:15-21:

"Nevertheless on some points I have written to you rather boldly by way of reminder, because of the grace given me by God [16]to be a minister of Christ Jesus to the Gentiles in the priestly service of the gospel of God, so that the offering of the Gentiles may be acceptable, sanctified by the Holy Spirit. [17]In Christ Jesus, then, I have reason to boast of my work for God. [18]For I will not venture to speak of anything except what Christ has accomplished through me to win obedience from the Gentiles, by word and deed, [19]by the power of signs and wonders, by the power of the Spirit of God, so that from Jerusalem and as far around as Illyricum I have fully proclaimed the good news of Christ. [20]Thus I make it my ambition to proclaim the good news, not where Christ has already been named, so that I do not build on someone else's foundation, [21]but as it is written, 'Those who have never been told of him shall see, and those who have never heard of him shall understand.'"

Paul describes his work as an apostle to the Gentiles again in the context of a reference to his plans of visiting Rome.[217] He speaks of the grace (χάρις, *charis*) that God had extended to him so that he may be a servant of Jesus Christ for

---

[215]Thus, for example, Best 1984, 20.
[216]Best 1984, 20.
[217]On this text see Chae 1998, 18-38, 51-71.

the nations (εἰς τὰ ἔθνη, *eis ta ethnē*)—that is, a missionary engaged in priestly service for the gospel. The term λειτουργός (*leitourgos*) describes the servant who acts as directed by a superior authority; in the context of Rom 15:16b the term has a cultic sense. The following elements are important.

1. Paul's mission among Jews and Gentiles aims at expanding the new people of God. Paul describes his missionary work as an act of sacrifice (Rom 15:16) "in which the apostle offers the Gentile nations as a sacrifice pleasing to God."[218] The cultic language is transformed by the eschatological fulfillment, as James Dunn asserts: "The division between cultic and secular (together with that between sacred and profane, clean and unclean . . .) has been broken down and abolished . . . as part of the breaking down of the (in large part cultically determined) distinction between Jew and Gentile."[219] The term ἱερουργεῖν (*hierourgein*), which occurs in the Greek Bible only here, is used by Philo and Josephus to describe the offering of sacrifices by a priest. Paul thus applies a priestly-cultic term to his missionary work, which takes place outside of the temple, outside of Jerusalem, outside of the Holy Land, indeed outside of the people of God *in the world.*

2. Paul states that the goal of his missionary work is "so that the offering of the Gentiles may be acceptable, sanctified by the Holy Spirit" (Rom 15:16b). The term προσφορά (*prosphora*) describes either the act of offering a sacrifice or the sacrifice itself. The latter meaning is in view here: the sacrifice probably is the Gentiles (genitive of apposition), or perhaps it is the sacrifice being offered by the Gentiles—that is, the worship of the Gentile Christians as fruit of the (priestly) missionary ministry of Paul. We notice again the transformation of traditional cultic categories and differentiations: the sacrifice that Paul refers to transcends the fundamental (cultic) distinction between Jews and Gentiles that prevented Gentiles from approaching the altar of sacrifices in the temple. This meaning does not change if the Gentiles are identified with the sacrifice: the law allowed only ritually clean sacrifices to be offered, a fact that would have excluded the Gentiles, who were regarded as fundamentally unclean.[220] The goal of Paul's missionary work is the conversion of pagans, polytheists, God-fearers. The goal of the Gentile mission is the "full number of the Gentiles" (Rom 11:25) that God has determined will be converted, a number that remains unknown to Paul.

3. Paul carries out his missionary work in dependence on the power of Jesus Christ. In Rom 15:18 Paul emphasizes the constant efficacy of Jesus in his preaching ministry when he asserts, "I will not venture to speak of anything except what Christ has accomplished through me to win obedience from the

---

[218] Wilckens, *Röm,* 3:118.
[219] Dunn, *Rom,* 2:860, following O. Michel, K. L. Schmidt, E. Käsemann, H. Schlier; for the comment that follows above see ibid.
[220] Dunn, *Rom,* 2:860-61.

Gentiles, by word and deed." The fact that Jesus the Messiah is active (κατειργάσατο, *kateirgasato*) explains why Gentiles become obedient to faith in Christ.[221] Paul's reliance on the continuing activity of Jesus Christ is also seen in his plans to go to Spain: despite the fact that the gospel probably had not been preached in every single city in Syria, Galatia, Macedonia or Achaia, he intends to leave the eastern Mediterranean regions and go to Spain, relying on the existing churches in these areas to proclaim the message of Jesus Christ in cities and villages that have not yet been reached with the gospel. Hans Conzelmann argues that Paul "is not concerned about winning individual souls but about 'world mission.'"[222] This view clearly is wrong: of course Paul is concerned about the salvation of individuals, but the apostle is willing and able to leave it to God how the gospel reaches the people who live in cities that he has not visited. Because the course and success of all missionary work depends on God and his son Jesus Christ, not on apostles, Paul is able to give God all the praise for all his successes, and he can appreciate the missionary work of other missionaries as complementing his own mission without having to regard them as rivals.[223]

4. Paul describes himself as a pioneer missionary (Rom 15:20-21).[224] He has a universal concept of mission, with pioneer missionary work as the central component: he aims at leading Gentiles who live in regions where the gospel had not yet been preached to faith in Jesus Christ. Like an *architektōn* who moves from city to city, contracted to work on major building projects, Paul travels to regions in which there was much work to do because the gospel had not been preached and no churches established.[225] Since it is problematic to build on alien foundations, Paul wants to open up new areas of pioneer missionary work. All the while Paul is concerned that his Gentile mission not become detached from its Old Testament and Jewish origins.[226] Paul establishes his strategy with Is 52:15, a text that speaks of the inclusion of those formerly excluded and thus explains why non-Jews are now "seeing" and "hearing" and "understanding" the good news.

5. The oral proclamation of the gospel is the central action of missionary work. The goal of universal missionary work is to be attained "by word and deed" (λόγῳ καὶ ἔργῳ, *logō kai ergō* [Rom 15:18]); the good news of Jesus Christ is "proclaimed" (εὐαγγελίζεσθαι, *euangelizesthai* [Rom 15:20]). The "word" (*logos*) is the word that the missionaries preach: the proclamation of the message of Jesus the Messiah and Savior, of the crucified and risen Son of God, is

---

[221]Wilckens, *Röm,* 3:118-19, with reference to Rom 1:5; 6:16; 16:19; 2 Cor 10:5; 1 Pet 1:2, 14, 22.
[222]Conzelmann and Lindemann 1995, 248.
[223]Escobar 1993, 58-59.
[224]Cf. Rom 1:1-7, 14-17; 9:1-5; 10:14-21; 11:1-32; 15:14-29.
[225]Derrett 1997, 134.
[226]Stuhlmacher (1981, 122), who posits here an unnecesary conflict with Mt 28:18-20. On the quotation of Is 52:15 see J. Wagner 2002, 332-36.

for Paul the central process of missionary work. This conviction corresponds to the priorities of the Jerusalem apostles (Acts 6:2, 4) and can be verified in the account of Luke in the book of Acts:

Acts 18:5: "When Silas and Timothy arrived from Macedonia, Paul was occupied with proclaiming the word, testifying to the Jews that the Messiah was Jesus."

Acts 20:20-21: "I did not shrink from doing anything helpful, proclaiming the message to you and teaching you publicly and from house to house, [21]as I testified to both Jews and Greeks about repentance toward God and faith toward our Lord Jesus."

Cf. 1 Thess 1:5: "Because our message of the gospel came to you not in word only, but also in power and in the Holy Spirit and with full conviction; just as you know what kind of persons we proved to be among you for your sake."

Cf. 1 Thess 2:8-9: "So deeply do we care for you that we are determined to share with you not only the gospel of God but also our own selves, because you have become very dear to us. [9]You remember our labor and toil, brothers and sisters; we worked night and day, so that we might not burden any of you while we proclaimed to you the gospel of God."

The primacy of the preaching of the word in Paul's missionary work is based on theological presuppositions, but it also has historical reasons. (a) Involvement in charitable activities as a central part of missionary strategy, which was quite significant for missionary work in the nineteenth and twentieth centuries, generally was unfeasible because of financial constraints. The Jerusalem church was poor and soon needed help from outside, and the church in Antioch evidently was unable to finance Paul's missionary ministry. (b) The pioneer situation of the early Christian churches implied that the believers who found themselves in a minority situation in the cities in which they lived, worked, worshiped and preached could rely only on the power of the truth of the message that they preached. (c) The oral proclamation of the gospel was not an end in itself. Paul was not content simply to confront Jews and Gentiles with the gospel: he wants to "save" people (1 Thess 2:16; 1 Cor 9:19-22; 10:33), he wants to lead them to obedience of faith (Rom 1:5; 15:18), he wants to help people move from listening and hearing to understanding and obeying (Rom 10:14-21), and he wants to establish and consolidate churches.[227] Still, the "action" that the verb *euangelizesthai* implies is primarily the active, verbal proclamation of the gospel.[228]

6. The reality of Paul's life is an integral part of his missionary work. When Paul states in Rom 15:17 that he boasts of his "work for God," the term "work" (ἔργον, *ergon*) probably does not refer to the "signs and wonders" of 15:19: the term *ergon* occurs sixty-eight times in Paul's letters and never refers to a mira-

---

[227]See Bowers 1987.
[228]Contra R. Cook 1982.

cle.[229] Rather, *ergon* refers to the entire scope of Paul's ministry and experience and to his behavior in his daily life as a missionary. It includes his humility, his endurance despite robust opposition and sometimes fierce persecution, his independence of the views of other people, his freedom from being concerned about his own reputation, his uncompromising focus on the truth, his refrainment from manipulation, his personal devotion to individual people with their specific needs.[230]

Col 1:24-29

Following a reference to the universal proclamation of the gospel whose "servant" he has become (Col 1:23), Paul describes central aspects of his missionary work.

Col 1:24-29: " I am now rejoicing in my sufferings for your sake, and in my flesh I am completing what is lacking in Christ's afflictions for the sake of his body, that is, the church. [25]I became its servant according to God's commission that was given to me for you, to make the word of God fully known, [26]the mystery that has been hidden throughout the ages and generations but has now been revealed to his saints. [27]To them God chose to make known how great among the Gentiles are the riches of the glory of this mystery, which is Christ in you, the hope of glory. [28]It is he whom we proclaim, warning everyone and teaching everyone in all wisdom, so that we may present everyone mature in Christ. [29]For this I toil and struggle with all the energy that he powerfully inspires within me."

1. As Jesus Christ suffered in his mission, Paul suffers as apostle of Christ. Sufferings are necessary not because of predestined quotas but because they are the inevitable corollary of missionary work. This was Paul's experience.[231]

2. The sufferings of Christ that Paul "completes" (ἀνταναπληρῶ, *antanaplērō* [Col 1:24]) in his own sufferings are not Jesus' suffering during the trial and on the cross through which he secured salvation for humankind,[232] suffering with which believers need to somehow connect their own trials. Paul appears to speak of Jesus' sufferings before Easter, interpreting them in terms of the messianic woes that are mentioned in the apocalyptic tradition.[233] Paul links "Christ's afflictions"—that is, the "sufferings of the Messiah"—with his suffering as an itinerant missionary. A play on words in Col 1:25 with the rare term *antanaplēroun* in 1:24 (the only occurrence in the New Testament) emphasizes that he has been commissioned by God to preach the word of God "fully" (*plērōsai*).[234] The context in Col 1:23, 28 clearly refers to Paul's missionary work. This means that

---

[229]See Cranfield, *Rom*, 2:759.
[230]Cf. Acts 20:18-24; 1 Thess 1:5-10; 2:1-12; see also the *peristasis* catalogues.
[231]See Cahill 1992, 143.
[232]Schweizer, *Kol*, 83.
[233]See Stettler 2000; see also O'Brien, *Col*, 78.
[234]See Cahill 1992, 144-45.

the messianic woes became historical reality in the suffering of Jesus the Messiah and continue in the missionary work of Paul.

3. As a "servant" (*diakonos*) of the church (Col 1:25), Paul is a "servant" of the gospel (Col 1:23). The ministry of the apostle in the early Christian church "is in its essence the office of proclamation. The church thus owes its existence to the fact that it is constituted by proclamation, as far as its historical reality is concerned. Proclamation is the essence of the church."[235]

4. The "office" (*oikonomia*) that Paul has received from God, the task that he carries out, is "to make the word of God fully known." He seeks to proclaim the word of God as the gospel of Jesus Christ, and he wants the gospel to have full missionary success.[236] In other words, Paul works as a servant of the gospel and of the church of Jesus Christ, preaching the word of God in the world among all nations energetically and effectively in the power of the Holy Spirit, with the goal that people accept the message of Jesus Christ and come to saving faith.[237]

5. Paul describes the process of preaching of the word of God with different verbs (Col 1:28): he "proclaims" (καταγγέλλομεν, *katangellomen*); that is, he announces the gospel in public. He "warns" (νουθετοῦντες, *nouthetountes*) people; that is, he admonishes concerning wrong behavior and instructs in proper behavior so that believers are fully and consistently oriented toward Jesus Christ.[238] He "teaches" (διδάσκοντες, *didaskontes*) people in all wisdom; that is, he explains the content, roots, and consequences of the gospel for the world and for individuals. Peter O'Brien comments, "Clearly for Paul and his colleagues evangelistic and missionary outreach was not effected by some superficial presentation of the saving message about Christ to the world, but rather was prosecuted through warning and intensive teaching in pastoral situations."[239] Paul acknowledges that the Christians in Colossae make progress in faith and in love (Col 1:4). However, as missionary, pastor, and teacher he is satisfied with nothing less than the full maturity of each individual believer, which will be completed only when Jesus Christ returns.

6. Missionary activity is hard work (κοπιῶ, *kopiō*) and regularly involves struggle (ἀγωνιζόμενος, *agōnizomenos* [Col 1:29]). Paul's missionary work is very hard work that demands his full attention and all his energy.[240] At the same time Paul emphasizes that the energy and the power for this arduous missionary work are not his own: "The power, the ἐνέργεια, ultimately is not his own but is the power that comes from his being in Christ." Paul never relies on his physical vitality, his rhetorical abilities, his missionary experience or his theological

---

[235]Hübner, *Kol*, 69.
[236]Hübner, *EWNT* 3:261 (*EDNT* 3:110); idem, *Kol*, 69; cf. Gnilka, *Kol*, 99; Wolter, *Kol*, 103.
[237]See O'Brien, *Col*, 83, with reference to 1 Thess 1:5-6; Eph 6:18-20; Col 4:2-4; 2 Thess 3:1-3.
[238]Cf. H. Stadelmann, *ThBLNT* 1:381.
[239]O'Brien, *Col*, 87-88; for the comment that follows above see ibid., 90.
[240]Hübner, *Kol*, 72; the quotation that follows above, ibid.

competence. As far as his missionary work and the success of his preaching is concerned, he relies solely on the power of God, which has become graciously available in Jesus Christ.

Summary

Paul's missionary self-understanding as an apostle of Jesus Christ can be summarized as follows. (1) God is the Kyrios, the Lord of all missionary work (1 Cor 3:5). God gives to each believer, each apostle, missionary, pastor and teacher particular tasks and particular (spiritual) gifts. Success in missionary work is solely due to God's power and grace, as only he grants growth (1 Cor 3:6-7). Paul relies in his missionary work consistently and solely on the power of Jesus Christ, the Son of God (Rom 15:18). (2) Effectiveness in missionary work and in church ministry does not depend on people or on programs, nor on rhetorical techniques or elaborate methods, but is the result of God's activity. Churches that arise from missionary work are not the possession of Paul or of other teachers: the church is and always remains "God's field, God's building" (1 Cor 3:9). (3) The crucified and risen Jesus Christ is the content of missionary preaching and thus the foundation, the criterion and the measure of church planting and church growth (1 Cor 1:23; 2:2; 3:11; 15:2). The decisive factor of missionary work, therefore, is not the missionary but Jesus Christ, who is proclaimed, not the messenger but the message. (4) Paul understands himself as a "servant" of God and of his word, as a servant of Jesus Christ and of the gospel, and as a servant of the church (1 Cor 3:5; Col 1:23, 25). This self-understanding excludes all self-reliance and self-interest and all boasting with regard to his missionary work and his successes. Missionaries are *diakonoi* whose life is completely and constantly devoted to serving their Lord. Missionaries who preach the gospel are, like clay jars, weak, unimposing, ultimately irrelevant (2 Cor 4:7). The suffering and the weaknesses of the missionaries whom God uses to proclaim the gospel and to establish new churches demonstrate that success and growth are solely the result of God's power, the effect of the truth of the word of God and of the power of the Holy Spirit (2 Cor 4:7-15; Col 1:24). (5) Paul understands his missionary work as public proclamation of the victory of God, who had conquered him, the persecutor of the messianic people of God, and who led him through the world in his triumphal procession (2 Cor 2:14-16). His self-understanding is fundamentally controlled by the encounter with Jesus Christ on the road to Damascus. Paul understands himself as an ambassador of Jesus Christ who speaks as a representative of the Messiah (2 Cor 5:20; 13:3; Rom 15:18). This status is all the reputation that he requires: he does not need to boast of himself or increase his importance with letters of introduction (2 Cor 3:1; 5:12). (6) Paul knows himself to be called by God to work as a pioneer missionary who "plants," who lays the foundation as an "expert master builder"—that is, one who establishes new communities of believers (1 Cor 3:6, 10; 9:10). The metaphors of building and planting and the military metaphors indicate that missionary work is hard work (Col 1:29): he does not spare himself, for as "servant" and "slave" he has no right to "take it easy." (7) The central process of missionary work is the oral proclamation of the good news about Jesus the Messiah and Savior (1 Cor 15:1-2, 11; Rom 10:14-17; 15:18; Col 1:28): faith comes from hearing the word of God that missionaries preached and that people heard and accepted. (8) The foundational rule of missionary work is consistent attention to the listeners: Jews have to be reached with the gospel as Jews, and Gentiles as Gentiles (1 Cor 9:19). All people without distinction need to hear the gospel: both the elites of the Greco-Roman cities and the foreigners and barbarians, both the educated and the uneducated (Rom 1:14). (9) The behavior of the missionaries is subject to the proclamation of the gospel: the missionary is willing to become "all things to all people" (1 Cor 9:22), with the proviso that the integrity of the gospel is the normative criterion for missionary accommodation (1 Cor 9:23). (10) Paul is not satisfied with the success of his mission: he wants to reach ever more people with the gospel in the entire world (1 Cor 9:19; Rom 10:18), even though sometimes few people come to faith, as was the case in the Jewish communities in which he preached (Rom 10:16). (11) Paul does not work alone; he is connected with other missionaries and coworkers: the loyalty to the Lord establishes the unity of the ministry of all those who serve the church. The pioneer missionary who "plants" and the preacher and the teacher in the church who "waters" are engaged in one and the same work, and they are dependent upon one and the same Lord: they are "one" (1 Cor 3:8a). (12) All missionaries, preachers and teachers engaged in building up the church are responsible to God for their actions and their motivations. The reality of this responsibility will become evident and have consequences on the day of judgment. There is missionary work and there is church ministry that will be rejected by God if the gospel was compromised in the course of such activity (1 Cor 3:12-15). Because God alone is the Lord of missionary outreach, the missionaries are responsible to God directly: each will receive his or her own reward "according to the labor of each" (1 Cor 3:8). As God is their master, their "employer," they are primarily and fully accountable to him. God alone, not the church or other workers, decides whether the work of the missionary, the pastor and the teacher is successful or unsuccessful.

25

CONTACTS, CONFERENCES
AND CONFLICTS

The relationship between Paul and the church in Jerusalem, the place of origin of the early Christian mission, was not without conflicts, although these were not as problematic as many scholars have thought. First, I will describe the historical context of the developments in Jerusalem after Easter and Pentecost.

1. The life and work of the Jerusalem church was guided and coordinated by the Twelve under the leadership of Peter from Pentecost in A.D. 30 until about A.D. 41, when a group of Elders with James as *primus inter pares* took over the leadership of the church in the Jewish capital (Acts 12:17; 15:13). Besides the Twelve, whom Jesus himself had called and commissioned, further preachers and teachers belonged to the leadership of the Jerusalem church: initially Stephen (Acts 6—7) and Barnabas (Acts 11:22; 14:4, 14; Gal 2:1, 9), soon James the brother of Jesus (Gal 1:19).[1]

2. Most Jewish Christians probably continued to keep the purity and food laws of the Torah in the first months and perhaps years after Pentecost. The followers of Jesus in Jerusalem lived as Jews: they prayed in the temple (Acts 3:1), they preached in Solomon's Portico on the temple mount (Acts 3:11; 5:21, 42), and they enjoyed the favor "of all the people" (Acts 2:47).

3. The formulation "those who believed were of one heart and soul" (Acts 4:32) characterizes the situation in the Jerusalem church in the first few months of its existence, not the relationship between the Jewish Christians and their Jewish contemporaries who did not believe in Jesus the Messiah. Although the apostles were popular among the general public in Jerusalem, the opposition particularly of the leading priestly circles led to repeated arrests (Acts 4:3; 5:18), a ban against speaking (Acts 4:17-18; 5:40), and mistreatment (Acts 5:40). The reason for the antagonism of the Sadducees (Acts 4:6; 5:17) and the members of the Sanhedrin, for their measures of suppression and for their actions against the leaders of the Jerusalem church was the apostles' message. The apostles pro-

---

[1]On James see Wolff, *Kor*, 2:83; Hengel 1985, 101; Lang 1996, 421.

claimed and defended the messianic identity of Jesus, the redemptive significance of Jesus as cornerstone (Acts 4:11) and of his death on the cross and his resurrection and exaltation as Lord and Savior (Acts 5:30-31), and of the beginning of the last days that the prophets had announced (Acts 5:32). The apostles stayed in Jerusalem despite the fact that they were Galileans and despite the fact that their lives were in danger, potentially as early as Jesus' arrest and crucifixion. This shows that they recognized and accepted the fundamental significance of Jesus. Otherwise they would hardly have risked their lives for the dissemination of the message of Jesus, the crucified and risen Messiah.

4. Not long after Pentecost, perhaps in A.D. 31 or 32, Stephen, one of the leaders of the Jerusalem church, publicly defended the view that the temple was no longer the place of holiness and sanctification since God had revealed himself in Jesus the Messiah. It is plausible to assume that not all Jewish Christians in Jerusalem agreed with Stephen's position. However, Luke's account does not indicate any divisions in the Jerusalem church over this question. If the church in Antioch, established perhaps as early as A.D. 32, reached Gentiles with the gospel at an early date, then the question of the circumcision of Gentile believers may have arisen at this time. However, Luke's account in Acts 11:19-26 does not provide any indications to that effect, and such an early date for the foundation of the church in Antioch is not certain (a date ca. A.D. 35 is equally possible).

5. When Paul visited Jerusalem in A.D. 33/34 for the first time after his conversion (Acts 9:27-30; Gal 1:18-19), he was introduced to the apostles by Barnabas. Paul acknowledged the authority of the Jerusalem apostles, but he had preached the message of Jesus Christ immediately after his conversion both in Arabia and in Damascus without consulting them (Gal 1:16).[2] During his visit Paul "went in and out among them in Jerusalem" (ἐκπορευόμενος, *ekporeuomenos* [Acts 9:28a]) and preached the gospel "boldly" (παρρησιαζόμενος, *parrēsiazomenos* [Acts 9:28b]) among the Jews, as he had done in Damascus (Acts 9:27). Clearly Paul was not merely a guest of the apostles: he participated in their missionary activities in Jerusalem.[3]

6. According to Luke's report in the book of Acts, the question regarding the identity of the community of the followers of Jesus became a public controversy for the first time in connection with the conversion of Cornelius, a Roman officer in Caesarea, around A.D. 37. The primary issue was the fact that Peter had abandoned obedience to the food laws during his mission to Caesarea. Peter defended himself to the Jerusalem church (Acts 11:5-17) after "those of the circumcision" (Acts 11:2)—that is, the circumcised Jewish Christians—criticized his

---

[2]Gal 1:16: προσανατίθεσθαι (*prosanatithesthai*) means "to consult, confer, communicate with." The interpretation in the sense of "consult for authoritative ruling or interpretation" (Dunn 1991, 128) is too strong. Cf. Longenecker, *Gal,* 33.

[3]See Barrett, *Acts,* 1:470.

behavior. Luke does not state that the issue of circumcision was raised in this theological discussion between Peter and the leadership of the Jerusalem church (cf. Acts 11:1). The phrase "those of the circumcision" (Acts 11:2) does not describe the position that the critics argued in this meeting; it is Luke's way of describing Jewish Christians at a time when uncircumcised Gentile Christians were no longer a novelty. The concern of Peter's critics was twofold: "Why did you go to uncircumcised men and eat with them?" (Acts 11:3). Luke does not report that the critics demanded that Cornelius be circumcised. Peter was able to convince his fellow apostles and the church at large with his report about the events in Caesarea (Acts 11:1, 18) that God has accepted the Gentiles *as Gentiles*. The summary of the agreement at the end of the meeting, formulated with the plural (τοῖς ἔθνεσιν, *tois ethnesin*)—"God has given even to the Gentiles the repentance that leads to life" (Acts 11:18)—indicates that the issue was not just Cornelius but Gentile believers as a whole. This means that the abandonment of the food laws of the Torah implied the renunciation of circumcision when Gentiles come to faith in Jesus Christ. C. K. Barrett argues, "It would make nonsense of the verse if it were supposed that the speakers were saying that God has granted them repentance and salvation on the assumption that they will now be circumcised. God has accepted Gentiles as Gentiles, and there is no hint that they should be circumcised."[4] Peter continued to maintain the position that he explained and defended in Jerusalem in the subsequent months and years when Gentiles were converted in Antioch and when he visited the capital of the province of Syria (Gal 2:12).

Some scholars describe the position of Peter (and of Paul) as "critical of the law" (*gesetzeskritisch*).[5] This terminology is not very helpful: neither Peter nor Paul criticized the Torah *as Torah;* rather, they argue for the salvation-historical fulfillment of the Torah by Jesus the Messiah. This fulfillment means, on the one hand, that considerable parts of the Torah no longer need to be practiced—for example, all commandments and regulations that stipulated the removal of guilt and sin and the restoration of holiness and purity, now made redundant because of Jesus' redemptive death on the cross. The emphasis that believers in Jesus the Messiah are no longer "under the law" is related to the conviction that he took upon himself the curse that the Torah pronounced on the sinner, with the result that all who have come to faith in him have been redeemed from the death sentence of the law. This "fulfillment" of the law in Jesus Christ must not be equated with an abrogation of the Torah as a whole (cf. Rom 3:31). Even Paul's mission among Gentiles was not "law free": he asserts that "before God" he is not without the law (μὴ ὢν ἄνομος θεοῦ, *mē ōn anomos theou*) since he remains committed to the law, which has been modified as a result of the redemp-

---

[4]See Barrett, *Acts,* 1:543.
[5]Recently Lang 1996, 421.

tive work of Jesus Christ (ἔννομος Χριστοῦ, *ennomos Christou* [1 Cor 9:21]).

7. The controversy continues with regard to the question of under what conditions converted Gentiles can and should be accepted into the messianic community of the people of God. This controversy caused the apostles to convene a conference in A.D. 48 to discuss and answer these matters. It was during this so-called apostolic council that James, Jesus' brother and the leader of the Jerusalem church for seven years, argued that the fulfillment of Scripture in the ministry of Jesus the Messiah and its ongoing reality in the new community of God's people support the praxis of Peter and Paul, who accept, without any further conditions, Gentiles who had come to faith in Jesus in the church.

8. Did James later insist on full obedience to the Torah, including the stipulation of circumcision, as a result of increasing pressure from outside, as some scholars suggest?[6] The information that Luke provides in the book of Acts renders this view very unlikely. Jewish Christians, "zealous for the law" (Acts 21:20), accuse Paul of teaching "all the Jews living among the Gentiles to forsake Moses," including abandonment of circumcision and the ancestral customs. James evidently is convinced that this charge is not based on fact (Acts 21:22). His suggestion that Paul should involve himself in a Levitical act of purification in order to be able to pay the costs for four Jewish Christians who had made a Nazirite vow (Acts 21:23-24) so as to demonstrate that he, Paul, does not stand for the abrogation of the Torah is not to be construed as an argument for a more conservative manner of Torah obedience. Rather, James wants to help Paul defend himself against false rumors and accusations.[7]

This is the prehistory of the subject "Gentile Christians and the Jerusalem church." The Christian community in Jerusalem was not unified in its theology.[8] Not a few scholars have argued that Luke downplays ruptures and conflicts as a result of his "harmonizing tendency,"[9] a view that is unconvincing. Luke is able to emphasize the unity of the Jerusalem church (Acts 4:32) and report in the same larger context internal conflicts in the church (Acts 6:1-7). Jürgen Roloff argues that Luke was unable to sustain his initial portrait of the church as a "place free of conflict."[10] However, the question is not whether *Luke* managed to remain consistent, but whether the *Jerusalem church* was able to retain its unanimity. The possibility that a newly established local church (or mission society or school) is "of one heart and soul" and then loses that condition is, clearly, not simply a feature of "Lukan ecclesiology" but rather a reality that can be witnessed in the history of the church more than once.

---

[6]Thus Lang 1996, 422.
[7]Thus Pesch, *Apg,* 2:220.
[8]Lang 1996, 421.
[9]For example, Hengel 1979, 105; Roloff 1991, 116.
[10]Roloff 1991, 116.

25.1 Agreements with the Apostles in Jerusalem

Paul and Barnabas visit Jerusalem, before embarking on their missionary outreach to Cyprus and to Galatia, bringing gifts from the church in Antioch to help alleviate the effects of a famine in Judea (Acts 11:27-30). This visit takes place in A.D. 44 and is to be identified with the second visit to Jerusalem that Paul mentions in Gal 2:1-10, when he is accompanied not only by Barnabas but also by Titus, an uncircumcised Gentile Christian.

Famine Visit and Consultation

Conventional exegetical wisdom assumes that Paul's visit to Jerusalem described in Gal 2:1-10 is identical with his visit to Jerusalem on the occasion of the apostolic council reported by Luke in Acts 15:1-29.[11]

Proponents of this identification argue as follows. (1) Both passages deal with the same topics: the acceptance of Gentiles into the church and the validity of the Torah. (2) There is agreement about who was present: Barnabas and Paul from Antioch, Peter and James from Jerusalem; and there is agreement about the roles of these persons. (3) There is agreement about the outcome of the conference: the gospel that Paul preaches was acknowledged and accepted, and stipulations of the law such as circumcision are not imposed upon the Gentile Christians.

This interpretation encounters at least the following difficulties.[12] (1) If we assume that the visit to Jerusalem of Gal 2:1-20 and the visit of Acts 15:1-29 are identical, the famine-relief visit of Acts 11:27-30 becomes a problem. Three solutions have been suggested: (a) The famine-relief visit was indeed a historical event. Since Paul met only the elders of the church, this visit to Jerusalem was not important enough to warrant being mentioned in Gal 2:1-10.[13] (b) Luke's report in Acts 11:27-30 is authentic information about a collection from the church in Antioch for the believers in Jerusalem, which, however, cannot have been brought from Antioch to Jerusalem by Paul.[14] (c) The passage Acts 11:27-30 is a composition by Luke, who created two visits (Acts 11:27-30 and Acts 15:1-29) out of one historical visit (Gal 2:1-10 = Acts 15:1-29).[15] None of these solutions is convincing. (2) The visit of Acts 15 took place in the context of an official "plenary assembly" of the leadership of the Jerusalem church, whereas the visit that Paul describes in Gal 2:1-10 was a private consultation during which only the "pillar apostles" were present. Since Peter and James were the principal leaders of the Jerusalem church and its missionary work, the result of the consultation represented an important agreement. (3) The apostolic council in Acts 15 decided to draw up an official document that was communicated in a letter to the churches outside of Judea, whereas Paul mentions in Gal 2:1-10 neither official agree-

---

[11]See the commentaries of Zahn, Conzelmann, Haenchen, Schneider, Pesch, Dunn, Longenecker, and more recently Barrett, *Acts,* 2:711; Zmijewski, *Apg,* 559; Jervell, *Apg,* 404 with n. 745; see also Stein 1993, 466-68; Wehnert 1997, 21-143 passim; Cineira 1999, 247-54.

[12]For the discussion that follows above see particularly D. Wenham 1993, 226-44; see also Trebilco 1993, 453-54; Witherington, *Acts,* 441-45.

[13]See Lightfoot, *Gal,* 127.

[14]See Schneider, *Apg,* 2:94; Roloff, *Apg,* 182-83; Zmijewski, *Apg,* 450; Jervell, *Apg,* 329.

[15]See K. Lake, in *Begs.* 5:201; Haenchen, *Apg,* 364 (ET, 378-79); Pesch, *Apg,* 1:356; Weiser, *Apg,* 1:276; Lüdemann 1987, 144 (ET, 137-38); Klinghardt 1988, 216-17.

ments nor demands made by Jerusalem Christians. The only "demand" is the request of the apostles that Paul support the poor Christians in Judea. Attempts to harmonize Gal 2:1-10 with Acts 15 generally favor Paul's report over against Luke's because of Luke's alleged tendency toward harmonization.[16] (4) The subject matter of the two texts is not identical: Acts 15 reports a discussion about conditions that converted Gentiles have to fulfill in order to be admitted to the church, particularly about circumcision. The visit described in Gal 2:1-10 concerned Paul himself and the gospel that he proclaimed, while circumcision is mentioned only in passing (Gal 2:3). Gerd Lüdemann suggests that Gal 2:7-8 reports an earlier agreement between Paul and Peter on the occasion of Paul's first visit to Jerusalem (Gal 1:18). This view requires an unnecessary literary-critical operation in Gal 2:1-10 and therefore has been repeatedly criticized.[17] (5) The results of the two events are different. The visit of Gal 2:1-10 did not result in a lasting solution: the question of table fellowship with Gentile Christians soon became a contentious issue again in Antioch, one reason being Peter's behavior (Gal 2:11-21); and the demands of Jewish Christians that Gentile believers should be circumcised became so intense that Paul was prompted to write the Epistle to the Galatians.

There is sufficient evidence to suggest that the famine-relief visit described in Acts 11:27-30 is identical with Paul's second visit to Jerusalem fourteen years after his conversion, described in Gal 2:1-10.[18]

The following exegetical observations are pertinent for the discussion. (1) The term "after" (ἔπειτα, *epeita*) in Gal 2:1 indicates in connection with Paul's review of his contacts with the Jerusalem church after his conversion (Gal 1:10—2:10) that Paul does not omit any information that is important for his argument. The Jerusalem visit in Gal 2:1-10 is the second visit mentioned by Paul, and in Luke's account Paul's second visit to Jerusalem after his conversion is the famine-relief visit. (2) Paul visited Jerusalem as the result of a "revelation" (Gal 2:2), a comment that is most easily understood as a reference to the prophecy of a famine in Judea uttered by Agabus (Acts 11:27-28), a Christian prophet from the Jerusalem church who had visited Antioch. (3) Both texts mention the material needs of the Christians in Judea, explicitly in Acts 11:27-30, as does Gal 2:10, where the present-tense verb *mnēmoneuōmen* includes the current situation ("that we should continue to remember the poor" [TNIV]), while the aorist verb *espoudasa* can be translated as a pluperfect ("the very thing that I had been eager to do all along"). (4) Some scholars object that Acts 11:27-30 displays no knowledge of a discussion about the modalities of the Gentile mission. This argument is not compelling, however.[19] Luke recounts in Acts 11:19-26 the pioneer missionary work of Paul and Barnabas in Antioch, a city in which many Gentiles were converted to faith in Jesus Christ. In other words, the context of missionary outreach to Gentiles is indeed present. And we should note that Paul's report of the meeting be-

---

[16]See Barrett, *Acts,* 2:xxxix-xli.

[17]Lüdemann 1980, 105-10; followed by A. Schmidt 1992, 149-52. See the critique in McLean 1991, 67-76; Suhl 1992, 430-47; D. Wenham 1993, 233.

[18]F. F. Bruce, "Galatian Problems 1: Autobiographical Data," *BJRL* 51 (1968-1969): 292-309; idem, *Gal,* 43-56, 106-28; Marshall, *Acts,* 205, 244-47; Witherington, *Acts,* 440-43; Longenecker, *Gal,* lxxii-lxxxiii; Trebilco 1993, 453-55; D. Wenham 1993, 226-43; Barnett 1999, 294-95; Reymond 2000, 101-2; Witherington 2001, 232-33. See also Böcher (1989, 330-31), who dates Gal 2:11-21 before the apostolic council (while identifying the latter with the conflict of Acts 15:1-2).

[19]For the discussion that follows above see D. Wenham 1993, 236-38.

tween himself, Barnabas, Peter, James and John in Gal 2:1-10 focuses not on circumcision but on Paul's missionary work among Gentiles and on the legitimacy of his work and his message. (5) It is indeed a difficulty that Acts 11:27-30 does not mention apostles, whereas Paul reports in Gal 2:1-10 a conference with Peter. This difficulty does not necessarily render my basic reconstruction untenable. The famine-relief visit of Acts 11 is set in the context of the persecution that Herod Agrippa I initiated against the Jewish Christians in Jerusalem: Acts 11:27-30 is followed by a report of the arrest and torture of believers and of the execution of the apostle James (Acts 12:1-2), followed by a report of the arrest of Peter, who later manages to escape (Acts 12:3-19); the subsequent report of further activities of Herod Agrippa and of his death (Acts 12:20-23) and a note about the continued growth of the Christian communities (Acts 12:24) is followed by the comment that Barnabas and Saul, after completing their mission in Jerusalem, returned to Antioch together with John Mark (Acts 12:25). We have seen in previous discussion (§15.4) that there was a change of leadership in the Jerusalem church around A.D. 41/42: the Twelve left Jerusalem, presumably as the result of the persecution initiated by Agrippa I, who targeted the leaders of the church. The leadership of the Jerusalem church was transferred to a group of Jewish Christians who are described as "Elders." The famine-relief visit of Paul and Barnabas was paid to these Elders, who had replaced the apostles; that is, it evidently took place after the departure of the apostles in A.D. 41/42. This reconstruction does not exclude the presence of Peter in Jerusalem at this point in time: he appears, together with the other apostles, in Jerusalem again in Acts 15:2. Peter might have been active in the relative vicinity of Jerusalem and Judea at this time—for example, in Caesarea, where he would not have had to be afraid of Herod Agrippa. It is less likely that Paul's meeting with Peter in Jerusalem was accidental, given Paul's assertion in Gal 2:2: Paul wanted to make sure that he "was not running, or had not run, in vain."

David Wenham cogently argues that Gal 2:1-10 makes excellent historical sense in the context of Acts 11. He emphasizes two major points.

1. Barnabas had been sent by the apostles from Jerusalem to Antioch with the task of coordinating and consolidating the successful missionary outreach that had prompted many Gentiles to become followers of Jesus. In other words, the apostles knew Barnabas as a reliable preacher and teacher. Paul was not exactly a dark horse: he had been in Jerusalem three years after his conversion, where he had fellowship with the apostles and participated in their missionary activities in the synagogues of the city. However, this encounter had taken place eleven years ago. In the intervening years Paul had been involved in outreach as an independent missionary in Syria and in Cilicia, and in the more recent past he had been co-opted by Barnabas as a leader of the mission in Antioch, for which the Jerusalem church felt responsible. When Paul and Barnabas visited Jerusalem again, bringing with them famine-relief funds from the church in Antioch, it is rather plausible that Paul and Barnabas and Peter and James and other leaders present in Jerusalem would discuss the new developments, including the conversion of numerous Gentiles in Antioch and the role of Paul.

2. The famine-relief visit in Acts 11:27-30 follows in the larger context of Luke's narrative after the comprehensive description of Peter's mission in Caesarea (Acts 10:1—11:18), which initially was controversial in Jerusalem. These

events had taken place some time ago: the Caesarea mission may date to A.D. 37, and the famine-relief visit to A.D. 44. It is entirely plausible, however, that the apostles would have conferred about the legitimacy of Paul's Gentile mission and about the priorities of Peter's mission in the context of the missionary activities of both preachers.

3. A third observation can elucidate that historical scenario of the Jerusalem consultation of A.D. 44 even further. Paul embarked soon after the famine-relief visit with Barnabas and John Mark on a missionary journey to Cyprus and to Galatia, probably in the spring of A.D. 45 (Acts 13:1—14:28). It is conceivable that Paul and Barnabas had planned this new missionary venture for some time. Luke's reference to prayer, fasting and the speaking of the Holy Spirit (Acts 13:2) by no means excludes a period of planning: the leaders of the church in Antioch may have asked God for a confirmation of their plans, whose realization implied that the two leading preachers and teachers would leave the church in Antioch, a world city and the capital of the province of Syria, to engage in missionary outreach in areas that had not been visited by Christians. In view of these plans it would have been natural and prudent to consult with the leading teachers in Jerusalem, particularly for Paul, who had not been in Jerusalem for eleven years and who intended to leave the direct sphere of influence of the Jerusalem church.

Many scholars argue, or assume, that a major reason for the (alleged) conflict between Paul and the Jerusalem apostles was the problematic nature of his claim to be an apostle. If the definition of "apostle," in the narrow sense of the word, refers to people who had traveled with Jesus before his crucifixion and had encountered Jesus after the resurrection, Paul's apostleship poses a problem, as he had not been a disciple of Jesus. How can Paul be an authentic witness to Jesus' resurrection? Wolfgang Bienert formulates the dilemma as follows: "How shall he recognize that the Risen One who reveals himself to him is nobody else than the Crucified One? Paul recognized the problem of his apostolic office implied in this question when he described himself as 'the least of the apostles.'"[20] Bienert argues that Paul had his authority to engage in missionary work among Gentiles confirmed by the Jerusalem apostles (Gal 2:8), while accepting his direct calling and commissioning by God himself (Gal 1:1) as the ultimate grounds for his apostleship, which also establishes "the peculiar freedom of his missionary work." The New Testament concept of the apostles was discussed earlier (§10.2). Luke and Peter emphasize that an apostle is a companion of Jesus from the time of John the Baptist to Jesus' ascension, and thus a witness of the resurrection (Acts 1:21-22). This understanding of *apostolos* is related in the book of Acts to the Twelve and thus to those who had been given the responsibility for the new movement of the followers of Jesus. The independence that Paul claims for his missionary work does not question this responsibility of the Jerusalem apostle: this was the very reason why Paul visited Jerusalem three years after his conversion with the goal of meeting Peter (Gal 1:18, with the verb *historein,* which suggests not simply a courtesy call but implies an element of respect[21]). Anthony Bash argues that Paul, Barnabas and

---

[20]W. A. Bienert, in Hennecke and Schneemelcher 1990-1997, 2:11; for the observations that follow above see ibid.

[21]See Karrer 1989, 214-15, contra Mussner, *Gal,* 95.

Titus visited Jerusalem as official "ambassadors" of the church in Antioch, submitting the request that the apostles establish and confirm the form and substance of the authentic gospel.[22] The fact that Paul emphasizes in Gal 1—2 the independence of his apostolic authority and mission renders this suggestion unlikely. I see no reason why the historicity of Acts 11:19-30 should be doubted.[23]

Paul asserts in Gal 2:2, "I went in response to a revelation and, meeting privately with those esteemed as leaders, I set before them the gospel that I preach among the Gentiles." The Greek verb that is translated as "to set before somebody," ἀνατίθεσθαι (*anatithesthai*), can mean "to submit to a deliberative body for its consideration," but also "to communicate something that is one's own, with a view to consultation"[24] and even "to bring a dedicatory gift."[25] If we link the latter meaning with Paul's description of James, Cephas-Peter and John as "pillars" (στῦλοι, *styloi* [Gal 2:9]), a possible allusion to the church as eschatological temple with the Jerusalem apostles as supporting columns,[26] the purpose of the consultation becomes clear: Paul wants to have his divine commission to preach the gospel affirmed in the center of the eschatological community of the Messiah, in the "eschatological temple" in Jerusalem.[27]

It follows that if this analysis is correct, there was no in-depth discussion of circumcision during the consultation that took place on the occasion of the famine-relief visit in A.D. 44. Luke's account in Acts 11:27-30 does not indicate that the participants in the meeting discussed the modalities of missionary work among Gentiles. Perhaps these had been sufficiently addressed in the context of Peter's missionary work in Caesarea: this is suggested by Acts 11:18 as well as by the vigorous emphasis on Peter's dream-vision, which communicated to him the divine revelation concerning the manner in which he should interact with Gentiles.

James Dunn suggests that Cornelius's conversion was not regarded as a problem in the Jerusalem church. (1) Cornelius was a devout God-fearer, which means that evidently he had adopted Jewish customs in various areas; that is, he was not a "pure" pagan. (2) Cornelius's conversion was accompanied by unambiguous manifestations of the Holy Spirit that even the most conservative Jewish Christians in Jerusalem could not dismiss: they had to acknowledge that God had allowed this specific Gentile a "short cut" into the people of God, without circumcision. In other words, Cornelius and other similarly converted Gentiles were accepted as exceptions that did not jeopardize the usual modalities of receiving Gentiles into God's covenant people. This changed as Gentile conversions became more the rule than the exception[28] This reconstruction is plausible at first sight, but it cannot be adopted without modification for the following reasons. (1) The closeness of

---

[22]See Bash 1997, 82-85.
[23]For a recent attempt to cast doubt on the authenticity of Acts 11:19-30 see Joubert 2000, 91-93.
[24]Dunn 1982, 466; followed by Martyn, *Gal*, 190.
[25]See Karrer 1989, 216.
[26]U. Wilckens, *ThWNT* 4:734-35 (*TDNT* 4:728-29); Barrett 1953, 10-16; Martyn, *Gal*, 205.
[27]See Karrer 1989, 216.
[28]Dunn 1991, 125-26. Similarly earlier Harnack 1924, 1:57 (ET, 1:51-52).

the God-fearers to the synagogues may explain why Jewish Christians found it somewhat easier to interact with new converts from this group versus new believers who had been "pure" pagans, who had worshiped idols and lived an immoral life. This does not explain, however, why Peter had to defend himself before the Jerusalem church on account of his contacts with Cornelius, as Luke reports in Acts 11:1-17. (2) The formulations in Acts 11:18 indicate that the story of Cornelius was regarded not as an isolated case but as paradigmatic for all conversions of Gentiles. It therefore is unlikely that the Jerusalem church would have accepted the admission of Cornelius into God's covenant people as an exception. (3) Luke's account in Acts 10:1—11:18 focuses not on the external manifestations of the Holy Spirit on the occasion of Cornelius's conversion but on the vision of Peter. This indicates that the admission of the converted Gentiles in Caesarea is established not primarily on the basis of the unambiguous manifestations of God's Spirit in this particular instance but with a new revelation from God.

I argued in §16.1 that Paul describes the admission of Gentiles into God's messianic covenant people through faith in Jesus Christ, without circumcision, with the term "mystery." It is plausible to assume, therefore, that we have to reckon with new developments between the conversion of Cornelius in A.D. 37 and the official discussion of the modalities of admitting Gentile believers into the people of God by the apostolic council in A.D. 48.

The Agreement of Gal 2:7-9

Before describing this new situation, we need to examine the agreement between Paul and Peter that was formulated, according to Gal 2:7-9, in the course of the consultation in A.D. 44.

Gal 2:7-9: "On the contrary, when they saw that I had been entrusted with the gospel for the uncircumcised [τὸ εὐαγγέλιον τῆς ἀκροβυστίας], just as Peter had been entrusted with the gospel for the circumcised [τῆς περιτομῆς] [8](for he who worked through Peter making him an apostle to the circumcised [ὁ γὰρ ἐνεργήσας Πέτρῳ εἰς ἀποστολὴν τῆς περιτομῆς] also worked through me in sending me to the Gentiles [ἐνήργησεν καὶ ἐμοὶ εἰς τὰ ἔθνη]), [9]and when James and Cephas and John, who were acknowledged pillars, recognized the grace that had been given to me, they gave to Barnabas and me the right hand of fellowship, agreeing that we should go to the Gentiles and they to the circumcised [ἵνα ἡμεῖς εἰς τὰ ἔθνη, αὐτοὶ δὲ εἰς τὴν περιτομήν]."

The interpretation of Gal 2:7-9 is disputed. Some scholars understand the agreement between Peter and Paul in terms of a division of the areas of missionary responsibility along geographical lines: Peter engages in missionary work in Jewish regions, Paul in Gentile regions.[29] Other scholars interpret in the sense of a division along ethnic lines: Peter preaches among Jews, Paul

---

[29]See Zahn, *Gal,* 107; Burton, *Gal,* 97-98; Schlier, *Gal,* 79-80; Mussner, *Gal,* 122; Haas 1971, 49-50; Stein 1993, 470; see the discussion in Haenchen, *Apg,* 448-49 (ET, 465-66). J. M. Scott (1995, 151-57) seeks to connect the "geography" of the agreement with "Japheth" in the table of nations in Gen 10.

among Gentiles.[30] Both alternatives are problematic.[31]

Scholars who support the ethnic interpretation argue that the term *ta ethnē* refers in Paul nearly always to Gentiles in contrast to Jews, and that we find Peter not only in Judea but also in "Gentile" regions: according to Gal 2:11-14, he was in Antioch, and according to 1 Cor 9:5, Peter and his wife were engaged in missionary journeys. An interpretation in terms of a "Jewish mission" and a "Gentile mission" excludes Paul from preaching in synagogues and bars Peter from preaching the gospel before Gentiles. This scenario is historically entirely implausible, and it founders on the existing evidence at least as far as Paul is concerned: according to 1 Cor 9:19-20, Paul preaches among Jews with the same intensity as among Gentiles, an assertion that Luke clearly and repeatedly illustrates in his account of Paul's missionary work in the book of Acts.[32]

A division of the areas of missionary responsibility along geographical lines would have been impractical: Jewish communities existed in all larger cities of the eastern Mediterranean region that Paul would not have wanted to exclude from hearing the good news of Jesus the Messiah, and Peter would have encountered in his missionary work in synagogues outside of Judea and Galilee Gentile God-fearers, *ethnē* whom surely he would not have wanted to exclude from hearing his preaching and teaching.

Christian Grappe suggests that the Jerusalem apostles understood the agreement in an exclusive ethnic sense, while Paul interpreted it in a geographical sense.[33] It is implausible, however, that Paul records in Gal 2:7-9 a misunderstanding: he speaks in Gal 2:9 of "fellowship" (*koinōnia*).

Lucien Legrand argues for a modified geographical suggestion that deserves attention.[34] He criticizes, with some justification, the Eurocentric or "Western" prejudices of many scholars who interpret Gal 2:9 and the agreement between Peter and Paul often in terms of the contrast between Jerusalem/Palestine ("the circumcision") and the Mediterranean world, particularly Europe ("the Gentiles"), ignoring the Asian regions east of Syria as well as Africa. This dismissal of non-European regions is hardly legitimate, given the geography of Judaism in the first century. Legrand suggests that the participants in the Jerusalem consultation that Paul describes in Gal 2:7-9 thought and talked in terms of *regions* that were from an *ethnic* point of view either "Judaized" or "non-Judaized" in a general "repre-

---

[30]See Betz, *Gal,* 100; Martyn, *Gal,* 202, 211-16; Lüdemann 1980, 96; E. P. Sanders 1983, 181; Best 1984, 17; more recently Reinbold 2000, 168-72.

[31]See Legrand 1995, 31. John Knox (1964, 3) suggested in his presidential address to the Society of Biblical Literature that we probably will never know what Paul wanted to say in Gal 2:7-10. This is too pessimistic.

[32]The arguments of Martyn (*Gal,* 211-16), who disputes this, are unconvincing.

[33]Grappe 1992, 266-67. Beckheuer (1997, 52-97) suggests that Paul and the Jerusalem apostles talked at cross-purposes.

[34]Legrand 1995, esp. 36-63.

sentative" sense, not in terms of statistical realities. The "Judaized world" was the
Diaspora, with Jerusalem as capital—that is, the eastern and the southern regions
(Asia and Africa) corresponding to the list of regions in Acts 2:9. The "non-Judaized world" was the West, where relatively few Jews lived (with the exception
of the large Jewish community in Rome). This solution of the difficulties raised
by Gal 2:9, at first attractive, ultimately is unconvincing for the following reasons.
(1) The number of Gentiles living in Asia and in Africa presumably was as large
as the number of Gentiles living in the West. Since we have no reliable data about
population densities or about the numerical strength of Jewish Diaspora communities, we are left with pure speculation. The argument that the participants at
the Jerusalem consultation did not "count heads" but thought "representatively"
would be more plausible if Legrand could offer evidence for the connection between "Gentiles" and "the West" or between "the circumcision" and "Asia and
Africa." (2) The scant information that we possess about Peter and his missionary
work after his departure from Jerusalem in A.D. 41 does not fit a localization of
outreach to "Judaized" regions: in the geographical list of 1 Pet 1:1, which Legrand cites, Galatia is not the only "exception": Cappadocia was also "non-
Judaized," and the number of Jews living in Pontus and Bithynia probably was
not higher than the number of Jews living in Macedonia or Achaia.[35] (3) The geographical list of Acts 2:9 describes not areas of missionary work but Jewish visitors to Jerusalem on the occasion of the Feast of Pentecost in A.D. 30 who had
contact with the apostles. If the list, as recorded by Luke in the second volume
of his account of the Christian movement, implies the existence of churches in
the regions that are listed, they can be linked not only with Peter and "Judaized"
regions but also with Paul: Peter may have been active as a missionary in five of
the regions (Judea, Cappadocia, Pontus, Asia, Rome), Paul in six regions (Phrygia, Pamphylia, Asia, Rome, Crete, Arabia), while the regions of Parthia, Media,
Elam, Mesopotamia, Egypt, Cyrene and Libya are linked neither with Peter nor
with Paul in the tradition of the early church.

Some scholars, assuming the inauthenticity of Jesus' missionary commission, often implicitly presuppose in their interpretation of Gal 2:7-9 that the
Jerusalem apostles were not interested in a universal and international mission. Many argue on the basis of Gal 2:7-9 that Paul was the only "missionary
to the Gentiles." It is telling that Ernest Best, who shares this view, sees a need
to warn against the conclusion that Paul and Peter preached different gospel
messages.[36] We have seen, however, that the view is unjustified that posits that
the Twelve were not commissioned to engage in international missionary
work that included Gentiles, or that they did not understand or obey such a
commission (see §§12.3; 14.1; 16).

---

[35]Legrand 1995, 42-43; for the point that follows above see ibid., 38-41.
[36]Best 1984, 18. See the similar emphasis earlier in Zahn, *Gal*, 101-2.

Another suggestion to explain the fact that there is a tension at least between Paul's missionary work and the formulations in Gal 2:7-9 is that the agreement between Peter and Paul was impractical because it was too rigid: a Jewish-Christian missionary who preaches to Gentiles can hardly ignore Jews who have not heard the message of the crucified and risen Messiah. This is the reason, some scholars suggest, why Paul abandoned the agreement.[37] This explanation is unconvincing. Paul had been a missionary for fourteen years before the Jerusalem consultation: he surely knew what was "practical" and what was impractical, as both Jews and Gentiles lived in Arabia, Syria and Cilicia, where he had preached the gospel.

Attention to grammatical details such as the interpretation of the Greek preposition εἰς (*eis*) in Gal 2:8, 9 does not appear to advance the discussion. Scholars who accept the historical reliability of the book of Acts seem to prefer the geographical interpretation (Luke regularly portrays Paul as preaching to Jews), while scholars who are skeptical concerning Luke's account seem to prefer the ethnic interpretation.[38]

First, we need to note that Gal 2:1-10 describes not a "division" or "separation" but a κοινωνία (*koinōnia*), a "close association involving mutual interests and sharing" (BDAG). The subject of the consultation was not the question of whether there should be two distinct, or separate, branches of missionary work: a mission to Jews for which Peter and the other Jerusalem apostles would be responsible, and a mission to Gentiles for which Paul would be responsible. Nor did the discussion focus on the question of whether the missionary work of the early church should be organized in a unified manner with a unified authority. Ferdinand Baur missed precisely this point when he argued that the Jerusalem apostles, rather than separating themselves from Paul's mission, would have joined his mission to the Gentiles had they accepted the theological viability of such a mission.[39] The issue was not whether Paul would "join" Jerusalem or whether Peter would "join" the missionary work of Paul. If my reconstruction of the involvement of the Twelve in missionary outreach to Gentiles is correct, they did not need to "join" Paul: they were actively preaching among Gentiles, proclaiming, as was Paul, the exclusive significance of Jesus, the crucified and risen Messiah, for the forgiveness of sins (following the speeches of Peter as summarized by Luke in the book of Acts). This common emphasis does not exclude the possibility, indeed the likelihood, that questions of practical behavior of Christians were answered in different ways, depending on the cultural and social contexts of Jerusalem and Judea, Caesarea and Antioch, Rome and Ephesus.

---

[37]Thus Best 1984, 18-19.
[38]See Legrand 1995, 35.
[39]Baur 1866, 142-43; followed by Barrett, *Acts,* 2:xl.

Josef Hainz comments, "The *fellowship* that was confirmed by a handshake is specifically defined in terms of being established on the mutual *recognition of the different expressions of the one gospel* and in terms of being realized in the collection that had been agreed upon."[40]

What does Paul mean by what he writes in Gal 2:2 with regard to the consultation with Peter: "in order to make sure that I was not running, or had not run, in vain"? Some scholars interpret the phrase μή πως (*mē pōs,* "in order that . . . not") in the sense that Paul was afraid that the Jerusalem apostles would decide against him, which would mean that the "false brothers" of Gal 2:4 were accepted and that the existence of the Gentile-Christian churches and the unity of the church would be jeopardized.[41] This interpretation is unlikely. Paul has no doubts about the message that he proclaims as a missionary. What would he have changed if the consultation had reached a different outcome (presupposing a concern of Paul)? Would he have given up establishing Gentile-Christian churches in obedience to his divine commission?[42] In what sense would he have stood before God empty-handed "if Jerusalem would make him choose between the unity of the church and the truth of the gospel"? Without a doubt Paul would have continued to engage in missionary work among Jews and Gentiles alike, and he would have preached the same message that he had proclaimed so far. It is possible that the concern to have been running "in vain" refers not to Paul but to the Gentile Christians in the churches that Paul had founded: if they gave in to the pressure of the false brothers who demanded their circumcision, they would abandon the gospel in the eyes of Paul.[43] The statement in Gal 2:2 can also be interpreted as an indirect question,[44] which eliminates the nuance of fearful concern, suggesting the following interpretation: Paul wants to consult with Peter because he wants to know whether the Jerusalem apostles agree with those who argue that his previous missionary work was in vain and that this would continue unless he changed his view about circumcision in particular and about the Torah in general.[45] I cannot detect a difference in the theological or missionary "perspective" of Paul and Peter in Gal 2:2.[46]

The reference to the "false brothers" in Gal 2:4 (NRSV and TNIV translate as "false believers," even though no one suggested that these troublemakers included women) is somewhat ambiguous. These people could be Jewish Chris-

---

[40]Hainz 1982, 134 (italics added); cf. idem 1981; 1994, 378. See earlier Zahn, *Gal,* 102; see also Legrand 1995, 59-61.

[41]See Schlier, *Gal,* 67; Dunn, *Gal,* 93-94; Longenecker, *Gal,* 48-49; Becker, *Gal,* 34; *NSS* 2:138.

[42]Becker, *Gal,* 34; the quotation that follows above, ibid.

[43]See Dunn, *Gal,* 93.

[44]Zahn, *Gal,* 83-84; Mussner, *Gal,* 103 with n. 16, following M.-J. Lagrange, O. Kuss and A. Oepke.

[45]See Mussner, *Gal,* 103.

[46]Differently Silva 1996, 151-52, 156-57; Schreiner 2001, 50.

tians who demand that Gentile Christians be circumcised, analogous to the situation described in Acts 15:1-2. If this is correct we would have to assume after all that the consultation between Paul and Peter in A.D. 44 explicitly dealt with the modalities of the Gentile mission. This difficulty is resolved if Gal 2:4-5 is interpreted as a parenthesis in which Paul informs the Galatian Christians in A.D. 48 (or later) that "false brothers" intruded *after* this consultation: they intruded into the center of the Gentile mission at the time, i.e., they visited the church in Antioch and demanded that all Gentile Christians should be circumcised.[47] This means that Titus was not taken along by Paul as a "test case." Rather, the fact that Titus was not circumcised indicates that the issue of circumcision never came up during the consultation of the year A.D. 44. The reconstruction of the sequence of events remains difficult, notwithstanding the interpretation of the details of the passage.

Second, Paul's account in Gal 2:8 indicates that the issue was not areas of missionary work but the effectiveness of the missionary work among Jews (Peter) and among Gentiles (Paul), which in both cases is completely dependent upon God (ὁ ἐνεργήσας . . . ἐνήργησεν, *ho energēsas . . . enērgēsen*). In Gal 2:7 the comparative particle καθώς (*kathōs*, "just as") expresses not a contrast between the two missionaries but a complementary relationship: the statement in Gal 2:8 does not describe Paul and Peter as opponents or the relative status of the two apostles.[48] The emphasis that both apostolic missions depend on the power of God confirms that the participants in the Jerusalem consultation of A.D. 44 acknowledged both the basic theological unity and the practical, specific unity of the early Christian mission—Paul, who wrote the account of the consultation in Gal 2, as well as the Jerusalem apostles, who recognized that God was active in the missionary work of Paul. The exchange about the "effects" of the power of God in the activities of the missionaries who were present at the consultation must have been specific, reporting the conversions of people, Jews and Gentiles, that could be explained only as the direct result of the power of God. If Paul followed the accommodation principle, formulated in 1 Cor 9:19-23 (see §24.3), in the eleven years of independent missionary work in Arabia, Syria and Cilicia, he naturally would have been concerned about and committed to missionary methods that were as effective and as goal-oriented as possible.[49]

Third, we should note that Paul clearly speaks of his own concerns (Gal 2:2) but he does not register any "wishes" of the Jerusalem apostles, with the exception of financial support for the poor Christians in Jerusalem (and Judea). The

---

[47]Bruce, *Gal*, 115-16, with reference to T. W. Manson, A. S. Geyser and B. Orchard; see also D. Wenham 1993, 233 n. 37 (as a possibility).

[48]See Mussner, *Gal*, 117 with n. 93.

[49]On the importance of the accommodation principle for Gal 2:7-9 see Carson 1986, 29.

behavior of the "pillars" is described as follows: "they added nothing . . . they saw . . . they recognized . . . they gave" (Gal 2:6, 7, 9). I do not find any evidence in the text to support the view that Paul was put under pressure by the Jerusalem authorities, pressure that Paul resisted and thereby singlehandedly rescued the unity of the church.

James Dunn argues that Paul's refusal to accommodate the wishes of the Jerusalem apostles (to have Titus circumcised) obscures their own identity as Jews and members of the covenant people. According to Dunn, the apostles were convinced that their status as Jews was elevated as a result of their faith in Jesus as Israel's Messiah, as representatives and leaders of the faithful remnant in Israel. Paul's insistence on abandoning circumcision gave an entirely different answer to the question of status.[50] There is no doubt that the renunciation of circumcision must have put the apostles in Jerusalem in a bad light; in view of the political situation and the nationalistic pressures of the late 40s, their very lives could be in danger. The historical reconstruction is problematic, however: if Peter indeed said in his speech before the Sanhedrin what Luke reports in Acts 4:12, then Peter and the other apostles in Jerusalem were unconcerned about issues of status. It may well be that they did not realize what consequences might result from not circumcising converted Gentiles and from the potential increase in conversions of Gentiles for their Jewish identity and for the identity of the local Christian communities. If not only Paul but also Peter and the other Jerusalem apostles preached the message of the crucified and risen Messiah, literally risking their lives, we may safely assume that they regarded the proclamation of the gospel of Jesus Christ to be more important than reflection about future developments of the Christian communities. Or to put it in theological terms: Christology, soteriology and active proclamation of the gospel had priority over ecclesiology.

Paul's concern at the Jerusalem consultation with Peter, which Paul seems to have initiated, was focused on the recognition of his missionary work and the churches that he established as being every bit as valid as the missionary work of Peter and of the other apostles and the churches that they established.

Fourth, the development of Paul's argument in Gal 2:6-9 indicates that the Jerusalem apostles committed themselves not to interfere in the missionary work of Paul and Barnabas and not to raise or support any demands,[51] with the exception formulated in Gal 2:10 that they should remember the poor believers in the Judean churches. This shows again that the issue was not the division of spheres of missionary influence but the recognition of the independent mission of Paul, who had worked for eleven years without direct contact with the Jerusalem apostles and who was in the process of planning missionary outreach with Barnabas to Cyprus and to Galatia.

We must keep in mind the larger historical context of the Jerusalem consultation that took place in A.D. 44 (Gal 2:1-10; Acts 11:27-30). Peter had served as the leader of the Jerusalem church and its mission for twelve years. He had

---

[50]Dunn 1991, 129.
[51]See Zahn, *Gal,* 106.

preached mostly before Jewish audiences, but also he had been involved in missionary outreach to Samaria and to cities in the coastal plain at an early date. If the evidence discussed in §15.4 and §16 has been analyzed correctly, Peter and the other apostles preached not only to Jews but also to Gentiles, increasingly so since two or three years after they had to leave Jerusalem in A.D. 41/42 because of the persecution initiated by Herod Agrippa I. It is unclear whether the change of leadership in the Jerusalem church from the Twelve to the Elders played a role in the consultation of A.D. 44; it is striking, however, that Jesus' brother James, who had taken over the leadership of the Jerusalem church after Peter's departure, is mentioned in Gal 2:9 before Cephas-Peter and John. It appears that the Twelve initially remained focused on Jerusalem despite their missionary work outside of Jerusalem and Judea. On the other hand, Paul had engaged in missionary work in Arabia immediately after his conversion and then for eleven years in Cilicia and in Syria. At the time of the Jerusalem consultation he was active in Antioch, where many Gentiles had come to faith in Jesus Christ (Acts 11:26). In all probability he was in the process of planning a missionary journey to Cyprus and Galatia (Acts 13—14). Paul understood himself as a pioneer missionary who wanted to work in areas in which no other missionaries were active (1 Cor 3:6, 10; Rom 15:23). We do not know whether he expected Peter or other missionaries to follow a similar basic strategy. There is no doubt, however, that the Jerusalem apostles acknowledged the validity, equality and independence of the missionary work of Paul, who was able to trace his proclamation of the gospel to a revelatory encounter with the risen Christ, just as the Twelve did (Gal 1:11-12; cf. Eph 3:5), and who was able to demonstrate that God's blessing was manifest in his missionary work (Gal 2:8). The account in Gal 2:7-9 does not describe a "concordate" between Peter the missionary to the Jews and Paul the missionary to the Gentiles, nor a concordate between the Jewish mission of Jerusalem and the Gentile mission of Antioch. The participants in the consultation of A.D. 44 certainly did not agree that Peter (or the Twelve) should not preach to Gentiles or that Paul (or Barnabas) should not preach to Jews. The main issue of this high-level consultation during the early phase of international missionary work in which missionaries from Jerusalem started to play an increasingly important role after the change of leadership in the Jerusalem church was the recognition and acknowledgment of the successful work of a missionary who had been active without regular contact with the Jerusalem church. The request by the apostles that Paul remember the poor believers in Judea established a closer relationship between Paul and the Jewish Christians in Jerusalem and Judea than hitherto had existed. The fact that Paul's visits to Jerusalem became much more frequent might indicate that Paul took their request seriously. The following table illustrates the sequence and the frequency of Paul's visits to Jerusalem.

31/32   Conversion of Paul and missionary outreach in Arabia and in Damascus

33/34   First visit (Acts 9:26-29): three years after Paul's conversion, then eleven years
         of missionary work in Syria and Cilicia

44   Second visit (Acts 11:27-30): consultation, eleven years after the first visit, then
         missionary work on Cyprus and in Galatia

48   Third visit (Acts 15:1-29): apostolic council, three years after second visit, then
         missionary work in Macedonia and Achaia

51   Fourth visit (Acts 18:22): three years after the third visit, then missionary work
         in the province of Asia and visit to Achaia

57   Fifth visit (Acts 21:15-17): collection visit, six years after fourth visit, arrest in
         Jerusalem and imprisonment in Caesarea

The Collection

Paul organized a collection (ἡ λογεία, *hē logeia*) for the church in Jerusalem
throughout the churches in Macedonia and Achaia and perhaps in the churches
in the province of Asia.[52] Paul risked his life for this initiative, and it was in connection with the collection that he was arrested in Jerusalem. Clearly the collection that Paul organized in the churches that he established demonstrates his
connectedness with the believers in Jerusalem.

The following factors are important.[53] (1) The collection demonstrates Paul's
concern for and devotion to the believers in Jerusalem. The collection was not
a legal obligation for Paul or for the Jerusalem apostles, and it was not simply
an initiative prompted by sociocultural customs.[54] The collection was a voluntary gift: Paul wanted to help the Christians in Jerusalem as an expression of
the fellowship between Jewish believers and Gentile believers. (2) The collection demonstrates the central significance of Jerusalem for Paul's missionary
work. Jewish Christians from Jerusalem had been responsible for repeated interference in Paul's mission, even during the time he brought the collection to
Jerusalem, interference that prompted Paul to a forceful reaction both in Antioch when he confronted Peter and in his letter to the Galatian churches. Despite this opposition, or precisely because of it, Paul traveled to Jerusalem with
a good number of representatives of the churches that he had established in
which Jewish Christians and Gentile Christians lived together. The gospel originated in Jerusalem, the Gentile Christians are "debtors" to the believers in Jeru-

---

[52]See 1 Cor 16:1-4; 2 Cor 8:1-15; 9:1-5; Rom 15:14-21; cf. Gal 2:10.
[53]See Gnilka 1996, 159-61; McKnight 1993; Everts 1993a, 297-99; Joubert 2000; Wedderburn
    2002. Less helpful is the tradition-historical synthesis in Beckheuer 1997, 270-75.
[54]Contra Joubert (2000, 116-53), who interprets the collection as "benefit exchange" and "social
    reciprocity"; however, see ibid., 207-8, where Joubert emphasizes the aspect of *koinōnia*.

salem (Rom 15:27), and God's revelation to Israel in the Scriptures was authoritative for Gentile Christians as well (cf. Rom 3:21). These are reasons why the
collection is "more than a pious work and a social deed, it is an act of faith that
documents the connection with salvation history."[55] Paul's statement in 1 Cor
16:5 shows that the apostle pondered in A.D. 54 whether he should bring the
collection to Jerusalem himself or not. When he wrote the comments in 2 Cor
1:15-16 and in Rom 15:26-27 in A.D. 55/56, he had decided to travel to Jerusalem despite the anticipated dangers. It is obvious that Paul regarded the relationship between the Jerusalem church and the Gentile-Christian churches as
extremely significant.[56] (3) The collection confirms the equality of Jewish Christians and Gentile Christians. The fact that Paul took uncircumcised Gentile
Christians to Jerusalem was meant not as a provocation but as a demonstration
of what Paul regarded to be self-evident: Jewish believers and Gentile believers
should have fellowship with each other.

Was the project of the collection successful? In his letter to the Christians in
Rome, written in Corinth shortly before his departure to Jerusalem, Paul voices
the possibility that the collection might be rejected (Rom 15:31). Some scholars
interpret the fact that Luke does not mention the collection in the book of Acts
as an indication that the gift was not accepted.[57] This conclusion is entirely hypothetical, and also it founders in light of the friendly welcome that Paul received from James and the Elders of the Jerusalem church, according to Luke's
report (Acts 21:17-18); the passing reference to the collection in Paul's speech
before Felix (Acts 24:17) also supports the likelihood that the financial contribution of the Gentile-Christian churches was accepted.[58]

Stephan Joubert takes Luke's account in the book of Acts seriously, but his
reconstruction of the history of the collection remains speculative. He suggests
that the Jerusalem church under the leadership of James was prepared to accept
the collection only if Paul submitted to purification rites and paid the costs for
the Nazirite vow of four members of the Jerusalem church who continued to
observe the Torah (Acts 21:23-24). According to Joubert, Paul accepted this
compromise and thus was able to enjoy briefly the status of public benefactor
of the Jerusalem church. The fate of the monies that Paul brought to Jerusalem
remains unclear after Paul's arrest in the temple.[59] This reconstruction ultimately
is unconvincing: Luke does not hint at such a deal between Paul and the Elders
of the Jerusalem church in Acts 21:18-26. On the contrary, Luke's account of

---

[55]Gnilka 1996, 160.
[56]Murphy-O'Connor 1996, 343; cf. Thiselton, *1 Cor,* 1326.
[57]See Pesch, *Apg,* 2:222; Roloff, *Apg,* 313; Zmijewski, *Apg,* 764; Witherington, *Acts,* 644; Jervell,
    Apg, 529-30; Lüdemann 1983, 94-98 (ET, 59-62, 249-50 n. 111); 1987, 245 (ET, 236-37); Gnilka
    1996, 302; Wedderburn 2002, 104 n. 27.
[58]See Marshall, *Acts,* 342-43.
[59]Joubert 2000, 212-15.

Paul's arrival in Jerusalem suggests that the funds that he collected in his churches from *both* Jewish Christians and Gentile Christians were accepted. The following factors regarding Acts 21:18-26 need to be noted. (1) James and "all the elders" extend a friendly welcome to Paul, who "greets" the leaders of the church, as Luke explicitly points out (Acts 21:19a). (2) Paul gives an extensive report of his missionary activities: "He related one by one the things that God had done among the Gentiles through his ministry" (Acts 21:19b). (3) Paul reports specifically the conversion of Gentiles (Acts 21:19b). Since the Jerusalem leadership was already familiar with Paul's theological position and practices as a missionary working among Gentiles, the fact that he was able to present an in-depth report indicates that neither Paul's presence nor the churches that were established in the course of his missionary work was regarded as problematic. (4) James and the Elders listen intently and praise God: they acknowledge as a result of God's blessing both the conversions that take place in Paul's missionary ministry and the churches that have been established.[60]

Johannes Munck argues in an influential study, written in response to the interpretation by Ferdinand Baur, that Paul never lost sight of Jerusalem, that indeed Jerusalem was the goal of his missionary work. Paul understood himself as a salvation-historical figure and he believed that the arrival of the messianic period in Israel depended upon his own ministry. Munck argues that Paul organized a collection in his Gentile Christian churches in fulfillment of Is 2, Mic 4 and particularly Is 60:5-6 in the hope that his decision to arrive in Jerusalem with the collection and to die there as had been prophesied would bring the fulfillment of the missionary task in Israel, causing Israel to come to faith in the Messiah.[61] This hypothesis cannot be substantiated from Paul's letters, however. Dieter Georgi wants to link the collection with the eschatological pilgrimage of the nations to Mount Zion: Paul regarded the collection as a sign of the last days. The organization of the collection and the journey to Jerusalem with the collection in hand was a provocative demonstration of Paul's conviction that the last days had finally begun, reversing the sequence of the events that were expected: the Jews (from the Diaspora) do not precede the nations on the way to Zion; rather, the Gentiles arrive in Jerusalem before the Jews. Georgi asserts, "The promised pilgrimage of the peoples had begun to materialize, but without—indeed, in spite of—the majority of the Jews."[62] This theory cannot be established on the basis of the primary sources either.[63]

---

[60]On the first point see Acts 21:18: πάντες τε παρεγένοντο οἱ πρεσβύτεροι; Acts 21:19: ἀσπασάμενος αὐτούς. On the second point see Acts 21:19: ἐξηγεῖτο καθ᾽ ἓν ἕκαστον. On the third point see Acts 21:19: ἐποίησεν ὁ θεὸς ἐν τοῖς ἔθνεσιν διὰ τῆς διακονίας αὐτοῦ. On the fourth point see Acts 21:20: οἱ δὲ ἀκούσαντες ἐδόξαζον τὸν θεόν.

[61]Munck 1954, esp. 298-99 (ET, 302-4).

[62]Georgi 1965, 72, 84-86; quotation, 85 (ET, 99-100, 117-20; quotation, 119).

[63]See the critique in Beckheuer 1997, 46, 48-49; also Gnilka 1996, 160.

In the weeks and months of the spring in A.D. 57, when Paul was involved in bringing the collection from Achaia and Macedonia via Ephesus to Jerusalem, he was planning a mission to Spain, which indicates that he expected neither a mass conversion of Israel nor apocalyptic events. Finally, we need to emphasize that we have no detailed information about the history of the collection project.[64]

The strategic significance of Jerusalem for Paul's missionary work cannot be compared with the close links between the early medieval missionaries and Rome and the pope.[65] There is no New Testament evidence that suggests that the early Christian missionaries were "obedient" to "the church" or to Peter. The Jerusalem church did not function as the "center" from which pastoral letters and directives were normative for the missionaries. In the New Testament the concept of the unity of the various communities of followers of Jesus is not focused on Jerusalem as center, which means that it cannot be used as explanation for the normative role of Rome for the early medieval missionaries.[66]

25.2 The Clash with Peter in Antioch

During the 40s Jewish Christians "from James" (τινας ἀπὸ ᾽Ιακώβου, *tinas apo Iakōbou* [Gal 2:12]) came from Jerusalem to Antioch, where they managed to put Peter under immense pressure that eventually caused him, against his theological convictions, to break off close table fellowship with the Gentile believers. Peter caved in because he feared the reaction of zealous Jews (φοβούμενος τοὺς ἐκ περιτομῆς, *phoboumenos tous ek peritomēs*) and their potential actions against the church in Jerusalem (Gal 2:12).[67] The "certain people from James" evidently demanded separation from Gentile Christians who did not follow the ritual and cultic stipulations of the Torah. Even Barnabas, who had engaged in missionary work in Antioch, on Cyprus and in southern Galatia together with Paul, was "led astray" to act, like Peter, in contradiction to his true convictions, withdrawing from fellowship with the Gentile Christians. When Paul returned to Antioch and realized what had happened, he confronted Peter "before them all" (ἔμπροσθεν πάντων, *emprosthen pantōn* [Gal 2:14]).[68]

The Delegation of James

The "people from James" presumably represented James, the brother of Jesus

---

[64]See Joubert 2000, 124-25.
[65]On this subject see Padberg 1995, 49-50, 69-75.
[66]Thus, evidently, Padberg 1995, 73 with n. 59.
[67]Bruce, *Gal*, 131; Longenecker, *Gal*, 74-75; Witherington, *Gal*, 155-56; Jewett 1971; Bockmuehl 2000, 75. The motif of personal weakness on the part of Peter can be excluded as an explanation in light of the harsh reaction from Paul; contra Mussner, *Gal*, 142; Painter 1997, 69; differently Martyn, *Gal*, 236-40.
[68]The literature on the "incident at Antioch" is enormous; on the history of research see Wechsler 1991; besides the commentaries, see recently Wehr 1996, 60-73; Bockmuehl 2000, 49-83.

and *primus inter pares* among the Elders of the church in Jerusalem, in Antioch in accordance with the task they had been given. There is no evidence that they only claimed, falsely, to speak with the authority of James. It is possible that they did not convey authoritative demands[69] but that they presented a plea for solidarity with the Jerusalem church in view of the difficult political situation.[70]

The delegation from James must be distinguished from Paul's opponents in Jerusalem, Galatia and Achaia: (1) from the "false brothers" (ψευδαδέλφοι, *pseudadelphoi* [Gal 2:4]) from Jerusalem who had traveled to Antioch; (2) from the man who confuses (ὁ ταράσσων, *ho tarassōn* [Gal 5:10]) the believers in Galatia, the agitators (οἱ ἀναστατοῦντες, *hoi anastatountes* [Gal 5:12]), the people who fear being persecuted by the Jews and thus demand that the Gentile Christians in Galatia be circumcised (Gal 6:12-13); (3) from the "super-apostles" (ὑπερλίαν ἀπόστολοι, *hyperlian apostoloi* [2 Cor 11:5-13]) in Corinth. In these three cases we are dealing with Jewish Christians who personally seek out Gentile Christians, demanding that they be circumcised and follow other Jewish halakic customs. Neither James nor the issue of table fellowship is mentioned in any of these three cases. The "false brothers" from Jerusalem in Antioch, the "agitators" in Galatia and the "super-apostles" in Corinth evidently were identical with the believers who are described in the apostolic decree as people who "have gone out from us, though with no instructions from us" (Acts 15:24). The incident at Antioch did not concern the question of the circumcision of Gentile Christians[71] or the praxis of Gentile mission as such; rather, it involved the question of table fellowship between Jewish Christians and Gentile Christians. According to Paul's account in Gal 2:11-14, he initiated a public debate with Peter, not with James.[72]

The delegation from James appears to have acted in accordance with the agreement of the Jerusalem consultation of Gal 2:7-9: they ask the Jewish Christians of the church in Antioch to withdraw from table fellowship with the Gentile believers. At stake was hardly the question of whether the food that was consumed during the communal meals was selected and prepared in compliance with the food laws of the Torah or other halakic stipulations: such difficulties could have been addressed by making the appropriate changes (cf. the decisions of the apostolic council). The reason why James sent envoys to the church in Antioch seems to have been informed by political considerations that were linked with the repeated persecutions of the Jerusalem church by the Jewish authorities in the 40s. James evidently sought to reach a modus vivendi with the Jewish authorities in Jerusalem, a project that is jeopardized by news that

---

[69]Thus N. Taylor 1992, 129-30.
[70]Bockmuehl 2000, 71; for the arguments that follow above see ibid., 71-82.
[71]See Pratscher 1987, 81 with n. 132.
[72]See Bockmuehl 2000, 72.

the church allows Jews (Jewish Christians) to live in close fellowship with Gentiles (Gentile Christians) in Antioch, the capital of the province.

If James provided a biblical basis for his position, the formulations presumably would have resembled the arguments of the hard-liner Rabbi Eliezer b. Hyrcanus (see §21.2). Markus Bockmuehl further suggests that James wanted to remain faithful to Jesus' program of realizing the eschatological vision of a national restoration of Israel.[73] This argument is less plausible, as it downplays the importance of, and denies the authenticity of, Jesus' missionary commission (Mt 28:19-20; Acts 1:18). Friedrich Lang argues that the reference to James in Gal 2:12 means that "the primitive church under James claimed to have the right of supervision over the Jewish Christian Diaspora."[74] This possibility cannot be excluded, but it remains hypothetical because we have no hard information about the notion of administrative responsibility in the early Christian churches.

The Reaction of Paul

Peter's dilemma becomes understandable, considering the historical situation and the political plight of the church in Jerusalem. In Paul's view, however, these motivations were insignificant in comparison with the project of the Gentile mission in general and the Gentile-Christian members of the existing churches in particular. Paul would not permit uncircumcised followers of Jesus, Gentiles who had come to faith in Jesus as Lord and Savior, to be made second-class Christians. And Paul was convinced that any differentiation between or separation of Jewish Christians and Gentile Christians contradicted the logic of the gospel and denied the efficacy of Jesus' sacrificial death on the cross. This is the apostle's argument in his letter to the Galatian Christians.

Paul's criticism of Peter (Gal 2:11, 14) does not lead to a rupture of the dialogue between the two apostles; on the contrary, Paul continues the conversation. He describes in Gal 2:15-21 the position that they have in common: he formulates in the first person plural ("we") and describes Peter as "jointly sharing the basic convictions about works of the law, faith and righteousness in Christ."[75] It therefore is "impossible to stylize the controversy in Antioch as a fundamental break" between Paul and Peter or between Paul and Jerusalem. The very fact that Paul repeatedly refers to Peter in Gal 1—2 implies and supports Peter's "presence" in the Gentile-Christian churches. In his letters to the Christians in Corinth and in Rome Paul does not even mention the incident in Antioch, even though he mentions Cephas-Peter repeatedly (1 Cor 1:12; 3:22; 9:5; 15:5). In 1 Cor 15:3-11 Paul emphatically appeals to Peter as guarantor of the

---

[73]Bockmuehl 2000, 75-78. It is debatable whether the early rabbinic tradition according to which Antioch belonged to Eretz Israel (cf. ibid., 61-70) is relevant for our discussion. On the theme of Jesus and the restoration of Israel see now Bryan 2002.

[74]Lang 1996, 432.

[75]Karrer 1989, 218; for the comment that follows above see ibid. See also Böcher 1996, 269.

early Christian message of the death and resurrection of Jesus.[76]

Hans Lietzmann argues that the clash between Paul and Peter in Antioch led to a church split: in the ensuing years Peter and his coworkers traveled through Galatia, Macedonia, Achaia and Rome and engaged in anti-Pauline propaganda.[77] This view has been thoroughly disproven: there is no hard evidence that Peter or coworkers of his visited Asia Minor, Macedonia or Achaia; the Cephas party in Corinth (1 Cor 1:12) does not seem to have been inspired by Peter directly; there is no evidence that Paul and Peter were competitors in the church in Rome; the areas of missionary work in which Peter and Paul were active did not overlap, if we take Luke's reports in the book of Acts into account. Martin Karrer remarks, "There is no evidence for any responsibility on [Peter's] part for the formation of groupings on a larger scale within the Pauline churches."

If my reconstruction is correct, there also was no break between Paul and Barnabas.[78] The two missionaries planned a joint visit to the churches in southern Galatia only a few months after the incident in Antioch (Acts 15:36). Their separation was caused not by the clash in Antioch, in which Barnabas played an inglorious role (Gal 2:13), but by the question of whether John Mark, who had abandoned them on their previous mission to Galatia, was a suitable companion for the planned visit to the Galatian churches (Acts 15:37-39). There is no reason to doubt Luke's account.

Clement of Alexandria links the apocryphal *Epistle of Barnabas,* written probably between A.D. 130 and 140,[79] with Barnabas, Paul's companion (*Strom.* 2.116.3; 5.63.1). This is implausible because its author describes, in the first person plural ("we"), the conversion to the Christian faith in terms of abandoning idolatry (*Barn.* 16:7). The epistle is relevant for the *Wirkungsgeschichte* of the historical Barnabas only because it claims Joseph-Barnabas as an authority for Christian freedom from Jewish ceremonial law: the author spiritualizes the Old Testament sacrifices (*Barn.* 2:1-10) as well as circumcision (*Barn.* 9:4-6), the food laws (*Barn.* 10:1-12) and the sabbath laws (*Barn.* 15:1-9). Bernd Kollmann observes that an author "who attributes pseudepigraphically such an interpretation of the Torah to the historical Barnabas cannot have regarded the Antioch incident as having any fundamental significance; he clearly places Barnabas on that side of early Christianity that is represented by Paul, characterized by freedom from the ceremonial law."[80]

---

[76]The view of F. C. Baur, who argued for a permanent break between Paul and Jerusalem, was very influential; see more recently, for example, Dunn, *Gal,* 130; Lüdemann 1983; R. A. Martin 1993, 187-98.

[77]Lietzmann 1958b, 2:284-91. For the critique that follows above see Karrer 1989, 211-13; quotation, ibid., 212; on Lietzmann see ibid., 287-91.

[78]Contra, for example, Kollmann 1998, 51-56; Kraus 1999, 166; Schnelle 2003, 137.

[79]Klaus Wengst (1984, 114-15) argues that *Barn.* 16:3-4 probably alludes to the construction of a Jupiter temple on the temple mount in Jerusalem during the reign of Emperor Hadrian in 130.

[80]Kollmann 1998, 65; cf. Paget 1994, 143-54; Hvalvik 1996, 119-28.

25.3 The Apostolic Council in Jerusalem

Luke reports in Acts 15:5 that Pharisees who had come to faith in Jesus Christ demanded that converted Gentiles be circumcised and keep the Mosaic law. This evidently was a new development that seems to have taken place after the Jerusalem consultation of A.D. 44, prompting a controversy both in the church in Antioch (Acts 15:1) and in the church in Jerusalem (Acts 15:5). Luke states that the demands of these Jewish Christians from Jerusalem provoked "sharp dispute and debate" (Acts 15:2a) between these Judeans and Paul and Barnabas, who had just returned from missionary outreach on Cyprus and in Galatia.[81] The church of Antioch decided to send Paul, Barnabas and some other Christians to Jerusalem "to discuss this question with the apostles and the elders" (Acts 15:2b). Luke's account indicates that the Twelve, the Elders of the Jerusalem church and other leading missionaries such as Paul and Barnabas organized a meeting at which these issues should be discussed: "When they came to Jerusalem, they were welcomed by the church and the apostles and the elders, and they reported all that God had done with them" (Acts 15:4). The meeting, often called the "Apostles' Council,"[82] took place in A.D. 48.

Most scholars think that the apostolic council in Jerusalem described in Acts 15 is the same meeting as the conference that Paul describes in Gal 2:1-10. As we have seen, however, it is historically more plausible to link the Jerusalem consultation of Gal 2:1-10 with the famine-relief visit of A.D. 44 (§25.1). If the early date that some scholars posit for the composition of Paul's Epistle to the Galatians is correct, then Paul may have written to the Galatian Christians before the events that Luke describes in Acts 15.

Daniel Schwartz points out that the apostolic council of A.D. 48 took place at roughly the same time as the conversion to Judaism of the royal family of Adiabene, usually dated to A.D. 43.[83] His suggestion that Luke had read Josephus's report of this conversion and that he adopted the question that is posed by the Izates story is unlikely and unconvincing.

The Prehistory of the Council

Before we examine the discussion that took place at the apostolic council, we need to raise again the question of when Jewish Christians demanded for the first time that converted pagans be circumcised. Most scholars think that Paul's mission in southern Galatia in A.D. 45-47 was one of the presuppositions of the council.[84] This reconstruction is plausible when we follow Luke's account in the book of Acts, which reports the events of the apostolic council (Acts 15:1-29) immediately after the report of Paul and Barnabas's mission to southern Galatia (Acts 13—14). This interpretation assumes, therefore, that the early Christian dis-

---

[81]Acts 15:2: γενομένης δὲ στάσεως καὶ ζητήσεως οὐκ ὀλίγης.

[82]Hübner (1996, 137) speaks of a *Heidenmissionssynode* ("Gentile mission synod").

[83]D. Schwartz 1996, 263.

[84]See, for example, Hengel 1979, 94; Lang 1996, 419.

cussion about circumcision was caused by the missionary praxis of Paul, who admitted, on theological grounds, converted Gentiles as "children of Abraham" into the people of God without circumcision. Scholars who adopt this line of interpretation assume that the apostolic council marks the final acceptance of the law-free Gentile mission by the Jerusalem church.[85]

However, this interpretation raises several difficult questions. (1) Did Paul abandon the traditional Jewish insistence on the circumcision of Gentiles who converted to faith in Yahweh only during his mission to southern Galatia in A.D. 45? This is quite unlikely in light of the fact that Peter accepted Cornelius as a Gentile believer without circumcision as early as A.D. 37. (2) Why was the question of whether or not converted Gentiles should be circumcised not discussed until at the apostolic council in A.D. 48, if Paul renounced circumcision for Gentile followers of Jesus Christ already during his missionary work in Arabia, Syria and Cilicia since A.D. 32/33, and if the church in Antioch included uncircumcised believers soon after the establishment of the church in A.D. 35? (3) Why was the circumcision of Gentile believers still an issue in Jerusalem if the conversion and acceptance of Cornelius, the Roman officer, had been discussed and acknowledged publicly (Acts 11:18)? Why was the issue not settled with Peter's speech during the apostolic council, in which he reminded the participants of Cornelius's conversion (Acts 15:7-11)? (4) Why was the demand from the converted Pharisees that Gentile believers be circumcised first "considered" (Acts 15:6) rather than immediately rejected by James and the Twelve?[86] (5) In what sense is James's argument that Scripture proves that the restoration of Israel is linked with the Gentile mission an answer to the question of whether uncircumcised Gentiles could be admitted to the church?

Luke's account in Acts 1—15 seems to suggest that the Jerusalem church retained a certain measure of authority and control over the missionary work in Syria until about A.D. 45—that is, until Paul and Barnabas departed for Cyprus and southern Galatia. This assumption is not necessarily historically accurate; it depends largely on the question of whether the early Christian mission split after the apostolic council or after the Antioch incident, and on the question of whether and in what way the churches that Paul established were independent from Jerusalem. And it is not entirely clear whether Luke describes the visit of Paul and Barnabas to Jerusalem (Acts 15) as an official "embassy" of the church in Antioch.[87]

The main concern of the Jewish Christians in Jerusalem certainly was not so much the question of who "controls" the newly established churches but rather

---

[85]See Haenchen (*Apg*, 446-47 [ET, 462-44]), who argues that Luke's account is "an imaginary construction answering to no historical reality" (463).

[86]Löning 1985, 2622; the quotation that follows above, ibid.

[87]Thus Bash 1997, 145-49.

the issue of how the ethical norms of the churches could be safeguarded in view of the rapid growth of the Gentile-Christian segment in the churches outside of Judea.[88] Jesus had made some "critical" comments about the nonethical commandments of Jewish tradition, in particular about food laws (Mk 7:15) and the sabbath (Mk 2:27-28), but he had insisted also that his followers practice a righteousness that surpasses that of the scribes and the Pharisees (Mt 5:20). Jesus had intensified the ethical standards of God's revelation by his emphasis that what is important is not only the external behavior of a person but also the hidden motivations and emotions of the heart (Mt 5:21-32). It was not easy for the Jewish believers to fulfill Jesus' precepts, and this must have been even more difficult for Gentiles, whose ethical standards were not highly regarded by Jews (cf. Rom 1:18-32). How could the apostles safeguard the ethical standards of the will of God in the new communities that included so many Gentile believers?

At the same time the Jerusalem Christians had been commissioned to preach the message of Jesus Christ in Judea. In a time when the nationalistic Zealot movement became increasingly active, the task of missionary outreach to Jews in Judea, Samaria and Galilee certainly did not become easier when news arrived that a large number of Gentiles in the Diaspora regarded themselves as members of the people of God without having been circumcised and without keeping all of the law.

The Jerusalem church recently had suffered under the persecution that Herod Agrippa I (A.D. 41-44) had initiated against the Twelve. The apostle James, son of Zebedee, had been executed, and Peter had escaped the same fate only with supernatural help (Acts 12:1-19). Many Christians had to flee Jerusalem during the persecution in which Stephen was killed, and many left Jerusalem permanently. The Twelve had returned, but they seemed to have lost most of the goodwill that they had enjoyed among the inhabitants of Jerusalem, perhaps on account of the acceptance of Gentiles into the new communities (e.g., Cornelius in Caesarea). Another cause for concern was the new wave of Zealot guerrilla activity that followed the death of Agrippa in A.D. 44, when Judea was again placed under Roman control. The Roman procurator Tiberius Julius Alexander (46-48) crucified James and Simon, the two sons of a Galilean man named Jude, who were leading Zealots (Josephus, *A.J.* 20.102). In this new round of Zealot activity the rebels took action not only against representatives of the Roman occupying power but also against Jews who were suspected of being collaborators.[89] The latter would have been found mainly among the priestly aristocracy, but it is plausible to assume that any Jew who built "bridges" to the Gentile world and argued for eliminating barriers would have provoked the wrath of patriotic Jews.

---

[88]See Bruce, *Acts,* 301.
[89]Josephus, *B.J.* 2.254-255; *A.J.* 20.186-187.

The political climate in Judea during the mid-40s presented the Jerusalem church with an ethical and strategic-political problem caused by the influx of uncircumcised Gentile believers in the new communities. Some members of the church suggested a simple solution: Gentiles who came to faith in Jesus the Messiah should be accepted into the church with the same conditions under which Gentiles become Jews: converted Gentiles should be circumcised and made to commit to following the commandments of the Mosaic law. This procedure would safeguard the ethical standards of the Christian communities, and it would allow the Jerusalem Christians to defend themselves against accusations of the Jewish nationalists. Presumably, some Jewish Christians would have found this solution attractive, particularly the former Pharisees who had been converted. It is not clear whether some of the Twelve, or some of the Elders, supported this solution. However, this group of "conservative" Jewish Christians managed to create a situation in the church in Antioch in which Peter compromised his convictions.

Representatives of this group of Jewish Christians, among them converted Pharisees (Acts 15:5), came to Antioch and told the Gentile Christians, "Unless you are circumcised according to the custom of Moses, you cannot be saved" (Acts 15:1). They made the same demand during the apostolic council in Jerusalem.

Jürgen Roloff argues that the statement in Acts 15:1 represents a leveling of the historical facts, compared with Acts 11:1-18, where the author described the acceptance of God-fearing Gentiles such as Cornelius into the church.[90] This analysis remains unconvincing: (1) The subject of the "full integration of law-free Gentiles without circumcision" was not discussed for the first time at the apostolic council. This issue must have been debated already during the discussion recorded in Acts 11:3-18: Cornelius and his relatives and friends were uncircumcised. (2) For Jews, who insisted that all members of God's people must continue to distinguish between ritually clean and unclean, the difference between God-fearing Gentiles who are uncircumcised and Gentiles who are uncircumcised and have no contact with a synagogue was negligible as far as the question of their "full integration" into the messianic community was concerned. (3) While it certainly is true that Acts 11:1-18 is concerned with the integration of only a few individual God-fearers into the church, it is equally true that the question of the quantity of converted Gentiles is an issue neither in Acts 11 nor in Acts 15.

The suggestions concerning the tradition history of Luke's account of the apostolic council in Acts 15:1-33 cannot be discussed in detail here.[91] Ernst Haenchen argues that Luke composed the text without using any sources, meaning without any historical traditions. Alfons Weiser follows Mussner, Pesch, Roloff and Schneider, arguing that Acts 15 contains "elements of traditions about the Jerusalem agreement (Gal 2:1-10) and about

---

[90]Roloff 1991, 120; the quotation that follows above, ibid.

[91]See Haenchen, *Apg,* 438-44 (ET, 455-60); Schneider, *Apg,* 2:175-92; Pesch, *Apg,* 2:71-75; Weiser, *Apg,* 2:367-77; quotation, 375; followed by Zmijewski, *Apg,* 558-63, 573-74; quotation, 573; Barrett, *Acts,* 2:709-12; quotation, 710; Jervell, *Acts,* 403-7; quotation, 403-4, 405, 406; see also Wehnert 1997, 33-82, 263-73 (historical reconstruction); quotation, 273.

the solution of the problems of the Antioch incident (Gal 2:11-14)"—the former are found in Acts 15:1, 2, 4, 5, 6, 12, 7, 13, 10, 11, 19, the latter in Acts 15:5, 23, 30, 20, 29, 23, 22, 27, 30, 31, 32. Josef Zmijewski is confident that "the 'Apostles' Council' certainly did not take place as Luke describes it in Acts 15." Jürgen Wehnert suggests that the Lukan composition follows "not the actual development of events . . . but the theological concept of a rectilinear expansion of Christianity guided by the Holy Spirit." He concludes that "the outline of the book of Acts cannot be used as framework for a history of early Christianity." C. K. Barrett is less skeptical: "Luke used all the sources that he could find, whether written or oral." Jacob Jervell agrees and states, "Luke had at his disposal the best traditions from diverse origins . . . Luke formulated the scene himself. But he did not add much material. . . . From the historical perspective, Luke's account is largely reliable." Ben Witherington analyzes Acts 15 without recourse to hypothetical tradition-historical reconstructions: "Luke probably had some brief notes or oral testimony . . . which he wrote up in his own way."[92]

The Proceedings of the Council

Luke's account of the apostolic council in Acts 15:6-29 allows us to reconstruct the following sequence of events of this important meeting in A.D. 48.

1. The Twelve and the Elders—that is, the apostles and the leadership of the Jerusalem church—convened a meeting (Acts 15:6) in which the following groups participated: (a) Conservative Jewish Christians who demanded that converted Gentiles be circumcised. The comment in Acts 21:20 may suggest that the influence of this group was increasing. The "Judaizers" who traveled to the new Gentile-Christian churches in Asia Minor and beyond may have been the "right wing" of these conservatives. (b) Paul and Barnabas, Peter and John, and James. They agreed on the basic theological question that converted Gentiles should be accepted into the messianic people of God without requiring a prior conversion to Judaism involving circumcision and the keeping of the law. And they also agreed on the practical question of how the fellowship of Jewish Christians and Gentile Christians should be organized and shaped in the local communities of the followers of Jesus.

Many scholars follow Ferdinand Baur, who argued that Peter and Paul represented opposite positions and that James supported a mediating position. According to this reconstruction, four groups need to be distinguished: (a) Conservative Jewish Christians who demand that Gentile Christians be circumcised. (b) James the brother of Jesus, who abandoned the demand for circumcision but argued that the Gentile Christians should observe some of the commandments of the Torah. (c) Peter, who was more liberal than James: he wanted to impose on the Gentile Christians neither circumcision nor the purity laws. (d) Paul, who was more liberal than Peter: he argued against requiring obedience to any of the commandments of the Torah.

2. A robust debate ensued (πολλῆς δὲ ζητήσεως γενομένης, *pollēs de zēteseōs*

---

[92]Witherington, *Acts,* 456; see also the commentaries of F. F. Bruce and I. H. Marshall, as well as Bauckham 1995b; 1996a.

genomenēs [Acts 15:7a]). Some participants, presumably the former Pharisees who had become believers in Jesus the Messiah, argued that the Gentile Christians should be "circumcised and ordered to keep the law of Moses" (Acts 15:5b).

3. Peter reminds the participants in the discussion in a longer contribution (Acts 15:7b-11), speaking in his role as missionary among Gentiles, of the events that transpired in connection with the conversion of Cornelius in Caesarea. He emphasizes that "God made a choice" (ἐξελέξατο ὁ θεός, *exelexato ho theos*) in the church (ἐν ὑμῖν, *en hymin*) already "in the early days" (ἀφ᾽ ἡμερῶν ἀρχαίων, *aph᾽ hēmerōn archaiōn*) that the Gentiles should hear the message of the good news and come to faith (Acts 15:7b), without making a distinction between Jews and Gentiles (Acts 15:8) and without imposing upon the Gentiles the yoke of the law (Acts 15:9), since Gentiles are saved just like Jews by the grace of the Lord Jesus (Acts 15:11). Peter thus emphasizes the common early Christian conviction that the death and resurrection of Jesus inaugurated the messianic time of salvation, the era in which God would gather the nations on Mount Zion. The ingathering of the Gentiles had to wait until Jesus had finished his ministry to the house of Israel and until he had died and been raised from the dead. Jesus had called the apostles from the very beginning as "fishers of people" (Mk 1:17), he had trained them to be able to fulfill this task (Mk 6:7-13), and he had confirmed their calling after Easter, expanding their commission to include the universal and international proclamation of the good news of the arrival of the kingdom of God, a message that they were to preach until the "restoration of the kingdom" to "Israel" would be complete (Acts 1:6, 8). The disciples had understood and accepted this task, demonstrated by the appointment of a twelfth disciple as a witness of Jesus' resurrection (Acts 1:21-22). The disciples were convinced that the proclamation of Jesus as the crucified and risen Messiah and Savior would prompt the nations to be included in the kingdom of God—the last event before the consummation, as prophesied in Scripture. As witnesses of Jesus the Messiah who preach among the Gentiles, they are a part of the fulfillment of God's plan of salvation.

The apostles, whose position Peter presents, according to Luke's account, thus were motivated by two factors. First, they were convinced that now only Jesus "saves," which means that sins are now forgiven only as a result of faith in Jesus (Acts 4:12). Second, they were convinced that Jesus is the promised Messiah (Acts 2:36), that the last days have arrived (Acts 1:6), that the time has come when the nations will be gathered (Acts 1:8), and that Jesus has given them a significant role in the gathering of the nations. And they were convinced that God does not demand that the nations are gathered to Zion by becoming Jews through circumcision and obedience to the Torah. François Refoulé notes that Peter's speech in Acts 15:7-11 is typically "Pauline" and suggests that Luke wants to portray Paul as an "orthodox" missionary who preaches the same message as that of Peter and James.[93] It seems, however, that this was not simply the literary intention of Luke as author of the book of Acts but that the theological agreement that he reports corresponds to historical reality.

4. Peter's speech reassured the participants in the meeting: "the whole assembly kept silence" (Acts 15:12a). The conservative Jewish Christians had to acknowledge the fact that the Gentile mission that Paul and Barnabas and the church in Antioch had been responsible for, accepting Gentiles into the messianic people of God without circumcision, was neither a Syrian aberration nor a project of Paul alone (if they indeed attacked Paul as early as A.D. 48). They were forced to acknowledge that Peter himself, the *primus inter pares* of the Twelve and the first leader of the Jerusalem church, supported and taught the same theological position.

5. After the assembly had become quiet, Barnabas and Paul gave a report about the work of God "among the Gentiles" (ἐν τοῖς ἔθνεσιν, *en tois ethnesin* [Acts 15:12])—that is, in Syria and in Cilicia, on Cyprus and in Galatia. They recounted "all the signs and wonders" that God had done in the context of their missionary work (Acts 15:12). Luke's account of the report given by Paul and Barnabas is somewhat "thin," a fact that may find its explanation in the intention of Luke, whose recollection of Cornelius's conversion is meant "to settle the dispute concerning Paul's mission. To follow up this intention he does not need the eloquence of Paul, who might have introduced the success of his mission into the discussion as a kind of decision by God. Luke certainly does not want to give the impression that a man, even a great apostle, has won the decision for himself and his work by means of a struggle. Even Peter, whose experience is quoted here as a 'classic' one, is not the final authority. It is not to be said even of him that he introduced conversion of the Gentiles into the church without regard for the law. This was done not *by* him, but *in* him, through God."[94]

6. Finally, James spoke, the brother of Jesus and the leader of the Jerusalem church (Acts 15:3). He argued in a longer contribution (Acts 15:14-21) that converted Gentiles must be accepted into the church because God has restored his people (at least in principle)[95] and that converted Gentiles should be expected to follow only certain rules. James explains with an interpretation of Amos 9:11-12 the missionary-theological position that all apostles who were present accepted.

The quotation from Amos in Acts 15:16-18 is not a simple literary citation but rather the result of competent exegetical work.[96] (a) The introductory words and the last phrases

---

[93]Refoulé 1993.
[94]Dibelius 1947b, 102-3 (ET, 117).
[95]See Turner 1996a, 312-14; 1997, 90.
[96]For the exposition that follows above see Bauckham 1995b, 455; quotation, ibid. See also Ådna 2000b; Stowasser 2001; Pao 2000, 137-38, 238.

come not from Amos 9:11-12 but from Hos 3:5; Jer 12:15; Is 45:21. These passages are connected with Amos 9:11-12 through content and wording (*gezerah shawah*). (*i*) The phrase μετὰ ταῦτα (*meta tauta*) evidently comes from Hos 3:5, where the restoration of the temple and seeking the Lord are also linked with the restoration of Davidic rule. (*ii*) The term ἀναστρέφειν (*anastrephein*) probably comes from Jer 12:15-16, a passage that also refers to the conversion of the nations in the last days and that also uses the metaphor of building. The statement that the Gentile nations that learn from Israel will "dwell [be built] in the midst of my people" (Jer 12:16 LXX: καὶ οἰκοδομηθήσονται ἐν μέσῳ τοῦ λαοῦ μου) asserts that they form, together with Israel, the eschatological temple to which Amos 9:11 refers. The phrase "booth [tent] of David" (Heb., סֻכַּת דָּוִיד, *sukkat dāvid;* Gk., ἡ σκηνὴ Δαυίδ, *hē skēnē Dauid*) refers in the context of passages such as Ps 27:5; 31:21; 42:5; 76:3 to the Jerusalem temple, and in the context of passages such as Is 1:8; 16:5 to the city of Jerusalem.[97] (*iii*) The phrase ποιῶν ταῦτα γνωστὰ ἀπ᾽ αἰῶνος (*poiōn tauta gnōsta ap᾽ aiōnos*) at the end of the quotation is an echo of Is 45:21, which gives the phrase ποιῶν ταῦτα (*poiōn tauta*) a different meaning: James uses this allusion to show that God's intention to integrate Gentiles into his eschatological people is older than these prophecies. In its original context Is 45:21 is another prophecy that the nations will turn to the God of Israel and receive salvation. Richard Bauckham concludes, "The allusions to three other prophetic passages which frame the main quotation from Amos put the latter in a context of prophecies which associate the eschatological conversion of the Gentile nations with the restoration of the Temple in the messianic age." (b) James adapts the quotation from Amos 9:11 to the context of the discussion at the apostolic council: he omits two phrases (καὶ ἀνοικοδομήσω τὰ πεπτωκότα αὐτῆς and καθὼς αἱ ἡμέραι τοῦ αἰῶνος); he changes the main verb (ἀναστήσω is replaced by ἀνοικοδομήσω and ἀνορθώσω); and he omits the phrase καθὼς αἱ ἡμέραι τοῦ αἰῶνος because it would create a conflict with the emphasis on the superiority of the eschatological temple over previous temples. These modifications facilitate the interpretation of Amos 9:11 in terms of the eschatological temple of the messianic period. (c) In regard to the selection of the text of Amos 9:12a, the Greek translation (ἐκζητήσωσιν οἱ κατάλοιποι τῶν ἀνθρώπων [Acts 15:17]) is very different from the Masoretic Text (לְמַעַן יִירְשׁוּ אֶת־שְׁאֵרִית אֱדוֹם, "in order that they may possess the remnant of Edom"; note that אֱדוֹם means "Edom," while אָדָם means "man, humanity"). The Greek version that is quoted in Acts 15:17 is either an alternate Septuagint reading or a deliberate adaptation of the text according to the hermeneutical rule *al tiqrē* (cf. the pesharim in Qumran). James uses the quotation from Amos 9:11-12 to provide an exegetical foundation for his theological position: the Gentiles are integrated into the eschatological people of God *as Gentiles,* without having to become Jews. The messianic temple—the "tent of David" (ἡ σκηνὴ Δαυίδ)—is interpreted as the community of the believers in Jesus the Messiah. The same self-understanding of the Jerusalem church as "temple" is the background for Paul's description of Peter, John and James as "pillar apostles" in Gal 2:9.

James quotes Amos 9:11-12 in order to establish from Scripture that the nations belong to Yahweh *as Gentiles* in the messianic era and that they worship God in the eschatological temple, which is equated with the community of the believers in Jesus the Messiah. There perhaps was no other text that demonstrated this conviction as clearly as did Amos 9:11-12.

---

[97]See Nägele 1995, 192-214; followed by Ådna 2000b, 153-54.

The speech of James in Acts 15:13-21 is "a historically reliable report of the decisive contribution of the brother of Jesus, who supported the circumcision-free Gentile mission."[98] The Gentiles who have been converted to faith in Jesus the Messiah are "a people from among the nations" and represent, together with the converted Jews, the people of God of the messianic period. What appears at first sight to be new is in fact grounded in an action of God that had been prophesied in the sacred Scriptures. François Bovon comments, "Since the novelty is rooted in God, it is not a new invention of the people but an ancient truth that is discovered or understood only now. It seems . . . to be clear, therefore, that Luke saw in the primitive church both the legitimate continuity with the people of Israel and a new creation of God in the midst of the fallen people."[99]

Jacob Jervell refuses even with regard to Acts 15:14 to speak of a "new people,"[100] asserting that "the people is Israel, and Luke uses the phrase 'the people from among the nations' only to describe the Gentiles in the church as a particular group that is therefore not a people, not a nation, but a group consisting of different, non-Jewish peoples." This interpretation is implausible.[101] The argument that the relationship of the Christian community to Israel, the fallen dwelling of David, becomes unclear is not cogent: the scriptural quotation in Acts 15:15-16 does not identify the character of the people of God as "Israel of the fulfilled time of salvation." Rather, it interprets the successful missionary work among both Jews *and Gentiles* as fulfillment of the prophecy of Amos, and thus it identifies the newly established communities in which Jewish believers and Gentile believers live together as the people of God.

7. The Twelve and the Elders, together with the delegation from Antioch and indeed the entire assembly, decided to accept the theological consensus that emerged in the contributions and arguments of Peter, Barnabas, Paul and James as a solution to the controversy (Acts 15:22). They further decided to communicate this consensus in written form to the church in Antioch through Judas-Barsabbas and Silas, "leaders among the brothers" (ἄνδρας ἡγουμένους ἐν τοῖς ἀδελφοῖς, *andras hēgoumenous en tois adelphois*), who would accompany Paul and Barnabas on their journey back to the capital of Syria (Acts 15:23) and who would be able to explain the decision orally (Acts 15:27). Both Judas, of whom nothing further is known, and Silas (Lat., *Silvanus*), who later was a coworker of Paul (Acts 15:40), were men who had the gift of prophecy (Acts 15:32).

The Decree
Luke quotes verbatim the document that was drawn up (Acts 15:23b-29). It con-

---

[98]Ådna 1997, 23; cf. idem 2000b, esp. 126-42.
[99]Bovon 1983, 350; followed by W. Radl ("Rettung in Israel," in Bussmann and Radl 1991, 56), who describes Acts 15:16-18 as "the central statement of the book of Acts."
[100]Jervell 1991, 19; the quotation that follows above, ibid.
[101]See Weiser, *Apg,* 2:386; Roloff, *Apg,* 232.

tains the following elements. (1) Introductory formula (Acts 15:23b) with reference to the senders ("the brothers, both the apostles and the elders") and to the addressees ("to the believers of Gentile origin in Antioch and Syria and Cilicia"). (2) Review of the prehistory of the decision (Acts 15:24-27): the apostles and the leadership of the Jerusalem church emphasize together that the Jewish Christians who had demanded that Gentile Christians be circumcised had not been authorized to formulate such a demand (Acts 15:24). They recount their reaction to the activities of these Jewish Christians: they have made a "unanimous" decision[102] and they acknowledged Barnabas and Paul, "who have risked their lives for the sake of our Lord Jesus Christ" (Acts 15:26). Their achievement for the cause of Christ can be seen not least in the fact that the church accepted their theological argumentation. The council decided to send Judas and Silas to Antioch so that they could explain orally the decision recorded in the document (Acts 15:27). (3) The decision (Acts 15:28-29) made by the Holy Spirit and by the apostles and elders corresponds to the contribution of James in terms of both its structure and its content: (a) they "impose no further burden" on the Gentile Christians (μηδὲν πλέον ἐπιτίθεσθαι ὑμῖν βάρος); (b) they shall "abstain from what has been sacrificed to idols and from blood and from what is strangled and from fornication."

Several suggestions have been offered concerning the interpretation of the stipulations of Acts 15:29:

1. They are practical regulations for a specific situation in which fellowship in the community between Jewish Christians and Gentile Christians had become a problem.[103] The basic demand for the Gentile Christians was that they abandon their former religion, their pagan gods and the spiritual defilement that accompanies idolatry (cf. Acts 15:20 with Acts 15:29). This explanation is not fully convincing because the stipulation that forbids idolatry does not simply seek to establish "practical harmony" between Jewish Christians and Gentile Christians.

2. The stipulations of the apostolic council correspond to the Noahic commandments that the Jews regarded as normative for humanity as a whole (see *Jub.* 7:20).[104] The concrete specifications of the Noahic commandments that we encounter in the rabbinic sources mention the prohibition of idolatry, blasphemy, murder, incest, stealing, perverting justice and eating flesh containing blood. The stipulations of Acts 15:29 contain only the first, third, fourth and seventh commands, which means that the parallel is not very striking. The explanation becomes somewhat more plausible if one regards the Western Text of Acts 15:29 to be original: since the prohibition against eating from what is stran-

---

[102]Acts 15:25a: ἔδοξεν ἡμῖν γενομένοις ὁμοθυμαδόν. For the comment that follows above see Zmijewski, *Apg,* 571.

[103]See Weiser, *Apg,* 2:384-85; Blomberg 1998, 410.

[104]See Flusser 1994, 583; O. Betz 1994, 27; Flusser and Safrai 1986, 173-92.

gled is omitted, the three remaining prohibitions against idolatry, fornication and blood (interpreted by David Flusser as murder) can be compared with the three cardinal sins that a Jew was not supposed to commit under any circumstances, according to a decision made by rabbinic authorities in Lydda around A.D. 120: idolatry, fornication and murder.[105] However, it is rather unlikely that the reading of the Western Text has priority in Acts 15:29.[106]

3. The stipulations should be interpreted against the background of the Old Testament polemic against idolatry.[107] The term *porneia* refers to temple prostitution, while the reference to strangled animals and blood refers to cultic practices of pagans. This interpretation can be criticized for two reasons. First, if the apostolic decree wanted only to direct the Gentile Christians to give up their former pagan practices and to worship the one true God, this concern could have been formulated more clearly and more easily. Second, the decree would not have said anything new and therefore would have been redundant because the renunciation of pagan practices certainly was part and parcel of the message of the missionaries who preached the gospel among Gentiles.

4. The stipulations of the decree correspond to the minimal demands that were obligatory for Jews even if their lives were in danger: idolatry, murder and incest.[108] However, the prohibition against eating from what has been strangled is missing from this list of minimal demands.

5. The stipulations of the apostolic decree should be interpreted in terms of the regulations that Lev 17—18 formulates for Gentiles who live among Jews as "foreigners" (גֵּרִים, *gērîm*): prohibited are (a) *porneia* (Lev 17:10, 12), specifically sexual relations between blood relatives; (b) what has been strangled (Lev 17:13), meaning eating from animals that have not been slaughtered in a ritually proper manner as well as from animals that had a defect; (c) blood (Lev 18:26) as ingredient in food.[109] If this is the conceptual background of the decree, then the agreement in Acts 15:29 represents a (cultic-ritual) compromise formula that aimed at facilitating the communal fellowship of Jewish Christians and Gentile Christians in "mixed churches."[110] However, the pragmatic desire to facilitate table fellowship between Jewish Christians and Gentile Christians alone does not suffice to explain the selection of the four stipulations in Acts 15:20, 29; for example, stipulations for the "foreigner" (*gēr*) such as the sabbath commandment (Ex 20:10; Deut 5:14) are missing. Richard Bauckham argues that the term בְּתוֹךְ

---

[105]See *Sifre Deut.* 41:85; *b. Qidd.* 40b; *b. Sanh.* 74a; *y. Sanh.* 3:21b; 4:35a.

[106]See J. Strange 1992, 87-105; Head 1993, 438-42; Bauckham 1995b, 459.

[107]See Witherington, *Acts,* 461-67; Pao 2000, 241-42.

[108]See *y. Šeb.* 35a.; *y. Sanh.* 21b; *b. Pesaḥ.* 25ab; *b. Sanh.* 74a. See Nägele 1995, 105-7.

[109]See Siegert 1974, 133-35; Klinghardt 1988, 158-80; Heiligenthal 1994, 585-87; Dunn, *Acts,* 204; Bauckham 1995b, 459-60; Wehnert 1997, 209-38 (who did not know Bauckham's study); Kraus 1999, 146-47.

[110]See Dunn, *Acts,* 202, 206-7; N. Taylor 1992, 140-42.

(*bĕtōk,* "in the midst of"), which occurs only in Lev 17—18,[111] links Jer 12:16/
Zech 2:11 (via the quotation of Amos 9:11-12) with Lev 17—18 and thus can
explain the selection of the stipulations in the apostolic decree.[112] The exegetical
argument of James "which created a link between closely related prophecies
and Lev 17—18 establishes that the Law of Moses itself contains just four commandments which do explicitly apply to precisely those Gentiles. . . . [They] are
not simply a pragmatic compromise, dealing with the problem of table fellowship in a context where it is not debatable that Gentile Christians do not have
to keep the Law. In the thinking of those who formulated them, the same exegetical case which demonstrates conclusively that Gentile Christians do not have
to keep the Law also shows that they do have to observe these four prohibitions."

Paul never quotes or refers to the apostolic decree in his letters, even in passages in which he discusses identical issues. Does this mean that the Jerusalem
apostles claimed to possess an authority with regard to the Gentile Christians
that Paul rejected?[113] This question implies, first, that the apostles had no right
to formulate a decision that would be normative for Gentile Christians, and second, that Paul would have rejected such authoritative claims in any case. However, we must remember that Paul does not appeal to his own authority either
when he discusses these issues, despite the fact that he defends his apostolic
status when it is attacked. He emphasizes in his letter to the Galatian Christians
that the gospel that he preaches is a result of a revelation of Jesus Christ, including the renunciation of circumcision for Gentiles. If Paul does not argue from
his own authority as an apostle, why should he appeal to the authority of the
Jerusalem apostles? If Paul, the Twelve and the Elders of the Jerusalem church
agreed theologically on most of the basic questions regarding missionary work
among Gentiles, he would not have gained much in the particular controversies
to which he responded if he had referred his readers to the results of the apostolic council.

Some scholars have argued that Paul's acceptance of the compromise of Acts
15 implied that he tolerated a "different gospel" for a transitional period.[114] This
view is implausible. The agreement that was reached at the apostolic council
in A.D. 48 was basically acceptable for Paul for the following reasons.[115] (1) Paul
was willing to live among Jews as a Jew (1 Cor 9:19-20).(2). Paul rejected *porneia* (1 Cor 6:9). (3) Paul directed the Corinthian Christians not to eat meat in

---

[111]As well as in Lev 16:29; Num 15:14-16, 29; 19:10, where the term refers to the temple cult,
however.
[112]Bauckham 1995b, 460-61; the quotation that follows above, ibid., 461-62.
[113]Thus Bruce 1985b, 655.
[114]See Wehr 1996, 74.
[115]See Marshall, *Acts,* 246 (omit the "not," which turns the meaning of the argument on its
head); Dunn, *Acts,* 197.

the presence of Jewish Christians if it was known that the meat had been offered to idols in a pagan temple (1 Cor 10:25-28). (4) Paul possibly supported
the same proviso with regard to meat that contained blood (Rom 14:13-21).
Theodor Zahn correctly asks whether Paul would have regarded the renunciation of meat sacrificed to idols, of blood, of nonkosher meat and of fornication
as a burden or as a contradiction to his statement in Gal 2:6: "And from those
who were supposed to be acknowledged leaders (what they actually were
makes no difference to me; God shows no partiality)—those leaders contributed nothing to me."[116]

Did the apostolic decree solve the question of how Jewish Christians and
Gentile Christians should live together? Markus Bockmuehl argues that although
the initiatives that are described in Gal 2:1-10 and in Acts 15 fully acknowledged
missionary work among Gentiles, they did not solve the questions that arise out
of the Gentile mission with regard to the specific issues of communal fellowship
between Jewish Christians and Gentile Christians.[117] The controversies in which
Paul was involved after A.D. 48 indicate that the outcome of the apostolic council as described by Luke in Acts 15 did not remove all difficulties. The third faction that Paul describes in Gal 2:4 as "false brothers" who had "infiltrated" the
church in Antioch (τοὺς παρεισάκτους ψευδαδέλφους, *tous pareisaktous pseud-
adelphous*), consistently conservative Jewish Christians who continued to insist
that Gentile Christians be circumcised and instructed to keep the law, did not
give up. Subsequent developments in, for example, Galatian churches, clearly
demonstrate that the dispute about the status of Gentile Christians persisted. By
the second and third centuries, however, the church generally accepted the stipulations of the apostolic decree.[118] Traugott Holtz concludes, "James, Peter and
Barnabas won not only in Antioch but in the early church as a whole."

The hypothesis of Ferdinand Baur, who argues that Peter and Paul split over
the question of the validity of the law and that their missionary activities developed in separate ways, therefore is not only one-sided but also false. The Antioch incident did not cause a permanent rupture of the unity of the Christian
movement. The direct and indirect contacts between Peter and Paul can be summarized as follows.

33/34	Jerusalem	Paul visits Peter in Jerusalem, after having engaged in missionary work in Arabia and in Damascus, three years after his conversion (Gal 1:18-19).
44	Jerusalem	Consultation with Peter, James and John in the context of the famine relief that the church in Antioch had organized for the believers in

---

[116]Zahn, *Apg*, 539-40; followed by Böcher 1989, 331.
[117]See Bockmuehl 2000, 81.
[118]Wehnert 1997, 145-208. For the quotation that follows above see Holtz 1986, 355.

Jerusalem, together with Barnabas, twelve years later (Gal 2:1-10; Acts 11:27-30), shortly before embarking on the missionary journey to Cyprus and to Galatia.

48	Antioch	Confrontation with Peter in Antioch because of Peter's abandonment of table fellowship with the Gentile Christians (Gal 2:11-14), probably in the summer of that year.
48	Jerusalem	Apostolic council in the Jewish capital, with the discussion demonstrating that Peter, Paul and James agree theologically in their evaluation of the Gentile mission; the apostles, elders of the Jerusalem church and the missionaries agree on basic practical details that should facilitate the fellowship of Jewish Christians and Gentile Christians (Acts 15:1-29), probably in the fall of that year.
54	Corinth	Paul expresses his high regard for Peter, his fellow apostle and fellow missionary, in his first letter to the Corinthians (1 Cor 3:21-23; 9:5; 15:5-8); if Peter visited Corinth some time after A.D. 42, he is not criticized by Paul.
60-62	Rome	Paul and Peter possibly were in Rome at the same time, perhaps both being prisoners; under Nero, both died for their faith; Peter expresses his high regard for Paul in his second letter (2 Pet 3:15-16)

25.4 Conflict with Jewish Opponents

Paul was involved in controversy and conflict in practically every city in which he worked as a missionary. Having been a rabbi who had persecuted Christians and dragged them before courts of law, he could hardly have been surprised. And Jesus had repeatedly pointed out that his disciples whom he called and trained to be "fishers of people" would encounter resistance and opposition, the parable of the sower being a prime example (Mk 4:1-20). Paul repeatedly was forced to hastily depart from the city in which he was active after he had become aware of planned attacks on his life. Luke's account of such incidents (Acts 13:50-51; 14:2, 5-6, 19; 17:5-9, 13-14; 18:6, 12-17; 21:27-36; 23:12-25; cf. 16:19-40; 19:23-41) is confirmed by Paul's own testimony (2 Cor 11:24-25; 1 Thess 2:2, 13-16). On five different occasions Paul was punished with the synagogue penalty of "forty lashes less one" (2 Cor 11:24). When traveling, he faced the danger of being attacked by Jews who wanted to eliminate him: he was nearly stoned in Iconium (Acts 14:5); he was stoned in Lystra but escaped with his life (Acts 14:19); he was protected by 470 soldiers that the Romans had provided for the journey from Jerusalem to Caesarea after news about a planned attack had surfaced (Acts 23:12-25).

Wolfgang Reinbold argues, as do many scholars who view the historical reliability of the book of Acts with suspicion, that Luke intensifies and exaggerates the conflicts with the Jews; he insists that the "emphasis on the opposition of the Jews in the book of Acts" needs to be corrected by scholars more consistently. Reinbold suggests that Paul's statements in 1 Thess 2:14-16 are a polemic that can be used for historical reconstruction only with great caution, moderating the assertions that Paul makes at many points. The five instances in which Paul received the "forty lashes less one" (2 Cor 11:24) were purely an "internal matter of the synagogues" and a punishment that Paul could easily have avoided because it was not related to his missionary preaching; rather, it was a consequence of his non-Jewish way of life.[119] However, the likelihood that Luke's account is historically authentic is indicated by the fact that the details of the various controversies and conflicts that Luke reports are quite diverse and certainly not "stylized."[120] It is preposterous to separate Paul's punishment with the "forty lashes less one" from his missionary work: Paul refers to these incidents in 2 Cor 11 in the context of a review of his ministry as an apostle of Jesus Christ.

We should note that Paul never links his opponents with Jerusalem; on the contrary, he speaks of Jerusalem always in positive terms.[121] This does not exclude the possibility, however, that his opponents were aware of, for example, the persecution that Herod Agrippa I had instigated against the leaders of the Christians in Jerusalem.

One of the most important texts in which Paul discusses the hostility of Jews against his mission and the message that he proclaims is 1 Thess 2:13-16:

"We also constantly give thanks to God for this, that when you received the word of God that you heard from us, you accepted it not as a human word but as what it really is, God's word, which is also at work in you believers. [14]For you, brothers and sisters, became imitators of the churches of God in Christ Jesus that are in Judea, for you suffered the same things from your own compatriots as they did from the Jews, [15]who killed both the Lord Jesus and the prophets, and drove us out; they displease God and oppose everyone [16]by hindering us from speaking to the Gentiles so that they may be saved. Thus they have constantly been filling up the measure of their sins; but God's wrath has overtaken them at last."

The authenticity of this passage is disputed,[122] but the arguments that are adduced to support the view that 1 Thess 2:13-16 is a non-Pauline interpolation are unconvincing.[123] Paul does not attack Jews as such: the charge that the Jews "displease God and oppose everyone" (1 Thess 2:15c) is not anti-Jewish and must be interpreted in a historical context, as the substantiation in 1 Thess 2:16b shows. The Jews "oppose everyone" (πᾶσιν ἀνθρώποις, *pasin anthrōpois*) be-

---

[119]Reinbold 2000, 208-9.

[120]See Botermann 1996, 132 with n. 417; Molthagen (1991) is still too skeptical.

[121]See W. Campbell 1993b, 514.

[122]Birger A. Pearson, "1 Thessalonians 2:13-16: A Deutero-Pauline Interpolation," *HTR* 64 (1971): 79-94; Daryl Schmidt, "1 Thess 2:13-16: Linguistic Evidence for an Interpolation," *JBL* 102 (1983): 269-79.

[123]See Holtz, *1 Thess*, 96-97, 111-13; Marshall, *Thess*, 11-13; Wanamaker, *Thess*, 29-31, 108-9; J. A. Weatherly, "The Authenticity of 1 Thessalonians 2.13-16: Additional Evidence," *JSNT* 42 (1991): 79-98; Schlueter 1995; Hvalvik 1996, 221-22.

cause they actively seek to hinder Paul from preaching the gospel to the Gentiles (τοῖς ἔθνεσιν, *tois ethnesin*), thus factually preventing the salvation of people on judgment day. The issue is not the Jews as a nation or as an ethnic group; rather, the problem that Paul discusses is the fact that Jews oppose God's ambassadors as they persecute the missionaries.[124]

Luke mentions four factors that motivated the Jewish opposition against Paul.

1. Jealousy. The word ζῆλος (*zēlos*) describes "a passionate commitment to a person or cause"; in Acts 13:45; 17:5 it designates particularly "hostility occasioned by ill-will," with obstinacy, passion and a sense of religious obligation playing a role as well.[125] Luke refers to the motif of jealousy for the Jews in Pisidian Antiocheia and for the Jews in Thessalonike (Acts 13:45: ἐπλήσθησαν ζήλου, *eplēsthēsan zēlou;* Acts 17:5: ζηλώσαντες, *zēlōsantes*). Both texts speak of the missionary success of Paul and his coworkers not only in the local synagogues but also in "the whole city" (Acts 13:44) and among "a great many of the devout Greeks and not a few of the leading women" (Acts 17:4). It is not clear whether Luke wants to assert that the Jews in Antiocheia and in Thessalonike were jealous because their own missionary efforts were less successful.[126] Jealousy on account of numerically superior successes of others or on account of better "poll results" is an inferior human sentiment that surely can be indulged in by Jews as well. However, since there is no hard evidence for a Jewish mission among Gentiles, this interpretation is unlikely. The "jealousy" could have been caused by the fear that the unexpected successes of the new apocalyptic Jewish "sect" might undermine the reputation of the local Jewish community and the good relations that they had with the city magistrates and with the population in general. And if women of the leading families of the city joined the new group after having connected with the synagogue, the fear of losing some of the legal protection and the political influence that the Jews enjoyed in the city might have played a role as well. Or perhaps the Jews were afraid that the success of a "liberal" Jewish sect that spoke of the impotence of the Mosaic law (cf. Acts 13:38) might jeopardize the efforts of the local synagogues to withstand the pressure of assimilation that was always a reality in Greek cities and to stand firm against syncretistic tendencies, goals that the Diaspora synagogues sought to reach by emphasizing the ethnic and religious particularities and traditions of the Jewish people.[127]

2. Fear of losing political influence. The Jewish magician Elymas sought to keep Sergius Paullus, the procurator of Cyprus, from converting to faith in Jesus Christ

---

[124]Hvalvik 1996, 223; cf. Holtz, *1 Thess,* 106.
[125]W. Popkes, *EWNT* 2:248 (*EDNT* 2:100), following A. Stumpff, *ThWNT* 2:879 (*TDNT* 2:876).
[126]Thus Haenchen, *Apg,* 488 (ET, 507); Barrett, *Acts,* 1:655; Hvalvik 1996, 220 with n. 25.
[127]See Dunn, *Acts,* 183, 227; Pesch, *Apg,* 2:45, 122-23; Roloff, *Apg,* 209, 259; Zmijewski, *Apg,* 518, 623.

by working against Paul and Barnabas when they engaged in missionary work in Paphos (Acts 13:8-11), evidently because he was afraid of losing his influence.[128]

3. Unbelief. Luke describes the opposition of the Jews in Iconium as "disobe-dience" (ἀπειθεῖν, *apeithein*)—that is, unbelief (Acts 14:2). The motivation for the opposition against Paul is the rejection of the theological convictions that Paul and Barnabas taught in the synagogue, preaching the message of the cru-cified and risen Jesus as Messiah and Savior. The reaction of the Corinthian Jews is recounted along similar lines: when the synagogue audience heard the mes-sage of Jesus, they refused (ἀντιτάσσειν, *antitassein*) to accept the messianic identity of Jesus and denigrated in a demeaning manner (βλασφημεῖν, *blasphēmein*) the teaching of the missionaries (Acts 18:6). In Ephesus it is again the unbelief of the majority of the Jews in the synagogue that prompts them to insult (κακολογεῖν, *kakologein*) the missionaries and their message (Acts 19:9).

4. Pressure from Jews from other cities. The Jews of Lystra stoned Paul after they had been "persuaded" (πείθειν, *peithein*) by Jews from Antiocheia and Ico-nium to reject the teaching of Paul and of Barnabas and to take action against them (Acts 14:19). Similarly, Jews from Thessalonike agitated crowds in Beroea, in whose synagogue people had listened attentively to Paul's teaching, with the result that Paul and his coworkers had to leave the city (Acts 17:13).

25.5 Conflict with Jewish-Christian Teachers in Asia Minor

Not long after Paul had established churches in southern Galatia—in Antiocheia, Iconium, Lystra and Derbe—Jewish-Christian teachers visited these communi-ties and demanded that the Gentile Christians submit to circumcision and keep the Mosaic law, including the Jewish feasts (Gal 3:2; 4:10; 5:2-12; 6:12). Even though the sources are not explicit, it seems that these teachers had invited themselves into the churches that Paul had founded.

These Jewish-Christian teachers who opposed Paul's teaching in the Galatian churches have been explained in terms of Judaizing libertarians,[129] Jewish gnos-tics,[130] Gentile Christians,[131] or Jews,[132] suggestions that are unconvincing.[133] They were Jewish Christians who demanded that the Gentile Christians be cir-cumcised.[134] Many scholars describe these "conservative" Jewish Christians as "missionaries"[135] who engaged in "missionary work" in the churches that Paul

---

[128]See Pesch, *Apg*, 2:24.

[129]See Lütgert 1919.

[130]See Schmithals 1965, 9-46.

[131]See Munck 1954, 79-80.

[132]N. Walter, "Paulus und die Gegner des Christusevangeliums in Galatien," in Vanhoye 1986, 351-56.

[133]See Mussner, *Gal*, 15-24; Longenecker, *Gal*, xci-xciv; Becker, *Gal*, 12; Lang 1996, 427-28.

[134]See Cineira 1999, 291-317.

[135]See, for example, Martyn 1985; Dunn, *Gal*, 10-11.

had established, propagating contrary doctrines as "foreign missionaries" in a "countermission."[136] This description is not very helpful if we understand the term "missionary" to refer to followers of Jesus who proclaim the message of Jesus the crucified and risen Messiah and Savior with the goal of leading Jews and Gentiles to faith in Jesus Christ and of establishing communities of believers. A "countermission" would have had a primarily or even exclusively negative purpose and could hardly be described as proclamation of "good news." The expression "foreign missionary" (*Fremdmissionar*) is strange and vague and does not clarify anything. If Jewish Christians traveled from Jerusalem to Galatia to visit the churches that Paul had established with the purpose of convincing Gentile Christians to submit to circumcision and to the Torah, they were not "missionaries" but "teachers."[137]

The Jewish-Christian teachers who visited the churches in Galatia probably came from Jerusalem. Cilliers Breytenbach suggests that the controversy in the churches in southern Galatia was caused by Galatian Jewish Christians who maintained their connection with the local synagogues after their conversion to Jesus the Messiah and who demanded that the newly converted Gentile Christians keep the commandments of the law, including circumcision.[138] Three considerations suggest, however, that the Jewish-Christian teachers came from outside, probably from Jerusalem. (1) Paul consistently distinguishes these opponents from the Galatian Christians to whom he addresses his letter (Gal 1:7-9; 3:1; 4:17; 5:7, 12; 6:12-13). (2) Paul refers to opponents of his proclamation who demand that Gentile Christians be circumcised and who are connected with Jerusalem (Gal 2:4, 12; 4:29). (3) The motivation of the Jewish-Christian teachers seems to be linked with the political situation in Judea, where the increasing activity of the Zealot resistance movement appears to have prompted Jewish Christians to try to avoid persecution "for the cross of Christ" (Gal 6:12) by insisting that converted Gentiles who are admitted into the people of God be circumcised and directed to keep the law, a measure that would allow Jewish Christians to refute the charge of betraying the Torah.[139]

Paul never explicitly indicates in his letter to the Galatians that the visiting teachers come from Jerusalem or from Judea. Jürgen Becker argues that an institution that might have threatened to persecute Jewish Christians could have existed only in Jerusalem and Judea.[140] This view overlooks the events that transpired in the cities of southern Galatia: Jews of Pisidian Antiocheia who resented

---

[136]See recently Becker, *Gal*, 10, 12.
[137]See Martyn *Gal*, 18, 117-26; Martyn, however, also characterizes them as "evangelists" (18, 121).
[138]Breytenbach 1996, 99-173.
[139]See Robert Jewett, "The Agitators and the Galatian Congregation," *NTS* 17 (1971): 198-212, esp. 205; followed by Bruce, *Gal*, 269; Longenecker, *Gal*, 291; cf. Martyn, *Gal*, 562 n. 55.
[140]Becker, *Gal*, 99.

the success of Paul's missionary work among the Gentile population not only cursed Paul and his message (βλασφημεῖν, *blasphēmein* [Acts 13:45]) but also instigated a persecution (ἐπήγειραν διωγμόν, *epēgeiran diōgmon* [Acts 13:50]) that caused Paul and Barnabas to depart from the city. Jews of Iconium took action against Paul because "a great number of both Jews and Greeks became believers" (Acts 14:1): they "stirred up" (ἐπήγειραν, *epēgeiran* [Acts 14:2]) the majority Gentile population, and "an attempt was made" (ἐγένετο ὁρμή, *egeneto hormē*) by the Jews and the city magistrates to mistreat Paul and Barnabas and to stone them (ὑβρίσαι καὶ λιθοβολῆσαι, *hybrisai kai lithobolēsai* [Acts 14:5]), resulting in the hasty departure of the missionaries. Jews from Antiocheia and Iconium make the effort to travel to Lystra to make sure that the population would not listen to Paul and Barnabas, instigating such antagonism that a crowd stoned Paul (Acts 14:19). If Jews of Antiocheia traveled to Lystra, a journey of 180 km, in order to "take care" of Paul and Barnabas, one may indeed speak in terms of an "institution" that could intimidate local Jewish Christians. It surely is no coincidence that Paul encourages the Christians in southern Galatia with the words "It is through many persecutions that we must enter the kingdom of God" (Acts 14:22).

The reference to the "false brothers" (ψευδαδέλφοι, *pseudadelphoi*) in Gal 2:4 who wanted to force Titus to be circumcised a few years earlier in Jerusalem allows us to identify a group of "conservative" Jewish Christians in Jerusalem (or Judea) who proactively worked against Paul and against his teaching that Gentile Christians do not need to be circumcised, demanding that the new converts be taught to submit to the Torah. It seems logical to link this group with those Jewish Christians who had been Pharisees before their conversion, a group that Luke mentions in connection with the apostolic council[141] who argued that Gentile Christians must be circumcised and taught to keep the Mosaic law (Acts 15:5).[142] The Jewish Christians who had traveled to Antioch, the capital of the province of Syria, to put pressure on Peter came "from James" (τινας ἀπὸ Ἰακώβου, *tinas apo Iakōbou* [Gal 2:12]), which presumably is a reference to Jerusalem. Paul's reference in the midrash (or allegory) on Hagar and Sara to the current persecution that the Galatian Christians have to endure (Gal 4:29) connects the "persecutors" also with Jerusalem (Gal 4:25). Paul seems to compare several situations, without, however, identifying them with each other: the consultation in Jerusalem (Gal 2:1-5), the incident in Antioch (Gal 2:11-14) and the current situation in the Galatian churches. What connects these situations is, on the one hand, the demand of Jewish Christians that Gentile Christians keep the Mosaic law and be circumcised and, on the other hand, their origin in or connection with Jerusalem.

---

[141]Acts 15:5: τινες τῶν ἀπὸ τῆς αἱρέσεως τῶν Φαρισαίων πεπιστευκότες.

[142]See, for example, Dunn, *Gal*, 98.

The activities of these Jewish-Christian activists may be connected with the attempt of the Jews in the city of Rome to push the (Jewish) Christians into illegality in order to avoid future measures of repression by the emperor. The edict of Claudius against the (Jewish) Christians of Rome in A.D. 41 was only six or seven years in the past when the Jewish-Christian teachers from Jerusalem traveled to the Galatian churches in A.D. 47/48. And the disturbances in the synagogues of the city of Rome that caused Claudius in A.D. 49 to order the expulsion of all Jews from Rome presumably were already underway. The scenario that David Alvarez Cineira suggests may well be a historically plausible reconstruction of the events: "The Jewish Christians in Jerusalem felt driven into a corner by the strategy of the Jews. The way in which the Pauline mission was being realized, without circumcision, became a real danger for all Christians. The believers in Jerusalem were aware of the fact that persecution by the Romans was a real possibility if the new Christian group were to be declared a *collegium illicitum*. . . . In view of this new situation the church in Jerusalem had to make an important decision: if the Christian movement presented itself as a new religion separate from Judaism, then it faced possible illegality. But if it remained within Judaism, then it could continue to engage in missionary work without problems. The Jerusalem church decided in favor of staying close to Judaism. This decision implied appropriate measures, namely, the insistence that followers of Jesus be circumcised and follow the Jewish feast calendar so that outsiders would continue to regard Christianity as a Jewish group."[143] It is unlikely, I suggest, that the entire Jerusalem church adopted this view and officially supported the activities of the Jewish-Christian teachers who opposed Paul—as well as the decision of the apostolic council of A.D. 48, which evidently was supported by the Elders of the Jerusalem church.

The Jewish-Christian teachers bring a twofold charge against Paul. (1) The message that Paul preaches is "of human origin" (κατὰ ἄνθρωπον, *kata anthrōpon* [Gal 1:11]); that is, he proclaims a message that is controlled by human norms rather than by divine revelation. (2) His gospel is "from a human source" (παρὰ ἀνθρώπου, *para anthrōpou* [Gal 1:12]); that is, it has been borrowed from other people and therefore is not of divine origin, which means that Paul cannot claim to have apostolic authority.[144] Paul's argumentation in Gal 3—4 suggests that the Jewish-Christian teachers focused on Abraham as "father" (Gen 17:4) in whom "all the Gentiles shall be blessed" (Gal 3:8). Evidently, they argue that when a Gentile wants to become a son of Abraham and an heir of

---

[143]Cineira 1999, 314.

[144]See Mussner, *Gal,* 64-65; Beker 1987, 44-45; Lang 1996, 428, following J. Jeremias, "Chiasmus in den Paulusbriefen" [1958], in Jeremias 1966, 276-89, esp. 285-86. Jeremias understands the outline of the Epistle to the Galatians as Paul's answer, constructed as a chiasm, to these two charges: Gal 1:13—2:21 answers the charge of Gal 1:12, and Gal 3:6—4:7, 21-31 answers the charge of Gal 1:11. See the critique in Longenecker, *Gal,* 21-22.

the promised divine blessing, he has to be integrated into God's covenant people by circumcision, just as Abraham accepted circumcision, and he has to be obedient to the commandments of the law, the normative revelation of God, as Abraham was consistently obedient to the will of God. This understanding of God's promises, of covenant and law seeks to integrate God's redemptive revelation in Jesus Christ into God's revelation in the law, subordinating the former to the latter.

It appears that the teachers from Jerusalem were edging on to victory. Paul felt compelled to write a strongly worded, formidable letter in which he warns the new believers in the churches in Galatia not to accept the teaching of these people. More importantly, he explains the "logic of the gospel" as good news of justification by faith in Jesus Christ alone, apart from works that the law required. Paul demonstrates and emphasizes that the grace of God, which was revealed in Jesus Christ and became effective in their lives when they repented and believed in him, removes all ethnic and social barriers. Paul interprets the pronouncements of the teachers about faith and promise, covenant and law, as, in the words of Friedrich Lang, "an all-out attack on the truth of the gospel. He argues: Abraham who *believed* God (Gen 15:6) is the 'father of all *who believe*' (Gal 3:9 [*sic*]). Everyone who believes in the *one* true seed of Abraham, Jesus Christ (Gal 3:16) who has redeemed us from the curse of the law (Gal 3:13) is Abraham's seed and heir according to the promise (Gal 3:29). . . . For Paul the combination of grace and righteousness according to the law amounts to a rejection of the substitutionary death of atonement of Christ (Gal 2:21)."[145] Justification by faith in Jesus Christ makes the believer a recipient of God's promise to Abraham, whether Jew or Gentile. Circumcision leads Gentile believers only into a new slavery. Faith in Jesus Christ enables the follower of Jesus to lead a life according to the will of God in the context of the conflict of flesh and Spirit: circumcision and obedience to the commandments of the law—that is, conversion to Judaism—is unnecessary. The story of Abraham, which evidently played an important role in the theology of the Jewish-Christian teachers, demonstrates, for Paul, not simply that justification by God takes place only as a result of faith in God's word; it also demonstrates that the Gentile believers are "sons of Abraham" and therefore fully valid members of the people of God. And it demonstrates that his missionary work among polytheists has a firm foundation in the sacred Scriptures.[146]

If James Dunn is correct, the Christian teachers who were active in Colossae and who challenged Paul, his fellow missionaries and the message that they preached, were not much different from his Jewish-Christian opponents in the

---

[145]Lang 1996, 430, 433.
[146]See Hansen 1989.

Galatian churches.[147] The "philosophy" that the opponents in Colossae promulgated in the church evidently was regarded as a supplement to the apostolic message of the gospel, not as a substitute. As Paul argued in his letter to the Galatians (Gal 2:19—3:1; 6:12-14), he contends here that the proponents of the teaching that threatens the church in Colossae do not properly understand the gospel of the cross (Col 2:8-15). As in Galatia, teachers who have come from outside into the church in Colossae impressed Gentile Christians with regulations and practices that they were supposed to follow (Col 2:16, 20-23). In both situations "human tradition" (κατὰ τὴν παράδοσιν τῶν ἀνθρώπων, kata tēn paradosin tōn anthrōpōn [Col 2:8])—a phrase that reflects Paul's verdict on the message of the controversial teachers—plays a central role that the newly converted Gentile Christians are expected to adopt, including Jewish feasts (Gal 4:10; Col 2:16), food laws (Gal 2:11-14; Col 2:21), veneration of angels (Gal 3:19; Col 2:18), elemental forces (στοιχεῖα τοῦ κόσμου, stoicheia tou kosmou [Gal 4:3; Col 2:8, 20]) and halakic regulations that are meant to control the flesh (Gal 2:11-14; Col 2:21). In contrast to the Jewish-Christian teachers who visited the Galatian churches and emphasized the necessity of circumcision, the opponents in Colossae do not seem to have focused on circumcision. However, the allusion to circumcision in Col 2:11, the allusion to the Jewish evaluation of Gentiles with the reference to the "uncircumcision of sinful nature" in Col 2:13, and the refusal to differentiate in the church between circumcised believers and uncircumcised believers (Col 3:11) make it likely that the issue of circumcision was indeed a part of the teaching of the Jewish-Christian activists in Colossae. It is impossible to say whether the Jewish-Christian teachers in Colossae were the same people as the teachers in the Galatian churches. This would suggest that this "conservative" group of Jewish-Christian teachers sustained their geographically expansive opposition against Paul's missionary work for ten to fifteen years between A.D. 47/48 (Galatians) and A.D. 60 (Colossians).

25.6 Conflict with Jewish-Christian Teachers in Corinth

Paul discusses in the last chapters of his second letter to the Corinthian Christians the activity and charges of external teachers who had visited the church in Corinth (2 Cor 10—13). These Christian teachers (2 Cor 11:4) claim to be apostles of Christ (2 Cor 11:13); they are Jews (2 Cor 11:22) who want to be "servants of Christ" (2 Cor 11:23) and who seek to substantiate their claims of apostolic dignity with letters of recommendation (2 Cor 3:1; 10:2; 11:5, 13). They boast about their extraordinary experiences with the Holy Spirit, visions, revelations, signs and wonders (2 Cor 11:18; 12:1-10, 12). And they claim to have the right to receive room and board and money from the church (2 Cor 11:8-9).

---

[147]Dunn, Col, 33-35, esp. 136-37; for the analysis that follows above see ibid. Wright (Col, 24-28) assumes a purely Jewish opposition.

Friedrich Lang summarizes the arguments that suggest that these preachers were Hellenistic Jewish Christians from Syria.[148] (1) The "different gospel" of the new teachers evidently is connected not with demands that Gentile Christians be circumcised and keep the cultic Torah but rather with a different concept of the Spirit (2 Cor 11:4). This seems to indicate that the message of the teachers had Hellenistic philosophical origins, which suggests Antioch in Syria (or Alexandria in Egypt) rather than Jerusalem as geographical origin. (2) The intruding teachers are proud about their rhetorical abilities (2 Cor 11:6-7), and they operate with letters of recommendation (2 Cor 3:1), characteristics that seem to make less sense for envoys from Jerusalem. (3) The robust attack against the teachers as "false apostles, deceitful workmen, masquerading as apostles of Christ" (2 Cor 11:13 RSV) can hardly refer to the Jerusalem apostles, with whom Paul agrees theologically (1 Cor 15:11). (4) The question of the Mosaic law plays no role in Paul's evaluation of the teachers who had come to Corinth. According to 2 Cor 13:3-10, the issue was what factors and characteristics are crucial for ministry: "weakness or divine power, suffering in following the crucified Lord or pneumatic abilities, specifically . . . the question of how the power of the risen Christ becomes effective in the proclamation and in the life of his apostles."[149]

It is a common assumption that the intruders in the Corinthian church were itinerant missionaries, and scholars point to the phrase "if someone comes to you" (εἰ ὁ ἐρχόμενος, *ei ho erchomenos* [2 Cor 11:4]) and to the intruders' activities: they proclaim Jesus, they convey the Spirit and they preach a "gospel" (2 Cor 11:4).[150] This assumption is not a foregone conclusion. We know that these preachers came to Corinth from other churches (with letters of recommendation), but we do not know whether they had established these churches. We know that they were Christian preachers who spoke of Jesus, the gospel and the Holy Spirit, but we do not know for certain whether they preached before unbelievers whom they sought to lead to faith in Jesus Christ. They may have been teachers who visited churches founded by other missionaries in order to influence them in accordance with their theological agenda. Some scholars therefore are more cautious and refer to these opponents as "preachers."[151] Wolfgang Reinbold suggests that they were Christians who traveled from church to church with letters of recommendation, and they did not intend to establish new churches.[152] David Alvarez Cineira points out that the available evidence does not allow us to say with certainty to which group these teachers belonged; he does not see a connection with the edict of Claudius issued in A.D. 48.[153] Ad-

---

[148]Lang 1996, 422-27.

[149]Lang 1996, 426.

[150]See Wolff, *2 Kor,* 213; Martin, *2 Cor,* 335; Thrall, *2 Cor,* 665; Lang 1996, 423.

[151]See Scott, *2 Cor,* 204-5; Lambrecht, *2 Cor,* 174, 180-81.

[152]Reinbold 2000, 108.

[153]Cineira 343-47.

olf Schlatter proposes, not very convincingly, that Paul refers in 2 Cor 11:4 to an apostle who wanted to visit the church in Corinth in order to mediate the dispute in the church.[154]

These "super-apostles" did not establish new churches; they wanted to change the theological outlook of (Gentile) Christians in existing churches. Friedrich Lang comments, "Since the apostolic mission of Paul to the Gentiles had been officially acknowledged by the Jerusalem agreement, his rivals directed their attack not against the teaching of the freedom from the law but against the 'weak' person and the authority of Paul in order to destroy if work in Corinth."[155] Paul asserts in 2 Cor 11:4 that these teachers preach "another Jesus" (ἄλλον Ἰησοῦν, *allon Iēsoun*), a "different spirit" (πνεῦμα ἕτερον, *pneuma heteron*) and a "different gospel" (εὐαγγέλιον ἕτερον, *euangelion heteron*). If we connect the terms "Jesus," "spirit" and "gospel," and if we take into account that circumcision and law do not figure as themes in Second Corinthians, then the position of the visiting teachers in the Corinthian church can be characterized, as Friedrich Lang does, as follows: "The intruders evidently maintain a view concerning the relationship between the crucified Jesus and the risen Christ, who is active through the Spirit, that is different from Paul's teaching when he founded the church. . . . They probably represent a different type of apostle, one who appealed to pneumatic abilities."[156]

I conclude this chapter by quoting 2 Cor 11:23-28, a text in which Paul describes the dangers and the suffering that he faced as a missionary:

"Are they ministers of Christ? I am talking like a madman—I am a better one: with far greater labors, far more imprisonments, with countless floggings, and often near death. [24]Five times I have received from the Jews the forty lashes minus one. [25]Three times I was beaten with rods. Once I received a stoning. Three times I was shipwrecked; for a night and a day I was adrift at sea; [26]on frequent journeys, in danger from rivers, danger from bandits, danger from my own people, danger from Gentiles, danger in the city, danger in the wilderness, danger at sea, danger from false brothers and sisters; [27]in toil and hardship, through many a sleepless night, hungry and thirsty, often without food, cold and naked. [28]And, besides other things, I am under daily pressure because of my anxiety for all the churches."

Paul did not enjoy speaking about these matters. He asserts that he has worked harder and been arrested more often than any other apostle, that he has been beaten frequently and that he often nearly died only because the visiting teachers in Corinth forced him to substantiate his apostolic legitimacy. If he must boast, he prefers to boast of the things that show his weakness (2 Cor 11:30) so that it will be evident that the power of Jesus Christ dwells in him (2 Cor 12:9).

---

[154]Schlatter, *Kor,* 631-35.
[155]Lang 1996, 427.
[156]Lang 1996, 423, 425.

26

MISSIONARY WORK IN ARABIA, SYRIA AND CILICIA

P aul started to preach the good news of Jesus, the crucified, risen and exalted Messiah, right after his conversion on the road to Damascus in A.D. 31/32. The popular view that Paul began to engage in independent missionary work only after his ministry in the church in Antioch (i.e., only after A.D. 44), about twelve years after his conversion, ignores important evidence from Paul's letters. We know little about the period between Paul's conversion and his missionary work on Cyprus and in southern Galatia. However, the New Testament sources provide sufficient evidence for us to reconstruct, at lease in broad outlines, his activity during this period.

26.1 Missionary Work in Arabia, Damascus and Jerusalem

Evangelism in Damascus

Luke reports that Paul spoke of his newly found faith in Jesus the "Son of God" in the synagogues of Damascus soon after his conversion (Acts 9:20, 22). The message of Jesus had been brought to Damascus probably by Jewish Christians from Jerusalem (see §20.5). The evangelistic activity of Paul in Damascus dates to the early weeks after his conversion, around A.D. 31/32.

Acts 9:19b-22: "For several days he was with the disciples in Damascus, [20]and immediately he began to proclaim Jesus in the synagogues, saying, 'He is the Son of God.' [21]All who heard him were amazed and said, 'Is not this the man who made havoc in Jerusalem among those who invoked this name? And has he not come here for the purpose of bringing them bound before the chief priests?' [22]Saul became increasingly more powerful and confounded the Jews who lived in Damascus by proving that Jesus was the Messiah."

Some scholars argue that Acts 9:20-22 is a Lukan composition that uses traditional elements; particularly the flight from Damascus, they say, is derived from

Pauline tradition.[1] However, it is indeed possible to reconstruct the course of events on the basis of comments in Paul's letters (Gal 1:15-17; 2 Cor 11:32-33) and Luke's brief account (Acts 9:20-25). The following seven stages emerge. (1) Paul began to speak about Jesus the Messiah in the synagogues of Damascus right after his conversion (Acts 9:19, 20, 22). (2) Paul initiated missionary work in Arabia-Nabatea, based in Damascus (Gal 1:17). (3) Paul returned to Damascus, where he continued to preach the gospel (Gal 1:17). (4) Paul evidently was so successful in his missionary activity in Damascus and Arabia that the local Jews sought to eliminate him (Acts 9:23-24). (5) The Jews of Damascus succeeded in winning the support of the ethnarch of the Nabatean king for plans to arrest Paul (2 Cor 11:32). (6) Paul managed to evade capture by escaping over the city walls (Acts 9:25; 2 Cor 11:33). (7) Paul went to Jerusalem—his first visit since his conversion three years earlier (Gal 1:18).

Paul reports that he did not confer with "any human being" (lit., "flesh and blood") after his conversion but went immediately to Arabia before returning to Damascus (Gal 1:16-17). It therefore is possible that the missionary activity in Damascus that Luke mentions in Acts 9:20 took place not before his sojourn in Arabia. It is more plausible, however, that he returned to Damascus after his stay in Arabia and resumed his earlier preaching activity there (Acts 9:22), causing the reaction of the Nabatean ethnarch, which forced him to leave Damascus.

Acts 9:23-25: "After some time had passed, the Jews plotted to kill him, [24]but their plot became known to Saul. They were watching the gates day and night so that they might kill him; [25]but his disciples took him by night and let him down through an opening in the wall, lowering him in a basket."

2 Cor 11:32-33: "In Damascus, the governor [ethnarch] under King Aretas guarded the city of Damascus in order to seize me, [33]but I was let down in a basket through a window in the wall, and escaped from his hands."

Evangelism in Arabia

Paul states in Gal 1:17 that he went to Arabia after his conversion. As we will see, there is sufficient evidence to suggest that Paul engaged in missionary activity in Arabia, which refers to the Nabatean kingdom east of the Jordan River, ruled at the time by King Aretas IV. Paul had lived as a student of Rabbi Gamaliel for several years and would have been able to see Arabia from the Psephinus Tower (Josephus, *B.J.* 5.159-160). Damascus was situated at the northern edge of Nabatea.

---

[1]See, for example, Weiser, *Apg,* 1:231; Burchard 1970, 150-55; Lüdemann 1987, 122-23 (ET, 116-18).

Arabia (᾿ Ἀραβία [see fig. 23]),[2] understood as a geographical term, designates the Syrian desert between the valleys of the Jordan and the Orontes rivers and Mesopotamia and the adjacent peninsula to the south between the Red Sea in the west and the Persian Gulf and the Indian Ocean in the east.[3] In Roman and in Jewish terminology Arabia was the region to the south of the Roman province of Syria; it included Moab and Edom and extended from the Hauran Mountains in the north to the regions east and west of the Gulf of Aqaba. Most of the inhabitants of Arabia were Nabateans, whose language was a precursor of modern Arabic. The nomadic Nabateans first appear in the central Negev as group that was distinguished from other Arab tribes.[4] The Nabateans settled during the third century B.C. in the old tribal region of Edom, while the Idumeans established themselves in the area south of Judea. In the second century B.C. the Nabateans established a Hellenistic-type kingdom with the capital in Petra, situated between the Dead Sea and the Gulf of Aqaba. Josephus calls the region *Arabia Petrea* (*B.J.* 1.267). Strabo, who provides the most extensive description of the Nabateans, speaks of "Arabia of the Nabateans" (16.4.21). King Ḥrtt/Aretas III (87-62 B.C.) paid the Roman general Pompey 300 talents in 63 B.C. and was rewarded with the autonomy of his kingdom, which became a vassal state of Rome. Emperor Trajan reorganized the region and placed Nabatea under direct Roman rule in A.D. 106 as *Provincia Arabia*.[5] The core region of Nabatea extended between the Dead Sea and the Red Sea, the southern border ran east of the Gulf of Aqaba, and the northern border varied, at times reaching as far as Damascus, as probably in the late 30s of the first century A.D.[6] There has been no satisfactory explanation as to why the Nabateans suddenly had sophisticated architecture at the end of the first century B.C. They built not only temples, aqueducts and military installations but also the highly decorated tombs of Egra and Petra.

In the first century the king and his family formed the head of the Nabatean kingdom. The second-highest official was called "brother of the king" (Strabo 16.4.21-26). Next came the administrators called ἔπαρχοι (*eparchoi*) or στρατηγοί (*stratēgoi*) (Josephus,

---

[2]Jean Starcky, "Pétra et la Nabatène," *DBSup* 7 (1966): 886-1017; Robert H. Smith, *ABD* 1:324-27; J. Pahlitzsch, *DNP* 1:945-48; Gordon D. Newby, *EDSS* 1:45-46; Glen W. Bowersock, "A Report on Arabia Provincia," *JRS* 61 (1971): 219-42; Teixidor 1977, 76-94; Bowersock 1983; MacAdam 1986. On the Nabateans see Schürer 1:574-86; Manfred Lindner, ed., *Petra und das Königreich der Nabatäer* (Munich: Delp, 1970); P. Hammond 1973; Schmitt-Korte 1976; Negev 1978; 1986; Wenning 1987; Kasher 1988; A. Negev, "Understanding the Nabateans," *BAR* 14 (1988): 26-45; A. Segal 1988; Michal Gawlikowski, "Les dieux des Nabatéans," *ANRW* II.18.4 (1990): 2659-77; D. A. Graf, "The Origins of the Nabateans," *Aram* 2 (1990): 45-75; Millar 1993, 387-436; Murphy-O'Connor 1993; R. Wenning, "Die Dekapolis und die Nabatäer," *ZDPV* 110 (1994): 1-35; Levy 1996; Hengel and Schwemer 1998, 174-207 (ET, 106-26); P. Richardson 1999, 62-67; Ball 2000, 31-47, 60-74, 198-205. See the *Bulletin of Nabataean Studies* (<http://www.iuo.it/BNS/BNS_01HomePage/BNS_HomePage.html>).

[3]See U. Borse, *EWNT* 1:358 (*EDNT* 1:149).

[4]The theory according to which the Nabateans, Itureans and other nomadic tribes of the Syrian desert moved from the far regions of Arabia to the west cannot be substantiated by hard evidence. These tribes probably were ethnic groups that had always lived in eastern Syria. See M. Gawlikowski, "The Syrian Desert under the Romans," in Alcock 1997, 37-54, esp. 41-42.

[5]*Provincia Arabia* is mentioned in several Greek texts from the Bar Kokhba period: 5/6Ḥev 12, 14, 15-18, 20, 22, 27, 37; 10Ḥev/Se 62, 64, 65. See Philip Freeman, "The Annexation of Arabia and Imperial Grand Strategy," in D. Kennedy 1996, 91-118. Freeman thinks that local factors were primarily responsible for the annexation.

[6]See Millar 1993, 56-57.

A.J. 18.112), who were responsible for the safety of their districts and for communication.[7] The army of the Nabatean kingdom consisted of around ten thousand soldiers, some of whom were stationed in the border regions—for example, in Leuke Kome on the Red Sea, in Domata (Gabba; mod. Jawf) in Wadi Sirhan, and in Madaba in the region bordering on the Decapolis. The administration of the kingdom relied on existing urban structures, while clan chiefs continued to rule over their respective tribes. Some Nabateans lived as nomads. Urban centers in Nabatea were (from north to south): Shahba (Philippopolis), Kanatha (Qanawat), Suweida (Dionysias), Bostra (mod. Busrâ ash-Shâm), Heshbon (Esbous), Medaba, Rabbathmoba (Arsapolis), Charachmoba (Kerak), Mampsis (Kurnub), Nesana, Khirbet et-Tannur, Petra and Oboda (Avdat)[8] in the Negev. Recent excavations indicate that Umm el-Jimal (25 km south of Bostra)[9] and Humeima were important centers as well. Important villages were Thaima and Mabsara near Petra, as well as ed-Dharih, where recent excavations uncovered a temple dating to the first century A.D. that stood on an unusually large platform (115 by 45 m).

Northern Nabatea was fertile: good quality wheat was cultivated in the Auranitis. Because the Nabateans had mastered the art of irrigation, they were able to cultivate wheat, vegetables and fruit in some of the desert regions. The Nabatean economy relied not on agriculture, however, but on trade. Petra, the capital, was a important trading center, situated at the crossroads of two major trade routes: the Hejaz route to Arabia and the royal route from Aqaba to Damascus; the latter road was fortified under Trajan between A.D. 111 and 114.[10] The Aramaic language, which the Nabateans also spoke, facilitated trade with the east; the Nabatean language can be regarded as an Aramaic dialect. Many people also spoke and wrote Greek, a fact documented by bilingual inscriptions found in the northern Hauran.[11]

The Nabateans worshiped many gods. Their main god was Dusares, a deity that possibly derives from the northern Arabian deity Illah; in the Greco-Roman period Dusares was identified with Zeus/Jupiter. Dusares was represented by a simple square block of stone. Other male gods included al-Kutba and Shailaqaum. The most important goddess was Allat, identified with Athene, Aphrodite, Venus, Ishtar/Astarte and Attargatis; other female deities included Manawatu and al-Uzza. As in the case of Hellenistic and Roman religious tendencies, other deities could be easily assimilated— so, for example, Baalshamin (Baʿal Shamim) of Phoenicia and Palmyra, Kos from Idumea, Isis from Egypt. An important cult center was Siaʿ near Kanatha, with at least two temples built on newly constructed terraces between 33 B.C. and A.D. 70.[12] Members of a tribe called Obaishat (Gk., Obaisenoi) built a temple dedicated to Baalshamin.

---

[7]Negev 1978, 568; John D. Grainger, "Village Government in Roman Syria and Arabia," *Levant* 27 (1995): 179-95.

[8]Avraham Negev, *The Architecture of Oboda: Final Report* (Qedem Monographs 36; Jerusalem: Hebrew University, 1997); idem, "Oboda: A Major Caravan Halt," *Aram* 8 (1996): 67-87.

[9]See Bert de Vries, ed., *Umm el-Jimal: A Frontier Town and Its Landscape in Northern Jordan* (JRASup 26; Portsmouth, R.I.: Journal of Roman Archaeology, 1998). In Umm el-Jimal between four hundred and five hundred inscriptions written in five languages have been discovered; in the early Byzantine period fifteen churches existed in the town. See D. Kennedy, in Humphrey 1995-2002, 2:101.

[10]See David F. Graf, "The *Via Nova Traiana* in Arabia Petraea," in Humphrey 1995-2002, 1:241-65; Graf emphasizes that the "new" Roman road was not a new route but rather "the formalization of the old Nabataean caravan route between Petra and Syria" (264).

[11]See R. Schmitt 1980, 205-9; Millar 1993, 394.

[12]See Jean-Marie Dentzer, "Six campagnes de fouilles à Siaʿ: Développement et culture indigène en Syrie méridionale," *Damaszener Mitteilungen* 2 (1985): 65-83; Gawlikowski 1989, 328-29.

The Jews regarded the Nabateans as descendants of Ishmael the son of Abraham, thus as kindred tribes.[13] The translators of the Septuagint identified the Nabateans with Nabaioth, the firstborn of the twelve sons of Ishmael.[14] Since the Idumeans, the "descendants of Esau," were converted (by force) to Judaism by John Hyrcanus (135/34-104 B.C.), the Arab Nabateans appeared "as the closest 'relatives' of the Jews who were still Gentiles and as sons of the patriarch." Kypros, the mother of Herod I, came from a royal Nabatean family, and Salome, Herod's sister, intended to marry the Nabatean prince Syllaios.[15] Herod Antipas, the tetrarch of Galilee and son of Herod I, was married to a daughter of the Nabatean king Aretas IV. There were Jewish communities in the Nabatean cities, documented by Jewish tombs, inscriptions and, for example, a sundial from Hegra (mod. Mada'in Ṣaliḥ) dated to the first century A.D. with the name of the Jewish owner (Manasseh bar Natan) inscribed on it.[16] The Nabateans surfaced even in the eschatological expectations of Israel: according to Is 60:6-7, "The first things to be consecrated to the service of YHWH in the sanctuary on the pilgrimage of the nations are the treasures of Midian and Ephah, and as sacrificial animals the herds of Qedar and Nebaioth, the Arab tribes in the south."

Is 60:6-7: "A multitude of camels shall cover you, the young camels of Midian and Ephah; all those from Sheba shall come. They shall bring gold and frankincense, and shall proclaim the praise of the LORD. [7]All the flocks of Kedar shall be gathered to you, the rams of Nebaioth shall minister to you; they shall be acceptable on my altar, and I will glorify my glorious house."

Paul evidently engaged in missionary work in Arabia-Nabatea soon after his conversion on the road to Damascus and his commission to preach the good news of Jesus to Jews and Gentiles.[17] This suggestion is based on the following considerations.

1. Paul states in Gal 1:17 that he obeyed God's call after his conversion on the road to Damascus, that he preached the gospel without first conferring with

---

[13]Hengel and Schwemer 1998, 180 (ET, 110); for the observations that follow above see ibid., 180-84 (ET, 110-13); quotation, 180.

[14]Cf. Gen 25:13; 28:9; 36:3; 1 Chron 1:29 LXX.

[15]On Kypros see Josephus, *B.J.* 1.181; *A.J.* 14.121; 15.184; on Salome see, e.g., *A.J.* 16.220, 225, 322.

[16]Negev 1978, 581; Sergio Noja, "Testimoni anche epigrafiche di Giudei nell'Arabia settentrionale," *BeO* 21 (1979): 283-16; Hengel and Schwemer 1998, 183 with n. 744 (ET, 112, 388-39 n. 585); the quotation that follows above, ibid., 181 (ET, 111).

[17]See Bruce, *Acts,* 190; Haenchen, *Apg,* 322-23 (334-35); Betz, *Gal,* 74; Bornkamm 1993, 48-49; Dietzfelbinger 1985, 143-44; Becker 1987, 108; Bruce 1993, 683; Murphy-O'Connor 1993; 1994; 1996, 81-85; Conzelmann and Lindemann 1995, 439; Levy 1996, 91-92; Hengel and Schwemer 1998, 174-207 (ET, 106-26); Bruggen 2000, 38-40; Hengel 2000; Reymond 2000, 91. For an earlier work see Pieper 1929, 83 n. 16. Briggs (1913) interprets "Arabia" as "the east" and sees Paul traveling to the Jews of Babylonia. Riesner (1994, 227-31 [ET, 256-60]) remains skeptical. Dollar (1993, 164-65) and R. A. Martin (1993, 111-14) reject this interpretation.

the apostles in Jerusalem and that he went to Arabia.

Gal 1:15-17: "But when God, who had set me apart before I was born and called me through his grace, was pleased [16]to reveal his Son to me, so that I might proclaim him among the Gentiles, I did not confer with any human being, [17]nor did I go up to Jerusalem to those who were already apostles before me, but I went away at once into Arabia, and afterwards I returned to Damascus."

2. Paul reports in connection with a review of his sufferings and toil as an apostle that the ethnarch of King Aretas in Damascus wanted to arrest him (2 Cor 11:32-33). Luke refers to this incident as well, but without mentioning Aretas (Acts 9:23-25).

2 Cor 11:32-33: "In Damascus, the governor [ethnarch] under King Aretas guarded the city of Damascus in order to seize me, [33]but I was let down in a basket through a window in the wall, and escaped from his hands."

Acts 9:23-25: "After some time had passed, the Jews plotted to kill him, [24]but their plot became known to Saul. They were watching the gates day and night so that they might kill him; [25]but his disciples took him by night and let him down through an opening in the wall, lowering him in a basket."

King Aretas is the Nabatean king Aretas IV Philodemos, who ruled from 9 B.C. to A.D. 40. Herod Antipas, who ruled in Galilee as tetrarch, married Aretas's daughter in A.D. 23 but later divorced her in order to be able to marry Herodias, the wife of his half-brother Philip (Josephus, *A.J.* 18.109-115). John the Baptist was executed in A.D. 28 as a result of his criticism of this marriage. The tensions between Aretas IV, who felt insulted but who also, and perhaps primarily, pursued political goals, and Herod Antipas intensified, eventually resulting in a war (A.D. 34-36) in which Aretas was victorious (some scholars date the war to A.D. 29). Josephus reports that some Jews interpreted the defeat of Herod Antipas as divine punishment for the execution of John the Baptist by Herod.[18]

    3. The fact that the Nabatean ethnarch intended to arrest Paul makes sense only if Nabatean officials regarded Paul and his activities as provocative and threatening to public safety. Paul himself does not indicate why he went to Arabia. We may assume, however, that he did not travel from Damascus to Arabia in order to seek fellowship with God in the solitude of the desert, like Moses and Elijah, or "to master the effects of the powerful upheaval he had experienced and to gain inner clarity."[19] Arabia was not simply a desert; there was a flourishing civilization particularly in northern Nabatea. It appears that Paul

---

[18]Josephus, *A.J.* 18.109-115, 120-126. See Schürer 1:344-50; Hoehner 1972, 255; Bowersock 1983, 65-68; Kasher 1988, 176-83; Hengel and Schwemer 1998, 182 (ET, 111).

[19]E. Meyer 1921-1923, 3:345; also rejected as a motif by Hengel and Schwemer 1998, 178 (ET, 109).

acted immediately in obedience to the divine commission to missionary service that he had received in Damascus, and that he preached the gospel "among the Gentiles" (Gal 1:16) in the region that was close to Damascus and distant enough from Jerusalem. He may have focused primarily on the God-fearers and sympathizers with the Jewish faith whom he could reach with the gospel in the synagogues of the Nabatean cities. The intervention of the ethnarch of King Aretas is plausible "if he had had a hint from his royal lord that he should seize the agitator who had caused offence in his missionary activity in the Nabataean kingdom."[20] The intervention of Nabatean officials suggests that Paul did not limit his preaching to Jewish audiences, but that he reached pagan Nabateans as well.

The episode that Paul refers to in 2 Cor 11:32-33 probably should be dated not to the weeks or months immediately following Paul's conversion but about three years later (i.e., in A.D. 33/34), when Paul traveled from Damascus to Jerusalem, visiting the Jewish capital for the first time after his conversion. This means that the phrase "after some time had passed" in Acts 9:23 should be interpreted in the light of Gal 1:18. According to Acts 9:23-25, the intended arrest of Paul in Damascus appears to have been engineered by Jews who opposed Paul. If 2 Cor 11:32-33 and Acts 9:23-25 refer to the same incident, we must assume that the Jews of Damascus collaborated with the Nabatean ethnarch in the city or that the latter asked the Jews for help because they knew Paul. The view that Paul engaged in independent missionary work and embarked on wide-ranging missionary journeys only after the apostolic council in A.D. 48[21] is mistaken. If my reconstruction is correct, Paul engaged in independent missionary work for ten years between his conversion in A.D. 32/33 and the beginning of his ministry in Antioch in A.D. 42-44.

No Roman coins have been discovered in Damascus for the years between A.D. 37 and A.D. 61. This seems to indicate "that Damascus was indeed not under direct Roman rule during this period but that the city had been given to Klietas IV and his successors Abias and Malchus II."[22] Rainer Riesner suggests that the arguments for Nabatean control of Damascus are not cogent: Damascus was under Roman control in A.D. 32/33, and the "ethnarch" of Aretas mentioned in 2 Cor 11:32-33 probably was the "head of the Nabatean trade colony in Damascus, who at the same time probably also represented the interests of the Nabatean state, and was thus a kind of consul."[23] Unless new primary source material surfaces, the question of the status of Damascus during this period remains open. Fergus Millar, who has written a well-informed study of the Near East during the Roman Empire, thinks that Nabatean control of Damascus is possible.[24]

If Paul's conversion took place in A.D. 31/32, then his missionary activity in Ara-

---

[20]Hengel and Schwemer 1998, 210 (ET, 128-29).

[21]Thus Betz 1994, 28.

[22]Bietenhard 1977, 256, with reference to Herod, who had received several cities of the Decapolis from the Romans.

[23]Riesner 1994, 70-79 (ET, 80-89); the quotation (ibid., 75 [ET, 85]) is from E. A. Knauf, "Zum *Ethnarchen* des Aretas 2Kor 11,32," *ZNW* 74 (1983): 147; see also Hengel and Schwemer 1998, 211 (ET, 129-30).

[24]Millar 1993, 56-57 with n. 3; see also Kasher 1988, 184-86.

bia would date to A.D. 32/33. Jerome Murphy-O'Connor reconstructs the following scenario. When Paul came to Arabia in A.D. 33, the tensions between the
Nabateans and the Jews had intensified. King Aretas had to reckon with the intervention of the Romans, perhaps even with the annexation of his kingdom.
Nabatea could not afford to appear weak; all signs of unrest had to be avoided.
The activities of a Jewish missionary who wanted to win the Nabatean population for "Jewish" (Christian) convictions certainly would have met with opposition. Paul, however, managed to evade the Nabatean authorities who wanted to
arrest him in Damascus.[25] The Damascene Jews were involved somehow in the
efforts to silence Paul (Acts 9:23). Some critics suggest that the Jewish opponents of Paul in Acts 9:23 were introduced by the redactor of Acts,[26] a view that
is entirely hypothetical. According to Luke's account in the book of Acts, Jews
repeatedly attempted to use Gentile authorities in the cities in which Paul was
active, hoping to repress his preaching of Jesus Christ (Acts 18:12-13). It therefore is quite possible that the Jews of Damascus regarded Paul's missionary
work in Arabia as a provocation that should no longer be tolerated. Martin Hengel suggests, "Paul's 'mission' in Nabataean Arabia was hindered and perhaps
even ended by political tensions between Aretas and Antipas as the only Jewish
ruler still ruling, and that therefore the apostle returned to Damascus, where he
had brothers in the faith whom he knew and who trusted him."[27]

Paul evidently spent several months in Arabia, presumably in the northern
part of the Nabatean kingdom south of Damascus—that is, the region of the
modern state of Jordan. In which cities might Paul have preached the gospel?
Jerome Murphy-O'Connor suggests that Paul was active as a missionary in the
cities of Shahba, Kanatha and Soada.[28] Traveling from Damascus to the south,
Paul first would have reached Selaima. Bostra, a day's journey south of Soada,
would have been another possible goal. Hans Bietenhard suggests that Paul
might have established a church in Pella, "which might have prompted the
Christians of Jerusalem to come here when they fled at the beginning of the Jewish revolt in A.D. 66."[29] Paul also may have traveled to Scythopolis, only a few
kilometers west of Pella. Martin Hengel surmises that Paul "visited the synagogues in the larger cities during his stay of about two years, above all in the
capital Petra."[30]

Selaima (mod. Sulem),[31] about 85 km south-southwest of Damascus, a three days' journey,

---

[25]Murphy-O'Connor 1993, 736.
[26]See Weiser, *Apg*, 1:232.
[27]Hengel and Schwemer 1998, 182-83 (ET, 112).
[28]Murphy-O'Connor 1993, 737.
[29]Bietenhard 1977, 255.
[30]Hengel and Schwemer 1998, 184 (ET, 113); cf. Hengel 2000, 49 (ET, 59).
[31]J.-P. Rey-Coquais, *PECS* 820-21; J. P. Brown, *BAGRW* 1066, map 69.

was situated in the northwestern edge of Trachonitis on the main road from Damascus to Bostra. Towns on the road between Damascus and Selaima included Nejha, Buraq, Sauara (mod. Suwarat el-Kebire) and Umm es-Zeitun. Selaima was Nabatean and belonged to the Roman province of Syria. Remains include Greek inscriptions and a large temple.

Shahba (Σαβα [?]; later Philippopolis; mod. Shahba)[32] was situated at the western end of Trachonitis on the western slopes of Mount Asalmanus (Jebel Druz; mod. Jebel al ʾArab), 8 km northeast of Selaima. The Roman emperor M. Iulius Philippus (A.D. 244-249) came from Shahba; east of the old town he founded Philippopolis, complete with a forum, theater and an imperial temple, and he granted the city the status of metropolis of the province. Philippus ended the disputes with the Persians and achieved for the empire a level of stability that was unusual for the third century. In A.D. 247/248 he celebrated, with spectacular games, the millennial anniversary of the founding of Rome. Fourth-century sources contain the remarkable news that Philippus was a Christian.[33] Many historians are skeptical because of his role in the games in the city of Rome, because of the fact that he had his father deified in Philippopolis (*IGR* III 1199, 1200), and because no pagan author mentions his Christian faith, not even Zosimus, who comments negatively on his Arab descent. However, the information provided by Eusebius (*Hist. eccl.* 6.34: Φίλιππον κατέχει λόγος Χριστιανὸν ὄντα) and references to contacts that Origen is supposed to have had with Emperor Philippus and his wife, Severa (*Hist. eccl.* 6.36.3), are indeed striking.[34] Glen Bowersock thinks that it is unlikely that Philippus was a practicing Christian, but he is convinced that this Roman emperor from Arabia was interested in the Christian faith, with which he probably came into contact in his hometown of Shahba or in Bostra. The reported contacts of Emperor Philippus with Christian theology are evidence for the spread of the Christian faith in Arab regions.[35] However, it is not possible to connect the church that may have existed in Shaba around A.D. 230-240 with Paul's missionary activity in this area in the first century. A funerary inscription documents the presence of Jews in the city in the third or fourth century A.D. (*IJudO* III Syr37).

Kanatha (Κάναθα; mod. el-Qanawat),[36] about 8 km south of Selaima (and 12 km south

---

[32]Will 1989, 238, 240; P. Leriche, in Dentzer and Orthmann 1989, 276; E. Frézouls, in ibid., 394-97; Gawlikowski 1989, 333; *The International Colloquium History and Archaeology of Mohafazat as-Sweida, Sweida, 29-31 October 1990* (Annales archéologiques arabes syriennes 41; Damascus: Directorate-General of Antiquities and Museums, 1997); Isaac 1993, 361-63; Ball 2000, 204-5; see also G. Amer and M. Gawlikowski, "Le sanctuaire impérial de Philippopolis," *Damaszener Mitteilungen* 2 (1985): 1-15; J. P. Brown, *BAGRW* 1065, map 69.

[33]Eusebius, *Hist. Eccl.* 6.34; Jerome, *Vir. ill.* 54; Orosius 7.20.2. See H. Crouzel, "Le christianisme de l'empereur Philippe l'Arabe," *Gregorianum* 56 (1975): 545-50; H. A. Pohlsander, "Philip the Arab and Christianity," *Historia* 29 (1980): 463-73; Bowersock 1983, 125.

[34]On contacts of Origen with Arab Christians see Eusebius, *Hist. eccl.* 6.19.15; 6.21.3-4; 6.33.1.

[35]Bowersock 1983, 126-27.

[36]A. Dietrich, *KP* 3:106; Schürer 2:138-42; Rey-Coquais 1989, 51; idem, *PECS* 191-92; J. Gippert, *DNP* 6:242-43; Kasher 1988, 175-76; G. Bowersock, in Dentzer and Orthmann 1989, 76; P. Leriche, in ibid., 276; E. Frézouls, in ibid., 393-94; Gawlikowski 1989, 331-32; Moors 1992, 236-46; Bowersock 1983, 42, 66, 100, 177; Ball 2000, 187-88. The Deutsche Archäologische Institut has carried out excavations in Qanawat since 1997; see *Damaszener Mitteilungen* 11 (1999); first results have been published in *Damaszener Mitteilungen* 12 (2000): 155-253. See <http://www.dainst.de/en/pro/qanawat.html>.

of Shahba), was situated on the important road from Damascus to Bostra. Pompey or Gabinius reconstituted the city as a Greek polis in the mid-first century B.C. Kanatha belonged at times to the Decapolis. After 23 B.C. Kanatha belonged to the province of Syria. When the Roman *Provincia Arabia* was established in A.D. 106, Kanatha was the only polis in the southern border area of the province of Syria. The significant ruins date to the first centuries A.D. The remains include the temple of Zeus Megistos and the theater (or odeion), which had a diameter of 46 m. The important Nabatean cult center of Siaʿ (see above) was located near Kanatha. King Herod I had been defeated near Kanatha in a battle against Arab troops (Josephus, *B.J.* 1.367-368). It seems that the Nabatean king Aretas IV moved around A.D. 34/35 across the Yarmuk River into the Hauran (i.e., the region around Kanatha); after the death of Herod Philip, the latter's tetrarchy was annexed into the province of Syria, which could have prompted Aretas to retaliate against Herod Antipas, who had divorced his wife, Aretas's daughter, and to regain the areas that had belonged to the Nabatean sphere of influence earlier, perhaps even the city of Damascus. Herod Antipas sent his own troops into the region, which, however, were defeated by Aretas, perhaps (also) on account of the "exiles" from Philip's tetrarchy in his army who eventually supported Aretas (Josephus, *A.J.* 18.114). If Paul preached the gospel in A.D. 32/33 in Nabatea, these disturbances still lay in the future. A Latin-Greek inscription found in Trevoux near Lugdunum (Lyon) in Gaul, dated between A.D. 197 and 212, mentions a merchant living in town whose name was Thaim, who also was called Iulianus and who originally came from Athila (mod. ʿAtîl) near Kanatha; he was a citizen and a council member (*bouleutēs*) of Kanatha and owned in Lugdunum a large trading post (ἐνπόριον ἀγορασμῶν, *enporion agorasmōn*).[37] Kanatha was the seat of a bishop in the fifth century at the latest.

Soada (Suweida; Dionysias; mod. Suweda, Soada)[38] was situated on the main road from Damascus to Bostra, about 8 km southwest of Kanatha. Nabatean traditions are documented for Soada. The oldest known monument of the region is a pyramid tomb found in Soada; the dedicatory inscription, dating to the first century B.C., is bilingual (*CIS* II.1, 162), which indicates that the population read and spoke both Aramaic and Greek. The building of a temenos and a nymphaeum document the urbanization of the city, dating to the time of Trajan. The bishop Severus of Soada attended the Council of Nicea in the fourth century.

Bostra (Βόσσορα; mod. Busra esh-Sham, Boṣra, Syria),[39] about 25 km south of Soada (120 km south of Damascus) at the end of the royal road, controlled the caravan routes into the Wadi Sirhan and to Damascus. Judas Maccabaeus conquered the city in the spring of 163 B.C. after the Gentile inhabitants wanted to massacre the Jewish citizens (1 Macc 5:26-28). The city was close to the border with the tetrarchy of Herod Philip. In the first century

---

[37] *IG* XIV 2532 = *CIL* XIII 2448; see Jean Rougé, in *Actes du 96ᵉ Congrès national des Sociétés savantes, Toulouse 1971* (Section d'archéologique 1; Paris: Bibliothèque nationale, 1976), 211-21.

[38] Bowersock 1983, 66, 100, 177-78; Gawlikowski 1989, 330; Millar 1993, 394, 413-14.[9]

[39] C. Colpe, KP 1:935; D. J. Wiseman, GBL 1:211; J. F. Healey, OCD 254-55; J.-P. Rey-Coquais, PECS 159-60; T. Leisten, DNP 2:755; Bowersock 1983, 60-61, 73, 76-78, 83-84, and passim;275; E. Frézouls, in ibid., 397-99; K. S. Freyberger, "Einige Beobachtungen zur städtebaulichen Entwicklung des römischen Bostra," *Damaszener Mitteilungen* 4 (1989): 45-60; Moors 1992, 246-49; Isaac 1993, 123-24, 349-51; Millar 1993, 391, 399; Ball 2000, 198-204; Pollard 2000, 41-42, 52, 79, 115; J. P. Brown, *BAGRW* 1060, map 69. Inscriptions: *IGLSyria* XIII (1982).

A.D. the Legio III Cyrenaica was stationed in Bostra. When the Nabatean kingdom was organized in A.D. 106 as the Roman province of Arabia, Bostra became the capital (the economic importance of Petra had declined by the first century). According to an inscription dated A.D. 93, one of the deities worshiped in the city was Dushara-ʾAra. The archaeological remains demonstrate that Bostra was a flourishing city of the Nabatean kingdom. The central colonnaded street was 900 m long; the hippodrome (440 by 134 m) could seat thirty thousand spectators. The theater (102 m in diameter) ranks with the theaters of Orange in France and Aspendos in Turkey as one of the most magnificent examples of ancient theaters. A Christian community is documented for Bostra for A.D. 250 at the latest: Eusebius mentions Beryllos, the "bishop [*episkopos*] of the Arabs in Bostra," who denied the preexistence of Christ and who was the subject of discussion at a synod in which Origen participated (Eusebius, *Hist. eccl.* 6.20.2; 6.33.1-3). The bishop Nikomachos of Bostra attended the Council of Nicea in the fourth century.

Pella (Πέλλα; Berenike; mod. Khirbet Fachl, Jordan),[40] about 30 km south of the Sea of Galilee, east of the Jordan River, on the west-east road from Caesarea via Scythopolis to Gerasa, is already mentioned in ancient Egyptian texts; Pella exported parts of chariots to Egypt in the thirteenth century B.C. After 332 B.C. Greek colonists from Macedonia settled in the city, which had been almost insignificant in the Israelite period. In 83 B.C. Alexander Jannaeus conquered the city and ordered its destruction (Josephus, *A.J.* 13.397). Pompey included Pella in the federation of the Decapolis cities in 63 B.C. (Pliny, *Nat.* 5.18.74), but only under the Roman governor Gabinius after 57 B.C. was the city rebuilt. Many of the public buildings were erected in the first century A.D.: an odeion, a nymphaeum, baths and a large temple. Pella minted its own coins since A.D. 82. Eusebius, relying on early traditions that have to be regarded as credible, reports that the Jewish Christians from Jerusalem left the Jewish capital at the beginning of the Jewish revolt in A.D. 66 and emigrated to Pella in the Decapolis (Eusebius, *Hist. eccl.* 3.5.3-4).[41] A sarcophagus that dates to the late first or early second century A.D., found below the

---

[40]C. Burchardt, "Pella Nr. 2," *KP* 4:601; G. Reinholdt, *GBL* 3:1152-53; L. L. Levine, *EAEHL* 4:939-40; J.-M. Fenasse, *DBSup* 7 (1966): 605-26; R. H. Smith, *NEAEHL* 3:1174-80; T. Leisten, "Pella 2," *DNP* 9:496-97; R. H. Smith, *Pella of the Decapolis* (2 vols.; Wooster, Ohio: College of Wooster, 1973-1989); Anthony W. McNicoll, ed., *Pella in Jordan I-II* (2 vols.; Mediterranean Archaeology Supplement 2; Canberra: Australian National Gallery; Sydney: Meditarch, 1982-1992); Thomas Weber, *Pella Decapolitana: Studien zur Geschichte, Architektur und Bildenden Kunst einer hellenisierten Stadt des nördlichen Ostjordanlandes* (Wiesbaden: Harrasowitz, 1993); Ball 2000, 195-96. See <http://www.archaeology.usyd.edu.au/research/pella>.

[41]See also Epiphanius, *Mens. pond.* 14 (PG 43:261); *Pan.* 29.7.8; 30.2.7 (GCS 25.1, 330, 335). On the historicity of the Pella tradition see Harnack 1924, 2:622-23, 631-37 (ET, 2:91-92, 97-105); S. Sowers, "The Circumstances and Recollection of the Pella Flight," *ThZ* 26 (1970): 305-20; B. C. Gray, "The Movements of the Jerusalem Church during the First Jewish War," *JEH* 24 (1973): 1-17; Smith, *Pella of the Decapolis,* 11:42-44, 47-48; Pritz 1988, 122-27; J. E. Taylor 1990, 315-16; Wander 1994, 267-70; Riesner 1995, 1842; S. Wilson 1995, 145-46; Ellis 1999, 25-26; Paget 1999, 747; D. G. Reid, *DLNT* 900-902. On the rejection of the historicity of the Pella tradition by Lüdemann (1983, 265-86 [ET, 200-13]), see C. Koester, "The Origin and Significance of the Flight to Pella Tradition," *CBQ* 51 (1989): 90-106. On the critique of Jozef Verheyden, *De vlucht van de christenen naar Pella onderzoek van het getuigenis van Eusebius en Epiphanius* (Brussels: AWLSK, 1988); idem, "The Flight of the Christians to Pella," *ETL* 66 (1990) 368-384, see J. Wehnert, "Die Auswanderung der Jerusalemer Christen nach Pella—historisches Faktum oder theologische Konstruktion?" *ZKG* 102 (1991): 231-55.

north apse of a church in the western part of town, perhaps documents the presence of the Jerusalem believers in Pella.[42] Around A.D. 150 the Christian apologist Aristo lived in Pella (Eusebius, *Hist. eccl.* 4.6.3). In the third century Beryll, the first known bishop of the Arab Christians, wrote the *Didaskalia.* Origen participated in several important synods.

Scythopolis (Σκυθόπολις, Beth Shean; mod. Beisan, Israel),[43] 14 km west of Pella in the Jordan Valley on the road from Acco-Ptolemais through the Jezreel Valley to Gilead, was also one of the cities of the Decapolis. In the first century A.D. Scythopolis clearly was a pagan city with odeion, bouleuterion, nymphaeum, basilica, theater, amphitheater (second century?), public baths and several temples; the colonnaded road (180 m long) was constructed in a later period. Jewish inhabitants lived in Scythopolis at least since 163 B.C. (2 Macc 12:29-31). After the sons of John Hyrcanus conquered Scythopolis in 107 B.C. (Josephus, *B.J.* 1.66), they forced the Gentile inhabitants into exile in accordance with the politics of the Hasmonean rulers. Scythopolis became a Jewish city, the pagan temples probably were destroyed or used for other purposes, and it can be assumed that the old Israelite name "Beth Shean" was reintroduced. In 102 B.C. the Jewish king Alexander Jannaeus and the Egyptian queen Cleopatra III met in Scythopolis to conclude a treaty (Josephus, *A.J.* 13.355). Pompey passed through Scythopolis in 63 B.C. on his way to Jerusalem and restored the city as a Greek polis. Presumably, many Jews had to leave the city to make room for the returning Greek settlers. The proportion of the Jewish population in Scythopolis increased in the subsequent years: Josephus reports that thirteen thousand Jews were massacred in A.D. 66 when the Gentile citizens took the initiative in the beginning of the First Jewish Revolt (Josephus, *B.J.* 2.466-468). If these figures are reliable, Scythopolis had the second largest Jewish community in Coele-Syria after Caesarea. Three ossuaries that have been discovered in Jerusalem contained the bones of Jews from Scythopolis; they document the linguistic integration of at least some Jews in Scythopolis: the inscriptions are written in Hebrew and in Greek. And thirty Jewish ossuaries that were discovered in the northern necropolis of Scythopolis were written only in Greek.[44] The cult of Zeus Olympios, the dynastic cult of the Seleucid rulers, is attested in Scythopolis as cult of Zeus Akraios and of Zeus Soter; also attested are the cults of Ares, Dionysos, the Dioscuri and of Tyche. The large temple (70 by 30 m)[45] evidently was dedicated to Dionysos. An altar inscription found in 1995 (dated to the second century A.D.) honors Dionysos as "Lord" (κύριος, *kyrios*) and, probably, Zeus as founder (κτίστης, *ktistēs*) of the city. The sacred grove in which the mas-

---

[42]See Smith, *NEAEHL* 3:1175.

[43]A. Negev, *PECS* 815-16; G. Foerster, *NEAEHL* 1:223-35; M. Avi-Yonah, "Scythopolis," *IEJ* 45 (1962): 123-34; Henri Seyrig, "Note sur les cultes de Scythopolis à l'époque romaine," *Syria* 39 (1962): 207-24; Baruch Lifshitz, "Scythopolis: L'histoire, les institutions et les cultes de la ville à l'époque hellénistique et impériale," *ANRW* II.8 (1977): 262-94; Gideon Fuks, "The Jews of Hellenistic and Roman Scythopolis," *JJS* 33 (1982): 407-16; Jésus-M. Nieto Ibáñez, "The Sacred Grove of Scythopolis," *IEJ* 49 (1999): 260-68; Leah di Segni, "The Basilica and an Altar to Dionysos at Nysa-Scythopolis," in Humphrey 1995-2002, 2:59-75; Ball 2000, 193-95.

[44]*CIJ* II 1372-1374. See Fuks, "The Jews of Hellenistic and Roman Scythopolis," 409-10.

[45]The first phase of the temple dates to the first century A.D., and the second phase to the second century, during which time the altar was erected (in A.D. 141/142, according to the dedicatory inscription). See di Segni et al., in Humphrey 1995-2002, 2:62-63. The inscription that is mentioned in the comment that follows above belongs to a second altar that the same person, Seleukos son of Ariston, erected.

sacre that Josephus mentions took place probably was dedicated to Dionysos; it was one of the most important cult places of Dionysos in Syria and Palestine. Scythopolis was also called Nysa, after the nymph to whom Dionysos was given by Zeus in order to be brought up in the grove carrying the same name (Diodorus Siculus 1.15.6).[46] In the early Roman period Scythopolis was a production site for oil lamps.[47] In the third and fourth centuries Christians died as martyrs in Scythopolis. Around A.D. 500 or 515 a basilica was built with the help of Anastasius (A.D. 491-518).[48] The mosaic floor of the monastery of Abba Justinus dates from September 522.[49]

We do not know whether Paul was active as a missionary in Pella or Scythopolis, since both cities did not belong to Nabatea. Pella and Scythopolis belonged to Judea, as did Gadara and Capitolias. Other cities of the Decapolis were Nabatean, such as Philadelphia (mod. Amman), Gerasa, Dium and Adraa.[50]

Gerasa (Γέρασα; mod. Jerash),[51] about 35 km southeast of Pella, an old city settled already in the Bronze Age, possibly was refounded as a Greek polis by Perdikkas, a general of Alexander the Great. The Hellenistic city was called Antiochia ad Chrysorhoam (in honor of Antiochos III or Antiochos IV). Alexander Jannaeus conquered the city before 76 B.C. When the province of Syria was organized by Pompey, Gerasa became one of the cities of the Decapolis. In the Roman period the city occupied both sides of the Chrysorhoas River (Wadi Jerash). A temple of Zeus Olympus, built between A.D. 22 and 43, was located in the southern section of the city. A Nabatean sanctuary also dates to the first century. The southern theater was built during the principate of Domitian. The monumental temple of Artemis was built after A.D. 150: the temenos measured 161 by 121 m, the columns with Corinthian capitals were 13.2 m high, and the temple building measured 24.1 by 13.3 m. The northern theater was smaller and served as assembly place of the city council. A benefactor named Theon, who erected three dedicatory inscriptions in the temple of Zeus in A.D. 69/70, either came from Egypt or was an assimilated Jew. The synagogue that was excavated in 1929 dates to the fourth or fifth century.[52] One of the famous sons of Gerasa was the neo-Pythagorean philosopher and mathematician Nikomachos, who wrote, around A.D. 100, an introduction to arithmetic ('Αριθμητική εἰσαγωγή) that was a standard text for a thousand years. The oldest church of Gerasa was built around A.D. 500,

---

[46]The localization of the site of Nysa mentioned by Diodoros is disputed; cities in Thrace, Ethiopia, Libya, Arabia, Scythia and India have been mentioned.
[47]See D. Adan-Bayewitz, in Humphrey 1995-2002, 1:180.
[48]See L. di Segni, in Humphrey 1995-2002, 2:167.
[49]*SEG* VIII 37. See L. Di Segni, in Humphrey 1995-2002, 2:167.
[50]See Bowersock 1983, 91-92.
[51]C. Colpe, *KP* 2:759-60; W. L. MacDonald, *PECS* 348-49; J. McRay, *ABD* 2:991-92; S. Applebaum and A. Segal, *NEAEHL* 2:470-79; T. Leisten, *DNP* 4:949-50; R. O. Fink, "Jerash in the First Century A.D.," *JRS* 23 (1933): 109-24; C. H. Kraeling, ed., *Gerasa: City of the Decaplis* (New Haven: ASOR, 1938); Iain Browning, *Jerash and the Decapolis* (London: Chatto & Windus, 1982); Rami G. Khouri, *Jerash: A Frontier City of the Roman East* (London: Longman, 1986); Fawzi Zayadine, ed., *Jerash Archaeological Project* (2 vols.; Amman and Paris: Department of Antiquities of Jordan, 1986-1989); E. Frézouls, in Dentzer and Orthmann 1989, 387; Moors 1992, 249-53; Ball 2000, 188-91; K. J. Rigsby, "A Suppliant at Gerasa," *Phoenix* 54 (2000): 99-107.
[52]Kraeling, *Gerasa,* 236-39, 318-23; most recently L. Levine 2000, 239-40, and passim.

while several other churches date to the fifth and sixth centuries. The fact that thirteen churches have been discovered in ancient Gerasa shows the significance of the city for the church in this period.

Philadelphia (Φιλαδέλφεια; Rabbat Ammon; mod. Amman, Jordan),[53] about 50 km south of Gerasa (90 km south of Bostra and 90 km southeast of Scythopolis), was the old Canaanite city of Rabbat Ammon, which had been defeated by King David (2 Sam 12:26-31). The city owed its name to Ptolemaeus Philadelphus, who ruled Palestine and Syria after 259 B.C. When the Seleucid kings gained control in Syria after 200 B.C., Philadelphia was given to the Nabateans, who had helped them in their battles against the Ptolemies. Zenon Kotylas and his son Theodoros, who ruled in Philadelphia around 125 B.C., probably were Nabatean vassals. The city played an important role in the trade with the interior of Arabia: merchants from Philadelphia transported goods that had been brought into the city by caravans from the regions to the west (through the Wadi Sirhan and the oasis Azraq) or from Petra to the south via Gerasa to Pella and Scythopolis, from where they were transported to the Palestinian coast. Pompey annexed Philadelphia in 63 B.C. into the province of Syria. There is not much literary or archaeological evidence for the city in the first century; the extant remains of the public buildings such as the agora, theater, odeion, nymphaeum and the large temple of Hercules date to the second century A.D. The main street of Philadelphia ran from west to east, reaching a monumental gate on eastern side of the city; a second colonnaded street ran from north to south. The public baths were located near the intersection of the two main streets. In A.D. 325 the bishop Kyrion from Philadelphia attended the Council of Nicea.

Petra (Πέτρα),[54] about 370 km south of Damascus, as the crow flies, in the southern part of Nabatea, was the capital of the Nabatean kingdom from 312 B.C. until the Romans organized in A.D. 106 the province of Arabia, which was administered from Bostra. Petra is surrounded by steep slopes and canyons into which monumental tombs were built. The cosmopolitan character of Petra is illustrated by the Hellenistic architecture of its theater, temple and colonnaded street, which now has been unambiguously dated to the time of Aretas IV; Michael Gawlikowski contends that the Hellenistic architecture of Alexandria

---

[53]J.-P. Rey-Coquais, *PECS* 703-704; M. Burdajewicz and A. Segal, *NEAEHL* 4:1242-52; Kasher 1988, 153-55, and passim; Millar 1993, 410-11; Pierre-Louis Gatier, "Philadelphie et Gerasa du Royaume Nabatéen à la Province d'Arabie," in *Géographie historique au Proche-Orient: Syrie, Phénicie, Arabie, grecques, romaines, byzantines* (ed. P.-L. Gatier; Paris: Centre National de la Recherche Scientifique, 1988), 159-70; Henry Innes MacAdam, "The History of Philadelphia in the Classical Period," in Northedge 1992, 27-45, 195-99; A. Northedge, "Archaeological Topography," in ibid., 57-59; A. Hadidi, "Amman-Philadelphia: Aspects of Roman Urbanism," in *Studies in the History and Archaeology of Jordan IV* (ed. S. Tell; Amman: Department of Antiquities, 1992), 295-98; Moors 1992, 253-54; Ball 2000, 191-93; S. T. Parker, *BAGRW* 1088, map 71.

[54]J. Starcky, *DBSup* 7 (1966): 886-1017; John F. Healey, *OCD* 1149; Walter Bachmann et al., *Petra* (Berlin: Vereinigung Wissenschaftlicher Verleger, 1921); Philip C. Hammond, *The Excavation of the Main Theatre at Petra, 1961-62: Final Report* (London: Quaritch, 1965); Bowersock 1983; Rami G. Khouri, *Petra: A Guide to the Capital of the Nabataeans* (London: Longman, 1986); Iain Browning, *Petra* (3rd ed.; London: Chatto & Windus, 1989 [1973]); Judith McKenzie, *The Architecture of Petra* (British Academy Monographs in Archaeology 1; Oxford: Oxford University Press, 1990); Fawzi Zayadine, ed., *Petra and the Caravan Cities* (Amman: Department of Antiquities, 1990); Millar 1993, 406-8; Jane Taylor, *Petra* (London: Aurum Press,

is best preserved in Petra.[55] Strabo remarks that his informant Athenodoros, a citizen of Tarsus, found many foreigners and aliens in Petra (16.4.21). However, the legends on Petra's coins are only in Nabatean. Greek and bilingual inscriptions are rare. In the rabbinic literature Petra is identified with Reqem; already Josephus had identified Petra with Reqem and with Qadesh (Josephus, *A.J.* 4.161), and he claimed to know that it was here that Aaron went up Mount Hor, where he was buried (Josephus, *A.J.* 4.82-83; according to Num 20:22, Mount Hor was near Qadesh).[56] Martin Hengel argues that these traditions would have prompted Paul to travel to Petra to preach the gospel, a suggestion that must remain hypothetical. The early Byzantine church that was discovered in Petra in 1990 dates to the fifth century; the church building had an archive, as between forty and fifty burnt scrolls demonstrate.[57]

Martin Hengel and Anna Maria Schwemer suggest that Paul traveled as far as Hegra (mod. Mada'in Ṣaliḥ), in the far south of Arabia near the southeastern border, pointing to traditions that link Hegra with Mount Sinai and with Hagar, Abraham's slave and concubine.[58] Whether such traditions would have informed Paul's missionary strategy remains hypothetical. The distance would not have been a problem, of course: if there are routes that local and other international travelers use, they would be used by missionaries as well.

The Nabatean cities were islands of Hellenistic language and culture in the midst of the Semitic population. Hans Bietenhard points out that in the cities of the Decapolis "Greeks and Syrians dominated over the Jews; they were Hellenistic cities that must have been familiar to Paul as far as their structure was concerned."[59] If Paul spent only a few months in Nabatea, it becomes less likely that he penetrated to the cities further south. After his return from Arabia, Paul preached again in Damascus. The Christian community of Damascus may have been the base of Paul's missionary activity in Nabatea.

Evangelism in Jerusalem

Paul returned to Jerusalem in A.D. 33/34, after he had been active as a missionary in Arabia and in Damascus. The reports in Gal 1:18-19 and Acts 9:26-

---

1993); Thomas Weber and Robert Wenning, *Petra: Antike Felsstadt zwischen arabischer Tradition und griechischer Norm* (Mainz: Zabern, 1997); Martha Sharp Joukowsky, ed., *Petra: Great Temple* (Brown University Excavations 1993-1997; Providence: M. S. Joukowsky, 1998); Laila Nehme and François Villeneuve, *Petra: Metropole de l'Arabie antique* (Paris: Seuil, 1999); Christian Augé and Jean-Marie Dentzer, *Petra: The Rose-Red City* (London: Thames & Hudson, 2000); Ball 2000, 63-73, 370-75; Jane Taylor, *Petra and the Lost Kingdom of the Nabataeans* (London: Tauris, 2001); Glenn Markoe, ed., *Petra Rediscovered: The Lost City of the Nabateans* (New York: Abrams, 2003). For the Brown University excavations see <http://www.brown.edu/departments/anthropology/petra>.
[55]M. Gawlikowski, in Alcock 1997, 49; cf. Judith McKenzie, *The Architecture of Petra* (Oxford: Oxford University Press, 1990).
[56]G. Schmitt 1995, 276; Hengel and Schwemer 1998, 184-85 n. 748 (ET, 389 n. 589).
[57]See Z. T. Fiema, in Humphrey 1995-2002, 1:293-303.
[58]Hengel and Schwemer 1998, 186-90 (ET, 113-16).
[59]Bietenhard 1977, 255.

30 about this first visit in Jerusalem after his conversion complement each other.

Gal 1:18-19: "Then after three years I did go up to Jerusalem to visit Cephas and stayed with him fifteen days; [19]but I did not see any other apostle except James the Lord's brother."

Acts 9:26-30: "When he had come to Jerusalem, he attempted to join the disciples; and they were all afraid of him, for they did not believe that he was a disciple. [27]But Barnabas took him, brought him to the apostles, and described for them how on the road he had seen the Lord, who had spoken to him, and how in Damascus he had spoken boldly in the name of Jesus. [28]So he went in and out among them in Jerusalem [ἦν μετ' αὐτῶν εἰσπορευόμενος καὶ ἐκπορευόμενος εἰς Ἰερουσαλήμ], speaking boldly in the name of the Lord [παρρησιαζόμενος ἐν τῷ ὀνόματι τοῦ κυρίου]. [29]He spoke and argued [ἐλάλει τε καὶ συνεζήτει] with the Hellenists; but they were attempting to kill him. [30]When the believers learned of it, they brought him down to Caesarea and sent him off to Tarsus."

The fact that Paul designates James the brother of Jesus in Gal 1:19 as "apostle" suggests that we should interpret the term "apostle" in Acts 9:27 as generalizing statement[60] unless one is prepared to assume contradictory statements or a free creation by Luke.[61] Paul emphasizes in Gal 1:19 in regard to the leaders of the Christian community in Jerusalem that he met only Peter and James during his first visit there.

The goal of Paul's visit to Jerusalem was to get to know Peter (Gal 1:18). Luke reports that Paul preached in the Christian community (Acts 9:28) and that he evangelized Hellenistic Jews in the Jerusalem synagogues (cf. Acts 6:9) whom he sought to lead to faith in Jesus as the Messiah (Acts 9:29). The use of imperfect-tense verbs in Acts 9:28-29 suggests that this preaching and missionary ministry by Paul was not a single action but happened over a longer period of time. In Gal 1:18 Paul states that he was in Jerusalem for fifteen days.

Paul does not provide details about the circumstances and the results of his preaching and teaching activity in Jerusalem. Luke notes discussions with Greek-speaking Jews (Acts 9:29) and the plan of an attack by Jews from Jerusalem who want to eliminate Paul. The plan was thwarted as Paul managed to escape with the help of believers. Paul made his way via Caesarea to Tarsus (Acts 9:30).

26.2 Mission in Syria and Cilicia

Paul writes in Gal 1:21-24 that after his return from Arabia and his departure from Jerusalem he went "into the regions of Syria and Cilicia," and that the Christians in the Judean churches knew that he proclaimed the gospel of Jesus

---

[60]See Bruce, Acts, 193; earlier Pieper 1929, 87-88.
[61]As, for example, Zmijewski (Apg, 388) does.

Christ.[62] Luke does not mention Paul's missionary activity in Syria and Cilicia in the years A.D. 34-42. However, he does report, in connection with his account of Paul's journey through Galatia and his missionary activity in Macedonia and Achaia that took place after the apostolic council in A.D. 48, that Paul and Silas first visited the churches in Syria and Cilicia, where they strengthened the believers (Acts 15:41).[63] Since Paul and Silas had started their journey in Antioch, Luke's comment must refer to further churches in Syria (besides Antioch) and to churches in Cilicia. I conclude, therefore, that Paul engaged in missionary work in Syria and in Cilicia after his return from Arabia and the departure from Jerusalem.[64]

Gal 1:21-24: "Then I went into the regions of Syria and Cilicia, [22]and I was still unknown by sight to the churches of Judea that are in Christ; [23]they only heard it said, 'The one who formerly was persecuting us is now proclaiming the faith he once tried to destroy.' [24]And they glorified God because of me."

Acts 15:36-41: "After some days Paul said to Barnabas, 'Come, let us return and visit the believers in every city where we proclaimed the word of the Lord and see how they are doing.' [37]Barnabas wanted to take with them John called Mark. [38]But Paul decided not to take with them one who had deserted them in Pamphylia and had not accompanied them in the work. [39]The disagreement became so sharp that they parted company; Barnabas took Mark with him and sailed away to Cyprus. [40]But Paul chose Silas and set out, the believers commending him to the grace of the Lord. [41]He went through Syria and Cilicia, strengthening the churches."

How long was Paul active as a missionary in Syria and in Cilicia? Assuming that Paul was converted on the road to Damascus in A.D. 31/32 and that he preached in Nabatea in A.D. 32/33, he could have engaged in missionary work in Syria and in Cilicia beginning in A.D. 33/34. If we date Paul's mission to Cyprus and Galatia to A.D. 45-47, then his mission to Syria and Cilicia (including the ministry in Antioch) can be dated between A.D. 33/34 and 44/45. This means that Paul proclaimed the gospel of Jesus Christ for twelve years in the province of Syria-Cilicia.[65]

---

[62]Gal 1:21, 23: ἦλθον εἰς τὰ κλίματα τῆς Συρίας καὶ τῆς Κιλικίας . . . ποτε νῦν εὐαγγελίζεται τὴν πίστιν ἥν ποτε ἐπόρθει.

[63]Acts 15:41: διήρχετο δὲ τὴν Συρίαν καὶ Κιλικίαν ἐπιστηρίζων τὰς ἐκκλησίας.

[64]This conclusion is shared by most scholars. Differently Raymond Martin (1993, 114-15), who suggests that Paul spent these fourteen to seventeen years reflecting about the consequences of his new-found faith for his theology. This suggestion is hardly more plausible than the argument that Paul became a "Hellenized Jew" only during this period (see ibid., 135-53).

[65]Hengel and Schwemer (1998, 245, 275, 337-38, 473-74 [ET, xii-xiii, 157, 179, 205, 222-23]) assume thirteen years for Paul's missionary work in Syria-Cilicia: from A.D. 36/37 to 39/40 in Tarsus, in A.D. 38/39 in Antioch, and from A.D. 41 to 46/47 in Syria and Phoenicia. Reymond (2000, 95 n. 16) has misunderstood Hengel and Schwemer.

Neither Paul nor Luke nor the later Christian tradition provides any information about which cities Paul preached in during the period A.D. 33-44, planting churches that he visited again in A.D. 48/49. Assuming that Paul visited the synagogues of the cities in which he began missionary work, as Luke reports in the book of Acts for the time after A.D. 44, we would find Paul at least in those cities of Syria and Cilicia in which Jews lived.

Missionary Work in Syria

As far as Syria (see fig. 24) is concerned, a region with a large Jewish population (according to Josephus, *B.J.* 7.43), Jewish communities are attested in Antioch, Apameia, Byblos, Berytus, Damascus, Dora, Palmyra, Phaene, Ptolemais, Sidon and Tyre.[66] The book of Acts provides (only) reference to Christian communities in Syria besides Antioch and Damascus: there was a church in Tyre that Paul visited for one week in A.D. 57 on his journey from Ephesus and Corinth via Ptolemais and Caesarea to Jerusalem (Acts 21:3); in Sidon Paul had "friends" (φιλοί, *philoi*) who were allowed to take care of him as he was transported as a prisoner from Caesarea to Rome (Acts 27:3).

We do not know whether the churches in Tyre and Sidon were established by Paul some time after A.D. 33, or whether they were founded by the Greek-speaking Jewish Christians who were forced to leave Jerusalem in A.D. 31/32 and who eventually reached Antioch, preaching the gospel. The fact that Paul stayed for one whole week with the Christians in Tyre possibly suggests that he knew the believers very well; it is also possible, of course, that the duration of Paul's visit might be explained by the timetable of the ship on which Paul and his coworkers traveled to Caesarea. The "friends" who care for Paul in Sidon may also presuppose that they knew each other well, although this is not a necessary conclusion. On Tyre and Sidon see §21.4.

Assuming that Paul traveled from Jerusalem to Syria and Cilicia along the Mediterranean coast, he could have preached the gospel in the cities in which the Hellenist Jewish Christians from Jerusalem had already preached: perhaps in Berytus, Aphaka, Byblos, Tripolis, Arka (Caesarea ad Libanum), Aradus (with Baetocaece), Antaradus, Balaneae, Paltus, Gabala, Laodikeia and Seleukeia on the Orontes River (see §22.4).

Assuming that Paul returned to Damascus after he left Jerusalem, using the Christian community in Damascus as his base for missionary work, he could have reached several cities in central Syria, traveling in a northerly direction. He could have journeyed northwest via Abila through the Marsyas Valley (mod. Bekaa Valley) and along the Orontes River via Heliopolis, Laodikeia ad Libanum, Emesa, Arethusa, Epiphaneia and Larissa to Apameia. Or he could have traveled after Laodikeia in a northwesterly direction along the foot of

---

[66]See Schürer 3:14-15.

Jebel Ansariyeh to Mariamme, Raphaneai, Marsya to Seleucia ad Belum, and from there to Apameia. The cities on the Orontes River had been founded for military reasons and were some 25-30 km distant from each other. On Syria see §22.5.

Abila (Ἄβιλα; mod. Suq Le Basi Barada, Syria)[67] was situated between Mount Hermon and the Anti-Lebanon Mountains, about 25 km north of Damascus on the road that ran across the mountains to Heliopolis in the Marsyas Valley and further north in the direction of Emesa; a western route ran across Mount Lebanon to Berytus on the Mediterranean. In the first decades of the first century A.D. Abila was the capital of the tetrarchy of Abilene, whose ruler was Lysanias (Lk 3:1). In A.D. 37 Emperor Claudius gave Abilene to Herod Agrippa I. An inscription documents a certain Seleukos son of Abgaros, "priest of the Goddess Roma and of the Deified Augustus Caesar, and priest of Zeus and Apis," who erected an altar dedicated to the "Greatest Heliopolitan Zeus" together with his brother Alexandros.[68] Ruins from the Hellenistic, Roman and Byzantine periods have been investigated by archaeologists since 1980.

Heliopolis (mod. Baalbek, Lebanon),[69] about 75 km north of Damascus on the plateau of the Bekaa Valley between Mount Lebanon and the Anti-Lebanon Mountains, was settled already in prehistoric times but became significant only in the late Hellenistic period. The region was controlled since the first century B.C. by the Itureans, who originally had lived on the slopes of Mount Hermon.[70] Heliopolis flourished in the Roman period. The city belonged to the territory of the *colonia* of Berytus (Colonia Iulia Augusta Felix), the only Roman military colony in Syria. Heliopolis owed its name to the cult of the sun-god Helios. The temple of Jupiter had truly monumental dimensions: the temenos was 400 m from east to west, and the 10 times 19 columns of the peristyle temple were 19 m high. It was built, as was the temple of Bacchus, on the orders of Augustus and finished in the second century. An altar consisting of four levels and 18 m high stood in front of the temple of Jupiter; two staircases led up to the platform on which the sacrifices were offered. The city owned further temples, a hippodrome and a theater. In the Byzantine period Heliopolis was a center of pagan resistance to the Christian faith for a long time.

Laodikeia (Λαοδίκεια ἡ πρὸς Λιβάνῳ; Laodikeia ad Libanum, ancient Kadesh; Tell Nebi

---

[67]H. Treidler, "Abila 2," *KP* 1:14; A. Negev, *PECS* 4; F. F. Bruce, "Abilene," *GBL* 1:7; W. H. Mare, *NEAEHL* 1:1-3; T. Leisten, *DNP* 1:16-17; Jones 1937, 256, 272, 283; Schürer 2:136-37, 567; Millar 1993, 310-11; Ball 2000, 197; J. P. Brown, *BAGRW* 1058, map 69. See <http://www.abila.org>.

[68]Youssef Hajjar, *La triade d'Héliopolis-Baalbek: Son culte et sa diffusion à travers les textes littéraires et les documents iconographiques et épigraphiques I-III* (3 vols.; Leiden: Brill, 1977-1985), 1:179, no. 165, quoted in Millar 1993, 311.

[69]H. Treidler, "Baalbek," KP 1:795; J.-P. Rey-Coquais, *PECS* 380-82; T. Leisten, *DNP* 2:383; J. Teixidor, in Dentzer and Orthmann 1989, 91; Will 1989, 230; Isaac 1993, 318-21, 342-43; T. Wiegand, *Baalbek. Ergebnisse der Ausgrabungen und Untersuchungen in den Jahren 1898 bis 1905* (3 vols.; Berlin: de Gruyter, 1921-1925); Godefroy Goossens, *Hiérapolis de Syrie* (Leuven: Bibliothèque de l'Université, 1943); Friedrich Ragette, *Baalbek* (Park Ridge, N.J.: Noyes, 1980); Y. Hajjar, "Baalbek, grand centre religieux sous l'Empire," *ANRW* 2.18.4 (1990): 2458-2508; A. Segal, *Qadmoniot* 32 (1999): 2-16; Ball 2000, 39-47, 321, 324, 336-38.

[70]J. F. Healey, *OCD* 776; W. Schottroff, "Die Ituräer," *ZDPV* 98 (1982): 125-52.

Mend, near Aqrabiyé, Syria),[71] on the upper Orontes River about 75 km north of Heliopolis, was founded probably by Seleukos I and flourished since the second century B.C. Ptolemaios called the city Skabiosa Laodikeia (5.14.16) because the unhealthy location in the valley promoted leprosy. Laodikeia was connected to the Roman road system.

Emesa (Ἔμεσα; mod. Homs),[72] 28 km north of Laodikeia on the east bank of the Orontes River, was the capital of an Arab kingdom since the second century B.C. The rulers in the first century A.D. were Sampsigeramus II (A.D. 14-48) and Azizos (A.D. 48-65); they were related through marriages to Herod Agrippa I and Agrippa II (Josephus, *A.J.* 20.139) and had become Roman allies. Emesa controlled a large territory that extended far into the desert. Remains from the Roman period have been found on the site of ancient Emesa. Descendants of the royal house of Emesa became emperors in the third century (Geta, Caracalla). We know next to nothing about the culture and the society of Emesa in the first century, apart from the fact that the rulers of Emesa possessed Roman citizenship, that they used the title "king" and that they could supply the Roman army with four thousand soldiers. Emesa was famous for a temple dedicated to the sun-god Elagabalus (*deus Sol invictus*), whose symbol was a black stone; the temple stood where today a large mosque stands; the temple is depicted on coins as a Corinthian peripteral temple with 6 times 11 columns. Heliodoros, the author of the last ancient Greek novel (Αἰθιοπικά, "Ethiopian Stories"), made use of efforts by Emperor Elagabal (A.D. 218-222) to elevate the cult of the sun-god of Emesa to the main deity of the Roman Empire. Emesa remained pagan for a long time. Eusebius mentions in connection with the great persecution the bishop Silvanus, who was responsible for the Christians "around Emesa"—that is, the Christians who lived in the villages in the territory of Emesa (τῶν ἀμφιτὴν Ἐμισαν ἐκκλησιῶν ἐπίσκοπος [*Hist. eccl.* 8.13.4]). The bishop Anatolios of Emesa attended the Council of Nicea.[73] A bishop Eusebius was active in Emesa after A.D. 341; one of his teachers was Eusebius of Caesarea. Around A.D. 400 the bishop Nemesios of Emesa wrote a treatise "On the Nature of Man" (Περὶ φύσεως ἀνθρώπου).

Arethusa (Ἀρεθούσα; mod. Restan),[74] about 25 km north of Emesa, on the Orontes River, was controlled by Apameia, as were Larissa and Seleucia ad Belum. The name "Arethusa" indicates that the city was founded by Greek and Macedonian settlers. In the first century B.C. Arethusa belonged to Emesa. Strabo mentions Arethusa as an example of good administration (16.2.10-11). A bishop Eustathios of Arethusa is attested for the fourth century.

Epiphaneia (Ἐπιφάνεια; the Old Testament Hamath; mod. Hama),[75] about 25 km north

---

[71]H. Treidler, "Laodikeia 2," *KP* 3:483; T. Podella, "Laodikeia 2," *DNP* 6:1132; Rey-Coquais 1989, 50; Grainger 1990, 106, 130-31, 161-62; J. P. Brown, *BAGRW* 1046 (map 68).

[72]C. Colpe, *KP* 2:257-58; idem, *DNP* 3:1008-9; Jones 1937, 261-63; R. D. Sullivan, "The Dynasty of Emesa," *ANRW* II.8 (1977): 198-219; idem, *AB* 2:496-97; Rey-Coquais 1989, 49, 51-52; idem, *PECS* 302; Grainger 1990, 106, 130-33, 178-83, 184-86; Millar 1993, 34, 71-72, 82-84, 119-20, 300-309; Ball 2000, 33-47.

[73]Harnack 1924, 2:657-58 (ET, 2:122-23); Gelzer, Hilgenfeld and Cuntz 1898, lxi.

[74]Rey-Coquais 1989, 50; Grainger 1990, 59, 102-3, 106-7, 178-79; Millar 1993, 302.

[75]H. Treidler, "Epiphaneia 2," *KP* 2:321; G. Lehmann and T. Leisten, "Epiphaneia 2," *DNP* 3:1149-50; Jones 1937, 232, 240, 262-63; Grainger 1990, 106, 130-31, 138-41; Millar 1993, 300; J. P. Brown, *BAGRW* 1043, s.v. "Amathe," map 68.

of Emesa on the Orontes River, was located at an important crossroads. The Old Testament mentions Hamath repeatedly (e.g., 2 Sam 8:9; 2 Kings 14:28; Is 10:9). Antiochos IV renamed the city Epiphaneia, a name that suggests a refoundation of the city by the Seleucids, perhaps around 200 B.C. The city flourished in the Roman period and is mentioned by Pliny (*Nat.* 5.82) and Ptolemaios (5.14.12). The bishop Manikeios of Epiphaneia attended the Council of Nicea in A.D. 325.

Larissa (Λάρι[σ]σα; mod. Shaizar),[76] about 20 km northwest of Epiphaneia on the Orontes River, was founded probably in 301 B.C.: the citizens recalled for a long time that they descended from a regiment of Thessalian cavalry of Alexander the Great (Diodorus Siculus 33.4a). The bishop Gerontios of Larissa attended the Council of Nicea.

Apameia ('Απάμεια; originally Pella; mod. Qalaat el-Moudiq),[77] about 25 km northwest of Larissa (about 115 km south of Antioch), on the Orontes River, was one of the four large cities in northern Syria that had been founded by Seleukos Nikator after 301 B.C. As a military and administrative center, Apameia was the main rival of Antioch around 198 B.C.; the war elephants of the Syrian army continued to be stationed in Apameia. Pompey destroyed the fortress. Augustus punished the city, which had supported Mark Antony. The city was refounded in the first century A.D. as Claudia Apamea; it controlled a good number of dependent cities and continued to be most important urban center between Damascus and Antioch (Strabo 16.2.10).[78] The population is estimated at 117,000 people. Coins demonstrate that the emperor Claudius took an interest in the city. Apameia had perhaps the largest theater in antiquity (145 m diameter). Remains of the agora, baths, nymphaeum, the temple of Tyche and the temple of Zeus Belos (see Dio Cassius 79.8.5) have been investigated. The central colonnaded street was 1,600 m long and 23 m wide and was flanked by stoas 10.5 m high (dating to the second century). Inscriptions document Syrian merchants from Apameia in Rome (*IGR* I 311, 317); a merchant named Aziz Agrippa, who came from Kafr Zebed, a village that belonged to Apameia, died in Trier in Germania (*IG* XIV 2558). Famous sons of the city include Numenius, an important neo-Platonic philosopher of the second century, and Poseidonios. A church dating to the fourth century was erected at the site of a large synagogue.[79] The bishop Alphios attended the Council of Nicea.

Mariamme (Μαριάμμη; mod. Mariamin, near Rafnije),[80] 28 km northwest of Emesa, was a polis (*IGLSyria* 2106). Pliny mentions the citizens of Mariamme as being independent (Pliny, *Nat.* 5.19.81-82). Bishops from Mariamme are attested since A.D. 451.

---

[76]Rey-Coquais 1989, 50; Grainger 1990, 39-44, 130-31, 168-69.
[77]J.-P. Rey-Coquais, *PECS* 66-67; J. Oelsner, "Apameia 3," *DNP* 1:824; J. C. Balty, *OEANE* 1:145-47; J. C. Balty, "Apamée de Syrie, archéologie et histoire," *ANRW* II.8 (1977): 103-44; G. W. Bowersock, in Dentzer and Orthmann 1989, 73, 76; J. Teixidor, in ibid., 84; P. Leriche, in ibid., 269-70; Rey-Coquais 1989, 49, 52; Will 1989, 228-29, 232-34; Grainger 1990, 38-39, 72-73, 126-28; Millar 1993, 236-39, 256-63, and passim; Ball 2000, 159-62; Noy and Bloedhorn, in *IJudO* III, 2004, 84-85. See <http://www.ccr.jussieu.fr/dga/Campagnes/Apamee/Presentation.htm>.
[78]See Grainger 1990, 128.
[79]See Brenk 1991b; L. Levine 2000, 240-42, and passim.
[80] E. Honigmann, PW 14.1 (1928): 1745-46; K. Ziegler, "Mariamme 3," *KP* 3:1024; T. Leisten, "Mariamme 3," *DNP* 7:892; Jones 1937, 267, 543; Grainger 1990, 104-6, 131, 184.

Raphaneai (mod. Rafniye),[81] situated on the eastern route from Tripolis and Arka to Apameia, was a city with close connections to Arados. The bishop Basianos attended the Council of Nicea.

Marsya (mod. Miszaf),[82] about 15 km northwest of Mariamme, was a city (*polis*) off the main road to Apameia.

Seleucia ad Belum (Σελεύκεια πρὸς Βήλῳ; mod. Skeilbieh),[83] about 10 km south of Apameia, is mentioned repeatedly in ancient sources (see Pliny, *Nat.* 5.19.82).

Using Antioch as a base of operations, Paul could have reached several cities in northern Syria with the gospel. Traveling in a northerly direction, he would have reached Platanoi and Alexandreia; in a northeasterly direction were Imma, Gindaros, Kyrrhos and Nikopolis, and in an easterly direction Litarba and Beroia.

Platanoi (Πλάτανοι; mod. Belen, Turkey),[84] 35 km north of Antioch, was situated about 2 km east of the Syriai Pylai ("Syrian Gates"; mod. Beylan Geçidi [elevation 700 m]), the pass across the Amanos Mountains from Syria to Cilicia. The pass that was used by many travelers curved in antiquity to the southeast (the modern road makes a wide arc to the east). The modern town obliterated practically all ancient remains. In the nineteenth century remains of the Roman road were still visible (the ruins that remain visible today are from the Osman period).

Alexandreia (ʿΑλεξάνδρεια ἡ μίκρα; ʾΑλεξάνδρεια κατ' ʾΙσσόν; mod. Iskenderun),[85] about 15 km north of Platanoi, was a port city on the southeastern end of the Gulf of Issos (Strabo 12.1.3; 12.2.7). The town was situated on a rock that towered about the beach (Esentepe [1,900 by 300 m]) and controlled the road that ran between Antioch and Tarsus. Alexandreia probably was founded not by Alexander the Great but by Seleukos Nikator. The city minted its own coins since Antiochos IV Epiphanes. Roman remains document roads, cisterns and houses with mosaics. Christians are attested for the second century; the first documented bishop that we know was Alexander in A.D. 188. The bishop Hesychios attended the Council of Nicea.

Imma (mod. Yenişehir, near Reyhanlı, Turkey)[86] was situated 40 km east of Antioch on the western slopes of Mount Koryphe (mod. Jebel Sheikh Barakat), at the junction where the road from Antioch branched off toward the north (via Gindaros and Kyrrhos to Nikopolis), the west (to Zeugma on the Euphrates River) and the south (via Chalkis ad Belum and Apameia).

---

[81]Jones 1937, 267; J.-P. Rey-Coquais, *Arados et sa pérée aux époques grecque, romaine et byzantine* (Paris: Geuthner, 1974), 100-111; Pollard 2000, 22-24, 38-41, 65-66, 268; J. P. Brown, *BAGRW* 1047, map 68.

[82]Grainger 1990, 106.

[83]W. Röllig, "Seleukeia No. 5," *KP* 5:85; Grainger 1990, 59, 106-7, 131, 138; not shown in J. P. Brown, *BAGRW* 1047, map 68 (not listed under the toponyms that have not been located).

[84]Hild and Hellenkemper 1990, 212; T. Sinclair, *BAGRW* 1033, map 67.

[85]H. Treidler, "Alexandreia 3," *KP* 1:245; T. S. MacKay, "Alexandria ad Issum," *PECS* 38; Hild and Hellenkemper 1990, 170-72; Jones 1937, 198-200; Hellenkemper and Hild 1986, 112-15; Grainger 1990, 36-37, 68, 105, 108-9, 129, 135.

[86]T. Sinclair, *BAGRW* 1031, map 67.

Gindaros (Γίνδαρος; mod. Jenderes, Syria),[87] about 22 km north-northeast of Imma on the road to Zeugma, is mentioned by Strabo as a polis. Gindaros was the capital of the district of Kyrrestike (Strabo 16.2.8).

Kyrrhos (Κύρρος; the ruin Kuros, near mod. Nebi Ouri, Syria)[88] was situated about 55 km north-northeast of Gindaros (90 km northeast of Antioch) in northern Syria on the border with Commagene, on the Oinoparas River (mod. Nahr Afrin) in a large and fertile plain. The city seems to have been founded before 301 B.C. by Macedonians; it minted its own coins since 150 B.C. Kyrrhos was at the crossroads of the road from Antioch to Zeugma and to Samosata. In the winter of A.D. 18/19 the Tenth Legion was stationed at Kyrrhos (Tacitus, *Ann.* 2.57.2). Remains include the acropolis, a temple and a large theater (115 m in diameter). The bridges dating to the early Byzantine period are still in use. The bishop Sirikios from Kyrrhos attended the Council of Nicea.

Nikopolis (Νικόπολις; mod. Islahiye, Turkey),[89] 40 km northwest of Kyrrhos on the eastern route from Antioch to Cilicia in the valley between Mount Amanos and the mountains in the east, belonged between A.D. 21 and 30 to Syria; otherwise it was part of Cilicia (Strabo 14.5.19), later of Armenia. The city, a local market center, is not mentioned often in contemporary sources.

Germanikeia (Γερμανίκεια; mod. Kahramanmaraş, Maraş),[90] about 70 km north of Nikopolis on an eastern branch of the Pyramos River (mod. Ceyhan Nehri) on the southern slopes of the Taurus Mountains in the region of Commagene in northern Syria, first belonged to Cilicia, later to Syria. Coins document a special relationship of Germanikeia with the city of Rome in the imperial period. The name of the city documents the gratitude of the Commagene King Antiochos IV to the emperor Caligula or Claudius, who restored in A.D. 38 or 41 the local dynasty as rulers of the kingdom of Commagene, which had belonged to the province of Syria since A.D. 17. The bishop Salamanes of Germanikeia attended the Council of Nicea.

Litarba (mod. el-Athareb, Syria)[91] was located about 30 km southeast of Imma on the southern slopes of Mount Koryphe (mod. Jebel Sheikh Barakat). The city was also called Litargon.

Beroia (Βερόη; mod. Aleppo, Halab)[92] was situated 30 km east of Litarba (about 100 km

---

[87] Grainger 1990, 108, 174-75, 184; Millar 1993, 231-32.

[88] E. Honigmann, PW 12.1 (1924): 199-204; K. Ziegler, "Kyrrhos 2," *KP 3*:421; J.-P. Rey-Coquais, *PECS* 473; J. Gippert, "Kyrrhos 2," *DNP* 6:1019-20; E. Frézouls, "Cyrrhus et la Cyrrhestique jusqu'à la fin du Haut-Empire," *ANRW* II.8 (1977): 164-97; P. Leriche, in Dentzer and Orthmann 1989, 270-72; E. Frézouls, in ibid., 390-93; Grainger 1990, 40-42, 83-87, 95-97, 134-35, 174-75, 185-86; Millar 1993, 33, 229; Ball 2000, 163-64; Pollard 2000, 261-62, and passim.

[89] E. Olshausen, "Nikopolis 5," *KP 4*:125-26; idem, "Nikopolis 5," *DNP* 8:938; Grainger 1990, 52-53, 68-69, 80-81, 134-35.

[90] H. Treidler, PWSup 9 (1962): 70-72; idem, *KP* 2:767; J. Wagner, *DNP* 4:966; Millar 1993, 228-29, 257.

[91] P.-L. Gatier, *BAGRW* 1032, map 67.

[92] Treidler, "Beroia 3," *KP* 1:869-70; Rey-Coquais, "Beroea," *PECS* 150; T. Leisten, "Beroia 3," *DNP* 2:579; Grainger 1990, 44, 68-69, 79-80, 132, 173-74; Millar 1993, 237, 257; Anette Gangler, "Die Topographie von Aleppo," in Fansa 2000, 87-93; Ball 2000, 162-63; Heinz Gaube, "Aleppo zwischen Alexander dem Großen und der Arabischen Eroberung," in Fansa 2000, 101-7.

east of Antioch) on the Chalos River (mod. Qweiq), on the road from Apameia via Chalkis (35 km) to Zeugma. Beroia was founded between 301 and 281 B.C., possibly by settlers from Macedonian Beroia (Beroea). Beroia was a leading city in northern Syria. The city is mentioned in 2 Macc 13:4: the high priest Menelaus from Jerusalem was executed here in 163 B.C. As a result of an ideal location and fertile territory the site has been settled until the present. The main street that ran through Beroia from east to west was 20-25 m wide; the agora was in the center of the city (at the site of the large synagogue of modern times) at the end of an aqueduct 13 km in length.

It is less likely that Paul engaged in missionary work in eastern Syria, in cities such as Palmyra, Resafa, Sura, Nikephorion, Karrhai, Edessa, Charax Sidou, Zeugma (Seleucia), Hierapolis, Barbalissos (listed from south to north). It would not have been difficult to reach these cities on the regularly traveled caravan routes. The fact, however, that we find Paul in Tarsus and in Antioch suggests that he concentrated on western and northern Syria, besides Cilicia.

The list of bishops who attended the Council of Nicea in A.D. 325 includes Marinos of Palmyra, Antiochos of Resaina, Aïthalas of Edessa, Bassos of Zeugma, Philoxenos of Hierapolis.[93]

Missionary Work in Cilicia

In Cilicia Jews are attested for Tarsus, Seleucia on the Kalykadnos River, Korykos and Olba-Diokaisareia.[94] If Paul preached the gospel in towns without Jewish communities, he may have been active in other cities as well.

Cilicia (Κιλικία [see fig. 25])[95] is the region in the southeast of Asia Minor between Pamphylia in the province of Galatia to the west[96] and the province of Syria to the east, the boundary running on the heights of the Amanos Mountains. The southern boundary was the Mediterranean, and the northern boundary was Lycaonia in the province of Galatia and the province of Cappadocia (essentially along the Taurus Mountains). Western Cilicia, so-called Rugged Cilicia (Cilicia Tracheia, the region Isauria), extended from Korakesion (mod. Alanya) to the territory of Soloi-Pompeiopolis (mod. Viranşehir), with the Taurus Mountains bordering on the Mediterranean. Eastern or Plain Cilicia (Cilicia Pedias; mod. Çukurova), extending from Soloi to Alexandreia kat'Isson (mod. Iskenderun), is characterized by a coastal plan between 20 and 70 km wide (Strabo 14.5.1).

---

[93]See Gelzer 1898, lxi.
[94]Schürer 3:33-34; Hild and Hellenkemper 1990, 84, 99.
[95]W. Ruge, "Kilikien," PW 11 (1921): 385-89; A. Kammenhuber, KP 3:208-9; H. Täuber, DNP 6:454-56; G. E. Bean and S. Mitchell, OCD 330-31; Hild and Hellenkemper 1990; Jones 1937; Afif Erzen, *Kilikien bis zum Ende der Perserherrschaft* (Leipzig: Noske, 1940); Magie 1950; Mitford 1980; Pekáry 1980, 650-55; Fritz M. Heichelheim, "Geschichte Kleinasiens von der Eroberung durch Kyros II. bis zum Tode des Heraklios I. (547 v.Chr-641 n.Chr.)," in *Orientalische Geschichte von Kyros bis Mohammed* (Handbuch der Orientalistik 1.2, sec. 4.2; Leiden: Brill, 1966), 32-98; Claude Mutafian, *La Cilicie au carrefour des empires* (2 vols.; Paris: Les Belles Lettres, 1988). Inscriptions: *I. KilikiaDF* (ed. G. Dagron and D. Feissel, 1987).
[96]The border ran in the valley of the Sedre Çayı river, 12 km north of Iotape and 22 km south of modern Alanya in a northerly direction toward the western edge of Suğla Gölü.

The rivers Kydnos, Sarus and Pyramos, originating in the Taurus Mountains, were unsuitable for shipping traffic. The Cilician plains are very hot in the summer months, capable of temperatures reaching 45°C; they are regarded as the hottest region of Asia Minor. The winter months bring cold and huge amounts of snow to the Taurus Mountains. The major road in Cilicia ran from Sardis and Ephesus in western Asia Minor through the Cilician Gates to Tarsus and in an easterly direction via Adana and Mopsuestia along the Gulf of Issos to Alexandreia and across the Amanos Mountains to Antioch, the capital of the province of Syria. The East Cilician plain was and still is among the most fertile regions of Asia Minor.

Cilicia was a province of the Assyrian Empire between 713 and 663 B.C. After the defeat of the Assyrians in 612 B.C. Cilicia became an independent kingdom until it was forced to accept Persian rule in 547 B.C. After the victory of Alexander the Great over the Persians in 333 B.C. Cilicia belonged to the Seleucid kingdom; the coast of the Tracheia was disputed between the Seleucids and the Ptolemies. When the Romans organized the province of Asia in 133 B.C., Cilicia Tracheia, together with Pamphylia and Pisidia, was annexed to Cappadocia. When Pompey reorganized the East in 68 B.C. and stopped the activities of pirates in Rugged Cilicia, the two Cilician regions were united with Lycia, Pamphylia and Pisidia and organized as the *Provincia Cilicia,* with Tarsus as the capital. In 51/50 B.C. M. Tullius Cicero was governor of the province, which consisted at that time of five administrative districts: Lycaonia, Pamphylia, Isauria, Cilicia and Cyprus. After the reorganization under Augustus in 29/25 B.C. Tracheia was again annexed to Cappadocia. When Cappadocia became an imperial province under Tiberius in A.D. 17, changes in territorial responsibility occurred again. The Cilician province was divided between Galatia and Syria, while client rulers controlled Tracheia. When Vespasian reorganized the East in A.D. 72, Tarsus became again the capital of the reestablished province of Cilicia.

These political developments, whose details need not be described here, must not divert our attention from the fact that the first century A.D. was a peaceful time interrupted only rarely by disturbances. This fact explains the increase in the population figures, together with the continuous development of the economy. The unusually large number of towns and villages during the Roman period suggests that (eastern and southern) Cilicia had a much higher population density than other regions in Asia Minor during this time.[97] The indigenous population seems to have been Grecized later than other regions of Asia Minor. The foundation of Hellenistic cities in Cilicia did not lead to a basic change of the ethnic identity of the Cilicians, and the foundation of Roman colonies (Ninica-Klaudiopolis and Mallos) likewise had little influence on the population. The most important cities of Cilicia were (in alphabetical order): Adana, Aigai, Anazarbos, Anemurion, Aphrodisias, Epiphaneia, Kastabala, Korykos, Mallos, Mopsuestia, Olba, Soloi-Pompeiopolis and Selinus. The main crops that were cultivated were wheat, olives, pomegranates, apricots, dates, figs, cornelian cherries, walnuts, hazelnuts, pistachios, mulberries, white onions, lettuce, saffron,[98] styrax trees (for the production of odorous substances and aromas for cultic activity, for the fumigation of vermin and for medicinal purposes), and the production of wine was important.[99] Animal husbandry (primarily goats and sheep), fishing and

---

[97]Hild and Hellenkemper 1990, 23, 99. Population density declined after A.D. 500.

[98]Soloi-Pompeiopolis was famous for saffron balsam or saffron oil (Pliny, *Nat.* 13.2).

[99]Pliny (*Nat.* 14.19) praises the raisin wine (*passum*) that seems to have been exported. The name of a particular Cilician wine was *Abatēs,* which also was used as laxative (Athenaios, *Deipnosophistai* 1.33).

forestry played an important role as well.[100] Due to the strategic location of Cilicia at the most important trade route between Asia Minor and Syria and between Europe and the Orient, trade and traffic were economically significant factors as well.

We may plausibly assume that Paul preached the gospel in Tarsus, his hometown, in the time between A.D. 33/34 and 42: Barnabas finds Paul in A.D. 42 when he looked for a theologically competent missionary who could help to consolidate and expand the Christian community in Antioch, the capital of Syria.

Tarsus (Τάρσος, Θαρσός; mod. Tarsus),[101] about 210 km northwest of Antioch, is among the largest prehistoric sites of the Ancient Near East; archaeologists discovered thirty-three layers of settlement from the early Neolithic to the Islamic periods. The center of the development of the city was a huge hill south of the foothills of the Taurus Mountains at the southern end of the pass through the Cilician Gates. Xenophon reports that it took four days to march from Tarsus to the Cilician Gates (*Anab.* 1.2.21-24). The Kydnos River (mod. Tarsus Çayı) ran through the city from north to south; high water levels in the spring often caused flooding (the old river bed probably is preserved in the Sehir Ark ["town moat"], a small brook in the old city). The port of the city was in the lagoon 7 km south of the city (Ῥῆγμα, *Rhēgma,* "cleft, breakage"), and the exit from the lagoon into the Mediterranean was 13 km south of Tarsus.[102] The literary tradition documents the great importance of the city in pre-Christian times. The Hittite settlement was called Tarša. Tarsus was the capital of the Cilician kings and of the Persian satrapy in this region. Scholars assume that the population spoke both Cilician and Persian in the third century B.C. There may have been a Greek colony in the city before 340 B.C., although there is no hard evidence of that as yet. The importance of Tarsus prompted Alexander the Great to station troops in the city. Tarsus became Hellenized in the Seleucid period; the population adopted the Greek language and culture. In the second century B.C. (perhaps since Antiochos IV Epiphanes) the city was called Antiocheia on the Kydnos (᾿Αντιοχεῖς ἀπὸ Κύδνου). Around 170 B.C. unrest ensued in Tarsus and Mallos after Antiochos IV had presented the city as a "gift" to his concubine Antiochis; he probably imposed additional financial burdens on the citizens with Antiochis as beneficiary

---

[100]It is unclear when cotton was introduced to Cilicia, the most important agricultural export of the region today. It is possible that this did not happen before the Arab period. See Hild and Hellenkemper 1990, 111.

[101]W. Ruge, "Tarsos," PW 4.A (1931): 2413-39; E. Olshausen, "Tarsos," *KP* 5:629-30; M. Gough, *PECS* 883-84; C. J. Hemer, *ISBE* 4:734-36; A. J. M. Jones and S. Mitchell, *OCD* 1476; Hild and Hellenkemper 1990, 428-39; Ramsay 1907, 85-255; Magie 1950, 1:272, 473; 2:1146-48; Jones 1937, 192-94, 207-8; H. Böhlig, *Die Geisteskultur von Tarsus* (FRLANT 19; Göttingen: Vandenhoeck & Ruprecht, 1913); Welles 1962; C. P. Jones, *The Roman World of Dio Chrysostom* (Cambridge, Mass.: Harvard University Press, 1978), 71-82; Pierre Chuvin, "Apollon au trident et les dieux de Tarse," *Journal des Savants* (1981): 305-26; Price 1984, 274 (nos. 143-56); Ziegler 1985, 21-32, 58, 67, 69, 71; S. Johnson 1987, 25-34; Hengel 1991, 180-93; Ziegler 1993, 19-24, 41-46, 149 and passim; Riesner 1994, 236-37 (ET, 266); Hengel and Schwemer 1998, 237-273 (ET, 151-77); Hölbl 2001, 240-41. Inscriptions: *CIG* III 4437-4438; *CIG* IV 9161-9162; *CIL* III 221-222, 230; *IGR* III 876-885; *I. KilikiaDF* 26-41. Excavations took place between 1934 and 1939; see Hetty Goldman, ed., *Excavations at Gözlü Kule, Tarsus* (3 vols.; Princeton, N.J.: Princeton University Press, 1950-1963); cf. Gates 1995, 248.

[102]Strabo 14.5.10-11. See Magie 1950, 2:1147; Hild and Hellenkemper 1990, 391, 428-39.

of the funds.[103] Since 64 B.C. Tarsus was the undisputed capital of the Roman province of Cilicia and the seat of the governors, one of them being Cicero. The Tarsians called their city Iuliopolis in honor of Caesar, who had promoted the city after the battle of Pharsalos (Cassius Dio 47.26). Mark Antony, who had met with Cleopatra in Tarsus, and Augustus promoted Tarsus as well: the city was granted autonomy and tax exemption (Cassius Dio 47.30-31) as well as control over the Kydnos River and the territory between the city and the Mediterranean.

The prosperity of the city was connected with the textile industry and its function as a trade center.[104] Tarsus was also known for a perfume (*pardarlium*) and nard oil (μύριον νάρδινον [Pliny *Nat.* 13.2]). Strabo describes in detail the flourishing literary and philosophical life in the city in the first century B.C. (14.4.12-15 [see §16.2 in the present work]). He praises the scholars (φιλόλογοι, *philologoi*) from Tarsus, many of whom were active in Rome, just as scholars from Alexandria taught in the capital of the empire. In regard to the first century A.D., the only primary evidences for Tarsus are the New Testament references to the Tarsian origin of the apostle Paul. The sophist Dio Chrysostom, in two speeches written at the beginning of the second century, reproached the Tarsians for neglecting philosophy and the requisite generosity and tolerance regarding the neighboring cities of Mallos and Aigai (*Or.* 33; 34).[105] Philostratus reports that Apollonios of Tyana studied in Tarsus a generation after Strabo, and that he was disappointed with the academic atmosphere of the city (*Vit. Apoll.* 1.7).

As a result of continuous settlement in Tarsus, hardly any ancient remains exist. The ruins of imperial baths (60 by 30 m) are located near the center of modern Tarsus. During excavation works for a parking garage, a street dating to the Hellenistic period was discovered; in 1993 archaeologists were able to expose the street at a length of 65 m. The street was still in use in Roman Tarsus. It consisted of black polygonal stone slabs; the sidewalks were constructed with white limestone. The drainage pipes that ran along both sides of the street were connected with a central sewage canal underneath the street that could be controlled by square manholes. Traces of a theater are located on the east slope of the Gözlü Kule. The stadium was located between the bus station (Garaj) and the American College. The city wall was built probably in the late Roman period. Literary and numismatic sources attest temples dedicated to Zeus (Baal), Tyche, Apollo Tarsios, Apollo Argeios,[106] Perseus, Heracles/Sandan,[107] Demeter, Athene, Dionysos, Asclepius, Artemis, Cybele and Helios. The temple for the *koinon* (provincial assembly) of Cilicia was built probably in A.D. 150. Tarsus was a center of the emperor cult, as attested by the temple of Hadrian. There were several philosophical academies in the city. Tarsus organized numerous games; coins document "sacred oikoumenical" games in the time of Hadrian. The citizens of Mallos, Adana and Aigai came to Tarsus to offer sacrifices. Dio Chrysostom described Tarsus as one of the three greatest cities in Asia Minor, together with Ephesus and Smyrna (ca. A.D. 100). An inscription, Luke's comment in Acts 6:9, and Philostratus attest the presence of Jews in Tarsus. *CIJ* II 931 (*IJudO* II 249): "Here lies Isaac, elder [of the assembly] of the Cappadocians, linen merchant from Tarsus"; the inscription was found in Jaffa. Acts 6:9 mentions a synagogue

---

[103]See Welles 1962, 50-52.

[104]Dio 34.21-22; P.Oxy. 109. See Magie 1950, 2:1147-48.

[105]See Welles 1962, 62-75.

[106]Plutarch, who was a priest in Delphi between A.D. 90 and 120, knew the Apollo cult of Tarsus (*Def. orac.* 41 [433B]). See Chuvin, "Apollon," 310-11.

[107]Gill 1991, 82-83; 1994a, 90.

of Cilician Jews in Jerusalem. Philostratus reports that some Jews had Tarsian citizenship under Titus, thus around A.D. 80 (*Vit. Apoll.* 6.34). Indirect evidence is provided by Philo, who refers to a letter of Agrippa I to Caligula that mentions the fact that Cilicia is among the provinces in which Jews live (Philo, *Legat.* 281).[108] An inscription dated to the sixth century attests the existence of a synagogue.[109]

Tarsus was a plausible goal for Paul's missionary efforts for at least five reasons. (1) Tarsus was his hometown, so his relatives, friends and acquaintances in the city would be not only a natural first audience but also a helpful base of operations. (2) The Tarsian citizenship that Paul probably possessed gave him protection,[110] a factor that had practical significance after his experience in Nabatea. (3) Tarsus was the most significant city in the region after Antioch.[111] (4) Tarsus had a Jewish community. (5) Because of its location on the Mediterranean and on the main road across the Taurus Mountains, Tarsus was ideal as a base for missionary activity not only in Syria and Cilicia but also for the regions to the north and west.[112]

There is no evidence of Tarsian Christians after Paul for two hundred years. For the third century we read of Iulietta and her son Kyriakos, whose hometown was Iconium and who suffered martyrdom in Tarsus under Diocletian, as did Kyriaina, who lived in Tarsus. The first documented bishop of Tarsus is Helenos, who appears between A.D. 260 and 280 as mediator in the struggle with the Novatians (Eusebius, *Hist. eccl.* 6.46.3; 7.5.1, 28.1, 30.5).[113] The bishop Theodoros attended the Council of Nicea in A.D. 325. The oldest documented church of Tarsus is the Hagia Sophia; on January 6, 1198, the archbishop of Mainz (Germany) and papal legate Konrad von Wittelsbach crowned Leon I King of Armenia in the church. The Hagia Sophia stood possibly at the site of the Ulu Cami Mosque, built in 1385 and still in use today.

Assuming that Paul preached the gospel of Jesus Christ in cities with Jewish communities, as reported by Luke for the period after A.D. 45, he could have engaged in missionary work and (presumably) planted churches at least in Anazarbos, Mallos, Soloi, Sebaste, Korykos, Seleukia and Olba (listed from east to west).

---

[108]Rabbinic traditions mention synagogues of Tarsians—for example, in Jerusalem: *b. Meg.* 26a [bar.]; *t. Meg.* 3:6 = *y. Meg.* 3:1 (73d); *b. Naz.* 52; *y. Šeqal.* 2:7 (47a); *Lev. Rab.* 35:12. See Schürer 3:33-34; Hemer 1989, 127 n. 75; Riesner 1994, 131 (ET, 148); Hengel and Schwemer 1998, 240-50 (ET, 160); L. Levine 2000, 53-54, 191, 461.

[109]*I. KilikiaDF* 36 (80-82); *IJudO* II 248 (527-30).

[110]Riesner 1994, 236 (ET, 266).

[111]Hengel and Schwemer 1998, 248-29 (ET, 157-58); cf. Riesner 1994, 236 (ET, 266).

[112]Riesner 1994, 236-37 (ET, 266).

[113]See also H. Delehaye, ed., *Synaxarium,* 185-86, 252, 821; cf. B. Kötting, "Julitta u. Kyriakos," *LThK* 5 (1960) 1203; Hild and Hellenkemper 1990, 428; Harnack 1924, 2:664, 730 (ET, 2:128, 180-81); Hengel and Schwemer 1998, 224-45 (ET, 157). On the Hagia Sophia church, referred to in the comments that follow above, see Hellenkemper and Hild 1986, 92-93.

Anazarbos (᾿Ανάζαρβος; mod. Anavarza Kalesi),[114] about 110 km east of Tarsus (45 km northeast of Mopsuestia) on the west bank of the river Sumbas Çai, a branch of the Pyramos River, was the largest city in the eastern Cilician plain. The site was settled in Hellenistic times, at the latest, and was controlled in the first century B.C. by the local dynasty of Tarkondimotos, who ruled in Hierapolis-Kastabala. After a visit by Augustus the city was refounded in 19 B.C. as Kaisareia. After the death of Tarkondimotos II the region came under direct Roman rule, with Anazarbos and Hierapolis-Kastabala as the major cities. Little is known about the history of Anazarbos in the first century A.D. The acropolis that towered 200 m above the plain evidently was fortified, and a temple of Zeus stood there. Remains of the ancient city include a large colonnaded street, baths, a theater (57 m in diameter), a stadium (210 by 64 m [second century]), an amphitheater (83 by 62 m [third century]), an aqueduct built around A.D. 90 and a large necropolis. The city below the acropolis seems to have been fortified only in the early Byzantine period. Temples attested by inscriptions have not been located as of yet. The inhabitants worshiped Aphrodite, Dea Roma and the deified emperor, a "goddess who answers" (θεᾷ ἐπηκόῳ, *thea epēkoō*),[115] Ge Hedraia (earth goddess), Kasalitis (= Aphrodite), Poseidon Asphaleios, Zeus Keraunios, Zeus Olybris, Zeus Olympios and Zeus Soter.[116] Anazarbos had a temple of Domitian at the end of the first century; a column that belonged to a temple displays the dedication ᾿Αυτοκράτωρ Καῖσαρ (*Autokratōr Kaisar* [*I. Anazarbos* 21]). The city issued coins in the second and first centuries B.C.; the imperial coinage begins in A.D. 48/49. The wreath of corn ears displayed on several coins reflects the fertility of the territory that the city controlled. Coins minted during Claudius's principate display Zeus as θεὸς πολιοῦχος (*theos poliouchos*) with Anazarbos's acropolis as a background with fortifications and temples; other coins praise the victories of Claudius.[117] Anazarbos became imperial temple warden (*neōkoros*) in A.D. 198. In the third century Anazarbos was so significant that the elite of the city believed that they could relieve Tarsus of its status as metropolis. As in Tarsus, linen weaving was an important industry in Anazarbos. A horseman named Antiochos, hailing from Anazarbos, had served with distinction in the Roman army for ten years and was buried near Mainz.[118] One of the famous sons of the city was the botanist Pedanius Dioscorides, who lived in the second half of the first century A.D.; he studied in Tarsus and traveled to Greece, Crete, Egypt and Petra to gather information about the medicinal use of plants, minerals and animal products. His five-volume *Materials of Medicine* (Περὶ ὕλης ἰατρικῆς), in which he describes about seven hundred plants and over one thousand drugs, was the standard pharmacological work of antiquity; the Latin translation from the sixth century received much use in the Middle Ages.[119] According to the *Acta Sanctorum,* which contains a topographically correct report, Tarachus, Probus and Andronicus died in the amphitheater of Anazarbos as martyrs, and under the emperor Numerian (A.D. 283/284)

---

[114]G. Hirschfeld, PW 1 (1894): 2101; M. Gough, "Anazarbos," *AnSt* 2 (1952): 85-150; idem, *PECS* 53-54; H. Treidler, *KP* 1:340; M. H. Sayar, *DNP* 1:675; Jones 1937, 204-9; Magie 1950, 1:275, 473; Price 1984, 272 (no. 144); Ziegler 1985, 58-62, 66-68, 74-81; Hellenkemper and Hild 1986, 128-29; Hild and Hellenkemper 1990, 178-85; S. Mitchell 1995a, 1:206, 219, 232; Syme 1995, 164. Inscriptions: *I. KilikiaDF* 98-119; Mustafa Hamdi Sayar, *Die Inschriften von Anazarbos und Umgebung* (IK 56; Bonn: Habelt, 2000), nos. 1-661.

[115]*I. Anazarbos* 35-39; all five inscriptions date to the first and second centuries A.D.

[116]*I. Anazarbos* 39-49. See Sayar 1993, esp. 321-22.

[117]Ziegler 1993, 22-23, 106 (nos. 29-46, tables 1-2); description, ibid., 221-23.

[118]*I. Anazarbos* 14.

[119]J. M. Riddle, *OCD* 483-84.

EARLY CHRISTIAN MISSION

Thalelaios suffered martyrdom. In the years following the Council of Nicea Athanasius, the student of Lucian, was bishop in Anazarbos (Philostorgius, *Hist. eccl.* 3.15).[120] Archaeologists have documented three churches in the city. The earliest Christian inscriptions are connected with the early Byzantine Church of the Apostles and with Christian tombs from the fifth and sixth centuries (*I. Anazarbos* 59, 646-657).

Mallos (Μάλλος; near mod. Kızıltahta),[121] about 70 km from Tarsus (30 km south of Adana) on the Pyramos River, was one of the oldest Cilician cities. The large ancient site is located on a hill between the modern village and the western river bank. The city is said to have been founded by Amphilochos, a hero and seer from Thebes who accompanied Mopsus from Troy to Cilicia (Strabo 14.5.16). People came to Mallos to consult an oracle that promulgated revelations in the name of Amphilochos, a practice that is documented still in the second century A.D. Alexander the Great had liberated Mallos from Persian control. Ptolemaios I captured the city after Alexander's death and sold the male population into slavery. After coming under Seleucid rule, the city was renamed Antioch on the Pyramos under Antiochos IV. In the second century B.C. Mallos had a magistrate with a *demiourgos*. When Pompey resettled former pirates, he brought some to Mallos as well. In the first century B.C. Italian settlers are attested in the city. One of the famous sons of the city was the grammarian Krates.

Soloi-Pompeiopolis (Σόλοι, Πομπηιόπολις; mod. Viranşehir),[122] a port city about 40 km southwest of Tarsus, had been founded around 700 B.C. by colonists from Rhodes. The city originally was called Soloi (Soli). In the Persian period Soloi had the right to mint its own coins. Alexander the Great purged the pro-Persian aristocracy of the city and imposed a new constitution. Famous sons of Soloi include Aratos (315-240 B.C.), one of the most important Hellenistic poets, whose *Phaenomena* was the most widely read poem after the *Iliad* and the *Odyssey,* and Chrysippos (280-207 B.C.), who replaced Kleanthes as head of the Stoa in 232 B.C. and who is regarded as the theoretical founder of Stoic orthodoxy. In the first century B.C. the Armenian king Tigranes forced most of Soloi's citizens into exile, dragging them off to his new city Tigranocerta. After his victory over the Cilician pirates, Pompey refounded Soloi as Pompeiopolis in 67 B.C. (Strabo 14.5.8); the era of the city begins in 66/65 B.C. The city walls were built probably at this time. Remains include a theater, a colonnaded street (14.5 m wide) and large baths. The martyrdom of a certain Tarachus confirms that there was a Christian community in Soloi at a relatively early date.[123]

Sebaste (Σεβαστή; mod. Ayaş),[124] about 45 km southwest of Tarsus on what used to be

---

[120]Harnack 1924, 2:731 (ET, 2:180).

[121]W. Ruge, PW 14 (1930): 916-17; H. Treidler, *KP* 3:935; M. Gough, *PECS* 547; M. H. Sayar, *DNP* 7:780; Jones 1937, 193, 197-201, 207-8; Magie 1950, 1:274; 2:1149-50; Hild and Hellenkemper 1990, 337; S. Mitchell 1995a, 1:206. Inscriptions: *I. KilikiaDF* 69-73.

[122]W. Ruge, PW 3.A (1891): 935-38; Magie 1950, 1:273-74, 300; 2:1148-49; E. Olshausen, *KP* 5:262; M. Gough, *PECS* 851; Hild and Hellenkemper 1990, 381-82; Ziegler 1993, 20-21, 68; Gates 1995, 248-49; S. Mitchell 1995a, 1:206. Inscriptions: *I. KilikiaDF* 23-25.

[123]Harnack 1924, 2:731 (ET, 2:180).

[124]W. Ruge, PW 5 (1905): 2228-29; Jones 1937, 201, 206-7; Magie 1950, 1:268, 475; 2:1143; Ernst Kirsten, "Elaiussa-Sebaste in Kilikien," in *Mélanges Mansel* (Ankara: Tarih Kuru-mu Basimevi, 1974), 777-802; G. E. Bean, *PECS* 294-95; Hellenkemper and Hild 1986, 69-73, 123-27; Syme 1995, 162. Inscriptions: *I. KilikiaDF* 20-23; Hild and Hellenkemper 1990, 400-401.

an island 200 m from the coast in antiquity,[125] originally was called Elaiussa, a cult center in the city territory of Korykos. The city is attested in the first century B.C.; the legend of a coin describes the town as "sacred and autonomous" (ἱερὰ καὶ αὐτόνομος, *hiera kai autonomos*). When Augustus granted King Archelaos I of Cappadocia a part of Cilicia—Korykos and other areas of Rugged Cilicia—Archelaos moved his residence to the island in 12 B.C. and renamed the city Sebaste in honor of his benefactor Augustus. The new city was at times more significant than Korykos. After A.D. 38 Sebaste belonged to Antiochos IV of Commagene (A.D. 38-72). Remains of the late-Hellenistic fortifications are preserved to the west of the site; on the slope to the east of the city remains of the necropolis, living quarters, a theater and a temple (32.90 by 17.60 m, with 6 times 12 columns), possibly dedicated to Zeus, have been discovered. The aqueduct was built in the first or second century A.D. In the early Byzantine period Sebaste had three Christian basilicas, one of which had been erected on the site of the (Zeus) temple.

Korykos (Κώρυκος; near Kızkalesi),[126] about 5 km southwest of Sebaste, was known as a port city since the second century B.C. Coins indicate that the city was surrounded by walls by the first century A.D. The citizens believed that they enjoyed the protection of the god Hermes: Oppian of Cilicia describes the city in the second century A.D. as Ἑρμείαο πόλις (*Hermeiao polis* [*Halieut.* 3.208]). Remains of temples, colonnaded halls and baths survive. In caves in the vicinity there was an ancient sanctuary of Zeus. Ten inscriptions were discovered in the necropolis that document Jewish inhabitants, two of which date to the first and second centuries.[127] Korykos, famous for its saffron production, flourished in the Roman period. Families from Antioch and the vicinity comprised the largest group of new settlers in the city.[128] The non-Jewish character of the Jewish inscriptions of the pre-Constantinian period prompt Margaret Williams to a threefold conclusion: the Jews of Korykos were culturally assimilated, they had joined the political mainstream and they intentionally supported integration into the Greco-Roman institutions. This changed in the fourth century, when the identification with their Jewish heritage is clearly expressed in funerary inscriptions.

Seleucia (Σελεύκεια ἡ Τραχεῖα; also ἡ πρὸς τῷ Ταύρῳ or πρὸς τῷ Καλυκάδνῳ; mod. Silifke),[129] on the Kalykadnos River (mod. Göksu) about 25 km southwest of Korykos, was

---

[125]The highest point of the former island is 28 m above sea level. The sedimentation process presumably had already begun in the Roman period, perhaps on the line of the Roman aqueduct.

[126]W. Ruge, "Korykos Nr. 4," *PW* 11 (1922): 1452; J. Ziegler, "Korykos Nr. 2," *KP* 3:311; T. S. MacKay, *PECS* 464-65; F. Hild, "Korykos 2," *DNP* 6:761; Jones 1937, 199-208; Magie 1950, 1:268; 2:1143; S. Mitchell 1995a, 1:218, 257; 2:220; Syme 1995, 209. Inscriptions: *MAMA* II 90-195 (Meriamlik and Korykos); *MAMA* III 197-788; *I. KilikiaDF* 16-19; Hild and Hellenkemper 1990, 315-20.

[127]*CIJ* II 785-794 = *MAMA* III, 205, 222, 237, 262, 295, 344, 440, 448, 607, 679; Ameling, *IJudO* II 232-43). See Margaret H. Williams, "The Jews of Corycus—A Neglected Diaspora Community from Roman Times," *JSJ* 25 (1994): 274-86, with reprint and translation of the inscriptions.

[128]*MAMA* III, 240, 248, 376, 388, 443, 445, 455, 477, 478, 507, 563, 642. See D. Feissel, "Remarques de toponymie syrienne, d'après des inscriptions grecques chrétiennes trouvées hors de Syrie," *Syria* 59 (1982): 319-43, esp. 321.

[129]W. Ruge, "Seleukeia Nr. 5," *PW* 2.A (1921): 1203-4; E. Olshausen, "Seleukeia Nr. 5," *KP* 5:85; T. S. MacKay, *PECS* 821-22; Hild and Hellenkemper 1990, 402-6; Magie 1950, 1:268; 2:1142; S. Mitchell 1995a, 1:77; 2:116, 152. Inscriptions: *MAMA* III 3-22; *CIG* IV 9206-9236; *I. KilikiaDF* 1-10; S. Şahin, "Inschriften aus Seleukeia am Kalykadnos (Silifke)," *EA* 17 (1991): 139-66.

located at an important crossroads, the junction of the road from Iconium via Laranda (mod. Karaman) and Ninica (mod. Mut) through the Kalykadnos Valley, of the road further to the north from Laranda via Olba, and of the road from Germanikopolis via Meydancik (near mod. Gülnar), connecting with the coastal road in Seleucia. Seleukos I Nicator had resettled the citizens of Holmoi, the ancient port city, in Seleucia, which became in the subsequent years the most important city in Rugged Cilicia. The ruins of the Roman city lie 2-3 m below the present ground level. A temple of Athene Kanetis stood on the acropolis. Remains of a temple, the theater and the stadium survive. One of the sons of the city was the philosopher Xenarchus, who visited Alexandria and Athens and was active in Rome as a teacher of Augustus and mentor of Strabo.[130] Seleucia became the center of the cult of Thecla, who is mentioned in the apocryphal *Acts of Paul* as having been converted through Paul's preaching in Iconium and who allegedly engaged in missionary work in Antioch (in Phrygia?)—where supposedly took place the conversion Queen Tryphaena, a relative of the emperor (Claudius)—in Iconium and in Seleucia, where she is said to have died: "And having thus testified, she went to Seleucia and enlightened many by the word of God; then she rested in a glorious sleep" (*Acts Paul* 3, 43). Thecla was venerated since the fourth century in a basilica that stood south of the city (mod. Meriamlik).[131]

On Cape Sarpedon, at the western end of the Bay of Taşucu about 10 km south of Seleucia, stood a famous temple of Apollo.[132] In A.D. 325 worshipers of Apollo attacked Christians of Seleucia, where Athanasius of Alexandria preached the gospel. In fragment P.5 of the Coptic *Life of Athanasius* we read, ". . . hewn into the rock containing a statue of Apollo. And the people who believed in Christ knew him [i.e., Athanasius]. The pagans mocked them saying, 'You cannot seduce us into abandoning our God because it is more mighty than all others.' But there was much demonic power in that temple and nobody was allowed to enter but the priests who knew its magic . . . and virgins [?] . . . and magicians. And no human being can count the abominations that were done in that temple. While they still built the righteous temple, that is the church of Christ, the seventh heaven that is on the earth, there was a festival in that country which they celebrated in the rock sanctuary of Apollo. Nearly the entire country gathered there."[133] In the Byzantine period a monastery dedicated to St. Theodore was built at the site of the temple.

Olba ('Ολβα; mod. Ura Mahallesi, Uzuncaburç),[134] about 30 km north of Seleucia in the mountains of Rugged Cilicia at 1,050 m above sea level, was at least since 400 B.C. the

---

[130]See Dueck 2000, 9.

[131]See Harnack 1924, 2:778 (ET, 2:227); on the possibility that this text contains reliable historical information see ibid., 1:361 (ET, 1:351: "the legend itself *may* contain some nucleus of historical truth"); cf. Anne Jensen, *Thekla—die Apostolin* (Freiburg: Herder, 1995), 80-112. Skeptical are Lipsius 1883-1890, 2.1:464-67; Schneemelcher 1987-1989, 2:202 (ET, 2:332-33); Hofmann 2000, 290-93.

[132]See Hellenkemper and Hild 1986, 44-47.

[133]Oskar Lemm, *Koptische Fragmente zur Patriarchengeschichte Alexandriens* (Mémoires de l'Académie Imperiale des Sciences de St.-Pétersbourg [7th series] 36.11; St. Petersburg: Eggers, 1888), 40-43, quoted in Hellenkemper and Hild 1986, 44-45 (my translation).

[134]W. Ruge, PW 17.B (1937): 2399-2400; T. S. MacKay, *PECS* 641-42; F. Hild, *DNP* 8:1158; Jones 1937, 210-13, 215; Magie 1950, 1:269, 434, 494, 502; 2:1143-44 n. 23; S. Mitchell 1995a, 1:94-95; Syme 1995, 162-63. Inscriptions: *IGR* III 843-853; *MAMA* III 55-112; *I. KilikiaDF* 11-15; Hild and Hellenkemper 1990, 239-40, 369-70.

center of a temple state whose priests had the title "great high priest" (ἀρχιερεὺς μέγας, *archiereus megas*). Augustus evidently confirmed the priest-king Ajax as toparch: Olba remained autonomous and was spared annexation into the new province of Cappadocia. Emperor Tiberius was honored in Olba as benefactor. In the first century A.D., M. Antonius Polemo ruled over Olba and the regions Kennateis and Lalasseis (possibly in the Kalykadnos Valley). The city, situated at the end of a fertile plain about 4 km east of the temple of Zeus, lost its autonomy in A.D. 72 when Cilicia became an separate province. Under Tiberius the settlement at the temple was refounded as a city called Diokaisareia, which flourished in the second and third centuries, as is indicated by the colonnaded street, the temple of Tyche, a theater, a gymnasium, city walls and an aqueduct. The large peripteral temple of Zeus Olbios (39.70 by 21.20 m) was built between 150 and 100 B.C. The information of Strabo that Ajax son of Teuker, who had fought in Troy, founded the temple (14.5.10) probably is a Hellenistic legend. The tower, which had at least five floors, was built probably around 200 B.C. as the residence of the priest-kings of Olba. A Jewish votive inscription from the fourth or fifth century perhaps indicates an earlier presence of Jews in Olba or Diokaisareia.[135]

Paul could have engaged in missionary work in other Cilician cities as well: east of Tarsus in the port cities Baiae, Issos, Katabolos and Aigai, and in Epiphaneia, Hierapolis, Mopsuestia, Adana and Augusta; west of Tarsus in the port cities Zephyrion, Palaiai and Aphrodisias, and in Anemurion at the southern tip of Asia Minor.

Baiae (Βαίαι; mod. Payas, Yakacık),[136] on Payas River (mod. Seyithane) about 20 km north of Alexandreia, was a port city on the Gulf of Issos. Remains of the ancient city include columns.

Issos (Ἰσσός; mod. Yeşil Hüyük),[137] a port city 18 km north of Baiae, marked the eastern border of Cilicia Pedias (Strabo 14.5.1). It was at Issos that Alexander the Great won a decisive victory against the Persian king Darius III in 333 B.C., after which the city was called Nikopolis. In the first century A.D. Issos was a village. The site of the ancient city is 500 m from the sea. Remains dating to the Bronze Age and the Hellenistic-Roman period include stones and ceramics.

Katabolos (Mutlubake in the early Byzantine period; mod. Muttalip Hüyük),[138] 17 km northwest of Issos, is one of the most impressive ancient sites of Cilicia, situated on a hill 30 m high right on the coast, 1.5 km from the Amanikai Pylai (mod. Karanlık Kapı), the pass across Mount Parion (mod. Misis Dağları). On the southeastern end of the pass are the ruins of a gate (3.30 m wide); in the eastern section traces of the Roman pavement are still visible. On the rocky outcrop to the north the foundations of a Roman bath and perhaps of a *mansio* are preserved. The site of Katabolos has been settled since the Neolithic period. The ancient ruins have not been investigated by archaeologists.

---

[135]*I. KilikiaDF* 14 = *IJudO* II 230 (Museum of Silifke, inventory no. 138).

[136]See Hild and Hellenkemper 1990, 206-7.

[137]H. Treidler, *KP* 2:1474; F. Hild, *DNP* 5:1145; J. F. Lazenby, *OCD* 771; Hild and Hellenkemper 1990, 277-78.

[138]Hellenkemper and Hild 1986, 101-2; Hild and Hellenkemper 1990, 174, 361-62.

Aigai (Αἰγαί; mod. Yumurtalık, Ayas),[139] about 27 km southwest of Katabolos on the western side of the Gulf of Issos, was the military port of the Syrian fleet in the third century B.C. It was still an important port in the Roman period, servicing the connections with Alexandreia (Iskenderun) and Seleucia (Samandağ) with a dockyard. After the battle of Pharsalos, Caesar promoted Aigai as well as Tarsus. The new era of the city began in 47 B.C.: Caesar was honored as founder of the city (κτίστης, *ktistēs*) along with Alexander the Great. The increase in the minting of coins in A.D. 39-43 evidently is connected with Emperor Caligula's plan to travel to Syria in A.D. 40 to suppress the unrest in Judea (see Philo, *Legat.* 248)—if he traveled by ship along the coast of Asia Minor, he may have visited Aigai—and it probably is also connected with the crisis between Rome and the Parthians. Aigai was famous for its temple of Asclepius, mentioned in the same breath with the Asclepieia of Epidauros and Pergamon; it was destroyed in A.D. 326 on the order of Emperor Constantine. Eusebius reports that for the aristocracy of the region the temple of Asclepius in Aigai was the symbol of pagan resistance against the Christian faith, which had so much success among the "simple masses" (*Vit. Const.* 3.55-58).[140] The bishop Tarkondimantos of Aigai attended the Council of Nicea in A.D. 325.

Epiphaneia (Ἐπιφάνεια; former Oiniandos; mod. Gözene),[141] about 12 km north of Issos, was given its name by Antiochos IV Epiphanes. Pompey settled defeated pirates in Epiphaneia (as in Mallos). The city had a colonnaded street, a theater (87 m in diameter), an imperial temple and an aqueduct. A certain Dionysios son of Alexandros donated a wheat market to the city. The increase in the minting of coins in A.D. 39-40 is to be explained as parallel to the phenomenon in Aigai. One of the two Byzantine churches of the fifth/sixth century was erected possibly on the site of a pagan building.

Hierapolis (Ἱεράπολις; earlier Kastabala [Καστάβαλα]; mod. Bodrum Kalesi),[142] about 25 km north of Epiphaneia (28 km southeast of Anazarbos), situated in a valley 3 km north of the Pyramos River, is mentioned for the first time as the town (Kastabala) where Alexander the Great rested before the Battle of Issos. The city minted its own coins as early as 200 B.C. Antiochos IV Hellenized the city and renamed it Hieropolis. In the first century B.C. Hierapolis was the capital of the territory ruled by Tarkondimotos, a former pirate, whom the Romans granted several areas on the Pyramos River. His successor, Tarkondimotos II, was given the title "king." The city flourished during the Roman Empire. A rock, 35 m high, in the center of the city served as the acropolis. The colonnaded main street, running from east to west, was 300 m long and 11.2 m wide. The most important sanctu-

---

[139]H. Täuber, *DNP* 1:315; Hild and Hellenkemper 1990, 160-64; Jones 1937, 201-4, 206-9; Magie 1950, 274, 1150-51; Ziegler 1985, 18, 50-51, 67-68, and passim; 1993, 68, 88-89, 149; G. Cohen 1995, 355-57. Inscriptions: *I. KilikiaDF* 74-82.

[140]Debord 1982, 35, 289. See Sozomenos, *Hist. eccl.* 2.5.5.

[141]H. Treidler, "Epiphaneia 1," *KP* 2:321; M. Gough, *PECS* 315; M. H. Sayar, "Epiphaneia 1," *DNP* 3:1149; Hild and Hellenkemper 1990, 249-50; Magie 1950, 1:280, 300; 2:1159; Jones 1937, 201, 203, 436; Hellenkemper and Hild 1986, 102-4, 127-28; Sayar 1993, 325-26; Ziegler 1993, 21, 68, 88; G. Cohen 1995, 365-66.

[142]W. Ruge, PW 10.2 (1919): 2335-36; M. Gough, *PECS* 392; H. Täuber, *DNP* 6:322; Hild and Hellenkemper 1990, 293-94; Magie 1950, 1:275-76, 377; 2:1151-52; Jones 1937, 202-5; Fritz Krinzinger and Wolfgang Reiter, "Archäologische Forschungen in Hierapolis-Kastabala," in Dobesch and Rehrenböck 1993, 269-81; Ziegler 1993, 21-22, 38-42; G. Cohen 1995, 366-68; Syme 1995, 153-60, 164. Inscriptions: *I. KilikiaDF* 120-123; see Sayar (1993, 323-24), who points out that there is a total of 120 inscriptions.

ary of Hierapolis was the temple of Artemis Perasia. Strabo reports that the priestesses of Artemis Perasia walked barefoot on burning coals without being hurt (12.2.7). In the second century A.D. the city had a stadium, a theater (excavated in 1987), monumental baths and perhaps a second colonnaded main street starting at the theater. The bishop Moyses attended the Council of Nicea. The ruins of the churches date to the fifth century.

Mopsuestia (Μοψουεστία; former Misis; mod. Yakapınar),[143] about 70 km east of Tarsus on the Pyramos River, on the main road from the West to the Euphrates, is said to have been founded by Mopsus, a seer from Thebes. At the time of Antiochos IV the city briefly was called Seleucia on the Pyramos. Despite its strategic location, Mopsuestia is for the first time mentioned in 95 B.C. (Appian, *Syr.* 69). The city suffered during disputes of the Seleucids over succession to the throne; in 95 B.C. Seleukos VI was burned to death in the gymnasium of the city. An inscription documents the Roman quaestor Lucullus, who in 87 B.C. confirmed for the temple of Isis and Sarapis the right of granting asylum. The era of Mopsuestia began in 68 B.C. By the first century a stone bridge crossed the Pyramos River. Excavations in 1955 and 1961 discovered remains from the Chalcolitic and Hittite periods. The Hellenistic-Roman city was located east of the hill that served as the acropolis. The city had a colonnaded street, a stadium, a theater and an aqueduct. The bishop Makedonios attended the Council of Nicea. A large Christian basilica (fifth century?) was located in the western section of the city. Between A.D. 392 and 428 the important theologian Theodore, who came from Antioch, was bishop of Mopsuestia; he was declared a heretic after the Council of Chalcedon in A.D. 451.

Adana ("Αδανα; earlier Antiocheia ad Sarum; mod. Adana),[144] about 40 km east of Antioch on the road to Mopsuestia, was situated in a fertile plain on the east bank of the Saros River (mod. Seyhan) about 32 km east of Tarsus, at the point where the road to Antioch crossed the river. Seven of the thirteen arches of the bridge in Adana date to the early second century A.D. The Seleucid city had lost some of its importance, which allowed Pompey to settle vanquished pirates in the city in 67 B.C. (Appian, *Mithr.* 96). The continuous settlement has obliterated nearly all traces of the Roman period. Excavations conducted by the Archaeological Museum of Adana after 1930 in the area of Tepebağ Höyüğü (in the city center, hardly recognizable today) documented the occupation in the Hellenistic and the Roman periods; since then no further discoveries have been made. The first known bishop was bishop Paulinos, who attended the Council of Nicea.

Augusta (Αὐγούστα; mod. Gübe),[145] about 10 km north of Adana on the east bank of the Saros River, was founded during the principate of Tiberius; the era of the city began in A.D. 20. The major increase in the minting of coins has not been explained satisfactorily as of yet. The remains of the theater, a basilica, baths and two colonnaded streets were

---

[143]W. Ruge, PW 16.1 (1933): 243-50; K. Ziegler, *KP* 3:1421; M. Gough, *PECS* 593-94; H. Täuber, *DNP* 8:391; Hild and Hellenkemper 1990, 351-59; Magie 1950, 1:273; 2:1148; Ziegler 1993, 21, 28, 68, 87-98; S. Mitchell 1995a, 1:224, 232; Syme 1995, 158. Inscriptions: *I. KilikiaDF* 83-97; Sayar 1993, 323-24, 326-27 (82 inscriptions in total).

[144]W. Sontheimer, *KP* 1:62; M. Gough, *PECS* 8; M. H. Sayar, *DNP* 1:103-4; Hild and Hellenkemper 1990, 154-58, 398; Magie 1950, 1:273, 280, 300; 2:1148; Ziegler 1993, 21-22. Inscriptions: *I. KilikiaDF* 42-61.

[145]M. Gough, "Augusta Ciliciae," *AnSt* 6 (1956): 165-77; idem, *PECS* 113; M. H. Sayar, "Augusta 8," *DNP* 2:291; Jones 1937, 206; Hellenkemper and Hild 1986, 102; Ziegler 1993, 21-22, 88-89, 149.

available for investigation by archaeologists before the site was inundated in 1955 after the completion of the Seyhan Dam. Coins with agonistic motifs date to the third century. The city was represented at the Council of Chalcedon in A.D. 451.

Zephyrion (Ζεφύριον; mod. Mersin),[146] a port city about 30 km southwest of Tarsus, was a polis already in the Greek and Persian periods (Pseudo-Skylax, *Periplus* 77). The ancient site was located between Vilayet Konaği, Halkevi and the Greek Orthodox church. Zephyrion appears to have been founded at the site of ancient Anchiale (perhaps mod. Yümüktepe, on the east bank of the Müftü Dere, 1.5 km northwest of the new city center of modern Mersin). During the principate of Diocletian a Christian named Dulas of Zephyrion died as a martyr.[147]

Palaiai (Παλαλίαι; mod. Tahta Limanı, Güverin Adaı in the northern harbor),[148] 22 km southwest of Seleucia ad Kalykadnum (10 km southwest of Taşucu), was a Cilician port city. The ruins of the small late Roman and early Byzantine city are located beside the small river. A significant ancient site is located on the rocky outcrop above the beach from which the Roman road from Seleucia descended to sea level. Perhaps both sites were called Palaiai. The apocryphal *Acts of Barnabas* claims to know that Barnabas from Jerusalem, Paul's early companion, preached the gospel in Palaiai (*Acts Barn.* 11).

Aphrodisias (Ἀφροδισίας; mod. Cape Ovacık Burnu),[149] about 45 km southwest of Seleucia, was situated on a peninsula on the southern coast of Rugged Cilicia; it had west and east harbors. The fortress dates to the fifth and fourth centuries B.C. The ancient site is located on Cape Zephyrion above the east harbor. Aphrodisias lost its status as polis during the Roman period, indicated by the fact that the city did not mint coins. The town seems to have belonged to the territory of Seleucia.

Anemurion (Ἀνεμούριον; mod. Eski Anamur),[150] about 90 km southwest of Aphrodisias on the northeastern side of Cape Anamur at the southernmost tip of Asia Minor, is mentioned for the first time in a list of ports from the forth century B.C. (*GGM* I 76). Anemurion was an important city in the first century B.C. In A.D. 52 Anemurion was besieged by the Isaurian Cietae, and was rescued by Antiochos IV of Commagene, who controlled the Cilician coast during this period. The Roman city was located on a stretch of slope 250 m wide and 1.7 km long. Remains include walls 8 m high with interior towers perhaps dating to the first century A.D., a theater (60 m in diameter), three large baths, an odeion or bouleuterion (second century), houses with mosaics, an aqueduct and (roof) cisterns. The imperial temple of Anemurion has not yet been located. On the west slope a large, well-preserved necropolis from the imperial period has 350 tombs. A funerary inscription from Korykos which probably dates before A.D. 212 mentions a Jewish family from Anemurion

---

[146]Christo M. Danoff, "Zephyrion," PW 10.A (1972): 227; M. Gough, *PECS* 999-1000; Hild and Hellenkemper 1990, 185-86, 464-65; Magie 1950, 2:1156.

[147]See H. Delehaye, ed., *Synaxarium,* 750.

[148]Hild and Hellenkemper 1990, 372.

[149]H. Treidler, "Aphrodisias 2," *KP* 1:1541; F. Hild, "Aphrodisias 2," *DNP* 1:837; Magie 1950, 2:1142, 1156; Hild and Hellenkemper 1990, 195-96.

[150]H. Treidler, *KP* 1:1539; J. Russell, *PECS* 58; F. Hild, *DNP* 1:698-99; Hild and Hellenkemper 1990, 187-91; Magie 1950, 2:1142; Rosenbaum, Huber and Onurkan 1967, viii-ix, 1-17, 87-90, 93-94; Hellenkemper and Hild 1986, 27-30; Syme 1995, 230 .

(*IJudO* II 233). According to the *Acts Barn.* 12, the apostle Barnabas was the first missionary to preach in Anemurion.

It appears that none of the roads in Cilicia were paved before A.D. 75. The earliest milestone, discovered near Olba at the foot of the Taurus Mountains, dates to A.D. 75.[151]

Paul possibly preached the gospel not only in cities but also in smaller towns, villages and hamlets, assuming that he did not always "need" a synagogue as an initial point of contact.[152] Jesus himself had preached in small settlements, villages and hamlets, as did the Twelve in the course of their missionary activity in Judea in the first months and years after Pentecost. The high population density of Cilicia (see above) would have provided many possibilities to reach people with the gospel of Jesus Christ. During a journey from the port city of Pompeiopolis to Seleucia 70 km to the south, Paul would have passed through the smaller port cities of Kalanthia, Kanythela and Lamos. From these towns, numerous villages could be reached. For example, from Kalanthia, the settlements Şaha, Bozburun and Koramşalı could easily be visited.

Kalanthia (Καλανθία; mod. Erdemli),[153] about 65 km southwest of Tarsus, was a village (κώμη, *kōmē*) on the Cilician coast. The ancient site was located in the northwestern section of the modern town. The large early Byzantine basilica is now used partly as a mosque.

Şaha,[154] about 5 km northwest of Kalanthia, was a larger Hellenistic-Roman village (κώμη) situated on a foothill of the Taurus Mountains, and belonged to Sebaste. To the west and to the east of the village a necropolis has been discovered with Roman sarcophagi and inscriptions.

Bozburun,[155] about 10 km northwest of Kalanthia, was located on an old route across the Taurus Mountains via Tetrapyrgia (Kemeryayla) to Lycaonia. Roman remains have been discovered.

Koramşalı, about 20 km northwest of Kalanthia, was another ancient settlement, located on the road leading to the north.

Lamos (Λάμος; mod. Limonlu),[156] about 10 km southwest of Kanytela, was a village (κώμη [Strabo 14.5.6]) on the west bank of the Lamos River (mod. Limonly Çayı) near the Mediterranean. Some remains from the Roman period have been discovered.

---

[151]French 1981-1988, 2:430, no. 461 (Yeğenli 4); cf. French 1994b, 53, 56.

[152]Karl Pieper (1929, 149-51), and many other scholars after him, maintained that Paul engaged in "urban mission, not in village or rural mission." This view may be historically correct, but it remains hypothetical because neither Paul nor Luke provides a complete picture of Paul's missionary methods.

[153]Hild and Hellenkemper 1990, 281.

[154]Hild and Hellenkemper 1990, 394.

[155]Hild and Hellenkemper 1990, 217, 311.

[156]Treidler, "Lamos 4," *KP* 3:467; Bean, *PECS* 480; Hild and Hellenkemper 1990, 330-31.

Kanytela (mod. Kanlıdivane)[157] was a larger Hellenistic-Roman settlement located in a quarry 60 m deep. The ancient village (κώμη) belonged to Sebaste. On the southwestern edge above the quarry stood a Hellenistic tower (*Dynastenwohnturm*) with three stories, with sixty to eighty houses in the vicinity. The village was linked with the road from Seleucia to Tarsus via a paved road. The settlement flourished in the Roman period, as is indicated by five early Byzantine basilicas.

Another example for the accessibility of smaller settlements are the Hellenistic and Roman villages, villas and hamlets in the hinterland of Korykos.

A Roman road ran from Korykos to the foothills of the Taurus Mountains in a northerly direction to Olba. The pavement, stone slabs measuring 2.20 by 2.60 m, is still intact in places.[158] "On the steeper inclines, which the modern road navigates with serpentines, the Roman road is constructed with wide steps; it was built not for carriages but for pedestrians and riding animals. We noted milestones at mile 1, mile 2 and mile 4" (*MAMA* III 198, 199a; *CIL* III S 12123). After about 3 km a paved road branched off to a village east of the Roman road; the foundation walls of numerous houses can still be seen. Just under 1 km further north were two Hellenistic towers[159] that served in the Roman period in part as the center of a large farm that had an olive press. After 500 m there was a small village with traces that date back to the Hellenistic period; 200 m further on was a farm building (polygonal layout). After 500 m one reached a route branching off toward the west to a rocky hill above the valley of the river Verev Deresi, with a settlement from the Roman period that was surrounded by a fortified wall. Continuing on the road with the farm building for 1.4 km, one encountered two farms on the right and left sides of the road; about 900 m further on the ruins of an ancient house with cistern are visible to the west. After 2.6 km two Roman round altars with inscriptions have been found. About 2 km further on there was another Roman farm. The houses of the Turkish settlement Hüseyinler, 1.2 km further on, still utilize Roman cisterns. After 1.6 km there is a Turkish farm with a Roman tomb, and after another 1.8 km one reaches a group of houses that date to the Roman period.

Some scholars point out that Paul seems to have worked alone as a missionary in Arabia, Syria and Cilicia for the period A.D. 32-42, even though Jesus and the early church sent out apostles and missionaries in pairs.[160] Martin Hengel observes of Paul's purported solitude, "It accorded with the character of his call, in which he was addressed and sent by the Kyrios as a sole individual, like the Old Testament prophets, and probably also with his inner temperament. He loved independence, yet if he had to, he could fit into a community, though he rapidly took a leading role in it because of his para-

---

[157]F. Hild, "Kanytelis," *DNP* 6:255; Hild and Hellenkemper 1990, 285-86.

[158]See Hellenkemper and Hild 1986, 66-68 (with journal entries of the authors).

[159]See Serra Durugönül, *Türme und Siedlungen im Rauhen Kilikien: Eine Untersuchung zu den archäologischen Hinterlassenschaften im Olbischen Territorium* (Bonn: Habelt, 1998), 78.

[160]Hengel and Schwemer 1998, 177 (ET, 109); the quotation that follows above, ibid., 177-78 (ET, 109); on Philip see ibid., 177 n. 719 (ET, 386 n. 563).

mount gifts." We should remember, however, that others worked as "solitary missionaries" as well: Philip preached alone in Samaria and in the cities on the coastal plain, and it is not clear whether Peter traveled with a companion after his departure from Jerusalem. And we should note that Paul always traveled with a team of coworkers after A.D. 45. Since neither Paul nor Luke reports the tactical details of Paul's missionary activity between A.D. 32 and 44, the suggestion that he worked initially as a "solitary missionary" remains hypothetical.

26.3 Missionary Work in Antioch

The church in Antioch had been founded by Greek-speaking Jewish Christians from Jerusalem who had left the Jewish capital because of the persecution in A.D. 31/32 (see §22.5). These Jewish Christians, who originally came from Cyprus and from Cyrene, extended their preaching beyond Jewish audiences to Gentiles as well (Acts 11:20). The church had grown rapidly in size, a development that continued when Barnabas came from Jerusalem to consolidate and lead work in Antioch (Acts 11:21-24). The fact that "a great many people" (ὄχλος ἱκανός, *ochlos hikanos* [Acts 11:24b]) were converted seems to have been the reason why Barnabas, evidently in A.D. 42, went to Tarsus to recruit Paul for the work in Antioch. It is fair to assume that the "mass conversions"[161] in Antioch included Gentiles (cf. Acts 11:20-21), and that Barnabas sought Paul's collaboration in Antioch for this very reason, appreciating Paul's experience in missionary work among Gentiles.

Paul's motivation to leave his missionary work in Cilicia and move to Antioch remains unclear. Martin Hengel and Anna Maria Schwemer suggest, "Perhaps the apostle's activity in Cilicia, as later in Corinth and Ephesus or then in the eastern Mediterranean generally, had come to a certain conclusion. Presumably the communities which he had founded had to some degree become independent. On the other hand, Barnabas, who must have regarded Paul as a missionary authority 'with equal rights,' must have convinced him, with theological agreements that were fundamental to him, that he was urgently needed in Antioch, at least at that very moment," perhaps because the situation in the capital of the province of Syria "became more critical, so that a theologian with Paul's competence in the scriptures, capacity to argue strongly, resolution and capacity for organization was urgently needed."[162] It is unclear whether the ecstatic experience that Paul refers to in 2 Cor 12:2, dating to around A.D. 42, played a role in Paul's move from Tarsus to Antioch.[163]

---

[161]Jervell, *Apg*, 324.
[162]Hengel and Schwemer 1998, 275, 332 (ET, 179-80, 218).
[163]Thus Zahn 1924, 2:644 (2nd ed. [1900], 2:635; ET, 3:462); Riesner 1994, 242, 285 (ET, 272, 320).

Barnabas and Paul worked together in Antioch for one year (Acts 11:26). The formulation "for an entire year" (ἐνιαυτὸν ὅλον, *eniauton holon*), in the larger context of the book of Acts, represents a relatively long time. Usually Paul spends less time in a city, with the exceptions of Corinth (eighteen months) and Ephesus (over two years). The expansion of the church in Antioch continued as Paul became active in the city: Barnabas, Paul and the other missionaries and teachers "taught a great many people" (διδάξαι ὄχλον ἱκανόν, *didaxai ochlon ikanon* [Acts 11:26c]). The term "teach" may refer to missionary teaching in the synagogues of Antioch, but it may also refer to the instruction of new converts and of the believers in the church—that is, the "great many people" of Acts 11:24 who had been converted through the missionary work of the Jewish Christians from Jerusalem. The term ὄχλος (*ochlos,* "a large number of people, crowd") refers in Acts 6:7; 11:24; 19:26 to people who have been converted, while in Acts 13:45 it designates the curious listeners in the synagogue of Pisidian Antioch; thus it is not a term of "missionary language" that always refers to mass conversions.[164] The comment in Acts 11:27d regarding the designation "Christians" used for the followers of Jesus in Antioch may indicate that the reference to "teaching" in Acts 11:27c describes the instruction of the believers in Antioch who were so active, or prominent, that they attracted the attention of outsiders, including the Roman authorities (see §22.5). It is plausible, however, to link the teaching activity of Paul in Acts 11:26c *also* with missionary work: (1) Paul's primary self-understanding since his conversion was that of a missionary. Since later phases of missionary work in a given city would necessarily involve teaching the new converts and the believers in the Christian community, taking time and energy that might otherwise be spent preaching to and conversing with unbelievers, Paul always would have availed himself of every opportunity to reach non-Christians with the gospel. (2) Assuming that Gentiles who attended the Jewish synagogues as proselytes and God-fearers were reached with the gospel, perhaps right from the beginning, and assuming that Barnabas and Paul were able to continue to teach in the synagogues of Antioch, we may conclude that they would have automatically reached non-Jewish unbelievers. (3) When the followers of Jesus were no longer able to meet in the synagogues, and thus had to assemble in a lecture hall or in private houses—Luke omits "organizational" details of the church in Antioch—Paul would have encountered unbelievers there as well; at least the churches that Paul established were always open for Jews and Gentiles who had not yet come to faith in Jesus Christ (see 1 Cor 14:22, 24).

Some scholars suggest that the Gentile mission of the early church that renounced circumcision had its origins in the missionary work in Antioch. Luke's

---

[164]Contra Jervell, *Apg,* 324; in Acts 14:21, another passage that he refers to, *ochlos* is not mentioned.

account in the book of Acts may indeed suggest that this was the case, particularly if we accept the traditional view that Luke was the companion of Paul,
the missionary to the Gentiles. The transition from a purely Jewish mission to
the Gentile mission was not an "event" that can be dated, but rather a process.[165] The Greek-speaking Jewish Christians from Jerusalem initially
preached to fellow-Jews (Acts 6:9). Philip's mission to the Samaritans (Acts
8:4-25), despite their status as apostates, can be regarded as outreach to members of Israel. Subsequently Philip preached the gospel in the coastal plain, in
Gaza, Ashdod and Caesarea (Acts 8:26, 40), cities that were predominantly
Gentile: this phase of the early Christian mission may already have initiated
the transition to the Gentile mission, possibly even before the conversion of
Cornelius in Caesarea. Martin Hengel points out, "Nor does Luke say anywhere in so many words that in Damascus or the Palestinian coastal region *no*
Gentiles at all (i.e., God-fearers) became Christians before Acts 10."[166] It seems
that Philip and other Greek-speaking Jewish Christians transitioned step by
step to a Gentile mission free of the law in this region, "whereby the expression 'free of the law' initially meant foregoing the demands of circumcision
and the observance of ritual law."[167] In terms of chronology, this process can
be dated only generally to the time between Stephen's death in A.D. 31/32 and
the persecution of the Jerusalem church under Herod Agrippa I in A.D. 41.
Rainer Riesner comments, "To that extent, Luke is probably oversimplifying
things when he explicitly mentions only Antioch as the locus of this new stage
(Acts 11:20), though he is no doubt correct in referring to the virtually inesti-
mable significance of this particular metropolis for primitive Christianity and
for the development of its mission. It was there that the first larger or largely
Gentile-Christian church emerged."[168]

Was the church in Antioch "the mother-church of Christianity among non-
Jews?"[169] I think not: the first Gentile about whose conversion we have information came to faith in Jesus Christ as a result of Peter's preaching, resulting
in a lively discussion in the church in Jerusalem about the modalities of this
first "Gentile mission" (Acts 11:1-18). Luke reports the origins of the church
in Antioch immediately after Peter's mission to Caesarea and the subsequent
discussion in Jerusalem, and he describes Barnabas as the personal link between Jerusalem and Antioch. It therefore is plausible to assume that the modalities of the Gentile mission in Antioch corresponded to the missionary

---

[165]See Hengel 1979, 63-70; B. Meyer 1986, 67-83; Schenke 1990, 186-97; Hengel and Schwemer
1998, 239-41 (ET, 155-57); for the comments that follow above see Riesner 1994, 96-97 (ET,
109-110).
[166]Hengel and Schwemer 1998, 241 (ET, 154).
[167]Hengel 1979, 70; also quoted in Riesner 1994, 97 (ET, 109).
[168]Riesner 1994, 97 (ET, 110).
[169]Thus Andreas Feldtkeller, "Syrien II. Zeit des Neuen Testaments," *TRE* 32 (2001): 588.

praxis of Peter, and perhaps of other Jerusalem missionaries, which had been acknowledged by the apostles and the church in Jerusalem. Antioch seems to have been the first city in which Gentiles were converted to faith in Jesus Christ in larger numbers. But the "mother-church" of the Gentile mission was Jerusalem.

27

MISSIONARY WORK IN ASIA MINOR, GREECE AND SPAIN

After Paul worked as a missionary during A.D. 32/33 in Arabia, A.D. 34-42 in Cilicia and in Syria, and A.D. 42-44 in Antioch on the Orontes, he traveled in the spring of A.D. 45, with Barnabas and John Mark, to Cyprus and from there to Pamphylia, Pisidia and Phrygia in the southern regions of the province of Galatia. They were able to establish several churches in this area between A.D. 45 and 47. After returning to Antioch in A.D. 48 and attending the apostolic council in Jerusalem that same year, Paul, with Silas and Luke, traveled in A.D. 49 through Syria, Cilicia and southern Galatia with the goal of starting missionary work in the province of Asia, presumably in Ephesus. Due to external circumstances, neither this project nor a mission to Bithynia could be realized. Eventually the missionaries reached Macedonia, where they preached and established churches in several cities before traveling via Athens to Corinth in Achaia, where Paul was active in the years A.D. 50-51. After a short visit in Jerusalem and in Antioch Paul, together with several coworkers, traveled to Ephesus, where he preached the gospel and established a church in A.D. 52-55. During this time churches in other cities were established as well in the neighboring regions. After a journey through Macedonia that took Paul to Illyria, he visited Corinth in the winter of A.D. 56/57 before returning in the spring of A.D. 57 to Jerusalem, where he was arrested. After a long imprisonment in Caesarea (A.D. 57-59) and in Rome (A.D. 60-62) Paul evidently was released, allowing him to travel to Spain, a missionary project that he had planned since A.D. 56. In A.D. 64/65 Paul appears to have engaged in missionary work with Titus on the island of Crete before he was arrested again. According to reliable early traditions, Paul died as a martyr in Rome under Nero.

The primary sources for the following description of the missionary work of Paul are Paul's letters and Luke's account in the book of Acts. We possess more information about the twelve years of Paul's missionary work on Cyprus, in Galatia, Macedonia, Achaia and in the province of Asia in the years A.D. 45-56 than about any other period in the history of the early church in the first century. And we know more about Paul than about any other missionary of the first century. The purpose of this chapter is to provide an extensive description of the stations of Paul's missionary work.

27.1 Missionary Work on Cyprus and in the Province of Galatia

Paul's missionary work on Cyprus and in southern Galatia (Acts 13:4—14:28) took place in A.D. 45-47. The route that Paul and his coworkers traveled can be summarized as follows.

Phase I: Missionary Work on Cyprus (Acts 13:4-12)

Antioch	⇒ Seleucia	13:4	25 km
Seleucia	⇒ Salamis (Cyprus)	13:5 (by ship)	220 km
Salamis	⇒ Kition		47 km
	⇒ Amathos		58 km
	⇒ Neapolis		10 km
	⇒ Kourion		16 km
	⇒ Paphos	13:6	50 km

Phase II: Missionary Work in Southern Galatia (Acts 13:13—14:21a)

Paphos	⇒ Attaleia (Pamphylia)	(by ship)	280 km
Attaleia	⇒ Perge	13:13	15 km
Perge	⇒ Ariassos ?		55 km
	⇒ Komama ?		35 km
	⇒ Lysinia ? (Pisidia)		60 km
	⇒ Ilyas		12 km
	⇒ Eudoxiopolis ?		23 km
	⇒ Apollonia ?		20 km
	⇒ Tymandos ?		15 km
	⇒ Antiocheia	13:14	60 km
Antiocheia	⇒ Neapolis		50 km
	⇒ Pappa		42 km
	⇒ Iconium	13:51	56 km
Iconium	⇒ Lystra (Lycaonia)	14:6	35 km
Lystra	⇒ Dalisandos		50 km
	⇒ Kodylessos		20 km
	⇒ Posala		14 km
	⇒ Ilistra		16 km
	⇒ Laranda		25 km
	⇒ Derbe (Lycaonia)	14:6, 20	25 km

Phase III: Consolidation of the Churches in Southern Galatia (Acts 14:21b-23)

Derbe	⇒ Lystra	14:21	150 km
Lystra	⇒ Iconium	14:21	35 km
Iconium	⇒ Antiocheia	14:21	148 km

Phase IV: Missionary Work in Perge and Return to Antioch (Acts 14:24-28)

Antiocheia	⇒ Perge	14:25	280 km
Perge	⇒ Attaleia	14:25	15 km
Attaleia	⇒ Antioch	14:26 (by ship)	480 km

Notes on the travel route. Barnabas, Paul and John Mark sailed from Seleucia, the harbor of Antioch,[1] about 100 km to Cyprus, disembarking in Samalis on the eastern tip of the island. Assuming that the missionaries traveled the road along the southern coast, they passed through Kition, Amathos and Kourion before reaching Paphos.[2] The distance from Salamis to Paphos is 175 km. From Paphos they sailed to Attaleia (mod. Antalya), the port of western Pamphylia. Attaleia is not mentioned at this point in the narrative (Acts 13:13), but it is mentioned in the account of the journey back to Syria. From Attaleia the missionaries traveled on a paved road to Perge (see fig. 26),[3] the capital of Pamphylia.[4]

The journey from Perge to Pisidian Antiocheia (160 km) is sometimes described as "difficult and dangerous,"[5] an evaluation that applies only if Paul took the most direct route. Unless we assume that Paul and Barnabas climbed the steep and high slopes of the Taurus Mountains between Lake Karalis (mod. Beyşehir Gölü) and Lake Eğridir[6]—the highest peak reaches 2,980 m—they would have chosen between two routes. (1) A westerly route that ran about 6 km east of Dağ (35 km north of Attaleia) through the Döşeme Boğazı pass[7] via the Roman colony was longer but easier. As new discoveries has shown, this road was part of the paved Via Sebaste that had been built fifty years earlier under Augustus. It is as good as certain that the Via Sebaste reached the Pamphylian plain in Perge and did not continue to Attaleia. This road existed already in the Persian and Hellenistic periods (Polybius 5.72.4). Possibly Alexander the Great took this route in 334 B.C. when he marched from Pamphylia to Sagalassos (mod. Ağlasun) in Pisidia (Plutarch, *Alex.* 18).[8] On the pass of Döşeme Boğazı stands a milestone with the following inscription: "Emperor Caesar Augustus, Son of God, Pontifex Maximus, consul for the eleventh time, designatus for the twelfth time, Imperator for the fifteenth time, having the tribunicia potestas for the eighteenth time, built the Via Sebaste [viam Sebasten . . . fecit]. His legatus pro praetore Cornutus Aquila supervised the construction. 139 [Roman miles]."[9] (2) An easterly route ran through the Kestros Valley (mod. Aksu) and along the southern shore of Lake Eğridir. This route was more difficult because it had to navigate deep valleys and the high slopes of the western Taurus Mountains.[10] The most straightforward reconstruction of the

---

[1]It was possible in antiquity to sail from Seleucia on the Orontes River all the way to Antioch, which was reached in one day; see Pausanias 8.29.3; Strabo 16.2.7. When the missionaries left, they boarded the ship in Seleucia (Acts 13:4); on their return they sailed all the way to Antioch (Acts 14:26).

[2]See Gill 1995b, 226-27, with a list of the milestones.

[3]The map in fig. 28 (southern Galatia, with the regions of Pamphylia and Pisidia) was produced on the basis of the map in French 1994a, x, and supplemented with cities mentioned by Brandt 1992 (see the map in the appendix).

[4]For the observations that follow above see French 1994b, 51-53, 55; Hansen 1994, 384.

[5]Schneider, *Apg*, 2:130 n. 22.

[6]By the Byzantine period a road ran directly from Attaleia to Prostanna and Akroterion on Lake Eğridir. The modern road near Bademli traverses a pass 1,390 m high.

[7]See the inscriptions published by S. Mitchell in *I. Pisidia* 166-172. It is possible that this was the site of Maximianoupolis, which sent a delegate to the Council of Nicea in A.D. 325 (thus the editors of the TIB volume on Lycia and Pamphylia; see *I. Pisidia* 168).

[8]French 1980, 707-8; Hansen 1994, 384. Undecided is Riesner 1994, 244-45 (ET, 274-75). Riesner refers to the notable fact that they "did not continue on into nearby Apamea. At this crossroad of the Via Sebaste the road forked toward Cotyaeum on the one hand, and Dorylaion on the other, and the missionaries would have encountered here a strong Jewish community (Cicero, *Flac.* 28-68)."

[9]*I. Pisidia* 166; cf. French 1981-1988, vol. 2, nos. 267, 292, 293.

travel route of Paul assumes that he took the road that ran further to the west: he probably traveled from Perge on the Via Sebaste, the easiest route into the interior of Asia Minor, passing by Termessos (see §18.3), traveling via Ariassos, Komama, Palaiopolis, Kormasa, passing by the imperial domain Tymbrianassus, and continuing via Lysinia, Ilyas, Baris, Eudoxiopolis, Apollonia and Tymandos to the colony Antiocheia. From Antiocheia Paul traveled via Neapolis at the northeastern edge of Lake Koralis and via Pappa to Iconium and to Lystra. The course of the Via Sebaste has not been entirely clarified in the triangle marked by Pappa (Tiberiopolis), Iconium and Lystra. Many scholars assume that the Via Sebaste passed through all three cities. Gertrud Laminger-Pascher believes that the remains of the road between Lystra and Pappa that Klaus Belke discovered between 1974 and 1978 are decisive, agreeing with the assumption that the Via Sebaste, as a road with strategic significance, connects cities using the shortest route.[11] This means that the Via Sebaste ran via Pappa, Kızılören Ovası, Camurluigret, Bulumya and Kilistra to Lystra. The road to Iconium branched off near Kızılvıran. Between Iconium and Lystra the Via Sebaste ran via Gödene, Bayat, Sarıkız and Hayırabat. There were Jewish communities both in Antiocheia and in Iconium (Acts 13:14; 14:1); for Lystra Luke does not mention a synagogue, but the fact that Jews from Antiocheia and Iconium visited Lystra indicates that there was a Jewish community there as well. The missionaries would have reached Derbe on an unpaved road that passed probably through Isauria, Dalisandos and Posala. For the return journey they traveled on the same road.

The distances listed in the table, all of which are approximate because the exact course of the Via Sebaste and of other ancient roads is not always known, add up to a total of 1,440 km (895 mi.) that Paul and his coworkers walked on foot. If we assume that travelers walked 15 Roman miles[12] (i.e., about 25 km or 15 mi.) per day, this corresponds to sixty days of walking. The stages of the journey that the missionaries traveled by ship add up to 980 km, for which seven days might be needed under favorable circumstances, or eighteen days under poorer conditions. This means that Paul and Barnabas traveled for seventy days during the mission to Cyprus and to southern Galatia.

In regard to the historicity of the mission to southern Galatia, Ernst Haenchen and Hans Conzelmann speak of a "model journey," interpreting Acts 13—14 as a redactional construct composed by the author of the book of Acts.[13] Jürgen Wehnert maintains that the missionary journeys that Luke "composed" should be regarded as redactional stylization whose historical value lies "only in the traditions that have been used"; he thinks that it is quite possible that the missions of Philip, Peter and Paul were "in reality parallel events," that "the missions of the individual actors that Luke portrays as one single journey fuse, from a historical point of view, the results of several missionary efforts."[14] There is no evidence to support this general skepticism, as has been demonstrated in studies by Colin Hemer, for example. Cilliers Breytenbach argues with regard to Paul's mission to Cyprus and Galatia, particularly on account of the excellent local information of the author of Acts, that "according to Conzelmann the author could have seen many things on a map and constructed a fictive journey. Considering the nature and the dissemination of

---

[10]Breytenbach (1996, 79-80) assumes that the missionaries took this more direct and more difficult road.

[11]Laminger-Pascher 1992, 122.

[12]One Roman mile corresponds to 1,478.5 m.

[13]Haenchen, *Apg*, 97-98 (ET, 86-87); Conzelmann, *Apg*, 80-82, 86-89 (ET, 98-100, 108-11); cf. Borse 1986; Dockx 1989.

[14]Wehnert 1997, 273-74.

ancient maps, this is highly unlikely. As far as I know, there is hardly any map even today that shows that Antiocheia is located near the border of Pisidia, that Iconium is located in the area in which Phrygian was spoken, and that Lystra and Derbe were located in Lycaonia. But the text of Acts implies such knowledge."[15]

The date of Paul's mission to southern Galatia is disputed. Some scholars suggest a date *after* the apostolic council in A.D. 48, primarily arguing that Gal 1:21—2:1 does not mention the outreach to Pamphylia, Pisidia and Lycaonia.[16] A date *before* the apostolic council is more plausible,[17] linked as it is with the question of whether the Galatians to whom Paul's letter is addressed were ethnic Galatians in northern Galatia or the churches in southern Galatia, and with the question of whether Gal 2:1-10 should be identified with Acts 15:1-30 or with Acts 11:27-30. The mission to Cyprus and to southern Galatia is not the result of the apostolic council, but rather part of its precondition.[18] From an exegetical and chronological point of view it is important to note that the statement in Gal 1:21 ("then I went into the regions of Syria and Cilicia") refers not to the missionary journey reported in Acts 13—14 but to the interval between Acts 9:31 and Acts 11:30—that is, the time between Paul's activity in Tarsus and his ministry in Antioch. Thus, if Gal 2:1-10 is identified with the Jerusalem visit of Acts 11:27-30 (famine-relief visit), for which there are good reasons,[19] the problem disappears: the mission to southern Galatia is not to be found in Gal 1:21—2:1, but rather it took place between Gal 2:10 and Gal 2:11; the temporal conjunction ὅτε *(hote,* "when") in Gal 2:11 is undetermined and leaves open the question of what happened between Gal 2:20 and Gal 2:11. And we should note that in Gal 1:21—2:1 Paul's intention is not to provide a complete enumeration of his missionary journeys but to highlight his independence from the Jerusalem apostles.

It has been difficult to consult good maps of Turkey—the result of political and military obstinacy.[20] Maps on the scale of 1:5,000, 1:10,000 and 1:25,000 are under lock and key (military maps of the Soviet Union have been offered on the internet for large sums). A still useful map is the 1:200,000 series that was produced in the nineteenth century and revised in the 1940s. Also useful is the Kiepert series (2nd ed., 1914), as well as newer 1:500,000 maps (Ryborsch). The classical map of W. M. Calder and G. E. Bean is no longer fully reliable. Excellent and up to date is the *Barrington Atlas of the Greek and Roman World* (2000) with maps in the scale of 1:500,000.

Missionary Work on Cyprus

Luke reports in Acts 13:4-12 how Barnabas and Paul, along with John Mark as "assistant" (ὑπηρέτης, *hyperetēs*), evangelized on Cyprus, and that they had an encounter with the governor Sergius Paullus.

---

[15]Breytenbach 1996, 86-88; quotation, 87. See also Pesch, *Apg,* 2:20-21, 29, 44, 50, 54-56; Roloff, *Apg,* 194-95; Zmijewski, *Apg,* 552-53; Fitzmyer, *Acts,* 136-37, 495; similarly Barrett, *Acts,* 1:600, 609, 664; Lüdemann 1987, 164; Riesner 1994, 242-47 (ET, 272-79); Murphy-O'Connor 1996, 95-96; Reinbold 2000, 88-103.

[16]See recently Zmijewski (*Apg,* 553), who refers to Bornkamm, Borse, Burchard, Haenchen, Kasting, Pesch, Schenke and Fischer, Suhl.

[17]See Roloff, *Apg,* 195; Weiser, *Apg,* 2:310, with reference to Kümmel, Wikenhauser and Schmid, Mussner, Hengel.

[18]Roloff, *Apg,* 195. For the comment that follows above see Bruce, *Gal,* 15-16.

[19]See Longenecker, *Gal,* lxxvii-lxxxiii; see also the discussion in §25.1 in the present work.

[20]D. H. French, "Isinda and Lagbe," in French 1994a, 53-92, esp. 84.

Cyprus (Κύπρος [see fig. 28])[21] was annexed by the Romans in 58 B.C. In the following years the island was a bartering object between Rome and the Ptolemies in Egypt, who had controlled Cyprus since 312 B.C. After the defeat of Mark Antony and Cleopatra in 30 B.C. Cyprus became a Roman province. Augustus reorganized Egypt as an imperial province in 22 B.C. Cyprus, the third largest island of the Mediterranean, is 227 km long and 95 km wide. The narrow headland of eastern Cyprus is only 96 km from the Syrian coast, and only 65 km from Cape Anemurion, the southern tip of Asia Minor. The dry and hot summers were dreaded in antiquity: "Do be careful, my dear Flaccus, of the excessive heat for which Cyprus is famous" (Martial 9.90.9). The amount of precipitation was among the lowest in the Mediterranean region. The forests made Cyprus an important exporter of wood for shipbuilding (Strabo 14.6.5). The copper that was mined on the slopes of Mount Troodos was named after the island (Gk., *Kypros*). Cyprus was divided into the four districts of Paphos, Salamis, Amathos and Lapethos. The most important cities[22] in Cyprus are, on the north coast (from east to west): Karpasia, Keryneia, Lapethus, Soloi and Marion, on the south coast (from west to east) Paphos, Kourion, Amathos, Kition and Salamis; cities in the interior include Tamassos, Idalion and Golgi. For the principate of Claudius, only the governorship of T. Cominius Proculus in A.D. 43/44 is documented, although T. Clodius Eprius Marcellus also may have been proconsul under Claudius (same date of rule to A.D. 58/59).[23]

Jewish colonies existed on Cyprus since the second century B.C. (1 Macc 15:23). In 30 B.C. Augustus granted half of the income from the Cypriot copper mines to Herod I and left the other half for Herod to administer (Josephus, *A.J.* 16.127-129). The Jewish population had increased to such a degree by the first century A.D. that Philo could describe Cyprus as an island that was "full of Jewish colonies" (Philo, *Legat.* 282).[24] Discoveries from the second century A.D. indicate that Jews lived not only in the cities but also in smaller settlements. Salamis evidently had several synagogues (Acts 13:5); epigraphical evidence indicates a synagogue in Golgoi, and there may have been synagogues in Lapethos and Karpasia as well. Some Jews had become quite wealthy (see Josephus, *A.J.* 18.131).[25] According to *y. Yoma* 4:5 (41d), the Jews of Cyprus regularly donated wine for the temple in Jerusalem that was used for the incense offering on the Day of Atonement.

Luke mentions Cyprus for the first time in Acts 4:36 in connection with his introduction of Joseph-Barnabas, a member of the Jerusalem church, who sold

---

[21]Eugen Oberhummer, PW 12.1 (1924): 59-117; Heinrich Chantraine, *KP* 3:404-8; E. Meyer et al., *DNP* 5:990-95; Mitford 1980; Vassos Karageorghis, *Ancient Cyprus: 7,000 Years of Art and Archaeology* (Baton Rouge: Louisiana State University, 1981); idem, *Cyprus from the Stone Age to the Romans* (London: Thames & Hudson, 1982); idem, ed., *Archaeology in Cyprus: 1960-1985* (Nicosia: Leventis, 1985); Franz G. Maier, *Cypern: Insel am Kreuzweg der Geschichte* (2nd ed.; Munich: Beck, 1982; English: *Cyprus from Earliest Time to the Present Day* [London: Elek, 1968]); Nobbs 1994; Hölbl 2001, 15, 18-19, 23, 59-60, 226.

[22]See Jones 1937, 371-73, relying on Ptolemaios.

[23]See Riesner 1994, 126 (ET, 143); the late date is supported by Mitford (1980, 1301). See Terence B. Mitford, *The Inscriptions of Kourion* (Philadelphia: American Philosophical Society, 1971), 169-70; Mitford refers to the fact that we know the names of forty-six proconsuls of Cyprus in the time after 22 B.C.—one-sixth of the total figure.

[24]See also Josephus, *A.J.* 13.284-287. See Schürer 3:68-69; M. Stern, "The Jewish Diaspora," in Safrai and Stern 1987, 154-55; S. Applebaum, "The Social and Economic Status of the Jews in the Diaspora," in ibid., 2:711-12.

[25]Applebaum, "Social and Economic Status," 711, with reference to Josephus, *A.J.* 18.131.

land in order to support the work of the church: he was a Diaspora Jew from Cyprus of Levite background. In Acts 11:19 Luke reports that some of the Greek-speaking Jewish Christians from Jerusalem who were forced to flee the Jewish capital after Stephen's death came to Cyprus, where they preached the gospel of Jesus Christ "to no one except the Jews" (μηδενὶ λαλοῦντες τὸν λόγον εἰ μὴ μόνον Ἰουδαίοις). Luke provides no geographical information about this early missionary work of these Jerusalem believers in A.D. 32/33, nor does he note the result of their evangelistic efforts.

Alfons Weiser argues that the mission of Jewish Christians from Jerusalem to Cyprus in Acts 11:19 is "pre-Lukan tradition" and therefore historical, while the missionary activity of Paul and Barnabas on Cyprus in Acts 13:4-12 should be regarded as a product of "the Lukan missionary concept."[26] This interpretation is entirely unconvincing. Luke does not assert in Acts 13:4 that Paul and Barnabas were the first missionaries to reach Cyprus. It is entirely plausible to accept that both Greek-speaking Jewish Christians from Jerusalem, some of whom came from Cyprus, like Barnabas himself, and Paul and Barnabas evangelized on Cyprus. Weiser's reconstruction presupposes the concept of "exclusive rights to missionary activity" in a particular region, which is anachronistic: ecclesiastical jurisdictions arose at a later point in church history.

Barnabas, a Diaspora Jew from Cyprus, felt responsible for missionary work on Cyprus at a later date as well (Acts 15:39). He surely knew the Jewish Christians from Jerusalem who had moved back to Cyprus in A.D. 31/32 after they had been forced to leave the Jewish capital (Acts 11:19-20). It is quite possible that relatives of Barnabas lived on the island. The fact that Cyprus was the first destination of Paul and Barnabas after their collaboration in Antioch is entirely plausible.[27]

Paul, Barnabas and John Mark, arriving from Antioch, disembark in Salamis on the east coast of Cyprus. Luke's account demonstrates local knowledge: Luke knows that the port city of Salamis was located across from Seleucia in Syria and that Paphos was on the other end of the island (Acts 13:4-6). Luke's comment in Acts 13:5 implies that Salamis had a large Jewish community with several synagogues: "When they arrived at Salamis, they proclaimed the word of God in the synagogues of the Jews [ἐν ταῖς συναγωγαῖς τῶν Ἰουδαίων, *en tais synagōgais tōn Ioudaiōn*])."

Salamis (ἡ Σαλαμίς; 6 km north of Famagusta),[28] attested since the eleventh century B.C.,

---

[26]Weiser, *Apg*, 1:274; cf. Lüdemann 1987, 157-58 (ET, 150-51). For the relevant argument supporting the historicity of Paul's mission to Cyprus see Breytenbach 1996, 85-86.

[27]Riesner 1994, 242 (ET, 273); for the observation that follows above see ibid.

[28]E. Oberhummer, "Salamis 3," PW 1.A2 (1920): 1832-44; E. Meyer, *KP* 4:1505-6; K. Nicolaou, *PECS* 794-96; Hector W. Catling, *OCD* 1347; Vassos Karageorghis, *Salamis in Cyprus: Homeric, Hellenistic, Roman* (London: Thames & Hudson, 1969); idem, *Salamis, die zyprische Metropole des Altertums* (Bergisch Gladbach: Lübbe, 1970); J. Taylor 1995, 1190-91. Excavations: V. Karageorghis, *Excavating at Salamis in Cyprus, 1952-1974* (Athens: Leventis, 1999).

had been the most important city of Cyprus, as indicated by the monumental royal tombs in the necropolis west of the city. Salamis had intensive contacts with Greece and Phoenicia. The most eminent king of Cyprus was Euagoras I (410-374 B.C.), who subjected the entire island to his rule. Nikokreon, the last independent king of Cyprus, was forced to commit suicide in 311 B.C. In the second century B.C. Salamis was the seat of the Ptolemaic governors. Salamis remained one of the most important cities of Cyprus in the Roman period, even though it was replaced as capital by Paphos after the city was severely damaged in an earthquake in 15 B.C. Salamis was rebuilt with financial help from Augustus, calling itself Sebaste Augusta; during the principate of Claudius the city was also known as Sebaste Claudia Flavia. Tiberius accorded the temple of Zeus in Salamis the right to grant asylum. The Second Jewish Revolt of A.D. 116/117 caused severe damage in the city. The extensive archaeological remains include the theater, a large gymnasium with adjacent buildings, sculptures and a monumental early Byzantine basilica.

Luke does not report the success, or lack of success, of the missionaries in Salamis. Two factors may indicate, however, that the missionary work of Paul, Barnabas and John Mark indeed succeeded to lead people to faith in Jesus Christ in Salamis and in other cities between Salamis and Paphos. (1) The verb "to go through" (διέρχεσθαι, dierchesthai) in Acts 13:6 ("when they had gone through the whole island as far as Paphos") may indicate that the missionaries did not simply travel from Salamis to Paphos but that they were engaged in missionary outreach. In Acts 8:4 the same verb conveys the meaning of missionary activity: "Now those who were scattered went from place to place [διῆλθον, diēlthon], proclaiming the word."[29] (2) The return of Barnabas and John Mark in A.D. 49 to Cyprus perhaps indicates that there were churches on Cyprus to whose consolidation and expansion they wanted to contribute; this would correspond to the task that Barnabas fulfilled in Antioch when the leadership of the Jerusalem church had sent him to Syria. The role that Barnabas has in the book of Acts suggests that he did not understand himself to be a pioneer missionary.

In A.D. 325 Gelasios of Salamis, Cyrillus of Paphos and Spyridon of Trimithus attended the Council of Nicea. Jerome provides the information that there were fifteen bishops in Cyprus around A.D. 400.[30] Sozomenos reports in the fifth century that there were bishops in Cyprus even in the villages, which suggests a large number of Christians on the island by that time.

If Paul and Barnabas stayed on the coastal road and traveled in a southwesterly direction, they reached Kition, another very important city of Cyprus.

---

[29]Barrett, Acts, 1:612. We should note that διέρχεσθαι is used in Acts 8:4 parallel to εὐαγγελί-ζειν, "to preach the good news," and thus is not a technical term describing missionary activity by itself.

[30]Jerome, Epist. 92. See Harnack 1924, 2:677 n. 5 (only in 4th ed.); for the comment that follows above see ibid., 677 (ET, 141).

Kition (Κίτιον; mod. Larnaka),[31] on the southern coast of Cyprus, is attested since the Mycenaean period. Around 800 B.C. colonists from Tyre brought the Phoenician culture to the city. In 333/332 B.C. "merchants of Kition" were granted the right to build a temple of Aphrodite Urania in Athens. After 312 B.C. Kition was ruled by the Ptolemies, as was all of Cyprus; Ptolemaic troops were stationed in the city. Inscriptions attest a theater, gymnasium, stadium and hippodrome. Famous sons of the city include Zenon (335-262 B.C.), the founder of the Stoa, and Apollonios (first century B.C.), a physician who wrote a commentary titled Περὶ ἄρθρων (*Peri arthrōn*, "On Joints"), a text included among the works of Hippocrates. The "Kittim" (כתים) mentioned in Gen 10:4 among the descendants of Javan and Japheth generally are identified with the Kition on Cyprus or with the entire island (see Is 23:1, 12; Josephus, *A.J.* 1.128).[32] In Num 24:24 and Dan 11:30 ships from Kittim are mentioned. Other islands in the Mediterranean besides Cyprus could be designated as Kittim as well. In 1 Macc 1:1; 8:5 the term "Kittim" describes the Greek peninsula. After the Romans had replaced the Greeks as "world power," it is the Romans who are described as "Kittim" in Jewish texts; Theodotion translated כתים in Dan 11:30 with Κίτιοι (*Kitioi*), whereas the Septuagint translated with Ῥωμαῖοι (*Rōmaioi*, "Romans").[33] The Kittim who are mentioned in Qumran texts[34] generally are identified with the Romans. The Vulgate translates Ezek 27:6 with *insulis Italiae* ("island of Italy").

Traveling from Salamis in a westerly direction, Barnabas and Paul would have reached, after 45 km, Tremithus, before reaching Kition. *Tremithus* (Τρεμιθοῦς; near mod. Tremetousia)[35] is attested since the Hellenistic period; it is mentioned by Ptolemaios as one of the cities of Cyprus (5.14.6). An inscription documents the worship of Apollo. The Roman road system linked Tremithus directly with Salamis and Kition. The bishop Spyridon of Tremithus attended the Council of Nicea.

Leaving Kition, the missionaries reached Amathos after a two-day journey as they traveled along the south coast of Cyprus towards Paphos.

Amathos (Ἀμαθοῦς; near mod. Ayios Tychonas)[36] is attested in inscriptions before the arrival of the Phoenicians. The city was an independent kingdom controlling about 150 towns and villages. King Androkles fought with his fleet in support of Alexander the Great during the siege of Tyre. He was the last king of Amathos. The famous temple of Aphro-

---

[31]E. Oberhummer, PW 11.1 (1921): 535-45; E. Meyer, *KP* 3:223; K. Nicolaou, *PECS* 456-58; R. Senff, *DNP* 6:491-92; Vassos Karageorghis, ed., *Excavations at Kition* (9 vols.; Nicosia: Department of Antiquities, 1974-1985); idem, *Kition* (London: Thames & Hudson, 1976); Kyriacos Nicolaou, *The Historical Topography of Kition* (Studies in Mediterranean Archaeology 43; Göteborg: P. Åström, 1976); Herscher 1995, 276-77.

[32]See Hamilton, *Gen*, 1:333-34; Wenham, *Gen*, 1:218-19; Westermann, *Gen*, 1:678.

[33]See J. M. Scott 1994, 520-21; 1995, 54-55.

[34]See, for example, 1QM I, 2, 4, 6, 9, 12; XI, 11; XV, 2; XVI, 3, 6, 9; XVII, 12, 14-15; XVIII, 2, 4; XIX, 10, 13; 1QpHab II, 12-13; III, 4-11; IV; VI, 1, 10; IX, 7; 4Q247 6. See D. W. Baker, *ABD* 4:93; T. H. Lim, *EDSS* 1:469-71.

[35]R. Herbst, PW 6.A2 (1937): 2290; K. Nicolaou, *PECS* 933.

[36]G. Hirschfeld, "Amathus 4," PW 1.2 (1894): 1752; C. Colpe, "Amathus 3," *KP* 1:291; E. Power, *DBSup* 2:1-23; K. Nicolaou, *PECS* 47-48; H. W. Catling, *OCD* 69; Jones 1937, 366-71; Herscher 1995, 280-81, 289; Pierre Aupert, *Guide d'Amathonte* (Sites et monuments 15; Athens: École française d'Athènes, 1996). The results of the excavations conducted since 1975 by French archaeologists are published in the series *Amathonte* (4 vols.; Athens: École française d'Athènes, 1981-1988).

dite of the city was granted the right of asylum by Tiberius in the first century.

The next stop could have been Kourion, another city on the coastal road in southern Cyprus.

Kourion (Κούριον, Κώριον, near mod. Episkopi)[37] was founded by colonists from Argos, according to Herodotus and Strabo. Remains include a theater, nymphaeum, a colonnaded hall, public baths (with mosaics), stadium, city walls, necropolis and an aqueduct. About 4 km west of the city was the temple of Apollon Hylates, also attested in inscriptions. Other deities worshiped in Kourion, according to epigraphical evidence, include Hera, Dionysos, Aphrodite, Demeter, Kore and the hero Perseutas.

Finally the missionaries reached Paphos, the only city that Luke mentions besides Salamis in Acts 13:4-12. Paphos was 150 km from Salamis.

Old Paphos (Παλαίπαφος; mod. Kouklia),[38] according to local tradition, was founded by Agapenor, the king of Tegea in Arcadia. The temple of Aphrodite in Paphos was the most famous Aphrodite sanctuary in antiquity. The goddess is said to have emerged from the sea at the site of the sanctuary, after having been born of the foam of the waves. Around 320 B.C. the port *New Paphos* (Νεάπαφος; mod. Kato Paphos)[39] was founded, 16 km from Old Paphos. The pilgrims and tourists who visited the temple of Aphrodite in Old Paphos used the harbor of New Paphos: Strabo relates that Old Paphos had only an achorage (ὕφορμος, *hyphormos*), while New Paphos had an harbor (λιμήν, *limēn* [14.6.3]). New Paphos replaced Salamis as capital of Cyprus after 15 B.C. The city had a theater, amphitheater, gymnasium and a mint. Remains of the temple of Apollo survive. Other deities that were worshiped in Paphos include Aphrodite, Artemis, Leto and Zeus. In the first century A.D. New Paphos was the seat of the Roman governor and the headquarters of the Roman garrison. During the time of Augustus the city received the honorific title "Augusta" after an earthquake (Cassius Dio 54.13.7).

Luke reports in Acts 13:6-12 an encounter between Paul and Barnabas with

---

[37]E. Oberhummer, PW 11 (1921): 2210-14; E. Meyer, *KP* 3:380; K. Nicolaou, *PECS* 467-68; R. Senff, *DNP* 6:936; Jones 1937, 365-70; Demos Christou, "Excavations at Kourion 1975-1984," in *Archaeology in Cyprus 1960-1985* (ed. V. Karageorghis; Nicosia: Leventis, 1985), 269-76; idem, *Kourion: Its Monuments and Local Museum* (7th ed.; Nicosia: Filokipros, 1996); Diana Buitron-Oliver and Bernard C. Dietrich, *The Sanctuary of Apollo Hylates at Kourion* (Studies in Mediterranean Archaeology 109; Jonsered: Aström, 1996), 286-87.

[38]Johanna Schmidt, PW 18.3 (1949): 937-64; E. Meyer, *KP* 4:484-87; K. Nicolaou, *PECS* 673-76; H. W. Catling, *OCD* 1108; R. Senff, *DNP* 9:284-85; Mitford, 1980, 1309-15; Franz G. Maier and Vassos Karageorghis, *Paphos: History and Archaeology* (Nicosia: Leventis, 1984); J. Taylor 1995, 1191-92. Since 1966 a team of Swiss and German archaeologists, under the leadership of Franz G. Maier and Marie-Louise von Wartburg, carries out excavations. Results are published in the series *Ausgrabungen in Alt-Paphos auf Zypern* (6 vols.; Konstanz: Universitätsverlag, 1977-2003). See <http://www.hist.unizh.ch/ag/paphos>.

[39]C. Gempf, *ABD* 5:139-40; R. Senff, *DNP* 9:285-86. Excavations have been carried out in New Paphos since the 1960s, particularly by Polish archaeologists. For the latest results see Herscher 1995, 282-85, 288. On the excavations in the area of the theater see <http://www.archaeology.usyd.edu.au/~robinson>.

Sergius Paullus and his Jewish court astrologer Elymas-Barjesus. The missionaries did not look for Elymas; they "found" him (Acts 13:6). It may well have been a confrontation with Elymas that led to the contact with Sergius Paullus. Luke uses the historically correct title ἀνθύπατος (*anthypatos* [Acts 13:7]): Sergius Paullus the proconsul was the governor of the senatorial province of Cyprus, which was ruled by a civil administration.[40]

Luke's account of the activity of Paul, Barnabas and John Mark in (New) Paphos can be classified in terms of its literary genre as a "missionary narrative" with the following elements: introduction of the scene, action (with or without result), complication, heightening of the complication (lengthening), resolution.[41] Other missionary narratives that Luke includes in his account of Paul's mission have essentially the same elements, although there is no stereotypical uniformity. It is particularly important to distinguish between the initial proclamation of the gospel (pioneer missionary work) and the subsequent missionary work.

The stylistic analysis by Cilliers Breytenbach risks forcing Luke's missionary narratives into the Procrustean bed of a uniform "generally known narrative model" by overemphasizing the common elements. If "the global course of action" is "nearly" (!) repeated in the various narratives, while the details differ, the question arises of whether these divergences and details must not be integrated into the scheme of the plot, and whether it is legitimate to interpret a "global scheme" of "the missionary narrative" as the "result of Lukan composition." If Paul repeatedly had similar experiences in different cities and in different local contexts, it is precisely the differentiating details that need to be taken seriously, rather than only the common elements being the focus. The differences of the various missionary narratives suggest, indeed, that Luke did not follow a fixed literary scheme. If Paul indeed preached the gospel in the synagogue of Antiocheia, it is not justified to "remove" Acts 13:15-43 as a passage that was "composed by the author" because it is, allegedly, "hardly connected with other pre-Lukan stories."[42] Similarly, in the account of Paul's mission to Iconium in Acts 14:1-7 the comment that "a great number of both Jews and Greeks became believers" (Acts 14:1d) must not be labeled as a "scene" and the assumption made that there was no "missionary success." If the miracle that Luke relates with regard to Paul's mission to Lystra in Acts 14:8-18 actually happened, I see no reason why the report of the miracle should not be integrated into this particular missionary narrative. If we do not want to dissolve the narrative cohesion of Luke's account entirely, we need to analyze both abbreviated narratives and extended narratives in the book of Acts.[43] At least Breytenbach demonstrates that the details that diverge from the scheme of the "missionary narrative" reflect specific local conditions in the cities in which the missionaries were active.[44]

---

[40]Cassius Dio 53.12-14; 54.4. See H. Balz, *EWNT* 1:249 (*EDNT* 1:104), with reference to PW 23 (1957): 1232-34, 1240-79.

[41]See Breytenbach 1996, 24, with a slight modification of the stylistic elements.

[42]Breytenbach 1996, 21.

[43]See Breytenbach 1996, 22-23 with n. 7, who criticizes Borse 1986 precisely for doing this.

[44]See Breytenbach 1996, 29-52 ("local color in Acts 13 and 14").

Sergius Paullus perhaps is identical with Lucius Sergius Paullus, who is mentioned in an inscription from Rome, where he is described as one of five curators of the Tiber River (*curatores riparum et alvei Tiberis*) who were responsible for regulating the flow of the Tiber during the principate of Claudius between A.D. 41 and 47.[45]

The text of the inscription reads as follows: "Paullus Fabius Persicus, Gaius Eggius Marullus, Lucius Sergius Paullus, Gaius Obellius Rufus, Lucius Scribonius (Libo?), custodians [*curatores*] of the river banks and of the bed of the Tiber in accordance with the authority of Tiberius Claudius Caesar Augustus Germanicus, their (?) princeps, by placing boundary stones marked out the bank from the ninth region [Trigario] to the bridge of Agrippa" (*CIL* VI 31545 = *ILS* II 5926).

Classical scholars[46] usually have less difficulties with this identification than do many New Testament scholars.[47] The identification is made difficult because Luke does not mention the *praenomen* of the governor and because the Tiber inscription does not date the tenure of Lucius Sergius Paullus. The position of his name in the inscription suggests that he was praetor at the time, which would fit a subsequent career as proconsul in a senatorial province.[48] Rainer Riesner argues that since the senate had about six hundred members at the time, and since "Sergius Paullus" is an extremely rare name, it is very unlikely that two different senators with the same name occupied a similar office within one generation.[49] Several scholars assume that this L. Sergius Paullus is identical with the Sergius who is mentioned as consul, together with Asprenas, in A.D. 70 during the principate of Vespasian (*CIL* VI 253).[50]

[45]This office had been introduced by Tiberius (Cassius Dio 57.14.8). For the discussion that follows above see Mitford 1980, 1300; S. Mitchell 1995a, 2:6-7; Nobbs 1994, 284-85 (with text and English translation of the inscription); see also Hemer 1989, 109, 227; *NewDocs* 4:138; Riesner 1994, 123-24 (ET, 139-41); Breytenbach 1996, 180 (with text and German translation).

[46]See Ramsay 1896, 74; E. Groag, PW 2.4 (1923): 1718; T. Mommsen, *ZNW* 2 (1901): 83 n. 3; idem, *Gesammelte Schriften* (8 vols.; Berlin: Weidmann, 1905-1913), 1.3.433 n. 3; Levick 1967, 112; S. Mitchell 1980, 1073-74; Nobbs 1994, 287, 289; S. Mitchell 1995a, 2:6-7.

[47]See Lüdemann 1987, 157 (ET, 151); J. Taylor 1995, 1193; cautious are Elderen 1970, 153-55; Schneider, *Apg*, 2:121 n. 27; Fitzmyer, *Acts*, 501-2; undecided is Barrett, *Acts*, 1:613-14; positive are Weiser, *Apg*, 2:316; Witherington, *Acts*, 399-400; Hengel and Schwemer 1998, 115 (ET, 69). Reinbold (2000, 92 n. 25) regards this hypothesis as "attractive" ("nicht ohne Reiz").

[48]The curator Paullus Fabius Persicus became consul in A.D. 34. He was a friend of Claudius and later became proconsul of the province of Asia.

[49]Riesner 1994, 123 (ET, 140, where the reference to G. A. Harrer, *HTR* 33 [1940]: 29 n. 32, is omitted); cf. Mitford 1980, 1301, no. 20.

[50]See E. Groag, PW 2.A (1923): 1718; S. Mitchell 1995a, 2:6; Nobbs 1994, 287; Breytenbach 1996, 39. See also Syme 1979-1991, 3:1328 n. 95; 5:473 n. 189, 551 n. 26; 677, n. 37; Syme identifies the consul Sergius with the son of the proconsul of Cyprus; cf. Riesner 1994, 124 with n. 30 (ET, 141 n. 30).

The following considerations support this identification.[51] (1) An inscription of Antiocheia discovered by W. M. Ramsay and J. G. C. Anderson in 1912, dating to A.D. 60-100, refers to a certain Lucius Sergius L. f. Paullus, who probably is the son of the aforementioned curator of the Tiber in Rome (Lat. *L. f.* stands for *Luci filius,* "son of Lucius").[52] A translation of the inscription reads as follows: "For L(ucius) Sergius Paullus the younger, son of Lucius, one of the four commissioners in charge of the Roman streets, tribune of the sixth legion called Ferrata, quaestor . . ." Unfortunately, the inscription is incomplete. The addition *f(ilio)* indicates that the father was still alive and that he was known in Antiocheia. (2) A second inscription of Antiocheia mentions a certain Sergia Paulla, evidently the daughter of L. Sergius Paullus, married to C. Caristanius Fronto, who was a member of one of the influential families of Antiocheias, praetor of Lycia and Pamphylia during the principates of Titus and Domitian, and consul in Rome around A.D. 90.[53] The translation of the text of the inscription, inscribed on a limestone that was erected on the agora of Antiocheia in A.D. 74, reads, "For the most esteemed Sergia Paulla, daughter of Lucius, wife of Gaius Caristanius Fronto the imperial legate of emperor Domitian Augustus, the propraetor of Lycia and Pamphylia." The family of the Sergii Paulli owned extensive real estate in the region of Vetissus (Emirler) in the province of Galatia in central Anatolia. This is attested by three inscriptions: (a) An inscription erected in A.D. 89 states that a freedman of the Sergii Paulli financed the building of a temple of Men from his own resources: "Lucius Sergius Corinthus built for the wise Men, as promised, both the temple and the surrounding area, at his own (cost). In the year 114" (*MAMA* VII 486). (b) A tombstone erected by Sergia Paullina in A.D. 112 reads, "In memory of Gnaeus Cornelius Severinus, the *decurialis viator,* from Sergia Paullina, the daughter of Lucius the wife of Cornelius Severus."[54] This Gnaeus Cornelius Severus was a freedman of her husband, the Spanish patrician and Roman senator and consul Gnaeus Pinarius Cornelius Severus.[55] (c) A funerary inscription from the vicinity of Antiocheia mentions a manager of the estate of Paullus: "Sergia Tryphera wife of Sergius Karpus the manager of Paullus. Sergius Karpus mourns with the mother and with Sergia Bella, the esteemed mother-in-law."[56] In the context of similar land holdings in this region, Stephen Mitchell assumes that the family of the Sergii Paulli had aquired real estate in this region in the Julio-Claudian period.[57] The family tree of the Sergii Paulli illustrates the family relationships:[58]

---

[51]See Nobbs 1994, 287; Riesner 1994, 124-25 (ET, 140-41); Breytenbach 1996, 38-45.

[52]Editio princeps: W. M. Ramsay, "Sergius Paullus and His Relation to Christian Faith," in *The Bearing of Recent Discovery on the Trustworthiness of the New Testament* (repr. of 4th ed.; Grand Rapids: Baker, 1953 [1920]), 151. Reprinted and translated in Breytenbach 1996, 185; for an interpretation see ibid., 40.

[53]Editio princeps: *JRS* 3 (1913): 262-66, and Ramsay, *Recent Discovery,* 154-55; for the text and a German translation see Breytenbach 1996, 187. See also Levick 1967, 112; Halfmann 1979, 109-10, no. 13.

[54]*MAMA* VII 319 = *RECAM* 355.

[55]See Halfmann 1979, 105, no. 9; Breytenbach 1996, 183.

[56]*MAMA* II 321. Sergius Karpus was a freedmen of the Sergii; see *MAMA* VII 330, 331.

[57]S. Mitchell 1980, 1073-74; Riesner 1994, 245 (ET, 276); Halfmann 1979, 30, 55-56, 101-2, 105.

[58]Riesner (1994, 373 [ET, 416]) and Breytenbach (1996, 45) reproduce the family tree in Halfmann 1979, 106, without agreeing with his theory that the Cypriot proconsul Quintus Sergius Paullus was a brother of Lucius Sergius Paullus. I follow Stephen Mitchell (1995a, 2:7), who argues that this inscription is irrelevant for the description of the Sergii Paulli in Antiocheia. The term "cos." is the Roman abbreviation for "consul."

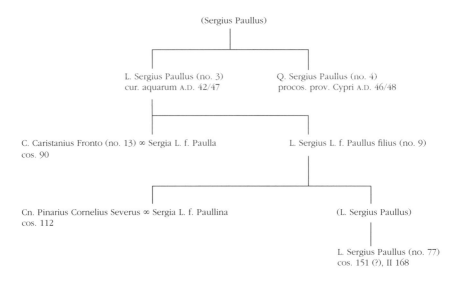

(Sergius Paullus)

L. Sergius Paullus (no. 3)   Q. Sergius Paullus (no. 4)
cur. aquarum A.D. 42/47   procos. prov. Cypri A.D. 46/48

C. Caristanius Fronto (no. 13) ∞ Sergia L. f. Paulla   L. Sergius L. f. Paullus filius (no. 9)
cos. 90

Cn. Pinarius Cornelius Severus ∞ Sergia L. f. Paullina   (L. Sergius Paullus)
cos. 112

L. Sergius Paullus (no. 77)
cos. 151 (?), II 168

Epigraphical sources possibly indicate that there were Christians in the family of the Sergii of Galatia. Although the identifications proposed by William Ramsay are partly hypothetical,[59] some scholars suggest that the "association" mentioned in twenty-three inscriptions discovered in Rome (*collegium quod est in domo Sergiae Paullinae*),[60] whose founder was L. Sergius L. f. Paullus (the consul of A.D. 70?), may have been a Christian house church. This *collegium* was continued by his daughter Sergia Paulla, who was married to Cornelius Severus, the consul in A.D. 112. A daughter of this Sergia Paulla married M. Acilius Glabrio, consul in A.D. 124, the son of Acilius Glabrio, who was executed under Domitian (A.D. 81-96), possibly because of his Christian faith (Cassius Dio 67.14.1-3).[61]

The proconsul Sergius Paullus is described as an "intelligent man" (ἀνὴρ συ-νετός, *anēr synetos* [Acts 13:7]). In view of his relationship to the magician Elymas, this comment does not imply a religious appraisal but describes his political wisdom: he invites Barnabas and Paul to come and present their message, evidently in order to establish whether it is subversive of not.[62]

It was during this hearing that Elymas-Barjesus "opposed them and tried to turn the proconsul away from the faith" (Acts 13:8). The status of Elymas as *ma-*

---

[59]Two further inscriptions that mention a Paul(l)us that have been identified with the proconsul Sergius Paullus of Acts 13:7 are no longer regarded as relevant because of palaeographical and chronological difficulties. The Soloi inscription (*IGR* III 930), found on the north coast of Cyprus, mentions a proconsul named Paulus but does not provide his *nomen* or *praenomen*. Today this inscription usually is dated to the time of Hadrian in the second century. The Kythraia inscription (*IGR* III 935 = *SEG* XX 302.9-11), mentions a proconsul named Quintus Sergius Paullus, who now is dated not to the time of Claudius but to that of Caligula.
[60]*CIL* VI 9148, 9149.
[61]Sordi 1986, 28, 185-86; cf. Riesner (1994, 124-25 [ET, 140-41]), who remains cautious.
[62]See Witherington, *Acts,* 400; Stenschke 1999a, 167.

gos can be compared with the role that philosophers and astrologers often played in aristocratic families.[63] Pliny reports that there were *magoi* on Cyprus (*Nat.* 30.2.11). Luke describes how Paul, under the inspiration of the Holy Spirit (Acts 13:9), unmasks Barjesus as "son of the devil" (Acts 13:10), pronouncing God's judgment against him, which caused Barjesus to become blind for a time (Acts 13:11). Upon witnessing these events, Sergius Paullus is converted.

The conversion of Sergius Paullus initially is linked with the miracle of judgment upon Elymas-Barjesus[64] but then is clearly tied to his reaction to the "teaching about the Lord" (Acts 13:12),[65] similar to the reaction of the citizens of Capernaum to the powerful preaching of Jesus (Lk 4:32). Some scholars suggest that the proconsul was not converted to faith in Jesus Christ, as there is no reference to baptism. If this criterion were applied consistently, we would have to conclude that no one on Cyprus and in southern Galatia was converted during the missionary work of Paul and Barnabas: Luke never mentions baptisms in Acts 13—14.[66] The fact that Paul and Barnabas visited "churches" in Lystra, Iconium and Antiocheia on the journey back to Syria (Acts 14:21, 23) demonstrates, however, that there were indeed a good number of people who had been converted, assuming that we can rely on Luke's account. Howard Marshall suggests that Acts 13:2 describes a conversion of Sergius but that it may have been of short duration, as Luke abruptly ends the narrative and provides no further details.[67] This conclusion does not follow necessarily, however. John Foster argues that Julian Apostata later refers to Cornelius in Caesarea and to Sergius Paullus in Paphos as the only examples for the argument that people who belonged to the aristocracy converted to the Christian faith.[68] More plausible is the suggestion of Martin Hengel that Sergius Paullus was not able to be baptized "on account of his political position and his senatorial status, despite his sympathy."[69] Unless we regard it as impossible for a Roman proconsul to come to faith in Jesus Christ, there is no reason to doubt the reliability of the Lukan account.[70]

There is an old Christian tradition, preceding Origen, that asserts that Saul of Tarsus changed his name after his encounter with the Cypriot governor Sergius Paulus and called himself *Paulos*,[71] in analogy to Scipio, who assumed the epithet *Africanus* after his victory

---

[63]J. Taylor 1995, 1195. Berger (1994b, 313) suggests that Barjesus could have been a Christian, a theory that is contradicted by Acts 13:8. On Barjesus see also Klauck 1996, 61-63.

[64]Acts 13:12a: τότε ἰδὼν ὁ ἀνθύπατος τὸ γεγονός.

[65]Acts 13:12b: ἐπίστευσεν ἐκπλησσόμενος ἐπὶ τῇ διδαχῇ τοῦ κυρίου.

[66]See Barrett, *Acts*, 1:619.

[67]Marshall, *Acts*, 220. Bruce (*Acts*, 265) leaves the question open.

[68]Foster 1948-1949.

[69]Hengel and Schwemer 1998, 115 (expansion of ET, 69).

[70]See Sordi 1986, 24, 28; also Stenschke 1999a, 306, 308.

[71]Origen, *Comm. Rom.* praef. (PG 14:836).

over Hannibal in Africa. This hypothesis is unnecessary: the formulation in Acts 13:9 with ὁ καί (*ho kaí*) is used in papyri in double names and can be translated as "alias." Most scholars attribute the change from Saul to Paul at this point in Acts to the redactional intentions of Luke: "Through this spectacular conversion of a Gentile from the upper classes, Paul proves himself as the apostle to the nations who now moves to the center of the story."[72]

The conversion of Sergius Paullus in Paphos could help explain why Paul and Barnabas evidently traveled from Paphos straight to Pisidian Antiocheia, given that his family owned estates in southern Galatia and had contact with Antiocheia (assuming that the identification with the Sergii Paulli of the Tiber inscription and of the Antiocheia inscription is correct).[73] William Ramsay suggested in connection with Gal 4:13 ("You know that it was because of a physical infirmity that I first announced the gospel to you") that Paul had contracted malaria in Pamphylia and that this was the reason why he traveled to southern Galatia, with its higher elevations.[74]

The likelihood that the Roman governor of Cyprus was converted to the Christian faith might by supported by another consideration. Paul evangelized in Cilicia and in Syria for fourteen years and in Antioch for two years, while he stayed on Cyprus only for a few months even though he did not have to cut short his missionary work there due to local opposition. Why did Paul leave Cyprus so soon? Perhaps he assumed that the conversion of the proconsul made a longer stay unnecessary, as the "success" on the highest level of society—the first such conversion in the history of the early Christian mission so far—would ensure the continuation of the expansion of the church on the island. And the recommendation that the proconsul possibly provided for contacting his relatives in Pisidian Antiocheia might have suggested that missionary work in this important Roman colony on the border of Phrygia and Pisidia should be started soon. The fact that Luke reports the conversion of an aristocrat surely is not evidence for a "bourgeois" prejudice on his part, as his description of the governors Felix and Festus indicates (Acts 24:26-27; 25:9): it is subordinated to his de-

---

[72]Riesner (1994, 127 [ET, 144]), who does not want to exclude the possibility that "the apostle may well have used his Roman name when dealing with the Gentile world." See, however, S. Mitchell 1980, 1073-74; 1995, 2:6.

[73]Thus S. Mitchell 1980, 1074 n. 134; Horsley, *NewDocs* 4:138; Riesner 1994, 124 (ET, 140); Lane Fox 1986, 293-94; Witherington 2001, 233. J. Taylor (1995, 1114, 1225) remains skeptical. Reinbold (2000, 183-84) does not seem to be aware of this suggestion. Keathley (1999, 71) believes that Paul and Barnabas went "wherever the road happened to lead," an assessment that is as frivolous as it as unconvincing.

[74]Ramsay 1896, 92-97; recently Reinbold 2000, 183-84 (unaware of Ramsay). See also Güttgemanns 1966, 162-65, 173-77. Martyn (*Gal,* 420) thinks that any speculation is superfluous. Goddard and Cummins (1993) interpret the "weakness" of Gal 4:13-14 as a reference to persecutions that accompanied the mission to Galatia, particularly the stoning in Lystra reported in Acts 14:8-20.

scription of the activity of the missionaries.[75]

Barnabas returned to Cyprus in A.D. 49 after his clash with Paul over the suitability of John Mark as a missionary (Acts 15:39). Barnabas took John Mark to Cyprus, where evidently he labored to consolidate the previous missionary work and the churches that had been established. The characterization of Barnabas in the book of Acts suggests that Luke regarded his mission to Cyprus as successful.[76] In Acts 21:16 Luke mentions that a certain "Mnason of Cyprus, an early disciple," who lived in Caesarea, was Paul's host when he returned from his mission to Ephesus. Luke provides no details about when and where Mnason heard the gospel.

These pieces of information from Luke are the earliest and for a long time the only evidence for the presence of Christians on Cyprus. There was news in the spring of 2000 that the fragment of an inscription on a marble slab, discovered by Italian archaeologists under the leadership of Filippo Guidice during excavations in Paphos, documents the presence of Paul in the city.[77] The text of the fragment is "LOY . . . OSTO," which Guidice reads as "[PAU]LOY [AP]OSTO[LOY]" or "[SAU]LOY [AP]OSTO[LOY]." The marble block was found in the ruins of an early Christian basilica that had been built above an earlier temple complex dedicated to the worship of Apollo, Artemis and Asclepius. The Christian basilica is dated to the time of Hilarion of Gaza (A.D. 291-371), who worked as a missionary on Cyprus. Guidice is convinced that the inscription is older, perhaps dating to the first or second century A.D. Further analysis must show whether this interpretation is plausible. Inscriptions dating to the third century that have been interpreted as attesting the presence of Christians on Cyprus are disputed in terms of both their Christian origin and their date.[78] Well documented is the presence of churches on Cyprus in the early fourth century: the bishop Kyrillos attended the Council of Nicea in A.D. 325.

Missionary Work in South Galatia

Barnabas, Paul and John Mark "set sail from Paphos and came to Perga in Pamphylia" (Acts 13:13). After the reorganization of the provinces in A.D. 43 by Claudius, Pamphylia formed a new province with Lycia and central and southern Pisidia (the northern border evidently was south of Lake Burdur).[79]

Pamphylia (Παμφυλία),[80] described by the Greeks as "land of all peoples," borders on Lycia in the west, only a few kilometers from Attaleia; to the east the border with Cilicia Tracheia ran between Laertes and Syedra; to the northeast was Isauria, and the northern

---

[75]See Beydon 1986.
[76]See Cara 2001, 151-54.
[77]J. Harris, "Putting Paul on the Map," *BAR* 26 (2000): 14.
[78]See Mitford 1980, 1374, 1381.
[79]See S. Mitchell 1995a, 1:79; 2:153-54.
[80]W. Ruge, PW 18.3 (1949): 354-407; E. Olshausen, *KP* 4:441-44; E. M. Blailock, *GBL* 3:1119-20; S. Mitchell, *OCD* 1102-3; W. Martini, *DNP* 9:216-19; Karl Graf Lanckoronski, *Städte Pamphyliens und Pisidiens I: Pamphylien* (Vienna: Tempsky, 1890; repr., Böblingen: Codex, 1966); Jones 1937, 127-33; Brandt 1992, 9-10; Nollé 1993, 297-317.

border with Pisidia was on the Taurus Mountains along the line Gündoğmuş (north of the port city of Korakesion [mod. Alanya]), Etenna (mod. Sırtköy), Beşkonak (south of Selge) and the area between Termessos and Attaleia. Pamphylia is divided by the rivers Kestros (Aksu Çayı), Eurymedon (Köprü Irmağı) and Melas (Manavgat Çayı), which entered the Mediterranean at Perge, Aspendos and Side. Apart from the area around Attaleia, Pamphylia is a fertile coastal region with a humid Mediterranean climate. The north is hill country, the foothills of the Taurus. The Mediterranean vegetation consists of evergreen maquis, of olive and citrus trees. The wealth of Pamphylia was connected with the rivers Kestros and Eurymedon, which were navigable in antiquity. The produce of the olive trees that were cultivated particularly in the northern part of the coastal plain was used for export. Rare plants were used to produce perfume and pharmaceuticals. The most important port was Side. According to Greek legends, Pamphylia was colonized by Greeks after the Trojan War. Greek colonization clearly began before 1000 B.C. Pamphylia never was a really independent political unit. The Persian king Cyrus II had taken over control of the region from the Lydians in the sixth century B.C. During the Persian period Perge, Aspendos and Sillyon minted their own coins. After Alexander's conquest Pamphylia was ruled by the Seleucids, and at times by the Ptolemies, until the kings of Pergamon dominated the region after 158 B.C. After 55 B.C. Pamphylia belonged to the new Roman province of Cilicia, after 49 B.C. to the province of Asia, after 36 B.C. to the Galatian kingdom of Amyntas, after 25 B.C. to the province of Galatia, after A.D. 43 to the new province Lycia-Pamphylia. When Paul came to Pamphylia for the first time in A.D. 45/46, the last reorganization was only two or three years in the past. The first legate was Q. Veranius II. (A.D. 43/44-47/48), succeeded by M. Calpurnius Rufus (A.D. 48-53?), Q. Petronius Umber and T. Clodius Eprius Marcellus.[81] Under Nero, Pamphylia was annexed to the new province Galatia-Cappadocia in A.D. 54. Vespasian united Pamphylia again with Lycia.

Lycia (Λυκία),[82] west of Pamphylia and south of Phrygia, extended from Olympos and Phaselis in the east to Telmessos and Daidala in the west; the northern border was near Oinoanda. Lycia, with the Taurus Mountains to the north, was linked with the north by two main roads: the most important route ran from the coast (coming from Attaleia and Phaselis) via Myra and Patara through the Xanthos Valley to Telmessos and Kalydna, reaching the east-west highway at Laodikeia. Lycia was under Ptolemaic rule at least since 277 B.C. In 197 B.C. Lycia was occupied by Antiochos III; after his defeat in the battle of Magnesia in 189 B.C. Lycia was given by the Romans to Rhodes. In 168 B.C. Lycia gained independence, which it maintained for two hundred years as a league of allied cities. Cities that minted federal bronze coins include Arykanda, Limyra, Myra,

---

[81]See Rémy 1988, 167-68; on Q. Petronius Umber see S. Mitchell 1995a, 2:154.
[82]G. Deeters, PW 13.2 (1927): 2270-91; S. Jameson, PWSup 13 (1973): 265-308; S. Mitchell, *OCD* 894-95; M. Zimmermann, *DNP* 7:559-62; Bean 1968; Pekáry 1980, 633-35; S. Jameson, "The Lycian League," *ANRW* VII.2 (1980): 832-55; Trevor R. Bryce, *The Lycians I: The Lycians in Literary and Epigraphic Sources* (Copenhagen: Museum Tusculanum Press, 1986); Kolb and Kupke 1992; M. Zimmermann 1992; Jürgen Borchhardt and Gerhard Dobesch, eds., *Akten des II. Internationalen Lykien-Symposions, Wien, 6.-12. Mai, 1990* (Vienna: Osterreichische Akademie der Wissenschaften, 1993); Pamela Gordon, *Epicurus in Lycia: The Second-Century World of Diogenes of Oenoanda* (Ann Arbor: University of Michigan Press, 1996); Ralf Behrwald, *Der lykische Bund: Untersuchungen zu Geschichte und Verfassung* (Bonn: Habelt, 2000).

Olympos, Patara, Phaselis, Telmessos, Tlos and Xanthos. In A.D. 43 Lycia was combined with most of Pisidia and Pamphylia to form a new province: Claudius had maintained that the Lycians misused the freedom that Rome had granted them, sympathizing with Rome's enemies in the east and killing Roman citizens. The first governor was Q. Veranius. When Lycia was annexed, the citizens of the Lycian cities were granted Roman citienzenship; the annexation was celebrated with a newly minted coinage. Claudius stationed only auxiliary troops in Lycia, in the first century A.D. the cohort Apula. When Vespasian reorganized the east, the union with Pamphylia and Pisidia was dissolved: Pisidia remained with the province of Galatia, while Lycia was combined with Pamphylia in the double province Lycia-Pamphylia.[83] The governors L. Luscius Ocrea and M. Hirrius Fronto Neratius Pansa are attested.

Paul, Barnabas and John Mark reached Pamphylia either at the port of Attaleia or they came directly to Perge, the capital of Pamphylia, which was linked with the Mediterranean at the time, probably by a connecting canal from the Kestros River.[84]

Attaleia (Ἀττάλεια; mod. Antalya)[85] was founded around 150 B.C. by Attalos II Philadelphos, probably at the site of an older settlement, when western Pamphylia was controlled by Pergamon. The Pergamene kings wanted to establish a second naval port on the south coast, besides Telmessos, and they hoped that Attaleia would become an economic competitor for the cities of Aspendos and Side in eastern Pamphylia. After the end of the Pergamene kingdom around 133 B.C. Attaleia seems to have been independent until 77 B.C., when it fell to the Romans. Pompey assembled his fleet in the port of Attaleia in 67 B.C. As far as Attaleia's port was concerned, it could not compete with Side. Compared with the other Pamphylian cities, Attaleia's reputation was relatively low. Augustus settled veterans in Attaleia as *sympoliteuomenoi Romaioi*—that is, as Roman citizens who belonged to the polis of Attaleia. The cult of Roma Archegetis.has to be understood in this context. Probably under T. Helvius Basila, governor of Galatia (A.D. 35-39), the colonnaded street was built. Remains of the ancient city are sparse: capitals of columns and ruins of the city walls (second century). Hadrian's Gate in the east, erected on the occasion of the visit of Hadrian to the city in A.D. 130, is the most impressive of the surviving ruins.

---

[83]Brandt 1992, 98-99. In the early second century Hadrian (or Antonius Pius) annexed most of Pisidia to Lyci-Pamphylia. The new province seems to have existed without further changes until the late third century.

[84]Strabo 14.42. See Magie 1950, 2:1134 n. 7; Riesner 1994, 246 n. 69 (ET, 276 n. 69).

[85]W. Ruge, PW 2.2 (1896): 2156; S. Jameson, PWSup 12 (1970): 125; Bean, *PECS* 111; S. Mitchell, *OCD* 211; W. Martini, "Attaleia 1," *DNP* 2:226; Magie 1950, 1:261, 291; 2:775, 1133 n. 4; Bean 1968, 41-45; Nollé 1993, 307-8, 310; G. Cohen 1995, 337-38; S. Mitchell 1995a, 1:77, 90-91, 102, 247; Sencer Şahin, "Bau einer Säulenstrasse in Attaleia (Pamphylien) unter Tiberius-Caligula?" *EA* 25 (1995): 25-27. In 1998 Sencer Şahin and Ender Varinlioğlu established at Akdeniz University in Antalya a research institute for Mediterranean languages and cultures with the goal of promoting epigraphical and historical-geographical research, particularly of Pamphylia and Lycia. They promised that results would be published in a speedy manner in *Epigraphica Anatolica* and other publications; see "Epigraphische Mitteilungen aus Antalya (EMA)," *EA* 31 (1999): 37-39.

Magydos (Μαγύδος),[86] only a few kilometers southeast of Attaleia, had some importance in the imperial period, as the coins and the buildings of the city indicate, due also to the artificially improved port that belonged to the largest harbors on the south coast of Asia Minor; the jetties were up to 340 m long. In 75 B.C. a customs post was established at Magydos, which was controlled by the *portorium Asiae* (*EA* 14 [1989] §9). Attested and in part surviving are harbor baths, agora, stoa, necropolis and aqueducts. Under the emperor Decius (A.D. 249-251), Nestor, bishop of Magydos, died as a martyr in Perge (according to another tradition, Nestor was bishop of Perge); at the same time a certain Konon of Nazareth was executed in Magydos after a trial before the governor of the province.[87] The bishop Aphrodisios of Magydos attended the Council of Nicea in A.D. 325. We do not know when the church in Magydos was established.

When Luke introduces Perge, he does not report a preaching activity of Paul and Barnabas, although this may be implied in the formulation "they came to Perge . . . they went on from Perge" (ἦλθον εἰς Πέργην . . . αὐτοὶ δὲ διελθόντες ἀπὸ τῆς Πέργης [Acts 13:13, 14]). Luke explicitly points out that the missionaries preached the gospel in Perge after they returned from Pisidian Antiocheia (Acts 14:25 [see below]). On the occasion of their first visit to the city Luke reports only that John Mark left Paul and Barnabas (Acts 13:13). The reasons for his departure remain unclear. Did John Mark resent that Paul had become the leader of the missionary advance, while his cousin Barnabas played second fiddle? Or did he object to the continuation of the missionary journey with the trip to southern Galatia? Or had he become tired? Or lost courage?[88] The suggestion that John Mark had reservations concerning Paul's missionary praxis among Gentiles[89] is implausible: John Mark evidently came along at the invitation of Barnabas and must have known not only his cousin but also his coworker in Antioch and their missionary praxis in the Syrian capital, where many Gentiles had come to faith.

Paul and Barnabas traveled from Perge on the Via Sebaste to the north. They crossed the provincial border of Lycia-Pamphylia and Galatia between Kormasa and Lysinia. The missionary activity of the following months concentrated on several cities in southern Galatia (see fig. 28) that were located on the Via Sebaste, the strategically important east-west route: Antiocheia, Iconium, Lystra and Derbe.

Pisidia (Πισιδία)[90] is the mountainous region in the western ranges of the Taurus Moun-

---

[86]W. Ruge, PW 14 (1928): 521; idem, PW 18.3 (1949): 393; Brandt 1992, 49, 106, 135; Mustafa Adak and Orhan Atvur, "Epigraphische Mitteilungen aus Antalya II: Die pamphylische Hafenstadt Magydos," *EA* 31 (1999): 53-68.
[87]H. Delehaye, ed., *Synaxarium,* 511, 515. See Adak and Atvur, "Epigraphische Mitteilungen," 65-66.
[88]See Marshall, *Acts,* 222.
[89]Roloff 1991, 122 n. 31.
[90]W. Brandenstein, PW 20.2 (1950): 1793-97; E. Olshausen and G. Neumann, *KP* 4:868-70; S. Mitchell, *OCD* 1186; H. Brandt, *DNP* 9:1043-45; Karl Graf Lanckoronski, *Städte Pamphyliens und Pisidiens II: Pisidien* (Vienna: Tempsky, 1892; repr., Böblingen: Codex, 1966); Levick

tains. The southern border with Pamphylia was described above; the eastern border with Isauria and Lycaonia ran along the line Neapolis (Sarkı Karaağaç, on the northeastern end of Lake Koralis), Pappa-Tiberiopolis (Yunuslar), Mistea (Beyšehir) and Etenna (Sırtköy); in the north the border ran from Apameia (Dinar) and Apollonia (Uluborlu) to Sultan Dağları (north of Yalvaç); the western border with Phrygia ran along the eastern side of Lake Askania (Burdur Gölü) to Karamanlı, Isinda (Korkuteli) and Termessos (Güllük Dağ). The landscape of Pisidia consisted of flat meadows on the mountain slopes (Yaylası) and basins (Ovası) with lakes; the region around Burdur, Isparta and Eğridir is regarded as the Turkish "lake district" (Göller Bölgesi). In northern Pisidia we find fir, cedar and spruce trees, and in central and southern Pisidia evergreen oaks, cotton and olives. As a result of the excellent water supply central Pisidia was a fertile region despite its high altitude. The Pisidians cultivated olives and wine, and they engaged in agriculture, animal husbandry and forestry. After the death of Alexander the Great, Pisidia belonged to the Seleucid kingdom, after 189 B.C. to Pergamon, after 133 B.C. to the kingdom of Cappadocia, after 100 B.C. to the Roman province Cilicia, after 39 B.C. to the Galatian kingdom of Amyntas. After the death of Amyntas in 25 B.C. Sulpicius Quirinius incorporated Pisidia into the province of Galatia. Augustus pursued a politics of Romanization in Pisidia: he founded military colonies in Antiocheia, Komama, Cremna,[91] Lystra and Olbasa,[92] and he fortified the Via Sebaste. Central and southern Pisidia evidently was incorporated into the province Lycia-Pamphylia in A.D. 43 when Claudius reorganized Asia Minor.[93]

Recent archaeological finds have made untenable the older view that Pisidia, an independent and mountainous region with a stubborn population, resisted the expansion of the Christian faith and remained for a long time a bastion of paganism. Two inscriptions attest the presence of Pisidian Christians in the second half of the second century at the latest: the Latin rescript that emperor Maximinus Daia sent in A.D. 312 to Pisidian Kolbasa demanding that the citizens force the Christians to leave the territory of the city, and an unpublished inscription from the territory of Komama that evidently refers to Christians.[94] The earliest Christian inscription in Cremna is found on a sarcophagus dating to the third or fourth century: "This is the grave solely of Alexandros and Patrikios. If somebody places another body in the grave he will have to give account at the eternal judgments of our master" (*I. Pisidia* 56).

The first city for which Luke reports missionary activity by Paul and Barnabas is Antiocheia. The localization in Acts 13:14 "to Pisidian Antiocheia" (εἰς Ἀντιόχειαν τὴν Πισιδίαν, *eis Antiocheian tēn Pisidian* [NRSV translates "to Antioch

---

1967; Pekáry 1980, 643-48; Belke and Mersich 1990; Brandt 1992; Schwertheim 1992; S. Mitchell 1995a, 2:151-57, and passim; Syme 1995, 177-92; on the Augustan colonies, ibid., 225-41. The inscriptions of central Pisidia, particularly Cremna, have been published recently (*I. Pisidia* [ed. Horsley and Mitchell, 2000]).

[91]The extensive surveys by Stephen Mitchell in Cremna conducted in the years 1985-1987 have uncovered hardly any traces of the early imperial period. The building activity after A.D. 230 was so dramatic that Mitchell speaks of a "cultural revolution." See S. Mitchell 1995b, 53, 79. Inscriptions: *I. Pisidia* 1-82.

[92]See Levick 1967, 48-50.

[93]S. Mitchell 1995a, 2:154.

[94]See S. Mitchell 1995b, 219. In Cremna the basilica dating to the time of Hadrian was transformed into a church probably at the end of the fourth century.

in Pisidia"]) does not assert that Antiocheia was actually located in Pisidia (thus erroneously Ptolemaios 5.4.9; Pliny, *Nat.* 5.24.94): the city belonged to Phrygia. The appellation "Pisidian" distinguishes this Antiocheia from the city of the same name on the Maeander River, also located in Phrygia: it describes the closeness of this Antiocheia to Pisidia. Strabo states unambiguously that this Antiocheia was located in Phrygia (12.6.4; cf. Ptolemaios 5.5).[95]

Phrygia (Φρυγία [see fig. 29])[96] is the region of the plateau of western central Anatolia. The ethnic boundaries of Phrygia cannot be described with precision. Strabo and Pliny knew that at the time of the old Phrygian empire and in the Persian period Phrygia extended from the upper Maeander Valley and the Hermos Valley in the west as far as the Salt Lake (Tata Limnē, Tuz Gölü) in the east, and in the south from the line marked by Iconium, Laodikeia Katakekaumene (Combusta) and Savatra to the Halys River and to Bithynia in the north. The descriptions by Strabo and Pliny of contemporary Phrygia omit the east with Galatia and Lycaonia.[97] In the Roman period Phrygia belonged in part to the province of Asia and in part to the province of Galatia. After the decline of the old Phrygian empire in the seventh century B.C. no autonomous political power controlled the Anatolian highlands until the Arab invasion in the eleventh century, with the exception of the eighty years between 270 and 189 B.C. when the Galatian kings ruled in central Anatolia. After the conquest by Alexander the Great, Macedonians settled in the region— for example, in Docimium, Philomelion and Lysias. In southern Phrygia cities and urban institutions developed during the rule of the Seleucids. Besides Zeus and various mother goddesses, the population venerated the Anatolian deity Men and various gods that were linked with righteousness, vengeance and justice, including the couple "Holy and Just." Stephen Mitchell believes that because the deities that the Phrygian population worshiped enjoined a strict moral code, "it is no coincidence that Jewish and early Christian communities flourished on Phrygian soil in the 2nd and 3rd cents. A.D."[98]

Antiocheia belonged to the Roman province of Galatia, as did all the other cities in which Paul and Barnabas preached the gospel during the following months.

Galatia (Γαλατία)[99] was originally the name of a region, connected with the Celtic ("Galatian") tribes that had invaded Greece and Macedonia in the third century B.C., to be

---

[95]In the New Testament text tradition Codex D and the Majority Text write Ἀντιόχειαν τῆς Πισιδίας (*Antiocheian tēs Pisidias*), with the genitive of possession indicating that the copyists assume that the city belonged to Pisidia, reflecting the political situation in the fourth century. See Levick 1967, 18, 33; Bruce, *Gal,* 6; Riesner 1994, 243 n. 45 (ET, 273 n. 45); Mitchell and Waelkens 1998, 5-6.

[96]W. Ruge, "Phrygia 1," PW 21.1 (1941): 781-868; S. Mitchell, *OCD* 1176-77; Olshausen, *DNP* 9:965-67; Haspels 1971; Pekáry 1980, 635-38; S. Mitchell 1995a; Laminger-Pascher 1989; Belke and Mersich 1990; Drew-Bear and Naour 1990.

[97]Cf. Strabo 12.5.4 with 12.8.13-17, and cf. Pliny, *Nat.* 41.84, with Ptolemaios 5.2.17.

[98]Mitchell, *OCD* 1177.

[99]Carl Georg Brandis, PW 7.1 (1910): 519-59; H. Volkmann, *KP* 2:666-70; S. Mitchell, *ABD* 1:264-65; W. M. Calder and S. Mitchell, *OCD* 621; K. Strobel, *DNP* 4:742-45; Mitchell, *RECAM* 13-30 (introduction); Belke 1984, 39-42, 93-110; Restle, in ibid., 43-47; Ramsay, *Gal,* 12-174; Stähelin 1907; Pekáry 1980, 641-43; S. Mitchell 1980, 111; Sherk 1980, 955-1052; S. Mitchell 1986; Rémy

stopped at the Battle of Delphi (279 B.C.), while three of the tribes crossed the Hellespont in 278 B.C. and migrated to Asia Minor: the Tolistobogii, the Trocmi and the Tectosages. Nikomedes, king of Bithynia, allowed them to settle in the rural, non-Hellenized areas of Pessinus, Ancyra, Gorbeus and Tavia (Tavium). The centers of the three tribes were large mountain fortresses: neither Pessinus, Ancyra, nor Tavia was inhabited by Celts/Galatians around 200 B.C. The territory of Galatia belongs to two large river systems: in the west the upper Sangarios River (Sakarya), and in the east the middle Halys River (Kızılırmak). The climate of Galatia is very hot in the summer, cold in the winter; the snowfalls begin in late November or early December and last until March. After the Galatians had supported the Romans in the Third Mithradatic War (74-64 B.C.), and after Julius Caesar was murdered in 44 B.C., Deiotaros, tetrarch of the Tolistobogii, succeeded in becoming king of all of Galatia. The most important Galatian cities were Ancyra, Pessinus, Tavium and Gordium. Amyntas, the last Galatian king, fortified Isaura Palaia (Bozkir, Aydoğmuş) as his residence. When he died in 25 B.C., Augustus created the new province of Galatia under a *legatus Augusti pro praetore;* Marcus Lollius was the first legate. The province consisted of the Galatian heartland around Ancyra, which became the provincial capital, much of eastern Phrygia, Pisidia, Pamphylia, Isauria, parts of Lycaonia, Paphlagonia (6/5 B.C.) and Pontus Galaticus (3/2 B.C.; further areas of Pontus were incorporated in A.D. 34/35 and 38). In A.D. 43 Claudius annexed Lycia, incorporating central and southern Pisidia into the new province of Lycia-Pamphylia. In A.D. 71/72 Vespasian created a huge consular province in central and eastern Anatolia consisting of Cappadocia, Galatia (without Pamphylia) and Armenia Minor. The province of Galatia thus was a product of administrative strategies of the Roman Empire "that showed no consideration for geographical and ethnographic boundaries but comprised the territory of Amyntas that had been created more or less arbitrarily. It was created on the basis of technical administrative reasons. It was inhabited by Paphlagoninas, Galatians, Phrygians, Pisidians, Isaurians, Lycaonians and Pamphylians, as well Roman colonists."[100] The Roman legates of the first century were Fronto (A.D. 25/26 or 29/30), Silvanus (A.D. 29/30-33/34), Titus Helvius Basila (A.D. 33-39), M. Annius Afrinus (between A.D. 49 and 54), L. Nonius Calpurnius Asprenas (A.D. 68/69-69/70) and Cn. Pompeius Collega (A.D. 76).[101] An inscription found in the temple of Roma and Augustus in Ancyra documents the governors under Tiberius.[102] The procurator M. Annius Afrinus evidently was the first Roman governor since the campaigns of P. Sulpicius Quirinius against the Homonadeis (between 6 B.C. and A.D. 4) who visited southern Galatia: he is mentioned on coins minted in Iconium, and he erected an inscription honoring Claudius in Lystra.[103]

The organization of the province of Galatia in 25 B.C. initiated a process of a thorough Hellenization of the Celtic tribes of Galatia, resulting in an increased urban culture in the region, particularly in northern Galatia, the heartland of the Celts. The old mountain fortresses of the Galatian princes were abandoned, and under Augustus the first larger urban centers were established. Pessinus (mod. Balıhisar), Ancyra and Tavium (mod. Büyük

---

1986; Rankin 1987; Brandt 1992, 96-100; Hansen 1994; Riesner 1994, 243-48; S. Mitchell 1995a, 2:151-57; J. M. Scott 1995, 181-201; Breytenbach 1996, 105-12; Strobel 1996; Bechard 2000, 233-79.

[100]Breytenbach 1996, 111.

[101]See Rémy 1988, 96-97; Stumpf 1991, 166-70. I follow S. Mitchell (1995a, 2:154), who interprets Q. Petronius Umbrinus as legate of the province of Lycia-Pamphylia; cf. Şahin, *EA* 24 (1995): 35.

[102]*CIG* 4039 = *OGIS* II 533; for discussion see S. Mitchell 1986.

[103]S. Mitchell 1995a, 1:79, with reference to Aulock 1976, nos. 253-256, and *MAMA* VIII 53.

Nefes Köy) were rebuilt as proper cities. Veterans of the Roman army were settled in Germa (mod. Babadat),[104] which became a *colonia.* Kinna (mod. Karahamzılı), about 80 km south of Ancyra, became a polis in the second century. The second factor that changed the life of the population of northern Galatia was the network of Roman roads that was expanded under the Flavians (i.e., after A.D. 69) to facilitate communication with the eastern border of the empire at the upper Euphrates River. The Roman road in north Galatia, running from west to east, linked Juliopolis, Ancyra and Tavium. North-south roads linked Gangra, Ancyra, Germa and Pessinus, and Ancyra, Aspona and Parnassus.[105] Archaeological discoveries show that smaller towns were established that owed their wealth and in many cases their existence to the network of Roman roads.[106] Some of the cults that are attested in Galatia are linked with Celtic names,[107] which does not mean, however, that the cult had a Celtic character: the inscriptions correspond to local Anatolian patterns that were connected with Celtic place or personal names. Most cults were Phrygian in origin.[108] Zeus and Men are mentioned quite often, usually connected with a local name.

As Paul and Barnabas traveled from Attaleia (or Perge) to Antiocheia, they passed through several cities that were located on the Via Sebaste.

Lyrba (mod. Orenkale, Varsak),[109] 13 km northwest of Perge at a road junction. A road further to the east runs directly to Komama; a more westerly route follows the road to Kibyra and Laodikeia and turns north about 2 km north of Termessos.

Ariassos (mod. Üçkapzı)[110] minted coins that document local games (*themides*). An inscription attests the worship of Zeus Megistos (*I. Pisidia* 119). Remains include the city walls, the aqueduct, a Christian basilica and the necropolis. We do not know when the church in Ariassos was established.

Komama (mod. Serefönü, Ürkütlü)[111] minted coins in the late Hellenistic period. The city probably was the capital of the region of Milyadum (Cicero, *Verr.* 1.95). Augustus refounded the city in 6 B.C. as a colony (Colonia Iulia Augusta Prima Fida Comama), probably not to keep the rebellious Pisidians in check, as some scholars assume (the city was not fortified), but as an economic center that could disseminate Roman influence in the region. In the second century A.D. Komama had between 6,000 and 9,000 inhabitants, in-

---

[104]See S. Mitchell 1995a, 1:87; cf. Robert 1962, 171-201, 377-413.

[105]See the maps in *RECAM* (appendix), and TIB 4 (appendix).

[106]See Mitchell, *RECAM* 15.

[107]*RECAM* 191 (Zeus Souolibrogenos), 203-204 (Zeus Bussurigios).

[108]Mitchell, *RECAM* 16 (introduction); see also ibid. on no. 201.

[109]W. Ruge, PW 13.2 (1927): 2498; S. Mitchell 1995a, 1:172; idem, *BAGRW* 1001.

[110]G. Hirschfeld, PW 2.1 (1895): 821-22; Bean, *PECS* 92; Magie 1950, 2:1317; Levick 1967, 15, 20; Armin Schulz, "Ariassos: Eine hellenistisch-römische Stadt in Pisidien," in Schwertheim 1992, 29-41; S. Mitchell 1995a, 1:196, 218 n. 139, 225. Inscriptions: *I. Pisidia* 109-137. The localization of Ariassos has been confirmed on the basis of a founders' inscription dated to A.D. 238 (*IGR* III 422 = *I. Pisidia* 117).

[111]B. Levick, PWSup 11 (1968): 859-71; G. E. Bean, *PECS* 460; Magie 1950, 1:462-63; 2:1323; Levick 1967, 20, 33, 39, 41, 48, 50-51, 94, 145-48, 188, 222. S. Mitchell 1995a, 1:90; 2:154. One of the original milestones of the Via Sebaste was found in Komama (*CIL* III 6974).

cluding 1,000 veterans. Among other deities, the inhabitants worshiped a veiled (Anatolian) goddess. Hardly any remains survive. About 15 km south of Komama was *Sibidunda* (mod. Bozova, former Zivint), where an inscription discovered in 1960 is (probable) evidence for a Jewish community.[112] Near Kozluca, 32 km north of Komama, the missionaries would have passed by a temple of Roma and Augustus.

Lysinia (Λυσινία; mod. Kayakent),[113] situated on the northwestern end of Lake Askanius (mod. Burdur Gölü), is mentioned for the first time by Polybius in connection with events of the second century B.C. (21.36.2). Lysinia minted coins and is attested on inscriptions.

Several cities between Komama and Lysinia, located a short distance off the Via Sebaste, would have been worthwhile goals of a more intensive missionary work in the area. *Kolbasa* (mod. Kuşbaba),[114] about 20 km northwest of Komama, is attested by coins that depict local games. *Kormasa* (mod. Gavur Ören, Boğaziçi),[115] about 20 km northwest of Komama, is first mentioned in connection with the march of Manlius in 189 B.C. (Polybius 21.36). Even though army veterans were stationed in the city, it evidently was never fortified with walls. *Tymbrianassos* (mod. Ören, Düver),[116] about 15 km north of Kormasa, situated a short distance after the junction of the road that branched off into the Lykos and Maeander Valley, was a village that belonged to an imperial estate.

Ilyas (ancient name unknown),[117] on the west side of Lake Burdur on the Pisidian-Pamphylian border, evidently was one of the more important cities of the region, considering the quality of the inscriptions and the stones used in the buildings. Visible remains include the ruins of a small temple and a gate with three arches.

Eudoxiopolis (probably mod. Keçiborlu),[118] 23 km north of Ilyas on the Via Sebaste, was an old city situated at the junction of several roads. The city is attested on a Roman milestone dated A.D. 198 (*CIL* III 14201). About 8 km south of Eudoxiopolis was *Baris* (mod. Farı mevkii, near Kılıç),[119] a city mentioned by Pliny (*Nat.* 5.42.147: "the region of the Milyae who live around Baris"). The site is covered with pieces of pottery, and coins mention local games. The bishop Pollion of Baris attended the Council of Nicea in A.D. 325. There is no information about when the church was established.

---

[112]*SEG* XIX 852; on the interpretation of the inscription, which mentions *Theos Hypsistos,* see Trebilco 1991, 136; S. Mitchell 1995a, 2:49.

[113]W. Ruge, PW 14.1 (1928): 40-41; H. Treier, *KP* 3:842; P. Weiss, *DNP* 7:609; Jones 1937, 130-31, 144; Magie 1950, 2:1158; G. E. Bean, *AnSt* 9 (1959): 78-81; idem, *PECS* 538; Levick 1967, 19, 39.

[114]S. Mitchell 1995a, 2:64. On neighboring Palaiopolis see idem, 1:218 n. 139.

[115]Magie 1950, 2:1138; G. E. Bean, *PECS* 462; S. Mitchell 1995a, 1:73. The identification of the site with Kormasa is confirmed by an inscription found in Boğaziçi (*SEG* XIX 777). Horsley and Mitchell discuss a possible identification with Ëgneş (*I. Pisidia,* 2).

[116]Magie 1950, 2:1326; G. E. Bean, *AnSt* 9 (1959): 84-85, no. 30; Levick 1967, 49-50; S. Mitchell 1995a, 1:67, 157.

[117]Ramsay 1895-1897, 1:322-23, 332-33; Bean, *AnSt* 9 (1959): 81-82; idem, *PECS* 408; Belke and Mersich 1990, 279.

[118]Ruge, PW 6.1 (1907): 929; Belke and Mersich 1990, 250, 297; Levick 1967, 39 n. 2.

[119]Magie 1950, 2:761; Levick 1967, 15, 54; Belke and Mersich 1990, 206; S. Mitchell 1995a, 1:225.

Apollonia (later Soziopolis; mod. Uluborlo),[120] about 20 km north of Eudoxiopolis, was situated west of Lake Eğridir on the western branch of the Via Sebaste, on a high rock in a commanding position. The city was founded by the Seleucid king Antiochos I. (294-261 B.C.); the Roman city was located on the slope beneath the fortress. Remains include buildings from the Roman imperial period. Inscriptions document a customs post in Apollonia, which was the last city of the province of Galatia before reaching the border of the province of Asia in Apameia.[121] Augustus settled veterans in Apollonia, but the local population was too strong or too influential to transform the city into a Roman colony. The citizens worshiped Men Askaenos, besides other deities, and had a temple dedicated to the worship of the emperor.

Tymandos (Τύμανδος; mod. Mandos),[122] on the river Hippophoras (Pupa Çayı) about 2 km east of the Via Sebaste. The city belonged originally to Phrygia but later was incorporated into Pisidia. A temple of Apollo is attested for Tymandus. Several manuscripts of the acts of the Council of Nicea mention a bishop Quintus of Tymandos.

Evangelism in Antiocheia

Paul and Barnabas preached the gospel in the summer of A.D. 46 in Antiocheia. As we have seen, Antiocheia belonged to the region of Phrygia; since it was located near the border to Pisidia, it was called "Pisidian Antiocheia" (*Antiocheia ad Pisidiam*). Augustus had refounded the city as a colony and settled army veterans here. Antiocheia was the most important colony in the south of the province of Galatia, in military, economic and political respects. This is one of the reasons why Antiocheia was the center of the imperial cult in the region.[123]

Antiocheia ('Αντιόχεια; mod. Yalvaç [see fig. 30])[124] was founded under Seleukos I Nikator (358-281 B.C.) or Antiochos II (261-246 B.C.) by Greek colonists from Magnesia on the Maeander (Strabo 12.8.14). The new city was intended to safeguard Seleucid interests

---

[120]G. Hirschfeld, "Apollonia 21," PW 2.1 (1895): 116; Magie 1950, 1:457, 463; 2:1315 n. 20; Levick 1967, 14-15, 17-18, 39, 124; Belke and Mersich 1990, 387-88; Price 1984, 270; G. Cohen 1995, 285-90; S. Mitchell 1995a, 1:20, 68, 77, 90-91, 104; 2:25; Witulski 2000, 186-87.

[121]*CIL* III Suppl. 12255 = *ZPE* 18 (1975) 13-14 = *I. Laodikeia* 102.

[122]W. Ruge, PW 7.A2 (1948): 1733-35; Belke and Mersich 1990, 408-9; S. Mitchell 1995a, 2:11 n. 6. Mandos lies 2 km southwest of Yassıören.

[123]See Witulski 2000, 189-90.

[124]G. Hirschfeld, "Antiocheia 15," PW 1.2 (1894): 2446; B. Levick, "Antiocheia 15 (Pisid.)," PW-Sup 11 (1968): 49-61; idem, *PECS* 60-61; S. Mitchell, *ABD* 1:264-65; idem, "Antioch 2," *OCD* 107; P. Weiss, "Antiocheia 5," *DNP* 1:765; B. W. R. Pearson, *DNTB* 31-34; Belke and Mersich 1990, 185-88; Ramsay 1907, 247-314; Jones 1937, 128-33; Magie 1950, 1:457-60, 464, 470; 2:1282-83, 1315-16 n. 21, 1319-20; Levick 1967, 18, 33-46, 72-78, 93-104, 111-29, 130-44; Brandt 1992, 61, 109-10, 123, 126, 128, 130-33, 139, 143, 145, 158; G. Cohen 1995, 278-81; S. Mitchell 1995a, 1:20, 38, 73-77, 89-90, 150-51, 70, 74-75, 78, 104, 178, 200, 228; 2:6-10, 35; Syme 1995, 224-41; J. Taylor 1995, 1200-1210; Breytenbach 1996, 45-50, 160-62; Taşlıalan 1997; Mitchell and Waelkens 1998; M. Christol and T. Drew-Bear, "Antioche de Piside capitale provinciale et l'oeuvre de M. Valerius Diogenes," *Antiquité Tardive* 7 (1999): 39-71; MacMullen 2000, 7, 9-10, 19-20, 27; Witulski 2000, 193-215; Taşlıalan 2001a; 2001b. See <http://www.pisidian.com>.

against the indigenous tribes. Antiocheia was a polis with demos, boule, strategoi and grammateis by 200 B.C. The city was supplied with water from the foothills of the Sultan Dağları via an aqueduct and clay pipes, conducting the water into large reservoir. The aqueduct, of which eleven arches have been preserved, began 11.5 km north of the city and evidently dates to the Hellenistic period. After the death of King Amyntas in 25 B.C., when much of eastern Phrygia and Pisidia was incorporated in the new Roman province of Galatia, Antiocheia was one of the cities that was refounded by Augustus as a Roman military colony (Cassius Dio 53.26.3); besides Antiocheia there were the cities of Cremna, Komama, Olbasa, Parlais and Lystra in Lycaonia. The refounding of Antiocheia as a Roman colony surely served military and strategic purposes rather than the goal of bringing Roman civilization into a region in which Hellenization allegedly had failed.[125] The official name of the city was Colonia Caesarea Antiocheia. Antiocheia was the starting point of the Via Sebaste, constructed in 6 B.C., which ran in the west via Lake Hoyran (Hoyran Gölü) via Apollonia to Lake Askania (Burdur Gölü) and to Komama in Pamphylia, and in the east via Neapolis via Mistea to Lystra and Iconium. Antiocheia was situated on a hill (785 by 990 m) that was part of the foothills of the Sultan Dağları, on the west bank of the Anthius River (mod. Yalvaç Çayı) between Lake Eğridir and Lake Akşehir (79 km southeast of mod. Afyon). A territory of about 1,400 km^2 (540 sq. mi.) belonged to the city, which occupied 46.5 ha (115 acres). Over fifty villages have been documented near Antiocheia.

The prominent temple of Men in which the Phrygian moon-god was worshiped until the fourth century A.D., located on Mount Karakuyu ("Black Well" [1,580 m]) about 4.5 km southeast of Antiocheia, belonged to the city territory.[126] The sanctuary, towering 400 m above the plain below, measured 72 by 43 m and was surrounded by colonnaded halls (sixty-six columns). Statues and votive steles covered with inscriptions stood on the paved plaza. The temple building proper, surrounded by thirty columns and accessed on the southwest side via ten steps, measured 18.5 by 8.6 m and consisted of three rooms. There was also a smaller temple (14.8 by 7.7 m), a stadium and dozens of houses that served as living quarters for the temple personnel and provided space for cultic meals and banquets. The temple of Men attracted worshipers from the wider region; attested are visitors from Synnada, Sagalassos and Adada.[127] The temple of Men and its territory, including the temple slaves, were placed under the control of a *curator acrae sanctuarii* in connection with the establishment of the Roman colony in Antiocheia.

Barbara Levick estimates that about three thousand veterans were settled in Antiocheia, a city that may have had some ten thousand inhabitants.[128] The high number of Italian immigrants is attested by the numerous Latin inscriptions (*CIL* III 6803-6865). Augustus stationed in Antiocheia and vicinity the Tenth Legion, a cavalry regiment (*ala Augusta Germaniciana*) and a cohort. A cavalry regiment, the *ala Antiochensium*, evidently was conscripted in Antiocheia.[129] The city was divided into seven districts in analogy to the city of Rome. The districts can no longer be identified in the city plan because the relevant inscriptions were not discovered *in situ:* the *vici* Venerius, Velabrus, Tuscus, Cermalus and

[125]See Brandt 1992, 110, contra Levick 1967, 51.

[126]See Mitchell and Waelkens 1998, 37-90.

[127]See Brandt 1992, 147-48, referring to *WE* 366, 373, 374, 376; for the comment that follows above see the inscription *CIL* III 6839-40.

[128]See Levick 1967, 93-94.

[129]See M. Christol and T. Drew-Bear, "Vétérans et soldats légionnaires à Antioche en Pisidie," in *Actes di IXe Rencontre franco-italienne sur l'épigraphie du monde romain 1995* (Rome: École française de Rome, 1999).

Salutaris derive their names from Rome's topography, and the *vici* Aedilicius and Patricius also are Roman.[130] Evidently Antiocheia was supposed to be a new Rome at the border of Phrygia and Pisidia.[131] New Roman settlers were incorporated in the *tribus Sergia;* a *tribus Romana* is also attested, which shows that the city was not only divided into Roman *vici* but also into Roman "tribes." The Italian colonists who settled in the Seleucid city after 25 B.C. presumably were given the confiscated lands of the temple of Men.[132] As a Roman city, Antiocheia had the usual institutions; the Greek *boule* was replaced by an *ordo decurionum.*[133] At the top of the city government were the *duoviri,* who since Caesar were the highest municipal magistrates as *duoviri de iure dicundo.* They were elected for one year from the decuriones, although they could be reelected (often after an interval). The older of the *duoviri* enjoyed seniority.[134] These highest magistrates were sometimes called, together with the two aediles that each had, *quattuorviri.* Luke's mention in Acts 13:50 of "the leading men of the city" (οἱ πρῶτοι τῆς πόλεως, *hoi prōtoi tēs poleōs*) refers to these members of the local aristocracy. The lower levels of Roman local government are attested in Antiocheia as well, the quaestors and the aediles,[135] as well as *grammateis* and *gymnasiarchai.*[136] Latin was spoken at official functions, such as occasions when the emperor, members of the local government or private persons were honored; for "private" communication Greek was spoken, particularly in religious contexts in which people sought "direct communication with the deity," and on tombstones whose inscriptions expressed the feelings of the surviving relatives.[137]

In the first half of the first century A.D., perhaps already in 2 B.C.,[138] an imperial temple dedicated to Augustus, emperor and founder of the colony, was built in the city center, at the eastern end of the *Tiberia Platea.*[139] Visitors entered the temple through a monumental gate with three arches and an inscription whose translation reads, "For the emperor Caesar Augustus, son of a god, pontifex maximus, consul for the 13th time, with tribunician power for the 22nd time, imperator for the 14th time, father of the country."[140] The sanctuary consisted of a large area (83 by 66 m) flanked by colonnaded halls 4.8 m

---

[130]Levick 1967, 76; Mitchell and Waelkens 1998, 8-9, 99-100, 222 (list with the epigraphical evidence); cf. MacMullen 2000, 13.

[131]Levick 1967, 78; Mitchell and Waelkens 1998, 9.

[132]Levick 1967, 51; Eugene N. Lane, "Men: A Neglected Cult of Roman Asia Minor," *ANRW* II.18.3 (1990): 2161-74; Brandt 1992, 109.

[133]Levick 1967, 76-7; idem, PWSup 11 (1968): 53-54.

[134]W. Waldstein, "Duoviri," *KP* 2:176-78, esp. 178.

[135]*ILS* 7199, 7200, 7202; *CIL* III 6845 (quaestors); *CIL* III 6833, 6839 (= *ILS* 7199, 7200).

[136]Levick 1967, 73, 82; MacMullen 2000, 141 n. 25.

[137]Levick 1967, 136.

[138]See Taşlıalan 2001b; Witulski 2000, 194; also Stephen Mitchell (see Witulski 2000, 194 n. 111, with reference to a communication by letter dated December 10, 1996).

[139]See Mitchell and Waelkens 1998, 113-73 (plan and reconstruction, figs. 23, 25); cf. the reconstruction of the temple in Taşlıalan 1997, 17. See also Klaus Tuchelt, "Bemerkungen zum Tempelbezirk von Antiochia ad Pisidiam," in *Beiträge zur Altertumskunde Kleinasiens* (FS K. Bittel; ed. R.M. Boehmer and H. Hauptmann; Mainz: Zabern, 1983), 501-22; Tuchelt, however, interprets the temple as a sanctuary dedicated to Men and Cybele; against this interpretation see Mitchell and Waelkens 1998, 157-67. On the imperial cult in Antiocheia see recently Witulski 2000, 193-215.

[140]Latin text: IMP • CAES[ARI • DI]VI • [F • A]VGVSTO • PONTI[F]ICI • M[AXIM]O COS • X[III • TRIB]VN[ICIAE] POTESTATIS • XXII • [IM]P • XIIII • P [• P •]. See Mitchell and Waelkens 1998, 147.

wide, which ended on the east side in a semicircular two-storied colonnaded hall (33 m in diameter, about 7 m high) that was built into the rock. The temple building proper stood exactly at the center of the semicircle on a platform (26 by 15 m) that was reached via twelve steps. The *cella* was reached by three further steps; in front of the *cella* stood four columns and probably an additional column on the right and on the left sides. The *cella* (12 by 10 m) was 8.9 m high (30 Roman feet) and consisted of a single room in which presumably a larger than life-sized statue of Augustus stood.[141] The architectural execution of the temple with its columns, architraves, friezes and sculptures depicting, among other motifs, defeated barbarians, was meant to constantly remind the citizens of the fact that Augustus, to whom the temple was dedicated, guaranteed the empire and the city a time of prosperity and security through his victories, family and rule. The feast that L. Calpurnius Longus donated to the city, perhaps around A.D. 50, may have been connected with the imperial cult.[142] The inscription that was erected to commemorate this occasion reads, "For Lucius Calpurnius, the son of Calpurnius Paullus, from the *tribus* Sergia, the priest, who was the first to promise the citizens of Antiochia from the overflowing harvest a festival [*munus*], who erected in two months [or: for a two-month period] a wooden amphitheater [*amphitheatrum ligneum*], who donated daily animal hunts of all kinds [*venationes cotidie omis generis*] and perfumed rain[143] and who had 26 [36] pairs of gladiators [*gladiatorum paria*] perform for eight days and who donated a free meal to the people [*cenam populo dedit*] for the completion of the festival." However, Men Askaenos remained the main deity of the city, whose description as τύραννος [*tyrannos*] expressed the conviction that he had absolute power over all areas of life, and whose description as σωτήρ [*sōtēr*] expressed the fact that many worshipers experienced him as "savior."[144] Other deities that are attested in Antiocheia are Asclepius, Demeter/Ceres, Dionysus, Zeus/Jupiter and Mercurius.[145]

The colony Antiocheia occupied the fourth place in Pisidia in the first century, after Selge, Termessos and Sagalassos, as far as the urban infrastructure was concerned. The city wall, possibly financed from imperial coffers, surrounded the entire city. The two main streets—the *Cardo Maximus* and the *Decumanus Maximus*—divided Antiocheia into three parts. The main entrance to the city was in the west; the monumental gate, with its four columns and three driveways, was dedicated in A.D. 129 to Hadrian and Sabina. People reached the city center on a main street that ran uphill; it was between 6 and 7.5 m wide, and semicircular stepped stone basins brought water down the middle of the street in decorative waterfalls. After 90 m the street turned right onto the *Decumanus Maximus,* passed after 120 m the theater that was to the left,[146] and reached after 200 m

---

[141]Mitchell and Waelkens 1998, 165, referring to the fragment of a huge foot with a sandal, discovered in 1924; for the comment that follows above see ibid., 164-66.

[142]Witulski 2000, 204-15, for the text and a translation of the inscription see 204-5. Editio princeps: W. M. Ramsay, "Studies in the Roman Province of Galatia VI," *JRS* 14 (1924): 172-205; see also *AE* (1926): 78; L. Robert, *Les gladiateurs dans l'Orient grec* (Amsterdam: Hakkert, 1940), 140, no. 92; Mitchell and Waelkens 1998, 224-25, no. 7.

[143]Witulski 2000, 205 n. 180, explains that this is a reference to "fragrant herbs that were strewn on the floor of the arena in order to mask the smell of the animal urine and excrement."

[144]On Men Tyrannos see Lane, *CMRDM* III, 76; on Men Soter see *CMRDM* I, 41, 72, 88, 91-92, 105, 107. See Breytenbach 1996, 161.

[145]Magie 1950, 1:470; Levick 1967, 55, 85-88, 97, 99, 125.

[146]In the course of the renovation of A.D. 311, during which the theater was enlarged, a tunnel was erected above the *Decumanus Maximus,* 56 m long and 8 m wide, to create space for additional rows of seating above the *Decumanus.*

the *Cardo*. The *Cardo Maximus* was the larger of the two main streets: it was a total of 400 m long and between 5 and 6 m wide. Continuing north on the *Cardo*, one reached after 70 m the *Tiberia Platea*, located on the right side of the *Cardo*.[147] The *Tiberia Platea* was a street 30 m wide and 85 m long, flanked by colonnaded halls in which small bars and restaurants evidently were accommodated. An inscription that was discovered in 1924 shows that both main streets of the city, together 880 m (2,973 ft.) long, were paved, or financed, in the first or second quarter of the first century A.D. by a certain T. Baebius T. f. Sergia Asiaticus.[148] In the north the *Decumanus* opened out into an elongated square (30 by 120 m), with a monumental nymphaeum at the northern end; this evidently is the square that was called *Augusta Platea*, the forum of the Roman colony.[149] West of the city, just outside the walls, was the stadium (190 by 30 m), which dated probably to the Hellenistic period.[150] Benefactions of the local elite seemed to have been rare: we hear of the donation of a weighhouse and of the promise of a landowner to donate an amphitheater (nothing is known about whether he fulfilled his promise). Hartwin Brandt observes, "The tradition of euergetism possibly was less important in Antiochia, with its Roman character, than in the Greek poleis."[151] The major phase of construction in Antiocheia was between 25 B.C. and A.D. 68; it appears that there was little building activity in the late first century and the second century, the period when urban development flourished in the Roman Empire.

Antiocheia's elite was represented in the senatorial families of the Caristanii and the Sergii, the *homines novi* who descended from the Italian colonists and who had succeeded in entering the *ordo senatorius* after serving as knights and officers.[152] The Sergii owned large amounts of land, with extensive property in Lycaonia and in western Galatia. C. Caristanius Fronto, who came from Antiocheia, was appointed senator in A.D. 73/74 as *adlectus in senatum inter tribunicios;* in A.D. 81-83 he was imperial legate of the province Lycia-Pamphylia, and in A.D. 90 he became consul.[153] He was married, as was mentioned above, to Sergia Paulla, who belonged to the family of the Sergii and who was the daughter or sister of L. Sergius L. f. Paullus, who probably was the son of L. Sergius Paullus, the proconsul whom Paul met on Cyprus.[154] Other leading families of the city that had estates in the vicinity included the Munatii, the Flavonii and the Iulii, as well as a certain Dottius Marullinus, an influential citizen who was officially honored in an inscription.[155] The relatively high number of senators from Antiocheia in the late first century and particularly

---

[147]Mitchell and Waelkens 1998, 218-21, with discussion of the two relevant inscriptions; first published by W. M. Ramsay, *JRS* 6 (1916): 106, no. 6; *JRS* 14 (1924): 17-205, no. 6.

[148]Latin text: T. Baebius T. f Ser(gia) / Asiaticus / aed(ilis) / III (mil) pedum d(e) s(ua) p(ecunia) / stravit. See Mitchell and Waelkens 1998, 150-51, 221. Editio princeps: D. M. Robinson, *TAPA* 57 (1926): 235, no. 71. The inscription was executed with bronze letters attached to the stone block.

[149]Mitchell and Waelkens 1998, 100-101, 220-21.

[150]Thus M. Taşlıalan; see Mitchell and Waelkens 1998, 110 n. 3.

[151]Brandt 1992, 110.

[152]See Halfmann 1979, 55.

[153]Brandt 1992, 154-55, with reference to Halfmann 1979, 101 (no. 3), 105 (no. 9), 109 (no. 13).

[154]See Levick 1967, 112.

[155]On the Munatii see *IGR* III 306, an inscription that mentions a certain Q. Munatius Eutyches, a *libertus*, as manager of an estate; see also *WE* 353, 360; *AE* (1967): 502; on the Flavonii, who supplied senators at the time of Marcus Aurelius, see *WE* 360; on the Iulii see *AE* (1960): 35; on Marullinus see *CIL* III 6835-6837; *AE* (1967): 117, no. 45. See Levick 1967, 113-17; Brandt 1992, 126.

in the second century attests to the vitality of the city and demonstrates that the leading citizens of Antiocheia could become rather wealthy. Agriculture played a central role, with the cultivation of wheat, fruit and nuts. In regard to professions, inscriptions of Antiocheia attest physicians, lawyers, teachers, philosophers, poets, actors, dancers, singers, musicians, gladiators, painters, merchants of vegetables and herbs, sellers of pastry.[156]

The existence of a strong Jewish community (Acts 13:14) indicates that the city was attractive for merchants.[157] Since Antiochos III (242-187 B.C. [Josephus, *A.J.* 12.147-153]) Jews lived in Phrygia and in Lydia. The presence of Jews in Antiocheia has not yet been confirmed through archaeological discoveries. Mehmet Taşlıalan, director of the Yalvaç Museum, excavated the large basilica in the western section of Antiocheia between 1985 and 1995 (see below) and is convinced that the synagogue of Antiocheia stood at this site.[158]

Luke devotes a relatively long section to the missionary activity of Paul and Barnabas in Antiocheia (Acts 13:13-52).[159] The central place of the Antiocheia narrative in Acts 13—14 underlines the importance of the episode.[160] Luke uses the mission to Antiocheia to give for the first time an extensive report of Paul's missionary preaching before a Jewish audience in synagogues (Acts 13:16-41[see below §28.3]). The missionaries came into contact with the following people or groups of people:

1. The officials of the synagogue (οἱ ἀρχισυνάγωγοι, *hoi archisynagōgoi* [Acts 13:15]).

2. Jews who meet on the sabbath in the synagogue (Ἰουδαῖοι, *Ioudaioi* [Acts 13:14, 43]), "men of Israel" (ἄνδρες Ἰσραηλῖται, *andres Israēlitai* [Acts 13:16]), "descendants of Abraham's family" (υἱοὶ γένους Ἀβραάμ, *huioi genous Abraam* [Acts 13:26]).

3. Devout proselytes (σεβόμενοι προσήλυτοι, *sebomenoi prosēlytoi* [Acts 13:43]); the adjective *sebomenoi* possibly indicates that the proselytes who became Christians previously had made special contributions for the Jewish community in Antiocheia or that they were in some other way connected with the synagogue. They could be described as "proselytes of the first category."[161]

4. God-fearers (οἱ φοβούμενοι τὸν θεόν, *hoi phoboumenoi ton theon* [Acts 13:16]; οἱ ἐν ὑμῖν φοβούμενοι τὸν θεόν, *hoi en hymin phoboumenoi ton theon* [Acts 13:26]), non-Jews who were a regular part of the synagogue community.

---

[156]Physicians: *SEG* VI 554, 563, 571; XXXI 1171; lawyers: *IGR* III 305; teachers: *WE* 360; philosophers: *ILS* 7777; *AE* (1933): 269; actors: *SEG* VI 562; XXXI 1283; dancers, singers, musicians: *SEG* VI 564; *AE* (1907): 65; a flute player who won competitions: *IG* VII 1776; gladiators: *AE* (1914): 266; painters: Lane, *CMRDM* I 217; merchants of vegetables: *SEG* XXXI 1162; sellers of pastry: Levick, *AnSt* 20 (1970): 43, no. 18.

[157]Thus Levick 1967, 58, 99, 189.

[158]M. Taşlıalan, "Pisidia Antiocheiaşı 1995 yılı çalışmaları," in *VII. Müze Kurtarma Kazıları Semineri: 8-10 Nisan 1996* (Ankara: Ankara Üniversitesi Basimevi, 1997), 221-51; idem 2001.

[159]Pilhofer (1999) is skeptical about the historicity of Luke's report, suggesting that Luke had no personal information at his disposal when he wrote Acts 13; similarly Reinbold 2000, 92-93.

[160]See Buss 1980, 17; Nelson 1982, 52.

[161]Wander 1998, 191, 197.

5. Sympathizers "of the first category": devout Gentile women of "high standing" in the city (τὰς σεβομένας γυναῖκας τὰς εὐσχήμονας, *tas sebomenas gynaikas tas euschēmonas* [Acts 13:50]) who were not part of the regular synagogue community but who were more than sympathetic regarding the Jewish faith.[162] There is solid evidence that aristocratic women in other cities were close to the Jewish faith.[163]

6. Sympathizers "of the second category": Gentile inhabitants of Antiocheia (πᾶσα ἡ πόλις, *pasa hē polis* [Acts 13:44]; τὰ ἔθνη, *ta ethnē* [Acts 13:48]), Greek listeners in the synagogue who did not belong to the regular group of "God-fearers and sympathizers."[164]

7. The "leading men of the city" (οἱ πρῶτοι τῆς πόλεως, *hoi prōtoi tēs poleōs* [Acts 13:50]), the members of the local elite in the municipal aristocracy, people who controlled public life in Antiocheia because of their social standing and the wealth that came from their estates. Luke does not indicate that Paul had contacts with these "leading men." If Paul came to Antiocheia as a result of his encounter with Sergius Paullus, the governor of Cyprus in Paphos, hoping that he could find similar access to the aristocracy of this Roman colony in the border region of Phrygia and Pisidia, the Jews of Antiocheia thwarted the potential of this plan, according to Acts 13:50.[165]

Luke emphasizes four elements in his description of the initial contact of Paul and Barnabas with the Jews in the synagogue: (1) reading from the Torah; (2) reading from the Prophets; (3) invitation of the *archisynagōgos* to Paul to address the worshipers; (4) Paul gives the homily. Lee Levine accepts the scene that Luke describes as credible and comments, "Once again, the synagogue served as an open forum for Jews of different background and persuasions."[166] Luke comments on the reaction to Paul's sermon initially with caution (Acts 13:42-44): Paul and Barnabas are asked to speak again about "these things" (λαληθῆναι αὐτοῖς τὰ ῥήματα ταῦτα) again the next sabbath (εἰς τὸ μεταξὺ σάββατον) in the synagogue (Acts 13:42). Luke does not specify who uttered this invitation. Since he mentions explicitly the dismissal of the visitors in the synagogue (Acts 13:43a), it appears that the two Jewish teachers are asked at the end of the service to come back and present further homilies: the invitation to return evidently is offered by the *archisynagōgos* (cf. Acts 13:15; Codex D wants to eliminate the ambiguity, introducing the Gentiles as those who ask the missionaries when they leave the synagogue to speak to them on the following sabbath). Luke

---

[162]Wander 1998, 197. Contra Wander (190), the text does not state that "the leading men of the city" (τοὺς πρώτους τῆς πόλεως [Acts 13:50]) belonged to the sympathizers of the Jews in Antiocheia.

[163]*CIJ* I 222, 462, 523; Josephus, *B.J.* 2.560; Cassius Dio 67.14.2.

[164]Wander (1998, 197) distinguishes (1) model God-fearers; (2) typical God-fearers; (3) sympathizers of the first category; (4) typical sympathizers; (5) further listeners who were present in the synagogue.

[165]See Breytenbach 1996, 48.

[166]L. Levine 2000, 111; on the historical reliability of the synagogue scenes see ibid., 108-9. On the *archisynagōgos* see also Rajak and Noy 1993.

notes in Acts 13:43b that "many Jews and devout converts to Judaism" (πολλοὶ τῶν Ἰουδαίων καὶ τῶν σεβομένων προσηλύτων, *polloi tōn Ioudaiōn kai tōn sebomenōn prosēlytōn*) "followed" (ἠκολούθησαν, *ēkolouthēsan*) Paul and Barnabas, initially quite literally.[167] Many of the synagogue visitors did not want to wait for the next sabbath; they wanted to learn more details and receive more explanations about Paul's message of Jesus as the Messiah. It seems that people soon were converted to faith in Jesus. Luke states with regard to the people who "followed" Paul and Barnabas that the missionaries "spoke to them and urged them to continue in the grace of God" (τῇ χάριτι τοῦ θεοῦ, *tē chariti tou theou* [Acts 13:43b]), indicating that some of the inquirers accepted the message of the revelation of God's grace in and through Jesus Christ.

On the following sabbath "almost the whole city" (σχεδὸν πᾶσα ἡ πόλις, *schedon pasa hē polis* [Acts 13:44]) gathered together: besides the Jews, proselytes and God-fearers in the synagogue, the whole town wanted to hear what the missionaries had to say. Many scholars interpret Luke's comment that "almost the whole city" gathered in terms of a rhetorical exaggeration, a hyperbolic comment that is meant to show that the missionaries had a large audience.[168] However, the qualification "almost"[169] and the description of the initially ambiguous reaction of the listeners suggest that critical prejudice is in play in the views such as those of Josef Pichler, who asserts that the "exaggerated formulation" creates "an ideal and typical scene that lacks any historical background."[170] Scholars who have never witnessed a mass scene in connection with the work of missionaries perhaps are unable to visualize such an event; however, such lack of experience or knowledge does not suffice to cast doubt on Luke's account. Contrary to the assumption of some scholars,[171] Luke does not assert that all the citizens of Antiocheia gathered in the synagogue. This is a deduction on the basis of the invitation in the synagogue (Acts 13:42) and on the basis of the presence of Jews in the crowd (Acts 13:45). Luke, however, merely depicts a large crowd that gathers "to hear the word of the Lord" (συνήχθη ἀκοῦσαι τὸν λόγον τοῦ κυρίου [Acts 13:44]). The synagogue of Antiocheia has not been located as of yet, but clearly it would not have been able to accommodate the approximately ten thousand inhabitants of the city, who may not even have found space in the theater (before the renovation of A.D. 300). It is not implausible to assume, however, that Paul had the opportunity to speak to a crowd numbering in the thousands within a week of his arrival in Antiocheia: he had arrived in the city possibly with a letter of introduction written by the Roman governor of Cyprus, and

---

[167]As in Acts 12:8, 9; 21:36. See Barrett, *Acts,* 1:654. The assumptions by Pichler (1997, 193) are superfluous.

[168]See Pesch, *Apg,* 2:45; Marshall, *Acts,* 229; Zmijewski, *Apg,* 518; Witherington, *Acts,* 414.

[169]The term σχεδόν (*schedon*) occurs only here and in Acts 19:26; Heb 9:22.

[170]Pichler 1997, 195; similarly Zmijewski, *Apg,* 518.

[171]See Roloff, *Apg,* 209; Pesch, *Apg,* 2:45.

he may well have had contact with the leading aristocratic families in the city during the first days of his visit. The crowd could have gathered in front of the synagogue, or perhaps in the *Tiberia Platea* in front of the temple of Augustus, or in the *Augusta Platea* at the northern end of the *Cardo Maximus,* or perhaps in the theater at the *Decumanus Maximus.*

Luke reports that "the Jews" reacted to the presence of the huge crowd with "jealousy" (ἐπλήσθησαν ζήλου, *eplēsthēsan zēlou*) and that they "contradicted" (ἀντέλεγον, *antelegon*) the proclamation of the missionaries (Acts 13:45). The term "the Jews" may refer to the leading officials of the synagogue. If Paul preached in the synagogue on that second sabbath, then the reference to the "contradiction" may describe a vociferous debate in front of the assembly in the synagogue. Luke further reports that the Jews "blasphemed" (βλασφημοῦντες, *blasphēmountes*) in the course of the debate: presumably they pronounced the curse of the law (Deut 21:22-23) against Jesus, who had been crucified; the missionaries and also Luke as a Christian author would have interpreted this as blasphemy against God himself, who had raised Jesus from the dead.[172]

Paul and Barnabas reacted to the opposition of the Jewish officials by pointing to God's plan of salvation: "It was necessary that the word of God should be spoken first [πρῶτον] to you. Since you reject it and judge yourselves to be unworthy of eternal life, we are now turning to the Gentiles" (Acts 13:46). If the Jews decide to reject and to oppose the word of God, which the missionaries claim to preach, henceforth they will turn to the Gentiles and preach to them. In his next comment Paul explains that such a turn to the Gentiles was prophesied in the Scriptures: "For so the Lord has commanded us, saying, 'I have set you to be a light for the Gentiles, so that you may bring salvation to the ends of the earth'" (Acts 13:47). The Jewish missionaries' preaching to the Gentiles fulfills God's commission to his Servant in Is 49:6, who was expected to restore Israel and to return the exiles to Israel (thus the Septuagint), and who was expected to bring salvation to the nations.[173] The phrase "light for the Gentiles" (φῶς ἐθνῶν, *phōs ethnōn*) in Acts 13:47 describes the messengers of the good news, here Paul and Barnabas.[174]

Wolfgang Stegemann argues that the phrase "light for the Gentiles" refers collectively to Israel, here specifically to the members of the synagogue in Antiocheia whom Paul and Barnabas supposedly regard as "representative of Israel among the nations," themselves included.[175] This interpretation is unconvincing. (1) Paul and Barnabas are the "we" subject of the previous sentence. (2) The phrase "light for the Gentiles" does not imply here

---

[172]Pesch, *Apg,* 2:45, with reference to Gal 3:13; 1 Cor 12:3; also Zmijewski, *Apg,* 518; for the comment that follows above see ibid., 519.

[173]Pesch, *Apg,* 2:46; cf. Bock 1998, 56-57; on the use of Is 49:6 see now Pao 2000, 96-101.

[174]Conzelmann, *Apg,* 86 (ET, 106); Haenchen, *Apg,* 398 (ET, 414); Pesch, *Apg,* 2:46; Schneider, *Apg,* 2:145; Roloff, *Apg,* 209; Buss 1980, 138-39.

[175]Wolfgang Stegemann, "'Licht der Völker' bei Lukas," in Bussmann and Radl 1991, 81-97, esp. 85; followed by Pichler 1997, 260.

a "special commissioning" of Paul and Barnabas; rather, it is a task that has been given to all the messengers of the Messiah. (3) Thus the description of Jesus as "light for the Gentiles" in Lk 2:32 is indeed relevant for Acts 13:47. C. K. Barrett rightly notes, "Paul is a light of the Gentiles only in virtue of the Christ whom he preaches; Christ is a light to the Gentiles as he is preached to them by his servants."[176]

Luke describes the success of the missionaries with a few sentences only: some Gentiles come to faith ("as many as had been destined for eternal life" [Acts 13:48]), not only in Antiocheia but also "throughout the region" (δι᾽ ὅλης τῆς χώρας, *di᾽ holēs tēs chōras* [Acts 13:49]). Paul and Barnabas evidently preached the gospel not only in the city of Antiocheia itself but also in the territory that the city controlled, including over fifty villages.[177]

Luke does not comment on the duration of Paul's stay in Antiocheia. The comment on the success of the misson in Acts 13:48-49 is immediately followed by the observation that the Antiochene Jews succeeded in using "the devout women of high standing" (τὰς σεβομένας γυναῖκας τὰς εὐσχήμονας) to prompt "the leading men of the city" (τοὺς πρώτους τῆς πόλεως) to take action against the missionaries. The "devout women of high standing" were those aristocratic women of Antiocheia who regularly attended the synagogue services, and "the leading men of the city" would have included the *duoviri,* the highest representatives of the local government who belonged to the elite families of Antiocheia and who played an important role in the cult of Men and presumably in the imperial cult as well. The leading Jews of Antiocheia possibly argued that the activities of the missionaries jeopardized the position of the main deity of the city, a development that was unavoidable if worshipers of Men accepted the message of Jesus Christ and followed the missionaries.[178] The "persecution" (διωγμός, *diōgmos*) that was instigated against Paul and Barnabas, eventually causing their departure from the city, seems to presuppose that the missionaries had success on a larger scale: perhaps a significant number of people in Antiocheia had come to faith in Jesus Christ. Luke does not provide any figures concerning the new community of followers of Jesus in this Roman colony. These events indicate, at any rate, that Paul and Barnabas did not spend merely a week in Antiocheia. When they revisit the city a few weeks or months later on their journey back to Syria, Luke reports that "they strengthened the souls of the disciples [μαθηταί, *mathētai*] and encouraged them to continue in the faith" (Acts 14:22), and that they appointed "elders" (πρεσβύτεροι, *presbyteroi*), meaning people responsible for the community of the followers of Jesus Christ (Acts 14:23).

Stephen Mitchell argues that Paul's missionary work in Antiocheia was without

---

[176]Barrett, *Acts,* 1:658.
[177]See Breytenbach 1996, 50.
[178]See Horsley, *NewDocs* 3:30-31; followed by Barrett, *Acts,* 1:660. This connection has been overlooked by Pichler 1997, 263-64.

lasting success, pointing to the fact that with the exception of the apocryphal *Acts of Paul* (*Acta Pauli et Theclae*), there are no documented traces of the presence of Christians in the city before the fourth century.[179] *Acts of Paul* mentions the martyrdom of a Christian woman named Thecla, who had been converted in the course of Paul's mission and is said to have been active as a Christian in Antiocheia. However, arguments from the "silence" of the sources are always precarious. Considering the fact that a church existed in Antiocheia in the first century after A.D. 46, that there were traditions about Christians of Antioch at the end of the second and at the beginning of the third centuries, and that church buildings were erected in the fourth century, the conclusion seems justified that there was a continuous presence of Christians in Antiocheia since the mission of Paul and Barnabas.

Three church buildings are documented in Antiocheia.[180] (1) The church that stood at the site of the temple of Men on Mount Karakuyu was a basilica (22 by 13 m) with a nave flanked by aisles on either side. The fact that the church was built with limestone blocks from the temple and the temenos of the Men sanctuary indicates that it was erected only after the temple of Men was no longer in use. Two large blocks with simple Latin crosses suggest that the church dates to the third century. The first bishop is attested around A.D. 300. (2) The central church of Antiocheia stood west of the *Cardo Maximus* opposite the *Tiberia Platea* in the city center behind a row of shops. The building measures roughly 42 by 25 m and dates probably to the fourth century. (3) The large basilica (Church of St. Paul) at the western edge of the city, measuring 70 by 26 m, is the largest church in the region that has been identified so far. The mosaic of the floor contains a reference to Bishop Optimus, who represented Antiocheia on the Council of Constantinople in A.D. 381. The later phases of the building cannot be dated. Mehmet Taşlıalan, who continued between 1985 and 1995 the earlier excavations of D. M. Robinson (1924), identified the church as Church of St. Paul on the basis of an inscription found on an altar (dating to the sixth century at the earliest);[181] He believes that the church stood at the site of the synagogue, implying that Paul preached at this site in A.D. 46.

After Paul and Barnabas left Antiocheia, they traveled first southeasterly and then in an easterly direction through Lycaonia.

Lycaonia (Λυκαονία)[182] bordered in the east on Cilicia and Cappadocia, in the south and west on Isauria, Pisidia and Phrygia, in the north on Galatia; it extended from Koropassos

---

[179]Mitchell, *ABD* 1:265.

[180]J. Öztürk and S. Mitchell, in Mitchell and Waelkens 1998, 201-18; Belke and Mersich 1990, 187.

[181]Text: [φ]ωνὴ Κ(υρίο)υ ἐπὶ τὸν ὑδά[των] // ' Ι(ησοῦς) Χ[ρίστο]ς Νήκᾳ // ὁ ἅγιος Παῦλος // ὁ ἅγιος Γρηγόρηος. Editio princeps: W. M. Calder, *JRS* 2 (1912): 98, no. 29; B. Pace, *Annuario della Scuola Archeologica di Atene* 3 (1916-1921): 55, no. 43; cf. M. Taşlıalan, "Pisidia Antiocheiası 1995 yılı çalışmaları," in *VII. Müze Kurtarma Kazıları Semineri: 8-10 Nisan 1996* (Ankara: Ankara Üniversitesi Basimevi, 1997), 221-51; idem 1997, 71 (fig.); see also Öztürk and Mitchell, in Mitchell and Waelkens 1998, 215 (with plate 143).

[182]W. Ruge, PW 13.2 (1927): 2253-65; H. Treidler, *KP* 3:807-8; F. F. Bruce, *ABD* 4:424-25; A. J. M. Jones and S. Mitchell, *OCD* 894; K. Belke, *DNP* 7:555-57; Belke 1984, 39-42, 93-110; Restle, in Belke 1984, 43-47; Pekáry 1980, 643; Laminger-Pascher 1984; 1989; idem, "Lykaonien und die Ostgrenze Phrygiens," *EA* 16 (1990): 1-13; idem 1992; S. Mitchell 1995a, 1:7-9, 116, 173-75, 208; 2:151-52, 155; Bechard 2000, 235-353.

(mod. Akhan), Garsaura (Archelais, mod. Aksaray) and Lake Ak in the east to a line running from Tyraion (Ilgın), Laodikeia Katakekaumenē (Ladik), Lystra (Zoldera/Hatunsaray) and Iconium (Konya) in the west.[183] The southern border was marked by the Taurus Mountains; the cities Ilistra, Laranda and Derbe belonged to Lycaonia; in the north the boundary was north of Iconium. Lycaonia did not have a river running to the Mediterranean; the line of the watershed or divide runs on the Taurus. In central Lycaonia was the Great Salt Lake (Tuz Gölü, Lake Tatta); the region to the southwest is salt steppe as far as Iconium. Lake Koralis (Beyşehir Gölü) is, as other lakes in the region, simply a basin collecting water from the rivers and brooks that run from the Taurus in a northerly direction; it is only 9 m deep.[184] Most Lycaonian cities are located in the area of the lakes. After the conquest by Alexander the Great, Lycaonia belonged to the Seleucid Empire, and after 188-133 B.C. to Pergamon. When Pergamon was defeated by the Romans in 133 B.C., and when the province of Asia was organized, the Romans granted the more distant regions to local rulers: Lycaonia was ruled by the sons of the Cappadocian king Ariarathes V. When Cicero was governor of Cilicia in 51 B.C., Antipater of Derbe ruled in eastern Lycaonia and also controlled Laranda as a vassal of the Romans. In 36 B.C. Lycaonia was given, together with Pisidia, to the Galatian king Amyntas; after the death of Amyntas in 25 B.C. Lycaonia remained in the province of Galatia, which Augustus had organized. Under Caligula southern Lycaonia was granted to Antiochos IV, king of Commagene, evidently including the region around Derbe and Laranda—about ten years before Paul and Barnabas visited the area.

Lycaonia is the classical land of the cult of Meter, attested in Çatal Hüyük already in 6780 B.C. In the Roman imperial period well-known cult sites included the sanctuary of Ma in Komama (mod. Ürkütli) and the sanctuary of Meter Zizimeme in Sisma (near Laodikeia Katakekaumenē, mod. Ladik).[185] According to Gertrud Laminger-Pascher, the strong religious attachment to the cult of Meter contributed to the preservation of the ancestral traditions, "to the preservation of the indigenous language as colloquial language, to the preservation of the old clan communities expressed in the numerous terms for the extended group of relatives, to the preservation of the old forms of administration in the village communities by a council of elders, the γεραιοί, as well as to the striking lack of inscriptions, urban decrees, edicts, inscriptions documenting games and victors. We conclude, therefore, that with the exception of the cities, Greek was only the written language and trade language as well as the language of the Christian church."[186] The Lycaonian language of the imperial period derives from a Luwian or Hittite dialect. A funerary inscription from the time of Tiberius (A.D. 14-37) on a limestone block depicting a sitting man and his wife[187] demonstrates that some Lycaonians were of Celtic origin: the identical *gen-*

---

[183]Iconium belonged not to Phrygia, as many have assumed, but to Lycaonia; see Laminger-Pascher 1992, 12; 1989, 6-8, with reference to Strabo 12.6.1; Cicero, *Fam.* 15.1.2; 15.2.1-2; 15.4.24; *Att.* 5.15.1; 5.20.1, 5; 15.21.9; Pliny, *Nat.* 5.25.95.

[184]See Belke 1984, 44.

[185]Laminger-Pascher (1992, 13) believes that the Lycaonian cult of Meter continued in the Christian cult of Mary that originated in Asia Minor.

[186]Laminger-Pascher (1992, 13), who continues, "We need to remember with regard to the lack of indigenous language monuments . . . that the language that people *speak* can only be *written* if they had learned to do that, and that school instruction in Asia Minor existed only in Greek, even in the imperial period, and that the stonemasons who manufactured the tombstones also could write only Greek, not even Latin" (ibid., n. 6).

[187]Text: Ρηγεῖνος Κορνήλιος Ναλημις καὶ Κορνηλία Μεδούσας γυνὴ αὐτοῦ ἀνέστησαν ἑαυτοὺς ζῶντας (*MAMA* VIII 36 = *I. Lykaonien* 232); the block was discovered in Kavak, a village 9 km southeast of Hatunsaray in the territory of Lystra.

tilicium (family name) of Cornelius/Cornelia suggests freed slaves; the patron's name probably was Reginus Cornelius, who was of Celtic origin; the husband, Nalemis, came from Isauria or Lycaonia; his wife, Medussas, also was of Celtic origin—"Reginus" and "Medussas" are Celtic names, while "Nalemis" is an indigenous name from Asia Minor. A recently published *ostotheke* from the region of Lake Trogitis (Suğla Gölü) documents for the second or third century A.D. a family with Roman citizenship that uses indigenous names (Armantos, Lanimanos, Lanimasis, Minnis, Mnimasis, Nannis, Opramobis, Oumen).[188]

Traveling from Antiocheia southeast through the Cillanian Plain, Paul and Barnabas passed through two cities before reaching Iconium.

Neapolis (mod. Iznebolu near Kıyakdede, north of Kıreli),[189] 29 km south of Antiocheia on the Via Sebaste running to Iconium, was situated at the northeastern edge Lake Karalis (Beyşehir Gölü) in the Cillanian Plain. The inscription of a recently published milestone from Kıyakdede dated 6 B.C. mentions Augustus.[190] Neapolis was founded by the Seleucids in the third century B.C. and presumably was a Greek polis. The city was occupied by the Roman Servilius Isauricus. Augustus settled veterans in Neapolis. Inscriptions attest a garrison of *stationarii* on horses who were responsible for the safety of the highways. No archaeological work has been done yet in Neapolis. One inscription documents a temple (*MAMA* VIII 350). The bishop Hesychios of Neapolis attended the Council of Nicea in A.D. 325. It is not known when the church was established.

Pappa (mod. Yunisler),[191] called Pappa-Tiberiopolis during the principate of Emperor Tiberius, also was located on the Via Sebaste between Antiocheia and Lystra. In Pappa a road branched off running south via Mistea (Klaudiokaisareia, mod. Beyşehir) and Etenna (Sırtköy)[192] to the Mediterranean port city Side (Selimiye). No archaeological remains survive except for stones and pagan and Christian inscriptions. One of the deities worshiped in Pappa was Men Askaenos. Inscriptions document that the highest position in the city was the office of priest of the imperial cult (*MAMA* III 332, 337), as in other cities. Since the time of Antoninus Pius (second century) at the latest Pappa had official (*homonoia*) relations with Antiocheia.

Evangelism in Iconium

Luke provides a brief account of the missionary activity of Paul and Barnabas in Iconium (Acts 14:1-7).

---

[188]Ebru Akdoğu Arca, "Epigraphische Mitteilungen aus Antalya III: Inschriften aus Lykaonien im Museum von Side," *EA* 31 (1999): 53-68 (see 70, no. 2).

[189]W. Ruge, "Neapolis 12," PW 16.2 (1935): 2126-27; E. Olshausen, "Neapolis 8," *KP* 4:32; idem, "Neapolis 7," *DNP* 8:775; Magie 1950, 2:1316-17; Robert 1962, 415; Levick 1967, 15, 39; G. Cohen 1995, 348-49; S. Mitchell 1995a, 1:85, 90, 122, 151, 157, 214. The earlier identification with Sarkıkaraağaç is erroneous; see S. Mitchell 1995a, 1:90 n. 109; contra Belke and Mersich 1990, 347, with the older identification. On the Cillanian Plain see S. Mitchell 1995a, 1:90, 157, 162.

[190]D. H. French, "Inscriptions in the Museums of Akşehir and Yalvaç," *EA* 29 (1997): 59-65, no. 3.

[191]W. Ruge, PW 18.3 (1949): 1130-31, 1360 n. 25; Belke and Mersich 1990, 355; Magie 1950, 1:463, 500; 2:1173; Levick 1967, 14, 39, 126, 165; S. Mitchell 1995a, 1:78, 95, 117; 2:25.

[192]On Etenna see W. Ruge, PW 6.1 (1909): 706-7; G. E. Bean, *PECS* 319-20; P. Weiss, *DNP* 4:159; Nollé 1992, inscription nos. 110-134.

Iconium ('Ikóviov; mod. Konya)[193] was an important city in the southern highlands of central Anatolia, the most important assize center in western Lycaonia, situated at the juncture of several important roads. Iconium is attested as a Phrygian city as early as 400 B.C. After being ruled by Lysimachos, the Seleucids and the kings of Pergamon, Iconium was incorporated by Pompey into the province of Cilicia. Cicero stayed in Iconium with his army in 52 B.C. when he received news about the invasion of the Parthians. Cicero regularly visited Iconium on his assize tours.[194] Mark Antony gave the city to the Galatian king Amyntas in 36 B.C. After the death of Amyntas in 25 B.C. Iconium was incorporated into the new province of Galatia. Augustus founded the colony *Iulia Augusta Iconium,* beside which the old polis continued to exist.[195] Iconium minted coins. The cavalry unit stationed in the city is attested by coins.[196] The theater was begun during the reign of Augustus. Emperor Claudius (A.D. 41-54) had considerable influence in the region, attested by the fact that Iconium was allowed to call itself a city. Pliny describes the city as *urbs celeberrima,* the most famous city of a tetrarchy with fourteen communities (*Nat.* 5.25.95).[197] The Roman governor of Galatia, M. Annius Afrinus, visited Iconium between A.D. 49 and 54; he is mentioned on coins of the city. The citizens of Iconium were divided into four tribes that were named after the deities worshiped in the city. Attested are a temple of Zeus Megistos (identified with Jupiter Optimus Maximus), an amphitheater and a stele depicting Perseus and Andromache. The theater, which dates to the Julian-Claudian period, was financed with both imperial and local (private) funds (*IGR* III 262, 1474). Besides Zeus Megistos, Artemis, Apollo, Poseidon, Pluto and Heracles, several Phrygian mother-goddesses were worshiped: one inscription mentions Boethene and the "mother of the gods" besides Apollo and Artemis Angdistis, describing them as "savior" (*MAMA* VIII 297). The imperial cult is attested by the reference to a priest of Tiberius (*IGR* III 1473). Luke's account in Acts 14:1 documents a synagogue.

Paul and Barnabas preached the gospel in Iconium to both Jews and Gentiles: Luke reports that they "went into the Jewish synagogue and spoke in such a way that a great number of both Jews and Greeks became believers" (Acts 14:1). This statement indicates that the missionaries preached in the synagogue to Jews and to sympathizers who were present there, evidently Greeks of the old polis of Iconium ('Ελλήνες, *Hellēnes* [Acts 14:1]). In contrast to Antiocheia, the opposion that forced the missioaries to leave Iconium came not from the local

---

[193]W. Ruge, PW 11.1 (1914): 990-91; A. Müfid Mansel, *KP* 2:1360; K. Belke, *DNP* 5:930; Belke 1984, 176-78; Magie 1950, 1:376, 396-97, 456, 547; 2:1308, 1312; Levick 1967, 4, 39, 78, 99, 154, 165, 183; S. Mitchell, "Iconium and Ninica: Two Double Communities in Roman Asia Minor," *Historia* 28 (1979): 409-38; idem 1995a, 1:64, 67, 73-74, 77, 79, 89-90, 95, 214; 2:3-4, 11-12, 23, 26, 28-29, 35-36, 155-56; Syme 1995, 226-40, 254-55, and passim; J. Taylor 1995, 1211-13; Breytenbach 1996, 50-52, 162-64.
[194]See L. W. Hunter, "Cicero's Journey to the Province of Cilicia," *JRS* 3 (1913): 73-97.
[195]S. Mitchell, *Historia* 28 (1979): 411-25. The Greek polis possibly was integrated into the Roman colony during the time of Hadrian.
[196]Text of the legend: COL E Q ICONIEN = Col[onia] Eq[questris] Iconien[sium]. See S. Mitchell, *Historia* 28 (1979): 414. Hans von Aulock (1976, 56-57, 81), interprets "E Q" as "e(x) [legione] q(uinta) [deducta]"—that is, as a reference to veterans of the *legio V. Gallica.* Breytenbach (1996, 163) follows Mitchell.
[197]Cf. Xenophon, *Anab.* 1.2.19.

Roman aristocracy in the Roman colony of Iconium but from the leading Jews and from Greeks living in the polis.[198] Luke gives no indication about the length of the missionaries' stay in Iconium. His reference to "disciples" and to "elders" that were appointed by Paul and Barnabas during their return journey (Acts 14:21-23) implies that a community of followers of Jesus had been established. When Paul traveled from Jerusalem and Antioch toward the province of Asia in the spring of A.D. 49, before the change of plans and the journey to Macedonia and Achaia, Paul and several coworkers visited the church in Iconium for the second time (Acts 15:41; 16:1). Three years later Paul presumably visited Iconium for the fourth time when he traveled from Syria to Ephesus (Acts 18:23).

One of the earliest larger church synods took place in Iconium between A.D. 220 and 240, with bishops from churches of Galatia, Cilicia and neighboring regions meeting (Cyprian, *Ep.* 75.7.5) to discuss the rebaptism of heretics (Eusebius, *Hist. eccl.* 7.7.5). Bishops of Iconium are documented since the beginning of the third century.[199]

Evangelism in Lystra

The work of the missionaries in Lystra is reported by Luke in Acts 14:8-20 with greater detail because of an incident in which Paul was nearly killed.[200]

Lystra (Λύστρα; mod. Zoldera, 1.5 km northwest of Hatunsaray),[201] about 34 km southwest of Iconium on the Via Sebaste, was founded probably by Augustus in 25 B.C., like Antiocheia, in a town that existed at the site, as a military colony named Colonia Iulia Felix Gemina Lystra, which is why it was called the "sister" ('Αδελφή, *Adelphē*) of Antiocheia; milestones have been discovered in Kavak, 9 km southeast of Hatunsaray. The epithet "Gemina" suggests that members of two legions were stationed in the colony: veterans of the Legio VII and of the Legio IV Macedonica.[202] Both Pliny (*Nat.* 5.42.147) and Ptolemaios (5.4.9) mention Lystra. In Acts 14:6 Luke describes Lystra and Derbe as "cities of Lycaonia." Lystra possibly had twelve *vici*.[203] The Roman governor M. Annius Afrinus probably was in Lystra between A.D. 49 and 54: he had an inscription erected in the city dedicated to Claudius (*MAMA* VIII 53). Coins and inscriptions document the veneration

---

[198]There is epigraphical evidence of a πρῶτος ἄρχων (*prōtos archōn*) in τῆ πόλε[ι τῶν Εἰκονιέων] (*tē polei tōn Eikonieōn* [*CIG* 4001; *IGR* III 262]). See S. Mitchell, *Historia* 28 (1979): 411-16.

[199]In A.D. 1190 Iconium was conquered by the army of the Third Crusade, led by Emperor Barbarossa.

[200]See, besides the commentaries, Breytenbach 1993; 1996; Gempf 1995; Fournier 1997; Stenschke 1999a, 178-93; Bechard 2000, 397-427 (with discussion of E. Haenchen, 400-406); on the question of historicity see Reinbold 2000, 95-99.

[201]Ruge, PW 14.1 (1928): 71-72; K. Belke, *DNP* 7:613; idem 1984, 200; Ramsay 1895-1897, 1:407-18; Magie 1950, 1:456, 463; 2:1320, 1324 n. 41; Levick 1967, 37-41, 51-53, 153-56, 183, 195-97; Laminger-Pascher 1992, 117-25; S. Mitchell 1995a, 1:76-78, 90; Syme 1995, 225-29, 237-38; J. Taylor 1995, 1216-21; Breytenbach 1996, 164-65.

[202]Laminger-Pascher 1992, 118. Coins minted in Lystra at the time of Augustus have the legend IMPE ΛVCVSTI COL IVL FEI CEM LVSTRA, or COL IVL FEL GEM LVSTRA.

[203]The relevant inscription is fragmentary: *JHS* 24 (1904:115, no. 158 = *CIL* III 14400a).

of Augustus, Ceres, Mercurius/Hermes, Minerva and Tyche.[204] The temple of Zeus mentioned in Acts 14:13 fits the information that we have about the worship of Zeus in the neighboring towns of Lystra: the cult of Zeus is attested in Kavak, Balük-Laou, Isaria, Antiocheia and Uasada.[205] More inscriptions have survived of Lystra than of any other colony that Augustus founded in Asia Minor.[206] Most inscriptions are funerary or other private inscriptions. The few official inscriptions include a Latin inscription that honors Augustus, the founder of the colony, probably shortly after his death in A.D. 15,[207] and a Greek inscription that was erected probably by the *vici* of Lystra. There was a direct connection to the Via Sebaste via Kilistra from Lystra running in a northwesterly direction; a road running south connected the city with Isaura Nova (Leontopolis); a road toward the southeast led to the route from Iconium via Barata to Laranda. Lystra's wealth was linked with this strategic location. According to Barbara Levick, Lystra was an active, prosperous city, a market town that paid little attention to its status as a Roman military colony.[208] Ancient and medieval pottery can be found on the site. In the village of Hatunsaray blocks with inscriptions and other ancient remains have been used as building material.

Lystra therefore was not as insignificant as William Ramsay, Barbara Levick and David Magie assumed.[209] (1) The city was not limited to the site of Zoldera, where the discoveries have been made, which should be seen as a fortification at the end of the Via Sebaste. Rather, the territory of Lystra extended as far as Hatunsaray. (2) The distribution of the inscriptions mentioning veterans[210] indicates that the number of veterans who received plots of land was so large that they could not all be accommodated in the colony and were settled on available land in the vicinity. (3) The territory that belonged to the *colonia* of Lystra included towns and villages on the following sites (from north to south): Kilisira, Hayırabat, Sarıkız, Kümse Ciftlik, Kavak, Eksile, Dinorna, Çeşme, Akvıran, Üçkese, Karahüyük Köy, Apasaraycık, Apa, Dineksaray, Alkaran, Balcıkhisar and Dorla.

Luke's account of Paul and Barnabas's missionary work in Lystra consists of three parts:[211]

Following an introductory summary that points to the missionary activity proper, the sequence of events in Acts 14:8-20a comprises three phases:

0.	14:7	Summary: Paul and Barnabas preach the gospel
1.	14:8-10	Healing of a lame man
2.	14:11-18	Misunderstanding of the citizens concerning the missionaries
3.	14:19-20a	Stoning of Paul

---

[204]Levick 1967, 99, 154, 155, 156 n. 3.

[205]See Breytenbach 1996, 32-37.

[206]*I. Lykaonien* 163-212 (Laminger-Pascher 1992, 125-49).

[207]Text: Divum Aug(ustum) / Col(onia) Iul(ia) fe / lix gemina / Lustra [leaf] / conse / cravit/ d(ecreto) d(ecurionum). *CIL* III 6786 = *MAMA* VIII 5 = I. Lykaonien 164. For the Greek inscription mentioned in the following comment see *JHS* 24 (1904) 113 no. 150.

[208]Levick 1967, 154.

[209]Ramsay 1907, 408, 418; Levick 1967, 52-53, 94, 154, 197; Magie 1950, 1:463. For the arguments that follow above see Laminger-Pascher 1992, 122-25.

[210]Veteran inscriptions from the first century A.D.: *CIL* III 6788; *MAMA* VIII 94; cf. *I. Lykaonien* 177, 288, 327.

[211]For the analysis that follows above see Fournier 1997, 56-76.

The rhetorical analysis by Marianne Fournier recognizes in Acts 14:8-20a a chiastic structure with antithetical parallelism, the center of which is a brief sketch of the missionaries' proclamation of the gospel:

A	14:8	Illness of the man
B	14:9-10	Healing through Paul
C	14:11-13	Desire of the citizens to honor the missionaries with sacrifices
D	14:14-15a	Protest of the missionaries
E	14:15b-17	Proclamation
D'	14:18a	Protest of the missionaries
C'	14:18b	Action of the missionaries to stop the citizens from offering sacrifices
B'	14:19	Stoning of Paul
A'	14:20a	Survival of Paul

Luke does not state how long Paul and Barnabas engaged in missionary work in Lystra. Therefore, we cannot link the narrative regarding the lame man chronologically with the course of the missionary activity in Lystra. Luke does not mention a synagogue; we do not know, therefore, where Paul and Barnabas preached. We cannot conclude, however, that therefore no Jewish community existed in Lystra:[212] Luke mentions in Acts 16:1-3 the Jewish mother of Timothy, who came from Lystra; the fact that she was married to a Greek man does not prove, of course, that she was the only Jewish person in the city.

We are given few details concerning the missionary activity of Paul and Barnabas. The reference to the Lycaonian language of the citizens[213] serves to inform the readers of the book of Acts that Paul did not preach only among "Greeks" but also to "barbarians" (cf. Rom 1:14), and that he was active not only in major cult centers such as Antioch, Corinth, Athens and Ephesus but also in rural regions such as the hinterland of Lycaonia.[214] Did Paul preach on the site of the temple of Zeus itself, or did Luke seek to evoke such a scenario? This cannot be deduced from the fact that Paul's preaching of the gospel to the lame man (Acts 14:9-10) is immediately followed by the attempt of the citizens of Lystra to offer sacrifices at the gate of the temple of Zeus, which was located outside of the city walls (Acts 14:11-13).[215] Luke concentrates entirely on the healing of the lame man and on the nearly fatal consequences for the missionaries.[216]

---

[212]Contra Zmijewski, *Apg*, 533.

[213]This is the only comment of this nature made by Luke. See also Bechard 2000, 413 with n. 133.

[214]Bechard 2000, 355-431.

[215]Contra Bechard 2000, 411.

[216]Roloff (*Apg*, 212) overinterprets when he says that Luke "introduces a totally new situation: the mission leaves the influence of the synagogue and turns to pagan people who have not been touched in any way by Israel's faith." There is no evidence that Paul faced a "totally new situation" as a missionary.

The presence of a lame man, presumably a beggar, suggests that Paul may have been preaching in the agora. This is also the place where we should picture the inhabitants who speak Lycaonian (Acts 14:11). The success of the missionary work in Lystra can be inferred from Acts 14:20: the "disciples" (μαθηταί, *mathētai*) whom Luke mentions are the people who have become believers in Jesus through the preaching of the missionaries.[217]

A man who had been crippled from birth listened to the preaching of Paul (ἤκουσεν, *ēkousen* [Acts 14:9a]). Paul saw that the man had the "faith to be made well" (Acts 14:9b NASB).[218] The verb σῴζειν (*sōzein*) signifies in the wider context of the reference to the illness of the man (Acts 14:8) initially "to heal," but in the immediate context of the man listening to the preaching of Paul (Acts 14:9a) it means also, and perhaps primarily, "to save."[219]

Marianne Fournier interprets the faith of the lame man in the context of Acts 14:15b-17 as faith in the living God: the apostles proclaimed God as sovereign and merciful, watching over the nations since creation and permitting them to go their own ways, including their worship of many deities; now, however, the living God requires something new from the nations: to turn away from the gods and acknowledge the presence and the actions of the living God alone. Saving faith is the acknowledgment of this living God. Gentiles who believe in the living God whom Paul preaches are offered salvation, before Jesus is even mentioned.[220] This interpretation makes three assumptions: (1) the rhetorical-literary sequence of the narrative units in Acts 14:8-18 reflects the exact chronological sequence of the events of the mission in Lystra; (2) Paul's address in Acts 14:15-17 is identical with his preaching activity mentioned in Acts 14:9; (3) Paul accepts "saving faith" without reference to Jesus Christ. The first assumption is hypothetical: the comment in Acts 14:9a may describe missionary activity that lasted for several weeks, during which Paul would have spoken of Jesus rather earlier than later. The second assumption demonstrates that it is problematic when rhetorical analyses are separated from the historical context: Paul does not mention Jesus in the speech in Acts 14:15-17 because he is addressing the specific situation in which he and Barnabas are about to be worshiped as gods (not as "saviors," which might prompt a reference to Jesus); in other words, Acts 14:15-17 does not represent a brief summary of the missionary preaching of the apostle. The third assumption is a theological and historical absurdity: for Paul the missionary there is never salvation apart from faith in Jesus Christ.

The initiative for the healing of the lame man is entirely Paul's: he recognized with prophetic insight that the man had come to faith and thus told him, "Stand upright on your feet" (Acts 14:10a). This command prompted the miracle, im-

---

[217]Zmijewski, *Apg,* 540. Jervell (*Apg,* 379) maintains that these Christians were not former pagans. This opinion owes more to Jervell's hermeneutical approach to the book of Acts than to a straightforward exegesis of the text.

[218]Acts 14:9b: ἔχει πίστιν τοῦ σωθῆναι; see BDF §400.2; Barrett, *Acts,* 1:675.

[219]Zmijewski, *Apg,* 534; for the comment that follows above see ibid.; see also Stenschke 1999a, 179-80.

[220]Fournier 1997, 81-84.

mediately, which was demonstrated right away: the man who had been crippled all his life "sprang up and began to walk" (Acts 14:10b).

The citizens of Lystra interpreted the miracle as proof of the supernatural character of the missionaries. They said to each other in Lycaonian: "The gods have come down to us in human form!" (Acts 14:11). They identified Barnabas with Zeus, perhaps because he had a more impressive appearance, and they identified Paul with Hermes, probably because he was the preacher (Acts 14:12). The priest of the Zeus temple that stood outside of the city walls "brought oxen and garlands to the gates; he and the crowds wanted to offer sacrifice" (Acts 14:13). The priest presumably was a member of the the local elite who had assumed the priesthood in the temple of Zeus for a defined period of time.[221] The gates (πυλῶνες, *pylōnes*) to which the priest wanted to bring "oxen and garlands" (ταύροι καὶ στέμματα, *tauroi kai stemmata*) probably were not the city gates but the gates of the temple: there, in the sacred precinct of the temple of Zeus, the sacrifices were to be offered.[222]

There might have been a local reason for this exaggerated reaction by the citizens of Lystra. There was a legend in neighboring Phrygia according to which two local gods, perhaps Tarchunt and Runt (or Pappas and Men), in the Greek version of the legend Zeus and Hermes, wander through the region as human beings. Nobody provides them with hospitality, until Philemon and Baucis, an older couple, share their supplies with the unrecognized gods, who reward the couple richly, eventually transforming them into sacred trees, while judgment falls on the other people (Ovid, *Metam.* 8.626-724). Some scholars suggest that Luke consciously alludes to this legend and has the Lycaonians, who do not want to make the same mistake again, react in the way they do.[223] A fragmentary inscription from Lystra possibly links Zeus, Hermes and perhaps Gē; a relief found in Lystra dedicated to Zeus Ampelites shows Zeus, Hermes and an eagle; in neighboring Sedasa an inscription dating to the third century also links Zeus and Hermes.[224]

The citizens of Lystra interpreted the miracle not as authentication of the missionaries and their message. Rather, they integrated the miracle into their traditional religiosity. They evidently had understood so little of the preaching and teaching of Paul and Barnabas that they saw their polytheistic and mythical traditions confirmed by the miracle.[225]

Barnabas and Paul tore their clothes (Acts 14:14a), a gesture of mourning and

---

[221]Gill (1994a, 82), who refers to *MAMA* VIII 12, an inscription that honors a former member of the magistrate of Lystra who officiated as a priest; for the observation that follows above see ibid., 84-85.

[222]See Bechard 2000, 408-10.

[223]See Lane Fox 1986, 100; Pervo 1987, 64-65; B. Winter 1991, 116, 129; Gill 1994a, 82; Klauck 1996, 73; Bechard 2000, 49-50, 292-301.

[224]*MAMA* VIII 1; L. Robert, *BCH* (1983): 539, 541; W. M. Calder, *Classical Review* 24 (1910): 76-81; cf. Hemer 1989, 111; Gill 1994a, 83-84; Bechard 2000, 49-50.

[225]Stenschke 1999a, 183.

shock.[226] The rushing into the crowd (Acts 14:14b) that accompanied the tearing of the clothes is an expression of self-humiliation. Paul and Barnabas clarified that they are not gods to be worshiped;[227] they are "mortals" just like the citizens of Lystra (Acts 14:15b). If the pagan audience did not sharply distinguish between gods and human beings, the missionaries emphasized this distinction as a corrective critique of their stance. The missionaries continued to explain who they were and what they wanted (Acts 14:15c-17).[228] (1) They bring good news: they themselves are not the message, but only messengers. They assert that it would be foolish to believe that they are somehow different from the inhabitants of Lystra. (2) The gods that are worshiped in Lystra, including Zeus and Hermes, are nothing, useless, deaf.[229] (3) The good news that they proclaim is the message that they no longer have to worship their useless gods because they can return to the only true and living God, who has created everything.

The expression "living God" (θεὸς ζῶν, *theos zōn*) often is used in the Septuagint "when the point is to emphasize the power of God over against the idols," particularly in narratives in which the heroes of Israel defeat their enemies with the power of the living God, the authors underlining the fact "that the κύριος as the living God is at the same time the only God."[230] The confession of faith in the one true and living God is the very foundation of the Jewish faith, not least in Diaspora Judaism.[231] According to the apocryphal text Bel and the Dragon, when Cyrus, king of the Persians, asked Daniel why he refused to worship Bel, Daniel answered, "Because I do not revere idols made with hands, but the living God, who created heaven and earth and has dominion over all living creatures" (Bel 5). The predicate "living" must be linked with those passages in which the living God of Israel is described as the source of life (in LXX: Ps 35:10; 41:2; 83:3; Jer 2:13; 17:13). And the predicate "living" indicates at the same time that the God of Israel, who is the creator of life, saves from death (*T. Ab.* A 17:11).

Paul and Barnabas told the citizens of Lystra that they should turn to the God of Israel, the God whom the Jews worshiped. (4) In the past God graciously had allowed the nations to go their own ways, to worship their own gods, even though he had always revealed himself through his good works: through the rain he gave them "fruitful seasons" (καιροὺς καρποφόρους, *kairous karpo-*

---

[226]See Gen 37:29, 33; 44:13; Num 14:6; *T. Jos.* 5:2; *T. Job* 19:2; *4 Bar.* 2:1-2, 8, 10; 9:9; Mk 14:63; Cassius Dio 48.37.7; Arrianus *Anab.* 7.24.3; Diodoros 17.35.5.

[227]See Breytenbach 1996, 57.

[228]See B. Winter 1991, 113-30; Fournier 1997; Stenschke 1999a, 185-90; Bechard 2000, 423-27.

[229]The adjective μάταιος (*mataios*), with the meaning "idle, empty, useless," often is used in Jewish literature of the Second Temple period to "describe" the gods (εἴδωλα, *eidōla*) of the pagans: *T. Ab.* A 1:7; *T. Dan* 4:1; *Let. Aris.* 134:4; 137:1; 139:6; 205:3; 321:5; *Sib. Or.* 3:29; 4:4; 5:83.

[230]Breytenbach 1996, 62. See Deut 5:26; Josh 3:10; 1 Sam 17:26, 36; 2 Kings 19:4, 16 = Is 37:4, 17; Dan 5:23. For the observations that follow above see Breytenbach 1996, 60-66.

[231]See Bel 5-6, 24-25; Tob 13:1-3; 2 Macc 7:33; 15:4; *Gk. En.* 5:1; *Jos. Asen.* 8:5; 11:10; 19:8; *T. Job* 37:2; *Sib. Or.* 3:763.

phorous) and thus filled them with the joy of nourishment (τροφῆς καὶ εὐφροσύνης, *trophēs kai euphrosynēs*). In other words, Paul taught the citizens of Lystra three truths about God and what God does:[232] (a) God is present in the works of creation, which are a silent witness of his goodness; (b) God in his goodness seeks to satisfy the needs of people, for whom he cares; (c) God wants people to experience joy in their hearts.

Paul and Barnabas proclaim God as the One who "does good" (ἀγαθουργῶν, *agathourgōn* [Acts 14:17]), "giving you rains from heaven and fruitful seasons" (Acts 14:18). Some scholars suggest that the background for this formulation is found is the veneration of Zeus as the god of vegetation in Phrygia and in Pisidia, who appears in the region as, for example, Zeus Kalakagathios (Ζεὺς Καλακαγάθιος [*SEG* VI 550])—that is, the god "who does what is good and fruitful." The cult of Zeus Bronton (Ζεὺς Βροντῶν), a patron of agriculture, that is attested in the vicinity is also linked with Hermes.[233] If this assumption is correct, the term *agathourgōn* in Acts 14:17 is an example of linguistic "contextualization" by Paul or by Luke.

Paul and Barnabas inform the people of Lystra that growth and food come from the living God, the God of Israel, not from Zeus.[234] Cilliers Breytenbach observes that with this teaching "the characterization of Israel's God in a missionary speech is adapted to the local veneration of Zeus and opposed to it. Because in the vicinity of Lystra, Zeus is worshiped in several cult places as god of heaven, as god of vegetation who determines the weather." It is unconvincing, however, when Breytenbach asserts that this evidence makes it "unlikely that the author of Acts uses an actual speech." He argues that the description of God as the God of creation who alone is responsible for the harvest that is sold on the market in Lystra diverges from "the Lukan narrative model of the missionary story," as befits the scene of the story. If this is indeed correct, the possibility cannot be denied that this contextualized adaptation is not the literary creation of the author of the book of Acts but rather the substantial content of an actual missionary speech given by Paul in Lystra.

Luke's report of the reaction of the two missionaries underlines the universality of Paul's missionary project: the apostle evangelizes not only the educated but also the rural population, not only Greeks but also "barbarians" who speak another language, not only in the centers of Greek culture but also in the politically unimportant hinterland of Lycaonia. At the same time Luke's report illustrates the integrity of the missionaries and their work by their reaction to the desire of the citizens of Lystra to honor them with sacrifices: Paul and Barnabas refuse to utilize the superstitious, uncritical piety of the Lycaonians.

---

[232]See B. Winter 1991, 117.

[233]*CIG* 5931; *SEG* II 481. See Breytenbach 1996, 69-73; 1993. On καλακαγάθιος see LSJ Suppl. 164.

[234]Breytenbach 1996, 73-75; the quotations that follow above, ibid.

As a result of this refusal, Paul learned the raw side of popular piety: Luke reports that some Jews who had arrived from Antiocheia and Iconium incited the citizens, who took action against the missionaries and stoned Paul (Acts 14:19).[235]

The missionary outreach in Lystra in A.D. 46/47 evidently led to the establishment of a church: Paul visited the believers in Lystra on the return journey from Derbe to Antiocheia (Acts 14:21-23), and then again two years later in A.D. 49 on the journey from Syria to the province of Asia (Acts 16:1-3). During the latter visit to Lystra, Paul recruited as a coworker Timothy, the son of a Jewish woman married to a Greek husband. Paul probably visited Lystra a fourth time when he traveled in A.D. 52 from Syria to Ephesus (Acts 18:23).

We have no further information about the history of the church of Lystra. The oldest Christian tombstone that has been found in Isauria or Lycaonia, dating to the first century A.D., comes from the territory of Lystra and mentions a certain Philtatos.

The inscription was found in Dorla, 33 km southeast of Hatunsaray (Lystra), on the hill on the western river bank. The text reads,[236]

]ιλλα ἐκόσμησεν τὸν μακάριον πάπαν τὸ[ν γ]λυκύτα-
τον καὶ πάντων φ[ί]λον

—————

Φίλτατος ὁ μα-
κάριος πάπας ὁ
θεοῦ φίλος

M   X

Translation: ". . . buried the blessed and dearest father [bishop] beloved by all.—The blessed father [bishop] Philtatos, beloved by God. In memory." The relief of the inscription shows, with excellent execution, a portal with an open central arcade and one arcade to the right and to the left with pointed roofs, supported by two richly decorated columns with capitals. Next to the gables is a rosette, and below the gables are two hanging leaf garlands and a large fish. In the archivolt lies an open writing tablet (*diptychon*), and above it a wreath of leaves is tied at the top. The first part of the inscription is located on the upper ledge above a double vine tendril; the second part of the inscription is in the wreath of leaves below the writing tablet. The deceased man was a certain Philtatos, who evidently was wealthy and educated. His title *papas* corresponds

---

[235]The stoning of Paul usually is accepted as historical, even by critics who regard the "abrupt introduction" of the Jews as fictitious. See Lüdemann 1987, 169, 171-72 (ET, 163, 165-66); Molthagen 1991, 49. Goddard and Cummins (1993) interpret the persecution that Paul experienced during the mission to Galatia as the "weakness" that Paul refers to in Gal 4:13-14; see ibid., 103 n. 29, for the argument that the preposition διά not only gives the (causative) reason for the missionary work in Galatia but also could express the attending circumstances of the mission to Galatia.

[236]See Kaufmann 1917, 251-52. There is a new edition of the inscription by Gertrud Laminger-Pascher, *I. Lykaonien* 408; for a discussion of the inscription see ibid., 215, 229-30.

to *episkopos*,[237] and this means that Philtatos was a leading Christian, perhaps the leader of the church.

Artemas, mentioned in Tit 3:12, is said to have been the first bishop of Lystra.[238] Bishops are documented since A.D. 381, and a bishop of Lystra attended the Council of Chalcedon in A.D. 451.

When Paul and Barnabas continued their journey on the Via Sebaste toward eastern Lycaonia, they passed through several towns that were not insignificant in which they could have preached the gospel of Jesus Christ.

Dalisandos (mod. Belören)[239] was situated, if the proposed identification is correct, about 50 km southeast of Lystra at the edge of the Isaurian highlands. The name of the city presumably is connected with the Cilician god Sandos. Marinus of Dalisandos attended the Council of Constantinople in A.D. 381. There is no further information about the church in Dalisandos.

Kodylessos (near mod. Güdelisin Harabeler),[240] between Iconium and Laranda, is attested by coins and an inscription. Roman and Byzantine pottery is evident at the site, despite the fact that the limestone blocks of the ruins that were still visible in 1890 were used for building houses for refugees.

Laranda (Λάρανδα; mod. Karaman),[241] 25 southwest of Derbe, is attested in the early Seleucid period (see Diodoros Siculus 17.22; Strabo 12.6.3). Laranda was situated at the junction of the old roads that ran from the west (Pisidia, Isauria) and north (Iconium) to five passes across the Taurus Mountains and to the Mediterranean coast. The plain of Laranda was fertile, and people settled here at an early date. In the first century B.C. Laranda belonged to the kingdom of Antipater, who ruled in Derbe. Eusebius mentions for the early third century a bishop Neon of Laranda (Eusebius, *Hist. eccl.* 6.19.18). The

---

[237]Thus Laminger-Pascher 1992, 215, 230, with the not fully convincing argument that because of the title πάπας the inscription should be dated to the first century, "since there existed no fixed ecclesiastical organization at this time." Since the term ἐπίσκοπος (*episkopos*) is used in the New Testament (Acts 20:28; Phil 1:1; 1 Tim 3:2; Tit 1:7) for "individuals who have a function or an office in the Christian community" (J. Rohde, *EWNT* 2:89 [*EDNT* 2:36]), the title πάπας is not certain evidence for a lack of organization in the structure of the church. William Ramsay, who discovered the inscription, as well as Kaufmann (1917, 252) date the inscription to the third century A.D.

[238]See Spicq, *ÉpPast*, 2:690; Belke 1984, 200.

[239]W. Ruge, PW 4.2 (1901): 2023-24; F. Hild, *DNP* 3:282; Hild and Hellenkemper 1990, 233-34. David French initially identified Dalisandos with Kara Sinir northwest of Güdelisin, and later in the Isaurian hill country to the southwest in Belören; see D. French, "The Site of Dalisandos," *EA* 4 (1984): 85-98.

[240]See Laminger-Pascher 1992, 32-33. Cf. *ETAM* 11, no. 67. For the inscriptions found in Güdelisin (nos. 1-14) see ibid., 33-36. On this identification see Belke 1984, 192; S. Mitchell, in *BAGRW* 1017. For the inscription mentioned in the comment that follows above see Laminger-Pascher 1984, no. 67.

[241]W. Ruge, PW 12.1 (1924): 793-94; H. Treidler, *KP* 3:492-93; K. Belke, *DNP* 6:11145; Belke 1984, 197-98; Ramsay 1890, 130, 336, and passim; Laminger-Pascher 1992, 54-60; S. Mitchell 1995a, 1:32, 84; 2:60, 155.

bishop Paulos of Laranda attended the Council of Nicea in A.D. 325. There is no information about when the church in Laranda was established.

Posala (mod. Özyurt, former Bosala)[242] was located 14 km east of Kodylessos.

Evangelism in Derbe

The city of Derbe is attested in the writings of Cicero, Strabo and Ptolemaios, but it became known particularly as a result of the missionary work of Paul.[243] Derbe was located on the road that linked Iconium, the most important city of the region, with Laranda.

Derbe (Δέρβη; mod. Devri Şehr, near Sudurağı)[244] is to be identified with the ancient site (mod. Devri Şehr) about 4 km north-northeast of Sidrova (Sudurağı); the older identification with the ruins near Bin Bir Kilise (Madenşehir [W. M. Leake, Smirnov]) or with Güdelisin (W. M. Ramsay) is no longer defended by scholars.[245] Presumably it was Pompey who installed Antipater son of Perilaus, who likely was of Macedonian origin, as ruler of a small vassal kingdom. Antipater ruled from Derbe and also controlled Laranda. After 31 B.C. the Galatian king Amyntas evicted Antipater from his princedom.[246] It is not entirely clear whether Derbe belonged to the province of Galatia (cf. Strabo 12.6.3). Neighboring Laranda was controlled at least since A.D. 41 by Antiochos IV, king of Commagene.[247] The population of Derbe spoke Lycaonian, as in Lystra (Acts 14:11), and in the first century Greek would have been understood as well. Derbe seems to have had a special relationship with Claudius. During his principate Derbe was renamed Claudioderbe; coins dating to the second century have this legend: "Clau[dia] Derb[e]."

The first attested bishop of Derbe attended the Council of Constantinople in A.D. 381. The city was destroyed by Timur Lenk in the late summer of 1402. Only a few remains of the ancient city survive. In Sidrova limestone blocks with inscriptions have been found, including tombstones of two early Byzantine bishops, one of whom is called *Michail episkopos Derbis.*

Luke reports that Paul and Barnabas preached the gospel in Derbe and "made many disciples" (Acts 14:20-21). One of the Christians of Derbe was Gaius: he

---

[242]See Belke 1984, 216.

[243]Cicero, *Fam.* 13.73; Strabo 12.1.4; 12.6.3; 14.5.24; Ptolemaios 5.6.16.

[244]W. Ruge, PW 5.1 (1903): 237; H. Treidler, *KP* 1:1493; J. D. Wineland, *ABD* 2:144-45; K. Belke, *DNP* 3:481; K. Belke 1984, 157; Ramsay 1896, 103-11; Jones 1937, 133, 136-37; Magie 1950, 1:375, 443, 456, 475; George Ogg, "Derbe," *NTS* 9 (1963): 367-70; Laminger-Pascher 1992, 61-66; Syme 1995, 234-35; J. Taylor 1995, 1221-24; S. Mitchell 1995a, 1:32, 72, 85, 96; 2:5, 152; 155; Breytenbach 1996, 165-66; Bechard 2000, 52-53, 256-57 with n. 72. Inscriptions: *I. Lykaonien* 59-63.

[245]See Michael H. Ballance, "The Site of Derbe: A New Inscription," *AnSt* 7 (1957): 147-51; *AnSt* 14 (1964): 139; these studies were crucial for the new identification. See also Wineland, *ABD* 2:144; Belke 1984, 157; Elderen 1970, 156-61; Hansen 1994, 385 n. 22; Riesner 1994, 247 n. 80.

[246]Levick 1967, 24, 28; S. Mitchell 1995a, 1:72; 2:152. Cicero calls Antipater his friend (Cicero, *Fam.* 13.73.2), while Strabo describes him as a bandit chief (12.2.4).

[247]S. Mitchell (1980, fig. 1 [after p. 1056]), Breytenbach (1996, 166) and others assume that Derbe belonged to Galatia. Other scholars remain unconvinced; see Ogg, *NTS* 9 (1963): 369-70; Sherk 1980, fig. 1 (after p. 960); I. Pill-Rademacher (*TAVO* B V 8 [1988]).

was one of Paul's coworkers in Ephesus (Acts 19:29) and accompanied Paul on his journey through Macedonia and Galatia (Acts 20:4).

Evangelism in Perge

After Paul and Barnabas returned from Derbe, Lystra, Iconium and Antiocheia in southern Galatia, they preached the gospel in Perge: "Then they passed through Pisidia and came to Pamphylia. When they had spoken the word in Perge [λαλήσαντες ἐν Πέργῃ τὸν λόγον], they went down to Attalia" (Acts 14:24-25).

Perge (Πέργη; mod. Aksu),[248] about 16 km northeast of Attaleia in the Pamphylian Plain on the Kestros River (mod. Asku), had been founded in the course of the Mycenaean colonization as a Greek city. In the Hellenistic period Perge belonged to the Seleucid Empire; in 188 B.C. the city was given by Antiochos III to Eumenes II from Pergamon. The yearly games that Strabo mentions were celebrated in honor of Artemis (Strabo 14.4.2) and attracted many visitors, particularly from the neighboring cities Selge, Aspendos and Side. The most important games of Pamphylia were the Pythian Games of Side and Perge. Famous sons of the city include the mathematician Apolloios, from the school of Euclid, who was active around 200 B.C. in Alexandria and Pergamon.[249] The temple of Artemis was surpassed in fame only by the temple of Artemis Ephesia in Ephesus. The right to grant asylum (*asylia*) of the temple seems to go back to the Hellenistic period: evidently it was confirmed by Emperor Tiberius in the context of an embassy to Rome of Apolloios son of Lysimachos (*I. Perge* 23), and it seems to have played a role in the diplomatic success of the ambassador Ti. Claudius Apolloius Elaibares during the principate of Claudius or Nero (*I. Perge* 58).[250] Perge flourished noticeably during the first century A.D., in contrast to other cities of Pamphylia. Sencer Şahin concludes from newly discovered inscriptions, "The city took decisive steps already in the first quarter of this [the first] century to adapt to the new world order of the Romans. The process of Romanization evidently took place in all areas of urban life. Not only the social structure was Romanized, first of all the elite; the architecture of the city was modernized in this sense as well. Very quickly a leading class of families developed in the city, for example the Plancii and the Iulii Cornuti, whose members were accepted into the Roman senate already in the middle of the

---

[248]W. Ruge, PW 19.1 (1937): 694-95; S. Jameson, PWSup 14 (1974): 375-83; E. Olshausen, *KP* 4:631-32; G. E. Bean, *PECS* 692-93; G. E. Bean and S. Mitchell, *OCD* 1139; Brandt 1992, 47-48, 101-2, 127-28, 134-35, 139, 146-47, 154-56, 158; Adnan Pekman, *The History of Perge* (Ankara: Basimevi, 1973); Sencer Şahin, "Studien zu den Inschriften von Perge I: Germancus in Perge," *EA* 24 (1995): 21-35; Breytenbach 1996, 166-67. Excavations: Arif Müfid Mansel, *Excavations and Researches at Perge* (Ankara: Türk Tarih Kurumu Basimevi, 1949). Inscriptions: Sencer Şahin, *Die Inschriften von Perge I* (IK 54; Bonn: Habelt, 1999); see also Merkelbach and Şahin, "Die publizierten Inschriften von Perge," *EA* 11 (1988): 97-169; C. P. Jones, "Old and New in the Inscriptions of Perge," *EA* 31 (1999): 8-17.

[249]Buchwald, *Tusculum-Lexikon*, 67. Apolloios was the author of the normative work on conic in eight books (Κωνικά), four of which survive in Greek and three in Arabic; the Greek volumes are the earliest extensive example of Hellenistic literary Greek (i.e., of Koine).

[250]See Kent Rigsby, *Asylia: Territorial Inviolability in the Greek World* (Berkeley: University of California Press, 1996), 449. 452; C. P. Jones, *EA* 31 (1999): 13-17. Differently S. Şahin, "Studien zu den Inschriften von Perge II: Der Gesandte Apolloios und seine Familie," *EA* 25 (1995): 1-23l; Şahin assumes a date during the reign of Domitian.

first century or shortly thereafter. . . . We observe a noticeable progress of the economy and a lively building activity in the city."[251] The old main streets were replaced by streets flanked with colonnaded halls, and during the reign of Domitian (and later of Hadrian) monumental gates were erected. In the first decades of the first century A.D. new markets were built—for example, the Sebaste Agora (Augustus market); under Claudius the Cornutus gymnasium was constructed, and under the Flavians the large South Baths were built. The tariff law of the province of Asia (νόμος τέλους ᾿Ασίας εἰσαγωγῆς καὶ ἐξαγωγῆς, *nomos telous Asias eisāgōgēs kai exagōgēs*) dating to A.D. 62, recently discovered in Ephesus, indicates that Perge belonged to the ports that were united in the *portorium Asiae,* which means that there was a customs post in Perge.[252] Perge competed with Side for the status of the most important city of Pamphylia. Johannes Nollé comments, "While Perge could point to its ancient temple with the right to grant asylum, Side referred with pride to its old alliance with Rome and to its role as a Roman naval base."[253] The decision of the emperor that both cities could use the title "First City of Pamphylia" did not bring an end to the quarrel, which reached its climax in the third century and later was reflected in the ecclesiastical organization of the church in Pamphylia. Emperor Tacitus (A.D. 275/276) granted Perge numerous advantages and elevated the city to the status of metropolis.[254]

Inscriptions document a gymnasium with palaestra and stadium (second century B.C.), and a temple of Artemis Pergaia, situated outside of the city walls, whose cult was popular in all of Pamphylia; this temple was a significant economic factor for Perge. During the imperial period Perge received a regular street plan, dominated by two large colonnaded streets with water canals running in the center of the street. As in other cities, building activity in Perge depended on the benefactions of wealthy citizens. In the first century we encounter C. Iulius Cornutus, who belonged to a senatorial family and was a benefactor for a gymnasium and a palaestra. The members of the noble family of the Plancii financed the renovation of the "founders' hall." Perge had the complete infrastructure of a flourishing city of the imperial period: a theater for fourteen thousand spectators, a stadium (234 m long), monumental city gates, baths, nymphaeum and aqueduct. The buildings of Perge document the enormous wealth of the city in the first century.[255] The high level of Greek education and culture in Perge is demonstrated by inscriptions that document the presence of physicians, philosophers, philologists, athletes, actors, poets, singers, mimes, musicians and dancers, some of whom were active in other regions—for example, Ephesus, Pergamon, Tlos, Thyatira, Sparta and Rome. The increased communication between cities and regions that flourished in the Roman Empire can be seen in the foreigners or aliens (ξενοί, *xenoi*) who are attested for Perge: worshipers from Side, Aspendos, Selge and Tarsus visited the temple of Artemis, and inscriptions document the presence of people from Termessos, Cremna, Klaudiopolis and Byzantion. The local population sometimes had a share in the wealth of Perge: inscriptions document an old family from the village of Lyr-

---

[251]S. Şahin, *EA* 24 (1995): 21.

[252]Engelmann and Knibbe 1989; cf. Martin Dreher, "Die *Lex Portorii Asiae* und der Zollbezirk Asia," *EA* 26 (1996) 111-127. On the *portorium* cf. F. Vittinghoff, "Portorium," PW 22 (1953): 346-399; G. P. Burton, *OCD* 1228.

[253]Nollé 1993, 311-12.

[254]See I. Kaygusuz, *EA* 4 (1984): 1-4 = *SEG* XXXIV 1306 = *EA* 29 (1997): 70, a monument with twelve acclamations inscribed on a pillar. See P. Weiss, "Auxe Perge," *Chiron* 21 (1991): 353-74. For a newly discovered pillar inscribed with an epigram in ten lines see R. Merkelbach et al., *EA* 29 (1997): 73-74.

[255]Brandt 1992, 102; for the comment that follows above see ibid., 145.

boton Kome (note the indigenous names Trokondas, Moas, Kotes, Les, Kille) in the territory controlled by Perge whose members were landowners in the first and second centuries A.D. and who financed local buildings and were connected with the temple of Apollo through the donation of land.[256] This inscription demonstrates that the local Pamphylian population was able to acquire considerable land holdings. The generosity of the local people indicates their desire to improve their social status, which also is "articulated in the directive, connected with the benefactions, to finance agonistic events in honor of the benefactors as well as village festivals from the produce of the donated lands."[257] Perge was famous for its silversmiths and goldsmiths, who were connected with the cult of Artemis Pergaia. The silversmiths had shops in the stadium. The impressive remains include city walls (third century, with four main gates), theater, stadium, baths, colonnaded street and sculptures (housed in the Archaeological Museum of von Antalya). The temple of Artemis Pergaia has not yet been located.

The presence of Jews in Perge has not been confirmed by inscriptions as of yet. Perge's status as one of the most important cities on the southern coast of Asia Minor makes it more than likely that a Jewish community existed in the city. The fact that Paul first preached in synagogues, at least during his mission to Cyprus and Galatia, seems to imply that Luke believed that there were Jews in Perge.

In 1988 an inscription dating to the first or second century from neighboring Aspendos (mod. Belkis) was published that perhaps can be linked with a Gentile who has been influenced by the Jewish faith, a God-fearer. The translation of the text of the inscription reads, "To the true God who is not made by hands. [In fulfillment of] a vow" (*IJudO* II 218).[258] Since the inscription is inscribed on small altar, it is not certain that it can be interpreted as proving the presence of Jews in the Pamphylian Plain during this period.

The church in Perge is the only church in Pamphylia for which we have evidence. The apocryphal *Acts of Paul* mention Christians in Perge.

"But when Paul departed from Myra and wished to go up to Sidon there was great sorrow among the brethren who were in Pisidia and Pamphylia since they yearned after his word and his holy presence, so that some from Perge followed Paul, namely Thrasymachus and Cleon with their wives Aline (?) and Chrysa, the wife of Cleon" (*Acts Paul* 5).[259]

At the time of the persecution under Diocletian in A.D. 304 there were at least twelve churches in Pamphylia. In the fourth century the bishop Kallikles was active in Perge.

---

[256]*SEG* VI 672-674 = *EA* 11 (1988): 151-154.
[257]Brandt 1992, 127-28.
[258]See Horst 1992; Wander 1998, 136; Ameling, in *IJudO* II, 2004, 458-61.
[259]Elliott 1993, 376; cf. W. Rordorf, in Bovon and Geoltrain, *Écrits apocryphes chrétiens*, 1146, as *Acts Paul* 6:1.

27.2 Missionary Work in Macedonia and Achaia

The mission to the provinces of Macedonia and Achaia that Luke reports in Acts 15:30—18:22 took place between A.D. 49 and 52. Paul traveled from Jerusalem via Antioch to Syria and Galatia, visiting together with several coworkers the churches that had been established two years earlier. Paul planned to reach the province of Asia, probably to begin missionary work in Ephesus. This plan could not be realized, nor could the alternate plan to reach Bithynia. After the missionaries received divine confirmation, Paul and his friends traveled to Macedonia and Achaia and preached the gospel at least in Philippi, Thessalonike, Beroea, Athens and Corinth.

Phase I: Visit of the Churches in Syria and Galatia

Jerusalem	⇒ Antioch	15:30, 40	540 km
Antioch	⇒ Platanoi		35 km
	⇒ Alexandria ad Issum	15:41 (Syria)	15 km
	⇒ Baiae	15:41 (Cilicia)	20 km
	⇒ Issos		18 km
	⇒ Katabolos		17 km
	⇒ Mopsuestia		35 km
	⇒ Adana		30 km
	⇒ Tarsus		40 km
	⇒ Cilician Gates		44 km
	⇒ Podandos		22 km
	⇒ Tynna		34 km
	⇒ Kybistra		50 km
	⇒ Sidamaria		40 km
	⇒ Derbe	16:1	30 km
Derbe	⇒ Lystra	16:1	150 km
Lystra	⇒ Iconium ?	16:4-5	35 km
Iconium	⇒ Antiocheia ?	16:4-5	148 km
Antiocheia	⇒ Tymandus ?		60 km
	⇒ Apollonia ?	16:6 (Phrygian Galatia)	15 km
	⇒ Aporidos ?		19 km
	⇒ Apameia ?		17 km
	⇒ Synnada ?		82 km
	⇒ Prymnessus ?		22 km
	⇒ Leontos Kome ?		30 km
	⇒ Meiros ?		30 km
	⇒ Cotiaeum ?	16:7	45 km
	⇒ Aizanoi ?		40 km
	⇒ Kadoi ?	16:8 (Mysia)	26 km
	⇒ Synaos ?		52 km
	⇒ Attea ?		110 km
	⇒ Hadrianothera ?		22 km
	⇒ Pionia ?		30 km
	⇒ Adramyttion		60 km
	⇒ Antandros ?		30 km
	⇒ Gargara ?		24 km
	⇒ Skamandreia ?		51 km
	⇒ Alexandria Troas		22 km

Phase II: Missionary Work in Macedonia

Alexandria

Troas	⇒ Samothrace	16:11 (by ship)	110 km
Samothrace	⇒ Neapolis	16:11 (by ship)	110 km
Neapolis	⇒ Philippi	16:12	16 km
Philippi	⇒ Amphipolis	17:1	60 km
Amphipolis	⇒ Apollonia	17:1	40 km
Apollonia	⇒ Thessalonike	17:1	65 km
Thessalonike	⇒ Beroea	17:10	75 km

Phase III: Missionary Work in Corinth (Achaia)

Beroea	⇒ Pydna	17:14	50 km
Pydna	⇒ Athens	17:15 (by ship)	450 km
Athens	⇒ Eleusis		20 km
	⇒ Megara		21 km
	⇒ Corinth	18:1	45 km

Phase IV: Return Journey to Jerusalem and Antioch

Corinth	⇒ Cenchreae	18:18	2 km
Cenchreae	⇒ Ephesus	18:19 (by ship)	350 km
Ephesus	⇒ Caesarea	18:22 (by ship)	1040 km
Caesarea	⇒ Jerusalem	18:22	100 km
Jerusalem	⇒ Antioch	18:22	540 km

Notes on the travel route. Paul had traveled the 540 km (335 mi.) from Jerusalem to Antioch several times before, on foot: presumably as a youngster when he left Tarsus to study in Jerusalem; after his conversion when he had returned from Nabatea to visit Jerusalem and moved to "Syria and Cilicia" (Gal 1:18-21); after the mission to Cyprus and Galatia when he traveled from Antioch to Jerusalem and back (Acts 15:2, 30).[260] Leaving Antioch, Paul took the usual road to Cilicia, Cappadocia and Galatia: he traveled via Platanoi, Alexandria ad Issum, Baiae, Issos, Katabolos, Mopsuestia and Adana to Tarsus (on these cities see §26.2; fig. 31). In the years between A.D. 49 and 52, when Paul traveled through Syria, Cilicia and Galatia to visit the churches there, engaging in missionary work in Phrygia/Galatia, Macedonia and Achaia, he traveled a total of 3,110 km (1,933 mi.) on foot and 2,060 km by ship. This corresponds to 145 days (ca. five months) of travel, with 125 days on foot and 20 days at sea.

Departure from Antioch

Before leaving Antioch, Paul and Barnabas separated. Barnabas wanted to take John Mark along again, a plan that was rejected by Paul because Mark had left them in Pamphylia and "had not accompanied them in the work" (Acts 15:38). After a sharp disagreement (παροξυσμός, *paroxysmos* [Acts 15:39]), Barnabas and Mark traveled to Cyprus, while Paul and Silas traveled north to southern Galatia.

    Jürgen Roloff suggests that the real reason for the disagreement between Barnabas and Paul was "without doubt" the fact that Barnabas had adopted the

---

[260]The road from Jerusalem via Antioch to Tarsus and to Constantinople is often called "Pilgrims' Road," following the *Itinerarium Burdigalense,* a documented pilgrimage to Jerusalem purportedly in the fourth century (Cuntz 1929).

theological position of the "Antiochene majority" opposing Paul (Gal 2:13), which prompted the "dissolution of the missionary partnership."[261] This interpretation is undermined by the primary sources. (1) Paul does not accuse his coworker Barnabas of maintaining an erroneous theological position in Gal 2:13; rather, he accuses him of "hypocrisy." In other words, Barnabas acted against his convictions when he gave in to the pressure of the Jewish-Christian delegation from Jerusalem: he had become weak, he was "led astray" (συν-απήχθη, *synapēchthē*), implying that his real, personal position was in agreement with Paul's. (2) The suggestion that Paul interpreted the clash with Barnabas as a split with Antioch that was permanent is unlikely: according to Acts 18:22, Paul returned to Antioch after his mission to Greece, spending "some time" in the Syrian capital (Acts 18:23). In 1 Cor 9:6 Paul speaks positively of Barnabas in connection with his description of his missionary praxis: "Or is it only Barnabas and I who have no right to refrain from working for a living?" There is no evidence for a permanent division or split. (3) If the connection of Gal 2:1-10 with the events of the famine-relief visit to Jerusalem (Acts 11:27-30) is correct (see §25.1), and if Paul indeed wrote the letter to the Galatians before the apostolic council, an assumption that is not necessary for the following explanation, Luke's account in Acts 15:22, 30, 35, 36 represents evidence that the crisis of Paul's relationship with Barnabas described in Gal 2:1-10 was later resolved. Roloff's charge that Luke downplays the harshness of the conflict by omitting the "theological components" and reducing it to "superficial events," thus personalizing the clash, can be turned against Roloff himself: he intensifies the conflict by introducing hypothetical assumptions, he fails to consider the possibility of a reconciliation between Paul and Barnabas and between Paul and "Antioch" that several New Testament texts suggest, he prefers a priori theological factors to personal factors, and he regards "obvious" elements as historically less relevant than factors that are not actually mentioned in the text.

Robert Cara shows that Acts 15:36-41 is "pro Paul" and that, at least from Luke's perspective, the behavior of Barnabas is negatively characterized.[262] (1) In Acts 15:37-38 Luke gives a reason why John Mark should not be taken along for the missionary work in the province of Asia that had been planned. Luke does not comment on the arguments of Barnabas, who evidently wanted to give John Mark another opportunity to join them as a missionary. (2) According to Acts 15:40, Paul and Silas were commended by the believers in Antioch "to the grace of the Lord" when they set out toward Galatia and Asia. There is no corresponding notice concerning Barnabas and John Mark. (3) According to Acts 15:41, Paul visits the churches in Syria and in Cilicia, fulfilling the wishes of the apostolic council (Acts 15:23). Luke clearly emphasizes here the "fellowship"

---

[261]Roloff 1991, 122. See earlier J. Bailey 1909.
[262]Cara 2001, esp. 64-79, 145-50.

between Paul and Jerusalem. Again there is no corresponding comment with regard to Barnabas. (4) Luke reports the specific activity of Paul: he "strengthened" the churches in Syria and Cilicia (Acts 15:41). Barnabas's mission to Cyprus remains unspecified. (5) Barnabas is positively characterized as missionary and church leader before Acts 15:36-41, with particular emphasis on his reliability and his function as a mediator.[263] However, this characterization is always linked with specific situations, and the character trait of communicating *paraklēsis* is primarily connected with his role as preacher, which in turn is generally connected with his role as mediator. This means, in other words, that the suggestion that Barnabas acted correctly when he wanted to encourage and help young John Mark, and that Paul, who (allegedly) began the quarrel, was wrong[264] has no basis in Luke's account in the book of Acts.

In Tarsus Paul and Silas presumably stayed with relatives or with Christians in the city who had been converted during his early missionary activity in Cilicia. From Tarsus the road to Galatia ran directly north through the Cilician Gates (αἱ Κιλικίαι πύλαι, *hai Kilikiai pylai* [cf. Strabo 12.2.7]), across the Taurus Mountains, through the valleys of the rivers Çakıt and Kırkgeçit, past Mount Medetsiz (3,524 m) and Mount Karanfil (3,059 m).

David French points out that the road through the Cilician Gates was paved but that the early chronology of the construction and the reparation of the road is uncertain, and suggests an alternative route further to the west that linked Seleucia on the Kalykadnos River with Laranda, the later capital of Lycaonia, and ran to Derbe and Lystra.[265] However, since it is unnecessary to assume that Paul would by necessity have preferred a paved Roman road, this suggestion remains hypothetical. The *Itinerarium Burdigalense* mentions two *mansiones* (Mansucrinae, Podandos) for the road between Tarsus and Tyana as well as a *mutatio* on the pass of the Cilician Gates (Pilas, as "fines Cappadociae et Ciliciae"). About 8 km north of Podandos a road branched off toward the west, following the valley of the Çakıt River; it crossed the Kılan-Dere pass near Tynna and continued to Kybistra in southeastern Lykaonia and via Sidamaria and perhaps Cinasınören to Derbe. The road from Derbe to Lystra was familiar to Paul from his mission to Galatia. The road from Iconium via Tyana and across the Cilician Gates to Tarsus was an old main route since at least the Persian period.[266]

Mopsukrene (Μόψουκρήνη; near mod. Kırıtlar),[267] between Tarsus and the Pylai Kilikias, was a Roman hamlet that still existed in the early Byzantine period. In the area of the set-

---

[263]Cara (2001, 105-43), who discusses Acts 4:36-37; 9:26-30; 11:19-30; 12:25—13:3; 13:4—14:28; 15:1-35.

[264]F. Spencer 1997a, 158; but see Cara 2001, 147-48.

[265]French 1994b, 56. The milestones that have been found in the region of Podandos and the Cilician Gates, dating to the early third century A.D., have been newly edited in *I. Tyana* 131-133 (I 288-290).

[266]See Seibert 1985, 21.

[267]W. Ruge, PW 16.1 (1933): 250; Magie 1950, 2:1154; Hild and Hellenkemper 1990, 359-60; Berges and Nollé 2000, 325-26, 367, 439-40.

tlement have been found Roman limestone sarcophagi dating to the second and third centuries, as well as cisterns, parts of columns, a small ancient quarry and a small necropolis.

The *Cilician Gates* (Πύλαι Κιλικίας, *Pylai Kilikias;* mod. Gülek Boğazı)[268] describe the narrow pass, 1,050 m above sea level, across the Taurus Mountains north of Tarsus at the point where the Kydnos River (mod. Tarsus Çayı) runs south toward the Mediterranean. This famous pass was used by numerous armies from Cyrus and Alexander the Great to the Crusaders. Caracalla widened the pass; the inscription in the rock on the east side of the pass dates to A.D. 217, as does a milestone found in Podandos that confirms that this part of the road was called *Via Tauri:* "Im(perator) Caes(ar) M(arcus) Aurelius Severus Antoninus . . . renovated the Taurus Road that had become dilapidated on account of its age by leveling mountains and by smashing rocks, and by widening the road including the bridges. From the (Cilician) Gates 15 M(iles)."[269] Curtius Rufus describes the narrowness of the pass through which the army of Alexander the Great marched as follows: "'The Gates' is what the natives call that very narrow entrance, and in its natural formation it resembles fortifications made by human hands. . . . The road barely allowed four armed men to walk abreast; a ridge of the mountain overhung a passage that was not merely narrow, but often broken by streams which crossed it, trickling from the roof of the mountains. . . . In this manner the army came to the city of Tarsus" (3.4.2, 12, 13).[270] Aelius Aristides states that the Cilician Gates lost their fright only as a result of the power of Rome (*Or.* 26.100). In 1902 the pass was about 5 m wide, 2 m of which were occupied by the Osman road. The location of the *mutatio* on the highest point of the pass had not been identified. The ancient pass is covered by the modern highway, which leaves only the rock with the Caracalla inscription visible. The passes across the Taurus Mountains were impassable during the winter months (Cicero, *Att.* 5.21).

Podandos (Ποδανδός; Hittite Pauwandas; mod. Pozantı),[271] 15 Roman miles north of the Cilician Gates on the east bank of the Çakit Suyu, was located in a wide and fertile valley. Pondandos controlled a junction of the north-south connection between Asia Minor and Syria. The region around Podandos was an imperial estate in the second century. The Crusaders knew the town under the name "Butrentum."

Tynna (Τύννα; mod. Zeyve, Porsuk),[272] settled already in ancient times, is mentioned by Ptolemaios (5.6). After the foundation of Faustinopolis, Tynna may have belonged to the territory of this city. Tynna belonged to the Cappadocian strategy of Cataonia. The Roman

---

[268]W. Ruge, PW 11.1 (1921): 389-90; H. Treidler, PWSup 9 (1962): 1352-66; R. P. Harper, *PECS* 745; F. Hild, *DNP* 6:457; Hild and Hellenkemper 1990, 38; S. Mitchell 1995a, 1:129, 164, 246; Berges and Nollé 2000, 12-18, 290-96 (inscriptions), 328-35, 447-57, 503-5.

[269]See French 1981-1988, 1:13, 33, 92 (no. 61) = *I. Tyana* 132. For the description that follows above of the road from Tarsus to Podandos see French 1991-1998, 1:17-19, and the maps in the appendix. See also Berges and Nollé 2000, 325-30.

[270]Berges and Nollé 2000, 447-48 (no. 140); for Aelius Aristides, mentioned in the comment that follows above, see ibid., 454-55 (no. 147).

[271]K. Bittel, PW 21.1 (1951): 1136-39; Magie 1950, 1:276; R. P. Harper, "Podandus and the Via Tauri," *AnSt* 20 (1970): 149-53; idem, *PECS* 718; S. Mitchell 1995a, 2:77; Berges and Nollé 2000, 16, 442-48, 494, 504.

[272]J. Friedrich, PW 7.A2 (1948): 1793-94; S. Mitchell, in *BAGRW* 1020, with reference to T. Drew-Bear, "Inscriptions de Cappadoce," *Anatolia Antiqua* 1 (1991): 131-42; Berges and Nollé 2000, 439-40, 504.

army maintained a military station in Tynna by the Flavian period. Remains of the ancient city have not survived.

Kybistra (Κύβιστρα; former Herakleia; mod. Ereğli),[273] about 90 km north of the Cilician Gates, was located in a fertile region and belonged to the Cappadocian kingdom since 220 B.C. at the latest. Cicero wanted to make a stand against Parthian invaders in Kybistra in September 51 B.C. (Cicero, *Att.* 5.20.2). Kybistra minted coins in the imperial period.

Sidamaria (mod. Ambar, Anbararasıı, Kurdish Serpek)[274] about 7 km southwest of Lake Ak (Ak Göl), about 50 km northeast of Laranda. The northern and the southern routes of the Via Sebaste meet in Sidamaria; the southern route leads to Lystra and Derbe. The council of the city dedicated public baths to Emperor Hadrian.

Cinasınören (ancient name unknown)[275] was a Roman city at a crossroads of only local significance. The road branching off to the north, often used in Byzantine times, runs to Constantinople, crossing a pass (Cinasın Geçidi) before reaching Akçaşehir after 11 km. The ruins are among the most extensive ancient sites in Lycaonia; no archaeological work has been done.

Paul left Antioch with the goal of communicating the decisions of the apostolic council in the churches of Syria and Cilicia (see §25.3). Luke's brief account in Acts 16:4-5 mentions only Derbe and Lystra. The formulation "they were passing through the cities" (Acts 16:4 NASB), which uses the definite article (τὰς πόλεις, *tas poleis*), and the information that "the churches were strengthened in the faith and increased in numbers daily" (Acts 16:5), may refer only to the cities of Derbe and Lystra mentioned in Acts 16:1, or it may refer to "those places" (ἐν τοῖς τόποις ἐκείνοις, *en tois topois ekeinois*)—that is, those cities in which synagogues and Christian communities existed, including at least Derbe, Lystra (Acts 16:1) and Iconium (Acts 16:2). Did Paul also visit Pisidian Antiocheia? The phrase "in those places" may suggest that he did: Antiocheia is as far from Iconium as it is from Derbe (about 130 km), and Luke had reported extensively about Paul's missionary work in the city (Acts 13:14-50; 14:21). The fact that Paul's mission to Antiocheia had been rather successful (see above) suggests that Paul would have wanted to inform the believers in this important Roman colony about the decisions of the apostolic council as well.

Luke notes with regard to the churches visited by Paul and Silas that the believers were strengthened in their faith and that "they increased in number daily" (Acts 16:5).[276] The growth of the churches presumably was the result of renewed

---

[273]W. Ruge, "Kybistra 4," PWSup 4 (1924): 1123; K. Strobel, *DNP* 6:956; Jones 1937, 179, 183; Magie 1950, 1:276, 375, 397; S. Mitchell 1995a, 1:32; Berges and Nollé 2000, 15-16, 309-10, 339, 453-54

[274]W. Ruge, PW 2.A2 (1923): 2208; Belke 1984, 126; Magie 1950, 1:622; Laminger-Pascher 1992, 99-107.

[275]Belke 1984, 126, 151-52; Laminger-Pascher 1992, 98 (no. 136).

[276]On the comment regarding the growth of the churches see Noordegraaf 1983, 95-98; Reinhardt 1995a, 245-55.

missionary preaching of Paul and Silas,[277] perhaps also the result of the missionary activity of the churches in these regions themselves.[278] Luke's reference to new church growth surely intends to demonstrate, at the same time, that the solution of the conflict concerning circumcision of Gentile believers reached at the apostolic council (Acts 15) had been successful.[279] And, finally, the new expansion of the church may possibly be connected with the appoiontment of new missionary coworkers (Acts 15:40; 16:1-3).

Plans for Missionary Work in the Provinces of Asia and Bithynia

A second goal of Paul's journey was the project of missionary outreach in the province of Asia (λαλῆσαι τὸν λόγον ἐν τῇ Ἀσίᾳ, *lalēsai ton logon en tē Asia* [Acts 16:6]). Which cities in the province of Asia did Paul want to visit? After Paul had been active in the provincial capitals of Tarsus (Cilicia), Antioch (Syria), Paphos (Cyprus) and Perge (Pamphylia), he evidently wanted to preach the gospel in Ephesus. A journey from Pisidian Antiocheia to Ephesus would have proceeded first toward the southwest to Apollonia and Apameia, then in a westerly direction to Sanaos at Lake Sanaos in the Maeander Valley, and via Laodikeia, Antiochia ad Maeandrum, Nyssa, Tralles and Magnesia ad Maeandrum to Ephesus, a journey of about 530 km, just about the same distance as the journey from Jerusalem to Antioch in Syria.

As Paul visited the churches in Lycaonia, Pisidia and Phrygia in southern Galatia, God prevented the missionaries from continuing their journey to the province of Asia (Acts 16:6b), perhaps in a dream-vision or through a prophetic message. The substitute plan of a mission to Bithynia had to be dropped as well (Acts 16:7b), presumably for the same reasons. In Bithynia the cities of Nicea, Nicomedia and Chalcedon would have been logical destinations for Paul (on these cities see §22.8).

Eventually the missionaries arrive in Alexandria Troas (Acts 16:8). The travel route of this period between Iconium or Antiocheia and Alexandria Troas is disputed.

Notes on the travel route. Luke makes three points in Acts 16:6 ("They went through the region of Phrygia and Galatia, having been forbidden by the Holy Spirit to speak the word in Asia") about events and plans whose chronological correlation is disputed. (1) The missionaries passed through the Phrygian and Galatian region; (2) the missionaries planned to preach the gospel in the province of Asia; (3) the Holy Spirit prevented the execution of this plan. Several questions arise: Is the journey through Phrygia/Galatia a (temporal, or logical) *result* of the abandonment of the plans to reach the province of Asia? Did the missionaries realize *during* the journey through Phrygia/Galatia that they had to abandon

---

[277]Zahn, *Apg,* 2:559. The expansion in Codex D of Acts 16:4 makes this point explicitly: "They passed through the cities and preached and presented the Lord Jesus with all boldness."

[278]See Reinhardt 1995a, 253.

[279]See Pesch, *Apg,* 2:97.

the plan to travel to the province of Asia? Or did the divine intervention take place only shortly before entering the province of Asia? How should we understand the reference to Phrygia and Galatia? Do the two terms refer to geographical regions (Phrygia was not a province)? Does this mean that Paul traveled to the "region Galatia" (i.e., to northern Galatia), where he preached the gospel and established churches in the cities of the Celts, perhaps in Pessinus and Ancyra? The last question, which many New Testament scholars answer in the affirmative, is connected with another question: To whom did Paul address his letter to the Galatians? If Paul wrote to ethnic Galatians, he must have established churches in northern Galatia in the region of Pessinus and Ancyra. If Paul did not visit northern Galatia, where the ethnic Galatians/Celts lived, he obviously addressed the letter to churches that he established during his missionary work in southern Galatia: the churches in Antiocheia, Iconium, Lystra and Derbe.

The main arguments for a journey of Paul through northern Galatia to the region of the Celtic Galatians are the following.[280] (1) The formulation τὴν Φρυγίαν καὶ Γαλατικὴν χώραν (*tēn Phrygian kai Galatikēn chōran*) in Acts 16:6a should be interpreted as a reference to Phrygia (Φρυγία, *Phrygia,* as noun) and to the "region" (χώρα, *chōra*) of Galatia. Thus, since the plan to travel to the province of Asia could not be realized (Acts 16:6b), the missionaries left Lystra and Iconium in the direction of Phrygia and then passed through Galatia until they reached the border of Mysia (Acts 16:7a), from where they wanted to travel to Bithynia (Acts 16:7b), a plan that the Holy Spirit prevented as well. (2) The aorist participle in Acts 16:6a (κωλυθέντες, *kōlythentes*) describes either (a) an action that took place *before* the event that is described with the main verb ("they went through"): "They went through Phrygia and Galatia after they had been forbidden by the Holy Spirit to preach in the province of Asia"; or (b) the reason for the event indicated with the main verb: "They went through Phrygia and the region of Galatia because the Holy Spirit had prohibited them." (3) The alternative route that we would have to assume for Paul—Phrygian Galatia, province of Asia, border region near Mysia, toward Bithynia, Mysia, Troas—is unconvincing. Kirsopp Lake argues that it is not conceivable that the Spirit would have allowed Paul to journey through the province of Asia but prevented him from preaching the gospel there.[281]

The main arguments against a missionary journey to northern Galatia are the following. (1) The formulation τὴν Φρυγίαν καὶ Γαλατικὴν χώραν (*tēn Phrygian kai Galatikēn chōran*) in Acts 16:6a should be interpreted as reference to a region (χώρα, *chōra*) that is both Phrygian and Galatian (Φρυγία, *Phrygia,* as adjective)—that is, the region that originally was Phrygian and belonged since 25 B.C. to the province of Galatia. This usage of Φρυγία (*Phrygia*) is supported by classical texts, and is confirmed by the use of a single article for both "Phrygian" and "Galatian" (τήν connects Φρυγίαν καὶ Γαλατικὴν as a unit).[282] Both Iconium and Antiocheia belonged to the Phrygian region that had been incorporated in Galatia. (2) (a) The aorist participle Acts 16:6a (κωλυθέντες, *kōlythentes*) can be understood in terms of simultaneousness: "They went through the Phrygian-Galatian region; [but] they were prevented [while they traveled] by the Holy Spirit from preaching the word in the province of Asia." This means that the "prevention" took place *during* the

---

[280]See recently Barrett, *Acts,* 2:766-69.
[281]Lake, *Begs.* 5:235-36; followed by Barrett, *Acts,* 2:767.
[282]See Hemer 1989, 112, 277-307; idem, in *NewDocs* 4:174; Bruce, *Acts,* 11; Mitchell, *ABD* 2:871; Riesner 1994, 253-54 (ET, 285-86); *NSS* 2:758; see also Breytenbach (1996, 113-14), who asserts that the evidence collected by Colin Hemer should suffice to eliminate the "error" of Kirsopp Lake.

journey through Phrygian Galatia. Since Iconium, mentioned in Acts 16:2, is the last stop that Luke reports, the reference to Phrygian Galatia relates to a journey of the missionaries after they left Iconium, traveling toward the west, during which Paul decided to abandon his plan of starting missionary work in the province of Asia. (b) Or the aorist participle can be understood in terms of a subsequent event: "They went through the Phrygian-Galatian region after the Holy Spirit had prevented them from preaching the word in the province of Asia."[283] In other words, the "prevention" took place *after* the missionaries spent time in the Phrygian-Galatian region: after the missionaries had left Iconium and traveled through Phrygian Galatia, with a presumed stopover in Antiocheia, continuing in the direction of the province of Asia toward the west, they realized that they had to give up their plans probably "where the highway forks off to Apamea, leading through the Lycus Valley to the Asiatic provincial capital Ephesus."[284] In geographical terms, the difference between these two options is nearly negligible: the question of whether the missionaries abandoned the province of Asia as a goal of their missionary journey between Derbe and Antiocheia or whether they did so 100 km southwest of Antiocheia has little significance. More important is the fact that an interpretation in the sense of a decision to abandon the mission to Asia prior to the journey through Phrygian Galatia (option b) suggests that Paul engaged in missionary work in Phrygian Galatia: after the missionaries had been prevented from preaching in the province of Asia, they decided to pass through the Phrygian-Galatian region, evidently with the intention of preaching the gospel in this area (see below). In both cases it remains an open question as to when Paul decided to start missionary work in the province of Asia: did he make this decision during the journey through southern Galatia, or earlier in Syrian Antioch? (3) The aforementioned objection by Kirsopp Lake is unconvincing: on the one hand, we do not know the specific circumstances that perhaps prompted the divine prohibition; on the other hand, there have continued to be situations that make missionaries realize that it would be wise to delay, or adapt, plans that had been made concerning missionary acticities without avoiding the particular city or region altogether. (4) Several factors make a mission of Paul to the Celtic-Galatian heartland unlikely.[285] (a) There is no hard evidence for Jews living in the region of (northern) Galatia in the first century A.D. The earliest evidence for Jews in the region comes from Kalecık, northeast of Ancyra, and dates to the third century.[286] This fact is explained by two factors: when the Seleucid kings settled Jews in the colonies, they had newly founded Asia Minor, and northern Galatia was the region of the Celts; and Jews usually settled along the main trade routes or in cities that were centers of trade—the expansion of the Roman roads in Galatia under the Flavian emperors dates to the late first

---

[283]*NSS* 2:758. Supporting the view of simultaneous action is Hemer 1989, 281-82; supporting the view of subsequent action are Ramsay 1893, 89; G. M. Lee, "The Aorist Participle of Subsequent Action (Acts 16,6)," *Bib* 51 (1970): 235-237.

[284]Riesner 1994, 253 (ET, 285).

[285]Riesner (1994, 250-53 [ET, 281-86]) and Breytenbach (1996, 99-173) have argued against the North Galatia theory (*Landschaftshypothese*); Becker (1997, 986-87) remains unconvinced. Many British scholars, such as William Ramsay in the nineteenth century and F. F. Bruce, Howard Marshall and Stephen Mitchell in the twentieth century, have long supported the "province hypothesis"—that is, a South Galatian address for Paul's letter to the Galatians.

[286]See A. R. R. Sheppard, "Pagan Cults in Roman Asia Minor," *ΤΑΛΑΝΤΑ* 12-13 (1980-1981): 77-101, esp. 94-97, quoted by Breytenbach (1996, 145-46 with nn. 89-90), who refers to private communications of Stephen Mitchell and Johan Strubbe, who know the unpublished material from Ancyra and Pessinus and confirm that there is no evidence for a Jewish presence in this region for the first and second centuries A.D.

century, and the urbanization of northern Galatia began only with Augustus. The activities of the Jewish-Christian agitators to whose positions Paul reacts in his letter to the Galatians become intelligible if we assume the existence of a synagogue into which the newly circumcised Gentile believers should be integrated.[287] (b) The "linguistic isolation" of northern Galatia would have made missionary outreach in this region even more challenging than usual. (c) The journey that the North Galatia theory presupposes leads through eastern Phrygia and the southern area of the Galatian region, an unpopulated area: immediately north of Iconium there is a steppe region. (5) An assumed journey through northern Galatia faces the difficulty of having to explain Acts 16:7, as Rainer Riesner argues: "Anyone in the area around Ancyra who wants to reach Bithynia does not turn in an almost right angle westward to the vicinity of the Mysian boundary. Even assuming that Galatia is referring only to the area around Pessinus, the mention of Mysia still does not really make sense. Bithynia lay immediately to the north, whereas Phrygian territory separated the city from Mysia in the west."[288]

The fourth argument is not completely convincing: (1) The reference to a lack of evidence for synagogues in northern Galatia is an argument from silence that, as such, is not fully compelling. And the hypothesis of visiting Jewish-Christian teachers who operated independently of a local synagogue is not totally implausible, considering the fact that Peter was active already in the first months after Jesus' crucifixion "independently" of institutional links with "the synagogue" or with the temple, when the issue of the integration of converted Gentiles was not yet a critical one. (2) The Celtic language was preserved in (northern) Galatia indeed for a long time. However, at least in the larger cities of Pessinus, Ancyra, Tavium and Germa, refounded under Augustus, people spoke not only Celtic but also Greek.[289] (3) The area between Ancyra and Iconium—the western areas of the province of Galatia and the eastern areas of the province of Asia—were densely populated at the time of the Roman Empire.[290] (4) The cities in northern Galatia would have been attractive goals for a missionary journey.

Ancyra (Ἄγκυρα; mod. Ankara)[291] is situated at the confluence of the rivers Bent Deresi (Hatip Çayı), Çubuk Çayı and İnce Su, which together form the Ankara Çayı River, which flows into the Sangarios River. Ancyra has prehistoric origins and was settled in the Hittite and in the Phrygian periods. The foundation of the city traces back to the Phrygian king Midas in the eighth century B.C. (Pausanias 1.4.5). In the third century B.C. Ancyra was the capital of the Galatian region of the Tectosages (Strabo 12.5.2). Augustus organized Ancyra as a polis and as capital of the province of Galatia founded in 25 B.C.; the era of the city begins on September 23 of 22 or 21 B.C. (as does the era of Pessinus and Tavium).[292] The games of the assembly (*koinon*) of the province of Galatia took place in Ancyra and Tavium. Ancyra was located at the most significant crossroads in central Asia minor, particularly since

---

[287]Breytenbach 1996, 146, 143.
[288]Riesner 1994, 251 (ET, 283).
[289]See S. Mitchell 1995a, 1:50, 88-89, 174-75.
[290]See S. Mitchell 1995a, 1:148.
[291]G. Hirschfeld, "Ancyra 1," PW 1.2 (1894): 2221-22; S. Mitchell, *PECS* 5455; idem, *OCD* 87; K. Strobel, *DNP* 1:707; Belke 1984, 126-30; Daniel M. Krencker and Martin Schede, *Der Tempel in Ankara* (Denkmäler antiker Architektur 3; Berlin: de Gruyter, 1936); Magie 1950, 1:455, 459; 2:1311 n. 12; Emin Bosch, *Quellen zur Geschichte der Stadt Ankara im Altertum* (Ankara: Türk Tarih Kurumu Basimevi, 1967); Price 1984, 267-68 (nos. 108-9); S. Mitchell 1986; 1995, 1:86-89, 101-14, 118-20, 214, 244; 2:13-14, 84-85.
[292]See S. Mitchell 1986, 21-22.

the Flavian emperors established the Euphrates border. Under Augustus the temple of Roma and Augustus (Sebasteion) was erected, as probably was the theater. No major building activities are known until Caracalla, during whose principate the monumental baths and a gymnasium were built; the Roman city wall dates to A.D. 270. Ancyra was one of the few cities that had more than twenty-five thousand inhabitants. When the Sebasteion was inaugurated, probably in A.D. 19, the *Res Gestae* of Augustus were inscribed in Latin and Greek on the walls of the temple; in A.D. 39 a new altar was erected, presumably in connection with the death of Tiberius and the accession of Gaius Caligula. Besides the Sebasteion there were sanctuaries of Aphrodite, Asclepius and Hygieia, Demeter, Dionysus, the Dioscuri, Hekate, Helios, Heracles, Hermes, Isis, Leto, Nemesis, Men, the muses, Sarapis, Tyche and Zeus Tavianos. Ancyra was a cultural center at least since the second century, as is documented by inscriptions honoring philosophers and philologists. It was easy to travel from Antioch in Syria to Ancyra. David French describes in detail the Roman road from Constantinople via Ancyra to Antioch; the road was built between A.D. 80 and 82 but followed the route of an earlier road.[293] Pliny comments on the dense traffic on this road (Pliny, *Ep.* 10.77.3). The bishop Markellos attended the Council of Nicea in A.D. 325.

Pessinus (Πεσσινοῦς; mod. Ballıhisar),[294] an old Phrygian city on the river Gallos, 16 km north of the Sangarios River (128 km southwest of Ancyra), was the largest trade center in western Galatia. At the time of Augustus, Pessinus was an old temple-city of the Anatolian cult of Cybele. The cult of the mother-goddess Magna Mater of Cybele (Strabo 12.5.3) was alive well into the early Byzantine period. In the second century B.C. the Celtic tribe of the Tolistoagii settled in the region. During the rule of the Galatian princes Pessinus became a priest-state but remained autonomous. Augustus refounded Pessinus as a polis in 22 B.C. The cults attested at Pessinus include Aphrodite, Apollo, Artemis, Asclepius, Athene, Attis, Demeter, Dionysus, Eros, Harpocrates, Helios, Heracles, Hermes, Hygieia, Isis, Cybele, Men, Nemesis, Nike, Poseidon, Sarapis, Tyche, Zeus, and the river-gods Gallus and Sagaris. Under Tiberius a temple dedicated to the imperial cult was erected in the southern part of Pessinus. In the vicinity of the city fifteen Roman cemeteries were discovered. The first documented bishop is Demetrius, who supported John Chrysostom. Bishops of Pessinus attended the Councils of Ephesus (A.D. 431 and 449) and Chalcedon (A.D. 451).

Tavium (mod. Büyüknefes),[295] about 140 km east of Ancyra, was the capital of the tribe of the Galatian Trocmi and cult place of Jupiter Tavianus. Augustus refounded the city as a polis in 22-20 B.C. Since the time of Nero the games of the provincial assembly (*koinon*) of Galatia were held in Tavium, alternating with Ancyra every four years. The city had the obligatory baths, a gymnasium, a temple of Zeus, a temple of Asclepius and other sanctuaries. Tavium was located at an important road junction with routes branching off to Ancyra, Amaseia and Neokaisareia, Sebasteia and Kaisareia.

---

[293]See French 1981-1988, vol. 1; on the dating of the Roman road, 1:32.

[294]W. Ruge, PW 19.1 (1937): 1104-13; W. L. MacDonald, *PECS* 693-94; E. Olshausen, *KP* 4:666-67; S. Mitchell, *OCD*, 1148; Belke 1984, 214-15; Jones 1937, 111-12, 118-21; G. Cohen 1995, 380; S. Mitchell 1995a, 1:54, 82-89; 2:14; Breytenbach 1996, 120-22. Excavations: John Devreker and Marc Waelkens, *Les fouilles de la Rijksuniversiteit te Gent à Pessinonte 1967-1973* (Dissertationes archaeologicae Gandenses 22; Brugge: De Tempel, 1984).

[295]W. Ruge, PW 4.A (1932): 2524-25; Magie 1950, 1:455, 459; 2:1311 n. 13; S. Mitchell, *PECS* 887; Belke 1984, 229-30; S. Mitchell 1995a, 1:82-89, 112, 116; 2:22.

Two main routes led from Pisidian Antiocheia to Ancyra and Tavium in northern Galatia.[296] (1) The peaks of Sultan Dağ, directly north of Antiocheia, reaching 2,531 m on Mount Toprak, would appear to preclude a direct connection toward the north. It was possible, however, to travel from Antiocheia on a road running in an east-northeasterly direction, just north of the temple of Men, across the mountains to reach Philomelion (mod. Akşehir) and connect with the larger road running south-east;[297] a road running east of Lake Akçaşehir led to Amorion,[298] and via Pessinus, Germa and Gordium one could reach Ancyra (a total of 310 km). A second route ran from Philomelion via a road further west via Çay on the southwestern end of Lake Eber and via Appola (mod. Çoğu) to Amorion.[299] Both these routes passed through the province of Asia in the region between Philomelion and Amorion, for roughly 110 km, or four days, of travel. There was a Christian community in Philomelion by A.D. 155 at the latest: the church in Smyrna informs the church in Philomelion in a letter written in A.D. 156 about the martyrdom of Polycarp, which had happened less than a year earlier: "The church of God that temporarily resides in Smyrna to the church of God that temporarily resides in Philemelium, and to all congregations of temporary residents everywhere, who belong to the holy and universal church" (*Mart. Pol.* 1:1).[300] (2) A more comfortable route to Ancyra that consistently avoided the province of Asia ran from Antiocheia via Iconium, 145 km to the southeast, and via Kongustos (mod. Altımekin, former Zıvarık)[301] toward the north (a total of 380 km). The fact that Paul continued his journey toward Mysia (via Dorylaion) suggests that Pessinus was the only Galatian city in the strict (Celtic) sense of the word that would have been a natural stop or goal for missionary work.[302]

Paul thus could indeed have reached the heartland of the Celts. Assuming for the sake of the argument that Paul traveled on one of these routes to northern Galatia, we do not know whether he actually preached in Galatian cities. It is risky to deduce a missionary activity solely from the verb διέρχεσθαι (*dierchesthai:* in Acts 16:6 supposedly a technical term for missionary work, as in Acts 8:4; 13:6).[303] In Acts 8:4 the verb *dierchesthai* is used

---

[296]See French 1981-1988, vol. 1, appendix; Belke 1984, appendix; Levick 1967, 7-16.

[297]See T. Drew-Bear, *BAGRW,* map 62.

[298]Amorion (mod. Hisar, former Hergan Kale) belonged in the Roman period to Phrygia (Strabo 12.8.13; Ptolemaios 5.2.17). Amorion was, besides Apollonia, a customs post on the border between the province of Galatia and the province of Asia (*AnSt* 38 [1988]: 180-81, no. 1). Roman soldiers were stationed in the city. Bishops of Amorion participated in the Councils of Ephesus (A.D. 431) and Chalcedon (A.D. 451). See G. Hirschfeld, PW 1.2 (1894): 1876; Belke 1984, 122-25; S. Mitchell 1995a, 1:68, 121, 141; G. Cohen 1995, 277.

[299]A road even further to the west, running into the province of Asia and passing through a much greater number of cities, ran through Phrygian Apollonia (Sozopolis, mod. Uluborlu) and Apameia (mod. Dinar), and from there toward the northeast to Metropolis (mod. Ayazinköyü), Synnada (mod. Şuhut), Prymnessus (mod. Afyon), Amorion, Pessinus, Germa and Gordium to Ancyra (about 340 km total).

[300]On the date of *Martyrdom of Polycarp* see Lightfoot, *Apostolic Fathers,* 1:646-722; Buschmann, *Das Martyrium des Polykarp,* 39-40. The author of *Martyrdom of Polycarp* does not, as Campenhausen (1974, 76) suggests, pursue a missionary purpose, but rather the pragmatic goal of helping the church know how to behave in the context of persecution, using the form of an evangelical norm of martyrdom, reinforcing the behavior of faithful Christians (Buschmann, *Das Martyrium des Polykarp,* 65).

[301]See Belke 1984, 153.

[302]Thus Breytenbach 1996, 118.

[303]Thus Pesch, *Apg,* 2:100.

parallel to εὐαγγελίζειν (*euangelizein,* "to preach the good news") and thus, taken by it-self, is not evidence for missionary proclamation.[304] In addition, if Paul had engaged in missionary work in northern Galatia, we would expect Luke at least to mention Paul preaching there, if not establishing churches in this region. This is a reasonable expecta-tion particularly if Paul's letter to the Galatians is indeed addressed to churches in north-ern Galatia, assuming that the author of the book of Acts knew this letter. And we must remember that the region around Ancyra is 200 km north of the route from Lystra, Ico-nium and Antiocheia to Mysia: it would have taken specific planning and deliberate effort to start missionary work there. Finally, the presence of Christians is attested at a relatively late date in Ancyra.[305]

The arguments for the second option, the South Galatia hypothesis (or "provincial hy-pothesis") are more convincing as a whole:[306] the phrase "the region of Phrygia and Ga-latia" in Acts 16:6 refers to the region of *Phrygia Paroreius*—that is, the region on both sides of the Sultan Dağ Mountains whose inhabitants were ethnically Phrygian. Parts of *Phrygia Paroreius* belonged to the province of Galatia (while other parts belonged to the province of Asia).[307]

I conclude with regard to Paul's plans and activities in the summer of A.D. 49: (1) The first goal of Paul's journey was to strengthen the churches that he had founded during his mission to southern Galatia (Acts 15:36, 41; 16:5) in Derbe, Lystra and Iconium Antiocheia, and to convey the decisions of the apostolic council (Acts 16:4). This goal was achieved successfully. (2) The second goal of the journey was new missionary outreach to the province of Asia, probably in Ephesus. It has proved impossible to reconstruct at what point this mission was planned. This goal was not achieved, because a divine intervention pre-vented the missionaries from preaching in the province of Asia. (3) It is un-likely that Paul engaged in missionary work in northern Galatia—that is, among the Greeks and the Celts living in the cities of the ethnic Galatians. The arguments that speak against the plausibility of a journey of Paul and his co-workers to the area around Pessinus and Ancyra are quite weighty. (4) Paul possibly preached the gospel in Phrygian Galatia, meaning the western part of South Galatia. (5) Due to divine intervention, the goal of a newly planned mission to Bithynia could not be realized. (6) Since missionary work in the west (province of Asia) and in the north (province of Bithynia) was not pos-

---

[304]See Riesner 1994, 250 (ET, 282).

[305]Differently Belke (1984, 127), who assumes, in the context of the North Galatian theory, that Christianization "probably goes back to apostolic times." The bishops Markellos and Basile-lios of Ancyra played a role in the theological discussions of the fourth century. See also S. Mitchell (1995a, 2:38 with n. 223, 2:62 with n. 56), who refers to the fact that hardly any Christian inscriptions of the pre-Constantinian period have been found in Northern Galatia.

[306]See Stuhlmacher 1992-1999, 1:226; Witulski 2000, esp. 82-224, with an interpretation of Gal 4:8-20 (Witulski's redaction-critical operations [ibid., 71-81] are as unconvincing as his inter-pretation of Gal 4:10 in terms of the emperor cult [ibid., 152-75]). Contra Pesch, *Apg,* 2:101; Barrett, *Acts,* 2:766-68; Fitzmyer, *Acts,* 578.

[307]See S. Mitchell 1995a, 2:3-4.

sible, and since Paul did not want to return to Syria, he traveled through Mysia to Alexandria Troas.

Notes on the travel route. In which cities of southern Galatia could Paul have preached the gospel? He left Lystra (Acts 16:1) and probably visited the churches in Iconium (Acts 16:2-4) and Antiocheia (cf. Acts 16:3, 4). The next geographical comment refers to a journey toward the north in the direction of Bithynia and Mysia (Acts 16:7). The following possibilities present themselves.

1. After visiting the church in Antiocheia, Paul concentrated his missionary efforts for some time on Phrygian Galatia, preaching the gospel in cities that he had not visited before. A new missionary venture to Bithynia was planned at a somewhat later date. Paul could well have spent time in the Phrygian region of Galatia without orienting himself toward the north. It is not impossible to assume that Paul wanted to stay in the same general area, waiting to see whether the original plan for missionary outreach to the province of Asia could be realized after all. Two options were available: (a) in the Cillanian Plain, missionary outreach in Neapolis and in Anabura; (b) northwest of Iconium, missionary outreach in Laodikeia Katakekaumene and in Tyraion, located on the main road to Cotiaeum.

On *Neapolis* see §27.1.

Anabura ('Ἀναβούρα; at the site of former Enevre Köyü)[308] is located in the Cillanian Plain, 6 km north of Lake Karalis, about 30 km south-southeast of Antiocheia. Strabo quotes information from Artemidoros, according to whom Anabura belonged to the cities of Pisidia together with Selge, Sagalassos, Cremna and Termessos (Strabo 12.7.2). The city maintained contacts with Antiocheia, as Men Askaenos was also worshiped in Anabura. Very few remains survive e.g., lids of sarcophagi.

Laodikeia Katakekaumene (Λαοδίκεια ἡ κατακεκαυμένη; Laodicea Combusta; mod. Ladik, Halıcı),[309] about 33 km north-northwest of Iconium, was founded by the Seleucid kings. The city belonged originally to Lycaonia; it is mentioned by Strabo at a town on the trade route from Ephesus to the east (14.4.29). The epithet *kekaumenē* possibly implies the presence of furnaces for smelting: vermilion and copper were mined in the area, and inscriptions attest the activity of goldsmiths.[310] For the second and third centuries private and imperial domains are documented at Laodikeia Katakekaumene. About 2.5 km southeast of the city was a temple; an inscription attests a priest of the *theoi Sebastoi*. Like Iconium, Derbe and Seleucia, Laodikeia Katakekaumene boasted a special relationship with Claudius: the city was allowed to call itself Claudiolaodicea. A theater, a nymphaeum and an aqueduct are attested. Some scholars link the family of C. Iulius Paulus, which an inscription of Laodikeia documents (*MAMA* I 34, 44), with

---

[308]G. Hirschfeld, "Anabura 2," PW 1.2 (1894): 2016-17; Belke and Mersich 1990, 182-83; Jones 1937, 133, 141; Magie 1950, 1:457; 2:1316; S. Mitchell 1995a, 1:90 with n. 109; 2:25. Enevre Köyü is located 12 km west-southwest of mod. Sarkikaraagac.

[309]W. Ruge, PW 12 (1924): 721-22; H. Treidler, "Laodikeia 3," *KP* 3:483; K. Belke, "Laodikeia 3," *DNP* 6:1132; Belke and Mersich 1990, 327-28; Ramsay 1890, 39, 343; Magie 1950, 1:456, 547; 2:1313; Levick 1967, 16, 52, 165; G. Cohen 1995, 346-48; S. Mitchell 1995a, 1:85, 95, 132, 214; 2:2, 26-27.

[310]*MAMA* I 24, 24a, 170, 171, 214, 215, 243, 281, 281a; cf. ibid., XIII-XIV.

Iulius Paullus, the senator from Pisidian Antiocheia.[311] Besides the old Phrygian gods and the usual Greek deities, the citizens also worshiped Men Askaenos. An inscription from the third century documents the presence of the Jews (*IJudO* II 227). The pre-Constantinian Christian churches in eastern Phrygia were particularly conspicuous in the area around Laodikeia Katakekaumene.[312]

Tyraion (Τυράϊον; mod. Ilgın),[313] about 40 km west of Laodikeia Katakekaumene, was also located on the old trade route from Ephesus to the Euphrates River. Tyraion was an important city as early as 401 B.C., when Cyrus marched through the area (Xenophon, *Anab.* 1.12.14). The city became Hellenized already in the Seleucid period. Pliny states that Tyraion marked the boundary between Phrygia and Lycaonia (Pliny, *Nat.* 5.25.95), Strabo calls it the easternmost city of Phrygia Paroreius (Strabo 14.2.29). Hot springs containing iron and sulfur were located about 2.5 km west of Tyraion.

2. Paul engaged in missionary work in Phrygian Galatia, but he planned a mission to Bithynia early on. If this plan was conceived during his visit to Antiocheia or shortly afterwards, an evangelistic activity in Phrygian Galatia would have focused on cities north or west of Antiocheia, depending on the route that he chose to travel toward the north. Again, two options would have presented themselves: (a) west of Lake Eğridir, which could be reached by a road that ran along the western shore of the lake, missionary outreach in Parlais, Prostanna and Seleucia Sidera; (b) cities located on the Via Sebaste north and west of Lake Eğridir in the direction of Apameia, missionary outreach in Tymandus, Apollonia and Aporidos.

If Paul continued to travel on the Via Sebaste after leaving Lystra, an assumption that is not necessary but plausible, the second option is more likely. Paul had passed through Tymandus and Apollonia previously on the occasion of his mission to southern Galatia. He might have decided to preach the gospel in these cities, which presumably he knew from overnight stays, making the best of the situation in which he had to postpone other missionary plans. Assuming that this reconstruction is correct, Paul entered the province of Asia in Apameia. The project of a mission to Bithynia suggests the continuation of the journey in the road leading to the north that runs past Synnada to Prymnessos. If Paul intended to reach Bithynia in Nikaia or Nikomedia, he presumably traveled as far as Cotiaeum, located on the northwestern border between Phrygia and Mysia;[314] perhaps he also reached Dorylaion,[315] an important crossroads located 60 km north-

---

[311]Halfmann 1979, 55, 116, no. 20; cf. J. Taylor 1995, 1205-7; S. Mitchell (1995a, 1:154 with n. 106) remains unconvinced.

[312]See S. Mitchell 1995a, 2:41.

[313]W. Ruge, PW 7.A2 (1948): 1800-1802; Belke 1984, 40, 155; Belke and Mersich 1990, 409-11; Magie 1950, 1:456; S. Mitchell 1995a, 1:85, 156.

[314]See French 1994b, 54.

[315]Ruge, PW 5 (1905): 1577; Belke and Mersich 1990, 238-42; Jones 1937, 37, 60, 65-67, 160; Magie 1950, 2:1000; Peter Frei, "Die epigraphische Erforschung des mittleren Porsuktales in Nordwestphrygien," in Dobesch and Rehrenböck 1993, 189-209, esp. 191-92; G. Cohen 1995, 299; S. Mitchell 1995a, 1:129, 132. The bishop Athenodoros of Dorylaion attended the Council of Nicea.

east of Cotiaeum.[316] Did Paul preach the gospel in these cities? The answer to this question is no, if we relate the divine prohibition of missionary activity in the province of Asia (Acts 16:6b) to all cities in the province. On the other hand, if Paul abandoned a planned missionary outreach to Ephesus only, the provincial capital, he could well have preached the gospel in these cities during the (hesitant) continuation of his journey toward the northeast of Asia Minor.

Parlais (ὁ Παρλαοῦ; near mod. Barla, now Kocapınar),[317] 3 km west of Lake Eğridir and 46 km southwest of Antiocheia, was one of the military colonies founded by Augustus in Pisidia (Colonia Iulia Augusta Hadriana). The evidence of inscriptions and coins suggests that Parlais was the least important Roman colony in southern Galatia. Perhaps only five hundred Roman colonists settled in Parlais, which was, however, integrated in the Pisidian road network. Hartwin Brandt observes that "the connections to the Via Sebaste are uncomplicated in the flat terrain, the Augustan colony presumably was linked by connecting roads with the main road."[318]

Prostanna (Προστανά; mod. Eğridir),[319] 32 km south of Parlais on the southern end of Lake Eğridir, had contacts with a Roman quaestor already in 113 B.C. The city had a nearly circular acropolis (200 m in diameter). Coins document a temple of Men; several public buildings are attested.

Seleucia Sidera (Σελεύκεια ἡ Σιδηρᾶ; mod. Asar Tepe, Selef),[320] 2 km north-northeast of the city of Bayat near (mod.) Isparta, was one of the cities founded by Antiochos I; it belonged to Pisidia. An inscription dedicated to Augustus has been discovered in the city (*CIL* III 6869). Under Claudius the new polis Claudioseleucia was founded in Seleucia, which maintained close official relations with Pisidian Antiocheia. The city was called "Sidera" in the fourth century. Excavations carried out in 1993 discovered remains of the Hellenistic wall, the theater, living quarters, a circular building that probably served a religious function, and the necropolis. The first bishop of Seleucia, Artemon, is said to have been appointed by the apostle Paul,[321] a tradition that cannot be confirmed.

On *Tymandus* and *Apollonia* see §27.1.

---

[316]See V. Weber 1920, 33; K. Lake, in *Begs.* 4:230; Haenchen, *Acts,* 466 n. 3 (ET, 484 n. 3), besides Cotiaeum; Bowers 1979, 508; Jewett 1997, 5-6.

[317]B. Levick, PWSup 12 (1970): 990-1005; Belke and Mersich 1990, 356; Levick 1967, 53-55, 94-95, 159-62; S. Mitchell 1995a, 1:77, 90; H. Brandt, "Parlais: Eine römische Kolonie in Pisidien," *EA* 24 (1994): 57-60.

[318]H. Brandt, *EA* 24 (1995): 59.

[319]Kirsten, PW 23.1 (1957): 899; M. Ballance, "The Site of Prostanna," *AnSt* 9 (1959): 125-29; E. N. Lane, "The Temple-Type of Prostanna," in Şahin et al. 1978, 540-45; S. Mitchell 1995a, 1:72.

[320]W. Ruge, "Seleukeia 6," PW 2.A1 (1929): 1204-5; E. Olshausen, "Seleukeia 6," *KP* 5:85; G. E. Bean, *PECS* 821; Belke and Mersich 1990, 378; Levick 1967, 17, 128; G. Cohen 1995, 349-50; S. Mitchell 1995a, 1:20, 78-79, 95; Ergün Lafli, "Sagalassos Red Slip Ware aus Seleukeia Sidera: Ein Beispiel der Verbreitung der sagalassischen Keramik im römischen Pisidien," *Forum Archaeologiae* 10 (1999): <http://farch.tsx.org>.

[321]*BHG* no. 2047; H. Delehaye, ed., *Synaxarium,* 557.

Aporidos (mod. Eldere),[322] on the eastern shore of Lake Aulokrene, was linked with Apollonia, 13 km to the west, via a road.

Apameia (ʼΑπάμεια Κιβωτός; Apameia Kibotos, Celaenae, mod. Dinar/Dimêr)[323] was founded after 280 B.C. at the Marsyas River by Antiochos I, who named the city after his mother. He resettled the inhabitants of the neighboring city of Celaenae, which had a long history as the most important royal residence of the Persians in Phrygia, at the main southern road to the east. The Romans gave the city to Pergamon after 188 B.C. Apameia was almost completely destroyed in the early first century B.C. by one of the numerous earthquakes; it was quickly rebuilt with the help of Mithradates. Sulla integrated the nominally autonomous city in 85 B.C. into the Roman province of Asia. Strabo describes Apameia as a large commercial city that was surpassed in Asia Minor only by Ephesus (12.8.15). In the Roman period Apameia was an assize center and the center of a large region—not only for Phrygia, Lydia and Caria but also for Cappadocia, Pamphylia and Pisidia. The largest Jewish communities of Phrygia existed in Apameia and the surrounding region, probably since 200 B.C. The original Jewish version of the first two books of the *Sibylline Oracles* were written very probably between 30 B.C. and A.D. 70 in Apameia.[324] According to *Sib. Or.* 1:261-267, Noah's ark landed in Phrygia on Mount Ararat at the source of the Marsyas River. A Jewish inscription dating to the third century A.D. attests that the (Jewish) reader of the tombstone acknowledged the validity of the Jewish law (τòν νόμον οἶδεν Ἐιουδέων [*CIJ* 774; *IJudO* II 179]).[325] When Apameia was again damaged by an earthquake in A.D. 53, Emperor Claudius granted the city a tax exemption for several years. A Christian community existed in Apameia by A.D. 243 at the latest. The earliest epigraphical evidence for the term ΙΧΘΥΣ (*ICHTHYS*) as a Christian codeword comes from Apameia (*MAMA* IV 31), as does the first attested use of the Christogram (the combined first two Greek letters of *Christos,* Χ and Ρ); the first line of the inscription *MAMA* VI 234 reads, ΖΩΕΠΔѮXΧPEI, perhaps to be read as ζῶν ἐποίησε δοῦλος Χρίστου Χριστιανòς Χριστιανοῖς (*zōn epoiēse doulos Christou Christianos Christianois*).[326] The bishop Tarsikios of Apameia attended the Council of Nicea in A.D. 325.

Metropolis (Μητρόπολις; mod. Tatarlı),[327] about 40 km northeast of Apameia in Phrygia, 6 km east of the ancient west-east road from Smyrna and Ephesus via Laodikeia

---

[322]G. Hirschfeld, PW 2.1 (1895): 175; S. Mitchell, in *BAGRW* 997, with reference to M. Christol, in M. Christol and T. Drew-Bear, *Un castellum romain près d'Apamée de Phrygie* (Denkschriften 189, Vienna: Österreichische Akademie der Wissenschaften 1987), 29-32.

[323]G. Hirschfeld, "Apameia 5," PW 1.2 (1894): 2664; Treidler, *KP* 1:419; J. P. Rey-Coquais, *PECS* 66-67; T. Drew-Bear, "Apameia 2," *DNP* 1:824; Ramsay 1895-1897, 2:396-450; Magie 1950, 1:125-36, 136, 542-43; 2:791 (on the road), 983-84; Macro 1980, 664; Trebilco 1991, 14, 85-103; G. Cohen 1995, 281-85; S. Mitchell 1995a, 1:20, 121, 141, 226 n. 197, 258; 2:33-34, 36, 40-41; Bechard 2000, 300-21.

[324]J. J. Collins, "The Development of the Sibylline Tradition," *ANRW* II.20.1 (1987): 421-59, esp. 442; Trebilco 1991, 96.

[325]See Ramsay 1895-1897, 1.2, no. 399; Trebilco 1991, 100.

[326]See E. Gibson 1978, 113, no. 40 = *MAMA* VI 234. The inscription *MAMA* IV 31 possibly dates between A.D. 200 and 225; see S. Mitchell 1995a, 2:41 n. 244.

[327]W. Ruge, "Metropolis 3," PW 15.2 (1932): 1495; K. Ziegler, "Metropolis 6," *KP* 3:1284; T. Drew-Bear, "Metropolis 6," *DNP* 8:140-41; Belke and Mersich 1990, 339-40; Magie 1950, 2:791; G. Cohen 1995, 313-14; Gates 1995, 239; S. Mitchell 1995a, 1:226 n. 197.

and Apameia to the Euphrates River. Metropolis belonged to the assize district of Apameia in the Roman period. The games that the city organized were called *Sebasta Caesareia*. The theater, renovated in Roman times, is very well preserved; otherwise, no remains survive.

Synnada (Σύναδα; mod. Şuhut),[328] about 26 km south of modern Afyon on a high plateau surrounded by mountains, one of the most important Phrygian cities, would also have been an attractive goal of missionary work. Synnada is attested since the Hellenistic period; it belonged to the *conventus iuridicus* of the province of Asia and thus hosted periodic court days. Synnada was the administrative center of large imperial estates in the area as well as of the marble quarries in Docimium (Dokimeion).[329] Cicero visited Synnada in 52/51 B.C. as governor. The games of the city were called *Panathenaia Atheneia*. Members of the influential family of the Lucii Arruntii lived in Synnada; a certain Arruntia Attice married Hyacintyus, a *tabularius* of the family of Nero.[330] Besides numerous other cults, a priest of *Hygieia* and of *Sophrosynē* is attested for Synnada. It appears that the soldiers of the Legio IV Flavia were stationed in the city, with responsibility for the safety of the main roads in the region. An inscription dating to the first or second century A.D. documents a Jewish community (*CIJ* II 759; *IJudO* II 214). The bishop Prokopios of Synnada attended the Council of Nicea in A.D. 325.

Paul could have traveled to Synnada via the Pentapolis, which included the cities of Eukarpia,[331] Otrus, Stektorion, Bruzos and Hierapolis. *Hierapolis* (Koçhisar, about 45 km north of Apameia) was the home of the bishop Aberkios (ca. A.D. 170), who was a successful missionary not only in the Pentapolis but also in Rome, and visited Syria and the region around Nisibis and Edessa east of the Euphrates River. The tombstone that he himself erected at the age of seventy-two is inscribed with an epigram consisting of twenty-two lines. Lines 3-4, 10-11 read, "Aberkios by name, I am a disciple of the pure Shepherd who feeds his flocks of sheep on mountains and plains [ὃς βόσκει προβάτων ἀγέλας ὄρεσιν πεδίοις τε]. . . . And I saw the plain of Syria and all the cities [ἄστεα πάντα], even Nisibis, crossing over the Euphrates."[332] The authenticity of the events depicted in the *Life of Aberkios*[333] is in part doubtful, but as a whole this text must be regarded as "an important document for the history of the church in the second century. . . . Aberkios, who was like the apostles, was an important personality." Aberkios represents one of the very few missionaries of the second century about whom we have information.

---

[328]W. Ruge, PW 4.A2 (1932): 1410-12; Magie 1950, 1:132; 2:791, 1001; Olshausen, *KP* 5:456-57; S. Mitchell, *OCD* 1463; Belke and Mersich 1990, 393-95; G. Cohen 1995, 322-25; S. Mitchell 1995a, 1:64, 85, 121, 178, 185, 191, 211, 225. Inscriptions: *MAMA* IV 14-35; VI 127-132.

[329]See Belke and Mersich 1990, 237-38; Magie 1950, 1002; G. Cohen 1995, 295-99. On a Jewish presence see Ameling, in *IJudO* II, 2004, 388-92.

[330]*MAMA* IV 53 = *I. GRIAsia* 61; on the Lucii Arruntii in Prymnessos see below.

[331]See Belke and Mersich 1990, 250-51; Ramsay 1895-1897, 1:678-79; G. Cohen 1995, 299-301.

[332]Newly edited, with discussion, in W. Wischmeyer 1980, 22-47. See Grégoire 1955-1957; K. Wegenast, *KP* 1:12-13; Bundy 1990; Merkelbach 1997b; Kant 2001; Ross 2001, 117.

[333]Theodor Nissen, *S. Abercii Vita* (Leipzig: Teubner, 1912); cf. Lightfoot, *Apostolic Fathers*, 2.1:493-97. The text was written after A.D. 363, as the reference to the emperor Julian shows, but it evidently is based on an older version that must have been written soon after Aberkios's death; see Merkelbach 1997b, 385 n. 7; the quotation that follows above, ibid., 399.

Prymnessos (Πρυμνησσός; mod. Sülün, former Suğlün),[334] 22 km north of Synnada, was located at an important road junction, a factor that would have been important for the dissemination of the gospel in the region. The road to northern Galatia via Pessinus and Germa passed through the city. The main deity of Prymnessos was the Phrygian goddess "Justice" (δικαιοσύνη), whose altar stood in the center of the city; she is depicted on coins with scales in her hand. Remains of the ancient theater survive on the slope at the eastern end of the city. In Sülün and the surrounding villages numerous Roman fragments and inscriptions have been found. One inscription dating to around A.D. 50 honors a certain Lucius Arruntius Scribonianus, the prefect of Prymnessos.[335]

Leontos Kome (mod. Gazlıgöl),[336] about 30 km north of Prymnessos on the upper Kaystros River, was a spa with a mineral spring.

Meiros (mod. Demirözü, former Malatça)[337] about 30 km north of Leontos Kome on the junction of the road running via Nakoleia to Dorylaion. Meiros is mentioned in inscriptions both as *katoikia* and as *polis.*

Cotiaeum (Κοττυάειον; mod. Kütahya),[338] about 45 km northwest of Meiros in a fertile plain on the upper Tembris River, was located at an important junction of the most westerly route of the north-south roads emanating from Dorylaion. No ancient remains survive; stone blocks of the ancient city, some with inscriptions, are used in buildings in Kütahya. The hill on which the fortress is located probably was the acropolis of Cotiaeum. Aelius Aristides, the famous rhetor born in Hadrianothera, received a solid rhetorical education in Cotiaeum in A.D. 132 in the school of the renowned grammarian Alexandros, later the teacher of Marcus Aurelius.[339]

Aizanoi (Ἀζανοί, Αἰζανοί; mod. Çavdarhisar),[340] on the Rhyndakos River (mod. Çavdarhisar Suyu), 54 km southwest of Cotiaeum, was known since Hellenistic times (Strabo 12.8.4). The city of Aizanoi originated from a temple of Zeus that was one of the most significant cult places in Asia Minor: a cave 3.5 km southwest of the city on the river Penkalas, a branch of the Rhyndakos River, was regarded as the birthplace of Zeus and had a Cybele sanctuary of Meter Steunene (Μήτηρ Στευνηνή). Eumenes II conquered the city in 184 B.C. and incorporated it into the Pergamene Empire. After 133 B.C. the city belonged to Rome. For the time of Augustus a high priest of the imperial cult is documented for

---

[334]E. Kirsten, PW 23.1 (1957): 1154-56; Belke and Mersich 1990, 364-65; Magie 1950, 2:791; Price 1984, 265, no. 89; S. Mitchell 1995a, 1:159, 191; 2:13, 18.

[335]*CIL* III Suppl. 7043 = *SEG* XXXVI 1200 = *I. GRIAsia* 135.

[336]W. Ruge, PW 12.2 (1925): 2057; T. Drew-Bear, in *BAGRW* 961.

[337]W. Ruge, PW 15.1 (1931): 359; Belke and Mersich 1990, 337-38.

[338]W. Ruge, PW 11.2 (1922): 1526-27; Belke and Mersich 1990, 312-16; Jones 1937, 38, 65, 67-68; Magie 1950, 2:1000; S. Mitchell 1995a, 1:179-80.

[339]See R. Klein 1981, 73-74.

[340]G. Hirschfeld, PW 1.1 (1893): 1131-32; R. Naumann, *PECS* 16; S. Mitchell, *OCD* 32-33; Belke and Mersich 1990, 201-3; Levick and Mitchell, in *MAMA* IX (1988), xvii-lxix; Jones 1937, 60, 65, 67; Magie 1950, 1:132, 544; 2:999-1000; S. Mitchell 1995a, 1:199-200, 214, 219 n. 146, 225; K. Rheidt, "Aizanoi: Bericht über die Ausgrabungen und Forschungen 1997 bis 2000," *Archäologischer Anzeiger* (2001): 241-267 In regard to the ongoing excavations carried out by the German Archaeological Institute see <www.dainst.de/de/pro/aizanoi>. Inscriptions: *MAMA* IX 1-589.

Aizanoi whose main qualification consisted of his financial resources. The city maintained close relations with the emperor, seeking his protection; the city council was described as φιλοσέβαστος (*philosebastos*), which is best translated as "loyal to the emperor." In one inscription Claudius is called "god, savior and benefactor" (Θεὸς σωτὴρ καὶ εὐεργέτης, *theos sōtēr kai euergetēs*).[341] Aizanoi was one of three cities in Asia Minor that was allowed to name its games after Claudius (*Sebasta Claudieia*). A certain Menogenes son of Nannas was granted Roman citizenship by Claudius; he was one of the wealthiest and most significant citizens of Aizanois. In the second century Aizanoi was the most important city in northern Phrygia, and its monumental buildings, erected between A.D. 125 and 175, could compare with those of Ephesus, particularly the large temple of Zeus, the temple of Meter Steunene, a second temple of Zeus (112 by 130 m; the building with sixteen surviving columns is the best preserved Ionic temple of Asia Minor), the theater and the stadium. The Jewish community of Aizanoi evidently was small.[342] The members of the city magistrate were called ἄρχοντες (*archontes*); the members of the executive called themselves στρατηγοί (*stratēgoi*). Inscriptions attest lawyers, painters, sculptors, musicians, gladiators and gymnasiarchs. The inscription *MAMA* IX 319, found on a funerary monument, begins with the letters ΠΖ: this may be a date (year 87 of the era of Aizanoi, thus A.D. 56/57), although that does not quite fit the style of the monument; or the letters may be an abbreviated reference to π[νεῦμα] ζ[ωῆς] (*p/neuma z/ōēs/*), the "Spirit of life," which would be a very early reference to Christians in Aizanoi. The Christian faith seems to have made only slow progress in the area: only a few Christian inscriptions dating to the fourth and fifth centuries have been found, in contrast to the numerous Christian inscriptions of the upper Tembris Valley. The later bishops of Aizanoi resided in the rebuilt temple of Zeus. The bishop Phristicius of Aizanoi attended the Council of Nicea in A.D. 325.

Since the plan to travel north[343] and to begin missionary work in Bithynia was prevented by "the Spirit of Jesus" (Acts 16:7b), Paul traveled through Mysia (Acts 16:8a).[344] Coming from Cotiaeum, he presumably passed through Kadoi, traveled along the upper reaches of the Makestos River (mod. Simav) in a westerly direction via Synaos, Hadrianothera and the port city of Adramyttion to Alexandria Troas.

Mysia (Μυσία),[345] a region in northwestern Asia Minor, received its name from the Mysians, the indigenous inhabitants of the area. Strabo found it difficult to describe the borders of Mysia: "It is difficult to mark the boundaries between the Bithynians and the Phry-

---

[341]*CIG* 3840 = *IGR* IV 581; *CIG* 3831a = *IGR* IV 584. *MAMA* IX 30 (second century) honors a certain Pollio, whose son venerated the emperors: εἰς εὐσεβείαν τ[ῶν] Κυρίων.

[342]*MAMA* IX 550b (Jewish symbols, without inscription). The funerary inscriptions *MAMA* IX 420, 430 mention a certain Mathias, but it is uncertain whether the name is Jewish ("Mathia," "Matha," and "Mathos" are Phrygian names). *MAMA* IX 421 mentions a certain Χελειδόν (*Cheleidon*), who perhaps was a Jew.

[343]If Paul decided in Antiocheia to travel north to Bithynia, he could have chosen the difficult route across the Sultan Dağ to Philomelion (Akşehir), and from there via Polybotos (Bolvadin) and Amorion (Hisar Köy) to Pessinus (175 km) and Germa (200 km).

[344]In Acts 16:8 the term *parelthontes* could also mean "to pass by," but most exegetes assume "travel through" Mysia (Codex D reads *dielthontes*); see BDAG 776, s.v. "παρέρχομαι 6"; Barrett, *Acts,* 2:770-71.

[345]F. K. Dörner, 3:1529-32; E. Schwertheim, *DNP* 8:608-10; Pekáry 1980, 613.

gians and the Mysians. . . . And it is agreed that each tribe is 'apart' from the others (in the case of the Phrygians and Mysians, at least, there is a proverb, 'Apart are the boundaries of the Mysians and Phrygians'), but that it is difficult to mark the boundaries between them" (Strabo 12.4.4). In the north Mysia bordered on the Propontis and the Hellespont, while the border with Bithynia in the east ran along the Rhyndakos River (mod. Orhaneli, Koca Dere) and the Mysian-Bithynian Mount Olympus; the border with Phrygia and Lydia to the south was in flux: parts of Mysia Minor were also called Phrygia Minor (see Ptolemaios 5.2.4); in the west Mysia bordered on the Aegean Sea. The region along the border with Phrygia was called Mysia Abrettene (Strabo 12.8.11), with the cities of Ancyra Sidera (mod. Boğaz Köy) and Synaos (mod. Simav) in the eastern Makestos Valley. The city of Kadoi, further to the east on the upper Hermos River, was located, according to Ptolemaios (5.2.16), in the border area of Mysia, Lydia and Phrygia.

Troas (Τρῳάς; or Troad),[346] the northwestern tip of Asia Minor with Troy as a major center, was the region through which the land traffic from Europe to Asia passed and that controlled the shipping traffic from the Mediterranean to the Black Sea. The importance of the region is reflected in the fact that Strabo provides an extensive description (13.1.1). The region of Troas was settled by Greek colonists in the eighth and seventh centuries B.C. In the seventh century it was controlled by the Lydians, who ruled in Sardis; in the fifth century it was controlled by the Persians. After the Battle of Granikos Troas became part of the sphere of influence of Alexander the Great; later the Seleucid and the Pergamene kings ruled the region before it became part of the Roman province of Asia in 129 B.C. The fact that none of the cities of Troas was granted the privilege of being temple warden (*neōkoros*) indicates that the Roman emperors were not very interested in the region.

Notes on the travel route. Paul presumably traveled on a southern route through Mysia, via Kadoi, Synaos, Attea, Hadrianothera and Pionia to the port city of Adramyttion, then along the coast via Antandros, Gargara and Skamandreia to Alexandria Troas.[347] Robert Jewett proposes the same route as far as Hadrianothera, and then assumes a more northern route through the hinterland of Troas (via Pericharaxis, Ergasteria, Argiza, Argyria, Polichna, Palaiskepsis, Skepsis, Kebren and Skamandros); he argues that the forced resettlement of the population from the port cities in the city of Alexandria Troas largely depopulated these cities, which would have reduced the attractiveness of the route for Paul.[348] Apart from the fact that such a forced resettlement has not been fully confirmed historically, we should recall that Paul evidently did not intend to preach the gospel during his journey through Mysia.

Kadoi (Κάδοι; Cadi; mod. Eski Gediz),[349] about 65 km southwest of Cotiaeum, is mentioned by Polybios in the second century B.C. (33.12.2). During the Roman period Kadoi is described as Mysian or as belonging to Phrygia Epiktetos (Strabo 12.8.12): the city was situated on the

---

[346]Ruge, "Troas 1," PW 7.A1 (1939): 525-83; Danoff, *KP* 5:975; D. Wormell and S. Mitchell, *OCD* 1555; J. M. Cook 1973; Burdick 1978; B. Tenger, "Zur Geographie und Geschichte der Troas," in Schwertheim 1999, 103-80. On Jews in Troas see Ameling, in *IJudO* II, 2004, 303-4.

[347]Burdick (1978, 38-40) opts for a "central" route via Skepsis.

[348]Jewett 1997, esp. 15.

[349]L. Bürchner, PW 10.2 (1919): 1477; H. Treidler, *KP* 3:42; E. Schwertheim, *DNP* 6:131; Belke and Mersich 1990, 285; Ramsay 1890, 120, 147, 168, and passim; Jones 1937, 44, 60, 81-82; Magie 1950, 2:1001; G. Cohen 1995, 213-14; S. Mitchell 1995a, 1:181.

border of Mysia, Lydia and Phrygia. The ancient city was located just east of the location of the city of Gediz, which was destroyed by an earthquake in 1970 (rebuilt on the plain 6 km to the south). The designation "Macedones Cadieni" (Pliny, *Nat.* 5.30.111) probably indicates that Kadoi originally was a colony of Macedonian veterans. Inscriptions dating to A.D. 157 and 179 confirm the existence of Christians in Kadoi: the figures of the deceased persons carry a circular object on which a cross is depicted, probably a symbol of the Eucharist; the stem of the grapes that are depicted in one of the reliefs end in a cross the shape of a T.[350] We do now know when the Christian community of Kadoi was established.

Synaos (Σύναος, Ζινᾶ; mod. Simav),[351] 93 km west-southwest of Cotiaeum, was the capital of the region Mysia Abbaitis. The acropolis of Synaos was located on the hill to the east. The cult of Mithras is attested for the Persian period. Synaos minted coins since the time of Nero at the latest. Inscriptions attest a Christian community in Synaos in the second or third century. Synaos was the seat of a bishop in the Byzantine period. About 15 km west of Synaos the road passed through Mysian *Ancyra* (mod. Boğaz Köy, former Kilise Köy), situated on the upper Makestos River on the border with Lydia, attested since the Roman period.[352] Robert Jewett mentions several towns between Synaos and Hadrianothera: Ancyra (in Mysia), Carsae, Didymoteiche and Achyraus.[353] The localization or the existence of some of these towns in the Roman period is uncertain.

Attea (Ovabayındır)[354] was situated 110 km west of Synaos on the northeastern foothills of Mount Temnon in the valley of the upper Makestos River. C. Foss and S. Mitchell record only one town from the Hellenistic period in the Makestos Valley between Ancyra/Synaos and Attea (near Sındırgı; the ancient name ended in [. . .]*aleia*).

Hadrianothera (Ἀδριανόθερα; mod. Balıkesir),[355] about 80 km, as the crow flies, northeast of Pergamon in the plain of Apias on the Makestos River, 22 km northwest of Attea. The city was founded by Hadrian, presumably at the site of an earlier city. The most famous son of the city was the orator Aelius Aristides (A.D. 117-181).[356]

Pionia (Πιονία; Pioniai; mod. Gömeniç),[357] attested already in pre-Hellenistic times, was situated on the upper Enbeilos River (mod. Kadıköy Deresi) on the road across the mountains between the Makestos Valley and Troas. The bishop Aetios of Pionia attended Council of Ephesus in A.D. 431.

---

[350]Inscriptions: T. Lochmann, *Bulletin du Musée Hongrois des Beaux-Arts* 74 (1991): 16, fig. 5; the inscription is housed in the Museum of Izmir; W. M. Calder, *AnSt* 5 (1955): 33-35, no. 2; idem, *MAMA* VII, xxxiv. See S. Mitchell 1995a, 2:38.

[351]Ruge, PW 4.A2 (1932): 1326-27; Belke and Mersich 1990, 395-96; Jones 1937, 89-90; Magie 1950, 2:782; S. Mitchell 1995a, 1:181; 2:29, 39.

[352]G. Hirschfeld, "Ancyra 2," PW 1.2 (1894): 2222; Belke and Mersich 1990, 184-85.

[353]Jewett 1997, 9-10.

[354]L. Bürchner, "Attaia 1," PW 2.2 (1896): 2154-55; C. Foss and S. Mitchell, *BAGRW* 844, with reference to H. Taeuber, "Bericht über eine epigraphische Forschungsreise in Südmysien/ Nordlydien," in *VII. Araştırma Sonuçları Toplantısı, Antalya, 18-23 Mayis 1989* (Ankara: Ankara Üniversitesi Basimevi, 1990), 220.

[355]L. Bürchner, PW 7.2 (1912): 2177; Jones 1937, 89; Magie 1950, 1:617; 2:1476; C. Foss and S. Mitchell, *BAGRW* 846.

[356]On Aelius Aristides see R. Klein 1981, 71-108; Swain 1998, 254-97.

[357]Ruge, PW 20.2 (1950) 1715-17. Inscriptions: *IK* 50, 93-97.

Adramyttion ('Αδραμύττιον; originally Pedasos; mod. Ören, former Karataş),[358] about 17 km south of Edremit, was offered by the Persian governor in 422 B.C. to a group of exiles from the island who had been evicted by the Athenians. Since this time the city was Greek and belonged to Troas (Strabo 13.1.4). Adramyttion had an excellent port with docks and harbor facilities. The road to the silver mines in the region ended in the city. During the Mithradatic Wars a certain Diodoros, who had claimed to be a philosopher of the Academy and a teacher of rhetoric, instigated a massacre among the citizens. In the first century B.C. the rhetorical school of Adramyttion was renowned (Strabo 13.1.66); its most famous representative was Xenokles, whom Cicero counted among the greatest orators of his time (Cicero, *Brut.* 316; cf. Strabo 14.2.25). The Romans organized Adramyttion as the capital of an assize district (Pliny, *Nat.* 5.123). Newly published honorary inscriptions document the prosperity and attractiveness of the city in the Roman period.[359] Adramyttion had a Jewish community (Cicero, *Flac.* 28): in 62 B.C. Jewish temple monies were confiscated in the city. Luke mentions "a ship of Adramyttion that was about to set sail to the ports along the coast of Asia," (Acts 27:2) which was used by Julius to transport his prisoners from Caesarea to Rome. Paul must have passed through Adramyttion earlier on his way to Alexandria Troas.

Antandros ("Άντανδρος; mod. Devren, Avcılar),[360] an ancient Aeolian city on the north side of the Gulf of Adramyttion, about 30 km northwest of Adramyttion, was a center of the timber trade from the forests on Mount Ida (mod. Kaz Dağı [1,774 m]) to the north. At the time of the Peloponnesian War Antandros paid tribute to Athens (Thucydides 4.52.75), before the Persians resumed control over the city. Antandros minted coins since the time of Titus. It was the seat of a bishop in the Byzantine period.

Gargara (Γάργαρα; near mod. Arıclı)[361] was situated 24 km west of Antandros in the western foothills of Mount Ida, on whose southern peak, called Mount Gargaron, stood a temple of Zeus (Homer *Il.* 8.48; 14.292). There was a town with the same name on the coast (Strabo 13.1.5) where the road branches off to the north. Citizens of Garagara are mentioned in inscriptions of Rhodes, Chios and Athens. Gargara minted coins in the first century.

From Gargara there were two routes to Alexandria Troas: one road ran north, at Skamandreia, west to Alexandria Troas (53 km); another road ran along the coast via Assos and Larisa (70 km). I assume the first road for my reconstruction.

Skamandreia (Σκάμανδρος; mod. Adatepe),[362] about 5 km northwest of Ezine on the Skamandros River, which empties into the Aegean Sea in front of Troy, is attested in pre-Hellenistic times. In Homer's writings Skamandros is a river-god (in the language of the gods, Xanthos son of Zeus) and an ancestor of the kings of Troy (Homer, *Il.* 14.434).

---

[358]G. Hirschfeld, PW 1.1 (1893): 404; E. Kirsten, *KP* 1:73-74; E. Schwertheim, *DNP* 1:127-28; Jones 1937, 33-34, 44, 47, 61, 69, 85-86, 89-90; Magie 1950, 1:83, 216-17; 2:905; S. Mitchell 1995a, 1:33. Inscriptions: *IK* 50, 127-149; E. Schwertheim, *EA* 19 (1992): 125-33.

[359]See E. Schwertheim, *EA* 19 (1992): 126.

[360]G. Hirschfeld, "Antandros 1," PW 1.2 (1894): 2346; W. Sontheimer, *KP* 1:367; E. Schwertheim, "Antandros 2," *DNP* 1:724; Jones 1937, 35, 85, 90; J. M. Cook 1973, 267-71.

[361]L. Bürchner, PW 7.1 (1910): 757-58; H. Treidler, *KP* 2:697; E. Schwertheim, *DNP* 4:784; Ramsay 1890, 166; Jones 1937, 35, 85, 90; J. M. Cook 1973, 255-61; G. Cohen 1995, 151-52.

[362]L. Bürchner, PW 3.A1 (1927): 425; J. M. Cook 1973, 354-56.

On *Alexandria Troas* see §27.3 According to 2 Cor 2:12, Paul preached the gospel in Alexandria Troas after he had left Ephesus.

When Paul and his coworkers avoided the Province of Asia as well as Ephesus the capital and Pergamon, the old royal city, avoiding travel on the large Roman roads—explained by Luke with reference to the Holy Spirit (Acts 16:6b, 7b)—this was possibly the consequence of the public and official hostility that Paul had encountered in Antiocheia, Iconium and Lystra and that had caused major difficulties for his missionary work.[363]

Why did Paul travel from eastern Mysia to Alexandria Troas? If he wanted to reach the closest port in order to sail home to Judea or to Syria, he could have reached Adramyttion on a more westerly route, or he could have traveled south to Perge or to Attaleia. If he wanted to reach the closest port for embarking on a mission to the regions on the Black Sea, he could have traveled to Kyzikos on the Propontis (Marmara Sea). Paul Bowers plausibly suggests that Paul did not arrive in Alexandria Troas as a clueless missionary who was running out of options for new areas for missionary work: rather, he traveled to Troas with purpose and resolve, seeing it as the point of departure for the newly planned mission to Greece. This suggestion is not contradicted by the dream-vision in which Paul is beseeched by a Macedonian man to "come over to Macedonia and help us" (Acts 16:9). Paul had been planning missionary outreach in the province of Asia, and then missionary outreach in the province of Bithynia, but he was hindered in both cases by the Holy Spirit from traveling to these regions. Luke probably wants to asserts in Acts 16:9 that the new plans of missionary outreach to Macedonia received divine confirmation during the visit to Alexandria Troas.[364]

Notes on the travel route. Paul sailed from Alexandria Troas to Neapolis; he could have traveled by land on the paved Roman road from Pergamon and Adramyttion to Lampsacus and taken a ferry across the Hellespont. From Neapolis Paul traveled on the Via Egnatia to Philippi. Construction of the Via Egnatia was begun in 145 B.C. and finished around 130 B.C. It ran from Byzantion (Constantinople) to the port cities on the Adriatic Sea, making it the quickest route from Rome into the East. In Thrace the Via Egnatia passed through Neapolis, Philippi, Amphipolis and Apollonia before reaching Thessalonike. After leaving Beroea, Paul was brought by local Christians "to the coast" (ἕως ἐπὶ τὴν θάλασσαν [Acts 17:14]), which indicates that he wanted to continue his journey by ship. The closest port city to Beroea is Pydna. After reaching Athens, Paul traveled via Eleusis (17 km) and Megara (16 km) to Corinth (45 km). After a year and six months (Acts 18:11) Paul returned via Cenchreae (Acts 18:18) by ship to Syria, with a stopover in Ephesus, where he preached but could not stay (Acts 18:19-21). After reaching Caesarea, he traveled to Jerusalem and to Antioch (Acts 18:22).

---

[363]Thus French 1994b, 57-58.
[364]See Bowers 1979. On the historicity of Acts 16:9-10 see Reinbold 2000, 122.

Neapolis (Νεάπολις; mod. Kavala),[365] a Greek colony founded in 650 B.C. by settlers from Thasos on the coast of Thrace in the northwestern region of the Gulf of Kavala, was located on the Via Egnatia between Mount Pangaion (mod. Pangion) to the southwest, on which gold was mined, and the Sapaike, the Nestos Delta to the northeast. In the fifth century B.C. Neapolis had close links with Athens. Philipp II conquered Neapolis around 350 B.C. and made the city the port of Philippi. In 42 B.C. Neapolis was the naval base for Brutus and Cassius. In the first century A.D. the city belonged to Philippi and was an important port on the route from Macedonia to Asia Minor. Remains of the temple of Parthenos survive; Parthenos was the goddess of Neapolis, probably a Hellenized version of Artemis Tauropolos (or Bendis) of Thrace. Paul and his coworkers enter Europe for the first time in Neapolis. There is no information about the establishment of the Christian community in the city. In the ninth century Neapolis was called Christopolis.

On *Philippi* see below.

Amphipolis (Ἀμφίπολις; mod. Amphipolis),[366] surrounded on three sides by the Strymon River, hence the name of the city, was a Greek city in an area of Macedonia that had belonged to Thrace. Amphipolis was founded by Athens in 437 B.C. as a colony controlling the access to the interior of Thrace. After 421 B.C. Amphipolis was independent, and in 362 B.C. it came under Macedonian rule. The famous gold coins of Philipp II were minted in Amphipolis. Several admirals of Alexander the Great came from Amphipolis, among them Nearchos. When Macedonia came under Roman control in 168 B.C., Amphipolis became the capital of the first Macedonian region. It seems that the city, which had been in decline for some time, flourished again under Augustus. Remains of the Hellenistic gymnasium survive. The large temple that is attested in literary sources has not been located as of yet. Amphipolis is mentioned repeatedly in the *Itineraria* as a station on the Via Egnatia. The origin of the Christian community in Amphipolis is unknown; the first bishop is mentioned in connection with the council of A.D. 553.

After 30 km Paul reached *Arethusa* (mod. Rendina),[367] an old city founded by Ionian settlers on the eastern shore of Lake Bolbe (mod. Volve), situated on the Via Egnatia at the western entrance to the Tempe Valley.

Apollonia (Ἀπολλωνία; Apollonia Mygdonia; mod. Polina, Apolonia),[368] about 40 km southwest of Amphipolis on the southern shore of Lake Bolbe on the Via Egnatia between Amphipolis and Thessalonike, minted coins since the time of Philipp V (221-179 B.C.) at the latest. Luke notes Paul's visit to the city (Acts 17:1). Apollonia was the seat of a bishop

---

[365]F. Hiller, "Neapolis 1," PW 16.2 (1935): 2110-12; C. Danoff, "Neapolis 1," *KP* 4:29-30; D. Lazarides, *PECS* 614; Papazoglou 1988, 403-4; M. Zahrnt, in Lauffer 1989, 314-15; Touratsoglou 1997, 357-71.

[366]G. Hirschfeld, PW 1.2 (1894): 1949-52; C. Danoff, *KP* 1:314-15; Lazarides, *PECS* 51-52; M. Errington, *DNP* 1:616; Alexandrov 1976, 14-15; Papazoglou 1988, 392-97; D. Müller, in Lauffer 1989, 109-10; Gill 1994c, 414; D. Lazarides, *Amphipolis* (Athens: Ministry of Culture, 1997); Touratsoglou 1997, 335-47.

[367]G. Hirschfeld, "Arethusa 8," PW 2.1 (1895): 679-80; C. Danoff, "Arethusa 9," *KP* 1:531-32; Alexandrov 1976, 17; Papazoglou 1988, 222-23; D. Müller, in Lauffer 1989, 127.

[368]G. Hirschfeld, "Apollonia 3," PW 2.1 (1895): 114; C. Danoff, "Apollonia 3," *KP* 1:449; M. Errington, "Apollonia 3," *DNP* 1:872; Alexandrov 1976, 16; Papazoglou 1988, 218-22; M. Zahrnt, in Lauffer 1989, 125; Gill 1994c, 413; M. B. Hatzopoulos, "Apollonia Hellenis," in *Ventures in Greek History* (ed. I. Worthington; Oxford: Clarendon, 1994), 159-88.

in the Byzantine period. It is not known when the church there was established.

On *Thessalonike* and *Beroea* see below.

Pydna (Πύδνα; near mod. Kitros),[369] like neighboring Methone a Greek city in Macedonia on the Thermaic Gulf in the Plain of Katerini, is mentioned for the first time by Thucydides (1.61; 2.137). After the conquest by Archelaos the Macedonian, the city, originally located near modern Makrygalios, was rebuilt 5 km to the southwest in the interior (near mod. Kitros); the harbor of Pydna was at Cape Atherida. The decisive battle on June 22 in the year 168 B.C. in which thirty-eight thousand Romans under Aemilius Paullus were victorious against forty-three thousand Macedonians under Perseus, the last Macedonian king, took place in the coastal plain immediately south of Pydna. Pydna was an insignificant provincial town during the Roman period.

On *Athens, Eleusis, Megara, Corinth* and *Cenchreae* see below.

Paul traveled 3,110 km (ca. 1,930 mi.) by foot and 2,060 km by ship during the period A.D. 49-52, visiting the churches in Syria, Cilicia and southern Galatia and engaging in missionary work in Phrygian Galatia, Macedonia and Achaia. This corresponds to 175 days of travel (almost six months): 155 days on foot, and about 20 days at sea.

After leaving Alexandria Troas in the province of Asia, Paul and his companions arrived by ship in Neapolis before traveling to Philippi. The first region of Europe that Paul visited in order to start missionary work was Macedonia.

Macedonia (Μακεδονία [see fig. 33])[370] formed the northern part of Greece. Lower Macedonia comprised the plain on the Thermaic Gulf (Gulf of Thessalonike) marked by the rivers Axios and Haliakmon as well as Pieria, consisting of four districts: the district Bottiaia with the cities Aigai (Edessa), Beroea, Pella and Kyrrhos; the district Pieria on the coast with the cities Methone, Pydna and Dion; the district Amphaxitis; the district Almopia. Eastern Macedonia comprised the area between the rivers Axios and Strymon as well as the Plain of Philippi, with the following regions: Mygdonia with the cities Sindos, Lete and Thermai; Bisaltia with the cities Argilos and Sintike, Krestonia; Anthemus with the city Thessalonike; the Plain of Philippi with the cities Philippi, Neapolis, Galepsos and Eion. Upper Macedonia comprised the regions Elimeia, Orestis, Lynkestis, Deuriopos, Dassaretis and Eordaia. The Greeks regarded the Macedonians, who maintained close relationships with the Illyrians and the Thracians, as barbarians, with the exception of the Macedonian royal family, whose Greek origins they acknowledged. Macedonia became the leading power of the Greek-speaking world under King Philipp II (382-336 B.C.) on the strength of its internal unity and formidable army. Alexander, the son of Philip, conquered the Persian Empire as he marched through Asia Minor and Syria to Persia, finally reaching India. Since Philipp II the Macedonian court was a center

---

[369]C. Danoff, PWSup 10 (1965): 833-42; idem, *KP* 4:1246; P. M. Petsas, *PECS* 745; Alexandrov 1976, 105; Papazoglou 1988, 106-8; D. Müller, in Lauffer 1989, 575-77.

[370]Fritz Geyer, PW 14.1 (1928): 638-771; Günter Neumann, *KP* 3:910-19; N. G. L. Lemprière, *OCD* 904-5; M. Oppermann, *OCD* 905; M. Errington et al., *DNP* 8:726-48; A. Weiser, *EWNT* 2:933-34 (*EDNT* 2:379); N. Hammond 1972-1988; Papazoglou 1979; Errington 1986; Papazoglou 1988; Gill 1994c; Touratsoglou 1997.

of Greek culture, which was exported into the eastern Mediterranean regions under the label "Hellenism." The Macedonians worshiped essentially the same gods as did the Greeks; the cult of Zeus was particularly popular, as were the cults of Artemis, Dionysus, the Dioscuri, Heracles, Helios, Selene, as well as the cults of several river-gods. The Diadochi Wars and the disputes of numerous candidates for the throne caused the decline of Macedonia. King Perseus lost a decisive battle in 168 B.C. against a Roman army in the Third Macedonian War and became a Roman prisoner. The senate of Rome divided Macedonia into four independent republics with the capitals Amphipolis, Thessalonike, Pella and Pelagonia. After the rebellion of Andriskos, Macedonia became a Roman province in 148 B.C., which included Illyrian regions, Epirus and Greece. Roman colonies were founded in Dyrrachium, Dion, Pella, Philippi, Kassandreia and Stoboi (Stobi). Macedonia was a senatorial province (without Greece) after 27 B.C. Between A.D. 15 and 44 Macedonia was administered together with Achaia by the imperial legate of Moesia, with Thessalonike as the new capital. In A.D. 44 Claudius organized Macedonia and Achaia as separate senatorial provinces. The capital of the province of Macedonia was Thessalonike.

Evangelism in Philippi

After disembarking from Neapolis, Paul, Silas and Timothy traveled to Philippi. Luke describes Paul's missionary outreach in Philippi in Acts 16:12-40, which probably took place in August and October of A.D. 49.

Philippi (Φίλιπποι; mod. Krenides)[371] was situated in eastern Macedonia in the Plain of Daton not far from the Gangites River, surrounded by Mounts Orbelos, Pangaion, Symbolon and Sapaike; the Plain of Daton was open only to the southwest. Philippi's wealth in wood for shipbuilding and in precious metals was proverbial. The mines for gold and silver on Mount Pangaion were mentioned earlier. The road from the east via Neapolis to Philippi crossed the pass called Stena Pylai between Mounts Symbolon and Sapaike. The city originally was called Daton, and had been founded around 360 B.C. by colonists from Thasos on a narrow spot between a swamp and the mountain near the ancient town of Krenides. In 350 B.C. King Philipp II conquered the city, which he fortified with city walls (3.5 km long); he settled new colonists in the city, which henceforth was called Philippi. The gold mines in the vicinity, which no longer yielded gold by the late Macedonian period, were discovered only recently. In 86 B.C. Philippi was conquered by the Roman consul L. Valerius Flaccus. In 42 B.C. Philippi, at the time a "small settlement" (κατοικία μικρά, *katoikia mikra* [Strabo 7, frg. 41]), was the site of the renowned battle between the forces of Brutus and Cassius (the murderers of Julius Caesar) and those of Mark Antony and Octavian (Augustus), one of the greatest battles of antiquity.

---

[371]Johanna Schmidt, PW 19.2 (1938): 2206-44; C. Danoff, *KP* 4:742-43; Avramea and Karanastassi 1993, 44-45; H. L. Hendrix, *ABD* 5:513-17; N. Hammond, *OCD* 1162-63; M. Errington and E. Wirbelauer, *DNP* 9:794-96; L. M. McDonald, *DNTB* 787-89; M. Zahrnt, in Lauffer 1989, 539-41; Paul Collard, *Philippes: Ville de Macédoine depuis ses origines jusqu'à la fin de la l'époque romaine* (2 vols.; Paris: Boccard, 1937); Papazoglou 1988, 39-43, 405-13, and passim; McRay 1991, 283-88; Gill 1994c, 411-12; Abrahamsen 1995, 7-25; Bormann 1995, 2-83; Pilhofer 1995-2000; Touratsoglou 1997, 373-81; Ascough 1998; Bakirtzis and Koester 1998, esp. the contributions by Chaido Koulouli-Chrysantaki and Charalambos Bakirtzis. Reports of the ongoing excavations of the École Française d'Athènes are published in *BCH*. Inscriptions: *CIL* III; Collart, *Philippes;* Pilhofer 1995-2000, vol. 2.

Philippi often is mentioned by Greek and Roman historical writers because of this bat-tle.[372]

The Roman settlement of Philippi began with Mark Antony, who founded the Colonia Victrix Philippensium in 42 B.C. and settled veterans of the Legio XXVIII. In 31 B.C., after the battle of Actium, Italian colonists were settled in the city by Augustus, who had to make room in southern Italy for settlements for his veterans, as well as veterans of the Praetorian Cohort (Cassius Dio 51.4.6); he refounded the city and in 27 B.C. renamed it Colonia Iulia Augusta Philipp[i]ensis.[373] In the two refoundations of Philippi at least one thousand colonists were settled in the city. However, Philippi was not a typical military colony or veterans' town.[374] Philippi possessed not only Roman citizenship but also Ital-ian citizenship, the *ius Italicum,* which could be granted to Roman colonies outside of Italy, resulting in tax exemption for the land of the citizens. The territory of Philippi covered 1,890 km^2. In the imperial period Philippi was the most important city in east-ern Macedonia. Inscriptions attest fifteen villages: Kalpapouritai, Satriceni, Mediani, Prouptosoureni, Iollitai, Scaporeni, vicani Sc[. . .], Nicaenses, Coreni, Zcambu, Tasibas-teni, Suritani, Aulonitai, Kerdozeis, Sceveni; in at least seven further villages ancient re-mains have been found. The port of the city, Neapolis, was also a *vicus* of Philippi, with busy maritime connections with Asia Minor, particularly Alexandria Troas.[375] Remains of the city walls built by Philipp II survive, as do the east gate (Neapolis Gate) and the west gate (Krenides Gate) on both ends of the *Decumanus Maximus,* the section of the Via Egnatia running through the city, of which some of the marble pavement survives. Other ancient remains include several temples (of Apollo Komaios and of Artemis), gymnasium, market buildings, shops and amphitheater (second century). The theater in the eastern section of the city goes back to Philipp II; it could seat eight thousand spec-tators. No remains survive of the triumphal arch 2 km west of the city, which had been erected in the first half of the first century A.D. as a symbol of the political significance of the Roman colony of Philippi. Two temples were found on the forum that were ded-icated to the worship of the emperor, dating to the second century, with earlier versions dating to the first century. Seven inscriptions attest *flamines* and *sacerdotes divae Au-gustae,* women officiating in the cult honoring Livia, the wife of Augustus; eight inscrip-tions document *seviri Augustales,* freedmen who were responsible for the festivities honoring Augustus for one year (one of the few possibilities for freedmen in Philippi to occupy a public function).[376] Open-air sanctuaries of Silvanus, Artemis Bendis, Cybele and Bacchus were discovered on the acropolis, as well as a temple of the Egyptian gods; the worship of Isis can be documented with certainty only for the second century, however. Besides Thracian influence, only Greco-Roman cults are attested for the first century A.D., a fact that leads Lukas Bormann to conclude that we should assume for Philippi "a religious identity influenced primarily by Roman religion in which the wor-ship of the princeps and his deified ancestors or predecessors was central, besides the

---

[372]The testimonies have been collected in Bormann 1995, 68-84.

[373]Both names are attested on coins: (1) A(ntoni) I(ussu) C(olonia) V(ictrix) P(hilippensium); see H. Gäbler, "Die erste Colonialprägung in Philippi," *ZN* 39 (1929): 260-69, plate 1; (2) COL(onia) AVG(usta) IVL(ia) PHIL(ippensis) IVSSV AVG(usti); see *BCH* (1935): 148, no. 42. See also Collard, *Philippes,* 224-27; Papazoglou 1988, 407; Bormann 1995, 12-19.

[374]Contra Becker 1992, 322-23 (ET, 305-6). For the observation that follows above see Boter-mann 1991, 299.

[375]See Bormann 1995, 27.

[376]Bormann 1995, 42-46; for the comment that follows above see ibid., 56-60, 66-67 (on O'Brien, *Phil,* 5).

traditional Greco-Roman pantheon."[377] The deities that were worshiped in Philippi include Apollo Comaeus, Artemis, Dionysos, the hero Aulonites, the Kabiroi, Zeus, the Egyptian gods Isis and Sarapis. Philippi had between five thousand and ten thousand inhabitants in the first century.[378]

Paul and his companions found a "place of prayer" (προσευχή, *proseuchē* [Acts 16:13]), a synagogue, at the river Gangites, about 3 km west of the city center.

Martin Hengel assumes that this "place of prayer" was a building. Authors including Apion, Kleomedes, Artemidoros and Juvenal always use the term προσευχή (*proseuchē*) when they refer to a synagogue.[379] The lack of early epigraphical evidence for a synagogue in Philippi does not allow the conclusion that there was no synagogue in the city and that Acts 16:13 is contracted by the evidence of the local archaeological finds.[380] Lukas Bormann believes that the reference to a Jewish "place of prayer" in Philippi is "a Lukan missionary scheme according to which Paul first turns to the Jews." This view is unconvincing, demonstrated by the fact that Luke does not use the term *synagōgē*, which customarily he does. Implausible is the view that the *proseuchē* was a house regularly used (only) by women[381] or a place of prayer in the open air.[382] The *proseuchē* at the river was a synagogue.[383] Luke's statement that Paul met only women might mean that the men and the women met at different times. Luke's comment that the missionaries regularly visited the *proseuchē* can hardly mean that they regularly participated in a womens' prayer meeting.[384] A new discovery in the west cemetery of Philippi yielded the first epigraphical evidence for Jews in the city: a funerary inscription dated to the third or fourth century documents a Jew named Nikostratos Aurelios Oxycholios.[385]

Lydia is introduced (like Cornelius) by name, profession and reference to her "house," and she is described as a God-fearer.[386] She is described further as a

---

[377]Bormann 1995, 63-64; for the list that follows above see Koukouli-Chrysantaki, in Bakirtzis and Koester 1998, 24-27.

[378]See Philhofer 1995, 1:76 with n. 76.

[379]Hengel 1971, 172-73.

[380]Contra Bormann 1995, 5-6 n. 16; the quotation that follows above, ibid.

[381]Thus Blue 1994, 152-52 n. 130.

[382]Thus H. Balz, *EWNT* 3:409 (*EDNT* 3:169).

[383]See I. Levine 2000, 108-9, 293, 473; Reinbold 2000, 124-25 with n. 33; on the location of the synagogue see Pilhofer 1995-2000, 1:165-74.

[384]See Binder 1999, 291 with n. 115.

[385]See Koukouli-Chrysantaki, in Bakirtzis and Koester 1998, 28-35; Pilhofer 2000, 339-40 (No. 387a/G813); *IJudO* I Mac12 (Museum of Philippi, inventory no. Δ 1529); another tombstone belonged to the grave of Simon Smyrnaios, probably a Jew as well (inventory no. Δ 1776).

[386]Acts 16:15: σεβομένη τὸν θεόν. Beginning in Acts 16, Luke uses the term σέβομαι (*sebomai*) for the phenomenon of the God-fearers. Wander (1998, 192) rejects the view that the author of Acts used another source; he argues that it is more plausible to assume that as the missionaries crossed over to Europe, Luke uses "the formulation that is more common for this cultural region and that is morally less ambiguous. φοβούμενος τὸν θεόν belongs to the Syrian-Palestinian linguistic realm, where the usage was more clearly understood than in other cultural contexts."

person who prayed on the Sabbath and was hospitable, gracious and humble.[387] In other words, Luke describes an ideal God-fearer. Lydia had a house, which means that she was well off.[388]

In Acts 16:15 Luke asserts, for the first time explicitly, that Paul entered the house of a pagan.[389] However, in contrast to Peter's visit to the house of the Roman Cornelius in Acts 10, this fact is not highlighted by Luke. Paul surely had been in houses of Gentiles before. Luke's comment in Acts 16:15 says more about Lydia than about Paul.

Lydia listened eagerly to what the missionaries had to say and came to faith in Jesus Christ (Acts 16:15b) because the Lord "opened her heart" (Acts 16:14b). We see again the theological conviction of Luke, which he shares with Paul: people come to faith only if and when God opens their heart, granting them repentance (Acts 11:18).[390] Lydia and her household were baptized (Acts 16:15). The context of the passages in the book of Acts that link a reference to a person and his or her "(whole) household" with baptism "restricts us to the conclusion that infants and small children are not included."[391]

Luke reports no further missionary activity of Paul in the city. This does not necessarily mean, however, that Paul preached in Philippi only in the synagogue outside of the city walls or that only Lydia and later the prison official were converted. The action of the city magistrates suggests a longer stay and a more extensive evangelistic activity in Philippi. Luke's reference to "brothers" (Acts 16:40) who met in Lydia's house suggests a house church in Philippi.

During the first weeks while Paul and his coworkers were preaching in the synagogue, a new situation arose when they encountered a slave girl who was demon-possessed. She followed the missionaries "for many days" (Acts 16:18), shouting, "These men are slaves of the Most High God, who proclaim to you a way of salvation" (Acts 16:17). Some scholars think that the girl broadcast to the citizens of Philippi the true meaning of the message that the missionaries preached and that Paul exorcised her demons because he did not want a pagan medium to announce the gospel. This interpretation is implausible. Paul drove out the demon because he was annoyed (Acts 16:18) not at the girl or the situation, but because the "message" of the slave girl was misleading.[392] The "Most

---

[387]Cf. Acts 16:15: "If you have judged me to be faithful to the Lord, come and stay at my home."

[388]Becker 1992, 323 (ET, 306); Gill 1994b, 114-15. Botermann (1991, 300) argues that the reference to a house has little significance because resident aliens would hardly have belonged to the elite of the municipal aristocracy of the city. On the purple trade in Philippi see Pilhofer 1995-2000, 1:174-82.

[389]See Wander 1998, 196.

[390]See Bengel, *Gnomon*, 501: "Cor clausum per se: sed Dei est, id aperire."

[391]Peter Weigandt, *EWNT* 2:1227 (*EDNT* 2:502); followed by Wolfgang Schrage (*1 Kor,* 1:156 with n. 329), who asserts that neither Acts 16:15 nor 1 Cor 7:14 provides any justification for the practice of infant baptism.

[392]See Trebilco 1989, 58-62; followed by Stenschke 1999a, 196-97.

High God" (*theos hypsistos* [see §18.4]) would have been understood as a reference to the God of Israel only in the synagogue where Paul proclaimed his revelation in Jesus Christ. Outside of the synagogue, in the forum of Philippi, for example, the term "Most High God" could refer to several "highest gods" depending on the personal religiosity of the individual citizen or on the professional reputation of the slave girl whose fortune-telling might have been linked with a "high god." Most citizens of Philippi would have linked "Most High God" with Zeus. Paul exorcised the demon that possessed the slave girl because he was "annoyed" about the misleading pronouncements that she made in public, implying the danger that his own proclamation could be misunderstood in a syncretistic context.

The owners of the girl who had been liberated through the exorcism saw "their hope of making money" dashed, and so they dragged Paul and Silas to the forum "before the authorities" (ἄρχονται, *archontai* [Acts 16:19]). The Latin term used in Philippi for the local authorities was *duoviri,* as is documented by numerous inscriptions found in Philippi. The charge leveled by the owners of the girl (Acts 16:20-21), who proudly describe themselves as Romans, is formulated in general political terms. They accuse Paul of being a troublemaker (in the Roman colony of Philippi). They accuse him of introducing new, illicit (Jewish) customs, arguing that for Romans the alteration of the *mores,* the ancestral customs, is tantamount to revolution.[393] Paul and Silas are described as newcomers, as Jews who are aliens (*peregrini*) and therefore possess neither influence (*potentia*) nor favor (*gratia*).

It is important to remember in this context that the image of Philippi in Roman historiography was dominated by the decisive battle between those who wanted to avenge the murder of Julius Caesar and those who murdered him. The name "Philippi" reminded Romans "of a turning point in Roman history at which the course of the subsequent development of the constitution of the state was determined by the force of arms. . . . Philippi represented one of the most important historical roots of the constitution of the Roman state, the principate of the Julian-Claudian dynasty—a fact that presumably was important not only for the self-understanding of the Roman citizens of Philippi but also for the knowledge of the entire Mediterranean world. . . . Since its refoundation by Augustus, Philippi was a city in which the Roman self-consciousness was formed as trust in the divine right and the inspired ability of the Julian-Claudian family."[394]

Paul and Silas were stripped of their clothing, beaten with rods and thrown into jail (Acts 16:22-24). Eighteen years earlier Paul himself had thrown followers of Jesus into prison (Acts 8:3); now he was in jail. For a long time the Romans regarded imprisonment (Lat., *carcer*) not as a punishment but as a security meas-

---

[393]See Unnik 1964; Rapske 1994a, 120-21; for the comment that follows above see ibid., 121, with reference to J. M. Kelly, *Roman Litigation* (Oxford: Clarendon, 1966), 44.
[394]Bormann 1995, 83-84.

ure. The magistrates employed incarceration as a police measure for the short-term penalizing of misbehaving individuals but mainly as a pretrial detention or as a custody until the time of implementation of the punishment.[395] Helga Botermann attributes the fact that Paul did not immediately confront the authorities with his Roman citizenship in protest against the *coercitio* to the tumultuous sequence of events.[396] If Brian Rapske is correct, Luke describes in Acts 16:22 not an illegal mob action, but rather the citizens of Philippi, including many Romans, siding with the accusation made by the owners of the slave girl.[397] Paul did not appeal to his Roman citizenship in the proceedings that the owners of the girl initiated against him with the support of the citizens of Philippi: he mentions the fact that he is a Roman citizen only after the trial and his release from prison (Acts 16:37). Rapske suggests a threefold explanation: practical, religious and missionary. (1) An appeal to his Roman *persona* would have caused legal complications requiring time to resolve, leading to unwanted delays. It was easy to prove one's Roman citizenship, which was registered in the *tabularium publicum* in one's hometown. In Philippi, over 1,000 km from his hometown of Tarsus, this would have been quite difficult for Paul. Roman citizens could have private copies made, usually attested by seven witnesses; such a *testatio* was engraved on the interior sides, covered with bright wax, of a diptych, a writing tablet consisting of two wooden tablets connected with a cord or with hinges.[398] At the end of the *testatio* were found the markings *q. p. f. c. r. e. ad k.,* with the letters *c. r. e.* standing for *c(iuem) r(omanum) e(sse).* Since Paul was accused as a Jew, and since he claimed as a Jew to possess Roman citizenship, he would have had to prove the correctness of his *testatio,* assuming that he carried such a document with him, by assembling witnesses from remote places, which would have cost time and money. Even if the authorities in Philippi did not question the *testatio,* the problem of time would not have disappeared: the trial probably would have had to be decided by the governor of the province, and the wait for his arrival in Philippi for the next court day could have taken a long time. Transporting the prisoner to the capital, Thessalonike, might have shortened the process only slightly. (2) In the context of the perhaps publicly anti-Jewish sentiments in Philippi, an appeal to Roman citizenship would have amounted to a negative qualification of Jewish identity, which is something that Paul surely wished to avoid: he never denied his Jewish heritage, and he preached a "Jewish message" with a "Jewish" Savior. (3) An appeal to his Roman citizenship could have been interpreted by the magistrates and the citizens of

---

[395]See T. Mayer-Maly, *KP* 1:1053-54; E. Bernecker, *KP* 1:1496-97; see also Rapske 1994a; esp. 115-34, on the trial in Philippi.

[396]Botermann 1993, 79.

[397]Rapske 1994a, 121-23; for the comments that follow above see ibid., 130-34.

[398]See W. H. Gross, *KP* 2:98-99. See F. Schulz, "Roman Registers of Births and Birth Certificates," *JRS* 32 (1942): 78-91; 33 (1943): 55-64; the comment that follows above, 56.

the city as an approval of Roman customs and rejection of Jewish traditions. This would have more than irritated new believers such as Lydia and other converted God-fearers and Jews who perhaps had converted to faith in Jesus. At the same time missionary work among the Roman citizens of Philippi would have been jeopardized if Paul had distanced himself from Jewish traditions and emphasized Roman identity, as the magistrate and Philippi's Roman citizens identified it. Therefore, Paul's silence concering his Roman citizenship during the initial legal proceedings in Philippi evidently was a carefully thought-out decision.[399]

While they were in prison, Paul and Silas gave testimony to their faith by prayers and the singing of hymns (Acts 16:25). When the city was shaken by an earthquake, the jailer was so disturbed that he expressed his religious sensitivity for the reality of the supernatural to Paul and Silas in the question "Sirs, what must I do to be saved?" (Acts 16:30). Since evidently he had mistreated the prisoners when he put them into the innermost cell and "fastened their feet in the stocks" (Acts 16:24), without washing their wounds (Acts 16:33) and without giving them any food (Acts 16:34), he obviously was afraid of the vengeance of their god.[400] The jailer's fear of the divine, seen in his falling to his knees before the missionaries, perhaps is expressed in the fact that he addresses them as *kyrioi* ("lords").

Some scholars suggest that the jailer was afraid for his life only in a "secular," or literal sense of the word: the prisoners are about to escape, prompting the jailer to fear for his life, which is why he contemplates committing suicide; the verb *sōzein* can mean "rescue" or "liberate" (from a misfortune).[401] This interpretation of Acts 16:30 makes it difficult, however, to explain why the jailer expects to receive from Paul and Silas an answer to his question that would solve his problem. The assurance that the faith of the jailer guarantees the rescue of his entire household (Acts 16:31) is not a decisive argument for the "secular" interpretation: Luke asserts in Acts 16:32 that Paul and Silas proclaimed the gospel to the entire household of the jailer. The jailer formulates his readiness to religious action with a typically pagan perspective: he wants to know what he should "do" (*poiein*)—that is, what (sacrificial) activity is necessary—to appease the god of the prisoners. Paul informs him that only faith in Jesus can rescue him: "Believe on the Lord Jesus, and you will be saved, you and your household" (Acts 16:31). Rudolf Pesch comments that Luke's account reflects the theological horizon of Paul, who emphasized that what is necessary for salvation is not "doing," but rather faith in the Lord Jesus Christ.[402] The continuation of the account indicates that Paul preached a missionary sermon to those who were present: "They spoke the word of the Lord to him and to all who were in his house" (Acts 16:32). If Luke intends the sequence of Acts 16:31 and 16:32 to describe historical reality, the interpretation of C. K. Barrett may well be

---

[399]Rapske (1994a, 134) comments, "Paul's earlier silence concerning his citizenship reflects a carefully considered choice rather than a novelistic dramatization or the expression of Luke's juridical naivete."

[400]See Rapske 1994a, 126-27, 263-64; Stenschke 1999a, 200-201.

[401]See Barrett, *Acts*, 2:797; Witherington 1998b, 153.

[402]See Pesch, *Apg*, 2:116; cf. Stenschke 1999a, 202.

correct: the missionaries encouraged the jailer to believe in Jesus and to acknowledge him as "Lord" *(kyrios)*, as highest authority, challenging him to believe in Jesus as the one whom God had raised from the dead (otherwise the crucified Jesus cannot be *kyrios*); as a pagan listener, the jailer must have linked the term *kyrios* with a category known to him—a cultic figure, a divine being who is offended because his servants (Paul and Silas) have been publicly mistreated, who is so powerful that he can send an earthquake for the rescue of his servants and who therefore can demand loyalty.[403] As a result of the earthquake and as a result of the explanation of the gospel by Paul and Silas (Acts 16:32), the jailer and evidently other members of his household accepted the message of the missionaries, came to faith and were baptized (Acts 16:33b). The jailer (*desmophylax* [Acts 16:27]) was neither a Roman official[404] nor a soldier with the rank of a centurion or a veteran[405] but probably a slave owned by the city who had been put in charge of the local prison.[406] Stationed in Macedonia, a demilitarized province since A.D. 14, were only smaller military units and individual soldiers who fulfilled administrative or security tasks. It is implausible in this context that a soldier would have been put in charge of a local prison. A veteran would not have regarded such a task as attractive. The administration of the city of Philippi had a purely civil character, as is demonstrated by the hierarchical structure from the magistrates (Lat., *duoviri;* in Acts 16:19: *hoi archontes;* in Acts 16:20, 22, 26, 38: *hoi stratēgoi*), to the police (Lat., *lictores;* in Acts 16:35, 38: *hoi rhabdouchoi*), to the jailer (Acts 16:23, 27, 36), to his servant (cf. Acts 16:29). Civil administrations tended to recruit the personnel in charge of the prison from among slaves who belonged to the city.[407] Several public slaves are documented for Philippi. Since the jailer occupied an elevated position in the city, the reference to his "household" (*oikos* [Acts 16:31, 32]) and his "house" (*oikos* [Acts 16:34]), implying a certain prosperity, cannot be used as an argument against this interpretation: some slaves achieved a certain level of wealth. The conversion of the jailer was evident not just in his acceptance of the message of the missionaries and baptism: he brought Paul and Silas from the inner prison into his (private) house (Acts 16:33a, 34a), washed their wounds (Acts 16:33b), gave them food (Acts 16:34b) and rejoiced (*ēgalliasato*) in his new-found faith (Acts 16:34c). The behavior of the jailer was, if not illegal, certainly most inappropriate: in his joy over his faith and in his desire to help his new friends he threw all consideration for his legal duties overboard.[408]

On the day after the earthquake the magistrates sent the "police"—their attendants, the lectors—to the prison under orders to release Paul and Silas (Acts 16:35-36). They evidently were convinced that the flogging and the imprisonment, as brief as that may have been, were punishment enough for the troublemakers. It was at this point that Paul informed the authorities that he and Silas possessed Roman citizenship (Acts 16:37). His wish that the representatives of the magistrate apologize publicly probably was fulfilled; they

---

[403]Barrett, *Acts*, 2:979.

[404]Contra Becker 1992, 323. According to Helga Botermann (1991, 299), the predicate "Roman" is to be reserved in these contexts for the representatives of the imperial government.

[405]Contra Bruce, *Acts*, 315.

[406]See Peterlin 1995, 144-50; Rapske 1994a, 261-64.

[407]See Rapske 1994a, 244-50.

[408]See Rapske 1994a, 390-92.

placated the missionaries (Acts 16:38-39), presumably because they did not want to incur trouble from the governor, to whom Paul and Silas might complain.[409]

Paul's letter to the Philippians informs about the subsequent history of the church in Philippi.[410] In this letter, written twelve years after the foundation of the church, Paul reminded the believers in Philippi of their "sharing in the gospel" (κοινωνία ὑμῶν εἰς τὸ εὐαγγέλιον, *koinōnia hymōn eis to euangelion* [Phil 1:5]) from the first day until the present, a "fellowship" that was demonstrated in the financial support of the church for Paul's missionary work, which included the gift that Epaphroditus recently had taken to Paul (Phil 2:25-30; 4:10-20). Some time between the establishment of the church in A.D. 49 and the imprisonment of Paul in Rome in A.D. 60-62, Jewish-Christian teachers came to Philippi who probably called themselves "workers" (*ergatai* [Phil 3:2]); that is, they perhaps were missionaries. They intended to convince the Gentile Christians to be circumcised (Phil 3:3-4), while their own personal behavior was anything but exemplary (Phil 3:17-21).[411] Paul wrote to the Philippians to warn them emphatically about these teachers (Phil 3:2-21). Another reason why Paul wrote this letter—perhaps the most important reason—was to exhort the Philippians to patient steadfastness and consistent unity: they should "stand firm in one spirit, striving side by side with one mind for the faith of the gospel" and not be intimidated by the opponents (Phil 1:27; cf. 1:28-30; 2:1-4; 4:2-3). Paul's final concern was to inform the Christians in Philippi about the situation of his imprisonment, about the well-being of Epaphroditus, their envoy who had become ill and nearly died, and about his plan to send Timothy to them and to visit Philippi himself in the future (Phil 1:12-20; 2:19-30).

Critical scholars generally assume the Epistle to the Philippians is a composite of several letters and that the redactional action that combined these letters should be dated to the post-Pauline generation. Lukas Bormann, in a monograph on the church in Philippi, distinguishes Letter A (Phil 4:10-23), Letter B (Phil 1:1—3:1 + 4:2-7) and Letter C (Phil 3:2—4:1 + 4:8-9).[412] The arguments in support of the unity of the canonical Epistle to the Philippians are more cogent, however.[413]

Philippi is attested as the seat of a bishop in the fourth century: the bishop Porphyrios attended the Council of Sardis (A.D. 343); he is portrayed in a mosaic of St. Paul's Church located south of the Via Egnatia and east of the forum, the oldest early Byzantine church

---

[409]David Alvarez Cineira (1999, 353-54) thinks that this is a Lukan construct but is unable to explain the motive that Luke might have had (ibid., 363).

[410]For the comments that follow above see O'Brien, *Phil*, 35-38.

[411]See O'Brien, *Phil*, 26-35, esp. 33-34, with a discussion of other suggestions concerning these teachers.

[412]See Bormann 1995.

[413]See Hawthorne, *Phil*, xxix-xxxii; O'Brien, *Phil*, 10-18; Cineira 1999, 321-23.

of Philippi.[414] The inscription of the mosaic reads, Πορ[φυ]ριὸς ἐπίσκοπος τὴ[ν κ]έντησιν τῆς βασιλικῆς Παῦλο[υ ἐπ]οίησεν ἐν Χρ[ιστ]ῷ; it refers to a building, allegedly dedicated by the apostle Paul, that was a precursor of the Apostle Paul Octagon, which was built during the reign of the emperor Arcadius (A.D. 395-408). Ernst Dassmann asserts that this inscription "surpasses in terms of age and certainty of dating all other archaeological testimonies that refer to Paul." The bishop Flavianos of Philippi was involved in removing the archbishop of Thessalonike from office during the Council of Ephesus (A.D. 431).

Evangelism in Thessalonike

Paul and his fellow missionaries traveled from Philippi via Amphipolis and Apollonia to Thessalonike, the old capital of Macedonia. Luke's account of the mission to Thessalonike is brief (Acts 17:1-9).

Thessalonike (Θεσσαλονίκη; mod. Thessaloniki [see fig. 34])[415] was situated at the northeastern end of the Thermaic Gulf at the foot of the Chortiatis Mountains (Mount Kissos). Thessalonike was the metropolis of Macedonia (Strabo 7, frg. 21). The poet Antipater of Thessalonike (first century B.C.) called the city "the mother of all Macedonia" (μήτηρ ἡ πάσης Μακεδονίας).[416] The city was founded by the Macedonian king Kassandros (316-297 B.C.), the son of Antipatros, one of the Diadochi, who needed a trade center for the expanding Macedonia. Kassandros combined the old city of Therme[417] with twenty-six other settlements (*synoikismos*), naming the new city in honor of his wife, Thessalonike, a half-sister of Alexander the Great (Strabo 7, frg. 21, 24). Thessalonike was built with a Hippodamian layout, the *insulae* measuring 102 by 58.5 m. The city was situated at the junction of the roads from Asia Minor to the Adriatic Sea and from the Balkans through the Axios Valley (mod. Vardar) to the Danube region. This and the fact that the city's harbor controlled the connections with the Bosporus soon led to Thessalonike becoming more important than the old Macedonian capital of Pella (mod. Pella, on the road to Edessa), about 40 km to the northwest. According to Strabo, Thessalonike was the most populous city of Macedonia (7.7.4); Livy describes it as "very populous city" (45.30.4). After Aemilius Paullus defeated Perseus, the last Macedonian king, Thessalonike became the capital of the second *regio* of Macedonia in 168 B.C. When the senatorial province of

---

[414]*I. MakedChr* 226; see Elliger 1978, 74-75; Dassmann 1989, 278; the quotation that follows above, ibid.

[415]E. Oberhummer, PW 6.A (1936): 143-48; C. Danoff, *KP* 5:761-63; M. Vickers, *PECS* 912-13; R. Riesner, *GBL* 3:1545-48; H. L. Hendrix, *ABD* 6:523-27; N. Hammond, *OCD* 1510; J. R. McRay, *DNTB* 1231-33; Alexandrov 1976, 139-47; Papazoglou 1988, 189-96, 205-12; D. Müller, in Lauffer 1989, 676-83; H. Koester 1994; Nigdelis 1994; Riesner 1994, 297-301 (ET, 337-41); G. Cohen 1995, 101-5; Touratsoglou 1997, 61-129; Brocke 2001; see also Ioannis Touratsoglou, *Die Münzstätte von Thessaloniki in der römischen Kaiserzeit 32/31 v. Chr. bis 268 n. Chr.* (Berlin: de Gruyter, 1988); Massimo Vitti, *Hē Poleodomikē Exelixē tēs Thessalonikēs apo tēn Hydrisē tēs eēs ton Galerio [The Urban Development of Thessaloniki: From the Foundation to Galerius]* (Athens: Archaiologikēs Hetaireias, 1996). Results of excavations are published in the journals *To archaiologiko ergo ste Makedonia kai Thrake, Makedonia* and *AAA.* Inscriptions: *IG* X 2.1 1-1019 (ed. Charles Edson, 1972); D. Papakonstantinou-Diamantourou will publish three hundred newly discovered inscriptions in a supplemental volume to *IG* X 2.1.

[416]*Anthologia Palatina* 4:428.

[417]See Papazoglou 1988, 190-96. The fleet and the land army of Xerxes had met at Therme in 480 B.C. before the Persians marched to the Thermopylae.

Macedonia was established in 146 B.C., which included Achaia, Epirus and parts of Illyria, Thessalonike was granted autonomous self-rule and became capital of the province and seat of the governor as well as of other supraregional offices such as the office of the Macedoniarch and of the high priest of the Macedonians. When the Via Egnatia was built in 125 B.C., linking Italy with Macedonia and the new province of Asia, Thessalonike became connected with the Roman network of long-distance roads. Cicero lived in Thessalonike in 59 B.C. during his exile; he mentions the *quaestorium* (Cicero, *Planc.* 41). Mark Antony and Octavian (Augustus) granted the city further privileges in 42 B.C., including self-government (*civitas libera*) and the right to mint coins; the mint that was discovered in the excavations of 1998 is situated on the northeastern end of the agora.[418] An arch was erected in the western section of the city to honor Octavian and Mark Antony. The city was governed by politarchs (πολιτάρχαι, *politarchai*), who were non-Roman magistrate officials of the city, five or six officials in the first century A.D.[419] The names of four of the *phylai* or "tribes" (Lat., *tribus*) of the city are known: Asklepias, Antigonis, Dionysias and Gnaias.[420] When Achaia and Macedonia complained to the emperor of high taxation, Augustus placed both regions under his immediate control in A.D. 15 (Tacitus, *Ann.* 1.76). In A.D. 44 Claudius organized Macedonia again as a senatorial province, with Thessalonike as the capital; at times the governor resided in Illyrian Dyrrhachium on the Adriatic Sea. Thessalonike became an important center of trade, with links to the Adriatic region, to the urban centers of Thrace and to the Black Sea region. An inscription dating to the first century A.D. documents an association for Roman merchants; a recently discovered inscription attests a professional and cult association of Aphrodite Epiteuxidia, evidently an association of seafaring merchants.[421] Inscriptions document dyers (*kallibaphoi*), the guild of purple dyers (*synētheia tōn porphyrobaphōn*) and blacksmiths.[422] The poets Antipatros and Philippos lived in Thessalonike in the first century A.D. The fact that the rhetorician Lucian (second century) stayed in Thessalonike indicates that the city was an attractive academic center. When Galerius became emperor in A.D. 305, succeeding Diocletian, he chose Thessalonike as his residence.

Major building activity continued until the fifth century. Only a few remains of ancient Thessalonike survive, including the Hellenistic acropolis and the harbor, in which warships were built at least in the second century B.C. The Sarapeion (excavated in 1920 and

---

[418]The granting of privileges in 42 B.C. was celebrated in a series of coins that had the following legend: Θεσσαλονικέων Ἐλευθερίας | Μ. Αντ(ώνιος) Αὐτ(οκράτωρ) Γ(αῖος) Καῖ(σαρ) Αὐτ(οκράτοω). On the mint see Touratsoglou, *Die Münzstätte von Thessaloniki*, 21; Papazoglou 1988, 206; Brocke 2001, 17 n. 33, 82.

[419]*IG* X 2.1 126, 133. The title *politarchos* has been critiqued by critical scholars as anachronistic; however, it is attested in more than thirty inscriptions—for example, an inscription at an arch on the western end of the Hodos Egnatia dating to the first century. See C. Schuler, "The Macedonian Politarchs," *Classical Philology* 55 (1960): 90-100; F. Gschnitzer, PWSup 13 (1973): 483-500; M. Hatzopoulos, "Les politarques de Philippopolis," in *Dritter Internationaler Thrakologischer Kongress* (FS W. Tomaschek; ed. H. Peschew et al.; 2 vols.; Vienna: Bulgarisches Forschungsinstitut in Österreich, 1984), 2:137-49; Papazoglou 1988, 50, 209-10; McRay 1991, 295; G. H. R. Horsley, "Politarchs," *ABD* 5:384-89; idem, "The Politarchs," in Gill and Gempf 1994, 419-31; idem, "The Politarchs in Macedonia and Beyond," *Mediterranean Archaeology* 7 (1994): 99-126; Brocke 2001, 259-65.

[420]*IG* X 2.1 183-185, 265, 278. See Brocke 2001, 156-57 with n. 28.

[421]*IG* X 2.1 32-33; E. Voutiras, "Berufs- und Kultverein: Ein ΔΟΥΜΟΣ in Thessalonike," *ZPE* 90 (1992): 87-96. See Brocke 2001, 76.

[422]*IG* X 2.1 758, 291, 391. See Brocke 2001, 81.

1939) consisted of several temples (the *naiskos* measured 11 by 8 m), altars, colonnaded halls and other buildings; over seventy inscriptions have been discovered in the Sarapeion; the excavated site has been covered by the city planners of modern Thessaloniki. The Roman agora (100 by 200 m) with a central court (65 by 146 m), the southern stoa with two rows of columns, the subterranean stoa (*cryptoporticus*) that was used as a warehouse, the odeion/bouleuterion with a capacity for 400 spectators, and the public library on the northeast corner date, as far as the architectural arrangement is concerned, to the second or third century A.D. Inscriptions (*IG* X 2.1 5; *SEG* XXIV 570) and stratigraphic analyses suggest that the agora of the first century was situated at the same location.[423] A street lined with shops and warehouses ran underneath the southern section of the agora in the second century. A brothel dating to the first century recently was discovered in the area of the agora, attested by a red pitcher whose spout is stylized as a phallus.[424] An inscription (*IG* X 2.1 31) documents the existence of a Caesareum built at the time of Augustus; it initially was dedicated to the cult of *Divus Iulius* but eventually was used for the imperial cult as well; a localization just north of the agora is regarded as more likely than the earlier localization north of the Sarapeion. The gymnasium, attested since the second century B.C., probably was located directly northeast of the agora. The Hellenistic theater/stadium probably was located north of the agora in the area of the Church of St. Demetrios. The Roman theater and stadium, in which gladiator fights and animal hunts were conducted, probably was located in the southeastern section of the old city near the Galerius palace, as is suggested by new finds, including parts of the spectator tiers of a building measuring 250 by 100 m. An inscription (*CIG* I 1068) documents Olympian and Pythian games in Thessalonike. The hippodrome was built in the fourth century in connection with the Galerius complex. Several main streets of modern Thessaloniki are located above the ancient street network—for example, the main east-west streets Egnatias and Dimitriu, as well as the street Ionos Dragumi, which leads to the harbor.

Rainer Riesner assumes that the Hellenistic-Roman city occupied an area of 130 ha (320 acres) and had 65,000 inhabitants, perhaps 100,000 if the villages are included that belonged to the territory of the city.[425] Christoph vom Brocke assumes 200 ha (perhaps 250 ha) for the city in the first century and suggests on the basis of a comparison with cities of similar size and on the basis of the capacity of the theater/stadium that Thessalonike had 20,000 to 30,000, at the most 40,000, inhabitants.[426] The population of Thessalonike consisted mainly of Thracians, Greeks, Macedonians and Romans.[427] The Thracians can be identified by their names (e.g., Manta, Momo, Doules, Torkos, Pyroulas); they were Hellenized by the first century but continued their religious practices, such as the veneration of the Thracian rider-god (*eques thrax*). It is unclear whether the Macedonian names attested in inscriptions (e.g., Parmenion, Lysanias, Neikandros, Korragos) are evidence for a Macedonian self-consciousness in Thessalonike in the first century, since the linguistic, cultural and religious links between Macedonians and Greeks were centuries old.[428] Despite the presence of Romans in the provincial government, which

---

[423]See Brocke 2001, 52-59; on the Caesareum, ibid., 59-60; on the theater/stadium, ibid., 60-64.

[424]See Brocke 2001, 131.

[425]Riesner 1994, 301 (ET, 341), with reference to the demographic assumptions in Broshi 1975, 5-7.

[426]Brocke 2001, 71-72; his critique (ibid., 73 with n. 243) of R. Riesner ignores the fact that Riesner's figure of one hundred thousand includes the people living in the villages of the city.

[427]On the population of Thessalonike see Brocke 2001, 86-101.

[428]See Brocke 2001, 93.

had its seat in Thessalonike, and among the merchants and traders, the city was thoroughly Greek, organized according to Greek patterns with a council (βουλή, *boulē*), assembly of the citizens (δῆμος, *dēmos*) and magistrates (πολιτάρχαι, *politarchai*), and minting (bronze) coins with Greek legends.[429] Nevertheless, the fact that only 2 percent of the inscriptions discovered in Thessalonike are in Latin does not reflect the true influence of Romans in the city.

Luke's account in Acts 17:1-9 was for a long time the only evidence for Jews in Thessalonike. Since Philo refers to Jewish colonies in Macedonia (Philo, *Legat.* 281-282), scholars rightly assumed that there must have been a sizable Jewish community in Thessalonike, the capital of Macedonia. An inscription (discovered in 1965 but published only in 1994) dating to the third century documents the existence of several synagogues in the city (*IJudO* I Mac 15). The text is inscribed on a marble sarcophagus that belonged to Marcus Aurelius Iakob Eutychios, a Jew who was a Roman citizen; his wife, Anna, was also called Asynkrition. The text of the inscription warns that anyone who places another deceased person into the sarcophagus must pay a penalty of 75,000 denarii to the synagogues (plural: ταῖς συναγωγαῖς, *tais synagōgais*).[430]

Luke's account of Paul's first visit to Thessalonike (Acts 17:1-9) consists of two parts. The first part (Acts 17:1-4) reports the beginning of the activity of the missionaries: Paul preached in the local synagogue on three sabbaths, seeking to convince the listeners on the basis of the sacred Scriptures that Jesus, who suffered (and died), is the promised Messiah. The listeners included not only Jews but also a great number of "devout Greeks" (Acts 17:4b):[431] that is, "sympathizers of the second category" who attended the synagogue services and showed interest in the Jewish faith; and also "not a few of the leading women" (Acts 17:4c):[432] that is, "sympathizers of the first category."[433] Luke briefly and summarily notes the success of Paul's missionary preaching: some Jews and a larger number of non-Jews—God-fearers, including several women who belonged to the local aristocracy—were persuaded, came to faith in Jesus Christ and joined Paul and Silas (Acts 17:4a).

Luke's comment that the new converts "joined" (προσεκληρώθησαν, *proseklērōthēsan* [Acts 17:4a]) Paul and Silas indicates the establishment of a church in the city. Paul reminds the Christians in Thessalonike in his letter written only a few months later that they had turned away from idols (εἴδωλα, *eidōla* [1Thess 1:9]).[434] This comment suggests that the majority of the new Christian community consisted of former polytheists.

---

[429]See Brocke 2001, 97; for the comment that follows above see ibid., 99.

[430]See Nigdelis 1994; inscription, 298, table 7; cf. Stavroulakis and DeVinney 1992, 159; Levinskaya 1996, 155-56; Brocke 2001, 205-33; Panayotov, in *IJudO* I, 2004, 95-98.

[431]Acts 17:4b: τῶν τε σεβομένων Ἑλλήνων πλῆθος πολύ.

[432]Acts 17:4c: γυναικῶν τε τῶν πρώτων οὐκ ὀλίγαι.

[433]See Wander 1998, 199.

[434]H. Hübner, *EWNT* 1:937 (*EDNT* 1:387); Brocke 2001, 114; for the comment that follows above see ibid.

Inscriptions and literary texts document for Thessalonike the cults (and temples) of Aphrodite, Aphrodite Homonoia, Athene, Apollo, Dionysos, Heracles, Kabiros, Nemesis, Zeus (Theos Hypsistos), Zeus Eleutherios; the Dioscuri; the nymphs; the Egyptian gods Isis, Sarapis, Osiris, Anubis and Harpocrates (attested by sixty-nine inscriptions); the Roman benefactors as well as the imperial cult.[435] The cult of Kabiros was one of the most important cults of Thessalonike. It was characterized by elementary demonic concepts and therefore is described by some authors as "god of the nocturnal fiends and chthonic treasures." The cult perhaps came originally from Phrygia and could be found in the entire Mediterranean world, with different local characteristics. In regard to the number and personal constitution of the Kaboroi: sometimes they appear as a triad, sometimes as a male pair; in Berytos seven Kabiroi were worshiped, in Samothrace four. Accordording to myth, two of the three Kabiroi decapitated their brother, wrapped the head in a purple cloth and buried it at the foot of Mount Olympus. It appears that it was this third brother who was worshiped in Thessalonike: he is depicted on the autonomous coinage since the time of Vespasian as youthful figure, clothed in a short chiton and holding a blacksmith's hammer in his left hand. It is possible that the cult of this Kabiros played an important role in Thessalonike already in earlier times, considering the fact that the Kabiroi were known in Larissa at least since 200 B.C.[436] In an inscription dating to the third century (*IG* X 2.1 199), the Kabiros is described as ἁγιώτατος πάτριος θεός (*hagiōtatos patrios theos*), as ancestral and "most holy" of all gods. Entirely hypothetical and not very convincing is the suggestion of Christoph vom Brocke that Paul's exhortation to "holiness" (*hagiasmos* [1 Thess 4:3-6]) is an allusion to the "most holy" (*hagiōtatos*) Kabiros. (1) This epithet is used for Kabiros in Thessalonike only in a single inscription, dating to the third century, which is too late to be used as "background" for the local history of the city in the first century. (2) The epexegetical infinitives in 1 Thess 4:3-6 that explain Paul's understanding of "holiness"—abstaining from fornication, honorable treatment of one's wife, refraining from greedy designs on one's fellow believer—deal with behavior that was hardly characteristic for the cult of the Kabiroi. (3) The identification of "holiness" or "sanctification" with the "will of God" alludes to Lev 11:44-45; 19:2; 21:8 rather than to the cult of Kabiros. (4) There is no cogent reason why the superlative *hagiōtatos* ("most holy") should be connected only with the noun *hagiasmos* and not also with the simplex *hagios* ("holy"), which is used in the Pauline writings seventy-six times, or with the word group *hagios, hagiazein, hagiasmos, hagiosynē* as a whole, attested ninety-six times—in both cases the "frequency" of *hagiasmos* in 1 Thess 4:3, 4, 7 disappears.

The cult of Dionysos also played a central role in Thessalonike, as is demonstrated by the fact that one of the local *phylai* was named after Dionysos. The temple of Dionysos has not been located as of yet. Inscriptions document private cultic associations that devoted themselves to the worship of Dionysos; most of their members seem to have been Roman citizens. Paul's exhortations in 1 Thess 5:5-8 not to be drunk at night

---

[435]See C. Edson, "Cults of Thessalonica," *HTR* 41 (1948): 143-204; K. P. Donfried, "The Cults of Thessalonica and the Thessalonian Correspondence," *NTS* 31 (1985) 336-56 (= Donfried 2002, 21-48); Brocke 2001, 116-42.

[436]Brocke 2001, 117-21; on the inscription *IG* X 2.1 199 see 120; on a possible connection to 1 Thess 4:3, 4, 7 see 121. On the cult of the Kabiroi see also W. Fauth, *KP* 3:34-38; Bengt Hemberg, *Die Kabiren* (Uppsala: Almqvist & Wiksell, 1950); Rex Witt, "The Kabeiroi," in *Ancient Macedonia II* (Thessalonike: Hidryma meleton Chersonesou tou Haimou, 1977), 67-80; Michèle Daumas, *Cabiriaca recherches sur l'iconographie du culte des Cabires* (Paris: Boccard, 1998).

but to be sober might well allude to practices of the cult of Dionysos.[437] Devotees to the cult of Isis celebrated the goddess as inventor of culture and custom, of agriculture, seafaring, writing and language, as teacher of building temples and of awe for the gods. A fragment of a revelatory speech of Isis has been found in Thessalonike (*IG* X 2.1 254) that evidently was displayed in other temples of Isis as well. In the *Kaisaros naos* (*IG* X 2.1 31), built at the time of Augustus, the citizens of Thessalonike worshiped Julius Caesar, who is described as *theos* in a series of coins minted in 28/27 B.C. Augustus was worshiped as *divi filius* ("son of god") in A.D. 41 and possibly already during his lifetime.[438] The imperial cult was linked with the worship of Roma, worshiped together with the "Roman benefactors" ('Ρωμαῖοι εὐεργέται, *Rōmaioi euergetai*). Inscriptions document the office of a priest and *agōnothetēs* of the imperial cult (ἱερεὺς καὶ ἀγωνοθέτης Αὐτοκράτορος Καίσαρος [*IG* X 2.1 31, 133]), who was responsible for organizing games that were celebrated in connection with the imperial cult.[439]

The second part of Luke's account (Acts 17:5-9) reports a riot scene in which the missionaries have no direct rule but nevertheless are forced to leave the city (Acts 17:10). Jews and local mobs accuse Paul of having turned "the whole world" (οἰκουμένη, *oikoumenē*) upside down through his worldwide preaching activity (Acts 17:6b).

Some scholars suggest that the author formulated this accusation "in line with his apologetic purpose"[440] and that it represents a "crass anachronism."[441] But one must read the text closely to see that such criticism is unwarranted: it is not Luke who says that the work of Paul turned "the whole world" upside down, but rather his Jewish opponents, who are prepared to use any measure, including the agitation of the mob in the marketplace, to discredit Paul and obstruct his activities (Acts 17:5). Their accusation against Paul is a charge that seeks to make him appear to be a criminal, using allegations from the traditional arsenal of polemics, slander and defamation.[442] The formulation "the whole world" surely is meant in a hyperbolic sense: by A.D. 50 Paul had preached the gospel only in Antioch and in Damascus as far as larger cities in the Roman Empire were concerned; he had not been in Alexandria or in Ephesus, in Corinth or in Rome. However, the phrase is not hyperbolic in an anachronistic sense, amounting to a mistake by Luke as a historian, but in an polemical sense, for which Paul's Jewish opponents are to be blamed. The charge of the opponents did not need to be grounded in reality to serve their goal of agitating: formulated as Luke reports it, it served its purpose of causing the magistrate of the city to take decisive action. Christoph vom Brocke analyzes

---

[437]See Riesner 1994, 333 (ET, 375); Brocke 2001, 128-29; on the cult of Isis see ibid., 135-36.

[438]See *IG* X 2.1 31, dated between 27 B.C. and A.D. 14 (C. Edson).

[439]See Brocke 2001, 140-41.

[440]Conzelmann, *Apg*, 103 (ET, 135); Schneider, *Apg*, 2:225; cf. Reinbold 2000, 130-31 with n. 56, with respect to the role of the Jews.

[441]Botermann 1993, 80, arguing that "it was impossible to speak in these terms in Thessalonike in A.D. 49 or 50." Cf. Botermann 1996, 171, stating that "Luke evidently did not have precise information about this station of Paul and thus he filled the gap with the charge brought [against Paul] later in Caesarea (Acts 24:5). Because when Paul was active in Europe for a few weeks only, nobody could maintain that he stirred up the entire Oikoumene. There was no edict of the emperor before A.D. 64 that he could have violated."

[442]See Wander 1998, 210 n. 18.

the proceedings against Jason against the background of the local historical realities in Thessalonike and formulates the following result: "The incensed crowd that gathered in front of the house of Jason initially intended to take Paul and his companions to the assembly of the people, probably to indict him here and have sentence passed on him (Acts 17:5b: ἐζήτουν αὐτοὺς προαγαγεῖν εἰς τὸν δῆμον). But since they could not get hold of him, they dragged Jason and some of the Christians who were present before the politarchs. . . . Evidently they had been given far-reaching executive powers with the result that the accused could be sentenced to post bail. . . . [Bail] possibly was ordered to guarantee the subpoena of the missionaries."[443] The local color of Luke's account suggests that the charge against Paul had been carefully planned, a clear indication of historical reliability. Rudolf Pesch argues, "The charge that was deliberately formulated in political terms was meant to impress the politarchs by asserting that the newcomers stirred up not just the city (as in Acts 16:20) but 'the world' (cf. Lk 2:1; Acts 24:5), and that they not only cause unrest but also they foment rebellion (ἀναστατώσαντες). In other words, the politarchs in the capital of the province are confronted also with the interests of the Roman officials of the province who reside here, the interests of the *Imperium Romanum,* whose proconsul would call the politarchs to account if they tolerated troublemakers in the city."[444] I cannot detect a reference to the edict of Claudius of A.D. 41 (or of A.D. 49) as a background for the action of the missionaries' Jewish opponents in Thessalonike, neither in Acts 17:5-9 nor in 1 Thessalonians.[445]

Jason, whom Luke does not describe in any detail, had accommodated Paul during this turbulent time and posted bail for him (Acts 17:5-9). The information that the agitated crowd went to the house of Jason, arresting him and several Christians who were present, suggests that the church in Thessalonike met in Jason's house.[446] Christoph vom Brocke surmises that Paul knew Jason before his arrival in Thessalonike: Lydia of Philippi may have initiated the contact with Jason—dealers in purple are attested for both Philippi and Thessalonike—and she may have helped the apostle to plan the continuation of his journey after leaving Philippi.[447] The presence of purple dyers in Thessalonike cannot elevate this hypothesis to historical probability, however. Others suggest that Jason may have been a (perhaps distant) relative of Paul: the apostle describes him, together with Lucius/Luke and Sosipater, as his συγγενεῖς (*syngeneis* [Rom 16:21]). This interpretation would explain why Luke does not describe Jason in greater detail, why Paul lived in his house and why he was willing to post bail for Paul. However, this interpretation of the term *syngeneis* is uncertain; most scholars interpret the term in the sense of "compatriots, kin."[448] We encounter Jason later

---

[443]Brocke 2001, 267.

[444]Pesch, *Apg,* 2:124.

[445]Contra Cineira 1999, 291-340.

[446]See Brocke 2001, 237; on Aristarchus and Secundus see ibid., 242-49.

[447]Brocke 2001, 236-37, with reference to *IG* X 2.1 291 (second century).

[448]See BAA 1541, s.v. "συγγενής"; BDAG 950, s.v. "συγγενής 2": "belonging to the same people group, compatriot, kin"; see also G. Schneider, *EWNT* 3:675 (*EDNT* 3:282); the commentaries on Rom 16:7, 21.

as a coworker of Paul in Corinth (Rom 16:21). Luke mentions the names of two other Christians from Thessalonike in Acts 20:4: Aristarchus and Secundus. Aristarchus is Paul's coworker in Ephesus, where he was arrested with a certain Gaius and taken to the theater. Evidently he accompanied Paul to Judea: he is with Paul when the apostle is taken as a prisoner to Rome (Acts 27:2), and according to Col 4:10-11, he was imprisoned with Paul.

Paul was forced to leave Thessalonike suddenly, while Timothy and Silas stayed in the city (Acts 17:14-15; 18:5) before following Paul, whom they meet in Beroea. When Timothy traveled via Athens to Corinth several weeks later to join Paul in his missionary outreach there, he is soon sent back to Thessalonike with a letter from Paul (1 Thess 3:5) in which the apostle addresses theological misunderstandings that had arisen in the previous weeks and months. It appears that Silas later returned to Thessalonike (2 Cor 11:9; Phil 4:14).[449]

Paul wrote 1 Thessalonians soon after the establishment of the church; he asks that the letter is read to "all brothers"—that is, all believers in the city (1 Thess 5:27).[450] Adolf von Harnack argues on the basis of the allegedly stronger Jewish character of 2 Thessalonians that this comment attests two Christian churches in Thessalonike that met in separate assemblies: a large Gentile-Christian community and a smaller Jewish-Christian community.[451] However, 2 Thessalonians is not more "Jewish" than 1 Thessalonians, and there is no evidence in any of the letters that there was a Gentile-Christian majority and a Jewish-Christian minority that were divided. The interpretation by Abraham Malherbe is more plausible: evidently several house churches had come into existence in Thessalonike, perhaps already during Paul's first stay in the city, in which the letter was to be read to all believers.[452]

Dieter Lührmann concludes from 1 Thessalonians that when Luke later wrote his account of Paul's mission to Thessalonike, he followed a traditional pattern and thus had Paul preach in the synagogue, while 1 Thess 1:9-10 and 2:14 suggest Gentile listeners for Paul and Gentile Christians in the church of Thessalonike.[453] The skepticism of this interpretation concerning Luke's account is unnecessary. A letter written to a Gentile-Christian church does not exclude the possibility that there were some Jewish Christians in Thessalonike as well.[454] On 1 Thess 1:9-10 see §28.2. Christoph vom Brocke suggests that the term *symphyletai* in 1 Thess 2:14 is a reference to the fact that the Christians in Thessalonike belonged to the political *phylai,* implying that they were full citizens of

---

[449]Michael Goulder (1992, 101-6) believes that Silas was responsible for the theological difficulties that prompted the writing of 2 Thessalonians. However, the silence about Silas in the book of Acts and in Paul's letters cannot be used to construct a historical hypothesis. See Malherbe, *Thess,* 70-71.

[450]1 Thess 5:27: ἀναγνωσθῆναι τὴν ἐπιστολὴν πᾶσιν τοῖς ἀδελφοῖς.

[451]Harnack 1910. For other explanations see Malherbe, *Thess,* 344.

[452]Malherbe, *Thess,* 344-45.

[453]See Lührmann 1990, 241-43.

[454]See Malherbe, *Thess,* 56, 353.

the city and thus belonged to the privileged elite.[455] This view convinces neither with regard to the interpretation of the term *symphyletai* nor with regard to his description of the social status of the Thessalonian Christians: Paul's exhortation that the believers live an upright life and work with their own hands in order not to be a burden to other people (1 Thess 4:11-12) suggests that the Christians in Thessalonike did not belong to the privileged class.

According to early Christian tradition, Aristarchus, Paul's coworker, was the first bishop of Thessalonike. The first securely documented bishop was Alexander, who attended the Council of Nicea. In the fifth century a church building (100 m long) stood in Thessalonike, above which the Hagia Sophia was built in the eighth century.

Evangelism in Beroea

After their hurried departure from Thessalonike, Paul and Silas arrived in Beroea (Acts 17:10), and they were joined by Timothy some time later (Acts 17:14; 1 Thess 3:1-5). Luke describes Paul's ministry in Beroea in Acts 17:10-14.

Beroea (Βέροια; mod. Veroia)[456] was situated on a terrace 188 m above the Haliakmon River on the southernmost of the three passes across the Bermion Mountains, belonging to the Macedonian region of Bottiaia. Macedonians had settled on the east slope of Mount Bermion around 700 B.C., as they did in Edessa about 40 km to the north. The first historical reference to Beroea is found in Thucydides (1.61.4) in the context of events that transpired in 432 B.C. After the battle at Pydna in 168 B.C., Beroea was one of the first cities that capitulated to the Romans. During the civil war Beroea was the military basis of Pompey around 49/48 B.C. (Plutarch, *Pomp.* 64). Beroea seems to have been the seat of the Macedonian provincial assembly (*koinon*) since the time of Augustus, headed up by the high priest of the imperial cult of the province and connected with athletic and musical games. Beroea flourished in the first century; the city was one of the cultural centers of the province. A colossal head of Medusa dating to the Hellenistic period was found near the east gate. Inscriptions attest the worship of Zeus Hypsistos, Heracles, Asclepius, Hermes and Kynagidas. About 10 km southwest of the city stood a temple of the Mother of the Autochthonous Gods, attested by inscriptions dating from the second to the fourth centuries. The worship of the Syrian goddess Atargatis and of Isis Lochia demonstrates that Beroea was open to outside influences.[457] The Jewish community of Beroea is first attested in Acts 17:10-12.[458] Remains of the agora, public baths, streets and the city wall survive.

Paul preached the gospel in the synagogue of Beroea (Acts 17:10). Luke reports

---

[455]Brocke 2001, 152-66.

[456]E. Oberhummer, "Beroia 1," PW 3.1 (1897): 304-6; H. Treidler, "Beroia 1," *KP* 1:869; P. M. Petsas, *PECS* 150-51; M. Errington, "Beroia 1," *DNP* 2:577; Papazoglou 1988, 141-48; A. B. Tataki, *Ancient Beroea: Prosopography and Society* (Meletemata 8; Athens: Research Centre for Greek and Roman Antiquity; National Hellenic Research Foundation, 1988); D. Müller and W. Günther, in Lauffer 1989, 703-4; Gill 1994c, 415-17; Touratsoglou 1997, 161-79.

[457]See Papazoglou 1988, 141.

[458]See Stavroulakis and DeVinney 1992, 197; L. Levine 2000, 108-9, 473. On the Jewish tombstones dating to the fourth and fifth centuries see Levinskaya 1996, 157; Panayotov, in *IJudO* I, 2004, 76-87, on the Jewish tombstones dating to the fourth and fifth century.

that the Beroean Jews were prepared to listen attentively to the message of the apostle, examining with the help of the Hebrew Scriptures whether it harmonized with the received revelation (Acts 17:11). Luke notes the conversion of many Jews (πολλοὶ ἐξ αὐτῶν) and "not a few Greek women and men of high standing" (Acts 17:12), whom evidently he reached with the gospel in the synagogue. The reference to "the brothers" in Acts 17:14 confirms the establishment of a Christian community through Paul's preaching. Little is known about the subsequent history of the Christians in Beroea. A bishop of Beroea is mentioned for the first time in connection with the Council of Sardis in A.D. 343.

The Jews of Beroea evidently had good contacts with the Jews of Thessalonike: when the latter heard that Paul was preaching in Beroea, they sent envoys to Beroea who stirred up the people in the city (Acts 17:13) in the hope that Paul would be identified as the cause of the disturbances and that the magistrate would take appropriate action. When the new converts in Beroea realized what was happening, they immediately took Paul to Pydna, the port of Beroea, and accompanied him by ship to Athens (Acts 17:14-15). Thus Paul's missionary outreach to the province of Achaia began in the spring of A.D. 50.

Achaia (Ἀχαΐα)[459] was a senatorial province since an edict of Augustus from 27 B.C. Between A.D. 15 and 44 Achaia was administered with Macedonia as an imperial province before being organized again as a separate senatorial province after A.D. 44. Achaia comprised Greece proper (Attica, Boeotia, Peloponnese) as well as Thessaly and southern Epirus. The province was governed by a proconsul, appointed by lot every year, whose seat was in Corinth. The interests of the emperor were looked after by several procurators. The city of Aigion was the seat of the provincial assembly, the *koinon* τῶν Ἀχαιῶν (Pausanias 7.24.4), and thus was the sacred center of the Peloponnese. The independent cities of the province included Athens, Sparta, Ellis and Delphi.

Evangelism in Athens

Paul waited in Athens for Silas and Timothy (Acts 17:15), who had stayed in Beroea (Acts 17:14), with Timothy having been active in Thessalonike as well (1 Thess 3:1-5).[460] They probably met Paul in Athens, who sent them back to Macedonia with new assignments: Timothy evidently went to Thessalonike (1 Thess 3:1-5), and Silas to Philippi (2 Cor 11:9; Phil 4:14).[461] They rejoined Paul in Corinth.

Did Paul have plans for missionary outreach in Athens? Or did he simply use

---

[459]C. G. Brandis, PW 1.1 (1893): 156-90; E. Kirsten and B. E. Thomasson, *KP* 1:32-38; Y. Lafond, *DNP* 1:62-70; A. J. S. Spawforth, *OCD* 6; B. Reicke, *EWNT* 1:447-48 (*EDNT* 1:185-86); Larsen 1938; Gill 1994d.

[460]Donfried (1991b) argues with regard to the difficulty of reconciling Acts 17:14-15; 18:5 and 1 Thess 3:1-3 that Timothy was never in Athens, suggesting that Luke's information is correct, while the "we" in 1 Thess 3:1 is a redactional plural: Paul was alone in Athens.

[461]Marshall, *Acts*, 281; Malherbe, *Thess*, 70. Differently Donfried (1991b), who believes that Timothy and Silas never visited in Athens.

his visit to the old "university city" as a tourist as an opportunity to preach the gospel? Luke provides an extensive account of Paul's stay in Athens (Acts 17:16-34),[462] a fact that might suggest that Paul's preaching activity in Athens was not incidental. The comment in Acts 17:17 ("So he argued in the synagogue with the Jews and the devout persons, and also in the marketplace every day with those who happened to be there") shows that Paul engaged in missionary work in Athens as he did in other cities: he preached in synagogues to Jewish audiences and in the Agora to Gentile audiences.

Athens (᾽Αθῆναι; mod. Athina, Athens [see fig. 35]),[463] about 6 km from the coast of the Saronic Gulf on the southwestern edge of the Attic Plain, was about five hundred years past its prime when Paul visited the city in the middle of the first century (about the same amount of time that Germany is past the Reformation and since Christopher Columbus first saw the land of the western hemisphere). The golden age of Athens was the Pentekontaetia, the Great Fifty Years from the end of the campaign of Xerxes (479 B.C.), who burned the Acropolis and almost completely destroyed the lower city, to the beginning of the Peloponnesian War (431 B.C.). The participation of the citizens in the democracy of the city was made possible not least by the per diem allowance that Pericles arranged for the poorer citizens who served as members of juries or of the city council. "At times more than 20,000 Athenians lived at public expense, including 6,000 judges, 500 council members, 550 watchmen, 700 lower officials, 700 federal officers, and a large number of people in the fleet and in the army as well as people who helped in the rebuilding of the destroyed temples."[464] The Sophists Protagoras, Prodikos, Hippias and Gorgias taught political theory, Herodotus and Thucydides wrote the history of Athens, the tragic poets Sophocles and Euripides and the comic poets Kratinos, Eupolis and Aristophanes composed plays for the theater, the sculptors Myron and Pheidias worked on their famous sculptures. This peaceful and fertile period was terminated by the Peloponnesian War, which was caused by disputes with the city of Corinth and was encouraged by Pericles for reasons of internal politics. One hundred years later the Athenians were decisively defeated by the Macedonian king Philipp II at Chaironeia (338 B.C.). However, Athens remained a center of Greek culture and education. In 335 B.C., fifty years after the foundation of the Academy by Plato, his student Aristotle established his own school (*Peripatos*), in 306 B.C. Epicurus established the *Kepos,* and in 301 B.C. Zenon began to teach in the *Stoa Poikile,* a colonnaded hall from which his

---

[462]Besides the commentaries see Stenschke 1999a, 203-24.

[463]J. Papastavrou, PWSup 10 (1965): 48-89; W. Zschietzschman, PWSup 13 (1973): 55-140; idem, *KP* 1:686-701; H. Volkmann, *KP* 5:1578-82; J. Travlos, *PECS* 106-10; O. Dickinson et al., *OCD* 203-5; J. McK. Camp, *OCD* 203-6; H. R. Goette and J. Niehoff, "Athenai 1," *DNP* 2:167-95; J. R. McRay, *DNTB* 139-40; Paul Graindor, *Athènes sous Auguste* (Cairo: Le Caire, 1927); idem, *Athènes de Tibère à Trajan* (Cairo: Le Caire, 1931); Day 1942; John Travlos, *Pictorial Dictionary of Ancient Athens* (New York: Hacker, 1980 [1971]); Cothenet 1978c, 52-55; Geagan 1979; J. Camp 1980; Shear 1981; *Athens in Prehistory and Antiquity* (Athens: Ministry of Culture, 1987); A. Wittenberg, in Lauffer 1989, 141-51; Gill 1994c, 441-48; Habicht 1994; 1995; Köhler 1996, 18-32; Maria Brouskari, *The Monuments of the Acropolis* (Athens: Ministry of Culture, 1997); Michael C. Hoff and Susan I. Rotroff, eds., *The Romanization of Athens* (Oxford: Oxbow Books, 1997); J. Camp 2001.

[464]H. Volkmann, *KP* 5:1581.

school received its name.[465] After the Chremonides' War Athens received limited autonomy in 261 B.C. Sulla conquered and plundered the city in 86 B.C. after the Athenians had sided with King Mithradates against Rome. Not until Emperor Valerian (A.D. 253-260) were the city walls were rebuilt.[466] After the murder of Julius Caesar the citizens of Athens celebrated Brutus and Cassius as murderers of the tyrant. However, the city profited from the defeat of Brutus and Cassius: Mark Antony was a friend of Greek culture and spent time in the city. After the Battle of Actium on September 2 in the year 31 B.C. the victorious Octavian visited Athens first. To honor Octavian-Augustus, who visited Athens repeatedly and helped finance the rebuilding of several temples and other buildings that had been damaged, the city erected a temple of Roma and Augustus on the Acropolis between 27 and 17 B.C.; an inscription honors Augustus as "Savior and Benefactor." The generosity of Augustus caused Athens to flourish again. The new period of prosperity was relatively short-lived, but Augustus's example motivated other wealthy non-Athenians to help Athens as well, including the Jewish king Herod I, whom the Athenians thanked by erecting several statues in his honor in the city, and C. Julius Nikanor from Syrian Hierapolis, who bought the island of Salamis and donated it to the Athenians. Statues of rulers of Thrace that were erected in Athens indicate that Augustus's donations of grain did not end the shortage of food in the city, requiring Athenians to maintain a close relationship with Thrace with its large wheat harvests.[467] Apart from several donations, neither Athens' culture nor politics appears to have produced major achievements in the first century after Augustus, probably a result of the difficult economic situation of the city. The economic predicament is reflected in the fact that the Garden of Hephaistos was no longer maintained and the cultic embassies to Delphi stopped.[468] The dramatic games of the Dionysia continued to be celebrated, however. After Augustus, Claudius was the most popular emperor. He financed a new monumental staircase leading from the city to the Propylaia of the Acropolis probably in A.D. 52, as well as a staircase from the old agora to the temple of Hephaistos, and the theater of Dionysos received a new stage (*skēnē*). The Athenians thanked the emperor for these donations by erecting several statues of Claudius, with inscriptions honoring the emperor as "Savior and Benefactor,"[469] and by worshiping him in the agora as Apollo Patroos.

The magistrates who were responsible de facto for the affairs in the city were the general of the *hoplitai* and the herald of the Areopagus on Ares Hill west of the Acropolis, on which the highest court of Athens met. The Areopagus ("Αρειος Πάγος, *Areios Pagos*), one of the ancient institutions of Athens, evidently functioned increasingly as city council (*ordo decurionum*). The Council of the Six Hundred no longer played a role in the first century. Several scholars visited Athens in the first century: Daniel Geagan mentions, other than Paul, particularly Plutarch.[470] The Romans admired Athens as the seat of the four philosophical schools: the Academy, the Peripatos, the Kepos and the Stoa.

---

[465] On the philosophical schools in Athens see Habicht 1994, 231-60.

[466] On the war of Cornelius Sulla against Athens and its aftermath see Habicht 1995, 303-13; on Athens during the civil war of 49-31 B.C. see ibid., 348-61.

[467] Geagan 1979, 382; for the comment that follows above see ibid., 385; see also Day 1942, 177-83.

[468] On the Garden of Hephaistos see D. B. Thompson, "The Garden of Hephaistos," *Hesperia* 6 (1937): 396-425; on Athens' relationship with Delphi, which was very close in the second century B.C., see Habicht 1995, 275-80.

[469] *IG* II² 3269, 3271, 3272, 3274.

[470] Geagan 1979, 387.

Athens was surrounded on three sides by mountains: Mount Parnes in the northwest, Mount Pentelikon in the northeast and Mount Hymettos in the southeast. The topography of the city was dominated by seven hills: in the center of the city was the Acropolis, the site of the ancient cults and festivals, with a monumental gate (the Propylaia, with a main hall and two side wings, one of which was the site of the Pinakotheke, which housed paintings). The Monument of Agrippa was to the left and the temple of Athene Nike was to the right. Other buildings on the Acropolis included the temple of Artemis Brauronia, the Chalkotheke (a large storeroom for dedications and weapons), the majestic Parthenon (70 by 30 m, with a peristyle of 35 columns 10.4 m high, with a wealth of sculptures: 92 metopes, 160 m of relief frieze and 50 marble sculptures depicting gods and heroes; the statue of Athene Parthenos, sculpted by Pheidias, stood in the *cella* [30 by 19 m] in the back of building: the statue reached 12 m high, and its clothes and helmet were made of gold weighing 1,140 kg), the Sanctuary of Pandion, the round temple of Roma and Augustus, the temple of Zeus Polieus, the Altar of Athene Polias, the Erechtheion (the "old temple"; the northwest hall was dedicated to Athene Polias and housed the most sacred statue of Athene that the city possessed, made of olive tree wood; the western hall was dedicated to the worship of Boutes, Hephaistos and Poseidon-Erechtheus) and the temple of Pandrosos (with the holy olive tree of Athene and an altar of Zeus Herkeios). The monumental staircase that Claudius commissioned as new access to the Acropolis was built in A.D. 52, two years after Paul's visit to the city.

West of the Acropolis was Ares Hill (*Areo Pagus* [115 m high]), the seat of a venerable council of elders named after the hill; this council was the supreme court of Athens, which met in the open air. John Camp describes the function of this council, which changed over the centuries, as follows: "Originally the council had great constitutional powers, which were eroded away over the years with the rise of democracy. The council was made up of retired magistrates and tended to be very conservative; the best modern parallel might be the British House of Lords, once extremely powerful and now reduced to little more than a ceremonial role. In the historical period, the Council of the Areopagos still served as a homicide court. In later times, Saint Paul addressed it in its role as the guardian of traditional Athenian ways."[471]

North of Ares Hill was the agora (200 by 250 m) surrounded on all four sides by buildings: on the west side was the Stoa Basileios (Hall of Zeus Eleutherios, about 18 by 7 m, with a large statue of Nike and a large altar of Zeus), the temple of Zeus Phratrios and Athene Phratria, the temple of Apollo Patroos, the Metroon, which served both as a sanctuary of the Mother of the Gods and as the archive building of the city, an altar dedicated to Zeus Agoraios in front of the Metroon, the New Bouleuterion (council building), and the Tholos (dining hall and headquarters of the senate). In the southwest

---

[471]J. Camp 2001, 265. For the discussion of the Athenian agora that follows see W. Zschietzschmann, PWSup 13 (1973): 85-88; R. E. Wycherley, *The Athenian Agora III: Literary and Epigraphical Testimonia* (Princeton, N.J.: American School of Classical Studies at Athens, 1957); Homer A. Thompson and R. E. Wycherley, *The Agora of Athens: The History, Shape and Uses of an Ancient City Center* (The Athenian Agora 14; Princeton, N.J.: American School of Classical Studies at Athens, 1972); Geagan 1979, 380-81; Shear 1981, 360-61; Travlos, *Pictorial Dictionary of Ancient Athens*, 1-27; John M. Camp, *The Athenian Agora: Excavations in the Heart of Classical Athens* (New York: Thames & Hudson, 1986; German: *Die Agora von Athen* [Kulturgeschichte der antiken Welt 41; Mainz: Philipp von Zabern, 1989]), esp. 153-161; idem 2001, 257-61; on the Roman market see Thompson and Wycherley, *The Agora of Athens*, 173; Travlos, *Pictorial Dictionary of Ancient Athens*, 28-36; J. Camp 2001, 192-93. See <http://www.attalos.com/index.html>.

corner stood the Strategeion, renovated by Augustus, which was the administrative center of the army general and the cult place of the hero Strategos. On the south side the agora was divided into two areas of unequal size by the Middle Stoa (147 by 17.5 m), the longest building in the agora; behind this generally modest colonnaded hall stood the Heliaia (seat of the city's most famous court of law) and the Eleusinion with a temple and a fountain house; the route of the Panathenaic procession to Eleusis passed by this structure. On the east side of the agora stood the Stoa of Attalos (112 by 20 m), which had two stories and housed shops, serving as the principal market building of the Greek city. On the northeast corner of the agora stood another court building. On the north side of the agora stood the Stoa Poikile, or "Painted Stoa," in which paintings and mementos were displayed that reminded the citizens of the victories of the city; this stoa was open to all Athenians, a popular meeting place for discussions and cultural activities, attracting such diverse persons as jugglers, sword-swallowers, beggars, fishmongers and philosophers; around 300 B.C. Zeno had his classroom in this stoa, prompting his contemporaries to call his followers Stoics. Next to the Stoa Poikile stood the temple of Hephaistos. On the northwest corner of the agora stood a temple and the Peribolos with the Altar of the Twelve Gods. During the Roman period the appearance of the agora was changed decisively: the public square was filled with buildings and monuments—a conquered city did not need democratic assemblies. In the first century B.C. the temple of Aphrodite Urania was built on the north side, and an annex was added to the Stoa of Zeus dedicated to the imperial cult, with Augustus worshiped as Zeus Eleutherios. The most impressive building erected in the old agora was the large Odeion of Agrippa, built by Augustus's son-in-law in 15 B.C. (51.4 by 43.2 m), with a marble orchestra seating one thousand people. In the center of the agora a temple of Ares was erected, transferred from Pallene, where it originally stood. The base of a column dating to A.D. 2 honors Gaius Caesar, Agrippa's son and Augustus's adoptive son, as "new Ares" (*IG* II^2 3250). At the southeast corner of the agora the old mint was replaced by a new temple that was constructed with eight columns from the temple of Athene in Sounion. Some time after 12 B.C. a new market was built about 75 m east of the agora, the Market of Caesar and Augustus, dedicated to Athene Archegetis, as the new commercial market of the city. The large Roman agora (111 by 98 m), a peristyle court with Ionic colonnades on all four sides, was accessed by two monumental gates; behind the colonnade on the east side was a row of shops; along the south side stood a small fountain; the gate at the west entrance (gate of Athene Archegetis) is still visible today.[472] East of the Roman agora was a square (about 100 by 50 m) with the Horologion, the so-called Tower of the Winds, an octagonal marble building (about 14 m high) with sundials incised on all eight sides, a large public latrine with roofed seats for seventy people, and the Agoranomion, the building of the market supervisors built under Claudius and dedicated to Athene Archegetis and the *theoi sebastoi*. The temple of Sarapis and the temple of Eileithyia, which Pausanias mentions (1.18.4-5), probably were located in this area as well.

The other hills of Athens were Anchesmos Hill and Lykabettos Hill in the northeastern part of the city. In the northwest was Pnyx Hill, the meeting place of the Athenian assembly, with the ancient bema, an altar of Zeus Agoraios and a temple of Zeus Hypsistos. In the southwest was Mouseion Hill with the Mouseion, the site of a Macedonian fort and of the marble grave of Philopappos. To the southeast was Ardettos Hill with the stadium (since 330 B.C.). To the south was the temple of Zeus Olympios, begun by the Seleucid

---

[472]Zschietzschmann, PWSup 13 (1973): 86; J. Camp 2001, 192-93.

king Antiochos IV Epiphanes in 174 B.C. and finished during the principate of Hadrian in A.D. 131/132. The temple of Dionysos and the temple of Heracles Pankrates stood in this general area as well. Plato's Academy was located 1.5 km west of the Dipylon Gate, surrounded by temples and altars. A gymnasium was located nearby.

The port of Athens was Piraeus (Peiraieus), a peninsula 6 km southwest of the city that had three natural harbors. Kantharos, the largest harbor, was flanked on the eastern side with five colonnaded halls (*emporion*) where traders and merchants displayed their goods and where bankers had their tables. The port tax of one drachma had to be paid to the temple of Zeus Soter and Athene Soteira. Zea, the second harbor, was the home of the Athenian warships. Mounychia was the smallest of the three harbors.[473]

Jews lived in Athens since the fourth century B.C., as epigraphical and literary evidence attests.[474] According to 2 Macc 6:1-2, Antiochos IV Epiphanes sent an "Athenian senator" (or "Geron an Athenian") to Jerusalem "to compel the Jews to forsake the laws of their ancestors and no longer to live by the laws of God; also to pollute the temple in Jerusalem and to call it the temple of Olympian Zeus, and to call the one in Gerizim the temple of Zeus-the-Friend-of-Strangers, as did the people who lived in that place." When Antiochos repented on his deathbed, he promised God that he would grant Jerusalem autonomy and make the Jews "equal to citizens of Athens" (2 Macc 9:14-15). In 105 B.C. the assembly of the Athenians decided to send a golden crown to the Jewish ruler Hyrcanus and to erect a bronze statue in his honor in the temple of the Demos of Athens (Josephus, *A.J.* 14.151-155). Herod I and his family were attracted by Athens (Josephus, *B.J.* 1.422-425). Jewish authors mention Athens repeatedly. Philo refers to a letter of Agrippa I to Caligula in which the presence of Jews in Athens in mentioned (Philo, *Legat.* 36). An Athenian inscription dating to the second century B.C. mentions a certain "Simon, son of Ananias"; an inscription dating to the first century A.D. mentions a certain "Ammia of Jerusalem"; an inscription from Piraeus mentions a certain "Demetrius son of Demetrius, the Jew."[475] The site of the oldest synagogue of Athens has not been located. In the fifth century A.D. a synagogue probably was located in the two rooms on the north side of the Metroon, where a menorah and a marble plate decorated with a palm branch has been discovered, linked with renovations dating to this period.[476]

Paul went to the synagogue in Athens and preached before Jews and God-fearers.[477] And he went daily to the agora to speak with those "who happened to be there."[478] Philosophical discussions in the agora were characteristic of the cultural life of Athens: Socrates was a model,[479] and the Stoa Poikile was a prime site for such activities. If Paul saw the temples that he mentions in his speech on the Areopagus (Acts 17:23) in the agora, then his "street preaching"[480] took

---

[473]See J. Camp 2001, 294-99.

[474]*CIJ* I 712-715; *IJudO* I Ach26-39. See Kraabel 1979, 507; Stavroulakis and DeVinney 1992, 31, 34; Levinskaya 1996, 158-62; Panayotov, in *IJudO* I, 2004, 144-64.

[475]*CIJ* I 715c, 715a, 715i (*IJudO* I Ach 33, 26, 40).

[476]Kraabel 1979, 505-7; J. Camp 1980, 30.

[477]Acts 17:17a: τοῖς Ἰουδαίοις καὶ τοῖς σεβομένοις.

[478]Acts 17:17b: πρὸς τοὺς παρατυγχάνοντας.

[479]Barrett, *Acts,* 2:828-29; Zmijewski, *Apg,* 638; cf. Hemer 1989, 116.

[480]See Schneider, *Apg,* 2:235 ("Straßenmission"); Zmijewski, *Apg,* 638.

place in the old agora, not in the new market of Caesar and Augustus.

Some scholars maintain that the people whom Paul met in the marketplace were "not his intended and primary target audiences."[481] This view is unconvincing: the formulation κατὰ πᾶσαν ἡμέραν (*kata pasan hēmeran,* "every day") indicates that Paul wanted to convince precisely these people, the non-Jewish citizens of Athens, of the truth of the gospel of Jesus Christ, including the Stoic and the Epicurean philosophers with whom Paul disputed in the agora. Luke emphasizes that Paul proclaimed the same message in Athens that he had proclaimed in other cities: "He was telling the good news about Jesus and the resurrection" (Acts 17:18).[482]

Paul observed that Athens had as many cult images or idols as a forest had trees (Acts 17:16).[483] If Paul stood on the Areopagus and looked down on the old agora, with the Acropolis towering behind him, he would have easily noted the great and famous temples of Athens. Centers of religious activity were the old agora, the Eleusinion and further temples between the agora and the Acropolis, on the Panathenaic Street and on the road to Dipylon. The numerous deities, heroes and political and ethical abstractions (such as Themis [Justice] and Eueteria [Prosperity]) were worshiped not only in the masterpieces of the Greek architects but also in numerous smaller sanctuaries and simple temples located on sidestreets and between houses and workshops. Deities worshiped in the streets included particularly Apollo Agyieus, the god of streets and gates; Hekate, the goddess of junctions; and Hermes, the great god of the roads, whose statues stood in several temples in the city as well as in many squares and streets. Somewhat like shopping for products in a modern supermarket, people could choose from among various versions of a god or goddess, depending on family traditions and personal taste: some worshiped the Whispering Hermes (Psithyristes), some the Three-Headed Hermes (Trikephalos), others the Four-Headed Hermes (Tetrakephalos), whose statue stood on a junction in the quarter Kerameikos, with the inscription "Hermes Tetrakephalos, the noble work of Telesarchides, you see everything."

The traditional gods were worshiped in several temples.[484] Zeus, the father of the gods, was worshiped on the Acropolis, in the stoa on the west side of the agora, on the altar in front of the stoa, as well as in other temples. Athene, the goddess of wisdom and the patron of the city, had three temples on the Acropolis and a small temple in the agora, and she was worshiped also in the bouleuterion and in the great temple of Hephaistos. Deme-

---

[481]See Wander 1998, 194.

[482]See Stenschke 1999a, 205.

[483]On the interpretation of κατείδωλος (*kateidōlos*) see Thompson and Wycherley, *The Agora of Athens,* 168 n. 266; for the comment that follows above see ibid., 168-69, with reference to Demosthenes 21.52; 59.39; Eustathios, *Commentarii ad Homeri Iliadem* 24.334; *IG* II² 4719, 4850, 4995; Aristophanes, *Vespae* 875.

[484]For the observations that follow above see J. Camp 1980.

ter, the goddess of vegetation and fertility, was worshiped in the Eleusinion, located on the road from the agora to the Acropolis. Apollo, the god of light and music, was worshiped in a temple located next to the Stoa of Zeus; a monumental statue of the god was discovered in the area of the agora. Artemis, the sister of Apollo and the goddess of hunting and of good counsel, was worshiped on the Acropolis as Artemis Brauronia and in the agora as Artemis Boulaia. Aphrodite, the goddess of love, was worshiped in at least two temples located above the agora on the way up to the Acropolis; over three hundred statues of Aphrodite have been discovered in excavations in the city. Other temples were dedicated to Ares, Asclepius, Dionysos, Hekate, Hephaistos, Hera, Heracles, Hermes, Hestia, Pan, Poseidon, the Twelve (Olympian?) Gods, the Phrygian Mother-Goddess; the Egyptian gods Isis, Sarapis, Harpocrates and Anubis; abstractions, including the Demos (the People of Athens) and Nike (Victory); the emperors, as well as heroes such as Theseus, Hippothoon, Antiochos, Ajax, Leos, Erechtheus, Aigeus, Oineus, Akamas, Kekrops, Pandion, Harmodios, Aristogeiton, Eurysakes, Epitegios, Strategos, Iatros and Kallistephanos. Shortly after 27 B.C. the Athenians erected a small, round Ionic temple east of the Parthenon on the Acropolis in which Roma and Caesar were venerated. A series of thirteen small altars, most of which were discovered in the vicinity of the agora, confirms the practice of the emperor cult in the lower city as well.[485] Emperor Claudius was worshiped as Apollo Patroos, and Tiberius was honored with an inscription that dedicated to him the large bronze quadriga dating to the second century B.C. that stood in front of the Stoa of Attalos.

According to Luke's account, Paul saw an altar in the city that displayed an inscription whose text read, "To an unknown god" ('Αγνώστῳ θεῷ, Agnōstō Theō [Acts 17:23]). Eduard Norden suggests in his book *Agnostos Theos* that the notion of an unknown god is completely "un-Greek" and "entirely incommensurable for Hellenistic speculation."[486] This interpretation has been challenged.[487] In his description of the ports of Athens, Pausanias mentions "altars of gods who are called Unknown" (βωμοὶ θεῶν ὀνομαζομέ-νων 'Αγνώστων, bōmoi theōn onomazomenōn Agnōstōn [Pausanias 1.1.4]). We do not know, however, which inscriptions were incised on these altars; they may have displayed inscriptions that simply read, Θεῷ (Theō), "for a god"; or Θεοῦ (Theou), "of a god"; or perhaps Θεῷ 'Αγνώστῳ (Theō Agnōstō), as in Acts 17:23. Another comment by Pausanias suggests that such inscriptions were formulated with plural nouns. In his description of the temples of Olympia he mentions a "temple of unknown gods" (πρὸς αὐτῷ δέ ἐστιν ἀγνώστων θεῶν βωμός, pros autō de estin agnōstōn theōn bōmos [Pausanias 5.14.8]). In the third century Diogenes Laertius claims to know that there were altars in various sections of the city of Athens "without name" (εὑρεῖν κατὰ τοὺς δήμους τῶν 'Αθηναίων βωμοὺς ἀνωνύμους, heurein kata tous dēmous tōn Athēnaiōn bōmous anōnymous [Diogenes Laertius 1.110]). Philostratus mentions a conversation of his hero Apollonios, a contemporary of Paul, in which he informs a certain Timasion that it is a sign of wisdom to say good things "about all gods" (περὶ πάντων θεῶν, peri pantōn theōn), "especially in Athens where altars are erected even for unknown gods" (οὗ καὶ ἀγνώστων δαιμόνων βωμοι ἵδρυνται, hou kai agōstōn daimonōn bōmoi hidryntai [Philostratus, *Vit. Apoll.* 6.3]). An altar that was discovered in 1909 in the temple of Demeter in Pergamon, dating to the second century A.D., displays the following fragmentary inscription (restoration by H. Hepding): θεοις αγ[νω-

---

[485]See A. S. Benjamin and A. E. Raubitschek, "Arae Augustae," *Hesperia* 28 (1959): 65-85; Shear 1981, 363-65. For the comment that follows above see the inscriptions *IG* II² 3269, 3273, 3274.
[486]Norden 1913, 83-84.
[487]For the discussion that follows above see Horst 1989a.

στοις] καπιτ[ων] δαδουχος (*theois ag[nōstois] kapit[ōn] dadouchos;* "Kapito the torchbearer [dedicated this altar] to unknown gods"). The arguments that have been advanced to dispute these texts as parallels to Acts 17:23 are not cogent.[488] An inscription found in the vicinity of Dorylaion (*MAMA* V 107) represents a second epigraphical piece of evidence for the altar inscription θεοῖς ἀγνώστοις (*theois agnōstois*), if the reconstruction suggested by Pieter van der Horst is correct. The fact that these literary and epigraphical parallels attest the altar inscription in the plural, "For unknown gods," while Acts 17:23 formulates with the singular perhaps can explained by the possibility that Paul, who argues in his speech for belief in one true God, reformulated the traditional plural forms deliberately in the singular, as Tertullian, Didymus and Jerome suggested.[489] The available literary and epigraphical evidence suggests that it is indeed possible that there was an altar in Athens carrying the dedicatory inscription "To an unknown god."

Paul experienced a twofold reaction to his preaching: some regard him as a charlatan, an unsystematic "rag-bag collector of scraps of learning" (σπερμολόγος, *spermologos*), while others speculate that "he seems to be a proclaimer of foreign divinities" (Acts 17:18c).[490] It appears that people who had listened more attentively to Paul's message thought that this Jewish orator wanted to introduce to the Athenians new deities, perhaps "Jesus and Anastasis," since he spoke of Jesus and the resurrection (Gk., *anastasis*).[491] Paul was taken to the council (βουλή, *boulē*) of the Areopagus, whose members promptly refer to their right (δυνάμεθα, *dynametha*) to examine Paul and make a decision in this matter concerning the question of new deities that can be worshiped in Athens (Acts 17:19).[492] The request by the members of the council of the Areopagus that Paul present his religious teaching was polite. Paul was not asked to "defend" his convictions; he did not stand as an accused intruder before the council. Rather, he was questioned as an orator who proclaimed deities that were new to the Athenians. The council assumed that if Paul found broad support for his religious teaching among the Athenian citizens, he could claim for the gods whom he proclaims a rightful place in the pantheon of Athenian gods; they expected that Paul would have to buy a piece of land in the city on which he would establish the new cult, at least build-

---

[488]See Horst 1989a, 194-98, with reference to O. Weinreich, "Agnostos Theos," *Deutsche Literaturzeitung* 39 (1913): 2949-64, esp. 2958-59; A. D. Nock, *Sallustius: Concerning the Gods and the Universe* (Hildesheim: Olms, 1988 [1926]), xc-xci n. 211; Nilsson 1941-1950, 2:355; contra Norden 1913, 56 n. 1; Haenchen, *Apg*, 500-501 n. 6. For the comment that follows above see Horst 1989, 198-200; the inscriptions of *MAMA* V were published in 1937.

[489]See Tertullian, *Comm. in Tit.* 1.12 (PL 26.607); Didymus, in Staab 1933, 37; Jerome, *Epist. 70 ad Magnum;* see Horst 1989a, 201; for the comment that follows above see ibid., 217.

[490]Acts 17:18: ξένων δαιμονίων δοκεῖ καταγγελεὺς εἶναι. For the definition of *spermologos* as "a rag-bag collector of scraps of learning" see B. Winter 1996, 80 n. 37.

[491]On the practice of introducing new gods to Athens see Robert Garland, *Introducing New Gods: The Politics of Athenian Religion* (Ithaca, N.Y.: Cornell University Press, 1992). The analysis that follows above relies on B. Winter 1996.

[492]Acts 17:19: γνῶναι τίς ἡ καινὴ αὕτη ἡ ὑπὸ σοῦ λαλουμένη διδαχή. See B. Winter 1986, 82-83; for the comments that follow above see ibid.

ing an altar for the necessary sacrificial activities; they surmised that Paul might donate financial resources for the celebration of a festival to honor the new gods at least once a year and perhaps even for the support of cult personnel.

Another interpretation focuses on Paul as an orator: the council of the Areopagus invited Paul to demonstrate his competence as an orator.[493] There is evidence from the eastern Mediterranean world that orators who spoke in public were invited by the magistrates of the cities to demonstrate their rhetorical abilities and their philosophical orientation. The orator usually was given one day's notice to prepare a declamation on a predetermined topic. The orator would compose the declamation, write it down, memorize it and present it without relying on notes. In the early imperial period such declamations often were copied and circulated in the city; there is evidence for this practice in connection with Athens.[494] Therefore, it is possible that the speech that Luke reports in Acts 17:22-31 is the summary of a written source. This social-religious scenario does not necessarily exclude the earlier political-religious interpretation.

Paul's speech before the council of the Areopagus, therefore, must not be separated from his preaching activity in the agora and the context in Acts 17:16-20 in general. This means that the speech that Luke records in Acts 17:22-31 should be understood not as a summary of Paul's usual missionary sermons before pagan audiences but as a speech in the specific context of Acts 17:16-20.

Because the council of the Areopagus, responsible for the preservation and maintenance of the customs of the city of Athens, met at different places since the fourth century B.C., it is not certain at which site Paul gave the speech that Luke reports.[495] The content of Paul's Areopagus speech will be discussed in full detail in §28.3 ("Dialogical Concentration").

Luke notes the success of Paul's missionary outreach in Athens in a brief comment (Acts 17:34): some people came to faith in Jesus, among them Dionysios, who was a member of the council of the Areopagus, a woman named Damaris, "and others with them" (καὶ ἕτεροι σὺν αὐτοῖς, *kai heteroi syn autois*). The comment in Acts 17:21 ("Now all the Athenians and the foreigners living there would spend their time in nothing but telling or hearing something new") perhaps is the background of the notice of success in Acts 17:34: some people ridiculed Paul (Acts 17:32a), while others refrained from making a judgment until they could hear more (Acts 17:32b), leading to the conversion of several Athenian citizens (Acts 17:34).[496] The fact that Paul describes the Corinthian Christian Stephanas and his household as "the first converts in Achaia" (1 Cor 16:15) does

---

[493]See B. Winter 1991, 114; for the analysis that follows above see ibid., 114-15 with n. 9.

[494]See B. Winter 1991, 114-15 with n. 9; 1997, 149-51, with reference to Dio Chrysostom, *Or.* 37.1; 51.29; Philostratus, *Vit. Soph.* 579; see also Russell 1983, 76-77. For the observation that follows above see Winter 1991, 115 n. 9.

[495]See J. Camp 2001, 195.

[496]See B. Winter 1996, 86-87.

not prove that the first conversions in Achaia happened in Corinth and that Luke's comment in Acts 17:34 is therefore erroneous because Paul's missionary work in Athens evidently was unsuccessful.[497]

David Gill believes that Dionysios and Damaris are "plausible inventions by the author to illustrate and lend particularity to his point that a few Athenians, but prominent ones, were converted to Christianity by Paul's speech."[498] He postulates that Luke had no detailed information about a visit of Paul to Athens and thus assumes that the entire scene is a creation of the author. It is indeed correct that the name "Dionysios" is frequently attested in Athens: of 8,306 men who are attested in literary and epigraphical texts for the history of ancient Athens, 1,103 are called by that name.[499] The fact that the name "Damaris" is unattested cannot be "explained" with the assertion that the name was invented by the author because it sounded "ancient and respectable." Colin Hemer sees the reference to Dionysios and Damaris in Acts 17:34 as an example of details that Luke mentions that are seemingly unnecessary for the report as such, whose inclusion in the report serves no theological purpose, and that perhaps belong to those cases where Luke mentions persons by name because they were well known in the early church.[500]

Paul's reference to Stephanas and his family as "first converts" (lit., "first fruits") in Achaia in 1 Cor 16:15 can be understood as referring to the establishment of a church: the church in Corinth was the first Christian community in Achaia, whereas the conversion of several individuals in Athens did not lead to the foundation of a church.[501] Or the term "Achaia" in 1 Cor 16:15 describes primarily Corinth as capital of Achaia.[502] And it must be noted that the term *aparchē* ("first fruits"), as it is used in the context of 1 Cor 16:16, describes not exclusively, perhaps not even primarily, a temporal priority but rather means "first" in the sense of "model," "pledge" or "promise" of further fruit—that is, additional conversions.[503]

The information about the history of the church in Athens between the first and the third centuries is sparse. Eusebius claims to know that Dionysios the Areopagite, who was converted as a result of Paul's preaching, was the first bishop of the church of Athens; his source is the bishop of Corinth whose name likewise was Dionysios (Eusebius, *Hist. eccl.* 3.4.10; 4.23.3). The *Apostolic Constitutions* state that the bishop of the church in Athens was appointed by the apostles, thus presumably by Paul (*Apos. Con.* 7.45). Christian apologists possibly petitioned Emperor Hadrian when he visited Athens in A.D. 124. Melito of Sardis (ca. A.D. 190) reports about a letter from Emperor Antoninus Pius (A.D. 138-161) to

---

[497]Contra Murphy-O'Connor 1996, 107; Reinbold 2000, 134; also Schrage (*1 Kor,* 4:453 n. 166), who warns readers not to "squeeze" history out of the book of Acts at this point. However, see Lindemann 1995, 247-48.

[498]D. Gill, "Dionysios and Damaris: A Note on Acts 17:34," *CBQ* 61 (1999): 484.

[499]P. M. Fraser and E. Matthews, *A Lexicon of Greek Personal Names,* vol. 2; cf. Gill, "Dionysos and Damaris," 484-85; for the comment that follows above see ibid., 486-87.

[500]Hemer 1989, 208-9.

[501]See Marshall, *Acts,* 291.

[502]See Barrett, *1 Cor,* 393; Fee, *1 Cor,* 829 n. 19; Thiselton, *1 Cor,* 1338.

[503]See Fee, *1 Cor,* 829; Thiselton, *1 Cor,* 1338; similarly Schrage, *1 Kor,* 4:454.

the city of Athens in which he instructs the city council not to tolerate disturbances directed against the Christians (Eusebius, *Hist. eccl.* 4.26.10). Dionysios, the bishop of Corinth (ca. A.D. 170) mentioned above, wrote a letter to the church in Athens in which he mentions two bishops who led the church of Athens during his time: Publius and Quadratus (Eusebius, *Hist. eccl.* 4.23.2-3).[504] Origen visited Athens in A.D. 230 and again in 240, finishing his commentary on Ezekiel there (Eusebius, *Hist. eccl.* 6.32.2). Origen writes, "For the Church of God, for example, which is at Athens, is a meek and stable body, as being one which desires to please God, who is over all things; whereas the assembly of the Athenians is given to sedition, and is not at all to be compared to the Church of God in that city" (*Cels.* 3.30). In A.D. 325 Bishop Pistos of Athens attended the Council of Nicea. We should also note that the "official" arrival of the Christian faith in Athens under Emperor Constantine in A.D. 325 had only minimal effects on the city, which remained pagan far into late antiquity.[505] In A.D. 529 Emperor Justinian prohibited non-Christian philosophers from teaching in Athens. The closure of the philosophical schools of Athens, which had existed for over nine hundred years, represented the terminal decline of Athens.

Assuming that Paul traveled on land from Athens to Corinth, he would have passed through Eleusis and Megara. We do not know, however, whether or not he preached the gospel in these cities.

Eleusis (ʾΕλευσίς; mod. Elefsina)[506] was situated about 22 km west of Athens on the Bay of Eleusis on the coastal road to Corinth. The site was settled in prehistoric times and belonged to Athens at least since the seventh century B.C.; together with Panakton and Phyle it was one of the fortresses that guarded western Attica. The famous sanctuary, dedicated to the cult of Demeter, was located on the eastern slopes of Mount Akris. E. Freund states that it was "already the Homeric Hymn of Demeter that promised to the initiates, the *mystai,* prosperity in the earthly life and a happy lot in the beyond—a promise that Greek religion otherwise did not know in such an individual manner."[507] The ancient sanctuary derived from a fertility cult in a cave. The square hall that was built at the behest of Pericles in the fifth century B.C. was the largest public building in Greece at the time. Small propylaia dating to the late first century B.C. led into the interior area of the sacred precinct. The temple building stood beside the cave of Pluto; it measured 52 by 52 m and had 6 times 7 interior columns. The unusual layout was linked with the function of the temple as initiation hall (Anaktoron, Telesterion) of the Eleusinian mysteries. The Great Mysteries included processions to Athens and back to Eleusis and sacred activities in the Telesterion (with room for three thousand people) taking place annually between the 14th and the 22nd of Boëdromion (beginning of October). On a terrace beside the Demeter sanctuary stood a Roman temple. There was a theater dedicated to Dionysos. The festivals that took place in the theater and in the temple of Demeter and Kore drew visitors from all over Greece. Apart from sections of the city walls and the east

---

[504]See Harnack 1924, 2:788-89 (ET, 2:232-33).
[505]J. Camp 2001, 229; for the comment that follows above see ibid., 237.
[506]O. Kern, "Eleusis 1," PW 5.2 (1905): 2336-38; E. Meyer, *KP* 2:245; H. Lohmann, *DNP* 3:983-86; G. E. Mylonas, *PECS* 296-98; Kevin Clinton, *OCD* 520; idem, "The Eleusinian Mysteries," *ANRW* II.18.2 (1989): 1499-1537; idem, *Myth and Cult: The Iconography of the Eleusinian Mysteries* (Stockholm: Svenska Institutet i Athen, 1992); G. E. Mylonas, *Eleusis and the Eleusinian Mysteries* (Princeton, N.J.: Princeton University Press, 1961); E. Freund, in Lauffer 1989, 210-13; J. Camp 2001, 283-89.
[507]E. Freund, in Lauffer 1989, 211.

gate (Asty Gate), few remains of ancient Eleusis survive.

Megara (Μέγαρα; mod. Megara),[508] about 20 km west of Eleusis, was the only city on the narrow strip that links Attica with the Peloponnese. The city that Pausanias describes extensively (1.40-43) was situated about 2 km from the coast at the foot of two low acropolises. In the eighth century Megara founded colonies on Sicily, at the Bosporus (Chalcedon, Byzantion) and on the Black Sea coast. The port of the city was Nisaia, connected with Megara by walls. In the civil war Megara was conquered by Calenus, the legate of Julius Caesar. In the imperial period Megara was a modest town; Pliny describes it as a Roman colony (Pliny, *Nat.* 4.34). According to the apocryphal *Acts of Andrew*, the apostle Andrew supposedly preached the gospel in Megara during his stay in Corinth; the family that he liberated from a demon helped him in his missionary work.[509] Megara was the seat of a bishop since the fourth century.

Evangelism in Corinth

Paul arrived in Corinth probably in February or March of the year A.D. 50 and engaged in missionary activity for over eighteen months (Acts 18:11, 18), leaving Corinth presumably in September of A.D. 51. Luke describes Paul's mission in Corinth in Acts 18:1-18.[510]

Corinth (Κόρινθος; mod. Archaia Corinthos [see fig. 36]),[511] situated in strategic position

---

[508]E. Meyer, PW 15.1 (1931): 152-205, 1295-96; idem, *KP* 3:1143-47; W. R. Biers, *PECS* 565; J. B. Salmon, *OCD* 951; K. Freitag, *DNP* 7:1139-42; R. Scheer, in Lauffer 1989, 431-15; Ronald P. Legon, *Megara: The Political History of a Greek City-State to 336 B.C.* (Ithaca, N.Y.: Cornell University Press, 1981).

[509]W. Schneemelcher, in Hennecke and Schneemelcher 1990-1997, 2:112.

[510]Riesner 1994, 180-87 (ET, 202-10). On Paul's mission to Corinth see, besides the commentaries, Koet 1996.

[511]A. W. Blyvanck and T. Lenschau, PWSup 4 (1924): 991-1036; E. Meyer, *KP* 3:301-5; H. S. Robinson, *PECS* 240-43; J. B. Salmon and A. J. S. Spawforth, *OCD* 390-91; J. Murphy-O'Connor, *ABD* 1:1134-39; Y. Lafond, *DNP* 6:745-51; J. R. McRay, *DNTB* 227-31; Edouard Will, *Korinthiaka: Recherches sur l'histoire et la civilisation de Corinthe des origines aux guerres médiques* (Paris: Boccard, 1955); Ferdinand Joseph de Waele, *Les antiquités de la Grèce: Corinthe et Saint Paul* (Les hauts lieux de l'histoire 15; Paris: Guillot, 1961); Cothenet 1978c, 55-60; Wiseman 1979; Elliger 1987, esp. 200-42; Murphy-O'Connor 1983; Lauffer 1989, 338-43; Engels 1990; B. Winter 1990; Clarke 1993, 9-39, 135-57; Gill 1993; Gregory 1993; C. Williams 1993; Gill 1994c, 448-53; Nicosj Papahatzis, *Ancient Corinth: The Museums of Corinth, Isthmia and Sicyon* (Athens: Ekdotike Athenon, 2000); Romano 2000, 83-104; B. Winter 2001. Excavations: *Corinth: Results of Excavations Conducted by the American School of Classical Studies at Athens* (20 vols.; Cambridge, Mass.: Harvard University Press; Princeton, N.J.: American School of Classical Studies at Athens, 1929-2003). Inscriptions: Lindley R. Dean, *Latin Inscriptions from Corinth* (New York: Archaeological Institute of America, 1918); Benjamin D. Merritt, *Corinth: Results of Excavations*, vol. 8.1, *Greek Inscriptions 1896-1927* (1931); Allen B. West, *Corinth: Results of Excavations*, vol. 8.2, *Latin Inscriptions 1896-1926* (1931); John H. Kent, *Corinth: Results of Excavations*, vol. 8.3, *The Inscriptions 1926-1950* (1966); see also the PHI CD-ROM. See <http://corinth.sas.upenn.edu>; D. G. Romano, *The Corinth Computer Project: Reconstructing the City Plan and Landscape of Roman Corinth;* D. G. Romano and B. C. Schoenbrun, "A Computerized Architectural and Topographical Survey of Ancient Corinth," *Journal of Field Archaeology* 20 (1993): 177-90.

about 10 km west of the isthmus on the junction of the routes linking the Peloponnese and Attica, was settled since around 900 B.C. Corinth had the most impressive acropolis (575 m high) in Greece, located south of the city. The city flourished since about 725 B.C. It minted coins since 600 B.C., which attests to the importance of trade and commerce. Corinth was known for its pottery industry (Corinthian vases), metal manufacture (a particular alloy was known as "Corinthian bronze") and carpet weaving. The city walls that encompassed the Acrocorinth with the temple of Aphrodite were 12 km in length, to which should be added another 4 km of walls that enclosed the road to Lechaeum, the harbor on the Corinthian Gulf. The second harbor of Corinth was Cenchreae, southeast of the city on the Saronic Gulf. During the Persian Wars Corinth served as the seat of the allied Greeks, the "Corinthian League." Changing alliances with and against Athens, Sparta and Thebes determined the history of Corinth during the fifth and fourth centuries B.C. During the reign of the Macedonian king Philipp II Corinth was again the seat of the newly established league of the Greek cities. Since Corinth was the most important center of the last resistance against Rome, the Roman senate decreed that the city be destroyed; after the works of art were removed and the population killed or sold into slavery, the Roman consul Lucius Mummius destroyed Corinth in 146 B.C. (Pausanias 7.16). The city remained deserted for a century, although some people evidently lived in the ruins (Cicero, *Tusc.* 3.22.53). The territory of the city was given in part to the city of Sikyon; for the most part it was Roman *ager publicus.* In 44 B.C. Julius Caesar refounded the city as Colonia Laus Iulia Corinthus.[512] Caesar settled the city with three thousand freed slaves (Strabo 8.6.23) and with veterans (Appian, *Lyb.* 136). The aristocratic families of the senate in Rome who decided the reestablishment of Corinth were prevented by existing laws from controlling the trade on the new east-west trade route that ran via Corinth; evidently they hoped that the freed slaves whom they settled in Corinth would be their go-betweens in the new commercial center on the Isthmus of Greece. Corinth the colony was intended to safeguard Roman control of the trade from Rome to the eastern Mediterranean.[513] It is likely that merchants (*negotiatores*) were among the early settlers as well.[514] People with Roman citizenship evidently arrived in the new colony at an early date: Julius Caesar had granted the freedmen the right to occupy magistrate positions in the colonies that he established and to become senators (*curiales* or *decuriones*), privileges that Augustus had rescinded; in the time after Augustus all magistrate officials in Corinth were Roman citizens.[515] One of the most important aristocrats of Corinth was Gnaeus Babbius Philinus, probably a freedman who belonged to the original colonists. During the principate of Augustus he was aedile, in A.D. 7-12 *duovir,* and later pontifex.[516] During the principate of Tiberius he built the so-called Babbius Monument on the west side of the forum, perhaps also the building on the southeast corner of the forum that may have been a library. A daughter of Babbius married M. Publicius Rusticus, one of the most prominent men of the

---

[512]Or *Laus Iulia Corinthiensis.* Cf. Strabo 8.6.23; Plutarch, *Caes.* 57; Cassius Dio 43.50.3-4; Appian, *Lyb.* 136. See Gill 1993; M. E. H. Walbank, "The Foundation and Planning of Early Roman Corinth," *JRA* 10 (1997): 95-130.

[513]C. Williams 1993, 33.

[514]See A. J. S. Spawforth, "Roman Corinth: The Formation of a Roman Elite," in *Roman Onomastics in the Greek East: Social and Political Aspects* (ed. A. D. Rizakis; Meletemata 21; Athens: Research Centre for Greek and Roman Antiquity; National Hellenic Research Foundation, 1996), 167-82.

[515]Engels 1990, 67-68; for the comment that follows abve see ibid., 68-69. On the leading officials of Corinth see Clarke 1993, 9-39 (with prosographic table in appendix A, 135-57).

[516]On Babbius see Clarke 1993, 141, no. 46.

city. Following the example of Rome, Roman Corinth was divided into "tribes" (*tribus*), of which the following are known: Agrippia, Atia, Aurelia, Calpurnia, Claudia, Domitia, Hostilia, Livia, Maneia, Vatinia and Vinicia.

Roman Corinth was rebuilt on the basis of the consistent axial layout of the streets of a Roman colony that divided the city into four quadrants of roughly equal size of 32 by 15 *actus*.[517] The twenty-nine streets (*cardines*) created twenty-nine blocks (*insulae*) in each city quarter, each 1 *actus* wide. The *insulae* at the west side of the two eastern quarters were reserved for Corinth's main street, the *Cardo Maximus,* which was 15.2 m wide and ran from north to south, ending in Lechaeum. Each of the twelve *decumani* of Corinth, the east-west roads, was about 6 m wide, and the *cardines,* the north-south streets, about 3.6 m. The area north of the city that extended to the gulf was controlled by Corinth as *territorium;* it was divided for agricultural use into sections 16 *actus* wide. Corinth flourished soon after its refoundation: many of the destroyed buildings were restored, including the temple of Apollo, the temple of Asclepius, the South Stoa, the Fountain of Peirene, the Fountain of Glauke and the theater; also, new buildings were erected with a distinctly Roman architecture (in contrast to Athens).[518] The fact that the cult of Roma practiced in Corinth only in the second century A.D. demonstrates the self-confidence of Corinth as Roman *colonia:* the cult of Roma was a political institution that enabled non-Roman populations to celebrate Rome and the Romans. The Pan-Hellenic games in nearby Isthmia were again controlled by Corinth, celebrated regularly since A.D. 50-60 in the temple of Poseidon (56 by 22 m) in Isthmia.[519] Members of the elites of other cities were willing to assume magistrate positions in Corinth and donate financial resources to the city as benefactors. By 27 B.C. Corinth was the administrative center of the senatorial province of Achaia. Roman Corinth was a center of commerce and services; its prosperity was based on trade (in which the ports Lechaeum and Cenchreae played an important role), on people passing through the city and on tourists.[520] Plutarch compares Corinth with Patrae and Athens, cities known for their moneylenders, and he reports that Corinth was known for its brokers (πραγμαζευζής, *pragmazeuzēs* [Plutarch, *vit. aere* al. 831a]). Strabo describes Corinth as wealthy "because of its commerce" (διὰ τὸ ἐμπόριον, *dia to emporion* [Strabo 8.6.20]) and refers to the two ports of Corinth as well as to the Isthmian Games, which brought large crowds into the city. Donald Engels estimates that Roman Corinth (including Lechaeum) had approximately eighty thousand inhabitants, a figure that David Romano regards as much too high for the period before the foundation of a second colony, the Colonia Iulia Flavia Augusta Corinthiensis, under Vespasian after A.D. 70. If we include the inhabitants of the five larger cities—Krommyon, Cenchreae, Tenea, Ayios Charalambos and Asprokambos—and of the forty-five smaller towns and villages that belonged to the territory of Corinth, another twenty thousand people should be added.[521] As Corinth assimilated the Italian immigrants and newly arriving Greeks, it be-

---

[517]The Roman linear measure of 1 *actus* corresponds to 120 Roman feet (*pedes monetales*) or 35.2 m. For the comments that follows above see David G. Romano, "Post-146 B.C. Land Use in Corinth, and Planning of the Roman Colony of 44 B.C.," in Gregory 1993, 9-30.

[518]For the comment that follows above see Gill 1993, 263.

[519]See Elizabeth R. Gebhard, "The Isthmian Games and the Sanctuary of Poseidon in the Early Empire," in Gregory 1993, 78-94.

[520]See Engels 1990, 22-39; C. Williams 1993, 31-32 with n. 3. D. P. Thompkins (*Bryn Mawr Classical Review* 1 [1990]: 20-33) agrees with Donald Engels that Corinth was primarily a merchant city, "in particular the entrepôt, comparable in Weber's eyes to modern financial capitals like London or Paris" (28).

[521]Engels 1990, 79-84, 178-81; Romano 2000, 103 n. 71.

came a Greek city again during the course of the first and second centuries. Of the 104 inscriptions that date before Hadrian, 101 are written in Latin and 3 in Greek; of the inscriptions dating to the time of Hadrian, 10 are written in Latin and 15 in Greek.

The *Cardo Maximus,* which ran through Corinth from north to south, the extension of the road running from the port of Lechaeum to Corinth, began at a monumental gate in the north of the city and led to the forum, the old agora (225 by 127 m). Before reaching the forum, a street branched off to the right, passing the market donated by Quintus Cornelius Secundus (with an interior colonnaded hall measuring 15 by 24 m) behind the basilica at the Lechaion Street to the North Market (58 by 46.5 m, with fifty rooms measuring about 2.9 by 4.4 m each) and to the North Stoa. The rooms of the North Market, which was built in the first quarter of the first century A.D., probably were offices for merchants and shipping brokers.[522] East of the *Cardo Maximus* at this point were the Baths of Eurykles; south of the baths were public latrines and a third market that stood at the site of a previous Greek temple (a courtyard with colonnaded halls and shops on two sides); after the earthquake in A.D. 77 the market was torn down and replaced by the so-called Peribolos of Apollo, an open courtyard (32 by 23.5 m) surrounded by colonnaded halls. From the basilica on the right and the market (the later Peribolos of Apollo) to the left, the *Cardo Maximus* ascended several steps to a monumental triumphal gate, rebuilt in the first century, that gave access to the large Roman forum (165 by 65 m). On the northeast corner of the forum stood the magnificent Fountain of Peirene with an open basin (9 by 6 m) and three apses. On the east side was a two-story basilica (38 by 23 m) decorated with statues of members of the imperial family, including statues of Augustus and his grandsons Gaius and Lucius, which is why it was called Julian Basilica. On the south side on the upper forum was the administrative center of the province. The building on the southeast corner dating to the early first century A.D. served administrative purposes as well, mostly as a *tabularium,* an archive for public and private documents; it is less likely that it was a library. The two-story South Stoa (164 by 25 m), with seventy-one Doric and thirty-four Ionic columns, was the largest public building in Greece, originally built in the fourth century B.C. and later restored by the Romans. The thirty-three shops in the southern part of the building were torn down in the first century and replaced by buildings of the Roman administration: the office of the *agōnothetēs* who organized the Isthmian Games, the office of the governor of the province (the statue of a procurator who held office during the time of Trajan has been found), the two-story South Basilica (38 by 23 m, beside the road to Cenchreae), the city council (*bouleuterion*), a public bath and the office of the *duoviri.* The most important Roman building phase dates to A.D. 50 and later (the year in which Paul arrived in Corinth). In Greek Corinth there was a low wall in front of the South Stoa on which over one hundred statues stood; Pausanius mentions statues of marble, bronze and wood of Aphrodite, Apollo, Artemis Ephesia, Athene, Dionysius, Hermes and Zeus; the statues probably were taken to Rome when Corinth was destroyed in 146 B.C. The forum was divided into the upper forum (with the South Stoa) and the lower forum by the Central Shops. In the center of this row of shops was a monumental speaker's platform (βῆμα, *bēma;* Lat., *rostrum*) on which the governor, for example, would speak; west of the Bema were three rooms (another eleven rooms were added ca. A.D. 100); on the eastern end of the row of shops was a round monument (9 m in diameter, with a column 2 m high). These small rooms (each about 2.2 by 3 m), decorated with frescoes, were used either by merchants of precious

---

[522]C. Williams 1993, 43.

metals or by bankers.[523] On the west side of the forum stood the temple of Venus Victrix (Temple F), the temple of Roma, the Senate and the Emperors (Temple G), the Fountain of Poseidon, the Babbius Monument with a temple (Temple K, perhaps the Pantheion that Pausanias mentions, or a temple of Apollo) and a temple of Tyche (Temple D, identified by some scholars as the temple of Hermes). On the north side of the forum was another stoa (101 by 9.2 m, with forty-seven Doric columns), which provided access to the temple of Apollo (100 by 80 m); the *naos,* the temple building proper (53.8 by 21.5 m), built in 540 B.C. and restored after 164 B.C., had a peristyle of thirty-eight columns that were 7 m each in height. Northwest of the forum, on the road to Sikyon, stood another temple (Temple C, identified by some with the temple of Hera Akraia); to the south was another large sanctuary (Temple D, measuring 120 by 90 m) whose temple was erected on a platform (44 by 23.5 m) at the time of Caligula at the latest; this sanctuary usually is identified as the temple of Octavia, although some scholars identify it as the Capitolium temple, in which the triad Jupiter Optimus Maximus, Juno and Minerva would have been worshiped.

To the northwest was a temple of Zeus, the large Fountain of Lerna, the sacred precinct of Asclepius[524] and, further to the south, the "old gymnasium" (Pausanias). To the west was a fourth market (30 m west of Temple E, with rooms measuring about 5 by 5.8 m each), the theater, with seating for fifteen thousand spectators, and the odeion, which could accommodate three thousand visitors (built after A.D. 70). East of the theater was a paved square (19 by 19 m); an inscription discovered during the 1929 excavations in the pavement[525] states that Erastus donated the pavement in gratitude for being appointed aedile: "Erastus in return for his aedileship laid [the pavement] at his own expense" (ERASTUS • PRO • AEDILIT[AT]E / S(UA) • P(ECUNIA) • STRAVIT).[526] This Erastus perhaps is identical with Erastus the city treasurer (*oikonomos tēs poleōs*) mentioned by Paul in Rom 16:23 and with Erastus the coworker of Paul mentioned in Acts 19:22 and 2 Tim 4:20.[527] The gymnasium was located in the southeastern quarter, Kraneion, frequented by Diogenes in the fourth century B.C. At the ascent to the acropolis was the pottery quarter, where there was a temple of Demeter and Kore that existed since the seventh century B.C., evidently restored soon after the foundation of the Roman colony.[528] In the course of the renovation the dining rooms of the old sanctuary, in each of which between seven

---

[523]C. Williams 1993, 37, with reference to Vitruvius (5.1.2), who asserts that offices of bankers should receive priority in the planning of a forum.

[524]See Mabel Lang, *Cure and Cult in Ancient Corinth* (Princeton, N.J.: American School of Classical Studies at Athens, 1977).

[525]The larger part of the inscription was found on a plate discovered in April 1929 *in situ;* in March 1928 and in August 1947 two parts of the right side of the damaged plate were found. See Clarke 1993, 47.

[526]T. L. Shear, "Excavations in the Theatre District and Tombs of Corinth in 1929," *AJA* 33 (1929): 525; *I. KorinthKent* 232 (Kent, ed., *Corinth,* 99); cf. D. W. J. Gill, "Erastus the Aedile," *TynBul* 40 (1989): 293-301; see also Clarke 1993, 46-56.

[527]Theissen 1974b, 236-45 (ET, 75-83). Clarke (1993, 55-57) argues for the historical possibility of this identification, which cannot be proven, however. Dassmann (1989, 283) remains skeptical, and many commentators reject the identification (e.g., Cranfield, Dunn, Meyer, Leenhardt, Michel, Murray, Wilckens).

[528]See Ronald S. Stroud, "The Sanctuary of Demeter on Acrocorinth in the Roman Period," in Gregory 1993, 65-73; Ronald S. Stroud and Nancy Bookidis, *The Sanctuary of Demeter and Kore: Topography and Architecture* (Princeton, N.J.: American School of Classical Studies at Athens, 1997).

and nine persons could dine—there was room for two hundred guests altogether—were replaced by a building that served other purposes. After the earthquake of A.D. 77 three small temples were erected on the upper terrace (Pausanias). On the acropolis stood the temple of Aphrodite (10 by 16 m), of which virtually nothing survives. There were at least three more temples of Aphrodite in the city, and there were two more temples of Aphrodite in Lechaeum and in Cenchreae. The cults of Isis and Sarapis (two temples) and of Cybele are attested as well. Coins attest the worship of the heroes Pegasus and Bellerophon; dedications have been discovered for the Roman abstractions Victoria and Concordia as well as for the Genius of the city of Corinth. The most important deities were Aphrodite and Poseidon. The Latin-speaking elite were active in the emperor cult: twenty of the thirty-two Latin inscriptions concern the imperial cult. Demeter and Kore were popular among the poorer population, as were Isis and Sarapis.[529]

The Jewish community in Corinth is attested by Luke's account in Acts 18 as well as by a lintel with the inscription "synagogue of the Hebrews" ([συνα]γωγὴ Ἐβρ[αίω]ν], *synagōgē Ebraiōn* [*CIJ* I 718; *IJudO* I Ach47]); although some scholars initially dated the lintel to the first century A.D., others prefer a date in the second/third or in the fourth century.[530] The designation "synagogue of the Hebrews" probably is linked with the fact that this synagogue was the first in Corinth (which could well have been older than the lintel in question) and therefore used the ethnic description; if the members of the synagogue originally spoke Hebrew or Aramaic, they (or their descendants) later would have used Greek.

Luke reports on Paul's missionary work in an introduction and three scenes. (1) In a historical introduction Luke narrates Paul's arrival in Corinth, his meeting with the Jewish couple Aquila and Priscilla, his work as an artisan, the regular missionary teaching in the synagogue, and the arrival of Silas and Timothy from Macedonia (Acts 18:1-5).[531] (2) The first scene depicts negative and positive reactions of the Jewish listeners to Paul's missionary preaching, Paul's departure from the synagogue, and the continuation of missionary work in the house of Titius Justus (Acts 18:6-8). (3) The second scene reports a vision in which Jesus Christ encourages Paul, asking him to continue missionary work despite the opposition and predicting the success of the mission, and it notes that Paul stayed and taught in Corinth for one year and six months (Acts 18:9-11). (4) The third scene narrates the charge with which Corinthian Jews seek to indict Paul before the Roman governor Gallio, Gallio's refusal to initiate trial proceedings, and Gallio's inaction when Sosthenes is beaten (Acts 18:11-17). The account ends with the comment that Paul stayed in Corinth "for a considerable time" before returning to Syria (Acts 18:18).

Luke notes first that Paul met Aquila in Corinth, a Jew who originally came

---

[529]Engels 1990, 106. On the imperial cult in Achaia see Regina Trummer, *Die Denkmäler des Kaiserkults in der römischen Provinz Achaia* (Dissertationen der Universität Graz 52; Graz: DBV, 1980).

[530]See Levinskaya 1996, 162-63; for the comment that follows above see ibid., 163-65. See also L. Levine 2000, 98 n. 132, 108-9, 282.

[531]Tannehill (1986-1990, 2:221) links Acts 18:5 with the first "scene," as does Koet (1996, 399). However, Paul does not begin his preaching activity in Acts 18:5, which is presupposed already in Acts 18:4.

from Pontus and had recently arrived from Italy with his wife, Priscilla (diminutive form of Prisca), "because Claudius had ordered all Jews to leave Rome" (Acts 18:2). If the edict of Claudius is dated between January 25 of A.D. 49 and January 24 of A.D. 50,[532] it is plausible to assume that Aquila and Priscilla arrived in Corinth in the fall of A.D. 49, before the closing of nagivation with the onset of winter. When Paul came to Corinth in the fall of A.D. 50, Aquila and Priscilla had been living in the city for about a year. The couple presumably were well off: they either owned in Corinth a branch of their artisan business in Rome, where they worked as "tentmakers" (*tabernacularii*)—that is, leatherworkers[533]—or they possessed the means to open a new workshop soon after their arrival in Corinth in which they employed other other people.[534] Luke's account implies that the two were already Christians when they lived in Rome: he does not link their conversion with Paul's missionary work.

Gerd Lüdemann argues that the tradition in Acts 18:2-3 "does not presuppose that the couple belong to the Christian church but explains Paul's association with them by referring to their shared craft," which makes the "historical conclusion" likely that the couple became Christians as a result of their encounter with Paul.[535] Lüdemann overlooks the fact that Luke explains the encounter between Aquila, Priscilla and Paul not with their common profession (Acts 18:3); rather, Luke states in Acts 18:2 that Paul "went to them" (προσῆλθεν αὐτοῖς, *prosēlthen autois*) without explaining Paul's action. Since the conversion of the couple is not mentioned in the context, it is more plausible to assume that they were already Christians.

Possibly Aquila and Priscilla were leading Christians in the church in Rome.[536] If so, and if we take into account the fact that the expulsion of the Jews from Rome was the result of the missionary activity of Jewish Christians there (see §22.6), then it is noteworthy that Aquila and Priscilla evidently did not engage in missionary work in Corinth: they are not described as founders of the church. David Alvarez Cineira suggests, "It is possible that the couple decided after they experienced the difficulties in Rome resulting from the Edict of Claudius to live in peace in their new home. . . . At the same time they had to look after the setting up of their workshop."[537] Other scholars assume that Aquila and Priscilla

---

[532]See §18.1. See also Riesner 1994, 139-80 (ET, 157-201); Cineira 1999, 196-216.

[533]See W. Michaelis, *ThWNT* 7:394-96 (*TDNT* 7:393-94); G. Schneider, *EWNT* 3:602 (*EDNT* 3:252); P. W. Barnett, *DPL* 925-27; Ronald F. Hock, "Paul's Tentmaking and the Problem of His Social Class," *JBL* 97 (1978): 555-64; idem, *The Social Context of Paul's Ministry: Tentmaking and Apostleship* (Philadelphia: Fortress, 1980).

[534]Pesch, *Apg*, 2:147; cf. Ollrog 1979, 26-27; Dunn, *Rom*, 2:890. Cineira (1999, 219-20), is skeptical, but without giving reasons.

[535]Contra Lüdemann 1987, 209 (ET, 201).

[536]Pesch (*Apg*, 2:147), who assumes that the church in Rome was a Jewish-Christian church; similarly Zmijewski, *Apg*, 656-57.

[537]Cineira 1999, 221; also Klauck 1981, 22.

preached the gospel in Corinth. Jürgen Roloff suggests that "there was already a small Jewish Christian group in Corinth around them before Paul arrived."[538] The presence of Aquila and Priscilla in Corinth indicates that there were Christians in Corinth before Paul's arrival in the city, which means that we cannot rule out the possibility that some Corinthians had been converted to faith in Jesus Christ, perhaps in the synagogue, as a result of the presence of this couple. On the other hand, Paul's assertions in 1 Cor 2:1-5; 3:6 suggest that he was the founder of the church in Corinth.

Initially, Paul lived with Aquila and Priscilla and was employed in their workshop, where he earned money for his support (Acts 18:2). Paul asserts in 1 Thess 2:9 that, contrary to the custom of Greco-Roman orators, he refused to look for a patron and benefactor who would finance him: he did not want to be dependent upon benefactors, who initially would be unbelievers, as this would bring more disadvantages than advantages for him as a pioneer missionary. Paul therefore earned his own support, unless other churches supported him financially.

Paul visited the synagogue in Corinth on the sabbath and taught the congregation with the intention[539] of persuading Jews and Greeks (ἔπειθέν τε Ἰουδαίους καὶ Ἕλληνας [Acts 18:4]) to believe in Jesus as the Messiah. The "Greeks" in Acts 18:4 are Gentiles who sympathized with the Jewish faith and attended the synagogue services or belonged to the more committed God-fearers. Luke describes Titius Justus, whose house was located right next to the synagogue, as a God-fearer (σεβομένου τὸν θεόν, sebomenou ton theon [Acts 18:7]). In Acts 18:8a Luke reports the conversion of the archisynagōgos Crispus and his family. The text does not say that the conversion of "many of the Corinthians" (πολλοὶ τῶν Κορινθίων, polloi tōn Korinthiōn [Acts 18:8b]) was caused by the conversion of Crispus:[540] the wave of conversions is explained by Luke with reference to the Corinthians "hearing" Paul (ἀκούοντες, akouontes), meaning that they listened to his missionary preaching, and with reference to the acceptance of his message (ἐπίστευον, episteuon), meaning that they came to faith in Jesus Christ and were baptized (ἐβαπτίζοντο, ebaptizonto [Acts 18:8b]). The new converts, citizens of Corinth, heard Paul teach in the synagogue—that is, God-fearers and sympathizers. They probably were people who had come into contact with Paul during the weeks and months that he had been active in the city—in the workshop of Aquila and Priscilla, perhaps in the agora, perhaps in the house of Titius Justus, where he was giving lectures on the Christian faith.

---

[538]Roloff, *Apg,* 270; cf. Murphy-O'Connor 1992b, 49.

[539]The verb ἔπειθεν (*epeithen*) is to be interpreted as a conative imperfect: "and he would try to convince Jews and Greeks" (NRSV; contra RSV: "and he persuaded Jews and Greeks"); in Acts 18:6 Luke reports robust opposition. Koet (1996, 401 n. 19) interprets in terms of an iterative imperfect, which does not significantly alter the sense.

[540]Contra Theissen 1974b, 235.

When Silas and Timothy "came down from Macedonia" (Acts 18:5 NASB), traveling through the mountains of northern Greece, they brought financial support from the Macedonian churches. This enabled Paul to preach and teach the Christian message not only on the sabbath but also during the entire week.[541] The intensification of missionary work led to more conversions. The fact that Luke notes the success only in Acts 18:8 does not prove that people were converted only after the move to the house of Titius Justus.[542] The notice about the intensive opposition of the Corinthian Jews seems to presuppose that Paul's preaching and teaching in the synagogue and, after the arrival of Silas and Timothy, before larger audiences throughout the week was successful.

Two reasons might explain why Luke does not link the notice about the success of Paul's mission in Acts 18:8 directly with Acts 18:5. (1) In Acts 18:5 Luke summarizes the content of Paul's preaching before Jewish audiences in Corinth with regard to the messianic identity of Jesus. The question of Jesus' messianic identity had provoked strong opposition already in Palestine, and later in southern Galatia and Macedonia; since Paul encountered the same kind of reaction in Corinth, it was natural to record first the reaction of the Jews and Paul's response. (2) By moving the comment on Paul's missionary success to the end of the second scene of his account, Luke emphasizes its effect.[543]

The opposition and the "blasphemies" (Acts 18:6)[544] of the Jews in Corinth were directed against Paul's proclamation of Jesus as the Messiah (Acts 18:5), presumably also against the conviction, which the apostle would not have hidden, that the "Greeks" whom Luke explicitly mentions as listeners can become members of the people of God without being circumcised (Gal 2:1-10). The "blasphemies" of Acts 18:6 describe, as in Acts 13:45; 26:11, the opinion of the opponents (and of Saul the Pharisee before his conversion) that the crucified Jesus was a criminal cursed by God.[545] Since Luke refers to a mixed synagogue congregation consisting of Jews and God-fearing Greeks in Acts 18:4, it cannot be excluded that the "blasphemies" of the Corinthian Jews should be understood in terms of a charge that Paul is guilty of blasphemy. If Paul taught the Gentiles in the synagogue audience that they can find salvation without circumcision and Torah, then some Jews easily could have accused Paul of blasphemy (cf. Acts 6:11, the accusation against Stephen). It was not simply the conviction that Jesus is the Messiah that provoked opposition, but the notion that a crucified person is the Messiah and the notion that the Mosaic covenant and the Torah, which had tied God's redemptive presence to Mount Zion and thus to Israel, its faith, its cult and its history, no longer guaranteed salvation.

---

[541]See Haenchen, *Apg*, 517 (ET, 538-39).
[542]Contra Schneider, *Apg*, 2:249-50.
[543]See Pesch, *Apg*, 2:149.
[544]Acts 18:6: ἀντιτασσομένων δὲ αὐτῶν καὶ βλασφημούντων.
[545]O. Hofius, "βλασφημία," *EWNT* 1:531 (*EDNT* 1:221), with reference to Deut 21:22-23.

Luke describes Paul's reaction to the Jews' opposition in Acts 18:6: "When they opposed and reviled him, in protest he shook the dust from his clothes and said to them, 'Your blood be on your own heads! I am innocent. From now on I will go to the Gentiles.'" Paul's action and statement are not an expression of judgment on Israel as a whole or on all Jews:[546] The gesture that is interpreted in the subsequent statement is reminiscent of similar actions by Old Testament prophets: it underlines the authority of Paul as a teacher and emphasizes the fact that he has fulfilled his obligation, proclaiming the word of God to the Jews in Corinth. The contextual background of Ezek 33:4 indicates that Paul issues here a warning to his listeners in the synagogue: the "watchman" has passed on the life-saving message, and now the listeners are responsible for their own fate. The turn to the Gentiles does not signify an abandonment of the Jews. Paul makes no negative statements about the Jews, but rather a positive statement about the Gentiles (Acts 18:6c). He continues to work among Jews in Corinth, leading them to faith in Jesus (Acts 18:8). And both Luke's account in the book of Acts and Paul's letters written to the Christians in Corinth speak about "the Jews" in a differentiated manner. Not all Jews reject the gospel, not "all Israel" opposes the missionaries.

After it had become impossible to continue to explain and teach his faith in the synagogue, Paul moved to the house of Titius Justus (Acts 18:7), a God-fearer who evidently had been converted earlier and lived right next to the synagogue. Paul, who evidently continued to live in the house of Aquila and Priscilla, continued his missionary work in Titius Justus's house, a fact that the Jews must have regarded as provocative. Luke reports that Crispus, the official of the synagogue (*archisynagōgos*), "became a believer in the Lord, together with all his household" (Acts 18:8).[547] Paul writes in 1 Cor 1:14 that he himself baptized Crispus. Luke mentions neither Gaius, who also was baptized by Paul and is mentioned as Paul's host in Rom 16:23, nor Stephanas and his family, the first converts in the province of Achaia (1 Cor 16:15), who probably were converted during the first weeks or months of Paul's missionary work in Corinth. The comment in Rom 16:23 suggests that a church met in the house of Gaius.[548] Some scholars suggest that the Titius Justus whom Luke mentions in Acts 18:7 is identical with the Gaius whom Paul mentions in 1 Cor 1:14 and Rom 16:23; his full (Roman) name would have been Gaius Titius Justus.[549] This possibility remains conjectural.

Many Corinthians (πολλοὶ τῶν Κορινθίων), along with Crispus, were con-

---

[546]Koet 1996, 402-11.

[547]Accepted as historical fact by, for example, Engels (1990, 107) and Reinbold (2000, 140).

[548]Klauck 1981, 34-35.

[549]See E. J. Goodspeed, "Gaius Titius Justus," *JBL* 69 (1950): 382-83; Blue 1994, 174-75; Reinbold 2000, 137-38.

verted to faith in Jesus Christ (Acts 18:8). Evidently they were non-Jewish inhabitants of the city—God-fearers, polytheistic Greeks and perhaps Roman citizens. The problems of the young church that Paul discusses in 1 Corinthians indicate that members of the local elite had become Christians as well: people who belonged to the wise and powerful (1 Cor 1:26; 3:18), who demanded high rhetorical standards of orators (1 Cor 2:1-5), who could afford legal proceedings (1 Cor 6:1-11), who visited prostitutes, probably in connection with banquets in the houses of their rich friends (1 Cor 6:12-18), who dined in the temples of the city (1 Cor 8:10), who covered their heads during the worship services of the church as signs of their superior social status, as priests did when they officiated in the temples (1 Cor 11:4), who had time for festive meals in the afternoons (1 Cor 11:21-22).[550]

The divine encouragement that Paul received in a dream during his missionary work in Corinth (Acts 18:9-10) presupposes the continued opposition of the Corinthian Jews. God directs Paul not to be silenced, but instead to preach without fear. God promises Paul physical protection and substantiates his encouragement of Paul with the assertion that there are "many in this city who are my people" (Acts 18:10). This formulation indicates divine foreknowledge of the success of Paul's missionary work in Corinth,[551] and it describes the divine election of people as members of the (new) people of God.

Philip Towner suggests that Acts 18:9-10 allows us to infer that Paul changed his missionary strategy at this point. During his missionary work in Galatia Paul first preached the gospel of Jesus Christ in the local synagogues, winning converts among Jews and God-fearers, which only provoked opposition and rejection from members of the Jewish community, prompting him to turn to the Gentiles and forcing him usually to abrupt departures. In Corinth he is directed by a word from the Lord to remain in the city despite continued opposition from the Jews: he continued his missionary work outside the synagogue, without excluding Jews as a matter of principle, however, over a longer period of time, preaching the gospel in the context of an inclusive theological understanding of the universal people of God.[552] This explanation does not seem to be warranted by the relevant New Testament texts or by the historical circumstances. It surely is correct that the command "speak and do not be silent" (Acts 18:9b) implies that Paul stays in Corinth. However, Luke never hints at the possibility that Paul was about to leave the city. In principle it is possible to assume that Paul changed his missionary tactics, which presumably he had followed for eighteen years, as the result of a divine revelation that he received in Corinth. But such a hypothesis needs a firmer foundation than suppositions based in implicit assumptions. In regard to the history of

[550]See Theissen 1974b; Gill 1990; B. Winter 1990; 2001.
[551]See Marshall, *Apg,* 296; Reinhardt 1995a, 255-63; for the comment that follows above see ibid.
[552]See Towner 1998; for the comment that follows above see ibid., 425-26. See also Cole 1988.

Paul's missionary work and missionary strategy/tactics, we must be careful not to base any reconstruction only on the book of Acts. Luke's account allows us to compare the period described in Acts 18—20, Paul's missionary work in Corinth and Ephesus (five years), only with Acts 11:25-26, Paul's missionary work in Antioch (three years) and with Acts 13—14, Paul's missionary work on Cyprus and in Antiocheia, Iconium, Lystra, Derbe and Perge (two years). For a fuller picture we must also consider Paul's missionary work in Arabia, Cilicia and Syria (ten years) immediately after his conversion—a period about which we have almost no specific information, which makes it impossible to reach reliable conclusions concerning any major changes of Paul's missionary strategy between Paul's so-called first and second missionary journeys.

Paul's opponents in Corinth began to initiate legal proceedings "when Gallio was proconsul of Achaia" (Acts 18:12). This formulation does not allow conclusions concerning the precise date of their action, but the context in Acts 18:11 seems to indicate that the presence of Gallio the proconsul created a new situation,[553] and it is plausible to assume that the Corinthian Jews thought that the new governor would be favorably disposed to their request.[554] The Gallio inscription that has been found in Delphi[555] allows us to date the proconsulship of L. Iunius Gallio[556] to the one-year period from July 1 of A.D. 51 to June 30 of A.D. 52.[557] Thus the "trial" before Gallio is to be dated probably to the summer of A.D. 51.[558]

---

[553]See Schneider, *Apg,* 2:253.

[554]See Haenchen, *Apg,* 514 (ET, 536); Hemer 1989, 119. The formulation Γαλλίωνος δὲ ἀνθυπάτου ὄντος τῆς Ἀχαίας is a genitive absolute that describes, however, "only an episode from the time of Paul's visit" (Schneider, *Apg,* 2:252). The roughly one hundred genitive absolutes in the book of Acts do not reflect a specific usage of the author; see BDR §423.2.

[555]See Émile Bourguet, *De Rebus Delphicis imperatoriae aetatis capita duo* (Montepessulano: Camillum Coulet, 1905), 63; A. Brassac, *RB* 10 (1913): 143-54; H. Pomtov, *SIG*³ II 801D; cf. W. M. Ramsay, *ExpTim* 7 (1909): 467-69; A. Deissmann 1925, 205-21. A new edition of the nine fragments has been provided by André Plassart, *Fouilles de Delphes III: Épigraphie 4.3* (Paris: Boccard, 1970), no. 286 (26-32; and plate 7). English and German translations are readily available in Murphy-O'Connor 1983, 173-76; Barrett and Thornton, *Texte zur Umwelt des Neuen Testaments,* 59, no. 53. For the publication history see Riesner 1994, 181-82 (ET, 203-4).

[556]See B. Reicke, *EWNT* 1:562 (*EDNT* 1:234); Elliger 1987, 231-37; especially Riesner 1994, 180-85 (ET, 202-7).

[557]See Jewett 1979, 72-75; Lüdemann 1980, 181-83; Pesch, *Apg,* 2:152, Barrett and Thornton, *Texte zur Umwelt des Neuen Testaments,* 59; Riesner 1994, 180-84 (ET, 202-207); cf. B. Reicke (*EWNT* 1:562 [*EDNT* 1:234]), who assumes an appointment in the fall of A.D. 51. Against a broad consensus, Slingerland (1991) argues that Paul's arrival in Corinth cannot be dated with reference to the Gallio inscription, suggesting that the available information allows us only to conclude that Paul arrived in Corinth in December of A.D. 47 at the earliest and April of A.D. 54 at the latest.

[558]See Pesch, *Apg,* 2:152, with C. Hemer and many others. Differently K. Haacker, "Die Gallio-Episode und die paulinische Chronologie," *BZ* 16 (1972): 252-55, esp. 254; Haacker argues that Luke could be referring to the end of Gallio's proconsulship, "when Gallio was still proconsul." On the historicity of Luke's account see Reinbold 2000, 141-43.

Gallio, whose original name was Lucius Annaeus Novatus, was the oldest son of M. Annaeus Seneca (the Elder), the Roman knight and orator from Cordoba in Spain, and thus the brother of Seneca, the philosopher and teacher of Nero.[559] Gallio had come to Rome with his father during the principate of Tiberius and followed the usual career path (*cursus honorum*), of which few details are known, however. He changed his name because of his adoption by the senator Lucius Junius Gallio, to be called Lucius Iunius Annaeus Gallio. Emperor Claudius appointed him proconsul of the province of Achaia for one year, as was the custom.

During the imperial period the proconsul (ἀνθύπατος, *anthypatos*) ruled a senatorial province; he was responsible primarily for the maintenance of public order. The legal basis for his governorship were imperial *mandata,* specifically formulated directives for his term of office, and he had to take into account the customs that applied in his province. In regard to the relationship between Roman proconsuls and the Jewish communities, the sources[560] for the eastern Mediterranean provinces document that the Roman authorities strove to maintain amicable relations with the Jews. They were allowed to live according to their own customs and traditions, and they were protected by the governors when citizens of the Greek cities attacked them. There is no evidence for a special status of the Jewish people in the Roman colony of Corinth.[561]

Paul's Jewish opponents evidently assumed that Gallio would be favorably disposed to their requests. They brought Paul to the "tribunal" (βῆμα, *bēma*), which most likely is identical with the building whose foundations can still be seen in the agora of Corinth. This was the first time that Paul was forced to defend himself before a proconsul rather than before municipal magistrates. The charge against Paul was formulated, perhaps deliberately, in an ambiguous manner: "This man is persuading people to worship God in ways that are contrary to the law" (Acts 18:13). The term "law" (*nomos*) could be a reference to the Mosaic Torah. Rudolf Pesch argues that from a Jewish point of view, "the accusation aims at the worship of the crucified Jesus as Messiah or at the worship of God who is said to be 'against the law' and who is said to affirm the curse of a crucified person, since Paul proclaimed his resurrection."[562] This interpretation raises the question of whether the Corinthian Jews could expect the Roman proconsul to coerce Jews to keep Jewish laws. Rather, they might have sought to get the proconsul to remove the (Jewish) Christians from the protection that the Jews of the city enjoyed by virtue of their affiliation with the local Jewish community as an officially tolerated *religio licita*. It is more plausible to

---

[559]On Gallio see particularly K. Haacker, *ABD* 2:901-3; J. Murphy-O'Connor, "Paul and Gallio," *JBL* 112 (1993): 315-17; Riesner 1994, 180-89 (ET, 202-11). On the subject "Paul and Seneca" see R. Gibson 2000.

[560]See Rajak 1984, 107-23. Cf. Josephus, *A.J.* 14.185-222, 256, 267; 19.280-291.

[561]See Botermann 1993, 77-78.

[562]Pesch, *Apg,* 2:150.

assume that Paul was accused of violating the laws of the state, similar to the accusations leveled against Paul and his proclamation of Jesus as the Messiah-King in Thessalonike (Acts 17:7). Paul was accused of instigating rebellion against the emperor and his rule over the world. Other scholars suggest that the Jews appealed to an edict of Claudius that guaranteed that the Jews be allowed to practice their customs without interference, arguing that Paul disturbed the peace of their community.[563]

Gallio received the Corinthian Jews and listened to their grievances. Before Paul could defend himself, Gallio stopped the proceedings (Acts 18:14a).[564] Evidently Gallio saw immediately that no "crime" (ἀδίκημα, adikēma) or "serious villainy" (ῥᾳδιούργημα πονηρόν, rhadiourgēma ponēron) had been committed, in which case it would be reasonable (κατὰ λόγον, kata logon) for him as the governor to admit a complaint (ἀνέχομαι τινος, anechomai tinos [Acts 18:14b]). Gallio clearly interpreted the accusation against Paul in terms of a possible violation against the laws of the state, and he recognized that the accused had not committed any such violation: the dispute is about "questions" or controversial "issues" (ζητήματα, zētēmata) concerning Jewish teaching, persons (Jesus and the question of his identity) or law, and thus concerning matters extra ordinem, which a Roman official need not get involved in.[565] Gallio did not want to become active as a judge in these matters (Acts 18:15); he was content to leave the controversy of the Corinthians Jews alone. As Winfried Elliger argues, "It did not fall into his jurisdiction since there was no danger for public security. This means that Gallio acted perhaps without reproach as a statesman, but the rebuff of the accusation by no means amounted to an endorsement of Paul."[566] Gallio "dismissed" the accusers and the accused "from the tribunal" (Acts 18:16).

Some scholars interpret the behavior of Gallio in Acts 18:12-18 as evidence of the pro-Roman and apologetic tendency of Luke the author. Gerhard Schneider argues, for example, "Gallio acts as Luke would like the Roman authorities to act concerning the Christians."[567] This interpretation, which presupposes the historical unreliability of Luke's account, is unconvincing. First, we need to note that the trial is reported as a Jewish affair; there is no hint in the text that the real aim of Luke is to portray the relationship between the Roman authorities and the Christian community. Second, the behavior of Gallio is not exceptional: he acts in agreement with the general practice of the Roman state—"anything else would be conspicuous, requiring an explanation."[568]

---

[563]See Sherwin-White 1963, 99-107.
[564]Gerd Lüdemann (1987, 205 [ET, 198]) thinks that "it is inconceivable that Paul could not have said anything," but he gives no reasons. However, if Gallio recognized the accusation of the Jews as the result of internal religious quarrels of the Jewish community and decided not to proceed with an official trial, then he did not need to hear the accused defend himself.
[565]See Sherwin-White 1963, 102.
[566]Elliger 1987, 236-37.
[567]Schneider, Apg, 2:253.
[568]Botermann 1993, 78.

It is unclear what happened immediately after the dismissal of the accusation made by the Corinthian Jews. Luke reports that "all of them" seized Sosthenes, the official of the synagogue, and beat him in front of the tribunal without intervention from Gallio (Acts 18:17). First, the identity of Sosthenes as second *archisynagōgos* after Crispus (Acts 18:8) is unclear. Was he a colleague of Crispus? Was he his successor? Is he identical with "Sosthenes the brother" mentioned in 1 Cor 1:1 as co-sender of Paul's letter? An affirmative answer to the last question would presuppose that Sosthenes probably had sympathies already for Paul's message at the time of the Gallio episode, that he later joined the Christian community, and that he became a coworker of Paul.[569] Second, the reference to the term *pantes* ("all of them") is unclear: the identity of who started the beating is obscure. Some scholars interpret *pantes* in terms of the crowd that is present in the agora in front of the tribunal—that is, the citizens of Corinth[570]—assuming that the beating is an anti-Semitic attack of the crowd that Gallio did not object to.[571] It is more plausible, however, to relate *pantes* ("all") in Acts 18:18 to *autous* ("them") in Acts 18:16: the Corinthian Jews clobbered the synagogue official, presumably because they believed that he had botched the attempt to have Paul and his followers tried and condemned by the governor,[572] perhaps because he had displayed sympathy for Paul and his message. Third, it is curious that Luke does not mention Paul in connection with the beating of Sosthenes. Several explanations are possible. If the attack was the result of anti-Semitic aggression, then it is plausible that the citizens of Corinth directed their belligerence against a presumably well-known representative of the Jewish community whose attempt to get the proconsul involved in Jewish affairs might have been regarded as pretentious. If the Jews themselves pummeled their *archisynagōgos,* we may assume that Paul enjoyed a certain protection immediately after the decision of Gallio to dismiss the case, or he might have left the tribunal quickly while the Jews "investigated" the cause of their failure by assaulting their officials. At any rate, the fact that Paul was accused by the Corinthian Jews in front of the Roman governor indicates that they no longer regarded Paul as belonging to the Jewish community of

---

[569]As a possibility in Marshall, *Acts,* 299; Pesch, *Apg,* 2:151; Schrage, *1 Kor,* 1:31. Gerd Lüdemann (1987, 208 [ET, 200]) rejects the discussion of such alternative explanations as illegitimate "historicization," as he excludes the possibility that Luke was an eyewitness or that he took the basic material of his account from the diary of a companion of Paul. This position becomes untenable if we allow the information that Luke reports to speak for itself and if we exercise caution with regard to the introduction of tradition-critical hypotheses.

[570]Haenchen, *Apg,* 515 (ET, 536-37); Schneider, *Apg,* 2:253; cf. Lüdemann 1987, 207 (ET, 199). This is the interpretation in several manuscripts (D E Ψ 0120, the Majority Text, as well as Syriac and Sahidic versions), whose text-critical value is not decisive, however.

[571]See Elliger 1987, 237, referring to Seneca, who described the Jews as a "most wicked race" (*gens sceleratissima*).

[572]H. Balz, "Σωσθένης," *EWNT* 3:780 (*EDNT* 3:325); Pesch, *Apg,* 2:151.

Corinth,[573] although it remains unclear whether they officially excommunicated him from the synagogue.

Paul's first letter to the Corinthians references events and developments in the Corinthian church in the time between Paul's departure from Corinth in September of A.D. 51 and the composition of his first letter to the Corinthian Christians six years later (see §28). Chrys Caragounis concludes from Paul's comments in 1 Cor 14:23-24, whereby unbelievers could "enter" (εἰσέλθῃ, *eiselthē*) a Christian meeting and be confused when the believers speak uncontrollably in languages that the unbelievers do not understand, that the church in Corinth met in a public venue: non-Christians would not just "enter" a private house in which Christians met.[574] He suggests that the church in Corinth may have rented a basilica, perhaps the basilica (64.7 by 22.8 m) at the road to Lechaeum dating to the first century A.D., arguing that the Christians described their churches since the fourth century as basilicas in remembrance of the rooms that they rented in the beginning of the Christian movement. The term *basilica* describes a Roman building form, commonly a long enclosed hall with several aisles, usually serving commercial, sometimes social, purposes.[575] Parallel situations might be Luke's report that Paul rented the school of Tyrannos in Ephesus for two years (Acts 19:9-10), and that he lived in a rented flat in Rome (Acts 28:30). This suggestion is attractive and historically plausible but remains hypothetical; it cannot be defended with reference to one verb in 1 Cor 14:24 (*eiselthē*). Unbelievers who are invited by friends who have become followers of Jesus to attend Christian meetings in their private homes also "enter" the Christian assembly. The historical connection between the Roman *basilica* and the architecture of the Christian churches (basilicas), which is attested in the entire Roman Empire since the time of Constantine, has not yet been explained.[576]

After Paul left Corinth, Apollo evidently played an important role in the life of the Corinthian church—a Jewish Christian from Alexandria in Egypt (1 Cor 3:6; Acts 18:24-28; 19:1). And it appears that the outreach of the Corinthian Christians led to the establishment of offspring churches in the vicinity: according to Rom 16:1-2, there was a church in Cenchreae, the second port of Corinth to the east, and 2 Cor 1:1 presupposes the existence of churches "throughout Achaia," as Paul writes, "Paul, an apostle of Christ Jesus by the will of God, and Timothy our brother, To the church of God that is in Corinth, including all the saints throughout Achaia."

---

[573]Botermann 1993, 76.
[574]Caragounis 1998, 259 with n. 62; for the comment that follows above see ibid., 258-59 n. 61.
[575]See W. H. Gross, *KP* 1:836-37; R. A. Tomlinson, *OCD* 235.
[576]See Gross, *KP* 1:836.

Cenchreae (Κεγχρεαί; mod. Kechries)[577] was the port of Corinth on the Saronic Gulf, about 11 km southeast of the city center and 4 km south of the temple of Poseidon on the isthmus. The city is mentioned repeatedly in Greek sources. Strabo describes Cenchreae as a "village" (8.6.4). The city flourished in the Roman period; it had perhaps 4,400 inhabitants[578] and belonged to the *territorium* of Corinth. Literary sources attest the worship of Aphrodite, Asclepius, Isis and Poseidon (Pausanias 2.2.3). The harbor was enlarged by artificial breakwaters; at the southwestern end the pier extended about 120 m into the gulf. At the quay (13 m wide) to the northeast of the pier stood large rectangular buildings; to the southeast, on a street 2.5 m wide, warehouses (50 by 25 to 30 m) dating to the first century A.D. were discovered. In the northern part of the city stood a simple colonnaded hall. The temple of Isis that is attested in literary sources stood south of the warehouses (today submerged); the temple of Aphrodite (?) was at the northeastern end of the harbor. The two churches that have been discovered in Cenchreae (with mosaics and baptistry) date to the fourth and fifth centuries.

Paul's extended missionary ministry in Corinth may have led to the establishment of churches in other cities of Achaia;[579] this possibility remains hypothetical, however. The suggestion that Paul uses the term "Achaia" in 2 Cor 1:1 in the sense of the region of ancient Achaia, a small area on the north coast of the Peloponnese,[580] is implausible: Corinth itself did not belong to this "old Achaia," and if Corinth was indeed the capital of the Roman province of Achaia, then a reference to Achaia that excluded Corinth would prove very confusing. On the other hand, Paul's second letter to the Corinthians is not a circular letter to several churches in the province of Achaia, but clearly a letter addressed to the church in Corinth. It is unclear why other churches in the region should also read the letter. However, this does not exclude the possibility that there were churches not only in Athens, Corinth and Cenchreae but also in other cities of Achaia established between A.D. 49 and 55.

27.3 Missionary Work in the Province of Asia

Paul preached the gospel in the province of Asia, mostly in Ephesus, from A.D. 52 to 55. Luke provides an extensive account in Acts 18:23—21:17.

Phase I: Visit to the Churches in the Provinces of Syria and Galatia

Antioch	⇒ Tarsus ?		210 km
	⇒ Derbe ?	Acts 18:23a (Galatia)	220 km

---

[577]F. Bölte, PW 11.1 (1921): 167-70; E. Meyer, "Kenchreai 2," *KP* 3:182; R. L. Scranton, *PECS* 446; R. L. Hohlfelder, *ABD* 1:881-82; J. B. Salmon, *OCD* 307; Y. Lafond, *DNP* 6:411; R. Scheer, in Lauffer 1989, 318; Robert L. Scranton and Edwin S. Ramage, "Investigations at Corinthian Kenchreai," *Hesperia* 36 (1967): 124-86. Excavations: R. L. Scranton et al., *Kenchreai, Eastern Port of Corinth* (4 vols.; Leiden: Brill, 1976-1978).

[578]See Engels 1990, 82.

[579]At Acts 18:27 Codex D speaks of "churches" in Achaia: ὃς ἐπιδημήσας εἰς τὴν Ἀχαίαν πολὺ συνεβάλλετο ἐν ταῖς ἐκκλησίαις.

[580]See Martin, *2 Cor,* 3. For the arguments that follow above see Thrall, *2 Cor,* 1:88.

	⇒ Lystra ?		150 km
	⇒ Iconium ?		35 km
	⇒ Antiocheia ?		148 km
	⇒ Tymandus ?		60 km
	⇒ Apollonia ?	Acts 18:23b (Galatia-Phrygia) ?	15 km
	⇒ Aporidos ?		19 km
	⇒ Apameia ?		17 km

Phase II: Missionary Work in Ephesus

	⇒ Homadena ?	Acts 19:1a (highlands)	26 km
	⇒ Eumeneia ?		18 km
	⇒ Sebaste ?		29 km
	⇒ Akmonia ?		22 km
	⇒ Temenouthyrai ?		40 km
	⇒ Blaundos ?		41 km
	⇒ Tarigya ?		100 km
	⇒ Diginda ?		4 km
	⇒ Daredda ?	Kaystros Valley	4 km
	⇒ Oumyrota ?		8 km
	⇒ Koloe ?		5 km
	⇒ Nikaia ?		15 km
	⇒ Hypaipa ?		12 km
	⇒ Larisa ?		25 km
	⇒ Metropolis ?		47 km
	⇒ Anokome ?		17 km
	⇒ Ephesus	Acts 19:1b	16 km

Phase III: Visit Corinth, Return to Ephesus

Ephesus	⇒ Cenchreae	2 Cor 2:1 (by ship)	350 km
	⇒ Corinth		2 km
	⇒ Cenchreae		2 km
Corinth	⇒ Ephesus	(by ship)	50 km

Phase IV: Missionary Work in Alexandria Troas

Ephesus	⇒ Alexandria Troas	2 Cor 2:12 (by ship)	320 km

Phase V: Visit to the Churches in the Province of Macedonia

Alexandria Troas	⇒ Neapolis	Acts 20:1; 2 Cor 2:13 (by ship)	220 km
	⇒ Philippi		16 km
	⇒ Amphipolis ?		70 km
	⇒ Apollonia ?		40 km
	⇒ Thessalonike	Acts 20:1-2a	65 km
	⇒ Beroea	20:1-2a	75 km
	⇒ Edessa	20:2a to Illyria? (Rom 15:19)	40 km
	⇒ Arnisa		40 km
	⇒ Herakleia		50 km
	⇒ Lychnidos		65 km
	⇒ Klaudanon		30 km
	⇒ Treiecto		30 km
	⇒ Clodiana		50 km

⇒ Dyrrhachium			50 km
⇒ Apollonia			80 km

Phase VI: Visit to the Churches in Achaia

⇒ Corinth		Acts 20:2b-3a (19:21) (by ship)	500 km

Phase VII: Return to Jerusalem

Corinth	⇒ Megara	Acts 20:3	45 km
	⇒ Eleusis		17 km
	⇒ Thebes		48 km
	⇒ Lebadeia		47 km
	⇒ Chaironeia		10 km
	⇒ Elateia		20 km
	⇒ Lamia		50 km
	⇒ Thaumakoi		35 km
	⇒ Larissa		60 km
	⇒ Herakleion		50 km
	⇒ Pydna		50 km
	⇒ Beroea	(20:4)	50 km
	⇒ Thessalonike	(20:4)	75 km
	⇒ Apollonia		65 km
	⇒ Amphipolis		40 km
	⇒ Philippi	20:6	70 km
	⇒ Neapolis		16 km
	⇒ Alexandria Troas	20:6 (by ship)	200 km
Alexandria Troas	⇒ Assos	20:13-14	53 km
Assos	⇒ Mytilene	20:14 (by ship)	45 km
	⇒ Samos	20:15 (by ship)	120 km
	⇒ Miletus	20:15 (by ship)	35 km
Miletus	⇒ Cos	21:1 (by ship)	80 km
Cos	⇒ Rhodes	21:1 (by ship)	150 km
Rhodes	⇒ Patara	21:1 (by ship)	100 km
Patara	⇒ Tyrus	21:3 (by ship)	620 km
Tyre	⇒ Ptolemais	21:7 (by ship)	50 km
Ptolemais	⇒ Caesarea	21:8 (by ship)	70 km
Caesarea	⇒ Jerusalem	21:15	100 km

Notes on the travel route. The route between Antioch (Acts 18:23a) and Ephesus (Acts 19:1c) is uncertain. The phrase διερχόμενος καθεξῆς τὴν Γαλατικὴν χώραν καὶ Φρυγίαν suggests that Paul visited two different areas: Lycaonian and Phrygian Galatia and Asian Phrygia (i.e., the region of Phrygia that belonged the the province of Asia).[581] The route in the "Galatian region" (Γαλατικὴ χώρα, *Galatikē chōra*) usually is reconstructed with the help of the route of the previous missionary outreach to Macedonia and Achaia. Indeed, when Paul strengthened "all the disciples" in the "Galatian region" (Acts 18:23b), he evidently visited existing churches, and the only churches between Antioch and Ephesus were in southern Galatia in Derbe, Lystra, Iconium and Antiocheia. The comment in Acts 19:1 (διελθόντα τὰ ἀνωτερικὰ μέρη, *dielthonta ta anōterika merē;* NASB: "Paul passed through the upper country"; NRSV: "Paul passed through the interior regions") is inter-

---

[581]Note the position of καί and the adverb καθεξῆς with the meaning "one after the other." See Hemer 1989, 120; Riesner 1994, 254 (ET, 285-86); French 1994b, 55, as a possibility.

preted in different ways. David French suggests that Luke uses this formulation to indicate that Paul realized the former plans of evangelizing in Bithynia, Pontus and Mysia that he had to abandon during the previous missionary journey.[582] Colin Hemer interprets the term τὰ ἀνωτερικά (*ta anōterika*) in the sense of "the traverse of the hill-road" that ran at high altitudes from Apameia to the Kaystros Valley (Καυστρου πεδίον; mod. Küçük Menderes) north of the Messogis Mountains (mod. Aydın Dağları) and to Ephesus.[583] This seems plausible. Since Paul did not know the Christians in Colossae and in Laodikeia personally (cf. Col 2:1), it is rather likely that he did not travel to Ephesus through the Lykos Valley and the Maeander Valley in A.D. 52, which he could have reached from Apameia if he had traveled in southwesterly direction via Sanaos: (1) this southern route did not run through Phrygia; (2) evidently Paul knew neither Colossae nor Laodikeia or Hierapolis. Hemer's interpretation, however, has to address the matter of the course of the route between Apameia and the Kaystros Valley: the route via Apameia, Homadena, Eumeneia, Sebaste, Akmonia, Temenouthyrai and Blaundos could indeed be described as a "high road"; from Blaundos (mod. Sülmenli) the Roman road ran south for 11.5 km before turning west (reaching the Hermos Valley after about 50 km and Sardis after another 50 km). At this point, near mod. Güllü, one needs to assume a road running toward the southwest across the eastern Tmolos Mountains (mod. Boz Dağları), perhaps along the line from Güllü to Aşağiçeşme, Bozalan, Sarıgöl, Uluderebent and Akpınar. The *BAGRW* maps neither document nor suggest such a route, which, however, does not prove that such a route did not exist; it is quite possible that the settlements in the eastern Tmolos Mountains, extending for about 30 km—Tarigya, Diginda, Daredda, Oumyrota, Koloe, Dios Hieron and Nikaia—had a connection to the east, as is the case for the Turkish villages in this area today.[584]

Some scholars have voiced doubts concerning the historicity of a journey of Paul from Corinth via Ephesus to Jerusalem in A.D. 51/52 and back to Ephesus in A.D. 52, as reported by Luke in Acts 18:20-23.[585] There is no reason, however, to doubt the authenticity of Luke's account. The hypothetical speculation about the redactional motives of Luke are more problematic and more contradictory than the difficulties presented by the details of Luke's account in Acts 18:18-23. Howard Marshall convincingly argues that there is no plausible explanation as to why Luke would include Acts 18:18-21 in his account if the events did not indeed happen as he reports.[586] The following survey describes the towns mentioned by Luke (and not described elsewhere) through which Paul and his coworkers traveled and in which he could have preached the gospel to people whom he encountered during overnight stays and rest stops.

Homadena (mod. Gümüşü)[587] was situated 26 km northwest of Apameia on the upper

[582]French (1994b, 54-55), concluding his discussion with the caution that "there can be no certainty."

[583]Hemer 1989, 120; followed by Riesner 1994, 254 (ET, 286); Barrett, *Acts,* 2:893.

[584]The distance from Tarigya in the east to Blaundos is about 100 km, a journey of three days. The *BAGRW* map does not indicate any ancient settlements between Blaundos and Tarigya.

[585]Recently Wehnert 1997, 96-97; Reinbold 2000, 144-45.

[586]Marshall, *Acts,* 299.

[587]W. Ruge, "Phrygia," PW 20.1 (1941): 781-868, esp. 831; Belke and Mersich 1990, 222.

Maeander River in Phrygia on the Roman road to Aizanoi.

Eumeneia (Εὐμένεια; also Fulvia; mod. Işıklı),[588] 18 km northwest of Homadena, was a new Hellenistic foundation of Attalos II around 150 B.C. The city is attested by coins and inscriptions. Since the Hellenistic period Eumeneia organized regular games, the *Eumeneia Philadelphia*. Around 35 B.C. Antony renamed the city Fulvia in honor of his wife; at this time a certain Zmertorix (a Celtic name!) was a member of the magistrate of the city. Inscriptions attest the worship of Apollo Propylaios and Men Askaenos. The Jewish community in Eumeneia that is documented for the third century A.D. presumably existed at a much earlier date. Inscriptions of the third century indicate that the Christian community of Eumeneia was very vital, a center of the Christian faith in southern Phrygia. We do not know when the church in Eumeneia was established. Stephen Mitchell believes that the number of Christians in Eumeneia likely surpassed the number of Gentile citizens already by A.D. 250.[589] Two bishops are attested between A.D. 250 and 300. Some historians link Eusebius's comment that all the citizens of a Phrygian city, including women and children and magistrates, were executed after the onset of the persecution of A.D. 303 because they refused to offer sacrifices to idols (Eusebius, *Hist. eccl.* 8.11.1) with the Christians of Eumeneia.[590]

Sebaste (Σεβαστή; mod. Selçikler, near Sivaslı),[591] 29 km northwest of Eumeneia in the Sindros Valley (mod. Banaz Çay), was one of the most important cities of Phrygia. Sebaste was founded probably under Augustus around 20 B.C. as the result of the combination of several villages in the area that followed the interpretation of an oracle of Apollo. Ruins of city walls date to the Hellenistic period; a funerary monument dating to the fifth century B.C. contains a tomb made of superior marble stones. Coins minted in Sebaste depict Dionysos, Heracles, Cybele, Men Askaenos, Perseus, Zeus and a river-god. Inscriptions document an *agoranomos* and a *stratēgos*. Christians are attested in Sebaste around A.D. 250; in the Byzantine period Sebaste was the seat of a bishop. It is not known when the Christian community was established.

Akmonia ('Ακμονία; mod. Ahat Köy),[592] 22 km north of Sebaste on the upper Sindros River at the road from Dorylaion to Philadelphia, belonged to the assize district of Apameia during the Roman period. Remains of the city walls survive; Roman and Byzantine stones are used in the buildings of the Turkish village. Akmonia minted its own coins since the first century B.C. The city was the seat of high priests of the imperial cult. Claudius was worshiped as "new Zeus." Akmonia spent about 34,000 denarii in one year for

---

[588]W. Ruge, "Eumeneia 1," PW 6.1 (1907): 1082; H. Treidler, "Eumenia 1," *KP* 2:427; T. Drew-Bear, *DNP* 4:250; Schürer 3:36; Belke and Mersich 1990, 251-52; Ramsay 1895-1897, 353-95; Jones 1937, 54, 71-73; Magie 1950, 12:984-85; G. Cohen 1995, 301-5; S. Mitchell 1995a, 1:40, 57, 225; 2:12, 25, 33-35, 40-41, 57-58.

[589]S. Mitchell 1995a, 2:40-41, 58.

[590]Ramsay 1895-1897, 1.2:502-5; S. Mitchell 1995a, 2:57-58, as a possibility; Lane Fox (1988, 771 n. 4) is skeptical.

[591]L. Bürchner and W. Ruge, "Sebaste 1," PW 2.A1 (1921): 951-52; E. Olshausen, *KP* 5:57; Belke and Mersich 1990, 376-78; N. Firatli, *PECS* 816; Ramsay 1895-1897, 2:5; Magie 1950, 472-73, 1334; S. Mitchell 1995a, 25, 33, 40-41, 47.

[592]Hirschfeld, PW 1.1 (1893): 1174; Schürer 3:30-32; Belke and Mersich 1990, 175-76; Ramsay 1895-1897, 2:621-31; Magie 1950, 1:132, 544; 2:999; Levick 1967, 106-7; Jones 1937, 71; Trebilco 1991, 58-84; G. Cohen 1995, 277; S. Mitchell 1995a, 1:113, 217, 257; 2:9, 33-36, 39.

olive oil that was used in the gymnasium, a fact that illustrates the size and the prosperity of the city. A Jewish community existed in Akmonia in the first century A.D., with most Jews living in a particular quarter near one of the city gates. The Jewish community of Akmonia evidently enjoyed a considerable reputation: an inscription dating to the first century A.D. honors three (non-Jewish) men who restored the synagogue that had been donated by Julia Severa.[593] One of these men, a certain P. Turronius Claudius, is described as *archisynagōgos* "for life" (διὰ βίου, *dia biou*). Julia Severa came from a prominent family—her son L. Servenius Cornutus became a member of the Roman senate during the principate of Nero—she was a member of the city council and a priestess of the imperial cult, and she is depicted on coins of the city. She was favorably disposed toward the Jews, was their benefactor and had donated funds to erect a synagogue.[594] She was active between A.D. 50 and 70, which means that the synagogue presumably was built during this period. It is unclear whether both she and the three men honored in the inscription were God-fearers and attended synagogue services. Numerous Jewish funerary inscriptions from Akmonia date to the third century A.D.; a certain Aurelius Frugianus had attained the offices of *agoranomos, sitonēs, paraphylax* and *stratēgos* (*MAMA* VI 335; *IJudO* II 173).

Temenouthyrai (Τεμένου θύραι; also Flaviopolis; mod. Uşak),[595] about 40 km east of Akmonia in the border area between eastern Lydia and northwestern Phrygia, belonging to Phrygia, was reached by a Roman road that passed by a temple of Zeus Orkamaneites (near mod. Banaz).[596] The city is attested by inscriptions dating to the first century A.D. It was a station at the Persian royal road and was one of the most important towns of the region of Mokadene on the upper Hippurios River. Trajan established the city Trajanopolis (mod. Ortaköy)[597] about 14 km east of Temenouthyrai, soon to overshadow its neighbor. The largest corpus of Montanist inscriptions, dating to A.D. 200-225, was found in Temenouthyrai. We do not know when the Christian community was established in the city.

Blaundos (Βλαῦνδος; former Mlaundos; mod. Sülümenli),[598] 41 km south of Temenouthyrai in the Hippurios Valley, was founded by the Seleucid rulers as a military colony, like other cities in Phrygia (or Lydia; it is disputed whether Blaundos belonged to Phrygia or to Lydia). Gaius Octavius donated a temple including colonnaded halls in the first century A.D.[599] The citizens also visited the temple of Apollo Lairbenos, which was situated on a hill overlooking the upper Maeander Valley about 15 km to the southeast as the crow flies;

---

[593]*MAMA* VI 264 = *CIJ* II 766 = *DF* 33 (improved text); *IJudO* II 168; also in Trebilco 1991, 58-59; see Schürer 3:31; Seager and Kraabel 1983, 180-81; Rajak 1996, 314; Binder 1999, 145-46, 286-88; L. Levine 2000, 111-12, 125-26, 399-401.

[594]See Schürer 3:31; Trebilco 1991, 58-60; Rajak and Noy 1993, 88; Binder 1999, 146, 287; L. Levine 2000, 111, 350, 480-81; *pace* Ramsay (1895-1897, 2:638-40, 647-51, 673), who assumed that she was Jewish. See now Ameling, in *IJudO* II, 2004, 348-55.

[595]J. Keil, PW 5.A1 (1934): 458-59; Magie 1950, 1:132; 2:999; E. Olshausen, *KP* 5:578; T. Drew-Bear, "The City of Temenouthyrai in Phrygia," *Chiron* 9 (1979): 275-302; S. Mitchell 1995a, 1:139, 176, 180, 188; 2:39. From Sebaste there was also a direct road to Temenouthyrai.

[596]See Drew-Bear and Naour 1990, 1943.

[597]W. Ruge, "Traianopolis 2," PW 6.A2 (1937): 2085-90; E. Olshausen, *KP* 5:918.

[598]W. Ruge, PW 3.1 (1897): 560; Magie 1950, 2:1001; S. Mitchell 1995a, 1:20, 180, 187; G. Cohen 1995, 290-92.

[599]*IGR* IV 717, 1700; *SEG* XL 1206; *I. GRIAsia* 168. The description of this temple as "Temple of Claudius" has no basis in the inscription. It is unclear which deity was worshiped in the temple.

a "sacred way" ascended the hill to the temenos and its large temple (27 by 12 m), which was built probably in the second century.[600]

Tarigya (mod. Akpınar) was situated about 100 km west of Blaundos on the eastern Tmolos Mountains (mod. Boz Dağları), south of a peak of 1,890 m.

Diginda (Δίγινδα; mod. Kayacık Asar)[601] was situated 4 km west of Tarigya in the upper Kaystros Valley (*Kilbianoi ano*).[602] The town is mentioned in inscriptions.

Daredda (Δάρεδδα; mod. Elbi), 4 km west of Diginda, also was situated in the upper Kaystros Valley on the eastern slopes of Mount Tmolos.

Oumyrota (Οὐμυρώτα; mod. Suludere)[603] was situated 8 km northwest of Daredda.

Koloe (Κολόη; mod. Kiraz)[604] was situated 5 km west of Oumyrota on the upper Kaystros River.

Nikaia (Νίκαια; mod. Türkönü) was situated 15 km southwest of Koloe. The city overlooked the plain of the upper Kaystros Valley.

Hypaipa (τὰ ῎Υπαιπα; mod. Datbei),[605] 12 km northwest of Nikaia on the road that ran from the north across the Tmolos Mountains from Sardis to Ephesus, was a Greek polis. A large temple dating to the Persian period is documented. A temple of Apollo Karios was located about 2 km north of the city.

Larisa (Λάρισα; near mod. Çatal)[606] was situated 25 km southwest of Hypaipa, north of the Kaystros River, on the road to Ephesus. Larisa belonged to Ephesus after the third century B.C. Coins of the city depict Apollo Larisenos.

Metropolis (Μετρόπολις; mod. Yeniköy)[607] was situated 47 km west of Larisa at the end of the Kaystros Valley on the eastern slopes of Mount Gallesion, about 20 km north of Ephesus. The city was of some significance in the late Hellenistic and in the Roman periods; it organized local games, the *Sebasta Caesareia*. Metropolis was the seat of a bishop in the Byzantine period.

Notes on the travel route. Paul's journey from Ephesus to Macedonia in the summer of A.D. 55, the journey to Illyria in the summer of A.D. 56, the journey to Achaia and Corinth in the fall of A.D. 56 and the journey back to Jerusalem in the spring of A.D. 57 will be discussed below.

---

[600] See *MAMA* IV 98; *SEG* XXXV (1985) 1378. Cf. S. Mitchell 1995a, 1:193. The inscription *MAMA* IV 335 (A.D. 248/249), which attests a Jew with the name "Aur. Phrygianos Menokritou" is not from Blaundos (contra *CIJ* II 760) but from Akmonia; see Nigdelis 1994, 303 n. 30.

[601] L. Bürchner, PW 5.1 (1903): 543.

[602] L. Bürchner, "Kilbianoi," PW 11.1 (1921): 383-84.

[603] See *IK* 17.2 323, no. 3713.

[604] L. Bürchner, "Koloë 1," PW 11.1 (1921): 1107.

[605] L. Bürchner, PW 9.1 (1914): 195-96; S. Mitchell 1995a, 1:181; 2:29.

[606] L. Bürchner, "Larisa 9," PW 12.1 (1924): 872; H. Treidler, "Larisa 7," *KP* 3:501.

[607] J. Keil, "Metropolis 8," PW 15.2 (1932): 1497; K. Ziegler, "Metropolis 5," *KP* 3:1284; S. Mitchell 1995a, 1:226.

Paul traveled at least 2,900 km (1,800 mi.) by foot and 3,200 km (almost 2,000 mi.) by ship between A.D. 52 and 55, engaging in missionary work in the province of Asia (and probably in the province of Illyria) and visiting churches in Macedonia and Achaia. This corresponds to a total of about 150 days of travel: 115 days on foot and perhaps 35 days on ships.

After Paul had attempted to reach Ephesus, the capital of the province of Asia, for several years, he finally was able to spend three years in the city and in the province, from the summer of A.D. 52 to the summer of A.D. 55. From his base in Ephesus, Paul also reached Alexandria Troas with the gospel, and possibly Miletus. While Paul was in Ephesus, his coworkers established churches in Laodikeia, Hierapolis and Colossae. After Paul left Ephesus, with the intention of visiting the churches in Macedonia and in Achaia, evidently he traveled to the province of Illyria in the summer of A.D. 56 to preach the gospel.

The province of Asia ('Ασία; Asia Proconsularis)[608] was organized in 133 B.C. after the death of Attalos III, the king of Pergamon, who had deeded his kingdom to the Romans. The elites of Lydia, Caria and Phrygia had mostly accepted the hegemony of Rome earlier. The province consisted originally of Mysia, Troas, Aeolis, Lydia, Ionia, the islands along the coast, most of Caria and a corridor through Pisidia to Pamphylia. In 116 B.C. several regions of Phrygia were added, and before 100 B.C. Lycaonia was annexed, followed in 82 B.C. by the area around Kibyra. After 80 B.C. the regions in the southeast were included in the new province of Cilicia, and between 56 and 50 B.C. the Phrygian districts of Laodikea, Apameia and Synnada were included as well. The victory of Augustus initiated a period of three hundred years of peace for the region. In the imperial period the province of Asia extended from Amorion and Philomelion in the east to the Mediterranean in the west; in the north it bordered on Bithynia, in the south on Lycia and in the east on Galatia.[609] After Galatia had become a Roman province in 25 B.C., Rome no longer stationed legionary troops in the province of Asia. Since Augustus, the position of proconsul of the province of Asia was one of the highest positions of a consular career.[610] Sextus Appuleius, a relative of Augustus, consul (29 B.C.) and governor of the province (25/24 and 24/23 B.C.),[611] was honored in a cult dedicated to him, as inscriptions from Klaros, Cotiaeum, Kyme, Metropolis, Pergamon and Troas attest, being worshiped as σωτήρ (sōtēr, "savior").[612] The main task of the proconsul was supervision of the local governments. The appendix to the customs law of the province of Asia lists for the year 17 B.C. twelve administrative districts (διοικήσεις, dioikēseis, Lat., conventus) of the province: the metropolis Ephesus is men-

---

[608]B. E. Thomasson, KP 1:636-37; W. M. Calder et al., OCD 189-90; Victor Chapot, La province romaine proconsulaire d'Asie depuis ses origines jusqu'à da fin du Haut-Empire (Rome: Bretschneider, 1904; repr., 1967); T. R. S. Broughton, Roman Asia Minor (Economic Survey of Ancient Rome 4; ed. T. Frank; Baltimore: Johns Hopkins Press, 1938), 503-916; Magie 1950; Pekáry 1980, esp. 613-38; Dräger 1993.

[609]See Sviatoslav Dmitriev, "Local Administration in the Province of Asia: The Problem of Roman Influence" (Ph.D. diss.; Harvard University, 2001 [non vidi]).

[610]See Dräger 1993, 22.

[611]See Stumpf 1991, 90-91.

[612]See H. Halfmann, "Ein neuer Statthalterkult in der Provinz Asia," EA 10 (1987): 83-89, esp. 86-87.

tioned first, followed by the capitals of the districts on the coast (Miletus, Halikarnassos, Smyrna, Pergamon, Adramyttion, Hellespont [with Kyzikos as capital]), and in the interior Sardis, Kibyra, Apameia, Synnada and Lykaonia (with Philomelion as capital). The islands were divided among different districts: Cos belonged to Halikarnassos, Samos to Miletus, Chios and Lesbos to Pergamon.[613] The governors in the first century A.D. until the year 70 were M. Plautius Silvanus (4/5), Q. Poppaeus Secundus (before 20), M. Aemilius Lepidus (26/27 and 27/28), P. Petronius (between 28 and 36), C. Calpurnius Aviola (37/38), C. Asinius Pollio (38/39?), P. Cornelius Lentulus Scipio (41/42); L. Pedanius Secundus (49/50 or 50/51), Cn. Domitius Corbulo (between 51 and 54), Marius Cordus (55?), M. Vettius Niger (between 56 and 58), P. Volasenna (62/63) and M. Acilius Aviola (65/66).[614] The Roman colonies Alexandria Troas and Parion enjoyed the greatest privileges: both cities were granted the *ius Italicum,* and Alexandria Troas also was granted tax autonomy. The Roman senate limited the right to extend asylum in A.D. 22/23 to eleven important temples in the province of Asia: Tacitus mentions Aphrodisias, Ephesus, Hierokaisareia, Cos, Magnesia, Miletus, Pergamon, Samos, Sardis, Smyrna and Stratonikeia.[615] In 29 B.C. Augustus allowed Ephesus and Pergamon to erect provincial cults that were dedicated to him or to Julius Caesar, his adoptive father. The temple of Dea Roma and Divus Caesar in Ephesus was the only supraregional sanctuary in the province of Asia. In A.D. 26 a temple of Tiberius, Livia and the Senate was built in Smyrna, followed in A.D. 40 by a temple of Apollo and Caligula in Miletus (rescinded one year later).

Lydia and Caria were two of the most important regions of the province of Asia (Mysia and Phrygia were discussed above). *Lydia* (ἡ Λυδία),[616] the region in western Asia Minor, bordered on Mysia to the north, on Phrygia to the east, on Caria to the south and on Ionia to the west. The main rivers of Lydia (Maeander, Hermos, Kaystros) flow into the Aegean. Strabo provides a detailed description of Lydia (13.4.3-9). The Lydian language is attested by several dozen inscriptions, most of which were found in Sardis. According to L. A. Borsay, the important cities of Lydia included Sardis, Tantalis, Hermocapeleia, Hierocaesarea, Tralles, Nysa, Cydrara and Celaenae; port cities were Miletus and Myus (south of the Maeander River), Ephesus and Erythrae (north of the Maeander), as well as Cymae, Pitane, Philadelphia, Thyatira, Magnesia and Hypaepa. Sardis was the capital of the Lydian kingdom. The political ascent of Lydia began with Gyges after 680 B.C.; the heyday of the rule of the Mermnades dynasty was the time of Alyattes (ca. 607-560 B.C.). After the defeat of Croesus by Cyrus in 547 B.C. Lydia came under Persian rule, with Sardis as seat of the satraps. After the conquest by Alexander the Great in 133 B.C. Lydia belonged to the empire of the Seleucid kings, after 190 B.C. to Pergamon, after 133 B.C. to the Roman province of Asia. Under Diocletian, Lydia became a Roman province, with Sardis as capital. *Caria* (ἡ Καρία),[617] the

---

[613]See Macro 1980, 671 with n. 26; Engelmann and Knibbe 1989, 103-9; Dräger (1993) adds Alabanda as thirteenth district.

[614]See Stumpf 1991, 99-103, 116-22, 134-46, 171-81.

[615]Tacitus, *Ann.* 3.61.1—62.3; 3.63.2-3; 4.14.1-2. See Dräger 1993, 28; G. Cohen 1995, 232-38.

[616]L. Bürchner and J. Keil, PW 13.2 (1927): 2122-2202; H. Treidler and G. Neumann, *KP* 3:797-800; H. Kaletsch, *DNP* 7:538-47; Laszlo Aaron Borsay, "Lydia, Its Land and History" (Ph.D diss.; University of Pittsburgh, 1965); Pekáry 1980, 623-26; Lindsay Mary Gee, "Lydia: A Cultural and Social History" (D.Phil. diss.; University of Oxford, 1993 [*non vidi*]); Schwertheim 1995; Roberto Gusmani, "Zum Stand der Erforschung der lydischen Sprache," in Schwertheim 1995, 9-19. Inscriptions: *TAM* V 1 (ed. P. Herrmann, 1981); G. Petzl, "Neue Inschriften aus Lydien," *EA* 26 (1996): 1-29; *EA* 28 (1997): 69-79; *EA* 30 (1998): 19-46.

[617]L. Bürchner, PW 10.2 (1919): 1940-47; W. Brandenstein, PWSup 6 (1935): 140-45; A. Kammenhuber, *KP* 3:118-21; H. Kaletsch, *DNP* 6:270-77; Pekáry 1980, 626-33.

region in southwestern Asia Minor, was south of Lydia, southwest of Phrygia and northwest of Lycia, with the cities Ephesus, Miletus and Priene. According to Herodotus and Thucydides, the original inhabitants of this region came from the Aegean islands.

Evangelism in Ephesus

Paul preached the gospel of Jesus Christ in Ephesus between A.D. 52 and 55. Luke provides an extensive report in Acts 18:23—21:17.[618]

Ephesus (Ἔφεσος; near mod. Selçuk [see fig. 38]),[619] on the Kaystros River (mod. Küçük Menderes [the Little Maeander]), was one of the most important metropolises of the Mediterranean world in the first century. Founded in the second millennium B.C., Ephesus had a colorful history, with Hittites, Mycenaeans, the sea people, Aeolians, Ionians, Dorians, Persians and Macedonians controlling the region. The oldest finds of the temple dedicated to the goddess Artemis [1] date to the eighth century B.C. The city founded by Androklos, son of king Kodros of Athens, at Mount Koressos (mod. Panayir Dağ) [3] was abandoned in the sixth century after the Lydian king Croesus besieged the city; the inhabitants were resettled near the temple of Artemis (Ephesus II). No ruins of old Ephesus survive. Alexander the Great came to Ephesus via Sardis in 334 B.C.; he introduced political changes, and he celebrated a grand festival of sacrifices to Artemis and organized a procession that demonstrated the significance of this most important temple in Asia Minor. Lysimachos, one of Alexander's deputies who ruled Thrace and western Asia Minor (323-281 B.C.) during the time of the Diadochi struggles, founded a new capital city (Ephesus III), named Arsionë (Arsinoeia) in honor of his wife, 1.5 km west of the old city: south of the Koressos acropolis at the western base of Mount Tracheia (mod. Panayir Dağ) and in the narrow valley south of Tracheia (Mount Pion) and northwest of Mount Lepre Akte (mod. Bülbül Dağ), with a wall 9 km in length surrounding the city [6]. Lysimachos also started to build the theater [45], with seats for twenty-four thousand spectators (on three levels with

---

[618]On Paul's mission to Ephesus see, besides the commentaries, Duncan 1930; Pereira 1983; Tannehill 1986-1990, 2:230-40; Baugh 1990; Schnackenburg 1991; Elliger 1992, 137-48; Günther 1995, 29-75; H. Koester 1995b; Thiessen 1995; R. Strelan 1996, 126-301; Fieger 1998; Schnabel 1999; see also T. C. Alexander 1990.

[619]L. Bürchner, PW 5.2 (1905): 2773-22; W. Zschietzschmann, *KP* 2 (1975): 293-96; V. Mitsopoulou-Leon, *PECS* 306-10; Oster 1992b; C. E. Arnold, *DPL* 249-53; P. Scherrer and C. Höcker, *DNP* 3:1078-85; Magie 1950, 1:46-47, 74-76, 91, 165-66, 216-17, 404-5, 564, 577-78, 636-37; 2:885-88; Alzinger 1974; Dieter Knibbe, "Ephesos—nicht nur die Stadt der Artemis," in Şahin et al. 1978, 489-503; Hemer 1986, 34-54; Akurgal 1987, 417-23; Baugh 1990; Oster 1990; Elliger 1992; Trebilco 1994, 302-57; G. Cohen 1995, 177-80; Günther 1995; H. Koester 1995a; White 1995; Karwiese 1995; Thiessen 1995; R. Strelan 1996; Fieger 1998; Schnabel 1999. On the archaeology of Ephesus see Scherrer 1995; Wiplinger and Wlach 1995; Wohlers-Scharf 1995; P. Scherrer, "Die historische Topographie von Ephesus," *Forum Archaeologiae* 4 (1997): <http://farch.tsx.org>; Manfred Kandler, ed., *100 Jahre Österreichisches Archäologisches Institut: 1898-1998* (Vienna: Archäologisches Institut, 1998). Excavations: *JÖAI* (since 1898), with supplemental volumes ("Berichte und Materialien," since 1998 "Ergänzungen"); SÖAI (since 1901); Anzeiger der Akademie der Wissenschaften in Wien; as well as Forschungen in Ephesos (since 1906). Inscriptions: *I. Ephesos* (ed. H. Wankel et al., 1979-1984) and *JÖAI;* see D. Knibbe, "Geschichte und Stand der epigraphischen Forschung in Ephesos," in Dobesch and Rehrenböck 1993, 265-68, esp. 267. See <http://www.oeai.at/ausland/ephesos.html>. The numbers in square brackets in the text that follows above refer to fig. 38.

twenty-two rows each), into the western flank of Mount Tracheia. And he built the agora [39] and the stadium [56]. The main gate [5] controlled the highway to Magnesia and to Miletus. The Ephesians settled in the new city only reluctantly; many continued to live in the old, narrow city near the temple of Artemis, although they used the new harbor that Lysimachos had built.

After 281 B.C. Ephesus was ruled in turn by Seleucid and Ptolemaic rulers. In 188 B.C. the Romans included Ephesus as military district in the kingdom of Pergamon. When King Attalos III died in 133 B.C., Rome founded the *provincia Asia* as the first Roman province in Asia Minor. Pergamon was the provincial capital, but Ephesus played an important role as the starting point of two large military roads into the interior, whose milestones were numbered *ab Epheso* since 126 B.C. When Julius Caesar arrived in Asia Minor in 48 B.C., in his fight with Pompey, he probably disembarked in Ephesus, where he issued decrees, reorganized taxation and lowered taxes. The grateful citizens honored him with a monument. The following inscription was found at a statue-base: "The cities in Asia and the [Demoi] and the Ethne (honor) Gaius Iulius, son of Gaius, Caesar, Pontifex Maximus and Imperator and Consul for the second time, the god appearing (descending) from Ares and Aphrodite and the savior of human life."[620] Mark Antony was in Ephesus in 41 B.C.; he regarded the city as the second most important city in the eastern Mediterranean region after Alexandria and seems to have had special plans for Ephesus.[621] During the imperial period Ephesus was an autonomous city, although the extent of the autonomy is disputed.[622] Ephesus was one of the largest cities of the Roman Empire, a residence city of the governor of the province of Asia, and therefore would not have totally escaped the influence and control of Roman police supervision and jurisdiction.[623]

Octavian (Augustus) stayed in Ephesus for several months after the autumn of the year 30 B.C., when he reorganized the East after his victory over Mark Antony. After his proclamation as emperor in 27 B.C.—his official Latin title, *Imperator Caesar Augustus,* was translated by the Greeks as Ἀυτοκράτωρ Καῖσαρ Σεβαστός (*Autokratōr Kaisar Sebastos*)—the assembly of the Greeks in Asia requested permission to honor him in temples as divine. Augustus allowed the province of Asia to erect a temple in Pergamon and worship him together with Roma, the divine personification of the Roman state. In Ephesus the citizens established a Sebasteion (temple of Augustus) in the Artemision. The following years witnessed a building boom in the city. The center of Roman Ephesus was built in the upper city of Lysimachos's Ephesus on the small plateau between the two peaks of Mount Pion (Panayir Dağ) and Mount Lepre Akte (Bülbül Dağ).[624] The inscriptions incised on the new public buildings were bilingual, and the Latin text was emphasized by the use of larger letters.[625] The oldest building (apart from funerary monuments) in Augustean Ephesus was the South Gate [38], which gave access to the agora, erected by the freedmen Mazaeus and Mithridates for the imperial house and the people of the city. This

---

[620] *I. Ephesos* II 251; German translation, *HGIÜ* III 511.

[621] See Karwiese 1995, 77.

[622] See E. Guerber, "Cité libre ou stipendiaire? A propos du status juridique d'Éphèse à l'époque du haut empire romain," *REG* 108 (1995): 388-409.

[623] See Selinger 1997, 259 with n. 81.

[624] See Karwiese 1995, 81. On the building program of the Roman period see P. Scherrer, "The City of Ephesos: From the Roman Period to Late Antiquity," in H. Koester 1995a, 1-25; on the first century A.D., 4-10.

[625] See D. Knibbe, "Die Inschriften von Ephesos," *Forum Archaeologiae* 4 (1997): <http://farch.tsx.org>.

gate, called the Triodos Gate,[626] named after the three roads that branched off at this point (to the Embolos, to the agora and to Ortygia west of the city), with three wide passages, was constructed as a Roman triumphal gate; the inscription, easily read even today, is bilingual.[627] The text reads, "To Imperator Caesar Augustus, son of god, pontifex maximus, consul 12 times, in his 20th year of tribunician power, and to Livia, wife of Caesar Augustus. To Marcus Agrippa, son of Lucius, consul three times, imperator, in his 6th year of tribunician power, and to Julia, daughter of Caesar Augustus. Mazaeus and Mithridates to their patrons. [and, in Greek] Mazaeus and Mithridates to their patrons and to the people." The so-called State Agora [11], built probably by Mark Antony in the first century B.C., was a large square measuring 160 by 58 m. The State Agora must be understood as a temenos: the surrounding stoas did not contain shops. Between A.D. 11 and 13 a monumental colonnaded hall, the Basilike Stoa [14], was built on the north side of the State Agora in the space between the Bouleuterion and the Prytaneion and the temple of Divus Iulius and Dea Roma, with the State Altar in the center of the square, a three-aisled stoa (168 m long) with sixty-seven columns and two stories, dedicated to Artemis, Augustus, Tiberius and the Demos of Ephesus; the building was donated by Gaius Sextilius Pollio and his family, who were prominent citizens; the annex on the east side of the building was a room in which Augustus and Livia were worshiped (*Kaisersaal*). The bilingual building inscription, dating between A.D. 11 and 14, begins with the words "To Ephesian Diana and to the Imperator Caesar Augustus, son of god, pontifex maximus, in his 30th year . . . of tribunician power, consul 13 times, imperator 29 times, *pater patriae,* and to Tiberius, son of Augustus, in his . . . year of tribunician power, consul two times, imperator . . . times, and to the city of the Ephesians. . . ."[628] At the northwest corner of the Basilike Stoa a monumental tomb of C. Sextilius Pollio was built in A.D. 14 [21]. The small temple on the west side of the State Agora, the "Temple of Isis," evidently was transformed into a temple of Dea Roma and Divus Caesar [13], who were worshiped by the Romans citizens outside of Rome (Cassius Dio 51.20.6). The Prytaneion [17], the "house of the sacred fire," was built in the first years of the first century A.D. north of the Basilike Stoa as the city temple of Artemis and the new seat of the council of the Curetes, the foremost cult commission of Ephesus. To the east of the Prytaneion stood the Bouleuterion [15]; between the two buildings was another sanctuary dedicated to Artemis and Augustus [16]. The city had two gymnasiums: the Upper Gymnasium east of the State Agora, and the Theater Gymnasium northwest of the theater. New water conduits were built, the *Aqua Iulia* and the *Aqua Troessitica,* and Pollio financed the construction of a two-story aqueduct. The official buildings of Roman Ephesus occupied the level plateaus in the valley between the two hills of the city; private houses were built on the slopes, reached via often steep alleyways [32, 33]. Pliny writes in A.D. 77 that Ephesus "grew up to Mount Pion" (*attolitur monte Pione* [Pliny, *Nat.* 5.31.115]). The so-called Slope House 2 was described above in §18.3 (see fig. 39).

After a devastating earthquake in A.D. 23[629] many buildings needed to be renovated or rebuilt. During the principate of Tiberius a stadium [56] was enlarged or newly built on

---

[626]On the newly discovered inscription that mentions the name of the gate see D. Knibbe, *JÖAI* 62 (1993): 123-24.

[627]*I. Ephesos* VII.1 3006 = *I. GRIAsia* 151; See Ehrenberg, Jones and Stockton 1979, no. 71; English translation in Braund 1985, no. 65. On the Tridos Gate see Alzinger 1974, 9-16.

[628]*I. Ephesos* II 404 = *I. GRIAsia* 154. The Greek inscription reads Ἀρτέμιδι Ἐφεσίαι instead rather than Deanae Ephesiae (*sic*). See Alzinger 1974, 26-37.

[629]See A. Hermann, "Erdbeben," *RAC* 5:1104.

the western slopes of Mount Pion. The harbor received a gate with three passages [46], constructed as a triumphal arch. A new market was built on the level square enlarged by terraces north of the Gate of Mazaeus and Mithridates: the grand Tetragonos Agora [39], measuring 110 by 110 m, with two monumental gates and surrounded by colonnaded halls (on the Triodos Gate see above). Ephesus competed during this time with Pergamon, Smyrna and Miletus for the right to build an official imperial temple and receive the title of temple warden (*neōkoros*); the aristocracy of Ephesus sent embassies to Rome and minted coins that depicted busts of Emperor Claudius and of his wife, Agrippina, with the legend θεογαμία (*theogamia,* "marriage of gods"), celebrating their wedding in A.D. 49 as divine event. Ephesus did not receive the status of *neōkoros* at this time, but it did succeed in getting the cistophoric coinage of the province of Asia to bear the cult image of Diana Ephesia along with the traditional references to the emperor and to the province.[630] During the principate of Nero building activity increased again: between A.D. 54 and 59 Claudia Metrodora and her (unknown) husband donated, on the east side of the Tetragonos Agora, a Doric hall (the so-called Neronic Hall [40]) that was dedicated to Artemis, the emperor and the Demos of Ephesus; this hall may have been the *auditorium,* the building in which the Roman governor and his council held their meetings.[631] The stadium was renovated, and the approach to the harbor was dredged in A.D. 62/63.

After A.D. 69 Emperor Vespasian made Ephesus the seat of the imperial control board of taxation. During the principate of Domitian, in A.D. 83/84, Ephesus finally received the title of temple warden (*neōkoros*); the temple of the Sebastoi (Emperors) of the Koinon of Asia [22] was erected west of the State Agora.[632] In the heroon [31], located between the Gate of Hadrian and the Octagon south of the Celsus Library, was the marble portrait of a sixty-year-old man (discovered in the excavations of 1978/1988) who has been identified as a priest of the imperial cult on the basis of the diadem on his head; he is identified with the skeletal remains found in the sarcophagus: "the features of the portrait, characterized by latent pain, harmonize with the changes of the skeleton by arthritis and spondylosis."[633] Peter Scherrer identifies this imperial priest with Tiberius Claudius Aristion, an Ephesian aristocrat known from other sources: he was *archiereus* (high priest) of the Imperial Temple of Asia and Ephesus in A.D. 88/89; *neōkoros* (temple warden) of the Imperial Temple of Asia in Ephesus in A.D. 89-91, asiarch and prytanis (president) of the Harbor Gymnasium in A.D. 91/92 (which he helped build), asiarch and grammateus (secretary) in A.D. 92/93, and he finished the Celsus Library after A.D. 114. Pliny calls him *princeps Ephesiorum (Ep.* 3.31.3, 7). The building activity during the principate of Domitian was hectic: new projects included the enlargement of the theater [45]; a surge tank near the State Agora [11]; a nym-

---

[630]See Karwiese 1995, 86.

[631]*I. Ephesos* VII.1 3003 = *I. GRIAsia* 155. See H. Engelmann, "Celsusbibliothek und Auditorium in Ephesos (IK 17 3009)," *JÖAI* 62 (1993): 105-11, esp. 106; R. Kearsley, in *I. GRIAsia, esp.* 198-201; for the relevant inscriptions (with translation) see ibid., 208-11.

[632]See Dräger 1993, 122-200; Friesen 1993; idem, "The Cult of the Roman Emperors in Ephesos: Temple Wardens, City Titles, and the Interpretation of the Revelation of John," in H. Koester 1995a, 229-50.

[633]Hilke Thür, "Porträt eines Kaiserpriesters und Mäzens aus Ephesos," *Forum Archaeologiae* 7 (1998): <http://farch.tsx.org>; cf. H. Thür, ed., *". . . KAI KOSMHSANTA THN POLIN . . ." ". . . und verschönerte die Stadt . . .": Ein ephesischer Priester des Kaiserkultes in seinem Umfeld* (SÖAI 27; Vienna: Österreichisches Archäologisches Institut, 1997). Spondylosis is osteoarthritis in the spine. On the temple of Hadrian mentioned in the discussion that follows below see Barbara Burrell, "Temples of Hadrian, not Zeus." *GRBS* 43 (2003): 31-50, esp. 40-48.

phaeum near the Pollio Monument and a fountain near the Memmius Mausoleum [23]; the paving of the Embolos ("Curetes Street" [25]); a new water conduit; the huge complex of the Harbor Baths [50], with the Halls of Verulanus [52] (200 by 240 m); the Harbor Gymnasium [51], with a building in which the official imperial cult was celebrated on the north side of the large palaestra (88 by 88 m). The sanctuary west of the agora [42], which possibly was dedicated to Egyptian gods (so-called Sarapeion), was built by C. Iulius Celsus, as was the Celsus Library [37] and the Olympieion [53], which used to be identified with the temple of Hadrian (as Zeus Olympios) but actually predates Hadrian and was located far from the temple that today is tentatively identified as his temple.

The prominent families of Ephesus included the Caristanii (influential Roman merchants),[634] the Carsidii, the Cusinii, the Pollio and the Vedii.[635] A certain Gaius Stertinius Orpex, a freedman, was *scriba librarius* around A.D. 50.[636] In the second part of the first century A.D. the physician Rufus was active in Ephesus. He had studied in Alexandria and had visited Caria and Cos. His treatise *On the Nomenclature of Parts of the Human Body* (Περὶ ὀνομασίας τῶν κατ' ἄνθρωπον μορίων), the oldest surviving anatomy, was based on an investigation of apes. He described kidney diseases, the male sex drive, gonorrhea, yellow fever, gout and bubonic plague, and he wrote about the manner in which physicians should ask questions of their patients.[637] The medical school of Ephesus had an excellent reputation, even though it could not compare with the more famous schools in Pergamon and Cos.

Ephesus had about two hundred thousand inhabitants.[638] Ephesus was linked with Sardis by the highway leading north through the Kaystros Valley; another frequently used road ran through the Maeander Valley in an easterly direction to Laodikeia and Hierapolis. Ships using the city's harbor came from the regions of the Black Sea, from Egypt and from Syria, from Greece and from Italy, from southern Gaul (France) and from Spain.

The cult of Artemis was dominant in the history of the city (see below). Coins, inscriptions and sculptures[639] further attest the worship of Aphrodite of Aphrodisias, Aphrodite Daitis, Aphrodite Hetaira, Apollo, Apollo Patroios, Asclepius, Athene, Concordia, Demeter, Dionysos, Dionysos Bakchios, Dionysos Oreiogyadon, Dionysos Phleus, Enedra, Eros,

---

[634] *I. Ephesos* III 634, 634a, V 1629; VI 2266; R. Kearsley, in *I. GRIAsia*, 29.

[635] Caristanii: *I. GRIAsia* 15 (probably not related to the Caristanii in Pisidian Antiocheia); Carsidii: *I. GRIAsia* 55; Cusinii: *I. Ephesos* VI 2551B; VII.2 4119-4120 (*I. GRIAsia* 21, 28); *I. Ephesos* III 659B, 716; IV 1122, 1034-1035; Pollio: *I. Ephesos* II 404, 405, 407; VII.1 3092 (*I. GRIAsia* 114-115, 152, 154); Vedii: *I. Ephesos* VI 2324; VII.1 76; *I. GRIAsia* 18.

[636] *I. Ephesos* VII.2 4123 = *I. GRIAsia* 24.

[637] Rufus, *Oeuvres de Rufus d'Ephèse* (ed. C. Daremberg and C. É. Ruelle; Amsterdam: Hakkert, 1963 [1879]); *Die Fragen des Arztes an den Kranken* (ed. Hans Gärtner; Corpus medicorum Graecorum supplementum 5.4; Berlin: Akademie-Verlag, 1962); see Henrike Thomssen, "Die Medizin des Rufus von Ephesos" (diss.; University of Munich, 1989); Amal Abou-Aly, "The Medical Writings of Rufus of Ephesus" (Ph.D. diss.; University of London, 1992; [*non vidi*]).

[638] Magie 1950, 1:585; White (1995, 40-43) assumes 180,000 inhabitants. For the observation that follows above see Schnackenburg 1991, 41 with n. 3.

[639] D. Knibbe, "Ephesos—nicht nur die Stadt der Artemis," in Şahin et al. 1978, 489-503; Oster 1990. On the coins see S. Karwiese, "Ephesos C. Numismatischer Teil," PWSup 12 (1970): 297-364. On the sculptures see Maria Aurenhammer, *Die Skulpturen von Ephesos: Bildwerke aus Stein; Idealplastik I* (Forschungen in Ephesos 10.1; Vienna: Verlag der Österreichischen Akademie der Wissenschaften, 1990); idem, "Sculptures of Gods and Heroes from Ephesos," in H. Koester 1995a, 251-80. On the Egyptian cults see J. C. Walters, "Egyptian Religions in Ephesos," in H. Koester 1995a, 281-309.

Ge Karpophoros, Hekate, Hephaistos, Heracles, Hermes, Hestia, Hygieia, Hypnos, the Kabiroi, Leto, Marsyas, Meter-Cybele, Meter Oreia, Nemesis, Pan, the mountain-god Pion, Pluto, Poseidon, Priapus, the gods of the Prytaneion, Satyrs, Silen, Telesphoros, Theoi Pantes, Theos Hypsistos, Triton, Tyche, Zeus Hyetios, Zeus Keraunios, Zeus Meilichios, Zeus Patroios, several river gods; the Egyptian gods Sarapis, Isis Panthea and Harpocrates; numerous heroes, including Ganymed, Heracles and Androklos, the mythical founder of the city whose heroon evidently was located in the city center, as well as the members of the family of the Roman emperor.

Ephesus owed its wealth to its harbor, which was the site of transshipment for all goods produced in the rich province of Asia, as well as for goods imported from the Far East (Babylonia, India) via the royal road or goods imported from the West (Spain, Italy and Rome).[640] The numerous pottery fragments that were found in the western section of the Tetragonos Agora during the excavations of 1988, ceramics of the type Eastern Sigillata B—sixty-four shards display the stamp of C. Sentius, a famous Arretine potter of the Augustan period—suggest that this was the site of a distribution center of fine red-gloss Roman tableware that evidently was produced in nearby Tralles.

Another important economic factor in the history of Ephesus was the temple of Artemis, which was one of "the seven wonders of the world" that attracted tourists from all areas of the Roman Empire, and which also functioned as a credit bank of Asia.

The temple of Artemis,[641] about 2.5 km east of the center of Ephesus, was rediscovered by John Turtle Wood on December 31, 1869. The pit that remained after the excavations of the year 1874, measuring 170 by 100 by 7 m, revealed the immense size of the temple. The temple of Artemis was four times as large as the Parthenon in Athens. The first sanctuary at the site was built around 800 B.C. The ruins that were discovered included the column bases of a temple with a peripteros in the center, measuring 9.50 by 13.3 m, with 4 by 8 columns; in the center of the peripteros was a rectangular structure measuring 3.7 by 1.7 m that is interpreted as an altar or as the base of a cult statue. Around 600 B.C. two main cults existed on the site: in the center of the so-called Temple C (D. G. Hogarth), and the so-called *hekatompedos* (i.e., 100 Ionian feet in length), the first building (34 by 16 m) at the site made with marble (A. Bammer); some scholars, however, interpret the *hekatompedos* as an altar of the temple of Croesus (M. Weissl). Numerous votive offerings of gold and ivory were found, as well as bones of sacrifices of pigs, donkeys, dogs, bears, lions and even humans. After A.D. 560 the Lydian king Croesus of Sardis built the Archaic Temple of Artemis, a great

---

[640]Heinrich Zabehlicky, "Preliminary Views of the Ephesian Harbor," in H. Koester 1995a, 201-21. For the observation that follows above see Susanne Zabehlicky-Scheffenegger, "Subsidiary Factories of Italian Sigillata Potters," in H. Koester 1995a, 217-28. On Tralles see Pliny, *Nat.* 35.160.

[641]See Anton Bammer and Ulrike Muss, *Das Artemision von Ephesos* (Mainz: Zabern, 1996); A. Bammer, "The Temple of Artemis—the Artemision of Ephesus," *Forum Archaeologiae* 4.8 (1997): <http://farch.net>; Michael Weissl, "Untersuchungen zur Topographie des Artemisions von Ephesos," *Forum Archaeologiae* 18.3 (2001): <http://farch.net>; Karwiese 1995; see also Elliger 1992, 128-36; R. Strelan 1996, 68-76.

marble temple also called the Temple of Croesus. This temple, surrounded by columns, measured 21 by 47 m and had no roof; the cult statue of Artemis Ephesia stood in a small *naiskos* at the eastern end of the temple. The Artemision of Croesus burned down on July 1, 356 B.C. The temple was rebuilt with the same dimensions, but it surpassed the archaic temple in terms of building materials and artwork. The stylobate—the top step of the steps that form the base of a Greek temple—of the new temple was elevated by 3 m, making the temple appear even more majestic. The number of columns at the entrance, decorated with reliefs over 2 m high, increased from 4 to 36. The *naiskos* was surrounded by a forest of 117 columns that were 17.5 m high. Sculptors and painters decorated the temple's interior and exterior. Apelles painted two pictures of Alexander the Great that were displayed in the Artemision; the second picture is said to have cost 20 talents of gold.

The temple of Artemis was controlled by an administrative board whose members had the title of νεωποιός (*neōpoios*); during the imperial period they exercised not only religious functions but also civil functions.[642] The *Artemisia,* the great festival in honor of the goddess Artemis, was celebrated in March/April, with sacrifices and athletic games and competitions in drama.[643] Xenophon of Ephesus, who wrote his *Ephesian Tale of Anthia and Habrokomas* in the second century A.D., describes the *Artemisia* as a festival during which families of Ephesus and the neighboring regions arranged the marriage of their children. Young women and young men of marrigeable age—Anthia was fourteen years old—walked in a festive procession in which cult objects of Artemis were carried along from the city to the temple, accompanied by the singing of hymns.[644] Numerous large and small "altars of Artemis" (Βωμὸς τῆς Ἀρτέμιδος, *Bōmos tēs Artemidos*) stood along the processional road (*via sacra*) from the city to the Artemision, which ran around Mount Pion (Tracheia; Panayir Dağ). The processions probably took place at night so that the devotees of the goddess could pray, offer sacrifices and sing hymns.[645] A second festival, the *Thargelion,* occurring in May/June, celebrated the birth of Artemis and of Apollo. The Curetes played a major role during this festival. Another festival, the *Daitis,* celebrated Artemis, whose statue was washed in the sea and subsequently rubbed with oil and newly clothed; in the imperial period this festival perhaps was combined with the *Thargelion.*[646] The cult statue of Artemis Ephesia was covered with woven clothes and genuine jewelry that could be removed and were renewed from time to time; only the face, neck, hands and feet of the sculptured figure of the goddess were visible. Thus, regarding extant examples of the statue of Artemis Ephesia, Robert Fleischer concludes, "The mysterious 'breasts' have nothing to do with real female breasts and hardly anything to do with fertility symbols. They belong to the removable wardrobe of the goddess just like the clothes and the jewelry. They are not a later addition but were there right from the beginning. . . . Their significance continues to be unclear."[647] During excavations that have been carried out since 1969, animal bones discovered in the

---

[642]*I. Ephesos* III 950, 957, 959, 961, 963; V 1579B; VI 2926; VII.1 3263; see Magie 1950, 1:60; 2:847-48; Horsley, *NewDocs* 4:127-29; Hemer 1989, 235-36; Lampe 1992, 66-69.

[643]See Oster 1990, 1708-9; R. Strelan 1996, 57-58.

[644]See Anderson, trans., *Xenophon of Ephesus;* Kytzler, ed., *Die Waffen des Eros;* cf. R. Strelan 1996, 58-59.

[645]D. Knibbe, "Via Sacra Ephesiaca," in H. Koester 1995a, 141-55, esp. 144; on the processions see 153-54. For a description of the buildings on Curetes Street, which was a part of the *via sacra,* including the heroon of Androklos, the founder of Ephesus, and of Arsinoë IV (Octagon) see H. Thür, "The Processional Way in Ephesos as a Place of Cult and Burial," in H. Koester 1995a, 157-99.

[646]Fleischer 1973, 124-25; R. Strelan 1996, 63-64.

[647]Fleischer 1978, 326; cf. idem 1973.

vicinity of the altar in the temple of Artemis confirm that the animals that were slaughtered as sacrifices included particularly goats, sheep, cattle and pigs, occasionally also donkeys, horses, dogs, cats, red deer, fallow deer, goitered gazelles and red foxes.[648] Anton Bammer describes the sacrificial rites as follows: "After the sacrificial animal had been decorated, it was led to the altar in a procession (πομπή). The procession was formed by the kanephoroi and musicians, followed by the sacrificial animal, the person offering the sacrifice (usually the priest), flute players and festive participants. The kanephoroi, young girls, carried sacrificial knives, ax, incense and sacrificial barley (οὐλαί) in baskets. The basket with the barley and the basin with the sacrificial water (χέρνιψ) were carried around the altar. Then a burning log was immersed in the water, and the participants, the sacrificial animal, and the altar were sprinkled with water. The participants put their hands into the water and sprinkled the sacrificial water as well. The barley was scattered on the ground, into the fire, and on the sacrificial animal. . . . Following a communal prayer, the priest cut some hair from the animal and threw it into the fire. The animal was killed, accompanied by the playing of the flute. The blood was allowed to run onto the altar, or it was caught in a bowl and spread onto the altar. Then the intestines (σπλάγχνα) were roasted and eaten, and the parts set aside for the gods (ἱερά, θεομορία), the thighs (μηρία) and meat from all parts of the animal were burned. The μηρία and the pelvic bone (ὀσφύς) were placed in the correct anatomical arrangement. . . . The sacrificial meat proper either was roasted and eaten right on the spot, or later it often was distributed and taken home."

Reproductions of the temple of Artemis made of silver have not been documented by archaeologists as of yet, but a miniature temple made of marble[649] and terracotta figurines[650] have been found. The cult of Artemis Ephesia[651] is attested for the Pisidian cities of Termessos and Cremna,[652] and in several cities on the northern coast of the Black Sea traces of the cult of Artemis Ephesia have been discovered as well.[653]

Dieter Knibbe comments on the numerous deities and cults that were worshiped and observed in Ephesus as follows:[654] "The religious 'infrastructure' of Ephesos consisted of an astonishingly rich inventory of deities and divine powers. Apart from Cybele, the indigenous goddess of Asia Minor, the deities that came with the Greek immigrants largely were adapted to the local circumstances on Ephesian soil; the same is true for later and late 'new-

---

[648]See Anton Bammer, Friedrich Brein and Petra Wolff, "Das Tieropfer am Artemisaltar von Ephesos," in Şahin et al. 1978, 107-57, esp. 108, 150-51; the quotation that follows above, 144-45.

[649]Wolfgang Oberleitner and Erich Lessing, *Funde aus Ephesos und Samothrake* (Katalog der Antikensammlung 2; Vienna: Kunsthistorisches Museum Wien, 1978), 56, no. 20; cf. Horsley, *NewDocs* 4:9; Trebilco 1994, 336-38.

[650]J. R. Coleman, "A Roman Terracotta Figurine of the Ephesian Artemis in the McDaniel Collection," *HSCP* 70 (1965): 111-15; cf. Trebilco 1994, 336.

[651]See Fleischer 1973; 1978, 324-58; Elliger 1992, 113-28; Christine M. Thomas, "At Home in the City of Artemis," in H. Koester 1995a, 81-117.

[652]See S. Mitchell 1995b, 55. In regard to the honorary inscription for Trokondas, the priest of Artemis Ephesia in Cremna, dating to the first half of the first century A.D., see now *I. Pisidia* 31 (= *SEG* XLII 1223). Trokondas, whose grandfather Hermaios and whose father, Osaeis, were priests of the Ephesian Artemis as well, has watched "with integrity" over the "solemn mysteries of the goddess" (ἱεροτελῆ μυστήρια τῆς θ[ε]οῦ), and he has celebrated her rites to increase her fame and glory" (εἰς αὔξησιν πλείονα ἀγειωχότα).

[653]M. Treister, "Ephesus and the North Pontic Area in the Archaic and Classical Periods," quoted in G. R. Tsetskhladze, "Greek Colonisation in the Black Sea Area," in Tsetskhladze 1998, 36.

[654]Knibbe, in Şahin et al. 1978, 502-3.

comers,' deities of the 'great pantheon' and popular deities of salvation. Their common characteristic, at least in official terms, was their subordinate status with regard to Artemis, who defended her primacy with jealousy and with success. It surely was not easy to stand one's ground over against this powerful competition [i.e., of Artemis]. The fact that this indeed happened to a large degree attests not only to the vitality of these deities . . . but also to the fact that Artemis was never able to do justice to the many religious demands—less and less over time." Knibbe adds that all these deities had nothing to offer that would effectively counter "the unpretentious teaching of Paul that ultimately was victorious a little over three centuries after his memorable preaching."

Jews are attested in Ephesus since the Seleucid period.[655] Josephus (*A.J.* 12.125) notes that the Jews of Ephesus received citizenship rights from Antiochos III (261-246 B.C.). Even though this comment is problematic because only individuals could receive citizenship rights in a Greek city, it does confirm the existence of a Jewish community in Ephesus.[656]

Josephus quotes several edicts, including an edict of the Roman consul L. Lentulus Crus issued in 49 B.C., that address the issue of exempting the Jews of Ephesus from military service; the problem involved marching on the sabbath and kosher food. This indicates that some Ephesian Jews possessed Roman citizenship.[657] When P. Cornelius Dolabella, the governor of the province of Syria during the reign of Julius Caesar, renewed this privilege in 43 B.C., it concerned not just the Jews in Ephesus to whom his letter was directed, and not just Jews who were Roman citizens, but all Jews of the province of Asia: they are permitted to live according to their ancestral customs and to assemble for worship.[658] Philo quotes a similar edict that G. Norbanus Flaccus, the proconsul of the province of Asia in 24 B.C. (?), addressed to the magistrates of Ephesus on behalf of Augustus.[659] These texts suggest that the Jews in Ephesus had a synagogue, a fact that Luke notes explicitly in his account in the book of Acts (Acts 18:19-21, 24-26; 19:8-9). Luke uses the singular "the synagogue" when he refers to the Jewish community in Ephesus; if, therefore, there was only one synagogue in the city (which is not a necessary inference), it must have been a large one because the Jewish community of Ephesus probably was of considerable size.[660] In 14 B.C. Herod I visited Ephesus during a journey through Asia Minor.[661] In view of the fact that over five thousand inscriptions have been discovered in Ephesus, it seems surprising that no epigraphical evidence has been found for a synagogue in Ephesus. This lack of evidence perhaps is due to the fact that many sections of the city remain unexcavated. The date of a fragmentary inscription that attests a *synagōgos* is uncertain.[662] The tombstone of a Jew with the name

---

[655]See Schürer 3:22-23, 88; Trebilco 1991 passim (cf. 310 s.v. Ephesus); Hengel 1993, 292-93; Levinskaya 1996, 143-48; Binder 1999, 279-82; Ameling, in *IJudO* II, 2004, 147-52.

[656]See Smallwood 1976, 121; Trebilco 1991, 168-69.

[657]Josephus, *A.J.* 14.225-227, 228-229, 230, 234, 237-240. In regard to the confusion in Josephus concerning the edicts that he refers to see Smallwood 1976, 127 with n. 24.

[658]Josephus, *A.J.* 14.223-227. See Smallwood 1976, 128 with n. 25.

[659]Philo, *Legat.* 314; cf. Josephus, *A.J.* 16.167-168, 172-173. See Smallwood 1976, 142 n. 87.

[660]See Binder 1999, 282.

[661]Josephus, *A.J.* 16.23-62. See D. Jacobson 2001, 23.

[662]*I. Ephesos IV* 1251. See H. Engelmann and D. Knibbe, *JÖAI* 52 (1978-1980): 50, no. 94; Levinskaya 1996, 146.

"Marcus Aurelius Mussius" (second century A.D.) and the tombstone of a Jewish "chief physician" (*archiatros* [second or third century]) have been found.[663]

Paul visited Ephesus for the first time during his journey from Corinth back to Antioch in Syria in the late summer of the year A.D. 51. He stayed in the city only for a short period of time, but he did preach in the synagogue. The Christian couple Aquila and Priscilla accompanied Paul from Corinth to Ephesus.

Acts 18:19-21: "When they reached Ephesus, he left them there, but first he himself went into the synagogue and had a discussion with the Jews. [20]When they asked him to stay longer, he declined; [21]but on taking leave of them, he said, 'I will return to you, if God wills.' Then he set sail from Ephesus."

Paul encountered an audience in the synagogue that was attentive and wanted to hear more. The Jews, presumably the officials of the synagogue, asked Paul to stay and continue to teach. Paul declined this invitation because he wanted to return to Antioch and to visit Jerusalem.

Priscilla and Aquila, who had arrived with Paul from Corinth (Acts 18:18), remained in Ephesus. After Paul left for Syria, they encountered Apollos, who was visiting Ephesus. Apollos, an educated Jew from Alexandria who was knowledgeable in the sacred Scriptures, taught in the synagogue of Ephesus accurately about Jesus, but he knew only the baptism of John (Acts 18:24-26a).

Scholars interpret Apollos as (1) a Jewish missionary with connections to the revival movement of John the Baptist;[664] (2) a disciple of John the Baptist who became a disciple of Jesus before the crucifixion and missed the outpouring of the Holy Spirit because he had left Judea,[665] or who perhaps was introduced to the theology of John the Baptist in Alexandria by one of his disciples;[666] (3) a Jewish follower of Jesus who had not yet become a Christian;[667] (4) an independent Christian missionary whose remedial instruction by Aquila and Priscilla is a motif that was freely created by Luke;[668] (5) a Christian missionary who held a particular doctrine of baptism: it is a rite of repentance (as in the revival movement of John the Baptist), and it implies a special bond between the person who is baptized and the person who baptizes.[669]

Apollos evidently was a Christian who lacked a deeper theological understanding in some areas. Luke asserts that Aquila and Priscilla instructed him "more accurately" with respect to "the Way of God" (Acts 18:26b).

---

[663]*I. Ephesos* V 1676 = *CIJ* II 746 (with a different interpretation of the name; *IJudO* II 33); *I. Ephesos* V 1677 = *CIJ* I 745. See Levinskaya 1996, 146-48.

[664]See H. Merklein, *EWNT* 1:328-29 (*EDNT* 1:136-37); Roloff, *Apg,* 279.

[665]See W. Michaelis, "Die sog. Johannes-Jünger in Ephesus," *NKZ* 38 (1927): 717-35.

[666]See Schumacher 1916, 11.

[667]See Schneider, *Apg,* 2:261.

[668]See H. Preisker, "Apollos und die Johannesjünger in Act 18,23-19,6," *ZNW* 30 (1931): 301-4.

[669]See Thiessen 1995, 43-60; followed by Dobbeler 2000a, 195-97.

When Paul returned to Ephesus a few months later, in the spring of A.D. 52, he encountered "some disciples" in the city (Acts 19:1-3).

Acts 19:1-3: "While Apollos was in Corinth, Paul passed through the interior regions and came to Ephesus, where he found some disciples. ²He said to them, 'Did you receive the Holy Spirit when you became believers?' They replied, 'No, we have not even heard that there is a Holy Spirit.' ³Then he said, 'Into what then were you baptized?' They answered, 'Into John's baptism.'"

Luke's reference to "disciples" (*mathētai*) is interpreted in various ways.[670] Scholars traditionally have interpreted them as disciples of John the Baptist.[671] Some scholars have suggested that Paul initially believed that these "disciples" were Christians, only to realize that this was not the case.[672] Scholars who interpreted these disciples as Christians usually saw them as "incomplete" Christians.[673] More recently some scholars interpret the disciples as Jewish Christians who had been converted as a result of Apollos's ministry.[674]

Axel von Dobbeler accepts this newer interpretation and suggests that Apollos's notion of baptism did not reckon with the impartation of the Holy Spirit: this is why Apollos apparently was not baptized by Aquila and Priscilla, because he was already baptized and had received the Holy Spirit, while Paul (re)baptized the "disciples" who had undergone baptism (analogous to the baptism of John) but had not received the Holy Spirit.[675] This interpretation is unconvincing: Luke appears to contrast the disciples with Apollos, he does not describe them as Apollos's disciples, and Apollos received the Holy Spirit (Acts 18:25) while the disciples had not even heard that the eschatological Spirit had been poured out.[676]

The term "disciples of John" is somewhat unfortunate because Acts 19:1-7 talks not about baptizers but about baptism.[677] But Luke links their status as "disciples" with John's baptism of repentance, a fact that makes it plausible to describe them as disciples of John. Apparently these "disciples" were not Christians:[678] the only piece of new information that made a second baptism necessary was the identification of the Coming One, of whom John had spoken, with Jesus Christ, and if this identification was new for the disciples, they could

---

[670]See Thiessen 1995, 61-70; Schnabel 1999, 367-72; Dobbeler 2000a, 197-202.
[671]See Conzelmann, *Apg,* 119 (ET, 159); Haenchen, *Apg,* 534 (ET, 556-57); Pesch, *Apg,* 2:163-66; Roloff, *Apg,* 280-81; Zmijewski, *Apg,* 680-85; Schnackenburg 1991, 44.
[672]See Marshall, *Acts,* 305-6; Roloff, *Apg,* 281; K. Haacker, "Einige Fälle von 'erlebter Rede' im Neuen Testament," *NovT* 12 (1970): 70-77, esp. 76-77; Lichtenberger 1987, 50.
[673]With regard to the intention of Luke see Käsemann 1970, 1:163 (ET, 141).
[674]See Menzies 1991, 268-77; Spencer 1992, 232-39.
[675]Dobbeler 2000a, 201-2.
[676]See Turner 1996a, 389.
[677]Thiessen 1995, 74; Dobbeler 2000a, 199.
[678]Pesch, *Apg,* 2:163-66; Turner 1996a, 390; for the argument that follows above see ibid.

not have been believers in Jesus. These "disciples" had been baptized by John and were waiting for the Messiah, of whom John had preached.[679]

Luke's comment about Paul's first brief visit to Ephesus in the late summer of A.D. 51 (Acts 18:19-21), linked with the notice about Apollos (Acts 18:24-26) and about the "disciples" in Ephesus (Acts 19:1-3), raises the question of who established the church in Ephesus. Who was the first pioneer missionary who preached the gospel of Jesus Christ in the city and established a community of believers?

Several recent studies argue that the origins of the church in Ephesus were linked not with the mission of Paul but with the ministry of Apollos.[680] Matthias Günther asserts categorically that "the Alexandrian Apollos was the influential figure at the beginning of Ephesian Christianity."[681] This position assumes either that the comment in Acts 18:19-21 (Paul preached in the synagogue in Ephesus) is redactional and possesses no historical value,[682] or that Paul's short visit in Ephesus during his journey to Jerusalem was unsuccessful.[683] However, there are good reasons to accept the report of Paul's visit to Ephesus, including his preaching in the synagogue, in Acts 18:19-21 as historically reliable.[684] (1) The formulation "he left them there [Priscilla and Aquila in Ephesus], but first he himself [αὐτὸς δὲ] went into the synagogue" (Acts 18:19) emphasizes that the couple stayed in Ephesus, where they continued to reside (Acts 18:26) after Paul had left the city (Acts 18:21b). Richard Strelan suggests that the Ephesian Jews might have had their place of assembly outside the city walls: Paul left Aquila and Priscilla in the city, where they owned a house and/or a workshop, and visited the synagogue outside the city.[685] (2) Luke's account of the origins of the churches in Antioch (Acts 11:19-30) and in Rome (Acts 28:14-15) indicates that he has no difficulty attributing the establishment of churches to other missionaries. The suggestion that Luke included the comment about Paul's preaching in the synagogue in Ephesus in Acts 18:19b in order to accord to Paul the honor of the first Christian sermon in the city is weak.[686] If Luke had such intentions, he simply could have omitted the reference to the "disciples" and to Apollos.[687] And the text in Acts 18:19b-21a does not actually state that Paul established a church.

The view that Paul's short visit to Ephesus and his preaching in the synagogue mentioned in Acts 18:19-21 were unsuccessful seems more conjectural than the result of careful analysis. The following factors need to be observed. (1) Paul

---

[679]On the reception of the Spirit by the "disciples" see Turner 1996a, 391-97.

[680]See Günther 1995, 35-37, 46, 205; H. Koester 1995a, 126; Thiessen 1995, 45, 53; R. Strelan 1996, 213, 227; Fieger 1998, 73.

[681]Günther 1995, 205. For the discussion that follows above see Schnabel 1999, 367-72.

[682]See Haenchen, *Apg,* 525 (ET, 547-48); Zmijewski, *Apg,* 669; Thiessen 1995, 32-33.

[683]See Barrett, *Acts,* 2:879.

[684]See R. Strelan 1996, 204-10; Schnabel 1999, 369-70; Fitzmyer, *Acts,* 633, 635; Barrett, *Acts,* 2:878.

[685]R. Strelan 1996, 206-7.

[686]See C. K. Barrett's critique (*Acts,* 2:878) of the reconstruction by Ernst Haenchen (*Apg,* 525 [ET, 547]).

[687]The theories of Matthias Günther (1995, 54-55) on Apollos are purely speculative; see Schnabel 1999, 370.

preached the gospel of Jesus Christ in the synagogue in Ephesus: the verb *dia-legomai* (Acts 18:19) describes, as in Acts 17:2, the missionary discourse or lesson in the synagogue in which the apostle sought to win the listeners to faith in Jesus as Messiah.[688] In contrast to Acts 17:4, however, Luke does not report in Acts 18:19 that the sermon in the synagogue had any success; the first notice concerning Paul having success in Ephesus comes in connection with the apostle's longer stay in Ephesus (Acts 19:8). (2) Luke describes Paul's departure in Acts 18:21 with the verb *apotassomai,* as in Acts 18:18, where Paul's farewell from the "brothers" in Corinth is described. Of course, *apotassomai* could refer to the Christians in Corinth in Acts 18:18 and to the Jews of Ephesus in Acts 18:21. However, since *apotassomai* occurs only twice in the book of Acts, and since Luke reports only farewells of Paul to Christians,[689] it seems preferable to interpret Acts 18:21 in terms of a farewell to Christians. (3) The comment that Paul was asked to "stay" (*meinai* [Acts 18:20]) also supports the possibility that Ephesian Jews were converted during Paul's brief stopover in the city: in all other passages in the book of Acts the term *menein,* applied in a local context with regard to people, always relates to Christian believers.[690] If the Ephesians who asked Paul to stay were only interested Jews who wanted to converse with him about his message, then this hardly explains the comment that Paul was asked "to stay for a longer time" (ἐπὶ πλείονα χρόνον, *epi pleiona chronon* [Acts 18:20]). This note also suggests that Ephesian Jews were converted during Paul's first visit. (4) The "brothers" (ἀδελφοί, *adelphoi*) who provide Apollos with a letter of recommendation to the "disciples" (μαθηταί, *mathētai*) in Corinth (Acts 18:27) are Ephesian Jews who have been converted through the ministry of Apollos (Acts 18:25b, 26a) and of Aquila and Priscilla (Acts 18:26b). The possibility cannot be excluded that some of the "brothers" had been converted earlier during Paul's brief visit to Ephesus.[691] If scholars are prepared to interpret Acts 19:24-27a in terms of a successful mission of Apollos in Ephesus, without Luke commenting on the result of Apollos's "burning enthusiasm" (Acts 18:25) and "bold preaching" (Acts 18:26) in the synagogue, then the possibility should not be rejected that the missionary sermon of Paul in the synagogue mentioned in Acts 18:19b could have convinced Jewish listeners to come to faith in Jesus the Messiah. (5) Luke is interested neither in a "victory" of Paul nor in claims to responsibility for the first missionary "success" in a city: he is interested in a description of the expansion of the gospel. Luke reports historical facts in his acount of the early Christian mission, and he can narrate complex dramatic scenes: in Acts 18:19—19:10 he integrated the missionary ministry of Priscilla

---

[688]See Barrett, *Acts,* 2:810, 878.
[689]Acts 18:18; 20:1; see also 13:3; 16:40; 17:10, 14; 20:36-38.
[690]Acts 9:43; 16:15; 18:3; 21:7, 8.
[691]Thus Marshall, *Acts,* 304; cf. Towner 1989, 427.

and Aquila and Apollos in Ephesus into the context of Paul's missionary strategy.

It thus appears that Paul was the first missionary in Ephesus, although other Jewish Christians had a large role in the first months in the history of the Christian community in Ephesus. Paul's missionary work in Ephesus thus had three phases:

1. Paul visited Ephesus in the late summer of A.D. 51 on the occasion of his journey from Corinth to Jerusalem for several days (or weeks?). He preached in the synagogue, probably with some success. The first Ephesians who believed in Jesus as Messiah and Savior were members of the local synagogue: Jews and perhaps God-fearers.

2. Paul returned to Ephesus probably in the early summer of A.D. 52. He was able to teach and preach in the synagogue for three months (Acts 19:8). The fact that he was able to teach in the synagogue "boldly" (παρρησιάζομαι, *parrēsiazomai,* "to express oneself freely, speak openly, fearlessly") for three months, thus at least twelve sabbaths, is surprising: in general Paul's visits to the local synagogues became impossible much sooner. The conclusion that Paul was very much interested in the conversion of Ephesus's influential Jewish inhabitants[692] is not very illuminating. Paul was always eager to lead Jews to faith in Jesus Christ, whether they were "influential" or not. A more plausible conclusion focuses on the officials of the synagogue in Ephesus: either they were open to Paul's message of the revelation of the kingdom of God in Jesus the Messiah (Acts 19:8), or they were at least willing to examine his message for an extended period of time. The synagogue parted ways with Paul after three months "when some stubbornly refused to believe and spoke evil of the Way before the congregation" (Acts 19:9a)—that is, when some of the Jews, possibly some of the officials of the synagogue, opposed Paul's message and ridiculed the followers of Jesus.

3. The next phase of Paul's mission to Ephesus lasted for two years: Paul left the synagogue with the "disciples," the new converts, and held meetings in the lecture hall (*scholē*) of a certain Tyrannos, teaching and "arguing" daily (καθ᾽ ἡμεραν διαλεγόμενος, *kath᾽ hēmeran dialegomenos* [Acts 19:9-10]). The Western Text adds the comment that this happened "from the fifth to the tenth hour,"[693] or from ten in the morning to four in the afternoon. This comment may represent information that was reliably handed down;[694] it is at least a plausible specification for a guild hall or a lecture hall. The name "Tyrannos" is frequently attested both in western Asia Minor and in Ephesus.[695]

---

[692]Schnackenburg 1991, 44.

[693]Acts 19:9: ἀπὸ ὥρας ε᾽ [πέμπτης] ἕως ὥρας δεκάτης (D [614 2147 2412] gig w sy^{h*}).

[694]Schneider, *Apg,* 2:265 no. c. For the comment that follows above see Schnackenburg 1991, 45 n. 16.

[695]See Hemer 1989, 120-21, 243.

Luke notes in Acts 19:20 that "the word of the Lord grew mightily and prevailed"; he implies large numerical successes for Paul's missionary work in Ephesus.[696] The comment in Acts 19:10b informs us that during the two years that Paul worked in Ephesus "all the residents of Asia [πάντας τοὺς κατοικοῦντας τὴν Ἀσίαν], both Jews and Greeks, heard the word of the Lord." Luke does not specify this piece of information in geographical terms or in terms of Paul's missionary tactics or methods. Luke's information is confirmed by a comment in 1 Cor 16:19, where Paul conveys to the Christians in Corinth greetings from "the churches of Asia [αἱ ἐκκλησίαι τῆς Ἀσίας, hai ekklēsiai tēs Asias]," in a letter that he writes in Ephesus. Paul informs the Corinthian Christians in the same context that God has opened "a wide door for effective work" in Ephesus (1 Cor 16:8-9). Paul began his missionary efforts in Ephesus in A.D. 52, and he wrote 1 Corinthians in the spring of A.D. 54: it appears that in the two or three years between A.D. 52 and 54 several churches were established in the province of Asia. Luke and Paul probably think of the churches in Laodikeia, Hierapolis and Colossae in the Lykos Valley on the upper Maeander River that were established by Epaphras (Col 1:3-8; 4:13), and perhaps of a Christian community in Miletus (see below). It is impossible to confirm (or deny) whether the churches in Smyrna, Pergamon, Thyatira, Sardis and Philadelphia (see §22.7) were also established during this period.

Paul had several coworkers from the province of Asia during his mission to Ephesus:[697] Epaphras (Col 1:3-8; 4:13), Philemon (Philem 1-2), Aristarchus from Macedonia (Acts 19:29; 20:4; 27:2; Philem 23), Gaius from Corinth (Acts 19:29; 1 Cor 1:14), Tychicus and Trophimus (Acts 20:4; Col 4:7). Aquila and Priscilla were part of Paul's team of missionaries in Ephesus right from the beginning, as was Timothy (1 Cor 16:10). Later Stephanas, Fortunatus and Archaicus visited Paul in Ephesus (1 Cor 16:17). According to Acts 20:31, Paul stayed in Ephesus for three years altogether.

The success of Paul's missionary work in Ephesus was demonstrated not only in the conversions of Jews and Greeks in the city and in the province but also in miracles that happened. Luke does not recount any of these miracles (Acts 19:11), but he does report that they caused a serious misunderstanding among the population in the context of their traditional magical views, prompting them to believe that "handkerchiefs or aprons that had touched his skin" would be able to heal illnesses (Acts 19:12a). Hans-Josef Klauck comments, "They seemed to have had a materialistic view of miraculous power that could be subtracted from the person of the miracle worker and be stored. The pieces of cloth assume the function of amulets and charms that customarily were used in ancient

---

[696]See Schnackenburg 1991, 44. On Acts 19:20 see also Noordegraaf 1983, 136-46; Reinhardt 1995a, 263-77.
[697]Cf. Schnackenburg 1991, 45-46.

magic."[698] Despite the fact that this was a misunderstanding of the views of Paul, further miracles took place, including exorcisms of demons (Acts 19:12b). When Jewish exorcists who were active in Ephesus used the name of Jesus in their activities, perhaps as an experiment with a new magical formula, they suffered public divine punishment (Acts 19:13-16), an event that "became known to all residents of Ephesus, both Jews and Greeks," who were awestruck (Acts 19:17a). Luke notes that "they were all seized with fear" (TNIV; NRSV: "everyone was awestruck") and that "the name of the Lord Jesus was praised" (Acts 19:17b): this comment seems to assert that many people submitted to the power that was demonstrated publicly in connection with Paul's ministry, implying that the missionary success became even larger.[699] These events caused many of the new converts to confess openly and publicly their own involvement with magical practices: they brought their magic texts to the church, worth 50,000 silver drachmas, and burned them publicly (Acts 19:18-19). The amount of 50,000 silver drachmas (denarii) corresponds to 200,000 sesterces, a huge amount: one day laborer would have to work 50,000 days (137 years) to earn this sum. It is impossible to calculate the number of believers in Ephesus on the basis of this figure: Luke may be describing the activities of the poorer Christians in Acts 19:18, and in Acts 19:19 the actions of the more wealthy believers, who could afford to buy magic texts.[700]

Wolfgang Reinbold considers that Paul and Timothy could have sold the magic books and "live from the proceeds for the rest of their lives and promote their missionary work"[701]— the Jewish-Christian missionaries would never have even dreamed of such an idea. Neither Jews, who follow the Torah, nor Christians, who proclaim the arrival of the kingdom of God and want to lead polytheists to faith in the true God and in his Savior, would ever seek to profit from occult practices or objects. Reinbold regards the comment in Acts 19:18-19 as redactional, a result of the theological interests of Luke, who wanted to declare the imminent end of sorcery and magic.

The collection of Greek magical papyri that Karl Preisendanz published, as well as Hans Dieter Betz's edition of Greek magical papyri and Demotic spells, provide authentic insights into the kind of material that was destroyed in the action that Luke describes in Acts 19:18-19. A large number of magical texts describe how to make amulets that protect against demons and how to concoct love charms. The text *PGM* IV 1390-1495 recommends dipping seven pieces of bread into the blood of gladiators or other heroes and throwing them together with some soil into the house of the person whom one wants to woo. Other texts describe charms meant to harm other people. The text *PGM* III 1-164 suggests that one should drown a cat while praying to the "cat-faced god" to seek vengeance and to harm enemies; the texts ends with the lines "This is the ritual of the cat that is useful for every ritual purpose: as curse against charioteers in the race, to summon

---

[698]Klauck 1996, 113; on the failed attempt at exorcism reported in Acts 19:13-16 see ibid., 114-16.
[699]See Roloff, *Apg,* 287; followed by Pesch, *Apg,* 2:173.
[700]See Witherington, *Acts,* 582.
[701]Reinbold 2000, 148.

dreams, as binding love charm or to sow discord and hatred." Many magic texts use *voces mysticae,* "semantically meaningless phonetic sequences that were an indispensable part of spells."[702] For example, the text *PGM* I 222-231 reads, "Indispensable invisibility spell: Take fat or an eye of a nightowl and a ball of dung rolled by a beetle and oil of an unripe olive and grind them all together until smooth, and smear your whole body with it and say to Helios: 'I adjure you by your great name, *borkē phoiour iō zizia aparxeouch thythe lailam aaaaaa iiiii oooo ieō ieō ieō ieō ieō ieō ieō naunax ai ai aeō aeō ēaō,'* and moisten it and say in addition, 'Make me invisible, lord Helios, *aeō ōaē eiē ēaō,* in the presence of any man until sunset, *iō iō ō phrixrizō eōa.'*"[703]

The immense success of Paul's missionary work in Ephesus is indirectly confirmed by the hostility that Paul experienced in the city. In 1 Cor 15:32 Paul asserts that he was in a very dangerous situation while in Ephesus; his comment that he "fought with wild animals in Ephesus" (ἐθηριομάχησα ἐν Ἐφέσῳ, *ethēriomachēsa en Ephesō*) can hardly have a literal meaning: a Roman citizen could not be sentenced *ad bestias* unless he had previously lost his citizenship rights—rights that Paul claims when he appeals to the emperor (Acts 22:25-29). In addition, hardly anyone ever survived a fight with wild animals, and Paul's extensive list of trials and sufferings in 2 Cor 11:23-33 probably would have included a reference to such a horrific experience had it actually happened.[704] The reference to a fight with wild animals metaphorically states that Paul had to "fight for his life"—evidently in a specific situation, perhaps in connection with the incident in which Aquila and Priscilla risked their lives for the apostles (Rom 16:3-4). Many scholars assume that Paul was thrown into prison in Ephesus,[705] a hypothesis that cannot be confirmed.

Another major incident happened evidently during the last months of Paul's mission to Ephesus, causing a general uproar in the city. A silversmith name Demetrios invited his colleagues from the guild of silversmiths to a meeting; he acted either as a large-scale entrepreneur in the manufacture and sale of devotional articles within the parameters of the rights of associations,[706] or as the dominant member of a guild whose interests coincided with those of his suppliers. Luke describes Demetrios as an "exponent of a guild that was interested in the temple for economic reasons only." The guild of silversmiths in Ephesus is attested in inscriptions.[707] The meeting that Luke mentions in Acts 19:23-40

---

[702]Klauck 1995-1996, 1:183.

[703]Betz, *Greek Magical Papyri,* 9; German translation in Klauck 1995-1996, 1:184.

[704]Schrage, *1 Kor,* 4:243; for the interpretation that follows above see ibid., 244.

[705]On the basis of Philem 22; Phil 1:12-26; 2 Cor 1:8-11. See Duncan 1930, 57-161; Stuhlmacher, *Philem,* 1975; Gnilka, *Phil,* 57-58; Weiser, *Apg,* 2:543; Schnackenburg 1991, 46; Becker 1992, 169 (ET, 159).

[706]Selinger 1997, 244-45. For the comment that follows above see Lampe 1992, 68.

[707]*I. Ephesos* II 425, 547, 585, 586; III 636; VI 2212, 2441; D. Knibbe and B. İplikçioğlu, *JÖAI* 55 (1984): 130-31; Horsley, *NewDocs* 4:7-10. The *neopoios* Demetrios who is mentioned in *I. Ephesos* V 1578 is not identical with the Demetrios of Acts 19:24; see Ramsay 1893, 113-34; Horsley, *NewDocs* 4:8; Lampe 1992, 66-69; Trebilco 1994, 336 with n. 203.

could have taken place in connection with the Artemis festival in March or April; according to 1 Cor 16:8, Paul wanted to stay in Ephesus until the Feast of Pentecost, which was celebrated in the beginning of June.[708]

Scholars dispute the historicity of the events described in Acts 19:23-40. Ernst Haenchen believes that the account is the creation of the author of the book of Acts, Gerd Lüdemann assumes that Luke tests his skills in inventing stories, "presenting his own theological ideas about the political harmlessness of the Christians and the missionary power of the Christian faith."[709] Gunther Bornkamm is convinced that the Lukan narrative is historically more or less worthless.[710] Jürgen Roloff asserts that the author has reworked traditions, but traditions that did not concern Paul but rather a later "critical situation from the early period of the church."[711] Helga Botermann argues that the skepticism of these New Testament scholars is a prejudice: "Should the chancellor have stayed at home and waited for the appearance of the proconsul in person in the assembly? Or should he have challenged the assembly to start a pogrom?"[712] Friedemann Quass, like Botermann a classical scholar, likewise regards the narrated events as essentially authentic; in regard to Acts 19:40 he refers to the inscription *I. Knidos* 71 as a parallel.[713] Reinhard Selinger, a legal historian, remarks that the author "does a magnificent job as a whole, with incoherent individual facts contradicting the total conception only in appearance. His conception is grounded in a realistic perception of the administrative structure of the city of Ephesos. Persons and offices are integrated in the narrative in a manner that is so close to reality that the sequence of events ensues with a certain consistency automatically. The historical and legal ambience of Ephesos is present in the Demetrios saga in such clear form and with such sharp contours that we are forced to presuppose of the author a large amount of detailed knowledge of the theory and practice of Greek city government."[714] The inscription *I. Ephesos* II 215 is an important parallel for the economic motives of the silversmiths and for their behavior as narrated in Acts 19:25-27: assemblies of the guilds of the bakers (*artokopoi*) in the agora of Ephesus provoked confusion and riots among the population (*dēmos*) in the city, "with the result that it happens that sometimes the *dēmos* falls into confusion and uproar because of the assembling together and insolence of the bakers at the agora."[715] The inscription *I. Ephesos* VI 2212 (published in 1980), dating to the time of Emperor Claudius or later, attests the association of silversmiths in Ephesus: "This tomb and the area around it and the subterranean vault belong to M. Antonius Hermeias, silversmith *[neipoios]*, and Claudia daughter of Erotion, his

---

[708]Bruce, *Acts,* 416; cf. Selinger 1997, 245 n. 22.

[709]Haenchen, *Apg,* 554 (ET, 577-78); Lüdemann 1987, 227-28 (ET, 219-20; John Bowden's translation of "Fabulierkunst" as "narrative skill" is incorrect: "fabulieren" means "to tell or invent stories, fable, romance").

[710]Bornkamm 1993, 95.

[711]Roloff, *Apg,* 291; cf. Molthagen 1991, 70; H. Koester 1995b, 126-31.

[712]Botermann 1996, 168 n. 545.

[713]Friedemann Quass, *Die Honoratiorenschicht in den Städten des griechischen Ostens* (Stuttgart: Steiner, 1993), 358, quoted in Botermann 1996, 168.

[714]Selinger 1997, 259.

[715]Horsley, *NewDocs* 4:9-10; cf. W. M. Buckler, in *Anatolian Studies Presented to W. M. Ramsay* (ed. W. H. Buckler and W. M. Calder; Manchester: Manchester University Press, 1923), 30-33; R. Merkelbach, "Ephesische Parerga (18): Der Bäckerstreik," *ZPE* 30 (1978): 164-65. For the comment that follows above see Horsley, *NewDocs* 4:7-8, no. 1.

wife. No one is to be put in this tomb except the aforementioned. If anyone does dare to put in a corpse or excise this text, he shall pay to the silversmiths at Ephesos 1000 denarii. Responsibility for this tomb rests with the association of silversmiths, and Erotion dedicated 50,000 denarii. The legacy was provided in the 6th month, on the appointed 8th day."

Demetrios the silversmith gave a forceful speech (Acts 19:25b-27) in which he asserted that the sale of reproductions of the temple of Artemis had been suffering and voiced his fear that there might be far-reaching consequences for his trade and for the cult of Artemis. Demetrios's speech, if we assume the historical authenticity of its content, implies the tangible success of Paul's missionary work in the city of Ephesus.[716]

Richard Strelan downplays the reference to Paul in Acts 19:26 when he asserts that the message of Paul was hardly new for the Ephesians because for many centuries Greek authors had made monotheistic statements and issued criticisms of idol images; he believes that the effect of Paul's message that Demetrios mentions refers only to citizens of Ephesus whose opinion Paul changed concerning the question of whether idol images made by human beings are gods, and he believes that the text does not indicate whether these people were indeed convinced by Paul.[717] This position is unconvincing. If Demetrios's complaint does *not* presuppose considerable success of Paul's missionary work in Ephesus, then only two options remain: either the author of the book of Acts has freely invented the scene (something that Strelan does not assume), or Strelan simply insists on his a priori opinion that Paul had no success among the Gentile citizens of Ephesus. This is the alternative: either Paul's missionary work in Ephesus was unsuccessful, in which case the episode of the silversmiths is not historical, or the silversmith episode is historical, in which case Paul's missionary efforts must have led to the conversion of a significant number of Gentiles in the city, a development that resulted in declining sales of religious devotional items or at least in the apprehension that such a decline in revenues was imminent.

Luke reports that Paul had friends among the "Asiarchs" (Ἀσιάρχαι, *Asiarchai*) who wanted to protect him and who advised him not to go into the theater while the citizens were in uproar because of Demetrios's speech (Acts 19:31).[718] The Asiarchs, attested in inscriptions,[719] are not identical with the high priests of the imperial cult in the province,[720] nor are they the delegates of the provincial assembly (*koinon*) of the province of Asia.[721] The Asiarchs were high officials of

---

[716]See Schnabel 1999, 375; Fitzmyer, *Acts,* 658; Barrett, *Acts,* 2:925-27; Zmijewski, *Apg,* 710-11.

[717]R. Strelan 1996, 137-38; for the critique that follows above see Schnabel 1999, 375-76.

[718]See Kearsley 1994; Gill 1994a, 81.

[719]See Lesslie Ross Taylor, "The Asiarchs," in *Begs.* 5:256-262; Magie 1950, 1:449-50; 2:1298; Sherwin-White 1963, 88-90; M. Rossner, "Asiarchen und Archiereis Asias," *Studii Clasice* 16 (1974): 101-42; Baugh 1990, 132-64; Rosalinde A. Kearsley, *NewDocs* 4:46-55; idem 1994, with text and translation of all relevant inscriptions (368-76).

[720]Contra Taylor, "The Asiarchs"; Rossner, "Asiarchen und Archiereis Asias," 106-7; Price 1984, 60.

[721]Contra Schneider, *EWNT* 1:415 (*EDNT* 1:172); Roloff, *Apg,* 293; Jervell, *Apg,* 491.

the city who introduced motions in the assemblies of the city council, dedicated buildings, built statues and organized festivals and games.[722] Were these Asiarchs whom Paul knew Christian believers? The formulation ὄντες αὐτῷ φίλοι (*ontes autō philoi*, "who were friendly to him") does not state this explicitly; it may simply describe a friendly disposition.[723] Luke's comment in Acts 19:31 implies, however, that Paul knew high officials in the city of Ephesus very well. Since there is no evidence that Paul sought official protection from the magistrates of Ephesus, we may assume that his acquaintance with the Asiarchs was the result of his missionary work. And it is safe to assume that Paul would have explained to them his message about Jesus the Messiah and Savior.

Gerhard Schneider argues that Luke uses the Asiarchs as "witnesses for the defense" of Paul: their intervention in support of Paul shows that they had no objections against him and his message as far as the state cult was concerned.[724] This interpretation is unconvincing: Jacob Jervell correctly observes, "This connection with the elite does not make the message incontestable. That is something that Luke would have had to express much more clearly, especially in connection with the breakup of the crowd assembled in the theater."[725] Doubts regarding their intervention for Paul are unnecessary: (1) The text does not say that *all* the Asiarchs wanted to help Paul; on the contrary, Luke states that "some" (*tines*) wanted to help the apostle.[726] (2) The text does not presuppose that the Asiarchs *immediately* thought of Paul when the commotion began.[727] (3) Why should it be strange or surprising that leading officials of the city of Ephesus were friendly toward Paul?[728] There is no valid reason to question the authenticity of Luke's note. If leading officials of Ephesus indeed knew Paul, if they were aware of his missionary work in the city and were sympathetic toward him, whether as converted Christians or as friendly discussion partners, then it remains entirely plausible from a historical point of view that they wanted to protect Paul amidst a riot that the magistrates could not tolerate for political reasons anyway.

Michael White links the development of the church in Ephesus with the openness of the city to aliens and foreigners.[729] The growth of the city of Ephesus and its population, mentioned in literary sources and documented by the history of building activity and by epigraphical sources, cannot be explained without reference to a considerable influx of aliens. The growth of Ephesus in the second and third centuries A.D. to two hundred thousand inhabitants requires a yearly influx of 1,769 non-Ephesians, who comprised 50 percent of the population after fifty years. White suggests that the strikingly positive attitude of the Asiarchs over against (the "Lukan") Paul in Acts 19:31 becomes plausible in this context.

The attempts of a Jewish official named Alexander to calm the crowd were

---

[722]See Kearsley 1994, 366.

[723]See Jervell, *Apg,* 491.

[724]Schneider, *Apg,* 2:277; cf. Haenchen, *Apg,* 555 (ET, 578).

[725]Jervell, *Apg,* 491.

[726]Contra Haenchen, *Apg,* 550 (ET, 574: "and indeed every one of them"); Zmijewski, *Apg,* 712.

[727]Haenchen, *Apg,* 550 (ET, 574); followed by Zmijewski, *Apg,* 712.

[728]Contra Zmijewski, *Apg,* 712.

[729]White 1995, 36-38; following E. Haenchen and G. Lüdemann. However, White refuses to evaluate the evidence of the book of Acts for the history of Ephesus in the middle of the first century A.D. (36).

unsuccessful (Acts 19:32-34). It is unclear what his specific intentions were and whether he was in any way connected with Paul. Luke describes what happened: "Some of the crowd gave instructions to Alexander, whom the Jews had pushed forward. And Alexander motioned for silence and tried to make a defense before the people. But when they recognized that he was a Jew, for about two hours all of them shouted in unison, 'Great is Artemis of the Ephesians!'" (Acts 19:33-34). Most scholars interpret the reaction of the Ephesians as anti-Semitic furor from the mob.[730] Some scholars suggest that Jews and Christians, most of them presumably of Jewish background, attempted to survive the riot in an alliance born of emergency and necessity.[731] Some identify Alexander with Alexander the coppersmith mentioned in 2 Tim 4:14, while others describe him as a Jewish Christian without assuming this identification.[732] Such considerations must remain hypothetical. Alexander's intervention does not calm the crowd. Reinhard Selinger remarks, "The people shout down the Jews; the Asiarchs (and later the secretary) protect the Christians. In the competition for the favor of patronal friendship in a pagan context, the Jews of Ephesus lost for the first time to the Christians."[733] This interpretation is correct as long we do not understand the reference to the "competition for the favor of patronal friendship" as an interpretation of the motives of Paul or of the Ephesian church.

The intervention of the secretary of the assembly of the people (grammateus, the chief executive officer of the city), one of the highest officials in the city,[734] transformed the agitated crowd in the theater into an assembly of the dēmos: he addresses the people as citizens of Ephesus (Acts 19:35). The grammateus faces "the legal problem that a riot is in progress in which uncontested matters are discussed and in which innocent people are held responsible."[735] According to Luke's report, the intervention of the grammateus focused on five elements. (1) He first analyzed the facts. He confirmed that the city of Ephesus was responsible for the cult of Artemis. He noted that the public order had been disturbed. He pointed out the danger that the citizens might do something reckless (propetēs)—that is, act illegally (Acts 19:35b-36). (2) He examined the accusations against Gaius and Aristarchus, or the accusations against the Christians,

[730]Conzelmann, Apg, 123 (ET, 166); Haenchen, Apg, 551-52 (ET, 574-75); Schneider, Apg, 2:277; Roloff, Apg, 293; Zmijewski, Apg, 730; Jervell, Apg, 492; Trebilco 1991, 24-25; Stegemann and Stegemann 1995, 285-87; Thiessen 1995, 103-5.
[731]See Setzer 1994, 54-57.
[732]See Lampe 1992, 71-74; also Meyer, Apg, 354-55; R. Strelan 1996, 148-50.
[733]Selinger 1997, 253.
[734]Claudia Schulte, Die Grammateis von Ephesos: Schreiberamt und Sozialstruktur in einer Provinzhauptstadt des römischen Kaiserreiches (Heidelberger althistorische Beiträge und epigraphische Studien 15; Stuttgart: Steiner, 1994); see also Magie 1950, 1:60; Lampe 1992, 61-62; Trebilco 1994, 351; Selinger 1997, 254-55 with n. 69; for the comment that follows above see ibid., 255-56.
[735]Selinger 1997, 257; for the analysis that follows above see ibid., 255-58.

who are accused of robbing the temple and blaspheming Artemis (Acts 19:37). Jews were often accused of *sacrilegium,* a charge that Roman legal texts treat as theft but was regarded as quite serious on account of its consequences: the disturbance of public order. (3) Since the accusation was groundless, the *grammateus* referred the plaintiffs, whom he did not address directly, to the court of competent jurisdiction—in this case, the proconsul and the appropriate assize days (Acts 19:38). (4) He suggested that any additional claims that the plaintiffs might have should be discussed in a future meeting of the *dēmos* (Acts 19:39). (5) Since he could not detect illegal activities on the part of Gaius and Aristarchus, and since therefore there was no immediate need to make a decision, the *grammateus* ordered the dissolution of the meeting in the theater, warning the crowd that public order must be reestablished because a tumult could have serious negative consequences for the city (Acts 19:40): as an autonomous city, Ephesus had no interest in appealing to the Roman proconsul.

Luke's report of the speech of the *grammateus* seems to reflect civil respect for pagan religious institutions (Acts 19:35-36): he formulates in Acts 19 no theological critique of the cult of Artemis, but rather an ethical critique of the devotees of Artemis.

Matthias Günther maintains that Paul failed as a missionary in Ephesus, and Richard Strelan is convinced that it is very unlikely that any pagans were converted in Ephesus.[736] These pessimistic assessments are unconvincing for several reasons. (1) Since Paul taught in the lecture hall of Tyrannos for two years, the suggestion that Paul did not get "a foot on the ground" is quite incomprehensible.[737] Paul was always willing to revise or to abandon his missionary plans (Acts 16:6-7); he even left Athens after a relatively short time. If he had had no success in Ephesus, he would not have stayed for two years. (2) Strelan argues that the vitality of the cult of Artemis and the religious satisfaction of the devotees of Artemis speak against the probability that Gentile citizens of Ephesus were converted. This view is convincing only if one could prove that neither Paul nor other missionaries had much success among Gentiles if the religiosity of the pagans was *not* in decline; if one could prove that even if this assumption does not apply to cities such as Antioch, Corinth and Rome, it does apply to Ephesus; and if one could prove that this assumption is correct not only for the first century but also for the second century. The mission-historical, geographical and chronological consequences of Stelan's position are unconvincing. (3) Strelan overlooks the fact that Paul's gospel message was problematic not only for "vital" pagans but also for the equally vital Judaism as well (cf. 1 Cor 1:23; Gal 5:11). If Strelan is correct, then Paul also would have been unsuccessful among Jews. (4) Strelan overlooks not only Acts 19:10 and Acts 19:18 but also the fact Luke's account of the riot instigated by the silversmiths in Acts 19:23-40 places not Paul in the center of the events but rather "the Way" (Acts 19:23), presupposing a larger number of Gentile Christians in Ephesus.[738]

---

[736]Günther 1995, 29-76; R. Strelan 1996, 129-53. For the discussion that follows above see Schnabel 1999, 372-78.

[737]Contra Günther (1995, 60), who provides no arguments for his radical destruction of the historical value of the passage, but simply follows Weiser, *Apg.*

[738]Richard Strelan (1996, 133-34) accepts the silversmith episode as basically historical.

Wolfgang Reinbold believes that Paul's missionary work in Ephesus was slow and that Paul was unable to establish a viable church that survived. He supports his position with five arguments.[739] (1) Paul lived in the house of Aquila and Priscilla, who were not Ephesian citizens, a fact that indicates that there was no one in Ephesus who had a house in which Paul could stay, in contrast to Philippi, where he stayed in the house of Lydia, and in contrast to Corinth, where he lived in the house of Titius Justus. (2) Paul engaged in missionary work in Ephesus for a longer period than in other cities, but the book of Acts has "not a single specific success" to report. (3) The church seems to have been so small that it could meet in Aquila's workshop for a longer period (1 Cor 16:19), in contrast to Corinth, where the church moved to the house of Titius Justus (Acts 18:7). (4) Paul repeatedly speaks of great difficulties during his time in Ephesus (1 Cor 16:9; 2 Cor 1:8-10). (5) The church in Ephesus evidently did not contribute to the collection for the Jerusalem church.

These arguments are unconvincing. (1) The first two considerations are based on an argument from silence: Luke does not state that Paul lived in the house of Aquila or that the church of Ephesus met there. In 1 Cor 16:9 a church is attested in the house of Aquila and Priscilla, while the formulation ἡ κατ᾽ οἶκον αὐτῶν ἐκκλησία (hē kat᾽ oikon autōn ekklēsia) suggests that several churches existed in Ephesus, the city from which Paul wrote 1 Corinthians.[740] The addition παρ᾽ οἷς ξενίζομαι (par᾽ hois xenizomai) in several manuscripts (D* F G it vg^cl) presupposes that Paul lived with Aquila and Priscilla, but this addition is secondary. This means that we have no reliable information about Paul's living arrangements in Ephesus, nor do we know where the first church met or how many house churches existed in Ephesus. Reinbold looks for situations that are comparable with Paul's missionary work in other cities, which is a curious inconsistency because he regards the Lukan "Grundmodell" of the Pauline mission—with its stages of preaching in the synagogue, (successes), opposition, separation—as redactional and thus of little historical value.[741] (2) The claim that Luke does not report specific successes of Paul's preaching in Ephesus is curious; Reinbold can defend that position only because he eliminates Luke's reference to the burning of magic books as a redactional creation of the author, and he regards the account of the episode in the theater, suggestive of an immense success of Paul's missionary work, as nothing more than "the recollection of a critical situation in the early period of the church."[742] Reinbold also regards the "summary success notices" in Acts 19:10, 17, 20 as redactional, and he believes that the reference to the elders of the church in Ephesus in Acts 20:17-18 is a creation of Luke. If a scholar removes all references to the dramatic effects of the missionary work of Paul both on the new converts and on the citizens of Ephesus and all summary statements that note the success of Paul's work as historically worthless, and does so without providing solid and objective historical arguments for such literary-critical operations, then the scholar invites the charge of methodological arbitrariness. Reinbold demands that the claim of "specific accomplishments" of Paul's mission in Ephesus would have to be proven with the names of converts. He is aware, of course, of three converts in Ephesus whose names are known: Epaenetus, "the first convert [first fruits] in Asia for Christ" (Rom 16:5), who probably came from Ephesus, the first city in the province of Asia in which Paul did missionary work, as well as Tychicus (Acts 20:4; Col 4:7) and Trophimus (Acts 20:4; 21:29). Reinbold accepts the connection of these converts with Ephesus but downplays their significance for Paul's

---

[739]Reinbold 2000, 151, with n. 138; similarly Günther 1995, 29-75; R. Strelan 1996, 23, 294-95.
[740]See Fee, 1 Cor, 835; Schrage, 1 Kor, 4:467.
[741]Reinbold 2000, 148, with regard to the mission in Ephesus.
[742]Reinbold 2000, 148 n. 124 (with a quotation from Roloff, Apg, 291); for the comment that follows above see ibid., 151 n. 138; on Acts 20:17-18 see ibid., 157.

missionary work in Ephesus when he states that with these men "we know only a few persons who probably were won by Paul in Ephesus." (Reinbold is correct, however, when he rejects the view of some scholars who suggest that the list of greetings in Rom 16:3-16 was addressed to Ephesus and thus contains the names of Ephesian Christians.) It is hard to imagine what Reinbold would accept as proof for a successful mission of Paul in Ephesus. (3) We have no information about the size of the church in Ephesus. The comment in 1 Cor 16:9 constitutes probable evidence for several house churches in the city. If "all the brothers" send greetings from Ephesus, where Paul writes 1 Corinthians (1 Cor 16:20), we indeed do not know how many Christians lived in Ephesus; however, in the context of 1 Cor 16:20 the phrase "all the brothers" clearly implies the existence of a church in Ephesus. The existence of a church in the city is further attested by the address in Eph 1:1 (at least in some manuscripts) as well as by the prophetic oracle addressed to the church in Ephesus in Rev 2:1-7; the fact that the first of the prophetic messages to seven churches in the province of Asia is addressed to Ephesus confirms the importance of the Ephesian church at least for the last decades of the first century. (4) The fact that Paul mentions difficulties that he experienced during his work in Ephesus does not exclude the possibility that his missionary activities were successful; on the contrary: trials, hostility, pressure and persecution usually are evidence for missionary "success." (5) The assumption that the church in Ephesus did not participate in the collection of funds that Paul organized in support of the church in Jerusalem can be maintained only if, as Reinbold claims, the list in Acts 20:4 should not be connected with the collection.[743] However, many scholars link the list of Paul's travel companions in Acts 20:4 ("he was accompanied by Sopater son of Pyrrhus from Beroea, by Aristarchus and Secundus from Thessalonica, by Gaius from Derbe, and by Timothy, as well as by Tychicus and Trophimus from Asia") with representatives of the individual churches who contributed to the collection[744]—including Trophimus, who came from Ephesus (cf. Acts 21:29), and Tychicus, who probably came from Ephesus as well.

We have no data that would allow us to characterize the church in Ephesus in more detail or to provide a sociological description of its members, apart from the information, which is neither novel nor surprising, that the church consisted of Jewish believers and of Gentile believers. The church in Corinth should not hastily be used as a pattern.[745] The city of Corinth was a Roman colony, a fact that implies that its citizenship very probably represented a somewhat different composition. The farewell speech of Paul before the elders of the church of Ephesus, given in Miletus, reported by Luke in Acts 20:17-36, does not provide much detailed information either. The comment that Paul proclaimed the gospel and taught "publicly and from house to house" (Acts 20:20) may indicate the presence of several house churches, but this is not a necessary conclusion. The reference to "the church of God" (Acts 20:28), formulated in the singular, may imply the existence of only one house church, or it may describe the community of all the believers in Ephesus irrespective of the number of meeting places they used. The disclaimer "I coveted no one's silver or gold or clothing" (Acts 20:33) may imply that some Ephesian

---

[743]Reinbold 2000, 151 n. 138; cf. ibid., 155-56.
[744]Zmijewski, *Apg,* 720; Pesch, *Apg,* 2:185-6; Marshall, *Acts,* 323; Witherington, *Acts,* 603.
[745]*Pace* Schnackenburg 1991, 47-48.

believers were wealthy, but Paul may simply be asserting that he had worked in Ephesus not to make money or to gain some other material advantage.

The history of the church in Ephesus after Paul left can be reconstructed, at least in its broad outlines, on the basis of several texts. (1) The farewell speech before the elders of the church of Ephesus, given in Miletus (Acts 20:17-36).[746] (2) The Epistle to the Ephesians, whose address in Eph 1:1, "to the saints who are *in Ephesus*," seems to have been added later (it is lacking in the earliest manuscripts), evidently was a general letter to the churches in the province of Asia. It therefore allows only general conclusions concerning the situation in Ephesus. (3) The First Epistle to Timothy, which presupposes the presence of Timothy in Ephesus (1 Tim 1:3). (4) The Second Epistle to Timothy, with a reference to Onesiphorus as a missionary coworker in Ephesus (2 Tim 1:16-18). (5) The prophetic message to the church Ephesus in Rev 2:1-7, which deals with the situation of the church in Ephesus and reflects details of the history of the city.[747] (6) The Gospel of John, the book of Revelation and the Epistles of John, if we accept the early Christian tradition that connects these texts with John the apostle and his ministry in Ephesus. Scholars who reject these earliest traditions and ascribe these texts to other authors often relate these texts to developments in churches in the province of Asia more generally. (7) The letter from Ignatius of Antioch to the church in Ephesus, written in Smyrna in the late summer of A.D. 113 at the latest (Eusebius, *Hist. eccl.* 3.36.5-6), addressed to Onesimus the bishop, to Burrhus the deacon and to a certain Crocus and to other Christians in Ephesus (Ign. *Eph.* 1:3; 2:1).

The history of the church in Ephesus still needs to be written, despite studies by Matthias Günther and Werner Thiessen.[748] There is no consensus regarding the identity and the message of the false teachers whom the farewell address of Miletus announces and who form the backdrop of the Epistles to Timothy and the Johannine literature. There is also no consensus regarding the question of whether there were "Pauline" and "Johannine" churches in Ephesus. Rudolf Schnackenburg suggests that there was both a "Johannine association of churches" with its center in Ephesus and "a large Pauline church" ("paulinische Großgemeinde") in Ephesus.[749] Questions of authorship and date of individual texts are as important in this discussion as is the question of how one should deal with the contradictions or the complementary nature of theological positions, ethical points of view and ecclesiologi-

---

[746]See, besides the commentaries, Schürmann 1962; Dupont 1966; H.-J. Michel 1973; Prast 1979; Pereira 1983, 199-202; Tannehill 1986-1990, 2:252-61; Aejmelaeus 1987; Gempf 1988, 268-340; T. C. Alexander 1990; Thiessen 1995, 143-247; Walton 2000. On the connections with Pauline material in the speech see Porter 1999, 117-18. With regard to the next point above and the text-critical problem of the address in Eph 1:1 see E. Best, "Recipients and Title of the Letter to the Ephesians: Why and When the Designation 'Ephesians'?" *ANRW* II.24.4 (1987): 3247-79; idem, *Eph*, 98-101; Lincoln, *Eph*, 1-4; Hoehner, *Eph*, 144-48 (who argues for Ephesus as the originally intended destination of the letter).

[747]See Ramsay 1904, 151-81; Hemer 1986, 35-56; also the commentaries.

[748]Günther 1995; Thiessen 1995; cf. Schnackenburg 1991.

[749]Schnackenburg 1991, 60.

cal measures of the early Christian missionaries, theologians and churches.[750]

The Second and Third Epistles of John attest for the late 80s or early 90s A.D. that traveling missionaries continued to be active, visiting churches (2 John 10; 3 John 5-8). However, the two letters are too short to provide any certainty concerning the identity and origins of these missionaries. Hans-Josef Klauck believes that "Johannine Christianity" never had much missionary success because it faced the "danger of divisions" in Asia Minor: "They did not fish with the net . . . but with the fishing rod. Missionary outreach to individuals and counseling of individuals was the order of the day."[751] Klauck appeals to Jesus' conversations with individuals in the Gospel of John (Jn 3—4) as evidence. This hypothesis is pure speculation that is unsupported by the scant and fragmentary pieces of information that we have. Justin Martyr, born around A.D. 100 in Shechem (Nablus) of pagan parents, was converted probably in Ephesus between A.D. 120 and 130. Justin describes his conversion as the belated result of a conversation with an old man whom he never saw again (Justin, *Dial.* 8.1). Eusebius claims to know that this dialogue took place in Ephesus (*Hist. eccl.* 4.18.6).[752]

Evangelism in Miletus?

When Paul visited Miletus in April of A.D. 57, he dialogued with the leadership of the church in Ephesus (Acts 20:15, 17-38). The location of this dialogue suggests that there was a church in Miletus. The possibility cannot be excluded that Paul visited Miletus while he was engaged in missionary work in Ephesus: Miletus could easily be reached within two or three days; it is also possible that coworkers of Paul brought the gospel to Miletus, or that he met citizens of Miletus who visited Ephesus and heard him preach there. Luke's account in Acts 20:17-38 implies that there was a house in Miletus in which Christians could meet, suggesting the existence of a church.

Miletus (Μίλητος; mod. Balat),[753] about 70 km south of Ephesus, could be reached on the

---

[750]See Schnabel 1999, 381-82.

[751]Klauck 1985, 204.

[752]See Karl Semisch, *Justin der Märtyrer: Eine kirchen- und dogmengeschichtliche Monographie* (2 vols.; Breslau: Scholz, 1840-1842), 1:18-21; T. Zahn, "Studien zu Justinus Martyr," *ZKG* 8 (1886): 1-84, esp. 46-48; cf. Harnack 1893-1904, 2.1:281; Skarsaune 1976; T. Heckel 1999, 311.

[753]H. von Gärtringen and M. Mayer, PW 15.2 (1932): 1568-1655; K. Ziegler and W. Zschietzschmann, "Miletos 2," *KP* 3:1295-98; G. Kleiner, *PECS* 578-82; K. L. MacKay, *GBL* 2:979-80; P. N. Ure et al., *OCD* 980; V. von Graeve, *DNP* 8:170-80; Magie 1950, 1:73-74, 90-91, 97-98, 100-101, 104, 469-70; 2:882-83 n. 79; Bean 1966, 219-30; Gerhard Kleiner, *Die Ruinen von Milet* (Berlin: de Gruyter 1968); Wolfgang Müller-Wiener, *Milet 1899-1980: Ergebnisse, Probleme und Perspektiven einer Ausgrabung* (Istanbuler Mitteilungen 31; Tübingen: Wasmuth, 1986); Vanessa B. Gorman, *Miletos, The Ornament of Ionia: A History of the City to 400 B.C.E.* (Ann Arbor: University of Michigan Press, 2001). Excavations: *Milet 1-6* (6 vols.; Deutsches Archäologisches Institut; Berlin: de Gruyter, 1903-1997 [vol. 4 deals with the theater, vol. 6 presents the inscriptions]); on the coins of Miletus see Barbara Deppert-Lippitz, *Die Münzprägung Milets vom vierten bis ersten Jahrhundert v.Chr.* (Aarau: Sauerländer, 1984); see the continuing reports in *Archäologischer Anzeiger*. See <http://www.ruhr-uni-bochum.de/milet>. The Foundation of the Hellenic World offers 3D-projections of individual buildings: <http://www2.fhw.gr/fhw/en/projects/3dvr/miletus>.

coastal road that passed west of Mount Mykale, running from Ephesus south via Phygela, Marathesion, Anaia and Maiandros in the Maeander Valley (mod. Büjük Menderes) and Priene to Miletus. A route of equal length ran between Mount Thorax and Mount Paktyes toward the southeast to the Maeander Valley and in southerly direction via Magnesia, Maiandros and Priene to Ephesus. According to legend, the city was founded by Miletos, son of Apollo, who fled from Minos, escaping with Sarpedon from Crete to Caria. Historically, Miletus, a Greek colony in Ionia, was founded in the eleventh century B.C. In the seventh century B.C. Miletus was the most important center of trade in Ionia. The city founded numerous colonies—for example, on the coast of the Black Sea.[754] Pliny calls Miletus "the capital of Ionia . . . the mother of over 90 cities scattered over all the seas" ("Ioniae caput . . . super LXXXX urbium per cuncta maria genetrix" [*Nat.* 5.31.112]). The importance of the city was based not least upon on its four harbors, which were situated on both sides of the peninsula on which Miletus was located. (Today the harbor of Miletus forms an inland lake; the Delphinium and the North Agora are often inundated until early summer.) The golden age of Miletus is linked with the philosophers Thales, Anaximander and Anaximenes and with the chronicler Hekataios (Strabo 14.1.7). In the sixth century Miletus was ruled by Croesus, king of Pergamon. At the end of the Ionian Revolt (499-494 B.C.) Miletus was destroyed and its inhabitants sold into slavery. The city was rebuilt after 479 B.C., and it was ruled by the Persians until the conquest by Alexander the Great in 334 B.C. Miletus came under Roman control together with Pergamon, and the city was granted autonomy in 38 B.C. In the first century A.D. Miletus belonged to the province of Asia. The city flourished under Trajan in the second century.

Miletus was built according to the rectangular or gridiron type of layout for city streets before Hippodamos (fifth century B.C.), who was a son of the city, dividing the city into regular quarters and city blocks (*insulae*). The Harbor Theater, with a front 140 m wide, was the largest theater in Asia Minor, seating fifteen thousand visitors. The stadium (192 by 30 m), the West Market, a temple of Athene (30 by 18 m), a heroon built like a temple, and the Eumenes Gymnasium (second century B.C.) were located between in the Theater Harbor and the inner city. The Faustina Baths were built in the second century A.D., with a palaestra measuring 62 by 64 m. In the Bay of Lions, named after the two marble lions to which a chain was attached that blocked the harbor, port facilities, two monuments and baths were discovered; Miletus's main boulevard ended in the harbor. East of the monumental gate stood the temple of Apollo Delphinios (50 by 60 m), the so-called Delphinium, the largest temple in the city and the starting point for the processions to Didyma; some of the roughly two hundred inscriptions that were found in this area date to the sixth century B.C. West of the boulevard was the North Agora, with a large colonnaded hall, the bouleuterion (35 by 24 m; built in 175-164 B.C., with a semicircular assembly hall), the market temple and a temple of Asclepius. The Baths of Capito were located east of the boulevard, the Hellenistic Gymnasium and the nymphaeum, which was rebuilt with monumental dimensions in the second century. The Market Gate, built in A.D. 162-165, was 29 m wide, with three arches and two stories. and stood at the other end of the boulevard (it is displayed in the Pergamon Museum in Berlin). On the west side of the grand South Agora, located opposite the bouleuterion and the nymphaeum, was a large storage building (196 m long). In the third century a temple of Sarapis (22 by 12 m) was built near the South Agora.

---

[754]See Tsetskhladze 1998.

The Jews were familiar with Miletus since the second century B.C. at the latest, so much so that the Greek translator of the book of Ezekiel smuggled the city into the text of Ezek 27:18 (translating the phrase "wool from Zahar" with "wool from Miletus").[755] An inscription in the theater confirms the existence of a Jewish community in Miletus; the inscription reads: τόπος Ειουδέων τῶν καὶ θεοσεβίον (*topos Eioudeōn tōn kai theosebion*, "place of the Jews who are also called God-fearers" [*CIJ* II 748; *IJudO* II 37]).[756] There has been a long debate over whether the inscription refers to "pious Jews" or to Jews and to the God-fearers as a second group. Bernd Wander connects this inscription with a comment by Cassius Dio (*Historia Romana* 32.17.1), who mentions in passing that the word "Jew" also describes all those who imitate the customs of the Jews (τὰ νόμιμα αὐτῶν . . . ζηλοῦσι) irrespective of their ethnic origins; he concludes that the inscription in the theater row very probably was donated by the pagan leadership of the theater. It is unlikely that they wanted to describe the Jews with an epithet emphasizing their piety. This means that there was a Jewish community in Miletus that included God-fearers who were regarded as Jews because they followed Jewish customs.[757] The Jews of Miletus were patrons of the Harbor Theater: the inscription reserves for the Jews of the city seats in the fifth row from the bottom in the second *kerkis* (i.e., in the second section from the west). The first German archaeologists identified a building as a synagogue, which has not been completely excavated; this identification generally is contested today.[758]

The temple of Apollo in Didyma, situated 15 km south of Miletus, belonged to the territory of the city. This famous temple, which competed with the temple of Apollo in Delphi, was destroyed by the Persian king Darius when he conquered Miletus. The rebuilding that was begun in the third century B.C. was not yet finished in the first century A.D. (and never was). A *via sacra* connected Didyma with Miletus.

If the gospel reached Miletus between A.D. 52 and 55, while Paul and his co-workers were active in Ephesus, it is possible that the origins of the church of Priene date to this period as well.

Priene (Πριήνη; mod. Güllübahçe, Turunçlar)[759] was situated 46 km south of Ephesus in the Maeander Valley on the south slope of Mount Mykale on the road between Ephe-

---

[755]Wool from Miletus was both famous and expensive; see P. Herrmann, "Milesischer Purpur," *Mitteilungen des Deutschen Archäologischen Instituts, Abteilung Istanbul (I)* 25 (1975): 141-47.

[756]H. Hommel, *Istanbuler Mitteilungen* 25 (1975): 167-95; W. Wischmeyer 1980, 22-47 (new edition and discussion); cf. Trebilco 1991, 158-59; Levinskaya 1996, 63-65, 148-49; Ameling, in *IJudO* II, 2004, 168-71.

[757]Wander 1998, 108-9. Cf. Kraabel 1979, 488-89; Seager and Kraabel 1983, 180.

[758]Kraabel 1979, 489; followed by Levinskaya 1996, 149.

[759]G. Kleiner, PWSup 9 (1962): 1181-1221; W. Zschietzschmann, *KP* 4:1131-33; Magie 1950, 1:78; Bean 1966 197-216; idem, *PECS* 737-39; J. M. Cook and A. Spawforth, *OCD* 1245; Frank Rumscheid, *Priene: A Guide to the "Pompeii of Asia Minor"* (Istanbul: Ege yay nlar, 1998). Excavations: Martin Schede et al., *Die Ruinen von Priene: Kurze Beschreibung* (Berlin: de Gruyter, 1964 [1934]); Armin von Gerkan, *Das Theater von Priene als Einzelanlage und in seiner Bedeutung für das griechische Bühnenwesen* (Munich: Schmidt, 1921). Inscriptions: *I. Priene* (ed. Hiller von Gaertringen, 1906); Donald F. McCabe et al., *Priene Inscriptions: Texts and List* (Princeton, N.J.: Institute for Advanced Study, 1987).

sus and Miletus. The city suffered under the Persians (Pausanias 7.2.10) and was visited by Alexander the Great in 334 B.C. An inscription at the south ante of the temple of Athene reads, "King Alexander dedicated the Temple of Athene Polias."[760] Priene was refounded in the fourth century B.C. and built according to the Hippodamian system with parallel streets and square *insulae* that consisted generally of four two-story houses with an interior courtyard (and no windows opening to the street). The excavations of 1894-1899 showed that the water installations, which included pipes, canals, cesspool and fountain, functioned far into the Byzantine period. Priene had the traditional infrastructure of a Greek city: an agora with stoas and shops, with an altar in the center that probably was dedicated to Hermes, and a temple of Zeus with the cult of Hera, Pan and Asclepius; a long colonnaded hall (116 m long), a bouleuterion (a square room with theater-style seating for 640 people), a prytaneion, two gymnasia (the Upper Gymnasium was refurbished as baths in the Roman period; the walls of the ephebeion in the Lower Gymnasium display the names of over seven hundred students), a theater (with a water clock) and a stadium (120 by 18 m). The old temple of Athene Polias was dedicated to Augustus after 27 B.C. (*I. Priene* 159).[761] A temple of Asclepius stood near the western city gate; a temple of the Egyptian gods with a large altar was located on the eastern edge of the city in which Isis, Sarapis, Anubis and Harpocrates were worshiped. Above the city was a temple of Demeter and Kore, with a square sacrificial pit on the southeast side of the temple. The harbor of Priene was already silted in the first century A.D. (Strabo 12.8.17); today the city is 12 km from the Mediterranean. The dating of the synagogue that was discovered in a remodeled house from the Hellenistic period (10.2 by 12.6-13.7 m, with a Torah niche in the east wall) is uncertain.[762] The Bishops' Church, dating to the Byzantine period, has three aisles.

If the gospel reached Priene and Miletus during this period, it is possible, at least from a geographical point of view, that there was missionary activity in other cities of the Maeander Valley.

Magnesia (Μαγνησία; Magnesia ad Maeandrum; mod. Tekke, near Ortaklar),[763] 22 km east of Ephesus at the foot of Mount Thorax in the Maeander Valley, was founded as Leukophrys by Aeolian settlers from Magnesia in northern Greece. The city was located on the main highway from the Aegean into the East. Magnesia had close connections with Smyrna; King Seleucus II had granted the Magnesians the citizenship rights of Smyrna because they had safeguarded the military presence of the Seleucids in the city. The temple of Artemis, built by Hermogenes in the third century B.C., stood on a large platform measuring 67 by 41 m. Magnesia flourished during the imperial period; it was one of the three cities of Asia Minor that Claudius permitted to name its games after him. Remains of the agora, odeion, gymnasium, theater and stadium survive.

---

[760] *I. Priene* 156 = *HGIÜ* II 260; for the edict of Alexander the Great concerning Priene see ibid.
[761] See Price 1984, 258 no. 43.
[762] Kraabel 1979, 489-91; L. Levine 2000, 232-33, 249, and passim; Ameling, in *IJudO* II, 2004, 172-74.
[763] L. Bürchner, "Magnesia," PW 14.1 (1928): 471-72; H. Treidler, "Magnesia 2," *KP* 3:885-86; G. E. Bean, *PECS* 544; W. M. Calder et al., *OCD* 912; W. Blümel, "Magnesia 2," *DNP* 7:695; Magie 1950, 1:78-79, 122-23; Bean 1966, 246-51; S. Mitchell 1995a, 1:219 with n. 146.

Tralles (Τράλλεις; mod. Aydın),[764] about 30 km east of Magnesia on the slopes of Mount Messogis, likewise was located on the main road into the East. The city was famous as the cult place of Zeus Larasios, a deity that continued to be worshiped until the third century A.D. The city was renamed Seleukeia during Seleucid rule. The kings of Pergamon built a royal residence in Tralles. In the first century B.C. the city was known for its rhetorical school. Tralles was severely damaged in an earthquake in 27 B.C.; because Augustus helped to rebuild the city, it called itself Kaisareia. Italian colonists were settled in the city, although Tralles was not granted the status of a Roman colony. The city was famous for its pottery. Today the site can be visited only with an escort because it is located within the confines of a military base. Travelers in the nineteenth century saw the ruins of a theater, stadium, agora and the gymnasiums; the only remains surviving today are three large arches of a gymnasium dating to the third century A.D. An inscription attests a synagogue, mentioning a certain "Capitolina, esteemed and Godfearer, made the stairs and the stairway, for her prayers and those of her children and grandchildren" (*CIG* 2924; *IJudO* II 27). Capitolina belonged to an important family: she probably was the wife or the sister of a proconsul, either a God-fearer who attended the synagogue or a proselyte who was honored because she contributed to the synagogue building more prominently than most others.[765] The letters of Ignatius of Antioch confirm the existence of a church in Tralles in the late first century.

Nysa (Νῦσα; mod. Sultanhisar),[766] just under 30 km east of Tralles (about 80 km east of Ephesus), founded as Athymbra by settlers from Sparta, was refounded by the Seleucid king Antiochos I. Acharaka (mod. Salavatlı), about 3 km from Nysa in the city territory, was the site of Charonion, the cave with the famous sulphur springs, and a temple of Pluto and Kore. Strabo, who describes the city (14.1.43-44), was educated in Nysa. The three-story library in the vicinity of the theater was built after Strabo's time. Remains of the agora, council building (*gerontikon*), theater, amphitheater and gymnasium survive. An inscription that possibly dates to the first century B.C. documents the existence of a synagogue in Nysa (*IJudO* II 26).

Antiocheia ad Maeandrum (Ἀντιόχεια ἐπὶ Μαιάνδρῳ; mod. Aliağaçiftliği, Kuyucak),[767] about 40 km east of Nysa, founded by Antiochos I, was located in Caria in the border region with Phrygia. According to Pliny (5.108), Antiocheia was established at the site of the cities of Symmaithos and Kranaos. Strabo describes Antiocheia as a city of medium size, with a bridge across the Maeander River and with a large territory on both sides of the river that was very fertile and produced large amounts of "Antiochene" dried figs (τὴν καλουμένην Ἀντιοχικὴν ἰσχάδα [Strabo 13.4.15]). Strabo mentions in the same context the frequent earthquakes in the region as well as the famous Sophist Diotrephes, who lived in Antiocheia and who had as his student the great orator Hybreas. Few remains of

---

[764]W. Ruge, PW 6.A2 (1937): 2093-28; E. Olshausen, *KP* 5:921-22; Magie 1950, 1:129-30, 379, 448-49, 469; 2:991-92 n. 29, 1331-32; G. E. Bean, *PECS* 931; W. M. Calder et al., *OCD* 1544-45; Bean 1971, 208-11; G. Cohen 1995, 265-68. Inscriptions: Fjodor B. Poljakov, *Die Inschriften von Tralleis und Nysa* (IK 36.1; Bonn: Habelt, 1989).

[765]See Wander 1998, 115; Ameling, in *IJudO* II, 2004, 141.

[766]W. Ruge, PW 17.2 (1937): 1631-40; E. Olshausen, "Nysa 3," *KP* 4:218; G. E. Bean, *PECS* 637; H. Kaletsch, "Nysa 3," *DNP* 8:1075-76; Magie 1950, 989-91; Bean 1971, 211-20; G. Cohen 1995, 256-59.

[767]H. Treidler, "Antiocheia 8," *KP* 1:387; G. E. Bean, *PECS* 61; H. Kaletsch, "Antiocheia 6," *DNP* 1:765-66; Belke and Mersich 1990, 185-88; S. Mitchell 1995a, 1:204 (fig. 35a: coin).

the ancient city survive. Coins of the city dating to the third century depict a bridge with six arches leading to a monumental city gate.

During this time several churches were established in southwest Phrygia near the border with Caria and Lydia in the wide valley of the Lykos River (mod. Çürüksu Çay): in Laodikeia, Hierapolis and Colossae.

The Lykos River[768] flows from southeast to northwest and empties south of Apollonia-Tripolis (mod. Yenice, near Buldan) into the Maeander River. The Lykos Valley is flanked in the north by the Çökelez Dağı Mountains, in the southwest by Mount Salbakos (Baba Dağı) and in the southeast by Mount Kadmos (Honaz Dağı). In the eastern Lykos Valley the city of Colossae controlled a smaller valley of a branch of the Lykos River. The two most important cities of the region were located in the main section of the plain: Laodikeia controlled the southern part of the valley, and Hierapolis the smaller northern part. The smaller cities of Trapezopolis and Attuda were located west of Laodikeia in side valleys.

Two passages in the letter to the Colossians mention the establishment of these churches by Epaphras:

Col 1:3-8: "In our prayers for you we always thank God, the Father of our Lord Jesus Christ, [4]for we have heard of your faith in Christ Jesus and of the love that you have for all the saints, [5]because of the hope laid up for you in heaven. You have heard of this hope before in the word of the truth, the gospel [6]that has come to you. Just as it is bearing fruit and growing in the whole world, so it has been bearing fruit among yourselves from the day you heard it and truly comprehended the grace of God. [7]This you learned from Epaphras, our beloved fellow servant. He is a faithful minister of Christ on your behalf, [8]and he has made known to us your love in the Spirit."

Col 4:12-13: "Epaphras, who is one of you, a servant of Christ Jesus, greets you. He is always wrestling in his prayers on your behalf, so that you may stand mature and fully assured in everything that God wills. [13]For I testify for him that he has worked hard for you and for those in Laodicea and in Hierapolis."

Evangelism in Laodikeia

Epaphras probably engaged in missionary work in Laodikeia during A.D. 52-55, when Paul worked in Ephesus, as Col 4:13 suggests.[769]

Laodikeia (Λαοδίκεια, Laodiceia ad Lycum; mod. Eski Hisar, at the edge of Denizli)[770] was

---

[768]For the description that follows above see Corsten 1997, 1.

[769]A less likely proposal is that of Kirkland (1995, 112), who suggests that Philemon was the missionary who brought the gospel to Laodikeia; Philemon is a less likely candidate, however.

[770]W. Ruge, "Laodikeia 5," PW 12.1 (1924): 722-24; H. Treidler, *KP* 3:482-84; Bean, *PECS* 481-82; M. Rudwick and C. J. Hemer, *GBL* 2:867-68; W. M. Calder and S. M. Sherwin-White, *OCD* 815; E. Olshausen, "Laodikeia 4," *DNP* 6:1132-33; Belke and Mersich 1990, 323-25; Ramsay 1895-1897, 1:32-83; Magie 1950, 1:127, 133, 391, 448, 469, 544, 564; 2:986-87 n. 23; Bean 1971, 247-57; S. Mitchell 1995a, 1:17, 219, 257; 2:33, and passim; Price 1984, 183, 185, 264-65 (nos. 87,

located 53 km east of Nysa, about 165 km east of Ephesus in the Lykos Valley at the foot of Mount Kadmos (Honaz Dağı). Laodikeia was situated on a flat hill at the southern edge of the plain at the confluence of the Maeander and the Lykos Rivers. The city was flanked in the west and in the east by the small rivers Asopos (mod. Gümüş Çayı) and Kapros (Başlı Çayı), which flowed into the Lykos River. The city originally was called Diospolis (Pliny, *Nat.* 5.29.105) or Roas. An inscription dating to 267 B.C. that was found in the city territory of Laodikeia attests for the period the still acute danger of invading Celtic tribes.[771] The city was organized by Antiochos II around 206 B.C. as a *demos* and named after his wife, Laodike. Laodikeia controlled the junction of two important roads: the main road from Ephesus via Apameia to the Euphrates River in the east, and the north-south route from Pergamon via Sardis, Philadelphia, Kibyra and Xanthos to the Mediterranean; only 40 km east of the city the road branched off to Attaleia in Pamphylia. Hierapolis was 11 km north of Laodikeia on the other side of the valley, and Colossae lay 15 km to the southeast. The far-reaching influence of Laodikeia can be seen in the fact that there was an association of citizens of Laodikeia in Panamara in Caria.[772] In 220 B.C. Achaios, the brother-in-law of Antiochos III, was crowned in Laodikeia three years after he had reconquered Seleucid areas that Attalos I of Pergamon had occupied (Polybios 4.46.4; 5.27-28). Laodikeia was besieged by the army of Mithradates in the First Mithradatic War (89-84 B.C.), and a generation later the city withstood the Parthians. At that time Laodikeia was the capital (*dioecesis*) of the assize district (*conventus*) of Kibyra. Cicero visited Laodikeia on July 31 in 51 B.C. as the new governor of the province of Cilicia,[773] and he stayed in the city from February to April of 52 B.C. (several Phrygian *conventus* had been incorporated in the province of Cilicia, including the assize district of Laodikeia). In the first century A.D. Laodikeia was one of the three cities of Asia Minor permitted to name its games after the emperor Claudius.[774] The city was severely damaged in earthquakes during the principates of Augustus (27. B.C.) and Nero (A.D. 60). After the earthquake of A.D. 60 the citizens of Laodikeia rebuilt the city without the help offered by the emperor: "In the same year, Laodicea, one of the famous Asiatic cities, was laid in ruins by an earthquake, but recovered by its own resources, without assistance from ourselves" ("Eodem anno ex inlustribus Asiae urbibus Laodicea tremore terrae prolapsa nullo a nobis remedio propriis opibus revaluit" [Tacitus, *Ann.* 14.27]). Cicero describes Laodikeia as an important center of finance and trade (Cicero, *Fam.* 3.5.4) and as a famous center of ophthalmology. An

---

88); Hemer 1986, 178-207; G. Cohen 1995, 308-11. Excavations: Jean des Gagniers et al., *Laodicée du Lycos: Le nymphée; campagnes 1961-1963* (Recherches archéologiques Série 1: Fouilles; Québec: Les Presses de l'Université Laval; Paris: Boccard, 1969). Inscriptions: Louis Robert, "Les inscriptions," in *Laodicée du Lycos* (ed. J. des Gagniers; Québec: Les Presses de l'Université Laval; Paris: Boccard, 1969), 247-389; *I. Laodikeia* (ed. T. Corsten, 1997); see also Ali Ceylan and Thomas Corsten, "Inscriptions from Laodikeia in the Museum of Denizli," *EA* 25 (1995): 89-92; Thomas Corsten and Thomas Drew-Bear, "Inschriften aus Laodikeia am Lykos und Eumeneia," *EA* 26 (1996): 31-42. Phrygian Laodikeia must not be confused with Laodikeia in Lykaonia (Laodikeia Katakekaumene), located a few kilometers north of Iconium.

[771]M. Wörrle, "Antiochus I., Achaios der Ältere und die Galater: Eine neue Inschrift in Denizli," *Chiron* 5 (1975): 59-87 = *I. Laodikeia* 1 (7-17): "Because Banabelos . . . and Lachares . . . bought the freedom of many of those who had been taken prisoner by the Galatians according to Achaios, they are to be praised and their benefaction shall be inscribed on a stele."

[772]See Thomas Corsten, "Das Koinon der Laodikener in Panamara," *EA* 25 (1995): 87-88, in an interpretation of the inscription *EA* 25 (1995), no. 2.

[773]See Stumpf 1991, 54-55.

[774]*REG* 19 (1906): 253-55, no. 148.

important product of the city was clothing made of shiny black wool (Strabo 12.8.16). Inscriptions dating to the second and third centuries mention wealthy shepherds (ποιμήν, *poimēn*),[775] clothes merchants (ἑιματιοπώλης, *heimatiopōlēs*),[776] fullers (γναφεῖς, *gnapheis*) and purple dyers (ἁπλουργοῖ, *haplourgoi*).[777] Textiles produced in Laodikeia were exported to Italy, Gaul and Africa.[778] Inscriptions document financial officers (ἑξεταστής, *exetastēs*), tax officials (δεκάπρωτοι, *dekaprōtoi*) and officials responsible for the sale of wheat (σιτώνης, *sitōnēs*).[779] An honorary inscription for M. Sestius Philemo dating to the first century A.D. documents Roman citizens in Laodikeia, probably merchants (*negotiatores*).[780] Another inscription honors Antonia, who belonged to the famous Zenon family from Laodikeia (see Strabo 14.2.24): she was the daughter of Lucius Antonius Zeno, "the greatest high priest of Asia, the priest of the city . . . the gymnasiarch"; this probably was the L. Antonius Zeno who is mentioned on coins of Laodikeia minted at the time of Nero. Antonia occupied several offices: she was temple warden (νεωκόρος, *neōkoros*) of a goddess in Laodikeia, high priest of Asia (ἀρχιέρεια τῆς Ἀσίας, *archiereia tēs Asias*), priestess (ἱέρεια), perhaps of the personified city (as her father), as well as gymnasiarch.[781] Antonius Polemon (ca. A.D. 90-145), the famous orator of the Second Sophistic who taught in Smyrna, also was a member of the Zenon family and came from Laodikeia.[782] The honorary inscription for the deceased Quintus Pomponius Flaccus dating to the first/second century, erected by the assembly of the province of Asia, the association of the Romans in the province and the people of Laodikeia, was mentioned earlier (§18.2): the honoree was strategos, administrator of the public funds, clerk of the market, guardian of the laws and night-strategos; he financed the installation of heating in two colonnaded halls (ἑκατέρους τοὺς θερμοὺς περιπάτους καύσαντ[α] πρῶτον καὶ μόνον), he distributed monthly oil during the festivals that were organized while he was clerk of the market, he carried the costs for registrations in the administrative records, he paid himself for his journey to Rome as envoy of Laodikeia, he helped finance "festivals of good news" (τὰ εὐαγγέλια, *ta euangelia*) that were celebrated upon the arrival of good news from the imperial family, he paid for the pavement of marble (probably in the agora in front of a statue of Zeus), and he donated oil to the city on another occasion.[783] The "Monument of the Gladiators" (Μνῆμα μονομάχων, *Mnēma monomachōn*), donated by Diokles son of Metrophilos, who was high priest and the official responsible for gladiator fights, probably dates to the first century.[784]

---

[775]*MAMA* VI 21 = *I. Laodikeia* 112.

[776]*I. Laodikeia* 51 (second century).

[777]*I. Laodikeia* 50. The attribute ἁπλοῦς (*haplous*) describes "cloth that was dyed with one color only in contrast to other purple clothes"; see Corsten (1997, 104), who suggests the translation "Schneckenpurpureinfachfärber," with reference to G. Steigerwald, *Byzantinische Forschungen* 15 (1990) 253-254.

[778]See J. Rougé, "Un negotiator Laudecenarius à Lyons," *ZPE* 27 (1977): 263-69.

[779]*I. Laodikeia* 47. On the *exetastēs*, who also was responsible for the inscribing of honorary decrees, see *I. Laodikeia* 2, 4, 5.

[780]*I. Laodikeia* 48 = *I. GRIAsia* 56.

[781]*I. Laodikeia* 53; for the coins see Andrew M. Burnett, Michel Amandry and Pere Pau Ripollès, *Provincial Coinage* (2 vols.; London: British Museum; Paris: Bibliothèque Nationale, 1992), vol. 1, nos. 2912-16, 2928; cf. ibid., 475-76; see Corsten 1997, 110.

[782]H. Gärtner, "Polemon 5," *KP* 4:972; see Reader 1996.

[783]*IGR* IV 860 = *I. Laodikeia* 82 (with a commentary by Corsten); see Robert, "Les inscriptions," in *Laodicée du Lycos* (ed. J. des Gagniers), 265-77.

[784]*I. Laodikeia* 73.

The plateau on which Laodikeia was located was surrounded by a wall, ruins of which survive on the east side of the city. Laodikeia had three city gates: the Syrian Gate stood in the east at the road that went to Syria, the West Gate controlled the road to Ephesus, and through the North Gate ran the road to Hierapolis. The Syrian Gate, of which fragments of the architrave with a Latin and Greek inscription are preserved,[785] was financed by the imperial freedman Tiberius Claudius Trypho and inaugurated by the proconsul Sextus Iulius Frontinus, who came probably from southern Gaul (later governor of Britannia from A.D. 73-77). Laodikeia had two theaters, both built into the northeast slope of the hill on which the city was located. The stadium stood on the southern side of the city, an *amphitheatron* whose normally open side had semicircular spectator stands.[786] The stadium, 370 m long, was donated in A.D. 79 by Nikostratos, a wealthy citizen of Laodikeia, and dedicated to the emperor Titus. The new stadium perhaps replaced an early structure destroyed in the earthquake of A.D. 60. About 100 m north of the stadium was the odeion or bouleuterion (five rows of seats survive). The large building in the southeast part of the city often has been identified as a gymnasium, but more likely it was a public bath (dedicated to the emperor Hadrian). A watertower (ἐκδοχεῖον, *ekdocheion*), of which walls 5 m high survive, stood next to this building.[787] The water supply of Laodikeia was a problem: the water had to be brought to the city from the small river Kapros (in the plain of Denizli) via a canal and two aqueducts; the northern aqueduct had thirty-five pillars, whose ruins can still be seen for several kilometers in the direction of Denizli. On a hill south of the city was a basin in which the water coming from the south was collected; the difference in elevation was overcome with a high-pressure water pipe that brought the water into the watertower. Several blocks of the water pipe display a funnel-shaped incision at the top that evidently was meant to make it easier to locate the blockage of the conduit that resulted from the strongly calciferous water. Beside the watertower stood a fountain and baths built by Hedychrus in the first century A.D.[788] Hedychrus, evidently a slave employed by the imperial family, had become wealthy after his manumission. In the center of the city was the nymphaeum (early third century). Coins attest an imperial temple for the time of Domitian. Hardly anything of the public buildings survives.

Inscriptions attest the worship of Zeus Megistos Soter, Zeus Patrios, Theos Hypsistos, Eros, Heracles, Hermes, Hestia and the deified emperors.[789] The dice oracle (*I. Laodikeia* 69) that probably stood in the agora mentions Ares, Athensa, Euphrosyne, Meter, Men Phosphoros, Zeus Katachthonios, Aphrodite and Hermes Tetragonos. Cicero's defense of Lucius Valerius Flaccus, the proconsul of the province of Asia in 62 B.C., documents a Jewish community in Laodikeia: it collected the temple tax in the district of Kibyra[790] and in the Jewish communities in the Lykos Valley and in the middle Maeander Valley (the twenty pounds of gold that were meant to be sent to the temple in Jeru-

---

[785] *IGR* IV 847; *MAMA* VI 2; *I. Laodikeia* 24; *I. GRIAsia* 170. The newest reconstruction of the inscription is offered by Corsten and Drew-Bear, *EA* 26 (1996): 31-40, no. 1; see Corsten 1997, 67-71. On Frontinus see Corsten and Drew-Bear, *EA* 26 (1996): 32-33; J. B. Campbell and N. Purcell, *OCD* 785. Pliny describes Frontinus as one of two most eminent men of the citizenry (Pliny, *Ep.* 5.1.5).

[786] Corsten 1997, 52.

[787] See *I. Laodikeia* 12, a fragment of the building inscription of the watertower. The inscription dates to the time of Domitian and documents the (re)building of the water reservoir after the earthquake of A.D. 60 as a private donation.

[788] *I. Laodikeia* 13.

[789] *I. Laodikeia* 24, 26, 61, 62A, 64-66, 70-72.

salem had been confiscated in Laodikeia [Cicero, *Flac.* 28, 68-69]). Josephus quotes a letter written by the administration of Laodikeia to the Roman proconsul Gaius Rabirius that dealt with the treatment of the Jews in the city during the time in which he was governor of the province of Asia (Josephus, *A.J.* 14.241).[791] This literary evidence for a Jewish community in Laodikeia has been confirmed by recently discovered inscriptions. A sarcophagus dating to the second or third century A.D., discovered in the vicinity of Laodikeia, displays an inscription that threatens grave robbers with the curses of the book of Deuteronomy, which suggests that Lucius Nonius Glyko, who was buried in the sarcophagus, was a Jew.[792] A recently discovered inscription that also dates to the second or third century mentions a woman with the name "Piste" (Πίστη), "who is also faithful to God" (καὶ θεῷ πιστή, *kai theō pistē*). The personal name "Piste" is often attested, but the description of the woman suggests that she was a Jew or a Christian.[793]

The foundation of a Christian community in Laodikeia during the apostolic period is attested by Col 2:1; 4:13, 15; Rev 1:11; 3:14.

The synod that met in Laodikeia between A.D. 165 and 175 discussed the date of Easter. At about the same time the bishop Sagaris died as a martyr; he was buried in Laodikeia (Eusebius, *Hist. eccl.* 4.26.3; 5.24.5). The bishop Nunechios of Laodikeia is listed as the first bishop among the church leaders from the province of Phrygia who attended the Council of Nicea.[794]

Evangelism in Hierapolis

Epaphras was active as a missionary in Hierapolis as well, as Col 4:12-13 suggests. Paul writes with regard to Epaphras, "Epaphras, who is one of you, a servant of Christ Jesus, greets you. He is always wrestling in his prayers on your behalf, so that you may stand mature and fully assured in everything that God wills. For I testify for him that he has worked hard for you and for those in Laodicea and in Hierapolis."

Hierapolis (Ἱεράπολις, mod. Pamukkale)[795] was situated on a terrace on the slopes of Mount Küçükçekelez (1,734 m; ancient name unknown), about 100 m above the plain in which the Lykos River empties into the Maeander River, 11 km north of Laodikeia. The city was located on the road that ran through the Hermos Valley via Sardis and Philadel-

---

[790]See N. P. Milner, *An Epigraphical Survey in the Kibyra-Olbasa Region, Conducted by A. S. Hall* (Oxford: British Institute of Archaeology at Ankara, 1998); Thomas Corsten et al., "Forschungen in der Kibyratis," *EA* 30 (1998): 45-78. One of the richest families of this region was the Calpurnii, who owned estates in Pisidia. Kibyra belonged to the province of Asia since the time of Augustus, and in A.D. 43 it was included in the new province of Lycia-Pamphylia; see Dirk Erkelenz, "Zur Provinzzugehörigkeit Kibyras in der römischen Kaiserzeit," *EA* 30 (1998): 81-95.

[791]See S. Mitchell 1995a, 2:32-33; T. Corsten, in *I. Laodikeia*, 193 (on no. 111).

[792]Ceylan and Corsten, *EA* 25 (1995): 91-92, no. 3 = *I. Laodikeia* 111; *IJudO* II 213.

[793]Ceylan and Corsten, *EA* 25 (1995): 89-90, no. 1 = *I. Laodikeia* 108.

[794]Belke and Mersich 1990, 323; S. Mitchell 1995a, 2:35.

[795]W. Ruge, "Hierapolis 3," *PW* 8.2 (1913): 1404-5; H. Treidler, "Hierapolis 1," *KP* 2:1129-30; M. Rudwick and C. J. Hemer, *GBL* 2:574; T. Drew-Bear, *DNP* 5:533; Jones 1937, 73-75; Ramsay 1895-1897, 1:84-119; Magie 1950, 1:47-49, 127-28, 142, 564; 2:987-88, 1020-21; Bean 1971,

phia south to Kibyra and from there to Xanthos on the Mediterranean coast. The origins of Hierapolis are linked with a temple of Cybele, as the name suggests ("*polis* of the *hieron*," meaning "city of the temple"). Hierapolis was founded probably in the Hellenistic period under Eumenes II in the third century B.C.; since the second century the city minted its own coins. One of the attractions of the city was a crevice in the area of the temple of Apollo, called Plutonium or Charoneion, from which poisonous fumes arose. Strabo describes oxen who died as a result of these fumes, and eunuchs of Cybele who were immune to the effects of the gases to a certain degree (Strabo 13.4.14). Other ancient authors mention the Plutonium as well. Italian archaeologists rediscovered the crevice in the back part of the temple of Apollo: three flat steps lead down to a paved room (2.7 m²), at whose back one can see fast-running water through a crevice 1 m wide; the fumes that arise from this crevice make one's eyes water and are capable of rendering a person unconscious.[796] The mineral-rich volcanic hot springs of Hierapolis originate in the Plutonium; the calcium carbonate in the water separates off to form a grayish-white limestone sediment on the rocks underneath the city that can be seen from a long distance (the mod. name "Pamukkale" means "cotton castle"). Few details are known about the history of the city. Neighboring Laodikeia cast a shadow over Hierapolis for a long time. After 129 B.C. the city belonged to the Roman province of Asia. It was severely damaged in several earthquakes (Strabo 12.8.16-17), particularly the earthquake of A.D. 60. Coins minted during the principate of Claudius attest a temple of the Imperial Family (γενεὶ Σεβαστῶν). Hadrian visited Hierapolis in A.D. 129.

Inscriptions show that Apollo was the main god of the city; the temple of Apollo was located in the city center. Also attested is the worship of Artemis Ephesia, Cybele, Men,[797] Pluto, Poseidon, the *Theoi Motaleōn* and Zeus (also under the Anatolian names "Bozius" and "Troius"). The temple of Apollo Lairbenos (27 by 12 m; near mod. Çavdarlı), located on a hilltop high above the valley of the upper Maeander River about 40 km north of Hierapolis, belonged to the territory of the city; it was visited by the citizens of Hierapolis and from the towns and villages controlled by the city, including Mamakome, Kroula, Motella, Blaundos and Dionysopolis.[798] The philosopher Epictetus was born in Hierapolis around A.D. 50 (Paul lived in Ephesus since A.D. 52); in his early years he was a slave of Epaphroditus, a freedman who had become the secretary of the emperor Nero. He was involved in uncovering the conspiracy of Piso in A.D. 65 and received military honors. After his manumission he studied under Musonius Rufus and taught as a Stoic popular philosopher in Rome until he was sent into exile by Domitian in A.D. 89; later he founded a philosophical school in Nikopolis in southern Epirus.

232-46; F. Kolb, *ZPE* 15 (1974): 255-70; Price 1984, 264, nos. 85-86; Belke and Mersich 1990, 268-72; A. Peres, ed., *Hierapolis di Frigia, 1957-1987* (Milano: Fabbri, 1987); M. J. Mellink, "Archaeology in Anatolia: Hierapolis," *AJA* 92 (1988): 130-31; 93 (1989): 132-33; 94 (1990): 150; G. Cohen 1995, 305-8; S. Mitchell 1995a, 1:187-88; 2:33; Amsler 1999, 521-42. Excavations: Carl Humann et al., *Altertümer von Hierapolis* (Jahrbuch des Kaiserlich-Deutschen Archälogischen Instituts 4; Berlin: Reimer, 1898); Eugenia Equini Schneider, *La necropoli di Hierapolis di Frigia* (Monumenti antichi 48.2; Rome: Accademia nazionale dei Lincei, 1972); Francesco D'Andria, ed., *Hierapolis: Scavi e ricerche* (3 vols.; Archaeologica 53-54, 99; Rome: Bretschneider, 1985-1991).

[796]Larry J. Kreitzer, "The Plutonium of Hierapolis and the Descent of Christ into the 'Lower-most Parts of the Earth' (Ephesians 4,9)," *Bib* 79 (1998): 381-93.

[797]See Eugene N. Lane, "A Men-Stele from Phrygian Hierapolis," *EA* 7 (1986): 107-9.

[798]Kevin M. Miller, "Apollo Lairbenos," *Numen* 32 (1985): 46-70. On Dionysopolis and the sanctuary of Apollo Lairbenos see Robert 1962, 127-49.

Hierapolis was known for its wool, as were other cities in the region. The wealth of the city derived from the dyeworks and from tourism connected with the thermal springs. The famous Hierapolitan marble was quarried in what is now Gölemezli, 11 km northwest of Hierapolis; marble used for local and less prestigious building programs, white to dark gray in color, was quarried north of the city. The main street of Hierapolis was flanked by colonnaded halls. Remains of the Hellenistic theater, large Roman theater (second century; capacity for 12,000 spectators), nymphaeum, several public baths, temples, the agora and city walls survive. The room in the middle of the baths north of the main gate was rebuilt as a church around A.D. 400 (45 by 22 m). Coins from the third century A.D. suggest a close relationship of the city with Ephesus (*homonoia*).

Several funerary inscriptions dating to the second and third centuries document the existence of a Jewish community in Hierapolis. The description as κατοικία (*katoikia*) suggests that the Jews had a recognizable identity in the life of the city.[799] The association of purple dyers and the council of the association of the producers of tapestries in Hierapolis were responsible for commemoration ceremonies that were conducted on Passover and on the Feast of Pentecost for deceased Jewish members.[800]

Papias, who was born in Hierapolis between A.D. 55 and 70, reports around A.D. 110 that "Philip the apostle dwelt at Hierapolis with his daughters" (Eusebius, *Hist. eccl.* 3.39.9).[801] Eusebius quotes a letter of Polycrates of Ephesus to Victor, who was bishop in Rome, in which Polycrates reports that the apostle Philip settled in Hierapolis with two of his daughters and that he is buried in Hierapolis (Eusebius, *Hist. eccl.* 3.31.3-4).[802]

The apocryphal *Acts of Philip* (fourth century) also refer to the ministry of Philip in Phrygian Hierapolis: he is described as an apostle (*Acts Phil.* 13—15), and he has attributes both of Jesus' disciple Philip, who was born in Bethsaida,[803] and of Philip the Hellenistic Jewish Christian of Jerusalem—that is, the "deacon" and evangelist Philip mentioned in the book of Acts.[804] Since Luke reports that Philip the evangelist had daughters who prophesied (Acts 21:8), and since Luke distinguishes Philip the evangelist from Philip the apostle (Acts 1:13), most scholars assume that the figure of Philip the evangelist and the figure of Philip the apostle were fused in the later tradition (see §20.2).[805] Frédéric Amsler

---

[799]See Elena Miranda, "La comunità giudaica di Hierapolis di Frigia," *EA* 31 (1999): 109-55; Ameling, in *IJudO* II, 2004, 398-440 (no. 187-209).

[800]*CIJ* II 775, 777 (*IJudO* II 205, 196). See Seager and Kraabel 1983, 181; Ameling, in *IJudO* II, 2004, 414-22.

[801]*Papias Fragment* 5 (Körtner and Leutzsch, eds., *Papiasfragmente,* 57). On the daughters of Philip see Zahn 1900, 170-71; Peter Corssen, "Die Töchter des Philippus," *ZNW* 2 (1901): 289-99; now Matthews 2002, 23-34 (on Eusebius, *Hist. eccl.* 3.39.9 see ibid., 28). Matthews, while not denying the presence of Philip and his daughters in Hierapolis, is interested more in traditions, less in history.

[802]Eusebius often mentions Philip; see *Hist. eccl.* 2.1.10-14; 2.15.2-3; 3.31.3; 3.39.9; 4.26.1; 4.27; 5.17.3; 5.24.2.

[803]See Mt 10:2-4; Mk 3:16-19; Lk 6:14-16; Jn 1:43-48; 6:5, 7; 12:20-22; 14:8-9; Acts 1:13.

[804]See Acts 6:5; 8:5-13, 26-40; 21:8-9.

[805]See A. de Santos Otero, in Hennecke and Schneemelcher 1990-1997, 2:425; Hengel 1993, 118, 324-25 (ET, 133-34); Dobbeler 2000a, 233. Matthews (2002, 2-3, 33-34, 48, 65, 171, 216) posits that there was but one Philip.

suggests that the Philip of *Acts of Philip* may have been a Christian from Phrygian Hierapolis who was assimilated with Philip the deacon and evangelist, who in turn was assimilated with Philip the apostle.[806]

Many scholars assume that Philip the evangelist moved from Caesarea to Hierapolis, perhaps in the mid-60s, as a result of anti-Jewish pogroms in Caesarea.[807] Bernd Kollmann states, "If Philip settled in the church of Hierapolis, which was Pauline in character, this again confirms the basic theological agreement with Paul that Acts 21:8-14 suggests."[808] It is possible that Papias personally knew the daughters of Philip in Hierapolis. The author of *Acts of Philip* claims to know that Philip and John the apostle brought to an end the worship of snakes in Hierapolis (*Acts Phil.* 7), which could have a historical background: the cult of Cybele, attested in Hierapolis, often is represented by the symbol of a snake.[809]

L. J. Kreitzer suggests that the Epistle to the Ephesians was "originally intended for the Christian congregation at Hierapolis within the region of Phrygia in Asia Minor and that it was written by an unnamed disciple of Paul who was a member of the church at Colossae."[810] There is no evidence, in Greek manuscripts or otherwise, that supports this hypothesis.

Philip was followed by Heros (or Stachys) as bishop of Hierapolis. At the beginning of the second century Papias was bishop in Hierapolis, and Apollinarius is attested as bishop between A.D. 161 and 180.[811] The church of the Martyrion of St. Philip was built in Hierapolis in the fourth or fifth century.

Evangelism in Colossae

When Paul wrote his letter to the Christians in Colossae, he had not yet visited the city (Col 2:1). The church evidently was founded by Epaphras his coworker (Col 1:7; 4:12-13).

---

[806]Amsler 1999, 6-9, 441-68.

[807]See Zahn 1900, 158-75; Körtner and Leutzsch, eds., *Papiasfragmente*, 96 n. 24; Hengel 1993, 324-25 (ET, 133-34); Hengel and Schwemer 1998, 85 n. 330 (ET, 350 n. 259); Dobbeler 2000a, 247-48; Hofmann 2000, 286-88; Kollmann 2000, 561-62; accepted by Matthews (2002, 32 n. 66). See also Kirkland (1995, 112, 115-18), who suggests that that Philip founded the church in Hierapolis.

[808]Kollmann 2000, 563.

[809]Belke and Mersich 1990, 268; cf. Amsler (1999, 299-312), who sees in this text "a polemic against the pagan cult of Cybele."

[810]L. J. Kreitzer, "Plutonium," *Bib* 79 (1998): 381; cf. Lincoln (*Eph*, 3-4), who argues that the letter originally was intended for the churches in Laodikeia and Hierapolis.

[811]On Papias see Zahn 1900, 109-57; William R. Schoedel, *ABD* 5:140-41; idem, "Papias," *ANRW* II.27.1 (1993): 235-70; Ulrich H. J. Körtner, *Papias von Hierapolis* (FRLANT 133; Göttingen: Vandenhoeck & Ruprecht, 1983); Armin D. Baum, "Papias als Kommentator evangelischer Aus-sprüche Jesu: Erwägungen zur Art seines Werkes," *NovT* 38 (1996): 257-76. On Apollinarius see Clemens Scholten, "Apo(l)linarios," *LThK* 1:826.

Colossae (Κολοσσαί; near mod. Honaz)[812] was located about 15 km east-southeast of Laodikeia in the Lykos Valley at the foot of Mount Honag Dağı (2,571 m; ancient name unknown). The acropolis was located on an isolated hill on the south bank of the Lykos River, flanked by small brooks to the west and to the east that flow into the Lykos. Colossae was an important city during the Lydian and Persian periods: Herodotus describes Colossae as a "large city" of Phrygia (πόλις μεγάλη, *polis megalē* [7.30]) at the time of Xerxes' march through Asia Minor in 481 B.C.; Xenophon describes Colossae in connection with events in 401 B.C. as an "inhabited city, prosperous, large" (πόλις οἰκουμένη καὶ εὐδαίμων καὶ μεγάλη, *polis oikoumenē kai eudaimōn kai megalē* [*Anab*. 1.2.6]). The city owed its importance to its location at the junction of two main roads through Asia Minor: the north-west route from Ephesus through the Maeander Valley via Apameia to the east, and the north-south route from Pergamon and Sardis via Kibyra and Oenoanda to Xanthos on the Mediterranean coast. The wealth of ancient Colossae was linked with the textile industry of the region: the wool of the sheep was particularly soft, as Strabo notes (12.8.16); wool dyed purple was described as "Colossian wool" (Pliny, *Nat.* 25.9.67; 21.9.27). After the north-south route was moved further west to Laodikeia, Colossae slowly declined. Strabo distinguishes Colossae and other towns, which he describes as πολίσματα (*polismata*), from Apameia and Laodikeia, which he calls "the largest city in Phrygia" (μέγισται τῶν κατὰ τὴν Φρυγίαν πόλεων, *megistai tōn kata tōn Phrygian poleōn* [12.8.13]). When Pliny describes Colossae as one of the "most famous cities" (*oppida celeberrima* [*Nat.* 5.41.145]), he indulges in historical reminiscence. Colossae was devasted in the earthquake of A.D. 60 (Tacitus, *Ann.* 14.27), and evidently it was rebuilt. In the ninth century the city was moved north about 4 km (Chonaz, mod. Honaz). The hill of ancient Colossae is 25 m high, measuring 250 by 150 m. Hardly any ruins survive; foundation blocks of the wall that surrounded the city can be seen all around the edge, and red pottery shards can be seen on the mound. Cisterns, a few coins and a few inscriptions can be found. On the east side of the mound one can still see where the theater was located, but nothing survives from the *skēnē* or the rows of seats. The necropolis was north of the hill. From the mound one can see the Lykos River to the north and Hierapolis to the northwest on the other side of the Lykos Valley.

Philemon and his slave Onesimus belonged to the church of Colossae (Philem 1:22; Col 2:1). Possibly a Scythian was a member of the church, perhaps a converted slave (Col 3:11).[813]

---

[812]W. Ruge, PW 11.1 (1921): 1119-20; K. Ziegler, *KP* 3:276; E. Green and C. J. Hemer, *GBL* 2:803-4; C. E. Arnold, *ABD* 1:1089-90; T. Drew-Bear, *DNP* 6:667-68; L. M. McDonald, *DNTB* 225-26; Belke and Mersich 1990, 309-11; W. J. Hamilton, *Researches in Asia Minor, Pontus, and Armenia* (London: Murray, 1842), 507-13; Ramsay 1895-1897, 1:208-34; S. E. Johnson, "Laodicea and Its Neighbors," *BA* 13 (1950): 1-18; Magie 1950, 1:47-48, 126-27, 564; 2:985-86 n. 22; Bean 1971, 257-59; B. Reicke, "The Historical Setting of Colossians," *RevExp* 20 (1973): 429-38; W. H. Mare, "Archaeological Prospects at Colossae," *NEASB* 7 (1976): 39-59. See also among the commentaries Lightfoot, *Col*, 1-22; Lohse, *Kol*, 36-38 (ET, 8-9); Barth and Blanke, *Col*, 7-8. Inscriptions: *MAMA* XI 15-18.

[813]Bengel, *Gnomon Novi Testamenti*, 806; Michel, *ThWNT* 7:450-51 (*TDNT* 7:450); D. Campbell 1996. This interpretation is rejected by Lohse, *Kol*, 208 with n. 2 (ET, 144 with n. 78); Wolter, *Kol*, 182; O'Brien, *Col*, 193. Silent on this possibility are the commentaries of Dunn, Barth and Blanke, Hübner, Gnilka, Schweizer; also Harnack 1924.

Col 3:11: "There is no longer Greek and Jew, circumcised and uncircumcised, barbarian [βάρβαρος], Scythian [Σκύθης], slave and free; but Christ is all and in all!"

Most scholars interpret the reference to the Scythian in terms of the archetype of barbarism, "the epitome of unrefinement or savagery."[814] Some scholars point out that the Scythian could be a slave,[815] or that the image of the Scythians among the Greeks was ambivalent: on the one hand, the Scythians were regarded as particularly barbaric people because of their lack of culture and their proverbial savagery, and on the other hand, they were idealized as an unspoiled and free primitive people.[816] The traditional interpretation suffers from several problems:[817] (1) The assumed antithesis between Greek identity and barbarism is not really found in Col 3:11: Paul does *not* say "there is no longer Greek and barbarian." (2) The words "barbarian" and "Scythian" are surrounded by three *antithetical* pairs: Greek/Jew, circumcised/uncircumcised, slave/free. This suggests that the terms "barbarian" and "Scythian" cannot simply be interpreted as *complementary* terms (the Scythian as the most savage barbarian). (3) Three of the pairs address ethnic realities: Greek/Jew, circumcised/uncircumcised, barbarian/Scythian, and the antithesis slave/free speaks of social barriers; we note that the pair barbarian/Scythian is not construed as an antithesis. (4) It is striking that in contrast to Col 3:11 the parallel passages Gal 3:28 and 1 Cor 12:13 have the contrast "Jew and Greek" followed by the contrast "slave and free." The evidence of Greek and Roman authors indicates that there were Scythian slaves in regions of the Mediterranean.[818] If we interpret the Scythian as a slave, Col 3:11 expresses a consistent contrast of eight terms as well as a chiasm (A-B-B-A): The Greeks/Jews are chiastically contrasted with the circumcised/uncircumcised, and the barbarians/Scythians likewise are contrasted with the slaves/free. Paul thus emphasizes the fact that the reality of the gospel transcends two types of ethnic barriers and two types of social barriers of society: converted Greeks and converted uncircumcised people are as much members of the messianic people of God as are Jews and circumcised people, and Scythians and slaves who have become Christians have the same identity in Jesus Christ as non-Greeks and free citizens. If Philemon and (his wife?) Apphia were free Phrygians, thus "barbarians"—both names are attested in Phrygia,[819] a fact that does not provide exegetical certainty—then we obtain a combination of ethnic, geographical and social differences. Paul speaks of barbarians with differing geographical and social backgrounds: slave owners from Phrygia (Philemon?), who are "local" barbarians; free citizens in Phrygia (or in Lydia and Pisidia); and slaves from Scythia, who are "foreign" barbarians from the uncivilized regions north of the Black Sea—all belong to the church because they share the same identity in Jesus Christ.

---

[814]BDAG, s.v. "Σκύθης," 932; cf. BAA 1514; Bruce, *Col,* 276; Lohse, *Kol,* 208 (ET, 144); Schweizer, *Kol,* 150; Gnilka, *Kol,* 190; Wright, *Col,* 139; Dunn, *Col,* 225-26; Barth and Blanke, *Col,* 416; G. Schneider, *EWNT* 3:612 (*EDNT* 3:256).

[815]Moule, *Col,* 121; O'Brien, *Col,* 193.

[816]See Wolter, *Kol,* 183.

[817]See D. Campbell 1996, 123-24.

[818]Plutarch, *Pomp.* 78.4; Dio Cassius 79.5.5—79.6.3; Strabo 11.6.2; Pliny, *Nat.* 4.80-81; Seneca, *Ep.* 80.9. For references to Scythians in northern regions of the Roman Empire (Sarmatae, in the Danube region, Moesians) see Tacitus, *Ann.* 12.17; Martial 7.80; Juvenal 9.1.42.

[819]For Philemon see MM 670; *NewDocs* 3:91; 5:144; for Apphia see MM 73. Cf. D. Campbell 1996, 132 n. 39; for the comment that follows above see ibid., 132. See also Fitzmyer, *Philem,* 86-87.

Paul, in his letter to Philemon, mentions his desire to visit Colossae (Philem 22). We do not know whether Paul was able to visit Colossae after his (assumed) release from his Roman imprisonment and after his (assumed) missionary work in Spain.

Archippus, Philemon and Apphia are said to have died as martyrs in Colossae, and Titus and Timothy spent some time in the church there.[820] In Colossae (and in Chonai) the cult of St. Michael is attested in the fifth century: the apostles John and Philip are said to have successfully prayed to the archangel Michael, who miraculously caused the appearance of a popular medicinal spring that led to the building of a chapel; the crevice at the site is attested already in the sixth century B.C. (Herodotus 7.30). A local synod that met in Laodikeia some time after A.D. 350 criticized the excessive veneration of angels. Churches where St. Michael was worshiped continue to be attested in Phrygia and in Pisidia in the first half of the fifth century. Ruins that were still clearly visible in the eighteenth century in the northeast section of the hill on the north bank of the Lykos River may have been the remains of the Church of the Archangel (Church of St. Michael), which was known throughout Asia Minor in the fifth century.[821]

Epaphras and other early Christian missionaries who were active in the Lykos Valley in the upper Maeander region could easily have reached Aphrodisias, a city with a large Jewish community.

Aphrodisias ('Αφροδισίας; mod. Geyre)[822] was situated 25 km east of Antiocheia on the Maeander in the valley of the Morsynos River (mod. Dandala Su), a tributary of the Maeander River in Caria, southwest of Mount Kadmos, north of which was the Lykos Valley. Aphrodisias was founded probably in the second century B.C. and originally was called Ninoe, a name that may be connected with the Babylonian goddess Ishtar. During the Hellenistic period the main deity of the city was Aphrodite, whose early identification with the Roman goddess Venus led to a close connection with Rome and with the family of Julius Caesar.

---

[820]*Menologium Basilianum* (PG 117:33c-d; 173d); H. Delehaye, ed., *Synaxarium,* 19-20, 247, 477.

[821]See Belke and Mersich 1990, 310.

[822]G. Hirschfeld, "Aphrodisias 2," PW 1.2 (1894): 2726; H. Treidler, "Aphrodisias 1," *KP* 1:1541; K. Erim, *PECS* 68-70; J. M. Reynolds, *OCD* 119-20; H. Kaletsch, *DNP* 1:836-37; Magie 1950, 1:132, 431-32, 473, 502; 2:1002 n. 38; Bean 1971, 211-31; Price 1984, 41, 83, 118-19, 137, 261 (no. 64); S. Mitchell 1995a, 1:81, 177, 195, 2:24, 32, 36, 118; Joyce Maire Reynolds, *Aphrodisias and Rome: Documents from the Excavation of the Theatre at Aphrodisias* (London: Society for the Promotion of Roman Studies, 1982); Kenan T. Erim, *Aphrodisias: City of Venus Aphrodite* (London: Muller, Blond & White, 1986); K. T. Erim, *Aphrodisias: A Guide to the Site and Its Museum* (Istanbul: Net Turistik Yayinlar, 1989 [1998]); Charlotte Roueché and Kenan T. Erim, eds., *Aphrodisias Papers [1]: Recent Work on Architecture and Sculpture* (JRASup 1; Ann Arbor: University of Michigan, 1990); R. R. R. Smith and K. T. Erim, eds., *Aphrodisias Papers 2: The Theatre, a Sculptor's Workshop, Philosophers, and Coin-Types* (JRASup 2; Ann Arbor: University of Michigan, 1991); Charlotte Roueché and R. R. R. Smith, eds., *Aphrodisias Papers 3: The Setting and Quarries, Mythological and Other Sculptural Decoration, Architectural Development, Portico of Tiberius, and Tetrapylon* (JRASup 20; Ann Arbor: University of Michigan, 1996). Inscriptions: *MAMA* VIII 72-160 (ed. W. M. Calder and J. M. R. Cormack, 1962); further inscriptions have been and continue to be published in *Aphrodisias Papers.*

Aphrodisias resisted Mithradates VI in 88 B.C. and received privileges that it retained until the third century A.D. Julius Caesar visited the city and donated a golden statue of Eros to the temple of Aphrodite. The citizens were *liberi* in the first century (Pliny, *Nat.* 5.29.109). Several events of the history of the city can be reconstructed on the basis of the inscriptions incised in the "archive wall" in the theater. Since the first century B.C. Aphrodisias was the center of a famous school of sculptors. The signature of Aristeias and Papias, who sculptured the two centaurs that stood in Hadrian's villa in Tibur, included a reference to Aphrodisias.[823] In Aphrodisias sculptures of gods, priests, philosophers and other men and women have been discovered. The only extant sculptured portrait of Pythagoras the philosopher was (re)discovered in Aphrodisias in 1990.[824] The valuable white marble came from at least seventy-eight quarries, all of which were only 2 km away from the city center.[825] Continuous archaeological work conducted since 1937 and since 1961 has excavated important buildings of the city: the temple of Aphrodite (first century; 8 by 13 columns),[826] the imperial temple (before A.D. 50; 14 by 90 m, with two colonnaded halls measuring 80 by 14 m each), bouleuterion, North Agora, South Agora, Stoa of Tiberius (216 by 69 m, with a pool in the center measuring 169 by 19 m and 85 cm deep),[827] theater (first century B.C.; capacity for 8,000 spectators), baths, nymphaeum, philosophical school, stadium (first/second century A.D.; 262 by 59 m; capacity for 30,000 spectators), tetrapylon (second century), atrium house (with mosaics), large private villa (later the seat of the bishop). The city walls (3.5 km long) date to the third century A.D. Chariton, who wrote the oldest Greek novel to have survived in its entirety, the romantic adventure novel *Chaireas and Kallirrhoe,* lived in Aphrodisias between the first century B.C. and the second century A.D.[828] Alexander, a commentator on the works of Aristotle in the second century A.D., came from Aphrodisias.

A few years ago no evidence of a Jewish community in Aphrodisias had surfaced. In the mid-1980s, two long inscriptions dating to the second century A.D. were discovered, listing the names and professions of a large number of Jews who lived in Aphrodisias.[829] A new regional survey in the area led to the discovery of a tomb depicting a menorah in the Işılar Valley, further evidence for Jewish inhabitants in the city.[830] This example suggests that there may have been large Jewish communities in other cities that simply have not been documented yet.[831] The veneration of pagan deities persisted in Aphrodisias far into the early Byzantine period—even after the city had become the seat of the bishop of Caria—probably due to the popularity of Aphrodite. The city came to be called Stavropolis or simply Caria (after the province) in order to erase the memory of Aphrodite. The bishop Ammonios attended the Council of Nicea in A.D. 325. The temple of Aphrodite was refurbished as a church, the Bishop's Church, in the fifth century, perhaps in connection with a visit of the emperor Theodosius II in A.D. 443.[832]

---

[823]See M. Floriani Squarciapino and P. Rockwell, in *Aphrodisias Papers 2,* 123-26, 127-43.

[824]See R. R. R. Smith, "A New Portrait of Pythagoras," in *Aphrodisias Papers 2,* 159-67.

[825]See P. Rockwell, "The Marble Quarries," in *Aphrodisias Papers 3,* 81-104.

[826]Reynolds et al., in *Aphrodisias Papers [1],* 37-88; Smith, in *Aphrodisias Papers 3,* 31-43.

[827]Smith, in *Aphrodisias Papers 3,* 13-23, 44-49; N. de Chaisemartin et al., in *Aphrodisias Papers 3,* 149-72.

[828]See E. L. Bowie, *OCD* 318-19.

[829]Reynolds and Tannenbaum 1987, 5-7; *SEG* XXXVI 970; NewDocs 9:73-80 (no. 25); IJudO II 14; for the Greek text with a German translation see Wander 1998, 235-39; for a discussion of the inscription see ibid., 121-27; W. Ameling, in *IJudO* II 2004, 71-112.

[830]See Gates 1995, 237.

[831]See Seager and Kraabel 1983, 181.

[832]See R. Cormack, "The Temple as the Cathedral," in *Aphrodisias Papers [1],* 75-88.

Other important cities close to Ephesus that would have been attractive targets for Paul and his coworkers included Smyrna, Pergamon, Thyatira, Sardis and Philadelphia. We know from Rev 2—3 that churches existed in these cities around A.D. 80-90, but we do not know which missionaries were responsible for the establishment of these churches (see §22.7). It is possible that Paul or his coworkers visited these cities during the three years that he worked in the province of Asia.

Evangelism in Alexandria Troas

Paul ended his long missionary work in Ephesus probably on account of an "affliction" that he and his coworkers experienced in the province of Asia: "We do not want you to be unaware, brothers and sisters, of the affliction we experienced in Asia; for we were so utterly, unbearably crushed that we despaired of life itself" (2 Cor 1:8). Before he could realize the planned visit to Corinth, he traveled to Alexandria Troas to preach the gospel there (2 Cor 2:12).[833] Paul did not stay very long: he was anxious because Titus failed to meet up with him in Troas, and so he left for Macedonia (2 Cor 2:13b). Still, the missionary work in Troas was successful: Paul speaks of a "door" that the Lord has opened in the city (θύρας μοι ἀνεῳγμένης ἐν κυρίῳ, *thyras moi aneōgmenēs en kyriō* [2 Cor 2:12b]); when he left Troas, there were people in the city to whom he "said farewell" (ἀποταξάμενος αὐτοῖς, *apotaxamenos autois* [2 Cor 2:13b]); and when he traveled to Jerusalem several months later, he and his companions stayed in Troas for an entire week and celebrated the Lord's Supper with the church on the first day of the week (i.e., on Sunday).[834] Paul's missionary outreach in Alexandria Troas is dated to the summer of A.D. 55.

Alexandria Troas (᾿Αλεξάνδρεια ἡ Τρωϊάς; mod. Eskistanbul, south of Dalyan)[835] was founded in 310 B.C. by the Seleucid king Antigonos I under the name "Antigoneia" by resettling the inhabitants of smaller towns—Larisa, Kolonai, Hamaxitos, Chrysa, Neandreia, Kebrene, Skepsios—in the southern Troad (Strabo 13.1.33, 47 [on the Troad see above]).[836] The Macedonian king Lysimachus, who defeated Antigonos, renamed the city

---

[833]2 Cor 2:12a: ἐλθὼν δὲ εἰς τὴν Τρωᾶδα εἰς τὸ εὐαγγέλιον. The preposition εἰς (*eis*) has a final meaning here; see Thrall, *2 Cor,* 1:183.

[834]See Llewelyn 2001, with a discussion of 1 Cor 16:2; Acts 20:7; Rev 1:10.

[835]W. Ruge, "Troas 2," PW 7.A1 (1939): 583-84; H. Treidler, "Alexandreia 2," *KP* 1:245; C. Bayburtluoğlu, *PECS* 39; S. Mitchell, *OCD* 62; Magie 1950, 1:69, 82, 92; 2:923, 947, 1334-35; J. M. Cook 1973, 198-204; C. J. Hemer, "Alexandria Troas," *TynBul* 26 (1975): 91-92; Burdick 1978, 50-53; Schwertheim and Wiegartz 1994, 157-95; G. Cohen 1995, 145-48; Schwertheim and Wiegartz 1996; Jewett 1997, 16-17; Ricl 1997, 1-21; Schwertheim 1999, esp. "Zur Gründung der römischen Kolonie in Alexandria Troas," 95-101. A survey on the site of ancient Alexandria Troas was conducted in 1994/1995. Inscriptions: E. Schwertheim, "Neue Inschriften aus Alexandreia Troas, Antandros, Skepsis und Kebren," in Schwertheim and Wiegartz 1996, 99-124; *I. AlexTroas* (ed. M. Ricl, 1997).

[836]See Ricl 1997, 4-11.

Alexandria Troas, built a new city wall, and allowed the citizens of Skepsios to return. Alexandria Troas controlled the trade with the northern Aegean regions because of its geographical location, and so the city quickly became one of the most important centers of trade in the Mediterranean world. The harbor was surrounded by a wall (2.5 by 1.7 km). A recently discovered inscription documents that Sextus Appuleius, consul in 29 B.C. and governor of the province of Asia in 23-21 B.C., was ritually venerated in the context of the local imperial cult.[837] Julius Caesar evidently supported Alexandria Troas: two inscriptions honor him as "divine."[838] The city was transformed into a colony of veterans of the Roman army between 41 and 30 B.C. (Colonia [Iulia] Augusta Troas/Troadensis) and was strengthened by Augustus.[839] It probably was Augustus who granted Troas the *ius italicum,* a privilege enjoyed by only one other colony in the province of Asia, Parium.[840] The importance of the Roman citizens can be seen in the fact that 44 percent of the inscriptions are in Latin; of the 144 individuals mentioned in the inscriptions, 121 are Roman citizens.[841] Many highly decorated officials and military figures settled in Alexandria Troas at an early date (*I. AlexTroas* 34-48), including a certain Quintus Lollius Fronto, who was honored for his illustrious career by forty-four African cities.[842] The city evidently offered excellent opportunities for advancing one's fortunes.[843] Troas had perhaps fifty thousand inhabitants.[844] Emperor Claudius was honored with three statues between A.D. 37 and 41, and Nero with at least one statue.[845] Inscriptions attest the worship of Apollo Patroos, Apollo Smintheus, Asclepius, Dionysos, Genius populi, Hosios and Dikaios, Theos Hypsistos and the river-god Skamander.[846] Remains of the aqueduct, a nymphaeum and large public baths from the time of Hadrian survive, and the *cavea* of the theater can still be seen. No remains of the Doric temple, stadium, agora or gymnasium survive.

Paul left Troas because his "mind could not rest" since Titus failed to arrive, causing him to leave for Macedonia earlier than planned (2 Cor 2:13). If the subsequent v. 14 is to be connected with v. 13, which is suggested by the particle δέ (*de*), then the thanksgiving and the triumphal procession mentioned in v. 14 may be a reference to the fact that God used him despite his hasty departure from Troas.[847]

---

[837]Helmut Halfmann, "Ein neuer Statthalterkult in der Provinz Asia," *EA* 10 (1987): 83-89. The inscription was discovered in the vicinity of Üvecik, about 14 km northeast of Troas.

[838]*I. AlexTroas* 13, 36.

[839]See *I. AlexTroas* 106 (funerary inscription of Gaius Cannutius, a soldier who had served in the Legio XXX Classica). The inscription *I. AlexTroas* 34 shows that a certain Gaius Fabricius Tuscus (*I. AlexTroas* 34) supervised the building activities that Augustus had initiated.

[840]Ricl 1997, 226-27 (Testimonia no. 119: *Digesta Iustiniani Augusti* L 15.7; L 15.8.9 [ed. Mommsen, 1870]).

[841]Ricl 1997, 14.

[842]*I. AlexTroas* 35.

[843]Schwertheim, in Schwertheim 1999, 99.

[844]Burdick (1978, 50) assumes between 30,000 and 100,000 inhabitants, referring to W. Leaf, *Strabo on the Troad* (Cambridge: Cambridge University Press, 1923), 236. J. M. Cook (1973, 383) suggest 30,000 to 40,000 inhabitants, a figure seen by Jewett (1997, 16 n. 65) as too low.

[845]*I. AlexTroas* 15-17 (Claudius), 18 (Nero).

[846]*I. AlexTroas* 62-77.

[847]See Perriman 1989, 39-40.

Missionary Work in Illyricum

Paul had decided toward the end of his time in Ephesus to visit the churches in Macedonia and Achaia before his journey back to Antioch and Jerusalem (Acts 19:21). After his situation in Ephesus had become so critical that he barely escaped with his life, he decided in the summer of A.D. 55 to realize these plans (Acts 20:1-3). Paul was in the process of concluding the collection that he had organized in the churches that he had founded; he planned to travel to Spain after taking the collected funds to the church in Jerusalem. In his letter to the Christians in Rome, which he writes in the context of these plans in Corinth, Paul notes that he preached the gospel "from Jerusalem and as far around as Illyricum" (Rom 15:19). I agree with those scholars who interpret this comment in terms of Paul having engaged in missionary work in the province of Illyricum. This mission must have taken place in the summer of A.D. 56: after Paul traveled from Ephesus and Alexandria Troas to Macedonia in the late summer of A.D. 55—he wrote 2 Corinthians during the late summer or early fall, perhaps in Philippi—he evidently did not travel directly to Achaia and to Corinth, but first visited Illyricum.

Paul says in Rom 15:19 that "from Jerusalem and as far around as Illyricum I have fully proclaimed the good news of Christ" (ἀπὸ Ἰερουσαλὴμ καὶ κύκλῳ μέχρι τοῦ Ἰλλυρικοῦ, *apo Ierousalēm kai kyklō mechri tou Illyrikou*). The interpretation of this formulation is disputed. Some scholars interpret the phrase in an exclusive sense: the geographical terms describe not areas in which Paul worked as a missionary but rather "the limits of missionary activity."[848] This interpretation is unconvincing because the phrase *apo Ierousalēm* designates the starting point of the preaching of the gospel by Paul.[849] When Paul visited Jerusalem in A.D. 33/34 for the first time after his conversion, he had a vision in the temple in which Jesus confirmed his call as apostle to the Gentiles, telling him that his testimony would be rejected in Jerusalem (Acts 22:17-18). This notice agrees with Paul's statement in Rom 15:19 that his missionary work started in Jerusalem.[850] The formulation οὐ παραδέξονταί σου μαρτυρίαν περὶ ἐμοῦ (*paradexontai sou martyrian peri emou*) in Acts 22:18 might indeed indicate that Paul presented the message of Jesus the Messiah to the rabbis whom he knew, to his fellow students and to the members of the synagogue that he used to visit: Luke reports in Acts 9:28-29 that he spoke "boldly" (παρρησιαζόμενος, *parrēsiazomenos*) in the name of the Lord and that he "spoke and argued" (ἐλάλει τε καὶ συνεζήτει, *elalei te kai synezētei*) with the Greek-speaking Jews during his visit to Jerusalem; in Acts 26:20 Luke again states that Paul proclaimed the message of Jesus (ἀπήγγελλον, *apēngellon*) during this visit to Jerusalem. The fact that Paul

---

[848]Käsemann, *Röm*, 380 (ET, 394), and other interpreters.
[849]Wilckens, *Röm*, 3:119-20.
[850]See Hengel 1979, 74-75; Riesner 1994, 233-34 (ET, 263).

visited Jerusalem repeatedly (Acts 9:26; 15:4; 18:22; 21:15-18; cf. 19:21; 20:16, 22) shows that the city in which the first Christian community existed was important to him. Paul's reference to the importance of Jerusalem for the progress of the gospel in Rom 15:19 demonstrates the error of the view that construes the references to Paul's visits to Jerusalem as a Lukan fabrication.[851] If the reference to Jerusalem in Rom 15:19 is to be understood in terms of a geographical localization of Paul's missionary work, then it is plausible to assume the same for the reference to Illyricum. The objection that neither Paul nor Luke mentions missionary work in Illyricum[852] is unconvincing: if Paul asserts that he preached in Jerusalem for some time, he indeed asserts in Rom 15:19 that he preached in Illyricum. It must be significant that Paul mentions Illyricum, and not Corinth, as the western limit of his missionary activities. Paul presumably does not refer to the region in Macedonia that was regarded as Illyrian in ethnic terms (see Strabo 7.7.4): Paul refers in Rom 15 to provinces (in Rom 15:24, 28 to Spain, in Rom 15:26 to Macedonia and Achaia). The fact that Paul uses an unusual Latinized form of the name of the province (Ἰλλυρικόν, *Illyrikon;* the traditional Greek terms were Ἰλλυρία, *Illyria,* and Ἰλλυρίς, *Illyris*)[853] confirms the suggestion that Paul reached the province of Illyricum on the coast of the Adriatic Sea.[854]

F. F. Bruce suggests that Paul traveled to Illyricum with the goal of familiarizing himself with a situation in which Latin was spoken as preparation for his planned outreach to Spain.[855] The reconstruction by Jerome Murphy-O'Connor is more comprehensive and more convincing in the context of the specific historical situation of Paul at the end of his mission to Ephesus. He argues that at the end of his stay in Ephesus Paul had not been involved in pioneer missionary work for several years because he had been caring for the church in Ephesus and dealing with problems in other churches that he had founded, particulary the church of Corinth. His coworkers, on the other hand, had founded new churches in several cities: in Colossae, Laodikeia and Hierapolis. And the church in Corinth had made peace with him, at least temporarily. "Now all were tranquil. A free summer was a golden opportunity to again seek virgin territory . . . the prospect must have been irresistible. In any case, Paul did not restrain himself. He went to Illyricum."[856]

---

[851]Thus correctly Riesner 1994, 214, 233-34 (ET, 242, 263).

[852]Wilckens, *Röm,* 3:119-20, and other commentators.

[853]Bowers 1976, 21 n. 3; Riesner 1994, 215.

[854]Thus Suhl 1975, 92-110, 342; Bruce 1977, 316-17; D. Gill, in Gill and Gempf 1994, 399, 410; Riesner 1994, 214-15, 263 (ET, 242-43, 295-96); Murphy-O'Connor 1996, 316-17, 322, 363; as a possibility: Cranfield, *Rom,* 2:761-62; Dunn, *Rom,* 2:864; Fitzmyer, *Rom,* 714.

[855]Bruce 1977, 317.

[856]Murphy-O'Connor 1996, 316; he dates Paul's mission to Illyricum a year earlier (A.D. 55), since he dates the departure from Ephesus one year earlier (A.D. 54). A visit to Illyricum also is assumed by Duncan 1930, 217-21; W. Metzger 1976, 42-44; as a possibility: Riesner 1994, 268-69 (ET, 301).

Illyricum (Illuricum; Ἰλλυρίς [see fig. 37])[857] was the region between the Adriatic coast and the Morawa River, from the region of Epirus to the Danube. The Indo-Germanic tribes that lived in this region formed an independent entity only after 250 B.C. The Romans conquered the region after many battles, and Illyricum became a Roman province under Julius Caesar. After the last revolts were crushed by Tiberius, Illyricum was divided into two provinces around A.D. 9, designated Dalmatia and Pannonia under the Flavian emperors. Dalmatia possibly was called *superior provincia Illyricum;* this province included Illyricum south of the Save River and extended east as far as the Danube. Illyricum was governed by imperial legates of consular rank, with the seat of the governor in Salonae. L. Arruntius Camillus Scribonianus, one of the legates of Illyricum, unsuccessfully revolted in A.D. 42. Scodra, Epetium and Tragurium were important cities. Agriculture and forestry as well as gold, silver and copper mines were major sources of income.

Notes on the travel route. If Paul indeed traveled to Illyricum after visiting the Macedonian churches in Philippi, Thessalonike and Beroea, then he would have passed through the following cities on the Via Egnatia:

Edessa (Ἔδεσσα; mod. Edessa),[858] 82 km west of Thessalonike on the western end of the Macedonian plain on the Via Egnatia, controlled the northernmost pass from the coastal plain on the Thermaic Gulf across Mount Bermion to Upper Macedonia. It was long believed that Edessa was identical with the city of Aigai that Homer and Pindar mention repeatedly.[859] As the result of new excavations since 1977, Aigai is now identified with a site near modern Vergina, 42 km south of Edessa and 10 km southeast of Beroea.[860] The acropolis of Edessa was located on a high plateau with famous waterfalls (of the tributary of the Lydias River), the site of modern Edessa. Since the first century B.C. Romans and Italians lived in the city. Augustus granted Edessa autonomy and the right to mint coins. The lower city of ancient Edessa has been investigated, particularly the ruins of the city walls and the city gates. The oldest Christian inscriptions of Macedonia were discovered in Edessa, dating to the second and third centuries, including the inscription of a bishop (his name has not been preserved) and a prayer for the dedication of a church.[861] We do not know when the Christian community in Edessa was established. The first bishop of Edessa

---

[857]N. Vulić, PW 9.1 (1914): 1085-88; J. Szilágyi, *KP* 2:1367-69; J. J. Wilkes, *OCD* 747; M. Šašel Kos, *DNP* 5:940-43; Aleksandar Stipcević, *The Illyrians History and Culture* (Park Ridge, N.J.: Noyes, 1977); J. J. Wilkes, "The Population of Roman Dalmatia," *ANRW* II.6 (1977): 732-66; Marin Zaninović, "The Economy of Roman Dalmatia," *ANRW* II.6 (1977) 767-809; Polomé 1983, 536-40; Selim Islami, *Les Illyriens Aperçu Historique* (Tirana: Académie des sciences de la RPS d'Albanie, Centre des recherches archéologiques, 1985); Wilkes 1992.

[858]E. Oberhummer, "Edessa 1," PW 5.2 (1905): 1933; C. Danoff, "Edessa 1," *KP* 2:197; P. M. Petsas, *PECS* 292-93; M. Errington, "Edessa 3," *DNP* 3:874; D. Müller, in Lauffer 1989, 205-7; Papazoglou 1988, 127-31; see also A. B. Tataki, *Macedonian Edessa: Prosopography and Onomasticon* (Meletemata 18; Athens: Kentron Hellenikes kai Romaikes Archaiotetos; Paris: Boccard, 1994); Touratsoglou 1997, 187-97.

[859]See P. M. Petsas, *PECS* 292.

[860]See E. N. Borza, *BAGRW* 762, with reference to Manoles Andronikos, *Vergina: The Royal Tombs and the City* (Athens: Ekdotike Athenon, 1984). Aigai was the old capital of Macedonia until King Archelaos (413-399 B.C.) moved to Pella. Aigai remained an important city for the royal dynasty, however, indicated by the fact that members of the royal family were buried there. See Papazoglou 1988, 128, 131-35; Touratsoglou 1997, 211-49.

[861]*I. MakedChr* 7-10, 23-59, nos. 1-54. See Pallas 1977, 83.

listed in the records of the church councils is a certain Isidoros, in A.D. 691.

Arnisa ("Αρνισα; near mod. Vegora Novigrad),[862] 40 km west of Edessa and 3 km south of Lake Begorritus (mod. Vegorritis), was the last city of the Macedonian kingdom in the Lynkos region that a traveler encountered before crossing over the Kirli Derven Pass to Illyricum.

Herakleia ('Ηράκλεια; near mod. Bitola, Macedonia),[863] about 50 km northwest of Arnisa in the Erigon Valley (mod. Crna), at the junction of the Via Egnatia with a road that ran via Stoboi north to the province of Dacia.[864] Strabo, in his description of the Via Egnatia, which he borrowed from Polybius, mentions Herakleia as an important town (7.7.4). Herakleia was founded probably by Philipp II, and it played an important role in the military campaigns of Julius Caesar (Caesar, *Bell. civ.* 3.79.3). In the first century A.D. veterans of the Roman army lived in the city, whose importance is documented by several inscriptions. Remains of the city walls, public baths, colonnaded hall, theater, two early Byzantine basilicas (fifth/sixth century) and the Bishop's Palace survive. Herakleia was the seat of a bishop since the fourth century.

Lychnidos (Λυχνιδός, Λυχνίς; Lychnitus; mod. Ohrid),[865] 65 km west of Herakleia on the northeastern shore of Lake Lychnidos, was an Illyrian city that became Macedonian in the Hellenistic period; it belonged to the Roman province of Macedonia. Remains of the ancient theater and of two early Byzantine churches survive; one of the churches was discovered underneath the church of St. Sophia. The bishop Zosimus (fourth century) is the first bishop attested.

Klaudanon (mod. Orake, Albania?)[866] was situated 30 km west of Lychnidos on the eastern end of the pass of the Via Egnatia across Mount Candaviae, on the upper Genusus River (mod. Shkumbini).

Treiecto (near mod. Mirake)[867] was situated 30 km west of Klaudanon in the valley of the Genesus River.

---

[862]W. Tomaschek, "Arnissa 1," PW 2.1 (1895): 1205; P. A. McKay, *PECS* 94, with a localization north of modern Petres. Against this identification is J. J. Wilkes (in *BAGRW* 751), who identifies the ancient site near modern Petres with the ancient city of Cellae, a town attested in the Roman and Late Roman periods on the Via Egnatia 8 km northwest of Arnisa; see also N. G. L. Hammond and M. B. Hatzopoulos, "The Via Egnatia in Western Macedonia I," *American Journal of Ancient History* 7 (1982): 128-49, esp. 134-35; D. Müller, in Lauffer 1989, 135. Papazoglou (1988, 161-64) argues for an identification of the ancient site in Vegora Novigrad with Kellai and for the localization of Arnisa with a site on the northeast shore of Lake Begorritus.

[863]F. Stählin, "Herakleia 4," PW 8.1 (1912): 424-29; E. Meyer, "Herakleia 2," *KP* 2:1034; J. Wiseman, *PECS* 385; M. Errington, "Herakleia 2," *DNP* 5:364-65; Papazoglou 1988, 259-68, and passim; H. Kramolisch and K. Braun, in Lauffer 1989, 264-65. Excavations: *Herakleja I-III* (3 vols.; ed. F. Papazoglou et al.; Bitola: Odbor za Herakleja, 1961-1967).

[864]Stoboi had a Jewish community at least since the second century A.D., as the inscription *SEG* XXXIV 679 documents. See §22.10.

[865]M. Fluss, PW 13.2 (1927): 2111-15; J. Szilágyi, *KP* 3:796; J. Wiseman, *PECS* 536; M. Šašel Kos, *DNP* 7:536; Alexandrov 1976, 81-82; Papazoglou 1988, 93-96; Wilkes 1992, 170, 172.

[866]J. J. Wilkes, in *BAGRW* 752, with reference to N. G. L. Hammond, "The Western Part of the Via Egnatia," *JRS* 64 (1974): 185-94, esp. 185-86.

[867]J. J. Wilkes, in *BAGRW* 756, with reference to Hammond, "Western Part," 187-88.

Clodiana (mod. Mafmutaga?)[868] was situated about 50 km west of Treiecto on the north bank of the Genesus River in the coastal plain.

Dyrrhachium (Δυρράχιον; former Epidamnos; mod. Durrës, Albania),[869] about 50 km northwest of Clodiana, was a Greek colony founded in 627 B.C. by Corinth and by Korkyra on the coast of Dalmatia (Illyricum). Appian relates the foundation myth in connection with his account of the civil war between Pompey and Julius Caesar (Appian, *Bell. civ.* 2.39). The city had its own treasure house in Olympia (Pausanias 6.19.8). Dyrrhachium was annexed by Rome after the first Illyrian War (Livy 29.12.3). In the Roman period Dyrrhachium was an important city: it was the best port for crossing from Italy (Brindisi) into Greece and was the starting point of the Via Egnatia, the road that crossed the new province of Macedonia linking Rome with the eastern provinces, built after 140 B.C., under the proconsul Gn. Egnatius, with a length of 535 Roman miles. Under Augustus, Dyrrhachium became a Roman colony with the *ius italicum*. Inscriptions document an aqueduct from the time of Hadrian, a temple of Minerva, a temple of Diana and a library.

Apollonia (mod. Pojan, Albania),[870] about 80 km south of Dyrrhachium on the Adriatic Sea near the mouth of the Aous River (mod. Vijosë) in southern Illyricum, was an old Greek city founded by colonists from Korkyra and Corinth around 588 B.C. Apollonia was located on the southern branch of the Via Egnatia (Strabo 7.7.4); it minted its own coins since the early fourth century B.C. and belonged to Rome since the death of Pyrrhos (297-272 B.C.). Cicero describes Apollonia as "urbs gravis et nobilis" (Cicero, *Fam.* 13.29.2). The city had a famous rhetorical school that Augustus attended before coming to power. Remains include the ancient city walls (4 km long), a triumphal arch, the theater, an odeion, several temples, a gymnasium (cf. Strabo 9.3.16) and a large hall, identified by some scholars as a library.

My reconstruction of Paul's movements assumes that the apostle traveled from Illyrian Apollonia by ship to Corinth (500 km, between five and ten days of travel). After visiting the churches in Macedonia and a short period of missionary work in Illyricum, he probably wanted to reach Corinth in late November or early December before the onset of the winter. If Paul decided to take the overland route and travel from Illyricum southeast via the region of Epirus to Corinth (485 km, about twenty-four days of travel), he would have passed through the following cities, presumably sharing the gospel as he traveled.

(1) *Byllis* (Βύλλις; mod. Hekal),[871] 35 km from Apollonia on the upper Aous River, attested in the Hellenistic period, was a Roman colony in southern Illyricum. Remains of two theaters, the agora and a gymnasium survive. (2) *Hekatompedon* (mod. Saraqinishti?),[872]

---

[868] L. Bürchner, PW 4.1 (1900): 62; J. J. Wilkes, in *BAGRW* 752; Hammond, "Western Part," 188; Alexandrov 1976, 36.

[869] A. Philippson, PW 5.2 (1905): 1882-87; E. Meyer, *KP* 2:187-88; P. C. Sestieri, *PECS* 311; D. Strauch, *DNP* 3:857-58; Alexandrov 1976, 50; Wilkes 1992, 110-11, 168, 212-13.

[870] G. Hirschfeld, "Apollonia 1," PW 2.1 (1895): 111-13; C. Danoff, "Apollonia 1," *KP* 1:448; P. Sestieri, *PECS* 70-71; E. Wirbelauer, "Apollonia 1," *DNP* 1:870-71; Alexandrov 1976, 16.

[871] E. Meyer, *KP* 1:978; N. G. L. Hammond, *PECS* 177; M. Šašel Kos, *DNP* 2:865; N. Ceka, "Le Koinon des Bylliones," *Iliria* 14 (1984): 61-89. The first four cities are in modern Albania.

[872] N. Hammond 1967, 209, 659; idem, *PECS* 380 (identification with Lekli; see, however, Wilkes, in *BAGRW* 753); Alexandrov 1976, 62.

47 km from Byllis on the upper Aous River at the confluence of the Elaion River (mod. Drin), was founded probably by Pyrrhos. (3) *Antigoneia* (mod. Lekli?),[873] 31 km from Hek-atompedon, was founded by Pyrrhos and is mentioned in connection with Rome's war against Philipp V in 198 B.C. (4) *Hadrianopolis* (mod. Sofratikë, near Libohovë),[874] about 10 km from Antigoneia on the upper Elaion River. (5) *Phanota* (mod. Ravene [near Vro-sina]?),[875] about 50 km southeast of Hadrianopolis on the Thyamis River (mod. Kalamas). (6) *Photike* (mod. Paramithia, Liboni),[876] 25 km south of Phanota on the hills between the Thyamis River and the Acheron Valley. (7) *Ephyra-Kichyros* ("Εφυρα; mod. Mesopota-mon),[877] 30 km south of Photike in the coastal plain (Bay of Elaia), the site where Odys-seus procured the poison for his arrows (Homer, *Od.* 1.259ff.). Remains of the temple of Persephone and of Hades, gods of the underworld (Pausanias 1.17.4-5), survive. (8) *Ni-kopolis* (Νικόπολις; Actia Nicopolis; mod. Palaio-Preveza),[878] about 35 km southeast of Ephyra, was founded by Augustus in 30 B.C. at the site where his troops had rested before the Battle of Actium (31 B.C.), situated on the other side of the peninsula. The city had a west harbor on the Ionian Sea and an east harbor on the Gulf of Ambrakai. Large areas in southern Epirus and of Acarnania belonged to the city territory (Strabo 7.7.5; 10.2.2; Pausanias 5.23.3). Nikopolis was a free city that minted its own coins. Augustus directed the Actian Games that were celebrated in honor of Apollo Aktios to be held at Nikopolis, and he integrated the games of the Delphic Amphictiony. During the principate of Nero, Nikopolis became the capital of the province of Epirus. Remains of the theater, stadium, amphitheater, odeion, gymnasium, baths and the impressive city walls survive. The Stoic philosopher Epictetus, who was a native of Phrygian Hierapolis, established a philosoph-ical school in Nikopolis after he was exiled from Rome in A.D. 89. (9) *Stratos* (Στράτος; mod. Stratos, Sourovigli),[879] about 70 km southeast of Nikopolis on the Acheloos River, was the most important city of Arcania. Remains of the city walls, agora, temple of Zeus Stratios (16 by 23 m; fourth century B.C.) and theater survive. An inscription documents a gymnasium. (10) *Pleuron* (Νέα Πλευρών; mod. Kato Retsina),[880] about 35 km south of Stratos on the lagoon of Mesologi in western Aetolia, was a new foundation after the de-struction of Old Pleuron in 230 B.C. Under Augustus, Pleuron was incorporated into the

---

[873]H. Treidler, "Antigoneia 4," *KP* 1:380; N. Hammond 1967, 278-79; idem, *PECS* 60 (identifica-tion with Saraqinishti); Alexandrov 1976, 15-16 (identification with Temnik); D. Budina, "An-tigonée (fouilles 1966-1970)," *Iliria* 2 (1972): 269-378; idem, "Antigonée d'Epire," *Iliria* 4 (1976): 327-46; G. Cohen 1995, 75-76; Wilkes, *BAGRW* 750.

[874]W. Ruge, "Hadrianopolis 2," PW 7.2 (1912): 2173; Soustal 1981, 146-48.

[875]E. Oberhummer, PW 19.2 (1938): 1788; E. Meyer, *KP* 4:709; N. Hammond 1967, 186-87, 676; idem, "Raveni," *PECS* 751.

[876]N. Hammond 1967, 73-74, 582; idem, *PECS* 709; Lauffer 1989, 509.

[877]A. Philippson, "Ephyra 7," PW 6.1 (1907): 20; E. Meyer, "Ephyra 3," *KP* 2:301; S. Dakaris, *PECS* 310-11; W. M. Murray, *OCD* 530; D. Strauch, "Ephyra 3," *DNP* 3:1091-92; N. Hammond 1967, 64-65, 478; R. Scheer, in Lauffer 1989, 218-19.

[878]F. Schober, "Nikopolis 2," PW 17.1 (1936): 511-15; E. Meyer, "Nikopolis 3," *KP* 4:124-25; Soustal 1981, 213-14; A. Weis, *PECS* 625-26; N. Purcell, "Nicopolis 3," *OCD* 1043; D. Strauch, "Nikopolis 3," *DNP* 8:936-37; N. Hammond 1967, 62; R. Scheer, in Lauffer 1989, 469-71; Evan-gelos K. Chrysos, ed., *Nikopolis I* (Proceedings of the First International Symposion at Nico-polis, 23-29 September 1984; Preveza: Demos Prevezas, 1987).

[879]W. Zschietzschmann, PW 4.A1 (1931): 331-35; E. Meyer, *KP* 5:395; N. Bonacasa, *PECS* 861-62; R. Scheer, in Lauffer 1989, 638-39. The inscription is *IG* IX 1.2^2 408.

[880]E. Kisten, PW 21.1 (1951): 239-40; E. Meyer, *KP* 4:928; N. Bonacasa, *PECS* 717-18; W. M. Mur-ray, *OCD* 1197; K. Freitag, *DNP* 9:1134; R. Scheer, in Lauffer 1989, 557.

colony Patrai. Remains of the mighty city walls (with seven gates and thirty-one towers), agora with a colonnaded hall 62 m long, theater, gymnasium and private houses survive. (11) *Patrai* (αἱ Πάτραι; Patrae; mod. Patras),[881] 35 km southeast of Pleuron on the other side of the Gulf of Patras on the Peloponnese in western Achaia, a port city since Mycenaen times, was refounded by Augustus in 14 B.C. as Colonia Augusta Aroë Patrensis, with the incorporation of neighboring towns including Pharai, Tritaia, Dyme, Pleuron and further areas in Aeolia. Besides Athens and Corinth, Patrai was among the most important cities of Greece (Strabo 8.7.5; Pausanias 7.18.2-4). Two inscriptions document Jews in Patrai.[882] Remain of the agora, amphitheater, odeion, a temple dating to the time of Augustus and city streets survive. The apocryphal *Acts of Andrew* claims to know that the apostle Andrew preached the gospel in Patrai after he had engaged in missionary work in Macedonia: he performed numerous miracles, healed the proconsul Lesbios, which resulted in the entire city accepting faith in Jesus, and received permission from Lesbios to destroy the idols in the city (*Acts Andr.* 22-24, 30-35).[883] The new proconsul Aegeates, who replaced Lesbios, whom the emperor had recalled and whose wife, Maximilla, had been converted as well, takes action against Andrew; on November 30 (year unknown) Andrew was crucified in Patrai. Some scholars assume that there was a Christian community in Patrai in the first century A.D.[884] Bishops of Patrai are documented since A.D. 347. (12) *Aigion* (Αἴγιον; mod. Aigion, Egio),[885] about 40 km east of Patrai on the Gulf of Corinth, was the site of the cult center of Zeus Homarios (in Helike, 8 km from the city) and, as a result the center of Achaia, the seat of the assembly of the Achaean Confederacy since 373 B.C. Twelve temples are attested for Aigion in the second century B.C., dedicated to Aphrodite, Apollo, Artemis, Asclepius, Athene, Demeter Panachaia, Dionysos, Hera, Kore, Poseidon, Soteria and Zeus Homagyrios (Pausanias 7.23.5-24.4). Aigion continued to flourish during the Roman Empire, as it was the cult center of the provincial assembly, but it was overshadowed by Patrai. Only a few ancient remains survive. (13) *Aigai* (Αἰγαί; mod. Akrata),[886] about 30 km from Aigion, was a member of the old Dodekapolis of Achaia; it later belonged to Aigion (Strabo 8.7.4). A temple of Poseidon is attested for Aigai. (14) *Sikyon* (Σικυών; mod. Vasiliko),[887] 45 km east of Aigai, was situated in the same fertile plain as Corinth about 20 km to the west. Old Sikyon had flourished in the sixth century B.C. but was destroyed in 303 B.C. in the time of the Diadochi. Sikyon was rebuilt on an acropolis 4 km from the coast. Sikyon had a leading role in the Achaean Confederacy. After the destruction of Corinth in 146 B.C. Sikyon was given most of the territory of the city of Corinth as well as the right to organize the Isthmian Games. Not much is known about Sikyon during the Roman period; presumably it was overshadowed by Corinth, its powerful neighbor, which had been refounded as a Roman colony. Pausanias

---

[881]E. Meyer, PW 18.4 (1942): 2191-22; idem, *KP* 4:549-50; P. Petsas, *PECS* 681-82; Lauffer 1989, 518-22; C. A. Morgan, *OCD* 1122; Y. Lafond, *DNP* 9:400-401; A. D. Rizakis, in *Alcock* 1997, 15-36; C. Auffarth, "'Verräter—Übersetzer'? Pausanias, das römische Patrai und die Identität der Griechen in der Achaea," in Cancik and Rüpke 1997, 219-38, esp. 226-35.

[882]*CIJ* I 716, 717.

[883]Jean-Marc Prieur and W. Schneemelcher, in Hennecke and Schneemelcher 1990-1997, 2:100, 109; J. K. Elliott 1993, 251-52, 254-55.

[884]See McDonald 1992, 961.

[885]Kirsten, *KP* 1:163-64; N. Bonacasa, *PECS* 21; Lafond, *DNP* 1:323; Lauffer 1989, 86-87.

[886]See E. Kirsten, "Achaia," *KP* 1:32-37, esp. 33.

[887]Geyer and Lippold, PW 2.A2 (1923): 2528-32; E. Meyer, PWSup 9 (1962): 1378; idem, *KP* 5:186-88; R. Stroud, *PECS* 839-40; J. B. Salmon, *OCD* 1403-4; J. Hopp, in Lauffer 1989, 615-18; Audrey Griffin, *Sikyon* (Oxford: Clarendon, 1982).

mentions temples dedicated to Apollo, the Dioscuri and Tyche Akraia (2.7.5). The ruins include the theater (at 120 m in diameter, one of the largest theaters of Greece), stadium, the large Gymnasium of Kleinias (the father of Aratos), a bouleuterion, colonnaded hall (45 by 22 columns, with twenty-one shops) in the agora, temples and baths.

Return to Jerusalem

Paul stayed "in Greece" for three months (Acts 20:3a), presumably in Corinth for most of the time. This was the apostle's third visit to Corinth (2 Cor 12:14; Acts 13:1; 20:3), which is dated to the winter of 56/57, perhaps from December to February. During these winter months Paul wrote the Epistle to the Romans. He originally planned to travel directly from Corinth to Jerusalem, which he wanted to reach for Passover, perhaps on a ship carrying other pilgrims.[888] When he heard that some Jews were planning to attack him, he decided to travel overland via Macedonia to Alexandria Troas (Acts 20:3, 5). As a result of this decision Paul was in Philippi for Passover on April 7 in A.D. 57 (Acts 20:6) and arrived in Jerusalem for the Feast of Pentecost, celebrated in A.D. 57 on May 29.[889] A traveler who left Corinth at the beginning of March could cover the approximately 750 km, about thirty days of travel, to Philippi easily by early April.

Notes on the travel route. Paul probably traveled from Corinth via Megara and Eleusis across the pass of Eleutherai between Mount Kithairon and Mount Pastra to Thebes; the main road to the north ran through the Kephistos Valley via Lebadeia, Chaironeia and Elateia to the coastal road that ran through the Thermopylae to the Plain of Spercheios and to Lamia. Paul would have continued through the Phurka Pass across Mount Antinitsa, reaching Larissa in the Thessalian Plain via Thaumakoi. The main route from Thessaly to Macedonia ran through the Tempe Valley along the east coast, past Mount Olympus and via Herakleion and Pydna to Beroea, Thessalonike and Philippi (Acts 20:3, 6). From Philippi Paul continued by ship to Alexandria Troas.

On *Megara* and *Eleusis* see above.

Thebes (Θῆβαι; mod. Thivai),[890] 47 km northwest of Eleusis, was the capital of Boeotia. The city is already attested in the fifteenth century B.C., with the Mycenaean palace of Kadmos on the acropolis of the city. Thebes controlled central Greece in the fifth and early fourth centuries B.C.; it was destroyed in 335 B.C. by Alexander the Great after the citizens had rebelled against Macedonian rule, and only the temples and the house of Pindar on

---

[888]Thus Ramsay 1896, 287; Bornkamm 1966-1971, 4:136; Bruce, *Acts,* 405; Haenchen, *Apg,* 559 (ET, 583); Schneider, *Apg,* 2:280-81; Pesch, *Apg,* 2:185; Riesner 1994, 269 (ET, 303); Barrett, *Acts,* 2:946.

[889]On the chronology see Riesner 1994, 195, 268-71 (ET, 218-19, 300-303).

[890]F. Schober and L. Ziehen, PW 5.A2 (1934): 1423-1553; E. Meyer, *KP* 5:664-69; P. Roesch, *PECS* 904-6; J. Buckler, *OCD* 1495; Koder and Hild 1976, 269-71; Paul Cloché, *Thèbes de Béotie des origines á la conquête romaine* (Namur: Secrétariat des publications, Facultés universitaires, 1952); Sarantis Symeonoglou, *The Topography of Thebes from the Bronze Age to Modern Times* (Princeton, N.J.: Princeton University Press, 1985); K. Braun, in Lauffer 1989, 662-67; G. Cohen 1995, 119-20.

the Kadmeia were left standing. The city was rebuilt in 316 B.C. but never regained its former significance. In the imperial period Thebes did "not preserve the character even of a respectable village" (Strabo 9.2.5); it was a small town limited to the Kadmeia. Hardly any traces of ancient Thebes survived, the result of both the repeated destruction and the continuous settlement of the site. The agora and the temple of Artemis Eukleia evidently were located east of the acropolis, and the theater of Sulla (86 B.C.) stood in the northeast part of the city. In the plain (northeast of the railway station) was a gymnasium, stadium, hippodrome, the temple of Poseidion Hippodromios and the temple of Heracles. Bishops of Thebes are documented in the fourth century.

Lebadeia (Λεβάδεια; mod. Levadeia),[891] about 50 km northwest of Thebes in the Plain of Kopais at the end of the Herkyna Gorge, was the site of the famous oracle of Trophonios, which was one of the five great oracles of Greece, extensively described by Pausanias (9.39.5-13; cf. Strabo 9.2.38). Mithradates destroyed the city in 86 B.C. It was rebuilt and flourished in the imperial period, particularly in the second century A.D., due to its strategic location and its cotton industry. Inscriptions document the worship of Artemis Argotis, Artemides Praeiai, Dionysos Enstaphylos, Hera Basilis, Zeus Basileus, Zeus Trophonius and the imperial cult. Pausanias mentions a temple of Apollo and a temple of Demeter. On the slopes of the acropolis were found ruins of the large temple of Zeus Basileus, which had been built with funds donated by Antiochos IV Epiphanes but was never finished. Greek archaeologists recently discovered the site of the oracle of Trophonios a few meters southwest of the temple of Zeus: a well 4 m deep and 2 m across, with a man-high cave at the bottom that was closed by a stone. In the rocks on the left bank of the Herkyna River niches are still visible in which statues of deities stood, as well as a chamber (4 by 4 m) with two benches, probably the sanctuary of Agathos Daimon and Agathe Tyche. The low tower of the medieval fortress evidently was erected on top of the temple of Trophonios.

Chaironeia (Χαιρώνεια; mod. Kapraina),[892] the most western city of Boeotia, was located at the point where the Kephisos River flows into Lake Kopais, about 10 km north of Lebadeia. The city became famous as the site of the decisive battle between the Macedonians under King Philipp II and the Greek cities under the leadership of Thebes and Athens on September 1 in 338 B.C.; the skeletons of 254 Thebans were found in a mass grave. Sulla defeated the army of Mithradates in 86 B.C. in the vicinity. The philosopher and biographer Plutarch (ca. A.D. 46-120) was born in Chaironeia; he was a priest in Delphi, visited Egypt and taught in Rome, but he lived in his hometown most of the time.[893] Inscriptions and literary texts document a temple of Zeus, a temple of Isis and the imperial cult. Remains of the city wall and the theater survive. Underneath the church Hagia Paraskevi the ruins of a Christian basilica with three aisles have been discovered.

---

[891]Eric Pieske, PW 12.1 (1924): 1048-52; E. Meyer, *KP* 3:526-27; P. Roesch, *PECS* 492; A. Schachter, "Trophonius," *OCD* 1556-57; E. Wirbelauer, *DNP* 6:1204-5; E. Vallas and N. Faraklas, *Athens Annals of Archaeology* 2 (1969): 228-33; John M. Fossey, "The Cities of the Kopaïs in the Roman Period," *ANRW* II.7.1 (1979): 549-91, esp. 571-75; Fossey 1988, 343-49; P. W. Haider, in Lauffer 1989, 373-76.

[892]E. Oberhummer, PW 3.2 (1899): 2033-36; E. Meyer, *KP* 1:1122-23; P. Roesch, *PECS* 215-16; J. Buckler, *OCD* 315; P. Funke, *DNP* 2:1084; Fossey, *ANRW* II.7.1 (1979): 578-82; idem 1988, 375-82; P. W. Haider, in Lauffer 1989, 160-62.

[893]The inscription *IG* VII 3422 probably honors Plutarch. A son or grandson of Plutarch is honored in the inscription *IG* VII 3423. On Plutarch see Swain 1998, 135-87.

Elateia ('Ελάτεια; mod. Drakhmani, Piperis),[894] about 20 km north of Chaironeia, was the largest city in the region of Phocis. Elateia controlled the main road from the Plain of Kephisos through the Thermopylae to the Plain of Spercheios, the only pass from Boeotia to Macedonia suitable for an army.[895] The city was destroyed by Xerxes in 480 B.C. and occupied by Philipp II in 339 B.C. It was granted autonomy by the Romans after 86 B.C. because it had supported Rome in the struggle against Mithradates. Only a few remains on the acropolis and the city walls survive. Pausanias mentions the agora, a temple of Asclepius and a temple of Athene Kranaia (10.34.1-8); the latter has been located about 3 km southeast of the town. Elateia was the seat of a bishop since A.D. 347 at the latest.

Lamia (Λάμια; mod. Lamia),[896] about 50 km from Elateia, on the north end of the Plain of Spercheios, controlled the roads from the south to Thessaly. The port in the Malesian Gulf was Phalara. Lamia was already settled in the prehistoric period; it came under Roman control in 190 B.C. During the imperial period Lamia belonged to the region of Phthiotis.

Thaumakoi (Θαυμακοί; Domokos Kastri),[897] a city in the region of Phthiotis on the north slope of Mount Othrys, was located on the most important pass to Thessaly. The citizens looked out on the Thessalian Plain. Remains of the city walls (900 m long) survive. About 2 km north of the city the remains of a temple were discovered. Thaumakoi was the seat of a bishop in the Byzantine period.

Larissa (Λάρισσα Πελασγίς; mod. Larisa),[898] about 60 km to the north in the eastern part of the Plain of Thessaly, on the banks of the Peneios River, was the most important city in Thessaly. The physician Hippocrates lived here for many years; he died in Larissa in 370 B.C. King Philipp II made Larissa his main city in Thessaly in 352 B.C.; it remained the leading city of the region into the imperial period. The acropolis was only 26 m high, with a temple of Athene Polias on top; the temple of Apollo Kerdoios with the city archives and the temple of Zeus Eleutherios with the federal archives were located in the lower city. There seems to have been a Jewish community in Larissa, but there is no clear evidence for the first century.[899] Remains of a theater are preserved on the south slope of the acropolis. The *Apostolic Constitutions* (4.46) suggest that there was a Christian community in Larissa as early as the first century, perhaps established by Macedonian Christians.[900] The bishop Achilleios, who lived at the time of Constantine I, is the first attested bishop of Larissa.

---

[894]A. Philippson, "Elateia 1," PW 5.2 (1905): 2236-37; E. Meyer, "Elateia 1," *KP* 1:232-33; S. S. Weinberg, *PECS* 295; Koder and Hild 1976, 153-54; J. Buckler, *OCD* 515; G. Daverio Rocci, *DNP* 3:960-61; K. Braun, in Lauffer 1989, 208-9.

[895]F. Stählin, PW 5.A (1934): 2398-23; E. Meyer, *KP* 5:743-46; P. MacKay, *PECS* 910.

[896]F. Stählin, "Lamia 8," PW 12.1 (1924): 547-60; E. Meyer, "Lamia 5," *KP* 3:465; B. Helly, *OCD* 812; Kramolisch, "Lamia 2," *DNP* 6:1080-81; Braun, in Lauffer 1989, 365-66.

[897]F. Stählin, PW 5.A (1934): 1331-32; E. Meyer, *KP* 5:654; T. S. MacKay, *PECS* 903-4; Koder and Hild 1976, 148-49; F. Hild, in Lauffer 1989, 200-201.

[898]F. Stählin, "Larisa 3," PW 12.1 (1924): 845-71; E. Meyer, "Larisa 3," *KP* 3:499-501; H. Kramolisch, "Larisa 3," *DNP* 6:1152-53; Koder and Hild 1976, 198-99; T. S. MacKay, *PECS* 485; H. Kramolisch and F. Hild, in Lauffer 1989, 367-69; B. Helly, *OCD* 816.

[899]Stavroulakis 1992, 135; see now *IJudO* I, 2004, 197-26. The Jewish inscription *SEG* XXXV 633 (*IJudO* I Ach14) dates to the fourth century A.D.

[900]McDonald 1992, 961, with referenced to 1 Thess 1:7-8.

Herakleion ('Ηράκλειον, Herakleia; Platamon),[901] on the Thermaic Gulf at the foot of Mount Olympus, was the southernmost town of Macedonia, reached through the Tempe Valley by travelers coming from the south via the city of Gonnoi (mod. Dereli).[902] The city had a temple of Athene Polias, a temple of Artemis and a temple of Asclepius. Plutarch mentions Herakleion as a port city in connection with events of 168 B.C. (Plutarch, *Aem.* 15).

On *Pydna, Beroea, Thessalonike, Apollonia, Amphipolis, Philippi, Neapolis* and *Alexandria Troas* see above.

In Beroea, Thessalonike and Philippi Paul visited the Macedonian churches that he had founded eight years earlier in A.D. 49/50. When Paul left for Asia Minor, Sopater the son of Pyrrhus from Beroea and Aristarchus and Secundus from Thessalonike joined his group en route to Jerusalem (Acts 20:4). Most of Paul's companions went ahead and waited for him in Alexandria Troas, where he joined them a week later (Acts 20:5-6). While his companions sailed ahead to Assos, Paul took the overland route and met them there (Acts 20:13-14).

Assos ('Ασσός; near mod. Behramkale),[903] situated impressively on the steep terraces of a volcanic cone 234 m high, controlled the coastal road in the southern Troad. The city was the port of call for ships that wanted to avoid the strong south currents at the coast and did not want to circumnavigate Cape Lekton. Assos had an artificial harbor, and the acropolis and the lower city were fortified. Remains of the theater, bouleuterion, gymnasium, agora and market stoas survive. A Doric temple of Athene, built in 520 B.C., stood on the acropolis. The fortifications date to the Persian period (fourth century B.C.), a time in which Assos was known for its philosophical school, founded by the Platonist Hermias. Aristotle (348-345 B.C.) lived for a time in Assos, and the Stoic Kleanthes (331-232 B.C.) was born there. Because of improved sailing techniques and the ascent of neighboring Alexandria Troas, the significance of Assos declined, and it became an agricultural center. The city came under Roman control in 133 B.C. In the early first century A.D. a certain Quintus Lollius Philetaerus, a member of one of the aristocratic families of Assos, was honored by the *demos* with a golden crown, a painted portrait and a marble statue.[904]

Mytilene (Μυτιλήνη or Μιτυλήνη)[905]was the largest city on the island of Lesbos, on the north coast of the island. The city is attested since 1200 B.C. It had two harbors, which

---

[901]L. Bürchner, "Herakleion 2," PW 8.1 (1912): 499; E. Meyer, "Herakleion 2," *KP* 2:1045; H. Errington, "Herakleion 2," *DNP* 5:380; Papazoglou 1988, 114-15; D. Müller, in Lauffer 1989, 267.
[902]Meyer, *KP* 2:844; MacKay, *PECS* 359-60; Koder and Hild 1976, 166; Lauffer 1989, 236-37.
[903]E. Oberhummer, PW 2.2 (1896): 1748-50; A. M. Mansel, *KP* 1:1542-44; H. S. Robinson, *PECS* 104-5; S. Mitchell, *OCD* 194-95; Schwertheim, *DNP* 2:112-13; Magie 1950, 1:83; 2:904-5; Cook 1973, 240-50; Burdick 1978, 45-50; S. Mitchell 1995a, 1:256. Excavations: Ümit Serdaroğlu et al., eds., *Ausgrabungen in Assos I-IV* (4 vols.; AMS 2, 5, 10, 21; Bonn: Habelt, 1990-1996); see Ü. Serdaroğlu, "Zur Geschichte der Stadt Assos und ihrer Ausgrabungen," in *Ausgrabungen in Assos I*, 1-6. Inscriptions: *I. Assos* (ed. R. Merkelbach, 1976).
[904]*I. Assos* 18 = *I. GRIAsia* 2; the inscription is bilingual.
[905]R. Herbst, PW 16.2 (1935): 1411-18; E. Meyer, *KP* 3:1544-46; D. Shipley and C. Roueché, *OCD* 1020; H. Sonnabend, *DNP* 8:650-53; Magie 1950, 1:84, 100, 416, 468, 511-12; W. Günther, in Lauffer 1989, 451-54.

were an important factor for the prosperity of the city: a deep commercial harbor protected by a mole to the north, and a smaller enclosed harbor for the navy to the south. The city was surrounded by walls (5 km in length) and was "well equipped with everything" (Strabo 13.2.2). Because of the ideal location and the acclaimed climate, famous and rich people visited Mytilene. Famous sons of the city included Alkaios the lyricist and the historians Hellanikos and Theophanes. After the city was taken over by the Romans in 80 B.C., Julius Caesar was personally involved, and the city lost its autonomy until 62 B.C. Mitylene continued to prosper in the imperial period. Remains of the city walls, theater and aqueduct (25 km long) survive. Bishops of Mytilene are documented since the fourth century.

Samos (Σάμος)[906] was only 1.3 km from the mainland, the peninsula of Mykale (mod. Samsun Daği). The city of Samos was located on the southeast coast of the island (near mod. Pythagorion). Greeks lived on Samos since 1000 B.C. The city developed as a commercial and cultural center and founded several colonies. In 660/650 B.C. Kolaios of Samos sailed to Spain; he reached Gades and the legendary Tartessos, which is confirmed by finds in the temple of Hera. During the seventh and sixth centuries the power of Samos reached its zenith. The palace of the ruler Polykrates (532-522 B.C.) has not yet been discovered. Julius Caesar, Mark Antony and Octavian visited Samos. Numerous statues of Roman emperors were found in the temple of Hera. A building inscription documents that Claudius rebuilt the temple of Dionysos, which had collapsed "because of age and an earthquake" ("vetustate et terrae motu").[907] Ruins of the temple of Hera, baths, theater, stadium, gymnasium and the aqueduct survive. The first bishop of Samos is documented for A.D. 390.

On *Miletus* see below; on *Cos* and *Rhodes* see above, §22.5.

Patara (Πάταρα)[908] was a port in western Lycia. The temple of Apollo Patroios in Patara was one of the most important cults of Apollo in the Greek world. The city enjoyed autonomy for a long time; after A.D. 43 it was controlled by the governor of the province of Lycia, who resided in Patara. During this time a complete list of the roads of the new province was incised in stone. The bishop Eudemos was active in Patara in the fourth century.

Paul and his companions visited Rhodes and Cos on their journey to Jerusalem (Acts 21:1). It is unlikely that they engaged in missionary work, as they stayed only one day. The argument that Paul stayed on Rhodes and Cos for only one day because there were no Jewish communities[909] is unconvincing: Paul wanted to reach Jerusalem as soon as possible and thus stayed in town only as long as his ship stayed in port.

---

[906]L. Bürchner, "Samos 4," PW 1.A2 (1920): 2162-2218; D. Graham Shipley, *OCD* 1351; idem, *A History of Samos 800-188* B.C. (Oxford: Clarendon, 1987); H. Kaletsch, in Lauffer 1989, 599-605. Excavations: R. C. S. Felsch et al., *Samos* (22 vols.; Deutsches Archäologisches Institut; Bonn: Habelt, 1961-1998).

[907]H. Freis, "Eine Bauinschrift des Kaiser Claudius aus Samos," *ZPE* 58 (1985): 189-91; *SEG* xxxv 949 = *I. GRIAsia* 171.

[908]Radke, PW 18.4 (1949): 2555-61; Marek, *DNP* 9:392-93; S. Mitchell, *OCD* 1121; G. E. Bean, *Lycian Turkey* (London: Benn, 1978), 82-91; G. Cohen 1995, 329-30.

[909]Stavroulakis and DeVinney 1992, 145.

Paul planned to travel to Rome after his visit to Jerusalem in connection with his plans to initiate missionary work in Spain (Rom 15:28). If Paul was born around the turn of the century,[910] then he was between fifty-seven and sixty years of age when he planned the mission to Spain in A.D. 57—an old man under the circumstances of the ancient world. When Paul arrived in Jerusalem, he was arrested, forcing him to postpone his plans for Spain.

27.4 Paul in Caesarea Maritima and in Rome

As a Prisoner in Caesarea

After Paul had been arrested in Jerusalem in A.D. 57, presumably soon after Pentecost, the Roman authorities took him to Caesarea, where the Jewish leaders accused him before the Roman governor Antonius Felix (see Tacitus, *Ann.* 5.9) of rebellion against the state (*seditio*) and of having desecrated the temple (Acts 24:5-6; 25:7).[911] Paul had to wait from A.D. 57 to 59, two years, for his case to be decided by Felix (Acts 24:26-27), who postponed a decision for political reasons, leaving it to his successor. Porcius Festus, who arrived in Caesarea probably in the summer of A.D. 59, wanted to bring the trial to a speedy resolution (Acts 25:6, 17). He consulted with the new high priest, Ismael b. Phiabi (A.D. 59-61), as well as with his predecessors, including the still powerful Ananias b. Nebedaios (A.D. 47-59) (Acts 23:2-5; Josephus, *A.J.* 20.205, 209), with the political Jewish elite (Acts 25:2) and with king Herod Agrippa II (A.D. 50-93), whom evidently he trusted more than the religious aristocracy, with whom he had his own problems (Acts 25:13-22; Josephus, *A.J.* 20.193). Paul insisted that he wanted to remain under Roman jurisdiction, refusing to be tried by the Sanhedrin in Jerusalem (Acts 25:10). He reminded the governor of his right as a Roman citizen to be tried by a higher court, and he appealed to the emperor (Καίσαρα ἐπικαλοῦμαι, *Kaisara epikaloumai* [Acts 25:11]). Paul had been brought before a Roman court several times in the past, and in each case he had been cleared of the charges brought against him. Evidently he was afraid that the new proconsul might hand him over to the jurisdiction of his Jewish opponents, who then would be both his accusers and his judges, and so he made sure that he would get a fair trial at a neutral location. The hearing before Festus and Herod Agrippa II, narrated at length by Luke (Acts 25:23—26:32), was intended to establish the relevant evidence.

During his imprisonment in Caesarea, probably in a room in the *praetorium* (i.e., in the Herodian palace), Paul was chained (cf. Acts 26:29), which is suggested by the command of Felix to the centurion "to keep him in custody, but to let him have some liberty" (Acts 24:23a). He was not in *custodia libera,* free

---

[910]Riesner 1994, 191 (ET, 213-14); similarly Légasse 1991, 31. According to Murphy-O'Connor (1996, 4), Paul would have been about ten years older.
[911]On Paul's trial in Caesarea see Dupont 1967a, 527-52; Tajra 1989; Rapske 1994a, 151-72.

or open custody, but "in a lightened form of military custody."[912] But he was allowed to receive family members and friends (Acts 24:23b).

In the course of the trial and the hearing in Caesarea Paul used every opportunity to explain and proclaim the message of Jesus the Messiah and the Savior. During the hearing before Felix he clearly hoped to convince the Roman governor of the truth of the message of Jesus Christ (Acts 24:24-25):

> Acts 24:24-25: "Some days later when Felix came with his wife Drusilla, who was Jewish, he sent for Paul and heard him speak concerning faith in Christ Jesus. [25]And as he discussed justice, self-control, and the coming judgment, Felix became frightened and said, 'Go away for the present; when I have an opportunity, I will send for you.' "

Paul explained his message of Jesus the Messiah and of the necessity of faith in Jesus as the one who was crucified and raised from the dead (Acts 24:24b). Luke relates that Paul pointed Felix to the ethical consequences of faith in Jesus Christ (Acts 24:25a), which indicates that Paul did not simply present an academic lecture but rather spoke to the procurator in personal terms. Focusing on the subjects of righteousness, self-control and the coming judgment, Paul "clearly addressed the specific situation of the governor."[913] The term δι-καιοσύνη (*dikaiosynē*) means, initially, "just behavior," which Paul could interpret in a legal sense ("justice") and at the same time in an ethical sense ("righteousness"). The term ἐγκράτεια (*enkrateia*) often was used since Plato to describe control over one's desires and lusts ("self-control" or "self-discipline"). Paul used the term probably to refer to Felix's behavior as a Roman official,[914] and perhaps to allude to the marital situation of the procurator, even though Luke does not hint at this connection: Drusilla was the third wife of Felix, a sister of Herod Agrippa II whom Felix had wooed away from Azizos, the king of Emesa, with the help of a magician from Cyprus (Josephus, *A.J.* 20.141-144). Paul's reference to the coming judgment (τὸ κρίμα τὸ μέλλον, *to krima to mellon*) indicates that he was not simply explaining ethical maxims to impress the procurator: he explained the way of life and the behavior that God demands, drawing upon central Jewish and Christian convictions that linked the final verdict on the behavior of human beings with the coming judgment of the world by God the Creator.

Ravi Zacharias interprets the three terms righteousness, self-control and judgment in terms of a three-stage process of missionary communication.[915] (1) Paul first established com-

---

[912]Rapske 1994a, 168-72; quotation, 172; on the place of imprisonment see ibid., 155-58.

[913]Zmijewski, *Apg,* 823.

[914]Pesch, *Apg,* 2:261-62; for the comment that follows above see ibid.; cf. Zmijewski, *Apg,* 823; Barrett, *Acts,* 2:1112-13.

[915]Ravi Zacharias, "The Touch of Truth," in *Telling the Truth: Evangelizing Postmoderns* (ed. D. A. Carson; Grand Rapids: Zondervan, 2000), 30-43.

mon ground (point of reference): as procorator and highest judge of the province of Judea, Felix had to ensure and maintain justice, as Roman jurisdiction and administration was based on the principle of *iustitia*—the term *ius* designated specifically the legality of private behavior, and abstractly the law in its entirety, "the entire jurisdiction with its diverse layers varying in origin, validity and application."[916] The definition by Celsus, *Ius est ars boni et aequi* ("Law is the art of the good and the just"), epitomizes the Roman concept of law. When Paul proclaimed the gospel of Jesus Christ, he also spoke about justice: the "justice" or "righteousness" that God the Judge freely gives to those human beings, sinners all, who believe in Jesus the crucified and risen Messiah and Savior. This message was foreign to Felix, but the term "righteousness" connects Paul the incarcerated missionary and Felix the powerful procurator. Paul therefore started his address with a subject that was of interest to both. (2) Paul proceeded to discuss a subject that was, in his eyes, a relevant topic for Felix (point of relevance): he talked about self-control. As a chained prisoner he himself was controlled by others, and as a follower of Jesus he knew himself to be under the control of Jesus the Kyrios, who produces the fruit of the Holy Spirit in those who believe in him, behavior that includes the reality of self-control (Gal 5:23). For Felix, *enkrateia* evidently is a problem: it is not a coincidence that Josephus writes extensively about Drusilla and Felix (Josephus, *A.J.* 20.141-144). (3) In the last part of his address Paul irritated Felix (point of disturbance): he did not simply entertain the procurator by declaiming about common interests and relevant subjects; rather, he proclaimed the hard truth about the reality of a final divine day of judgment on which all people, including the Roman procurator, must give an account of their behavior. Despite all the legal maneuvers that Paul used to secure his release from imprisonment, for which his private conversations with the procurator provided an ideal venue, he remained faithful to the responsibility of maintaining theological integrity: he did not pass over the reality of the wrath of God to be manifested fully and irresistibly on judgment day, even in his address to the powerful Felix (cf. Rom 1:18—3:20). Paul refused to avoid speaking about the day of judgment because it is this very reality that reveals the consequences of the lack of self-control and the practice of unjust behavior and at the same time establishes as good news the message of Jesus, the messianic Savior who forgives the sins of lack of self-control and of personal unrighteousness (cf. Rom 3:21—5:21).

Felix "became frightened" because as a Roman he did not know how to respond to arguments about life after death and about a divine forum before which all persons must give an account of their deeds, and perhaps because he felt personally implicated. He promised Paul that they would meet again (Acts 24:25). Felix kept the promise, as "he hoped that money would be given him by Paul, and for that reason he used to send for him very often and converse with him" (Acts 24:26). This means that Paul had repeated opportunities over the next two years (Acts 24:27a) to speak with the Roman governor about his case and about his message of Jesus Christ—opportunities that he used not only as an accused prisoner who sought release but also as a missionary who strove to convince others of the truth of the gospel.

When Paul appeared before Festus, Felix's successor, and Herod Agrippa II,

---

[916]D. V. Simon, *KP* 3:11. For the quotation that follows above see Celsus, in Ulpianus, *Digests* 1.1.1 *pr.*

who wanted to establish the evidence in the Jewish leaders' case against Paul for the upcoming trial in Rome, he again not only defended himself but also explained his message of Jesus the crucified and risen Savior (Acts 26:17-18, 20, 22-23). When Festus declared that Paul, the undaunted prisoner, was out of his mind (Acts 26:24), Paul directly addressed King Agrippa and challenged him to believe in the message of Jesus Christ:

Acts 26:25-27: "But Paul said, 'I am not out of my mind, most excellent Festus, but I am speaking the sober truth. [26]Indeed the king knows about these things, and to him I speak freely; for I am certain that none of these things has escaped his notice, for this was not done in a corner. [27]King Agrippa, do you believe the prophets? I know that you believe.'"

Paul concludes with the prayer that, "whether quickly or not," Agrippa and all the other listeners "might become such as I am—except for these chains" (Acts 26:29); that is, that they might come to faith in Jesus the crucified and risen Savior. Luke does not report Agrippa's reaction.

Paul was limited in terms of his geographical reach during his two years of imprisonment in Caesarea during A.D. 57-59; he had to abandon his plans to preach the gospel in Spain, at least for the time being. But he had regular contact with several of the highest representatives of the Roman imperial administration. The last time that this had been possible was twelve years earlier, in A.D. 45, during his missionary work in Paphos when Sergius Paullus, the governor of Cyprus, had heard and responded to the gospel; the encounter with Gallio, the governor of the province of Achaia in Corinth, had been only brief. In Caesarea Paul had contact with Roman soldiers, centurions and tribunes (Acts 21:32, 37), and he presented the gospel to two Roman governors and to the king of Judea (cf. Mk 13:9).

Paul very probably wrote the Epistle to the Philippians during his imprisonment in the city of Rome.[917] Other candidates for the place of composition of the letter are Ephesus[918] and Caesarea.[919] One of the arguments that is said to rule out Caesarea is that the situation described in Phil 1:14-18 does not fit Caesarea:[920] (1) Caesarea was a political backwater whereas Phil 1:13 speaks of "the whole praetorium" in which Paul's imprisonment became known, as it did to "everyone else." (2) The many "brothers" of Phil 1:14 who became emboldened by Paul's imprisonment "to speak the word with greater boldness and without fear" presuppose a larger center of Christians than Caesarea presumably was. I find this to be unconvincing. With regard to the first point of the argument, we must recall that Caesarea was the seat of the Roman governor in the province of Judea. There is no question that Caesarea was not as important as Antioch, Alexandria or Rome, but nevertheless it was the most important city after Jerusalem in this region of the Roman Empire.

---

[917]Recently O'Brien, *Phil,* 20-26; Fee, *Phil,* 34-37; Ellis 1999, 275-76.

[918]Duncan 1930; Gnilka, *Phil,* 18-24; Carson, Moo and Morris 1992, 320-21.

[919]Lohmeyer, *Phil,* 3-4; Hawthorne, *Phil,* xli-xliv.

[920]See O'Brien, *Phil,* 24.

If the *praetorium* in Caesarea heard the gospel of Jesus Christ as a result of Paul's presence in the city, then this was very significant indeed for Judea, in at least two respects: if the Roman governors, who were not always friendly toward the Jews, maintained a constructive relationship with a Jewish teacher, this would be advantageous for general political reasons; also, if the Roman governor in Judea was favorably disposed toward the followers of Jesus, perhaps even accepting faith in Jesus, this would have immense implications for the "center" of the church in Jerusalem. The second point of the argument is unconvincing because we have no information about the size of the church in Caesarea. We should not forget that the church in Caesarea evidently was the center of missionary activity in the coastal plain (cf. Acts 8:40; 21:8). And nobody knows how large a city must be for evangelists to exist who preach the gospel as the result of problematic reasons (Phil 1:15, 17). It therefore is not impossible to link the situation implied in Phil 1:14-18 with Caesarea. This does not mean, however, that the Epistle to the Philippians was indeed written in Caesarea rather than in Rome. The arguments for a composition of the letter in the city of Rome are more convincing.

The Journey to Rome

During the sea voyage from Caesarea to Rome (Acts 27:1—28:16)[921] Paul and his companions—Luke mentions in Acts 27:2 Aristarchus and himself (as source of the we-account)—came to Sidon, where Paul had "friends" (φίλοι, *philoi*), evidently Christian friends, who take care of him (Acts 27:3). Headwinds forced their ship to sail around Cyprus and put in at Myra in Lycia, where Paul's party changed ships (Acts 27:4-5).

Myra (Μύρα)[922] was a port city on the coast of Lycia, settled since the fifth century B.C. The temple of Eleuthera is regarded as the largest and architecturally most beautiful building discovered in Lycia. Inscriptions that were accidentally discovered in 1998 document several citizens of Myra in the first centuries B.C. and A.D. whom the city had honored with monuments that stood probably in the gymnasium.[923] The ephebes donated the statue of Ptolemaios the gymnasiarch, and eight members of a cultic association honored the young Hermapias, who had become a hero, with a statue.

The apocryphal *Acts of Paul* claims to know that Paul "taught the word of God in Myra" and healed a man named Hermokrates of dropsy (*Acts Paul* 4). This led to all sorts of complications that eventually resulted in the resuscitation of a dead person and the healing of a blind person. Wilhelm Schneemelcher assumes that the author used some local legends that inspired him to write this episode.[924] It is theoretically possible that Paul had an opportunity in Myra to preach the gospel while

---

[921]On the historical reliability of Acts 27 see now Reiser (2001), who accuses twentieth-century New Testament exegesis of "a nearly dogmatic skepticism" that has caused a loss of real knowledge (72-73).

[922]W. Ruge, PW 16.1 (1933): 1068-89; M. Zimmermann, *DNP* 8:594-95; Jones 1937, 99-102, 107-8; Jürgen Borchardt, ed., *Myra: Eine lykische Metropole in antiker und byzantinischer Zeit* (Istanbuler Forschungen 30; Berlin: Mann, 1975); M. Zimmermann 1992, 101-22, 219-30.

[923]S. Şahin, "Epigraphische Mitteilungen aus Antalya I," *EA* 31 (1999): 40-51, nos. 11-14.

[924]W. Schneemelcher, in Hennecke and Schneemelcher 1990-1997, 2:203 (ET, 2:334-35).

the Roman officer who was responsible for him and the other prisoners arranged for the continuation of the transport to Rome.[925] It remains hypothetical, however, to assume that Paul engaged in missionary work in Myra and therefore was the missionary who brought the gospel to Lycia, as Basileios of Seleukeia asserts.[926]

An inscription found in Arykanda documents that the provincial assembly of Lycia asked the emperors Galerius Valerius Flavius Constantinus and Valerius Licinnianus Licinnius in A.D. 311 to prohibit the Christian cult and to direct the people to offer the ancestral sacrifices (*TAM* II 785).[927] This request indicates pagan religious convictions and cults were still firmly anchored at least in the elites of the Lycian cities around A.D. 300.[928] A Jewish community is attested for Tlos, a city in the interior of western Lycia (*CIJ* II 757; *IJudO* II 223). It is not known when the Christian community was established.

The ship that Paul's party boarded made only slow progress due to adverse winds, sailing past the island of Cnidus; the next port that they could reach was Kaloi Limenes ("Fair Havens"), a port on Crete near the city of Lasaea (Acts 27:8). Since the harbor was not suitable for staying over the winter, the centurion insisted they continue the journey and sail to Phoenix, a port further west on the south coast of Crete. This plan came to nothing as the ship drifted in the direction of North Africa, pushed by a wind from the northeast (Gk., *Eurakylōn,* from *euros,* "east," and *aquilo,* "north").[929] After fourteen days at sea the ship stranded on the coast of Malta (Acts 2:27-44).

While the stranded party stayed on Malta for three months (Acts 28:1-11) in the winter of A.D. 59/60, they had contact with the people living on the island (Acts 28:2-6), including contact with Publius, the "leading man of the island" (Acts 28:7), one of the important local officials who accommodated the ship-wrecked party for three days. During this time Paul healed the Publius's father, who had become ill with fever and dysentery (Acts 28:8), which led to further healing of sick people on the island (Acts 28:9). Luke does not mention any missionary activity of Paul: he reports that the healed citizens bestowed "many honors" on the Christians and that they gave them provisions when they were about to set sail (Acts 28:10), but he does not refer to any conversions. It can be assumed, however, that Paul prayed for the sick in the name of Jesus Christ and that he explained who Jesus was and why faith in Jesus was necessary.[930]

---

[925]See F. Kolb, in Kolb and Kupke 1992, 31.

[926]PG 85:552. For S. Jameson ("Lykia," PWSup 13 [1973]: 294), this claim is "probably exaggerated."

[927]See S. Jameson, "Lykia," PWSup 13 (1973): 294.

[928]F. Kolb, in Kolb and Kupke 1992, 31.

[929]See C. J. Hemer, "Euraquilo und Melita," *JTS* 26 (1975): 100-111, esp. 102; idem 1989, 141-42; recently Reiser 2001, 63-64, with reference to the large twelve-part compass-rose, 8 m in diameter, dating to the third century, that was discovered in Thugga (Dougga) in North Africa, in which the wind from the east-northeast is called Euraquilo (*CIL* VIII, Suppl. IV 26652).

[930]See Rapske 1994a, 360; Stenschke 1999a, 236.

A Christian community is attested for Crete only for the post-Constantine period. The local tradition maintains that Paul converted the people on the island and that St. Publius was the first bishop. The bishop Acacius, who attended the Council of Chalcedon in A.D. 451, is the first documented Christian leader of the Christians on Crete.

As a Prisoner in Rome

Paul's situation in Rome as a prisoner of the Roman state is described in Acts 28:16-31 and can be reconstructed from his letters written during this time: the Epistles to the Philippians, to the Colossians, to Philemon and to the churches in the province of Asia (the Epistle to the Ephesians).[931] Paul received permission from an official who reported to the *praefectus praetorii* to stay in rented private quarters (Acts 28:16) that evidently were spacious enough to receive a larger number of visitors (Acts 28:23). Paul was chained to a soldier (Acts 28:20), as was customary in such situations. Otherwise he was not greatly restricted in what he could do: he was able to invite and receive the Jewish leaders of the city of Rome (Acts 28:17), he was able to invite them to a second meeting (Acts 28:23), and was able, for two years, to welcome "all who came to him, proclaiming the kingdom of God and teaching about the Lord Jesus Christ with all boldness and without hindrance" (Acts 28:30-31).

Luke summarizes in Acts 28:23-28, 31, for the last time, the context of Paul's missionary preaching:

Acts 28:23-31: "After they had set a day to meet with him, they came to him at his lodgings in great numbers. From morning until evening he explained the matter to them, testifying to the kingdom of God and trying to convince them about Jesus both from the law of Moses and from the prophets. [24]Some were convinced by what he had said, while others refused to believe. [25]So they disagreed with each other; and as they were leaving, Paul made one further statement: 'The Holy Spirit was right in saying to your ancestors through the prophet Isaiah, [26]"Go to this people and say, You will indeed listen, but never understand, and you will indeed look, but never perceive. [27]For this people's heart has grown dull, and their ears are hard of hearing, and they have shut their eyes; so that they might not look with their eyes, and listen with their ears, and understand with their heart and turn—and I would heal them." [28]Let it be known to you then that this salvation of God has been sent to the Gentiles; they will listen.' [30]He lived there two whole years at his own expense and welcomed all who came to him, [31]proclaiming the kingdom of God and teaching about the Lord Jesus Christ with all boldness and without hindrance."

Paul explained to the leaders of the Jewish community in Rome who visited him for an entire day the message that he proclaimed and that was the cause for the legal proceedings that brought him as a prisoner to Rome. Presumably, in one respect he hoped that he could convince the *prōtoi* of the Jews in Rome to be favorably disposed toward his cause because they might play a role in his up-

---

[931]On Paul's stay in Rome see Lichtenberger 1996, 2149-54; on Paul's imprisonment see Rapske 1994, 173-91.

coming trial—something that he could justifiably assume. It was this very purpose that would have prompted Paul to explain and substantiate the validity of his message of the kingdom of God "from the law of Moses and from the prophets" (Acts 28:23). The phrase "the kingdom of God" is, in Luke's account in the book of Acts, a summary of the Christian message:[932] Paul sought to convince his visitors that the crucified and risen Jesus is the Messiah and fulfills the meaning and the promises of the law and the prophets.[933] The reaction is mixed: some Jews "were convinced"—that is, they converted to faith in Jesus as the Messiah—while others rejected Paul's teaching (Acts 28:24-25). Before the participants in the "conference" departed, Paul used the quotation from Is 6:9-10 to explain the fact that not all Jews accept the Messiah whom he proclaims (Acts 28:26-27). Paul's conclusion as formulated in Acts 28:28 is not meant to state that God disowned Israel as his people: Paul links the quotation from Is 6:9-10 about the hard-heartedness and stubbornness of God's people (Acts 28:26b-27) with allusions to Ezek 2:3-5 and Ezek 3:4-7 in order to enhance this charge. The entire passage Acts 28:25c-28 is a prophetic indictment that is formulated with the help of the critique of the prophets Isaiah and Ezekiel—with the hope of provoking the Jews of Rome to repent and believe in Jesus the Messiah.[934]

Luke concludes his account with the comment that Paul taught "about the Lord Jesus Christ with all boldness and without hindrance" (Acts 28:31b). Carsten Burfeind correctly points out that "what Peter proclaims in Jerusalem, Paul proclaims in Rome: Jesus is κύριος and χριστός *as the Risen One*."[935] Some scholars suggest that Luke wants to emphasize that Paul, teaching about the *kyrios Iēsous Christos* in Rome, deliberately and provocatively engaged in missionary proclamation "in polemical contrast to the claims to power of all pagan deities and in particular in contrast to the *kyrios Kaisar* of the imperial cult."[936] Indeed, since the reference to Jesus' title as Lord (*kyrios*) and Messiah (*Christos*) in Acts 28:31 is linked with a reference to the kingdom of God (*basileia tou theou*), a term rarely used in the book of Acts, it is plausible to assume that there is a political dimension to Paul's missionary proclamation as reported by Luke.

Paul asserts in the letter that he writes to the Christians in Philippi during the time of his imprisonment in Rome that the gospel was becoming known "throughout the whole praetorium" (Phil 1:13)—that is, probably among the Praetorian Guard:[937] among the imperial bodyguards or among the Praetorian cohorts, of which nine thousand men were stationed in the city of Rome. Pre-

---

[932]Acts 1:3; 8:12; 14:22; 19:8.

[933]See Barrett, *Acts*, 2:1243.

[934]See Sandt 1994; now particularly Pao 2000, 101-9.

[935]See Burfeind 2000, 89, with reference to Acts 2:36.

[936]Roloff, *Apg*, 55, referring to Rev 17:14; 19:16; Burfeind 2000, 89; for the comment that follows above see ibid., 90-91.

[937]Lightfoot, *Col*, 99-104; O'Brien, *Phil*, 93; cf. G. Schneider, *EWNT* 3:348 (*EDNT* 3:145).

sumably, Paul came into contact with the Praetorians in connection with his house arrest. When Paul adds that the circumstances of his imprisonment and thus the gospel of Jesus Christ have become known "to everyone else" (Phil 1:13), he refers probably to pagans who received information about the reasons for the imprisonment of Paul the Roman citizen of Tarsus and Jerusalem, thus being exposed to the gospel.[938] According to Phil 4:22, there were followers of Jesus in "the emperor's household" (οἱ ἐκ τῆς Καίσαρος οἰκίας, *hoi ek tēs Kaisaros oikias*), probably among the freedmen and slaves of the imperial household. We have no information about the circumstances in which they came into contact with Christians and their message about Jesus Christ.

Paul likely received a release in A.D. 62, after two years of imprisonment.[939] Unless Paul's case was heard by Emperor Nero himself, the apostle would have to appear before Sextus Afranius Burrus,[940] who came from Gaul (Narbonensis) and had been appointed by Claudius in A.D. 51 as sole prefect of the Praetorian Guard, an office that he held until his death in A.D. 62 and that he used to exercise a moderating influence on Nero together with Seneca.[941] Burrus was replaced as *praefecti praetorio* by Tigellinus and Faenius Rufus.

The main argument for the assumption that Paul was released from Roman custody is the content and tone of the Second Epistle to Timothy, in which he speaks of his isolation in custody (2 Tim 1:16-17; 4:11, 16), comments that do not fit the imprisonment of A.D. 60-62 but rather suggest a second, later imprisonment. A second argument is that early Christian texts assert that Paul was indeed in Spain and preached the gospel (see below).

Michael Prior argues in a study on 2 Timothy (whose Pauline authenticity he wants to prove) that Paul, contrary to the common assumption, is not writing a "farewell letter," but that he is rather confident of the future: he asks Timothy to come as soon as he can (2 Tim 4:9), if possible before the onset of winter (2 Tim 4:21), to bring John Mark with him because he is useful in Paul's ministry (ἔστιν γάρ μοι εὔχρηστος εἰς διακονίαν [2 Tim 4:11]), to bring Paul's cloak, books and parchments (2 Tim 4:13); he reminds Timothy of how the Lord supported him during the first trial (2 Tim 4:16-17a), and he expresses his confidence that through his ministry "the message might be fully proclaimed and all the Gentiles might hear it" (ἵνα δι᾽ ἐμοῦ τὸ κήρυγμα πληροφορηθῇ καὶ ἀκούσωσιν πάντα τὰ ἔθνη [2 Tim 4:17b]), and that the Lord will rescue him "from every evil attack" (2 Tim 4:18a). Prior argues that Paul evidently was "preparing an apostolic team for further missionary activity" and that this picture is disturbed only by the "dark pessimism" of 2 Tim 4:6-8, which is due mostly, however, to a faulty interpretation of the terms σπένδομαι and ἀνάλυσις (2 Tim 4:6). According to Prior, the verb *spendomai*, "to be poured out as a li-

---

[938]See O'Brien, *Phil*, 94.
[939]See Spic, *ÉpPast*, 140-41; Sordi 1986, 26; Prior 1989, 73-84, 90; Murphy-O'Connor 1996, 359-60.
[940]See Sordi (1986, 36 n. 8), who dates Paul's imprisonment in Rome to A.D. 58.
[941]P. von Rohden, "Afranius 8," PW 1 (1893): 712-13; M. Leglay, "Afranius 3," *KP* 1:108; A. Momigliano and M. T. Griffin, *OCD* 33; Griffin 2000, 67-69.

bation," does not refer metaphorically to the death of the apostle as a sacrifice, but rather to his absolute dedication to his apostolic service; and the noun *analysis* refers not to Paul's imminent death (NRSV, TNIV: "my departure"; NLT: "the time of my death is near") but to his "release."[942] Prior's interpretation of 2 Tim 4:6 is unconvincing: the apostle evidently expected his death when he wrote 2 Tim 4.[943] Equally unconvincing is Prior's suggestion that Luke's description of the conditions of Paul the prisoner in Acts 28:16-31 indicates that all the Christians of Rome rejected Paul, that Paul's project of a mission to Spain presumably failed as a result, and that the missionary work that Paul planned in 2 Tim 4 evidently took place not in the West but somewhere in the East.[944] The fact that Paul knew many of the believers in the Roman church (see the greeting list in Rom 16) suggests that Paul was accepted by the Roman Christians. The fact that Luke does not mention believers in Rome in his account in Acts 28 does not prove that Luke wanted to gloss over an inglorious sojourn of Paul in the capital of the Empire; rather, it can be understood as a result of Luke's narrative decisions: he focuses his description entirely on the mission of Paul and omits any references to Roman governmental institutions and to Roman Christians.[945] The traditional interpretation is more plausible: in 2 Timothy, Paul presupposes a second imprisonment in Rome, and he is not optimistic about its outcome. A mission to Spain would have to be dated before this second incarceration.

27.5 Missionary Work in Spain

Paul mentions Spain as the next goal of his missionary work in his letter to the Roman Christians, which he writes at the end of his outreach in the province of Asia during his visit to Corinth. He plans to travel via Rome to Spain after the upcoming visit to Jerusalem:

Rom 15:23-29: "But now, with no further place for me in these regions, I desire, as I have for many years, to come to you [24]when I go to Spain [ὡς ἂν πορεύωμαι εἰς τὴν Σπανιαν, *hōs an poreuōmai eis tēn Spanian*]. For I do hope to see you on my journey and to be sent on by you [ὑφ᾽ ὑμῶν προπεμφθῆναι ἐκεῖ, *hyph᾽ hymōn propemphthēnai ekei*], once I have enjoyed your company for a little while. [25]At present, however, I am going to Jerusalem in a ministry to the saints; [26]for Macedonia and Achaia have been pleased to share their resources with the poor among the saints at Jerusalem. [27]They were pleased to do this, and indeed they owe it to them; for if the Gentiles have come to share in their spiritual blessings, they ought also to be of service to them in material things. [28]So, when I have completed this, and have delivered to them what has been collected, I will set out by way of you to Spain [ἀπελεύσομαι δι᾽ ὑμῶν εἰς Σπανίαν, *apeleusomai di᾽ hymōn eis Spanian*]; [29]and I know that when I come to you, I will come in the fullness of the blessing of Christ."

Why did Paul plan to begin missionary work in Spain? The Greek and the Hebrew notion that the "end of the earth" was located in Gades or in Tarshish

---

[942]Prior 1989, 91-112; quotation, 111; on 2 Tim 4:17 see ibid., 113-39.

[943]See Marshall, *PastEp*, 805-7; Mounce, *PastEp*, 577-78; Johnson, *1-2 Tim*, 431, all of whom argue against Prior.

[944]Prior 1989, 113-65, esp. 130-38.

[945]Marshall, *Acts*, 420; Dunn, *Acts*, 349-50; Jervell, *Apg*, 621, 623; similarly Pesch, *Apg*, 2:313; Witherington, *Acts*, 787, 793. Differently Roloff, *Apg*, 372; Barrett, *Acts*, 2:1235-36.

probably played an important role.[946] However, there is no evidence for the suggestion that Paul viewed a mission to the "end of the earth" in Spain as the eschatological climax that would usher in the end of the world. Paul's geographical movements that we have traced in this chapter suggest that a mission to Spain would have been not an endpoint for the apostle but only another step on the way of the gospel to further unreached regions.

Rainer Riesner argues that the fact that Paul evidently did not plan a mission to Gaul, the province located between Italy and Spain, finds its explanation in Is 66:19, a text that Paul read as an expression of his missionary program and that directed him to go to Spain and thus reach the "end of the world."[947] James Scott argues that Spain, as the westernmost part of the territory of Japheth, should be regarded as the "end of the earth," which Paul, who understood himself as missionary of "Japheth," interpreted as a divine directive to plan missionary outreach to Spain.[948] Since there is no unambiguous evidence in Paul's letter to support these suggestions, they remain hypothetical.

The fact that Paul "omitted" Gaul and Germania, Roman provinces west and north of the city of Rome that were closer than Spain, does not constitute a major problem for Paul's missionary planning: he initially passed over the province of Asia and traveled from Galatia to Macedonia and Achaia.

Spain (Σπανία; Lat., Hispania, Spania [see fig. 40])[949] had contacts with the eastern regions of the Mediterranean world already by 1000 B.C. when Phoenician traders from Tyre and Sidon founded Gades and other cities on the south coast of Spain, including Mainake

---

[946]Bowers 1976, 53-62; for the comment that follows above see ibid., 62-63. The "utopian" interpretation of Dewey (1994) is interesting from a literary point of view but quite irrelevant for Paul as a missionary who wants to reach people with the message of Jesus Christ. See also Wander 2001.

[947]Riesner 1994, 272-73 (ET, 305).

[948]J. M. Scott 1995, 142, 155-56, 175-76.

[949]P. Schulten, PW 8.2 (1913): 1965-2046; R. Grosse, *KP* 2:1185-89, H. Volkmann, *KP* 5:1606-7; W. J. Heard, *ABD* 6:176; S. J. Keay, *OCD* 1429-30; P. Barceló et al., *DNP* 5:618-31; Rostovtzeff [1929] 1957, 1:211-15; G. Alföldy, *Fasti Hispanienses: Senatorische Reichsbeamte und Offiziere in den spanischen Provinzen des Römischen Reiches von Augustus bis Diokletian* (Wiesbaden: Steiner, 1969); Hartmut Galsterer, *Untersuchungen zum römischen Städtewesen auf der iberischen Halbinsel* (Madrider Forschungen 8; Berlin: de Gruyter, 1971); A. Garcia y Bellido, "Die Latinisierung Hispaniens," *ANRW* I.1 (1972): 462-500; Pedro Bosch-Gimpera, "Katalonien in der römischen Kaiserzeit," *ANRW* II.3 (1975): 572-600; F. Diego Santos, "Die Integration Nord- und Nordwestspaniens als römische Provinz in der Reichspolitik des Augustus. Von der konsularischen zur hispanischen Ära," *ANRW* II.3 (1975): 523-71; Antonio Tovar and José M. Blázquez Martínez, "Forschungsbericht zur Geschichte des römischen Hispanien," *ANRW* II.3 (1975): 428-51; Nicola Mackie, *Local Administration in Roman Spain A.D. 14-212* (London: British Institute of Archaeology, 1983); Dewey 1994; Simon J. Keay, *Roman Spain* (Berkeley: University of California Press, 1988); J. Richardson 1996, esp. 127-78; J. M. Laboa, "Spanien," *TRE* 31 (2000): 610-35; MacMullen 2000, 50-84; Adolfo J. Domínguez and Carmen Sánchez, *Greek Pottery from the Iberian Peninsula: Archaic and Classical Periods* (Leiden: Brill, 2001).

(Malaga) and Abdera. Later Greek settlers from Phokaia founded Rhode, Emporion and Artemision (Dianium). The driving force of this colonization were the rich mineral deposits on the Iberian Peninsula. After the Carthaginians had lost Sicily and Sardinia to Rome, they conquered large parts of Spain and founded Carthago Nova as new capital. The Romans defeated Carthage in 204 B.C. and occupied Spain, and in 197 B.C. the new provinces Hispania Citerior (along the east coast) and Hispania Ulterior (the southeast coast and the Guadalquivir Valley) were founded. In the course of the reorganizations of 29 B.C. and 19 B.C. the province of Hispania Ulterior was divided between the senatorial province of Baetica with Corduba as capital and the imperial province of Lusitania with Emerita Augusta as capital; the northern region of Spain continued to be administered as the province of Hispania Citeror with Tarraco as capital.The historiographical sources for the imperial period are scant; there were no major historical events that they relate.[950] Gold and silver were mined in Spain, and wine, olive oil and fish sauce were exported. Since the time of Augustus, Spain had a system of Roman colonies and municipalities linked by a dense network of roads. Many Roman senators of the first century who who were born in the provinces came from Spain. Famous Spaniards included Seneca, Quintilian and Martial, as well as the later emperors Trajan, Hadrian and Marcus Aurelius.

For a Jew from Tarsus, Spain was at the "end of the earth," with the city of Gades as the westernmost endpoint. However, Spain was anything but unreachable or remote. Spain could easily be reached overland on the developed network of Roman roads;[951] the journey by ship was quicker and more comfortable. When Paul speaks in Rom 15:24 about his plan of starting missionary outreach in Spain, the term Σπανία (*Spania*) describes either the imperial province of Hispania Citerior (Tarraconensis) or the entire Iberian Peninsula.

The question of whether or not Paul actually reached Spain depends upon the reliability of the early Christian sources that assert or imply that he was released from Roman custody. The earliest piece of evidence is comment *1 Clement; Canon Muratori* also knows of a mission of Paul to Spain, as do the apocryphal *Acts of Peter.*

1 Clem. 5:5-7: "Because of jealousy and strife Paul pointed the way to the prize for endurance. ⁶Seven times he bore chains; he was sent into exile and stoned; he served as a herald in both the East and in the West [κήρυξ γενόμενος ἔν τε τῇ ἀνατολῇ καὶ ἐν τῇ δύσει, *kēryx genomenos en te tē anatolē kai en tē dysei*]; and he received the noble reputation for his faith. ⁷He taught righteousness to the whole world, and came to the limits of the West [ἐπὶ τὸ τέρμα τῆς δύσεως ἐλθών, *epi to terma tēs dyseōs elthōn*], bearing his witness before the rulers. And so he was set free from this world and transported up to the holy place, having become the greatest example of endurance."

Canon Muratori, lines 35-39: "For the 'most excellent Theophilus' Luke ³⁶summarises the

---

[950]Tovar and Blázquez Martínez, "Forschungsbericht zur Geschichte des römischen Hispanien," 434.

[951]See Radke 1973, 1667-84. On the roads in Spain see Pierre Sillières, *Les voies de communication de l'Hispanie méridionale* (Paris: Boccard, 1990); Fatás Cabeza et al. 1993; J. Richardson 1996, 160-62; Cepas et al. 1997.

several things that in his own presence [37]have come to pass, as also by the omission of the passion of Peter [38]he makes quite clear, and equally by (the omission) of the journey of Paul, who from [39]the city (of Rome) proceeded the Spain."[952]

Acts of Peter 1 (ca. A.D. 180-190): "When Paul was at Rome confirming many in the faith . . . Quartus [a member of the guard who had come to faith] persuaded Paul to leave the city and to go wherever he pleased. Paul said to him, 'If such be the will of God, he will reveal it to me.' And Paul fasted three days and besought the Lord to grant what was good for him, and in a vision he saw the Lord who said to him, 'Paul, arise, and be a physician to the Spaniards!' At this he related to the brethren what God had commanded him, and without hesitation he made ready to leave the city. When Paul was preparing to leave, there was a great lamentation among the brethren because they thought they would never see Paul again." (See also the later passage *Actus Vercellensis* 1:1.)

Clement of Rome implies in his letter to the church in Corinth, written at the end of the first century, that Paul preached the gospel in Spain: the term δύσις (*dysis*), "West," sometimes is used for Gaul and Britain, but usually it designates Spain.[953] This cannot be dismissed as a projection from Rom 15:25 designed to enhance the reputation of the apostle: if Paul's letter to the Romans were the only source for Clement's comment, presumably he would not speak in general terms of the "limits of the West" but rather would use the word "Spain" to describe Paul's mission to the West.

There is no reason to doubt that the phrase "the limits of the West" in *1 Clem.* 5:7 refers to Spain.[954] Among earlier scholars Adolf von Harnack, Theodor Zahn, J. B. Lightfoot and Ceslas Spicq accepted the historicity of these early Christian references to a mission of Paul in Spain, as have, more recently, Colin Hemer, Harry Tajra, George Knight, Earle Ellis, Jerome Murphy-O'Connor and others.[955] Earle Ellis argues that the release of Paul from Roman custody is a historical fact that should be the basis for any critical reconstruction of the history of the early church.[956] The formulation of the comment in *1 Clem.* 5:7 does not seek to convey explicit historical information but rather alludes to Paul's ministry in Spain more indirectly, which makes the comment "rather unsuspicious" because no special interest to invent a particular fact about Paul's ministry can be detected. Ellis argues for a mission of Paul to Spain from the phrase "end of the earth" in Acts 1:8 and from the

---

[952]Translation by W. Schneemelcher, in Hennecke and Schneemelcher 1990-1997, 1:28-29 (ET, 1:42-45).

[953]Josephus, *C. Ap.* 1.67; Tacitus 4.3; Strabo 1.2.31; 1.4.6; 2.1.1; 2.4.3-4; 3.1.2; 3.5.5; Philostratus, *Vit. Apoll.* 5.4; 4.47; Pliny, *Nat.* 3.1.3-7; Livy 21.43.13; 23.5.11. See Ellis 1991, 282-83.

[954]See recently H. Löhr 2001, 207-9, contra Lindemann, *Die Clemensbriefe,* 39; idem 1979, 78.

[955]Harnack 1893-1904, 1:239-40; Zahn 1924, 1:442-54 (ET, 2:60-67); Lightfoot, *Apostolic Fathers,* 1.2, 30; Spicq, *ÉpPast,* 1:126-46; Hemer 1989, 390-404; Tajra 1989, 196; Knight, *PastEp,* 15-20; Ellis 1991, 284-85; Murphy-O'Connor 1996, 361; cautiously positive are Hengel and Schwemer 1998, 403 n. 1660 (ET, 476 n. 1373); H. Löhr 2001, 207-12; as a possibility, Wander 2001; Jewett (1979, 45) remains skeptical. Wolfgang Metzger (1976, 16-20) accepts that Paul was released from Roman custody and that he preached the gospel on Crete, but he does not think that Paul was in Spain.

[956]Ellis 1999, 278-82. For the comment that follows above see H. Löhr 2001, 212.

fact of a second Roman imprisonment of Paul, which implies, in the context of Paul's plans as described in Rom 15:24, 28, that Paul must have been in Spain after the release from his first Roman imprisonment.[957]

The existence of a Jewish community in Spain in the first century A.D. is uncertain: the available evidence documents synagogues only for the third and fourth centuries. A funerary inscription (*I. WEuropeJud* I 188) discovered in Mérida that mentions a Jew may date as early as the first century: "Alucius Roscius C(ai) l(ibertus) h(ic) s(itus) e(st) Iudeus [. . .]" ("Alucius [?] Roscius, freedman of Caius, a Jew, lies here . . .").[958] Josephus reports in *B.J.* 2.183 that Caligula exiled Herod Antipas to Spain, while he asserts in *A.J.* 18.252 that Herod was exiled to Lugdunum in Gaul, perhaps Lugdunum Convenarum, a city in Gaul on the border with Spain.[959] Josephus's information does not presuppose a Jewish community in Spain, however. Rabbi Meir is said to have spoken about Jews returning from the diaspora in Gaul and Spain (*Lev. Rab.* 29:2). In A.D. 305 the Council of Elvira prohibited Spanish Christians from living in the houses of Jews, dining in their presence and blessing the produce of their fields.[960] This (unfortunate) decision attests a sizable Jewish community in Spain for the late second century. A rabbinic tradition claims to know that a temple weaver emigrated to Spain after the destruction of Jerusalem in A.D. 70 (*m. B. Bat.* 3:2).[961] A tradition that circulated among Spanish Jews and that dates to around A.D. 800 at the latest (*Seder 'Olam Zuta*) links the presence of Jews in Spain with the destruction of the temple in Jerusalem by Titus in A.D. 70.[962] An amphora, discovered in the sea near the island of Ibiza and dating to the first century A.D. at the latest, that displays Hebrew characters documents trade relations with Jews but not necessarily a Jewish community on Ibiza. The earliest unambiguous archaeological evidence for Jews in Spain is a funerary inscription from Adra/Abdera from the third century

---

[957]Ellis 1991, 285-86.

[958]For *I. WEuropeJud* I 188 see M. Williams 1997, no. 25. For the inscription *CIJ* I² 665 = *I. WEuropeJud* I 179, found in Abdera, see M. Williams 1997, no. 35. See generally Simon R. Schwarzfuchs, "Spanien," *EncJud* 15:220-21; J. M. Blázquez, "Relaciones entre Hispania y los Semitas (Sirios, Fenicios, Chipriotas, Cartagineses y Judios) en la Antiguedad," in *Beiträge zur alten Geschichte und deren Nachleben* (FS F. Altheim; ed. R. Stiehl and H. E. Stier; Berlin: de Gruyter, 1969), 42-75; Bowers 1975; Schürer 3:84-85; M. Koch 1977; Solin 1983, 749-52; Ellis 1991, 285-86. The older literature is listed in Bowers 1975, 395-96 n. 1.

[959]See H. Crouzel, "Le lieu d'exil d'Hérode Antipas et d'Hérodiade selon Flavius Josèphe," in *Studia Patristica* (ed. F. L. Cross; TU 107; Berlin: Akademie-Verlag, 1970), 275-80; Hoehner 1972, 262 n. 1; Bowers 1975, 398.

[960]For the text of the Council of Elvira see Karl Joseph von Hefele, ed., *Histoire des Conciles d'après les documents originaux* (12 vols.; Paris: Letouzey, 1907 [1869-1878]), 1.1, 212-64, esp. *canones* 49, 50, 78; cf. Schürer 3:84 n. 123.

[961]See S. Applebaum, "The Organization of the Jewish Communities in the Diaspora," in Safrai and Stern 1987, 464-503, esp. 482.

[962]Bowers 1975, 399; for the comments that follow above see ibid., 396-97.

A.D. that mentions a Jewish girl with the name "Salo[mo]nida" (*CIJ* I 665).[963] A bilingual inscription found in Tarragona attests an *archisynagōgos* in the fourth or fifth century A.D.[964]

Some scholars argue that Paul's intention to start missionary work in Spain is the best piece of evidence for the existence of a Jewish community on the Iberian Peninsula, since Paul generally first preached to Jews and God-fearers in the synagogues.[965] This argument is not necessarily convincing: there is no evidence to prove that Paul would preach in a city only if it had a synagogue. Paul Bowers surveyed the late evidence for the existence of Jewish communities in Spain as well as the evidence of the lists of Jewish communities that do not include countries or cities west of Rome. He concludes that there were no Jews in Spain during the first century.[966] Bowers argues that the statement in Rom 10:18—the message of the gospel has gone out into the entire world, and as a result the Jews cannot claim that they had had no opportunity to hear the gospel (Rom 10:14-21)—confirms the suggestion that there were no Jews in Spain in the first century.[967] However, a lack of Jewish communities would not necessarily have prevented Paul from starting missionary work in Spain: according to Rom 1:14, Paul saw himself as having been sent not only to Jews and Greeks but also to barbarians.[968]

Paul could converse in Greek with the people who came from the eastern Mediterranean world living in the cities of Spain, particularly with the freedmen and slaves in the urban centers of Baetica and on the Levantine coast.[969] We know with regard to a later period that "the first dissemination of Christianity reached for the most part these lower classes, as is attested particularly by the Christian funerary inscriptions written in Greek, not only by the names of the deceased, of their relatives and of those who are responsible for the dedications but also by the state of the language: it could be described as 'vulgar Greek' . . . on account of the frequent mistakes." The Latin-speaking elites in the Spanish

---

[963]The other Jewish inscriptions that were found in Spain are *CIJ* I 660c (Tarragona, date uncertain); *CIJ* I 661 (Tortosa, date uncertain); *CIJ* I 660d (Pallaresos, fourth century); *CIJ* I 665a (Emeria, fourth to eighth century, probably from a synagogue); *CIJ* I 662-664 (Elche, date uncertain).

[964]J.-M. Millás, "Una nueva inscriptión judaica bilingüe en Tarragona," *Sefarad* 17 (1975): 3-10; G. Alföldy, *Die römischen Inschriften von Tarraco* (Madrider Forschungen 10; Berlin: de Gruyter, 1975), no. 1075.

[965]Ellis 1991, 285-86; cf. earlier Jackson and Lake, *Begs.* 1:158; Baron 1952, 1:170; Haas 1971, 37; Safrai and Stern 1987, 169-70.

[966]See *Sib. Or.* 3:271; Strabo, according to Josephus, *A.J.* 14.115; Philo, *Flacc.* 45-46; Josephus, *B.J.* 2.398; 7.43. See Bowers 1975, 401; also Dewey 1994, 324-26.

[967]Bowers 1975, 402; followed by Jewett 1988, 144.

[968]See Wander 2001, 193.

[969]See Sebastián Mariner Bigorra, "Hispanische Latinität und sprachliche Kontakte im römischen Hispanien," *ANRW* II.29.2 (1983): 819-52; the quotation that follows above, ibid., 841-42.

cities spoke Greek as well.[970] Thus the older argument that Paul would not have been able to find Spaniards with whom he could have conversed in Greek[971] is disproved. Paul possibly had contacts with Spain through Christians living in Rome, or he had information that such contacts could be established through the Roman church.

Some scholars suggest that Paul desired to preach the gospel in Tarraco, the capital of the province of Hispania Citerior on the northeast coast of Spain.[972] This is a plausible assumption, but there were other attractive goals for missionary work as well: from Tarraco on the northern east coast he could easily have reached Barcino, Emporion, Rhoda, Ilerda, Celsa, Caesaraugusta and Dertosa; on the southern east coast, Saguntum, Valentia, Saetabis, Ilici and Carthago Nova; on the south coast, Abdera, Sexi, Malaca (and Corduba in the interior), Carteia and Iulia Traducta; on the Atlantic south coast, Gades, Hasta Regia and Hispalis.

Tarraco (mod. Tarragona)[973] was the most important city in Spain, from a political perspective, during the imperial period. The presence of Romans at the site of an old Iberian settlement begins with Scipio around 218 B.C. Julius Caesar granted Tarraco the status of colony (Colonia Iulia Urbs Triumphalis) in 45 B.C. Augustus, who had recuperated from an illness in Tarraco, made the city the capital of the province of Hispania Citerior (Hispania Tarraconensis) in 27 B.C. In A.D. 15 Tiberius permitted the city to build a temple of Divus Augustus (Tacitus, *Ann.* 1.78). The prosperity of the city derived from sea trade, wine production and linen weaving. The infrastructure of Tarraco included the imperial temple, a forum, a theater and a circus (built during the principate of Vespasian). The survey of the territory of Tarraco that was concluded in 1990 revealed that the city controlled about 3,300 villages and hamlets in the early Roman period. Archaeologists estimate that Tarraco had between 10,000 and 15,000 inhabitants and that about 66,000 people lived in the villages in the territory of the city. According to local tradition, Paul preached at the site of the chapel that stands in the courtyard of the cathedral and is built on Roman foundations; Paul is said to have appointed Prosperus, the first bishop of the city.[974] *Barcino* (mod. Barcelona),[975] just under 100 km north of Tarraco, was founded by Augustus as Co-

---

[970]The population living in the rural areas continued to speak the Iberian and Celtic-Iberian dialects for a long time. On the languages spoken in Spain see Jürgen Untermann, "Hispania," in Neumann and Untermann 1980, 1-17; idem, "Die althispanischen Sprachen," *ANRW* II.29.2 (1983): 791-818.

[971]See recently Wander 2001, 192-93.

[972]See Breytenbach 1996, 152 n. 23.

[973]A. Schulten, PW 4.A2 (1932): 2398; K. Abel, *KP* 5:528-29; J. Arce, *PECS* 882-83; S. J. Keay, *OCD* 1476; Xavier Aquilué at al., *Tarraco: An Archaeological Guide* (Tarragona: El Mèdol, 1992); Josep-Maria Carreté, Simon Keay and Martin Millett, *A Roman Provincial Capital and Its Hinterland: The Survey of the Territory of Tarragona, Spain, 1985-1990* (JRASup 15; Ann Arbor: Journal of Roman Archaeology, 1995); bibliography, ibid., 283; Cepas et al. 1997, 151-55. Inscriptions: Géza Alföldy, *Die römischen Inschriften von Tarraco* (Berlin: de Gruyter, 1975).

[974]See Dassmann 1989, 276.

[975]R. Grosse, *KP* 1:823-24; J. Maluquer de Motes, *PECS* 142-43; Keay, *OCD* 233; Cepas et al. 1997, 44-49.

Ionia Iulia Augusta Paterna Faventia around 15 B.C. The impressive city walls and the excellent harbor guaranteed the importance of the city in the early imperial period. *Emporion/Emporiae* (mod. Empúries),[976] an old trade center (Gk., *emporion*) on the coast about 250 km north of Tarraco, incorporated several older towns, including Palaiopolis, which had been founded by colonists from Massilia (mod. Marseille) around 500 B.C., the "new city" of Neapolis and the Iberian settlement of Indike. Julius Caesar settled Roman veterans in the city in 45 B.C. The Greek city had a temple of Asclepius, a temple of Sarapis, a small agora and a colonnaded hall.

Rhoda (mod. Ciutadella de Roses),[977] around 270 km north of Tarraco, located on a small peninsula in the eastern foothills of the Pyrenees, was founded around 800 B.C. by settlers from Rhodes. Cato the Roman senator began to quell the Iberian rebellion in Rhoda in 195 B.C. *Ilerda* (mod. Lleida),[978] about 90 km west of Tarraco on the Sicoris River (mod. Segre), was founded in the third century B.C. Ilerda was a *municipium* in the early imperial period (Pliny, *Nat.* 3.24). *Celsa* (mod. Velilla del Ebro),[979] about 185 km west of Tarraco on the Iberus River (mod. Ebro), played an important role for the Romanization of the Iberus Valley. The city was founded in 42 B.C. at the site of an Iberian settlement (Colonia Victrix Iulia Lepida). *Caesaraugusta* (mod. Zaragoza),[980] about 240 km west of Tarraco on the south bank of the Iberus River, was founded by Augustus between 25 and 15 B.C. as Colonia Caesaraugusta at the site of the Iberian town of Salduba. The square layout of the city (895 by 513 m) can still be recognized in the Old City of Zaragoza. The city was the seat of a bishop as early as A.D. 250. *Bilbilis* (mod. Cerro de la Bámbola), located 75 km to the southwest, was the hometown of Marcus Valerius Martialis (ca. A.D. 40-102), the poet who became famous for his Latin epigrams; in A.D. 64 he went to Rome, where he became a protégé of the younger Seneca, the most eminent Spaniard in Rome. *Calagurris,* about 120 km to the northwest in the Iberus Valley, was the hometown of Marcus Fabius Quintilian (A.D. 35-98), the famous orator and educator of princes at the court of Domitian; he was the first orator to be paid from the Roman *fiscus* (during the principate of Vespasian). Pliny the Younger was one of Quintilian's students. His main work on rhetoric, the renowned *De institutione oratoria,* written around A.D. 88, treats in twelve books the five traditional elements of rhetoric: invention (finding and organizing the relevant material), arrangement, style, memorization and delivery, and he describes the nature, value, origin and function of rhetoric as well as different types of oratory. *Dertosa* (mod. Tortosa),[981] a coastal city about 80 km south of Tarraco on the mouth of the Iberus River, is described by Livy as a "very rich" city (Livy 23.28.10). The full name of the city was Hibera Iulia Ilercavonia Dertosa. Coins of the city minted under Augustus attest a *colonia,* and coins minted under Tiberius attest a *municipium,* which suggests that there may have been two towns existing simultaneously, perhaps on the north bank and on the south bank of the Iberus River. According to the local tradition, Paul appointed a certain Rufus as the first bishop of the city.[982]

---

[976]Grosse, *KP* 2:262-63; Maluquer de Motes, *PECS* 303; Keay, *OCD* 524; Rosa Plana Mallart, *La chora d'Emporion: Paysage et structures agraires dans le nord-est Catalan à la période préromaine* (Paris: Les Belles Lettres, 1994); Cepas et al. 1997, 71-75.

[977]Maluquer de Motes, *PECS* 754-55; Cepas et al. 1997, 130.

[978]Grosse, *KP* 2:1362-63; Keay, *OCD* 747; Barceló, *DNP* 5:931; Cepas et al. 1997, 91.

[979]A. Beltrán, *PECS* 210-11; Fatás Cabeza et al. 1993, 91.

[980]Grosse, *KP* 1:1003; Beltrán, *PECS* 181-82; Keay, *OCD* 271-72; Barceló, *DNP* 2:923-24; Fatás Cabeza et al. 1993, 73-75.

[981]Grosse, *KP* 1:1495-96; Barceló, *DNP* 3:484; Cepas et al. 1997, 69.

[982]See Dassmann 1989, 276.

On the southern east coast, the following coastal cities were important: *Saguntum* (Ζάκανθα; mod. Sagunto)[983] was an old Iberian city that had friendly relations with Rome since 231 B.C. Hannibal's siege of the city started the Second Punic War. The Scipio brothers rebuilt the destroyed city, and Augustus granted it the status of *municipium.* It was a center of pottery production. Saguntum had a theater (first century A.D.; capacity for 10,000 spectators), a circus (probably second century; capacity for 10,000 spectators) and several temples. *Valentia* (mod. Valencia)[984] was founded in 138 B.C. by Iunius Brutus as a colony of war veterans. Several Roman armies who campaigned in the interior disembarked in Valentia, including the army of Pompey in 75 B.C. *Saetabis* (mod. Xátiva),[985] about 30 km inland, situated on the north-south connection from Tarraco to Carthago Nova, is described by Pliny as *municipium Augustum.* The city was known for its linen industry (Pliny, *Nat.* 3.25; 19.9). *Ilici* (mod. Alcudia de Elche)[986] was an old Iberian city that was called Helike in the Hellenistic period. Pliny describes Ilici as a *colonia immunis* (Pliny, *Nat.* 3.19). *Carthago Nova* (mod. Cartagena)[987] was founded in 221 B.C. by Hasdrubal at the site of the old Iberian city Mastia as a base of the power of Carthage in Spain. The city had one of the best harbors in the Mediterranean. Scipio Africanus conquered the city in 209 B.C.; it became a Roman colony probably around 42 B.C. (Colonia Urbs Iulia Nova Carthago) and minted its own coins since the first century B.C. (a total of forty-three series of Latin coins). The city owed its importance to its harbor, the silver mines 20 km to the east, the production of rope and the fishing industry. Archaeological remains include the amphitheater (underneath the bullring), the theater, streets, private houses and the late Roman city walls. Coins and literary sources attest a temple of Augustus and a temple of Asclepius.

The following cities were important on the south coast (from east to west): *Abdera* (Adra)[988] was an old Phoenician city at the foot of Mount Solorius. Abdera was a *municipium* in the Roman period. *Sexi* (mod. Almuñécar)[989] also was a Phoenician foundation from the eighth century B.C. that became a *municipium* in the early Roman period (Sexi Firmum Iulium). Sexi was known for its fish sauce; coins show Heracles with two tuna. Remains of a monument, an aqueduct and *columbaria* survive. *Malaca* (mod. Malaga)[990] also was a Phoenician foundation; it came under Roman control in 205 B.C. In the first century A.D. Malaca continued to be an important city for the trade with Africa (Strabo 3.4.2). A bronze tablet found in 1851 contains chapters 51-69 of the *Lex municipii Malacitani* of A.D. 81-84, a written version of the law of the city after Malaca had become a *municipium* under Vespasian. Remains of the theater survive. The first bishop is documented for A.D. 306.[991] *Corduba* (mod. Córdoba),[992] only 150 km from Malaca, an old Ibe-

---

[983]K. Abel, *KP* 4:1500; D. Fletcher, *PECS* 783; Keay, *OCD* 1346.

[984]M. E. Aubet, *KP* 5:1092; D. Fletcher, *PECS* 952-53; Keay, *OCD* 1576.

[985]A. Schulten, PW 1.A2 (1920): 1727; W. Sontheimer, *KP* 4:1495.

[986]Schulten, PW 9.1 (1914): 1061; Grosse, *KP* 2:1363-64; Barceló, *DNP* 5:935; Fear 1996, 73-75, 95-97.

[987]Grosse, *KP* 1:1063; Beltrán, *PECS* 202-3; Keay, *OCD* 296; Barceló, *DNP* 2:998-99.

[988]Grosse, "Abdera 2," *KP* 1:6; H.-G. Niemeyer, *DNP* 1:12; Fear 1996, 194, 206, 248.

[989]K. Abel, *KP* 5:154; Keay, *OCD* 1398; Fear 1996, 56, 60, 117, 230.

[990]Grosse, *KP* 3:923-24; R. Teja, *PECS* 546-47; J. J. van Nostrand, *OCD* 914; Barceló and Niemeyer, *DNP* 7:762-63; Fear 1996, 107-8, 184-86, 199, 202-3.

[991]See Adolf Schulten and Pedro Bosch Gimpera, *Fontes Hispaniae Antiquae* (2nd ed.; 9 vols.; Barcelona: Librería Bosch, 1922-1959), 8:59-60.

[992]Grosse, *KP* 1:1304-5; J. M. Roldán, *PECS* 239-40; Keay, *OCD* 389; Barceló, *DNP* 3:161-62; Robert C. Knapp, *Roman Córdoba* (Berkeley: University of California Press, 1983); Fear 1996, 41-45, 170-226.

rian city on the Baetis River (mod. Guadalquivir), was refounded as a Roman city in 169 or 152 B.C.; it became a colony under Augustus (Colonia Patricia). Corduba was the capital of the province of Hispania Ulterior, and since 27 B.C. was the capital of the senatorial province of Hispania Baetica, one of the richest western provinces of Rome, which exported gold, silver, olive oil and fish sauce. Cordoba was the center of intellectual life in Roman Spain. Seneca the Elder (ca. 55 B.C.-A.D. 40) came from Corduba. His history of Rome has not survived. His son Seneca the Younger (ca. 4 B.C.-A.D. 65) was born in Corduba as well. Caligula regarded Seneca's brilliance as an insult, so that the latter nearly lost his life in A.D. 39. Claudius sent him to exile in Corsica in A.D. 41; he returned in A.D. 49 to become praetor and Nero's teacher. After A.D. 54 he was Nero's adviser and, for all practical purposes, managed the affairs of state. He retired after A.D. 59 and devoted himself to philosophy; he wrote tragedies, ethical-philosophical letters and treatises about ethical themes. He was forced to commit suicide in A.D. 65. The bishop Hosios (Ossius), who attended the Council of Nicea in A.D. 325, was a dominant figure of the church in the West. Other cities on the south coast include the following: *Carteia* (mod. El Rocadillo, near Roque)[993] was a naval base in the Second Punic War. It was the first newly founded city outside of Italy in a permanent Roman province to be granted the status of *colonia Latina* (in 171 B.C.). The city was known for its fishing industry. Several authors assume that Carteia was the site of the legendary city of Tartessos (Strabo 3.2.14; cf. Pliny, *Nat.* 3.7; Pausanias 6.19.3), which sometimes was mistaken for Gades. Tartessos was an old Phoenician city situated between the branches of the Odiel and Quadalquivir Rivers; it was the center of the export of copper, silver and iron ore mined in Spain; Tartessos sometimes is identified with the city of Tarshish mentioned in the Old Testament as a place where precious metals are mined (Jer 10:9; Ezek 27:12; 38:13) and the place to which the prophet Jonah wanted to flee (Jon 1:3; 4:2); Is 23:4-6 links Tarshish with Sidon and Tyrus.[994] Remains of the city walls, theater, baths, a temple as well as sculptures survive. *Iulia Traducta* (mod. Algeciras, near Gibraltar),[995] also called Iulia Ioza (Strabo 3.1.8), was founded as a colony (Colonia Iulia Traducta) under Augustus at the site of the older city of Tingentera. The name probably is connected with the fact that some of the inhabitants who were settled in the city came from the North African cities of Zelis (Algiers) and Tingis (Tanger). Pliny dates the foundation of the colony to the time of Claudius (Pliny 5.2), which suggests to some scholars that the citizens of the first colony returned to Africa at this time. Iulia Traducta was the home town of Pomponius Mela, who wrote a Latin description of the inhabited world (*De chorographia*) in A.D. 43/44.[996] This work is the oldest surviving geographical text of the Romans.

The following cities were located on the southwest coast of Spain: *Belo* (mod. Bolonia)[997] was granted the status of a *municipium* under Claudius. During this time several monumental buildings were erected in the city. On the north side of the paved forum (33 by 30 m) stood a *capitolium* with three temples and a monumental nymphaeum, on the south side stood a basilica (30 by 20 m), and on the east and west sides were colonnaded

---

[993]Grosse, *KP* 1:1062; C. Fernandez-Chicarro, *PECS* 437; Keay, *OCD* 294-95; Barceló, *DNP* 2:998; Fear 1996, 36-37, 58-59, 170-226.

[994]Schulten, PW 4.A (1932): 2446; Abel, *KP* 5:531; Blázquez, *PECS* 884; Keay, *OCD* 1476.

[995]C. Fernandez-Chicarro (*PECS* 422), who identifies Iulia Traducta with Tarifa, 22 km southwest of Algeciras. See now R. C. Knapp, *BAGRW* 423.

[996]N. Purcell, *OCD* 1218; Olshausen 1991, 75.

[997]Fear 1996, 44-45, 113-14, 173-77, and passim.

halls. *Gades* (mod. Cadiz)[998] was an old Phoenician colony founded around 1100 B.C. (*gadir* means "fortress"). The Greek city (Γαδεῖρα, *Gadeira*), located on an island that today is linked with the mainland (San Sebastian), was also called Aphrodisias, Erythreia or Hera, named after the temple of Venus Marina and the cave with an oracle at the site. On an island 18 km to the south was the temple of Heracles, visited by Hannibal, Julius Caesar and Apollonios of Tyana. The practice of offering human sacrifices in the temple of Moloch was abolished by Julius Caesar (Cicero, *Balb.* 43). The larger island to the east was the site of Roman Gades (Didyma), the endpoint of the Via Augusta, which ran from southern Gaul via Gallia Narbonensis and Valentia to Gades.[999] Caesar granted Gades Roman citizenship (Urbs Iulia Gaditana), which was confirmed by Augustus (Colonia Augusta Gaditana). The senator L. Cornelius Balbus, who came from Gades, built the new city and a new harbor. At the time of Augustus, Gades probably had over half a million inhabitants. The local population who came from rural areas maintained their old, non-Roman traditions.[1000] The prosperity of the city depended on sea trade, the fishing industry and agriculture. Strabo claims to know that Gades built the best ships on the Mediterranean Sea and on the Atlantic Ocean, and that it was second only to Rome in population (Strabo 3.5.3). With favorable winds, a ship could reach Rome in seven days. The export of fish extended as far as Palestine (*m. Šabb.* 22:2; *m. Mak.* 6;3).[1001] Remains of the theater, amphitheater and circus survive. Gades was the hometown of Lucius Iunius Moderatus Columella, who between A.D. 60 and 65 wrote a book about agriculture (*De re rustica*); his critical work on the astrologers did not survive. For the Greeks, Gades was the proverbial "end of the world" (Diodoros Siculus 25.10.1: Γάδειρα . . . κεῖται μὲν εἰς τὰ ἔσχατα τῆς οἰκουμένης, *Gadeira . . . keitai men eis ta eschata tēs oikoumenēs*),[1002] a notion that persisted as late as the tenth century.[1003] Earle Ellis is convinced that Paul sailed directly to Gades after his release from Roman imprisonment.[1004] *Hasta Regia* (mod. Cortija el Rosario),[1005] was an old Iberian coastal town about 60 km north of Gades. According to Pliny (3.11), the city was a colony (Colonia Hasta Regia). *Hispalis* (mod. Sevilla),[1006] situated on the mouth of the Guadalqivir River, is mentioned for the first time in the sources as a base for Julius Caesar, who granted the city the status of a colony in 45 B.C. (Colonia Iulia Romula). Hispalis was the most important port for the export of olive oil and metals from the richest province of western Spain. Hispalis possibly had two forums. Remains of a temple, public baths and private houses survive.

It is possible that Aquila and Priscilla were to have an important role in the mis-

---

[998]Strabo 3.5.3-10. See A. Schulten, PW 7.1 (1910): 455-57; Grosse, *KP* 2:654-56; J. M. Blázquez, *PECS* 341-42; Keay, *OCD* 618; Barceló and Niemeyer, *DNP* 4:730-32; Fear 1996, 39-41, 66-67, 109-10, 170-226, 231-37.

[999]See Radke 1973, 1674-84.

[1000]See Polomé 1983, 523.

[1001]See S. Applebaum, "Economic Life in Palestine," in Safrai and Stern 1987, 670.

[1002]See Strabo 3.5.5; Philostratus, *Vit. Apoll.* 5.4.

[1003]Suidas, *Lexicon,* s.v. "Γάδειρα"; cf. A. Adler, ed., *Suidae Lexicon* (5 vols.; Lexicographi Graeci 1; Leipzig: Teubner, 1928-1938 [Stuttgart, 1967-1971]), 1:502, no. 7 = Schulten and Bosch Gimpera, *Fontes Hispaniae Antiquae,* 9:432. See also Georgios Sphranztes in the fifteenth century; cf. Schulten and Bosch Gimpera, *Fontes Hispaniae Antiquae,* 9:439.

[1004]See Ellis 1999, 279-82.

[1005]Grosse, "Hasta 5," *KP* 2:955; Fernandez-Chicarro, *PECS* 379; Fear 1996, 42, 64, 110, 205.

[1006]Grosse, *KP* 2:1184-85; Keay, *OCD* 712; Barceló, *DNP* 5:617; Fear 1996, 42-43, 45-46, 67-68, 170-226.

sionary work in Spain: Paul's greetings in 1 Cor 16:19 presuppose that the couple was in Ephesus until shortly before the third visit in Corinth in the spring of A.D. 56, and Paul's greetings in Rom 16:3-4 imply that the couple was in Rome in the spring of A.D. 57. Aquila and Priscilla evidently moved from Ephesus to Rome in the fall of A.D. 56 or early spring of A.D. 57. Gerd Lüdemann suggests that the return of Aquila and Priscilla to their former home city was of considerable significance for Paul's plans of future missionary work: "Evidently—along with others mentioned in the list of greetings, Christians known to Paul—they were to prepare the base for Paul's future missionary work in Spain, namely, the community in Rome, for Paul's coming and ensure that he had a warm welcome there."[1007] This suggestion is quite plausible, even though it cannot be confirmed by specific evidence.

Leonard Curchin infers from Paul's plans to go to Spain that there must have been small Christian communities existing in Spain already in which Paul wanted to preach.[1008] This hypothesis is unsubstantiated by any solid evidence, and it is implausible as a explanation for the plans of Paul the pioneer missionary and apostle to the Gentiles. However, Curchin's considerations in regard to the nature of the first contacts between Christians and non-Christians in Spain are relevant. If Paul indeed was in Spain, presumably he would have initiated his missionary activities along the lines that Curchin suggests. Two population groups were prime targets for the initial proclamation of the gospel: the Jewish communities and the Greek settlers. Curchin refers to Jewish coins of the first century A.D. that have been found in Emporiae and in Iluro-Mataró (the Jewish inscriptions from Tarraco, Emeria and other cities are of a later date). Several centuries before Paul's time Greek settlers had an established presence on the east and the south coasts of Spain. The fact that the church in Spain spoke Greek until the late second century might indicate that the first Christian communities originated among the Greeks.

Robert Jewett suggests that the "matter" (πράγμα, *pragma*) in which the church in Rome is asked to support Phoebe (Rom 16:2) is the upcoming mission to Spain: Phoebe provides financial support as "patron" for the mission to Spain. Jewett further argues that the long roster of names in Rom 16:3-16 lists Christians who are living in Rome from whom Paul expects support for his mission to Spain.[1009] This suggestion is attractive but hypothetical. Would Paul be prepared to argue with the cultural concepts of patronage and benefaction in a letter that he writes in Corinth, while he soundly and consistently rejects such patronage in Corinth for himself as a pioneer missionary? In my view, this is unlikely.

The first explicit reference to Christians in Spain comes from Irenaeus, the

---

[1007]Lüdemann 1987, 210 (ET, 202); 1980, 200-201 (ET, 174-75).

[1008]Leonard A. Curchin, *Roman Spain: Conquest and Assimilation* (London: Routledge, 1991), 173-74; for the comments that follow above he refers to L. García Iglesias, *Los judíos en la España antigua* (Madrid: Cristiandad, 1978), 50-68.

[1009]Jewett 1988, 151-54.

bishop of Lyon: "For the churches [ἐκκλησίαι, *ekklēsiai*] which have been planted in Germany do not believe or hand down anything different, nor do those in Spain, nor those in Gaul, nor those in the East, nor those in Egypt, nor those in Libya, nor those which have been established in the central regions of the world [i.e., in Palestine with Jerusalem]" (Irenaeus, *Haer.* 1.10.2). J. M. Laboa asserts that there is "no Spanish church that regards itself as a direct foundation by Paul."[1010] As a result, some scholars assume that the first Christian communities in Spain were established in the second century.[1011] These considerations do not prove, however, that Paul cannot have been in Spain: the evidence of Irenaeus allows a Pauline mission to Spain, and the evidence of local tradition is ambiguous, as the local tradition of the churches in Tarraco and in Dertosa indeed has it that Paul was active in Spain.

Paul cannot have been engaged in missionary work in Spain for a very long period of time: he seems to have returned to the eastern Mediterranean world within a year or so after his arrival. We do not know the reason for the early interruption of missionary work in Spain. Lack of success can hardly have been the reason:[1012] even though he never had the kind of success among Jewish audiences that he hoped for, he continued to preach in the synagogues. Paul surely would not have decided after one summer in Spain that he should leave these Roman provinces because few people had been converted to faith in Jesus Christ. It may have been news from the Aegean region about a situation that urgently needed his attention. Paul's age may have played a role: he was between 60 and 65 years of age in A.D. 63/64, and since a 60-year-old man had a life expectancy of 69 years,[1013] Paul was an old man not only in regard to his age but also in regard to his physical constitution, it perhaps being comparable to that of an octogenarian. He may have decided to spend the last few years of his life in the eastern regions of the Mediterranean world to deal with unsolved conflicts or some unforeseen situation.

27.6 Missionary Work on Crete

The First Epistle to Timothy and the Epistle to Titus document a second period of missionary activity by Paul in the Aegean region, dating to the time after Paul's release from his (first) Roman imprisonment.[1014] If Paul was indeed in

---

[1010]J. M. Laboa, "Spanien," *TRE* 31 (2000): 610; cf. Wander 2001, 179 n. 19.

[1011]R. Konetzke, "Spanien," *RGG* 6:223; O. F. A. Meinardus, *BA* 41 (1978): 62; Jewett 1979, 131-32; 1988, 147.

[1012]Contra Murphy-O'Connor 1996, 362-63.

[1013]See B. Frier, "Roman Life Expectancy: Ulpian's Evidence," *HSCP* 86 (1982): 213-51; Ann Ellis Hanson, "Ancient Illiteracy," in Beard et al. 1991, 186 n. 99.

[1014]See Eusebius, *Hist. eccl.* 2.22.1-2; Harnack 1893-1904, 1:480-85; Schlatter, *Die Kirche der Griechen,* 397-410, 402-3; Jeremias, *Tim/Tit,* 2-3; Spicq, *ÉpPast,* 1:138-46; Knight, *PastEp,* 17-20, 53-54; Ellis 1999, 283-84. John Robinson (1976, 73-84) dates the second Aegean mission to the time before Paul's imprisonment in Caesarea.

Spain, this Aegean mission would date after the mission to Spain. A brief comment in Tit 1:5 implies (if we assume Pauline authenticity for the Epistle to Titus) a mission to Crete by Paul: "I left you behind in Crete for this reason, so that you should put in order what remained to be done, and should appoint elders in every town, as I directed you."[1015] Evidently there were Christian communities in several cities on Crete by the time the Epistle to Titus was written. The text does not state, however, the identity of the pioneer missionary who had founded these churches. Luke mentions Jewish pilgrims from Crete who visited Jerusalem on the occasion of the Feast of Pentecost in A.D. 30 (Acts 2:11): if some of these pilgrims came to faith as a result of Peter's proclamation of the gospel of Jesus the Messiah during Pentecost, then the gospel could have been brought to Crete by these new Jewish believers as early as A.D. 30.[1016] An alternative scenario is that coworkers of Paul— at least Titus—worked as missionaries in the cities of Crete, asking for the apostle's help in consolidating the new churches around A.D. 63. There is no explicit reference to Paul himself establishing the churches on Crete.

There were large Jewish communities on Crete. Philo states in his report of the letter of Herod Agrippa I to Caligula that the Greek islands are "full" of Jewish communities, mentioning Crete in this context (Philo, *Legat.* 282). One of the wives of Josephus came from one of the first Jewish families of Crete (Josephus, *Vita* 427).[1017] Tacitus mentions Jewish communities on Crete as well (Tacitus, *Hist.* 5.11). A mission to Crete would have been a logical project for the early Jewish Christian missionaries.

If Paul arrived on Crete from a westerly direction—the distance from Rome to Crete is 1,300 km —then presumably he would have disembarked in Kydonia on the northwest coast of the island. Traveling west, he would have reached the city of Polyrrhenia. Other cities on the north coast of Crete were Rhithymna, Knosos, Chersonasos, Lyktos and Olous. There were fewer cities on the south coast; Hierapytna and Gortyn would have been attractive cities to visit.

Kydonia (Κυδωνία; mod. Khania)[1018] was the third-largest city of Crete (Strabo 10.4.7). Kydonia had a good harbor and was situated in a fertile plain. For a long period of time the city controlled the Diktynnaion, the sanctuary of Britomartis (later fused with Artemis), the Cretan mountain goddess, located about 40 km northwest of the city on the Dikte Mountains. The city led the opposition to Rome in the first century B.C. Because Kydonia supported Augustus against Mark Antony, it was granted autonomy in 30 B.C. Other than some graves, hardly any ancient remains survive.

[1015]W. Metzger 1976, 29-30; for the comments that follow above see ibid.
[1016]As a possibility, see Mounce, *PastEp,* 386.
[1017]See also Josephus, *A.J.* 17.327; *B.J.* 2.103.
[1018]E. Mayer, *KP* 3:391; D. J. Blackman, *PECS* 472; H. Sonnabend, *DNP* 6:959; R. Scheer, in Lauffer 1989, 167-68.

Polyrrhenia (Πολυρρηνία; mod. Epano Palaiokastro),[1019] 35 km west of Kydonia, located on an isolated hill in the Plain of Kisamos. The city is mentioned nearly exclusively by ancient geographers.[1020] Polyrrhenia lost its preeminent position in western Crete in the second century B.C. to Kydonia, which is why it supported the Roman conquest of the island, a course of action that Rome honored: Polyrrhenia was allowed to mint coins and was granted control over the Diktynnaion.

Rhithymna (ʹΡίθυμνα; also Arsinoë; mod. Rethymnon),[1021] located east of Kydonia, was an old city that is mentioned by Greek and Roman geographers (Pliny, *Nat.* 4.12.59). A temple of Artemis Rhokkaia is attested.

Knosos (Κνωσός; mod. Knossos, near Makryteikhos),[1022] 4 km south of the coast near Herakleion, was the center of Minoan culture, with a huge palace built around 2000 B.C. (destroyed around 1400 B.C.). Knosos was the most powerful city of Crete during the Hellenistic period. When it resisted the invasion of the Romans in the first century B.C., Gortyn became the capital of the island and of the new province in 64 B.C. Augustus founded a colony in Knosos (Colonia Iulia Nobilis Cnosus). Remains of the agora, a basilica, baths and a small amphitheater survive.

Chersonasos (Χερρόνησος; mod. Limin Khersonisos)[1023] minted coins since the fourth or third century B.C. The city had a temple of Britomartis (Strabo 10.4.14), one of the main gods of Crete; the temple is depicted on many coins of the city. Ruins of the theater and the amphitheater could still be seen in the nineteenth century.

Lyktos (Λύκτος; mod. Xidas),[1024] situated about 15 km south of Chersonasos in the mountains, is described as the oldest city of Crete (Polybios 4.54.6). The cult of Zeus is said to have included human sacrifices. Lyktos had close connections with Sparta. When the city resisted Knosos in 219 B.C., it was completely destroyed, and later it was rebuilt. After 67 B.C. Lyktos was under Roman control. It remained one of the important cities of Crete.

Olous (ʹΟλοῦς; Elounta),[1025] a coastal city in eastern Crete on the Bay of Mirabello, had close connections with Rhodes in the third and second centuries B.C. Coins suggest that Zeus Tallaios was the main god of the city. Asclepius and Britomartis were worshiped as well; Olous is said to have had an archaic image of the goddess Britomartis made by Daidalos. Most of the ancient ruins are submerged today.

Hierapytna (ʹΙεράπυτνα, ʹΙεράπετρα; mod. Ierapetra),[1026] located in the east of the south

---

[1019]E. Meyer, *KP* 4:1011-12; D. J. Blackman, *PECS* 722-23; Scheer, in Lauffer 1989, 559.

[1020]See Strabo 10.4.13; Polybios 4.53.55, 61.

[1021]L. Bürchner, PW 1.A1 (1914): 923-24; E. Meyer, *KP* 4:1419; D. J. Blackman, *PECS* 754.

[1022]E. Meyer, *KP* 3:260-61; K. Branigan, *PECS* 459; L. F. Nixon and S. Price, *OCD* 354; Sonnabend, *DNP* 6:617-18; H. Buhmann, in Lauffer 1989, 332-34.

[1023]L. Bürchner, "Chersonesos 4," PW 3.1 (1899): 2251; D. J. Blackman, *PECS* 221.

[1024]E. Meyer, *KP* 3:821-22; Branigan, *PECS* 538; Sonnabend, *DNP* 7:577-78; Beister, in Lauffer 1989, 399-400.

[1025]E. Kirsten, "Olus 2," PW 17.2 (1937): 2504-8; E. Meyer, *KP* 4:278; D. J. Blackman, *PECS* 645-46; Sonnabend, *DNP* 8:1168; H. Beister, in Lauffer 1989, 216.

[1026]E. Meyer, *KP* 2:1130-31; D. J. Blackman, *PECS* 391-92; Sonnabend, *DNP* 5:533-34; Beister, in Lauffer 1989, 268-69.

coast of Crete, originally seems to have been the port of Oleros, but it increased in significance during the third century B.C. The city, the last refuge of Crete's freedom fighters, surrendered in 67 B.C. to the Roman army under Metellus. Inscriptions, two harbor basins, two theaters, an amphitheater, public baths and several temples attest that Hierapytna prospered during the imperial period. The main gods of the city were Athene, Apollo, Hera, Zeus and Egyptian deities. Remains of one of the two theaters, amphitheater and tombs survive. In the Byzantine period Hierapytna was the seat of the bishop of eastern Crete. Titus is said to have appointed the first bishop.

Gortyn (Γόρτυνς; Gortyna, Ag. Deka),[1027] 16 km from the south coast in the Plain of Mesara (Strabo 10.4.7), was one of the most important cities of Crete in the third century B.C., with a temple of Athene on the acropolis (seventh century B.C.), a temple of Apollo Pythios and a temple of Asclepius. The famous "Law of Gortyn," the longest extant Greek inscription, is a codification of family, inheritance and proprietary laws. Since Gortyn had allied itself with Rome at an early date, the city became the capital of the new province of Creta et Cyrene. The infrastructure of Roman Gortyn included the praetorium of the governor, theater, amphitheater, circus, odeion, nymphaeum, public baths and a temple of Isis and Sarapis. Gortyn is mentioned in 1 Macc 15:23 as a city with a Jewish community. An inscription attests a woman named Sophia as "elder and ruler of the synagogue" (πρεσβυτέρα κὲ ἀρχισυναγώγισσα, *presbytera ke archisynagōgissa*), functions that evidently she held personally.[1028] According to local tradition, Titus, Paul's coworker, was the first bishop of the city; the church Haghios Titus was built in the sixth century. The first documented bishop is Philippos in the second century.[1029] Ten Christians of Gortyn were killed around A.D. 250 in the persecution under Decius.

Paul directed Titus to appoint elders "in every town" in which a Christian community existed and to "put in order what remained to be done" (Tit 1:5); that is, Titus presumably was to instruct the Christians of Crete in the biblical norms and criteria of Christian behavior. The churches evidently had been established not long before, and chronological considerations suggest that they can hardly have been founded by Paul's preaching alone.[1030] Paul did not stay long on Crete. His letter to Titus with specific instructions for the churches in the cities of Crete was delivered by Zenas, a lawyer, and Apollos (Tit 3:13), who were on their way to another destination; the southern direction of their journey and the presence of Apollos might suggest Alexandria as destination.[1031] Paul informed Titus that he would be replaced by Artemas or Tychicus (Tit 3:12). According to 2 Tim 4:12, Tychicus went to Ephesus, probably to replace Timothy. This suggests that Artemas (short form for "Artemidoros") went to Crete.[1032] The

---

[1027]E. Meyer, *KP* 2:855-56; K. Branigan, *PECS* 362-63; V. Ehrenberg at al., *OCD* 643; Sonnabend, *DNP* 4:1159-61; H. Buhmann, in Lauffer 1989, 237-39; Hölbl 2001, 132.

[1028]See Horst 1988; L. Levine 2000, 482.

[1029]See Michaelis le Quien, *Oriens Christianus* (3 vols.; repr., Graz: Akademische Druck und Verlagsanstalt, 1958 [Paris: Ex Typographia Regia, 1740]), 2:526-27 and 2:257-58 [1] 30.

[1030]See Mounce, *PastEp*, 386, with reference to J. P. Meier, "Presbyteros in the Pastoral Epistles," *CBQ* 35 (1973): 323-45, esp. 338.

[1031]Mounce, *PastEp*, 458. Marshall (*PastEp*, 344) declines to suggest a hypothesis.

New Testament provides no further evidence about Artemas.

27.7 Paul's Last Journeys

The last travels of Paul before his second arrest have to be reconstructed on the basis of brief comments in the Second Epistle to Timothy and in the Epistle to Titus. There can be no certainty concerning the details of this reconstruction. Paul probably traveled from Crete to Nikopolis (500 km)—that is, Actia Nicopolis— which since the principate of Nero was the capital of the province of Epirus (between the provinces of Illyricum and Achaia [on Nikopolis see §27.3]).[1033] Titus, whose replacement Paul announced in Tit 3:12, was active in Dalmatia (2 Tim 4:10)—that is, "upper" Illyricum north of Nikopolis. Paul intended to spend the winter in Nikopolis. It is possible that a church was established in the city.[1034] Paul evidently left Nikopolis and traveled to Macedonia (900 km), and from there to Alexandria Troas in the province of Asia (850 km), where he lived in the house of Carpus, where he left the cloak, books (*biblia*) and parchments (*membrana*) that Timothy later is directed to bring to Rome (2 Tim 4:13). Paul had visited Alexandria Troas repeatedly;[1035] on this occasion he probably was en route to Ephesus, where he had promised to meet Timothy, who was responsible for the churches in the area (1 Tim 3:14). Paul may have been arrested in Alexandria Troas, or perhaps in Ephesus, or perhaps in Miletus (cf. 2 Tim 4:20b). On the way to Rome for his trial he seems to have passed through Corinth (2 Tim 4:20a).

Final note on Paul's journeys. The following table shows the distances and travel times that Paul covered as a missionary, including the visits to Jerusalem in A.D. 44 and 48, the mission in Arabia,[1036] the mission in Syria and Cilicia,[1037] the mission in southern Galatia, the mission in Macedonia and Achaia, the mission in the province of Asia, the mission in Spain,[1038] the mission on Crete[1039] and the travels of the final years before the second Roman imprisonment.[1040]

[1032] Spicq, *ÉpPast,* 2:689-90; Marshall, *PastEp,* 341; Mounce, *PastEp,* 457.

[1033] See Marshall, *PastEp,* 341-42; Mounce, *PastEp,* 457-58.

[1034] McDonald 1992, 961.

[1035] Cf. Acts 16:8, 11; 20:5-6; 2 Cor 2:12.

[1036] Assuming a journey from Damascus to Bostra, Philadelphia and Jerusalem, a distance of about 300 km.

[1037] Assuming a journey from Jerusalem to Damascus; a journey in Syria to Abila, Emesa, Apamea, Antiochia and Kyrrhos; a journey in Cilicia from Tarsus to Adana, Mopsuestia, Anazarbus, Mallos, Korykos, Seleukia ad Kalykadnum and back to Tarsus; a journey from Tarsus to Antiochia—a total of 1,800 km. This is a low figure: Paul presumably traveled much more frequently during the ten years that he worked in Syria and in Cilicia.

[1038] Assuming a journey from Rome to Tarraco, Barcino, Emporiae, Rhoda, Ilerda, Celsa, Caesaraugusta and back to Rome, a total of 1,800 km by ship and 1,000 km on land.

[1039] Assuming a journey from Rome to Kydonia and along the coastal road to Rhithymna, and by ship to Knosos, a total of 1,300 km by ship and 120 km on land.

[1040] Assuming a journey from Knosos on Crete to Epirus and Illyricum (Nikopolis), overland to Macedonia (Thessalonike), by ship to Alexandria Troas and overland to Ephesus, a total of 900 km on land and 1,700 km by ship.

Arabia	300 km land (12 days)		:: 300 km	12 days
Syria/Cilicia	1,800 km land (70 days)		:: 1,800 km	70 days
Jerusalem (A.D. 44)	1,080 km land (45 days)		:: 1,080 km	45 days
Galatia	1,440 km land (60 days)	980 km sea (10 days)	:: 2,420 km	70 days
Jerusalem (A.D. 48)	1,080 km land (45 days)		:: 1,080 km	45 days
Greece	3,110 km land (125 days)	2,060 km sea (20 days)	:: 5,170 km	145 days
Asia	2,900 km land (115 days)	3,210 km sea (35 days)	:: 6,110 km	150 days
Spain	1,000 km land (40 days)	1,800 km sea (15 days)	:: 2,800 km	55 days
Crete	120 km land (5 days)	1,300 km sea (14 days)	:: 1,420 km	19 days
Last journeys	900 km land (35 days)	1,700 km sea (17 days)	:: 2,600 km	52 days

These figures yield the following approximate totals: Paul traveled at least 25,000 km (15,500 mi.) as a missionary, about 14,000 km (8,700 mi.) of that by land (for comparison: Alexander the Great traveled about 32,000 km or 19,900 mi.).[1041]

27.8 The Missionary Work of Coworkers in Dalmatia (and Gallia?)

Paul organized missionary outreach in the province of Dalmatia during the last months of his life. Titus evidently was responsible for this project. And Crescens, another coworker of Paul, possibly went to Gaul.

The Missionary Work of Titus in Dalmatia

Paul informs Timothy in his last letter, presumably written in A.D. 66/67 from prison in Rome, that Titus went to Dalmatia (2 Tim 4:10c). Paul evidently assumes that Timothy knew what Titus was doing in Dalmatia. The negative comment on the behavior of Demas—he left Paul because he was "in love with the present world" and went to Thessalonike (2 Tim 4:10a)[1042]—suggests that Titus went to Dalmatia in the context of Paul's missionary project.

[1041]On Alexander see Elmer C. May, *Ancient and Medieval Warfare* (Wayne, N.J.: Avery, 1984), 29.

[1042]Demas probably did not abandon his faith (differently Mounce, *PastEp*, 589-90): he seems to have left Paul because he did not want to risk martyrdom; presumably he continued to be active as a Christian, perhaps even as a missionary; see Spicq, *ÉpPast*, 2:810-11; Marshall, *PastEp*, 816.

Dalmatia (Dalmatae)[1043] was a Roman province since A.D. 9, when Tiberius divided Illyricum into two provinces after he had crushed the last rebellion in the region; under the Flavian emperors the two provinces were called Dalmatia and Pannonia; Dalmatia possibly was known as *superior provincia Illyricum*. In A.D. 67 the term "Dalmatia" described the region between the border with Macedonia and the Titius River (mod. Kerka), but sometimes the term was used for all of Illyricum. Important cities in Dalmatia included Saslona, Scodra and the capital, Delminium.

Scodra (mod. Shkodra, Albania)[1044] was situated on the southeastern end of Lake Labeatis (Lake Shkodra), about 30 km northeast of the coastal city of Olcinium (mod. Ulcinij, Montenegro), on the coastal road that ran through Illyricum and Dalmatia, about 110 km north of Dyrrachium. Scodra was the capital of the Illyrian kingdom that was annexed by the Romans in 200 B.C. After 167 B.C. Scodra was a Roman garrison. During the imperial period Scodra became a Roman colony (Colonia Claudia).

Narona (mod. Vid, Croatia),[1045] about 230 km northwest of Scodra on the north-east road through Dalmatia, situated 20 km from the coast on the Naro River (mod. Neretva). The inhabitants of Narona included Thracians and Illyrians, as well as Greeks, Italians and people from Asia Minor. The city is mentioned in the sixth century B.C. as a center of the trade between the Mediterranean world and the Balkan region (Strabo 7.5.5). Coins document commercial relations with Italy, Greece, the Aegean islands and Gaul. Since about 50 B.C. Narona was a center of Roman Dalmatia; between 47 and 27 B.C. the city was granted the status of a colony (Colonia Iulia Narona). Veterans were settled in the city since the time of Tiberius. The rise of Salona as capital of the province caused the decline of Narona in the first and second centuries A.D., accelerated by the silting of the Naro River. Narona boasted of temples dedicated to Jupiter, Ceres, Diana, Mercurius, Neptune, Venus and Isis, as well as Augustus and Livia. The infrastructure included a forum, public baths and theater. There is no information about the origins of the Christian community in the city.[1046]

Salona (mod. Solin near Split, Croatia),[1047] about 130 km northwest of Narona on the Salon River (mod. Jader), was one of the most important port cities on the Adriatic Sea. The city was the seat of the governor and of the provincial assembly. The originally Thracian and Illyrian city became a Greek colony in the fourth century B.C. Around 150 B.C. Salona was occupied by Dalmatian tribes, and in 78 B.C. it was recaptured by a Roman proconsul. Between 47 and 44 B.C. it became a Roman colony (Colonia Martia Iulia Salonae). After A.D. 9 Salona was the capital of the province of Dalmatia. Being at the crossroads of the network of Roman roads, the city flourished quickly. In the second century Salona had about sixty thousand inhabitants. The emperor Diocletian, whose home town was Salona,

---

[1043]J. Szilágyi, *KP* 1:1364-68; F. A. W. Schehl and J. J. Wilkes, *OCD*, 426-27; M. Šašel Kos, *DNP* 3:282-86; J. J. Wilkes, *Dalmatia* (London: Routledge, 1969); idem, "The Population of Roman Dalmatia," *ANRW* II.6 (1977): 732-66; Marin Zaninović, "The Economy of Roman Dalmatia," *ANRW* II.6 (1977): 767-809.

[1044]J. Fitz, *KP* 5:51; Alexandrov 1976, 112; J. J. Wilkes, *BAGRW* 755, map 49.

[1045]M. Fluss, PW 16.2 (1935): 1755-56; J. Szilágyi, *KP* 3:1574; M. Zaninović, *PECS* 609; E. Olshausen, *DNP* 8:715-16; P. Kos, *BAGRW* 294, map 20.

[1046]Note the early Christian inscription *CIL* III 1891.

[1047]J. Fitz, *KP* 4:1521; M. Zaninović, *PECS* 799; J. J. Wilkes, *OCD* 1350. For the presence of Jews, see *IJudO* I, 2004, 24-29. See also P. Kos, *BAGRW* 296, map 20.

lived in a villa 5 km from Salona after his resignation in A.D. 305. Remains of the theater, amphitheater (second century), temples and baths survive. There was a Christian community in Salona since the second or third century.

Missionary Work of Crescens in Gallia?

Paul informed Timothy in his last letter from prison in Rome that Crescens went to Galatia (2 Tim 4:10b). The Greek word Γαλατία (*Galatia*) can describe (1) the Roman province of Galatia in central Asia Minor; (2) the region of the Celtic Galatians in the north of the province of Galatia; (3) the Roman province of Gaul (Gallia; mod. France). Several New Testament manuscripts clarify the matter by reading in 2 Tim 4:10 εἰς Γαλλίαν (*Gallian*)[1048] rather than εἰς Γαλατίαν (*Galatian*). Some scholars assume that it was already the author of 2 Timothy who interpreted the Greek term *Galatia*—if this was the original reading—as a reference to the province of Gaul, even before the subsequent manuscript tradition and the later tradition of the church read *Gallia*.[1049]

A mission to Gaul certainly would not have proved a precarious adventure. Rainer Riesner correctly points out that "precisely the fact that southern Gaul had already been Hellenized, and that compared to Spain it was far more likely to have a significant number of Jews, would have made this region attractive to Paul." Gaul could be easily reached by ship, and there was a well-developed network of Roman roads in southern France.[1050]

Massalia (Μασσαλία; Massilia; mod. Marseille),[1051] about 600 km northwest of Rome, was founded around 600 B.C. by Greek colonists from Phokaia. Massalia in turn established numerous colonies on the Ligurian and Iberian coasts: Nikaia (mod. Nizza), Antipolis (mod. Antibes), Emporion (mod. Ampurias) and Mainake (near mod. Malaga). The existence of a treasure house of Massalia in Delphi indicates that the city maintained close contacts with Greece. Pytheas of Massalia sailed as far as Thule (Iceland, or the Faeroe Islands) in 325 B.C. Strabo describes a temple of Artemis Ephesia and a temple of Apollo Delphinios on the acropolis of Massalia, and he also notes the stability of the aristocratic administration of the city (Strabo 4.1.4-5). The harbor included a shipbuilding yard. Mas-

---

[1048]The manuscripts ℵ C 81 104 326 *pc* vg[st.ww] sa bo[pt], and also Eusebius and Epiphanius.

[1049]Particularly Spicq, *ÉpPast,* 2:811-13. A mission to Gaul is assumed in Zahn 1886, 145; J. B. Lightfoot 1893, 432; Kelly, *PastEp,* 213; Holtz, *Pastoralbriefe,* 195; Hasler, *Tim/Tit,* 79-80; as a possibility in Mounce, *PastEp,* 590; Riesner 1994, 271 (ET, 304). Marshall (*PastEp,* 816) remains skeptical. For the quotation that follows above see Riesner 1994, 271 (ET, 304).

[1050]See Radke 1973, 1667-74.

[1051]H. G. Wackernagel, PW 14.2 (1930): 2130-52; H. Volkmann, *KP* 3:1066-68; F. Salviat, *PECS* 557-58; A. Rivet and J. F. Drinkwater, *OCD* 935; Y. Lafond, *DNP* 7:983-86; Michel Bats, *Le territoire de Marseille grecque* (Publications de l'Université de Provence 1; Aix-en-Provence: Université de Provence, 1986); idem, ed., *Marseille grecque et la Gaule: Actes du Colloque d'histoire et d'archéologie et du Ve Congrès archéologique de Gaule meridionale (Marseille, 18-23 novembre 1990)* (Études massalietes 3; Aix-en-Provence: Université de Provence, 1992); S. Loseby, *BAGRW* 223, map 15. On the Roman reorganization of Gaul see MacMullen 2000, 85-123.

salia had a close relationship with Rome at an early period. The city supported Pompey against Julius Caesar, who conquered the city in 49 B.C. and gave a large part of its territory (with the exception of Nikaia) to Arelate (mod. Arles), although the city managed to maintain its independence. The importance of Massalia declined in the subsequent decades but remained a center of Greek culture and learning. Strabo relates that Massalia turns the Gauls into φιλέλληνες (*philellēnes,* "friends of the Greeks") and teaches them to write their treaties in the Greek language, and that some noble Romans prefer to come to Massalia to study rather than going to Athens (Strabo 4.1.5). Massalia had a forum, baths, stadium and theater. Under Nero, the city walls that had been destroyed in 49 B.C. were rebuilt by the physician Krinas. Remains of the Greek theater (south of the old harbor), a temple of Cybele, other temples, the agora, city wall and harbor facilities survive. Scholars who think that a successful missionary ministry of Crescens in Gaul is unlikely assume that the Christian community of Massalia was established in the second century, at about the same time that the churches in Lugdunum and Vienne were founded.[1052]

Narbo (mod. Narbonne),[1053] about 240 km east of Massalia, originally was an old Celtic-Iberian settlement on the banks of the Atax River (mod. Aude), the capital of the Elysicii tribe. In 118/117 B.C. the Romans established the first Roman colony in Gaul (Colonia Narbo Martius) at the site in order to protect the road to Spain. Under Augustus, Narbo became the capital of the province of Gallia Narbonensis. Claudius founded a second colony in the expanding city (Colonia Iulia Paterna Claudia Narbo Martius decumanorum). Narbo was the seat of the proconsul and of the imperial cult; it had a forum (60 by 85 m), a capitol, warehouses, a theater, an amphitheater (121 by 93 m), temples and public baths. An altar in the forum displayed an inscription of the laws and the calendar of the festivals celebrated in honor of Augustus (*CIL* XII 4333). The inhabitants worshiped Jupiter, Mars, Mercurius, Vulcanus, Hercules, Silvanus, Belenus, Larrasco, Bona Dea and Cybele.

Lugdunum (Λούγδουνον; mod. Lyon),[1054] 340 km north of Massalia on the confluence of the Arar River (mod. Saône) and the Rhodanus River (Rhône), was founded in 61 B.C. by Rome at the site of two old Celtic settlements in order to establish a Roman presence in the central Rhône Valley. In 43 B.C. Lugdunum was granted the status of a colony (Colonia Copia Claudia Augusta Lugdunum), with veterans of Roman armies settled in the city (Tacitus, *Hist.* 1.65.2). In 12 B.C. Lugdunum became the seat of the provincial assembly and the center of the imperial cult. Lugdunum was the religious, administrative, financial and commercial center of the three provinces of Gaul (Lugdunensis, Belgica, Aquitania) and of Germania, the most important city in the northwestern part of the Roman Empire. Numerous roads converged in the city. Since 15 B.C. the imperial mint was located in Lug-

---

[1052]See Volkmann, *KP* 3:1067, with reference to *CIL* XII 489.

[1053]M. Leglay, *KP* 3:1570-71; M. Gayraud and Y. Solier, *PECS* 607-8; J. F. Drinkwater, *OCD* 1026; Y. Lafond, *DNP* 8:708-9; Raymond Chevallier, "Gallia Narbonensis: Bilan de 25 ans de recherches historiques et archéologiques," *ANRW* II.3 (1975): 686-828; Michel Gayraud, "Narbonne aux trois premiers siècles après Jésus-Christ," *ANRW* II.3 (1975): 829-59; idem, *Narbonne antique des origines à la fin du IIIe siècle* (Paris: Boccard, 1981); A. L. F. Rivet, *Gallia Narbonensis: With a Chapter on Alpes Maritimae; Southern France in Roman Times* (London: Batsford, 1988), 130-35; R. W. Mathisen and H. S. Sivan, *BAGRW* 394, map 25.

[1054]F. Cramer, "Lugdunum 1," *PW* 13.2 (1927): 1718-23; M. Leglay, *KP* 3:770-71; idem, *PECS* 528-31; A. Rivet and J. F. Drinkwater, *OCD* 891; Y. Lafond, *DNP* 7:487-89; R. Chevallier, "Gallia Lugdunensis: Bilan de 25 ans de recherches historiques et archéologques," *ANRW* II.3 (1975) 860-1060; Christ 1992, 119, 157, 449, 588; E. Betrand, *BAGRW* 249, map 17.

dunum, partly due to a concentration of Roman troops in the region. Series of Roman copper coins depicted Lugdunum's altar of Roma and Augustus on the reverse, which thus was well known to the people living in the western part of the Roman Empire. The two columns (10.5 m high) that flanked the altar were made of marble from Syene in Egypt. Lugdunum had between 50,000 and 100,000 inhabitants. The emperor Augustus visited the city repeatedly, and the emperor Claudius was born there. After the fire of A.D. 65 (Tacitus, *Ann.* 16.3) and after the unrest of A.D. 68-69 the city flourished again very quickly. Remains include the theater (16-14 B.C.; capacity for 4,500 spectators), amphitheater (A.D. 19), odeion (capacity for 3,000 spectators), the Augustan forum (140 by 61.5 m), a temple of Cybele (82 by 50 meters), the industrial quarter with potteries, bronze foundries, glassmaker workshops, as well as the aqueduct and over one hundred mosaics. In A.D. 177 at the latest a Christian community existed in Lugdunum that maintained contact with the church in Ephesus. In A.D. 178 the church appointed Irenaeus of Ephesus as bishop.[1055]

The extant sources provide no information about early Christian missionary work in Germania. There would have been logical targets of missionary travels: Cologne, founded in 38 B.C. by Agrippa as *oppidum* and elevated probably before A.D. 5 as *Ara Romae et Augusti,* was the religious and political center of the province of Germania, "a city in the sense of the Roman Mediterranean culture."[1056] In A.D. 43—the twelve apostles had just left Jerusalem and Paul worked as a missionary in Antioch in Syria—Roman troops massed in Cologne before the invasion of Britain. In A.D. 50—Paul preached the gospel in the province of Achaia—Cologne became a colony. A Jewish community existed in Cologne by A.D. 312 at the latest.[1057]

[1055]On the church in Lugdunum in the second century see recently Hayes 2002, 130-36. On Irenaeus see Robert M. Grant, *Irenaeus of Lyons* (Early Church Fathers; London: Routledge, 1997). On the theology of missions of Irenaeus see Tiessen 1993.

[1056]Otto Doppelfeld, "Das römische Köln," *ANRW* II.4 (1975): 715-82, esp. 719.

[1057]Cf. Codex Theodosianus 16.8.3: "Imp. Constantinus A. Decurionibus Agrippiniensibus: Cunctis ordinibus generali lege concedimus, Iudaeos vocare ad curiam." See Polomé 1983, 512; Solin 1983, 754; Schürer 3:85 with n. 128.

28

MISSIONARY TACTICS AND COMMUNICATION

P aul planned his missionary initiatives in the context of a general strategy that controlled his tactical decisions.[1] The survey of Paul's missionary work in the previous chapter has shown that the apostle did not slavishly follow plans that he had made, nor did he simply follow the internal guidance of the Holy Spirit without reflection or without consultation with others. In this chapter I will discuss, first, the tactical missionary procedures that informed Paul's work in the Greek cities and in the Roman colonies of the provinces in the Eastern Mediterranean: his preaching and teaching in the synagogues before Jewish audiences, proselytes and God-fearers; his missionary preaching in marketplaces before polytheists; his teaching in lecture halls and in private homes before mixed audiences, to simple people and to aristocrats. Second, I will discuss extensively communication aspects of Paul's missionary work: the sending of envoys, the establishment of initial contacts, the proclamation of the gospel, the persuasiveness of the message, methods of missionary proclamation, the credibility of the envoy, the disposition of the listeners, the conversion of people and the establishment of communities of believers. A third area of discussion concentrates on the forms and on the content of Paul's missionary preaching: pioneer preaching to Jewish audiences (christological communication), pioneer preaching to Gentile audiences (theological communication), the explanation of the gospel (dialogical concentration), the proclamation of Jesus as Messiah and Lord (ideological confrontation), the defense of the gospel (apologetic confrontation) and the encouragement of the Christian communities (pastoral concretization). Fourth, I will survey the available information about organizational issues: centers of missionary work, teams of missionaries and coworkers, support of the missionaries and finances. Fifth, I will discuss the missionary work of the Christian communities: the lack of exhortations to active missionary participation, the evangelism of the local communities, conduct in the family, conduct in worship

---

[1]See §16.3 on the definition of "strategy" and "tactics."

services, conduct in society, the willingness to suffer, the eschatological responsibility of believers and the Epistle to the Romans as a missionary document.

28.1 Tactical Missionary Procedures

Paul understood his missionary task as being directed first to the Jews and then
to the Gentiles, both from a "theoretical" theological point of view and from a
concrete evangelistic point of view. At the same time he interpreted the call and
the commission that the Risen Lord had extended to him as a directive to reach
non-Jews with the message of Jesus Christ. Paul was both a missionary to Jews
and a missionary to Gentiles: "For I am not ashamed of the gospel; it is the
power of God for salvation to everyone who has faith, to the Jew first and also
to the Greek" (Rom 1:16).

The cultural background and the social position of Paul suggest that his missionary activities of preaching and teaching were concentrated on specific locations in the infrastructure of Greek and Roman cities. What this meant specifically can been seen in the example of Philo, the Jewish philosopher of religion
in Alexandria, Egypt.

Christian Noack distinguishes five ideal-typical locations for the teaching activity of Philo:[2]
(1) the synagogue, with the reading of Scripture, exposition of Scripture (sermon), use of
library and adjacent school; (2) the private philosophical school, with private library, di-
dactic conversation (diatribe), dialogue and lecture (interpretation of texts); (3) the public
lecture hall (gymnasium, ephebes) for orators and philosophers; (4) the private villa of a
wealthy citizen, with lectures that served philosophical education; (5) the agora, where
philosophers publicly presented their teaching (Philo, *Spec.* 1.319-323). Philo was active
as a teacher of Alexander his nephew—that is, a philosophical educator in the private
houses of his extended family. His teaching activity took place not in the gymnasium but
in the synagogue, whose function could be compared to that of the gymnasium. Philo's
expositions of the Torah could have been delivered before a circle of teachers and students in one of the function rooms of the synagogue, or perhaps in the main hall of the
synagogue at a time when there was no service; this activity was similar to the exegetical
lectures in the philosophical schools. Philo also may have presented some of his texts in
private homes that had private libraries.

Geographical Missionary Strategy?

The notion that the missionary activity of Paul remained within the borders of
the Roman Empire[3] is not entirely correct. If Paul went to Arabia immediately
after his conversion to preach the message of Jesus Christ in the cities of the
Nabatean kingdom (§26.1), then he showed little concern for the borders of the
Imperium Romanum during the first phase of his missionary work. Since his
mission to Syria and Cilicia (§26.2) took him to the north and to the west (from

---

[2]Noack 2000, 27-29; he interprets Philo's activity in terms of missionary outreach.
[3]See, among many others, Haacker 1988a, 64.

the perspective of Jerusalem), the geographical localization of his missionary work in "the Roman Empire" is a commonplace identification that is not very telling: the mission to Spain (§27.5) aimed at "Roman" regions, just as a mission to Gaul, Germania or Britannia would have remained within the outer boundaries of the empire. And we must remember that the borders of the Roman Empire, even where they were marked in a precise manner—for example, along the Rhine River or along the Limes in Germania—are not key features for the description of the history of the *Imperium Romanum.*[4]

Did Paul pursue a systematic missionary strategy? Henri Clavier and other scholars suggest that the "missionary plan" of the apostle Paul was born, developed, specified and adapted in the course of the events as they unfolded.[5] Paul's statement in Rom 15:19—"from Jerusalem and as far around [κύκλῳ, *kyklō*] as Illyricum I have fully proclaimed the good news of Christ"—suggests that when Paul evaluated his ministry of the last thirty-five years in A.D. 56/57, he saw a geographical "order" that can indeed be described in terms of a "plan" of his missionary strategy. The term *kyklos* that connects Jerusalem with Illyricum and, in the context of Rom 15:24, also with Rome and with Spain perhaps describes the upper half of a circle in whose lower half—from Jerusalem via Egypt and the Cyrenaica to Numidia—other missionaries are active.[6] This does not yet prove, however, that Paul pursued a detailed geographical plan in terms of his missionary strategy.

Roger Aus and Rainer Riesner suggest that Paul understood his missionary ministry against the background of Isaiah's prophecies of Yahweh's eschatological salvation that reaches the Gentiles (Is 66) and that his missionary strategy should be interpreted against this background.[7] Aus suggests that the reference to the "full number of the Gentiles" (Rom 11:25) should be connected with the plans for a mission to Spain (Rom 15:22-24, 28-29) in the context of the identification of the city of Tarshish in Is 66:19 with Spain. Aus argues that Paul became convinced that Jesus the Messiah would return if he brought converted Spaniards together with other representatives of the Gentile-Christian churches to Jerusalem so that "all flesh" (Is 66:23), including the unbelieving Israel (Rom 15:26), would be saved.

It surely is plausible to assume that Paul was familiar with Isaiah's vision of Is 66 and that he interpreted his missionary ministry within this eschatological framework. However, it is implausible to argue that Paul understood himself as

---

[4]See John C. Mann, "The Frontiers of the Principate," *ANRW* II.1 (1974): 508-33, esp. 531.

[5]Clavier 1970, 177; earlier Richter 1929, 26-27; also Haas 1971, 83-84; cf. Keathley 1999, 71: "The new place apparently was dictated by the direction the road followed rather [than by] the deliberate choice of the missionary team."

[6]See Dunn, *Rom,* 2:864.

[7]Aus 1979; Riesner 1994, 216-25 (ET, 245-53). Aus and Riesner arrived independently at their conclusions; see Riesner 1994, 217 n. 55 (ET, 245 n. 55).

the decisive figure of the last days, as the one and only missionary to the Gentiles, as the only apostle who related Is 66 to his missionary ministry. The speech by James during the apostolic council (Acts 15:14-21) demonstrates that the Jewish Christians of Jerusalem also related statements of the Old Testament prophets to the contemporary conversion of Gentiles, interpreted as their eschatological fulfillment. It therefore is very likely that not only Paul but also other early Christian missionaries understood Is 66 as an integral component of their divine commission and as being fulfilled in their missionary work. Another problem with Aus's interpretation is the fact that the identification of Spain with the Tarshish of Is 66:19 is not certain: *Jub.* 9:12 identifies Spain with Meshech, and Josephus identifies Spain with Tubal in eastern Anatolia (*A.J.* 1.124), while he identifies Tarsis (Θαρσίς) with Tarsus in Cilicia (*A.J.* 1.127).[8]

Paul did not see himself as the only missionary to the Gentiles (1 Cor 9:5). Thus the suggestion is hardly plausible that Paul alone regarded the fulfillment of the missionary commission of the risen Lord to go from Jerusalem to the ends of the earth as his personal task.[9] Paul engaged in missionary work "from Jerusalem to Illyricum" (Rom 15:19), and he planned to go to Spain (Rom 15:24). This does mean, however, that he saw himself as the only missionary in the northern regions of the Mediterranean world: he knows other missionaries, and he never hints at plans to start missionary outreach in Moesia or in Scythia, in Gaul or in Germania—all well-known regions, in part Roman provinces, in the northern Mediterranean region.

Rainer Riesner similarly argues that Paul understood his calling in analogy to the eschatological mission of the Servant of Yahweh in the book of Isaiah. The mission of the Servant includes the "end of the earth" (Is 49:6), and he takes the message of God in the eschaton specifically to Tarshish, Put, Lud, Meshech, Rosh, Tubal, Javan and the distant coastlands (Is 66:19). Paul explains in Rom 11:25-27 the "mystery" that God revealed to him. It includes the point that the "full number of the Gentiles" is the condition for Israel's eschatological salvation, in fulfillment of Is 66:19. In this text the prophet speaks of the proclamation of the glory of God among the nations "that have not heard of my fame or seen my glory." This is the presupposition for the Jews living in the Diaspora to return "as an offering to the Lord" to Jerusalem (Is 66:20). Riesner argues that Paul evidently understood his divine calling first as winning the "full number of the Gentiles" that God had predetermined (Rom 11:25) through his missionary work carried out in areas "where Christ was not known" (Rom 15:20) as he "fully proclaimed" the gospel of Jesus Christ "from Jerusalem and as far around as Illyricum" (Rom 15:19). The "survivors to the nations" that the prophet mentions in Is 66:19 as messengers who are sent to

---

[8]See J. M. Scott 1995, 142 n. 34; Riesner 1994, 222 (ET, 248).
[9]See, among many others, I. H. Marshall 1990, 45.

the nations first go to Tarshish (Tarsus) and then reach in a semicircular movement in a northwesterly direction: Put (Cilicia), Lud (Lydia), Meshech (Mysia), Tubal (Bithynia), Javan (Greece, Macedonia) and the distant coastlands (the regions in the far west, Spain).[10] Riesner suggests that the geographical framework of Is 66:19 explains why Paul planned a mission to Spain but not a mission to Gaul.

This explanation is very attractive against the background of Paul's self-understanding and in the context of the significance of the Old Testament for his theology. However, it cannot ultimately explain the geographical movements of Paul, as Riesner himself implies when he adds this caveat: "The assertion here is not that the Pauline missionary plans were from the very outset oriented toward Isa. 66:19, nor that this prophecy represents the only or even most important basis for the routes taken by the apostle." A first problem with this explanation is the fact that the two geographical endpoints that Paul mentions in Rom 15:19 cannot be connected with Is 66:19. A second problem is the envoys of Is 66:19: in the context of Is 66:18-20 they evidently are Gentiles who have survived God's judgment—a notion that can hardly be applied to Paul, a Diaspora Jew. Riesner sees the problem but merely points to the lack of agreement among scholars, who variously interpret the priests and Levites of the last days in Is 66:21 as Jews or Gentiles or both, and he refers to the Jewish exegesis that attempts to avoid the exegetical conclusion that Is 66:21 refers to Gentiles.[11] Whether this suggests that "it is possible that Paul associated these statements with eschatological Jewish emissaries such as himself" seems doubtful, however. A third problem is the geographical identifications. Put usually is identified with Libya or with Cyrene in North Africa. It seems unlikely that Paul abandoned this tradition and followed the book of Judith, which relates "Put and Lud" to Cilicia (Jdt 2:23). The identification of Meshech with Mysia and of Tubal with Bithynia—two areas for which Paul planned missionary work that never was carried out—is selective: in the Jewish tradition Tubal is also identified with Iberia/Spain (Josephus) and with Europe from Bulgaria to France (*Jubilees*), and Meshech is identified with Cappadocia (Josephus), Spain/France (*Jubilees*) and Illyricum (Hippolytus).[12] And the first sixteen years of Paul's missionary work in Nabatea, Syria and Cilicia remains without explanation. A fourth difficulty is the fact that Is 66:18-20 is never mentioned in the New Testament explicitly.[13]

James Scott suggests that the apostles divided the world along the "borders"

---

[10]Riesner 1994, 216-24 (ET, 245-53); the quotation that follows above, ibid., 224-25 (ET, 253).

[11]Riesner 1994, 220-21 (ET, 248-49); the quotation that follows above, 221 (ET, 249). On the identification of Put see ibid., 222-23 (ET, 251), with reference to LXX Jer 26:9; Ezek 27:10; 30:5; 38:5; Nah 3:9; Josephus, *A.J.* 1.132.

[12]See J. M. Scott 1995, 48-49 (table 3).

[13]Thus the critique by J. M. Scott 1995, 146-47; cf. Wander 2001, 185.

of the regions in which the descendants of Noah lived who are listed in the table of nations in Gen 10, with Paul "receiving" the territory of Japheth. Scott argues that this is why Paul preached the gospel "from Jerusalem to Illyricum" (Rom 15:19) and why he wanted to go to Spain (Rom 15:22-24, 28-29): he engaged in missionary work in Asia Minor and in Europe, the territory in which Japheth and his descendants settled.[14] This hypothesis seems plausible from a tradition-historical perspective. It founders, however, on account of the very diverse geographical identifications in the Jewish (and early Christian patristic) tradition, and also on account of the details of Paul's actual missionary work. The following five objections seem decisive. (1) Scott must ignore the first fourteen years of Paul's missionary work for his hypothesis to work, the years during which Paul preached the gospel in Arabia and Syria. Paul's "independent" mission did *not* begin after the apostolic council in A.D. 48; rather, it began in A.D. 32/33, immediately after his conversion, when he went to Arabia/Nabatea and to Syria and Cilicia. Arabia was not part of the territory of Japheth; it belonged to the descendants of Mizraim—that is, the descendants of Ham.[15] Of course, we could argue with Scott that the Pauline "Japheth missionary program" became "evident" only after the apostolic council and after the separation from Barnabas, when Paul traveled to Macedonia and to Achaia (Acts 15:36—18:22). Scott's hypothesis is easier to correlate with Paul's geographical movements after Acts 15:36, but it "loses" the sixteen years or so of missionary work between A.D. 32/33 and A.D. 48. (2) Paul's plan to preach the gospel in the region of Lydia during the mission to the province of Asia (Acts 16:6) is a problem for Scott because Lud was a son of Shem (Gen 10:22). Since the Holy Spirit prevented Paul from preaching the gospel in the province of Asia (Acts 16:6), and since Paul, as a result, avoided this "Semitic enclave" in Asia Minor, the hypothesis survives. The fact that Paul stayed in Ephesus for several years during his subsequent mission to the province of Asia is not a problem for Scott only because he connects the city of Ephesus as an Ionian colony with Javan, one of the sons of Japheth. He maintains that Paul's missionary work in the province of Asia (i.e., Lydia) was a more indirect ministry, apart from the church-planting efforts in the city of Ephesus—Paul writes to Philemon and to the church in Colossae without having established the churches in this area himself. This is unconvincing: it is entirely possible that Paul preached the gospel in other cities in the province of Asia besides Ephesus during this three-year stay in the province. The information that Paul and Luke relate does not provide systematic or complete geographical data. Paul's statement in Col 1:7 ("Epaphras . . . is a faithful minister of Christ on our be-

---

[14]J. M. Scott 1994, 522-44; 1995, 135-80. On Scott's hypothesis see §16.2 in the present work.

[15]Gen 10:6. See Scott 1995, 166; on the Arabs see ibid., 139 n. 23; for the comment that follows above see ibid., 174.

half"[16]) suggests that he regarded Epaphras's missionary work in the Lykos Valley as his responsibility.[17] And Scott cannot explain why Paul failed to go to Bithynia, which, after all, belonged to the territory of Japheth. (3) If my previous reconstruction is correct that Paul went to Crete after his return from Spain, then he left "Japheth" and went to "Ham"—the Cretans were regarded as descendants of Mizraim (Egypt) who belonged to Ham (Gen 10:6).[18] (4) The only identifications of Japheth's descendants that are not controversial in the Jewish and the Christian patristic traditions are those of Javan with Ionia (or the Greeks) and of Madai with the Medes—we hear nothing about Paul planning to preach the gospel in Media, east of Syria. (5) Several descendants of Japheth—Togarma, Magog, Tubal, Meshech—are identified with northern Europe in the Jewish and the Christian patristic traditions—that is, regions such as the Ukraine, Bulgaria, Romania, Germany and France. Again, we hear nothing about Paul planning to reach Moesia, Thrace, Germania, Gaul or Scythia (except the possibility that Crescens, Paul's coworker, went to Gaul). The suggestion that Paul understood his missionary work as a "Japheth mission" thus remains hypothetical and, in my opinion, unconvincing.

The basic strategy of Paul was simple: he wanted to proclaim the message of Jesus Christ to Jews and Gentiles in obedience to a divine commission, particularly in areas in which it had not been proclaimed before (Gal 2:7; Rom 15:14-21). The planning for the implementation of this goal likewise was relatively simple: he traveled on the major Roman roads and on smaller local roads from city to city, preaching the message of Jesus the Messiah and Savior and gathering new converts into local Christian communities. This is what he did in Arabia, in Syria, in Cilicia, on Cyprus, in the provinces of Galatia and Asia, in the provinces of Macedonia and Achaia, and presumably in Spain and on Crete. What Harvie Conn says with regard to Luke in general applies to Paul in particular: "The book of Acts deals almost entirely with cities; missionary work is almost limited to them."[19]

When it proved impossible for Paul to reach a region for which he had planned missionary outreach, as was the case with the project of traveling to the provinces of Asia, Bithynia and Mysia (Acts 16:7-8), his strategy did not break

---

[16]The reading ἡμῶν, "on our behalf" ($\mathfrak{P}^{46}$ ℵ* A B D* F G 326* 1505) is better attested than the reading ὑμῶν, "on your behalf" (ℵ² C D¹ Ψ 075 33 1739 1881 𝔐 lat sy co). Hübner (*Kol,* 48) argues that there is no substantial reason to prefer the reading ὑμῶν, "on your behalf"; likewise the commentaries of Lightfoot, Abott, Dibelius/Greeven, Lohse, Gnilka, Schweizer, O'Brien, Pokorný, Wolter, Barth and Blancke, Dunn, and also many translations. However, NA²⁷ and UBS⁴ prefer ὑμῶν; see Metzger, *Textual Commentary,* 552-53.

[17]Thus also J. M. Scott 1995, 175 n. 186; for the comment that follows above see ibid., 175 n. 187.

[18]See J. M. Scott 1995, 166.

[19]Conn 1985, 417; for a contextualized application see idem, "A Contextual Theology of Mission for the City," in Engen et al. 1993, 96-104. See also Bruce 1993, 687.

down: there were other cities in other regions that needed to hear the gospel. Paul was prepared to leave the "tactical selection" of locations for missionary work to God's sovereignty. He was willing to change plans. He depended not upon personal decisions but upon God's guidance. The transition to Europe was not part of his missionary plans at the time (cf. Acts 16:9), and yet he spent three years in Macedonia and Achaia.

Roland Allen emphasized in an older and influential study that Paul's missionary strategy focused on the urban centers, on the centers of Roman administration, of Greek culture and of Jewish presence, to ensure that the gospel would radiate from the churches in the cities to the rural areas.[20] Paul indeed preached in the centers of several Roman provinces: in Antioch in Syria, probably in Tarsus in Cilicia, in Paphos on Cyprus, in Perge in Pamphylia, in Thessalonike in Macedonia, in Corinth in Achaia, in Ephesus in the province of Asia. He planned to use the church in Rome as a base for his mission to Spain. Still, Paul's missionary outreach cannot fully be described as a "metropolis mission." Consider the following points. (1) We do not possess enough information about the first fifteen years of Paul's missionary work in Arabia, Syria and Cilicia to prove or disprove such a strategy for the years between A.D. 32/33 and 45. And we must recall that during those years Paul preached the gospel in Syria, and he became active in the metropolis of Antioch only after being asked by Barnabas to join him. (2) In regard to the thirteen years of Paul's missionary work between A.D. 45 and 57, we need to remember that Paul evidently did not visit Ancyra, the metropolis of the province of Galatia. And apparently he bypassed other important cities as well: Side in Pamphylia, Termessos and Sagalassos in Pisidia, Cybistra in Lycaonia. (3) Passages such as Acts 13:48-49 show that Paul's missionary work was not limited to cities but also reached into the cities' territory (χώρα, chōra), the people living in villages: "When the Gentiles heard this, they were glad and praised the word of the Lord; and as many as had been destined for eternal life became believers. Thus the word of the Lord spread throughout the region [χώρα, chōra]."

Missionary Work in Synagogues

Paul always understood himself as a Jew, even and especially as a missionary among the Gentiles. He accepted the Jewish jurisdiction of the synagogues for himself, as is demonstrated by the fact that he was punished five times with the "forty minus one" lashes (2 Cor 11:24).[21] Seen from a mission-tactical point of view, Gentiles who believed in Israel's God were the best candidates for successful evangelism. This alone suggested that a Jewish-Christian missionary to the Gentiles should begin missionary work in the local synagogue, where

---

[20]Allen 1977 [1912], 13; cf. recently Di Berardino 1999, 235.
[21]See Botermann 1993, 76.

he would encounter not only Jews but also Gentiles: proselytes, God-fearers and sympathizers who were attracted by the ethical monotheism of the Jewish faith. As Theodor Zahn asserted well over a century ago, "The synagogue presented itself to the Christian missionary as the bridge linking Israel and the Gentiles, a bridge that could be crossed and that sometimes proved rather solid and safe. It took several months in Ephesus and in Corinth until Paul was forced to leave the synagogue and settle firmly and forever on the pagan side. And he was always able to draw some Jews across, sometimes eminent members and surely always the best elements of the Jewish community, who formed the nucleus of the young community of Christians together with the God-fearing Greeks who had converted in the synagogue first to the Jewish then to the Christian preaching."[22]

Many Gentiles who converted to faith in Jesus Christ, perhaps the majority of the non-Jewish believers, came from the group of the God-fearers and the Gentile sympathizers with the Jewish faith. This can be inferred from the fact that Paul could presuppose as a matter of course that the believers in the churches that he had established, at least the leading pastors and teachers, were familiar with the Septuagint as sacred Scripture and with Jewish customs.[23]

Stephen Mitchell argues that "the transformation of the pagan world to Christian monotheism" is hardly conceivable without the pagan God-fearers in the synagogues who had a monotheistic notion of God.[24] This evaluation surely is correct, but we must remember that the center of the Christian message was not simply the monotheistic understanding of God alone but the proclamation of Jesus Christ, the crucified Savior of all people. It was indeed helpful for Paul and the other early Christian missionaries to encounter in the synagogues henotheistic or monotheistic pagans. However, the fact that the proclamation of the good news of salvation through faith in Jesus Christ "transformed" the pagan world must have had another reason (see §33).

Missionary Work in Houses

The success of the early Christian mission and the life of the new churches was closely connected with the private house. In the ancient world the Greek term *oikos* (Lat., *familia*) described the "house as living space and familial domestic household," and as such it became the "base of missionary work, foundational center of a local church, location of the assembly for worship, lodging for the missionaries and envoys, and at the same time, of course, the primary and de-

---

[22]Zahn 1886, 138-39. Zahn's reference to the "best elements" ("die besten Elemente") cannot be substantiated from the New Testament texts and is not entirely free of Christian prejudices.
[23]Hengel, introduction in Feldmeier and Heckel 1994, x; cf. S. Mitchell 1999, 121-22.
[24]S. Mitchell 1998, 64. On Mitchell's identification of the God-fearers with the devotees of Theos Hypsistos see §18.4.

cisive place of Christian life and formation."[25] The following reasons explain why the early missionaries chose private homes as meeting places for the new Christian communities.[26] (1) The houses of converted Jews and Gentiles were immediately available as meeting places. They did not have to be remodeled or refurbished, as the meetings of Christian believers did not require any special architectural features. (2) Jews were accustomed to meeting in private houses, both in Palestine and in the Diaspora. Jews, proselytes and God-fearers who converted to faith in Jesus Christ thus would not have been surprised about the choice of private homes as meeting places for religious activities. (3) A private home provided excellent conditions for important elements of the meetings of Christian believers: familial fellowship and common meals during which the Lord's Supper was celebrated. (4) Private houses allowed Christians to meet in a relatively inconspicuous manner, which became a pressing necessity as soon as the local synagogues no longer tolerated believers in Jesus the Messiah.

Jürgen Becker summarizes the importance of the "house" for Greco-Roman society and for the early Christian mission as follows: "The ancient house with the *pater familias* as its head was the decisive building block of the polis and of the state in the Roman Empire. . . . One's destiny and the risks of life (social and political career and decline, education, choice of profession, illness, age, consequences of war, natural catastrophes, etc.) were largely tied to one's family, supported by the family rather than warded off . . . by public welfare. The Roman state was not a welfare state, despite the fact that it cared for the veterans of its army and provided food for the poor. As a result the ancient house had a considerable amount of independence in legal, social and religious matters, particularly in the form of the father of the family, supported by the state. . . . It needs to be emphasized in this connection that the house, with the exception of only very few larger structures of production, was the basic economic form of antiquity, and it had enormous significance as a religious place as well. . . . The transition from religious piety in the house to private cults—the latter were not limited to the family but were practiced in private houses with a focus on the family—is well attested in the legal form of the private associations. From the standpoint of the later historian, the fact that Christianity organized itself with this focus on the house must be regarded as a particularly fortunate decision. This movement could not even imagine at the time ever having a formative voice in the affairs of state and society, it being an officially despised minority, people who waited for the imminent end of the world. The private house gave them a free space with particular qualifications for self-determination, linked with the opportunity to integrate religious services with everyday life in the world according to their own ideas, with the advantage of utilizing an existing infrastructure with its traditional structure of close personal, economic, social and religious relationships."

The fundamental importance of the private house and of the family is illustrated by Paul's exhortation to Christian wives not to divorce their Gentile husbands

---

[25]See Becker 1987, 125; quotation, ibid., 125-26. See also "Houses" in §18.3 of the present work.
[26]See Blue 1997, 92. On this topic see also Gehring 2000; with a summary of his concusions, 478-92.

but rather to continue living with them (1 Cor 7:13-14), accepting the likelihood that their husbands would continue to worship pagan deities in the house and in the various temples of the city, that they would continue to perform the traditional priestly duties in the local temples, and that they might continue to frequent the brothels. Paul maintained that Christians should remain within the context and the confines of their social setting as much as possible and not look for other solutions.[27]

The preaching by the early Christian missionaries led to the conversion not only of individuals but also sometimes of entire families or "houses"—in Philippi the "house" of Lydia the merchant of purple cloth and the "house" of the prison official (Acts 16:14-15, 32-34), in Corinth the "house" of Crispus the synagogue ruler and the "house" of Stephanas (Acts 18:8; 1 Cor 1:16; 16:15). The households of newly converted believers were important centers of Paul's missionary work, and they were centers of the life of the newly established communities of believers, who met in "house churches."[28] The comment that Stephanas and his household "devoted themselves to the service of the saints" (1 Cor 16:15)[29] suggests that Christians were meeting in his house, that he was responsible for a house church.

The term "house church" (ἡ κατ᾽ οἶκον ἐκκλησία, *hē kat᾽ oikon ekklēsia*) occurs four times in the New Testament. Paul uses this expression for the church that met in the house of Aquila and Priscilla in Ephesus and later in Rome, for the church that met in the house of Philemon in Colossae, and for the church that met in the house of Nympha in Laodikeia or in Hierapolis (1 Cor 16:19; Rom 16:5; Philem 2; Col 4:15). Roger Gehring comments that "at least during the early years, the triclinium (sometimes together with the forecourt . . . or the atrium) represented a more or less ideal space for the teaching and preaching activity, the catechetical baptismal instruction and other missionary activities of the church."[30] Rainer Riesner suggests that Paul generally would have chosen the leaders of the house churches from among the members of the educated upper class, since "he would hardly have appointed Christians with only minimal education as teachers."[31] These early Christian teachers were "the tradents of the Jesus tradition, besides the apostles and their 'students.' "

Jerome Murphy-O'Connor concludes on the basis of the architectural features of the Roman atrium house and the Greek peristyle house (see fig. 39), whose largest room could accommodate between thirty and forty people, that the

---

[27]See Klinghardt 1988, 61.
[28]See Banks 1980; Klauck 1981; Bieritz and Kähler 1985, 484-86; Branick 1989; Weiser 1990, 73-84; Blue 1994; 1997; Gehring 2000. On the significance of the private house for missionary strategy see Branick 1989, 18-20.
[29]1 Cor 16:15: τὴν οἰκίαν Στεφανᾶ . . . εἰς διακονίαν τοῖς ἁγίοις ἔταξαν ἑαυτούς.
[30]Gehring 2000, 480.
[31]Riesner 1988, 65; the quotation that follows above, ibid.

Christian house churches had about that same number of members.[32] In some exceptional cases it was possible that up to one hundred people could gather in private houses with large rooms. He further suggests that a house church might also have met in the workshop in a house that was accessible from the street. Aquila and Priscilla, the Jewish-Christian leatherworkers, owned such workshops in Corinth, in Ephesus and in Rome. Such a workshop could accommodate between ten and twenty Christians.[33] The existence of a house church required that there be a patron who either owned the house or rented the house's workshop.[34] Paul mentions several such patrons: Erastus, Crispus, Stephanus, Gaius, Philemon and Apphia, Nympha[35] and Phoebe.

Thus the early Christian house churches existed in the context of the hierarchical social structures of Roman society, in which the *pater familias,* the father of the household, had legal and familial authority over members of the family, relatives and slaves.[36] Gerd Theissen describes the reality of the early Christian communities in this context with the term "primitive Christian love-patriarchalism."

Gerd Theissen writes that this early Christian love-patriarchalism "takes social differences for granted but ameliorates them through an obligation of respect and love, an obligation imposed upon those who are socially stronger. From the weaker are required subordination, fidelity, and esteem. . . . Its historical effectiveness is rooted not least of all in its ability to integrate members of different strata. Members of the upper classes could find a fertile field of activity, so that ancient Christianity never lacked for distinguished leadership figures—beginning with Paul. But the lower strata were also at home here. They found a fundamental equality of status before God, solidarity and help in the concrete problems of life, not least of all from those Christians who enjoyed a higher station in life. Christian brotherhood probably would have been more radically carried out within socially homogeneous groups. That is much easier, however, than realizing a measure of brotherhood within communities which are sharply stratified socially. It was here that primitive Christianity's love-patriarchalism offered a realistic solution."[37]

The early Christian "household code" in Col 3:18—4:1; Eph 5:22—6:9; 1 Pet 2:18—3:7 shares many similarities with the ethical instruction of Hellenistic popular philosophy and of the neo-Pythagoreans with regard to the mutual privileges and obligations in the "house," an ethical instruction that represents a mediating position between a rigorous patriarchalism and an extreme emancipation. However, the early Christian elements are more prominent than the similarities with Greco-Roman ethical exhortations for the family. Consider the

---

[32]Murphy-O'Connor 1983, 156.
[33]Murphy-O'Connor 1992b.
[34]See Jewett 1994, 47.
[35]See Hofmann 2000, 290.
[36]See Meeks 1983, 76.
[37]Theissen 1974b, 268-69 (ET, 107-8). The term "love-patriarchalism" *(Liebeskommunismus)* was coined by Ernst Troeltsch.

following three areas. (1) The direct address of all groups that belong to the "house," including wives, children and slaves, highlights the personal value of the "subordinates." (2) The repeated motivation of specific ethical behavior with reference to the Lord Jesus Christ demonstrates that Paul does not simply adopt social traditions and that he does not give advice and exhortation based on laws of nature or on reason. Rather, he places all persons of the "house" under the authority of Jesus Christ and reminds all of their corresponding responsibilities. (3) The emphasis of Jesus Christ as Lord of all members of the household "relativizes the precedence and the subordination that characterize the human realm."[38]

The first Christians in the city of Rome—at least the two house churches that Paul mentions in Rom 16:14-15—evidently included freedmen, slaves and Greek immigrants (note the names of the Christians that Paul lists); patrons are not mentioned. Robert Jewett infers from this that some house churches that did not have a patron as a sponsor met in tenement houses (*insulae*), perhaps in a workshop on the ground floor or in an apartment in the upper floors that could be combined with an adjacent unit by removing the temporary partitions. Jewett argues that the leadership model of such a tenement church that met without a patron was "charismatic" and "egalitarian." In the house churches the mutual support of the believers depended on the patron and the patron's financial capabilities. In the tenement churches the mutual support was realized probably in the communal meals that Jude and Ignatius describe as *agapē*, or "love feast" (Jude 12; Ign. *Smyrn.* 6:2; 7:1; 8:2).[39] Jewett suggests that what we find in the tenement churches is not "love-patriarchalism" but "love communalism."[40] This suggestion seems plausible if we disregard Jewett's evaluation of the patron as leading authority of the house churches, which might well be somewhat exaggerated, and if we disregard his limitation of the terms "charismatic" and "egalitarian" to the tenement churches. The question of whether believers met in "tenement churches" hinges on the question of whether it was possible to provide sufficient space for a congregation by combining two or more apartment units. Roger Gehring disputes this possibility. He points out that the walls inside the tenement houses were built with blocks of limestone or with wood, which could not be quickly or easily removed whenever the need arose.[41] Another factor renders Jewett's suggestion tenuous: in his description of the *insulae* of Os-

---

[38]Weiser 1990, 78, 79. Birkey (1991, 71) sees a "revolutionary equalization of racial, class, and sexual distinctions." This cannot be substantiated from the New Testament texts.

[39]See Bo Reicke, *Diakonie, Festfreude und Zelos in Verbindung mit der altchristlichen Agapenfeier* (Uppsala: Lundequistska Bokhandeln, 1951); W.-D. Hauschild, *TRE* 1:748-53.

[40]Jewett 1994, 49-50; cf. Gehring (2000, 263-64), who summarizes Jewett's position.

[41]Gehring 2000, 266 with n. 207; for the relevant evidence see ibid.; see especially James E. Packer, *The Insulae of Imperial Ostia* (MAAR 31; Rome: American Academy, 1971), 177-82; for the comment that follows above see ibid., 73.

tia, James Packer points out that the units of the tenement houses should not be understood as apartments in the modern sense of the word, with the exception of the larger units. Since the tenement units were very small and had only minimal facilities—no bathroom and no toilet—the units of an *insula* probably were not used to receive friends for a visit.

Contacts with Aristocrats

Luke reports that Paul repeatedly had contacts with members of the ruling elites, some of whom were converted to faith in Jesus Christ or were friendly toward him. Examples include Sergius Paullus the proconsul of Cyprus (Acts 13:6-12), the "prominent women" in Thessalonike and in Beroea (Acts 17:4, 12), and the Asiarchs in Ephesus (Acts 19:31); we might also mention Lydia the merchant of purple cloth in Philippi (Acts 16:13-15).[42]

Luke's reference to the high social position of these people does not serve a political agenda: he reports the hostile acts of "the God-fearing women of high standing and the leading men" of Antiocheia (Acts 13:50) and of governors who keep Paul in custody despite the fact that they know him to be innocent (Acts 24:27; 25:9). The high social position of the people with whom Paul has positive encounters is subject to Luke's description of the progress of the early Christian mission: (1) Persons of high social status have houses in which the new communities of believers can meet. (2) Aristocrats with whom Paul maintains friendly contacts are able to protect Paul and the local Christians in politically critical situations. (3) The gospel reaches not only the lower classes and the poor but also the upper classes and the rich. As far as the gospel of the crucified Savior is concerned, all people are equal.

The Duration of Missionary Work in Cities

In regard to Paul's missionary work in Arabia, Syria and Cilicia in the twelve years from A.D. 32/33 to 44, generally we have no information about how much time Paul spent in the cities in which he preached the gospel. There are two exceptions. When Paul visited Jerusalem for the first time after his conversion, he stayed for fifteen days, during which he preached the gospel (Gal 1:18; Acts 9:28-29). However, this visit presumably was not intended to be a "missionary visit." In regard to Paul's ministry in Antioch in Syria between A.D. 42 and 44, Luke reports that Paul stayed "for a whole year." Since we have no information in which other cities of Arabia, Syria and Cilicia Paul worked as a missionary and in which cities churches could be established, it is impossible even to venture an educated guess about the duration of Paul's missionary work in the individual cities.

In regard to Paul's mission on Cyprus and in southern Galatia from A.D. 45

---

[42]See Gill 1994b, 108-9.

to 47, we possess no specific data either. Luke reports the establishment of at least four churches during these two years: in Antiocheia, Iconium, Lystra and Derbe (and perhaps in Perge). If we subtract the time needed for travel, Paul would have spent an average of five months in each city. However, since Luke relates no specific information about the establishment of churches in the cities on Cyprus in which Paul and Barnabas preached the gospel, and since presumably they spent a considerable amount of time on the island, we may be justified in assuming that Paul spent perhaps three months in the cities of southern Galatia as a pioneer missionary.

Paul's missionary work in Macedonia and Achaia lasted three years, from A.D. 49 to 51. He established at least four churches: in Philippi, Thessalonike, Beroea and Corinth. Luke reports that Paul stayed in Corinth for "a year and six months" (Acts 18:11), although it is unclear whether these eighteen months relate to Paul's entire stay in the city or only to the time before the Gallio episode, after which Paul continued his ministry in the city: according to Acts 18:18, Paul stayed "for a considerable time" (ἡμέρας ἱκανάς, *hēmeras hikanas*) after Gallio had refused to take action against him.[43] The second option seems more plausible, which means that Paul's work as a pioneer missionary in Corinth lasted from February or March of A.D. 50 to September A.D. 51.[44] This leaves the following time frame for the missionary work in Philippi, Thessalonike and Beroea: Paul was active in Philippi perhaps for three months from August to October A.D. 49, in Thessalonike for two or three months from October to November (or December) A.D. 49,[45] in Beroea for three months from December A.D. 49 to January A.D. 50, and in Corinth for twenty months from February A.D. 50 to September A.D. 51.

Paul's mission in the province of Asia between A.D. 52 and 55 focused on Ephesus, where he preached and taught for about three years (Acts 20:31): he taught for three months in the synagogue (Acts 19:8), for two years in the lecture hall of Tyrannos (Acts 19:10), and then "for some time longer" (χρόνον, *chronon* [Acts 19:22]).[46]

We have no specific data for Paul's mission to Spain and to Crete. If we assume that Paul engaged in missionary work in Spain in A.D. 63-64, then either he visited very few cities or he concentrated on one particular city for a longer period, perhaps Tarraco. The same assumption applies to a possible mission to Crete in A.D. 64-65.

These chronological data are generally too fragmentary to allow a reconstruc-

---

[43]See K. Lake, *Begs.* 5:464; Haacker 1972, 252-55; Riesner 1994, 185-87 (ET, 208-9); Barrett, *Acts,* 2:876.
[44]Riesner 1994, 187 (ET, 210).
[45]Riesner 1994, 321-23 (ET, 362-64).
[46]See Riesner 1994, 189-94 (ET, 212-18).

tion of Paul's tactical decisions concerning the duration of his pioneer missionary work, or to speculate about changes in his tactical approach. A precise reconstruction is also made difficult by the fact that Paul often was forced to
depart in haste or prematurely from a city in which he had started missionary
work, reacting to the pressure from local synagogues and magistrates who put
his life in danger at least in some places. Luke reports premature departures
from Antiocheia (Acts 13:50-51), Iconium (Acts 14:5-6), Lystra (Acts 14:19-20),
Philippi (Acts 16:19-40), Thessalonike (Acts 17:5-10), Beroea (Acts 17:13-14) and
Ephesus (Acts 20:1). In regard to Ephesus, we may safely assume that Paul probably would have left the city relatively soon, even without the complications
caused by the riot of the silversmiths, since he had spent three years in the city.
We do not know, however, how long Paul would have stayed in Antiocheia,
Iconium, Lystra, Philippi, Thessalonike and Beroea if he had not been forced to
leave. Luke does not report a premature departure from Antioch (Acts 13:1-3),
Salamis (Acts 13:5), Paphos (Acts 13:12-13), Derbe (Acts 14:21), Perge (Acts
14:25), Athens (Acts 18:1) and Corinth (Acts 18:18). When Paul left the church
in Antioch, it presumably was easy for this influential church, with strong ties
to the church in Jerusalem, to cope with the departure of Paul and Barnabas.
Paul's departure from Corinth after two years of preaching and teaching is understandable as well. The departure from Paphos on Cyprus may have been motivated by the conversion of the proconsul, who could provide protection for
the newly established church, and it possibly was connected with letters of recommendation that Sergius Paullus wrote to his relatives in Pisidian Antiocheia,
which might have suggested a swift departure.

   This leaves only Salamis and Paphos on Cyprus, Derbe in Lycaonia, Perge in
Pamphylia, and Athens in Achaia as examples for a "short-term mission" of Paul.
This evidence renders implausible the suggestion of Dan Cole, that Paul
changed his tactical procedure in connection with his mission to Corinth, tran-
sitioning from short-term missions to longer periods of missionary work in the
same city.[47] The arguments that Cole adduces in support of his hypothesis remain unconvincing. Corinth and Ephesus were indeed strategically located cities, but the same is true of Pisidian Antiocheia, which was an ideal base of operations for missionary work in Phrygia and Lycaonia, and Perge was strategic
for missionary activities in Pisidia and Lycia. The cosmopolitan character of
Corinth and Ephesus made these cities a logical choice for long-term missionary
work. But Athens was cosmopolitan as well, in the first century still a meeting
place of scholars, students and tourists from "around the world."

   Oscar Cullmann and Dieter Zeller, among others, suggest that the early
Christian conviction of the imminent return of Jesus Christ, a conviction that

---

[47]Cole 1988; cf. Towner 1998; for the considerations that follow above see Cole 1988, 22-25.
See also §28.2 in the present work regarding Paul's missionary work in Corinth.

Paul shared (1 Cor 7:29-31; 1 Thess 4:15-17), was a motivating factor in Paul's missionary work.[48] Ernst Käsemann has the "impression" that Paul's mission must be understood from the perspective of his conviction of the imminent end of the world, a conviction that caused Paul to be "a possessed man" who was "pursuing a feverish dream."[49] This hypothesis, for which there is no specific evidence in any New Testament text, cannot explain the long-term missionary work in Antioch, Corinth and Ephesus. There is no evidence for the view, which this hypothesis implies, that Paul modified his eschatological expectations after his ministry in Corinth. Ultimately, there is no explanation for the disparate durations of Paul's visits to the cities in which he initiated missionary activities.

The Question of the Salvation of the Jewish People

The question of the salvation of the Jewish people is perhaps not immediately relevant for the tactical decisions of Paul's missionary work, but it is a critical question for his theology of mission that ultimately is highly significant for the evaluation of the place of Jews in the early Christian missionary enterprise. The question is this: When Paul writes in Rom 11:26a, "and so all Israel will be saved" (καὶ οὕτως πᾶς Ἰσραὴλ σωθήσεται, *kai houtōs pas Israēl sōthēsetai*), does he prophesy a future conversion of the Jewish people? Scholars of diverse theological persuasions and political agendas argue that Paul was convinced that the Jewish people would accept faith in Jesus the Messiah at or before the parousia, the return of Christ. Many evangelical scholars view the salvation of Israel as an integral part of God's plan of salvation, particularly scholars and popular authors who work in the context of dispensational theology, while many liberal historical-critical scholars emphasize the continuing status of Israel as God's elect people, particularly scholars who work in the context of a "theology after Auschwitz."

In Germany the synod of the regional Protestant Church in the Rhineland accepted in January 1980 a declaration that argued that the election of Israel and of the Jewish people as God's covenant people is grounded in God's faithfulness, that Israel's election therefore cannot be repealed, and that the church is incorporated in Israel, God's covenant people, through Jesus Christ. The synod asserted that the designation "people of God" uniquely describes the Jewish people, and that it is explicitly differentiated from the designation "covenant of God," in which the church has been incorporated.[50] Jacob Jervell interprets Rom 11:26 in terms of a "general amnesty" that Paul extends to the

---

[48]Cullmann 1936; Zeller 1982a, 185-86.
[49]Käsemann 1963, 244 (ET, 241). See also the critique in Adloff 1986, 15.
[50]The declaration is reprinted in *EvTh* 40 (1980): 260-76; also in *Kirche und Israel* 1 (1986): 71-73. See B. Klappert and B. Starck, eds., *Umkehr und Erneuerung: Erläuterungen zum Synodalbeschluß der Rheinischen Landessynode 1980* (Neukirchen-Vluyn: Neukirchener Verlag, 1980), 264-81. On the discussion about this declaration see Sänger 1994, 14-35,

Jewish people.[51] Wolfgang Kraus writes in a recent dissertation that the mode of Christ's gift of salvation for Israel and for the Jews is "not connected with missionary proclamation of the gospel. [Paul refers even less to missionary work among Jews by Gentile Christians.] What we have is nothing less than the acknowledgment of the savior from Zion, i.e., of the Christ of the parousia. This acknowledgment is, according to Pauline categories (2 Cor 5:7), not 'believing' but rather 'seeing.' . . . Paul thus expects Israel to receive eschatological salvation not 'sola fide' but still 'sola gratia' and 'solo Christo.'"[52] In other words, there is a *Sonderweg* to salvation for the Jews: they do not need to believe in Jesus as the Messiah today, as they will "see" Jesus as the returning Messiah in the future. Winfrid Keller suggests in a study on Rom 11:25-27 that the phrase "all Israel" should be understood in a diachronic sense—that is, as a reference to all Israelites and Jews from Abraham to Jesus' parousia. He argues that "election and promise have soteriological efficacy insofar as God's faithfulness guarantees salvation [in his election and in his promise]. The Jew receives the promise of salvation because he is a Jew, because all Jews are chosen in the Fathers and are thus 'God's beloved.' The path of the Jew leads to salvation because of divine election. We recognize thus in Judaism *an independent path to salvation*. . . . Jesus Christ will extend the salvation that he procured through his death and resurrection to 'all Israel' when he returns at the parousia. This is precisely how Paul understands the fulfillment of the promise, the corroboration of the election and the demonstration of God's faithfulness. . . . This is in a fundamental sense the path to salvation proper, the 'normal path' pure and simple: God fulfills his original promise through Christ. We also could put it this way: the path of the Gentiles, the path of the church, is an *additional path to salvation*."[53]

The exposition by Erich Zenger, an Old Testament scholar, demonstrates how problematic this position is. He deplores the "messianic delusion of the Christians" and believes that the "messianic question" is still open. He argues that God's covenant must be understood in such a way that "the Jews can live in it *without* Jesus Christ and the Christians *with* Jesus Christ."[54] The New Testament scholar Ekkehard Stegemann believes that "the faith of Christians" must be connected with "the faith of the people of God," and that Christians "must not proscribe for the Jewish people what role Jesus of Nazareth has in the history of salvation *of Israel*." He argues that Christians can escape the charge of being anti-Jewish only when they express their confession of Jesus as the Messiah in such a way that "on the one hand we claim its validity only for us, but not for the Jewish people, while not forgetting on the other hand that we owe it to the Jewish people."[55] In a contribution to a volume of essays on the question of conversion to Judaism, Pinchas Lapide, a Jewish theologian and philosopher of religion, comments on Christian missionary efforts among Jews. He argues that Paul's sentence in Rom 11:26 summarizes the essential truth that "all Israel will be saved"—without baptism or faith in Jesus, which are not mentioned by Paul. Lapide asks, what is for him, a rhetorical question: "For whom or for what would Christians

---

[51]Jervell 1984, 36-40; cf. idem 1991, 23.

[52]Kraus 1996, 322 (the part of the quotation within brackets, 322 n. 347). Similarly, for example, Gundry Volf 1994, 161-95.

[53]Keller 1998, 283; for an analysis of the phrase "all Israel" see ibid., 223-41.

[54]E. Zenger, "Vom christlichen Umgang mit messianischen Texten der hebräischen Bibel," in Stegemann 1993, 129-45; quotations, 131, 145.

[55]W. Stegemann, "Jesus als Messias in der Theologie des Lukas," in Stegemann 1993, 21-40; quotations, 22-23, 39.

want to evangelize Jews?"[56] In other words, when Christians engage in missionary work, they should leave Jews in peace because Jews continue to be the chosen people of God and do not need conversion, just as Saul was not "converted" but was "called" by "his" Jewish Messiah as an apostle (to the Gentiles).

Such statements and evaluations are congenial in the context of the Jewish-Christian dialogue, especially if they are formulated by German theologians. However, they are not legitimate interpretations of the early Christian faith as formulated and proclaimed by Paul and the apostles. Jesus himself, as well as Paul and Luke, Peter and Matthew, James and John shared the conviction that the salvific reality of God's covenant with Israel depends on the individual Jew's reaction to Jesus the Messiah. Daniel Chae has demonstrated for Rom 11:26 that it is impossible to interpret Paul's statements in terms of a *Sonderweg* or independent path to salvation for the Jewish people.[57] Paul argues in the Epistle to the Romans for the equal status of Gentiles and Jews with regard to their sin (Rom 1:18—3:20), with regard to their justification through acceptance of and faith in God's salvific revelation in Jesus the Messiah alone (Rom 3:21—4:25), and with regard to their new status of believers in Jesus Christ (Rom 5:1—8:39). In Rom 9—11 Paul argues that Jews and Gentiles have equal status in God's plan of salvation. After Rom 5:1 Paul no longer distinguishes between Jews who believe in Jesus Christ and Gentiles who believe in Jesus Christ: all believers, regardless of their ethnic or religious origins, form together the one community of followers of Jesus. Paul's argumentation in Rom 9—11 can be succinctly analyzed as follows.

1. Paul asserts in Rom 9:1-5 several facts that are relevant for his subsequent exposition.[58] (a) Paul mourns on account of the unbelief of the Jews. Their lack of faith is not a historical accident that has no significant consequences; rather, it has resulted in their being cut off from God's salvation. (b) The list of Jewish privileges in Rom 9:4-5 summarizes precisely the basic categories of Jewish self-definition that Paul has demonstrated in Rom 1—8 have been transferred to the Messiah, the "representative" of God's people. Now, as a result of the identity and the work of the Messiah, these privileges have been transferred to all who are "in him"—that is, all who are followers of Jesus and believe in him as the Messiah and Savior, whether they are Jews or Gentiles. Sonship, glory, covenants, law, worship, promises, patriarchs: all these are characteristics of the community of believers in Jesus Christ. (c) Not all elements of the list in Rom 9:4-5 are programmatic for the argument in Rom 9—11. The decisive statement

---

[56]Lapide 1995, 17 ("Zu wem oder zu was wollen Christen dann eigentlich Juden missionieren?"); for the comment that follows above see ibid., 16.

[57]Chae 1997, 215-88, esp. 280-82; summary, 285-88; followed by Köstenberger and O'Brien 2001, 185-91.

[58]The analysis that follows above draws from N. T. Wright 1992, 231-57.

is the last element: "and from them, according to the flesh, comes the Messiah, who is God over all, blessed forever. Amen" (Rom 9:5b). The phrase "over all" highlights the absolute, salvation-historical priority of Jesus the Messiah over both Jews and Gentiles. If Jews cling to their inherited, traditional privileges but reject Jesus the Messiah, they miss God's eschatological, universal salvation; they place themselves in opposition to God's basic promise to Abraham that "in him" all nations will be blessed. It is for this very reason that Paul always proclaimed the message of Jesus the Messiah in the synagogues of the cities where he began his missionary outreach.

Günter Wasserberg argues that Paul is portrayed in the book of Acts as a failing missionary among Jews.[59] He suggests that the author portrays Paul as a Jew, faithful to the Torah, for whom the Jewish customs continue to be the basis of his life after his conversion to faith in Jesus Christ; he is arrested at the end as a "faithful temple Jew." Wasserberg contends, "Luke does not tire of portraying Paul his narrative figure as a Jew with integrity who happily complies with Jewish tradition and faith. For Luke, Paul is not an innovator but the herald of Israel's very own hope which has become realized in Jesus' resurrection for the benefit of *all* people. It is because of this Jewish promise that he always visits the synagogue first whenever possible in order to proclaim Jesus to the Jews and with him *their* salvation that they hope for. He usually has some initial success among the Jews, but then he again and again has the experience that those for whom the salvation was primarily announced resist Jesus' salvation. . . . Thus the Lukan Paul proves to be—and this is nothing but a tragedy—a failing missionary among Jews." Wasserberg's characterization of "the Lukan Paul" as a missionary among Jews is one-sided and unconvincing. He does not cross-check Luke's description of Paul as a missionary among Gentiles: Paul is opposed not only by his fellow Jews but also by pagans—the Roman governor in Caesarea keeps Paul in custody even though he knows him to be innocent, and at the end of the book of Acts Paul is in Rome as a prisoner. Was Paul more successful as a missionary among Gentiles than as a missionary among Jews? It actually is impossible to answer that question: both Jews and Gentiles found faith in Christ through Paul's preaching, and if "success" is measured by statistical data, then we must admit that we have no figures for the number of converted Jews and converted Gentiles. Therefore it is impossible to speak of a "failure" of Paul's missionary outreach to Jews. We must keep in mind that according to Luke's account, Paul's preaching and teaching in the synagogues always led to the conversion of Jews who formed the nucleus of the new community of believers in Jesus the Messiah and Savior.

2. In Rom 9:6-29 Paul discusses God's faithfulness with regard to the covenant and the promises, in particular the specific problem of whether the unbelief of the Jews proves that God has failed to keep his fundamental promises to Israel his people. Paul's argument has three parts. (a) Paul emphasizes in Rom 9:6-13 that the succession from Abraham to Isaac rather than Ishmael and to Jacob rather than Esau is in agreement with God's promises. God did not promise Abraham that *all* of his biological descendants would be members of his cove-

---

[59]Wasserberg 1998, 306-57; the quotation that follows above, ibid., 356.

nant. There was a "twofold Israel" right from the beginning: an "Israel (merely) according to the flesh" and the "true Israel" of the promise (Rom 9:6). It is God's grace that counts, not biological descent. The connection with Rom 4 shows that Abraham's true "seed" in Rom 9:7 is not only a member within ethnic Israel: according to Rom 4:16, the "seed" is a worldwide family. (b) In Rom 9:14-18 Paul answers the question that follows from the previous argument: Is God not unjust if he limits the "seed" of Abraham? Paul advances a historical argument: he reminds his readers of the time of the exodus from Egypt, particularly of the episode of the golden calf. At that time the entire nation was guilty before God, when Moses asked God for forgiving grace. Israel may indeed be the people of God, but it is a people of the flesh. God acts righteously, and this means that as the Judge he punishes sin, and as the God of the covenant he preserves the glory of his name, even and especially in view of the failures of his people. (c) In Rom 9:19-29 Paul argues that God the Judge will carry out his righteous judgment, and that he withholds his judgment in the present time so that more people may be saved. God is always just in his dealings with humankind; he treats nobody preferentially. God has not betrayed his promises; rather, he has fulfilled them precisely in the present time, when Israel's leaders have rejected the Messiah. Scripture had always said that God cannot accept Israel in its present condition: Israel needs to be refined through a process of judgment and grace, exile and restoration. It is not God who has failed; Israel has failed. The reference to the "vessels of wrath" (NASB; NRSV: "objects of wrath") in Rom 9:22 does not prove that God is arbitrary after all, saving some and condemning others. God can demonstrate the "riches of his glory" (Rom 9:23) only by solving the problem of sin. God the Creator and the Judge solves the problem of sin by concentrating evil in one place, where he destroys it. He sends his devastating wrath of judgment not on the entire people but on his representative, the Messiah. As Israel became the place where God concentrated sin, it became a "vessel of wrath." If Israel rejects the crucified Messiah and clings to its privileged status as the ethnic covenant people of God, then Israel rejects God's revelation of his eschatological covenant righteousness and remains a "vessel of wrath."

3. In the central section Rom 9:30—10:21 Paul continues to discuss Israel's case and the paradoxical fact that it corresponds to the promises and the warnings of Scripture. Paul now argues that Gentiles have been brought into the family of the covenant people through God's actions in the present time. Israel is presently transformed from an ethnic people into a worldwide family by the Messiah and by the proclamation of his gospel. Paul's argument can be described in four steps. (a) In Rom 9:30-33 he states that Gentiles are accepted into the people of God, while Israel stumbles. Israel stumbled because it strove for righteousness in the wrong way: "Israel, who did strive for the righteousness that is based on the law, did not succeed in fulfilling that law. Why not? Because they did not strive for it on the basis of faith, but as if it were

based on works. They have stumbled over the stumbling stone" (Rom 9:31-32). When Israel regards the Torah as a document of national privileges that Israelites deserve automatically, God's law is misused: the law always can be fulfilled only by faith. When Israel clings to the Torah as national privilege, the rejection of Jesus the Messiah is the logical consequence. But if Israel rejects Jesus the Messiah, it remains stuck with the terrible fate that the Messiah, as representative of his people, wanted to take upon himself—the fate of being the place where sin is concentrated and judged by God. However, even in these catastrophic events God's plan is revealed: when Israel rejected Jesus the Messiah, God enabled the Gentiles to gain access to his covenant people. (b) In Rom 10:1-13 Paul explains the path to salvation that God had predetermined, a path that corresponded to his covenant. Israel sought to establish a "righteousness of its own," insisting on its status as the chosen covenant people, while rejecting God's covenant plan: Israel rejected the Messiah, who always had been "the goal of the law" (τέλος νόμου, *telos nomou* [Rom 10:4]), thus rejecting the climax and fulfillment of God's covenant. The rejection of the Messiah and the misuse of the Torah (as national privilege) by Israel were the two sides of the same coin: for the Jews, the scandal of the cross was that it broke the Jewish insistence on nationalist guarantees of salvation. The covenant that God had granted to Israel was intended to restore the life that humankind had forfeited since Adam and the fall. Israel was meant to be the instrument of the restoration of "Adam," and Israel's Messiah had been sent to bring this national task to a victorious conclusion. As the Torah condemns Israel, and with Israel its Messiah (Gal 3:13), Israel is made righteous. God has acted in this manner so that the sin of the world would be removed by the Lamb that he himself provided. It is in this sense that the Messiah, crucified on Golgotha, is the goal of the Torah. In Rom 10:5-8 Paul declares that the "doing of the law" demanded by Lev 18 is fulfilled, according to Deut 30, when people—whether Jews or Gentiles—hear the good news of the Messiah and accept it by faith. In other words, faith in Jesus the Messiah is the "keeping the law" that Lev 18 speaks of. It is through this "doing" that God gives to people a new heart, as he had promised, with the result that people have the law on their lips and in their heart. (c) In Rom 10:4-18 Paul speaks of the Gentile mission. He shows that Israel's rejection of the gospel is not something strange; rather, it was prophesied in the Scriptures, as the warnings in Deut 32 and Is 65 demonstrate. At the same time Israel's rejection of the gospel is organically, if paradoxically, linked with the promised acceptance of the Gentiles into the people of God. (d) In Rom 10:19-21 Paul again speaks about Israel's obstinacy, returning to the beginning of his argument (cf. Rom 9:30-31). An important term for his argument is "jealousy," which will be significant for his subsequent argument in Rom 11. Paul finds in Deut 32:21, 43—texts that he explicitly quotes in Rom 10:19; 15:10—a prophecy of Israel's lack of faith and of Israel's restoration as well as a prophecy of God's intention to provoke the people of Israel to jealousy by accepting the Gentiles.[60]

4. In Rom 11:1-24 Paul concludes his discourse on Israel's lack of faith in Jesus the Messiah. He raises and answers two questions. (a) In Rom 11:1-10 he gives an answer to the question of whether *any* Jews can be saved: yes, Jews can (still) be saved, for God has not rejected his people. Paul himself is saved; being a Jew, he is part of the "remnant" that the prophets said would be saved. Paul emphasizes that this "remnant" has been chosen by God's grace and is saved by God's grace, not on the basis of ethnic descent or of the "works" of Jewish privileges. In other words, the "remnant" does not consist of a small number of Jews for whom "national righteousness" has positive effects after all, guaranteeing salvation on the day of judgment as the result of "works." Whoever does not belong to this "remnant" is hardened. According to Jewish tradition and theology, people are "hardened" when they reject the grace and the patience of God. Hardening leads to just condemnation in the final judgment. (b) In Rom 11:11-24 Paul poses a second question: Is it possible that *more* Jews can be saved? Possibly some Gentile Christians, perhaps in Rome, believed that the entire Jewish people is hardened permanently and that Jews no longer can find salvation. Paul had already emphasized in Rom 1:16 that his missionary work seeks to address "Jews first" and also Greeks. In Rom 14—15 he exhorted the "strong" (probably mostly Gentile Christians), who have no scruples about eating nonkosher meat, to accept and support the "weak." The Christian community in Rome perhaps was in danger of declaring itself as a non-Jewish association (to escape the odium of Jewish exclusivity that Greeks and Romans often sarcastically reproached?) (a) In Rom 11:11-16 Paul emphasizes that the world was saved in that Israel took upon itself the sin of Adam, and that therefore these is no reason why Israel cannot still be saved now. In Rom 11:13-14 Paul states his goal: "Now I am speaking to you Gentiles. Inasmuch then as I am an apostle to the Gentiles, I glorify my ministry in order to make my own people jealous, and thus save some of them." He understands his Gentile mission, which is his primary calling, as a means for the salvation of Israel. He hopes that Jews will see how their privileges (Rom 9:4-5) are taken over by Gentiles (Rom 9:30-31); if they become "jealous" (Rom 10:19), they might give in and decide to join God's eschatological salvation. Paul writes in Rom 11:15, "For if their rejection is the reconciliation of the world, what will their acceptance be but life from the dead!" When a Gentile joins the eschatological people of God, it is a *creatio ex nihilo*, a creation out of nothing; when a Jew comes to faith in Jesus the Messiah, it is like a resurrection. (b) In his allegory of the olive tree (Rom 11:17-24) Paul explains his assertions in Rom 11:11-16. Gentile Christians must not boast over against Jewish unbelievers: if they do, they establish a reverse

---

[60]Hays 1989, 164; W. Campbell 1993a, 445; J. M. Scott 1993, 802-4.

"national righteousness" that would fall under the same verdict as the Jewish "model" (Rom 11:21). This means that the possibility always exists that Jews can come to faith in Jesus Christ and be "grafted in" again. The statement in Rom 11:23 is decisive: "if they do not persist in unbelief." The salvation of Jews in the present and in the future is dependent on their coming to faith in Jesus the Messiah. Paul's main concern is to make sure that the church in Rome understands that the Jews are not irrevocably lost for the gospel.

5. In Rom 11:28-32 Paul summarizes God's plan of salvation. God always wanted to "reject" Israel, meaning to concentrate his judgment of sin on Israel—in the suffering Servant of God—so that the world could be saved. This does not mean, however, that God's promise of a family to Abraham excludes the Jews. The Jews had to realize that they are "in the flesh"—that is, descendants of Adam who need salvation by God's grace. Paul asserts that the Jews receive God's mercy through the process of jealousy and imitation that he had described. And this process is in progress "now" in the present: "they have now been disobedient in order that, by the mercy shown to you, they too may now receive mercy" (Rom 11:31). Paul hopes that there will be a constant and increasing stream of Jews who by God's grace and by faith in Jesus join the salvation of the Messiah. For Paul, a purely Gentile-Christian community of God is inconceivable—just as a purely Jewish people of God would contradict God's promise to Abraham.

6. Rom 11:25-27 needs to be understood in this general framework. The exhortation of Rom 11:25a ("So that you may not claim to be wiser than you are, brothers and sisters, I want you to understand this mystery") is connected with the preceding assertion: Gentile Christians must not be arrogant toward Jews. The reason for this exhortation is the "mystery" (μυστήριον, *mystērion*). The term "mystery" is disputed with regard both to its tradition-historical background and to its meaning in this passage.[61] Some scholars suggest that in Rom 11:25-26 Paul quotes a new prophetic revelation that he received from God. If this is correct, surely it would have to be interpreted in a way that would not contradict his argument since Rom 9:1 (or since Rom 1:16!). It is anything but certain, however, that Paul uses the term *mystērion* to pass on a new revelation. It is more likely that the apostle summarizes here the result of his salvation-historical, theological-christological argumentation.[62] If indeed Paul summarizes his exposition of God's paradoxical plan of salvation at the end of his discussion in Rom 9—11 (rather than proclaiming a totally new insight), he asserts this: instead of judging the people who rejected his messianic Son immediately, God made possible a time of hardening during which his salvation can reach the ends of the earth—a time that will end with God's judgment of the world. During this time Gentiles

---

[61]For a survey of the (mostly German) discussion see Keller 1998, 68-127.
[62]Similarly Keller 1998, 124-25.

will join the people of God "until the fullness of the Gentiles has come in" (Rom 11:25b NASB).

The phrase "the fullness of the Gentiles" (τὸ πλήρωμα τῶν ἐθνῶν, *to plērōma tōn ethnōn;* NRSV: "the full number of the Gentiles")[63] hardly refers to a divinely fixed number of Gentiles who will be converted: it is unclear how such a number can be made to agree with God's intention that the conversion of the Gentiles is linked with the hardening of Israel. Nor is the interpretation in terms of the conclusion of the Gentile mission convincing: the missionary work among Gentiles will be concluded only with Jesus' return; there is no criterion that would justify an earlier conclusion of the Gentile mission. Paul uses the phrase "fullness of the Gentiles" to express his expectation "that the prophetic promise of the pilgrimage of the nations to Zion will be fulfilled, that God's will for the Gentiles to find salvation proves to be effective." How will this promise be fulfilled? Winfrid Keller surmises that Paul did not have to think about how this would happen, "since he proclaims the realization of God's commitment to salvation that had been promised by the prophets."[64] This is unconvincing: Paul is a missionary and certainly would have reflected on the question of when and how this prophecy would be fulfilled. The answer to the question of how the "fullness of the Gentiles" will "come in" as the fulfillment of God's promise was not difficult to find: the prophecy of the pilgrimage of the nations to Zion is specifically fulfilled in the present Gentile mission of the apostles, which will end only when Jesus returns to establish his kingdom.

Paul writes, "And so all Israel will be saved" (Rom 11:26a). The conjunction καὶ οὕτως (*kai houtōs*) in all likelihood should be understood not in a temporal sense, suggesting that the Jews will be converted after the Gentiles have been converted, but rather in a modal sense: Paul interprets a specific process as the salvation of Israel. The phrase "all Israel" (πᾶς Ἰσραήλ, *pas Israēl*), interpreted in the context not only of Rom 9:1—11:24 but also of Paul's theology as a whole, can hardly mean "all Jews"—whether all Israelites and all Jews since Abraham or all Jews of the generation that lives at the time of Christ's return. Paul uses the expression "all Israel" as a reference to the "elect Israel"—that is, in the context of Rom 9—11 the Jews who have come to faith in Jesus the Messiah—or the term "Israel" has a different referent in Rom 11:26a than in Rom 11:25b: since Rom 9:6 Paul has argued with a programmatic differentiation of two "Israels," and since Rom 3:21 he has systematically transferred privileges and attributes that traditionally belonged to ethnic Israel to the Messiah and his people, consisting of both Jews and Gentiles who believe in Jesus the Messiah and Savior. It therefore is exegetically possible that the phrase "all Israel" in Rom 11:26a implies a (polemical) redefinition of (ethnic) Israel, as in Gal 6:16.[65] If this is correct, then the phase "and so all Israel will be saved" means the following: God's

---

[63]For the discussion on this term see Keller 1998, 158-82; the quotations that follow above, 174.
[64]Keller 1998, 174.
[65]See N. T. Wright 1991, 246-51; Beale 1999, with reference to Is 54:10, as well as Ps 84 (LXX); 1QH XIII, 5; *Jub.* 22:9. See also Phil 3:2-11, where the church is described as "the circumcision." For arguments against this interpretation see Chae 1997, 274.

method of saving "all Israel" consists of hardening ethnic Israel—that is, not immediately judging the Jews who reject Jesus the Messiah—so that a period of time is made possible during which the good news of salvation is carried to the Gentiles; during this period it remains God's will that the present "remnant" of Jews believing in Jesus the Messiah becomes larger—that is, more Jews are saved—by the process of "jealousy," which should lead Jews to faith in Jesus the Messiah. Gerhard Lohfink comments that "all Israel" will be saved because Jews can finally believe in Jesus the Messiah "on account of the messianic attractiveness of the Gentile church."[66] This statement is correct if we speak of "the church" and not of the "Gentile church," as Paul neither established nor argued for Christian communities consisting of Gentiles only, but rather churches that consisted of Jewish believers and Gentile believers.

Some scholars regard Paul's reference to God's election of Jews who have come, and who will come, to faith in Jesus the Messiah as an inadequate answer to the question of whether God's promises to his people are still valid. Wilfrid Keller argues that Paul needs a different, better answer: Paul affirms in Rom 9:4-5 that God's promises apply to all Jews, and he intercedes for Israel in Rom 9:2-3 and 10:1, which is superfluous if the answer of Rom 9:6-13 is final.[67] This argument is not cogent. First, Paul's statement in Rom 9:4 does not say that *all promises* are still valid, and it does not say that the promises applied to *all Jews*. Paul merely states that "the promises" are part of the privileges that God gave to Israel, implying particularly God's promises to the patriarchs (cf. Rom 9:5; 4:13-22) and messianic promises (cf. 2 Cor 1:20).[68] The "covenants" (διαθῆκαι, *diathēkai*) that are mentioned in Rom 9:4 before the reference to the "promises" include repeated announcements of divine judgment, both in the Sinaitic covenant and in the prophets. This is why it is rather unlikely that Paul interpreted the "promise" as conversion of "all Jews," including the Jews who reject Jesus the Messiah. Second, the passage about the election of the Jews who believe in the gospel of Jesus Christ in Rom 9:6-13 leaves open the question of how many Jews will come to faith in Jesus the Messiah in the future. Indeed, Paul does not regard the subject of "the conversion of the Jewish people" to have been exhausted with his exposition about God's election: he is an active missionary who continues to preach before Jews, he mourns because of the unbelief of many of his Jewish contemporaries, and he intercedes before God, praying for their salvation. However, his mourning and intercession do not push him "to give an answer that goes beyond what he has said so far."[69] Rather, they push him to continued missionary activities among Jews, and his upcoming visit to Jerusalem has to be understood in this context of his missionary concern for the Jewish people as well. Similarly, Paul's reference to the hardening of the majority of Israel (Rom 11:1-10) does not force him to give a new answer: in Rom 11:11, 14 he answers the question of what will happen to this majority in the future[70] by pointing to God's intention of provoking Israel to jealousy by the Gentiles who are converted to faith in the Messiah and therefore receive salvation, so that "some" of Israel will be saved.

---

[66]G. Lohfink 1982, 165.
[67]Keller 1998, 130-32.
[68]See Cranfield, *Rom,* 2:464; Sass 1995.
[69]Keller 1998, 132.
[70]*Pace* Keller 1998, 133.

F. W. Maier argues that Paul's ministry as a missionary to the Gentiles "is ultimately and essentially aimed at Israel's salvation."[71] This view exaggerates: for Paul, the salvation of Gentiles surely is as important as the salvation of Jews. It would be wrong, however, to dispute that Paul engaged proactively in missionary work among Jews.[72]

Most scholars assume that the quotation in Rom 11:26b-27—a mixed quotation that combines Is 59:20-21 with Is 2:3 (and/or Mic 4:2; cf. Is 27:9; Jer 31:34)— refers to the parousia, the return of Jesus Christ. The Old Testament passages that Paul quotes refer, in their original context, to the last, great renewal of the covenant, the final end of the dispersion, and the blessing that will flow to the nations after Israel has been vindicated. The Old Testament sometimes describes this eschatological blessing as the law going out to the nations (cf. Mic 4:2-3). Paul might well assert with the combination of Old Testament passages that he quotes that what the law was not able to do is now happening through Jesus Christ and through the Holy Spirit (replacing the departure of the Torah with the coming of the Savior). This interpretation accords with the argument in Rom 9:30—10:13. This means that Paul presumably speaks not of Christ's return but rather of the Gentile mission in which the Savior comes to the nations. If this interpretation is correct, then Paul is exhorting the Gentile Christians not to stand in the way of this fulfillment of Scripture: the conversion of more Jews is nothing less than the result of the covenant faithfulness and the righteousness of the one true God. And this is precisely what Paul celebrates in the praise uttered in Rom 11:33-36.

The long passage Rom 9—11 thus describes neither exclusively God's judgment of unbelieving Israel nor exclusively God's mercy for Israel, but both, as is indicated by the quotation from Deut 32: the Gentile mission continues despite Israel's unbelief, leading to the conversion of Gentiles and to the establishment of churches and making Jews jealous who then are converted to faith in Jesus the Messiah as well.[73] The eschatological pilgrimage of the nations to Zion does not *follow* the restoration of Israel, as was expected, but rather *precedes* it: the nations do not come to faith in Israel's God because they see the glory of Israel; rather, "Israel" is converted because the Jews see the salvation and the glory that the Gentiles have found in Jesus Christ. The view that Paul, like Jesus, did not expect a "restoration" of "all Israel" in terms of every single Jew being granted salvation is in agreement with the Old Testament and the Jewish traditions concerning the righteous in Israel who receive God's mercy and salvation—as a holy "remnant" of the elect who are obedient to God's revelation.[74]

---

[71]F. Maier 1929, 129-30.

[72]Contra Lübking 1986, 111-12; also contra Keller (1998, 193-94), who rejects an "indirect Israel mission of Paul."

[73]W. Campbell 1993a, 445; for the comment that follows above see ibid.

[74]M. Elliott 2000; see the summary of his conclusions in §9.2 in the present work.

Summary

Paul pursued a comprehensive *international* missionary strategy: he wanted to preach the gospel of Jesus Christ in provinces and regions, in cities and towns in which no other missionary had preached before. Paul pursued a comprehensive *social* missionary strategy: he wanted to reach both Jews and pagans, Greeks and barbarians, the educated and the uneducated. Whether Paul pursued a comprehensive *geographical* missionary strategy is unclear, unless we are content to assert that he moved from Damascus to Jerusalem, from Antioch to Paphos, from Pisidian Antiocheia to Ephesus, and from Corinth via Rome to Spain. The mission in Arabia, Syria and Cilicia lasted twelve years, the mission on Cyprus and to Galatia two years, the mission in Macedonia and Achaia four years, the mission in the province of Asia three years. There were eminent cities in these provinces and regions that were important for a comprehensive missionary strategy but that Paul evidently did not visit. Shall we assume, as some scholars suggest, that Paul developed a comprehensive geographical strategy around A.D. 44 during his ministry in Antioch, after missionary work in Arabia, Syria and Cilicia for twelve years? Perhaps, but such a scenario must remain hypothetical.

The picture that Luke provides of Paul's missionary work in the book of Acts agrees with the information that Paul provides in his letters. We find the same combination of prayer, planning, divine guidance and rational decisions that become necessary and can be explained in the context of specific historical situations.[75] Paul makes plans for missionary travels, but he knows himself to be dependent on God's "permission" to carry out these plans.[76] He acts as the result of revelations,[77] he prays for successful visits in the cities in which he preaches the gospel.[78] And he finds that not all plans can be realized.[79]

28.2 Communication Aspects of Paul's Missionary Work

Missionaries need practicable methods that the communication structure of the contemporary society provides if they want to have any prospect of success among people who have never heard the gospel. Reinhold Reck provides a helpful description of the options of available communication patterns in the first century: "the natural dissemination of ideas in connection with the varied mobility of the people, the transmission in the context of the relationships of everyday life, proclamation in established cult centers, the attractiveness of the mysterious in connection with the self-presentation of the cults in public litur-

---

[75]For the observations that follow above see I. H. Marshall 1990, 44-47.
[76]Cf. 1 Thess 3:1; 2 Cor 1:15-16; Phil 2:24; 1 Cor 16:7.
[77]Cf. Gal 2:2; Acts 16:9.
[78]Cf. 1 Thess 3:10; Rom 1:10-12; 15:30.
[79]Cf. 1 Thess 2:18; Rom 1:13; Acts 16:6-7. See I. H. Marshall 2000b, 101-2.

gies, and last but not least the declamations of the itinerant preachers. Three of these concepts are central for the praxis of Paul's initial evangelism: life as an itinerant preacher, the Diaspora synagogues as cult centers, and the everyday relationships in his work as a craftsman. The dissemination by general mobility will play a role for the Pauline churches, but not for the apostle himself; and can describe his missionary praxis as public liturgy only in metaphorical speech (e.g., Rom 15:16; Phil 2:17; 2 Cor 2:14)."[80]

Standard communication models help us to illustrate the situation in which Paul finds himself as a pioneer missionary (see fig. 42).[81] The model of mass communication developed by B. H. Westley and M. S. MacLean distinguishes five elements. The source or communicator (A) focuses on a "universe" of possible objects or events in the environment ($X_{1-\infty}$) and formulates a message (X′) that is transmitted via a gatekeeper or opinion leader (C) to a receiver or audience (B). The gatekeeper (e.g., a journalist) sends the message in connection with his or her knowledge of reality (X_{3c}) to the audience (X″). The audience or receiver sends feedback (f_{BA}) to the source of the communication. At the same time there is feedback from the gatekeeper to the source (f_{CA}) and from the receiver to the gatekeeper (f_{BC}). In the communication model of C. E. Shannon and W. Weaver, a further element plays a role: noise (D). The transmission of a message generally is accompanied by disturbances, unwanted stimuli that can influence the accuracy of the message—for example, static interference during a phone conversation, called "noise" in human communication.

Reck summarizes the communicative situation that Paul faced as follows: "The *sending* occurs through a primary *communicator* who uses a messenger as a *personal medium*. The central active process of communication is the *proclamation* which has to converge with *hearing* as the receptive act of communication in order for communication to take place, i.e., so that the message can be conveyed. Between *hearing* and *believing* we have the intracommunicative processes of selection, reduction, interpretation and reception; the act of believing is a communicative act as decisive *intra*personal turnabout with a *trans*communicative result (the *calling* on the Lord). The chain of communication is initiated by the sending."[82]

Paul's letters and Luke's account in the book of Acts allow us to describe the following elements of communication in Paul's missionary work: (1) the sending of envoys; (2) establishing contact; (3) the proclamation of the gospel; (4) the persuasiveness of the message; (5) methods of missionary proclamation; (6) the credibility of the envoy; (7) the disposition of the listeners; (8) the conversion

---

[80]Reck 1991, 166. On the role of mobility see also Di Berardino 1999.
[81]See Burgoon, Hunsaker and Dawson 1994, 26-31; see also Maletzke 1988, 3-15, 56-60; Badura 1995.
[82]Reck 1991, 167.

of listeners. The forms and the content of Paul's missionary sermons, in whose outline and delivery we see the processes of selection, reduction and interpretation at work, will be discussed later (§28.3).

The Sending of Envoys

Paul understands himself as a messenger of the gospel who has been called, sent and empowered by God and Jesus Christ. The basic texts in which Paul clearly expresses this conviction are 2 Cor 5:18-20 and Rom 10:14-17:

2 Cor 5:18-20: "All this is from God, who reconciled us to himself through Christ, and has given us the ministry of reconciliation; [19]that is, in Christ God was reconciling the world to himself, not counting their trespasses against them, and entrusting the message of reconciliation to us. [20]So we are ambassadors for Christ, since God is making his appeal through us; we entreat you on behalf of Christ, be reconciled to God."

Rom 10:14-17: "But how are they to call on one in whom they have not believed? And how are they to believe in one of whom they have never heard? And how are they to hear without someone to proclaim him? [15]And how are they to proclaim him unless they are sent? As it is written, 'How beautiful are the feet of those who bring good news!' [16]But not all have obeyed the good news; for Isaiah says, 'Lord, who has believed our message?' [17]So faith comes from what is heard, and what is heard comes through the word of Christ."

The word of God reaches the people through messengers who proclaim the message of Jesus Christ, of his messianic identity and his life, of his death on the cross and of his resurrection on the third day, of his exaltation to the right hand of God. Paul relates in Rom 10:14-17, in a chain syllogism, the worship of Jesus Christ as Lord to believing, believing to hearing, hearing to proclamation, and proclamation to the sending of the messenger. Not every hearing leads to faith, but Paul insists that with the sending and with the obedient going of the messengers—the missionaries—everything has been done that makes it possible for people to call on Jesus Christ as Lord. The messengers of faith who have been sent by God—the apostles—have proclaimed the gospel by preaching the good news of Jesus Christ before live audiences. This is not surprising in light of the possibilities for communication in the first century. We have no reliable information about whether the early Christian missionaries used written texts as a means of missionary communication (see §30.2). The letters that Paul wrote, at least those that have survived, were not intended to convince Jews or pagans of the truth of the gospel; rather, Paul wrote for Christians in order to establish them more fully and more consistently in the gospel and in the behavior that should result from their faith in Jesus the Messiah and Savior. Still, Peter Müller is right when he emphasizes that the impression that Paul gives priority to the spoken word over against the written word is not entirely correct: according to Rom 10:5, 19, Paul can speak of Moses "in the mode of writing as well as in the mode of speaking. Scripture is not totally and exclusively scripture, and the spoken word is not merely spoken."[83] The message of the messengers sent by Jesus Christ is the "word of Christ" (Rom 10:17), the "word of faith" (Rom 10:8). In the spoken word of the missionaries the exalted Christ himself is being heard. Their message is a "living word that hits home . . . and at the same time in it and through it the word of Christ."

Establishing Contact

Paul speaks deliberately and specifically of the "entrance" to the people or the "acceptance" (εἴσοδος, *eisodos*) by the people who hear his proclamation of the gospel (1 Thess 1:9). Paul obviously reflected upon the factors and the conditions that come into play during the process of establishing initial contacts with Jewish and Gentile listeners. Relevant texts are 1 Thess 1:9; 1 Cor 2:1-2; 16:8-9; 2 Cor 2:12; Gal 4:14; Col 4:3.

1 Thess 1:9: "For the people of those regions report about us what kind of welcome we had among you, and how you turned to God from idols, to serve a living and true God."

1 Cor 2:1-2: "When I came to you, brothers and sisters, I did not come proclaiming the mystery of God to you in lofty words or wisdom. [2]For I decided to know nothing among you except Jesus Christ, and him crucified."

2 Cor 2:12: "When I came to Troas to proclaim the good news of Christ, a door was opened for me in the Lord."

Gal 4:14: "Though my condition put you to the test, you did not scorn or despise me, but welcomed me as an angel of God, as Christ Jesus."

Col 4:3: "At the same time pray for us as well that God will open to us a door for the word, that we may declare the mystery of Christ, for which I am in prison."

Acts 13:5: "When they arrived at Salamis, they proclaimed the word of God in the synagogues of the Jews. And they had John also to assist them."[84]

Acts 17:17: "So he argued in the synagogue with the Jews and the devout persons, and also in the marketplace every day with those who happened to be there."

In regard to Paul's initiation of contacts with Jews and Gentiles in his endeavor to proclaim the gospel of Jesus Christ, these and other texts establish the following conceptual factors.

   1. Paul was conscious of the significance of the initial contact with people. The term "entrance" (εἴσοδος, *eisodos*) in 1 Thess 1:9 could describe the apostle's entire visit in the city of Thessalonike, as in 1 Thess 2:1.[85] Here it refers more

---

[83]P. Müller 1994, 423; the quotation that follows above, ibid., 425.
[84]Cf. Acts 13:14; 14:1; 17:1, 10, 17; 18:4, 19; 19:8.
[85]Thus Wanamaker, *Thess,* 84

likely to his active behavior during his first sojourn in the city only a few months earlier.[86]

2. Paul first visited the local synagogue, presenting himself as an experienced interpreter of Scripture. He used the reading from the Law and the Prophets and the synagogue sermon as opportunities to proclaim Jesus of Nazareth as the Messiah. Paul (and Luke in Acts) rejects the legitimacy of being sidelined, or expelled, by the representatives of the local synagogue.[87] The former student of Rabbi Gamaliel always reckons with the possibility that he can expound the Law and the Prophets for the synagogue congregation. With only one exception (Acts 20:7), all sabbath passages of Acts are related to Paul preaching in synagogues.[88] Paul anticipates that some among the audience in the synagogues will accept his message. In every instance representatives of the synagogue take action against him. However, despite repeated mistreatment and abuse, Paul continues to attend and participate in synagogue services. This is implied in his statement in 2 Cor 11:24: "Five times I have received from the Jews the forty lashes minus one."

Matthias Klinghardt believes that it was only when God-fearers or pagans were converted that Jews reacted against the early Christian mission; that is, the preaching of early Christian missionaries before Jewish audiences was not problematic.[89] He refers to Paul's missionary work in Thessalonike that proceeded without interruption for three weeks (Acts 17:2-4a): attacks are recorded only after the reference to missionary success among Gentiles (Acts 17:5: after 17:4b). Klinghardt maintains that the economic and political significance of the God-fearers for the synagogues was less problematic than the notion of their full membership in the people of God, on grounds of purity and identity. However, this interpretation is contradicted by the repeated arrests of the leading apostles and of other Christians who proclaimed the gospel of Jesus as the Messiah in Jerusalem mostly, or even exclusively, before Jewish audiences (Acts 4—12). When Paul visited Jerusalem after his conversion and argued the messianic identity of Jesus in the local synagogues before Greek-speaking Jews, he encountered essentially identical reactions as later during his ministry in the Diaspora: Jews plot to kill him, which forces him to leave the city in a hurry (Acts 9:28-29). Klinghardt's thesis founders because of the facts as recorded by Luke.

Wolfgang Reinbold labels Luke's record as "stylized" and treats it as historically worthless.[90] He fails to recognize the fact that the mode of initial contacts in missionary situations indeed is often repetitive, as is true of many "actions" of preachers, pastors and other church workers. People do not always react as individuals in completely unique ways. Common and similar patters of behavior and experience do indeed develop and exist. Reinbold's assertions concerning the "modalities" of Paul's missionary work[91] ultimately

---

[86]See Malherbe, *Thess,* 118; Klauck 1992a, 21-22.

[87]Klinghardt 1988, 234-36.

[88]Cf. Acts 13:14-15; 16:13; 17:2; 18:4.

[89]Klinghardt 1988, 235-36.

[90]Reinbold 2000, 117-63.

[91]Reinbold 2000, 182-225; on "first contacts" see 183-95; quotation, 195; on the "means" of Paul's missionary work see 195-225.

are unrealistic. He traces "first contacts" between Paul and non-Christians to illness (Gal 4:13-14), work (Acts 18:3; 1 Thess 2:9), loose personal contacts in synagogues (Acts 16:11-15), local Christians such as Aquila and Priscilla (Acts 18:1-3; 1 Cor 16:19), imprisonments (Phil 1:12-14; Acts 16:25-34) and travel companions from existing churches (1 Cor 16:6; 2 Cor 1:16; Rom 15:24)—that is, to "accidental acquaintances, relatives, families, colleagues, small groups of interested people and the like"; Paul did not deliver missionary sermons in synagogues. According to Reinbold, Paul used the following "means" to win "neophytes": existing local churches in which non-Christians hear the gospel (1 Cor 14:23-25), his teaching in private homes (Acts 18:11; 19:9), miracles (2 Cor 12:11-12) and personal contacts (Philem 10; Gal 4:13-14). According to Reinbold, Paul did not preach in the marketplaces of cities that he visited (see below under point 4). Apart from the fact that it remains unclear what the difference between "first contacts" and "means of missionary work" is supposed to be, the conclusion that Reinbold proposes is such a precipitous theory that historical reality plunges into the abyss of preconceived assumptions. If we eliminate contacts that presuppose the presence of Christians in a city, all that Reinbold has left are accidental encounters at the places where Paul lives or works or accidental encounters in prisons and synagogues. Since Paul understood himself to be an *apostolos,* an envoy sent by Jesus Christ to convince people of Jesus' messianic identity and of the reality of God's revelation in him, and since he knew of Jesus' proactive, determined and purposeful movements in Galilee, it is a case of special pleading to assume that he would have relied on accidental encounters in his quest to share his faith with others.

3. Paul's behavior and demeanor as an "orator" evidently surprised and confounded educated Gentiles both at the point of initial contact and afterwards. In 1 Cor 2:1 Paul reminds the Christians in Corinth of the events that took place when he first visited the city: "When I came to you, brothers and sisters, I did not come proclaiming the mystery of God to you in lofty words or wisdom." Paul's forceful remarks in the context of this passage (1 Cor 1:18—2:5) are best understood against the background of orators of the Second Sophistic who also were active in Corinth. Well-known examples are Favorinus of Arles (b. ca. A.D. 90) and Herod Atticus of Athens (b. A.D. 101), and we should add, as Bruce Winter argues, the Jewish-Christian teachers with whose influence Paul interacts in his first letter to the Corinthian Christians.[92] The phrase in 1 Cor 2:1 "when I came to you" (κἀγὼ ἐλθὼν πρὸς ὑμᾶς, *kagō elthōn pros hymas*) refers to the behavior of the Sophists. A Sophist orator could attain to great fame if he managed to establish himself in *politeia* and *paideia*. The first visit of a Sophist in a city gave him the opportunity to provide the citizens with a taste of his oratory. Favorinus, an orator in Corinth at the time of Hadrian, reminded the Corinthians of his first visit in the city, when he proved his rhetorical skills and established friendly relations with the citizens and the municipal authori-

---

[92]For the observations that follow above see B. Winter 1997, 147-65. See also Schnabel 2002c, 59-63. On the Sophist Polemon, who was active in Smyrna in the second century, see Reader 1996. On the Second Sophistic see Thomas Schmitz, *Bildung und Macht: Zur sozialen und politischen Funktion der zweiten Sophistik in der griechischen Welt der Kaiserzeit* (Zetemata 97; Munich: Beck, 1997); Swain 1998.

ties.[93] When Aristides visited Smyrna for the first time (A.D. 176), the citizens came out to greet him. The most gifted young people offered themselves as students, a date for a lecture by Aristides was set, and an invitation was formulated. Before the day on which the lecture was to take place Aristides had a "dream" in which he was told to declaim in the council chamber at ten o'clock that very day. He was able to arrange this impromptu appearance on very short notice. Even though hardly anyone had heard of this turn of events, the council chamber was so packed "that it was impossible to see anything except men's heads, and there was not even room to shove your hand between the people." Aristides delivered the preliminary speech sitting down, and he presented the ensuing declamation standing up. The excited audience was spellbound throughout his delivery, so much so that "every man counted it his gain, if he should bestow some very great compliment on me." Aristides' "dream" probably was prompted by a rival Sophist, "an Egyptian" who happened to present a declamation in the odeion on that particular day with two days' notice. Aristides thus was able to carry off a complete victory over the Egyptian, whose event attracted only seventeen people.[94] This story confirms what other sources tell us: the Sophist orators wanted to impress their audiences with their declamations, both the young men of the leading families of the city and invited guests and other people who would pay for the experience of listening to the oratory. The first "coming" of a Sophist to a city evidently followed certain conventions, as he sought to establish his reputation as an orator. If he was successful and found acceptance, he could profit financially.

Paul, in the eyes of the citizens of Corinth, initially was an orator looking for audiences. However, compared with the conventions of the Sophists, Paul's conduct was unconventional. It is important to note that Paul asserts that his conduct was deliberate:

1 Cor 2:1-5: "When I came to you, brothers and sisters, I did not come proclaiming the mystery of God to you in lofty words or wisdom (ἦλθον οὐ καθ᾽ ὑπεροχὴν λόγου ἢ σοφίας). ²For I decided to know nothing among you except Jesus Christ, and him crucified. ³And I came to you in weakness and in fear and in much trembling. ⁴My speech and my proclamation (ὁ λόγος μου καὶ τὸ κήρυγμά μου) were not with plausible words of wisdom (οὐκ ἐν πειθοῖς σοφίας λόγοις), but with a demonstration of the Spirit and of power (ἀλλ᾽ ἐν ἀποδείξει πνεύματος καὶ δυνάμεως), ⁵so that your faith (ἡ πίστις ὑμῶν) might rest not on human wisdom but on the power of God."

---

[93]The Corinthian speech of Favorinus is found in Dio Chrysostom, Or. 37 (Corinthiaca). See A. Barigazzi, Favorino di Arelate: Opera (Florence: Lelice Le Monnier, 1966); B. W. Winter, "Acts and the Pauline Corpus I," in Winter and Clarke 1993, 197-205; M. W. Gleason, "Favorinus and His Statue," in Making Men: Sophists and Self-Presentation in Ancient Rome (Princeton, N.J.: Princeton University Press, 1995); B. Winter 1997, 132-37; Swain 1998, 43-46.

[94]Aristides, Or. 51.29-34. See Russell 1983, 76-77; B. Winter 1997, 149-50; Swain 1998, 295.

The term ἡ πίστις (*hē pistis*) in 1 Cor 2:5 takes up a rhetorical term: Paul spe-cifically addresses the expectations of his listeners in terms of his rhetoric during their first encounter in the city. Aristotle linked *pistis* in terms of "confidence" or "conviction" with the combined application of three proofs: τὸ ἦθος τοῦ λέγον-τος (*to ēthos tou legontos*), τὰ πάθη (*ta pathē*) and ἀπόδειξις (*apodeixis*).[95] (a) The orator persuades by *ēthos* when he delivers his speech in a manner that demonstrates that he is worthy of the listeners' trust. For Aristotle, this was the most effective means of proof. The term *ēthos* describes the goal of the orator to prove his good character and thus his credibility. In order to be believed, in order to be successful, he needs to convey a sympathetic picture of himself as a credible and likable person. In order to achieve this he must identify and study the particular qualities of his listeners so that he can anticipate their reactions to his declamation. (b) The term *pathos* describes the feelings of the listeners that can be utilized strategically in order to guarantee the effectiveness of the ora-tion. Aristotle describes ten *pathoi,* the circumstances in which they might be evoked, the type of person in whom they can be evoked, and against whom they can be directed. (c) The term *apodeixis* describes "clear proofs" (Quintil-ian). This involves the method by which an orator can prove what is not certain by referring to what is certain: specific arguments. Paul, in 1 Cor 2:4, uses not only the term *apodeixis* but also the term *dynamis* (δύναμις, "power"), which is used by Isocrates and Aristotle in their definitions of rhetoric: rhetoric is the "power" to detect the means of persuasion; rhetoric is the "power of speaking" (δύναμις τοῦ λέγειν, *dynamis tou legein*). Quintilian speaks of *vis persuadendi,* and Dio Chrysostom describes the gift of oratory as *dynamis*. In 1 Cor 2:4 Paul uses the verb *peithein* (πείθειν, "persuade"), which often is used in definitions of rhetoric.

Paul provides in 1 Cor 2:1-5 an autobiographical account of his coming into the city of Corinth and of the methods of his proclamation. He explains his mis-sionary preaching on the occasion of his first contact with the Corinthians: he proclaims the message of the cross not with "the wisdom of words" (1 Cor 1:17), because he does not want to show off his eloquence but rather wants to boast in the Lord Jesus Christ. Paul writes, "When I came to you, brothers and sisters, I did not come proclaiming the mystery of God to you in lofty words or wisdom" (1 Cor 2:1), emphasizing that he dispenses intentionally with the superiority of the art of rhetoric when he preaches the gospel. He had no interest in being the center of attention or in being praised by others. The participle *katangellōn* (καταγγέλλων) indicates the reason for this attitude: his task was the proclama-tion of the message of Jesus as the Messiah, "and him crucified" (1 Cor 2:2). This message required no *dialexis,* no discussion (on the level of style or *lexis*) con-cerning his own person, nor did it need a eulogy (*enkomion*) on the greatness

---

[95] Aristotle, *Rhet.* 1.1.1356a; see B. Winter 1997, 153.

of the city of Corinth. He needed no subject that a critical audience might suggest for a declamation that he would accept in order to receive the approval of the citizens of the city. The subject matter on which he spoke had been determined long before he arrived. And he did not allow himself to be distracted by any other subject when he initiated contact with the citizens of Corinth for the first time whom he wanted to bring to faith in Jesus Christ.

Paul's renunciation of rhetorical techniques must not be confused with a "weak" public appearance, however. The view is incorrect that public speaking was not Paul's forte and so he resorted to other means of communication.[96] Equally wrong is the argument that the (alleged) lack of success of Paul's speech on the Areopagus in Athens proves that he lacked the rhetorical education and expertise that both the cultural elite and the citizens more generally expected:[97] rhetorical brilliance can never "guarantee" the "success" of a Christian missionary sermon. According to 2 Cor 10:1, 10-11, Corinthian Christians reproached Paul for writing strong and audacious letters while being personally subservient (*tapeinos*) and weak (*asthenēs*), his oral talks being contemptible, having no merit (*exouthenemēnos*). Another accusation, put forward by some Christians in Corinth, was that he was "untrained in speech" (*idiōtēs tō logō* [1 Cor 11:6])—that is, an amateur, managing only a botched job when he speaks. Paul emphasizes against such criticism that these accusations are aimed, in the final analysis, against Jesus Christ himself: the "meekness and gentleness of Christ" (2 Cor 10:1) consist, according to Phil 2:1-11, in self-abasement. Paul's behavior as a missionary, as a teacher who speaks in public, is characterized by humility because Jesus Christ's conduct and demeanor likewise were characterized by humility.[98]

4. Paul establishes contacts with the citizens in the agora, the commercial center—in Greek cities the political and commercial center, in Roman cities or colonies (such as Athens and Corinth in the first century) the political and religious center. We possess only one explicit piece of evidence for this tactical decision: Paul's first contacts with the citizens of Athens as reported in Acts 17:17. Paul went "every day" (κατὰ πᾶσαν ἡμέραν, *kata pasan hēmeran*) to the marketplace and spoke "with those who happened to be there" (πρὸς τοὺς παρατυγχάνοντας). The present participle *paratynchanontas* implies that going to the agora and speaking with passersby was a routine that the apostle adopted regularly.[99]

There is no reason to dispense with Acts 17:17 as a stylized picture of Paul used by the author, who allegedly wanted to allude to the Athenian Socrates.[100] Wolfgang Reinbold

---

[96]Contra Young 1989, 82.
[97]Contra Siegert 1993, 55-56.
[98]See P. Müller 1994, 432.
[99]Barrett, *Acts,* 2:829.
[100]Contra Reinbold 2000, 200; the quotation that follows above, ibid., 202. His only argument is a reference to Stowers 1984, 80-81.

engages in pure speculation when he writes, "At best one may ask whether Paul occasionally had conversations in the agora with strangers and disputed with them in the style of the Cynics. It is impossible to discount such a possibility. If such contacts took place, they would not have played a major role in the mission of the apostle of the Gentiles." Reinbold claims to know that Paul's ministry as miracle worker and missionary took place "in small settings," namely, "in families, houses, small groups, (small) *ekklesiai,* etc.," and he concludes, "The mission of the historical Paul was characterized by microcommunication, not by public or semipublic speeches, sermons or similar appearances."[101] The fact that Reinbold qualifies this hypothesis with the phrase "in der Regel" ("usually") and points to public accusations and interrogations such as in Acts 18:12-17—situations that Paul himself did not initiate—indicates that he is not interested in consistent historical verification of his theories. "Microcommunication" cannot explain the public accusations, the legal proceedings and the personal attacks against Paul in Corinth and in other cities of the Greco-Roman world. Invariably influential citizens reacted against Paul's activities as provocative and dangerous. Paul came under pressure not simply as a result of "opposition and counteractions" but because of specific people, leading citizens of their cities, who would hardly have been bothered by activities "behind closed doors."[102] Reinbold underestimates the public character both of the gospel message that Paul proclaimed and of the local Christian communities. His view that "if the circumstances were particularly fortunate," the church grew simply as a result of personal contacts between the apostle and local people, "with evidently no other means or methods being necessary," demonstrates a fundamental lack of insight into missionary work.

Paul seeks to make contact with the population of a city, outside of the synagogues of the Jewish community, in the agora, which was the place where he could reach a large and diverse audience, including the decision makers of the city, notably before noon. However, it would be inappropriate to interpret Paul's preaching activity in the agora as "mass evangelism," particularly if one thinks of the organized mass rallies of evangelists such as George Whitefield and Billy Graham. On the other hand, it is equally wrong to assume that Paul preached the gospel mainly in his workshop during his free time.[103] Paul clearly was not a missionary who preached only when he could find time for it.

5. Paul repeatedly had contacts with imperial officials and local magistrates,[104] members of the aristocracy whom he sought to acquaint with the gospel of Jesus Christ. On one occasion he may have deliberately visited representatives of the aristocracy in connection with his missionary work. If my reconstruction of Paul's acquaintance with the family of the Sergii Paulii during his mission in Cyprus and Galatia (§27.1) is historically accurate, then he may have traveled from Paphos on Cyprus to Antiocheia in (southern) Galatia with the goal of contacting the Pisidian branch of this aristocratic family. The

---

[101]Reinbold 2000, 104, 205; for the remark that follows above see 205 with n. 31.

[102]Contra Reinbold 2000, 206, 207; the quotation that follows above, ibid., 204.

[103]Contra Young 1989, 82.

[104]Gill 1994b, 108. Gill does not evaluate the relevant evidence in terms of Paul's missionary work.

initial contact with Sergius Paullus, the Roman governor of Cyprus, seems to have been initiated by Sergius as a result of the Jewish-Christian missionaries' confrontation with Elymas, the Jewish astrologer at his court. According to Acts 13:7, 12, Sergius Paullus listened to the preaching of Paul, showing interest, and came to faith being "astonished at the teaching about the Lord." However, in regard to the mission in Antioch (Acts 13:13-52), Luke does not report any contacts with the Sergii Paulii. On the contrary, he recounts that the Jews who rejected Paul's message were successful in inciting "the leading men of the city" (οἱ πρῶτοι), the local aristocracy, against Paul and Barnabas (Acts 13:50). Another contact with a proconsul is reported for Corinth: the Jews of the city accuse Paul before Gallio, the proconsul of the province of Achaia (Acts 18:12-16). According to Luke, Paul did not even have an opportunity to defend himself, as Gallio refused to hear the case: if Paul had been given an opportunity to speak, surely he would have explained the message of Jesus Christ that he proclaimed and that had instigated the accusations against him (Acts 18:14).

In the context of his report of Paul's mission in Ephesus, Luke relates that the apostle had friends among the Asiarchs, the prominent magistrates of the city. They were prepared to protect Paul during a period of unrest in the city that was prompted by his missionary activity (Acts 19:31). It is plausible to surmise that this acquaintance was related in some way to Paul's missionary activity in Ephesus.

After his arrest in Jerusalem Paul was a prisoner of the Roman Empire, accused by leading Jews of having broken the law. Paul defended himself before Felix, the Roman governor, who gave him an opportunity to explain his message of Jesus Christ (Acts 24:24). Luke reports that Paul spoke about the topics of justice/righteousness, self-control and the coming judgment (Acts 24:25)—topics clearly relevant for the specific situation of the governor.[105] When Paul was asked to speak before Festus, the proconsul, and Herod Agrippa II, the Jewish king, he not only defended himself (Acts 26:1-23) but also challenged Agrippa to believe in his message (Acts 26:27) after Festus had responded to Paul's discourse on resurrection from the dead by declaring him insane, "out of his mind" (Acts 26:24).[106] Paul concluded his presentation with a prayer that "all" who were listening to him might come to faith in Jesus, the crucified and risen Savior, "whether quickly or not" (Acts 26:29). Paul's move from a speech of defense to a missionary appeal not only underlines the courage of the apostle but also demonstrates his conviction that a successful mission among Jews was still possible.[107] On Malta Paul has friendly (φιλοφρόνως, *philophronōs*) contacts

---

[105]Zmijewski (*Apg,* 823) interprets Luke as taking up the "main subjects of the post-apostolic proclamation"; cf. Haenchen, *Apg,* 632 (ET, 660-61).

[106]See Weiser, *Apg,* 2:655.

[107]Tannehill 1992, 257, 266-67.

with Publius, the "chief man of the island," who had given shelter to the ship-wrecked prisoners and crew (Acts 28:7).

According to 2 Tim 4:17, Paul used his trial in Rome as an opportunity to explain the gospel: "The Lord stood by me and gave me strength, so that through me the message might be fully proclaimed and all the Gentiles might hear it. So I was rescued from the lion's mouth." The context of 2 Tim 2:16 suggests that Paul refers to his (second) trial in Rome, in about A.D. 64,[108] specifically to his defense in the *prima actio,* the preliminary proceedings in which the legally relevant material was presented (rather than to a period of evangelism after his first trial in Rome in A.D. 62—that is, to his mission in Spain.)[109]

These texts show that Paul did not have a mission strategy that sought to initiate (or consolidate) missionary work by establishing contacts with the powerful elites of the cities or provinces in which he preached the gospel, with the exception, perhaps, of the first causes of the mission to Pisidian Antiocheia.

The conversion of Constantine and the legalization of the Christian communities brought about fundamental changes in this regard, changes that became evident in the missionary work of the early medieval church in which basic strategic procedures included establishing close ties with the political overlords of the territory or country to be converted.[110] The social structure of the Anglo-Saxon and Frankish regions prompted missionaries such as Willibrord to establish ties with the leaders of the tribe or region in which they wanted to establish churches in order to be able to initiate and to safeguard opportunities for missionary work. The early medieval missionaries demonstrated flexibility in such endeavors. Whether their behavior was contextually "adequate"—that is, whether it was *necessary* to preach the gospel of Jesus Christ in cooperation with (pagan) political rulers—is a question that cannot be addressed here. The actions of Gallio in Acts 18:12-16 demonstrate, however, that the tolerant attitude of Roman magistrates in the first century made such a strategic "adaptation" by Paul or other early Christian missionaries unnecessary.

6. Paul did not visit pagan temples with the purpose of proclaiming the gospel before worshipers present in the temple precincts. There is no evidence for such tactics in the early Christian texts, nor is such a strategy likely. Paul was intimately familiar with Greco-Roman society; he had a realistic view of the political, social and religious power structures of Greek and Roman cities.[111] The Christian missionaries and the small Christian communities, often threatened by local actions of (Jewish) opponents, had to abstain from provocative actions if they wanted to be tolerated in the Greek and Roman cities, with their fundamentally forbearing culture and society of the first century. Further, the reli-

---

[108]See Spicq, *ÉpPast,* 2:818-19; Mounce, *PastEp,* 595.

[109]Contra Prior 1989, 125-39; see Marshall, *PastEp,* 824.

[110]Padberg 1995, 49-52, 95-102; for the observations that follow above see ibid., 51-52.

[111]See Padberg 1995, 111-12, commenting on the first contacts of the early medieval missionaries who sought to reach the central locales of the religious and political life of the regions in which they wanted to establish churches.

gious-social structures of the cities suggest that missionary actions in a specific temple would reach only a portion of the population, as many citizens would frequent other temples in worshiping other gods.

The early medieval missionaries took calculated action against pagan sanctuaries: they profaned images of deities, altars and sacred groves and springs, and they destroyed temples and cult places.[112] When Paul accuses Jews in Rom 2:22 of "robbing temples"—that is, of illegally removing objects from temples of pagan shrines[113]—or of trading objects that have been stolen from pagan temples,[114] this has a rhetorical meaning in the context of Rom 2. Paul seeks to prove that there is an unmistakable disparity in contemporary Jewish society between the claims being made and the reality of everyday behavior. It is precisely for this reason that Paul could never have used force in order to advance the gospel among pagans.

Nor did Paul carry objects with him that could have enhanced the acceptance of him or his message on account of structural similarities with pagan phenomena. We hear nothing of prayers or liturgical hymns that may have impressed pagans being recited and sung in public. The only steps that Paul took to mitigate the unbridgeable contrast between pagan religiosity and Christian faith were rhetorical in nature: He strove to take into account the categories of thought and the possibilities of linguistic expression of his listeners as he formulated his missionary sermons. The speech to the council of the Areopagus in Athens (see §28.3) is an impressive example.

The early medieval missionaries carried with them mobile altars, containers for consecrated oil and for sacrificial substances, crosses, pictorial representations of Christ on boards, relics and priestly garments. They often entered pagan territories with supplicatory processions during which hymns of confession, hymns of praise and petitions were sung.[115] They endeavored to use their appearance as a picture of the royal dignity and authority of Christ in the sense of a "realization of holiness." If there are certain initial correspondences between pagan religiosity and the Christian faith—the history-of-religions school never tires of pointing out such "parallels"—then Paul evidently made no strategic or methodological allowances for them.

7. The historical context of Old Testament and Second Temple traditions does not force us to expect that Paul would be at pains to consider the religious beliefs of his pagan listeners deliberately and extensively. Paul Wernle sug-

---

[112]Padberg 1995, 146-51. German medieval scholars use the term *Tatmission* (missionary work by actions); the term *Gewalttatmission* (missionary work by violent actions) would be more adequate.

[113]Michel, *Röm,* 131; Dunn, *Rom,*1:114-15. See Str-B 3:113-15.

[114]Käsemann, *Röm,* 66-67 (ET, 71); Wilckens, *Röm,* 1:150. Many commentators interpret this remark in terms of a metaphor: Paul accuses the Jews of robbing God of things that belong to him; see G. Schrenk, *ThWNT* 3:255-56 (*TDNT* 3:256); Cranfield, *Rom,*1:169-70; Fitzmyer, *Rom,* 318.

[115]Padberg 1995, 113-25; for the observations that follow above see ibid., 124-25.

gested that the apostle Paul lacked one of the primary "virtues" that a missionary needs for his or her "profession": an open-minded interest in "the world and the people." Wernle argues, "The colorful variety of countries and seas, and nations and cities passed him by almost without a trace. He divides all of humanity into two groups, Jews and Gentiles, and on the basis of language, the Gentiles perhaps into Greeks and barbarians. Further differences remain unacknowledged. He knows the Jews very well, because he is a Jew himself. The Gentiles, however, are a 'mass of perdition' that he never really became acquainted with. He had no firsthand knowledge of their state cult or of their mystery religions. What he writes about pagan vices in his Epistle to the Romans might be found in any Jewish reader: every Jew believed that pagans were capable of these things. He did not know the first thing about Greek philosophy; his indifference concerning the outside world was aggravated in these areas by the Jewish inhibitions concerning unclean contacts."[116] The following considerations will show that this viewpoint is a serious misjudgment of the historical reality of Paul's life and of the intellectual sophistication of his missionary theology.

Paul belonged to a tradition that had no "neutral" interest in the religion and the customs of non-Jews, a fact that explains why there are no objective descriptions of pagan religiosity in Jewish literature, with the exception, perhaps, of Philo, the Jewish philosopher of religion from Alexandria. Note the following facts. (a) The authors of the Old Testament know specific pagan deities and the practices linked with their cults—for example, the cult of Moloch, in which parents sacrificed sons and daughters, a cult that was practiced at the time of King Josiah in the Hinnom Valley outside Jerusalem.[117] Much more frequent, however, than such specific references are negative summary value judgments of pagan deities as *ʾelîlîm,* a term that sounds like *ʾelōhîm,* the standard epithet for "god," but is derived from the adjective *elîl* ("insignificant, trivial, empty") and therefore means "nonentities."[118] Other Hebrew terms used for pagan deities include *gĕlalîm* ("dung"),[119] *šiqqûz* ("abomination"),[120] *tôʿebâh* ("abomination"),[121] *hebel* ("idols, things that do not really exist"),[122] *šeqer* ("lie, illusion")[123] and *šāwʾ* ("what is worth-

---

[116]Wernle 1909, 6.

[117]Ex 13:2, 11-15; 22:9-30; 34:19-20; 2 Kings 17:31; 23:10; 2 Chron 28:3; 33:6; Ezek 20:26; on the Moloch cult in the Hinnom Valley see 2 Kings 23:10.

[118]Lev 19:4; 26:1; Deut 32:21; Ps 97:7; 115:4-7; 135:15-17; Is 2:8, 18, 20; 10:10, 11; 19:1, 3; 31:7; 41:29; 57:12; Jer 2:11; 5:7; 10:3; 16:20; 51:17-18; Hab 2:18. See *HALOT* 1:56; Preuss 1971.

[119]Jer 50:2; Ezek 22:3-4. See *HALOT* 1:194.

[120]Deut 29:16; 1 Kings 11:5, 7; 2 Kings 23:13, 24; Is 66:3; Jer 4:1; 7:30; 13:27; 16:18; 32:34; Ezek 5:11; 7:20; 11:18, 21; 20:7-8, 30; 37:23; 2 Chron 15:8. See *HALOT* 4:1646.

[121]Deut 32:16; 2 Kings 23:13; Is 44:19; Jer 16:18; Ezek 5:11. See *HALOT* 4:1703.

[122]Deut 32:21; 1 Kings 16:13, 26; 2 Kings 17:15; Ps 31:7; Jer 2:5; 8:19; 10:8, 14-15; 14:22; Jon 2:9. See *HALOT* 1:236.

[123]Is 44:20; Jer 10:14; 16:19. See *HALOT* 4:1649.

less").[124] In Deut 32:17 and Ps 95:5 LXX the pagan deities are identified with demons. Against the background of these traditions and in the context of the Old Testament convictions about YHWH, Paul would perceive no need to portray the details of pagan deities and cults. Paul postulates, as a Jew, that all non-Jews must believe in the one and only God, the creator of the heavens and the earth, and the Father of Abraham and of Israel, and he proclaims, as a follower of Jesus, that all non-Christians must believe in the one God and Father of Jesus Christ. In view of the early Christian belief in the exclusive salvific significance of God's revelation in Jesus Christ, finer distinctions among specific phenomena of pagan religiosity are hardly relevant. Generalized judgments do not reveal indifference on Paul's part regarding pagan religion but rather correspond to Old Testament and Jewish tradition.[125] (b) The later rabbinic texts do not display specific interest or knowledge of pagan cultic practices either. It seems that the rabbis who compiled the Mishnah and the Tosefta in Galilee took hardly any notice of pagan realities in the Decapolis and in the coastal cities. They basically ignored all non-Jews and all heretics.[126] (c) We must not overlook the fact that Roman authors do not manifest much interest in peoples living in territories beyond the control of Rome,[127] although many do provide detailed descriptions of various cults and cultic practices. (d) Luke localizes the missionary activity of Paul outside of Palestine generally in synagogues, which means that the question of the potential relevance of non-Jewish religious cults and phenomena seldom applies in the historical situations that he describes.[128]

8. Luke has no focused interest in describing contacts with Greco-Roman institutions. This may have political-tactical reasons. His composition of Acts has no primary political purpose e.g., in the sense of an apology for the movement of the *Christianoi*. When he describes contacts with Romans, he portrays them in general as positive. Luke also knows that aggressive attacks against polytheistic religious phenomena would hardly benefit the early Christian missionaries, which was probably the reason why they seem not to have engaged in open anti-pagan polemics in their missionary activities.[129] More important, however, are theological reasons.[130] Luke reports a confrontation between Paul and a pagan medium during Paul's missionary work in Philippi, but the exorcism of the demon functions mainly as exposition for the confrontation of the missionaries with the judicial authorities of Philippi, a situation in which Luke seems much

[124]Ps 31:7; Jon 2:9; Jer 18:15. See *HALOT* 4:1425.
[125]See Hanson 1985, 144-45.
[126]See M. Goodman 1996, 507-8; cf. the evidence presented in Hadas-Lebel 1979. On the discussion about the *minim* see §22.2 in the present work.
[127]Stroumsa 1996, 339.
[128]Löning 1985, 2628.
[129]Grant 1986, 22.
[130]For the remarks that follow above see Löning 1985, 2620-21, 2631-32.

more interested. In his narration of Paul's mission in Ephesus Luke relates another confrontation with pagan religiosity. We note that Luke passes over the priests of Artemis (assuming that they were involved in the events in the first place) and focuses on Demetrios the silversmith as an exponent of a guild that has only economic interests in the temple of Artemis. In his narration of the speech of the town clerk Luke shows a certain degree of respect for pagan religious institutions (Acts 19:35-36); he formulates not a theological but (implicitly) an ethical critique of the cult of Artemis. In his description of Paul's mission in Lystra and in Athens Luke focuses more extensively on the discussion of pagan religiosity. Some scholars speak of a "theoretical deficit"[131] when Luke portrays the polytheism of Lystra's population (Acts 14:8-18) as "a form of salvation-historical ignorance" and thus as obsolete, or when he labels, in Acts 17:16-34, the Epicurean and Stoic philosophers derisively as "intellectual snobs," speaking from a "disparaging distance," establishing a "certain continuity" between pagan religiosity and the Christian faith by poetry (Acts 17:28), institutionally independent of pagan religion, only to pour scorn on polytheism and all its concrete phenomena (Acts 17:16; cf. 17:24-25). For Luke, pagan religiosity is not a positive moral authority, and that is why he does not discuss it more extensively or more "objectively." The situation is different with regard to the Jewish faith and Jewish religious practices because of the salvation-historical continuity between the Jewish and the Christian faiths.[132]

9. We have seen[133] that Christian authors of the second century were independent of the literary traditions of their contemporaries in regard to foreign peoples, and that they could arrive at their own understanding of nations, as, for example, the people living in India. If this is true for Clement of Alexandria, it cannot be ruled out that Paul of Tarsus had a comparable interest in other religions and peoples. Guy Stroumsa argues that two factors were responsible for this interest in and openness to other peoples and their traditions among Christian theologians.[134] First, there is the religious "universalism" of the early Christians, their conviction that all nations were created by the one true God, the God of Israel and the Father of Jesus Christ, and that the human race therefore could be understood as a unity, as all people needed salvation. The second factor was the Christians' cultural "relativism," their distance from the literary and philosophical traditions of their time. At the same time Paul and the other early Christian missionaries were convinced that their main task was the proclamation of God's revelation in Jesus Christ, leading to the forgiveness of sin and to salvation. "Thus they were less interested in their past than in the process of

---

[131]Löning 1985, 2636; the quotations that follow above, ibid., 2632, 2633.
[132]Thus correctly Löning 1985, 2636.
[133]"The Geographical Perspective of the Apostles" in §16.2.
[134]Stroumsa 1996, esp. 340-41, 346-47, 354-58.

their transformation and in their new mode of being as Christians."[135] Further-more, we must remember that Paul passed dozens of pagan temples and statues of deities daily in Antioch and in Tarsus, in Philippi and in Athens, in Corinth and in Ephesus. He possessed a great deal more in-depth knowledge about the various deities and cults than do specialists in comparative religion in the twenty-first century. In Athens he "observed with sustained attention" (*theōrein* [Acts 17:16]; BDAG) the numerous images of deities in the city, he "looked care-fully" at their sanctuaries (*anatheōrein* [Acts 17:23]), he saw the altars, among them an altar with the dedication "To an unknown god" (Acts 17:23).

10. Paul focuses his analysis of the situation of the people to whom he pro-claims the gospel on the person and fate of Adam and on the person and fate of Jesus Christ. First, Paul asserts that what can be said about Adam can be said about all human beings.[136] Adam's life was ruined because he desired something that went beyond the life that God had given him, a desire that led to an act of disobedience against the explicit will of God; in the same way the human ego is marked by "all kinds of covetousness" (πᾶσαν ἐπιθυμίαν, *pasan epithymian*) that leads to death (Rom 7:8). Adam refused to acknowledge the goodness and the sovereignty of his Creator; similarly, humankind refuses to acknowledge the one true God (Rom 1:18-23). The consequences of this defiance become evident in the behavior of people: idol worship and immorality, manifold perversions and universal malice. Since Adam, all human beings have sinned as Adam sinned, and since sin rules over the human race, death has moved through all human generations (Rom 5:18-19; 1 Cor 15:21-22, 56).[137] The argument in Rom 1:18-32 and in Rom 2:1—3:20 (summarized in Rom 3:23) shows that Paul does not dis-tinguish between pagans who sin and Jews who sin. Paul's analysis is a theolog-ical analysis. This is evident not only in the content of the argument in Rom 1:18-23 but also in the fact that Paul substantiates his position with quotations from Scripture (Rom 3:10-18). At the same time his analysis is an anthropological and sociological one, as the details in Rom 1:24-32 and in Rom 2:1-11 demonstrate.

Second, Paul treats people always as "addressees of the gospel."[138] Paul had

---

[135]Padberg 1995, 32, formulated with regard to the early medieval missionaries, but equally rel-evant for the missionaries of the first century. Padberg demonstrates that the missionaries of the seventh and eighth centuries employed the verdicts on pagan religiosity found in the Old and New Testament, that they rarely commented on the situation of pagans before their con-version, that they mentioned pagan religious practices only summarily and stereotypically, that they hardly ever mentioned the names of pagan deities, that they did not interact with the content of pagan religiosity, and that they showed no interest in establishing constructive contacts in conversations about the Christian faith (ibid., 32-41).

[136]For the remarks that follow above see Barrett 1962, 1-21, esp. 19-20; see also Dunn 1998, 79-101.

[137]On the concept of sin in Paul's theology see recently Martin Karrer, "Sünde IV: Neues Testa-ment," *TRE* 32 (2001): 375-89, esp. 379-81.

[138]Eichholz 1972, 41; for the remarks that follow above see ibid., 41-48; quotation, 42; cf. Eich-holz 1959.

accepted God's call to proclaim the gospel to Jews and Gentiles. The gospel of Jesus Christ was the one reality that controlled both his life and his thinking. He knew himself to be so totally obligated to God and bound to proclaim the gospel that he was willing to become "all things to all people" in order to win them for Jesus Christ (1 Cor 9:19-23). In 1 Cor 1:18-31 Paul describes the gospel as "word of the cross" in terms of God's decision for all people. This implies that every human being receives his or her "profile" from the gospel. Paul "profiles" everybody in the context of the gospel. Georg Eichholz describes the gospel that Paul proclaims as the "apocalypse" of every human being: "The gospel defines human beings. It exposes them. Jews come to understand, in the light of God's action in Jesus Christ, the hopelessness of their existence before God, and non-Jews grasp that their lives are mortgaged to their guilt before God." As people encounter the gospel—rather, as the gospel encounters people—they are confronted with the decision to say yes or no to the gospel and thus to God's "decision" for the human race. The gospel is "God's power for salvation to everyone who believes" (Rom 1:16; cf. 1 Cor 1:18, 24). As a result, the decision that people make—their reaction to the gospel message—has eschatological and apocalyptic consequences.[139] The encounter between the gospel and people reveals that people have their distinctive presuppositions about God (1 Cor 1:22-25). These presuppositions differentiate humankind as Jews and pagans: Jews expect God to reveal himself in power and glory, whereas Greeks link the divine with wisdom. Despite such cultural and religious differences between Jews and Gentiles, Paul reduces all people to a common denominator: all people miss the reality of the one true God; neither pagans nor Jews can comprehend the reality of God as he has revealed himself in the cross of Jesus Christ. For Jews the cross is a stumbling block, while for pagans it is folly. But it is at the cross that God has revealed himself: at the cross God demonstrated his love for people, in Jesus Christ God spoke to humankind, in Jesus Christ God gave himself for people without demanding prior accomplishments. And it is exactly this fact that neither Jews nor pagans can understand. Jews expect that God effects salvation in visible displays of power, particularly in the messianic days when the righteous will be redeemed and the unrighteous will be judged. For Jews it is next to impossible to imagine that one can encounter God, the sovereign and invisible Creator of the world, in the weakness of the cross, that the cross is the triumph of God's grace. And Greeks can detect no wisdom in the human concreteness of the cross: the story of a crucified savior is a foolish, a pointless story. In other words, Paul asserts that people possess no hermeneutical parameters that enable them to grasp the reality of God. The cross of Jesus Christ, the center of Paul's theology, cannot be integrated into the presupposi-

---

[139]Eichholz 1972, 58; for the remarks that follow above see ibid., 58-60. For a critique of Rudolf Bultmann's anthropological hermeneutic see ibid., 44-48.

tions of human reasoning or reflection, whether Jewish, Greek or Roman. People come to know God only when they abandon their preconceived notions about God, when they relinquish their criteria and their standards for divine behavior and action, when they let God be God.

E. P. Sanders suggests that Paul argues from "solution to plight," that Paul's critique of pagan and of Jewish religion is not primarily an anthropological critique but a christological and soteriological critique. According to Sanders, Paul is convinced that God effected salvation in Jesus Christ for all people, for both pagans and for Jews, and this is why the law can no longer save, why all people, without any exception, are sinners.[140] "Since salvation is only in Christ, therefore all other ways toward salvation are wrong." In the context of the Jewish salvation-historical thinking of Paul, this analysis is helpful as far as Jews are concerned: Paul never abandoned the convictions that God revealed himself in Israel (cf. Rom 9:4-5), and that the law and its commandments are holy, just and good (Rom 7:12)—that is, God's own revelation (cf. *hagios/hagia*), which is always merciful (*dikaia*) and useful as well as practicable (*agathē*) for imperfect people. At the same time Paul shares the early Christian conviction that Jesus is the promised Messiah sent by God whose death and resurrection procure salvation, first and foremost for Israel, then also for pagans. This means that if God "now" (νῦν) effects salvation and righteousness—that is, forgiveness of sins and deliverance from judgment through the person and work of Jesus the Messiah—independently of the law (Rom 3:21-26), then salvation and righteousness can no longer be effected through sacrifices and other cultic practices in the temple. And this means that salvation no longer comes through keeping the law. With regard to Paul's view of pagan religiosity, however, the view of Sanders is flawed: pagans are sinners not because God's salvific revelation is now focused in an exclusive manner on Jesus Christ, all pagan cults thus being exposed as a mistaken way to find salvation. Rather, Paul is convinced, as are all Jews, that pagans have always been looking for salvation in the wrong places, since there is no salvation outside of Israel. Gentiles thus always had "a problem," a "plight" for which they had no solution. Paul evaluated pagan religiosity after his conversion no differently than before it: Gentiles live in "darkness" because they deny the reality of the one true God, who provides salvation only in Israel. They can find salvation "now," in the days of the Messiah, not through integration into the nation of Israel by circumcision and obedience to the commandments of the Mosaic law but rather, in keeping with the prophets' prediction of the coming of the nations to Zion in the last days, through reconciliation with the one true God, made possible by God himself on account of faith in Jesus, the crucified Messiah who rose from the dead.

---

[140]E. P. Sanders 1977, 442-511; the quotation that follows above, 482; followed more recently by Donaldson 1997, 107-64.

11. Paul, missionary and theologian, provides in Rom 1:18-32 a fundamental description of pagans.[141]

Rom 1:18-32: "For the wrath of God is revealed from heaven against all ungodliness and wickedness of those who by their wickedness suppress the truth. [19]For what can be known about God is plain to them, because God has shown it to them. [20]Ever since the creation of the world his eternal power and divine nature, invisible though they are, have been understood and seen through the things he has made. So they are without excuse; [21]for though they knew God, they did not honor him as God or give thanks to him, but they became futile in their thinking, and their senseless minds were darkened. [22]Claiming to be wise, they became fools; [23]and they exchanged the glory of the immortal God for images resembling a mortal human being or birds or four-footed animals or reptiles. [24]Therefore God gave them up in the lusts of their hearts to impurity, to the degrading of their bodies among themselves, [25]because they exchanged the truth about God for a lie and worshiped and served the creature rather than the Creator, who is blessed forever! Amen. [26]For this reason God gave them up to degrading passions. Their women exchanged natural intercourse for unnatural, [27]and in the same way also the men, giving up natural intercourse with women, were consumed with passion for one another. Men committed shameless acts with men and received in their own persons the due penalty for their error. [28]And since they did not see fit to acknowledge God, God gave them up to a debased mind and to things that should not be done. [29]They were filled with every kind of wickedness, evil, covetousness, malice. Full of envy, murder, strife, deceit, craftiness, they are gossips, [30]slanderers, God-haters, insolent, haughty, boastful, inventors of evil, rebellious toward parents, [31]foolish, faithless, heartless, ruthless. [32]They know God's decree, that those who practice such things deserve to die—yet they not only do them but even applaud others who practice them."

Paul emphasizes in this long section several fundamental convictions about non-Jews. (a) Pagans know the truth—that is, the rightful claims of God the Creator—but they suppress the truth and the reality of God (Rom 1:18). (b) God has revealed to all people the truth and the reality of his being, everything that "can be known about God" (Rom 1:19). (c) The invisible attributes of God can be contemplated by rational perception. God has revealed himself, since the beginning of creation, in his works and actions in creation and in history, and thus he has given to humankind the possibility of clearly perceiving him (Rom 1:20).[142] (d) The pagans have refused to acknowledge God as the Creator, they have not given him thanks for his blessings (Rom 1:21a); rather, they have worshiped mute idols instead of the living God (Rom 1:23; cf. 1 Cor 12:2). Paul follows Old Testament and Jewish tradition in applying the first commandment of the Decalogue as a basic criterion for critically reviewing pagan religiosity: there is no God beside YHWH, who is both the Creator and the Father of Jesus Christ.[143]

---

[141]See the commentaries; also Bussmann 1971, 109-23; Pak 1991, 27-78; Ndyabahika 1993; for connections between Rom 1:18-32 and the modern missionary experience see Walls 1970.

[142]See Michel, *Röm,* 99-101.

[143]U. Heckel 1994, 283, with reference to 1 Thess 1:9; 4:5; 1 Cor 12:2; 8:4-6.

Ulrich Heckel suggests that Paul's reference to the "mute idols" (1 Cor 12:2) is a "polemical distortion of the historical realities."[144] This critique is unfounded. The "significance of ecstasy in the Greek, but also in the ancient Near Eastern, world" has not turned mute idols into deities that speak; a more plausible parallel is oracles through which people believed they could hear gods speak. Paul joined the prophets of the Old Testament and the rabbis of the Jewish tradition in refusing to interpret such "speech" of pagan deities as the voice of the true and living God. When Paul refers to idols as mute gods, he does not provide a historical or religious-psychological analysis; rather, he adopts the verdict of Scripture concerning the illusion of pagan gods as nonentities. Seen from a "neutral" academic perspective, this verdict may be called "polemical," but surely it is not a "distortion of historical realities," unless Heckel believes that Apollo or Isis existed, historically, as deities who spoke.

(e) As a result, the life of pagans turned meaningless and aimless. Their thinking, indeed the center of their personality can be described as "darkness": their "heart" (kardia), the seat of reasoning (nous), of thought and will, has become dark because they did not allow their thinking to be illuminated by the light of God's self-revelation (Rom 1:21b). (f) The pagans claim to be wise, without recognizing that they have become fools (Rom 1:22), particularly through their claim that they could be wise apart from the revelation of the one true God, who created the world. (g) In their refusal to acknowledge the presence of God's reality with its "atmosphere of radiating light and power,"[145] and in their refusal to participate in God's glory as the "image of God," the pagans turned this glory "into the likeness of an image of his creatures" and accepted the transient nothingness of idol images that depict people and animals (Rom 1:23). This argument agrees with a broad biblical and Jewish tradition.[146] Paul puts this more precisely in Rom 1:25: the pagans worship "the creature" rather than the one true God, the Creator of the heavens and the earth. Did Paul know that statues of deities were not the object of worship proper, at least in theory, but that they represented dedicatory gifts and symbolic representations? Porphyrius, the last great defender of pagan religiosity, who hailed from Tarsus, attacked the "surprisingly ignorant" (ἀμαθεστάτους, amathestatous) people who were unaware of this difference.[147] Paul does not discuss this objection explicitly; presumably, he would argue with reference to God's invisibility, glory and immortality (cf. Rom 1:20, 23).[148] We do not know whether he would have used the argument, later employed by Athenagoras, Origen, Eusebius, Athanasius and other theologians, that although educated pagans may be aware of this difference, the vast majority of idol worshipers are not.[149] This is not impossible, since

---

[144]U. Heckel 1994, 283; for the remarks that follow above see ibid.

[145]Wilckens, Röm, 1:107; for the remark that follows above see ibid., 107-8.

[146]Ps 106:20 LXX; Jer 2:11; Is 44:9-20; Wis 11:15; 12:24; 13:10-14; 14:8; 15:18-19.

[147]Porphyrius, Peri agalmaton 1; see further Celsus, in Origen, Cels. 7.62.

[148]Dunn, Rom, 1:63.

[149]Hanson 1985, 147.

Paul knew—vastly better than we do today—from constant personal observation the views, motivations and feelings of the people "in the street" in Tarsus, Perge, Corinth and Ephesus. (h) The life of pagans in its specific ethical and social reality is the consequence of this rebellion against the truth of God, who continues to be present in his creation as he judges the Gentiles (cf. the phrase *dio paredōken autous,* "therefore God gave them up," in Rom 1:24, 26, 28). God's wrath and the self-destruction of men and women are closely connected: "Men and women pay for their perversion of the truth of God, and the community and fellowship of people suffers as well."[150] (i) Pagans live their lives in sinful contradiction to nature (Rom 1:24-27): because they worship the form of self-produced images instead of the one true God in his invisible but recognizable glory (Rom 1:25), their bodies are robbed of honor through disgraceful passions (*pathē atimias* [Rom 1:26a]); this becomes evident in homosexual behavior, which exchanges the divine order for a self-imposed and unnatural one (Rom 1:26b, 27).

Jewish tradition regarded immorality as the most serious vice as well.[151] In lists of moral misdemeanors, Paul often mentions immorality first.[152] The harsh indictment of immorality in the biblical tradition is influenced by several factors: the notion of clean and unclean; the prohibition of mixed marriages between Israelites or Jews and polytheists; the demarcation from Canaanite fertility cults, which often were sexually permissive; the comparison of idolatry and of apostasy from YHWH with adultery.

(j) The reasoning of the pagans lacks norms and moderation (*adokimos nous*) because they exclude God from everyday life.[153] They are no longer able to distinguish between right and wrong, and thus by necessity they do "things that should not be done" (Rom 1:28). Everything becomes possible, and they do not even recognize that they destroy themselves.[154] God allowed the pagans to leave the restricted area protected by his good and perfect will and gave them up to their self-chosen desires. This can be observed in countless specific modes of behavior: injustice and wickedness, greed and corruption, envy and murder and strife and deceit and craftiness, gossip and slander, hatred of God and arrogance, pride and smugness, in ever new inventions of evil, disobedience of parents, foolishness and instability, heartlessness and mercilessness, and in the active support of all these vices (Rom 1:19-32). Peter characterizes a similar enumeration with the phrase "what the Gentiles like to do" (*boulēma tōn ethnōn* [1 Pet 4:3]).

---

[150]Michel, *Röm,* 104. On the structure of Rom 1:18-32 see Dunn, *Rom,* 1:53.
[151]See S. Erlandsson, *ThWAT* 2:612-19 (*TDOT* 4:99-104); Str-B 3:64-74; Dabelstein 1981, 53-55; U. Heckel 1994, 284-85; for the remarks that follow above see ibid.
[152]Rom 1:24-27; 1 Cor 5:10, 11; 6:9, 10; 10:8; 2 Cor 12:21; Gal 5:19; 1 Thess 4:3; Eph 5:3; Col 3:5; cf. 1 Tim 3:2.
[153]Michel, *Röm,* 106.
[154]Note N. T. Wright 1997, 89: Paul "saw paganism as a self-destructive mode of being human."

The Greek tradition knows similar lists of vices, particularly the Stoic philosophical-ethical tradition.[155] However, the numerous parallels in both the Old Testament tradition[156] and the Jewish traditions,[157] and the important tradition of the "two-way motif" in Deut 27—30, as well as the numerous New Testament parallels[158] make it highly unlikely that Paul borrowed his evaluation of immoral behavior from Greek tradition. Detailed studies on the ethics of Paul have shown that he follows Old Testament structures, as is clearly seen in, for example, his conviction that identity determines, or should determine, behavior.[159] Neither the "virtues" that Paul lists in other passages nor the "vices" that he attacks are autonomous actions of a person that could be characterized as his or her "virtues" or "vices"; rather, they are specific signs, concrete evidence, consequences of the power of the "flesh" in the case of vices and of the power of the Holy Spirit in the case of virtues.[160]

The list of vices demonstrates that Paul (and other early Christian theologians) endorsed a very critical diagnosis of the values, ideologies and ways of life of their pagan contemporaries.[161] The "provisional value of paganism" that some scholars see is hardly a prominent feature of Rom 1.[162] The negative assessment of pagan life, thought and spirituality explains the rarity of positive or neutral statements about pagans or pagan society. We find such positive statements exclusively in ethical contexts where Paul reminds the church, constructively, of social norms for proper behavior (see below). It is unwarranted, however, to accuse Paul of a selective perception of reality that prompts the missionary "to describe only those impressions of pagans that make Christianity appear all the more radiant."[163] Two facts argue against such a charge. First, Paul can describe the behavior of Christians in rather negative terms as well. Second, Paul, as a missionary, does not engage in a dialogue with pagans about religious convic-

---

[155]Plato, *Gorg.* 525; *Resp.* 4.441c; Musonius, *Frag.* 16; Cicero, *Tusc.* 4.11-27; Epictetus, *Diss.* 3.1.24-35; 3.20.5-6; Diogenes Laertius 7.87, 92-93, 110-112; Horace, *Epod.* 1.1.33-40.

[156]Ex 20—21; 34:14-26; Lev 19; Deut 27:15-26; Hos 4:1-2.

[157]Wis 14:25-26; 4 Macc 1:26-27; 2:15; *T. Reu.* 3:3-6; *T. Levi* 14:5-8; 17:11; *T. Jud.* 16:1; *2 En.* 10:4-5; *3 Bar.* 8:5; 13:4; Philo, *Sacr.* 32 (with 149 items!); *As. Mos.* 7:4-7; *Jub.* 21:21; *Sib. Or.* 3:36-40; 1QS IV, 9-11.

[158]Mk 7:21-22; Rom 13:13; 1 Cor 5:10-11; 6:9-10; 2 Cor 12:20-21; Gal 5:19-21; Eph 4:31; 5:3-4; Col 3:5, 8; 1 Tim 1:9-10; 2 Tim 3:2-5; Tit 3:3; 1 Pet 4:3; Rev 22:15.

[159]Rosner 1994, 121, as a conclusion of his incisive study of 1 Cor 5—7 (ibid., 61-121). Cf. Käsemann (*Röm*, 46 [ET, 50]), who also is critical of a derivation of Paul's critique of pagan behavior in Rom 1 from Stoic philosophy.

[160]Martyn (*Gal*, 496, 532), who rejects the term "catalogue of vices/virtues."

[161]Söding 1990b, 147.

[162]Contra Wildhaber 1987, 162-63. N. T. Wright (1997, 81) finds in Paul "a radical and deep-rooted affirmation of the goodness of the created world," a statement that he does not link with paganism directly. In view of the radical manner in which Paul regards the world and humanity as *hamartōlos*, "sinful"—creation itself is waiting for salvation (Rom 8:18-22)—Wright's assessment is overly positive.

[163]Padberg 1995, 36, with regard to early medieval missionaries; he notes, however, that the authors of the medieval biographies (*vitae*) of missionaries did not aim at discriminating against paganism per se; rather, they sought to follow biblical guidelines (ibid., 37).

tions, sentiments and practices;[164] rather, he seeks to help pagan men and women find personal, existential liberation from servitude to false gods and come to faith in the one true God and Father of Jesus Christ, who alone can forgive their sins.

Kathy Gaca asserts that Paul adopted and reformulated in Rom 1:18-32 the Hellenistic-Jewish polemic against the ignorance of the pagans, who believe in a plurality of deities despite the fact that the majesty and the power of the Creator is apparent in creation.[165] Gaca argues that Paul does not treat pagans as religious outsiders who do not understand the argument from creation for the existence of God; rather, he regards pagans as people who know God's revelation in the works of creation but who suppress this knowledge. The pagans are blind; indeed they are apostates, rebels against the true God, whom they have deserted.[166] Gaca suggests that Paul's discussion of the "status" of Greek and other polytheistic cultures in Rom 1:18-32 led, in the argumentation of Tatian, Clement, Origen, Athanasius, Augustine, Gregory of Nazianzus and John Chrysostom at the end of the second century, to an antipagan polemic that argued for a ban on non-Christian cults and practices. It is easy to agree, at least from a modern democratic perspective, that the administrative prohibitions against pagan cults by Christian emperors in the late fourth century were problematic: the Christian faith spreads as a result of its inherent power of conviction, not as a result of force. At the same time we should note the following three points. (*i*) The Christians of the first centuries were not interested in entertaining good "pagan-Christian" relations as some kind of ecumenical dialogue. Rather, they wanted to convert pagans to faith in Jesus Christ because they were convinced that this was the only way for them to find forgiveness for their sins and to have eternal life. We must remember that the Christian critique of pagan religiosity in the second and third centuries was so radical that pagans accused Christians of "atheism." And the Christian critique did not stop short of the cult(s) of the Roman emperors. Christians of the first centuries were willing to sacrifice their lives for these convictions. (*ii*) The argumentation of Paul in Rom 1:18-32 differs little from the argumentation in, for example, Wis 13—14 in regard to the current "status" of pagans before God: they serve nameless and lifeless idols, which is "the beginning and cause and end of every evil" (Wis 14:27); God's punishment will fall upon them "because they thought wickedly of God in devoting themselves to idols, and because in deceit they swore unrighteously through contempt for holiness" (Wis 14:30). (*iii*) Paul's argument in Rom 1:18-32 does not justify an administrative ban on pagan practices, since he does not plead for a prohibition of the Jewish faith in Rom 2:1-29. Finally, we should note that the main point of Rom 1:19-20 is not God's "active revelation" to humankind[167] but rather the determination that people have no excuse when they face God's judgment, since they have defied God's self-revelation in their thinking and their actions.[168]

Paul does not want to unmask people who worship pagan deities as dangerous

---

[164]See Marshall 1992b, 37-42.
[165]See Wis 13:1-14:31; Josephus, *C. Ap.* 2.250-254; Philo, *Spec.* 1.15; *Opif.* 45; *Ebr.* 45; *Sib. Or.* 3:669-70, 207-208, 300-362.
[166]Gaca 1999, 165-98, esp. 171-72, 196.
[167]Contra Gaca 1999, 172, 196.
[168]See Wilckens, *Röm,* 1:105.

rebels against whom one should take action. Nevertheless, there is no doubt that Paul explains the polytheistic cults of the Greco-Roman world not only as the religious ignorance of the "Greeks and barbarians" but also with reference to a deliberate rebellion against God that leads not only to the worship of idols but also to immoral behavior. In Rom 5:12-21 Paul links the sin of humankind with the sin of Adam: the latter cannot be explained with ignorance, since it consisted of deliberate disobedience against his better judgment. If Paul indeed adopts the Hellenistic-Jewish argument about the ignorance of the pagans, intensifying it in terms of an argument about rebellion and apostasy, he takes up an important topos of Old Testament tradition. At the same time he takes seriously the person and the actions of the individual pagan: everyone, the pagan included, is responsible for his or her actions. Paul's conclusion that "all" have sinned is, however, clearly not the result of his anthropology and not simply a development of the Jewish axiom of God's impartiality; rather, it is the result of his conviction that "righteousness" comes only through faith in Jesus Christ (Rom 3:21-26).[169]

In Eph 2:1-3 Paul describes pagan society as an abysmal "space that is controlled by powers and principalities."[170]

Eph 2:1-3: "You were dead through the trespasses and sins [2]in which you once lived, following the course of this world, following the ruler of the power of the air, the spirit that is now at work among those who are disobedient. [3]All of us once lived among them in the passions of our flesh, following the desires of flesh and senses, and we were by nature children of wrath, like everyone else."

The terms that Paul uses to describe non-Jews[171]—"unjust" (adikos), "unbelieving" (apistos), "nations, Gentiles, polytheists" (ethnē), "uncircumcised, Gentiles" (akrobystia)—imply various negative connotations: lawlessness, sin, unbelief, hostility against God, idolatry, moral dereliction, nonmembership in the people of God. At the same time Paul uses the terms adikos and apistos for Jews as well, Jews who refuse to accept Jesus as the Messiah. Thus these terms express a theological verdict. The terms "uncircumcised/circumcised," "Jew/Greek" and "Israel/nations" are connected with the ethnic-religious criterion that Jews traditionally used to classify people. Paul, however, evens out these contrasts: polytheists become "children of Abraham" when they believe in Jesus Christ, and Jews lose the status of "true children of Abraham" when they refuse to believe in Jesus Christ as the Messiah. As apostle to the nations, Paul demonstrates again and again how Old Testament pronouncements of salvation for Israel become

---

[169]See Wilckens, Röm, 1:92; Perkins 1986, 372.

[170]G. Lohfink 1982, 167.

[171]For the analysis that follows above see Dabelstein 1981, 15-39, 40-60; see also U. Heckel 1994, 270-74.

pronouncements of salvation for pagans if and when they come to faith in Jesus Christ. The terms "Greek" and "barbarian" are not described negatively, apart from lack of faith in Jesus Christ,[172] although both "Greeks" and "barbarians" belong, of course, to the *ethnē* and thus are part of the "old aeon."

Gerald Downing argues that Paul and his coworkers offered the gospel as "fulfillment" of important ideals of Cynic popular philosophy when they preached before pagans, particularly before audiences that had little or no contact with the synagogue.[173] Downing claims that assertions such as Gal 3:28—"There is no longer Jew or Greek, there is no longer slave or free, there is no longer male and female," with the conclusion "for all of you are one in Christ Jesus"—reminded pagan listeners in Galatia of the Cynic vision of a society in which all people are *kosmopolitai* (κοσμοπολῖται), "citizens of the world," a society in which ethnic differences are as irrelevant[174] as the differences between freeborn and slave[175] or between men and women.[176] Downing asserts that the "formula" in Gal 3:28 would have had more than Cynic overtones in the missionary proclamation of Paul: the apostle assembled people around a crucified and risen Jew, Jesus, and there were allusions to Jewish convictions as well.[177] But he believes that Paul's listeners must have understood the break with social conventions asserted in Gal 3:28, which pagan audiences must have heard, not simply as a vision but as a specific way of life, as some kind of Cynic philosophy. Despite possible parallels with Cynic convictions and lifestyles, Downing's reconstruction of a more-or-less deliberate missionary tactic of Paul seems implausible. The following facts are important. (*i*) The suggestion that Gal 3:28 played a role in Paul's missionary proclamation in pioneer situations remains unproven. (*ii*) Paul's assertion in Gal 3:28 does not represent a break with all social conventions. His exhortations for slaves (1 Cor 7:21-22; Col 3:22-25) show that slaves who came to faith in Jesus Christ remained slaves in their everyday lives; his exhortations for women (1 Cor 14:34; Col 3:18; Eph 5:22-24) assert that converted wives should continue to be obedient to their husbands. (*iii*) Paul expected a radical break with traditional conventions only with regard to the distinction between Jews and non-Jews, with the Jews being primarily affected by Paul's position, while there would have been no change or, if the regulations of the apostolic decree from Acts 15 applied, very little change for non-Jews in regard to their relationship with Jews. In other words, the first coupling in Gal 3:28 is not so much a "promise" for non-Jews as it is a "threat" for Jews. (*iv*) In regard to the alleged allusions to the vision and the praxis of the Cynics, Paul's Greek audience would hardly have been reminded of specific Cynic communities in which one could find a new identity. The Cynic vision of an ideal society was far removed from the reality of the early Christian communities.

The picture that arises from Paul's letters is confirmed by the Pauline speeches

---

[172]Whether this proves that Paul was "open" to Hellenistic culture, as Dabelstein (1981, 39) suggests, is another matter.

[173]Downing 1996, esp. 457-62; see also Malherbe 1987, 8.

[174]Diogenes Laertius 6.63; cf. 6.1; Lucian, *Demon.* 34; Pseudo-Anacharsis 2; Pseudo-Diogenes 7; Dio Chrysostom, *Or.* 10.4-6; 9.1.

[175]Diogenes Laertius 6.74-75; Pseudo-Crates 34; Dio Chrysostom, *Or.* 14.10; 15.32; Lucian, *Hermot.* 24.

[176]Pseudo-Crates 29; Diogenes Laertius 6.12; Musonius 3.

[177]Downing 1996, 461.

in Acts.[178] Paul asserts that while Israel, as God's people, possesses a history in which God intervened directly and visibly (Acts 13:16-25; cf. 7:2-53), the history of the nations is almost entirely "empty." God has not intervened in their history: "he allowed all the nations to follow their own ways" (Acts 14:16).[179] At the same time "he has not left himself without a witness" (οὐκ ἀμάρτυρον, *ouk amartyron*): he did good, "giving you rains from heaven and fruitful seasons, and filling you with food and your hearts with joy" (Acts 14:17). Paul asserts, similarly, in Acts 17:24-29 that God has created everything in the world (Acts 17:24); he gives "to all mortals life and breath and all things" (Acts 17:25); he made from Adam all nations and gave them territories to live in, seasons and geographical boundaries (Acts 17:26); he is not far from anybody (Acts 17:27), because all people live "in him" (Acts 17:28) and are his offspring (Acts 17:29). But the nations have not accepted this testimony from God, thus their history is essentially a history of idolatry (Acts 14:15; 17:24-25: 29) and ignorance (Acts 17:30). The nations do not know the Creator, because they have no promises.

The generally negative, sometimes even polemical, characterization of the pagans is, however, never turned against specific persons. The apostle to the nations does not give the people whom he seeks to reach with the good news of Jesus Christ a dressing-down. This is also seen in the fact that Paul "no longer uses the traditional subjects of the Jewish polemic against pagans in order to achieve an external segregation from pagan neighbors; rather, he uses it to address grievances within the Christian community."[180] The vice lists are no "pagan code" (*Heidenspiegel*); they are aimed not against pagans but against crass sinners in the church.

12. Paul's discussion of the Corinthian Christians' (mis)understanding of the Lord's Supper possibly indicates his knowledge of pagan mystery cults and his ability and willingness to critically engage their religious ideology.[181] Phenomenologically, the celebration of the Lord's Supper and the meals of some mystery religions indeed share some analogies: when Christians eat bread that has been broken and drink from the cup of blessing, they have "fellowship" with the body and blood of Christ, they make themselves aware of the reality of the presence of Jesus Christ; in the celebrations of the mystery cults the initiated dine in the "presence" of the deity. In both situations the celebrants remind themselves of the origins of faith and identity, seeking to release the salvific power that is

---

[178]For the remarks that follow above see Jervell 1991, 17; and especially Stenschke 1999a, 166-230.

[179]Acts 14:16: πάντα τὰ ἔθνη πορεύεσθαι ταῖς ὁδοῖς αὐτῶν.

[180]Heckel 1994, 293; cf. ibid., 285-86, with reference to 1 Cor 5:1-13; for the remark that follows above see ibid., 287, with Dabelstein 1981, 85, contra Conzelmann, *1 Kor,* 128; Lang, *Kor,* 75.

[181]For the discussion that follows above see Söding 1990a. On the mystery cults see §18.4 in the present work. For a corresponding discussion by Clement of Alexandria, Tertullian, Arnobius and Eusebius see Hanson 1985, 166-70.

connected with the mythic origins. If Christians are open to influences of the rites and the thinking of the mystery cults as a result of such similarities, they may easily be tempted to understand participation in the Lord's Supper as a means of becoming immune against all religious temptation, believing that eating the eucharistic elements is the only thing relevant for salvation, with the result that love for brother and sister becomes secondary and is degraded to being simply one of many options.[182] Thomas Söding defines sacraments, in terms of their central characteristic, as "actions and objects, originally belonging to the realm of the profane, that refer, in the context of a hierophany, a self-manifestation of the divine (like symbols) to the realm of transcendent holiness and, more importantly, that convey at the same time, and effectively, the power of the transcendent, thus regenerating human (and cosmic) life." If we accept this definition, it is possible to speak of sacramentalistic tendencies in the Corinthian church that were influenced directly or indirectly by convictions of the Hellenistic mystery cults. When Paul speaks of the "communion" or "association" (*koinōnia*) with the crucified and risen Lord in 1 Cor 10:16, he uses a key term of the mystery religions.[183] However, he understands *koinōnia* differently: the Lord's Supper, celebrated by Christians, is not concerned with "deification" that secures immortality; rather, it aims at "strengthening believers through the Spirit in their fellowship with the risen and crucified Lord, confirming their participation in his theocentricity and pro-existence, and introducing them into right relationship with God, with one another and with other people." The Lord's Supper does not represent "the repeated realization of a transhistorical, holy and elemental event"; rather, it is the work of God's Spirit, who "actualizes the form-giving origin in the historical event of the ministry and the self-sacrifice of Jesus, brought to universal salvific effectiveness through the resurrection of the crucified Lord by its transforming power." Paul exhorts the Corinthian Christians in this context not to become "companions [*koinōnous*] of demons" (1 Cor 10:20); that is, he asserts that Christians cannot participate in cultic communal meals in pagan temples. Paul does not declare pagan cults "rationalistically as a figment of the mind and hocus-pocus,"[184] he does not simply demythologize and criticize pagan myths,[185] but rather he points to the danger of falling into the controlling domination of demonic powers.[186]

Thomas Söding suggests that Paul seeks to express "the salvific event of the Lord's Supper in language that originally belongs to the mystery cults," motivated by missionary con-

---

[182]Söding 1990a, 144 with n. 12; for the definition of sacrament that follows above see ibid., 143.

[183]See Klauck 1986, 260-61; Söding 1990a, 142; the quotations that follow above, ibid., 144-45. See also N. T. Wright 1997, 87-88.

[184]Correctly Schrage, *1 Kor,* 2:445.

[185]Thus Söding 1990a, 144.

[186]Schrage, *1 Kor,* 2:445-46.

cerns for pagan audiences, in order to help them understand "on the basis of their own religious traditions" the Lord's Supper of the Christian community before he teaches them the truth about the promise that the mystery cults held forward.[187] This suggestion is unlikely: the language in 1 Cor 10:16 is thoroughly Jewish and Jewish Christian, and *koinōnia* is a characteristic Pauline expression,[188] which, however, does not rule out a polemical interaction with Hellenistic convictions.

We do not know whether Paul explained all pagan religious phenomena in terms of demonic activity, as did Clement of Alexandria in the second century, Origen in the third century and other church fathers since, who adopted the Greek notion of *daimones* in their philosophy of religion while at the same time identifying demons, without exception, as evil.[189]

13. The encounter with Jewish audiences during Paul's first missionary contacts that generally took place in the local synagogues was initially unproblematic. Jewish teachers—particularly teachers with a rabbinic education and presumably primarily teachers who had studied in Jerusalem—had the opportunity in the synagogues of the Diaspora to preach on scriptural texts (see "Missionary Work in Synagogues" in §28.1). Since there were no comparable models for traveling missionaries in Second Temple Judaism, the one notable factor concerning Paul was that he was a Jewish teacher who visited synagogues in the Diaspora with the goal of convincing Jews of the truth of his teaching without having been sanctioned by the the Sanhedrin in Jerusalem. The Jews presumably were surprised about the missionaries' initiative and personal commitment. There is evidence for this regarding Peter's teaching activity in Jerusalem: the members of the Sanhedrin were astonished that these followers of Jesus, who did not have rabbinic training and who did not belong to the Jewish elite, had the courage to defend themselves and to proclaim their convictions with boldness (Acts 4:13). The fact that Jewish teachers championed divergent doctrines was not a fundamentally novel experience for the missionaries' audiences: the Jewish exegesis of the Second Temple Period was accustomed to a difference of opinions, and the discourse of the rabbis proceeded in controversial discussions.

Paul's Jewish listeners must have regarded at least four aspects of his teaching as extraordinary: (a) his conviction that the long-awaited Messiah had arrived, fulfilling the prophets' promises of salvation; (b) his message that Jesus the Messiah had been sentenced to death on the cross, that he died and that he rose from the dead; (c) his assertion that faith in Jesus the Messiah is now the only valid condition and criterion for receiving God's forgiveness of sins and redemption in the last judgment; (d) his emphasis that the messianic era of salva-

---

[187]Söding 1990a, 144, 145.
[188]See Thiselton, *1 Cor,* 757; Schrage, *1 Kor,* 2:431-32.
[189]Clement, *Protr.* 2.10.1-41.4; 3.42.1-43.4; 4.55.5-56.1; 10.103.2; Origen, *Cels.* 3.24-33. See Hanson 1985, 164-66.

tion had dawned and that Gentiles therefore come to faith in Israel's God and are incorporated into God's people without being circumcised and without keeping the purity and food laws of the Torah because they believe in Jesus the Savior.

The first two points provided good topics for robust discussion. The third point put into question the Jewish listeners' status as God's elect people who enjoy God's holy presence that forgives sins, and it was utterly astounding because it tied divine salvation to a human being—here everything depended on the question of whether Jesus was indeed the Messiah as the heavenly Son of Man and Son of God. The fourth point jolted the centuries-old social structure of the Jewish people: the notion that God granted individual pagans salvation is not surprising in view of God's sovereign grace extended to Gentiles in Israel's history—an argument that Paul made in his sermon in the synagogue in Antiocheia (Acts 13:17-19). However, the missionaries' conviction that the crucified Jesus of Nazareth was the Messiah and that faith in this crucified Messiah is necessary for salvation was utterly startling, indeed bizarre for Jewish audiences in the synagogues. Jews regarded this message as scandalous (*skandalon* [1 Cor 1:23]). This emphasis, as well as the missionaries' teaching that pagans who believe in Jesus the Messiah are incorporated into God's people without circumcision, repeatedly provoked massive disagreement that disturbed the communication process and eventually caused the interruption and the breaking off of contact. The message of the missionaries that God's messianic revelation and salvation take place no longer along the traditional fault-line between Jews and Gentiles but rather within both Jews and Gentiles was extraordinary indeed.[190]

The patterns of reaction that Luke reports in the book of Acts cover the entire range from neutral listening to positive acceptance to emphatic rejection.[191] For Paul's missionary work in Pisidian Antiocheia, Luke reports in elaborate detail the whole range of reactions (Acts 13:42-50). In other passages his account is more summary.

1. Synagogue officials ask Paul to return on the following sabbath to explain his message further:
    Antiocheia (Acts 13:42); Thessalonike (Acts 17:2); Beroea (Acts 17:11); Corinth (Acts 18:4); Ephesus (Acts 19:8); also in Rome (Acts 28:17-23)

2. The Jewish king acknowledges the persuasive power of Paul's missionary sermon and affirms that Paul and his message are not politically dangerous:
    Herod Agrippa II in Caesarea (Acts 26:28, 32)

3. Jews are affected by the miracles that happen in the ministry of the missionaries:
    Ephesus (Acts 19:17)

---

[190]See Stenschke 1999a, 287.
[191]Note the literary analysis in Tyson 1992, 132-45; see extensively Setzer 1994, 44-82.

4. Jews accept the message that Paul preaches and come to faith in Jesus the Messiah of Israel, including (sometimes) rulers of synagogues:
Antiocheia (Acts 13:43); Iconium (Acts14:1); Derbe (Acts14:21); Thessalonike (Acts 17:4); Beroea (Acts 17:12); Corinth (Acts 18:4); Rome (Acts 28:24); Crispus in Corinth (Acts 18:8)

5. Jews are jealous because of Paul's success, because the influence of the Jewish followers of Jesus grows and because the converted Gentiles joined the missionaries:
Jerusalem (Acts 5:17); Antiocheia (Acts 13:45); Thessalonike (Acts 17:5)[192]

6. Jews contradict Paul, they initiate a controversy in the synagogue, articulating opposing viewpoints:
Antiocheia (Acts 13:45); Corinth (Acts 18:6); Ephesus (Acts 19:9); Rome (Acts 28:24)

7. Jews utter blasphemies, probably against Jesus, presumably pronouncing the curse of the Torah (Deut 21:22-23) upon the crucified Jesus:[193]
Antiocheia (Acts 13:45); Corinth (Acts 18:6)

8. Jews in Diaspora synagogues incite the Gentile population of the city, sometimes officials of the magistrate, and initiate a persecution:
Antiocheia (Acts 13:50); Lystra (Acts 14:19); Iconium (Acts 14:5); Thessalonike (Acts 17:5-8, 13)

9. Jews in Diaspora synagogues accuse the missionaries, sometimes together with the Gentile citizens, of activities hostile to the state:
Thessalonike (Acts 17:6-7); Corinth (Acts 18:12-13)

10. The actions that some Jews instigate with the help of Gentile citizens lead in five cases to the missionaries being flogged (2 Cor 11:24), in one case to stoning,[194] and repeatedly to narrow escapes (2 Cor 11:26):
Antiocheia (Acts 13:50); Lystra (stoning: Acts 14:19; 2 Cor 11:25); Iconium (Acts 14:2, 5-6)

11. Jews accuse Paul before the tribunal of a Roman governor of inciting the citizenry to rebellion against the civil authorities (*seditio*) and of profaning temples:
Jerusalem/Caesarea (Acts 24:5-6; 25:7)

12. Jews want to kill Paul:
Jerusalem (Acts 22:22; 23:12-15; 25:3, 24)

These patterns of reaction can be explained by the mentality of the Jewish lis-

---

[192]Jervell, *Apg*, 205, 362; Roloff, *Apg*, 209. Pesch (*Apg*, 2:45) suggests that the Jews' "jealousy" should be interpreted against the background of their "zeal for the law." This suggestion may be correct in a theological sense, but it does not explain the historical event.

[193]Pesch, *Apg*, 2:45, with reference to Gal 3:13; 1 Cor 12:3; also Zmijewski, *Apg*, 518. Cf. the behavior of Paul the persecutor in Acts 26:10-11.

[194]See J. Sanders (1996, 1951-52), who downplays Luke's account of Paul being stoned.

teners. Mentality is always produced by actions, and it is reflected in typical behavioral patterns. When Jews become convinced by Paul's preaching that Jesus is the Messiah, they join him and the new community of believers in Jesus, and they are willing to endure opposition and persecution. When Jews reject Paul's message, they have little choice but to take action against Paul and try to silence him because they (have to) act according to the rules of Scripture concerning the handling of false prophets, seducers of the people and blasphemers.

An analysis of Paul's letters isolates five reasons why Paul was persecuted by his fellow Jews.[195] Paul was put under pressure by Jews and more often than not persecuted physically because (a) he preached faith in Jesus the crucified and risen Messiah as necessary for salvation; (b) he argued for a radical reevaluation of the privileges of the chosen people of God that fundamentally defined and described the identity of pious Jews; (c) he encouraged, indeed exhorted, Jewish believers to ignore important parts of the Torah, such as the purity laws and the food laws; (d) he did not teach the necessity of circumcision as prerequisite for membership in the people of God; (e) he allegedly abrogated all ethical norms and standards since the Torah no longer played a central role for him.

14. When Paul preached before Gentile audiences, he would not have caused any protest during the initial contact with regard to his convictions about pagan religion and existence that were summarized above (point 10): pagans would have heard such evaluations of their religious convictions from the local Jews. They already had heard the claim that their gods are nothing compared with the reality and the truth of the God of Abraham, Isaac and Jacob. They probably were astonished, just like their Jewish fellow citizens, with regard to the proactive initiative and the courageous personal commitment of the Christian missionaries because they were unfamiliar with any cult that deliberately promoted geographical expansion.

Gentile listeners would have regarded at least four emphases of Paul's teaching as extraordinary: (a) the exhortation not only to believe in the one true God of the Jews, but also to accept the offer of grace by one single mediator of salvation; (b) the message that this mediator of salvation was a crucified man from provincial Judea; (c) the claim that this Jesus returned from the dead; (d) the expectation that they would gather in a new community that is being established in the city in which neither ethnic origin nor social status plays any role.

Gentiles were familiar with the conviction that there is only one true God from the local Jews and, at least in the case of the educated citizens, from some philosophers. However, the claim that there is only one single mediator of salvation was extraordinary: neither the gods nor the emperors nor the heroes that people worshiped demanded exclusive loyalty, although the notion of exclusive

---

[195]See Kruse 1992, with reference to 1 Thess 2:15-16; Gal 1:13-24; 2:15-21; 4:29; 5:11; 2 Cor 11:24, 26, 30-33; Rom 3:7-8; Phil 3:4-8.

salvation would have reminded them of the religious convictions and praxis of the Jews. The information that the mediator of salvation whom Paul talked about in his speeches was a human being would not have been curious for Gentile listeners, since they worshiped heroes and gods with human traits. However, the insistence that Jesus, the exclusive mediator of salvation, was a Jew must have been provocative for many Gentiles. And they would have regarded Paul's emphasis that Jesus was executed by crucifixion and that the salvation that God offers is the result of precisely this death was complete nonsense (*mōria* [1 Cor 1:23]). Gentiles would have been able theoretically to acquiesce to the idea of a hero coming back from the dead, but it was quite far-fetched to suggest a glorious resurrection for a prophet and teacher who had been rejected by his own people and who had been sentenced to death by the governor of a Roman province and executed by crucifixion. Luke reports the following patterns of reaction by Gentile audiences.

1. God-fearing Gentiles who sympathized with the Jewish faith listen willingly and attentively:
   Lydia in Philippi (Acts 16:14)

2. Pagans listen willingly to what Paul and his fellow missionaries have to say:
   Sergius Paullus in Paphos (Acts 13:7); governor Felix in Caesarea (Acts 24:24)

3. Pagan philosophers take the initiative to dialogue with Paul about his teaching:
   Epicureans and Stoics in Athens (Acts 17:18-20, 32)

4. Pagan officials of provincial administrations and of city magistrates acknowledge that Paul does not teach any subversive doctrines:
   Gallio in Corinth (Acts 18:14-16); the secretary in Ephesus (Acts 19:35-40); governor Felix in Caesarea (Acts 25:25; 26:31)

5. Pagans are deeply affected by miracles that happen in the ministry of the missionaries:
   Sergius Paullus in Paphos (Acts 13:12); the citizens in Ephesus (Acts 19:17)

6. Pagans are so impressed by the miracles that the missionaries cause that they want to worship them and honor them as gods in human form:
   the citizens in Lystra (Acts 14:11-13)

7. Pagans are stunned by the content and the claims of the Christian message:
   governor Felix in Caesarea (Acts 24:25)

8. God-fearing pagans who sympathized with the Jewish faith come to faith in Jesus, including aristocratic women and men:
   Antiocheia (Acts 13:43, 48, 49); Iconium (Acts 14:1); Derbe (Acts 14:21); Lydia in Philippi (Acts 16:14); aristocrats in Thessalonike (Acts 17:4); aristocrats in Beroea (Acts 17:12); Corinth (Acts 18:4, 7)

9. Pagans come to faith in Jesus, including a Roman governor and a member of the

"council for education and science"[196] in Athens:
> Sergius Paullus in Paphos (Acts 13:12); citizens in Derbe (Acts 14:21 [?]) and Philippi (Acts 16:33-34); Dionysios in Athens (Acts 17:34); citizens in Corinth (Acts 18:8) and Ephesus (Acts 19:18)

10. Pagans who have come to faith in Jesus rejoice in the preaching of the missionaries and are filled with joy:
> Antiocheia (Acts 13:48, 52); Philippi (Acts 16:34)

11. God-fearers who attend the synagogue reject the teaching of the missionaries and their offer of salvation:
> Antioch (Acts 13:48)

12. Pagan philosophers make fun of the message that the missionaries proclaim:
> Athens (Acts 17:32)

13. Pagans often ridicule and reject the proclamation of Jesus the crucified Savior:
> Corinth, and generally (1 Cor 1:23)

14. Pagans initiate legal proceedings against Paul, accusing him of disturbing the peace and of illegal introduction of alien Jewish customs:
> Philippi (Acts 16:20-21)

15. On some occasions pagans are motivated by the financial loss that the activities of the missionaries have caused:
> the owners of a medium in Philippi (Acts 16:16-19); the producers of religious articles in Ephesus (Acts 19:23-27)

16. Pagans organize a protest meeting against the missionaries:
> Ephesus (Acts 19:29-34)

17. Praetors have Paul flogged by their lictors and thrown into prison:
> Philippi (Acts 16:22-23)

These patterns of reaction can also be explained by the mentality of the Gentiles—for example, the curiosity of the Athenian philosophers or the religious excitement of the citizens of Lystra after the astounding miracle that the missionaries caused. It is plausible not only from a historical perspective—temples were important economic factors in Greco-Roman cities—but also from the perspective of pagan mentality that economic losses became the cause for "official" actions of Gentiles against the missionaries. Compared with some Jewish reactions, it is striking that the sources do not report plans by pagans to eliminate Paul. This accords with the tolerant attitude about religious affairs of the Roman authorities and of the population: people with particular spiritual needs could worship any deity or hero who appeared useful and helpful. As long as the au-

---

[196]Roloff, *Apg,* 267, with regard to Dionysius.

thorities knew that Paul did not endanger the public order in the city, they could leave him to his activities, particularly when he preached in the synagogue. When the sources convey the impression that the Gentile listeners generally treated Paul and his coworkers with respect, interest and curiosity, this corresponds to the religious mentality of ancient paganism.

15. Paul evaluates the worldview and the moral notions of pagan philosophy and religiosity critically. However, he also can exhort Christians to take into account the views of non-Christians.[197] As Thomas Söding argues, this is the background for Paul's conviction "that even though the lifestyle of the Christians often provokes controversy, it is ultimately convincing and attractive (1 Thess 4; cf. 1 Pet 2:12). He presupposes that the Gentiles can find their way to the Christian message on the basis of their best religious, philosophical and ethical traditions. Christians must not block this path despite all hostility."[198]

16. On some occasions miracles played a role in connection with the initial contacts that missionaries had with the local population. The role of miracles was an ambiguous one, however. In some situations the miracle left those who witnessed it perplexed. Since they could not dispute that a miracle happened, they did not know what to do with the missionaries: the leading Jews in Jerusalem did not dare to take action against Jesus' disciples (Acts 4:15-17; 5:12-13). In other situations the miracle convinced the listener of the truth of the missionaries' message: Sergius Paullus, the governor of Cyprus, came to faith in Jesus when he saw the punitive miracle that struck Elymas, his astrologer (Acts 13:12). Paul never described miracles as events that can be effectively utilized in missionary tactics or as a conclusive argument for the truth of the gospel. This is not surprising for two reasons: in the first century the "market" was saturated with miracles, at least in the context of specific cults and deities (e.g., Asclepius)—the occurrence of a miracle was no reason to consider abandoning one's traditional gods or convictions. Furthermore, miracles sometimes were connected with magic, a connotation that would make an interpretation of the miracle in terms of a proof for the validity of the gospel problematic.[199]

17. Was Paul convinced that people who do not believe in Jesus the Messiah and Savior are "lost" and will be condemned on judgment day? The answer to this question is yes, if indeed the gods worshiped by pagans do not exist (1 Cor 8:4-6; cf. 10:20-21), if the pagans therefore are "without God in the world" (Eph 2:12), and if Jesus Christ is the only mediator between God and humankind (1 Tim 2:5). Not a few scholars have resisted this conclusion, sometimes with a

---

[197] 1 Thess 4:12; 1 Cor 10:32; Col 4:5; see also the references to what is "good" in 1 Thess 5:15; Rom 12:9; 13:3; 14:16; 15:2; 16:19; also the formulations "as is fittng" and "your acceptable duty" in Col 3:18, 20; Rom 12:2; and "whatever is true, whatever is honorable, whatever is just, whatever is pure" in Phil 4:8. See Unnik 1960b; Schnabel 1985, 319, 326.

[198] Söding 1990b, 148.

[199] See Hanson 1985, 170-71.

general reference to God's love, sometimes with a more specific reference to the "times of human ignorance" that Paul talks about (Acts 17:30), to the demonstration of God's mercy in the cycles of nature and the harvests that people reap (Acts 14:16-17), or to the light that God's universal revelation in creation sheds on people (Rom 1:19-21; cf. Jn 1:9). Paul never explicitly discusses the question of whether this knowledge of the creation from divine revelation in nature suffices for "noble pagans" to be spared in God's judgment: in Rom 1:19-32 the reference to the knowledge of God from the works of creation serves the argument that no human being has a valid excuse before God and that therefore all people are helplessly exposed to God's wrath and judgment. Paul uses his reference to the "times of ignorance" to define for the philosophers of Athens in his audience no category of human beings (which would have to include the audience!) that would be exempted from the coming judgment; rather, Paul refers to the Savior whom God had appointed.

The Proclamation of the Gospel

The task of the herald in the Greco-Roman world helps us understand Paul's proclamation of the gospel. Reinhold Reck characterizes the responsibilities of the herald as "one-way communication par excellence: essentially independent of the reception, it still looks for and needs the recipient and thus implies a complementary factor."[200] The term "herald" (κῆρυξ, *kēryx*) describes in the context of ancient society one who calls out in a clear and audible manner a message that has been given by a ruler or by the state to convey to the constituency, who thus makes the message known. Lothar Coenen observes, "The κῆρυξ is always subject to an extrinsic authority whose spokesman he is. He transmits, while being himself untouchable, the message and the viewpoint of his patron. He himself thus has . . . no room for any negotiation. His task is, at any rate, an official one . . . which is the reason why he is also the person who made court sentences public. What he makes public becomes effective as he calls it out."[201] Paul describes himself as *kēryx* in 1 Tim 2:7; 2 Tim 1:11, and he often employs the verb *kēryssein* to describe the basic process of the oral proclamation of the gospel of Jesus Christ.[202] The proclamation of the gospel consists in the communication of a message that Paul and the other early Christian missionaries have been entrusted with by God and by Jesus Christ, a message that they thus convey under divine authority and with personal intrepidness.

I will describe the content of Paul's missionary message more extensively later (§28.3). According to the criteria of both ancient rhetoric and modern per-

---

[200]Reck 1991, 169.

[201]L. Coenen, *ThBLNT* 2:1755-56.

[202]Rom 10:8, 14, 15; 1 Cor 1:23; 9:27; 15:11, 12; 2 Cor 1:19; 4:5; 11:4; Gal 2:2; 5:11; Phil 1:15; Col 1:23; 1 Thess 2:9; 1 Tim 3:16; cf. Acts 19:13; 20:25; 28:31.

suasion research,[203] the successful communication of a message depends on the persuasiveness of the message, the method of delivery, the credibility of the messenger and the disposition of the listeners. The following discussion is devoted to these issues.

The Persuasiveness of the Message

The content of the message that Paul proclaims is the gospel, the good news of Jesus the Messiah and Savior. Luke's account in the book of Acts allows us to describe the central content of the missionary speeches of the early Christian missionaries, summarized in a more-or-less detailed manner depending on the specific audiences: the death and resurrection of Jesus, the identity of Jesus as Messiah and Kyrios and Savior, the expected return of Jesus. Relevant texts from Paul's letters include 1 Thess 1:9-10 and Rom 15:20-21.[204]

1 Thess 1:9-10: "For the people of those regions report about us what kind of welcome we had among you, and how you turned to God from idols, to serve a living and true God, [10]and to wait for his Son from heaven, whom he raised from the dead—Jesus, who rescues us from the wrath that is coming."

Rom 15:20-21: "Thus I make it my ambition to proclaim the good news, not where Christ has already been named, so that I do not build on someone else's foundation, [21]but as it is written, 'Those who have never been told of him shall see, and those who have never heard of him shall understand' [Is 52:15]."

The offer of salvation as general liberation from guilt and sin, the offer of hope for a perfect existence after death, the offer of fellowship with people from all walks of life and all classes of society—these were attractive and powerful convictions that Paul put forward (although the last emphasis would be attractive for members of the lower classes only). Despite the attractiveness of these important elements of the early Christian preaching, the central emphasis of the apostles' proclamation was a "scandal" and "nonsense" for Jewish and Greek audiences (1 Cor 1:18-23; 2:14; 3:19). Reinhold Reck is correct when he points out that Paul's concept of communication "includes a surplus compared with modern models, namely, the sovereign work of the Holy Spirit." He describes this as the "deep dimension" of the work of God: the gospel ultimately is accepted and believed by listeners only because God himself is effectively present in its proclamation.[205] Paul knows and explicitly asserts that God is the real, the primary communicator: apostles are envoys, messengers who have been "sent" and thus are the medium or channel of the message; they themselves are not

---

[203]See Reck 1991, 25-27; for the observation that follows above see ibid., 169-78.

[204]See Reck 1991, 169-72.

[205]Reck 1991, 180; see also Howell 1998a, 77-84, with reference to 1 Thess 1:5-6; 4:8; 5:16-24; 2 Thess 1:11; 2:13.

the source of the message. Paul expresses this conviction in 1 Thess 2:13 and 2 Cor 5:18-21:

1 Thess 2:13: "We also constantly give thanks to God for this, that when you received the word of God that you heard from us, you accepted it not as a human word but as what it really is, God's word, which is also at work in you believers."

2 Cor 5:18-21: "All this is from God, who reconciled us to himself through Christ, and has given us the ministry of reconciliation; [19]that is, in Christ God was reconciling the world to himself, not counting their trespasses against them, and entrusting the message of reconciliation to us. [20]So we are ambassadors for Christ, since God is making his appeal through us; we entreat you on behalf of Christ, be reconciled to God. [21]For our sake he made him to be sin who knew no sin, so that in him we might become the righteousness of God."

We may call this, with Reinhold Reck, the "multidimensional" reality of the effective proclamation of the gospel: Paul preaches the message of Jesus Christ not just verbally and cognitively: it also is linked with the "demonstration of the Spirit and of power."[206] The terms *apodeixis* ("demonstration") and *dynamis* ("power") refer not to "the impact of the arguments" or the "power of the sermon on the hearts" but rather to "manifestations that the contemporaries of the apostle experienced as wondrous and extraordinary."[207] In Rom 15:18-19 Paul speaks more specifically of "the power of signs and wonders" linked with "the power of the Spirit of God"—that is, miraculous events that accompanied the proclamation of the gospel and are signs of the reliability of the apostolic message. This aspect of Paul's communication of the gospel is "not simply method, because it remains tied to the work of the Holy Spirit."[208] In 1 Cor 2:4-5 the "demonstration of the Spirit and of power" is linked with God's miraculous power, but it is not identical with a "proof by miracles," as Paul had rejected the latter in 1 Cor 1:22-23: "for Jews demand signs and Greeks desire wisdom, but we proclaim Christ crucified, a stumbling block to Jews and foolishness to Gentiles." Wolfgang Schrage is correct when he explains that the greatest miracle "which only the liberating and transforming power of the Spirit of God can perform happens where people who have been affected by the apostolic message (cf. 1 Cor 14:24-25) are snatched away from their rebellion or self-assurance and come to faith."[209]

This understanding of the "demonstration of the Spirit and of power" can be illustrated with Paul's missionary outreach in Thessalonike. Paul had to leave the city two or three months after his arrival because the situation had become

---

[206]Cf. 1 Thess 1:5; Gal 3:5; 1 Cor 2:4-5; 4:19-20; 2 Cor 6:7; 12:12; Rom 15:18-19.
[207]See Holtz, *1 Thess,* 47, on 1 Thess 1:5, rejecting the interpretation of E. von Dobschütz.
[208]Thus correctly Reck 1991, 173; on this subject see also Kelhoffer 2000, 275-77.
[209]Schrage, *1 Kor,* 1:234.

too dangerous. Paul left behind in the city Timothy, a young believer and new coworker, who before long followed him to Beroea and to Athens before Paul sent him back to Thessalonike, where he stayed for a short time before leaving the city again to join Paul in Corinth (Acts 17:10, 14, 15; 1 Thess 3:1-5). Despite this difficult early stage of the history of the church in Thessalonike, Paul asserts the following in his first letter to these believers in Macedonia, written only a few months after the establishment of the church:

1 Thess 1:5-6: "Our message of the gospel came to you not in word only, but also in power and in the Holy Spirit and with full conviction; just as you know what kind of persons we proved to be among you for your sake. [6]And you became imitators of us and of the Lord, for in spite of persecution you received the word with joy inspired by the Holy Spirit."

The effectiveness of the proclamation of the gospel came not from the method of missionary preaching but from God's Spirit, who convinced citizens of Thessalonike of the truth of the gospel and prompted them to become followers of Jesus and join the community of believers in the city, despite the fact that they were put under immense pressure by their Jewish friends to reject the message of the missionaries and the missionaries themselves. Surely it was precisely this reliance upon and confidence in the work of the Holy Spirit that allowed Paul to involve young and inexperienced coworkers such as Timothy in pioneer situations and entrust them with demanding responsibilities.[210]

The search for other factors that can explain the success of Paul's missionary work is understandable from a human perspective, but in Paul's view it is misguided from a theological perspective. For example, George Shillington argues that Paul's success in winning pagans for the gospel is linked with the fact that he abandoned the traditional characteristics of his Jewish heritage that controlled the boundary of acceptance (and exclusion) of all the members of the people of God—including ethnic Jews as well as the proselytes who came from a pagan background—and instead preached Jesus the Messiah "as God's universal, dynamic center of life and thought that meshed spontaneously with the cultural particularity of his Gentile converts."[211] He suggests that Paul "did not require them to deny their culture, to abandon their heritage, to learn a new language, to be circumcised, to eat certain foods and not others, to observe certain days and not others, to attend feasts, to present offerings." This is only half of the truth, and it misses completely the new reality that conversion to Jesus Christ effects. When a polytheist man in Ephesus, for example, was converted to faith in Jesus Christ, he did not simply accept a "universal, dynamic center of life and thought" (whatever that may mean), but rather he began to believe

---

[210]Howell 1996, 107-8, 216.
[211]Shillington 1991, 126; the quotation that follows above, ibid., 128.

in a "particularistic" Jewish Savior who was executed on a particular wooden cross and was raised specifically on the third day after the execution. He no longer visited the temple of Artemis Ephesia, and he no longer participated in the sacrificial rites of her cult or in processions celebrated in her honor. When the street on which he lived was decorated for the Artemisia celebrated in March or April, he stayed away. When he passed by the Basilike Stoa at the State Agora, he did not worship Augustus. When he visited the baths, he did not bow before the statue of the goddess there. He no longer dined in the temple, he no longer observed the traditional rituals on the doorstep of his house, he removed the statues of deities from the cult niche in his living room. In other words, the Gentile convert without doubt abandoned publicly, often conspicuously, a considerable part of his "culture" and his "heritage" after he came to faith in Jesus Christ.

Methods of Missionary Proclamation

Paul disassociates himself from certain methods of public speech. It is obvious and unsurprising that he, a Hellenistic Jew, is knowledgeable of rhetorical methods. A passage such as 2 Cor 11:4 demonstrates that Paul certainly was aware of the problematic nature and the appropriateness of rhetorical methods for the proclamation of the gospel:

2 Cor 11:4: "For if someone comes and proclaims another Jesus than the one we proclaimed, or if you receive a different spirit from the one you received, or a different gospel from the one you accepted, you submit to it readily enough."

In this text Paul describes the active process of communication as "proclaiming Jesus," and the (active) reception of the message as "accepting the gospel." The third factor of communication, inserted between communication and reception, is "receiving the Spirit." This third factor is, evidently, decisive. Paul insists that the method of communication that he practices corresponds with the content of the message that he proclaims. He describes his basic attitude as a missionary in several passages.[212] The longer passage in 1 Thess 2:3-12 and the succinct formulations in 1 Cor 2:2-5 are preeminent examples.[213]

1 Thess 2:3-8: "For our appeal does not spring from deceit or impure motives or trickery, [4]but just as we have been approved by God to be entrusted with the message of the gospel, even so we speak, not to please mortals, but to please God who tests our hearts. [5]As you know and as God is our witness, we never came with words of flattery or with a pretext for greed; [6]nor did we seek praise from mortals, whether from you or from others, [7]though we might have made demands as apostles of Christ. But we were gentle among you, like a nurse tenderly caring for her own children. [8]So deeply do we care for you that

---

[212]Cf. 1 Thess 2:3-12; 1 Cor 4:14-16; 2 Cor 4:1-2; 7:2; 11:7-11; 12:14; Gal 4:19; Phil 4:17.
[213]See, besides the commentaries, Denis 1957; Reck 1991, 174-75.

we are determined to share with you not only the gospel of God but also our own selves, because you have become very dear to us."

1 Cor 2:2-5: "For I decided to know nothing among you except Jesus Christ, and him cru-cified. ³And I came to you in weakness and in fear and in much trembling. ⁴My speech and my proclamation were not with plausible words of wisdom, but with a demonstration of the Spirit and of power, ⁵so that your faith might rest not on human wisdom but on the power of God."

1. In 1 Thess 2:3-8 Paul disassociates himself from deception, cunning, cajol-ery and "apostolic strong-arm stuff" (R. Reck) as *methods,* and from praise and from pleasing people (Gal 1:10) as well as from greediness (cf. 2 Cor 2:17) as *motivations* of missionary proclamation. He emphasizes his role as trustee (1 Thess 2:4; cf. 1 Cor 4:1), the openness of his ministry (2 Cor 4:2) and his re-sponsibility before God, expressed in love for the people to whom he preaches the gospel. This means that the communication of the Christian mes-sage not only happens on the cognitive level but also remains tied to the "communication of life"; that is, it is personal and thus, in the end, defenseless. "Thus the method becomes part of the message, and the message assumes shape and form in the method: the method communicates in an analogous-nonverbal manner what the message contains digitally-verbally in the word."[214]

2. The dedication of the missionary preacher is the counterpart of God's ac-tion in Jesus Christ that possesses final and exclusive significance: the mission-ary "solicits" and is "zealous" (Gal 4:18; 2 Cor 11:2). The relationship with Jesus Christ is both the goal of proclamation and the heart of the life of the missionary, which explains why the "solicitation" of the apostle does not aim at binding the listener to the messenger (Gal 4:17). Reinhold Reck explains, "The authenticity of the proclamation of the gospel is closely correlated with the manner of its communication, although it may not be automatically discernible from the methods. Because a wrong message can also be proclaimed with great zeal, as the right message can be communicated with improper methods. The decisive criterion is, in the final analysis, the content, which stipulates at the same time the goal of the proclamation."[215]

3. In 1 Cor 2:2-5 Paul asserts that he rejects the three traditional methods that could be used in the context of Greek and Roman rhetoric to convince audiences of the truth of a message. Paul reminds the Corinthian Christians that he proclaimed the gospel in their city "in weakness and in fear and in much trembling" (1 Cor 2:3).[216] The description of Scopelian the Sophist phi-

---

[214]Reck 1991, 175. On 1 Thess 2:8 see also Gillman 1990.
[215]Reck 1991, 176.
[216]1 Cor 2:3: κἀγὼ ἐν ἀσθενείᾳ καὶ ἐν φόβῳ καὶ ἐν τρόμῳ πολλῷ ἐγενόμην πρὸς ὑμᾶς.

losopher (late first century) by Philostratus provides a striking contrast to Paul's self-portrayal.[217] Scopelian argued in his disputation (διάλεξις, *dialexis*) "with great skill," as he required no time to prepare a speech on the suggested topic but started immediately to declaim in an "extremely melodious voice" with "charming pronunciation" and striking "covert allusions." Paul, on the other hand, was anti-*ēthos* and anti-*pathos:* he renounced efforts to project a positive picture of himself, and he refrained from playing on the feelings of the listeners. Was Paul incapable of delivering a skillful rhetorical oration? Did he suffer from physical or psychological disadvantages? Paul emphasizes that his behavior was a deliberate decision. We should accept Paul's assertion: the Corinthians knew him too well for him to have duped them. Paul did not aim his proclamation of the gospel at having his audiences react with shouts of "Bravo!" or "Marvelous!"[218] Paul points out that the success of his proclamation was not the result of rhetorical power of persuasion (1 Cor 2:4): "My speech and my proclamation [ὁ λόγος μου καὶ τὸ κήρυγμά μου, *ho logos mou kai to kērygma mou*] were not with plausible words of wisdom [οὐκ ἐν πειθοῖς σοφίας λόγοις, *ouk en peithois sophias logois*]." There was "proof" (ἀπόδειξις, *apodeixis*), but not in the manner of traditional rhetoric: the Corinthians were witnesses of the work and the power of the Holy Spirit, "with a demonstration of the Spirit and of power (ἀλλ᾽ ἐν ἀποδείξει πνεύματος καὶ δυνάμεως, *all' en apodeixei pneumatos kai dynameōs*)." The fact that the Corinthian believers had been persuaded to accept the gospel as truth—with the message of Jesus the crucified and risen Messiah as the central emphasis—is the supernatural proof for the validity of his proclamation. In 1 Cor 2:5 Paul explains why he renounces traditional rhetorical methods: "so that your faith [ἡ πίστις ὑμῶν, *hē pistis hymōn*] might rest not on human wisdom but on the power of God." The term "faith" (*pistis*) can also mean "conviction." Paul acted in deliberate opposition to Sophist rhetorical methods because he did not want to be mistaken for a Sophist orator and because he did not want people's applause for his rhetorical prowess to obscure the message that he proclaimed. When Dio Chrysostom, who also assumed a consciously anti-Sophist position, visited Corinth, he intended to punish his audience by denying their expectations.[219] Paul's goal, on the other hand, is not simply to deny the Corinthians a rhetorical spectacle: he wants to use a method of proclamation that corresponds with his "message of the humiliated and crucified God" so that the Corinthians may grasp the existential significance of this message.

4. The message of the cross cannot be adapted to aesthetic needs or expectations of the missionaries' audience. Paul preached Jesus as the "new Adam"

---

[217]Philostratus, *Vit. soph.* 519. For the analysis that follows above see B. Winter 1997, 157-58.
[218]See B. Winter 1997, 158, with reference to Epictetus, *Diss.* 3.23.23-24.
[219]Dio Chrysostom, *Or.* 47.1. For the remark that follows above see Winter 1997, 161.

and "Savior of humankind," as the "Son of God" and "firstborn of the dead"—
terms and categories that could indeed be packaged as attractive religious content. However, Paul never dispensed with linking the salvific significance of
Jesus with his death on the cross: "For I decided to know nothing among you
except Jesus Christ, and him crucified" (1 Cor 2:2). It was impossible, in the first
century, to speak in an aesthetically pleasing manner about a man who had
been executed on a cross by the Roman authorities. The reality of crucifixion
was so gruesome and so demanding of explanation that rhetorical competence
and brilliance were of little help.

5. The weakness and simplicity of Paul's preaching corresponds with the personal weakness for which some Christians blamed him (2 Cor 10:10), a weakness that he mentions repeatedly.[220] In the context of his critique of the Second
Sophistic in Corinth,[221] Paul deliberately relinquishes the use of rhetorical
means: he operates "without the wisdom of words" (οὐκ ἐν σοφίᾳ λόγου, *ouk en
sophia logou* [1 Cor 1:17]) because that robs the cross of its message. Paul does
not want to convince his audiences of the truth of his message by the use of
ēthos, pathos and *apodeixis.* He is concerned that their *pistis,* their (faith) conviction, rest not on human wisdom but on the "power of God" (ἐν δυνάμει θεοῦ,
en dynamei theou [1 Cor 2:5]). The "power of persuasion" lies not in rhetorical
techniques but in God himself and in the good news of his crucified and risen
Messiah. Since rhetorical techniques may conceal the content of the message,
Paul declares them unusable: they would only divert the attention of the listeners away from the message of the crucified God and focus it on Paul or Apollos
or other preachers.[222] Authentic evangelism does not consist in the simple reci-
tation of Scripture. At the same time authentic evangelism does not rely on
methods, because even the best method cannot contextualize the scandalous
offense of the cross of Jesus Christ.

The Credibility of the Envoy

Personal credibility is an important factor when an orator visits a city for the
first time and seeks to establish contact with the citizens, and it is an important
factor for missionaries who start to preach the gospel in a city as well as for the
leaders of the Christian community who continue to evangelize among their
fellow citizens. When Paul came into a city as a pioneer missionary, knowing
nobody, the issue of personal credibility played a different role in the two social places in which he sought to win people to his message of faith in Jesus
Christ. In the synagogue he had credibility because of his training as a rabbi in
Jerusalem under Gamaliel and because of his competence in interpreting Scrip-

---

[220]Cf. Gal 4:13; 1 Cor 2:3; 4:9-13; 2 Cor 12:7-10; 13:9; 1 Thess 2:2.
[221]See B. Winter 1997, 113-244.
[222]B. Winter 1997, 187.

ture. Pagans would have been impressed by his Roman citizenship if they were aware of it (something that we should not assume), by his many travels, by the miracles they saw (if miracles indeed happened), by his character as a man who behaved in an exemplary manner, by his astounding personal commitment to his preaching and teaching and by his immense courage. However, in view of the competition of various philosophical schools and religious cults in the first century, this initial credibility would have been quickly compromised or even nullified by the content of Paul's message, which focused on a crucified Jew as the Savior of the world.

Paul's dispute with the "super-apostles" in Corinth is relevant for the question of Paul's credibility.[223] Paul emphasizes that ultimately he pursues his missionary work—despite his zeal and commitment, despite his concern that he may have worked in vain (1 Thess 3:5; Gal 2:2; 4:11; Phil 2:16)—independently of whether or not he has "success" and independently of whether or not he receives recognition and praise (Gal 1:10; 1 Thess 2:6). He pursues his missionary work motivated by his conviction that God called him to proclaim Jesus as the Messiah and Savior (1 Thess 2:4; 1 Cor 9:16). As Reinhold Reck explains, "Paul has no other option than to rely on the persuasive power of the truth. This is why he fights with arguments and with dialogue, although his rhetoric is not inept. The basic issue was to proclaim the gospel in its provocative simplicity against all the wisdom of the world, against all edifices of ideas, philosophies and religious traditions." When Corinthian believers expected him to display the customary rhetorical competence of contemporary orators, when they criticized him for the "weakness" of his presentations (2 Cor 10:10; 11:6), he affirmed his missionary praxis. The weakness of his personal appearance, for which his Christian opponents reproach him and to which Paul himself repeatedly refers, "corresponds to the weakness and the simplicity" of the Christian message.[224]

In order to assert his personal credibility Paul refers to his behavior and ministry: his lifestyle with the missionary travels, the homelessness and the economic independence,[225] to his personal relationship with the people who have come to faith in Jesus Christ through his preaching (1 Thess 1:4—3:10), and to the historical origins of the local Christian community. He rejects recommendations by others, including letters of recommendation (2 Cor 3:1-3). Paul is concerned that at least the Christians know that his missionary work is not a moneymaking business.[226]

---

[223]See Reck 1991, 176; for the observations that follow above see ibid., 176-78; quotation, 176-77.

[224]Reck 1991, 177.

[225]Cf. 1 Thess 2:9; 1 Cor 4:11-12; 9:6-18; 2 Cor 6:5; 11:7-10, 27.

[226]Reck 1991, 178, with reference to 2 Cor 2:17; 1 Thess 2:5.

Paul did not adapt his behavior as a preacher to the forms and structures familiar to his contemporaries—for example, the conduct and demeanor of the Hellenistic itinerant orators or the Sophist philosophers. Paul's conduct was controlled by the nature of the gospel and the resulting consequences for personal behavior, risking isolation, loneliness and social discrimination. The authority of the preacher of the gospel is important for the authority of the gospel. Traugott Holtz is correct when he argues, "In the path of approach to the truth stands its representative . . . the messenger can block the access to his message. The world can easily avoid the claims of the gospel if it can get hold of the messenger."[227] The apostle who proclaims the gospel remains a stranger because of the strangeness of its message—not in external demeanor or appearance, but in terms of the integrity of his person and his willingness to be a servant. As Holtz maintains, "The true messenger becomes, for the world, a part of his true message. Paul gave to the world not only a word, he also gave himself."

The Disposition of the Listeners

The subjective disposition of listeners concerns motivating factors that increase or jeopardize the acceptance of the message.[228]

In Acts 26:18 Luke provides a general description of the Jews in the context of the third account of Saul/Paul's conversion (Acts 26:9-20) that is characteristic not only for Luke but also for Paul, as the parallels with Rom 1:18-32 show.

Acts 26:15-18: "I asked, 'Who are you, Lord?' The Lord answered, 'I am Jesus whom you are persecuting. [16]But get up and stand on your feet; for I have appeared to you for this purpose, to appoint you to serve and testify to the things in which you have seen me and to those in which I will appear to you. [17]I will rescue you from your people and from the Gentiles—to whom I am sending you [18]to open their eyes so that they may turn from darkness to light and from the power of Satan to God, so that they may receive forgiveness of sins and a place among those who are sanctified by faith in me.' "

Paul emphasizes the following convictions.[229] (1) The Gentiles' eyes are closed, and ultimately only God can open them.[230] What they must understand in order to find salvation they cannot comprehend. Since they are blind, they do not see the darkness in which they live, nor do they understand the powers that control them. (2) The Gentiles must turn from darkness to light. They need the light of God's revelation in order to recognize their situation and grasp the truth of the one true God, who alone can grant salvation. Pagan cults and religious rites are as ineffectual as the best pagan insights and motifs are futile. The Gentiles have

---

[227]Holtz, *1 Thess,* 95; the quotation that follows above, ibid.
[228]Reck (1991, 178), whose comments are rather sparse.
[229]For the discussion that follows above see, besides the commentaries, Stenschke 1999a, 245-55.
[230]For Luke see Stenschke 1999a, 275-317.

no "light," and they cannot illuminate themselves. (3) The Gentiles must be liberated from the power of Satan to faith in the true God. The darkness in which the Gentiles exist is not neutral territory, since they are controlled by Satan. Luke and Paul do not see the Gentiles' blindness as being caused by the work of Satan—that is, as demon possession. When Luke refers to manifestations of demonic power, the Gentiles are always helplessly at the mercy of these powers.[231] (4) The Gentiles need to turn to God. The gods that they worship in their homes and in the temples are not true deities. The Gentiles are strangers to the living God. They need to abandon the gods of their cities and families and turn to the only true God, who alone can grant salvation. (5) The Gentiles need forgiveness of their sins. The sacrifices and rituals that they offer more or less regularly in the temples and at home cannot atone for their moral lapses and cannot appease the deity. (6) The Gentiles have no salvation. They belong to "those who are sanctified" (*hoi hēgiasmenoi*) only when they believe in Jesus Christ and receive from him forgiveness of sins.

Conversion

Paul understood his mission in terms of having been called by Jesus the Messiah to contribute with his proclamation to the Gentiles' turning (*epistrephein*) "from darkness to light and from the power of Satan to God" (Acts 26:18). Paul's own conversion is not a prototype of conversions in the early church, as is demonstrated by the experience of the Twelve.[232] Surely the conversion experiences of many of the people whom Paul led to faith in Jesus Christ were not as dramatic as his own.

When Paul speaks of conversion in his letters, he generally describes it in fundamental terms. He asserts that when Jews "turn to" (*epistrephein*) the Lord, God removes "the veil" that had been over their eyes, preventing them from understanding how the Scriptures point to Jesus of Nazareth (2 Cor 3:16). When polytheists are converted, they "turn to God from idols, to serve a living and true God" (1 Thess 1:9). In regard to the believers in the churches in Galatia, Paul wonders why, after having turned to God and come to faith in Jesus Christ, they "turn back again to the weak and beggarly elemental spirits" (Gal 4:9). Luke refers in his account of Paul's missionary work to "conversion" (*epistrophē, epistrephein*) more frequently (Acts 13:38; 17:30; 20:21; 26:18, 20).[233] It is questionable that this indicates that Paul spoke of conversion only rarely, as his letters represent only a small portion of the linguistic "register" of the apostle. In his

---

[231]Lk 8:27-39; Acts 8:7; 13:10; 16:16; 19:12. See Stenschke 1999a, 240-43, 248-51, 263.

[232]See Peace 1999, esp. 17-101 (Paul), 105-281 (the Twelve). On the theme of conversion in Paul's theology see Prümm 1962; Dunn 1998, 326-28; see generally Nock 1933; Dupont 1960; Burkhardt 1978; Frend 1980; R. Black 1985; Bardy 1988; France 1993; Matson 1996.

[233]Dunn 1998, 326; for the comment that follows above see ibid., 326-28; quotation, 328.

letters Paul writes to Christians for whom consistent commitment to Christ is a more significant topic than conversion, which they have already experienced. In his missionary speeches before Jews and Gentiles who had not (yet) come to faith in Jesus Christ, Paul surely challenged his listeners to "turn" to God and come to faith in Jesus as the Messiah and Savior, as did John the Baptist and Jesus of Nazareth in their own way. Without doubt Paul was convinced that existence as a follower of Jesus has a definite, clear beginning. As James Dunn observes of Paul, "He simply took it for granted that his audiences were made up of individuals who had gone through a significant transition in their experience. They had responded to Paul's (or his team's) preaching, made some kind of confessional commitment to Jesus as Lord, and been baptized in Jesus' name. They had experienced God's grace and had become members of a group whose mutual interdependence and ethos were expected to characterize their whole lives."

Paul interprets conversion and its consequences as a "demonstration of the Spirit and power" (1 Cor 2:4; cf. 1 Thess 1:5). Turning to God and to Jesus Christ presupposes acknowledging God's salvific revelation in sending Jesus into the world and to the cross. As Peter Stuhlmacher explains, this acknowledgment of God's work of salvation "happens according to Rom 10:9 through the confession by which each individual believer turns to and submits to God and his Messiah. The ὁμολογία [homologia, "confession"] implies the acknowledgment that the believer stands before God as a transgressor who can win his salvation not by his own ability but only through God's grace and through the help of the Kyrios (cf. Gal 2:16; 1 Cor 1:26-30). . . . According to Paul, Jews and Gentiles receive justification by faith alone, not by works of law (Rom 3:28). God enables them to come to faith through the gospel and gives them forgiveness of sin and new life through Christ."[234]

The joy of newly converted Gentiles that Luke reports in connection with conversions in Antiocheia (Acts 13:48, 52) and Philippi (Acts 16:34) was linked with Paul's message that the prophecy of Is 49:6 was presently being fulfilled in the arrival of the messianic time of salvation in which the Gentiles receive salvation (Acts 13:47-48). Their joy was prompted also by the reception of the Holy Spirit (Acts 13:52). Paul's preaching of the gospel in the house of the pagan prison official in Philippi leads to conversions that are accompanied by rejoicing (ἠγαλλιάσατο, ēgalliasato [Acts 16:34]). Luke reported previously that the converted Samaritans were filled with "great joy" (πολλὴ χαρά, pollē chara) after they had listened attentively in the city to Philip's preaching, which was accompanied by miracles (Acts 8:8). The Ethiopian official who came to faith through his dialogue with Philip and who asked to be baptized continued his travels joyfully (χαίρων, chairōn [Acts 8:39]). In his gospel Luke repeatedly asserts that the arrival of Jesus

---

causes joy[235]—joy that is connected with liberation from anxiety about what to eat and what to drink (Lk 12:29; 17:28), buying and selling, planting and building (Lk 17:28). It is a joy that comes when Gentiles recognize that God has revealed the way to life in Jesus the Savior, and when they believe in the gospel, and when they are enabled to live in the presence of God without having to be afraid of God (Acts 2:28).[236] Such supernatural joy—a gift of God's Spirit that transcends the moaning of human existence in the world (Rom 8:22) and the suffering of the present age (Rom 8:18), and that proves its worth as joy in the midst of suffering (Rom 8:31-39)—was something unfamiliar to the Gentiles.[237]

The missionary preaching of the early Christian missionaries prompted the converted Gentiles not only to a change of mind but also to a change of behavior that might well have been noticeable at the very first meal after they started to believe in the one true God and in Jesus the only Savior: newly converted Greeks in Lystra would have abstained from the three ritual libations that they traditionally offered to the god or gods worshiped in the house—for example, the *agathos daimon*—and converted citizens in Corinth the Roman colony would have left the *patella* empty where they used to honor the Penates with sacrifices.[238]

Paul also comments on psychological consequences of conversion, on immediate personal feelings that the converts experienced, surely in varying degrees. According to Gal 4:14b-15, the new converts in Galatia were so impressed by their experience that they welcomed Paul "as an angel of God" and were willing even to tear out their eyes for Paul. Albrecht Oepke describes the conversion experience in this context as a "suggestive overflow of unimagined emotional and volitional powers."[239] The demeanor of Paul the missionary had nothing to do with this reaction: he arrived in southern Galatia with a "physical infirmity," a condition that initially put them to the test (Gal 4:13-14a). In 1 Cor 14:25 Paul speaks of Gentiles who attend the Christian meetings and are so affected by the word of God that they fall on their faces, worship God and confess that God is present. The context is the reaction of non-Christians to prophetic speech in the Christian meeting that makes them "visible,"[240] disclosing the secrets of their hearts and announcing the truth about their lives (1 Cor 14:24), but Paul's description probably can be applied to similar effects of early Christian

---

[235]Lk 1:14, 44, 47, 68; 10:17, 20; 13:17; 15:7, 10, 23; 24:11, 41, 52; Acts 5:41; 8:9, 39; 11:23; 13:48, 52; 15:3, 31; 20:24 (χαίρω, χαρά); Lk 1:14, 44; 10:21; Acts 2:26, 46-47; 16:34 (ἀγαλλιάω, ἀγαλλίασις).

[236]See Stenschke 1999a, 370. A. B. du Toit ("Freude I," *TRE* 11:584-86, esp. 585) maintains that Luke is the "evangelist of joy."

[237]On the subject of joy in paganism see O. Michel, "Freude," *RAC* 8:348-418, esp. 350-71.

[238]On the domestic cults see Klauck 1995-1996, 1:60-62.

[239]Oepke 1920, 205.

[240]Schrage, *1 Kor,* 3:413 ("durchsichtbar").

missionary preaching. When Gentiles—in the cultural context of the Greco-Roman world—hear the missionaries announce the coming judgment of God and are convicted of their guilt and sin, they prostrate themselves on the ground as a sign of homage and submission that is extended to high officials, rulers and divine beings when a petition is made.[241] Pagans recognize and indeed sense the presence of deity not just in terms of rational acceptance,[242] as the emphasized adverb *ontōs* ("certainly, in truth" [1 Cor 14:25]) shows, but with every fiber of their being. That is why they fall to the ground—not in the sense of an uncontrollable emotion[243] or of a hypothetical *proskynesis* rite that the early church might have practiced,[244] but rather as a spontaneous expression of acknowledging the reality of God's presence, of being convicted by God's word, as a cry for the forgiveness of sins.[245] Oepke links this passage with Rom 8:15 and Gal 4:6 and asserts, "When they had cast themselves in this manner on God's mercy, the Spirit continued to work in them, under the conviction by the Word, the sacred consciousness of God's children, indeed coming on them as Spirit of sonship who calls out 'Abba, Father.'"[246]

These passages do not allow us to reconstruct the process of the conversion event with a diagnosis of feelings. There is no doubt, however, that Paul linked the reception of the Holy Spirit with the conversion experience: "Anyone who does not have the Spirit of Christ does not belong to him" (Rom 8:9b; cf. Gal 3:2). And there seems to be no doubt that the reception of the Spirit was an event that could be felt: surely joy as a "fruit of the Spirit" (Gal 5:23) was the palpable, visible experience that accompanied the reception of the Spirit in places besides Thessalonike (1 Thess 1:6). In Antiocheia the new believers were "filled with joy and with the Holy Spirit" (Acts 13:52), and the converted Ethiopian likewise was "filled with joy" when he continued his journey (Acts 8:39). Albrecht Oepke describes the "undescribable elation" that the new converts experienced, possessing what nobody else had: forgiveness of sins once and for all, salvation in the final judgment, adoption into God's family. It is important to note at the same time that the faith of the new converts must not be confused with mystical sentiments: the faith that Paul preached had a specific content, focused on the one true God of Israel,[247] on Jesus the Messiah, Lord and Savior,[248]

---

[241]On προσκυνέω (*proskyneō*) see H. Greeven, *ThWNT* 6:759-67 (*TDNT* 6:758-66); J. M. Nützel, *EWNT* 3:419-23 (*EDNT* 3:173-75).

[242]See Schrage, *1 Kor,* 3:413 with n. 237.

[243]And surely not comparable to the practice of "being slain in the Spirit" as found in some Pentecostal traditions.

[244]Schrage, *1 Kor,* 3:414.

[245]Thiselton, *1 Cor,* 1130.

[246]Oepke 1920, 205; for the observations that follow above see ibid., 205, 208-9, 210-11.

[247]Acts 16:34; 1 Thess 1:8.

[248]Acts 14:23; 16:31; 18:8; 20:21; 24:24; 26:18; Rom 3:22, 26; Gal 2:16, 20; 3:22, 26; Eph 3:12; Phil 3:9; Col 2:5.

on Jesus' death and resurrection,[249] and on the gospel.[250]

The "first love" (ἡ ἀγάπη ἡ πρώτη, *hē agapē hē prōtē*) of Rev 2:4, whose abandonment the risen Lord includes in his indictment of the church in Ephesus, should not be understood in terms of the immediate psychological effects of conversion. In the context of "the works you did at first" (τὰ πρῶτα ἔργα, *ta prōta erga*) that the church is exhorted to "do" (ποίησον, *poiēson*) again after repenting (Rev 2:5), the expression "first love" can hardly be akin to the emotional excitement of two people who have "fallen in love" in terms of an intense feeling of devotion to Jesus Christ as "bridegroom." Rather, coming after the introduction to the Lord's message for the church in Ephesus, in which he introduces himself as the one "who holds the seven stars in his right hand, who walks among the seven golden lampstands," the charge of having abandoned the "first love" likely refers to the fact that the Christians in Ephesus have neglected their missionary involvement, their task and function as light of the world and witness to the world.[251]

Luke's account in the book of Acts of the missionary successes of Paul and of his team underscores the fact that the people who hear the gospel preached and are converted to faith in Jesus Christ come from all social groups. Luke singles out several persons for some of the social groups that the missionaries encounter.[252]

1. Jews (Acts 13:43: Antioch; 14:1: Iconium; 17:4: Thessalonike; 17:10-12: Beroea; 18:4: Corinth; 19:8-10: Ephesus)

2. Leading Jews: Crispus the synagogue ruler in Corinth (Acts 18:8)

3. Proselytes of the "first category" (Acts 13:43: Antioch)

4. God-fearers (Acts 13:16, 26: Antioch; 16:15: Philippi; 17:4: Thessalonike)

5. Sympathizers of the "first category" (Acts 17:4: Thessalonike; 17:12: Beroea)

6. Sympathizers (Acts 14:1: Iconium; 18:4.8: Corinth)

7. Gentiles (Acts 13:48-49: Antioch and the surrounding regions; 14:4: Iconium; 14:21: Derbe; 18:8: Corinth; 19:10: Ephesus and surrounding regions; 17:34: Athens)

8. Roman aristocrats: Sergius Paullus the proconsul of Cyprus (Acts 13:12)

9. Roman officials: the prison official in (Acts 16:30-34)

---

[249]1 Cor 15:11; Rom 10:9.
[250]Phil 1:27; cf. 1 Cor 15:2.
[251]Thus Beale, *Rev*, 230.
[252]See Wander 1998, 199.

10. Leading Greeks: Dionysius, a member of the Areopagus in Athens (Acts 17:34)

Luke's account has a twofold focus: the conversion of proselytes, God-fearers and sympathizers, and the conversion of Jews.

Establishing Communities of Believers

The communication process of Paul's missionary work did not end with the oral proclamation of the good news of Jesus Christ and the conversion of individuals: the apostle established churches, communities of men and women who had come to faith in Jesus the Messiah and Savior and who had been baptized in the name of Jesus Christ.[253] The fact that Paul himself did not regularly baptize new converts (1 Cor 1:13-17) and that he did not describe his missionary task in terms of baptism (1 Cor 1:17a) does not mean that he was interested only in the conversion of individuals. It is a matter of course for Paul that new converts belong to a local church, a local community of believers in Jesus. His repeated visits to churches that he had established in the course of earlier missionary travels are proof of the importance that he accorded to the establishment and development of local meetings of Christians. The existence of local churches was a central element in his understanding of the missionary task.

When Paul writes letters to the Christians in the cities in which he had engaged in missionary work, he does not write to individuals—for example, the leaders of the church—he writes to the congregation as a whole. For Paul, the existence of local churches is a confirmation of his apostolic ministry (1 Cor 9:2; 2 Cor 3:1-3). He describes himself as a teacher "in every church" (1 Cor 4:17). His rulings on theological and ethical questions are relevant for "all the churches" (1 Cor 7:17; cf. 11:16; 14:33; 16:1). He speaks of his "anxiety for all the churches" (2 Cor 11:28; cf. 12:13).

The specific challenges of establishing new churches and consolidating and developing existing churches as messianic communities were enormous. The integration of Jewish Christians and Gentile Christians was not easy, as Jewish believers needed to overcome not only ancient psychological barriers and legal traditions but also ways of behavior in everyday life stipulated in the Scriptures. Equally challenging was the integration of freeborn citizens and slaves, followers of Jesus who were to respect and love each other as "brothers" and "sisters." This mutual love among the Christians, whether Jews or Greeks, whether male or female, whether freeborn or slave, was to be demonstrated in the practice of greeting each other—presumably not only in private in the Christian assembly but also in public on the streets of the city or in the marketplace—with a kiss (Rom 16:16; 1 Cor 16:20; 2 Cor 13:12; 1 Thess 5:26). We should note that men

---

[253]Emphasized by Bowers 1987, 187-88; see also Pieper 1929, 211; Haas 1971, 110-16.

and women kissing in public was hardly a common cultural practice in the Greco-Roman world![254] For Paul, the following processes of church planting were central.

1. Theological instruction of believers. When Paul taught Jews who had been converted to faith in Jesus the Messiah, he could rely on their knowledge of the Scriptures. He entered new territory, however, when he explained the significance of Jesus' death on the cross and when he insisted that they have integrated fellowship with their pagan brothers and sisters, including the very practical matter of eating together. Paul would have had to promote change in practical theological matters as well: when Jewish Christians continued to circumcise their children (a plausible assumption), they needed to understand that circumcision was no longer a sign of membership in God's covenant people. Jewish Christians had to be instructed to recognize the central significance of Jesus' death on the cross as the normative criterion for the authority of God's revelation in the Torah of the "old" covenant. They had to understand, for example, that the purity laws and the food laws of the Torah were no longer valid because holiness had been established and granted by Jesus Christ once and for all, allowing the true integration of Jewish believers and Gentile believers. Paul's theological instruction of Gentile Christians could refer to some elements of pagan conceptions of the divine and to the need of salvation, but only in very general terms. Basically everything that Paul needed to say about God and his revelation in the history of Israel, about Jesus the Messiah and the forgiveness of sins that he had made possible, and about the identity of the followers of Jesus as the eschatological people of God was novel and unprecedented.

2. Ethical instruction of believers. Instruction concerning moral behavior was imperative for Gentile Christians, who had to learn the ethics of the revealed will of God in theory and in practice. In the course of his ethical instruction Paul could refer to some of the religious and philosophical traditions of the Greco-Roman world, but in many areas he had to train the new Gentile converts in new ways of behavior—for example, with regard to prostitutes or homosexual activities (Rom 1:24-27; 1 Cor 6:12-19). The ethical instruction of the missionaries had immediate and inevitable social consequences. Because of religious reasons, and often because of ethical reasons, the Gentile Christians were no longer able to visit the theater, the amphitheater or the circus, as the performances were integrated into a traditional pagan religious framework and promoted values that the new converts more often than not were leaving behind. Depending on the specific local situation, Christians could no longer visit the public baths, at least those Christians

---

[254]See William Klassen, "The Sacred Kiss in the New Testament: An Example of Social Boundary Lines," *NTS* 39 (1993): 122-35.

who were scrupulous in terms of public nudity. The performance of professions that were linked with traditional social obligations, including the acceptance of many public offices, at least became difficult.[255] Christoph Burchard observes correctly that to become a Christian implied in some respects a loss of, or removal from, culture. Paul exhorts the Christians in the city of Rome, "Do not be conformed to this world, but be transformed by the renewing of your minds, so that you may discern what is the will of God—what is good and acceptable and perfect" (Rom 12:2). We should note, however, that Paul does not argue for an apartheid of Christians and non-Christians. He clarifies that Christians need not fear contact with pagans: a Christian woman does not have to divorce her pagan husband (1 Cor 7:16); a Christian can, with a clear conscience, eat meat sold on the open market (1 Cor 10:25-26); Christians should ensure that unbelievers can attend their gatherings (1 Cor 14:23-24); Erastus could remain in office as treasurer for the city of Corinth (Rom 16:23).

3. Ecclesiological instruction. Paul had to instruct the new believers in new forms of religious gatherings and in new modes of behavior. Jewish Christians, who were no longer able to visit the local synagogue, had to get used to meeting in a private home for worship, perhaps a house owned by a Gentile man or woman who had become a Christian. For Gentiles, integration into the new community was more radical, as Meinrad Limbeck explains: the Gentile Christians had essentially no way "to express their new faith in forms that they were familiar with from dealing with their gods: there were no temples and no altars where priests offered sacrifices and invited the people to dine with the deity. In the houses in which they gathered there was no image—neither of God nor of Jesus Christ his son—in front of which the individual believer could pray and express with incense and dedicatory offerings his personal thankfulness and reverence. And Christians organized no processions or games in honor of their god in which the former Gentiles could have participated in festive celebration. The forms through which they could, together with other Christians, express their faith in God were baptism, the Lord's Supper (which did not require particular purification rites or particular implements, types of behavior or clothes) and prayer. For the 'nations' Christ was the end of their ancestral religion."[256] When certain Jewish Christians demanded that converted Gentiles practice circumcision (Gal 5:2-3; 6:12-13) and observe the festivals of the Jewish calendar (Gal 4:10; Col 2:16) and certain stipulations concerning food and the worship of angels (Col 2:16-23), Paul consistently and vehemently rejected all such attempts to "enrich" the spiritual life of the Christians. When support-

---

[255]Burchard 1984, 30; for the comment that follows above see ibid. ("Christwerden bedeutete eine bestimmte Entkulturation").
[256]Limbeck 1989, 53; for the remark that follows above see ibid., 53-54.

ers of these attempts described these practices as "humble worship" (Col 2:18, 23), Paul argued that "these have indeed an appearance of wisdom in promoting self-imposed piety, humility, and severe treatment of the body, but they are of no value in checking self-indulgence" (Col 2:23). And he argued that the spiritual reality that the believers have been made part of by Jesus Christ (Col 2:17) constitutes a "whole body, nourished and held together by its ligaments and sinews," and that it "grows with a growth that is from God" (Col 2:19).

When persons of high social standing are converted, their behavior concerning the *humiliores,* the freedmen and the slaves, had to be transformed. The challenge of this issue can be illustrated by the exhortation that Paul gives to the Christians in the city of Corinth. Members of the Corinthian elite were used to covering their head with their toga when they officiated at religious activities in the local temples, but now they are instructed to refrain from such ostentatious actions when they pray or speak prophetically (1 Cor 11:4) in the Christian assembly lest they dishonor their "head" Jesus Christ.[257] In 1 Cor 1—6 Paul reproaches the Corinthian believers for adopting the secular ("fleshly") concepts of Roman society in their understanding of leadership in the Christian community. He criticizes their loyalty to particular persons, their emphasis on status, their boasting with regard to people, their preference for the wisdom of leading personalities in society and for successful orators, their tolerance of the sexual immorality of a church member of high social standing, and their willingness to take other believers to court. The Corinthian believers must learn and understand that leading Christians, including the apostles whom they like to quote, do not distinguish themselves through wealth or personal authority, through status symbols and the prestige that the citizens of Roman Corinth so strongly emphasize. Rather, they are "servants" and correspond to the "workers" in agriculture and the "construction workers"—that is, people who work with their hands and whom the socially "superior" Romans despise. They are not esteemed patrons (1 Cor 3:5-9); rather, they are people who have been placed "last of all, as though sentenced to death," like the prisoners who come last in a Roman triumphal procession (1 Cor 4:8-13).

Troy Martin argues that the conversion of Gentiles to the gospel that Paul proclaimed implied that the new converts abandoned the conventions of the pagan eras and the pagan calendar and adopted the Jewish (liturgical) calendar.[258] However, several arguments of Paul that Martin adduces in support of his hypothesis are hardly relevant for calendar questions: the fact that Paul argues with the Feast of Passover in 1 Cor 5:6-8,

---

[257]Gill 1990. For the observations that follow above see Clarke (1993, 109-18), who refers to 1 Cor 1:20-21, 26; 2:6-8; 3:3-4. See also the important study of B. Winter 2001. On questions of leadership in the church see Clarke 2000, 145-208.

[258]T. Martin 1996, 106-11, 119.

the fact that he preached the gospel in synagogues on the sabbath (Acts 13:14, 44; 17:2), or the fact that he sailed from Philippi after the Feast of Unleavened Bread with the goal of reaching Jerusalem for the day of Pentecost (Acts 20:6.16). More significant is the fact that Paul linked the collection that he organized for the Christians in Jerusalem with the "first day after the sabbath" (κατὰ μίαν σαββάτου, *kata mian sabbatou* [1 Cor 16:2]), evidently the day on which the church met; this agrees with Luke's comment in Acts 20:7 that the church in Alexandria Troas met on the first day of the week. However, these two passages only demonstrate that these two churches had their meetings on the first day of the week,[259] a practice that is connected not so much with the Jewish calendar as with the celebration of Jesus' resurrection. The list in Col 2:10, which includes a reference to the new moon and to the sabbath, clearly reflects not the calendar practices of the church but the controversial concerns of the Jewish-Christian teachers who confuse the believers in Colossae. If Paul could advise the Corinthian Christians to buy meat offered on the open market without them having to investigate its origins, he probably was not concerned about weaning them from the traditional use of pagan religious names for the days of the week and the months of the year. We must recall that the reality of the ancient calendars was confusing and not uniform. (a) The lunisolar year (tracking both the sun and the moon) that was based on exact scientific calculations evidently had limited consequences for the calendar in the Greco-Roman world. Since the cities in Greece handled the insertion of days for the coordination of the calendar with the moon cycle differently, calendrical chaos was the result. Some measure of uniformity was achieved in the East when the Julian Calendar was introduced in 46 B.C. (b) The years were counted using different eras—the Seleucid era (312 B.C.), the era of Pompey (323 B.C.), the Foundation era (of the city of Rome) *ab urbe condita* (753 B.C.), the Olympiads (776 B.C.), or the Cistophoric era (of the autonomy of a city). (c) The Greek names of the months were derived from pagan deities of cultic festivals. In the Attic calendar five months are named after (former) feasts of Apollo; the seventh month of the Athenian calender that began with the summer solstice (i.e., January/February) was called Gamelion, a name that derived probably from a feast of Hera Gamelia, who was known as a goddess of women and as a patron of marriage.[260] It is doubtful whether Paul was concerned about or even interested in these calendar traditions. It was important that the newly converted followers of Jesus abandon, in a consistent manner, their old loyalties to the gods they had worshiped before their conversion. Less important was the matter of whether they should deliberately work on the day of a pagan Feast to demonstrate that they had renounced the worship of that god and to prove their integration into the messianic people of the one true God of Israel. It is highly unlikely that Paul would have expected Gentile Christians to celebrate the Jewish Feast of Passover.

4. Paul did not neatly distinguish between theological, ethical and ecclesiological instruction. The integration of these perspectives can be seen in the way in which

---

[259]See Llewelyn 2001.

[260]W. Sontheimer, "Kalender," *KP* 3:61-63; idem, "Monat, Monatsnamen," *KP* 3:1405-8; idem, "Gamelion," *KP* 2:689; H. Kaletsch, "Zeitrechnung," *KP* 5:1473-89; P. Kuhlmann, "Zeitrechnung," *DNP* 15; J. D. Mikalson, "Calendar, Greek," *OCD* 273-74; H. J. Rose and S. Price, "Calendar, Roman," *OCD* 274; E. J. Bickerman, *Chronology of the Ancient World* (London: Thames & Hudson, 1980 [1968]); A. E. Samuel, *Greek and Roman Chronology: Calendars and Years in Classical Antiquity* (Handbuch der Altertumswissenschaft 1.7; Munich: Beck, 1972).

he discusses various issues in 1 Corinthians that resulted from the religious pluralism in the city of Corinth and presented a challenge for the local Christians.[261]

a. Paul insists that when Corinthian Christians compare the rhetorical capabilities of Paul and Apollos, they make the mistake of being "of the flesh" (σαρκικοί ἐστε, *sarkikoi este*) and of "behaving according to human inclinations" (κατὰ ἄνθρωπον περιπατεῖτε, *kata anthrōpon peripateite*)—that is, of being controlled by the standards of current philosophical schools, such as the Sophists (1 Cor 3:3). Paul argues that (*i*) all Christian teachers belong, without exception, to the church and not vice versa (1 Cor 3:21-22); (*ii*) Christian teachers should be evaluated not with regard to their status but with regard to their function (1 Cor 3:5-8); (*iii*) all Christian teachers are servants of Christ and stewards of God's revelation for the benefit of the church (1 Cor 4:1); (*iv*) he consciously renounced impressive rhetorical fireworks in order to ensure that their faith rests squarely on the power of God (1 Cor 2:1-5); and (*v*) he did not attempt to win followers for himself when he preached and taught in Corinth, but instead he acted like a father whose children they are (1 Cor 4:15), brothers and sisters all, because they all believe in Jesus Christ the Son of God and thus belong together to God's family. Paul therefore challenges the Christians in Corinth to critically rethink the influences of the Greek and Roman traditions of education and erudition of their city and of their society, abandoning their criteria and norms in important respects.

b. If the Corinthian Christians maintain fellowship with the young man who is living in an incestuous relationship with his (step)mother and continue to "boast" (1 Cor 5:2, 6)—presumably with regard to the high social status of the man living in sin[262]—then they continue to function within the customs of Roman society, in which profitable social relationships with people of high social standing are more important than having moral integrity or obeying existing laws (1 Cor 5:1). Paul demands that the Corinthian Christians cease contact with this man, even if this means breaking with the social etiquette of the day (1 Cor 5:1-13). We should note that under Roman law both this man and his stepmother would be sentenced to exile on an island, his possessions confiscated, and his social status repealed.

c. Corinthian Christians who belonged to the local elite continued to use the Roman legal system for their power struggles and quarrels about "the smallest cases" (κριτήρια ἐλάχιστα, *kritēria elachista* [1 Cor 6:2]), as was the custom for rich Roman citizens who regarded personal insults or disagreements as sufficient to initiate *inimicitiae* before a civil court.[263] Paul argues that the failure to

---

[261]For the analysis that follows above see B. Winter 1990; 2001.

[262]Clarke 1993, 73-88; B. Winter 2001, 53-57.

[263]B. Winter 2001, 64-67, with reference to D. F. Epstein, *Personal Enmity in Roman Politics 218-43 B.C.* (London: Routledge, 1989).

put the Christian faith into practice is so evident that they should be ashamed (1 Cor 6:5). Christians must not allow the quarrels about power, influence and prestige that characterized Roman society to influence their own behavior (1 Cor 6:1-8).

d. Corinthian Christians, specifically members of the elite of the city who had the financial resources to finance a lifestyle corresponding to their high social status, evidently lived according to the motto "All things are lawful for me" (πάντα μοι ἔξεστιν, *panta moi exestin* [1 Cor 6:12]; πάντα ἔξεστιν, *panta exestin* [1 Cor 10:23]). This slogan served to rationalize the permissive lifestyle that they indulged in at banquets where the "dessert" of the meal included prostitutes and their services (1 Cor 6:13). Perhaps Paul thinks specifically of young men who received at the age of eighteen the *toga virilis,* and with full legal age the right to attend banquets on their own (note that Paul accuses them in 1 Cor 6:13 of *porneia,* "immorality" or "fornication," rather than *moicheia,* "adultery").[264] Paul rejects this attitude of ethical laissez-faire with strong words: people who behave in this way cannot inherit the kingdom of God (1 Cor 6:8-10); people who think and act in this manner have not understood that God's revelation in the person of Jesus Christ and in the power of the Holy Spirit have created an entirely new situation for the believer that is characterized by purity, holiness and righteousness (1 Cor 6:11) and by the presence of the risen Lord (1 Cor 6:14) and the Holy Spirit (1 Cor 6:19). Paul insists that they cannot attend, besides such private banquets (1 Cor 6:12-20; 15:32-34), public banquets held in the local temples (1 Cor 8:1—11:1), perhaps in connection with the Isthmian Games, where they eat, drink, dance (1 Cor 10:7) and fornicate (1 Cor 10:8), justifying their behavior with the slogan "All is permitted" (1 Cor 10:23). Christians who insist on the social "right" to recline at banquets in the temple (1 Cor 8:10)—for example, the banquet that Lucius Castricus Regulus organized as president of the Isthmian Games on the occasion of the return of the games from Sikyon to Corinth, inviting all Roman citizens of the city (*epulumo omnibus colonis*),[265] possibly in A.D. 51, the year in which Paul lived in Corinth—imply that status, entertainment and amusement are more important than the fellowship of believers in Jesus Christ. In the community of the followers of Jesus the principle of not giving offense to a brother or sister applies (1 Cor 8:13); and also, the encouragement and support of a brother and sister are more important than one's own rights, prompting the believer to be willing to renounce his or her own rights (1 Cor 10:23-33), a principle that the orientation to Jesus Christ makes the most important obliga-

---

[264]B. Winter 2001, 89-91, with reference to A. Booth, "The Age of Reclining and Its Attendant Perils," in *Dining in a Classical Context* (ed. W. J. Slater; Ann Arbor: University of Michigan Press, 1991), 105-20.

[265]*I. KorinthKent* 153. See B. Winter 2001, 94, 276-78.

tion (1 Cor 11:1). Paul rejects the philosophical principle that everything is permitted (for members of the elite), that nobody has the right to criticize the lifestyle of another person: this principle does not apply to Christians, members of the people of God. Prominent Christians of high social standing must not rely on their traditional privileges or think of themselves as exceptions, especially not with the slogan "All is permitted," irrespective of the Roman laws in the city of Corinth or the traditional customs of society.[266] The *ekklēsia* of the believers in Jesus Christ does not allow the ethical behavior of the powerful, rich and prominent Christians to be any different from the life of the other believers.

e. Some newly converted members of the elite brought their status symbols into the meetings of the congregation (1 Cor 11:2-16): they pulled their toga over their heads when they prayed (1 Cor 11:4), a custom that they followed when they officiated at cultic and liturgical activities in the temples of the city and that emphasized their high social status.[267] Paul demands that such behavior stop: it dishonors Jesus Christ, the head of the *ekklēsia,* where social differences no longer matter. Some wives come into the assembly without wearing the traditional head-covering that symbolized marriage (1 Cor 11:5), perhaps intending to imitate the women of the new "Roman elite." Paul insists that they dishonor their spouses with this behavior, which is why it cannot be tolerated in the congregation of God's people, where marriage and family have an important function instituted by God.

f. It seems that some Corinthian Christians used the name of Jesus in curses against rivals, continuing their preconversion habit of trying to vanquish hated rivals (in political or economic matters, in love or in sport), cursing other people in the name of Jesus (1 Cor 12:3a: Ἀνάθεμα Ἰησοῦς, *Anathema Iēsous*). The phrase *anathēma Iesous* usually is translated as "Let Jesus be cursed!" but there is no consensus as to what Paul specifically condemns with his assertion in 1 Cor 12:3a.[268] As scholars complete the parallel phrase *kyrios Iēsous* in 1 Cor 12:3b with the copula *estin* ("is"), reading "Jesus is Lord," it is possible, indeed plausible, likewise to complete the phrase *anathema Iēsous* with the copula *estin,* reading "Jesus is a curse," which means, "Jesus shall curse." This interpretation is supported by the fact that Paul speaks in the immediate context of 1 Cor 12:2 of the pagan past of the Corinthian believers and of the irresistible power of the mute idols.[269] In Corinth archaeologists have found twenty-seven curse tablets,

---

[266]B. Winter 2001, 109, 120.

[267]Gill 1990. For the comments that follow above see B. Winter 2001, 139-40.

[268]See Thiselton (*1 Cor,* 918-24), who presents twelve interpretations. Schrage (*1 Kor,* 3:123-24), without reviewing other options, interprets the phrase in terms of a "blaspheming cursing of Jesus."

[269]B. Winter 2001, 174-83; on ancient pagan (and later Christian) curses see ibid., 167-73; see also K. Preisendanz, "Fluchtafeln (Defixion)," *RAC* 8:1-29; Hendrik S. Versnel, "Beyond Curs-

most of them in the temple of Demeter and in the temple of Persephone, that have yet to be published.[270] The gods invoked in the curses belong to the realm of the earth or the underworld: people asked Hermes, Persephone/Kore, Hekate, Hades/Pluto, Ge and Demeter to curse their rivals or enemies. It is possible that some newly converted polytheists thought that they could "use" Jesus, who was victorious over death and Hades through his own death and resurrection, to harm rivals or enemies. Coptic Christian texts, funerary inscriptions from Asia Minor and funerary inscriptions from Corinth dating after A.D. 250 demonstrate that Christians of later periods used curses to harm other people. Paul scathingly rejects such a practice in 1 Cor 12:3. People who have been saved through faith in Jesus Christ and who have received the Spirit of God cannot curse others: believers use the gifts of the Spirit to nurture fellow believers and to benefit all people who do not yet believe in Jesus Christ.

Summary

Paul's specific missionary procedures can be summarized as follows. (1) Paul generally arrives in a city with a team of coworkers. (2) He establishes contact with the local Jewish community and the local synagogue, which may be able to provide him with hospitality and opportunities to find work. (3) He begins his missionary work with preaching and teaching in the synagogue; not only was this an obvious and therefore practical "tactic" of a Jewish rabbi and missionary, but also it expressed his acknowledgment of the salvation-historical priority of the Jews over the Gentiles. (4) The missionaries more often than not were forced rather quickly to relocate their activities from the synagogue to another venue, if and when the leading officials and the members of the synagogue no longer tolerated both Paul and the Jews who had accepted his teaching about Jesus the Messiah, among them many God-fearers and Gentile sympathizers of the Jewish faith. The new community of believers in Jesus that thereby was established met in rented lecture halls or in private houses of wealthy citizens who had been converted to the gospel of Jesus Christ. (5) Paul often comes under immense pressure from Jewish synagogue officials and members of the magistrate of the cities in which he preaches, being accused of disrupting law and order. Sometimes Paul leaves the city in a hurry, but sometimes he stays and endures physical mistreatment

---

ing: The Appeal to Justice in Judicial Prayers," in *Magikas Hiera: Ancient Greek Magic and Religion* (ed. C. A. Faraone and D. Obbink; Oxford: Oxford University Press, 1991), 60-106; John G. Gager, *Curse Tablets and Binding Spells from the Ancient World* (Oxford: Oxford University Press, 1992); Klauck 1995-1996, 1:179-81.

[270] On the finds in Corinth, to be published by David R. Jordan, see D. R. Jordan, "A Survey of Greek *Defixiones* Not Included in the Special *Corpora*," *GRBS* 26 (1985): 151-97; Ronald S. Stroud, "The Sanctuary of Demeter on Acrocorinth in the Roman Period," in Gregory 1993, 65-73, esp. 72; B. Winter 2001, 164-65.

and public punishment. (6) Paul gathers the new believers in house churches, and they meet regularly to worship God, to be instructed in God's word and for mutual support.

28.3 Form and Content of the Missionary Proclamation

What content did Paul preach in his missionary speeches and sermons? It is somewhat difficult to summarize the apostle's missionary preaching from his own writings. As C. K. Barrett observes, in Gal 4 Paul "provides a fascinating account of his first encounter with the Galatians and of his reception by them, but in this chapter we have not a word of what Paul said in his preaching. The epistles can indeed be described as written preaching, but they are not mission preaching."[271] Jacob Jervell believes that even in the book of Acts Paul's missionary preaching has all but disappeared.[272] This view is overly pessimistic. In my discussion of Paul's missionary self-understanding (§24.3) important and central elements of his missionary message have already been analyzed.

Lutz von Padberg studied the early medieval missionary movement and developed a typology of sermons even though very few sermons survive and even though the available sources contain mostly stereotypical formulations as well as phrases that are clearly removed from reality. He distinguishes six types of sermons of the early medieval missionaries.[273] (1) The summary sermon introduced the listeners to the central truths of the Christian faith. (2) The situational sermon used unexpected situations or experiences of the listeners that illustrated the truth of the Christian message. (3) The constructive, positive sermon conveyed biblical perspectives, such as the good news of the eternal joys of heaven. (4) The moralistic sermon emphasized the ethical claims of the Christian faith. (5) The antithetical sermon offered the pagans the gospel as an uncompromising alternative to their traditional faith and thus allowed the missionary to immediately explain the essence of the gospel. (6) The dogmatic sermon explained in detail theological truths, proceeding mostly by argumentation.

The following analysis of Paul's missionary preaching as narrated by Luke in the book of Acts and as illustrated by Paul's letters focuses on the content of his sermons. We can distinguish the following types of sermons: (1) christological communication as pioneer preaching to Jewish audiences ("exegetical sermon"); (2) theological communication as pioneer preaching to Gentile audiences ("summary sermon"); (3) dialogical concentration in terms of a detailed explanation of the gospel ("situational sermon"); (4) ideological confrontation with the proclamation of Jesus as Messiah and Lord ("antithetical sermon"); (5) apologetic confrontation as defense of the gospel ("dogmatic sermon");

---

[271]Barrett 1995, 156; cf. idem 1991, 8; see also Donaldson 1994, 169.
[272]Jervell 1984, 53.
[273]Padberg 1995, 125-40, esp. 128-34.

(6) pastoral concretization when Paul encourages the Christian communities ("constructive sermon").[274]

Christological Communication: Pioneer Preaching to Jewish Audiences

Paul's missionary preaching in synagogues can be illustrated by his sermon in Pisidian Antiocheia (Acts 13:16-41). This is the first and the longest sermon of Paul that Luke reports in the book of Acts. It resembles, as Rudolf Pesch explains, "Stephen's speech with its review of salvation history (Acts 7:2-53), and Peter's speeches before Jews with their proclamation of Jesus (Acts 2:22-36; 3:12-26). This speech by Paul is unique because it ends with the Pauline doctrine of justification and a reference to the Gentile mission as the work of God that divides Israel (Acts 13:38-41)."[275] The threefold address of the audience (Acts 13:16b, 26a, 38a) divides the speech into three parts, which can be linked with the traditional rhetorical parts of the *narratio* (explanation of the issue), *argumentatio* (proofs) and *peroratio* (conclusion).[276]

I. Review of Salvation History (Acts 13:16b-25): Narratio

13:16b	Address of the "Israelites"
13:17-25	Witnesses of God's promise in the history of the people of Israel
13:17-20a	1. From the *election* of the patriarchs to the preview of the exile
13:20b	2. Comment on the period of the judges
13:21-22	3. The period of the kings: Saul and David
13:23	4. The fullfilment of the *promise* given to David in the mission of Jesus
13:24-25	5. John the Baptist

II. Proclamation of the Significance of Jesus (Acts 13:26-37): Argumentatio

13:26	1. The relevance of the gospel for the audience
13:27-29	2. Discussion of the culpable behavior of the citizens of Jerusalem

---

[274]The "moralizing sermon" is missing in the typology of Paul's sermons, nor is it in the background of the Pastoral Epistles. I. H. Marshall (*PastEp*, 98-107) provides an explanation of the contingent aspects of the Pastoral Epistles in terms of the coherent theological, christological and soteriological center of early Christian theology.

[275]Pesch, *Apg*, 2:29-30. On Acts 13:16-41 see, besides the commentaries, Dumais 1976; Pillai 1979; Buss 1980; Bottino 1990; Pichler 1997; also Bolt 1998, 204-7.

[276]Pichler 1997, 124-31; cf. Schneider, *Apg*, 2:130; Pesch, *Apg*, 2:30-32; Fitzmyer, *Acts*, 507-8. Jervell (*Apg*, 354-58) divides the sermon in the three sections: Acts 13:17-25, 26-31, 32-41. Weiser (*Apg*, 2:322-23) and Zmijewski (*Apg*, 494) identify four parts: Acts 13:16-25, 26-31, 32-37, 38-41. Buss (1980, 26-31) finds five sections: Acts 13:16a-23, 24-26, 27-31, 32-37, 38-41. It makes no sense, however, to link Acts 13:26 with the section on John the Baptist in Acts 13:24-25. Wilckens (1974, 54) divides the text into six parts.

13:30	3. Announcement of the resurrection of Jesus
13:31	4. Note about Jesus' postresurrection appearances
13:32-33a	5. Paul and Barnabas as proclaimers of the fulfillment of the promise
13:33b-37	6. Proof from Scripture for Jesus' resurrection: Ps 2:7; Is 55:3; Ps 16:10

III. Call to Repentance (Acts 13:38-41): Peroratio

13:38-39	1. Forgiveness of sins and the justification of the believers
13:40-41	2. Warning not to ignore the work of God, using Hab 1:5

Some scholars regard this passage as a Lukan construction that combines various sources and comments on several biblical passages. Martin Dibelius argues that the first part of the sermon (Acts 13:16-22) "has no connection with the missionary—and there is certainly none with the content of the missionary sermon."[277] This suggestion becomes unnecessary if we take Acts 13:15 seriously: Paul was asked by the synagogue officials to preach in the synagogue service on the passages of the reading from the Law and from the Prophets. The two texts that were read on this occasion probably were Deut 4:25-46 (*parashah*, reading from the Torah) and 2 Sam 7:6-16 (*haftarah*, reading from the Prophets).[278] We also should note that consistent connections can be observed between the missionary situation in Acts 13 that Luke reports and implies[279] and the theology of Paul. Matthäus Buss demonstrates in a careful analysis of the first part of the speech (Acts 13:16-23) that Dibelius's view is untenable. He concludes, "This introduction mentions the darker sides of Israel's past history only by way of allusion and is to be understood as a *captatio benevolentiae* for the Jewish listeners who are present. . . . Paul is in new missionary territory that can still be open or closed to the new message."[280]

1. In the first part of the sermon Paul provides a review of salvation history, framed by the notion of Israel's election (Acts 13:17) and the notion of God's promise for Israel (Acts 13:23). He characterizes Israel's history as being planned and ordered by God with Jesus the Messiah as its goal. Paul's review of salvation history before the synagogue audience, hearing the message of Jesus the Messiah for the first time, is deliberately positive. The inclusion of personal names— Samuel, Saul, David, John—probably is intended to tell the audience that God focused his salvation on one redeemer figure.[281] And David is highlighted "because he is, on account of his obedient service, in a unique way the *typos* of Jesus the redeemer."

2. In the second part of the sermon Paul explains the fulfillment of God's

---

[277]Dibelius 1949, 143 (ET, 166); similarly Roloff, *Apg,* 203; Zmijewski, *Apg,* 495-500.

[278]Bowker 1967-1968; cf. Dumais 1976, 72-78, 281-325; Pesch, *Apg,* 2:32; Barrett, *Acts,* 1:624; Witherington, *Acts,* 408-9. Zmijewski (*Apg,* 495-96) rejects this suggestion.

[279]Pesch (*Apg,* 2:42) refers to the lack of specific emphases that Paul specified in his discussion with his opponents. See also Pillai 1979, 67-111.

[280]Buss (1980, 48), who nevertheless characterizes the speech as representing an "ideal type" (ibid., 146).

[281]Buss 1980, 47; the quotation that follows above, ibid.

promise to Israel in the life, death and resurrection of Jesus. Paul's proclamation of Jesus is controlled since Acts 13:23 by the theme "Jesus the Savior of Israel." The inhabitants of Jerusalem and the leading representatives of Israel rejected Jesus. They did not recognize who Jesus was; they did not understand the significance of the words of the prophets whose prophecies they regularly heard in the temple and in the synagogue. However, the listeners who are sitting in the synagogue of Antiocheia do not yet belong to the people who heard about Jesus and rejected him. Paul emphasizes that Jesus' rejection by the Jews in Jerusalem was part of God's plan. He contrasts the actions of Israel's leaders with God's actions: God raised Jesus from the dead and he appeared to his followers for many days. Paul substantiates this point with three quotations from Scripture:[282]

First quotation: Paul quotes Ps 2:7 (Acts 13:33) to explain that God has fulfilled the promise that he gave to the patriarchs (cf. Acts 13:23)—the promise of the reading from the prophets in 2 Sam 7:12-16—now in the present time, as he has raised Jesus from the dead. Jesus' resurrection is the fulfillment of Ps 2:7, a text connected with 2 Sam 7:12 (σπέρμα, *sperma,* the "seed" of David) and with 2 Sam 7:14b (υἱός μου . . . γεγέννηκά σε, *hyios mou . . . gegennēka se*) through the phrase "begotten son" (υἱός μου . . . γεγέννηκά σε). Psalm 2 describes the opposition of the nations and their rulers against the Lord's Anointed One, the ruler of God's people. In its original context Ps 2:7 refers to the legitimacy of Israel's king as "son of God"—that is, as ruler who enjoys God's care and protection. In some traditions of Second Temple Judaism, Psalm 2 was interpreted in terms of the Messiah (see *Pss. Sol.* 17:26). The early Christians interpreted Psalm 2 in terms of Jesus (cf. Acts 4:25-26; Lk 3:22; Heb 1:5; 5:5), probably as a result of the voice of God heard at Jesus' baptism. Thus 2 Sam 7:12 is relevant for Paul in two respects: the "raised seed" is Jesus, the "son" of Ps 2:7 whom God had "raised" from the dead. Paul asserts that Jesus is the messianic Son of David and the Savior of Israel, whom Scripture had promised and whom God had begotten.

Second quotation: In Acts 13:34b Paul quotes Is 55:3. He asserts that Jesus' resurrection from the dead corresponds to God's claim in Is 55:3 LXX. This text is linked with 2 Sam 7:15a ("my grace," LXX: τὸ δὲ ἔλεός μου, *to de eleos mou*) through the term *hasdī* "steadfast love for David" (LXX: τὰ ὅσια Δαυίδ, *ta hosia David,* "the holy of David," meaning the promise of salvation for David), and with 2 Sam 7:16a ("will be made sure forever," πιστωθήσεται) through the term τὰ πιστά (*ta pista,* "unswerving"). In the context of Is 55:3 God assures Israel of his covenantal faithfulness, of the reliability of the promise given to David. Rudolf Pesch comments, "As an interpretation of 2 Sam 7:14-16, the goal of the quotation of Is 55:3 and of the specified reference to resurrection 'no more to return to corruption' is to assert that the rule of Jesus, whom God had raised from the dead, 'will last forever' (2 Sam 7:16). The salvific promise given to David . . . proves reliable in the rule of Christ, who is enthroned in heaven."[283]

Third quotation: In Acts 13:35 Paul quotes Ps 16:10. He asserts in Acts 13:34 that when

---

[282]See Marshall, *Acts,* 226-28; Pesch, *Apg,* 2:38-39; Bock 1998, 50.
[283]Pesch, *Apg,* 2:39.

Jesus was raised from the dead, he assumed a new form of existence that made it impossible for him to experience death again and the corruption of the body. The quotation from Is 55:3 is linked through the term τὰ ὅσια Δαυίδ (*ta hosia David*) with Ps 16:10 (τὸν ὅσιόν σου, *ton hosion sou,* "your holy one"); Ps 16 is also connected with 2 Sam 7:12-13, stating in Ps 16:10, "For you do not give me up to Sheol, or let your faithful one see the Pit" (LXX: ἰδεῖν διαφθοράν, *idein diaphthoran*); and 2 Sam 7:12b asserts, "When your days are fulfilled and you lie down with your ancestors, I will raise up your offspring [σπέρμα, *sperma*] after you, who shall come forth from your body, and I will establish his kingdom." Also, Ps 16:10 is linked with the subject of Paul's sermon through the term "corruption" (διαφθορά, *diaphthora*): Paul proclaimed that Jesus, who had died, "did not see corruption" because he was raised from the dead. Rudolf Pesch comments, "Paul thus interprets the promise to David (2 Sam 7:12-16), whose reliability God himself confirmed (Is 55:2), in this sense: as David knew . . . God does not let 'his holy one' (i.e., the messianic seed of David) 'see corruption.'"[284] Paul argues that this passage cannot refer to David himself: David "served his own generation" (Acts 13:36a) and then died, thus he "experienced corruption" (Acts 13:37). Jesus, however, "experienced no corruption" because God raised him from the dead (Acts 13:37).

The numerous quotations from and allusions to Old Testament passages, formulations and expectations fit the communicative situation of a sermon or an exegetical lecture in a synagogue. Klaus Haacker is correct when he explains that "before this congregation Paul can speak the language in which he thinks when he develops his deepest theological insights."[285] The scriptural quotations do not just correspond to the historical situation of a synagogue sermon; they also demonstrate Paul's intention to integrate the life of Jesus into the course of the history of Israel, the people of God, and they demonstrate Paul's conviction that ultimately God himself is the subject of salvation history and of Jesus' history.[286] By referring to Jerusalem in the section on Jesus (Acts 13:27, 31), Paul clarifies that God's salvation reached its climax in the Holy City.

3. In the third section of the sermon Paul formulates the decisive proclamation of salvation through Jesus the Messiah. He argues that Jesus, whom God had raised from the dead, is the one through whom God forgives sins, a forgiveness that now is offered to the congregation in the synagogue of Antiocheia. Paul argues that it is only through faith in the risen Jesus that people can have the right relationship with God. The forgiveness of sins that God offers in Jesus is valid for "all" sins (ἀπὸ πάντων, *apo pantōn*), from which the law could not free them, and it justifies "all who believe" (πᾶς ὁ πιστεύων, *pas ho pisteuōn* [Acts 13:39]).[287] This last assertion, "all who believe," implies the Gentiles also, which is why Paul warns his synagogue audience of the danger of despising

---

[284]Ibid.
[285]Haacker 1988a, 68.
[286]Buss 1980, 80-81.
[287]On the "Paulinism" of this passage see Pichler 1997, 251-53 (cf. ibid., 267-354); contra Horn 1983, 284; Wehr 1996, 132, following Schille, *Apg,* 177; Pesch, *Apg,* 2:42.

God's gift and thus fulfilling Hab 1:5, where the prophet asserts, "Look at the nations, and see! Be astonished! Be astounded! For a work is being done in your days that you would not believe if you were told." This passage speaks of Israel's failure to recognize the invasion of the Chaldeans as God's judgment. Paul applies the prophecy to the danger that the Jews may not grasp that Jesus is the Savior sent by God. The "work" (ἔργον, *ergon*) that God has done is the resurrection of Jesus, an event that many refuse to believe.[288]

Paul argues for the significance of Jesus' resurrection in four steps.[289] (a) Jesus' resurrection is the climax of salvation history. God, who had revealed himself in the history of Israel through mighty acts, has sent the Savior to his people, Jesus (Acts 13:23), whom he raised from the dead (Acts 13:30). (b) Jesus' resurrection represents the fulfillment of God's promise in Ps 2 and thus confirms Jesus as the Son of God. And it represents at the same time the fulfillment of the promise in Is 55:3 and thus brings God's gracious gifts, which no one can destroy—through the risen Son, who cannot experience corruption, according to Ps 16:10 (Acts 13:32-37). (c) Jesus' resurrection is the basis for God's forgiveness of sins and for the justification of everyone who believes in Jesus (Acts 13:38-39). (d) Jesus' resurrection is the amazing act of God that many do not want to believe, a fact that prompts Paul to warn the audience not to despise the work of God (Acts 13:40-41). Karl Löning comments on the way in which Luke refers to the people of Israel: "Luke speaks of Israel's past primarily in terms of revelatory history as the realization of Israel's hope through the promises of the prophets, which are transmitted as Scripture. Luke speaks of Israel at the time of Jesus and the apostles primarily in terms of soteriology as the people that loses its identity, grounded in its messianic hope, in the debate about Jesus, and as the people that is at stake in the dispute about the recognition of Jesus as the Messiah of the promise."[290]

Was it necessary for Paul in his missionary preaching to Jewish audiences to first awaken a consciousness of Jews being sinners? Albrecht Oepke answered this question in the affirmative, in the context of his (Lutheran) interpretation of the self-consciousness of the Jewish people imagining circumcision and the law to be "external" privileges that Paul's arguments in Rom 2 destroy.[291] Scholars today no longer dispute that even the most conservative Jews had a deep sense of being sinners, as the final paragraphs of Qumran's *Rule of the Community* (1QS XI) demonstrate. Paul did not need to convince his Jewish listeners that they were sinners. What he needed to demonstrate in his missionary sermons before Jews

---

[288]See Pillai 1979, 71-73.

[289]Cf. Hansen 1998, 300-306. On Jesus' redemptive death and resurrection in Paul's proclamation see now Hurtado 2003, 126-33.

[290]Löning 1985, 2609, formulated as a critique of H. Conzelmann's scheme of three periods (time of Israel, time of Jesus, time of the church).

[291]Oepke 1920, 65-66; on the "propaedeutics of preaching to Jews" see ibid., 76-82; on Paul's "salvific preaching to Jews" see ibid., 108-19.

was the messianic identity of Jesus. The question of whether or not Jesus was the Messiah decided the validity of the message that God forgives sins through Jesus and provides rescue on judgment day through Jesus. The acknowledgment that Jesus is the Messiah and the acceptance that his death brings salvation implied the conclusion that Israel's salvation no longer rests on being God's covenant people as a result of circumcision and the sacrifices in the temple that God had stipulated for Israel in the law as the means of restoring the holiness that had been lost as the result of sin. Thus a "propaedeutics" that would demonstrate to Jews that they are sinners needing salvation was unnecessary. Paul could move immediately *in medias res* and explain the identity and the work of Jesus of Nazareth.

Luke provides ample evidence for the fact that Paul's missionary proclamation in the synagogue was focused on the history of Jesus. This corresponds to Paul's assertion that the message of "Jesus crucified" is the missionary message pure and simple (1 Cor 1—2; 15:1-14; Rom 1:1-4).[292] (1) Luke repeatedly points out that Paul preached "the kingdom of God" (Acts 19:8; 20:25: in Ephesus; 28:23, 31: in Rome). Luke never explains this expression in the book of Acts; that would be unnecessary because his readers know from the first volume of his work that Jesus preached the kingdom of God, a message that he continued to emphasize after his resurrection (Acts 1:3) and that the Jerusalem missionaries preached as well (Acts 8:12: Philip in Samaria). Luke's readers therefore understand that Paul preached Jesus' message of the dawn of the kingdom of God, which the Twelve and the Seventy preached (Lk 9—10), as did the Jerusalem missionaries. (2) Paul proclaims the history of Jesus that begins with John the Baptist (Acts 13:23-31), as Peter does (Acts 10:36-38). (3) The "teaching of the apostles" which is the focus of the preaching activity of the Twelve and of other preachers in Jerusalem (Acts 2:42), and which has priority over all other tasks of the leaders of the church (Acts 6:2), is connected with the history of Jesus' ministry from John the Baptist to Jesus' resurrection (Acts 1:21-22). (4) Luke describes the ministry of Jesus in detail in the first volume of his work. Luke himself was one of the early followers of Jesus, but he researched the history of Jesus' ministry, carefully consulting eyewitnesses (Lk 1:1-4). For Luke, the message proclaimed by Peter and Paul, the two main characters in the book of Acts, clearly is controlled by the history of Jesus that he recorded in his earlier book. David Wenham correctly concludes, "Paul did not preach theological abstractions or credal formulae, but the story of Jesus."[293]

Theological Communication: Pioneer Preaching to Gentile Audiences

Gentiles who came into contact with Paul in synagogue services heard the same

---

[292]For the analysis that follows above see D. Wenham 2000, esp. 88-93.
[293]Wenham 2000, 90. On the literary connections between the Gospel of Luke and the book of Acts see also Marshall 1993.

message that the Jewish audience heard: the message of Jesus, who was crucified and was raised from the dead, the Messiah sent by God who forgives sins
and provides rescue from God's coming judgment. Gentile audiences heard
Paul speak for the first time in a lecture hall in the city, during a meeting in a
private home, or outside in the open air of the agora. Such listeners perhaps had
just come from, for example, the temple of Athena in Thessalonike. Or they had
just participated in a banquet of the devotees of Sarapis, and then a friend invited them to an evening meeting in the house of a Christian. Or they still had
an invitation in their pocket that read, "The god calls you to a banquet being
held in the Thoereion tomorrow from the ninth hour."[294] Perhaps they had combined the veneration of Athena and the Sarapis banquet during the day. Pagans
would have welcomed the message of a savior from sins; it could easily be integrated into the diversity of the religious options in the city.

However, the assertion that forgiveness of sins could be obtained exclusively through faith in Jesus Christ needed to be explained. Such an explanation had to convince the listeners that there is only one true God: if there is
only one true God, there is probably only one true savior from sins. One may
call this "propaedeutical preaching."[295] To polytheists, Paul first needed to
speak about the God of Israel as the only true God before he could speak
about Jesus the Lord and Savior. In Athens Paul preached both in the agora
and in the synagogue "the good news about Jesus and the resurrection" (Acts
17:18). This clearly shows that Paul, when he preached to pagans, did not dispense with explaining the person, ministry and salvational significance of
Jesus Christ.

The text 1 Thess 1:9-10 often is mentioned as an example of Paul's missionary preaching to pagans in pioneer situations. Adolf von Harnack characterized
this text as a "mission-preaching to pagans in a nutshell."[296] Since Ulrich Wilckens's study on the missionary speeches in Acts, many interpreters regard 1 Thess
1:9-10 as a summary of Paul's initial missionary preaching to pagans. Another
foundational text is 2 Cor 11:4, in which Paul formulates the essential content
of proper missionary proclamation as he interacts with the message and behavior of false apostles. Another important text is 1 Thess 4:2-7, in which the phrase
"as we have already told you beforehand and solemnly warned you" (1 Thess
4:6) refers to subject matter that Paul emphasized during his first visit in Thessalonike as a missionary.

---

[294]P. Köln 57: καλεῖ σε ὁ θεὸς εἰς κλείνην γεινο(μένην) ἐν τῷ Θοηρείῳ αὔριον ἀπὸ ὥρ(ας) θ´;
for the translation see *NewDocs* 1:5, no. 1c; see also Klauck 1995-1996, 1:119.

[295]Oepke 1920, 65; on the "propaedeutics of preaching to pagans" see ibid., 82-108; on "preaching salvation to pagans" see ibid., 19-160.

[296]Harnack 1924, 1:117 (ET, 1:89). For the comment that follows above see Wilckens 1974, 81.
See also Schneider 1969, 65-66; Howell 1998a, 71-72.

1 Thess 1:9-10: "For the people of those regions report about us what kind of welcome [*eisodos*] we had among you, and how you turned to God [*epestrepsate pros ton theon*] from idols [*apo tōn eidōlōn*], to serve a living and true God [*douleuein theō*], ¹⁰and to wait for his Son from heaven, whom he raised from the dead—Jesus, who rescues us [*ton ryomenon*] from the wrath that is coming."

1 Thess 2:13: "We also constantly give thanks to God for this, that when you received the word of God that you heard from us [*logon akoēs par' hēmōn tou theou*], you accepted it not as a human word [*logon anthrōpon*] but as what it really is, God's word [*logon theou*], which is also at work in you believers [*energeitai en hymin*]."

2 Cor 11:4: "For if someone comes and proclaims another Jesus than the one we proclaimed, or if you receive a different spirit from the one you received, or a different gospel from the one you accepted, you submit to it readily enough."

1 Thess 4:2-7: "For you know what instructions we gave you through the Lord Jesus. ³For this is the will of God, your sanctification: that you abstain from fornication; ⁴that each one of you know how to control your own body in holiness and honor, ⁵not with lustful passion, like the Gentiles who do not know God; ⁶that no one wrong or exploit a brother or sister in this matter, because the Lord is an avenger in all these things, just as we have already told you beforehand and solemnly warned you. ⁷For God did not call us to impurity but in holiness."

According to these texts, the following factors are of foundational importance for Paul's missionary preaching to pagans.[297]

1. The active entrance of the apostle and the passive acceptance by the listeners (εἴσοδος, *eisodos*). In 1 Thess 1:9-10 Paul does not state which "proofs" he used to convince his listeners, nor does he indicate the first "point" that he made in his (first) sermon. Paul informs about the goal, not the means, of his missionary preaching.[298] He does not write about the details of his "entrance." He does not need to, because the Christians in Thessalonike would remember the specifics.[299] In 1 Thess 2:13 Paul provides more details about his missionary preaching in Thessalonike: he proclaimed his message not as "human word" but as "God's word," which is at work in the listeners (1 Thess 2:13).

2. Paul proclaims the God of Israel as the one true God (1 Thess 2:13). Since the Gentile Christians in Thessalonike evidently turned away from the deities they had worshiped, Paul must have spoken of the futility of idol worship. Paul's description of, and the reasoning for, the break with the idols mentions only the goal of conversion: to worship the one true God. This means that the abandonment of the idols and the turning to the one true God happen simultaneously—it is one and the same process. The break with the pagan deities is not the result of a theoretical insight into monotheism; rather, it takes place in

---

[297]On 1 Thess 1:9-10 see, besides the commentaries, Pesce 1994, 63-91.
[298]See Barrett 1991, 9.
[299]See Holtz, *1 Thess,* 56.

the context of a pagan turning to the one true God.[300] It is impossible to say whether Paul spent more time and rhetorical energy on a discussion of the pagan deities worshiped locally and on the problem of the veneration of a plurality of deities, or on arguments supporting the reality of the one true God, the God of Israel. It is fair to assume that Paul's emphasis depended on the requirements of the particular situation. In any case, Rom 1:18-32 demonstrates that Paul could write, and surely speak, with extraordinary commitment and with rhetorical refinement about pagan religiosity and its consequences for society and for the individual. And the Areopagus speech in Acts 17:22-31 shows that Paul was able to lecture with penetrating logic in a philosophically informed manner about false and valid concepts of God.

3. Paul recounts the life and ministry of Jesus of Nazareth and proclaims the significance of his death and resurrection as central events that make the message that he proclaims *good* news: in Jesus Christ, God forgives the sins of the people and now invites Gentiles to become members of the people of God through faith in him. The use of the name "Jesus" in 1 Thess 1:10, without an explanatory addendum such as a title, indicates that Paul talked about Jesus of Nazareth as a person in space and time. Paul proclaimed Jesus not as a mythical hero or as a philosophical or pneumatic principle[301] but as a historical person who lived and suffered, who died and was raised from the dead. The reference to the resurrection (1 Thess 1:10) serves "to identify the promised Son of God with the historical person. . . . People who turn to the God who is proclaimed in the gospel message gain the certain salvific hope of eschatological salvation through Jesus the Son of God, who has been shown by God to have broken through the barrier of death into life that is eschatologically safe and sound."[302] In 1 Thess 1:10 Paul does not answer the question of *how* Jesus saves. The answer to this question is given by Paul in other passages—for example, in 1 Cor 1:17-18, where he describes the message that he proclaims as the "message about the cross": God forgives sins through Jesus Christ because Jesus died on the cross, taking the place of the sinners, taking upon himself their death sentence and thus atoning for their guilt.[303] Jesus died on the cross *as a substitute* for the sinner and, at the same time, *for the benefit* of the sinner who believes in Jesus as the messianic Savior.[304] In two letters that probably were both written within a few months of the foundation of the churches in Thessalonike and Galatia, Paul speaks of the "kingdom of God" (*basileia theou* [1 Thess 2:12; Gal

---

[300]Holtz, *1 Thess,* 61.

[301]Against such suggestions see Oepke 1920, 58.

[302]Holtz, *1 Thess,* 60, 61-62.

[303]Cf. Rom 1:16-17; 3:25-26; 5:9; 6:3-9; 8:3, 32; 1 Cor 1:18, 24; 5:7; 2 Cor 5:19-21; Gal 1:4; 3:13; Eph 1:7; 2:13; 5:2; Col 2:10; Phil 2:8; 3:18.

[304]See Helmut Merklein, "Die Bedeutung des Kreuzestodes Christi für die paulinische Gerechtigkeits- und Gesetzesthematik," in Merklein 1987, 1-106, esp. 23.

5:21]), an expression that rarely occurs in Paul's letters.[305] This indicates that Paul must have spoken in his first missionary sermons about God's kingly rule that has dawned with the coming of Jesus Christ. In the political contexts of the *Imperium Romanum,* of the claims of the Roman emperors and the realities of the imperial cult, whose significance increased continuously, this was a potentially dangerous conviction. Clearly, this emphasis on the kingdom of God was so intricately connected with the message about the person and significance of Jesus Christ that Paul did not dispense with it in his sermons before pagan audiences. In his instruction of new believers he would have been able to build on this emphasis, probably in connection with immoral behavior, which is incompatible with membership in God's kingdom (see the list of vices and the warning in Gal 5:19-21).[306]

4. In his missionary sermons Paul spoke of the expectation that Jesus, the Son of God who had been raised from the dead, would return and save the people who believe in him, rescuing them from God's coming judgment of the world, a salvation that brings final reconciliation with God (2 Cor 5:20). As Albrecht Oepke argues, the summons to "be reconciled to God" receives its power and emphasis "from the reference to the coming universal catastrophe that was announced as the arrival of Christ for the redemption of believers and for the punishment of those who refused to be saved. This gospel shows, by its testimony of the crucified and resurrected Christ, the way to salvation from the coming wrath of God and is thus indeed 'a power of God for the salvation of all who believe' (Rom 1:16)."[307]

5. Paul explains the necessity of conversion, which consists of two components: turning away from the futile pagan gods (ἀπὸ τῶν εἰδώλων, *apo tōn eidōlōn*) and turning to the one, true, living God of Israel (ἐπεστρέψατε πρὸς τὸν θεόν, *epestrepsate pros ton theon*). According to 1 Thess 2:13, the dynamic of the event, or process, of conversion is connected not with the force of the arguments that are used (οὐ λόγον ἀνθρώπων, *ou logon anthrōpōn*) but with insight into the divine origin of the message (καθώς ἐστιν ἀληθῶς λόγον θεοῦ, *kathōs estin alēthōs logon theou*).

6. The goal and the purpose of the conversion of pagans is "faith in God" (1 Thess 1:8). In the book of Acts Luke regularly uses the verb *pisteuein* to describe the break with the pagan deities and the conversion to the one true God, who has revealed himself in Jesus Christ. The expression "to believe" or "to come to faith" describes the "new orientation of people's existence."[308] Paul uses the terms *pistis* ("faith") and *pisteuein* ("to believe") more often than does any other

---

[305]Rom 14:17; 1 Cor 4:20; 6:9-10; 15:50; Eph 5:5; Col 4:11. See D. Wenham 1995, 34-97.
[306]Haufe 1985, esp. 467-68; see earlier Oepke 1920, 69.
[307]Oepke 1920, 62-63.
[308]Brandenburger 1988, 186.

New Testament author. For Paul, faith in Jesus Christ is the great alternative to
life in bondage to the pagan deities.[309] Faith in the one true God as faith in Christ
is not a prior achievement demanded of the listener. As faith that comes from
"hearing" (Gal 3:23, 25; cf. Rom 10:17), it is "a gift from God that liberates people
from the rule of sin established by the law for a new life under the rule of
Christ," and it is "the new life in the Spirit mercifully made possible by God in
Christ through the gospel that remains (together with ἀγάπη and ἐλπίς) forever
(1 Cor 13:13)."

7. Paul speaks in his missionary sermons of the obedience that God demands
of all people, an obedience that characterizes the lives of those who have been
reconciled with God through faith in Jesus Christ on the basis of the power of
the Holy Spirit and in the context of their gratitude for what God has done in
their lives. Paul's missionary sermons included references to the fact that pagans
are to "serve" the one true God (δουλεύειν θεῷ, douleuein theō), and that they
can do so through faith in Jesus. It is fair to assume, on the basis of repeated
reminders in Paul's letters, that he also emphasized that faith in God is acted out
in love for God and in love for other people, that the driving power of faith is
the Holy Spirit, and that the fruit of faith is the "work produced by faith" (ἔργον
τῆς πίστεως, ergon tēs pisteōs) as effected by God's Spirit (1 Thess 1:3).[310] The
term "to serve" (douleuein) is, in the Septuagint, "the most common term for the
service of God, not in the sense of an isolated act, but in that of total commitment to the Godhead."[311] Paul uses the term douleuein to refer to obedience to
God and generally to the behavior of followers of Jesus, who no longer seek
fulfillment and fortune for themselves, who live committed to God and to the
benefit of others, as Jesus was sent by God the Father into the world in order
to serve humankind. The goal of turning to the one true God is all-encompass-
ing worship, enacted and accomplished in all facets of life—a life according to
the will of God. This new life that pagans receive upon believing in God's revelation in Jesus Christ is ruled by the Holy Spirit, and it becomes visible in a
lifestyle characterized by purity and sanctity, specifically in changed ways of behavior in family and in business, with regard to friends and acquaintances, in
the house and outside of the house. After referring to the pagan Thessalonians'
turning to God, Paul mentions (with two final infinitives: douleuein theō zōnti . . .
kai anamenein ton huion autou) their service of God and the expectation of
Jesus, the risen Son of God, thus explaining the significance of their conversion
(1 Thess 1:9-10).[312] Traugott Holtz explains, "Their turning to God took place so

---

[309]Stuhlmacher (1992-1999, 1:342), who refers to the "godlessness" of the pagans; the quotations that follow above, ibid., 1:344, formulated with regard to both Jewish and pagan audiences.

[310]See Stuhlmacher 1992-1999, 1:347.

[311]K. H. Rengstorf, ThWNT 2:270 (TDNT 2:267); Holtz, 1 Thess, 58.

[312]1 Thess 1:9-10: δουλεύειν θεῷ ζῶντι καὶ ἀληθινῷ καὶ ἀναμένειν τὸν υἱὸν αὐτοῦ.

that they serve the living and true God and wait for his Son. These are not processes that happen in succession, neither in the perception of the believing Thessalonians nor in Paul's summons to faith."[313]

Did Paul always preach the same sermon when he addressed pagans? Ulrich Wilckens suggests the existence of a "missionary sermon that was fixed both in terms of its content and in terms of the sequence of subject matter."[314] He submits that such a scheme can be found in 1 Thess 1:9-10; Acts 14:15-17; 17:22-31, as well as in Heb 6:1.

In regard to 1 Thess 1:9-10, Ulrich Wilckens observes, "First comes the 'conversion,' that is, the total break with polytheism and the turning to serve the one true God. Then there is the turn to the eschatological future. The converts are to expect the future coming of the Son of God from heaven. This expectation is the only reference to the present status of the convert. A brief review points to the resurrection of the Son of God from the dead as a decisive act of God in the past, on which the expectation of his return is based. Finally he mentions the name 'Jesus' and refers to his function at his future coming. He will be the one who 'saves' the converts from the future wrath. The resurrection and the future coming of Jesus are the only christological data, with the reference to the coming of Jesus as the decisive statement which is substantiated by the reference to the resurrection."

This thesis was highly influential. Jürgen Roloff writes in his commentary on Acts 17:22-31, "The main interest of the narrator was to show how Paul modified the monotheistic propaedeutics that the missionary scheme *demanded* for the specific situation of the conversation with pagan philosophers."[315] Rudolf Pesch asserts that the speech in Acts 17:22-31 "follows the traditional scheme of the early Christian missionary sermon (that expanded the Jewish-Hellenistic missionary sermon christologically), which thus cannot be deconstructed."[316] The hypothesis of a scheme for the early Christian missionary sermon has been criticized for good reasons.[317] (1) The texts that have been used as a basis for the reconstruction of such a scheme are rather disparate, in terms of both subject matter and the sequence of the topics. Acts 14:15-17 refers only to "turning to the living God," while the break with idolatry is not explicitly stated but only implied in the context. Acts 17:22-31 refers only "to comprehending God and turning to him."[318] Only 1 Thess 1:9-10 speaks of "serving God" and of the expectation of the coming of Jesus the Son of God, a text that has a unique "profile" just as the other texts. (2) Attempts to anchor such a scheme in tradition

---

[313]Holtz, *1 Thess,* 55-56.
[314]Wilckens 1974, 81; see generally ibid., 72-100; the quotation that follows above, ibid., 81-82. Wilckens refers to A. Seeberg, *Katechismus der Urchristenheit* (Leipzig: Deichert, 1903 [1966]), 82-83; Dibelius, *Thess,* 6-7.
[315]Roloff, *Apg,* 256 (italics added).
[316]Pesch, *Apg,* 2:132. See also Bussmann 1971, 39-56; Pak 1991, 3-25; Eckert 1992, esp. 289-97.
[317]See Munck 1962-1963; Holtz, *1 Thess,* 55-57; Wanamaker, *Thess,* 84-85.
[318]Holtz, *1 Thess,* 55; for the remark that follows above see ibid., 56.

history have been unsuccessful. For example, G. Friedrich interpreted 1 Thess 1:9-10 as a baptismal hymn of Hellenistic Jewish Christians that was composed by missionaries who had been influenced by the theology of the Q community.[319] The fact that 1 Thess 1:9-10 is not poetic in form makes this suggestion implausible. (3) We must remember that if Paul was converted only a few years after Easter, then there is hardly any "pre-Pauline" period worth speaking about in which the scheme of a missionary sermon could develop.[320] (4) It was Albrecht Oepke who earlier pointed out that "the fixed formula does not tend to be the fertile soil in which the blossom of life springs up; it is, rather, the cup in which it is preserved. . . . There was no generally binding formula from which one would have to derive the missionary sermon."[321]

Dialogical Concentration: Explanation of the Gospel

The speech on the Areopagus (Acts 17:22-31) is a key passage in the book of Acts. Whether it is the "climax of the book"[322] is questionable, however, as the central emphasis is not the gospel of Jesus Christ as such but the nature of the God whom Paul proclaims. We should also note that the interpretation of the speech must not divorce the text from the context in Acts 17:16-21 and analyze it in isolation. Martin Dibelius does just that and concludes that the speech is a "monotheistic sermon" that becomes "Christian" only at the end, and even then the name of Jesus is not mentioned.[323]

Luke first notes that Paul spoke to Jews and God-fearers in the synagogue of Athens (διελέγετο, dielegeto [Acts 17:17a]). Paul proclaimed the message of Jesus the Messiah and Savior to Jews, proselytes and God-fearers who attended the synagogue services, and he explained and substantiated his teaching in discussions after the services. Second, Luke notes that Paul also spoke to the people who happened to be in the marketplace "every day" (ἐν τῇ ἀγορᾷ κατὰ πᾶσαν ἡμέραν, en tē agora kata pasan hēmeran [Acts 17:17b]). Paul, in other words, engaged in missionary activity on the street.[324] In Acts 17:18 Luke reports that Paul "was telling the good news about Jesus and the resurrection." The verbal form that Luke uses (εὐηγγελίζετο, euēngelizeto [imperfect tense]) emphasizes the durative aspect of Paul's missionary preaching: over an extended period of time he taught the message of Jesus and his resurrection (and by implication of his death) in Athens in public

---

[319]G. Friedrich, "Ein Tauflied hellenistischer Judenchristen: 1. Thess 1,9f," ThZ 21 (1965): 502-16. For a critique see T. Holtz, " 'Euer Glaube an Gott': Zu Form und Inhalt von 1 Thess 1,9f," in Schnackenburg et al. 1978, 459-88; idem, 1 Thess, 55-57.

[320]Hengel 1983a, 30-47.

[321]Oepke 1920, 73-74.

[322]Thus Dibelius 1939, 29 (ET, 26).

[323]Dibelius 1939, 30 (ET, 27).

[324]Schneider (Apg, 2:235) and Zmijewski (Apg, 638) speak of "Straßenmission."

places, with the result that philosophers who lived in the city heard about Paul's teaching.

At some point Epicurean and Stoic philosophers discussed (συμβάλλειν, *symballein*) with Paul the deity that he proclaimed (Acts 17:18). They brought him to the Areopagus and asked him to explain the "new teaching" that he presented (ἡ καινὴ αὕτη ἡ ὑπὸ σοῦ λαλουμένη διδαχή, *hē kainē hautē hē hypo sou laloumenē didachē*), which involved "strange ideas" (ξενίζοντα τινα, *xenizonta tina*) (Acts 17:19-20). According to Luke's account, Paul gave a speech that traditionally is regarded as an example of early Christian missionary preaching to pagans. In the context of Acts 17, however, Paul's speech at most is a special case of missionary preaching to Gentiles: the philosophers and the council members of the Areopagus asked Paul to give an account of the deity that he preaches. In other words, Paul did not explain his message of Jesus the Savior of the world when he spoke before the council of the Areopagus; rather, he explained his concept of God. It is not only the contextual framework but also the flow of the argumentation of the speech itself that indicates that the only topic is the concept and the knowledge of God.[325] Stanley Porter argues that the "balance" of the speech is "completely wrong" because it lacks a christological section.[326] This assessment is incorrect. Paul explains in his dialogue with the philosophers and council members *one* of the themes that he presented in his public teaching activity: his doctrine of God.

The reference to "dialogue" is meant in a general sense of "conversation" in which Paul takes up the themes and formulations of his discussion partners—in the case of Acts 17, Hellenistic philosophers. The definition of "dialogue" championed by the World Council of Churches (WCC) since the conference of its central council in Addis Ababa in 1971 implies a different perspective, particularly the section "Dialogue with People of Living Faiths." The Indian theologian Stanley Samartha, who had an increasingly important role in the WCC, emphasized that the dialogue between people of different faiths should try not only to become more sensitive to the convictions, questions and hopes of others, but also "to become sensitive to the work of the Holy Spirit in the entire world, not only within the religions but also in the secular faiths and ideologies."[327] This "dialogue" is based on the assumption that God and Jesus Christ speak through all religions and ideologies in similar ways.[328]

This understanding of "dialogue" with non-Christians is foreign to the New Testament.[329] The controversy dialogues in the Gospels are "dialogues" of Jesus with people who have different convictions. These dialogues are prompted by Jesus' proclamation and statements that lead to conversations but never to a dialectical "cognitive progress"

---

[325]See Holtz, *1 Thess*, 55.

[326]Porter 1999, 124.

[327]S. Samartha, "Die Grenzen werden fließend," *Evangelische Kommentare*, October 1972, 293.

[328]For a critique of the WCC's dialogue program see Beyerhaus 1975.

[329]For the comments that follow above see Marshall 1992b.

of Jesus, whose authority is never questioned or "refined." Paul indeed employed the style of the diatribe, raising real or rhetorical questions that he then answers;[330] he took up the formulations of his (Christian) opponents and accentuated some parts of his teaching in the context of such "dialogues" (e.g., the stronger emphasis on the sovereignty and superiority of Jesus Christ in Col 1:15-20). However, Paul never abandoned his conviction that the sole criterion for valid knowledge and relevant truth that must be proclaimed is always God's revelation in Jesus, the crucified and risen Messiah (1 Cor 1:23-24; 2:2), and never the insights of others, let alone his own, subjective insight. Howard Marshall perceptively comments, "The problem of transmitting the message [of the gospel] is a problem of *communication* or translation in which the message must be put in such a way as to be intelligible and applicable to the receptor. It is not a problem of *discovery* in which the evangelist hopes that the 'receptor' will help him by means of dialogue to discover what the gospel is."[331]

Before I discuss details of the Areopagus speech, a survey of its content in the context of the historical situation (see §27.2) will be helpful. The council of the Areopagus wanted to know whether Paul intended to introduce "foreign" gods, deities unfamiliar to the Athenians. The council initiated this inquiry to gather information that they would need if a new altar or temple were to be built, or if there were to be changes made in the city's festival calendar.[332] The council members must have been somewhat perplexed after hearing Paul's polite introduction (*captatio benevolentiae* [Acts 17:22b-23a]) and after the *exordium*. First, Paul pointed out that he does not intend to introduce new gods to the citizens of Athens but essentially proclaims the nature of the deity whom they already honor at the altar with the inscription "To an unknown god" (Acts 17:23). Second, he pointed out that he is not the spokesman of a god seeking to acquire a piece of land to erect an altar or a sanctuary for the cultic veneration of that god. He stated that the god whom he proclaims does not live in shrines made by human hands (Acts 17:24) and does not need festivals: his god does not need to be served, because he is the creator of all being (Acts 17:25-26). Paul asserted that he is not applying for the admission of a new deity to the pantheon of the city of Athens, a procedure that would require the recommendation of the council and the permission of the *dēmos* of Athens. Paul argued that the God whom he proclaims "is not far from each one of us," as the poets already said (Acts 17:27-28); in other words, his God needs no formal introduction because he is already "here." The God whom he proclaims to the citizens of Athens is not just another deity that could be added to the pantheon. Paul indeed wants something, but it is not the council's legal endorsement of the introduction of the God whom he proclaims in the city: he wants them, and everyone else, to repent because God has already fixed the day of judgment and the rules for the verdict

---

[330]See Bultmann 1910, and the critical discussion in Stowers 1981.
[331]Marshall 1992b, 46.
[332]B. Winter 1996, 80-83; for the analysis that follows above see ibid., 84-89.

to be pronounced, and he has appointed the judge.[333] The members of the council suddenly realized that they were no longer investigating Paul and his deity, but that they themselves were being "investigated"—including the Epicurean and Stoic philosophers among them who permitted the people to worship idols despite their teaching that questioned the reality of idols.

Martin Dibelius argues that the Areopagus speech must be interpreted in philosophical terms rather than historically, and that Luke speaks not of nations, eras of peoples and borders of states "but of the cosmopolitan human race, the ordering of its life according to the seasons and to its appropriate habitations and of man's search after God which this ordering of life inspires."[334] He further argues that Luke presents Stoic concepts, particularly the notion of God's relationship with humankind and of God's proximity to human beings,[335] and that Luke thus contradicts Pauline theology.[336] This position found many supporters,[337] but it is a view that few scholars defend today. German scholars generally argue that Acts 17:22-32 is not the abstract of a historical speech that Paul delivered but rather a literary text created by the author of the book of Acts, who wanted to demonstrate that the gospel possesses relevance for the intellectual elites of his day.[338]

The following points disprove the hypothesis of Martin Dibelius, Hans Conzelmann and other scholars who argue that the Areopagus speech reflects the thinking of the author Luke rather than the theology of the apostle Paul.[339] (1) The stylistic-critical isolation of the Areopagus speech has no literary-critical foundation. It represents a hermeneutical a priori that some scholars no longer question. Dibelius allows that the speech is "directly" prepared by the preceding context of Acts 17:17, 20-21;[340] he pleads ignorance concerning the question whether the author "was able to rely occasionally upon his own or someone else's memory" but claims at the same time that the speech is a complete creation by the author "with the primary intention of guiding his readers rather than extending their knowledge of history"—a claim that is not supported by any hard evidence. The suggestion that Luke relies on primary source material and wants to impart historical knowledge is much more plausible than Dibelius's hypothesis. Dibelius contends that the speeches of the book of Acts cannot be understood as authentic reproductions of actual speeches and must be interpreted as literary productions of the author,[341] and he maintains that the missionary speeches represent a tradition "that has nothing to do with historiography in ancient times" because they contain, in compressed form, the content of the gospel.[342] This view founders on the analysis of the individual speeches and their context in the

---

[333]B. Winter 1996, 85; for the comment that follows above see ibid., 85-86.

[334]Dibelius 1939, 31-38; quotation, 38 (ET, 28-37; quotation, 37).

[335]Dibelius 1939, 45-53 (ET, 43-54).

[336]Dibelius 1939, 54-60 (ET, 57-64); cf. ibid., 57 (ET, 61): "Paul would never have written in this way."

[337]See Conzelmann, *Apg*, 104-13, esp. 111-13 (ET, 138-48, esp. 146-48); Schneider 1969, 62-64.

[338]See Haenchen, *Apg*, 508 (ET, 528); Plümacher 1972, 97-98; also Reinbold (2000, 133), whose assertion that the contrary opinion is "seldom argued today" (133 n. 65) shows that he either does not know or simply ignores Anglo-Saxon research into Acts 17; see also Horst 1989a, 188-89.

[339]See Bock 1993; Lindemann 1995.

[340]Dibelius 1939, 62 (ET, 67); the quotations that follow above, ibid., 65 (ET, 70).

[341]Dibelius 1949, 120, 162 (ET, 138-39, 184).

[342]Dibelius 1949, 142 (ET, 166).

book of Acts. (2) Paul emphasizes different convictions, depending on the audience that he is addressing. The speeches in Acts show that he adapts his preaching to his listeners, which agrees with Paul's statements in 1 Cor 9:20-22. (3) Paul seeks to establish some common ground with his listeners on the Areopagus in Acts 17:22-31, as is demonstrated by the *captatio benevolentiae* and the phraseology of his arguments. However, at the same time he criticizes the religious practices of the Athenians. His pronouncements on pagan religiosity and idol worship correspond to statements in his letters, particularly Rom 1:19-21a. The "Lukan" Paul in Acts 17:22-31 speaks fundamentally no differently than the Paul of the Epistle to the Romans. (4) Bertil Gärtner analyzed the Old Testament background of formulations and concepts of the Areopagus speech.[343] Some scholars emphasize similarities with Hellenistic-Jewish monotheistic sermons. Rudolf Pesch argues that "the borrowing from Greek philosophy for the *interpretatio Graeca* of the biblical revelation (including the reception of the quotation from Aratus—also found in Acts 17:28— in the Hellenistic-Jewish eclectic writer Aristobolos) is present here in a remarkable denseness related to the situation."[344] We find both in Paul's Areopagus speech: points of contact or agreement (*Anknüpfung*) and points of contradiction (*Widerspruch*). Paul distinguishes between religion and revelation as on a razor's edge, referring to the common notions and rejecting the elements that are contradicted by the revelation of Scripture. (5) We must remember Luke's comment in Acts 17:16 that Paul was provoked by the countless idols that he saw in Athens. (6) The call to repentance shows that the "Lukan" Paul by no means acknowledges the religiosity of his pagan listeners as a valid path to salvation. (7) Finally, the Areopagus speech must not be isolated from the context in Acts 17:16-21, which describes the situation in which the speech was given.[345] The "pioneer mission" took place in the agora, where Paul proclaimed the message of Jesus Christ. The speech on the Areopagus was delivered before a select, philosophically trained audience. Pesch concludes that Luke gets us close to the "historical Paul" and probably "to his missionary ability to link, by agreement and contradiction, a theology of creation with his salvation-historical proclamation of Christ."[346]

1. The elements of agreement are in the foreground in Paul's Areopagus speech. He "picks up" his listeners, among them Epicurean and Stoic philosophers (Acts 17:18), where they are in terms of concepts and language. Paul selects from Old Testament and Jewish theological and apologetic traditions such motifs as could be immediately understood by the Stoic and Epicurean philosophers, including terminological allusions and quotations.[347]

The Stoics. (a) The Stoics argued that the gods were immortal. Leading Stoic philosophers such as Cleantes, Chrysippos and Posidonius wrote books about

---

[343]Gärtner 1955; see Pao 2000, 193-208, on the points of contact with the book of Isaiah.

[344]Pesch, *Apg,* 2:132; for the comment that follows above see ibid. See also Schneider 1981; Gempf 1988, 112-34; 1993.

[345]Emphasized by Lindemann 1995, esp. 241, 248.

[346]Pesch, *Apg,* 2:142.

[347]For the analysis that follows above see B. Winter 1991, 117-24, with a discussion of A. J. Malherbe, " 'Not in a Corner': Early Christian Apologetic in Acts 26:26," in *Paul and the Popular Philosophers* (Minneapolis: Fortress, 1989), 147-163; D. L. Balch, "The Areopagus Speech: An Appeal to the Stoic Historian Posidonius against Later Stoics and the Epicureans," in Balch et al. 1990, 52-79.

the nature of the gods.[348] Balbus, in a discussion with a rival school of thought, asserted that the Stoics follow a fixed order in their discussion: first they prove that the gods exist, then they discuss their nature and show how they order the world before they explain how they care for the well-being of humankind. Paul argues similarly: as the Creator, God is the Lord of heaven and of the earth (Acts 17:24a), he gives life to human beings and everything they need to live (Acts 17:25b), and he cares for people as he determines the "times of their existence and the boundaries of the places where they would live" (Acts 17:26b). (b) The Stoics discussed the gods in their plurality and diversity, but they also were able to speak of "god" in the singular. Cleantes, the successor of Zenon, the founder of the Stoic school of philosophy, begins his hymn to Zeus with these lines: "Most glorious of the deathless gods, called by many a name: Great King of Nature, Changeless One, All-Powerful! You are the just ruler of all that is. We hail you as mortals hail you everywhere. Hail, Zeus! We are your children. And because of all the things that live and move on earth's broad ways, you gave the form of gods to us alone, I shall always praise and celebrate your power."[349] The Stoic philosophers in Paul's audience would not have been bothered by Paul's use of the word "god." On the other hand, Paul would have been concerned with the Stoic's easy transition from "god" to the "gods." (c) The Stoic concept of God was not so much personal as essentially pantheistic: they argued that the substance of God (οὐσία θεοῦ, *ousia theou*) is "the entire world and the heavens."[350] Seneca conceived that "God is near you, with you, in you." Paul asserted, according to Acts 17:28a, "In him [*en autō*] we live and move and have our being." If Paul's Stoic listeners related the phrase *en autō* in a spatial sense to God ("in him"), then they could interpret this triadic formulation in terms of the life, movement and being of humankind "in god" in a pantheistic sense as "the immanence of man in the all-pervasive deity."[351] Paul's quotation in Acts 17:28b from the Cilician poet Aratus, "For we too are his offspring," could also be interpreted in *this* sense as a pantheistic statement. (d) The Stoics believed in divine providence. They argued that the gods rule the world by their providence, and that this can be proved from the divine wisdom and power, from the nature of the world, from the miracles of nature and from the gods' care for human beings. Paul could agree with those convictions: "The God who made the world and everything in it, he who is Lord of heaven and earth . . . he himself gives to all mortals life and breath

---

[348]See Diogenes Laertius 7.148 (Zeno). For the comment by Balbus that follows above see Cicero, *Nat. d.* 2.3.

[349]Testimonia in *Stoicorum veterum fragmenta* (ed. H. von Armin; 4 vols.; Leipzig: Teubner, 1903-1924), 1:103-39; German translation in Barrett and Thornton, *Texte zur Umwelt des Neuen Testaments,* 82-83 (no. 77).

[350]Diogenes Laertius 7.14 (Zeno); the quotation that follows above, Seneca, *Ep.* 41.1.

[351]Pesch, *Apg,* 2:139.

and all things. From one ancestor he made all nations to inhabit the whole earth, and he allotted the times of their existence and the boundaries of the places where they would live" (Acts 17:24a, 25-26). (e) The subject of judgment was not foreign to the Stoics: at the end of his speech Paul refers to the divine judgment that would come upon all people who remain in their ignorance despite the availability of better information (Acts 17:31).

The Epicureans. (a) The Epicureans argued for the animated nature, immortality and bliss of God. These are concepts and terms that Paul uses.[352] (b) Epicurus believed that the knowledge of God is apparent, a function of human reason. Thus the Epicurean philosophers in Paul's audience would have understood his argument that the "unknown god" can be known (Acts 17:23). (c) The Epicureans argued that the gods do not live in temples that people had built. Plutarch urges that "one should not build temples of the gods."[353] They rejected the superstition of their contemporaries and discussed, for example, the psychological effects of false faith and of demeaning cultic practices. Paul agrees with this conviction when he writes, "The God who made the world and everything in it, he who is Lord of heaven and earth, does not live in shrines made by human hands." (Acts 17:24). (d) The Epicureans rejected sacrifices for the gods, arguing that a god does not need human things.[354] Paul agrees when he tells his audience on the Areopagus that God "is not served by human hands, as though he needed anything, since he himself gives to all mortals life and breath and all things" (Acts 17:25).

In his presentation to the Areopagus, initiated by the Epicurean and Stoic philosophers of Athens, Paul employs convictions, arguments and formulations that they were familiar with and acknowledged as valid. Exegetes and missiologists often use the term "contextualization" for this dimension of Paul's Areopagus speech, a term that has become a household word in mission studies.[355]

2. The elements of contradiction are found in the subtext of some parts of the speech and on the surface in other parts of the speech. Paul discourses about the one true Creator God of biblical revelation as an introduction to the proclamation of Jesus the Savior of salvation history. In the Areopagus speech Paul is not just "positive" and inclusive,[356] and he speaks not only of a continuity between the biblical revelation and pagan poets and philosophers; he disputes his contemporaries' understanding of God, particularly against the background of Isaiah's polemic against the pagan gods.[357]

---

[352]1 Thess 1:9; Rom 1:23; 1 Tim 1:11. On Epicurean concepts see Diogenes Laertius 10.123 (Epicurus).

[353]Plutarch, *Stoic. rep.* 1034b: Ἔτι δόγμα Ζηνωνός ἐστιν ἱερὰ θεῶν μὴ οἰκοδομεῖν.

[354]See Philodemus, *Pros eusebeias,* frg. 38; Plutarch, *Stoic. rep.* 1052a; cf. Plato, *Tim.* 33d, 34b.

[355]See, for example, Osei-Bonsu 1990, 133-37; Dumais 1981, 82-84.

[356]Contra Samuel 1986.

[357]See Pao 2000, 193-208.

Paul criticizes pagan religiosity in at least the following seven respects. (a) The reference to the "unknown god" (Acts 17:23) can be understood as a contradiction to pagan religious convictions, seen in the horizon of Is 45:15, 18-25.[358] In this passage the monotheistic confession "Truly, you are a God who hides himself, O God of Israel, the Savior" (Is 45:15) is followed by a speech of Yahweh that seeks to convert people to worship the one true God and aims at disproving the notion that God hides. (b) Paul acknowledges that Gentiles, including the philosophers, seek God (Acts 17:27). The optative mood of the verb (εὕροιεν, *heuroien*) in the indirect interrogative sentence indicates, however, that Paul thinks that it is doubtful whether they will indeed find God as God wishes. The Jewish author of Wis 13:6 voiced similar doubts. (c) Biblically trained ears could recognize in Paul's comment that God "is not far from each one of us" (Acts 17:27c) the conviction that Paul does not speak positively of the "nearness" of pagans to God. And if the phrase *en autō* (Acts 17:28a) is understood in an instrumental sense as "by him," then the triadic formulation in Acts 17:28a is not an argument for humankind's kinship with God but rather a creation-theological statement, even though it is expressed in Hellenistic philosophical terminology.[359] (d) The quotation from Aratus in Acts 17:28 is not just an accommodation to the philosophical convictions of his audience; it is "very aptly chosen, as the statement that humankind is the gods' offspring can again be placed within the biblical horizon of the theology of creation: people are God's offspring because he has created 'the one ancestor' from whom he made humankind (Acts 17:26a) as the 'image of God' (Gen 1:26-27; cf. Ps 8:6-7). The attempt to integrate the 'ignorant' knowledge of the poets into the truth of the revelation proves possible on the basis of the theology of creation (Acts 17:24ab)." The reference to the one ancestor (Acts 17:26a) is not a recourse to a general mythic tale that the Stoics or Epicureans know but rather a reference to the biblical and Jewish tradition of the beginning of creation and the creation of Adam, the first human being, by God, the Creator of the world. (e) The critique of temples (Acts 17:24) is reminiscent not only of Epicurean arguments but also of the emphasis of the prophets that everything belongs to the one true God, the Lord (Is 66:1-2). (f) The critique of sacrifices (Acts 17:25) also reminds the biblically informed reader of scriptural convictions and statements (Is 42:5; Job 32:8). (g) The critique of idols (Acts 17:29) is a clear indictment[360] of the popular piety with which the Stoic and the Epicurean philosophers had come to an arrangement. Both philosophical schools had accommodated their theoretical convictions to the religiosity of the populace so that people could continue to participate in the cultic activities of the

---

[358]Schneider 1981, 300-303.
[359]Pesch, *Apg,* 2:139; the quotation that follows above, ibid.
[360]Contra Roloff, *Apg,* 265.

cities.[361] Epicurus was convinced that popular piety was misguided, but he did not try to prevent adherents of his philosophy from participating in the local cults. An Epicurean text, written around A.D. 50, asserts that piety cannot be proven by the offering of sacrifices, but it goes on to say that offering to the gods is permitted because it is in agreement with religious traditions (P.Oxy. 215). Plutarch accuses the Stoics of contradicting themselves because they visit the mysteries in the temples, and ascend the acropolises to honor the idol statues, and lay down wreaths in the sanctuaries despite their convictions (*Stoic. rep.* 1034b-c). Paul uses the quotation from Aratus as an argument (οὐκ ὀφείλομεν νομίζειν, *ouk opheilomen nomizein*) against such a rapprochement with the religious pluralism of Greco-Roman culture. If we as human beings indeed come from God, then it is impossible to portray and worship God in the form of statues made of gold, silver or marble. Nor is the critique of idols merely a philosophical argument; it takes up Old Testament and Jewish traditions that rendered rather polemical and sarcastic verdicts.[362] For Paul, the critical discussion of Greco-Roman pluralism was an essential element of his explanation and proclamation of the gospel.[363]

It is on the basis of this critique of contemporary religiosity, particularly the Greco-Roman pluralism of gods and cults, of temples and mysteries, that Paul calls his audience to repent and turn to the one true God. He asserts that "God has overlooked the times of human ignorance" (Acts 17:30), thus noting that God has been forbearing. The phrase "times of ignorance" probably expresses Paul's conviction that the religious pluralism of the Athenians makes them guilty before God: one cannot ignore truth for long without being responsible for one's behavior. With this specific rejection of religious pluralism, implying quite practical consequences, Paul walked on very thin ice, considering the fact that the cultic veneration of the deceased emperors was an essential and increasingly important element of Roman culture in the larger cities. Like Isaiah (see Is 46:8), Paul criticizes the idols and then calls upon people to repent: "While God has overlooked the times of human ignorance, now he commands all people everywhere to repent" (Acts 17:30). Paul not only makes the philosophical and logical argument for the necessity of abandoning religious pluralism but also establishes the necessity of changing religious convictions and cultic activities with a reference to the divine judgment "by a man" (Acts 17:31a). Paul emphasizes, in agreement with passages such as Ps 9:9; 96:13; 98:9, that God will judge the *oikoumenē,* and, in agreement with early Christian teaching, that God has already appointed a judge who will carry out the divine judgment. According to Luke's account, Paul avoided mentioning the name of Jesus, perhaps because he

---

[361]See B. Winter 1991, 122, 126-30.
[362]Cf. Is 40:18-19; 44:9-20; 45:15-24; 46:5-7; see also Wis 13.
[363]B. Winter 1991, 129.

wanted to avoid the impression that he proclaimed "foreign divinities" (Acts 17:18).[364] When Paul points out that this judge was a man who had lived, died and was raised from the dead by God (Acts 17:31b), the reaction of the audience was divided: some listeners wanted to hear more, while others scoffed. The notion of life after death was foreign for both the Epicureans and the Stoics, who taught the "art of dying" meant to teach people to accept their mortality.[365]

This analysis shows that Paul's speech before the council of the Areopagus is characterized by agreement and contradiction, carefully calibrated with regard to the specific audience on Ares Hill. Paul does not want to explain a "new teaching" to the philosophers and council members of Athens "that seeks to expand their enlightened knowledge, but a teaching that transcends that knowledge."[366] Paul employed concepts and formulations that reflected Hellenistic ones, and at the same time he referred to the convictions and formulations of the Old Testament prophets and Jewish apologists. C. K. Barrett describes the Areopagus speech, in deliberate exaggeration, as "not natural but revealed theology. He who wrote Acts 17 learned his theology not from the Greeks but from the Bible."[367] It is for this reason that I cannot detect an "exchange of gifts" in the Areopagus speech.[368] Granted that Paul speaks "a new language" that is adapted to the new cultural situation of Acts 17:22-29, there is, nevertheless, no evidence in the text of the Areopagus speech or in Luke's intentions in general to support the view that the speech "prepares the future by enriching the monotheistic kerygma with pantheistically colored formulae" that point theology toward mysticism. The point of contact, or agreement, consists in the fact that Paul uses a vocabulary that is famliar to his listeners but that gives a new meaning to old words, "a meaning that is related to the old one, so that there may be a point of contact, but also different, so that the new message is communicated."[369]

Paul's message to the council of the Areopagus can be succinctly summarized as follows. (1) Paul explains the historical truth of the one true God and argues the futility of attempting to cast God in idol images (*eidōla*) in view of the nature of God as the almighty Creator of the world and in view of his relationship to humankind. (2) Paul proclaims that this one true and sovereign God, who cares for human beings, offers repentance and faith. (3) Paul announces that God has fixed a day of judgment at which a man who has been raised from the dead will be the judge, and he emphasizes that this historical and eschatological reality

---

[364]See Pesch, *Apg,* 2:140.

[365]See Haacker 1988a, 71.

[366]Pesch, *Apg,* 2:137.

[367]Barrett (1989, 27-28 [ET, 158]), who then assumes, however, that the speech "probably came not from Paul but from a non-Pauline branch of the Gentile mission."

[368]Contra Czajkowski 1988, 32; for the comments that follow above see ibid., 32-33.

[369]Barrett 1989, 31 (ET, 160-61), with reference to John Riches (1980), who showed this for the Gospels.

requires abandoning the worship of the old gods and turning to worship the one true God alone. Paul is unafraid to point to the resurrection of the dead despite that fact that, presumably, he knows that the doctrine of the resurrection is laughable to the Greeks, who think dualistically. As Rudolf Pesch points out, "This speech is necessary before the Athenian listeners so that it remains evident that the 'unknown God' is not made known through philosophical enlightenment but that he has revealed himself through his salvation-historical action and that he is now made known as the one 'God, who grants salvation not as the final intensification and transcendence of human existence but as the result of a new eschatological act that creates life out of death.'"[370]

Paul could not say everything in this speech before the council of the Areopagus, not only because he was interrupted but also because he focused consistently on the subject that he had been invited to address. That is why he describes Jesus as Judge but not as Savior. Klaus Haacker comments, "The life and the ministry of Jesus can be understood only in the context of the presuppositions of the biblical witness concerning *God*. This is the reason why the pioneer preaching before pagans who have not been exposed to biblical influences is essentially preaching about *God*. The fact that Jesus constitutes the path to God does not mean that it is Christology that opens the way to theology. God as Creator and Lord, humankind created in the image of God (God as Father), the prohibition of images—the unprepared pagans first need to hear the Old Testament foundations of the New Testament."[371] In the course of providing his listeners "instruction in the theology of Israel" Paul uses the intellectual, philosophical and linguistic traditions of his audience: as bridgehead for the proclamation of Jesus the Savior of the world, since he knows their religious customs and their educational values, and as signal, since he takes them seriously as discussion partners who are willing to listen to his teaching.

Paul does not seek to prove the existence of God with the help of gradual introduction to the theology of creation of biblical revelation, in contrast to the later cosmic religiosity of scientists such as Isaac Newton, Johannes Kepler and Albert Einstein, who sought to ground the rational claims of a science that proceeded *more geometrico*.[372] In these attempts to connect the world with the divine, God is not much more than the guarantor of the objective perceptibility of nature that follows objective laws.

When we compare the derisive rejection and the polite indifference of Paul's listeners at the Areopagus with the much more positive initial reaction of the Jewish audiences in the synagogues, we see that for Luke as the author of the book of Acts, biblical revelation and the Jewish faith are *praeparatio evangel-*

---

[370]Pesch, *Apg,* 1:140, with a quotation from Roloff, *Apg,* 266.
[371]Haacker 1988, 71; for the comment that follows above see ibid.
[372]See Max Jammer, *Einstein und die Religion* (Konstanz: Universitätsverlag Konstanz, 1995).

ica, whereas pagan philosophy and natural theology are not trailblazers for the gospel.[373]

At the end of Paul's Areopagus speech his conviction becomes obvious that people who approach God, the one true God, also approach Jesus, or rather must go through Jesus. As Darrell Bock comments, "When one looks to God, Paul says, one will find Jesus."[374] If God demands that all people of the *oikoumenē,* Athenians included, render account of their life on the day of judgment before Jesus the Judge, it ultimately is impossible to distinguish between God's action and the action of Jesus. The reference to the resurrection of the Judge whom God has appointed to judge the world alludes to the significance and to the centrality of Jesus. In other words, as Paul makes known the "unknown God," he speaks of both the one true God and of Jesus, as he does in 1 Cor 8:5-6: "Indeed, even though there may be so-called gods in heaven or on earth—as in fact there are many gods and many lords—yet for us there is one God, the Father, from whom are all things and for whom we exist, and one Lord, Jesus Christ, through whom are all things and through whom we exist."

The statement in Acts 17:30 "while God has overlooked the times of human ignorance" is relevant for the discussion of the question of whether a lack of knowledge of the gospel protects the ignorant—those who have never heard the gospel—from God's condemnation.[375] The term "ignorance" (ἄγνοια, *agnoia*) is also used by Luke in Acts 3:17, where Peter asserts in his sermon in Solomon's Portico that the Jewish leaders of Jerusalem chose Barabbas and killed Jesus "in ignorance," despite that fact that Jesus is "the Author of life" and Barabbas was a murderer. In Lk 23:13-23 Luke emphasizes that the actions of the Jewish leaders were deliberate, even though they did not understand what they did. This is why according to Acts 3:19, Peter called them to repent, asserting that Jesus will return (Acts 3:21). These subjects correspond to Luke's account of Paul's Areopagus speech in Acts 17:30-31. At the same time Peter's speech in Acts 3:12-26 shows that ignorance is not an excuse: the ignorant need to repent as well. As far as Paul's theology is concerned, Rom 10:2-3 demonstrates that the apostle was convinced that zeal for God combined with ignorance concerning Jesus constitutes no excuse, or defense, in God's judgment. Darrell Bock remarks, "When Paul speaks to 'those who have never heard,' lack of knowledge is no excuse. All must respond to the returning King who will surely sit in judgment on the last day."[376]

Some missiologists object that Paul's Athenian audience has just heard the gospel, and the situation of people who have never heard the gospel is different. However, if people who have never heard of Jesus are not responsible for their unredeemed status and thus have a valid defense in the last judgment, then Paul's preaching puts them in a precarious situation: if ignorance protects against God's judgment, surely it is preferable for the listeners to remain ignorant so that they have a chance of surviving the day of judgment. After Paul has explained his message of the one true God and the Judge whom he has appointed, their salvation depends on their reaction. This position therefore leads to the

---

[373]Stenschke 1999a, 223.
[374]Bock 1993, 120-21.
[375]See Bock 1993, 121.
[376]Bock 1993, 122; for the argument that follows above see ibid.

absurd conclusion that it would have been better for Paul not to have mentioned Jesus.

When Paul states in Rom 1:19, "For what can be known about God is plain to them, because God has shown it to them," he does not assert that "general" revelation suffices to obtain salvation.[377] The positive statement of Rom 1:19 must be understood in the context of Paul's statements in Rom 1:18-19, a "negative" introduction, and Rom 1:20-21, a "negative" conclusion. Paul explains why Gentiles are without excuse with regard to their idol worship. The statements in Rom 2:7, 13-15, 26-27 do not assert that people—Gentiles, for example—can be saved by good works. Some of the church fathers, as well as the Swiss reformer Ulrich Zwingli, related the statement to "enlightened" Gentiles who lived before Jesus. Statements such as Rom 3:20, 28; 4:5 demonstrate, however, that Paul could not have taught the possibility of salvation on the basis of works. And it is implausible to assume that Paul contradicted himself.[378] Some scholars interpret Paul's statement in a hypothetical sense with reference to the Gentiles,[379] while others interpret it in terms of Gentile Christians who do good works,[380] an interpretation that is less likely, however.

Ideological Confrontation: The Proclamation of Jesus as Messiah and Lord

Paul proclaimed Jesus as the Messiah of the Jewish people and the Kyrios of the world not only to Jewish audiences but also in his missionary sermons to polytheists. Clearly this statement by Richard Lipsius, a scholar from an earlier era, is a misjudgment: "As the apostle of the nations he preached the savior of the world rather than the Jewish Messiah."[381] Luke summarizes Paul's proclamation in the last verse of the book of Acts by pointing out that the apostle proclaimed "the kingdom of God" and taught "about the Lord Jesus Christ with all boldness and without hindrance" (Acts 28:31). The term "kingdom" and the phrase "kingdom of God" (basileia tou theou) occur in Acts only rarely.[382] Such terminology, however, Luke uses repeatedly to summarize Paul's missionary preaching to Jewish audiences. The direct association of kyrios and christos is also rare; it occurs for the first time in Peter's sermon at Pentecost.[383] Carsten Burfeind observes, "What Peter preaches in Jerusalem, Paul proclaims in Rome: Jesus is as the risen one κύριος and χριστός."[384] The frequency of christos as a designation for Jesus in Paul's letters to Gentile-Christian churches (383 occurrences)[385] is remarkable, as is the central significance of this title in statements about the death

---

[377]See A. Spencer 1993, 125-35.

[378]Contra Räisänen 1983, 99-108; E. P. Sanders 1983, 123-32.

[379]See Moo 1993, 142-45.

[380]See Cranfield, Rom, 1:151-58, 172-74; Bock 1993, 123 with n. 6; thus quite early Augustine.

[381]Lipsius 1897, 182.

[382]Acts 1:3 (Jesus); 1:6 (the Twelve); 8:12 (Philip); 14:22 (Paul and Barnabas); 19:8; 20:25; 28:23, 31 (Paul).

[383]Acts 2:36; cf. 10:36; 11:17; 15:26; 28:31.

[384]Burfeind 2000, 89.

[385]F. Hahn, EWNT 3:1149 (EDNT 3:479). Text-critical decisions on the omission or inclusion of the title christos in New Testament Greek manuscripts influence this statistic. For the comment that follows above see ibid., 1158-59 (EDNT 3:482-83).

and the resurrection of Jesus,[386] about his preexistence, earthly existence and exaltation,[387] as well as in statements about the church as his body and about Christ being "in you" or "in us."[388] Also relevant is the fact that Paul speaks of Jesus as *christos* in statements about his missionary activity of proclamation as well.[389] For the earliest followers of Jesus in Jerusalem, Jesus was the bringer of salvation. Paul acknowledged this conviction in his conversion in Damascus, he accepted it as his own conviction and he proclaimed it in his missionary preaching, substantiating and explaining what *christos* ("messiah") means. The confession of Jesus as messianic bringer of salvation was the crucial characteristic of the new movement, one of the main reasons why the followers of Jesus in Antioch were called *christianoi,* identified as the people who belong to Jesus as *christos.* It is not surprising that the conviction that Jesus is the Messiah had a central function in the early Christian creedal tradition that also shaped Paul's convictions, a tradition that he cites and formulates in his letters.[390] The decisive element in this conviction was the assertion that the Messiah/*Christos* died. Ferdinand Hahn comments, "This confession was associated on the one hand with the soteriological interpretation of death as the suffering of atonement, and on the other with the reference to Jesus' resurrection. Further, christological statements were associated with this. The living presence of the resurrected Jesus was understood, with the help of Ps 110:1, as exaltation and installation in the heavenly office of king, and his parousia as the institution of royal dominion at the consummation of salvation. . . . To this was added the idea that in Jesus' entire history and person the OT promises of salvation were fulfilled." The fundamental and central significance of the conviction that Jesus is the Messiah—the bringer of salvation sent by God who is Kyrios at God's right hand after his death and his resurrection—explains why Paul, whether addressing Jewish or pagan audiences, did not dispense with explaining this conviction in his missionary preaching.

The proclamation of Jesus as Messiah was potentially dangerous. Since in Jewish expectations the Messiah, as Son of David, was understood in a political sense as king and ruler, and since the early Christians expected Jesus to return as king, this emphasis in missionary preaching touched upon the claims of the imperial family in Rome. The link between *basileia tou theou* and *kyrios christos*

---

[386]Cf. Rom 5:6, 8; 6:3-4, 9; 8:11, 34; 10:7; 14:9, 15; 15:3; 1 Cor 1:23; 2:2; 8:11; 15:3-5, 12-17, 20, 23; Gal 2:19, 21; 3:1, 13; Eph 5:2.

[387]Preexistence: 1 Cor 10:4; 11:3; earthly existence: Rom 9:5; 2 Cor 5:16; exaltation: Rom 8:34; 10:6; Col 3:1.

[388]Cf. Rom 8:10; 1 Cor 1:13; 3:23; 12:12; 2 Cor 10:7; 13:5; Gal 2:20; 3:29; 4:19; 5:24; Col 1:27; 3:3; Eph 2:5; 3:17; 4:12, 15.

[389]Cf. Rom 15:18, 20; 1 Cor 1:17, 23; 2:2; 15:12; 2 Cor 1:19; 4:5; Gal 4:14; Phil 1:15, 17, 18; Col 4:3; Eph 3:4. On Paul's Christology see recently Hurtado 2003, 98-153.

[390]Hahn, *EWNT* 3:1165 (*EDNT* 3:485-86); the quotation that follows above, ibid.

hints at a political dimension of Paul's missionary proclamation.[391] Some scholars assume that Paul might have announced in the capital of the Roman Empire, in a deliberately provocative manner, the political implications of the universal salvation that God made possible exclusively in Jesus Christ, specifying consequences for the imperial house or for the senate. This assumption is both unrealistic and anachronistic, formulated at conference tables in the secure ivory towers of modern scholars whose lives are not in danger. We must remember that according to Luke's report, Paul does not speak to Roman officials but to "all who came to see him" (Acts 28:30b), which in the context of Acts 28:17-28 refers to Jews living in Rome.[392]

Martin Karrer suggests that *christos* is an ideal term for missionary work.[393] He submits a threefold argument. (1) In the New Testament the designation *christos* had little to do with the expectation of a Davidic king or with a messianic priestly or prophetic figure, since the Jewish concept of the "anointed one" did not correspond to a real historical figure. (2) The term *christos* has been transferred to Jesus primarily in the context of practices of anointing—for example, in the temple cult—and thus has nothing to do with Old Testament notions of the "anointed one." Karrer asserts, "As the sphere of God's blessing radiates from the cult surrounding the Holy of Holies, according to Israel's inherited faith, it now radiates, according to the new experience of faith, from him whom Christians believe to be the anointed one." (3) Since proceedings involving anointing were widely known in the Greco-Roman world, and since the anointed object was regarded as holy (i.e., close to the deity), the early Christian missionaries were able to explain the significance of Jesus with the designation *christos* without automatically implying Jewish notions of the royal anointed figure, which indeed would have been politically dangerous. Karrer's hypothesis is unconvincing for the following reasons. (1) It has not been possible to cite references in non-Jewish Greek texts that use the designation *ho christos* for a person. The masculine term χριστός (*christos*), used as a noun, occurs only in the Septuagint and in other Jewish texts.[394] (2) The title *christos* cannot be derived from general proceedings in the Jerusalem temple involving anointment. (3) Pagans in the first century found it difficult to understand the designation *christos*. This becomes evident in, for example, the misunderstanding involving the name *Chrēstos* (see Suetonius, *Claud.* 25.4). Neither the use of oil in pagan cults nor the anointing with ambrosia in Greek and Roman myths would have helped pagan listeners "take a step toward understanding this most important

---

[391]See Burfeind 2000, 89-91.
[392]Contra Burfeind (2000, 88), who speaks of Rome as Paul's "forum."
[393]Karrer 1991, 406; the quotations that follow above, ibid.
[394]Zimmermann 1998, 6 n. 28, with reference to Hengel 1992, 444. For the argument that follows above see Zimmermann 1998, 7 n. 28. For a critique of Martin Karrer see also Stuhlmacher 1992-1999, 1:113.

title of Jesus" and thus facilitate the missionary proclamation.[395]

As Paul consistently and with emphasis designates Jesus as *Christos,* he had to explain this title in terms of its Old Testament and Jewish background. In the course of such an explanation the three main outlines of messianic concepts in Second Temple Jewish theology could be highlighted: royal, priestly and prophetic. These concepts surface in, for example, the eschatological faith of the Essenes. These messianic convictions could be emphasized in various ways, and they could be merged.[396] In the context of his missionary proclamation, as far as we can reconstruct his evangelistic preaching, Paul emphasizes the following elements.

1. Jesus, the Savior and the coming Son of God, died on the cross as a sacrifice for sins. Several foundational texts, which probably take up traditional early Christian confessions of faith, emphasize this conviction.

1 Thess 5:9-10: "For God has destined us not for wrath but for obtaining salvation through our Lord Jesus Christ, [10]who died for us, so that whether we are awake or asleep we may live with him."

Gal 1:4: "[The Lord Jesus Christ] gave himself for our sins to set us free from the present evil age, according to the will of our God and Father."

Gal 2:20: "And it is no longer I who live, but it is Christ who lives in me. And the life I now live in the flesh I live by faith in the Son of God, who loved me and gave himself for me."

1 Cor 15:3: "For I handed on to you as of first importance what I in turn had received: that Christ died for our sins in accordance with the scriptures."

1 Cor 1:17-18: "For Christ did not send me to baptize but to proclaim the gospel, and not with eloquent wisdom, so that the cross of Christ might not be emptied of its power. [18]For the message about the cross is foolishness to those who are perishing, but to us who are being saved it is the power of God."

1 Cor 2:2: "For I decided to know nothing among you except Jesus Christ, and him crucified."

2. The coming Son of God is Jesus the Messiah, the Savior expected by the Jewish people. Paul must have given "instruction in Judaism" to pagan listeners who had had no prior contacts with the local synagogues.[397] The summons to renounce false gods and to turn to the one true God implies a reference to the Jewish faith. It was the God of the Jews, the God of Israel's sacred Scriptures, who had a Messiah—the one true God who was almighty, who intervened in

---

[395]Thus correctly Hengel and Schwemer 1998, 350 n. 1433 (ET, 456-57 n. 1189).
[396]Zimmermann 1998, 478.
[397]I owe the following analysis to Barrett 1991.

history, who was different from the divine supreme power of the Epicureans and from the divine immanence of the Stoics, the God who had chosen the strange people of the Jews and who had made their history the peculiar place of his interventions and revelation, the God who had given specific promises to the Jews that he would fulfill in the future. Paul's letter to the Christians in Galatia demonstrates that he spoke about Israel in his missionary sermons.[398] Some visiting Jewish Christians demanded that the non-Jewish Christians in Galatia be circumcised in order to qualify as full members of Abraham's family and thus of God's people. These visiting teachers seemed to have had some success, so much so that Paul was forced to write the letter to the Galatian Christians, which features some rather harsh language. This situation suggests that Paul included in his first missionary sermons a focus on Israel: evidently he was not at all surprised that the Galatian Christians want to belong to "Abraham's family." He was surprised only that they let themselves be convinced that circumcision was a necessary prerequisite for inclusion among Abraham's descendants. That is why Paul wrote the following sentences.

Gal 3:7, 9, 13-14: "So, you see, those who believe are the descendants of Abraham. . . . [9]For this reason, those who believe are blessed with Abraham who believed. . . . [13]Christ redeemed us from the curse of the law by becoming a curse for us—for it is written, 'Cursed is everyone who hangs on a tree' [Deut 21:23]—[14]in order that in Christ Jesus the blessing of Abraham might come to the Gentiles, so that we might receive the promise of the Spirit through faith."

3. Jesus, the coming Son of God, is the Savior because of his death on the cross. The significance of the term *estaurōmenos* ("crucified") was understood all too well in the first century. Paul therefore needed to explain why, if Jesus was not executed as a wicked slave, political usurper or rebel who had taken up arms, he was crucified. Paul had to give a report about Jesus' life. The historical question of why Jesus had to die on the cross was not easy to answer. And the theological question of why God the Father sent his Son Jesus to the cross was even more difficult: God is not evil, so why did his divine Son, Jesus the Savior, have to die such a violent death? If Jesus' mission was the implementation of God's mission, the cross on which Jesus died makes a statement about the nature of God. C. K. Barrett comments, "If the Crucified is not somehow God, as his Father also is, then the Father is inflicting suffering on an inferior—and this is monstrous."[399] He continues: "Simply to tell the story of the Cross poses all the questions about God, and on this basis the preacher could detach his hearers from their old belief (or unbelief) and lead them in a new direction. The Cross questions all conventional philosophical arguments, including the traditional Chris-

---

[398]See Donaldson (1994, esp. 176-84), who argues against Betz, *Gal*, 2-3, 8-9, and others.
[399]Barrett 1991, 12 (ET, 1995, 159); the quotation that follows above, ibid., 13 (ET, 1995, 159-60).

tian arguments, for the existence of God. The philosophical problem of verification is a real one, and the Cross means that God refuses to verify himself, to come down from the Cross and so to prove his case. It contradicts the cosmological and the teleological proof, for there is no event so disorderly, none that runs more plainly contrary to the notion of purpose in the ordering of the universe. It is the contradiction of the moral argument too. . . . It is not easy to believe in God. That is why Christian thought about God does not begin with Plato and Aristotle, with the consideration of creation (cosmology) or the consideration of history (teleology), but with the preaching of the Cross. It is in the obedience of Jesus that God is known, in the suffering of Jesus that God is glorified. Every other god is an idol. . . . We can never be content with a god who wound up this watch of a universe and left it to tick. We need a God who wrestles with rebellion and overcomes resistance with love, a God who speaks to us from outside ourselves, so remote that we can confuse him with the thunder, yet speaks in language that we can understand, because we see him in one who would rather be the friend of sinners and die than give them up and live."

The proclamation of Jesus, the crucified *Christos,* the messianic Savior, confronted Greek and Roman audiences with a faith that stood in stark contrast both to the old ideology of the polis, with its egalitarian structures that ultimately excluded the weak and the aliens, and to the new ideology of the *Imperium Romanum,* with its hierarchical structures that emphasized the divinity of the emperor and other members of the imperial family. Faith in and allegiance to a crucified God, a Jewish Savior of the world, was as scandalous and nonsensical as the suggestion that a new community of people might be formed in which neither ethnic nor social differences play any role, a community in which everything and everyone is focused on faith in the God of Israel and on allegiance to the crucified Savior sent by him, on sacrificial love for all fellow believers and for all fellow citizens, and on the expectant hope of the return of Jesus and the restoration of a world unmarred by any imperfection.

Apologetic Confrontation: The Defense of the Gospel
Paul re-presented, specified and applied his message in dialogue with the churches in Galatia, Achaia, Macedonia and in the province of Asia that he had established, and with the church in the province of Asia and with the church in Rome that other missionaries had established—in his letters to the Christians in southern Galatia, Thessalonike, Corinth, Philippi, Ephesus, Colossae and Rome. Paul reformulated his message usually in his confrontation with Jewish-Christian opponents who criticized his teaching on the basis of their convictions concerning the salvation-historical priority of Israel and concerning the Torah as normative divine revelation, and who wanted to rectify what they regarded as the erroneous, one-sided or loose teaching of Paul, helping the Gentile converts to become true members of the people of God. These Jewish-Christian teachers

probably came from Jerusalem. They were particularly concerned about Paul's theological convictions and ecclesiological praxis of admitting converted Gentiles into the eschatological and messianic community of salvation without requiring circumcision and obedience to the Mosaic law, particularly the purity laws and the food laws.

For Paul, the basic fact was not his own missionary work or his missionary theology, but the gospel of Jesus Christ—the conviction that Jesus was the promised Messiah, that Yahweh the God of Israel had revealed himself now, in the last days, in Jesus Christ, and that God had provided for the salvation of humankind in Jesus' death and resurrection. Paul specified his theology of the justification of all people by faith alone in Jesus Christ in his letters "not to legitimize the Gentile mission, but as an authentic interpretation of the Christ event, which has eschatological salvific significance, providing the foundation for the universality of the proclamation of the gospel."[400] Paul evidently was convinced of the universality of the church's mission since the days of his conversion. And this conviction was not dependent upon his own calling as apostle to the Gentiles. Thomas Söding observes, "The mission among the Greeks follows from the eschatological salvific significance of Jesus' death and resurrection, as does the equal membership of the Gentile Christians in the church of God, as Paul asserts with Jewish Christian traditions in Jerusalem and in Antioch (1 Thess 1:9-10; 2:11-12; 5:9-10). Paul's doctrine of justification is the radical consequence of this insight of faith. What is at issue is not merely the pragmatic argument that the Gentile mission can be much more successful without the requirement of circumcision and without an obedience to the law that includes the food laws and the purity laws. What is at stake is the conviction that the promise to Abraham in Gen 12:3 is fulfilled, which, in the context of Paul's 'canonical' reading of the Torah, cannot be separated from the promise of righteousness by faith in Gen 15:6." After the coming of Jesus the Messiah, the justification of sinners is separated from obedience to the law. Since God has conquered sin and death, the consequence of sin, at the cross and in the resurrection of Jesus, humankind can overcome sin and find justification and righteousness before God only through faith in the God who has raised Jesus the Messiah and Savior from the dead as the "firstborn" of the dead. Since faith in God who raises from the dead relies exclusively on God's grace, revealed in the cross and resurrection of Jesus, and since God's eschatological grace reaches all sinners, Israel as well as the nations, the righteousness by faith that was promised to Abraham and has become a reality in Jesus Christ is universal in scope. What Scripture has "foreseen" (Gal 3:8a) has happened: the "fullness of time" has arrived, and God's promises have become reality in the sending of his Son (Gal 4:4). The

---

[400]Söding 2000, 414; the quotation that follows above, ibid., 422.

faith that God had promised "has come" (Gal 3:25): this means that in the present time all "who believe" are blessed together with Abraham, who believed in God's promise, Jews as well as Gentiles (Gal 3:8-9). And this means that both Jews and Gentiles who believe in Jesus Christ and to whom God therefore gives the Spirit of his Son are adopted as children of God (Gal 4:5-6).

In Paul's letters to the Thessalonians, the question of the future of believers is the central theological issue. The Gentile Christians had heard Paul speak about the future return of Jesus Christ when he preached the gospel a few months earlier in Thessalonike. They were bewildered when some believers died (1 Thess 4:13). Paul emphasizes that God's salvific action applied to all believers in Jesus, whether they are alive or whether they are deceased (1 Thess 5:9-10). He emphasizes that all believers will experience Jesus' return with their bodies, both the believers who are alive and the believers who have passed away (1 Thess 4:15-18). He teaches that when Jesus Christ returns, all believers, whether "awake" or "asleep," will "live with him" (1 Thess 5:10). In 1 Thessalonians, written only a few weeks or months after the establishment of the church in Thessalonike, we see Paul as a missionary "who is completely devoted to his church, which is still weak. He has not forgotten his theology. However, his theology is expressed mostly in terms of pastoral counseling. His dedication to the church is total. Each statement of the apostle, each sentiment that the letter reveals, is focused on the church and its life in Christ. . . . This undivided dedication to ministry for the congregation is complemented by a sharp focus on the character of this ministry, consistently denying any suspicion of dishonesty in the witness and his behavior."[401] When some visiting Christian prophets and some letters written by other Christian teachers created confusion in the church in Thessalonike regarding the imminence of Jesus' return, Paul clarifies that Jesus cannot come back yet, since the evil (one) through which Satan expresses his power has not yet been eliminated (2 Thess 2:1-12).

In his letter to the churches in southern Galatia Paul substantiates and defends the "truth of the gospel" (Gal 2:5, 14) against Jewish-Christian teachers who probably have come from Jerusalem and who demand that the Gentile believers be circumcised. They seek to disparage Paul by accusing him of lacking the full authority of an apostle. Paul's response is formulated with language that could not be clearer. He asserts that the teaching of these opponents represents "a different gospel" that must be rejected at all costs (Gal 1:6-9). He defends his status as an apostle with the argument that although there are differences in logistics between his mission and the missionary work of the Jerusalem apostles, particularly the mission of Peter, they preach the same gospel (Gal 1:1; 1:11—2:10). In the middle section of his letter Paul expounds his conviction that now,

---

[401]Holtz, *1 Thess*, 281. On the charge of dishonesty, raised probably by non-Christians, see 1 Thess 2:1-12.

in the present time that has been newly qualified by Jesus the Messiah, "a person is justified not by the works of the law but through faith in Jesus Christ" (Gal 2:16). As a result of this new reality, the Mosaic law is shown to be incapable of guaranteeing salvation (Gal 2:15—3:18): the function of the Torah as prison warden and as *paidagōgos*, guardian and guide, has come to an end with the arrival of Jesus Christ (Gal 3:19—4:7). Paul argues that submission to the demands of circumcision and full obedience to the Torah is tantamount to submission to the enslaving powers of the world that the Gentile believers served before their conversion (Gal 4:8-20). And Paul argues that the "heavenly Jerusalem" is superior to the "present Jerusalem," and that the Gentile Christians, who have been set free from sin and from the law, are already children of Sarah the freewoman and thus members of the people of God (Gal 4:21-31). In the last two chapters of his letter Paul emphasizes that the problems of the "flesh"— issues of wrong and immoral behavior on the part the believers—cannot be solved with the help of the law; they are solved in the continuing union with the death and resurrection of Jesus Christ, in the liberation from bondage that Jesus the Messiah has effected, and in the power of the Holy Spirit, who produces "fruit" in the life of the believer acceptable to God (Gal 5:1—6:16).

In his first letter to the Corinthians Paul interacts with the concepts and behavioral patterns of believers who continue to be influenced and controlled by the social realities of the Roman colony of Corinth. This is evident in their emphasis on wisdom and rhetoric (1 Cor 1:18—4:21), in their tolerance of the serious sexual misconduct by a member of the church with high social standing (1 Cor 5:1-13), in vexatious litigation (1 Cor 6:1-11), in encounters with prostitutes, probably on the occasion of banquets in the houses of wealthy friends (1 Cor 6:12-20), in visits to pagan temples in which they reclined for meals (1 Cor 8:10; 10:7-8, 14-22), and in the ostentatious demonstration of their high social status in the meetings of the church (1 Cor 11:4, 17-22). Paul emphasizes, against such erroneous and problematic patterns of behavior, the reality and efficacy of the "word of the cross" (1 Cor 1:18), which is God's wisdom and power (1 Cor 1:24; 2:4-5). He argues that the gospel as the "word of the cross" prohibits commitment to any particular missionaries and teachers, that it excludes expectations of rhetorical brilliance, and that it bars immoral and selfish behavior. Paul also discusses one-sided theological positions in the Corinthian (house) churches that have already caused problematic behaviors or will do so if left uncorrected. An overly enthusiastic understanding of the Holy Spirit caused excesses in the meetings of the congregation with an unhealthy and unwarranted overemphasis on glossolalia (speaking unlearned languages) and on prophetic speech (1 Cor 12:1—14:40). It led to an exaggerated understanding of Christian freedom that devalues the human body and declares marriage and sexual intercourse in marriage as sinful (1 Cor 7:1-40). And, combined with an overrealized eschatology, it prompted a denial of the future resurrection of the body (1 Cor

15:1-58).[402] This means that in this letter to the Christians in Corinth Paul argues against both erroneous teaching in the church and wrong behavior caused by pagan standards and customs and by one-sided theological positions. Wolfgang Schrage comments, "Paul is thus forced not just to explain his theology of the cross: he also needs to remind the church of 'the ways' of the cross (1 Cor 4:17) and admonish them with regard to the purity of the church (1 Cor 5) and the eschatological responsibility of believers (1 Cor 6:1ff), instruct them with regard to the proper attitude concerning sexuality (1 Cor 6:12ff), marriage and celibacy (1 Cor 7) and meat sacrificed to idols (1 Cor 8—10), and call them to μίμησις [*mimēsis,* 'imitation'] (1 Cor 11:1 etc.) and οἰκοδομή [*oikodomē,* 'edification'] (1 Cor 14:26). This is why he contrasts love both with knowledge (1 Cor 8:1) and with religious individualism in the church service (1 Cor 13), and why he confronts the deplorable state of affairs at the Lord's Supper not only with the παράδοσις [*paradosis,* 'tradition'] which is focused on salvation, but also with the concept of brotherhood, understood in an ethical sense. Even when he discusses the denial and the hope of the resurrection, he emphasizes the practical consequences (1 Cor 15:58)."

In his second letter to the Corinthians Paul defends himself against some particular member of the church or a group within the church who oppose him with personal insults, with the charge of unfulfilled promises that he allegedly made, and by denying his apostolic authority and credibility (2 Cor 1:12-24; 10:1-13:10). His apostolic authority is also questioned by Christian teachers who have visited the church (2 Cor 10:10; 11:4, 12-15, 21-23). Paul defends his conduct as a missionary and teacher of the church in regard both to the travel plans that he had to change (2 Cor 1:12—2:13) and to his apostolic authority (2 Cor 2:14—7:16). He substantiates his apostolic authority primarily with reference to his life and suffering and with reference to the existence of believers in Corinth as proof for his competence as an apostle (2 Cor 2:14—3:6; 10:12-18). He argues that his ministry as a "servant of the new covenant" brought the Corinthians the transforming reality of God that the old covenant lacked (2 Cor 3:7-18). Paul repeatedly emphasizes the legitimacy of his apostleship (2 Cor 4:1-6; 10:7-11; 11:1-12), referring to the trials and the suffering that he constantly experiences (2 Cor 4:7—6:13; 11:23-33). He defends his apostolic status not because he is concerned about his own reputation, but because of the Christians in Corinth (2 Cor 12:19): Jesus Christ himself speaks in the gospel that he proclaims (2 Cor 13:3), and the power of God is at work in his mission and life (2 Cor 13:4), which means that the church can continue to exist and be edified only when its members are reconciled with Paul and thus acknowledge his message of the revelation of God's glory in the crucified and risen Jesus Christ (2 Cor 11:4; 12:21; 13:1-10).

In his letter to the Romans, written in the winter of A.D. 56/57 in Corinth on

---

[402]Schrage, *1 Kor,* 1:56; the quotation that follows above, ibid., 1:62.

the journey to Jerusalem, where he wanted to hand over the collection, Paul writes a "statement of accountability" (*Rechenschaftsbericht*)[403] about his theological convictions and arguments. The apostle anticipated a policy discussion during his visit to Jerusalem about his message of God's salvific revelation in Jesus Christ for all people, both Jews and Gentiles. In his letter to the believers in Rome, whom he wants to recruit as partners in his next project of a mission to Spain, Paul explains the message of Jesus Christ, which he has been set apart to proclaim (Rom 1:1-5) and which represents the common tradition of early Christian confession.[404] Paul constructs his exposition of the gospel in the form of a dialogue with a Jewish discussion partner who formulates the fundamental objections of his Jewish-Christian opponent against the gospel of the revelation of the righteousness of God without works of law. Ulrich Wilckens explains, "Paul makes a real effort in his letter to the Gentile Christian church in Rome to conduct the *dialogus cum Judaeo,* including not only his discussion until Rom 11 but also his emphasis on Jerusalem in Rom 15:27, because this subject matter allows him to invalidate the arguments against his Gentile Christian mission which soon will be leveled against him in Jerusalem and which probably caused some reservation about him in Rome. His existing and his future missionary work faces dangers in both cities."[405] Paul therefore explains, in this longest letter of his, who Jesus is and what he did as God's Messiah and Savior for Jews and for the nations, making atonement for sins and granting salvation through his death on the cross and his resurrection on the third day.[406]

In his letter to the Ephesians, probably a letter to all the churches in the province of Asia Minor, Paul exhorts the Gentile Christians (Eph 2:11) who are proud on account of their good works to remember that it is God's grace alone that grants salvation, and that everything that they have, including their good works, is the result of God's grace (Eph 2:8-10). He reminds the believers who may have become conceited of their past as pagans—"without Christ, being aliens from the commonwealth of Israel, and strangers to the covenants of promise, having no hope and without God in the world" (Eph 2:12). Paul exhorts them to remember that God creates from Jewish Christians and from Gentile Christians "one new humanity" as he reconciles "both groups to God in one body through the cross" (Eph 2:15-16) and as he proclaims "peace to you who were far off and peace to those who were near" (Eph 2:17).

In his letter to the Philippians Paul probably interacts with Jewish-Christian teachers who visited the church in Philippi and attempted to convince the Gentile Christians to submit to circumcision (Phil 3:3-4), despite the fact that their

---

[403]Stuhlmacher, *Röm,* 13 (ET, 8); on the early Christian confessional tradition, ibid., 14 (ET, 9).
[404]Cf. Rom 1:3-4; 3:25-26; 4:25; 6:17; 8:3; 10:9; 13:8-9; 14:17; 15:14-15.
[405]Wilckens, *Röm,* 1:46.
[406]See Stuhlmacher, *Röm,* 16 (ET, 11).

own personal behavior was anything but beyond reproach (Phil 3:17-21).[407] Paul emphasizes that perfection is not achieved through the adoption of certain Jewish doctrines or practices; rather, it is a goal that believers in Jesus Christ will reach only in God's future. Paul evidently is less concerned about minor differences in the understanding of Christian faith and practice: "Let those of us then who are mature be of the same mind; and if you think differently about anything, this too God will reveal to you" (Phil 3:15). What matters most for Christians is to "press on toward the goal for the prize of the heavenly call of God in Christ Jesus" (Phil 3:14).

In his letter to the Christians in Colossae Paul evidently discusses the attacks of local Jews who criticize, with enormous self-confidence, the convictions of the (Jewish) Christians as well as their worship practices and everyday behavior.[408] The main danger facing the Christians in Colossae was to have their conviction clouded about what they already possess as believers in Jesus Christ, and to miss the importance of realizing practically and specifically their faith in Christ in their everyday behavior (Col 2:6-7). Paul reminds them of the fullness of divine blessing that Jesus has procured and made available through his death on the cross (Col 2:8-15). He warns against the claim that there are spiritual experiences beyond the union with Jesus Christ by faith that allow the believer to leave the cross of Christ behind: matters of food and drink, of festivals and sabbath celebrations, of the worship of angels and visions and ascetic practices can never compete with God's salvific revelation in Jesus Christ and in the Christian community, in which the future is not merely a shadow but has already become reality (Col 2:16-19). Paul warns against the claim that the observance of Jewish food laws and purity stipulations is necessary for life in the community of Jesus the Messiah (Col 2:20-23). In the second part of the letter Paul describes the lifestyle that results from faith in Jesus Christ. Believers in Christ have died with Christ and have been raised with him, so that their life is determined by this heavenly perspective where Jesus Christ sits at the right hand of God (Col 3:1-4). This christological, theological and eschatological dimension has consequences for the everyday behavior of believers, signifying the abandonment of their former pagan customs and vices and the adoption of the praxis of life in the Christian community, which is characterized by mutual love and support (Col 3:5-17). Faith in Christ also influences the behavior of husbands and wives, parents and children, freemen and slaves (Col 3:18—4:1). Finally, Paul emphasizes the importance of constant prayer and intercession, and he advises the believers to be wise in their dealings with their pagan fellow citizens: they should aim at conversations about their faith that are "gracious and effective" so that

---

[407]See O'Brien, *Phil,* 26-35, esp. 33-34.
[408]Dunn, *Col,* 33-35; for a discussion of alternative explanations of the "Colossian heresy" see ibid., 23-33; for the comments that follow above see ibid., 136-37.

they will have "the right answer for everyone" (Col 4:6 NLT).

In his letters to Timothy and to Titus, Paul interacts again with Jewish-Christian teachers who are active in the churches that Paul established.[409] Opposition from these teachers continues to grow because they are active in the meetings of the local congregations and in the private houses of Christians. Paul asserts that their propaganda is nonsense and that they are engaged in foolish controversies.[410] The comment that these teachers seduce Christians (2 Tim 3:13; cf. Tit 1:10) indicates that the "nonsense" that they propagate has a modicum of plausibility and thus convinces some believers. Their teaching deals with the Mosaic law, which they interpret in an allegorical manner with Jewish myths and with circumcision,[411] with ascetic practices related to marriage and food.[412] They deny a future resurrection (2 Tim 2:18), they emphasize the participation of women in the teaching ministry of the churches with the result that they neglect their children (1 Tim 2:11-15), and they possibly downplay the importance of missionary work among Gentiles.[413] Their teaching implied or resulted in the displacement of Jesus Christ from his central position as Savior and as mediator between God and humankind, as speculations and discussions distracted the Christians from the truly important matters.[414] Paul therefore attacks these teachers particularly on account of their immoral behavior (Tit 1:18; 2 Tim 3:1-5), which was demonstrated in, for example, their hope of achieving financial gain through their teaching (1 Tim 6:5-10; Tit 1:11). Paul warns the Christians, through Timothy and Titus, to recognize the danger that these teachers represent and to reject them; otherwise these believers would return to being the kind of people they were before their conversion.[415] In the Pastoral Epistles the Pauline convictions of God's salvific revelation in Jesus Christ are applied to the situation in the churches,[416] which greatly concerns Paul, especially the question of church order: the apostle directs Timothy and Titus to work toward the consolidation of the leadership in the local congregations, of the elders and the deacons. And he emphasizes the necessity of acknowledging and agreeing with the early Christian tradition that the teachers in the churches must preserve.

Pastoral Consolidation: Encouragement of the Christian Communities

Paul's missionary praxis consisted not solely in the evangelistic proclamation of

---

[409]See Marshall, *PastEp,* 40-51; the summary that follows above, 42-44.

[410]1 Tim 6:3-5; Tit 1:10; 3:9; 2 Tim 2:14-16; 2:23.

[411]1 Tim 1:4, 7; Tit 1:14; 2 Tim 4:4; on circumcision see Tit 1:10.

[412]1 Tim 4:3; cf. Tit 1:15; 1 Tim 2:15; 5:23.

[413]Marshall, *PastEp,* 45, with reference to 1 Tim 2:4-6, 7; 4:10; Tit 2:11; cf. 1 Tim 3:16.

[414]See Marshall, *PastEp,* 51.

[415]Cf. 1 Tim 3:1-13; 5:6, 11; Tit 1:6-7; 2 Tim 2:22. See Marshall, *PastEp,* 43.

[416]See Marshall, *PastEp,* 92-108.

the gospel to Jews and Gentiles and in the establishment of churches. There is a third phase of Paul's missionary: the apostle consistently accompanied the local congregations on their way to dynamic maturity in which the creative energy of the Christian community finds expression in the fruit of the Holy Spirit. Some New Testament scholars think that Paul's missionary methods were characterized by a restless rush and hectic movements. Günther Bornkamm writes in his influential book on Paul, "It is perfectly astonishng to see how short a time he took in traversing the extensive fields where he worked, and how quickly he left scarcely founded churches and traveled farther, instead of taking time to care for them and train them. . . . The great goal of carrying the gospel to the ends of the earth kept him always on the move and gave him no rest."[417] Michael Green perceives, probably in light of the effective praxis of many evangelists and the exciting expansion of the church in the twentieth century, that Paul traveled from city to city with the intention of conquering new territories for the gospel, leaving the new converts behind after providing them with a minimum of instruction.[418]

Such views ignore the fact that Paul's mission to Corinth and Ephesus lasted in each case for over two years, before he started new missionary initiatives in regions in which the gospel had not been preached before. The "travel motif" that is deduced from the book of Acts and that often controls the scholarly interpretation of Paul's missionary work needs serious qualification.[419] Paul's visits in churches that he had established previously demonstrates the reality and the importance of the apostle's "anxiety for all the churches" (2 Cor 11:28) in his understanding of the missionary task. Paul visited the south Galatian churches in Antiocheia, in Iconium and in Lystra three times after the initial visit during which the congregations were established: on the occasion of the return journey from Derbe to Syria (Acts 14:21-28), during the journey from Antioch toward the province of Asia that eventually took the missionaries to Europe (Acts 15:36; 16:1-5), and on the occasion of the journey from Antioch to Ephesus (Acts 18:23). The fact that on the two latter occasions Paul undertook the long journey from Antioch in Syria to Ephesus in the province of Asia by foot suggests that en route he probably visited churches in other cities in Syria and in Cilicia as well, presumably at least in Tarsus. After Paul was forced to leave Thessalonike in a hurry, he "longed with great eagerness to see" the believers there "face to face" and thus attempted "again and again" to return to Thessalonike, only to be blocked by Satan (1 Thess 2:17-18). When the church in Corinth was unable to deal with difficulties that had arisen, Paul interrupted his missionary work in Ephesus and traveled to Corinth (2 Cor 6:1). When he was engaged in very promising missionary work in Troas, where God had given him an "open door" (2 Cor 2:12), he was restless because

---

[417]Bornkamm 1993, 73-74 (ET, 54-55).
[418]M. Green 1970, 169.
[419]See Marshall 2000b, 103.

the situation in the Corinthian church was still confused and because he had not received the news that he had been waiting for—so much so that he ended his missionary work in Troas and traveled to Macedonia to meet Titus and to reestablish contact with the church in Corinth (2 Cor 2:13). There is no evidence, however, that Paul ever ended his missionary work in a city on his own initiative in order to start a new project in unreached areas—apart from his mission to Corinth and Ephesus, two cities in which he stayed for over two years.[420]

Kristlieb Adloff formulates, in a lecture on "the missionary existence of the apostle Paul," important thoughts on the subject "Paul and time." He observes, "Paul had time. The second letter to the Corinthians can wait. He had waited for the reply of the Corinthians, even though this period of waiting meant pain and distress (2 Cor 2:4, 12-13; 7:5). But it is precisely this 'even though' that the Corinthians need to understand and appreciate (2 Cor 1:12ff.; 2:4; 12:15). Why did Paul not come to Corinth, as he had promised (2 Cor 1:15-23)? Why did he leave after his 'interim visit' (2 Cor 2:1; 12:14, 21; 13:1-2) without having accomplished anything? Why did he prefer the mortal danger in Ephesus (2 Cor 1:8)? Why did he write letters during his absence (2 Cor 10:1, 11; 13:2, 10), letters that are weighty and strong (2 Cor 10:10) and erudite (2 Cor 11:6), letters that people can interpret and understand as they choose (2 Cor 1:13)? The answer is this: because these letters provide the church time (2 Cor 1:23), because they constitute a gaining of time for many, thus belonging to the eschatological service of God's freedom that blackmails no one and does violence to no one (2 Cor 11:20-21), encouraging everybody, first of all the weak (2 Cor 11:29), to rejoice and to praise the good of all consolation (2 Cor 1:3-11)."[421]

The theological, ethical and spiritual consolidation of the churches was a fundamental concern of Paul. This is apparent already in his self-understanding as a missionary (see §24.3), and it is demonstrated by the function of the team of missionary coworkers that Paul organized (see §28.4). When Paul sent missionary coworkers into other cities, he always sent them to existing churches that he established. When Paul left Macedonia and went to Achaia in order to begin missionary work in Corinth, he left Timothy and Silas in Beroea, sending them later to the congregations in Philippi and Thessalonike (Acts 17:14; 1 Thess 3:1-8). Timothy and Titus repeatedly played an important role in the development and consolidation of the church in Corinth.[422] At a later period Timothy was sent a second time to Philippi (Phil 2:19-24), while Tychicus went to Colossae (Col 4:7-9). Paul Bowers summarizes Paul's missionary travels in this context with good sense: "There is no restless rushing from one new opening to another but rather a methodical progress concerned both with initiating work in new areas and at the same time with bringing the emergent groups in those areas to stable maturity."[423]

---

[420]See Bowers 1987, 192-93.
[421]Adloff 1986, 17.
[422]1 Cor 4:17; 16:10-11; 2 Cor 2:13; 7:6-7, 13-15; 8:6, 16-17, 23; 12:18. The hypothesis of Fellows (2001), that Titus and Timothy are one and the same person, is unconvincing.
[423]Bowers 1987, 189-90; similarly Knox 1964, 7; P. Beasley-Murray 1993.

Mauro Pesce describes in a recent study the complementary function of pioneer missionary work and the ministry of consolidating the churches.[424] We have ample primary sources for this phase of Paul's missionary ministry—the Pauline letters—in contrast to the first phase of pioneer missionary work. Pesce discusses in detail (1) the use of Scripture, which Paul constantly quotes or alludes to; (2) the spiritual growth of the believers; (3) the role of Christian prophecy; (4) the eschatological understanding of political power. He emphasizes particularly Paul's concern for the "liturgical assembly" of the local congregation. Paul seeks to strengthen the gifts of the individual believer as they work together for the welfare of the entire congregation, which consists on the one hand in a better understanding of the nature of God and of the work of Jesus Christ, and on the other hand in an increasingly deeper realization of their status as "resident aliens" in society. Pesce's description needs to be supplemented by two areas.[425] First, Paul often emphasizes the nature of the church as the body of Christ.[426] The Holy Spirit always plays an important role in Paul's exhortation of the believers, but the Spirit is always present as the Spirit of Jesus Christ. Second, Paul reminds the churches of the role of the local congregation as a concrete representation of the "words of life" that they offer to the world (Phil 2:14-16). The missionary responsibility of the local congregations will be discussed below.

28.4 Organizational Issues

Paul's missionary work was an integral part of the early Christian mission. Paul's missionary ministry was not the separate action of an apostle who perhaps was more enthusiastic than other apostles. Rather, while Paul preached the gospel and established churches, the Twelve and other missionaries also preached the gospels and planted churches.

Some scholars suggest that there were different types of missionary work in the early church. Their reconstructions remain hypothetical and speculative, however. François Bovon distinguishes three types of missionary outreach.[427] (1) The missionary praxis of Jesus himself, adopted by the first missionaries in Palestine and in Syria, Jewish Christians who worked in teams of two, renouncing personal possessions, traveling from town to town and from house to house and proclaiming the imminent arrival of the kingdom (Mk 6; Lk 10). Presumably these were the Jewish-Christian missionaries who opposed the Pauline missionary organization (2 Cor 10—13; *Didache*). (2) The missionary praxis of Hellenistic Jewish Christians who initially concentrated their missionary work on the

---

[424]Pesce 1994; on ministry in the local congregations as "the second phase of apostolic activity" see ibid., 31-34, 93-256. See also Bowers 1987, 188-97; Fleming 1993.

[425]See J. Murphy-O'Connor, *RB* 103 (1996): 295.

[426]Rom 12:3-8; 1 Cor 10:16-17; 12:12-27; Eph 1:22-23; 2:15-16; 4:4, 16; Col 1:24; 2:19; 3:15.

[427]Bovon 1982, esp. 369-73.

local Christian community in Jerusalem and then in Antioch. They based their missionary work on a central ("mother") church and sought to establish new churches, traveling even to Gentile cities (Acts 13:1-13). They attended the synagogue services in the Gentile cities that they visited and proclaimed Jesus as the Son of God who sits at the right hand of God the Creator. They invited the Gentiles who were present in the synagogues to turn to the living God and to believe in Jesus the Son of God as Savior. (3) The missionary praxis of Paul, which has been shaped on the one hand by the mission of the Hellenistic Jewish Christians with whom he collaborated for ten years in Antioch, and on the other hand by the methods of the first missionaries whose itinerant travels from town to town and whose renunciation of possessions he adopted. He relies on local congregations as centers of his missionary work, like the Hellenistic missionaries. At the same he does not understand his mission as the result of being commissioned by a local congregation, as he asserts that he has been called to be an apostle by Jesus Christ himself. And Paul did not rely on one center alone, as did the Hellenistic missionaries with regard to Jerusalem and Antioch. Rather, he established new bridgeheads for his missionary work during his travels that led him from province to province.

This typology of the early Christian mission is implausible. (1) The reconstruction of a first Jewish-Christian mission immediately after Easter in Palestine and in Syria, based on the missionary discourses in the Gospels, remains hypothetical and problematic from a source- and literary-critical point of view. First, the missionary discourses cannot be eliminated from the authentic Jesus tradition as easily as many critical scholars suggest. Second, Luke's account in the book of Acts contains no traces whatsoever of such a mission. It is true that Luke reports selectively. However, when he connects the beginning of the early Christian mission with Peter, John and evidently the Twelve, expanded by the evangelistic activity of Stephen and Philip, which represents a new phase but remains connected to and controlled by the church in Jerusalem and its leaders, there seems to be no room, historically speaking, for another missionary movement—unless we assume that Galilean followers of Jesus organized an independent mission that Luke ignores. Theoretically, Bovon's hypothetical reconstruction, which remains dependent on literary-critical operations, is a possibility. However, a historical reconstruction that assumes an initially unified Jewish mission organized by the Jerusalem church that eventually was transformed to include missionary outreach to Gentiles seems more plausible. Such a reconstruction has the advantage of being supported by historical source material in the book of Acts. Third, Bovon cannot prove, or disprove, whether these first (anonymous) Jewish-Christian missionaries relied on a local congregation as center of their mission, nor can he discount the possibility that they sought to reach not only fellow Jews but also Gentiles. (2) The assumption that the Hellenistic Jewish-Christian missionaries understood themselves as envoys of a local congregation presumably is correct, as far as Stephen and Philip are concerned, even though Luke does not comment on this aspect of their self-understanding: Stephen and Philip were entrusted with caring for the widows. They were not commissioned to preach the gospel in Jerusalem or in Samaria. Luke does not relate the reasons for their transition from a charitable ministry to an active missionary ministry. On the other hand, we must not play off the connection of the Hellenistic Jewish-Christian missionaries with a local congregation against Paul's missionary praxis. Paul indeed understood himself to have been commissioned as an apostle to the Gentiles by Jesus Christ himself. At the same time he regularly visits the churches in Jerusalem and in Antioch and gives an account of what God does in his missionary outreach. Paul was not an "autonomous" missionary, as far as we know (our knowledge concerning his missionary praxis in Arabia and Syria/Cilicia is extremely limited). Finally, it is unrealistic when Bovon constructs a contrast between this mission that relied on a local congregation as center and the mission of the first missionaries who traveled in pairs from town to town: how should we conceive, specifically, of the missionary praxis of the Hellenistic missionaries if they would not have left their "church center"? (3) Bovon's third point is largely correct, which demonstrates the concept that forms the basis for my reconstruction of the early Christian mission and follows closely Luke's report in the book of Acts: if Paul was willing and able to combine elements from different "types" of missionary work, there is no convincing reason to deny the possibility, indeed the likelihood, that the same is true for the missionary efforts of the church in Jerusalem, the missions of Peter, Stephen, Philip and other Jewish-Christian missionaries who eventually came to Antioch and started new missionary projects from there. Finally, the contrasts that Bovon assumes with regard to the Pauline mission are not cogent: the itinerant travel from town to town must have characterized the Hellenistic Jewish-Christian missionaries as well if they wanted to establish churches outside of the "church center." And Paul's self-understanding as an apostle commissioned by Jesus Christ himself constitutes no contrast to reliance on a local Christian community, a fact that is underscored by Paul's regular visits to Jerusalem.

Centers of Missionary Work

Obviously, the following discussion of "centers of missionary work" (see §30.1) does not assume that the mission of the early church relied on office buildings with directors, consultants and secretaries who formulate programs, coordinate the missionaries' work and secure financial resources for the missionary organization. Understood in *that* sense, there was not a single headquarters of the early Christian church and its mission, although the community in Jerusalem came somewhat close to being the headquarters of the Christian movement during the twelve years from A.D. 30 to 42.

Paul regularly visited the church in Jerusalem and Antioch, but he was not dependent upon geographical places or on persons, including the Jerusalem apostles, as he clarified in Gal 1—2.[428] Paul based his missionary outreach at different times on different centers: perhaps Damascus and Tarsus, briefly Jerusalem, certainly Antioch, Corinth and Ephesus, and, at least in intent, Rome.

1. Damascus. During the first months after Paul's conversion Damascus may well have been the center of his missionary outreach to Arabia. However, since we have virtually no information about this period in Paul's ministry, this assumption must remain hypothetical. Damascus, the city of Paul's conversion, of his first experience of a Christian community and of his first missionary activity (Gal 1:21), evidently played no role in his later ministry. Several reasons may explain this fact.[429] (a) Biographical context: the main cities in Paul's life, up to that point and during the later years, were Tarsus, Paul's hometown and the center of his missionary work in Cilicia, and Jerusalem, the "university town" where he had lived for many years. (b) The communicative infrastructure of the Roman Empire: the regions east of Damascus were border areas of the empire. (c) Missionary responsibilities: after Paul was forced to flee from Damascus, he may have arranged in Jerusalem for another apostle to become "responsible" for the missionary work centered in Damascus.

2. Tarsus. During the second period of Paul's missionary activity, in the approximately ten years of his missionary work in Syria and in Cilicia between A.D. 33 and 42, his hometown of Tarsus presumably was the center of his ministry. Since we have no information about this period—the earliest Christian sources do not even provide information on whether Paul established a church in Tarsus during this time—this assumption remains hypothetical. However, when Barnabas wanted to recruit Paul in A.D. 42 for the work in Antioch, he knew that he would find him in Tarsus (Acts 11:25).

3. Jerusalem. Paul asserts in Rom 15:19 that he proclaimed the gospel *apo Ierousalēm*—that is, beginning in Jerusalem. Three factors explain why Jerusalem was central for Paul's missionary work.[430] (a) Theological reasons: Jerusalem is the city of David and thus the center of the people of God, and in the messianic period it was the destination of the pilgrimage of the nations. (b) Historical reasons: Jerusalem is the city in which took place the decisive events responsible for the existence of the church—the city in which Jesus the Messiah died on the cross and was raised from the dead on the third day. Thus Jerusalem remains the center of the people of God, reconstituted in the mission of the Twelve as the messianic people of God, noteworthy in view of the fact that the Twelve were mostly Galileans. Paul grew up and studied in Jerusalem, and this may be

---

[428]See Townsend (1986, 100-101), who overemphasizes Paul's independence, however.
[429]For the first two reasons see Reck 1991, 209 n. 181.
[430]See Reck 1991, 209-210; cf. earlier Haas 1971, 53-55.

one of the reasons why he repeatedly visited Jerusalem. (c) Practical reasons: the Christian community of Jerusalem presumably was the largest church, where all the information about the work of the apostles, the evangelism of other missionaries and the establishment and growth of churches came together. Jerusalem was the city where one would most readily encounter one of the Twelve, at least during the first twelve years after Jesus' resurrection. Before embarking on the mission to Cyprus, Paul and Barnabas organized a private consultation with the leaders of the Jerusalem church (Gal 2:1-10). After the mission to Cyprus and southern Galatia, Paul returned with Barnabas to Antioch, "where they had been commended to the grace of God for the work that they had completed" (Acts 14:26), while Paul, upon the conclusion of the mission, sailed to Macedonia and Achaia and then to Caesarea, from where he traveled to Jerusalem, a detour of perhaps 250 km: "When he had landed at Caesarea, he went up to Jerusalem and greeted the church, and then went down to Antioch" (Acts 18:22). After the mission to the province of Asia, Paul also traveled directly to Jerusalem (Acts 21:15-17), the primary reason being the collection that he had gathered for the needy Jerusalem believers. Jerusalem never was a natural transit point for travelers: the capital of Judea was difficult to reach; roads led to Jerusalem only because the city was Israel's capital since the time of King David.[431] For Paul, Jerusalem was the acknowledged center of the followers of Jesus.

Why was Jerusalem not the operational base for Paul's missionary work? The fact that some Jews in Jerusalem threatened his life cannot have been the main reason,[432] since he continued to visit Jerusalem after his missionary travels and he insisted on going to Jerusalem even when Christian prophets warned him not to go (Acts 21:11-14). The reason seems to have been the agreement with the Twelve, particularly Peter and John, to coordinate their missionary efforts: as long as Paul operated in the east of the Mediterranean world, Antioch was a preferable center for his missionary work—an international metropolis and a city in which he had preached and taught for several years.

4. Antioch in Syria. The first Christian community in which Jewish Christians and Gentile Christians lived together without apartheid was the church in Antioch. The church was well suited as a base for new missionary initiatives. Antioch, the capital of the province of Syria, was the third largest city of the Roman Empire, with a large Jewish community.

After his conversion and after his return from Arabia, Paul preached the gospel in cities in Syria and Cilicia, but he seems to have avoided Antioch. We have no information about the success of Paul's mission to Syria and Cilicia. There is

---

[431]Emphasized in Fischer et al. 1996, 6-7. Jerusalem never was a city through which caravans passed.
[432]Contra Reck, 210 with n. 184.

no reason, however, to assume that Acts 13 constitutes a "break" concerning the missionary success of Paul's ministry. Paul's statements in Gal 1—2 do not hint at such a break, nor do they indicate a "new commission" in Antioch.

Why did Paul not choose one of the churches that he established in Syria and Cilicia as his "home church" and as a permanent base of operations? The following reasons may offer an explanation: (a) Geography: Tarsus, a provincial capital and strategically located, would have been a good choice, but Antioch was a large metropolis whose location was even more strategic. (b) Connections: the churches that Paul established may not have had direct connections with Jerusalem that could be maintained while Paul preached the gospel in other regions. (c) Coworkers: Paul perhaps had not yet been able to recruit coworkers who could support him on his missionary travels, while in Antioch Barnabas was available, who at the same time represented the connection to Jerusalem that always was important for Paul. (d) Size: perhaps the churches that Paul had founded in various cities in Syria and Cilicia were too small to serve as a base for missionary operations.

Paul worked in Antioch from A.D. 42 to 44, and he planned his mission to Cyprus and to southern Galatia with Barnabas in Antioch. The church in Antioch evidently was willing to send two of their most active and experienced leaders off to missionary work in other regions (Acts 13:1-2). Several scholars argue that Paul left Antioch in order to begin an independent missionary ministry.[433] It is indeed correct that Paul no longer worked as an "apostle of the church in Antioch" since his mission to Macedonia and Achaia, after the separation from Barnabas, but as an apostle who substantiated his apostolic authority with reference to a direct divine commission. Paul evidently did not intend to use the church in Antioch as a permanent base of operations: after the conclusion of the mission to the province of Asia, Paul wanted to leave the eastern Mediterranean world and go to Spain, a project that apparently implied that he would no longer return to Antioch. However, when Paul informs the elders of the church of Ephesus in Miletus that he would not see them in the future (Acts 20:38), his statement does not have to be understood as a basic strategic decision, as it may have had other reasons: in A.D. 57 Paul was at least fifty years old, and, given life expectancy in the first century, he may not have anticipated many more years to live.

5. Corinth. Paul stayed in Corinth for over two years (Acts 18:11), and he interacted with the Corinthian church with letters, envoys and repeated visits. The reference to churches in Achaia (Acts 19:21) is evidence for the possibility that during Paul's stay in Corinth other cities in the province were reached with the gospel. The city of Cenchreae is one example.

6. Ephesus. During the three years between A.D. 52 and 55 when Paul preached and taught in Ephesus, thousands of people in the province of Asia

---

[433]See, for example, Stuhlmacher 1981, 122; W. Campbell 1990, 81-97.

evidently were reached with the gospel (Acts 19:10). Several churches were established during this period in the Lykos Valley: in Colossae, Hierapolis and Laodikeia. It is possible, though uncertain, that during this time the churches in Smyrna, Philadelphia, Thyatira, Sardis and Pergamon were established as well.

7. Rome. According to Paul's plans, the church in Rome was to have an important role for the mission to Spain beginning in A.D. 58. It is unlikely, however, that Rome would have been a "center of operations," as he apparently looked (only) for help from Roman Christians, presumably with regard to contacts with Spanish cities and to Latin-speaking coworkers.

8. Jerusalem, Antioch, Tarsus, Corinth and Ephesus were centers of the early Christian and the Pauline mission, but buildings there played a minor role or perhaps none at all. The only buildings in which Christians met for which we have any information for the first century are mentioned with respect to Jerusalem: the upper room and the house of Mary (see §15). Besides the "shepherds," Paul mentions teachers (*didaskaloi*) as important workers in the churches, implying that the early Christian teachers in these centers had an important function not only for the local congregation but also, presumably, for the training of new missionaries.

Teams of Missionaries and Coworkers

Paul surrounded himself with a circle of coworkers, a team of fellow missionaries whose composition frequently changed.[434] Of the approximately one hundred names that are connected with Paul in the book of Acts and in the Pauline letters, thirty-eight people are coworkers of the apostle.

Paul uses nine different designations for the coworkers in the list that follows below: "brother" (*adelphos*), "apostle, envoy" (*apostolos*), "servant" (*diakonos*), "slave, fellow slave" (*doulos, syndoulos*), "partner, companion" (*koinōnos*), "the one who works" (*ho kopiōn*), "soldier, fellow soldier" (*stratiōtēs, systratiōtēs*), "fellow prisoner" (*synaichmalōtos*), "fellow worker" (*synergos*).[435] Other expressions used for some of Paul's coworkers include "prophet" (*prophētēs*), "teacher" (*didaskalos*), "traveling companion" (*synekdēmos*), "shepherd" (*poimēn*), "evangelist, proclaimer of the gospel" (*euangelistēs*), "minister, servant" (*leitourgos*), "manager, administrator" (*oikonomos*), "helper, assistant" (*hypēretēs*).[436]

---

[434]See Ellis 1971; Cothenet 1978a, 28-29; Ollrog 1979; Meeks 1983, 51-73; Ellis 1993; Schnabel 1997; Maness 1998; Dickson 2003, 86-132; earlier Zahn 1886, 145-50.

[435]Brother: Acts 25:22; Rom 16:23; 1 Cor 1:1; 16:12; 2 Cor 1:1; 2:13; Eph 6:21; Phil 2:25; Col 1:1; 4:7, 9; 1 Thess 3:2; Philem 1; apostle: Acts 14:4, 14; Rom 1:1; 16:7; Phil 2:25; 1 Thess 2:7; servant: 1 Cor 3:5; 2 Cor 3:6; 6:4; Eph 6:21; Col 1:7; 4:7; (fellow) slave: Phil 1:1; Col 1:7; 4:7, 12; 2 Tim 2:24; partner: 2 Cor 8:23; Philem 17; the one who works: Rom 16:6, 12; 2 Tim 2:6; (fellow) soldier: Phil 2:25; 2 Tim 2:3; Philem 2; fellow prisoner: Rom 16:7; Col 4:10; Philem 23; fellow worker: Rom 15:21; 16:3, 9, 21; 1 Cor 3:9; 2 Cor 8:23; Phil 2:25; 4:2-3; Col 4:10-11; 1 Thess 3:2; Philem 1, 24.

[436]Prophet: Acts 13:1; 15:32; teacher: Acts 13:1; traveling companion: Acts 19:29; shepherd: 1 Cor 9:7; Eph 4:11; evangelist: 2 Tim 4:5; Eph 4:11; minister: Phil 2:25; Rom 15:16; manager: 1 Cor 4:1-2; cf. Tit 1:7; helper: 1 Cor 4:1.

In the following list the more frequently mentioned coworkers are listed first (nos. 1-8); many of them are mentioned in the prescripts of Paul's letters. The coworkers who are mentioned less often placed in the second section of the list in alphabetical order (nos. 9-38).

Coworker	Hometown	Location of Missionary Work
1. Barnabas	Jerusalem	Antioch, Cyprus, Galatia[437]
2. Timothy	Lystra	Macedonia, Achaia, Thessalonike, Ephesus, Corinth[438]
3. Luke	Antioch (?)	Antioch (?), Macedonia, Philippi[439]
4. Aquila	Rome	see Priscilla
5. Priscilla	Rome	Corinth, Ephesus, house church in Rome[440]
6. Silas/Silvanus	Jerusalem	Macedonia, Achaia[441]
7. Titus	?	Antioch, Corinth, Crete, Dalmatia[442]
8. Tychicus	Asia	Colossae, Ephesus, Crete[443]
9. Achaicus	Corinth	Ephesus (1 Cor 16:17)
10. Andronicus	?	?, then Rome (Rom 16:7)
11. Apphia	Colossae	see Philemon (Philem 2)
12. Apollos	Alexandria	Achaia, Corinth, Ephesus, Crete[444]
13. Archippus	Colossae	Colossae (Col 4:17)
14. Aristarchus	Thessalonike	Ephesus, Jerusalem, Caesarea[445]
15. Clemens	Philippi	? (Phil 4:3)
16. Crescens	?	Rome, Galatia or Gaul (2 Tim 4:10
17. Demas	?	Rome (Col 4:14; Philem 24; 2 Tim 4:10)
18. Epaphras	Colossae	Ephesus, Colossae, Laodikeia, Hierapolis[446]
19. Epaphroditus	Philippi	Rome (Phil 2:25-30)
20. Erastus	Corinth	Ephesus, Macedonia (Acts 19:22)
21. Euodia	Philippi	Philippi (Phil 4:2-3)
22. Fortunatus	Corinth	Ephesus (1 Cor 16:1)
23. Junia	?	?, then Rome (Rom 16:7)
24. Jesus Justus	?	? (Col 4:11)
25. John Mark	Jerusalem	Antioch, Cyprus, Rome[447]

---

[437]Acts 11:19-26; 13-14.

[438]Acts 17—18, 1 Thess 3:1-6; Acts 19:22; 1 Cor 16:10-11; 1 Tim 1:3.

[439]See the "We-Passages" in the book of Acts.

[440]Acts 18:26; 1 Cor 16:19; Rom 16:4.

[441]Acts 15:40; 16:19; 17:4, 10, 15; 18:1; 2 Cor 1:19; 1 Thess 1:1; 2 Thess 1:1; 1 Pet 5:12.

[442]2 Cor 7:6-7, 13-15; 8:6; Tit 1:5; 2 Tim 4:10.

[443]Col 4:7-9; Eph 6:21; 2 Tim 4:12; Tit 3:12.

[444]Acts 18:27; 1 Cor 3:5—6:9; 16:12; Tit 3:13.

[445]Acts 19:29; 20:4; 27:2; Col 4:10-11; Philem 24.

[446]Col 1:7; 4:12; Philem 23.

[447]Acts 12:25; 15:37-40; Col 4:10-11; 2 Tim 4:11.

26. Mary	?	?, then Rome (Rom 16:6)
27. Onesimus	Colossae	? (Philem 13)
28. Quartus	?	Corinth (Rom 16:23)
29. Persis	?	?, then Rome (Rom 16:12)
30. Philemon	Colossae	Laodikeia ? (Philem 1)
31. Phoebe	Cenchreae	Corinth, Rome (Rom 16:1)
32. Sosthenes	?	Ephesus (1 Cor 1:1)
33. Stephanas	Corinth	Achaia, Corinth, Ephesus (1 Cor 16:15.17)
34. Syntyche	Philippi	Philippi (Phil 4:2-3)
35. Trophimus	Ephesus	Macedonia, Achaia, Asia[448]
36. Tryphaena	?	?, then Rome (Rom 16:12)
37. Tryphosa	?	?, then Rome (Rom 16:12)
38. Urbanus	?	?, then Rome (Rom 16:9)

The large number of coworkers is remarkable simply because we have no such information concerning any of the other apostles. Thus Wolf-Henning Ollrog remarks, "The fact that Paul surrounded himself with so many coworkers has no parallel in the early Christian mission."[449] However, since we have hardly any specific information about Peter's missionary work after A.D. 42, this evaluation is not very helpful. We simply have no detailed evidence for the missionary praxis of the Twelve after A.D. 42.

Only some of Paul's coworkers can be connected with specific phases of Paul's missionary initiatives. The following picture, painted with a broad brush, emerges:

Missionary Initiatives	*Coworkers of Paul*
Arabia	?
Cilicia	?
Antioch	Barnabas, John Mark, Titus, Luke (?)
Cyprus	Barnabas, John Mark
Galatia	Barnabas
Macedonia	Luke, Silas/Silvanus, Timothy
Achaia	Timothy, Priscilla and Aquila, Erastus, Aristarchus (?)
Asia	Aristarchus, Epaphras
Macedonia/Asia	Erastus, Timothy, Trophimus
Caesarea	Aristarchus, Epaphras, John Mark, Luke, Timothy, Trophimus
Rome	Aristarchus, Demas, Epaphras, Jesus Justus, John Mark, Luke, Timothy, Titus[450]
Spain	perhaps Aristarchus, Epaphras, John Mark, Jesus Justus
Rome	Demas, Crescens, John Mark, Luke, Tychicus

---

[448] Acts 20:4; 21:29; 2 Tim 4:20.

[449] Ollrog 1979, 228.

[450] Acts 20:4; 27:2; Col 4:10-14; Philem 23-24 (assuming that the letters to the Colossians and to Philemon were written from Rome).

Some missionaries were relatively constant members of Paul's missionary team, particularly Timothy. Other missionaries worked with Paul for a certain period of time but also worked independently of Paul as missionaries—for example, Barnabas, Silas/Silvanus and Apollos. Some coworkers were more consistently dependent upon their home churches than others.[451] The authority of the individual coworkers of Paul's missionary team was not primarily a function of their personality but rather was dependent, according to Joachim Gnilka, on the question of "how the ministry of these men engaged in and extended the apostolic work and gospel. . . . Authority, primarily, is not conveyed by the church but is the result of the apostolic form."[452]

The circle of Pauline coworkers included a considerable number of women. Andreas Köstenberger estimates that 18 percent of Paul's fellow missionaries were women.[453] In the list of greetings in his Epistle to the Romans Paul mentions the following female coworkers who are now residing in Rome: Phoebe (Rom 16:1-2), Priscilla (Rom 16:3), Mary (Rom 16:6), Junia (Rom 16:7), Tryphaena and Tryphosa (Rom 16:12) and Persis (Rom 16:12). Other women whom Paul's description reveals to be coworkers are Apphia (Philem 2) and Euodia and Syntyche (Phil 4:2-3). Their participation in Paul's missionary work is indicated by the prefix *syn-* ("with"): they have struggled "with" Paul for the gospel (Phil 4:3). They evidently preached the gospel along with Paul.[454]

Timothy embodies a good example of the central elements of missionary cooperation with Paul.[455] Timothy apparently was converted in the course of Paul's missionary activities in Galatia in A.D. 46, presumably during his mission to Lystra (Acts 14:6-20). Three years later Paul recruited him as a coworker when he was en route to the province of Asia, eventually diverted to Macedonia and Achaia (Acts 16:1-3). When Paul had to leave Thessalonike in a hurry because some local Jews threatened his life, he moved with Silas to Beroea, where they started a new missionary initiative (Acts 17:10), while Timothy evidently stayed in Thessalonike. He seems to have traveled to Beroea a few weeks later to reunite with Paul (Acts 17:14). When Paul was forced to leave Beroea because some Jews from Thessalonike stirred up trouble there as well, Timothy stayed in the city with Silas (Acts 17:14). A few weeks later he went to Athens to join Paul (Acts 17:15), who sent him back to Thessalonike with the task of caring for the new church (1 Thess 3:1-5). Two or three

---

[451]Maness (1998, 3, and passim) argues that the different factors of missionary cooperation with Paul cannot be reduced to one single principle.

[452]Gnilka, *Kol,* 242. To Gnilka's "men" we should add "and women."

[453]Köstenberger 2000a, 225. See also Wendy Cotter, "Women's Authority Roles in Paul's Churches: Countercultural or Conventional?" *NovT* 36 (1994): 350-72.

[454]Liefeld 1987, 292; for the comment that follows above see ibid.

[455]See J. Gillman, *ABD* 6:558-60; Mounce, *PastEp,* lvi-lix; Bruce 1995, 29-34; Maness 1998, 21-26, 83-87, 119-22, 143-44.

months later Timothy traveled to Corinth with good news about the church in Thessalonike (1 Thess 3:6) and with the request to deal with questions that had arisen in the church (1 Thess 4:9, 13; 5:1). If the traditional localization of the Pastoral Epistles is reliable, Timothy carried the responsibility for the churches in the province of Asia, perhaps after A.D. 62, when Paul had been arrested.

Barnabas (see §22.5), whose home church was Jerusalem, engaged in missionary work in Antioch, on Cyprus and in Galatia. After the separation from Paul he went to Cyprus with John Mark. He seems to have engaged in missionary work in the Aegean region in subsequent years.[456]

Luke may have belonged to the persecuted Hellenistic Jewish Christians from Jerusalem who originally came from Cyprus and Cyrene and who reached Antioch after they had been forced to leave the Jewish capital, reaching Jews and Gentiles with the gospel (Acts 11:19-20). If so, Luke had been responsible, along with other Greek-speaking Christians of the Jerusalem church, for the missionary initiative among Gentiles.[457] And, if that is correct, Luke would have been active in Antioch along with Paul between A.D. 42 and 44. Luke apparently was a physician (Col 4:14).

Paul's comment in Col 4:14 concerning "Luke the beloved physician" has prompted some scholars to view Luke as Paul's personal physician, at least during his imprisonment in Caesarea and/or in Rome. There is no evidence for this suggestion, however. Still, Luke's profession was unusual for the first century, which presumably is why Paul mentions it without placing any particular emphasis on the fact.

The account of Paul's mission to Cyprus and southern Galatia (Acts 13—14) contains no "We-Passages"; rather, Luke describes the preparation for this new missionary initiative (Acts 13:1-3) and the report that the returning missionaries gave in the congregation (Acts 14:27). The assumption that Luke was active in Antioch can be easily explained.[458] Perhaps Luke was active as a physician and was unable at this time to go to Cyprus and Galatia. When Barnabas and John Mark started their own missionary initiative on Cyprus, Luke joined Paul on the journey through Galatia and during the missionary work in Macedonia (cf. the We-Passages in the book of Acts).

Luke seems to have played an imported part in the missionary work in Phil-

---

[456]Acts 11:25-26; 13:1—14:28; 15:36-39; 1 Cor 9:6; Col 4:10. On Barnabas see J. Schmid, *RAC* 1:1207-17; J. B. Daniels, *ABD* 1:610-11; G. M. Burge, *DPL* 66-67; R. J. Bauckham, "Barnabas in Galatinas," *JSNT* 2 (1979): 61-70; Bruce 1979, 49-85; Roberts 1993; Bruce 1995, 15-22; Hengel and Schwemer 1998, 314-36 (ET, 205-21); Kollmann 1998; Maness 1998, 7-16, 76-80, 111-16, 141-42; Reinbold 2000, 84-106; Cara 2001; Öhler 2003.

[457]See Wenham 1991b, 38.

[458]R. Glover, "'Luke the Antiochene' and Acts," *NTS* 11 (1964): 97-106, esp. 102; followed by Wenham 1991b, 35.

ippi and in the consolidation of the church there.[459] We may assume, on the basis of the We-Passages, that he arrived in Philippi with Paul in the course of the mission to Macedonia and Achaia in A.D. 50 (Acts 16:12). In A.D. 57 he traveled with Paul from Corinth to Jerusalem (Acts 20:6). Before this departure Paul had spent three months in Greece (Acts 20:2-3), and he had written his letter to the Romans while staying in Corinth over the winter, in which Luke/Lucius conveys greetings as well (Rom 16:21). This indicates that Luke did not stay in Philippi for eight years but had contacts at least with Corinth.[460] Luke reports Paul's imprisonment for two years in Caesarea in the third person, which indicates that he was not with Paul during this time (unless the greetings mentioned in Philem 24; Col 4:14; 2 Tim 4:11 are sent from Caesarea, which is unlikely, however). When Paul traveled to Rome as a prisoner of the Roman state, Luke seems to have accompanied him (Acts 27:1—28:16).

Silas/Silvanus[461] was a Jewish-Christian prophet from Jerusalem who was involved in formulating and communicating the letter that recorded the results of the apostolic council of A.D. 48 (Acts 15:22-23). He evidently possessed Roman citizenship (Acts 16:37-38). Silas accompanied Paul during the missionary activities in Macedonia and Achaia, with responsibilities in the work in Thessalonike, Beroea, Philippi and Corinth. The important role that he plays in the book of Acts as well as the fact that he is mentioned by Paul before Timothy indicates that he was an eminent missionary and coworker. He was a co-sender of the Epistles to the Thessalonians (1 Thess 1:1; 2 Thess 1:1). We have no information about his whereabouts after his work in Philippi and Beroea between A.D. 50 and 52. If he is indeed identical with the Silvanus mentioned in 1 Pet 5:12, who carried the First Epistle of Peter to the churches in northern Asia Minor in the mid-60s,[462] then he might have been active as an independent missionary during the ten years between A.D. 52 and 62. The sources do not describe him as an apostle.[463]

Titus was an important coworker of Paul.[464] According to Gal 2:3, the

---

[459]W. Reinbold (2000, 120-21, 215) follows the many critical scholars who refuse to connect the We-Passages in the book of Acts or the comment in 2 Tim 4:11 with the historical Luke, with the result that he knows little else about Luke other than "he supported the Apostle in prison (in Caesarea?)" (ibid., 215).

[460]See Wenham 1991b, 37.

[461]G. Schneider, *EWNT* 3:580-82 (*EDNT* 3:243-44); John Gillmann, *ABD* 6:22-23; Goppelt, *1 Petr,* 347-49; Malherbe, *Thess,* 70-71, 97-98; Elliott, *1 Pet,* 91, 93, 871-74; B. N. Kaye, "Acts' Portrait of Silas," *NovT* 21 (1979): 13-26; Ollrog 1979, 17-20; J. H. Elliott 1980; Trebilco 1989; Ellis 1993, 185-86; Bruce 1995, 23-28; Maness 1998, 17-21, 80-83, 116-19, 142-43.

[462]See E. Randolph Richards, "Silvanus Was Not Peter's Secretary: Theological Bias in Interpreting διὰ Σιλουανοῦ . . . ἔγραψα," *JETS* 43 (2000): 417-32.

[463]The comment in 1 Thess 2:9, with the reference to physical work, refers only to Paul; see Holtz, *1 Thess,* 79-80; Malherbe, *Thess,* 144; differently Ellis 1993, 186.

[464]John Gillman, *ABD* 6:581-82; Mounce, *PastEp,* lix-lxii; Barrett 1969; Ollrog 1979, 33-37; Bruce 1995, 58-65; Maness 1998, 28-34, 88-91, 122-25, 144-45.

(chronologically) first New Testament text to mention Titus, Paul took Titus to Jerusalem when he traveled from Antioch to the Jewish capital in A.D. 47 in order to bring the famine-relief money that had been collected and, apparently, to obtain a private consultation with the apostles. The apostles did not require Titus to be circumcised, implying that he was a Gentile Christian, perhaps a God-fearer who had been converted to faith in Jesus Christ. He seems to have worked with Paul and Barnabas in Antioch between A.D. 45 and 47. It is unclear whether Antioch was his hometown; he may have been converted in the course of Paul's missionary work in Syria and Cilicia between A.D. 34 and 42. At the end of Paul's mission to Ephesus (A.D. 52-55) Titus appears as a coworker who was responsible for the practical aspects of organizing the collection for the "poor" in Jerusalem in the churches that Paul had established.[465] Wolf-Henning Ollrog suggests that Paul recruited Titus only "as a coworker for a very specific task, the collection."[466] This is unlikely, as the following considerations show. (1) When Paul was engaged in missionary work in Ephesus and corresponded with the church in Corinth, Titus evidently was one of the most important fellow missionaries of Paul, who entrusted him with the delicate task of taking the "letter of tears" (2 Cor 2:4) to the Corinthian church and to help achieve reconciliation between the Corinthian Christians and Paul.[467] It is not surprising that Paul describes him as "my partner and coworker in your service" (2 Cor 8:23).[468] (2) Titus was accompanied by a brother "who is famous among all the churches for his proclaiming the good news" (2 Cor 8:18), as well as a second brother "whom we have often tested and found eager in many matters, but who is now more eager than ever because of his great confidence in you" (2 Cor 8:22), implying a similar, if not superior, reputation and giftedness for Titus. (3) According to 2 Tim 4:10, Titus was active in Dalmatia, meaning that he was engaged in missionary work in Illyricum.[469] According to Tit 1:4-5, Titus was responsible for the new churches on Crete, at least since Paul's imprisonment in A.D. 57.

Apollos was a Jewish Christian from Alexandria.[470] As was pointed out earlier, we do not know whether he was converted in Alexandria, which would imply the presence of Christian missionaries in Egypt at a relatively early date, or whether he was converted during a visit to some other city, perhaps Jerusalem.

---

[465]Cf. 2 Cor 8:6, 10, 16-17; 12:17-18.

[466]Ollrog 1979, 95.

[467]Cf. 2 Cor 2:13; 7:6-7, 13-14; 8:6, 16, 23; 12:18. See Thrall, *2 Cor,* 1:186; differently Reinbold 2000, 220-21.

[468]2 Cor 8:23: κοινωνὸς ἐμὸς καὶ εἰς ὑμᾶς συνεργός.

[469]See Spicq, *ÉpPast,* 813.

[470]L. D. Hurst, *ABD* 1:301; Schumacher 1916; Ellis 1971, 438-39; Hunter 1976; L. D. Hurst, "Apollos, Hebrews and Corinth," *SJT* 38 (1985): 505-13; Wolter 1987; Beatrice 1995; Bruce 1995, 51-57; Maness 1998, 34-38, 91-94, 125-28, 145-46.

Apollos seems to have been active always independently of Paul, despite the fact that Aquila and Priscilla were both his and Paul's coworkers at different time periods. On one occasion Paul encouraged Apollos to go to Corinth with other "brothers," a comment that does not imply that Apollos was formally "sent" by Paul. At a later time Paul asked Titus to help Apollos, who was visiting Crete, with everything that he needs.[471]

Epaphras, the "missionary of the Lykos Valley," founded the churches in Colossae, Laodikeia and Hierapolis (Col 1:3-8; 4:13), presumably in the context of Paul's missionary work in Ephesus, thus between A.D. 53 and 56.[472] If this traditional assumption is correct, it seems plausible to assume that Epaphras was directed by Paul to start a missionary initiative in the Lykos Valley. Since Paul generally began his missionary work in the local synagogue, it is unlikely that he would have anticipated a different beginning for the missionary activities in the important cities of the Lykos Valley.[473] This assumption is supported by the fact that the heretical teaching that created confusion in the church in Colossae had at least strong Jewish influences and might have been entirely based on Jewish teachings,[474] indicating that the church in Colossae had Jewish-Christian beginnings. If this is correct, we may safely assume that Epaphras was a Jewish believer: there is no evidence in the New Testament that Jews were converted through the preaching of a Gentile-Christian missionary. The comment in Col 4:12 ("Epaphras, who is one of you, a servant of Christ Jesus, greets you") does not make this assumption impossible.

Erastus was the city treasurer (οἰκονόμος τῆς πόλεως, *oikonomos tēs poleōs*) in Corinth, probably holding the rank of a quaestor (Rom 16:23). If the identification with the Erastus in the inscription on the pavement of the road near the theater in Corinth is reliable, he also was an aedile, implying that he was a full citizen of Corinth, possessing Roman citizenship.[475] His financial contributions to the city of Corinth indicate that he was wealthy. According to 2 Tim 4:20 and Acts 19:22, he was at times one of Paul's coworkers—for example, during his mission to Macedonia.

Andronicus and Junia probably are a couple: an analysis of the Greek New Testament manuscript evidence in Rom 16:7 indicates that Paul refers not to a man named Junias (or Junianos) but to a woman named Junia.[476] Junia and An-

---

[471] Acts 18:24-27; 19:1; 1 Cor 1:12; 3:4, 5, 6, 22; 4:6; 16:12; Tit 3:13.

[472] Pokorný, *Kol*, 15, 36, 163; cf. Murphy-O'Connor 1996, 174-75, 234-35. Scholars who assume that the Epistle to the Colossians is pseudepigraphic cannot utilize this information to discuss the organization of Paul's missionary work and have to plead ignorance (see, e.g., Reinbold 2000, 217, 225).

[473] See D. Wenham 1991b, 15.

[474] See Wright, *Col*, 24; Dunn, *Col*, 23-53.

[475] Theissen 1974b, 245 (ET, 83); see the discussion in Clarke 1993, 46-57.

[476] See, besides the commentaries, Eisen 1996, 50-51; Köstenberger 2000a, 229-30; Reinbold 2000, 40; Bauckham (2002, 165-86), who identifies Junia with the Joanna of Lk 8:3; 24:10.

dronicus, probably Junia's husband, were Jews (συγγενεῖς, *syngeneis*). Both were converted before Paul, thus prior to A.D. 32/33, and both were imprisoned with Paul (Rom 16:7); the circumstances of this imprisonment are unknown. Paul says that "they are prominent among the apostles" (ἐπίσημοι ἐν τοῖς ἀποστόλοις, *episēmoi en tois apostolois* [Rom 16:7]). Many scholars argue that this formulation does not identify Andronicus and Junia as apostles;[477] some suggest that Paul's formulation merely asserts that they were prominent "among" the apostles, meaning that they were well-known to the apostles.[478] Even if this interpretation were correct, it remains true that Andronicus and Junia were Jewish-Christian missionaries.[479] The couple must have engaged in missionary work with Paul at some point in time, which is the only plausible background for their imprisonment with Paul. Some scholars suggest that they were the founders of the church in Rome.[480] This suggestion must remain hypothetical; we should note that there is no local tradition of the church in the city of Rome that supports this suggestion.[481]

Earle Ellis suggests that συγγενεῖς (*syngeneis*) in Rom 16:7, 11, 21 signifies not "compatriots" in the sense of "fellow Jews" but rather "kin" or "relatives," meaning that Andronicus and Junia, as well as Herodion, Jason, Sosipater and Lucius, were blood relations of Paul.[482] From a linguistic point of view this suggestion is not compelling. The term συγγενής (*syngenēs*) indeed often means "belonging to the same extended family," but in many other texts it means "belonging to the same people group."[483] Ellis concludes from the fact that Andronicus and Julia were converted before Paul (Rom 16:7) that they belonged to Paul's relatives who lived in Jerusalem (cf. Acts 23:16), and that they were active in the city of Rome as missionaries of the Jerusalem church. Ellis identifies Jason in Rom 16:21 with the Jason of Thessalonike (Acts 17:5-9), Sosipater in Rom 16:21 with the Sopater of Beroea (Acts 20:4), and Lucius in Rom 16:21 with Luke the physician and companion of Paul. He concludes that Paul utilized contacts with relatives in his mission to Thessalonike and Beroea, assuming that these relatives helped Paul in his missionary enterprise after their conversion to the Christian faith—for example, by opening their houses for new converts and new churches. It is indeed correct that there is evidence for extended Jewish families whose relatives lived in several cities of the Mediterranean world, who had been taken to cities as slaves, or who settled in other cities as merchants, or who joined Diaspora synagogues for other reasons. Ellis's identifications and hypothesis therefore cannot be rejected out of hand. However, historical possibilities and historical probabilities are not the same. Since Paul describes in Rom 9:3 the unbelieving Jews as οἱ συγγενεῖς μου κατὰ σάρκα (*hoi syngeneis mou kata sarka*), clearly re-

---

[477]See earlier Harnack (1924, 1:335 [ET, 1:321]), who, however, reads "Junias"; Wilckens, *Röm,* 3:135-36; recently Reinbold 2000, 40-41, 110.

[478]Burer and Wallace 2001; see the critique in Bauckham 2002, 172-80.

[479]Käsemann, *Röm,* 398 (ET, 414); Wilckens, *Röm,* 3:135; Köstenberger 2000a, 231; Bauckham 2002, 166-81. The doubts of Reinbold (2000, 110) are unconvincing.

[480]F. Watson 1986, 101; Bauckham 2002, 181, as a plausible possibility.

[481]See Reinbold 2000, 110.

[482]Ellis 1993, 186; for the comments that follow above see ibid.; see also idem 1999, 260-61.

[483]BDAG 950; G. Schneider, *EWNT* 3:675 (*EDNT* 3:282).

ferring to his fellow Jews, it is more plausible to assume the same meaning for οἱ συγ-γενεῖς in Rom 16:7, 11, 21.[484]

Epaphroditus came from Philippi and was the envoy of the church in Philippi who brought the financial support of the church to Paul during his imprisonment in the city of Rome (Phil 2:25; 4:18). Paul reports that Epaphroditus became ill and that he was sent back to Macedonia after he had become well (Phil 2:26-29). Paul describes him as "my brother and coworker and fellow soldier" (Phil 2:25) who "came close to death for the work of Christ" (Phil 2:30). The terms "coworker" (*synergos*) and "fellow soldier" (*systratiōtēs*) in Phil 2:25 suggest that Epaphroditus was not merely a messenger who carried the Philippians' gift to Rome, but rather that he was actively involved in Paul's missionary activities.[485] Epaphroditus was a coworker on Paul's team of missionaries.

Priscilla and Aquila are repeatedly mentioned by Luke and Paul.[486] This Jewish-Christian couple were among the Jews who were forced to leave Rome because of Claudius's edict of A.D. 49 expelling Jews from the city. In the fall or winter of A.D. 49 they evidently arrived in Corinth, where they collaborated with Paul in his preaching and teaching activities, as is indicated by the repeated references of Luke, and they also provided Paul with the opportunity to earn money for his support in their workshop. Aquila came originally from the province of Pontus on the Black Sea (Acts 18:2) and owned a business as tentmaker or leatherworker.[487] It is plausible to assume that Christians met in their house in Corinth. Some scholars describe their house in Corinth as "germ cell of the Corinthian city mission."[488] It is possible that Aquila and Priscilla were independent missionaries, a "missionary couple" who were closely associated with Paul[489] after they had engaged in missionary outreach in Corinth

---

[484]Thus essentially all commentators; see Käsemann, *Röm,* 398 (ET, 414); Barrett, *Röm,* 2:788; Moo, *Rom,* 559 n. 25, 921 n. 21. The interpretation of Wilckens (*Röm,* 3:135) is ambiguous: he translates *syngeneis* as "blood relations" ("Blutsverwandte") and identifies them as "Jewish Christians."

[485]Ollrog 1979, 99; contra Reinbold 2000, 216. On Epaphroditus see also Dickson 2003, 315-17.

[486]Acts 18:2-3, 18, 26; 1 Cor 16:19; Rom 16:3-5; 2 Tim 4:19. See P. Lampe, "Aquila," *ABD* 1:319-20; idem, "Prisca," *ABD* 5:467-68; Klauck 1981, 21-26; Bruce 1995, 44-50; Maness 1998, 38-44, 94-97, 128-30, 146; Cineira 1999, 217-24; Hofmann 2000, 288-89; Köstenberger 2000a, 227-28. See also the feminist study by Ingeborg Kruse, *Und Priska ließ sich nicht beirren: Frauengeschichten aus dem frühen Christentum* (Gütersloher Taschenbücher 541; Gütersloh: Gütersloher Verlaghaus, 1994), 50-56.

[487]F. W. Danker suggests that *skēnopoios* in Acts 18:3 should be interpreted as a "maker of stage properties" for theatrical productions (BDAG 928-29), although he is aware of Jewish objections against the theater; cf. Schürer 2:54-55. Reinbold (2000, 221-24) generally is overly skeptical.

[488]Hofmann 2000, 288.

[489]Harnack 1924, 1:85, 380 (ET, 1:79, 370).

even before Paul's arrival. Two years later the couple accompanied Paul to Ephesus (Acts 18:18-19), where, again, a church meets in their house (1 Cor 16:19). Some scholars suggest that Priscilla was, with her husband Aquila, "co-leader" of the house church in Ephesus.[490] Paul's comment in 1 Cor 16:19 does provide sufficient evidence for this conclusion, however: Paul conveys greetings from Aquila and Priscilla "together with the church in their house." Conclusions concerning ecclesiological structures remain speculative. Quite unlikely is the suggestion that Priscilla was the sole leader (or "bishop") of a house church,[491] not the least because Aquila is mentioned first in this passage. In Acts 18:26 Aquila and particularly Priscilla are mentioned as teachers of Apollos from Alexandria. By A.D. 56 Aquila and Priscilla are back in Rome, with a house church meeting in their home (Rom 16:3.5).

Phoebe[492] was a Gentile woman, as her name suggests, who had come to faith in Jesus Christ. She came from Cenchreae, the eastern harbor of Corinth. Paul describes Phoebe in Rom 16:1 as *diakonos,* a term that could suggest missionary activity, as passages such as 1 Cor 3:5; 2 Cor 3:6; 6:4; 11:15, 23 demonstrate.[493] It is unlikely that she was the "leader of the church" or "an official teacher and missionary," as has been suggested.[494] The term *prostatis* that Paul uses in Rom 16:2 after *diakonos* to describe her role can mean "patron" or "benefactor," which implies that Phoebe was a wealthy woman of high social standing who used her resources to support the work of the church and the mission of Paul. The example of Claudia Metrodora from Chios demonstrates the opportunities that a wealthy woman had. Claudia lived in the first century and occupied several high offices in Chios: she gave banquets for the city, she was four times gymnasiarch, three times agonothete of the Heraklea Romaia games and the Kaisareia games, priestess of the deified Livia, and she financed a hall in Ephesus dedicated to Artemis, to the emperor and to the *dēmos* of the city.[495] Since the term *prostatis* can describe, in a nontechnical sense, a person in a supportive role, an "assistant," it is possible that Paul simply states that Phoebe supported needy Christians.[496] Many scholars today are prepared to accept the first, technical meaning of *prostatis* in Rom 16:2. It is a plausible assumption that the church in Cenchreae met in her

---

[490]See Hofmann 2000, 289.

[491]See Eisen 1996, 204-205; rejected by Hofmann 2000, 289 n. 22.

[492]See Jewett 1988, 148-55; K. Romaniuk, "Was Phoebe in Romans 16.1 a Deaconess?" *ZNW* 81 (1990): 132-34; R. R. Schulz, "A Case for 'President' Phoebe in Romans 16.2," *Lutheran Theological Journal* 24 (1990): 124-27; M. Ernst, "Die Funktionen der Phöbe (Röm 16,1f) in der Gemeinde von Kenchreai," *Protokolle zur Bibel* 1 (1992): 135-47; C. F. Whelan, "Amica Pauli: The Role of Phoebe in the Early Church," *JSNT* 49 (1993): 67-85; Kearsley 1999, 201-2; Köstenberger 2000a, 228-29.

[493]See Holmberg 1978, 99-102.

[494]See Jewett 1988, 149; Fiorenza 1983, 171.

[495]See Kearsley 1999, 198-201, 208-11.

[496]See H. Balz, *EWNT* 3:426 (*EDNT* 3:176-77).

house.[497] Paul recommends Phoebe to the church in Rome as an important co-worker. Robert Jewett suggests that the "matter" in which the Roman church is asked to support Phoebe is the project of a missionary initiative to Spain that she finances as a "patron."[498] This suggestion must remain hypothetical.

The Greek terms that Paul uses to describe his coworkers indicate at least some aspects of the kind of work they were involved in as members of his missionary team.[499]

1. The most frequently used terms are συνεργός (synergos, "coworker") and ἐργάτης (ergatēs, "worker"), generally used to describe coworkers who travel with Paul. The term ergatēs generally describes "one who is engaged in work," and specifically the person who works for money, the "worker" or "laborer," including slaves.[500] The term synergos describes the "fellow worker," the person who works alongside another laborer. Some scholars maintain that ergatēs is a technical term for early Christian missionaries.[501] There is no clear evidence for this suggestion, however: Christians who have leadership responsibilities in the local congregation also "work." Paul describes himself and his fellow missionaries as "God's coworkers" (1 Cor 3:9), as he knows that the efficacy of the gospel in terms of people being converted to faith in Jesus Christ depends on God alone (1 Cor 2:5), while recognizing that he and others are called to engage in the work of preaching and teaching the gospel. The activities of the missionary team day in and day out, every month of the year, year in and year out, indeed represent "work" that often is difficult: continuously studying the Scriptures, proclaiming the gospel in public and in private, answering questions from the audience, caring for the new converts, interacting with local opponents, traveling to various cities, searching for living quarters for the members of the missionary team, obtaining food and drink. In 1 Cor 9:1-14 Paul establishes, with a dominical saying, the right of missionary workers to "live by the gospel" (1 Cor 9:14), meaning the right to be supported by the existing churches—a right that he renounces for his own ministry. The same Jesus tradition probably is the background for Paul's statement in 1 Tim 5:18: "the laborer deserves to be paid." In the context of 1 Tim 5:17 this saying is applied to Christian workers in the church "who labor [hoi kopiōntes] in preaching and teaching." The term κόπος (kopos; verb: κοπιᾶν, kopian) describes an "activity that is burdensome," hence "work, labor toil." It describes not just the physical labor by which Paul earns his living expenses (1 Thess 2:9; 2 Thess 3:8) but all labor that he undertakes as a missionary (2 Cor 6:5; 11:23, 27). Thus kopos is a term for missionary work (1 Cor 3:8; 2 Cor 10:15; 1 Thess 3:5) and for work

---

[497]Theissen 1974b, 250 (ET, 89).
[498]Jewett 1988, 151-53.
[499]See Ellis 1971, 8-15.
[500]R. Heiligenthal, EWNT 2:122 (EDNT 2:49).
[501]See Georgi 1964, 49-51 (ET, 40); Haraguchi 1993, 178.

in the local church (1 Cor 15:58; 1 Thess 1:3; 1 Tim 5:17).[502] The "workers" whom Paul mentions in his letters describe a specific group of coworkers who presumably have been recruited by Paul himself.

2. Paul's coworkers are "servants" (διάκονος, *diakonos*). This term often is used in conjunction with *synergos*.[503] The term ὑπηρέτης (*hyperetēs*), "helper" or "assistant," evidently is a synonym.[504] Missionary work is always "service." The main focus in Paul's use of the term *diakonos* seems to be the preaching and teaching ministry.[505] The oral proclamation of the gospel is the fundamental, central process of missionary work. Thus the importance of the Christian διδάσκαλος (*didaskalos*, "teacher"), whose role is that of the preacher in the local congregation. The characteristic feature of the *didaskalos* was the preaching and teaching ministry in the congregation, rather than traveling to other cities. In Gal 6:6 Paul instructs the churches in southern Galatia should give to their teachers (ὁ κατηχῶν, *ho katēchōn*) a "share in all good things," meaning that they should support them financially.[506]

3. Coworkers are also called "the brothers" (οἱ ἀδελφοί, *hoi adelphoi*). Paul usually employs the term *adelphos* to describe "fellow Christians," the brothers and sisters in the people of God. In some texts, however, he uses the term specifically for individual coworkers of a group of coworkers.[507] Because of the general meaning "fellow Christian" it is difficult to specify a particular meaning for the application of the term to missionary coworkers. The suggestion that the term "brothers" serves to describe the recipients of several of Paul's letters[508] remains hypothetical.

The missionary work of Paul's coworkers should not be interpreted as an inferior substitute for Paul's own presence and ministry. Robert Funk writes in an influential essay that the apostolic authority and effectivity was tied first to the apostle's personal presence (*parousia*), second to the presence of the apostle mediated by envoys, and third to the letters that he writes to churches in lieu of his presence.[509] This "typology" of three forms of apostolic "presence" perhaps

---

[502]See A. von Harnack, "Κόπος (Κοπιᾶν, Οἱ Κοπιῶντες) im frühchristlichen Sprachgebrauch," *ZNW* 27 (1928): 1-10; F. Hauck, *ThWNT* 3:827-29 (*TDNT* 3:827-30); Fendrich, *EWNT* 2:760-61 (*EDNT* 2:307-308); M. Seitz and F. Thiele, *ThBLNT* 1:62-64 (ET, 262-63). The hypothetical tradition-historical considerations in Haraguchi 1993 are not particularly helpful.

[503]Cf. 1 Cor 3:5, 9; 16:15-16; 2 Cor 6:1, 4; cf. 2 Cor 11:23-29.

[504]Cf. 1 Cor 4:1; cf. Acts 13:5; 15:40; 1 Cor 3:5, 22-23. See K. H. Rengstorf, *ThWNT* 8:543 (*TDNT* 8:543); G. Schneider, *EWNT* 3:957 (*EDNT* 3:400).

[505]See Georgi 1964, 31-38 (ET, 27-32) (the self-designation of Paul's opponents); Ellis 1993, 185.

[506]See F. Hauck, *ThWNT* 3:809 (*TDNT* 3:809); H. W. Beyer, *ThWNT* 3:639 (*TDNT* 3:639); J. Hainz, *EWNT* 2:752 (*EDNT* 2:304); Mussner, *Gal,* 403; Martyn, *Gal,* 551.

[507]Cf. 1 Cor 16:19-20; Gal 1:2; Eph 6:23-24; Phil 1:14; 4:21-22; Col 1:2; 4:15; cf. Acts 12:17; 15:40; 16:1-2; 18:27; 19:26-27, 30; 28:15; 3 Jn 10; Rev 22:9.

[508]Ellis 1971, 19-22, with regard to 2 Thessalonians.

[509]Funk 1967. For a critique see M. Mitchell 1992; for the comments that follow above see ibid.

is helpful for analytical purposes, but it is unwarranted to maintain that the desired and greatest effectivity was tied to the personal, physical presence of the apostle, with envoys and letters representing only an inferior substitute. We saw in the discussion of the "envoy" (see §24.3, on 2 Cor 5:20) that the messenger fully represents the sender, that the messenger is engaged in the work of the patron with the latter's full authority and therefore must be accepted and treated according to the status of the patron with dignity and respect. John succinctly formulates the general principle that characterized the formal and the informal relationships in Greco-Roman society when he reports Jesus as saying, "Whoever receives one whom I send receives me; and whoever receives me receives him who sent me" (Jn 13:20). What is true for the sending of Jesus by God and for the sending of the disciples by Jesus is true not only for the sending of the apostle Paul by Jesus but also for Paul's sending of Timothy, Titus, Onesimus and Epaphroditus. Paul directs the churches to receive these messengers as they would receive him.[510]

1 Cor 16:10-11: "If Timothy comes, see that he has nothing to fear among you, for he is doing the work of the Lord just as I am; [11]therefore let no one despise him. Send him on his way in peace, so that he may come to me; for I am expecting him with the brothers."

2 Cor 7:6-7, 15: "But God, who consoles the downcast, consoled us by the arrival of Titus, [7]and not only by his coming, but also by the consolation with which he was consoled about you, as he told us of your longing, your mourning, your zeal for me, so that I rejoiced still more. . . . [15]And his heart goes out all the more to you, as he remembers the obedience of all of you, and how you welcomed him with fear and trembling."

Philem 17: "So if you consider me your partner, welcome him [Onesimus] as you would welcome me."

Phil 2:29: "Welcome him [Epaphroditus] then in the Lord with all joy, and honor such people."

As Paul's envoy, Timothy can speak directly for Paul because he knows him and his message and because he teaches nothing that Paul himself would not teach: "For this reason I sent you Timothy, who is my beloved and faithful child in the Lord, to remind you of my ways in Christ Jesus, as I teach them everywhere in every church" (1 Cor 4:17). The role of Timothy in Thessalonike and of Titus in Corinth is hardly a "weak substitute" for Paul's presence: they perform important tasks that Paul himself will not or cannot perform at that particular time. Margaret Mitchell reconstructs the following sequence of events of the "embassies" of Timothy and Titus on the basis of 1 Thess 3 and 2 Cor 7.[511]

---

[510]M. Mitchell 1992, 644, 646-47.
[511]M. Mitchell 1992, 655-56; the quotation that follows above, ibid., 662. For a critique of Mitchell's definition of "envoy" see Bash 1997, 32-35.

1. Prehistory
    A. Paul explains why he cannot come: 1 Thess 2:17-18; 2 Cor 1:15—2:13
    B. Paul announces the sending of an envoy: 1 Thess 3:1-5
    C. Paul describes his waiting for the envoy's return: 1 Thess 3:1; 2 Cor 2:12-14; 7:5

2. Past History—Return of the Envoy
    A. Announcement of the arrival of the envoy: 1 Thess 3:6; 2 Cor 7:6
    B. Restatement of the envoy's message: 1 Thess 3:6; 2 Cor 7:7
    C. Response of Paul—comfort and joy: 1 Thess 3:7; 2 Cor 7:6-7, 13

3. Present History
    A. Paul confirms his initial response: 1 Thess 3:9; 2 Cor 7:9, 13, 16

Mitchell comments on the role of the "envoys" whom Paul sends from among his coworkers to the churches as follows: "Hardly mere substitutes for the universally preferable Pauline presence, these envoys were consciously sent by Paul to play a complex and crucial intermediary role that he could not play, even if present himself."

An analysis of the available evidence about Paul's coworkers who support him in his missionary work allows us to summarize their specific tasks as follows.

1. Some coworkers participated in the missionary activities that Paul had initiated in a particular city. Stephanas, the "first convert in Achaia," who had devoted himself and his family (*oikos*) "to the service of the saints" (1 Cor 16:15), apparently engaged in a *diakonia* in Corinth and the surrounding areas that went beyond practical assistance to include preaching and teaching activity, as is indicated in the ensuing sentence: "I urge you to put yourselves at the service of such people, and of everyone who works and toils with them" (1 Cor 16:16): the verbs *synergein* and *kopian* often refer to missionary preaching and teaching in Paul's vocabulary.[512] The term ἀπαρχή (*aparchē*, "first fruits") thus describes not exclusively and perhaps not even primarily a chronological or sequential priority, but "first" in the sense of "constituting a *sample, pledge,* or *promise* of more to come"—that is, more conversions in Achaia.[513] Stephanas and his "house" represented the nucleus of the growing church in Corinth and in Achaia. The loyal work and the committed witness of this family are the beginning, the foundation and the promise of the growth of the church.[514]

E. E. Ellis interprets *aparchē* in light of Ex 22:28-29 LXX as "the consecrated first-born who,

---

[512]Fee, *1 Cor,* 830; Schrage, *1 Kor,* 4:455.
[513]Thiselton, *1 Cor,* 1338; cf. Fee, *1 Cor,* 829; Schrage, *1 Kor,* 4:454.
[514]Schrage, *1 Kor,* 4:160, on 1 Cor 15:20.

like the Levites, are set apart for the work of God"[515]—that is, in terms of the firstborn son, who is obliged to serve. This interpretation is attractive but founders on the use of this term in other passages in Paul's letters.[516] If we assume that Paul refers in 1 Cor 16:15-16 to a more local ministry of Stephanas, then W. H. Ollrog's comment concerning the temporary character and the "constant fluctuation in the team of co-workers"[517] is not helpful. Not particularly helpful either is W. Schrage's explanation of the phrase ἔταξαν ἑαυτούς (*etaxan heautous*) in 1 Cor 16:15, which he translates as "they appointed themselves (independently)," commenting that "they have not been commissioned by the apostle or by the church at any rate. . . . They represent the beginning of a church organization . . . that knows no fixed institutional forms. The ecclesial structures arise by themselves, which is striking, although they may have been set in motion by the apostle."[518] The phrase *etaxan heautous* surely cannot carry the full weight of such far-reaching conclusions. A. T. Robertson and A. Plummer interpret the phrase in terms of a "self-imposed duty," while Jakob Kremer interprets it to mean "their faith urged them to serve."[519] Paul's concern in 1 Cor 16:15-16 is not offices or institutions in the church but rather the mutual love of all believers (1 Cor 16:14) who grow in their faith (1 Cor 16:13), a love that influences and controls all ministries (1 Cor 16:15) and all submission (1 Cor 16:16). As R. Hays comments, "That is how authority works in a community where believers are subject to one another in love (cf. Eph 5:21): people volunteer to serve and thereby gain the esteem of others in the community."[520]

Paul repeatedly mentions local coworkers who teach and preach in the local congregations and who establish churches in the surrounding areas, as the example of Epaphras's mission to the cities of the Lykos Valley demonstrates.[521] It is safe to assume that Paul trained these local coworkers during his initial stay in the city or during later visits.

2. Other coworkers, particularly Timothy, Titus and Tychicus, accompanied Paul on his missionary travels. They worked independently as well, when Paul sent them to other churches, to consolidate newly emerging congregations, to convey letters, or to help solve problems. Or they were responsible for the teaching ministry in the congregations while Paul was absent.[522] Timothy, taught and trained by Paul, had become so competent that the apostle describes him not only as "our brother" but also as "coworker for God in proclaiming the gospel of Christ" who is able to strengthen and encourage the believers in Thessalonike (1 Thess 3:2). Paul commends Timothy to the be-

---

[515]Ellis 1978, 19-20; cf. idem 1993, 187. Schrage (*1 Kor,* 4:453 n. 163) finds a similar interpretation in T. Beza, *Testamentum Novum, sive Novum Foedus Jesu Christi* (1638) 2:168.

[516]Fee, *1 Cor,* 829 n. 18.

[517]Ollrog 1979, 123.

[518]Schrage, *1 Kor,* 4: 454-55.

[519]Robertson and Plummer, *1 Cor,* 392; Kremer, *1 Kor,* 376; see also Fee, *1 Cor,* 827-28; Thiselton, *1 Cor,* 1339.

[520]Hays, *1 Cor,* 290.

[521]Gal 6:6; Phil 1:1; 4:2-3; 1 Thess 5:12-13; 2 Thess 3:6-11. For Epaphras see Col 1:7-8; 2:1; 3:16; 4:12, 16. See Ellis 1993, 187.

[522]Ellis 1993, 187; for the comments that follow above see ibid.

lievers in Corinth as "my beloved and faithful child in the Lord" who is able "to remind you of my ways in Christ Jesus, as I teach them everywhere in every church" (1 Cor 4:17). Titus is sent to Corinth at a later time on a very sensitive mission; he acts "with the same spirit" and takes "the same steps" as the apostle Paul (2 Cor 12:18). Tychicus was involved in the transport of letters to the churches in Asia Minor (Eph 6:21-22; Col 4:7); at a later date he was capable of replacing Titus as the missionary and teacher responsible for the churches on Crete (Tit 3:12) and to represent Paul in the church in Ephesus (2 Tim 4:12).

3. The majority of Paul's coworkers came from the new churches that the apostle had established. Some of them came to Paul as "delegates" of their home churches (Col 1:7; 4:12-13; Philem 13): they represent their churches as ἀπόστολοι ἐκκλησιῶν (*apostoloi ekklēsiōn* [2 Cor 8:23; cf. Phil 2:25]) and thereby acknowledge as members of the body of Christ their responsibility in building up the kingdom of God.[523] Their participation in Paul's mission "makes up" what their churches owe to Paul (1 Cor 16:17; Phil 2:30). The churches participate through their envoys in Paul's mission.[524] Wolfgang Schrage is correct when he observes that the role of the coworkers "cannot be determined only along psychological lines on the basis of the need for fellowship, nor along organizational lines in terms of maximizing the missionary effectiveness, nor along pedagogical lines in terms of training workers for the time after Paul. Rather, Paul emphasizes the co-responsibility and the participation of the churches because he regards missionary work and ministry as a function of the entire church (thus the great fluctuation in his team of coworkers)."[525]

4. Right from the beginning Paul integrated newly converted believers into his missionary team, giving them—at times, rather quickly—responsibilities in his preaching and teaching ministry. Timothy is a good example: he became responsible for the church in Thessalonike only three years after his conversion.[526]

5. One of the tasks that Paul's coworkers were responsible for was baptizing new converts (1 Cor 1:14-17).[527] Paul reminds the Corinthian believers that he baptized only a few converts when he established the church in their city: Crispus and Gaius and, yes, the household of Stephanas as well. He contends, stating his basic conviction, that "Christ did not send me to baptize but to proclaim the gospel" (1 Cor 1:17a). This means that all the other Corinthians who were converted in A.D. 51-52 must have been baptized by his coworkers.[528] Hans

---

[523]Ollrog 1979, 229.
[524]Stuhlmacher 1981, 123.
[525]Schrage, *1 Kor,* 1:101.
[526]See Howell 1996, 215-16.
[527]Emphasized in R. Cook 1981, 487-88.
[528]Richard Hays (*1 Cor,* 24), believes that Paul left the responsibility for baptizing new converts to Gaius, Crispus and Stephanas.

Conzelmann asserts that "baptism can be administered by anyone"[529]—a nonchalant statement that does not explain Paul's serious assertion. And Thomas Schmeller is completely off course when he asserts in this context that the Pauline mission "does not claim to convey everything that is necessary to being a Christian."[530]

Did Paul downplay Christian water baptism? Many scholars protest against such a conclusion.[531] Surely correct is the observation that Paul does not formulate the sentence in 1 Cor 1:17 as an expression of a "theological disregard of baptism," and it is equally feasible to see that 1 Cor 1:17 is rhetorical, a hyperbolic formulation, in the context of 1 Cor 1. Paul clearly did not despise water baptism: he did baptize the Corinthians Crispus, Gaius and Stephanas with his household. On the other hand, it is equally obvious from Paul's statement in 1 Cor 1:17 that baptism has neither salvific nor strategic missionary significance.[532] Paul's words in 1 Cor 1:17 are not simply rhetorical; rather, he formulates a fundamental theological principle.[533] Paul defends his missionary praxis "not pragmatically, but theologically"—but not on the basis of a charisma that Wolfgang Schrage thinks is necessary for baptizing people. Schrage asserts, "Even an apostle is not an ecclesiastical all-round man. The charisma sets limits even for him."[534] There is no evidence to support this interpretation, neither in 1 Cor 1 nor in Paul's understanding of the gifts of the Spirit. Missionaries do not need a "charisma" to baptize new converts. The fact that Paul entrusted his coworkers and, soon enough, the new Christian communities with the responsibility of baptizing new converts has nothing to do with "proper self-knowledge and self-limitation." Clearly, Paul implies that baptism is *not directly* linked with God's gift of salvation, which people are granted through faith in the gospel of Jesus Christ alone. The "eschatological salvation" through Jesus' death on the cross and the "exclusive commitment" to Jesus Christ do *not* "become irreversibly effective in baptism." According to Paul, this happens in the acceptance of the gospel of Jesus Christ, in personal reliance on Jesus' death and resurrection, in the conversion to the one true God and his salvific revelation in the crucified and risen Jesus, who is Messiah, Lord and Savior.[535] It is unlikely that Paul would have agreed with Otfried Hofius's understanding of baptism: "Baptism is an effective-causal event because Christ *himself* acts in baptism, imparting and granting salvation that results from his death."[536] If baptism effectively and causally imparts salvation, then missionaries would be *forced* to baptize new converts because their goal is to help people find salvation. Similarly problematic is the interpretation of Karl Müller, who writes in an older study that Paul's missionary goal—to lead all nations to the obedience of faith—requires "that all people receive the 'Sacramentum fidei,' that is, holy baptism."[537] But that is exactly what Paul avoided: baptizing new converts.

---

[529]Conzelmann, *1 Kor,* 55 (ET, 36); cf. Schmeller 1997, 269.

[530]Schmeller 1997, 269.

[531]Conzelmann, *1 Kor,* 55 (ET, 36-37); Fee, *1 Cor,* 63; Merklein, *1 Kor,* 1:165; Schrage, *1 Kor,* 1:156-57; for the comment that follows above see Lang, *Kor,* 22.

[532]This stands in contrast to the early medieval mission, in which baptism as such increasingly became the goal of missionary work; see Padberg 1995, 48-49.

[533]Contra Schrage, *1 Kor,* 1:157; the quotation that follows above, ibid.

[534]Schrage, *1 Kor,* 1:157; the quotations that follow above, ibid., 1:157, 162.

[535]Beasley-Murray 1968, 237; Dunn 1970, 119; cf. Hays, *1 Cor,* 24.

[536]Hofius 1994, 146 n. 42.

[537]K. Müller 1956, 29.

6. Paul involved coworkers in the writing of his letters: Timothy,[538] Tertius,[539] Silvanus,[540] Sosthenes[541] and "the brothers"[542] are mentioned in eight of the thirteen Pauline letters as co-senders. Timothy alone is mentioned in six letters. However, it is difficult to assess their contribution because secretaries who were involved in the composition of letters could write down a dictated letter, or they could participate in composing the content.[543]

7. Paul expected coworkers to minister in dangerous situations in which it was too risky for him to stay in a particular city. When Paul was forced to leave Philippi and Thessalonike in a hurry, his coworkers stayed in the city or revisited the city a few weeks later.

8. Paul expected his coworkers to travel hundreds of kilometers on foot or by ship, perhaps alone sometimes. One example is the travels of Timothy and Titus from Ephesus to Corinth. The journeys of the early Christian missionaries are not simply a literary "motif" that "reminds the readers of the fact that the work is carried out by itinerant apostles," as Gottfried Schille suggests,[544] but rather a concrete reality in a time in which travel was dangerous.

9. Paul maintained intensive and regular contacts with his coworkers, as is seen in the information about the efforts of coworkers and the greetings in his letters. The following reasons provide an explanation. (a) The numerous personal relationships and commitments evidently played an important role in coping with the pressures and difficulties of missionary life, particularly the hardship of the homelessness of the missionaries. (b) The individual intercession in prayer for one another was important. Despite the fact that several phrases that talk about mutual prayer support seem formulaic, the differences in content indicate that this was by no means a rote praxis. Praying for one another, as an "interior perspective"[545] of missionary work, was important for the missionaries' personal relationship with God, but it also maintained and deepened mutual friendship and commitment.

10. Some scholars assume that a "Pauline school" was responsible for the composition of several Pauline letters that are deemed inauthentic: 2 Thessalonians, Colossians, Ephesians, 1-2 Timothy and Titus.

Peter Müller remarks that the term *Paulusschule* ("School of Paul") should be understood not in terms of an organized educational institution localized in a city such as Ephesus or Corinth but as a "phenomenon of tradition and actualization of Paul's dis-

---

[538]1 Thess 1:1; 2 Thess 1:1; 2 Cor 1:1; Phil 1:1; Col 1:1; Philem 1.
[539]Rom 16:22.
[540]1 Thess 1:1; 2 Thess 1:1.
[541]1 Cor 1:1.
[542]Gal 1:2; 1 Cor 16:20.
[543]See E. Richards 1991; Ellis 1993, 188; 1999, 38-39, 326-27.
[544]Schille 1961, 205.
[545]Padberg 1995, 82.

ciples" that assumed different shapes and forms in the various churches that were loyal to Paul.[546] Müller believes that it was the specific situation of the churches that owed their existence to Paul and adopted Paul's theological thinking that caused the production of deutero-Pauline writings, such as 2 Thessalonians and Colossians. This description of a *Paulusschule* implies that it vanishes if the allegedly deutero-Pauline letters prove to be authentic letters of Paul after all. The evaluation of some of the traditionally Pauline Epistles as pseudonymous and thus inauthentic presupposes that the differences between, say, 2 Thessalonians and Colossians on the one hand and the authentic Pauline letters on the other hand are too great to be reconciled with Paul's theology, while at the same recognizing that there are similarities that suggest some kind of relationship with Paul. Such reconstructions stand or fall with the interpretation of individual passages. Müller asserts with regard to 2 Thessalonians that its apostle—like Paul himself—is committed to the church with his entire existence, but there is no evidence for any apostolic activity beyond the church, as the missionary dimension is made difficult because of apocalyptic expectations, thus receding into the background, confirmed by the fact that this letter, unlike Gal 1:16, does not refer to a mission to the nations.[547] This argumentation is exegetically unconvincing. In 2 Thess 3:1 the author asks the readers to pray for him "so that the word of the Lord may spread rapidly and be glorified everywhere, just as it is among you," reminding the Thessalonians of the pioneer missionary work in their city at the time of the foundation of the church, and noting the continuation of missionary work in other regions and cities and expressing the hope that this continuing missionary ministry might be successful. And the author underscores the responsibility of the church in Thessalonike for these missionary initiatives, primarily in prayer. In 2 Thess 3:8 the author again and more specifically reminds the readers of his missionary ministry in Thessalonike: "And we did not eat anyone's bread without paying for it; but with toil and labor we worked night and day, so that we might not burden any of you." It is incomprehensible how Müller sees only "silence concerning a continuing missionary task" in 2 Thessalonians.[548] The case for this letter being authentically Pauline is strong.[549]

We must remember that the term μαθητής (*mathētēs,* "student, pupil" or "disciple, adherent") does not occur in Paul's letters. The term τέκνον (*teknon,* "child") was used by later rabbis for a "disciple,"[550] but Paul uses it in the sense of "child" for people who have been converted to faith in Jesus Christ in the course of his ministry[551] or for coworkers such as Timothy (1 Cor 4:17; 1 Tim 1:2) and Titus (Tit 1:4).[552] It is safe to assume that the missionary coworkers who belonged to Paul's team at various times and in different places studied the content of the gospel and learned how to formulate and preach the message of Jesus Christ. It may be the case that Paul organized a "school" in a more formal

---

[546]P. Müller 1988, 325; for the comment that follows above see ibid.

[547]P. Müller 1988, 193-227, 236-37.

[548]P. Müller 1988, 236.

[549]See Wanamaker (*Thess,* 17-28) and Malherbe (*Thess,* 349-75), who conclude that 2 Thessalonians is authentically Pauline.

[550]Cf. *m. 'Abod. Zar.* 2:5; see Str-B 3:559, 765-66.

[551]Gal 4:19; 1 Cor 4:14; 2 Cor 6:13; Philem 10.

[552]See Ellis 1971, 3.

sense of the word, but this possibility remains hypothetical. It is an entirely different question whether his coworkers, or other Christians committed to Paul, wrote letters and published them under the pseudonym "Paul." There are solid and convincing reasons to believe that this was not the case.[553]

Missionary Journeys

The notion of three missionary journeys of the apostle Paul has become so commonplace that it controls the outlines of the book of Acts in modern Bible translations and the legends of maps included in Bibles. Johann Bengel may have been the first to speak of three missionary journeys of Paul, in a preface to the book of Acts in his *Gnomon Novi Testamenti.*[554] Most commentaries on Acts written in the nineteenth century refer to three missionary journeys of Paul.

The term "missionary journey" as applied to the missionary initiatives of the early church in the first century is not entirely wrong. However, it clearly is problematic with regard to Paul: the fact that during his mission to Cyprus and Galatia the apostle stayed only a few months in the cities in which he preached the gospel was not the result of a particular strategy or praxis of missionary ministry in terms of a "journey"; rather, it reflects that he had to leave most of the cities in which he was active in a hurry and under pressure from the local citizenry. The same applies to the mission to Macedonia. The fact that Paul lived and worked in Corinth for two years and in Ephesus for over two years proves that the term "journey" does not offer a helpful analytical concept for a description of Paul's missionary praxis. And we do not know whether Paul organized his missionary work in the ten years between A.D. 32 and 42 in Syria and Cilicia in terms of "journeys" or whether he stayed in some cities for longer periods of time.

Paul's travel companions during his return journey from the mission to Ephesus mentioned in Acts 20:4 are a special case because they accompany him as representatives of the churches that he had established, bringing the collection from the Jewish- and Gentile-Christian churches to Jerusalem.

Macedonia	Sopater, son of Pyrrhus from Beroea; Aristarchus and Secundus from Thessalonike
Galatia	Gaius from Derbe, Timothy from Lystra
Asia	Tychicus and Trophimus (probably) from Ephesus

It is striking that there are no representatives from Corinth (Achaia) and from Philippi.[555] Rudolf Pesch suggests that the representatives from Corinth and Philippi possibly belonged, like Timothy, to the group that did not travel by ship to Alexandria Troas ahead

---

[553]See recently Baum 2001.

[554]Bengel, *Gnomon Novi Testamenti,* 410-11. see Townsend 1986, 103.

[555]Ollrog (1979, 54-55) suggests that Luke introduced Timothy into the list; for a critique of this view see Reinbold 2000, 154 n. 151.

of Paul but joined Paul on his journey through Macedonia, celebrating Easter in Philippi.[556] If we add to the group mentioned in Acts 20:4 two delegates from Corinth and two delegates from Philippi—perhaps Lucius and Jason, who are mentioned in Rom 16:21 between Timothy and Sosipater—we would have twelve representatives of churches. Pesch comments, "Paul wanted to underline the unity of the church with twelve travel companions who consisted of Jewish Christians and Gentile Christians, a goal that he pursued with the collection as such." A different solution suggests that Luke was the representative of the church in Philippi and that Paul may have regarded himself as the "collection representative" of the church in Corinth.[557]

Paul's travel companions on this journey, which served to hand over the collection (which is not mentioned by Luke) to the Jerusalem church, were representatives of churches that Paul had established. It is unclear whether all of these men were also missionary coworkers of Paul, either at this point in time or later.

Support and Finances

Paul insists in 1 Cor 9:4-6, with decisive argumentation, that as an apostle he has the right to be supported in his ministry.[558] The questions that Paul raises in this text are rhetorical, expecting a positive answer in every case.

1 Cor 9:4-6: "Do we not have the right to our food and drink? ⁵Do we not have the right to be accompanied by a believing wife, as do the other apostles and the brothers of the Lord and Cephas? ⁶Or is it only Barnabas and I who have no right to refrain from working for a living?"

Paul substantiates the right to receive support in the following verses. (1) Paul refers to soldiers and their pay, to vineyard workers and their harvest, and to shepherds and the milk from the animals in their flock. In other words, he argues from the realities of everyday life (κατὰ ἄνθρωπον, kata anthrōpon [1 Cor 9:8a]). (2) He argues from the law (ὁ νόμος ταῦτα λέγει, ho nomos tauta legei [1 Cor 9:8b-9]). (3) He argues with reference to the support that the priests in temples receive (οἱ τὰ ἱερὰ ἐργαζόμενοι, hoi ta hera ergazomenoi [1 Cor 9:13])—in other words, from the cultic praxis of Judaism and of the Greco-Roman world. (4) He argues from a saying of Jesus (ὁ κύριος διέταξεν, ho kyrios dietaxen [1 Cor 9:14]). (5) He refers to the reality of missionary work and ministry in churches (εἰ ἡμεῖς ὑμῖν τὰ πνευματικὰ ἐσπείραμεν, ei hēmeis hymin ta pneumatika espeiramen [1 Cor 9:11]).

1 Cor 9:7-14: "Who at any time pays the expenses for doing military service? Who plants a vineyard and does not eat any of its fruit? Or who tends a flock and does not get any

---

[556]Pesch, Apg, 2:186; the quotation that follows above, ibid., 2:187 n. 13.

[557]Marshall, Acts, 324; Witherington, Acts, 603. Reinbold (2000, 155-56 n. 156) does not discuss this suggestion, which makes it easier for him to disconnect Acts 20:4 from the collection.

[558]Pratscher 1979, 284; Tassin 1992, 465-66; cf. Everts 1993, for the following analysis; see also Dickson 2003, 178-213.

of its milk?[8]Do I say this on human authority? Does not the law also say the same? [9]For it is written in the law of Moses, 'You shall not muzzle an ox while it is treading out the grain' [Deut 25:4]. Is it for oxen that God is concerned? [10]Or does he not speak entirely for our sake? It was indeed written for our sake, for whoever plows should plow in hope and whoever threshes should thresh in hope of a share in the crop. [11]If we have sown spiritual good among you, is it too much if we reap your material benefits? [12]If others share this rightful claim on you, do not we still more? Nevertheless, we have not made use of this right, but we endure anything rather than put an obstacle in the way of the gospel of Christ. [13]Do you not know that those who are employed in the temple service get their food from the temple, and those who serve at the altar share in what is sacrificed on the altar? [14]In the same way, the Lord commanded that those who proclaim the gospel should get their living by the gospel."

Paul has the right to be supported financially by the church, just as Simon Peter, James and the other apostles are so supported. Paul's argument for this right is supported in Phil 4:15, where he uses with the phrase εἰς λόγον δόσεως καὶ λήμψεως (*eis logon doseōs kai lēmpseōs*), a commercial technical term that many scholars find difficult to translate: the gift of the Philippian Christians represents the "give" (*dosis*) and "take" (*lēmpsis*) in the sense of the "settlement of an account" (*eis logon*) by a "financial contribution" (*koinōnein*).[559]

Phil 4:15-16: "You Philippians indeed know that in the early days of the gospel, when I left Macedonia, no church shared with me in the matter of giving and receiving, except you alone. [16]For even when I was in Thessalonica, you sent me help for my needs more than once."

A purely legal and financial interpretation assumes that Paul tells the Philippian Christians that he had a right to receive their financial support: he brought them the gospel, and they "pay" with their contribution, which is an "obligatory payment."[560] This interpretation is one-sided and cannot be supported by evidence from Greek texts regarding the meaning of the terms that Paul employs. Peter Marshall has demonstrated that Paul's formulation occurs in connection with the subject of "friendship." Paul confirms that he has received the Philippians' financial gift and expresses his gratefulness: he readily accepts the gift as an expression of their care and support, and he reminds them, and himself, of the mutual exchange of services and devotion.[561] In 2 Cor 11:8-9 Paul informs the Corinthian Christians of an apparently larger financial gift that Silas and Timothy

---

[559]See BDAG, s.v. "λόγος 2b": "in settlement of a mutual account (lit. 'of giving and receiving,' 'of debit and credit')"; BADG, s.v. "λόγος 2βd": "in Abrechnung des Gebens u. Empfangens, in gegenseitiger Abrechnung." On εἰς λόγον see P.Oxy. 275.19, 21; Thucydides 3.46; Polybius 11.28.8. See P. Marshall 1987, 157-64; also Reumann (1993, 439-42), whose hypotheses concerning the literary (Phil 2:6-11) and argumentative (in 2 Cor 8—9) contributions to Paul's ministry (ibid., 442-56) are unconvincing.

[560]Thus Pratscher 1979, 286.

[561]P. Marshall 1987, 163-64; followed by O'Brien, *Phil*, 534.

brought from Macedonia, probably from Philippi, when they joined him in Corinth.

2 Cor 11:8-9: "I robbed other churches by accepting support from them in order to serve you. ⁹And when I was with you and was in need, I did not burden anyone, for my needs were supplied by the friends who came from Macedonia. So I refrained and will continue to refrain from burdening you in any way."

Lukas Bormann investigated the relationship between Paul and the Philippians against the background of Hellenistic and Roman social conventions. He argues that neither Dieter Georgi's model of the religiously and ethically eminent personality nor Peter Marshall's model of the Hellenistic ideal of friendship (φιλία, *philia*) is persuasive.[562] Bormann contends that the Greek tradition of benefactors and benefactions explains Paul's statements more convincingly—that is, an interpretation that sees the financial contribution of the Philippian Christians as a *beneficium,* a "beneficial deed that the giver engages in voluntarily and that aims solely at the benefit of the recipient."[563] He points out that Paul would have seen himself as a debtor to the Philippians as a result of their gift, which explains why he was reluctant to accept it. According to Bormann, the clearest parallel for what transpired is the patronage system of the Hellenistic world: Paul the patron represents the common cause, which is the gospel, to the outside world, while the Philippians—the "emancipated clients"—cannot help him as the apostle waits for his trial in distant Rome.[564] Josef Hainz argues against this interpretation: he points out that there is no evidence in Phil 4:10-20 for Bormann's suggestion that Paul was unnerved as a result of the Philippians' gift. Hainz restates his earlier position, correctly so I believe: Paul and the Philippian Christians are linked with each other by *koinōnia,* the committed fellowship of the church founder and the church members "which arises out of mutual sharing and participation and which thus is realized anew again and again."[565] The "partnership in the gospel" of the Philippian Christians (Phil 1:5 TNIV) has been "established by the gospel in which they mutually participate, and it is related to the gospel which they serve in their own ways"—Paul through his missionary work that led to the establishment of the church, and the Philippians through their personal support of the gospel.

Mark Kiley argues that because the Epistles to the Colossians and to the Ephesians, 2 Thessalonians and the Pastoral Epistles do not mention any financial transactions in support of missionary work, this proves their pseudonymity.[566] This argument is as curious as the nonsensical argument that the reference to God in these letters proves that they are authentically Pauline.

Paul was willing to accept financial support for himself and his team of missionaries (2 Cor 11:9; Phil 4:18) because additional funds allowed him to focus more fully on his missionary work. The deprivations that Paul repeatedly mentions

---

[562]Bormann 1994, 164-71, 187-88, 203-11, arguing against Georgi 1965, 47, 83, and P. Marshall 1987.
[563]Bormann 1994, 171-81; quotation, 175.
[564]Bormann 1994, 187-223.
[565]Hainz 1994, 388; the quotation that follows above, idem 1982, 94-95.
[566]Kiley 1986, 46-51.

were linked, in part, with financial needs and emergencies. In pioneer situations a lack of finances would have meant difficulties and uncertainties regarding lodging and food. The suggestion that Paul would have been able to open a workshop in the cities that he visited as a missionary[567] is incorrect: he needed to find Jewish contacts who could provide him with opportunities to work and earn money. The intensity of missionary work depended on whether Paul was forced to support himself and his team financially by working as a "tentmaker" or whether he could devote himself totally to preaching and teaching the gospel while relying on financial support from existing churches. Luke's comment in Acts 18:5 illustrates this nexus.

Acts 18:5: "When Silas and Timothy came from Macedonia, Paul devoted himself exclusively to preaching, testifying to the Jews that Jesus was the Christ." (NIV)

The gift from Macedonian Christians, presumably the Christians in Philippi, meant that Paul no longer was required to earn his living with his own hand, working for several hours during the week. He now was able to intensify and maximize his missionary activities.[568]

There were times when Paul had to earn his livelihood by manual labor as a "tentmaker" or "leatherworker."[569] Paul does not follow the pre-Easter instructions about money and support that Jesus gave to the Twelve before their short-term mission to the towns in Galilee (Mt 10:9-10), but he explicitly quotes Jesus in 1 Cor 9 when he discusses the matter of financial support for missionaries. This confirms that the dominical saying in Mt 10:9-10 had limited significance in a specific historical setting. Despite his manual labor, Paul repeatedly has financial difficulties—for example, during his mission to Corinth (2 Cor 11:9)—apparently because he had to support not only himself but also his team of co-workers.

Some scholars assume that Paul supported himself by manual labor because he was concerned that "low-income people would stay away from the church, afraid of the costs that they could not pay."[570] This hypothesis is less than convincing. Somewhat more plausible is the assumption that Paul had to secure his missionary plans financially because self-help in terms of plucking grain was impossible in the cities.[571] However, this explanation cannot fully explain 1 Cor 9:4-14 either.

We need to take seriously the reasons that Paul himself mentions: he does

---

[567]Lührmann 1990, 242.
[568]Bornkamm 1993, 86 (ET, 69); Theissen 1989, 251.
[569]Cf. 1 Thess 2:9; 1 Cor 4:12; Acts 18:3; 20:34. See Pratscher 1979, 286-87; Schmeller 1997, 270-71.
[570]Klauck, *1 Kor,* 66.
[571]See Theissen 1974-1975, 212 (ET, 38).

not want to be a burden to anyone (1 Thess 2:9; 2 Cor 11:9), he wants to avoid any appearance of flattery and greed (1 Thess 2:5), he does not want to be mistaken for an itinerant philosopher, and he does not want to fall prey to the accusations of opponents in the churches (1 Cor 9:12; 2 Cor 11:12).[572] Why, then, did Paul accept financial support from the Philippian Christians but not from the believers in Corinth?

Evidently there are two situations in which Paul deliberately and emphatically refused to accept financial support. First, as a pioneer missionary who preaches the gospel in cities that have not been reached by other missionaries, he would not accept money (or logistical support) from people—unbelievers—who first need to hear the gospel.[573] When he arrived in a city as a missionary, he had no adherents who could support him. He would have had to find wealthy Jewish or Gentile patrons who were willing to support him as a visiting rabbi or as a visiting orator or philosopher. This would have signified a compromise of the gospel; Paul at least would have lost the freedom to preach the gospel to all people with all the consequences that the message of the crucified and risen Jesus Christ has for the personal behavior of the wealthy citizens as well. Paul seems to refer to the issue of depending on local patrons and benefactors in the following texts:

1 Thess 2:5-6: "As you know and as God is our witness, we never came with words of flattery or with a pretext for greed; [6]nor did we seek praise from mortals, whether from you or from others."

1 Cor 9:18: "What then is my reward? Just this: that in my proclamation I may make the gospel free of charge, so as not to make full use of my rights in the gospel."

2 Cor 11:7: "Did I commit a sin by humbling myself so that you might be exalted, because I proclaimed God's good news to you free of charge?"

A second reason for Paul's refusal to accept financial support is illustrated by the situation in Corinth, as Wilhelm Pratscher explains: "Paul refuses to accept the support of a church as long as his acceptance of such support could disturb or destroy his missionary work in that particular church or the gospel that he brings on account of the agitation of opponents."[574] Some Christians in Corinth insisted that Paul should have accepted their financial support (1 Cor 9:1-18; 2 Cor 2:17), as they insisted that Paul should have maximized his success more aggressively through more brilliant rhetorical means (see 1 Cor 1:17—2:5). These are perhaps the same believers who thought that Paul owed them details about his travel plans (2 Cor 1:17). Paul emphasizes with regard to this kind of think-

---

[572]See Barnett 1993.
[573]Pratscher 1979, 290-92.
[574]Pratscher 1979, 294; cf. Everts 1993a, 296, 299.

ing that the content and the success of his missionary preaching as well as the modus operandi of his missionary work are dependent upon God alone, both with regard to rhetorical techniques or the lack thereof and with regard to his travels and his financial independence.[575] This means that Paul's assertion in 1 Cor 4:12 cannot be limited to the initial period of Paul's missionary activity in a city.[576] Also, Paul's statements in 1 Cor 4:12 and 1 Cor 9:1-27 indicate that he had to work, or wanted to work, to support himself at later periods during his one and a half years in Corinth in order to avoid becoming a burden to others.[577] But Paul does accept the financial gift of the Philippian Christians: their gift evidently was free of any specific expectations, it was unproblematic, and it helped him in his missionary activities. He refuses to be supported by the Corinthian Christians because financial gifts are a controversial issue in the church in Corinth and because he does not want to be roped in by Christians who seek to influence and control his behavior as a missionary. What he expects of the Corinthian Christians is prayer support (2 Cor 1:11) and loyalty (2 Cor 5:11—6:13; 10-13).

28.5 The Missionary Work of the Christian Communities

Paul understood himself as a missionary to the Gentiles: the churches that he established consisted of, besides Jewish Christians, to a large extent people who converted to faith in Jesus Christ from paganism. The Christian churches were not clubs of like-minded people who had common interests; they consisted of Jews and Gentiles of different religious convictions and divergent ethical traditions who were united in their faith in the eschatological revelation of Israel's God in Jesus the Messiah and Savior, and who were called to align their everyday life and behavior in accordance with these new convictions. This new reality in the new community of believers presented the missionaries and the first leaders of the congregations with the challenge of helping the converted polytheists be transformed into followers of Jesus and members of the people of God. With regard to converted Jews and proselytes, Paul could assume in the area of ethical behavior a comprehensive knowledge and an existing praxis of the will of God as revealed in sacred Scripture. With regard to the converted God-fearers and sympathizers who had attended synagogue services, Paul could assume some knowledge of Scripture, but not necessarily with practical obedience to the will of God; otherwise, they presumably would have fully converted to Judaism. Converted polytheists would not automatically have abandoned moral traditions and practices that were problematic for Jews and for mature Christians, nor would they have automatically renounced all superstitions

---

[575]See Young 1989, 76-79.
[576]See Schrage, *1 Kor,* 1:33, with reference to Suhl 1975, 117 with n. 23.
[577]See Pesch, *Apg,* 2:148; Young 1989, 77.

or magical practices when they were converted. Martin Hengel has correctly pointed out that it is in these areas that we have to reckon with a direct "pagan influence" in the earliest churches established by the missionaries, specifically in the area of "the old, old human sins of these former 'God-fearers' from their pagan past in the ethical realm, sins that they would not have automatically shed in the synagogue, as the old familial and social obligations continued to exert their influence."[578] Laxness with regard to sexual behavior, ties to pagan temples and cults and notions of the magical or mysteries-like effect of the sacraments continued to affect Gentile Christians and thus the churches, as is indicated by the vice lists that Paul includes in his epistolary exhortations. Did Paul expect that the Christians of the churches that he established would actively preach the gospel to non-Christians?

The Lack of Exhortations to Active Missionary Participation

It is striking that the numerous, often rather specific exhortations that Paul addresses in his letters to the churches that he established or knows do not include appeals to be active in mission and evangelism and to work toward winning additional inhabitants of their cities and of the surrounding villages to faith in Jesus Christ. This silence has been variously explained.

1. Some scholars refer to Rom 15:19-23 and argue that Paul's missionary program received its profile from the conviction of the imminent return of Jesus Christ and hence did not aim at actively involving the newly founded churches in the mission of the church. Paul Althaus comments, "The nations stand before God and his judgment as a whole. They are complete entities. If only a few members of a nation, in this last generation, have accepted the Word, all have been reached, the entire nation is responsible. This is all the apostle aimed at. This is the reason why his work is finished in the East."[579] This explanation is implausible. There is no evidence that Paul's conviction that Jesus' return might be imminent influenced his missionary strategy, at least not with regard to the "speed" of his missionary initiatives. The three years of his mission to Ephesus can hardly be reconciled with an alleged "eschatological haste."

2. Some scholars, including contemporary missionary leaders, suggest that the new converts would have been motivated by their conversion and by God's Spirit to engage in missionary activity as a matter of course, which made it unnecessary for Paul to challenge them with appeals to be involved in evangelistic outreach.[580] This explanation is unconvincing. The moral behavior of

---

[578]Hengel 1994a, x.
[579]Althaus, Röm, 147; cf. Käsemann, Röm, 380 (ET, 395); Hultgren 1985, 125-45; Legrand 1990, 119-21.
[580]See Würz 1922, 57; Allen 1977, 93-94; Schlunck 1937, 45; M. Green 1970, 148-49, 236-66, 275; Gilliland 1983, 187-88; Howell 1996.

new converts is also a consequence of the conversion and the work of the Holy Spirit, as is their regular and continuous prayer life, and yet Paul includes repeated appeals and exhortations to live consistently as followers of Jesus in everyday life and to pray without ceasing.

3. Some scholars argue that the church is missionary in character, which explains the lack of appeals to engage in missionary outreach. This explanation, somewhat similar to the second view just discussed, is defended by Douwe van Swigchem, who argues as follows.[581] (a) The churches display interest in news about the missionary work of the apostles and support them through prayer, financial gifts, provision of coworkers and care for the newly established congregations.[582] (b) The churches clearly distinguish between members of the church and outsiders and regard the outsiders not as enemies but as people who have not (yet) come to faith in Jesus Christ—that is, potential converts.[583] (c) The apostles describe the moral behavior of the Christian believers as light that attracts non-Christians.[584] (d) The apostles expect that the churches imitate the apostolic missionary activity.[585] (e) The apostles admonish the churches to follow the example of Jesus Christ, which includes the proclamation of the gospel despite opposition.[586] (f) There are five passages in which Paul and Peter explicitly challenge the churches to be active in missionary ministry.[587] (g) The apostles praise the churches for their missionary involvement, which explains why they did not need to formulate appeals: the churches were already in the process of reaching out to non-Christians.[588] (h) Luke and Paul describe the evangelistic activity of individual church members with the terms "word of the Lord" (*logos tou kyriou*) and "gospel" (*euangelion*).[589] (i) The asssemblies of the churches have a secondary evangelistic function.[590] (j) The motivation of the mission of the church consists in the experience of God's mercy, in the lordship of Christ, in the glory of God and in the eschatological vision of the visible consummation of the kingdom of

---

[581]Swigchem 1955. See the description of his position in Ridderbos 1975, 432-35; Plummer 2001, 29-33.

[582]Swigchem 1955, 23-39, with reference to Rom 1:8; 15:18-32; 16; 1 Cor 16:9, 15-18; 2 Cor 8:16-19; 2:12; Gal 1:23-24; Eph 6:21-22; Phil 1:12; 2:22; 4:10; Col 4:2-4, 7-9; 1 Thess 1:7-10; 5:25; 2 Thess 1:4; 2 Tim 1:15; 4:10.

[583]Swigchem 1955, 40-77; cf. Rom 6—8; Gal 4:8; 1 Thess 1:8-9; 4:5; 5:9; 2 Thess 1:6, 8-10; 1 Pet 2:11.

[584]Swigchem 1955, 78-108; cf. Rom 12:17-21; 13:1-8; 1 Cor 11:5-16; 2 Cor 3:1-3; Phil 2:15; Col 4:4-6; 1 Thess 4:12; Tit 2:5, 8, 10; 3:1-2; 1 Pet 2:9-13.

[585]Swigchem 1955, 109-17; cf. 1 Cor 4:16; 9:19-23; 11:1; Phil 3:17; 1 Thess 1:6.

[586]Swigchem 1955, 117-23; cf. Rom 15:3; 1 Cor 11:1; Eph 4:32; 5:2; Phil 2:5-11; Col 3:13; 1 Thess 1:6; 1 Pet 3:13-19.

[587]Swigchem 1955, 123-30; cf. Eph 6:15; Phil 1:27; Col 4:5-6; 1 Pet 3:15; 4:16.

[588]Swigchem 1955, 130-41; cf. 1 Thess 1:8; Rom 1:8; Phil 1:5, 14.

[589]Swigchem 1955, 141-63; cf. Acts 8:4; 13:49; 19:10, 20; Rom 10:15; 1 Thess 1:8; 2 Thess 3:1.

[590]Swigchem 1955, 189-98; cf. 1 Cor 14; Eph 5:14; 1 Tim 2:1-3; Eph 6:23; 1 Pet 5:14.

God.[591] Swigchem's study suffers from weaknesses similar to those pointed out for the second view: the texts that he adduces do not always support his claims, and he does not distinguish the "missionary" effects of the life of the church on outsiders from the consciousness of being responsible for organizing and maintaining missionary outreach among unbelievers.

4. Some scholars suggest that Paul's missionary self-understanding "cannot be easily transferred to other missionaries and other ecclesial situations."[592] The missionary obligation of the churches consists primarily in being attractive for unbelievers[593] and in supporting Paul's mission by the provision of coworkers.[594] Paul Bowers explains the lack of missionary instructions for the churches with two factors. (a) Paul had a personalized understanding of mission: he was convinced that God fulfills the missionary task that he entrusted to the Twelve by select individuals whom he calls.[595] (b) In view of the fact that there was neither an active mission to Gentiles by Jews nor Greco-Roman models for the expansive propagation of religious convictions linked with a geographical strategy, we should not assume that Paul, or the early church, had a complete missionary theology and missionary strategy.[596]

The arguments of Paul Bowers are important and need to be reviewed in detail.[597] (a) Paul's exhortation to the Corinthian Christians to imitate him (1 Cor 9:1—11:1) includes a reference to his missionary work, which, however, merely serves to illustrate the humility that the "strong" should have in their controversy with the "weak." (b) When Paul writes in 2 Cor 5:18—6:2 that "we are ambassadors for Christ," he distinguishes between himself and the other apostles ("we") from the churches and the church members ("you"). (c) The metaphor of growth and of the church as a building under construction (Eph 2:19-22; Col 1:6, 10) refers to the development of spiritual maturity rather than to numerical growth. The meaning of the term "evangelist" (Eph 4:11) must not be limited to church members who are involved in missionary outreach; rather, the term includes the task of nurturing the believers. (d) The metaphor of the church as a body (1 Cor 12; Eph 4:16; Col 1; 2:19) is not connected with the relationship of the church with unbelievers in the sense of an active instrument of independent missionary ministry; rather, it emphasizes the indispensability of each member for the life of the entire church. (e) Several Pauline statements that often are re-

---

[591]Swigchem 1955, 221-40.

[592]Zeller 1982a, 164.

[593]Greeven 1958, 66; Bowers 1976, 119-20; idem 1991, 105, 111; Bosch 1991, 168.

[594]Ollrog 1979, esp. 130-31.

[595]Bowers 1976, 120-21; 1991, 103-4. On the "eschatological herald" as representing one dimension of Paul's view of mission see Dickson 2003, 153-77.

[596]Bowers 1980; cf. Marshall 2000a, 262.

[597]Bowers 1976, 103-21; 1991. For the discussion that follows above see also Marshall 2000a, 253-54; Plummer 2001, 42-43.

garded as evidence for a missionary ministry of local congregations are, according to Bowers, not conclusive. In 1 Thess 1:8 Paul does not describe the Thessalonian Christians as people who carry the gospel to unbelievers; rather, they themselves are the message. The same applies to Rom 1:8 and 2 Cor 3:2. When Paul challenges the believers in Philippi to "shine like stars in the world" and to "hold fast to the word of life" (Phil 2:15-16), we should note that the term ἐπέχοντες (*epechontes*) describes not the proclamation of the word of God to outsiders but the necessity of adhering to the word of God. In Col 4:5-6 the church indeed appears in an evangelistic role; however, the sense is not that of an active missionary outreach along the lines of the model of Paul's missionary work but rather that of being attractive to outsiders. In other words, the local church is a stationary rather than a mobile witness of the gospel.

Paul Bowers protests, particularly in personal conversations, if his position is interpreted in terms of a repudiation of any missionary activity of local churches in the first century. In the context of the evangelical movement (to which Bowers belongs, having been active in Africa for many years), with its strong emphasis on mission and evangelism, including the view that "every Christian is a missionary," Bowers is correct to emphasize that careful exegetical work consists in listening carefully to what the texts really say without constantly hearing what we want to hear. It is true that Paul never assigns the task of evangelism and missionary outreach to the local Christian community as such. The function of the *ekklēsia,* as Paul describes it, is connected with the coming together of believers in Jesus Christ for worship, fellowship and edification. The metaphor of the body—the church as the "body of Christ"—speaks about "vertical" (or "interior") growth rather than "horizontal" growth.[598] The conclusion that individual believers do not and cannot have an evangelistic task would be problematic, however. The reaction of several New Testament scholars shows that the position held by Bowers can easily be misunderstood and that some texts can and probably should be interpreted differently than he does.[599] However, the studies by Bowers provide a necessary correction to the popular notion that the pivotal impetus of the early Christian mission was the work of "normal believers" who "gossiped the gospel" in everyday life and in the context of their normal familial and professional relationships, representing a "total mobilization" of the early church.[600]

5. Another explanation for the missing "missionary commissions" in the Pauline letters refers to the possibility that the concept of missions both of Paul and of the early church was still developing,[601] or that Paul's ecclesiology was

---

[598]O'Brien 1995, 130; for the comment that follows above see ibid.
[599]O'Brien 1995, 110-30; Ware 1996; Marshall 2000a; Plummer 2001.
[600]Recently D. S. Lim 1997, 355.
[601]Marshall 2000a, 262-63.

simply focused on the spiritual growth of the young churches.[602] However, we will see that Paul's alleged silence about a missionary responsibility of the local church is not absolute. General considerations and several specific texts show that Paul indeed assumed that Christians would be involved in missionary outreach at least on the local level, and that the churches are integrated in various ways in his missionary work. These considerations and texts will be discussed in the following paragraphs.

General Considerations

The following general exegetical evidence suggests that Paul reckoned with the missionary activity of local churches and individual Christians in the local congregations.

1. Matthew, Luke and John link their reports about Jesus' resurrection appearances with a missionary commission that the risen Lord gave to the disciples (see §12.3). This missionary commission is formulated differently, but the central notion is the same: the disciples who had been called to be trained as "fishers of people" are now directed to engage in this "profession" after Easter. They are directed to go to the people, indeed to all nations as far as the ends of the earth, to proclaim the good news of Jesus Christ and to train those who accept their message as disciples of Jesus. These missionary commissions are indeed given to the Twelve (or the Eleven). We need to note at the same time, however, that the authors of the Gospels, who provide an account of the ministry of Jesus for the local churches, see the entire church of the messianic people of God represented in the Twelve. This means that if the Twelve go their separate ways in fulfillment of Jesus' missionary directive, then the "Great Commission" now applies to the local communities of followers of Jesus established by the ministry of the Twelve.[603] Luke reports in his Gospel a missionary outreach not only of the Twelve but also of seventy-two "missionaries," and when he repeats Jesus' missionary commission in Acts 1:8, he does so against the background of a larger group of followers of Jesus. When Matthew links the missionary commission with the end of the world, he indeed understands the Eleven as missionaries, but also he assumes a missionary responsibility of the entire church and of the local churches. And John closely links discipleship with the concept and the reality of "sending." The authors of the Gospels evidently do not limit Jesus' missionary commission to the Eleven or the Twelve, but regard missionary outreach as an obligation of the church. If this is true for the authors of the Gospels, who write for existing churches, it is a plausible assumption that this is true also for Paul, who establishes new churches.

2. In the book of Acts Luke describes the church in Antioch as actively in-

---

[602]O'Brien 1995, 130.
[603]See Marshall 2000a, 256; for the argument that follows above see ibid.

volved in the sending of missionaries (Acts 13:1-2). This means that we have to reckon with local congregations that sent missionaries to regions that had not yet been reached with the message of Jesus Christ and that stay in contact with these missionaries—at least for the time of Luke. Since there is no plausible reason to doubt the historicity of Luke's account in Acts 13:1-2, we have to conclude that Paul was active for two or three years in a church that was conscious of a missionary responsibility, willing to free leading preachers and teachers of the congregation to start missionary work in distant regions. And we should note that the missionary work of the Jewish Christians from Jerusalem who preached the gospel in Samaria, in the cities of the coastal plain, on Cyprus and in Syria (Acts 8:4-40; 11:19-26) was not different, according to Luke's account, from the later missionary work of Paul and his coworkers.[604]

3. The logic of the gospel implies not only a commitment to Jesus Christ but also a commitment to the progress of the gospel in the world.[605] In the introductory paragraph of his long letter to the Christians in Rome (Rom 1:1-17) Paul describes, first, his personal involvement in the gospel: he was chosen by God to be an apostle "called by God to preach his Good News" (Rom 1:1 TEV); the goal of his ministry is "to bring about the obedience of faith among all the Gentiles" (Rom 1:5); his ministry of the gospel is tireless (Rom 1:9); he wants to come to Rome and preach the gospel there as well (Rom 1:15); he is not ashamed of the gospel, because "it is the power of God for salvation to everyone who has faith, to the Jew first and also to the Greek" (Rom 1:16). Second, Paul describes at the same time the role and function of the gospel in salvation history. The gospel had been announced beforehand in the sacred Scriptures (Rom 1:1-2); the content of the gospel is Jesus Christ the Son of David and the Son of God, who was raised from the dead (Rom 1:3-4); the goal of the gospel is the lordship of the risen Messiah over the new people of God, which includes converted Gentiles (Rom 1:5); the gospel is the saving power of God, who fulfills his promise to Abraham (Rom 1:16-17). One of the reasons that Paul writes to the Christians in the city of Rome is to provide them with a fuller understanding of the saving power of the gospel in a world that has rebelled against God and stands powerless before God the Judge, and to help them understand better the faithfulness of God with regard to the covenant promises that he had given to Abraham and that implied the integration of the nations into the people of God. In this context Peter O'Brien observes, "The dynamic of the gospel's logic meant for these believers in Rome and for other Christians, including ourselves, a deeper commitment to its ongoing, powerful advance, as well as to the person at its centre, Jesus Christ, God's Son."[606] Paul speaks of the powerful dynamic of

---

[604]See Marshall 2000a, 257.
[605]O'Brien 1995, 53-77; followed by Marshall 2000a, 255.
[606]O'Brien 1995, 76-77.

the gospel that is part of the nature of the gospel—the term εὐαγγέλιον (*euangelion*) often is a *nomen actionis*[607]—in the key texts Rom 1:16 and 1 Cor 1:17-25, asserting that the gospel is *dynamis theou,* the power of God that affects Jews and Gentiles and saves them as they believe in Jesus the Messiah and Savior.

4. Some scholars suggest that Paul understood his role as a central and exclusive key figure in the mission to the Gentiles, rendering a missionary function of the local congregation superfluous.[608] Paul's letters do not support this view. The apostle reckons with the possibility that he might die before the task of proclaiming the gospel to Jews and Gentiles is completed (Phil 1:12-26). Paul plans to initiate missionary work in Spain, but he knows that the realization of this goal depends on whether or not he returns from Jerusalem unharmed (Rom 15:22-33). This indicates that he is aware of the fact that missionary work in further regions of the world does not depend on him alone. His announcement that he intends to preach the gospel in the city of Rome (Rom 1:13), an intention that he realizes after his arrival as a prisoner (Phil 1:12-13; Acts 28:17-31), shows that the existence of a church in a particular city does not make further missionary work superfluous.

5. Some scholars point out that Paul worked as a missionary in large cities with the hope that the gospel would be carried from these centers to adjacent areas by the churches that he establishes or by individual Christians from these congregations.[609] There is no hard evidence to support this assumption, but it is more plausible than the view that Paul regarded the missionary ministry in the large cities as representative for the entire province, believing that if one main urban center had been reached with the gospel, then the entire province had been reached. The example of Pisidian Antiocheia shows that the geographical component of Paul's missionary strategy cannot be reduced to a single factor.

6. Paul knows other Christians who are involved in missionary work: the apostles (1 Cor 9:5; 12:28-29) and the Christians in the city of Rome who are not legitimized by some specific "title" (Phil 1:14-18). Paul even tolerates problematic motivations on the part of Christian missionaries: "What does it matter? Just this, that Christ is proclaimed in every way, whether out of false motives or true; and in that I rejoice. Yes, and I will continue to rejoice" (Phil 1:18).

7. It is difficult to distinguish between the activities of the local church and the work of missionaries in the historical context of the first century, as Howard Marshall points out,[610] a fact that every pioneer missionary today can easily confirm. After Paul had established the churches in Corinth and Ephe-

---

[607]Cf. 2 Cor 2:12; 10:14; Gal 2:7; Phil 1:5; 2:22; 4:15.

[608]For this argument see Marshall 2000a, 258-59. Paul Bowers does not hold this view, which is found in the interpretation of Rom 15:19 by Oscar Cullmann, Johannes Munck and others.

[609]See Bosch 1991, 130; Marshall 2000a, 259.

[610]Marshall 2000a, 261-63.

sus, he did not leave immediately; he taught the new believers and established them in the faith, while he continued to preach the gospel to anyone he could reach. In other words, he remained a missionary even when he was a "shepherd" and a "teacher" for a year or two (Eph 4:11). Paul repeatedly visited many of the churches that he had founded, and it is safe to assume that he preached the gospel during these visits not only in the assembly of the local congregation but also before unbelievers. He planned to visit the church in Rome, but he also wanted to proclaim the gospel in the city (Rom 1:15; 15:15-16). When Paul, based in an existing church, continued to preach the gospel in the city, surely he did so not as a soloist but in concert with the congregation.

The Evangelism of the Local Communities

When Paul discusses the behavior of the Corinthian Christians, he notes in passing that outsiders attend the meetings of the congregation: "If, therefore, the whole church comes together and all speak in tongues, and outsiders or unbelievers enter, will they not say that you are out of your mind? But if all prophesy, an unbeliever or outsider who enters is reproved by all and called to account by all" (1 Cor 14:23-24). It evidently was a common occurrence that unbelievers attended the worship services and teaching sessions of the Christian communities. The meetings of the local churches were "no esoteric or exclusive gatherings of a closed society."[611] We have already noted the suggestion by Chrys Caragounis that the verb εἰσέλθῃ (*eiselthē*, "enters") in 1 Cor 14:24 implies that the congregation met not in a private house but in a public venue, perhaps in a rented basilica.[612] Even though this suggestion is hypothetical, it cannot be completely excluded: when the followers of Jesus met, they did not say or do anything that outsiders could not hear or see.

Paul praises the missionary commitment of the church in Thessalonike, which he had founded only a few months earlier:

1 Thess 1:8: "For the word of the Lord has sounded forth from you [ἀφ᾽ ὑμῶν γὰρ ἐξήχηται ὁ λόγος τοῦ κυρίου] not only in Macedonia and Achaia, but in every place your faith in God has become known, so that we have no need to speak about it."

The verb ἐξήχηται (*exēchētai*) describes not merely the news of conversions in the city of Thessalonike that other Christians have heard, but the "sound" of their evangelistic proclamation of the gospel, the "word of the Lord," which is underscored by the anteposition of *aph᾽ hymōn* ("from you"). Paul hardly describes the news about the conversion of people as the content of the "word of

---

[611]Schrage, *1 Kor,* 3:411. Note the discussion on public worship as "mission-commitment" in Dickson 2003, 293-308.

[612]Caragounis 1998, 258-59 with n. 61-62.

the Lord."[613] Abraham Malherbe comments, "Paul sketches a picture of active preaching by the Thessalonians in Macedonia and Achaia and beyond."[614]

Paul thanks the church members in Philippi for their "fellowship in the gospel" (κοινωνία εἰς τὸ εὐαγγέλιον, *koinōnia eis to euangelion* [Phil 1:5]). The phrase *eis to euangelion* describes "an active participation of the congregation, their involvement in the gospel, their cooperation in the preaching of the gospel" in the sense of "a direct participation in preaching, a passing on of the gospel that they had accepted" besides the financial support (Phil 4:15-16) and the prayers (Phil 1:19) of the Philippian Christians.[615] Since Paul refers in Phil 1:12 to the "progress of the gospel" (προκοπὴ τοῦ εὐαγγελίου, *prokopē tou euangeliou*), the "fellowship of the gospel" is centrally connected with this "progress": the believers in Philippi contribute to the "progress of the gospel" through their financial support of the apostle and through their own missionary activity in Philippi. Paul mentions the following situations of this "progress": the gospel became known "throughout the whole imperial guard [praetorium] and to everyone else" as a result of his imprisonment (Phil 1:13); most of the believers in Rome became "confident in the Lord" and thus dared "to speak the word with greater boldness and without fear" (Phil 1:14); although some believers proclaim the gospel out of problematic motives, Paul nevertheless rejoices that "Christ is proclaimed in every way" (Phil 1:18); if the upcoming trial has a positive outcome and he is released, he rejoices because he can continue to engage in "fruitful labor" (Phil 1:22), doing missionary work and leading people to faith in Jesus Christ.[616]

Paul writes in Phil 1:6 of the "good work" (ἔργον ἀγαθόν, *ergon agathon*) that God has begun among the Philippians, a work that he will bring to completion, describing their "fellowship in the gospel" as God's own work.[617] If the term *ergon* refers to the faith and salvation of the Philippians believers that become visible in their missionary involvement (among other areas), then Paul asserts that the proclamation of the gospel to unbelievers is a natural consequence of the salvation that Jesus Christ granted and that is experienced and realized in the church. Paul compares the believers in Philippi, who are living in "the midst of a crooked and perverse generation," to lights that "shine like stars in the world."

Phil 2:14-17: "Do all things without murmuring and arguing, [15]so that you may be blameless and innocent, children of God without blemish in the midst of a crooked and perverse generation, in which you shine like stars in the world [ὡς φωστῆρες ἐν κόσμῳ, *hōs phōstēres en kosmō*]. [16]It is by your holding fast [ἐπέχοντες, *epechontes*] to the word of life

---

[613]Correctly Ware 1992; 1996, 327-28; Marshall 2000a, 259; Plummer (2001, 88-92), who argues against Bowers 1976, 112-14; 1991, 98-99.

[614]Malherbe, *Thess,* 117, with reference to Henneken 1969, 62-63.

[615]Gnilka, *Phil,* 45; cf. O'Brien, *Phil,* 62-63; Fee, *Phil,* 82-84; also Peterman 1997, 101.

[616]See O'Brien, *Phil,* 125; also Plummer 2001, 105-11.

[617]Gnilka, *Phil,* 46; cf. O'Brien, *Phil,* 64; Fee, *Phil,* 87.

that I can boast on the day of Christ that I did not run in vain or labor in vain. [17]But even if I am being poured out as a libation over the sacrifice and the offering of your faith, I am glad and rejoice with all of you."

The following considerations show that Paul refers not only to the perseverance of Christians in an evil world but also to the task of evangelism.[618] (1) The word order: the expression "in the world" is followed by the phrase "holding fast to the word of life." (2) The description of the gospel as the "word of life," an expression that Paul uses only here, reminds the believers in Philippi in the context of Phil 2:15 that the people who live in the world are "dead" and live in darkness and need to receive the "life" of the gospel. (3) The context of Dan 12:1-4 that the phrase "stars in the world" alludes to, particularly Dan 12:3: "Those who are wise shall shine like the brightness of the sky, and those who lead many to righteousness, like the stars forever and ever." (4) The verb ἐπέ-χειν (*epechein*) generally is used in the sense of "hold fast,"[619] but in classical texts it often means "present, offer,"[620] a meaning that can be assumed for Phil 2:16.[621] Gordon Fee comments, "By their attitudes and behavior they are to be clearly distinguishable from, and in opposition to, the world around them, while they are also to be God's messengers, bringing the word of life to the dying."

The fact that Paul mentions the evangelistic activity of believers in Rome (assuming a Roman imprisonment of Paul) in Phil 1:14 in passing indicates that it was a given for Paul that individual Christians preached the gospel in their city.[622]

In 1 Cor 10:31—11:1 Paul describes himself as an example for the Corinthian Christians. In this context it is important to note that Paul subordinates his behavior, which always intends to serve the glory of God and to avoid being an unnecessary stumbling block, to missionary purposes, both in the church and among unbelieving Jews and Gentiles:[623]

1 Cor 10:31—11:1: "So, whether you eat or drink, or whatever you do, do everything for the glory of God. [32]Give no offense to Jews or to Greeks or to the church of God, [33]just as I try to please everyone in everything I do, not seeking my own advantage [σύμφορον, *symphoron*], but that of many, so that they may be saved [ἵνα σωθῶσιν, *hina sōthōsin*]. [11:1]Be imitators of me, as I am of Christ [μιμηταί μου γίνεσθε καθὼς κἀγὼ Χριστοῦ, *mimētai mou ginesthe kathōs kagō Christou*]."

---

[618]Fee, *Phil*, 247; for the quotation that follows above see ibid. See also Marshall 2000a, 259-60; Dickson 2003, 133-52; differently O'Brien, *Phil*, 296-98.

[619]See BDAG 362, s.v. "ἐπέχω 1"; Gnilka, *Phil*, 153; O'Brien, *Phil*, 297.

[620]LSJ 619, "ἐπέχω II": "hold out to, present, offer"; "ἐπέχω III": "hold or direct towards, aim at."

[621]See Ware 1996, 289-303; cf. Lohmeyer, *Phil*, 109-10; Marshall 2000a, 259; Plummer 2001, 108-9 with n. 8 (citing additional literature).

[622]See O'Brien 1995, 115.

[623]Schrage (*1 Kor*, 2:476), who, however, relates the imitation of 1 Cor 11:1 to the "praxis of love" of the apostle. See also Dickson 2003, 226-61, on "mission-commitment as social integration" in 1 Cor 5:9-10; 10:31—11:1.

The "example" that Paul implies in 1 Cor 11:1 has a missionary intention: the work of Jesus Christ procured life for others as he willingly accepted humiliation and death (cf. Phil 2:6-11); therefore, Paul works so that Jews and Gentiles will be saved, and the believers in Corinth should work in the same manner.[624]

The "messengers" whom the churches send out (2 Cor 8:23; Phil 2:25) represent the missionary responsibility of the Pauline churches. Paul writes the following with regard to Epaphroditus, whom the church in Philippi sent to Rome to support Paul, and whom he sends back to Philippi:

Phil 2:25, 29-30: "Still, I think it necessary to send to you Epaphroditus—my brother and co-worker and fellow soldier, your messenger [*apostolos*] and minister [*leitourgos*] to my need. . . . [29]Welcome him then in the Lord with all joy . . . [30]because he came close to death for the work of Christ, risking his life to make up for those services [*leitourgia*] that you could not give me." (TEV v. 30: "because he risked his life and nearly died for the sake of the word of Christ, in order to give me the help that you yourselves could not give.")

The church in Philippi was unable to serve Paul directly because he was imprisoned in Rome. The term *leitourgia,* to be interpreted here independently of the cultic meaning that it has in the Septuagint ("service of God in the temple"), describes the "service," the help and support, that the church extended to the apostle through their messenger. Paul thinks particularly of the financial gift that Epaphroditus brought to Rome.[625]

Gerald Peterman studied Phil 4:10-20 in the context of Greco-Roman conventions in the context of "gift-exchange." He shows that Paul did not become obligated to the Philippian Christians in terms of social conventions because he accepted their money and their envoy. On the contrary, because he accepted their gift, they became partners in the gospel— it was not only the apostle who profited (Phil 4:18), for they too realized a profit (Phil 4:17). The investment of their gift yields spiritual dividends for them, as it is God himself who will reward them (Phil 4:19).[626]

Since Paul does not sit idly in prison awaiting his trial but is actively preaching and teaching the gospel (Acts 28:30-31), the Philippian church supports him not only by providing food during his imprisonment—prisoners in Roman jails had to be brought food by relatives or friends[627]—but also by assisting him in his missionary work.

In the list of ministerial roles in Eph 4:11 Paul mentions "evangelists"

---

[624]O'Brien 1995, 103; Marshall 2000a, 260; Plummer 2001, 123-33; Thiselton, *1 Cor,* 797.
[625]O'Brien, *Phil,* 344; Fee, *Phil,* 283-84; Peterman 1997, 119. Differently H. Balz (*EWNT* 2:860 [*EDNT* 2:348]), who interprets it in terms of the "true Christian service." Gnilka (*Phil,* 164) interprets it, less plausibly, in terms of attitude and personal commitment.
[626]Peterman 1997, esp. 121-61; summary, 157-59.
[627]See Rapske 1994, 209-16.

(εὐαγγελισταί, *euangelistai* [see §19.1]) after apostles and prophets and before pastors and teachers as leaders in the church. Georg Strecker believes that the lower position of the evangelists in the list means that they are not primarily missionaries but rather are believers who serve church through the preaching of the gospel.[628] However, if this proclamation of the gospel takes place before unbelievers—for example, in the villages that belong to the territory of a city or in neighboring cities—then these evangelists would establish communities of believers. It therefore is not easy to distinguish them consistently from missionaries. The *charismata* that the Holy Spirit gives to the church for "building up the body of Christ" (Eph 4:12) include the charisma of evangelistic service. The orientation of this charisma toward the nurture of the church does not diminish the primary meaning of the word: evangelists, particularly if they are not at the same time pastors and teachers, *also* proclaim the gospel of Jesus Christ, and they do so perhaps primarily before people who have not yet heard the gospel or who have not yet come to faith in Jesus Christ.[629]

In Eph 6:10-20 Paul describes the existence of the believer as a battle against the powers of evil. He specifies two reactions to the attacks of Satan, who attempts, together with the cosmic powers and spiritual forces under his control, to harm believers. (1) Believers must resist temptation, which they can do because they are protected by the armor of God (Eph 6:10-11). (2) Believers should preach the gospel.

Eph 6:10-20: "Finally, be strong in the Lord and in the strength of his power. [11]Put on the whole armor of God, so that you may be able to stand against the wiles of the devil. [12]For our struggle is not against enemies of blood and flesh, but against the rulers, against the authorities, against the cosmic powers of this present darkness, against the spiritual forces of evil in the heavenly places. [13]Therefore take up the whole armor of God, so that you may be able to withstand on that evil day, and having done everything, to stand firm. [14]Stand therefore, and fasten the belt of truth around your waist, and put on the breastplate of righteousness. [15]As shoes for your feet put on whatever will make you ready to proclaim the gospel of peace [ὑποδησάμενοι τοὺς πόδας ἐν ἑτοιμασίᾳ τοῦ εὐαγγελίου τῆς εἰρήνης, *hypodēsamenoi tous podas en hetoimasia tou euangeliou tēs eirēnēs*]. [16]With all of these, [or: 'in all circumstances'] take the shield of faith, with which you will be able to quench all the flaming arrows of the evil one. [17]Take the helmet of salvation, and the sword of the Spirit, which is the word of God [τὴν μάχαιραν τοῦ πνεύματος, ὅ ἐστιν ῥῆμα θεοῦ, *tēn machairan tou pneumatos ho estin rhēma theou*]. [18]Pray in the Spirit at all times in every prayer and supplication. To that end keep alert and always persevere in supplication for all the saints. [19]Pray also for me, so that when I speak, a message may be given to me to make known with boldness the mystery of the gospel, [20]for which I am an ambassador in chains. Pray that I may declare it boldly, as I must speak."

The identification of footwear with being "ready to proclaim the gospel of

---

[628]G. Strecker, *EWNT* 2:176 (*EDNT* 2:70).
[629]See Marshall (2000a, 261), who argues against Bowers 1991, 96.

peace" (Eph 6:15) refers to the proclamation of the gospel. The term *hetoimasia,* used only here in the New Testament, refers not to "firmness" of the footwear that guarantees the stability of the soldier in battle[630] but to "readiness" in the common meaning of the word. Paul asserts that believers who are equipped with God's armor can be certain that they are prepared for all eventualities. The connection with the feet refers to active readiness. The genitive construction *hetoimasia tou euangeliou* is best interpreted in terms of an objective genitive: Paul speaks of "the readiness or preparation of the outward-going movement required for the proclamation of the good news of peace."[631]

Four arguments support this interpretation. (1) The term *hetoimasia* signals an attitude of being ready for action, and the term *euangelion* is used by Paul often as a *nomen actionis* referring to the proclamation of the gospel. (2) The context of Is 52:7 that Paul alludes to supports this interpretation: "How beautiful upon the mountains are the feet of the messenger who announces peace, who brings good news, who announces salvation, who says to Zion, 'Your God reigns.'" (3) The allusion to Is 52:7 in Eph 2:17 is linked with the proclamation of the gospel by Jesus Christ, who proclaims peace to Jews and Greeks as a result of his salvific death on the cross. (4) The parallel passage Col 4:6 encourages the Colossian believers to make sure that their conversations with outsiders are "seasoned with salt."

Joachim Gnilka interprets the phrase as "active readiness to be engaged in the cause of the gospel" but goes on to assert that "the perspective of the letter does not introduce the missionary-expansive aspect of the gospel, which is why it cannot be discovered in this passage."[632] This view results less from exegesis than from the assumption of a late date for the allegedly pseudonymous Epistle to the Colossians in the second or third generation of Christians, around A.D. 90. The collocation of feet, readiness and gospel clearly implies the active proclamation of the gospel.

The one reference to a weapon for battle shows that the struggle of the Christian believer is not merely defensive but offensive as well: the "sword of the Spirit" (*machaira tou pneumatos*) is identified with the "word of God" (*rhēma theou*) (Eph 6:17). The sharp, short sword (*machaira*) was the most important weapon for close-range combat. A "defensive" interpretation[633] does not make sense: the short sword was an offensive weapon. The apostle does not want to "immunize" the Christians against the influences of pagan society, nor does he call them "to a decisive realization of Christian existence."[634] Paul describes in Eph 6:15, 17 the primary offensive action of Christians in the fight against the attacks of Satan: the active proclamation of the good news of Jesus' death on the cross, by which

---

[630]Thus Best, *Eph,* 599-600.

[631]Best, *Eph,* 599 (an interpretation that he rejects); O'Brien, *Eph,* 476-77; for the arguments that follow above see ibid. *NSS* (2:168) interprets it in terms of a genitive of purpose, suggesting the same meaning: "zum/für das Evangelium (näml. es zu verbreiten)."

[632]Gnilka, *Eph,* 311, 312; similarly Schnackenburg, *Eph,* 284; Roels 1962, 217-18.

[633]Note Best, *Eph,* 603: "ῥῆμα θεοῦ . . . must be a word which protects the user from destruction by the powers."

[634]Schnackenburg, *Eph,* 276.

he defeated all evil powers, and of his resurrection to life. This message is made effective and powerful by God's Spirit.[635] The word of God is wielded by the Holy Spirit as "sword"; it is the proclamation of the gospel in a world dominated by evil powers, so that people are liberated from Satan's control and find salvation. Paul challenges the Christians in the province of Asia to remain steadfast against temptations and at the same time to aggressively proclaim the gospel.

In 2 Tim 4:5 the apostle exhorts Timothy, who carries the responsibility for the churches in Ephesus and other cities in the province of Asia, to "do the work of an evangelist." In the context of 2 Tim 4 the "work" (*ergon*) of an evangelist is closely connected with teaching and with exercising leadership in the local congregation.[636] The leaders of the congregations are called to proclaim the gospel, evidently before people who have not yet heard the message of Jesus Christ; that is, they are encouraged to engage in missionary ministry. The congregations should not wait for traveling missionaries to pass through; rather, they should take it upon themselves to make sure that people hear the gospel. The believers who are responsible for "evangelizing" are, first of all, men who have preaching and teaching responsibilities in the church, and surely women, such as Priscilla, who can explain the gospel and the Scriptures. Alastair Campbell closes his study on "evangelist" in the New Testament with three conclusions: "There was never an office of [evangelist], but there were of course many who spread the gospel and founded churches. . . . Evangelism was never a specialist ministry of people called evangelists. There were of course people who showed themselves called to particular ministries of evangelism and who were recognized by others as gifted in a special way. . . . The work of an evangelist was inseparable from explaining the scripture, that is, from the work of a teacher."[637]

Conduct in the Family

A Christian who is married to an unbelieving spouse faces a missionary situation, albeit one that is open, as Paul states: "Wife, for all you know, you might save your husband. Husband, for all you know, you might save your wife" (1 Cor 7:16). Joachim Jeremias argues on the basis of linguistic parallels that the repeated phrase τί οἶδας (*ti oidas*) should be translated as "perhaps," which means that the phrase is not an expression of resignation but rather formulates the missionary confidence of the apostle, who asserts that "perhaps you can save" your husband or wife.[638] Wolfgang Schrage comments, "Even though the linguistic parallels may

---

[635]See O'Brien, *Eph*, 481-82; Lincoln, *Eph*, 451; Fee 1994, 728-29; O'Brien 1995, 124-25; Plummer 2001, 112-17.
[636]Marshall, *PastEp*, 804; A. Campbell 1992, 127-28.
[637]A. Campbell 1992, 173.
[638]Jeremias 1954, esp. 297.

not necessarily demand an interpretation in the sense of a more optimistic 'perhaps,' an expression of resignation contradicts the missionary confidence of the apostle. . . . The institutions and structures of the world are not meant to cultivate the inner life and the peace of mind of the Christians, but they serve as moments of truth and missionary obligation of the Christians."[639]

The instructions for men and women in 1 Tim 2:8-15 perhaps should be interpreted in a missionary context as well. Paul directs the women in the churches to live their lives as believers who are saved and want to stay saved in such a manner that they bear children and "continue in faith and love and holiness, with modesty" (1 Tim 2:15). The link between the salvation of the women in the church and childbearing has prompted widely differing explanations. A connection with missionary commitment is suggested by Royce Gruenler, who links the exhortation in 1 Tim 2:15 with the reference to Eve in 1 Tim 2:13-14: Eve's sin consisted not only in her disobedience to God's commandment but also in her abandonment of "being one flesh" with Adam when she acted independently of her husband. For Eve, repentance *also* meant returning to her husband and bearing children who would constitute generations of blessing until the arrival of the one who would crush the head of the serpent once and for all, as God had promised. Married Christian women are exhorted, in correspondence to Eve's behavior, to behave as married women and to bear children—descendants who can continue the line of blessing. In this sense married Christians who bring new life into the world are important "evangelists" and "missionaries."[640]

The exhortation to the "older women" in Tit 2:3-5 may be motivated by missionary concerns as well: the are called "to be reverent in behavior, not to be slanderers or slaves to drink; they are to teach what is good, so that they may encourage the young women to love their husbands, to love their children, to be self-controlled, chaste, good managers of the household, kind, being submissive to their husbands, so that the word of God may not be discredited." Their behavior should not discredit, but rather promote, the evangelistic efforts of the church.[641]

The exhortation to Christian slaves has a missionary component as well. They are called "to be submissive to their masters and to give satisfaction in every respect; they are not to talk back, not to pilfer, but to show complete and perfect fidelity, so that in everything they may be an ornament to the doctrine of God our Savior" (Tit 2:9-10). Slaves who have become believers and therefore "free" in Jesus Christ are exhorted, as are all Christians, to put

---

[639]Schrage, *1 Kor,* 2:112.
[640]See Gruenler 1998, 216-18.
[641]Padgett 1987, 40-51; Towner 1989, 195-96; Marshall, *PastEp,* 250, with reference to Is 52:5; Ezek 36:20-36. Keener (1992) does not discuss a missionary dimension of the text.

into practice the reality of the gospel in everyday life (cf. Rom 12:1-2),[642] and to be aware of the fact that the credibility of the gospel preached in connection with the missionary activities of the local church would be discredited if they display a rebellious attitude.[643] As William Mounce remarks, "The slaves' motivation is to make the gospel as attractive as possible for those around them."

Conduct in Worship Services

Paul admonishes the Christians in Corinth to make sure that their meetings are characterized by clear, intelligible teaching empowered by God's Spirit[644] that makes sense to visitors, so that these unbelievers are able to feel the effect of the message on their conscience and recognize the presence of God.

1 Cor 14:14-15: "For if I pray in a tongue, my spirit prays but my mind is unproductive. [15]What should I do then? I will pray with the spirit, but I will pray with the mind also; I will sing praise with the spirit, but I will sing praise with the mind also."

The related text Zech 8:23 contains a missionary component as well: "Thus says the LORD of hosts: In those days ten men from nations of every language shall take hold of a Jew, grasping his garment and saying, 'Let us go with you, for we have heard that God is with you.'"

The meetings of the congregations therefore are opportunities for missionary witness. These opportunities do not happen incidentally or automatically: Christians must grasp these situations consciously as a task that influences their behavior in the meetings of the congregation.

In 1 Thess 3:12 Paul prays that the love of the believers in Thessalonike "for one another and for all" might increase. He reminds them that they should not allow the new community and fellowship that they enjoy as new converts to be hardened into a "closed group" that insulates itself against society in such a way "that acts of love no longer emanate from it so that other can experience the message of Christ as salvation."[645]

Paul directs Timothy to make sure that the behavior of the believers in the congregations is conducive to the spread of the gospel. The myths and endless genealogies upon which some Christians concentrate when they interpret the Scriptures (1 Tim 1:8-9) only provoke useless speculations. Christians should be concerned with matters that are profitable for "divine training" (NRSV) or for "advancing God's work" (TNIV) (οἰκονομία θεοῦ, *oikonomia theou*

---

[642]Marshall, *PastEp*, 261.

[643]Towner 1989, 196; Plummer 2001, 142-45; Mounce, *PastEp*, 416; the quotation that follows above, ibid.

[644]Stuhlmacher 1981, 125. On 1 Cor 14:24-25 see also Rebell 1988.

[645]Holtz, *1 Thess*, 144.

[1 Tim 1:4]),[646] which includes the sound teaching of God's plan of salva-tion,[647] as is indicated by the phrase *oikonomia theou*.[648] In 1 Tim 1:5 Paul for-mulates the "aim of such instruction," which is "love that comes from a pure heart, a good conscience, and sincere faith." In the context of the myths and the meaningless talk (1 Tim 1:4, 6) the term "love" (ἀγαπή, *agapē*) is related primarily to the congregation and to fellow believers:[649] Timothy is directed to instruct the teachers and preachers in the churches to make sure that their ministry promotes the loving commitment of believers to one another. In 1 Tim 1:11 Paul emphasizes that the gospel that God has revealed is the stan-dard for his own interpretation and proclamation of the law, the gospel that has been entrusted to him at his conversion, which he describes in the next section (1 Tim 1:12-16). Paul, faithful to the task that God has given him, has endeavored to preserve the content of the gospel against false teaching and an erroneous "spinning" of the law. Paul's reference to his responsibilities in connection with the gospel can hardly be separated from his calling to pro-claim the gospel to unbelievers.[650]

Paul always understood himself as a missionary, also during times of a pro-longed preaching and teaching ministry in a local church, and Timothy had been his coworker on his missionary team for many years. When Paul, in a long section, reminds Timothy of his conversion and his call to "ministry" (διακονία, *diakonia* [1 Tim 1:12]), it seems impossible to eliminate the apostle's fundamental self-understanding as a missionary. We should also note that he refers in 1 Tim 1:15 to the coming of Jesus Christ into the world "to save sinners," and that he speaks of his conversion in 1 Tim 1:16 as a model for others. Surely it is one-sided to describe 1 Tim 1:11-17 as a "missions statement" and to interpret the Pastoral Epistles as a whole in a missionary perspective in terms of a "missionary mandate of the church" that is the consequence of Jesus' mission into the world and that becomes visible in the lifestyle of Christians.[651] Nevertheless, it remains true that a church that avoids useless debates and erroneous interpretations of Scripture and that lives in accordance with Jesus' sending into the world will be involved in missionary ministries.

This concern is evident in the exhortation in 1 Tim 2:1-4 to pray for all peo-ple, including "kings and all who are in high positions" who exercise authority and whose task it is to maintain and safeguard a stable society. The motivation

---

[646]Roloff, *1 Tim*, 66; following Spicq, *ÉpPast*, 323-24; Schlatter, *Die Kirche der Griechen*, 37-38; see more recently Marshall, *PastEp*, 367-68.

[647]See Knight, *PastEp*, 75-76; Marshall, *PastEp*, 367.

[648]See Dibelius and Conzelmann, *Pastoralbriefe*, 15; Merkel, *Pastoralbriefe*, 19; also LÜ; EÜ; GN; NASB: "administration of God."

[649]See Marshall, *PastEp*, 369.

[650]See Lips 1979, 42; differently Marshall, *PastEp*, 384.

[651]Gruenler 1998, 216, 224-25.

of these prayers is the goal that the spiritual life of believers and their witness of "God our Savior" will thrive, for God "desires everyone to be saved and to come to the knowledge of the truth."[652] The believers in the province of Asia know, of course, that for people to be saved there must be missionary preaching and teaching.

The final qualification for a church overseer mentioned by Paul in 1 Tim 3:7 can be seen in a missionary context as well: "He must also have a good reputation [μαρτυρία, *martyria*] with outsiders, so that he will not fall into disgrace and into the devil's trap" (TNIV). The substantiation of this criterion is formulated from a "defensive" perspective: slander and actual moral improprieties and failures damage the reputation and destroy the credibility of an overseer. However, this criterion is connected with the apostle's interest throughout 1 Timothy in the role of the church in God's plan of salvation "for all people" (1 Tim 2:1-6; 4:9-10) and thus is linked with the effectiveness of the mission of congregations.[653] The "good reputation" (*martyria*) of the overseers determines the witness (*martyria*) of the church: both the overseers and the congregation are committed to the obligation "to let God's universal salvific will become visible in an unfeigned manner."

Conduct in Pagan Society

For Paul, the behavior of believers in everyday life has a missionary component. As Traugott Holtz comments, "What happens in the church is not a matter of indifference that does not concern anyone. The church promotes or hinders by its existence and life the course of the gospel and the destiny of other churches. . . . A successful church is a mighty missionary power."[654] Paul implies this truth in several passages.

2 Cor 3:3: "You show that you are a letter of Christ, prepared by us, written not with ink but with the Spirit of the living God, not on tablets of stone but on tablets of human hearts."

Phil 2:14-15: "Do all things without murmuring and arguing, [15]so that you may be blameless and innocent, children of God without blemish in the midst of a crooked and perverse generation, in which you shine like stars in the world."

1 Thess 1:8-9: "For the word of the Lord has sounded forth from you not only in Macedonia and Achaia, but in every place your faith in God has become known, so that we have no need to speak about it. [9]For the people of those regions report about us what kind of welcome we had among you, and how you turned to God from idols, to serve a living and true God."

---

[652]See Knight, *PastEp*, 116-17; Oberlinner, *1 Tim*, 68; Marshall, *PastEp*, 432; Mounce, *PastEp*, 82-83. Merkel (*Pastoralbriefe*, 24-25) misses this emphasis.

[653]Marshall, *PastEp*, 484; also Roloff, *1 Tim*, 162; the quotation that follows above, ibid.

[654]Holtz, *1 Thess*, 64; see generally Dickson 2003, 226-61.

In 1 Timothy the apostle calls Christians to lead a "quiet and peaceable life" and to be "good citizens," not with the goal of maintaining a quietistic life in a private corner of society, but with the intention of safeguarding continued missionary activity and effectiveness.

1 Tim 2:1-7: "First of all, then, I urge that supplications, prayers, intercessions, and thanksgivings be made for everyone, [2]for kings and all who are in high positions, so that we may lead a quiet and peaceable life in all godliness and dignity. [3]This is right and is acceptable in the sight of God our Savior, [4]who desires everyone to be saved and to come to the knowledge of the truth. [5]For there is one God; there is also one mediator between God and humankind, Christ Jesus, himself human, [6]who gave himself a ransom for all—this was attested at the right time. [7]For this I was appointed a herald and an apostle (I am telling the truth, I am not lying), a teacher of the Gentiles in faith and truth."

The goal of the prayers for the emperor and the magistrates of the cities in which the Christians live is not the emperor's health or the stability of the Roman Empire as such. Rather, Christians who pray for the authorities of state and city implore God "to let them create the necessary free space in which the expansion of the gospel is possible."[655]

It is somewhat surprising that there is no evidence in Paul's letters that prayer plays a direct role in the missionary endeavors of apostles, evangelists or other believers who seek to reach unbelievers with the gospel. Paul's intercession for unbelieving Jews (Rom 10:1) is the only exception.[656] However, we should note that Paul mentions in his prayers of thanksgiving the missionary activity of the congregation (Rom 1:8; Phil 1:3-5; 1 Thess 1:2-8), he asks churches to pray for his missionary initiatives (Eph 6:19-20; Col 4:2-4; 2 Thess 3:1-2), and he prays that God may make the believers "increase and abound in love for one another and for all," which surely includes unbelievers who attend their meetings (1 Thess 3:12).[657] These passages demonstrate that the issue of successful missionary work indeed played a role in the prayers of the apostle and of the churches.[658]

Willingness to Suffer

For Paul, the willingness to endure opposition and persecution is tantamount to participation in the battle for the gospel. Peter Stuhlmacher observes, "There is a clear correspondence between the missionary gospel of the crucified Christ, the existence and the suffering of Paul as a witness, and the life of the Pauline churches."[659] Traugott Holtz writes in the context of his interpretation of 1 Thess 1:2-10, "According to Paul, suffering is an integral part

---

[655]Lampe and Luz 1987, 213 (who assume pseudonymous authorship).
[656]Carson 2000, esp. 176. On the subject "prayer and missions" see also Howell 1998a, 87-91.
[657]See Malherbe, *Thess,* 213.
[658]See Carson 2000; Plummer 2001, 160-65.
[659]Stuhlmacher 1981, 126.

of the life of the church and its members; indeed its essence is linked with joy. This is the challenge for the church today. We need to rethink, in the light of this text, the aspirations of the modern church and its ministers to conform to the world and to quickly and loudly complain if its word is rejected or attacked."[660] Another important text in this regard is Phil 1:27-30.

Phil 1:27-30: "Only, live your life in a manner worthy of the gospel of Christ, so that, whether I come and see you or am absent and hear about you, I will know that you are standing firm in one spirit, striving side by side with one mind for the faith of the gospel, [28]and are in no way intimidated by your opponents. For them this is evidence of their destruction, but of your salvation. And this is God's doing. [29]For he has graciously granted you the privilege not only of believing in Christ, but of suffering for him as well—[30]since you are having the same struggle that you saw I had and now hear that I still have."

Paul again connects "striving for the gospel"—that is, involvement of the believers in Philippi for the expansive growth of the church—with opposition from non-Christians and with "struggle" (*synathlein, agōn* [Phil 1:27, 30]) and "suffering" (*paschein* [Phil 1:29]).[661] The word group *agōn/agōnizomai* describes in Paul's letters[662] tireless work and committed involvement for the expansion of the gospel and the strengthening of the faith of the Christians—work that is as intensive and intentional as a wrestling match. The conflicts and suffering that Paul mentions in this connection are linked not just with the personal suffering of the apostle on account of the weakness of believers and churches. They also are linked in a more comprehensive context with the missionary proclamation of the gospel. The church, at least in Philippi, is involved in this struggle and in the conflicts and sufferings that missionary work entails.

Eschatological Responsibility

The missionary commitment of the church is linked with an eschatological responsibility (1 Cor 3:8, 13-15; cf. Rom 14:7-12). The same applies to the participation of the local congregations in the missionary work of the apostle. In Eph 3:10 Paul refers to a "mission" of the church before the invisible world.

Eph 3:8-10: "Although I am the very least of all the saints, this grace was given to me to bring to the Gentiles the news of the boundless riches of Christ, [9]and to make everyone see what is the plan of the mystery hidden for ages in God who created all things; [10]so that through the church the wisdom of God in its rich variety might now be made known [γνωρισθῇ, *gnōristhē*] to the rulers and authorities in the heavenly places."

The powers that Jewish teachers as mediators of divine wisdom propagate in the churches of Asia Minor (Col 2:8, 16-18, 20-23) are not a source of revelation;

---

[660]Holtz, *1 Thess,* 63; see also Plummer 2001, 172-98.
[661]O'Brien, *Phil,* 152, 161-62, with reference to Pfitzner 1967, 109-12, 126-29.
[662]Cf. 1 Cor 9:25; 1 Thess 2:2; Col 1:29; 2:1; 4:12; 1 Tim 4:10; 6:12; 2 Tim 4:7.

on the contrary, it is the church that renders witness to the abundance of God's wisdom before the powers. This witness before the invisible world consists primarily in the unity of the community of the followers of Jesus as his body, in which Jews and Gentiles live together, signaling the beginning of the universal reconciliation of all things (Eph 1:9-10).[663] The church of Jesus Christ, with its integration of former pagans (Eph 1:6), exposes the authorities and powers to the wisdom of God, who planned their submission: they lose their power over that part of humanity—the world of the Gentiles—which they thought they could rule without restraint.[664]

The Letter to the Romans as a Missionary Document

The fundamental missionary perspective of Paul's understanding of the nature of the church is underscored by the fact that he writes to the Christian community in Rome, a church that he had neither established nor visited, on the occasion of his plans for a new missionary initiative to Spain.[665] Paul had not been involved in the origins of the church in the city of Rome, but he wants to recruit the believers in Rome to support him in the new missionary work in Spain. His "horizon" is not described and limited by "his" churches that he had founded: there is no "church of Paul," which explains why the apostle is "not concerned about *his* relationships and connections. His proximity to the Christians in Rome . . . is fundamentally established by the fact that the *one* Lord has 'called' both Paul and the Christians in Rome (Rom 1:1, 7)." This calling includes a missionary commitment: Paul does not have to tell the Roman Christians why a mission to Spain is an important initiative or why they should participate in this mission.

The Epistle to the Romans can be read as a "missionary document."[666] In the historical situation of the winter of A.D. 56/57 when Paul travels from Greece to Spain, where he wants to begin a new missionary initiative, with a detour to Jerusalem, he writes a long letter to the Christians in the city of Rome to recruit them to be a part of the team that will preach the gospel of Jesus Christ in the provinces of Spain.

Robert Jewett interprets the Epistle to the Romans as a "document of missionary diplomacy," with Paul writing to the house churches in the city of Rome in order to unite them and gain their cooperation for the upcoming mission to Spain; Paul expects the Roman Christians to support Phoebe, who has moved from Corinth to Rome as benefactor of the mission.[667] The focus of this analysis is one-sided, concentrating on one of many subjects

---

[663]See Turner 1995, 145-48.

[664]Schnackenburg, *Eph*, 142.

[665]Eichholz 1961, 16-18; for the comment and quotation that follow above see ibid., referring to Adolf Schlatter; see also Howell 1998b.

[666]For the survey that follows above see Schrenk 1954; see earlier Colenso 1861; more recently W. Campbell 1990.

[667]Jewett 1992; on Phoebe see idem, 1988.

that Paul discusses in the letter. There is insufficient evidence to warrant Jewett's conclusion that the Epistle to the Romans belongs to the genre of "documents of missionary diplomacy." In the following discussion, when I read the Epistle to the Romans as a "missionary document," that is not an appraisal of its genre; rather, I am focusing on Paul's theology, which he—the missionary to Jews and Gentiles alike—formulates here in a "systematic" manner not found anywhere else.

Charles van Engen argues that the Epistle to the Romans should be read as a document written by Paul as leader of a missionary team, and that he writes to a "mission church," a church that should be involved in missionary outreach just like all other churches.[668] This view, while attractive, cannot be substantiated from the text.

The following emphases of Paul's Epistle to the Romans are significant in terms of a "theology of missions" in connection with Paul's historical concern to prepare himself and the Roman Christians for missionary outreach in Spain.

1. Paul emphasizes the international and universal scope of his missionary ministry "from Jerusalem and as far around as Illyricum" (Rom 15:19) and to Spain (Rom 15:24a, 28). And he asserts that the responsibility of the Roman Christians has the same comprehensive scope: "For I do hope to see you on my journey and to be sent on by you, once I have enjoyed your company for a little while" (Rom 15:24b). The strategy of the early Christian mission focuses on the conversion of people no matter where they live or who they are—Paul reminds the Christians in the capital of the Roman Empire of this fact.

2. Missionary work and theological reflection about the gospel are mutually dependent. Gottlob Schrenk observes, "Centers of mission come into existence solely as a result of the fact that their members themselves fully carry out the message. This requires incisive, in-depth epistemological work."[669] Paul the missionary cannot be separated from Paul the theologian: Paul, the missionary who is on his way to a new missionary initiative in Spain, expects the Christians in the city of Rome to understand his longest and most intensively theological letter.

3. Paul writes in Rom 1—3 about the nature of sin and its consequences not merely for a fictitious Gentile or Jewish dialogue partner. He describes at the same time for the Roman Christians the foundations of their faith. Only Christians who look to their past with repentance and thereby are continuously liberated from their past are qualified coworkers among the people of the world, who still live in bondage.[670] The gospel demonstrates the "solidarity" of sinners, both Jews and pagans: in view of God's revelation in Jesus Christ, no one can escape God's judgment. A church that is active in mission and evangelism does not discharge itself from this solidarity. Missionary work presupposes that Christians remind themselves of the sin and bondage from which they have been liberated and redeemed.

---

[668]Engen 1993, 191-93.
[669]Schrenk 1954, 83.
[670]Schrenk 1954, 87.

4. The salvation-historical foundation of the gospel and of the mission of God's people has specific and practical consequences for the tactical procedures of missionary work: God addresses Jews first (Rom 1:16; 2:9-10; 9—11). The Gentile mission must never emancipate itself from missionary outreach among the Jews. Did Paul expect the Gentile Christians in the house churches in the city of Rome—probably the majority of the believers in the capital of the empire at the time of the composition of this letter—to bring the gospel of Jesus the Messiah to the Jews living in Rome? Many theologians answer this question in the negative, arguing, "after Auschwitz," that non-Jews have no business trying to convert Jews to the Christian faith. A positive answer seems to be more likely, however. We must remember Paul's motto for local congregations: "There is no longer Jew or Greek, there is no longer slave or free, there is no longer male and female; for all of you are one in Christ Jesus" (Gal 3:28). This motto is not merely a theological statement; it is the expression of a salvation-historical eschatological truth that has tangible consequences for the fellowship of the followers of Jesus: if Jews reach Gentiles with the gospel, there is no reason why a converted Gentile should not explain to a Jewish friend or neighbor his or her faith in Jesus as Israel's Messiah and the Savior of the world. Of course, Gentile Christians would have had no opportunities to proclaim the gospel in the synagogues. Nevertheless, there were other opportunities for contacts between Gentiles and Jews—opportunities in which the priority of the Jews as members of God's chosen people would have been an important conviction for the Gentile Christians as they sought to explain the gospel.

5. The missionary work of Paul and of the church is focused on the proclamation of God's salvation in Jesus, the crucified and risen Messiah (Rom 3:21-31). Sin can be forgiven only when God himself removes his wrath; guilt can be atoned for only when God himself procures and grants salvation. The message of God, the Creator and Judge who grants salvation to sinners, of Jesus the Messiah, who was sent into the world as a sin-offering and died on the cross in the place of sinners (Rom 8:3), is always a missionary message. The identity of the church that confesses Jesus as Kyrios consists in the reality of having received the gift of God's righteousness and of having become a part of the mission of the Son of God, who came into the world to save sinners. For this reason the church can be and should be a community that is involved in Jesus' mission.

6. Paul narrates the history of humankind from Adam (Rom 1:18-32; 5:12-21) and Abraham (Rom 4:1-25) to Jesus Christ, who has solved the problem of sin that dominated the world since Adam (Rom 5:1-21). God had chosen Abraham and his descendants, the people of Israel, to begin to solve the problem of sin in the world. Gentile Christians have become children of Abraham as a result of their faith in Jesus, the promised Savior (Rom 4:11), which means that they have been incorporated into the "world project" of salvation, whose immediate climax is the death and resurrection of Jesus Christ.

7. The missionary message is neither philosophy nor hermeneutical theory: it represents a reality that is connected with the praxis of everyday life and with the continuous task of dealing with persistent sin and temptation. The justification by faith in the crucified and risen Jesus Christ that Paul preaches and describes becomes a reality in the life of the believer who lives in the power of God's Spirit (Rom 6:1—8:39).

8. Missionary work always takes the specific situation of the audience into account. This is one of the reasons why Paul describes the "situation" of Israel (Rom 9:1—11:32). When missionaries offer salvation in their proclamation of the good news of Jesus the Messiah and Savior, Israel's unbelief becomes a problem: if God's people of the old covenant, the chosen descendants of Abraham, do no believe in Jesus the Messiah and Savior, then the missionary message of Jesus' followers is either wrong or weak, some might argue. Paul therefore provides theological, historical and practical insights into the condition of the Jews as seen from God's perspective.[671] Paul not only speaks of the goals of God's plan of salvation but also emphasizes the responsibility of the people who hear the gospel preached to them (Rom 10:14-15). And he underscores the responsibility of the (Gentile) Christian churches to provoke the Jews to jealousy, prompting them to come to faith in Jesus the Messiah as a result of the concrete realization of the messianic salvation that God has granted them in Jesus Christ and that receives visible form and shape through the work of God's Spirit (Rom 11:11-15).

9. The apostle and the church can be effective in mission and evangelism only when God's love is realized in their midst, and that means in the life of every believer (Rom 12:1—15:29). Paul does not formulate a Christian halakah that always and precisely knows beforehand how Christians must behave. Paul emphasizes and explains fundamental theological, christological and pneumatological realities. His emphasis on love (Rom 12:9-10), particularly the love of one's enemies (Rom 12:19-21), is not a coincidence: believers who are active in mission and evangelism often are attacked by "the evil one," as the Christians in Rome know all too well. As they "overcome evil with good" (Rom 12:21) as members of God's people who have experienced the salvation effected by Jesus Christ and who live by the power of the Holy Spirit, they can continue to be involved in the project of the eternal God "to bring about the obedience of faith" among the Gentiles (Rom 16:26).

---

[671]Schrenk 1954, 99.

29

SUMMARY

Paul, whose Jewish name was "Saul," came from a Jewish Diaspora family that lived in Tarsus in Cilicia. He had studied under the eminent rabbi Gamaliel in Jerusalem and had been involved in official proceedings against the followers of Jesus in A.D. 30/31. He came to faith in Jesus in A.D. 31/32 on the road to Damascus, accepting the conviction of Jesus' followers that Jesus of Nazareth was indeed the promised Messiah. This theological turn, prompted by God himself and by Jesus, who appeared to him as he traveled to Damascus to arrest Christians, caused a dramatic turn in the biography of Saul, the energetic rabbi from Jerusalem. Instead of continuing to study and teach the Scriptures in Jerusalem (and perhaps other cities, including Damascus), he understood himself to be called by the risen Lord to go to Jews and Gentiles and proclaim the message of salvation that was now available (only) in Jesus Christ. This divine commission meant that he would travel to cities outside of Jerusalem and Judea in order to preach and teach about Jesus, the Messiah and Savior.

Evidence in Paul's letters demonstrates that Paul started to fulfill this commission without delay: after his conversion sometime in A.D. 31/32, he preached the message of Jesus, the crucified, risen and exalted Messiah, in Damascus and soon in the cities of the Nabatean kingdom. We have no detailed information about Paul's missionary activities during this period, but the available evidence suggests that this first phase of Paul's missionary work was rather successful: the ethnarch of the Nabatean King Aretas IV wanted to arrest Paul, forcing him to leave Arabia and travel via Damascus to Jerusalem. An unsuccessful ministry would not have caused the kind of upheaval that prompted the Nabatean king to act. Paul's preaching the message of Jesus the Messiah in the synagogues of Jerusalem caused unrest again, with the result that the Christians in Jerusalem advised Paul to leave the city.

During the next ten years, perhaps from A.D. 33 to 42, Paul engaged in missionary work in Syria and Cilicia. Details for this second phase of his missionary activity are lacking as well. Several events that Paul mentions in 2 Corinthians seem to date to this period—for example, the synagogue punishment of the "forty minus one" lashes that he suffered five times, and several incidences of shipwreck that he survived (2 Cor 11:24-25). The visionary experience that Paul mentions in 2 Cor 12:2, which transported him to the "third heaven," must have taken place around A.D. 41, during this same period of time. We do not know in which cities of Syria and Cilicia Paul preached the gospel, nor do we know in which cities he was able to establish Christian communities. A good number of Syrian and Cilician cities were of regional and transregional importance, and many of them had a Jewish community—Paul easily could have reached two dozen cities in Syria and Cilicia with the gospel of Jesus Christ. Luke merely notes, in passing, that there were churches in Syria and Cilicia when the missionaries informed the Christians in these areas about the decisions of the apostolic council in A.D. 48 (Acts 15:41).

Barnabas from Cyprus, one of the leading teachers of the Jerusalem church who coordinated the missionary outreach and the consolidation of the church in Antioch, recruited Paul for the work in the capital of the province of Syria. Information about this third phase of Paul's missionary ministry during the years A.D. 42-44 is limited. Luke's comment in Acts 11:26 that Paul and Barnabas taught a large number of people suggests that many citizens of the Syrian metropolis were converted to faith in Jesus and joined the church.

Paul and Barnabas were commissioned in A.D. 45 by the church in Antioch to start a new missionary initiative on Cyprus, which led the missionaries eventually to southern Galatia. They established churches at least in the cities of Antiocheia, Iconium, Lystra and Derbe in the province of Galatia, and perhaps also in Salamis and Paphos on Cyprus and in Perge in Pamphylia. This fourth phase of Paul's missionary ministry is the first for which we possess more information, provided by Paul's Epistle to the Galatians and by Luke's account in the book of Acts.

Paul planned a new missionary initiative after the apostolic council in A.D. 48, aiming to reach the province of Asia in western Asia Minor, probably Ephesus, after visiting the churches in Syria, Cilicia and southern Galatia. Due to divine warnings, presumably connected with (unknown) external circumstances, this project could not be realized, nor could the mission to Bithynia in northern Asia Minor. After the arrival in Alexandria Troas at the western end of Asia Minor, the missionaries decided to cross the Aegean Sea and start missionary activities in Macedonia. Paul established churches in Philippi, Thessalonike and Beroea in the summer and fall of A.D. 49. During a visit by Paul to Athens, several Athenians were converted, including people of high social status, but there is no clear evidence that proves that Paul established a church in this renowned "university town." Beginning in February or March A.D. 50 Paul preached for nearly two years in Corinth in Achaia. Along with Luke's report in the book of Acts, Paul's letters to the Christians in Philippi, Thessalonike and Corinth provide information about this fifth phase of Paul's missionary ministry.

Paul worked as a missionary in Ephesus between A.D. 52 and 55, evidently with much success. At the same time he had to deal with a crisis in the church in Corinth involving theological, moral and ecclesiological problems during this period, which he did through letters, envoys and a short visit. Paul probably traveled to the province of Illyricum in the summer of A.D. 56, perhaps as preparation of the planned missionary outreach in Spain, which was a Latin-speaking province as well. After another visit to Corinth in the winter of A.D. 56/57, Paul traveled to Jerusalem with representatives of the young churches in Achaia, Macedonia, Asia and Galatia, taking a collection to the needy Christians in the Jewish capital that the churches had gathered. Paul's letters to the Corinthians and Luke's account in the book of Acts inform us about this sixth phase of Paul's missionary ministry. The Epistle to the Ephesians, evidently written to all the churches in the province of Asia, provides no information about the establishment of the church in Ephesus.

Paul was a prisoner of the Roman state in Caesarea (A.D. 57-59) and in Rome (A.D. 60-62), where very probably he was released. Early church traditions suggest that Paul traveled to Spain after his release from prison, preaching the gospel, perhaps in A.D. 63/64. Since Paul visited Crete around A.D. 64/65, according to comments in 1 Timothy and Titus, and since he was executed in Rome in A.D. 67 at the latest, the time he spent in Spain and on Crete cannot have been extensive. The information that Paul's letters to Timothy and Titus and the early patristic literature provide about this seventh and last phase of Paul's ministry is scant. We do not know whether or in which cities of Spain and Crete Paul preached or established churches.

Statistical information about the distances that Paul traveled is, of course, estimated, especially because we have no geographical information about the first twelve years of his missionary work in Arabia, Syria and Cilicia. A conservative estimate indicates that Paul traveled about 25,000 km (ca. 15,500 mi.) between his conversion in A.D. 31/32 and his execution in A.D. 67, including 14,000 km (ca. 8,700 mi.) on foot, a distance that required some 660 days of overland travel.

Paul and his message did not go undisputed, particularly his teaching that pagans receive forgiveness of sins and integration into the people of God by faith in Jesus Christ alone, without circumcision or the obligation to keep the food and purity laws. My analysis of the relevant texts in Paul's letters and in the book of Acts have shown that the differences that many scholars since F. C. Baur posit between Paul and Peter and between Paul and James are exaggerated. Paul avoided Jerusalem during the first few years immediately after his conversion. When he visited Jerusalem for the first time after his conversion, probably in A.D. 33/34, Barnabas introduced him to the other apostles who were present in the city; Luke reports that Paul "went in and out" among the leaders of the Jerusalem church (Acts 9:28a) and preached the gospel "boldly" (Acts

9:28b) in the synagogues of the city. Evidently Paul was not just a guest of the apostles: he participated in their missionary activities. Interrupting the work in Antioch in Syria for which Barnabas had recruited him, Paul visited Jerusalem in A.D. 44, just before embarking on his mission to Cyprus and Galatia, in order to take to the Christians in Jerusalem the famine-relief funds that the Christians in Antioch had organized (Acts 11:27-30). This visit corresponds with Paul's second visit to Jerusalem after his conversion, mentioned in Gal 2:1-10, during which he consulted with Peter about his missionary work and message (Gal 2:2). It appears that the subject of the circumcision of converted Gentiles was not a major issue at this encounter. This question became an issue after the conversion of Cornelius the Roman officer in A.D. 37, an issue that was settled in A.D. 48 during the apostolic council that "officially" discussed the modalities of the acceptance of Gentile Christians into the people of God. The question of the circumcision of converted Gentiles became contentious after numerous Pharisees and possibly some Essenes had come to faith in Jesus the Messiah who then tried to influence the church in this matter. Many scholars assume that Paul's consultation with Peter in A.D. 44 was the occasion on which the apostles divided the Roman world into areas of missionary responsibility. This is not the most plausible scenario. It appears that Paul wanted to consolidate the apostles' acknowledgment of the effectiveness of his missionary work among Gentiles, as Peter's work among Jews had been effective—missionary success always being dependent only on God (Gal 2:8). The decisions of the apostolic council in A.D. 48 were unanimously supported by Peter, James and Paul (Acts 15:1-29). Paul later asserted that he could live like a Jew among Jews (1 Cor 9:19-20); he rejected *porneia* (1 Cor 6:9) and advised the Gentile Christians in Corinth not to eat meat in the presence of Jewish Christians if it was known to have been offered to idols (1 Cor 10:25-28), and apparently he held a similar view about meat that contained blood (Rom 14:13-21). However, the apostolic council did not solve all the difficulties once and for all: the third faction, which Paul describes as "false brothers" who "slipped in" (Gal 2:4), consistently conservative Jewish Christians, continued to insist that converted Gentiles be circumcised and be made to keep at least the food and purity laws of the Torah. These teachers promulgated their position actively in the churches that had been established in the context of Paul's missionary work. Paul's Epistle to the Galatians is a direct result of their agitation.

In his missionary work Paul relied solely upon the power of Jesus Christ, who causes Jews and Gentiles to accept his message of Jesus the Messiah and Savior. People are converted and churches are planted solely by the *dynamis* of the gospel of Jesus Christ (1 Cor 3:5-7; Rom 1:16; 15:18). Missionary success depends not on people or programs, and not on rhetorical skills or refined methods, but rather on God's power and work alone. This is why missionaries, preachers and teachers are merely "servants" of God, and why the church is

"God's field, God's building" (1 Cor 3:9) and never the possession of a particular missionary, preacher or teacher. The content of missionary proclamation is the crucified and risen Jesus Christ, who thus is the ground and the measure of church planting and church growth (1 Cor 1:23; 2:2; 3:11; 15:2). Paul sees himself as a servant of God and of his word, of Jesus Christ and the gospel, and of the church (1 Cor 3:5; Col 1:23, 25). He has devoted his entire life to serve the Kyrios. Like other missionaries and preachers, he resembles a fragile clay jar: he is weak, unimpressive, insignificant (2 Cor 4:7), which proves that his missionary success and the growth experienced by the churches that he planted are solely the result of God's power, the effect of the truth of the gospel of Jesus Christ, the consequence of the work of the Holy Spirit (2 Cor 4:7-15; Col 1:24). Paul sees his missionary ministry as a proclamation of the victory of God, who had defeated him, the former persecutor of the people of God, leading him through the world in triumphal procession (2 Cor 2:14-16). As an apostle commissioned and sent by Jesus Christ, he preaches and teaches as a representative of the Messiah (2 Cor 5:20; 13:3; Rom 15:18). Paul sees himself called to work as a pioneer missionary who "plants" and who lays the foundation as a "skilled master builder"—establishing churches in cities in which no missionary had worked before, preaching and teaching the gospel of Jesus (1 Cor 3:6, 10; 9:10).

Because the pioneer missionary who "plants" and the preacher who "waters" are involved in one and the same task and are dependent upon one and the same Lord (1 Cor 3:8), Paul can work with other missionaries, preachers and teachers, some of whom he recruits in the new churches. The common loyalty to and dependence upon the one Lord establishes the unity of all ministries and ministers who serve the people of God. We know about forty coworkers of Paul by name, missionary preachers and teachers who proclaimed the gospel, baptized new converts, taught new believers, organized churches and traveled in order to maintain contact with other churches.

The metaphors of planting and building also show that missionary ministry is taxing work (see Col 1:29). Missionary work is not "fun." Paul does not spare himself. As a *doulos,* a "slave" of Jesus Christ, he has no right to spare himself or to take it easy.

The central process of missionary work is the oral proclamation of the good news of Jesus, the crucified and risen Messiah and Savior of the world (1 Cor 15:1-2, 11; Rom 10:14-17; 15:18; Col 1:28). Faith comes from preaching, from the message about Jesus Christ proclaimed to audiences.

The basic rule of missionary work is, for Paul, the consistent commitment to the listener, whom he takes very seriously. Jews need to be reached with the gospel as Jews, and likewise Gentiles as Gentiles. The one decisive factor is that people are won for faith in Jesus Christ (1 Cor 9:19). This basic rule controls Paul's behavior: he can live as a Jew among Jews, and he can live like a Gentile among Gentiles (1 Cor 9:20). Paul's behavior reflects his conviction that all people need to hear the gospel: the elites of the Greco-Roman world in the cities as well as uncultured barbarians, the educated and the ignorant (Rom 1:14). However, the behavior of Paul the missionary is controlled not by the circumstances in which he preaches and teaches but by the gospel and the necessity to proclaim it: he is willing to "become all things to all people" (1 Cor 9:22), with the integrity of the gospel as the controlling criterion for any accommodation (1 Cor 9:23). Paul is never content with existing missionary "successes," nor does he give up when only a few people are converted: he constantly strives to reach more people with the message of Jesus Christ (1 Cor 9:19; Rom 10:18), and he never gives up hope that more Gentiles, and more Jews (Rom 10:16), will come to faith in Jesus Christ.

Paul pursued an international missionary strategy: he sought to preach the gospel of Jesus Christ in provinces and regions, in cities and in towns in which no missionary had worked before. The question of whether Paul followed a comprehensive geographical strategy remains open. Paul's missionary work traced a semicircle in the eastern and northern parts of the Mediterranean region: he preached the gospel in Arabia, Syria and Cilicia east and northeast of Jerusalem, on Cyprus and in Galatia, Asia, Macedonia and Achaia north of Jerusalem, and in Rome and Spain northwest of Jerusalem. Suggestions that Paul's geographical movements stemmed from Old Testament passages or Jewish interpretation of the table of nations in Gen 10 remain hypothetical. There is no question, however, that Paul deliberately planned missionary initiatives, sometimes years ahead of their realization, but always remained open to divine guidance and the exigencies of historical circumstances: he prays, he acts as a result of dream-visions, and he realizes that not all plans can be carried out.

Paul generally arrived with several coworkers in a city (although we must recall that we have no information in this regard for the first ten years of his missionary activity). He established contacts in the Jewish community and the local synagogue who could provide hospitality and opportunities for work—at least when his companions were Jewish (Christians). The missionary initiative began with sermons, teaching sessions and lectures in the synagogue. This was not so much a particular "strategy" as it was a logical procedure—practical, and at the same time a reflection of his conviction that Jews have a salvation-historical priority over Gentiles. Paul was forced more often than not, and usually rather quickly, to relocate his activities outside the synagogue when synagogue officials or other members of the Jewish community refused to tolerate his activities any longer. The nascent community of believers in Jesus Christ met in rented lecture halls or in the private homes of wealthy citizens who showed an interest in the gospel or who had been converted to the Christian faith. Paul organized the communities of followers of Jesus Christ in house churches that met regularly to worship God, study the Scriptures, receive the teaching of the gospel, pray and provide mutual support.

My analysis of the content of Paul's missionary sermons has shown that the apostle adapted his terminology to the specific audiences and to the demands of specific situations. I described the pioneer preaching before Jews as "christological communication," illustrated by Paul's sermon in the synagogue in Pisidian Antiocheia (Acts 13:16-41): Paul presents the message of Jesus the Messiah in the context of a sermon that interprets the Scripture that has been read, arguing for Jesus' resurrection from the dead. Paul seeks to show that Jesus' resurrection is the basis for God's forgiveness of sins and for the justification of the individual sinner who believes in Jesus (Acts 13:38-39). The evidence in the book of Acts shows that Paul's missionary sermons in the synagogue focused on the story of Jesus, which coincides with Paul's emphasis that the proclamation of "Jesus crucified" is the missionary message pure and simple (1 Cor 1—2; 15:1-14; Rom 1:1-4).

The pioneer missionary preaching before Gentiles, which I described as "theological communication," can be illustrated by and reconstructed from Paul's summary in 1 Thess 1:9-10. The Gentiles appreciated Paul's message of a savior who liberates them from their sins, although it would have been easy for Gentiles to integrate this savior into the pluralistic diversity of the superabundant religious resources of the Greco-Roman world. Paul's message that it is exclusively faith in Jesus, a crucified Jew who was raised from the dead, that brings forgiveness of sin sounded nonsensical and needed explanation. Such an explanation required that Paul convince his Gentile listeners that there is only one true God, the God of the Jewish people: if there is only one true God, there is probably only one savior who forgives sins. To Gentile audiences Paul had to speak first of the God of Israel as the one true God before he could speak of Jesus Christ. The comment in Acts 17:18 that Paul preached in Athens both in the synagogue and in the agora "the good news of Jesus and of the resurrection" shows that Paul did not dispense with an explanation of the person, ministry, death and resurrection of Jesus to Gentile audiences.

The Areopagus speech (Acts 17:22-31) is not an example of a typical missionary sermon to Gentiles; rather, it is an example of the "dialogical concentration" of Paul's message (situational sermon). The council of the Areopagus wants to know whether Paul seeks to introduce alien gods—that is, deities that the Athenians did not yet worship and that therefore might need an altar or a sanctuary or a festival in the calendar of the city. Paul asserts, after a polite introduction, that he has no intention of introducing new gods to Athens but that he proclaims, essentially, the nature of the deity that the Athenians honored with the altar dedicated to the "unknown god." He explains that he is not a herald who seeks to obtain a piece of land for his God in order to build an altar or a sanctuary for cultic veneration, because his God does not live in temples that people have built. This means that he does not seek the introduction of a new deity into the pantheon of Athens, which would require a recommendation of the council and a favorable decision by the *dēmos* of the city. The God whom Paul proclaims is "not far from each one of us"—a truth found in the words of their poets—and therefore needs no formal introduction. Paul does not introduce a new god alongside the gods that the Athenians worship. He wants something else entirely: he wants to convince the Athenians, including the members of the council and the Epicurean and Stoic philosophers who are listening, to turn to the only true God and worship him alone, since this God has already fixed a day of judgment, determined the ground rules and the criteria for the judgment of the world, and appointed the judge. Interpreted against this background, Luke's account of Paul's speech before the council of the Areopagus is both plausible historically and intelligible in terms of missionary praxis. Paul's speech is characterized by elements of agreement and elements of contradiction: he uses phrases and formulations with which the Athenian cultural and political elite can identify. At the same time he never speaks of any deity other than the God of Israel, the Creator of the world and the Lord of history to whom all human beings are responsible: this God has appointed the one man who has been raised from the dead to decide in the end who has salvation and who does not.

Paul used certain terms and formulations in his missionary preaching, some of which were provocative for Jewish listeners and some of which were potentially dangerous in the context of Gentile audiences. I called this the dimension of "ideological confrontation." To Jewish audiences Paul argued that Jesus, who had been rejected by the Jewish leadership and was executed by Roman crucifixion, was the promised Messiah. To Gentile audiences Paul argued that Jesus is the Kyrios, the Lord of the world, who is in the process of establishing his kingdom. The emphasis that Jesus is the Messiah was potentially dangerous in a Gentile context as well, since Jewish expectations generally understood the coming Messiah in political terms as king and ruler. Thus the proclamation of Jesus as Messiah and Kyrios affected the claims of the emperors in Rome. There is no evidence that Paul proclaimed, with a deliberately provocative focus, the political implications of Jesus the Messiah, Savior and Kyrios in the cities of the *Imperium Romanum,* drawing out the consequences for the imperial family or for the senate or for emperor worship in the cities of the East. Nevertheless, he was unafraid to use formulations that could be misunderstood in ways that were potentially dangerous. Clearly, Paul was convinced that the gospel of Jesus Christ must be fully explained in terms of all relevant and significant details of the message of salvation, even though this might put his life in danger.

Paul preached and taught, explained and defended the gospel of Jesus Christ in continuous dialogue with the churches. I called this aspect of his missionary ministry "apologetic confrontation." This is abundantly illustrated in his letters to the churches in Galatia, Achaia, Macedonia and Asia that he established, and in his letters to the churches in Rome and in the province of Asia that other missionaries had founded. It generally was the confrontation with Jewish-Christian teachers that forced Paul to formulate the gospel message more precisely and more stringently. These teachers deduced from the salvation-historical priority of Israel that the Torah continues to be God's normative revelation, not only for Jewish believers in the Messiah but also for Gentile believers, who therefore must submit to circumcision and follow the food laws and the purity stipulations of Scripture. These Jewish-Christian teachers, who probably belonged to the church in Jerusalem, were particularly antagonized by Paul's basic theological conviction, which informed his praxis in the new churches, that God incorporates Gentiles into his new messianic people without circumcision and without obedience to the Torah. The activity of these teachers in the churches in southern Galatia prompted Paul to write the intense and robust Epistle to the Galatians. Paul's closely argued theological, historical and ethical explanation and exposition of the gospel message in his Epistle to the Romans presupposes the same general background. The situation in other churches raised other questions—for example, in Thessalonike the matter of Jesus' return, and in Corinth problems caused by the behavior of socially elite church members that was caused by one-sided and, in part, erroneous theological positions.

Paul defends and explains the gospel of God's revelation in Jesus Christ that he preaches in his letter, but also he specifies concisely and in detail the consequences that emerge from the gospel for the life of the church and of the individual believer. The missionary praxis of the apostle consisted not just in the evangelistic proclamation of the gospel before Jews and Gentiles and in the establishment of churches: Paul accompanied those local congregations born as a result of his missionary ministry on their way to the dynamic maturity of faith in which the fruit of the Holy Spirit is realized. Paul did not rush through the cities and regions of the Mediterranean world; he invested much time and energy in the theological, spiritual and ethical consolidation of the local churches. We have noted this reality in Paul's understanding of his calling, in the long durations of missionary initiatives in some cities, in his team of missionary coworkers and their activities, and in the long letters that he wrote to the churches.

The churches consisted of Jewish Christians and Gentile Christians who came from different religious background and different cultural and ethical traditions. When Jews and proselytes were converted to faith in Jesus Christ, Paul could reckon with the knowledge of biblical revelation and with the praxis of the will of God. When God-fearers and sympathizers who had attended synagogue services became Christians, Paul could assume some basic knowledge of Scripture but not necessarily behavior that corresponded to the ethics of the people of God. Converted polytheists would not have abandoned immediately or fully their superstitious beliefs, sexual looseness and magical practices after their conversion. Thus the issue of the everyday behavior of believers, the actualization of life in Jesus Christ and in the power of the Holy Spirit, was an important missionary subject for Paul. This can be observed in his repeated and numerous exhortations about behavior in the family, in the meetings of the church and in society.

Paul does not direct the churches to initiate missionary projects in other regions of their province or the Roman Empire: this is primarily the task of the apostles and of other missionaries whom the churches have commissioned. But Paul commends and praises the missionary commitment of individual churches. And he hopes that the believers' conversations and lifestyle in everyday situations will contribute to and support God's desire that more Jews and more Gentiles hear the gospel of Jesus Christ, accept it by faith and join the church, which thus continues to grow.

PART VI

GROWTH

Consolidation and Challenges of the

Early Christian Churches

30

REALITIES OF THE
EARLY CHRISTIAN MISSION

The texts of the New Testament are primary sources for the reconstruction of the early Christian mission, and they are genuine witnesses of the reality of the early Christians churches and their missionary activities in the second half of the first century. Before I describe the theology of the four Gospels with regard to their connection with the initiatives of the missionaries, I will summarize the evidence regarding the centers of the early Christian mission.

30.1 Centers of the Early Christian Missionary Movement

Jerusalem

Jerusalem, the Jewish capital and the center of the Jewish communities in the Mediterranean world of the Second Temple period, was the center for the followers of Jesus the Messiah for just under forty years: from the death and resurrection of Jesus of Nazareth in April A.D. 30 and the Feast of Pentecost at which the disciples under the leadership of Peter publicly preached Jesus as the Messiah until the beginning of the Jewish revolt against the Romans in A.D. 66/67 when the Christians from Jerusalem left the capital and fled to Pella in Transjordan.

The movement of people who believed in Jesus as Messiah, Son of God and Savior spread from Jerusalem to the ends of the known world (Acts 1:8). The first missionary sermon by a follower of Jesus—Peter's speech on the Feast of Pentecost on May 27 in A.D. 30 (Acts 2:14-36, 38-39)—was delivered to Jews from Jerusalem and Judea and Jewish pilgrims from Parthia, Media, Elam, Mesopotamia, Cappadocia, Pontus, Asia, Phrygia, Pamphylia, Egypt, Libya, Rome, Crete and Arabia (Acts 2:9-11). We do not know how many of these Diaspora Jews were among the three thousand people converted that day. It is entirely possible that the news of Jesus the Messiah reached some of these regions already in A.D. 30, perhaps Alexandria in Egypt, Damascus in Syria, Rome in Italy or Jewish communities in Mesopotamia. When Greek-speaking Jewish Christians had to leave Jerusalem in A.D. 31/32, Christian communities were established through their preaching in Samaria and in Syria—for example, in Antioch, the metropolis of the eastern Mediterranean world. And we have no way of knowing where and how many churches were established through the international mission of the Twelve when they left Jerusalem in A.D. 42—Peter apparently engaged in missionary work in the northern and eastern regions of Asia Minor, and Thomas probably went to India.

The Jerusalem church should not be understood as an institutionalized center of the numerous Christian communities born during these years: the churches in Syria and Cilicia, in Galatia and in the province of Asia, in Macedonia and in Achaia, in Rome and in North Africa were established and developed independently of a "center" that exercised control.[1] The conservative Jewish-Christian teachers who traveled to the new churches in Syria, Asia Minor and Greece to demand that the Gentile believers be circumcised and keep the food laws, probably identical with or connected to the "men from James" (Acts 15:1), came from Jerusalem, but they do not seem to have been authorized by the leadership of the Jerusalem church. The leading Christian missionaries, preachers and teachers all agreed at the apostolic council in A.D. 48—Luke reports the contributions of Paul, Barnabas, Peter and James to the discussion—that all people, Gentiles included, receive salvation by faith in Jesus Christ and are accepted into the people of God without circumcision (Acts 15:11, 19, 28). The apostolic council was not the result of an initiative by the leadership of the Jerusalem church that assumed responsibility for the modalities of the Gentile mission; rather, it stemmed from the initiative of the church in Antioch (Acts 15:2). The church in Jerusalem was the central institutional authority neither for the missionary work of the apostles and other disciples nor for the new churches that were established during this time.

Still, Jerusalem was the center for the first Christians, not only because this was the city in which Jesus had last taught, where he died and where God raised him from the dead on the third day, but also because the Twelve initially stayed in Jerusalem, because they represented the leadership of the messianic people of God, and because the "teaching of the apostles" (Acts 2:42) was the foundation of the faith of the Christians. Because the apostles lived in Jerusalem, the Jesus tradition was "located" in Jerusalem as well. This tradition, initially an oral one that might have received written form at an early date, was taught in Jerusalem and soon translated into Greek. It was more important than the literary production of the early Christians: the only New Testament texts that were written in Jerusalem are the brief Epistle of James and the even shorter Epistle of Jude. If the Gospel of Matthew was written before A.D. 70, and if an origin in

---

[1]Arnold 1997, 144-45. James Scott (2000) underestimates this reality.

Judea for it cannot be excluded,[2] then presumably the Jerusalem church played some role in its composition.

Antioch

The second center of the early Christian movement was Antioch on the Orontes River, the metropolis of Syria, a world-class city with over 250,000 inhabitants.[3] Antioch was strategically located on the large roads from Asia Minor into the East, and there was a large and influential Jewish community in the city. The Christian community in Antioch was established at an early date, perhaps as early as two years after Pentecost, around A.D. 32. The leaders of the church were Jewish Christians from Jerusalem (Acts 13:1); Barnabas was active in Antioch since A.D. 35. The followers of Jesus seem to have come to the attention of Roman officials for the first time in Antioch, as the designation *christianoi* suggests (Acts 11:26). Paul was active in Antioch from A.D. 42 to 44. After A.D. 45 Antioch was the base of operations for his missionary work in Asia Minor and in Greece, and after A.D. 49 it was the center for Barnabas's mission to Cyprus.

If the early date for the composition of Paul's Epistle to the Galatians in A.D. 48 is correct, this would be the only early Christian text whose composition in Antioch is certain.[4] Many scholars assume that the Gospel of Matthew was written in Antioch, perhaps in the 80s or 90s (see §30.2), a plausible but still hypothetical assumption.[5] Ignatius, the *episkopos* of the church in Antioch, wrote in the late summer of A.D. 113, at the latest, letters to six churches, although not in Antioch itself but on the way to his martyrdom: from Smyrna came the letters to the churches in Ephesus, Magnesia, Tralles and Rome, and from Alexandria Troas came the letter to the churches in Philadelphia and Smyrna as well as to Polycarp.

Corinth

A third center evidently was Corinth, a possibility that is suggested by the extended period of nearly two years of missionary work in the city (Acts 18:11), as well as by the fact that Paul maintained intensive contacts with this church through letters, envoys and repeated visits. The reference to churches in Achaia

---

[2]See the colophon of the manuscripts K 126, 174; cf. Jerome, *Vir. ill.* 3, and other church fathers. A Judean provenance is assumed by M. Albertz, W. C. Allen, A. Schlatter, T. H. Robinson, J. Schniewind, W. Michaelis, A. Wikenhauser, M. Hengel (as a possibility), Ellis 1999, 288-92. See Davies and Allison, *Mt,* 1:138, 139-40. Most scholars assume Syria or more specifically Antioch as the place of origin.

[3]See J. B. Polhill, "Antioch's Contribution to Christianity," *Faith & Mission* 18 (2000): 3-20.

[4]Differently Klaus Berger (1994a), who places the composition of all New Testament texts except for the Epistle of James under the rubric "Antioch." See the critique in Hengel and Schwemer 1998, 432-33 with n. 1781 (ET, 491).

[5]See recently Luz, *Mt,* 1:73-75 (ET, 90-92); Davies and Allison, *Mt,* 1:143-47.

(Acts 19:21) might suggest that Corinth was the base for missionary activities in the region. Apart from Paul's Epistles to the Corinthians, we have little information about the church in Corinth. Paul wrote his Epistle to the Romans while staying in Corinth in the winter of A.D. 56/57.

Ephesus

A fourth center was Ephesus, the capital of the province of Asia, strategically located for missionary work in the Aegean region. When Paul worked in the city between A.D. 52 and 55, thousands of people were reached with the gospel in the entire province (Acts 19:10). Ephesus probably was the base for the missionary outreach in two directions: (1) for the mission in the Maeander Valley west of Ephesus, in the course of which the churches in Magnesia and Tralles were established, which Ignatius mentions, and for the mission in the Lykos Valley on the upper Maeander, in the course of which the churches in Colossae, Laodikeia and Hierapolis were founded; (2) for the mission to the regions north of Ephesus, which led to the foundation of the churches in Smyrna, Philadelphia, Thyatira, Sardis and Pergamon. After Paul left Ephesus, Timothy and the apostle John were active in Ephesus.

Paul was in Ephesus when he wrote the First Epistle to the Corinthians. The Epistle to the Ephesians evidently was written to all churches in the province of Asia and thus was addressed to the church in Ephesus as well. Timothy was active in Ephesus when Paul wrote his first letter to him (1 Timothy). The early tradition that the apostle John was active in Ephesus allows us to connect the composition of the Gospel of John, the book of Revelation (written on the island of Patmos) and the Johannine Epistles with that city.

Rome

A fifth center of the early Christian movement was Rome, the capital of the *Imperium Romanum*. The Christian community in the city of Rome evidently was established at an early date in the context of the local synagogues, apparently without the help of an apostle. Peter probably visited Rome at an early date, perhaps soon after A.D. 42. Paul had plans to visit Rome since before A.D. 57; he eventually arrived as a prisoner in A.D. 60 and was forced to stay, under house arrest, presumably until A.D. 62. Paul wrote the Epistle to the Romans in the winter of A.D. 56/57, perhaps twenty years after the church had been founded. Paul's letter confirms the existence of several house churches in the city (Rom 16). After the fire of Rome in A.D. 64 the Christians there were made scapegoats, persecuted and brutally murdered. Paul and Peter died in Rome as martyrs, probably in A.D. 67.

Peter wrote his letter to the churches in northern Asia Minor while staying in Rome (1 Peter). The Gospel of Mark probably was written in Rome as well. Clement, the third *episkopos* of the church in Rome, wrote a letter to the church in Corinth some time after A.D. 96. The *Shepherd of Hermas* was written in Rome in the first half of the second century, a text that calls the Christians to repentance. The church of Rome probably maintained a central archive, around A.D. 150, in which texts written by the apostles were collected.[6]

Alexandria

Since we have no information about the origins of the church in Alexandria, we cannot even speculate about Alexandria as a center of the early Christian mission in Egypt and in North Africa.[7] Suggestions that the Gospel of Matthew[8] and the Gospel of John[9] were written in Alexandria are speculation. The numerous New Testament papyri discovered in Egypt suggest that the church in Alexandria was an important center of missionary work and theological reflection at least in the second and third centuries.

30.2 Consolidation of the Churches

The letters of the apostles Peter, John and Paul served the consolidation of the existing churches. The authors of the four Gospels pursued the same goal. We have already noted that the canonical Gospels need to be taken into account in the description of the early Christian missionary movement (§22.1). The authors of the Gospels wrote for Christian communities, which means that these texts are not "missionary treatises" that seek to convince non-Christians of the truth of the good news of Jesus Christ. However, the authors of the Gospels wrote in the context of churches whose leaders were actively involved in missionary work among Jews and Gentiles. This is a fact that scholars often forget when they analyze the Gospels: despite all the controversies about theological questions that did exist, the early Christian churches were not theological seminars in which literary experts discussed and debated the fine points of biblical interpretation. Rather, they were communities that continuously grew through the addition of new converts, attracted by members of the congregation who had talked about their faith in their families or in the workshop or on the street in the neighborhood, or convicted by missionary sermons that they heard in the synagogues or in the marketplace or in the meetings of Christians. The authors of the Gospels wrote their long texts in order to deepen what Christians in the various congregations knew about the person and ministry of Jesus of Nazareth—congregations that preached and taught about Jesus in their private meet-

---

[6]See C.-J. Thornton 1991, 47-55; Arnold 1997, 151.

[7]*Pace* Arnold 1997, 149-50.

[8]S. G. F. Brandon, *The Fall of Jerusalem and the Christian Church* (London: SPCK, 1951 [1957]). See the critique in Davies and Allison, *Mt,* 1:139.

[9]Joseph N. Sanders, *The Fourth Gospel in the Early Church* (Cambridge: Cambridge University Press, 1943), 85-86; H. C. Snape, "The Fourth Gospel, Ephesus and Alexandria," *HTR* 47 (1954): 1-14. See Schnackenburg, *Joh,* 1:133.

ings and in public venues. As the early Christians studied and preached the gospel of Jesus Christ, these authors wrote "gospels" to consolidate and expand their knowledge.[10]

The Missionary Theology of Matthew

Matthew is clearly and consistently interested in the missionary ministry of those who believe that Jesus is Israel's Messiah.[11] The addressees of the First Gospel sometimes are linked with Christians in Galilee,[12] but usually with churches in Syria.[13] It is highly unlikely that Matthew wrote his Gospel for a single church, which would have been a house church of perhaps fifty members. Matthew narrates the history of Jesus for several churches that presumably had loose contact with each other.[14] Earle Ellis believes that the Gospel of Matthew was written in Jerusalem as the Gospel of the mission of James the brother of Jesus some time before he was killed in A.D. 66/67, when the leaders of this mission fled to Pella at the beginning of the First Jewish Revolt.[15]

Eusebius quotes from the five-volume work of Papias (ca. A.D. 130-140) the comment that Matthew wrote a collection of *ta logia* that were orally translated (into Greek).[16] This notice apparently alludes to the Gospel of Matthew, as the expression *ta logia* does not merely designate the sayings of Jesus but *pars pro toto* the entire Gospel. In the time of Papias this oral translation of the original Aramaic Gospel of Matthew evidently was no longer necessary, presumably because the Greek Gospel of Matthew had been disseminated in the meantime in the churches of Asia Minor.[17] It is disputed, however, whether Papias's information about an original Aramaic version of the Gospel of Matthew is historically reliable. An Aramaic version of the First Gospel would have been an important text for the early Christian mission in Syria and the territories of Babylonia; the Greek version could have been read in all regions of the Mediterranean world.

Matthew begins his history of Jesus with Abraham and David (Mt 1:1) and with the history of Israel condensed in the genealogy in Mt 1:2-17, which culminates in Jesus the Son of David, the "Emmanuel," the "God with us" (Mt 1:23)—the Son of God, in whom God's presence in Israel becomes a reality.

---

[10]See Senior 1984, 74-81.

[11]See Bieder 1964, 7-18; Frankemölle 1982; A.-J. Levine 1988; J. Harvey 1998b; McKnight 1992, 261-62; Wong 1992; LaGrand 1995; Ukpong 1995; Köstenberger and O'Brien 2001, 87-109; Cousland 2002, 288-93; Smillie 2002; Wilk 2002, 83-153; also Saldarini 1994, 68-83, 99.

[12]See Overman 1990; Hertig 1997.

[13]Stanton 1994.

[14]See Stanton 1994; generally Bauckham 1998.

[15]Ellis 1999, 288-92.

[16]Eusebius, *Hist. eccl.* 3.39.16: Ματθαῖος μὲν οὖν ʽΕβραΐδι διαλέκτῳ τὰ λόγια συνετάξατο, ἡρμήνευσεν δ' αὐτὰ ὡς ἦν δυνατὸς ἕκαστος.

[17]See Armin Baum, "Ein aramäischer Urmatthäus im kleinasiatischen Gottesdienst: Das Papiaszeugnis zur Entstehung des Matthäusevangeliums," *ZNW* 92 (2001): 257-72.

Matthew concludes his history of Jesus with the commission given to the Twelve to make all nations disciples of Jesus, continuing and expanding the ministry of Jesus while experiencing Jesus' presence (Mt 28:16-20).[18] Matthew wants to strengthen his readers in the conviction that "the work that Jesus completes *for Israel* as 'Messiah' leads into his ministry *for the nations* as 'Son of Man'; for Jesus is the son of Abraham who leads Israel's history of election to its goal and who thus fulfills God's promise to make Abraham into a 'large nation' that exists as a light for the nations. On the other hand, his ministry as Son of Man is based on his work as Messiah; Jesus is 'Lord' of the nations only on the basis of his mission to Israel."

Matthew emphasizes in Mt 28:16-20 two subjects: the authority of Jesus and the teaching of Jesus. Both subjects had been highlighted in the previous sections of Matthew's Gospel. Oscar Brooks suggests that the author, who knew the missionary commission before he wrote the Gospel, apparently wanted to write a book that is in harmony with Jesus' call to international mission, and this is why he consistently refers to Jesus' authority and provides an extensive account of Jesus' teaching.[19] The observation that Matthew emphasizes Jesus' authority and teaching is correct, but Brooks's interpretation reduces the assertions of Mt 28:16-20 to an unnecessary minimum and ignores many subjects that Matthew also emphasizes in his Gospel. In my view, it is implausible to describe the motivation of the author of the First Gospel on the basis of Mt 28:16-20. Ulrich Luz suggests that the call to teach the commandments of Jesus in Mt 28:20 implies "an indirect but very important statement about the significance of the Matthean book," which contains Jesus' commandments, "which are to be proclaimed as 'gospel of the kingdom' to all nations." He argues that Matthew's understanding of the missionary proclamation of the Christians "renders his book indispensable. We might speak of a 'self-canonization' *in nuce.*"[20] This interpretation is unconvincing. If the missionary commission can indeed be understood as a commission from the historical Jesus to his disciples, Luz's suggestion is superfluous. And there is no evidence in the last forty words of the Gospel of Matthew that would suggest that the author wanted to make his book indispensable: the First Gospel contains much more than "commandments of Jesus" that the disciples are directed in Mt 28:20 to teach—the Gospel of Matthew cannot be reduced to Jesus' commandments. Clearly, however, Matthew's conclusion of his Gospel describes the reality of the early Christian missionary movement, a reality that the author himself and the churches for whom he wrote are familiar with, a reality that is reinforced by the reminder of Jesus' great missionary commission, which remains valid for the church in the future.

---

[18]Wilk 2002, 81-89; the quotation that follows above, ibid., 151.
[19]Brooks 1981.
[20]Luz, *Mt,* 4:455, with an acknowledgment of a suggestion of M. Mayordomo-Marín.

The Missionary Theology of Mark

If Mark's Gospel is indeed the first of the four canonical Gospels, then it is highly significant that he narrates the history of Jesus with the goal of inviting "the acclamation, the recognition of the true dignity of Jesus."[21] The entire movement of Jesus—from the preparation of the "way of the Lord" by John the Baptist (Mk 1:1-8) to his "going ahead" after his resurrection (Mk 16:7); his role as "beloved Son" (Mk 1:11; 9:7; 12:6) of the Father, who sent Jesus of Nazareth in Galilee as his last messenger (Mk 12:6); his ministry as the "Son of Man," who is anointed by God's Holy Spirit and is victorious when Satan tempts him; his proclamation of the dawn of the kingdom of God; his miracles, his controversy disputes, his great successes; the early and constant rejection; his death, which comes into view at an early stage (Mk 2:20); his journey from Galilee to Jerusalem to the temple, where he acts as the messianic prophet; his path to suffering and to his death on the cross (Mk 14—15) as the path to the resurrection, where his path leads into the path of the church—Mark asserts in Mk 1:1 that his book summarizes the foundations and the content of the *euangelion* of Jesus Christ. And Mark is aware of his "missionary and catechetical responsibility" for the Christian church, as Rudolf Pesch notes: "The entire history of Jesus has become the content of the gospel. The entire book of Mark is a *missionary book.*"

Mark's missionary interest surfaces in the very title of the Gospel: "The beginning of the good news of Jesus Christ, the Son of God" (Mk 1:1).[22] This formulation has been compared with the calendrical inscription of Priene dating to 9 B.C.,[23] where we read in lines 40-41, "The birthday of the god [Augustus] first brought to the world the good tidings residing in him" (ἦρξεν δὲ τῶι κόσμωι τῶν δι᾽ αὐτὸν εὐανγελίων ἡ γενέθλιος τοῦ θεοῦ). In both texts the term *euangelion* ("good news, good tidings"; pl., *euangelia*) is used; both texts speak of a "beginning" (Mk 1:1 uses the noun *archē;* the inscription uses the verb *archein*); both texts link the good tidings with a divine figure—in Mk 1:1 with Jesus the "Son of God" (*huios theou*), and in the inscription with the "god" (*theos*) Augustus, described a few lines earlier as "savior" (*sotēr*). Many inscriptions, coins and papyri describe Augustus as "son of god" (*divi filius*).[24] When Mark begins his

---

[21]Theissen 1974a, 212; Pesch, *Mk,* 1:60. For the comments that follow above see Pesch, *Mk,* 1:59-60; quotations, ibid., 1:62, 61. See generally Hahn 1963, 95-103; Stock 1982; Senior and Stuhlmueller 1983, 211-32; Kato 1986; LaVerdiere 1990; Schnabel 1994; Rhoads 1995b; Köstenberger and O'Brien 2001, 73-86.

[22]On the text-critical questions see Peter M. Head, "A Text-Critical Study of Mark 1.1, 'The Beginning of the Gospel of Jesus Christ,'" *NTS* 37 (1991): 621-29; differently Adela Yarbro Collins ("Establishing the Text: Mark 1:1," in Fornberg and Hellholm 1995, 111-27), who regards υἱοῦ θεοῦ as a later addition.

[23]*I. Priene* 105 = *OGIS* II 458; see Deissmann 1923, 313, and figs. 68, 69; Ehrenberg, Jones and Stockton 1979, 81-83, no. 98; Braund 1985, 56-58, no. 122. On the comparison with Mk 1:1 see Evans 2000; idem, *Mk,* lxxxi-xciii, whose analysis I follow.

[24]See T. Kim 1998. See §18.4 in the present work.

book about Jesus, the Messiah of Nazareth, using words that remind his readers of central elements of the imperial cult, which had become increasingly popular since Augustus, he expresses his conviction that the message of Jesus Christ is the only "good tidings," and that Jesus the Messiah from Israel is the only true "Son of God," whose significance is relevant for the entire world.[25] The fact that Mark begins his Gospel with such a categorical "beat of the drum" in the very first line perhaps can be explained by the fact that Mark possibly wrote his Gospel around A.D. 68/69, after Nero's death, during the disturbances linked with the power struggle for Nero's succession. Craig Evans comments, "The Markan evangelist presents Jesus as the true son of God and in doing so deliberately presents Jesus in opposition to Rome's candidates for a suitable emperor, savior, and lord. . . . Jesus was indeed the Son of God, humanity's true Savior and Lord. Mark's purpose is to narrate the story of Jesus in such a way that such a confession will appear compelling and plausible to Jews and Romans alike."[26]

The Gospel of Mark clearly links the universal dimension of the significance of Jesus of Nazareth with the cross, as Florian Wilk explains: "While Jesus limits contacts with non-Jews to the unavoidable minimum (Mk 7:24), encountering rejection (Mk 5:14-17) and partial or unwitting acknowledgment (Mk 15:2-27), two 'Gentiles' recognize his distinctive dignity as God's agent as well as that dimension of his ministry that was grounded in this dignity but transcends Israel (Mk 7:25-30; 15:[29-]37-41). This dimension consists primarily in the fact that his ministry is fulfilled in his *death*. Because it is his death, as death 'for many' (Mk 10:45; 14:24), that establishes the eschatological 'house of prayer'—replacing Israel's temple—*for all nations* (Mk 11:12—12:12), a house to which the disciples of Jesus, who proclaim the gospel in the entire world (Mk 13:10; 14:9), invite 'Gentiles' as well as Jews so that they who are the 'elect' will be saved at the parousia (Mk 13:20)."[27]

The Missionary Theology of Luke

Luke wrote not only an account about the history of Jesus but also a second volume in which he narrates the missionary work of the earliest followers of Jesus.[28] The outline of his Gospel in terms of the two large sections, Lk 3:1—9:50 and Lk 9:51—24:53, demonstrates that "Luke interprets Jesus' earthly ministry primarily as an expression of his identity—he is the Messiah and therefore the Son of God and the Son of Man—as well as preparation for his 'departure'

---

[25]Evans 2000, 70, 80-81.

[26]Evans, *Mk*, lxxxix, xciii, and idem, 2000, 80-81.

[27]Wilk 2002, 71.

[28]On Luke's missionary theology see Lohse 1954; Bieder 1960; Hahn 1963, 111-19; 1984; S. Wilson 1973; Karris 1979; Bovon 1983; Bosch 1989; McKnight 1992, 262-63; Talbert 1991; Dollar 1993; Larkin 1998a; 1998b; T. Lane 1996; Marshall 2000b; Köstenberger and O'Brien 2001, 111-59.

(Lk 9:31) through suffering to glory (Lk 24:27). His ministry is in this sense the *presupposition* of the eschatological reconstitution of the people of God, which is the goal of his sending (Lk 3:16-17). This goal is realized, however, only as the disciples become witnesses of the redemptive events after his ascension, proclaiming in the name of Jesus and on the basis of his suffering and resurrection repentance for the forgiveness of sins (Lk 24:46-53)."[29] When Luke describes Jesus' views and statements about the temple and its cult, the sabbath, the law and Jewish piety and customs, he often reflects the early Christian conviction that God's redemptive revelation in Jesus Christ defines in a new manner in what sense Jews belong to the people of God. The events of salvation connected with Jesus are the "glory of the people of Israel" (δόξα λαοῦ Ἰσραήλ, *doxa laou Israēl* [Lk 2:32]). However, since Jesus' mission to Israel newly constitutes the people of God, his mission is the foundation of missionary work among the nations, as the message that the disciples preach among both Jews and Gentiles is based on the life, death and resurrection of Jesus, calling all people to repentance and the forgiveness of sins (Lk 24:46-49).[30] Thus the "glory of Israel" becomes the "light for revelation to the nations" (φῶς εἰς ἀποκάλυψιν ἐθνῶν, *phōs eis apokalypsin ethnōn* [Lk 2:32]).

In the second part of his two-volume work, the book of Acts, Luke describes what is, for him, clearly a fundamental feature of the nature of the church.[31] The church of Jesus Christ is a missionary community of believers whose witnesses are empowered by the Spirit of God and carry the message of Jesus Christ "to the ends of the earth" (Acts 1:8), helping Jews and also Gentiles find the salvation that has been procured by Jesus Christ.[32] The missionary project of the Jerusalem apostles and other preachers—Luke focuses particularly on the mission of Peter and the mission of Paul—encounters opposition, rejection and open persecution that lead to the imprisonment and the killing of some missionaries. However, the course of the gospel cannot be stopped, since God himself is active through his Spirit in the proclamation of the gospel by the apostles.

Luke evidently does not include in his account all the information that he possesses about the missionary initiatives of the early Christians. In regard to the missionary activities of the Twelve, whose names he lists twice in his work, Luke focuses exclusively on Peter and his missionary ministry in Jerusalem, Samaria, the coastal plain and Caesarea Maritima in the twelve years between A.D. 30 and 42. Luke remains silent about the geographical scope of the next twenty-five years of Peter's mission, A.D. 42-67, from his departure from Jerusalem until

---

[29]Wilk 2002, 227.

[30]See Wilk 2002, 233; for the comment that follows above see ibid.

[31]Lampe and Luz 1987, 212. On the unity of the Gospel of Luke and the book of Acts see Marshall 1993.

[32]Köstenberger and O'Brien 2001, 157.

his martyr's death in Rome. Apart from accounts of missionaries of the early church such as Stephen in Jerusalem and Philip in Samaria and in the cities of the coastal plain, Luke focuses on Paul. Here again he reports selectively: he is silent about Paul's missionary work in Arabia and Syria/Cilicia during the first ten years after his conversion and commission, A.D. 32/33-42, concentrating instead on his activities during the years A.D. 42-57 in Antioch, on Cyprus, in Galatia, Macedonia, Achaia and Ephesus in the province of Asia.

For Luke, Jerusalem is the center of the mission among Jews and Gentiles, "the irreplaceable salvation-historical starting-point of all missionary work, chosen by God."[33] The goal of the missionary work of the church is not Rome, the capital of the Empire, but the courageous proclamation of the gospel of Jesus Christ among all nations "to the ends of the earth" (Lk 24:47; Acts 1:8). At the same time the missionaries preach the gospel to Jews in the synagogues. The view that "by Luke's time the Christian mission was directed solely to the Gentiles,"[34] held by Ernst Haenchen and others, is a serious misjudgment.

The open ending of the book of Acts highlights for the last time the continuous progress of the gospel from Jerusalem to the Gentile world, which cannot be stopped by anything, not even Paul's imprisonment in Rome. Luke describes Paul the prisoner, who is under house arrest in Rome, as God's missionary teacher who has been sent to the Gentiles (Acts 28:28) and who proclaims to Jews and Gentiles the kingdom of God and the message of the Lord Jesus Christ "with all boldness and without hindrance" (Acts 28:31). Luke perhaps uses this open ending to involve his readers in the task of world mission, a task that remains the responsibility of the church until God's visible kingdom arrives.[35] (1) The "missionary manifesto" of Acts 1:8 has not been completed with Paul's arrival in the city of Rome: the "ends of the earth" have not been reached at the end of the book of Acts. (2) The second volume of Luke's work ends in Acts 28:30-31 with a summary that describes the progress of the Christian faith in the capital of the Roman Empire. Since Luke generally uses summaries as transitions to further events, he tells his readers "between the lines" that the mission of the church is "to be continued"—not in a third book, but in the continued witness to Jesus Christ by the apostles and the missionaries of the church. (3) Luke's silence about the outcome of Paul's trial could indicate, in the context of the author's rhetorical technique, that Paul the witness and defender of the faith serves as a model for the readers.

Luke addresses his two-volume work to a certain Theophilus (Lk 1:3; Acts 1:1), about whom he provides no further information.

---

[33]Bieder 1964, 23; for the comment that follows above see ibid., 24-25.
[34]Haenchen, *Apg*, 112 (ET, 112); cf. Jervell 1965.
[35]For the arguments that follow above see Rosner 1998, 230-32.

Lk 1:1-4: "Since many have undertaken to set down an orderly account of the events that have been fulfilled among us, [2]just as they were handed on to us by those who from the beginning were eyewitnesses and servants of the word, [3]I too decided, after investigating everything carefully from the very first, [or: 'for a long time'] to write an orderly account for you, most excellent Theophilus, [4]so that you may know the truth concerning the things about which you have been instructed."

Acts 1:1-2: "In the first book, Theophilus, I wrote about all that Jesus did and taught from the beginning [2]until the day when he was taken up to heaven, after giving instructions through the Holy Spirit to the apostles whom he had chosen."

Joseph Tyson seeks to read the Gospel of Luke and the book of Acts using the question of the "model reader" (cf. the work of Umberto Eco) whom the text "produces" and presupposes, and he shows that the "model reader" resembles the Gentile "God-fearers" in the book of Acts. The information that Luke provides about places, persons, languages, events, measures, money, religious practices and literature can be combined into the following portrait of Luke's "model reader."[36] Luke's model reader (1) is an educated person who possesses at least a rudimentary knowledge of the geography of the eastern Mediterranean world and knows the larger and more significant Roman provinces; (2) probably speaks only Greek but knows several phrases and names in other languages; (3) knows the standard Greek and Roman measures and coins; (4) is familiar with public personalities, particularly Roman emperors; (5) is familiar with political events in the East, including events that affected the Jewish communities; (6) knows pagan religious traditions and Judaism, rejects some pagan practices and finds the Jewish religious life attractive, but is not well informed about some important aspects of Jewish life and thus probably is not a Jew; (7) knows the Jewish Bible in its Greek translation and acknowledges its normative status; (8) knows, though perhaps not very well, the Christian church and its leaders.

The God-fearers whom Luke repeatedly mentions in the book of Acts correspond to this portrait: pious Gentiles who are attracted by the Jewish faith but have not joined the synagogue by circumcision. The little information that we have about Theophilus ("beloved by God," or "loving God") corresponds to this portrait as well. He knows something about the Christian faith: according to Lk 1:4, he has "received instruction" (κατηχήθης, *katēchēthēs*) concerning the "reports" (λόγοι, *logoi*) of Jesus, but he does not belong to the "us" (ἡμῖν, *hēmin* [Lk 1:1, 2]) of the Christian believers who are convinced about the certainty of the Christian faith.[37] If we read Luke's two-volume work in this perspective, it

---

[36]See Tyson 1992; 1995, 24-25.

[37]See Nolland (*Lk*, 1:11), who points to the "generally secular and historiographical tone of the preface" in Lk 1:1-4 and thus endorses the "neutral" interpretation of κατηχεῖν and λόγοι in the sense of "to convey information orally" and "reports" rather than the "Christian" meanings "to teach" and "messages, teachings."

becomes possible to interpret it in terms of an evangelistic treatise addressed to God-fearers. This can be supported by the partially positive and partially negative treatment of Jewish religiosity—for example, the assertion in Acts 13:38-39 that the observance of the Torah does not make one righteous and thus is not effective. If this analysis is correct, then Luke challenges the God-fearers to abandon their love of Judaism and recognize that the Torah and the prophets point to Jesus and find their fulfillment in him, that the Jews have rejected Jesus as the Messiah, that obedience to the Torah does not guarantee salvation, and therefore that they should come to faith in Jesus as Messiah, Lord and Savior.[38]

Other scholars understand Theophilus as a baptismal candidate, as a new believer or as the leader of a house church.[39] Robert Karris points out that the churches that Luke has in mind as readers are missionary churches—churches that send missionaries to Jews, seeking to convince them that Jesus is the fulfillment of God's promises; churches that send missionaries to Gentiles, seeking to convince them that Jesus is the only Savior; churches whose missionary work and everyday existence are characterized by danger and suffering, putting them in need of encouragement and support.[40]

Florian Wilk summarizes the keynote concept of the Synoptic Gospels as follows: "The Synoptics agree that Jesus' mission to Israel initiates the realization of God's eschatological will to effect salvation for all people."[41] Wilk believes, however, that the authors of the Synoptic Gospels give "divergent answers that can hardly be harmonized with each other" to the following questions: "What happens to Israel's special relationship with God? What is the nature of the relationship to the nations for which Israel is being prepared by Jesus' earthly ministry? In what way does his death benefit both Jews *and* Gentiles? In what manner do the witnesses of the risen Christ remain connected with Israel? What is the relationship between Jews and Gentiles in the post-Easter church?" Wilk argues that Luke, with his model of the reconstitution of the Jewish people of God into which non-Jews can be integrated, "stands, as it were, between Mark, who situates the church of the believers in Christ in the 'house of prayer for all nations,' and Matthew, according to whom the disciples maintain their status as children of Abraham by conveying, as carriers of the light of the nations, the blessing of Abraham to the 'Gentiles' and by accepting them into their fellowship."

In my view, there is no compelling reason why these different emphases cannot be "harmonized." Wilk argues that it is "particularly" controversial "in what manner Jesus remains linked with the Jewish people as the one who has been exalted at the right hand of God and in what sense, therefore, discipleship remains under Jewish influence after Easter."[42] The following considerations show that this position is unconvincing. (1) Wilk's methodological decision to disregard the historical dimension of the life and message of the "historical Jesus" is rather unfortunate. The Gospels can and should be read, of course, as liter-

---

[38]Tyson 1995, 38.

[39]For the last suggestion see L. Alexander 1993a, 191-98. See also Fitzymer, *Acts,* 195.

[40]Karris 1979; summary, ibid., 96-97.

[41]Wilk 2002, 253; for the comments and quotations that follow above see ibid.; similarly ibid., 285-86, 291.

[42]Wilk 2002, 286.

ary, narrative texts of authors who write for a specific readership. However, since we have no information about their readers or about the specific historical intentions of the authors—all reconstructions remain hypothetical—any reflection about "post-Easter" situations and concerns remains hypothetical as well. This means that what Wilk cannot "harmonize" are perhaps only his historical-critical reconstructions. (2) Jesus' "connectedness" ("Verbundenheit") with the Jewish people is characterized by continuity *and* discontinuity. The same is true for Peter and James, for Stephen and Barnabas, as well as for Paul. These continuities and discontinuities are not solely the consequences of theological, hermeneutical and practical decisions, but are variously accentuated in different ways in different situations. Jesus is attacked by Pharisees, and yet he accepts invitations from Pharisees to attend banquets in their homes. Luke reports the same type of ambivalent experiences of Peter and Paul in the book of Acts.

The Missionary Theology of John

Jesus' mission and the mission of the church have a central role in the Gospel of John.[43] Teresa Okure argues that the subject of missions in the Fourth Gospel is connected with a tendency of the churches that John addresses to neglect their missionary involvement. Both the rhetorical structure of the Gospel and many individual rhetorical elements support the pastoral-missionary concerns of the author. The disciples who are John's readers had to be reminded of Jesus' uniqueness as God's eschatological mediator of salvation and how that therefore requires total dependence upon Jesus. Okure observes, "The missionary emphases in the Gospel suggested that an attitude of boasting, a tendency to behave as if they owned the mission, and pride in a variety of forms must have constituted a special weakness of the Johannine audience."[44] This scenario may be historically plausible, but any reconstruction that "mirror-reads" a text remains hypothetical. Karl Bornhäuser and other scholars suggests that John wants to evangelize (Diaspora) Jews and proselytes; that is, the Fourth Gospel intends to show unbelievers what it means to belong to the community of the Messiah and to participate in its mission to the world.[45] Some scholars connect the Gospel of John with a mission to the Samaritans[46] or more generally with

---

[43]See Bornhäuser 1928; Oehler 1936; 1941; Davey 1961; Hahn 1963, 135-45; Bieder 1964, 40-52; Kuhl 1967; McPolin 1969; Bühner 1977; Popkes 1978; Schnackenburg 1984; Viviano 1984; Ruiz 1987; Okure 1988; Ghiberti 1990a; McKnight 1992, 263-64; Mlakuzhyil 1993; Frey 1994; Towner 1995; Köstenberger 1995; 1998a; Erdmann 1998; Köstenberger and O'Brien 2001, 203-26. Differently K. Kuhn 1954; Schneider 1982, 203.

[44]Okure 1988, 228-84; quotation, ibid., 287. Okure rightly demands that the relationship of many critical scholars to the Gospel of John needs to be de-gnosticized and de-mythologized (ibid., 309).

[45]Bornhäuser 1928; cf. Oehler 1936; 1941; Oepke 1941; W. C. van Unnik, "The Purpose of St. John's Gospel," in *Studia Evangelica I* (ed. K. Aland; TU 73; Berlin: Akademie-Verlag, 1959), 382-411; J. A. T. Robinson, "The Destination and Purpose of St. John's Gospel," *NTS* 6 (1959-1960): 117-131; more recently Carson, *Jn*, 87-95; Köstenberger 1998a, 206-10.

[46]John Bowman, "The Fourth Gospel and the Samaritans," *BJRL* 40 (1958): 298-308; Edwin D. Freed, "Did John Write His Gospel Partly to Win Samaritan Converts?" *NovT* 12 (1970): 141-46.

non-Christian readers of the Hellenized world.[47] Benedict Viviano believes that the Fourth Gospel is a "missionary project" in terms of a "large-scale apologetic enterprise" that could be interpreted as "an expanded and improved version of the great missionary speeches in Acts: chapter 13 to the Jews, chapter 17 to the Athenians."[48] Rudolf Schnackenburg and other scholars assert, on the other hand, that the Fourth Gospel is a text written for the Christian community with the intention of providing Christians "with a deep vision of Christ" and to strengthen them "in their struggle for faith and their attempt to preserve their own faith."[49] It is unnecessary, in my view, to decide whether the Gospel of John is a "missionary document" or a "community document" as long as we recognize that Christians belonged to the intended first readers, and that the concern for active missionary outreach among Jews, Samaritans and Gentiles belongs to the main themes of the book. The promotion of the faith of Christians through an exposition of the nature and the "work" of Jesus always implies a missionary component. And the active propagation of faith in Jesus Christ among unbelievers always strengthens the faith of Christians.[50]

Xavier Levieils concludes from the Jewish character of the Johannine writings that the Christian community that came into being in Palestine reached Gentiles in Asia Minor and integrated the new converts in their community, an important impetus being the influence and pressure of the churches in Asia Minor that were influenced by Pauline theology. He suggests that the crisis that surfaces in the Johannine Epistles is connected with this coexistence and with the specific theological convictions of the Jewish and the "Greek" members of the church.[51] This hypothesis depends on the hypothetical reconstruction of historical developments and tradition-historical connections. It at least demonstrates the importance of missionary activity for the author and for the readers of the Johannine writings.

Whereas the Synoptic Gospels emphasize the salvation-historical priority of Israel or of the Jews before the Gentiles, John emphasizes the significance of Jesus as the bringer of God's revelation into the world. Jesus is the light of the world (Jn 8:12; 9:5; cf. 1:4) and the Savior of the world (Jn 3:17; 4:42; 6:33, 51; 11:27; 12:20-23). The suggestion that the "Johannine community" was characterized by a basic contrast to the "evil world," without the possibility of finding a way from one realm to the other, founders on specific statements in the Gospel of John.[52] (1) The prologue refers to the antithesis of light and darkness (Jn 1:5) only after references to creation (Jn 1:1-4). (2) John underscores the fact that God has not

---

[47]See Dodd 1953, 9.

[48]Viviano 1984, 387.

[49]Schnackenburg, *Joh,* 3:245 (ET, 3:217); cf. Conzelmann 1967, 362 (ET, 332).

[50]Note Okure 1988, 294: "In Johannine terms the Gospel is a missionary document, precisely because it is a community document."

[51]Levieils 2001.

[52]For the analysis that follows above, with a critique of Schottroff 1970, 228-96, see Schnelle 1991, esp. 38-39.

abandoned his creation: he sent his Son into the world (Jn 3:16; 10:36); Jesus is the Son of God, who has come into the world (Jn 11:27), gives life to the world (Jn 6:33) and is the light of the world (Jn 9:5). (3) The Johannine dualism must be understood not in a protological sense but as a logical consequence of Christology. The person of Jesus Christ decides the issue of salvation (Jn 3:16-17; 8:12; 12:46; 10:28), which means that people who refuse to believe in him remain in darkness. It is, in other words, unbelief that turns the world into God's enemy (Jn 1:10; 7:7; 8:23; 9:39; 14:17; 16:9). (4) The existence of the community of disciples in the world is not an unavoidable fate; rather, it is the express will of the Father (Jn 17:15). As the Son has brought the Father's revelation and thus salvation into the world, it is now the Christian community that proclaims to the world the message of Jesus Christ, which alone brings salvation. This takes place in the missionary initiatives of the church, a mission that overcomes the world as the place of unbelief as Jews and Gentiles come to faith in Jesus the Messiah and Savior.

It remains true, however, that John's notion of the world is negative.[53] For John, the term κόσμος (*kosmos*) often means "humanity in general."[54] When *kosmos* refers to the world as "place," it usually designates the world as the place where human beings live: Jesus came "into the world," which means that he came to people.[55] The statements about Jesus coming "into the world" indicate that John presupposes another dimension of existence that is different from the "world" of human beings. The world of humankind is "from below," whereas Jesus comes "from above" (Jn 8:23). It is, however, not just the identity of Jesus—and of all those who believe in him—that differs from the identity of the world. What Jesus offers to the world is also different from what the world has to offer: the peace that Jesus gives is different from the peace that the world gives (Jn 14:27). Finally, the *kosmos* into which Jesus has come had a beginning and will come to an end (Jn 17:5.24; 1 Jn 2:17), as the world, including all human beings and all powers that operate in the world, are temporal and transitory. A major emphasis of John with regard to the identity of the world is the state of affairs of the world, described as darkness without life, as blindness without knowledge, as lack of orientation without meaning.[56] The world is the place of sin that needs to be carried away (Jn 1:29). The world is the place where Satan, the "ruler of the world," dominates, controlling all desires, motivations and initiatives.[57] In other words, the world is a dangerous place, both for human beings in general and also for believers in Jesus Christ.

---

[53]Occurrences of the term κόσμος in John's Gospel and Epistles are as follows: Gospel, 78; 1 John, 23; 2 John, 1. For the observations that follow above see Towner 1995, 107-10.

[54]See Jn 1:10; 3:16; 4:42; 8:12; 9:5. See BDAG, s.v. "κόσμος 6a."

[55]See Jn 1:9; 6:14; 7:4; 1 Jn 4:1, 9. For the comments that follow above see Towner 1995, 108.

[56]See Jn 3:19; 8:12; 9:5, 35-41.

[57]See Jn 8:44; 12:31; 14:30; 16:11; 17:15; 1 Jn 2:15-16; 5:19.

In his Gospel, John focuses his exposition entirely on the mission of Jesus.[58] Jesus the only and preexistent Son of God (Jn 1:14, 18), sent by God to reveal God in the world and to take away the sin of the world (Jn 1:18, 29, 36; 3:16). This is the "work" (ἔργον, *ergon*) that the mission of Jesus accomplishes (Jn 4:34; 17:4). The "works" (ἔργα, *erga*) that Jesus performs[59] are "signs" (σημεῖα, *sēmeia*) of his messianic authority as the Son, who reveals the Father and brings to the Jews the salvation that God promised according to the Scriptures. For this reason the "hour" of Jesus' death is the hour of his glorification (Jn 12:23; 13:31-32; 17:1). Jesus is the promised messianic shepherd (Ezek 34:23-24; Zech 13:7-9), who, in contrast to the leaders of the Jews, gives his life for the sheep and thus leads them safely to green pastures (Jn 10:1-15). The new flock initially consists of Jews but eventually includes "other sheep" as well (Jn 10:16). The new people of God established by the Father's revelation in the Son is defined no longer by ethnic identity but by faith in Jesus: all those who hear Jesus' voice belong to the flock that is God's people, whether they are Jews or Gentiles, so that "there will be one flock, one shepherd" (Jn 10:16). The mission of the disciples is a function of the mission of Jesus, derived from his mission (Jn 17:18; 20:21) and subordinated to his mission: the disciples have been called by Jesus (Jn 1:35-51), they have been commissioned by Jesus (Jn 20:21-23), they follow Jesus (Jn 1:37; 21:22), they reap where they have not labored (Jn 4:38), they see fruit that they themselves have not produced (Jn 15:8, 16), and they give witness not of themselves but of Jesus (Jn 15:27). Their mission takes place "in the world," which hates them because it hated Jesus as well (Jn 15:19).

Teresa Okure interprets Jesus' conversation with the Samaritan woman (Jn 4:1-42) in terms of the unique and exclusive role of Jesus' mission, upon which the mission of the disciples depends. The following observations are pertinent. (1) John underscores the priority of Jesus' mission with the help of his dramatic narrative technique. The disciples are absent when Jesus speaks with the woman (Jn 4:2, 8, 27). This absence of the disciples highlights the fact that Jesus and the Father are the real "workers" in the work of missionary outreach.[60] (2) John states explicitly that Jesus is the exclusive mediator of salvation from the Father (Jn 4:1-26). He demonstrates this with regard to the woman (Jn 4:28-42), to the disciples (Jn 4:31-38) and to the Samaritans (Jn 4:28-30, 39-42). (3) In the explanatory section Jn 4:28-42, Jesus' entire mission appears as the subject that unifies the entire chapter: Jesus alone does the work (Jn 4:34) of the Father, and he completes this work. The disciples also have been sent, but what they reap is the harvest of the work of Jesus and the Father (Jn 4:38). And the Samaritans recognize that the real "evangelist" was not the woman, but Jesus (Jn 4:42). John

---

[58]For the survey that follows above see Köstenberger and O'Brien 2001, 203-26.
[59]See Jn 5:20, 36; 7:3, 21; 9:3, 4; 10:25, 32, 33, 37, 38; 14:10, 11, 12; 15:24.
[60]Okure 1988, 286.

develops the unique role of Jesus in God's mission and the dependence of the disciples upon Jesus in the farewell discourse (Jn 13—17) and in Jn 21.[61] Jesus reveals himself as the one who sustains the disciples in their everyday lives[62] and makes their mission fruitful,[63] while he offers himself as the model of humility that should characterize the missionary initiatives.

The disciples' dependence on Jesus and his mission is, at the same time, a dependence of the missionaries on the listeners whom they seek to lead to faith in Jesus Christ. Jesus' conversation with the Samaritan woman in Jn 4 shows[64] that the listeners determine the language and method used in missionary work. As Jesus makes himself "dependent" upon the woman, who constantly changes the subject, so the Christian missionaries are totally committed to the people who have not yet recognized who Jesus is and who have their own agendas and interests. Jesus' self-revelation is the central feature at the end of the conversation. The disciples likewise must be willing to wait and to be open for Jesus' self-revelation. This openness is to be understood in terms of faith in the Son, whom the Father has sent (Jn 6:29; 20:31). Without this faith it is impossible to receive the gift of eternal life, which the Father grants through the Son (Jn 3:16; 10:10; 17:2-3; 20:31). Since this initial faith is not the final goal, Jesus exhorts his disciples to remain steadfast in the faith and to let their faith become a living reality in everyday life, characterized by mutual love and humble ministry. It is this love, expressed in the unity of the believers, that is the authentic witness of the believing community of the followers of Jesus, who exemplify the reality of the new order that has been established through Jesus' mission.

Hubert Ritt argues that Jn 4:1-42 demonstrates that the missionary initiative to proclaim and pass on the Christian faith is connected with a woman, which proves for the Gospel of John that "women continue to have free space for ministry. There is no evidence of androcentric (focused on men) tendencies in the (institutional) development of the ministries."[65] This interpretation owes more to modern feminist concerns than to the evidence of the text.

The discourse about the good shepherd and the sheep (Jn 10:1-18) is fundamentally significant for the early Christian mission, which reaches both Jews and Gentiles with the good news of Jesus the Messiah and Savior and assembles the believers in Jesus in communities in which all followers of Jesus worship God together. Jesus speaks of sheep, a sheep pen with a gate, a gatekeeper, a shep-

---

[61]Okure 1998, 287 (summary).

[62]Note the metaphor of the vine and the branches in Jn 15:1-8, and the meal after the miraculous catch of fish in Jn 21:1-14.

[63]This he does by sending the Holy Spirit, by praying for his disciples, by providing the miraculous catch of fish.

[64]See "Conversations with Individuals" in §9.2.

[65]Ritt 1989, 305.

herd, thieves and strangers in order to paint a picture that emphasizes the contrast between the true shepherd and the thieves and strangers (Jn 10:1-5).[66] The true shepherd can be recognized by the fact that he uses the gate to enter the sheep pen and by the fact that he calls the sheep by name and they recognize his voice. The exposition of this metaphor connects two elements of the picture with an "I am" saying to Jesus. (1) Jesus is "the gate for the sheep" (Jn 10:7). He alone is the door into the sheep pen of the flock that is the people of God. Only those who enter through Jesus into God's people will be saved (Jn 10:7-10). (2) Jesus is "the good shepherd" (Jn 10:11). The sheep belong only to him: he is the true shepherd because he gives his life for the sheep (Jn 10:11-19). There are two kinds of sheep that recognize Jesus' voice and for which he gives up his life as the true shepherd: the *probata ta idia* (Jn 10:4, 12), which are the sheep from the (Jewish) people of God, and the *alla probata* (Jn 10:16), which are the sheep "that do not belong to this sheep pen" (of the Jewish *laos*). Because the shepherd gives up his life for all sheep, the circle of the recipients of salvation is expanded beyond Israel as the people of God. This means that Jesus' substitutionary death creates from the sheep from Israel that recognize the voice of the shepherd and from the other sheep "one flock" with one shepherd (γενήσονται μία ποίμνη, εἰς ποιμήν, *genēsontai mia poimnē, heis poimēn* [Jn 10:16]). This one flock under the care of the one shepherd "is not an already existing, given entity but results only from Jesus' death for the sheep."[67] John points the Gentile-Christian readers of his Gospel indirectly but unquestionably to the inclusion of Gentiles in the universal community of Israel's king through Jesus' death and resurrection (Jn 1:49; 12:13).

Teresa Okure interprets Jn 13—17 as Jesus' commentary on the missionary task, in the context of the possibility that these chapters represent the Johannine version of the Synoptic missionary discourses (Mt 10; Lk 9-10).[68] Without evaluating this hypothesis in detail, I will summarize the missionary elements of these chapters following Okure's analysis. (1) Missionary work requires humility. Jesus warns of self-glorification (Jn 13:16; 15:16) and illustrates his meaning when he washes the feet of the disciples (Jn 13:12-17). His prayer to the Father emphasizes his dependence (Jn 17:4), an important function of humility. (2) The scope of missionary work is universal. Jesus directs his own mission to the world (Jn 1:9-10; 3:16-17; 10:36; 12:47; 17:18), and the same applies to the disciples (Jn 17:18). Mission signifies the revelation of the Father (Jn 1:18; 17:6). The mission of the disciples is not merely the continuation of Jesus' mission but is "concurrent with it in its completed phase, the harvest phase."[69] The disciples

---

[66]For the interpretation that follows above see, besides the commentaries, Frey 1994, 245-49.
[67]Frey 1994, 247; for the comments that follows above see ibid., 249.
[68]Okure 1988, 196-219; for the discussion that follows above see ibid.
[69]Okure 1988, 200.

are sent into the same world into which Jesus was sent, and they are sent in the same way in which Jesus was sent (Jn 17:18; 20:21). (3) The mission of the disciples does not add any essential feature to Jesus' mission: the "finished work" of Jesus (Jn 19:30) is complete in all its dimensions—the disciples reap the harvest of Jesus' work. The disciples do not stand between Jesus and the believers: rather than speak "about Jesus" in their proclamation, they bring the people "to Jesus" so that they can hear Jesus' voice (Jn 1:29-36, 41, 45; 12:22; 21:8, 10-11). Both the acceptance of the word and the missionary sermon constitute the participation in the work of Jesus' completed mission (Jn 4:10, 14, 21, 23-24, 38, 42; 21:9-13.). (4) The mission of the disciples is integrally linked with fellowship. The focus on the disciples as a group underscores Jesus' uniqueness in mission: although he accomplished the work of the Father by himself (Jn 4:34; 17:4), the missionary effectiveness of the disciples is connected with their cooperative activity as a community.[70] This means, first, that Jesus gives the mission of the Father to a group of people, not to individuals, so that the veracity of the believers' witness can be verified (Jn 20:30). Second, the necessity of a group underlines Jesus' role as the only shepherd and guide of the flock (Jn 10:6; 12:32), and as the only way, truth and life of the believers (Jn 14:6). Third, the focus on the group reduces the risk that individuals will behave as if they own the mission: the glory belongs to the Father alone (Jn 15:8; 17:4, 22). (5) In Jn 15:1-8, 16 Jesus emphasizes that the disciples must be entirely dependent upon him as witnesses of his mission. The metaphor of the vine and the branches underlines the centrality of Jesus and the constant dependence of the disciples on him. John underscores, first, that the disciples receive their identity from Jesus. The personal life and the missionary fruitfulness of the "branches" depend on their "remaining" in the vine (Jn 15:5). The role of the disciples is important: only the branches of the vine carry fruit. But without the care of the Father (Jn 15:1-2) and without the work of Jesus, the disciples would neither live nor bring fruit (Jn 15:4-5). The primary, empowering reality is the work of Jesus and of the Father—the disciples only need to bring fruit. The nature of the disciples' mission is harvesting (καρπὸν φέρειν, *karpon pherein* [Jn 15:4, 16]). Second, the function of bringing fruit is the gift of being chosen by Jesus, rather than a role given to the disciples directly by the Father (Jn 5:16). The disciples are responsible to Jesus, as Jesus is responsible to the Father.[71] Finally, John emphasizes, as does Luke (Lk 24:48-49; Acts 1:8), the connection between the Spirit of God and the Gentile mission (Jn 16:8-10).

Jesus' surprising saying in Jn 14:12 is also related to the mission of the disciples:

---

[70]See Jn 4:31-38; 13:35; 15:27; 17:20-23; 15:16; 17:20; 21:1-14.

[71]Note the passage about the bread of life (Jn 6:56-57), with the distinction between "remaining in" Jesus, the personal dimension (Jn 6:56), and "living because of" Jesus, the missionary dimension (Jn 6:57).

"Very truly, I tell you, the one who believes in me will also do the works that I do and, in fact, will do greater works than these, because I am going to the Father."[72] The works that Jesus does are his miracles, events caused by God. The "greater works" that Jesus promises to his disciples who believe in him do not signify more remarkable miracles than those that Jesus performed: in John's Gospel the restoration of sight to a man born blind and the resurrection of Lazarus from the dead are entirely climactic events of Jesus' ministry, not only as visible events but also as signs that demonstrated that Jesus is the light of the world and the life of the world. Jesus in no way suggests that the disciples will perform even more dramatic miracles than these. According to Jn 5:20, the Father will show the Son "greater works than these," referring to the resurrection to life and to the judgment (Jn 5:21-29)—there are no greater "works" than these! In Jn 14:12 the prerequisite for the greater "works" is Jesus' glorification in his death and resurrection. The "greater works" thus refer to the continuing mission of the exalted Son through his disciples.[73] The greater works are the result of the life, death and resurrection of Jesus as the harvest in which the disciples reap: "Very truly, I tell you, unless a grain of wheat falls into the earth and dies, it remains just a single grain; but if it dies, it bears much fruit" (Jn 12:24). Thus the "greater works" that Jesus promises to the disciples are their missionary activities, in which Jesus' life, death and resurrection assume an ever greater effect and scope—the present and future salvation of the people who believe in Jesus and the continuously expanding growth of the church in the cities, regions and provinces of the world. Those who believe in Jesus are sent by Jesus, as Jesus has been sent by the Father (Jn 20:21).

Jesus' statement in Jn 14:12 provides the following exposition of the missionary theology that characterizes the faith of the followers of Jesus. (1) Authentic faith that depends on Jesus implies the conviction that the mission of the disciples as a task of the community of believers is never finished, that the mission of the Father will reach its goal despite all opposition, and that the mission of the Son is carried out and becomes effective through the authority that Jesus grants to his disciples. (2) Authentic faith is missionary faith. Faith that is dependent upon Jesus and relies on God is not, however, fixated on quantifiable expansion or on success that can be counted. Even though the reference to "greater" works does not necessarily exclude the element of ascertainable quantity, it focuses in the context of Jesus' life, death and resurrection on the offer of eternal life to people (Jn 17:2) and on the conviction of the unbelieving world (Jn 16:8-11).[74] Faith that relies on Jesus aims at visible success but knows that even in the "greater works" that happen it is always Jesus who is at work (Jn

---

[72]For the comments that follow above see Schnabel 1991; see also Köstenberger and O'Brien 2001, 218-19.

[73]See Barrett, *Jn,* 460; Brown, *Jn,* 2:633; Schlatter, *Joh,* 295.

[74]See Schnackenburg, *Joh,* 3:81 (ET, 3:71-72).

14:13). (3) Miracles can indeed happen in the mission of the community of the disciples. They are, however, as in Jesus' mission, not the genuine cause of authentic faith, but rather are "signs" that point to Jesus as the revealer and giver of life. A merely external faith in miracles does not understand the language of the sign: since it does not lead to authentic faith in Jesus, which is unconditional, it therefore is inadequate faith (Jn 4:48; 6:26, 36). The external faith that relies on miracles, on "seeing" the works of Jesus, because his word seems insufficient is a faith that is inferior (Jn 10:37-38; 14:10-11) and needs further growth and clarification.[75] Authentic faith relies on Jesus' word without needing the verification of "seeing" miracles. Thus Jesus says to Thomas, "Have you believed because you have seen me? Blessed are those who have not seen and yet have come to believe" (Jn 20:29). This beatitude is, with Jn 13:17, one of only two beatitudes in the Fourth Gospel. Genuine faith is grounded in the word of the Son, whom the Father has sent into the world, and in the mission of the disciples genuine faith relies on the apostolic word. Thus Jesus prays for those "who will believe in me through their word" (Jn 17:20). John repeatedly emphasizes that faith comes from "hearing"[76]—but not all people who have heard Jesus have come to faith, particularly if their first and foremost "evaluation" of Jesus consisted in "seeing," as the example of Nicodemus illustrates.[77]

John reports, in connection with the decision of the Jerusalem authorities to eliminate Jesus, a prophecy of Caiaphas the high priest (Jn 11:49-50), which he explains (Jn 11:51-52) and repeats on the occasion of Annas's interrogation of Jesus (Jn 18:14). Caiaphas had said, "It is better for you to have one man die for the people [*hyper tou laou*] than to have the whole nation [*holon to ethnos*] destroyed" (Jn 11:50). John interprets this cynical advice as unwitting prophecy: Caiaphas prophesied the substitutionary death of atonement of Jesus, who died vicariously for the people (*hyper tou ethnous*), and not only for his one *ethnos* but also "to gather into one the dispersed children of God" (Jn 11:51-52).[78] The author of the Fourth Gospel, who writes probably after the destruction of Jerusalem, implies that the "rational" argument that the high priest offered in A.D. 30 proved to be foolish in light of the events of the Jewish revolt in A.D. 66-70: the Romans came, Jerusalem was conquered, the temple was destroyed and most of the priests had been liquidated. For John, the reverse conclusion applies, as Jörg Frey suggests: "In contrast to the fears of the members of the Sanhedrin, Jesus' redemptive ministry did not constitute a competition for the political power of the Romans nor a provocation to take action, despite his messianic royal dignity." The Greek word *laos* that is used in Caiaphas's advice tradition-

---

[75]See Schnackenburg, *Joh*, 1:346, 521 (ET, 1:517, 571-72).
[76]Emphasized by C. Koester 1989.
[77]See Jn 3:9; 6:14-15, 41, 60; 8:59; 12:34; cf. 2:23-25.
[78]For the interpretation that follows above see Frey 1994, 238-45; quotation, 241-42.

ally is used for Israel as the people of God—that is, the Jewish people—while *ethnos* characterizes the Jews as a national-political entity. John transposes these meanings in his interpretation of Caiaphas's "prophecy": Jesus died for the Jewish *ethnos,* but not only for that; he also died for the *laos* as the new people of God, the new community of those who accept God's salvation. This new eschatological people of God includes parts of the Jewish *ethnos:* the "true Israelites," such as Nathanael, who acknowledge Jesus as Israel's king (Jn 1:47-49); but the new *laos* includes others as well, the "scattered children of God" (τὰ τέκνα τοῦ θεοῦ τὰ διεσκορπισμένα, *ta tekna tou theou ta dieskorpismena* [Jn 11:52]).[79] The new people of God is constituted "no longer on the basis of descent but on the basis of participation in the redemptive effect of Jesus' death by faith." Jesus had already emphasized in a debate with a Jewish audience that descent from Abraham no longer guarantees the reception of God's salvation (Jn 8:30-45). The "scattered children of God" are not simply the Gentile believers: they are "the sum total of those who are 'gathered into one' by Jesus' death, those who participate in the salvation that results from his substitutionary death—that is, the entire λαός that is newly constituted by Jesus' death."

Michael Labahn suggests that the wine miracle in Cana in Jn 2:1-12 and the healing of the official's son in Jn 4:46-54 can be traced back to a presumably fixed written tradition that can be described as a "missionary broadsheet" or leaflet that "celebrates Jesus as divine epiphany who reveals his power in people who are about to die."[80] He surmises that the story of the transformation of water into wine was an epiphany miracle, at the most primitive level of the development of the tradition, in which an appearance of Jesus as God for the salvation of his devotees was celebrated. According to Labahn, influences of the Dionysus myth as well as the fact that Roman emperors were celebrated as "new Dionysus" suggest that this miracle story has a polemical point: as a result of the integration into the framework of Jn 2—4, "the miracle no longer reads as a testimony of Jesus' divinity but as a report of his ministry in union with the Father." In other words, the miracle story was transformed into a "devotional story" whose focus "is no longer the mission but the edification and the preservation of the Johannine community."[81] The narrative of the healing of the official's son in Capernaum, at the earliest stage of the tradition, emphasizes the significance of Jesus as miracle worker who works for the benefit of human life, interpreting it as life that God grants. The fact that the faith of the official and of his family or community is highlighted at the end of the miracle story implies that the missionary motif is decisive.[82] Similarly, the narrative of the healing of the lame man at the pool in Jn 5:1-18, a demonstration of Jesus as powerful and sovereign miracle worker, can be read at the earliest level of the tradition in terms of a missionary function.[83] Finally, the narrative

---

[79]Frey 1994, 239-40, 242-43; the quotations that follow above, ibid., 243, 245.

[80]Labahn 1999, 120-212, esp. 122, 166; quotation, 166.

[81]Labahn 1999, 134-67; quotations 166, 167.

[82]Labahn 1999, 168-212; summary, ibid., 211-12.

[83]Labahn 1999, 213-64, esp. 242, 263; also 477. Labahn suggests that an "interior" or paraenetic function is possible as well: "Jesus grants a new quality of life through the liberation from sickness and/or guilt *which needs to be preserved in the life as a Christian*" (263).

of the healing of the blind man in Jn 9:1-41 had a missionary intention as well at the earliest stage of the tradition: "The story emphasizes Jesus as miracle worker. The community can present itself to outsiders with this kind of praise and proclaim Jesus as powerful man who works miracles. . . . The act of the healing of the blind man shows that messianic hopes and expectations have been fulfilled in the coming and in the ministry of Jesus."[84] Labahn correctly concludes that the miracles stories of the Gospel of John do not reveal an antidocetic intention, as Udo Schnelle had maintained: John has no "Christology of glory" that forces him to combine in the miracle stories the elements of the divinity and the humanity of the messenger. He argues, "The author of the Fourth Gospel can portray and understand the ministry and the incarnation of the eschatological revealer only by indicating that the divine doxa of the preexistent Son shines through his ministry, and this happens in the miracles, in which the goal of the sending is actualized, the gift of life for those who belong to him."[85] This is not the place to discuss the tradition-historical and form-critical analyses of Labahn, who, like so many other historical-critical interpreters of the Fourth Gospel, "knows" surprisingly well which details of the texts are projected back onto the "stage of the historical Jesus." Still, Labahn demonstrates the presence of geographical (Palestinian) "local color" in some of the passages that he discusses. He also shows that John is not interested in a merely symbolical understanding of Jesus' miracles,[86] and that (although this was not his intention) missionary purposes and ecclesiastical goals are not mutually exclusive: the new life that God offers and makes possible through liberation from illness and guilt by Jesus, his Son made flesh, must prove itself in the life of Christian believers as well.

It is worth mentioning the hypothesis here of J. D. M. Derrett, who suggests that the reference to the drinking of Jesus' blood and the eating of his flesh in Jn 6:47-60 has parallels in Theravada Buddhism, which, in his view, indicates that the author of this text expected that his exposition would be intelligible for Buddhists as well.[87]

Albrecht Oepke's summary conclusion about the theology of the Fourth Gospel remains valid:[88] "The witness of Christ in the Gospel of John is the living attestation of God's revelation, as remote from rigid dogmatism as from syncretistic accommodation. In this sense it remains a missionary model for all times."

The First Epistle of John interacts with the activity and doctrines of false teachers who originally belonged to the church (1 Jn 4:1). These teachers believe that the proclamation of the atoning death of Jesus Christ is insufficient, and they claim to have achieved a state of spiritual perfection. Peter Stuhlmacher comments in this context, "According to the Epistles of John, missions does not only mean to proclaim Christ, but also to resist false teaching concerning Jesus Christ and to resist the lack of love of these 'Christian' heretics who disguise themselves behind the name of Jesus."[89]

Many scholars interpret 3 Jn 3, 6, 8, 12 as alluding to itinerant missionaries

---

[84]Labahn 1999, 305-77, esp. 373, 477; quotation, 337.
[85]Labahn 1999, 480-82; quotation, 481-82; contra Schnelle 1987.
[86]Labahn 1999, 477, 479, 482 (summary).
[87]J. D. M. Derrett, "St. John's Jesus and the Buddha," *Journal of Higher Criticism* 6 (1999): 161-74.
[88]Oepke 1941, 26.
[89]Stuhlmacher 1981, 130.

who follow Jesus' missionary stipulations and preach Jesus Christ, influenced by Johannine Christology.[90]

3 Jn 5-12: "Beloved, you do faithfully whatever you do for the friends, even though they are strangers to you; [6]they have testified to your love before the church. You will do well to send them on in a manner worthy of God; [7]for they began their journey for the sake of Christ, accepting no support from non-believers. [8]Therefore we ought to support such people, so that we may become coworkers with the truth. [9]I have written something to the church; but Diotrephes, who likes to put himself first, does not acknowledge our authority. [10]So if I come, I will call attention to what he is doing in spreading false charges against us. And not content with those charges, he refuses to welcome the friends, and even prevents those who want to do so and expels them from the church. [11]Beloved, do not imitate what is evil but imitate what is good. Whoever does good is from God; whoever does evil has not seen God. [12]Everyone has testified favorably about Demetrius, and so has the truth itself. We also testify for him, and you know that our testimony is true."

The "elder" (*presbyteros*) writes 3 John to Gaius because a certain Diotrephes refused to provide hospitality for traveling missionaries. Adolf von Harnack assumes an extensive missionary ministry that was organized by the presbyter (John) in the central church (Ephesus) that sent out numerous missionaries to other parts of Asia Minor. He suggests that the mission of the presbyter represents the "church of the Spirit" (*Geistkirche*), which commissions charismatic itinerant missionaries, authorized by the presbyter but not subject to a fixed organization. Diotrephes represents the "church of the office" (*Amtskirche*), which was in the process of becoming pervasive and which mistrusted the itinerant preacher. Diotrephes was, in Harnack's view, the first "monarchic bishop" whose name has been preserved.[91] Walter Bauer believes that Diotrephes was the heretical bishop of a local congregation who excommunicated other Christians, which is criticized by the presbyter.[92] Ernst Käsemann holds the opposite view: Diotrephes was an orthodox bishop while the presbyter was an excommunicated elder of Diotrephes' church who spread heresies.[93] We should note, however, that the text of 3 John refers neither to heresy nor to excommunication. The only conclusions that the text allows are that Diotrephes claimed a position in the church that he does not deserve in the eyes of the presbyter. It is unclear whether there was a more fundamental ecclesial or institutional controversy.[94]

There seems to be no doubt, however, that the presbyter (John) sent missionaries to other areas who visited other cities and towns (and perhaps villages). They did not seek support from the Gentiles (3 Jn 7), but they expected to re-

---

[90]Stuhlmacher 1981, 131, with reference to Theissen 1973; cf. Schnelle 1991, 41 n. 13.

[91]Adolf von Harnack, *Über den dritten Johannesbrief* (TU 15.3; Leipzig: Hinrich, 1897), 21.

[92]Bauer 1934, 96-97.

[93]E. Käsemann, "Ketzer und Zeuge," in Käsemann 1970, 1:168-87.

[94]Conzelmann and Lindemann 1995, 325; cf. Marshall, *EpJn,* 88-90; Brown, *EpJn,* 107.

ceive room and board from the existing local congregations and their representatives, including Gaius, even though initially they were not known to the
churches that they encountered during their travels (3 Jn 5). The behavior of
Diotrephes seems to have been an exception, however. He possibly disagreed
with the rigorous attitude of the presbyter with regard to the opposing teachers,
for whom Diotrephes perhaps had sympathies.[95]

Martin Hengel suggests that we should describe these itinerant Christians perhaps not as
missionaries "since the unique form of missions which was dominant at the time of Paul
had long passed. They no longer visited synagogues and they no longer preached publicly as Paul allegedly did on the Areopagus in Acts 17 or in the *Acts of the Apostles,* which
glorify the preaching situation of the apostles. Missionary work around A.D. 100 was carried out primarily through individual contacts and conversations, as the story of Justin's
conversion through a mysterious old teacher shows, and through invitations to the services of the house churches. The traveling brethren evidently did not seek specific contacts with pagans unless they showed interest in the life and the teaching of the Christians.
They presumably wanted to strengthen the churches and help them maintain unity." This
hypothesis rests more on speculation than on the evidence of the texts, it cannot be substantiated through statements in 2—3 John, nor is it very plausible. If the number of Christian churches had increased throughout Asia Minor as it did in Pontus and Bithynia by
A.D. 111/112, so much so that the Roman governor became concerned and tried to curb
the activities of Christians (Pliny, *Ep.* 10.96.8-10), it seems impossible to explain this
growth merely by "individual contacts and conversations" and the evangelism of the
house churches in their meetings. The fact that we have little evidence for missionaries
in the second century A.D. who engaged in missionary work along the lines of Peter and
Paul or Philip and Barnabas does not prove that they did not exist.

The book of Revelation, written probably in the last two decades of the first century, demonstrates, albeit indirectly, that the missionary commitment at least of
the author has not diminished. The vision of the innumerably large crowd of
people "from every nation, from all tribes and peoples and languages" (Rev 7:9)
who praise God and the Lamb does not correspond to the empirical reality of
the church at the end of the first century.[96] This vision is an echo of God's promise to Abraham and Jacob that their descendants would be so numerous that no
one could count them.[97] The vision asserts more than that the promise to Abraham has found its fulfillment in the community of the followers of Jesus, as
Heinz Giesen explains: "When John speaks of a multitude that no one could
count, he cannot merely think of the Christians of his time. They are only a small
minority. Rather, the seer looks into the future with hope. He knows that the

---

[95]Hengel 1993, 124-33 (ET, 34-39); the quotation that follows above, ibid., 133 (an expansion
of ET, 38).
[96]Bauckham 1993a, 223; for the caveat that follows above see ibid. See generally Miller 1998;
Köstenberger and O'Brien 2001, 243-49.
[97]See Mounce, *Rev,* 162; Beale, *Rev,* 426-27; Osborne, *Rev,* 318; Bauckham 1993a, 223. Cf. Gen
13:16; 15:5; 16:10; 22:17; 26:4; 32:12; Hos 1:10; *Jub.* 13:20; 14:4-5; Heb 11:12.

Lamb who ransoms people from every tribe and language and people and nation (Rev 5:9) will be successful. Speculations whether the author expects a
mass conversion shortly before the end[98] are not very likely. We will see that the
seer reckons indeed with a longer time period before the end."[99]

Richard Bauckham interprets several passages in the book of Revelation in
terms of a Christian reinterpretation of the Old Testament and Jewish traditions
of the holy war (Rev 5:5-6; 7:2-14; 14:1-5).[100] The census in Rev 7:4-8 alludes to
the repeated census of Israel in the Old Testament whose goal it was to ascertain
the military power of the people of God (Num 1:3, 18, 20; 26:2; 1 Chron 27:23;
2 Sam 24:1-9). Men were counted who were capable to serve in the military. In
the parallel passage Rev 14:1-4 John speaks of men who were virgins. The *War
Scroll* of Qumran (1QM), which describes the messianic war in the last days,
divides the army of the people of God according to the twelve tribes of Israel.
The Jewish vision of the restoration of the twelve tribes of Israel included the
expectation that Israel would participate in the final war, in which God's enemies will be finally and utterly defeated (Is 11:14; Mic 5:6-9). Whether we agree
with all details of this interpretation or not, Bauckham's conclusions are plausible. John uses military metaphors and traditions to emphasize two truths. (1)
The decisive battle in God's holy war against evil, which includes Rome, the
seemingly invincible world power, has already been won through the faithful
witness and the sacrificial death of Jesus the Lamb of God (Rev 5:5-6). (2) The
followers of Jesus therefore are called to participate in this war and in this victory in the same manner, as they follow the Lamb "wherever he goes" (Rev
14:4): by courageously proclaiming the gospel of God's redemptive revelation
in Jesus Christ, even if it means martyrdom, "they have conquered him [the ac-
cuser] by the blood of the Lamb and by the word of their testimony, for they
did not cling to life even in the face of death" (Rev 12:11).

John emphasizes that the existence of the local congregations is safeguarded
by Jesus Christ, who loves them and has made them "to be a kingdom and
priests" (Rev 1:5-6) and his "bride" (Rev 19:7-8, 9; 20:9; 21:2-3, 9; 22:17).[101] In Rev
1:11 and in the prophetic messages in Rev 2—3 John speaks specifically of Ephesus, Smyrna, Pergamon, Thyatira, Sardis, Philadelphia and Laodikeia. In Rev 7:1-
17 John interrupts the narration of the judgments of the seven seals to show that
the followers of the Lamb have no reason to fear the coming day of God's judgment or the trials and judgments that God inflicts upon the earth in the time between the first coming of the Lamb and his return. John assures the believers that
God has sealed them with his protective seal, promising to preserve them for his

---

[98]Thus Räisänen 1995c, 152.
[99]Giesen, *Offb*, 1997.
[100]Bauckham 1988; followed by Beale, *Rev*, 422-23.
[101]See McIlraith 1989.

kingdom (Rev 7:1-8). In order to encourage the believers and the churches he shows them the effect and result of God's seal in the next vision of the redeemed followers of Jesus from all nations, who stand in God's presence and rejoice in the salvation and the blessing of God's new world (Rev 7:9-17).

Many interpretations have been offered for the figure of the 144,000; the following are among the more plausible suggestions. (1) They are Jews or Jewish Christians.[102] This interpretation means, however, that only Jews or Jewish Christians receive God's seal and that the Gentile Christians have to make do without it. In view of the meaning of God's seal—God provides protection of his people from the dangers of the last days to preserve them for participation in God's kingdom—this is hardly plausible. (2) They are martyrs of the end times.[103] This interpretation seems to be supported by Rev 14:4. However, the enumeration of all twelve tribes of Israel and the symbolism of the number "twelve" emphasize the notion of completeness—the martyrs constitute only a (small) part of the community of believers. (3) They are the entire people of God, in the sense of all followers of the Lamb.[104] This is the most plausible explanation, and the following arguments are relevant. (a) The effect of the seal must be as extensive as the dangers of the end times. (b) According to Rev 9:4, the church as a whole is sealed as protection against the attacks of the demonic powers. (c) In Rev 13:16-17 it states that all people will be required to accept the mark of the beast. This means that John assumes that the world is divided into two camps: those who accept God's seal, and those who accept the seal of the beast, who is God's enemy. (d) The vision of the 144,000 and of the innumerable multitude in Rev 7 has parallels to the vision of the Lion and the Lamb in Rev 5. As John *hears* that the Lion of Judah and the Root of David have been victorious (εἷς ἐκ τῶν πρεσβυτέρων λέγει [Rev 5:5]) and *sees* the Lamb that has been slaughtered (εἶδον ἐν μέσῳ τοῦ θρόνου [Rev 5:6]), he *hears* the number of those who were sealed (ἤκουσα τὸν ἀριθμὸν τῶν ἐσφραγισμένων [Rev 7:4]) and *sees* a multitude that nobody could number (εἶδον . . . ὄχλος πολύς [Rev 7:9]). Richard Bauckham concludes that the relationship between the 144,000 and the innumerable multitude is the same as the relationship between the Lion and the Lamb.[105] He refers to the following connections between the Lion and the 144,000 and between the Lamb and the innumerable multitude: the Lion *from the tribe of Judah* (ἐκ τῆς φυλῆς Ἰούδα [Rev 5:5]) corresponds with a list of those who have been sealed from the tribes of Israel, with those *from the tribe of Judah* (ἐκ φυλῆς Ἰούδα [Rev 7:5]) listed first; the Lamb who stands (ἀρνίον ἑστηκός [Rev 5:6]) and who has redeemed people from every tribe, language, people and nation (ἐκ πάσης φυλῆς καὶ γλώσσης καὶ λαοῦ καὶ ἔθνους [Rev 5:9]) corresponds with the multitude from all nations, tribes, peoples and languages (ἐκ παντὸς ἔθνους καὶ φυλῶν καὶ λαῶν καὶ γλωσσῶν [Rev 7:9]) that stands before the Lamb (ἑστῶτες ἐνώπιον τοῦ θρόνου καὶ ἐνώπιον τοῦ ἀρνίου [Rev 7:9]). Bauckham concludes that the 144,000 are the "Israelite" army of the military Davidic Messiah, while the international multitude represents the followers of the Lamb who was slain. He comments, "Having rejected nationalistic militarism from his picture of the Messiah in 5:5-6,

---

[102]This view is particularly popular in the dispensational interpretations of J. F. Walvoord, J. D. Pentecost, R. L. Thomas; see also Kraft, *Offb*, 126-27.

[103]See, for example, Caird, *Rev*, 96-97.

[104]See recently Beale, *Rev*, 404-23. The interpretation by Miller (1998, 235) in terms of missionaries who are commissioned to a final worldwide mission is unconvincing.

[105]Bauckham 1993a, 216, with reference to G. B. Caird and J. P. M. Sweet; followed by Osborne, *Rev*, 313.

John is now equally rejecting it from his picture of the Messiah's followers, whose victory must be of the same kind as that of their leader."[106]

The 144,000 "out of every tribe of the people of Israel" (ἐκ πάσης φυλῆς υἱῶν Ἰσραήλ, *ek pasēs phylēs hyiōn Israēl* [Rev 7:4]) thus represent the "servants of our God" (δούλους τοῦ θεοῦ ἡμῶν, *doulous tou theou hēmōn* [Rev 7:3]),[107] without any limitation to a particular people. John's figure of 144,000, composed of 12 by 12 by 1,000, describes the community of the followers of the Lamb as the new Israel.[108] The twelve tribes symbolize the people of God, while the figure 1,000 stands for completeness of the people of God.

The list of the twelve tribes in Rev 7:4-8 is unique in the Old Testament and Jewish tradition: Judah is moved to the first position (Reuben was the firstborn son), the tribe of Dan is omitted altogether, Manasseh is included (while Joseph is not replaced by Ephraim but remains in the list along with Manasseh). The "promotion" of the slave women's sons, who are moved en bloc from their usual final position to the top of the list—after Judah, the tribe from which the Messiah came, and Reuben the firstborn—is striking. This move may symbolize, according to Christopher Smith, that Gentiles (Gentile Christians) are incorporated in the people of God.[109] At any rate, it is unlikely that the 144,000 represent a Jewish "remnant" who will be saved in the future: the symbolic meaning in terms of "completeness" of the new covenant people of God is more plausible.

Thus the multitude of the 144,000 is identical with the "a great multitude that no one could count, from every nation, from all tribes and peoples and languages, standing before the throne and before the Lamb" (Rev 7:9). Wilhelm Hadorn remarks, "The 144,000 who have been sealed thus represent the two parts of the church who form together the true Israel, with the Jewish Christian church forming the foundation and providing the form—thus the twelve tribes—and the Gentile Christian church bringing in the full number of the people of God which was originally a people of twelve tribes, according to God's will."[110] This "completion" of the people of God requires and implies the active missionary commitment and engagement of the church.

   John emphasizes in the central vision Rev 11:1-14—part of the intermezzo between the events of the sixth trumpet (Rev 9:13-21) and the seventh trumpet (Rev 11:15-19)—that the suffering church has not been relieved of its responsibility to actively and boldly proclaim the gospel of the victory of the Lamb of

---

[106]Bauckham 1993a, 216.

[107]Cf. Rev 2:20; 11:18; 19:2, 5; 22:3, 6.

[108]Cf. Rev 1:5-6; 21:10-21; Gal 6:16; Rom 9:6-8; 11:26; 1 Cor 10:18.

[109]C. R. Smith 1990; cf. idem, "The Tribes of Revelation 7 and the Literary Competence of John the Seer," *JETS* 38 (1995): 231-18; cf. Hengstenberg, *Offb,* ad loc.; Osborne, *Rev,* 313. On C. R. Smith's interpretation see R. Bauckham, "The List of the Tribes in Revelation 7 Again," *JSNT* 42 (1991): 99-115.

[110]Hadorn, *Offb,* 93.

God. The vision of Rev 11:1-14 should be interpreted symbolically, as indicated by the identification of the two witnesses with two olive trees and with "the two lampstands that stand before the Lord of the earth" (Rev 11:4; cf. 1:12-13, 20; 2:1, 5). John compares the church to the temple, while the city represents the world as the enemy of God, and the two witnesses represent the community of the followers of Jesus who bear witness to their crucified Lord in fulfillment of its commission to be a witness of Jesus Christ in the last days of the tribulation.[111] The two lampstands stand "before the Lord of the earth" (Rev 11:4); that is, they are in God's presence in the temple. This means that the community of the followers of the Lamb, as the new Israel, as God's spiritual temple, draws its strength to witness in the time of tribulation from the presence of God in its midst—that is, from the Holy Spirit, who empowers its testimony. The missionary community of the crucified Lord can indeed be harmed by the attacks of the "beast" (Rev 11:7-10). In the end, however, the believers are immune to the deadly consequences of Satan's attacks (Rev 11:11-12).[112]

The book of Revelation concludes with the vision of the heavenly Jerusalem, the city of God, and of God's presence among his people, descending upon the earth in the time of the consummation. The nations of the earth are prominently mentioned in this vision.

Rev 21:1-4, 22-27: "Then I saw a new heaven and a new earth; for the first heaven and the first earth had passed away, and the sea was no more. [2]And I saw the holy city, the new Jerusalem, coming down out of heaven from God, prepared as a bride adorned for her husband. [3]And I heard a loud voice from the throne saying, 'See, the home of God is among mortals. He will dwell with them as their God; they will be his peoples, and God himself will be with them; [4]he will wipe every tear from their eyes. Death will be no more; mourning and crying and pain will be no more, for the first things have passed away.' . . . [22]I saw no temple in the city, for its temple is the Lord God the Almighty and the Lamb. [23]And the city has no need of sun or moon to shine on it, for the glory of God is its light, and its lamp is the Lamb. [24]The nations will walk by its light, and the kings of the earth will bring their glory into it. [25]Its gates will never be shut by day—and there will be no night there. [26]People will bring into it the glory and the honor of the nations. [27]But nothing unclean will enter it, nor anyone who practices abomination or falsehood, but only those who are written in the Lamb's book of life."

Rev 22:1-2: "Then the angel showed me the river of the water of life, bright as crystal, flowing from the throne of God and of the Lamb [2]through the middle of the street of the city. On either side of the river is the tree of life with its twelve kinds of fruit, producing its fruit each month; and the leaves of the tree are for the healing of the nations."

Mathias Rissi interprets the vision of the New Jerusalem with the open gates in Rev 21:24-25 as a symbol for the availability of God's grace, and he interprets

---

[111]See Mounce, *Rev*, 22-24; Beale, *Rev*, 572-75; Satake 1966, 129-32.
[112]Beale, *Rev*, 576-77.

the vision of the consummated world in Rev 22:1-5 as a symbol of God's unconditional grace at the end of time that will become a reality in terms of universal salvation. He comments, "The lake of fire, or the second death, is now done away with, for Israel, the nations, and the kings of the earth have entered into the fullness of the light of the divine glory. Revelation exhibits a hope that embraces the entire creation."[113] In a more recent study Rissi observes, "God's dealings with the world aim at bringing the nations to the knowledge of himself. . . . The seer dares to believe far beyond any restrictions of salvation to those who already believe and to see all as being grasped by redemption at the end. 'All nations' encompasses the totality of the Gentiles. . . . Healed from the sickness of their sin and freed from the curse, they will be servants of God and of the Lamb in Paradise." Richard Bauckham has presented the most extensive discussion on the nations in the book of Revelation.[114] He links the content of the scroll of the vision in Rev 5:1-9 that was opened in Rev 10:1-10 with the missionary witness and the death of the faithful followers of the Lamb portrayed in Rev 11:1-13. This passage presents, according to Bauckham, the central prophetic interest of the author with regard to the arrival of God's kingdom on the earth—God's strategy to take the prophetic witness to all "peoples and tribes and languages and nations" (Rev 11:9; cf. 10:11) and to save the nations from the control of the beast and bring them under his own redemptive dominion (cf. Rev 14:14-16; 15:3-4). God's strategy is twofold: the sacrificial death of the Lamb (Rev 5:6) and the prophetic and sacrificial witness of his followers who have been saved from all nations (Rev 5:9). According to Bauckham, the subject of the conversion of the nations reaches its climax and conclusion in the vision of the New Jerusalem in Rev 21:3-4 and Rev 22:2-3, where "all nations"—besides the historical Israel (the Jews) and the eschatological Israel (the community of Jesus' followers)—will live as covenant peoples in God's presence on the new and perfect earth.

This interpretation implies a redemptive universalism that is unconvincing.[115] The statements of judgment in the book of Revelation, particularly in Rev 19:11-21; 20:1-3, 7-15; 21:8, 27; 22:11-12, 15, clearly express John's conviction that only the followers of Jesus will escape God's judgment that is linked with Jesus' return. It is only the members of God's new covenant people who remain on God's newly created earth; it is only they who form the new redeemed and per-

---

[113]Rissi 1966, 97 (ET, 81); cf. idem 1965, 136-37; the quotation that follows above, idem 1995, 40-41. A similar position is argued by Dieter Georgi, "Die Visionen vom himmlischen Jerusalem in Apk 21 und 22," in *Kirche* (FS G. Bornkamm; ed. D. Lührmann and G. Strecker; Tübingen: Mohr-Siebeck, 1980), 351-72.

[114]Bauckham 1993a, 238-337; cf. idem, *The Theology of the Book of Revelation* (Cambridge: Cambridge University Press, 1993), 84-108.

[115]For a discussion of Bauckham's study see Schnabel 1998; idem 2002d; for the comments that follow above see ibid. On Rev 21:1—22:5 see also Mathewson 2002.

fected humanity. The catalogue of vices in Rev 21:8, the conditions mentioned in Rev 21:27 for access to the city of God, and the statement in Rev 22:15 about the people excluded from eternal salvation make it clear that unrepentant sinners have no place in the New Jerusalem.[116] The covenant that God grants to humanity in Rev 21:3 is described in Rev 21:7 as the believers' fellowship with God in the consummation of divine salvation: "Those who conquer will inherit these things, and I will be their God and they will be my children." The *anthrōpoi* and the *laoi* of Rev 21:3 thus are characterized as the followers of the Lamb: the "nations" are the believers in Jesus who came from all nations.[117] The reference to the nations does not eliminate the limitation that the redeemed community consists of Christians, who come from all nations. As John speaks of the new heavens, the new earth and the new city of God, he assures the believers who have been converted from among all tribes, languages, peoples and nations to faith in Jesus the crucified Savior that they will enjoy God's presence and have fellowship with God after Jesus' return and after the judgment. The expectation of the future immediate presence of God on earth with the followers of the Lamb is confirmed with a new and final covenant that applies only to the conquerors—those believers who are faithful to Jesus and his witness. Since the consummation of salvation has not yet become a reality, John reminds Christians of the importance of being faithful to God and his Messiah.

The vision of "the river of the water of life" that flows from the throne of God and of the Lamb (Rev 22:1), flanked on both sides by the "tree of life" with "twelve kinds of fruit, producing its fruit each month" (Rev 22:2), whose leaves are "for the healing of the nations" (εἰς θεραπείαν τῶν ἐθνῶν, *eis therapeian tōn ethnōn* [Rev 22:2b]) is not a prophecy of the future conversion of the nations. On this point I disagree with Richard Bauckham, who argues that all nations of the earth will inhabit the New Jerusalem and will be healed of their idolatry and other sins so that they will never again come under the curse of God's judgment.[118] As in Rev 21:3, the reference to the nations does not annul the limitation that the redemptive community consists of believers ransomed by the Lamb (Rev 5:9).[119] The "nations" that are "healed" in Rev 22:2 are the people who have been liberated from the curse of the wrath of God (Rev 22:3). All those who have "conquered," who have persevered and have preserved in their lives the victory won by the Lamb of God in the current time of tribulation in which Satanic powers struggle against God, will be given permission "to eat from the tree of life that is in the paradise of God" (Rev 2:7). John never prophesies the conversion of all human-

---

[116]See Bauckham 1993a, 313 n. 100, against the universalism ("Allversöhnung") of Rissi 1966.

[117]See Gundry 1987; Giesen, *Offb*, 455; Müller, *Offb*, 351; for the comment that follows above see ibid.

[118]Bauckham 1993a, 316-18.

[119]See Giesen, *Offb*, 474.

kind or universal success of the missionary proclamation of the church. He prophesies the final victory of Jesus Christ over the evil powers that resist God and over people who follow the "beast" (Rev 19:11-21). He prophesies the judgment and eternal condemnation of Satan, of his assistants on earth and of all people who let themselves be deceived by them (Rev 20:7-15). And John prophesies the eternal destruction of "the cowardly, the faithless, the polluted, the murderers, the fornicators, the sorcerers, the idolaters, and all liars" (Rev 21:8; cf. 21:27).

The people who will live in God's new world and who come "from every tribe and language and people and nation" are the people who have come to faith in Jesus, who died as God's ransom for their sins, and who therefore belong to God (Rev 5:9). They are the people who have been given white garments as a result of Jesus' atoning death (Rev 7:14; 12:11). They are the people who worship the one true God and the Lamb (Rev 7:9-10; 21:9; 22:3) and whose names are therefore written in the book of life (Rev 20:12, 15; 21:27). They are the people who are victorious in the time of tribulation (Rev 21:7). They are the people who are different from the godless (Rev 22:11). They are the people who displayed patient endurance and kept God's commandments and remained faithful to Jesus (Rev 14:12). When the new and perfect world of God, in which there will be no more night and no more tears, has become a reality, then all missionary work will have come to an end.[120] All the people who live in God's new creation, indeed "every creature in heaven and on earth and under the earth and in the sea, and all that is in them," will sing grateful praise "to the one seated on the throne and to the Lamb" and will worship his "blessing and honor and glory and might forever and ever!" (Rev 5:13).

The Missionary Theology of Peter

The missionary theology and the ministry of Peter as reported in the book of Acts were discussed earlier (see §21). The following description focuses on the Epistles of Peter, which, however, do not address the issue of missionary work explicitly, thus making the term "missionary theology" somewhat rhetorical.[121]

We should note, first, that Peter reminds the Christians in Asia Minor of their pagan past.[122] They lived in "ignorance" and were controlled by "desires" (1 Pet 1:14; 4:2) and ancestral traditions (1 Pet 1:18). The malice, guile, insincerity, envy and slander that they must get rid of (1 Pet 2:1) are every bit as much pagan behaviors as licentiousness, passions, drunkenness, revels, carousing and detestable idolatry (1 Pet 4:3). They used to live in "darkness," whereas now they live in the "marvelous light" of the presence of God (1 Pet 2:9). They once

---

[120]See Köstenberger and O'Brien 2001, 249.
[121]See Bieder 1950; Swigchem 1955; Senior and Stuhlmueller 1983, 297-98; Steuernagel 1986; P. Robinson 1989; Köstenberger and O'Brien 2001, 228, 230-31, 237-43.
[122]See Bieder 1950, 3-4; P. Robinson 1989, 179.

were "not a people," but now they are "God's people" (1 Pet 2:10). On the one hand, Peter reminds the Gentile believers in Asia Minor of their preconversion past to emphasize how they should live now; on the other hand, as their relatives, friends and neighbors continue to live in that manner, Peter's reminder of their past implicitly encourages them—in the midst of the opposition and ostracism that they presently face—not to give up the hope that their polytheistic fellow citizens might one day experience the new birth "into a living hope through the resurrection of Jesus Christ from the dead" (1 Pet 1:3). Peter reminds his readers of the fact that they "believe" (πιστεύουσιν, *pisteuousin*) in Jesus as the foundation stone of God's eschatological temple, while their contemporaries do "not believe" (ἀπιστοῦσιν, *apistousin* [1 Pet 2:7]). The fact that Peter formulates with present participles perhaps indicates that there is still hope for the world.[123] People who do not believe at present can become people who do believe. Christians are "living stones" out of which God builds his spiritual temple (οἰκοδομεῖσθε, *oikodomeisthe* [1 Pet 2:5]); the present tense of the verb indicates that the church, the local congregation, is never "finished"—again a sign of hope that unbelievers can come to the "living stone," Jesus (1 Pet 2:4).

Donald Senior comments, "One of the major contributions of 1 Peter is the robust sense of Christian mission he conveys. Even though these fragile communities are embedded in a hostile environment and suffering abuse, he does not prescribe reaction or caution. The Christians are not to flee the world but to participate in it (2:13). They are not to condemn or berate the world, but to treat it with respect, even gentleness, all with the hope that in its own time, the world will join the Christians in glorifying God."[124]

The missionary task is difficult not simply because of opposition, ostracism and persecution, but more fundamentally because of their identity as Christians. They are "strangers in the world" (παρεπιδήμοι, *parepidēmoi* [1 Pet 1:1; 2:11 TNIV]) and "foreigners" or "resident aliens" (πάροικοι, *paroikoi* [1 Pet 2:11]). The First Epistle of Peter is a "missionary document" precisely because it raises the most fundamental question about the church: How should Christians live in a non-Christian society as a new community of people who have a discernibly different lifestyle?[125] The cause of the "strangeness" and "alienness" of Christians and Christian communities in their relationship to society at large is their identity as people of God, a status that results from God's election. As Hans Bietenhard notes, "The internal distance from society (as deliberately different behavior and as experienced rejection) is a characteristic of the church. This calling and this purpose are the reason for the exhortation to refrain from sinful desires (1 Pet 2:11), i.e.,

---

[123]See P. Robinson 1989, 180; on 1 Pet 2:5 see ibid., 180-81.

[124]Senior, *1-2 Pet,* 7. The final comment alludes to 1 Pet 2:12. In my view, this passage speaks not about the conversion of the Gentiles but about their forced acknowledgment of God on the day of judgment.

[125]P. Robinson 1989, 177, with reference to Swigchem 1955.

to live according to the stipulations and laws of their true homeland."[126]

The Old Testament background of this concept is Abraham and the patriarchs, whom the author of the Epistle to the Hebrews describes as examples for Christians (Heb 11:13). Abraham lived as a foreigner in the promised land because he was, on account of his faith, the citizen of the future heavenly city (Heb 11:9-10): "All of these died in faith without having received the promises, but from a distance they saw and greeted them. They confessed that they were strangers and foreigners [*xenoi kai parepidēmoi*] on the earth" (Heb 11:13). The background of the application of this Old Testament concept to the church is the mission of Jesus, which led him to the cross. John summarizes Jesus' life thus: "He came to what was his own, and his own people did not accept him" (Jn 1:11); and he records these words of Jesus with regard to his followers: "If the world hates you, be aware that it hated me before it hated you. If you belonged to the world, the world would love you as its own. Because you do not belong to the world, but I have chosen you out of the world—therefore the world hates you" (Jn 15:18-19).[127]

Some scholars suggest that the terms *parepidēmoi* and *paroikoi* in 1 Pet 1:1; 2:11 describe the status of the Christians before their conversion as people who lived at the margins of society: at least some Christians belonged, before their conversion, to the (literal) foreigners and resident aliens in a city, an historical reality that later was interpreted metaphorically, used as a description of the situation of *all* Christians in society.[128] This hypothesis is unconvincing. (1) It is entirely possible, even likely in many cases, that people who were socially marginalized as *parepidēmoi* and *paroikoi* and who lived as "strangers" in the midst of the houses (*oikoi*) and the homelands (*dēmoi*) of their contemporaries found a new "house" (the church as *oikos*) and a new "home" (*dēmos*) when they came to faith in Jesus Christ and were incorporated in the Christian community.[129] However, the sociological perspective is generally one-sided. A well-known systemic problem of functionalistic sociological explanations is the unwillingness to acknowledge religious convictions and religious praxis as independent social factors. It underestimates the (new) alienation that is created by the conversion to faith in Jesus Christ and by a Christian way of life. It surely is possible that some Christians were socially disadvantaged before their conversion and belonged to the category of the "resident alien" or "foreigner," but it is certain that Christians were marginalized because of their Christian identity. Peter writes, "You have already spent enough time in doing what the Gentiles like to do, liv-

---

[126]H. Bietenhard, *ThBLNT* 1:519.

[127]See Volf 1994, 17.

[128]J. H. Elliott 1981, 37-49, 67-84; idem, *1 Pet,* 313, 461-62, 481-82. For a critique see Volf 1994, 17-18; cf. Achtemeier, *1 Pet,* 174-75.

[129]Elliott, *1 Pet,* 458. For the critique that follows above see Volf 1994, 18, 28 with n. 11.

ing in licentiousness, passions, drunkenness, revels, carousing, and lawless idolatry. They are surprised that you no longer join them in the same excesses of dissipation, and so they blaspheme" (1 Pet 4:3-4). (2) The argument that the terms *parepidēmoi* and *paroikoi* are used in the Septuagint nearly always in a literal sense suggests little: in Ps 118:19 and 2 Chron 29:15 the terms describe the transitoriness of human life. Philo uses *paroikos* in a figurative sense.[130] A metaphorical sense is attested in Eph 2:19 and Heb 11:13. And we should note that the combination of *parepidēmoi* and *paroikoi* occurs only in Gen 23:4 and Ps 38:13 (LXX). This evidence suggests that a metaphorical meaning of these terms in 1 Pet 1:1; 2:11 is quite possible, without the assumption that the original meaning was literal. (3) Peter repeatedly applies terms that describe Israel—in our context, Abraham—to the Christian community, which evidently is also the case with regard to *parepidēmoi* and *paroikoi*.

The witness of the churches and of individual believers is, according to 1 Peter, primarily the witness of persistent faith in the midst of a hostile world.[131] In Pet 5:1 the author describes himself as "a witness [*martys*] of the sufferings of Christ"—he has seen how Jesus suffered, he is an eyewitness.[132] Because eyewitnesses speak of the things that they have seen, Peter's description should also be understood in the sense that he gives witness of the sufferings of Christ; that is, he speaks of Jesus Christ as a witness. What is even more important for the readers of Peter's letter is the fact that this witness leads to participation in the suffering and thus to glory.[133] He participates in Christ's passion by suffering himself.[134] As he will participate in the future glory (1 Pet 5:1b), he participates now in the sufferings of Christ—he is not only an eyewitness (*Augenzeuge*) or a witness of the word (*Wortzeuge*), but also a witness of action (*Tatzeuge*).

The mere existence of the Christian believers—former polytheists who now are "a chosen race, a royal priesthood, a holy nation, God's own people" (1 Pet 2:9a)—is proof of God's mercy, the result of the death and resurrection of Jesus Christ. This proof is relevant not only for believers themselves but also for non-Christians: believers are called to "proclaim" (*exangellein*) to unbelievers "the mighty acts of him who called you out of darkness into his marvelous light" (1 Pet 2:9b).[135] Peter exhorts the believers to "always be ready to make your defense [πρὸς ἀπολογίαν, *pros apologian*] to anyone who demands from you an accounting for the hope that is in you" (1 Pet 3:15). The term *apologia* signifies that they should be prepared to

---

[130]Philo, *Conf.* 77.19-81; *Cher.* 119-121. See Feldmeier 1992, 60-72.

[131]P. Robinson 1989, 177. Cf. 1 Pet 1:6-7; 2:18-25; 3:13-18; 4:1-6, 12-19; 5:8-10.

[132]In the sense of "eyewitness" according to Selwyn, *1 Pet*, 228; Reicke, *EpPet*, 129; cf. Achtemeier, *1 Pet*, 323.

[133]Goppelt, *1 Petr*, 323.

[134]Brox, *1 Petr*, 229; for the comment that follows above see ibid. The meaning "blood witness," referring to a martyr in the modern sense of the word, is not yet in view.

[135]See Steuernagel 1986, 11.

give an account of the objective foundation of their Christian faith and identity.[136] For example, they should be prepared to explain that sins can be forgiven because God, the Father of Jesus Christ, is merciful and because Jesus has died and has been raised from the dead (1 Pet 1:3). They should be able to explain that Christians have the hope of life after death, when they will receive "an inheritance that is imperishable, undefiled, and unfading" (1 Pet 1:4). They should be willing to speak of their experience of the power of God in their everyday life, which enables them to endure the hostility and opposition that they encounter (1 Pet 1:5-6). They should be willing and able to speak of Jesus Christ, whom they have not seen but still love, not least because he gives them "an indescribable and glorious joy" (1 Pet 1:8). They should be able to explain the grace that God offers when Jesus Christ is revealed (1 Pet 1:13). They should be able to explain why they have given up their previous way of life and why they are now "holy" as God is holy (1 Pet 1:14-17). They should be able to explain how they have been saved through the "precious blood of Christ," who died on the cross (1 Pet 1:18-19). They should be able to explain why the world, which has a beginning, will come to an end (1 Pet 1:20). They should be able to explain their faith in the God who raised Jesus from the dead and soon will raise all people from the dead (1 Pet 1:21). They should be able to explain the meaning of the "new birth" that they have experienced, and the meaning of the "living word of God" that they have heard and in which they are instructed in their weekly meetings (1 Pet 1:23-25). Peter exhorts the women in the church who are married to pagan husbands to be a witness through their everyday behavior, as there is always hope that their husbands might be "won," even if they refuse to let their wives speak about their faith, making their witness with "words" impossible for the time being (1 Pet 3:1).

30.3 Continuous Expansion

The lack of information about the missionary activities of the churches at the end of the first century should not lead us to conclude that the churches "after Paul" did not have a missionary strategy or missionary methods, implying that the Christian faith spread in the postapostolic period "more or less accidentally through the personal contacts of individuals."[137] Peter Lampe and Ulrich Luz, who hold this view, maintain that these "itinerant prophets take to the road on the basis of their personal 'charisma'—they leave their homes not because churches have officially commissioned them, but because they personally feel called to this task. There is no planned missionary 'program' behind their existence." The primary sources provide no evidence that would warrant this conclusion. We simply do not possess the primary sources that we need to formu-

---

[136]See Bieder 1950, 12.

[137]Lampe and Luz 1987, 213; the quotation that follows above, ibid., 214-15; similarly Hengel 1993, 133 (ET, 38).

late a reliable description of the missionary work of the church at the end of the first century and into the second century.

Missionary Work at the End of the First Century

There is no doubt that Christians continued to speak about their faith in their personal contacts with relatives, friends, neighbors and business partners, and that people were converted to faith in Jesus Christ as the result of such conversations. Both Paul and Peter emphasized the missionary significance of behavior within the family[138] and of conversations with non-Christians.[139] Christian parents bring their children up in the faith.[140] This will not have been different after A.D. 67, when Paul and Peter died in Rome.[141] In the second century Celsus, a pagan, confirms the spread of the gospel by ordinary Christians.

Celsus, frg. III 55: "We see, indeed, in private houses workers in wool and leather, and fullers, and persons of the most uninstructed and rustic character, not venturing to utter a word in the presence of their elders and wiser masters; but when they get hold of the children privately, and certain women as ignorant as themselves, they pour forth wonderful statements, to the effect that they ought not to give heed to their father and to their teachers, but should obey them; that the former are foolish and stupid, and neither know nor can perform anything that is really good, being preoccupied with empty trifles; that they alone know how men ought to live, and that, if the children obey them, they will both be happy themselves, and will make their home happy also. And while thus speaking, if they see one of the instructors of youth approaching, or one of the more intelligent class, or even the father himself, the more timid among them become afraid, while the more forward incite the children to throw off the yoke, whispering that in the presence of father and teachers they neither will nor can explain to them any good thing, seeing they turn away with aversion from the silliness and stupidity of such persons as being altogether corrupt, and far advanced in wickedness, and such as would inflict punishment upon them; but that if they wish (to avail themselves of their aid), they must leave their father and their instructors, and go with the women and their playfellows to the women's apartments, or to the leather shop, or to the fuller's shop, that they may attain to perfection; and by words like these they gain them over."

Christian merchants contributed to the spread of the gospel through their behavior at business transactions. Justin writes in the second century in his *Apology for the Christians* that Christian businesspeople are unfailingly patient even when others seek to cheat them (Justin, *1 Apol.* 16).

Since Paul was not the only missionary who "traveled" with a missionary strategy and program between A.D. 44 and 60, and since the "pillar apostles" were not the only itinerant missionaries who visited city after city and town after town to preach the gospel of Jesus Christ and to establish Christian communi-

---

[138]See 1 Tim 6:1; Tit 2:9-10; 1 Pet 3:1-2.
[139]See Col 4:5-6; 1 Tim 3:7; 2 Thess 1:11-12; 1 Pet 3:15.
[140]See Eph 6:4; 2 Tim 1:5; cf. Col 3:20.
[141]Lampe and Luz 1987, 213; cf. Honig 1951, 64.

ties, as the example of Philip and Barnabas shows, there is no reason to assume that the martyrdom of Peter and Paul in the city of Rome signified the end of strategic and programmatic missionary work.

We should not downplay the significance of references to traveling missionaries in the second century. The *Didache,* a Christian document written around A.D. 100, knows of itinerant preachers who are supported by the churches (*Did.* 11-13).

Did. 11-13: "Whosoever then comes and teaches you all these things aforesaid, receive him. But if the teacher himself be perverted and teach another doctrine to destroy these things, do not listen to him, but if his teaching be for the increase of righteousness and knowledge of the Lord, receive him as the Lord. And concerning the Apostles and Prophets, act thus according to the ordinance of the Gospel. Let every Apostle who comes to you be received as the Lord, but let him not stay more than one day, or if need be a second as well; but if he stay three days, he is a false prophet. And when an Apostle goes forth let him accept nothing but bread till he reach his night's lodging; but if he ask for money, he is a false prophet. Do not test or examine any prophet who is speaking in a spirit, 'for every sin shall be forgiven, but this sin shall not be forgiven.' But not everyone who speaks in a spirit is a prophet, except he have the behaviour of the Lord. From his behaviour, then, the false prophet and the true prophet shall be known. And no prophet who orders a meal in a spirit shall eat of it: otherwise he is a false prophet. And every prophet who teaches the truth, if he do not what he teaches, is a false prophet. But no prophet who has been tried and is genuine, though he enact a worldly mystery of the Church, if he teach not others to do what he does himself, shall be judged by you: for he has his judgment with God, for so also did the prophets of old. [12]But whosoever shall say in a spirit 'Give me money, or something else,' you shall not listen to him; but if he tell you to give on behalf of others in want, let none judge him.

"Let everyone who 'comes in the Name of the Lord' be received; but when you have tested him you shall know him, for you shall have understanding of true and false. If he who comes is a traveller, help him as much as you can, but he shall not remain with you more than two days, or, if need be, three. And if he wishes to settle among you and has a craft, let him work for his bread. But if he has no craft provide for him according to your understanding, so that no man shall live among you in idleness because he is a Christian. But if he will not do so, he is making traffic of Christ; beware of such.

[13]"But every true prophet who wishes to settle among you is 'worthy of his food.' Likewise a true teacher is himself worthy, like the workman, of his food. Therefore thou shalt take the firstfruit of the produce of the winepress and of the threshing-floor and of oxen and sheep, and shalt give them as the firstfruits to the prophets, for they are your high priests. But if you have not a prophet, give to the poor. If thou makest bread, take the firstfruits, and give it according to the commandment. Likewise when thou openest a jar of wine or oil, give the firstfruits to the prophets. Of money also and clothes, and of all your possessions, take the firstfruits, as it seem best to you, and give according to the commandment" (translation by K. Lake).

Irenaeus, who writes in the second century, mentions the mobility of the Christian believers:

Haer. 4.30.3: "Yea, moreover, through their [the Romans'] instrumentality the world is at peace, and we walk on the highways without fear, and sail where we will."

Eusebius relates that the Alexandrian teacher Pantaenus traveled to India at the end of the second century and encountered Christians who possessed the Gospel of Matthew written in Hebrew (*Hist. eccl.* 5.10.1-4).

Eusebius, *Hist. eccl.* 5.10.1-4: "About that time, Pantaenus, a man highly distinguished for his learning, had charge of the school of the faithful in Alexandria. A school of sacred learning, which continues to our day, was established there in ancient times, and as we have been informed, was managed by men of great ability and zeal for divine things. Among these it is reported that Pantaenus was at that time especially conspicuous, as he had been educated in the philosophical system of those called Stoics. They say that he displayed such zeal for the divine Word, that he was appointed as a herald of the Gospel of Christ to the nations in the East, and was sent as far as India. For indeed there were still many evangelists of the Word who sought earnestly to use their inspired zeal, after the examples of the apostles, for the increase and building up of the Divine Word. Pantaenus was one of these, and is said to have gone to India. It is reported that among persons there who knew of Christ, he found the Gospel according to Matthew, which had anticipated his own arrival. For Bartholomew, one of the apostles, had preached to them, and left with them the writing of Matthew in the Hebrew language which they had preserved till that time. After many good deeds, Pantaenus finally became the head of the school at Alexandria, and expounded the treasures of divine doctrine both orally and in writing."

Origen, who writes in the third century, knows missionaries who travel from one region to the next:

Origen, *Cels.* 3.9: "But since he is manifestly guilty of falsehood in the statements which follow, let us examine his assertion when he says, 'If all men wished to become Christians, the latter would not desire such a result.' Now that the above statement is false is clear from this, that Christians do not neglect, as far as in them lies, to take measures to disseminate their doctrine throughout the whole world. Some of them, accordingly, have made it their business to itinerate not only through cities, but even villages and country houses, that they might make converts to God. And no one would maintain that they did this for the sake of gain, when sometimes they would not accept even necessary sustenance; or if at any time they were pressed by a necessity of this sort, were contented with the mere supply of their wants, although many were willing to share (their abundance) with them, and to bestow help upon them far above their need. At the present day, indeed, when, owing to the multitude of Christian believers, not only rich men, but persons of rank, and delicate and high-born ladies, receive the teachers of Christianity, some perhaps will dare to say that it is for the sake of a little glory that certain individuals assume the office of Christian instructors. It is impossible, however, rationally to entertain such a suspicion with respect to Christianity in its beginnings, when the danger incurred, especially by its teachers, was great; while at the present day the discredit attaching to it among the rest of mankind is greater than any supposed honour enjoyed among those who hold the same belief, especially when such honour is not shared by all. It is false, then, from the very nature of the case, to say that 'if all men wished to become Christians, the latter would not desire such a result.'"

A final comment takes up the matter of the early Christian technique of producing books: it seems that Christians adopted at a very early date the form of the papyrus codex,[142] which had been developed from private notebooks. Rainer Riesner links this development, which seems to have taken place in the second century, with the "mobility of a missionary movement," arguing that one reason for the preference of the codex form might have been the ease with which books produced in this format—versus the more cumbersome papyrus scroll—could be taken along on journeys.[143]

The Churches in the First and Second Centuries

At the end of the apostolic period, around A.D. 90-100, written and, in a few cases, archaeological sources[144] attest Christian communities for the cities listed in the following table or strongly suggest that churches existed in a particular city (the latter are listed in the third column with a question mark). The fourth column lists churches that are attested by A.D. 200. The list is organized in the alphabetical order of the Roman provinces and the regions that did not belong to the Roman Empire. The churches in Judea, Galilee and Samaria are listed first as marking the origin of the early Christian missionary movement.[145]

The Churches in the First and Second Centuries

Roman Provinces/Regions	Churches Established in the First Century	Churches Attested c. A.D. 200
Galilee	Capernaum	Shikhin?
	Bethsaida?	Sepphoris?
	Cana?	Tiberias?
	Kochaba?	
	Nazareth?	
Judea	Jerusalem	
	Caesarea	
	Joppa	
	Lydda	
	Ptolemais-Acco	
	Azotos-Ashdod?	Azotos-Ashdod?
Samaria	Samaria-Sebaste	
	Sichem-Neapolis?	
	Sychar?	
Achaia	Corinth	Aegina
	Cenchreae	Lakedaimon
	Athens?	Megara
	Megara?	Patras
	Patras?	

---

[142]See Martin Hengel, *Die Evangelienüberschriften* (Heidelberg: Winter, 1984), 41.

[143]Riesner 1988, 495, with reference to Roberts 1949, 162.

[144]Note the archaeological evidence for Christian house churches in Capernaum and Bethsaida.

[145]For Asia Minor see the list in Blanchetiere 1981, 44-48; for a list of the churches that existed around A.D. 200 see ibid. 49-61. See also S. Mitchell 1995, 2:37-43, Harnack 1924, 2:621-927 (ET, 2:89-306); *TAVO* 6.2 (Siegfried Pirker), in Mittman and Götz, *Tübinger Bibelatlas* (revised and updated, 1997).

Roman Provinces/Regions		Churches Established in the First Century	Churches Attested c. A.D. 200
Africa	Proconsularis		Carthage
			Scilium
	Numidia		Madaura
	Mauretania		Iol Caesarea
Asia	Lydia	Ephesus	
		Miletus	
		Magnesia	
		Philadelphia	
		Sardis	
		Smyrna	
		Thyatira	
		Tralles	
	Pergamon	Pergamon	
	Phrygia	Hierapolis	Temenouthyrai
		Colossae	
		Laodikeia	
	Mysia		Kadoi
			Parium
			Ankyra Sidera?
			Synaos?
	Troas	Alexandria Troas	
Cappadocia			Kaisareia
	Melitene		Melitene
Crete-Cyrene			
	Crete	Gortyn?	Knossos
	Cyrene	Cyrene?	
		Berenike?	
		Ptolemais?	
		Teucheira?	
Cyprus		Paphos	
		Amathus?	
		Kition?	
		Kourion?	
		Lapethos?	
		Salamis?	
		Tamassos?	
Dalmatia		?	Salona?
Egypt		Alexandria?	
			Alexandreia
			Arsenoïte
			Athribis
			Nikious
			Oxyrhynchus
Epirus		Nikopolis	

Roman Provinces/Regions		Churches Established in the First Century	Churches Attested c. A.D. 200
Ethiopia		Meroë?	
Galatia			
	Phrygia	Antiocheia	Apameia-Kibotos
			Ardabau
			Eumeneia
			Hierapolis
			Kadoi
			Kumane
			Otrous
			Pepuza
			Philomelion
			Tymion
			Synnada
	Lycaonia	Derbe	
		Iconium	
		Lystra	
	Isauria		Laranda
	Galatia		Ancyra
Gaul		?	Lugdunum
			Vienne
Illyricum		Dyrrhachium?	
India		Taxila?	
		Muziris?	
		Barbarikon?	
		Poduke/Arikamedu?	
Italy		Rome	Naples?
		Puteoli	
		Herculaneum?	
		Pompeii?	
Kephallenia			Same
Macedonia		Beroea	Larissa
		Philippi	
		Thessalonike	
Pamphylia-Lycia			
	Pamphylia	Attaleia	
		Perge	
	Lycia	Myra?	
Parthia			
	Adiabene	Arbela?	Nisibis
	Babylonia		Dura-Europos?
			Ktesiphon?
	Osroëne	Edessa?	

Roman Provinces/Regions		Churches Established in the First Century	Churches Attested c. A.D. 200
Pontus-Bithynia			
	Bithynia	Amisos?	Amastris
			Sinope
	Pontus	Nikomedia?	Nikomedia
Rhodes			Rhodes
Scythia		Chersonesos?	
		Gorgippia?	
		Neapolis?	
		Olbia?	
		Pantikapaion?	
Sicily			Syracuse?
	Malta	?	
Spain			Tarraco?
Syria-Cilicia			
	Syria	Alexandreia	
		Antioch	Edessa
		Damascus	
		Sidon	
		Tyre	
		Tripolis	
		Apameia?	
		Arethusa?	
		Berytos?	
		Byblos?	
		Emesa?	
		Laodikeia ad Libanum?	
		Larissa?	
		Seleucia?	
	Nabatea	Kanatha?	
		Pella?	
		Petra?	
		Shahba?	
		Soada?	
	Cilicia	Tarsus	
		Anazarbos?	
		Mallos?	
		Soloi?	
		Sebaste?	
		Korykos?	
		Seleukia?	
		Olba?	
Thrace		Byzantion?	Anchialus
			Debeltum

31

MISSION AND PERSECUTION

Opposition from Jewish and Gentile fellow citizens did not suppress the commitment of the early Christian missionaries, nor were they intimidated by local or state officials. The first persecution, instigated by the authorities in Jerusalem against the followers of Jesus in A.D. 31/32, led to missionary expansion that brought the gospel to the coastal regions, to Samaria and to Antioch, the capital of the province of Syria.

31.1 Causes of the Conflicts

Conflicts with pagan fellow citizens[1] were caused by misunderstandings, lack of understanding, preconceptions, irritations and provocations. The conversion of Gentiles "usually meant a profound aggravation, if not the large-scale loss of the relationships that had constituted their personal identity, social acceptance and social security; it leads to a form of life that is rejected, slandered and threatened by those with whom they had hitherto been connected." The proclamation of a crucified and risen Savior invariably provoked ridicule and rejection, as Paul states in 1 Cor 1:23 without any illusions. The fact that often it was simple and uneducated people who accepted the Christian message was employed in the standard argument, still in use in the fourth century, that the faith of the followers of Jesus was a religion of the ignorant. Already Paul had to deal with this kind of ridicule when he speaks of the gospel as "God's foolishness" and of the fact that among the Christians "not many of you were wise by human standards, not many were powerful, not many were of noble birth" (1 Cor 1:25-26). Comments by Suetonius, Tacitus, Pliny and Justin indicate that "ignorance, mistrust, disappointment about the life of a convert, probably also xenophobia" poisoned the atmosphere: the Christians were regarded as "adherents of obscure and orgiastic rites, as people who hate and despise humankind, as atheists, as superstitious, as arsonists, as poisoners of wells, as child killers."[2]

Paul often speaks of trials and suffering that believers have to endure, often

---

[1]For the summary that follows above see Söding 1990b, 141-46; quotation, 146.
[2]Söding 1990b, 142 with n. 16; cf. Benko 1980.

immediately after their conversion.[3] He mentions his own suffering as a missionary even more frequently.[4] In his letter to the churches in Asia Minor, Peter speaks of the ignorance, ridicule, slander and rejection they experience from their fellow citizens.[5] One of the reasons for this rejection of the lifestyle of the believers was that it differed conspicuously from the values and behavioral patterns of their pagan contemporaries.[6] John knows Christians who have been imprisoned, he had himself been sentenced to exile on the island of Patmos, and he knows that some Christians have been killed because of their faith and he anticipates that the same fate threatens other believers as well.[7] Thomas Söding comments, "Mostly the oppression remained limited to everyday discrimination and defamation. But there was also denunciation and accusation before state authorities that could become dangerous for Christians; in some places riots took place."[8] The riot instigated by the silversmiths in Ephesus (Acts 19:23-40) is one example.

The emperor cult and the weekly meetings of the Christians represented particular dangers.[9] The pagan citizens of the cities in which the Christians lived were unaccustomed to formal religious services in the temples they visited. Pagan religiosity was largely individualistic. The devotee of a particular god or goddess decided on the basis of felt needs, or the mood of the day, when to visit the temple of the deity, when to offer a sacrifice, or even to which deity to pray. The deities that a city venerated officially were an exception, including the cults devoted to the deified members of the imperial family and the deceased emperors, who were worshiped at annual festivals. The only regular weekly meeting (*ekklēsia*) known to the Greeks and Romans at which the attendance of all members of the religious community was expected was the service of the Jewish community. They must have become suspicious when they heard that the followers of Jesus, who were not registered as a traditional association (*collegium*), used the political term *ekklēsia* for their meetings—something that the Jews did not do. When Augustus came to power, he quickly moved against the associations that he regarded as a danger: they were prohibited from meeting more than once a month; the Jews were granted an exception with regard to the sabbath.[10] The weekly meetings of the Christians

---

[3]See Phil 1:29; Rom 5:3; 8:17-27, 35; 12:14, 17-21; 1 Thess 1:6; 2:14; 3:1-6.
[4]See 1 Thess 2:2; Phil 1:7, 12-17; 2:17; 4:11, 14; 1 Cor 4:12-13; 2 Cor 4:8-12, 16-17; 6:3-10; 7:4; 11:23-29, 32-33; 12:10; Gal 5:11; 6:12.
[5]See 1 Pet 1:6-7; 2:12; 3:14, 16; 4:1, 4, 12-16, 19; 5:9-10.
[6]See 1 Pet 2:12; 3:1-6, 16; 4:1-5, 15-19. See Söding 1990b, 142; cf. Brox, *1 Petr,* 24-34.
[7]See Rev 2:10; 13:7-10 (imprisonment); 1:9 (exile); 2:10, 13; 12:11; 13:7-10; 14:13; 17:6; 18:24; 20:4 (martyrdom).
[8]Söding 1990b, 142-43.
[9]For the comments that follow above see B. Winter 2000, esp. 288-93.
[10]See Olivia F. Robinson, *The Criminal Law of Ancient Rome* (London: Duckworth, 1995), 80.

could easily be interpreted as the seditious activity of a *collegium* devoted to the memory of a Jew who had been crucified by Roman authorities. The decision of Gallio, the governor of the province of Achaia, in A.D. 52 not to investigate the accusations against Paul in a trial but to dismiss them as a religious debate within the Jewish community was not a precedent that Christians outside of Achaia could appeal to. And Gallio's successor, exercising his *imperium,* could easily arrive at a different decision if he thought it more opportune. It is not a coincidence, therefore, that Paul emphasized the Jewish origins of the movement of the believers in Jesus (Acts 24:10, 14; 26:4-6, 22) in his trial before Felix, the governor of Judea, to whom he had been accused as "a pestilent fellow, an agitator among all the Jews throughout the world, and a ringleader of the sect of the Nazarenes" (Acts 24:5). The attempt of Jews to distance themselves from Christians again failed, not least because the Christian who was forced to defend himself in this trial was a Jew.

In regard to the emperor cult, Bruce Winter suggests that the claims made on provincials by the cult already during the time of the Julian-Claudian emperors usually is underestimated.[11] The Jews were exempt from participation in the emperor cult, which basically was expected of everyone (Cassius Dio 51.20.6-7), because they offered a sacrifice for the emperor in the temple in Jerusalem. In the urban centers the high point of the emperor cult was an annual festival, usually celebrated on the emperor's birthday: the citizens donned white festive garments and, adorned with garlands, marched in a procession to the imperial temple, passing by houses decorated in honor of the emperor. Festive banquets were given, athletic and musical contests were held, incense was burned before statues of the emperor. It was not easy to "excuse" oneself from these civic obligations, which is exactly what Paul expected when he directed the Corinthian Christians not to attend banquets in pagan temples (1 Cor 8:4-6; 10:21). Simon Price documented the imperial cult for nearly two hundred cities in Asia Minor, attested by altars, temples or imperial priests mentioned in inscriptions.[12] In the New Testament twenty-three of these cities in which the imperial cult played an important role are mentioned: Adramyttium, Antiocheia (Phrygia), Assos, Chios, Colossae, Cos, Derbe, Ephesus, Hierapolis, Iconium, Laodikeia, Miletus, Mitylene, Patara, Pergamon, Perge, Philadelphia, Rhodes, Samos, Sardis, Smyrna, Tarsus, Thyatira. Bruce Winter remarks, "For Christians the imperial cult simmered like a volcano, eventually erupting after Paul was dead. It posed a definite problem for converts of his day."[13]

---

[11]B. Winter 2000, 292-93; cf. idem 1994; see also Price 1984; Friesen 1993.
[12]Price 1984, xxi-xxvi (maps), 249-74 (catalogue). For the comment that follows above see Klauck 1995-1996, 2:70.
[13]B. Winter 2000, 293.

31.2 The Reaction of Christians

How did Christians react to these conflicts? Thomas Söding describes the follow-ing patterns of reaction that are attested by the New Testament documents.[14]

1. The pressure from pagan society prompted an intensification of the fellow-ship and solidarity within the Christian community, caused by mutual love and service and constantly deepened. Paul's exhortations to the Christians in the city of Rome in Rom 12:12-16 illustrate this point in an impressive manner.

Rom 12:12-16: "Rejoice in hope, be patient in suffering, persevere in prayer. [13]Contribute to the needs of the saints; extend hospitality to strangers. [14]Bless those who persecute you; bless and do not curse them. [15]Rejoice with those who rejoice, weep with those who weep. [16]Live in harmony with one another; do not be haughty, but associate with the lowly; do not claim to be wiser than you are."

2. The exposition and intensification of the Christians' theological identity as fol-lowers of Jesus and as community of God prompted by the external pressure helped the church to interpret correctly the conflict with society. Söding ex-plains, "It is only from the center of the gospel that it is possible to recognize where it is worthwhile to fight and to suffer and where false fronts are set up. It is only by concentrating on their Kyrios that Christians can react to the con-troversies into which they are dragged in such a manner that the will of God becomes clearer for them and for their opponents."[15] This explains why Peter encourages the Christians in Asia Minor who face opposition and oppression by reminding them of the redemptive work of Jesus Christ, who also suffered,[16] and of the grace of their calling,[17] reconfirming their hope for their ultimate salvation at the return of Jesus Christ.[18]

Already Jesus of Nazareth had emphasized that following him meant not only learning and working with him but also living with him—and eventually suffer-ing with him.[19] This suffering may include daily discrimination,[20] persecution,[21] imprisonment and torture,[22] and death.[23] When Paul explains that believers in Jesus have died and been crucified with Jesus Christ in order to be raised with him (Rom 6:1-14), he implies first of all a theological meaning: believers have "died" with regard to the power of sin that brings the death sentence upon the

---

[14]Söding 1990b, 146-53 (organizing the material differently).
[15]Söding 1990b, 147; for the comment that follows above see ibid.
[16]See 1 Pet 1:11; 2:21-24; 3:18-22; 4:1, 13; 5:1.
[17]See 1 Pet 2:7-10, 25; 3:7, 15; 5:10, 12.
[18]See 1 Pet 1:3-9, 13, 21; 3:5, 7; 5:10.
[19]Mk 8:34-38/Mt 16:24-28/Lk 9:23-27; Lk 14:27/Mt 16:24. See Söding 1990b, 151.
[20]Mk 6:11/Mt 10:14/Lk 9:5; Lk 10:10; Mk 13:13/Mt 24:9-10/Lk 21:17.
[21]Lk 6:22-23/Mt 5:11-12; Lk 6:27-28/Mt 5:44; Mk 4:17/Mt 13:21; Mk 10:30; Mt 5:10; 10:23.
[22]Mk 13:9-13/Mt 24:9-14/Lk 21:12-19; Lk 6:28-29.
[23]Mk 13:12/Mt 10:21/Lk 21:16; Mk 10:38-39/Mt 20:22-23.

sinners, which means that they can never downplay sin in their everyday lives in view of the forgiveness of sins, which they have received through faith in Jesus Christ. But the suffering with Christ characterizes the entire existence of the Christian, as Paul states in Rom 8:16-17: "if children, then heirs, heirs of God and joint heirs with Christ—if, in fact, we suffer with him so that we may also be glorified with him."

3. The antagonism of pagan society is understood as eschatological tribulation, as an unavoidable reality of the messianic period, the time between the first and the second advents of Jesus the Messiah. This explanation of why Christians should understand and accept their suffering can be found in Jesus' sayings, in the letters of Paul and Peter, and particularly in the book of Revelation.[24]

4. The antagonism of society underlines that the acceptance of the gospel of Jesus Christ creates a gap between Christians and the values and behaviors of pagans, and it underscores that the exhortation not to assimilate to "this world" (Rom 12:2) is critically important. The so-called catalogues of vices provide a vivid example of the Christians' critical diagnosis of values, ideologies and behavioral patterns. Their critical distance was grounded not only in relevant experiences and observations about the Gentiles but also, as Söding asserts, in "the theological conviction that their basic orientation leads astray because the coordinates of their thinking and acting is off base. This in turn rests on the theological verdict, shared by Jews and Christians, that the thinking, the acting and the self-understanding of the Gentiles is confused because their relationship to God is distorted."[25]

5. Followers of Jesus accept suffering for his sake and for the sake of the gospel (Mk 8:35; 10:29). This acceptance is specifically demonstrated in patient endurance,[26] in the refusal to strike back violently,[27] and in praying for one's persecutors.[28] "The acceptance of suffering in following Jesus is, in the final analysis, an expression of obedient confidence in God."[29]

6. The hostile reaction of society does more than just create a distance between Christians and society: it also enables Christians to turn to the world in a new way, as Söding points out: "The gospel, if they take it seriously, does not lead Christians out of the world. It does not seduce them to bypass reality in a religious fervor or to asperse the life and the world of the Gentiles as something

---

[24]Mt 10:17-25; Lk 12:11-12; Lk 17:22-37; Mt 24:3-22/Mk 13:3-13/Lk 21:7-24; Jn 13:16; Rom 8:17-27; note also the use of the term *thlipsis* in Rom 5:3; 8:35; 12:12; 2 Cor 1:8; 6:4; 7:4; 8:2; Phil 1:17; 4:14; 1 Thess 1:6; 3:3-7; 2 Thess 1:4.6-7; also Rev 13:7-10, 15-18.

[25]Söding 1990b, 147, with reference to Rom 1:26-32; Phil 2:15; Wis 14:12, 27.

[26]Rom 12:12; 1 Cor 13:7; 1 Thess 1:3; 2 Thess 1:4; Heb 10:32, 36; Rev 1:9; 2:2, 3, 19; 3:10; 13:10; 14:12.

[27]Mt 5:38-42/Lk 6:29-30; Mk 10:42-45/Mt 20:25-26/Lk 22:25-27.

[28]Lk 6:28/Mt 5:44; Rom 12:14; 1 Cor 4:12.

[29]Söding 1990b, 152.

born of the devil. Rather, it relies on the (pneumatic-charismatic) ability to evaluate reality in a sober manner, and also to discern the spirits."[30] This is why Paul can assume that the lifestyle of Christians, who take into account the views of non-Christians in their behavior, is ultimately convincing and attractive (1 Thess 4:1-12). In this manner the oppression and persecution of Christians is to become an opportunity for witnessing to the truth of the gospel.[31] Jesus himself referred to the necessity of proclaiming the gospel to all nations in the context of hostility and official persecution.

Mk 13:9-11: "As for yourselves, beware; for they will hand you over to councils; and you will be beaten in synagogues; and you will stand before governors and kings because of me, as a testimony to them. [10]And the good news must first be proclaimed to all nations. [11]When they bring you to trial and hand you over, do not worry beforehand about what you are to say; but say whatever is given you at that time, for it is not you who speak, but the Holy Spirit."

John interrupts his narration of the judgments of the seven trumpets with the vision of the two witnesses (Rev 11:1-14) in order to remind the churches in Asia Minor of their obligation to preach the gospel—an obligation and a task that continue even when the lives of the missionaries are in danger.

---

[30]Söding 1990b, 148, with reference to 1 Cor 12:10; 1 Jn 4:1.
[31]Söding 1990b, 152.

PART VII

RESULTS

The Identity, Praxis and Message
of the Early Christian Mission

32

THE SELF-UNDERSTANDING OF THE
EARLY CHRISTIAN MISSIONARIES

The first missionaries of the early church in the first century were Jews who had become convinced that Jesus was the expected Messiah and that his death and resurrection were the climax of God's redemptive action promised for the last days, deciding the salvation of all human beings—the salvation of their fellow Jews as well as of all the pagans. Jesus had called and trained the Twelve from the beginning as "fishers of people" for an active involvement in the proclamation and dissemination of the good news of the dawn of the kingdom of God. After Easter the Twelve were commissioned to proclaim the news of God's new, redemptive revelation in Jesus Christ to all nations, from Jerusalem to the ends of the earth. Soon more preachers and teachers of the first Christian community joined in this task: Stephen and Philip, unnamed Greek-speaking Jewish Christians from the Jerusalem church, Barnabas and John Mark, and within a year or two after Easter Saul/Paul, the Jerusalem-trained expert in the interpretation of the Scriptures.

The early Christian missionaries were convinced that the salvation of their Jewish contemporaries depended on their acceptance of God's redemptive revelation in Jesus Christ—that is, on their faith in Jesus the Messiah and Savior. They were convinced that Gentiles, whether proselytes or God-fearers or sympathizers with the Jewish faith, could receive forgiveness of sins, salvation and adoption as God's children by faith in Jesus the Lord and Savior, as redemptive faith in the one true God of Israel.

The apostles had learned from Jesus to proclaim the good news that they had been directed to announce in cities, towns and villages. They had learned that the verbal proclamation of the good news had priority over other forms of influencing people, including the performance of miracles. After Easter they had received Jesus' promise of his presence "from Jerusalem to the ends of the earth," and at Pentecost they had received the Holy Spirit of God's powerful presence. They witnessed the fact that God caused mighty deeds to happen in their ministry, as they had happened in Jesus' ministry before them. We have seen that the early Christian missionaries did not leave the implementation of their missionary commission to accidental developments and random opportunities; rather, they planned the details of their missionary work. This became evident particularly in the missionary ministry of Paul, who planned new initiatives of missionary outreach but also was able to react in a flexible manner to changing circumstances.[1]

32.1 Missionary Work Among Jews

For three years the Twelve had traveled with Jesus through the towns and villages of Galilee and some of the neighboring territories, including Judea and Jerusalem (§10). They had witnessed his ministry among the Jewish population of preaching and teaching as well as his ministry of healing people who were sick and liberating people who were oppressed by demons (§9). They had been sent out by Jesus on a tour through the Galilean countryside with the directive to preach and heal among the "lost sheep of the house of Israel" (§10.3). After Jesus' resurrection they were directed to begin an international missionary ministry that should commence in Jerusalem and in Judea (§14.1), preaching the good news of God's redemptive salvation in Jesus the Messiah to their fellow Jews (§12.3). Accordingly, they had been trained theologically and practically to preach and teach the good news after Pentecost in Jerusalem (§§15.2; 19.1; 21.1; 22.1), in Judea (§§21.1; 22.1), in Galilee (§22.2) and in Samaria (§§20.2; 22.3). The praxis of the apostle Paul, who started his missionary outreach in any given city by teaching in the local synagogue, indicates that even the eminent missionary to the Gentiles engaged in missionary work among the Jewish people. Paul explains this by referring to the salvation-historical priority that the Jews enjoy (Rom 1:16; §§24.3; 28.1) and to the commission that he received from the risen Lord (Acts 9:15; §24.1-2).

The early Christian missionaries were Jews: Peter and James, Stephen and Philip, Paul and Barnabas, John Mark and Timothy—the Twelve and the Greek-speaking Christians of the Jerusalem church who were the first preachers to reach Syria. The first Christian communities in Jerusalem, in Damascus and initially in Antioch consisted of Jewish Christians. Most if not all churches that were established in the first century outside Palestine originated in converted Jews who had come to faith in Jesus the Messiah after hearing the gospel preached in their local synagogues. As disciples and followers of Jesus of Nazareth, as believers in Israel's Messiah, it was inconceivable for the early Christian missionaries to exclude their fellow Jews from the proclamation of the good news of God's decisive and redemptive revelation in Jesus the Messiah.

32.2 Missionary Work Among Gentiles

The early Christian mission among Gentiles—God-fearers, sympathizers with

---

[1]For the summary that follows above see also Schnabel 1997.

the Jewish faith and polytheists—was not an invention of Paul of Tarsus. The project of the Gentile mission that planned and worked for the conversion of pagans to faith in the one true God and in Jesus the Lord and Savior has its roots in the teaching and ministry of Jesus himself (§12). Understood against the background of God's promises through the prophets, Jesus' proclamation of the fulfillment of time and the arrival of the kingdom of God (Mt 4:17; Mk 1:14-15)—a message that he directed his disciples to proclaim as well (Mt 10:7/Lk 10:9)—caused, with salvation-historical and theological necessity, the move to the nations, whose pilgrimage to Mount Zion and whose conversion to the one true God was expected by Israel. In the Sermon on the Mount Jesus formulated in basic statements his expectation that the true Israel will be the salt of the earth and the light of the world (Mt 5:13-16). When Gentiles approached Jesus, he did not rebuff them but rather extended to them the same healing and liberation granted to the Jewish people in Galilee and Judea. He announced that the arrival of the kingdom of God signifies the arrival of the time in which the Gentiles are included in the blessings of God's gracious rule, and that the day of judgment and God's new creation will arrive only after the good news of the kingdom of God has been proclaimed in the entire *oikoumenē* (Mk 13:10). After his victory on the cross and after his resurrection Jesus commissioned the Twelve to go and teach and make disciples of all nations, from Jerusalem to the ends of the earth (§12.3).

The project of the Gentile mission was not contested as such in the Jerusalem church (§16.1). The hotly debated issue was the conditions under which converted Gentiles should be admitted to the messianic people of God (§25.1-3). The evidence that we have for the missionary activity of the Twelve among Gentiles (§16.1-3) leads to the conclusion that the conversion of the Ethiopian aristocrat through the witness of Philip (§20.3) and the conversion of the Roman centurion in Caesarea through the preaching of Peter (§21.2-3) were not exceptions: the Twelve evidently heard and heeded Jesus' directive to engage in an international missionary outreach in the literal sense of the word. Peter probably traveled to the regions in northern Asia Minor after A.D. 42, visiting Antioch, perhaps Corinth and certainly Rome (§21.4). Other missionaries from the Jerusalem church brought the gospel to the cities on the Palestinian and Syrian coast (§22.4), to the cities of Cyprus and Syria (§22.5), perhaps to cities in Italy (§22.6), Asia Minor (§22.7), Egypt and North Africa (§22.11), and to Babylonia and India and perhaps to Scythia (§22.12). After his conversion Paul knew himself to be called by God and by the risen Lord as an apostle to the Gentiles (§24), a calling that he fulfilled in coordinated collaboration with the apostles in Jerusalem (§25.1), in the regions and cities between Arabia, Syria and Cilicia in the East (§26) and Spain in the West (§27.5), on Cyprus and in Galatia (§27.1), in Macedonia and in Achaia (§27.2) and in the province of Asia (§27.3). Even as a prisoner of the Roman state he continued to preach and teach the gospel of Jesus Christ (§27.4).

32.3 Missionary Work in Cities and Villages

As they reflected about Jesus' missionary commission and planned its actual implementation, the early Christians certainly would have regarded the praxis of Jesus' ministry as the model for their own ministry. They confessed Jesus not only as Messiah but also as Kyrios: his behavior was the model and the standard for their own behavior. Jesus had worked as prophetic preacher and teacher, but contrary to the rabbinic model, he did not wait for people to come to him (although that happened as well); instead, he traveled through the towns, villages and hamlets of Galilee (Mk 6:56), encountering people where they lived and worked (§9.2). Several comments that describe Jesus' itinerant ministry (Mk 6:6; 9:35; Lk 4:43) probably indicate that he planned his geographical movements. The Twelve would have followed this example: they could not leave the missionary outreach to Judea, Samaria and the further distant regions to the vicissitudes of personal preferences, but rather would have organized and planned their travels.

Luke's account of Paul's missionary ministry provides practically the only available information that confirms that the early Christian missionaries—Paul, at least—planned their work in the service of the crucified and risen Kyrios in geographical and tactical terms. Paul started his missionary work in any given city in the synagogues, where he preached and taught. The synagogues were the natural bridgeheads for a Jewish teacher who wanted to target Gentile audiences as well. Paul made and maintained contacts with representatives of the local elite, both in the synagogue and in the Greek and Roman cities. When people had come to faith in Jesus Christ, he organized them in new communities as *ekklēsiai* that met regularly, usually in the private homes of new converts. This was basically the only possibility in the context of the political and legal conditions of the Roman Empire and of autonomous cities to gather groups of like-minded people without official registration and acknowledgment (§28.1).

Jesus preached not only in towns and cities but also in villages and small hamlets. He reached all kinds of people with his message of the arrival of the kingdom of God: men and women, adults and children, pious Pharisees and lawless sinners, conservative teachers of the law and Sadducees whose theology was problematic, representatives of the Jewish establishment and people with bad reputations, sympathizers and opponents. The "dragnet" of his ministry reached "fish of every kind" (Mt 13:47). The early Christian missionaries faced the challenge of proclaiming the gospel in the same manner, without differentiating between people deemed worthy and people deemed unworthy. The fact that the authors of the Gospels note the full range of Jesus' social contacts strongly suggests that the early church never forgot his wide-ranging outreach, and that at least its leaders regarded this as important and, presumably, acted in the same manner. The fullest available information concerning this issue is, again, the missionary work of Paul: he describes himself as "a debtor both to Greeks and to barbarians, both to the wise and to the foolish" (Rom 1:14), which means that he was prepared to interact with highly cultured Greeks and Romans as well as with uncivilized people, with the educated as well as with the ignorant (§24.3). Paul preached to semi-nomadic Arabs (§26.1) and to the highest representatives of the Jewish commonwealth and of the Roman state (§27.4), to the superstitious population in remote Lystra (§27.1) and to the intellectually sophisticated philosophers in the "university town" of Athens (§27.2), to the Jews who lived in Jerusalem and kept the Torah (§26.1) and to the Greeks who lived in the Roman colony of Corinth and frequented the pagan temples (§27.2). And he reached both men and women with the gospel, as his team of coworkers documents (§28.4).

32.4 Expectations, Plans, Goals

Israel's prophets spoke of a future time in which the nations would stream to Mount Zion in Jerusalem, to the house of the God of Israel, in order to worship the one true God and learn his will (Is 2:2-5/Mic 4:1-5; Zech 8:20-23), a time in which God's chosen Servant would carry God's salvation to the ends of the earth (Is 49:1-6; §5.4). Jesus' proclamation of the dawn of the kingdom of God absorbed the expectation of the prophets that God would establish his rule over his creation in judgment and in gracious salvation in the days of the Messiah. His proclamation was characterized, however, by a new understanding of God's messianic rule compared with the Jewish expectations. The traditional components of Israel's identity—the temple and the Torah, the sabbath and the food and purity laws, the nation and the land—played no role at all, or at least no central role, in Jesus' teaching and behavior (§9.1). This new understanding of the dawn of God's messianic kingdom also included a reversal of the direction in which the nations of the earth were expected to find the salvation of the God of Israel: rather than waiting for the arrival of the nations in Jerusalem, Jesus directs his disciples to go from Jerusalem out to the nations (§12.3). The expected movement from the periphery to the center, from the ends of the earth to Mount Zion, is replaced by a movement from the center—the city of Jerusalem, where Jesus the Messiah died and was raised from the dead—to the periphery of the ends of the earth. Stationary communication (Israel stays at home in Jerusalem) becomes mobile communication: just as Jesus traveled through Galilee and the neighboring territories visiting cities, towns and villages, the disciples are directed and expected to travel through the cities and towns of the Jews, Samaritans and Gentiles until they reach the ends of the earth. This is the movement that we observe in Luke's account in the book of Acts and in the evidence provided by Paul's letters and by other documents relevant for the activity of the apostles in the first century: the apostles carry the good news of salvation that the God of Israel is granting through faith in Jesus, the crucified and risen Messiah and Savior, from Jerusalem to Damascus, Antioch, Rome, Alexandria, Athens, Corinth, Ephesus, Spain, probably to India and perhaps to Scythia, and there is at least one believer in Jesus in Ethiopia who rejoices in the forgiveness of sins that he has received.

There was no parallel in antiquity for the project of a group of people who operated in an international framework and scope, not in the religious, the philosophical or the political realms. Jesus evidently did not leave behind detailed instructions about the implementation of the missionary outreach among the Gentiles. However, the leading Jewish Christians in Jerusalem, soon joined by Paul the teacher from Tarsus and Jerusalem, carried out, with great courage, consistent personal commitment and amazing flexibility, the project that Jesus the Messiah had entrusted into their hands (and feet). They were aware of the necessity of preserving the unity of faith and practice in the churches that they established, a concern that received visible expression at the apostolic council in A.D. 48. The early tradition that the Twelve left Jerusalem twelve years after Easter, around A.D. 42, embarking on the international missionary work that Jesus had commissioned them for, probably is based on reliable historical information. The missionary work of Paul and his team of fellow missionaries, about which we possess more information than about the missionary work of the Twelve, illustrates the international travels in striking detail: Paul preached and taught in Arabia and Syria, in Cilicia and Galatia, in Macedonia and in Achaia, in the province of Asia and in Spain, in world-class cities such as Antioch and Ephesus, in regional centers such as Tarsus and Corinth, and also in unimportant towns in the Nabatean kingdom and in the hinterland of Lycaonia (§§26; 27). Neither the lack of suitable models for an international operation nor the religious thought patterns of the pagans in the Greek and Roman cities, neither political dangers nor social, cultural or psychological barriers, neither organizational nor personal challenges (§16.5) prevented the apostles from proclaiming the gospel of Jesus Christ in Jerusalem, in Judea, in Samaria and in regions toward the ends of the earth.

The basic strategy of the early Christian missionaries was simple: they wanted to reach as many people as possible and lead them to faith in Jesus the Messiah, Lord and Savior before he returns to execute God's judgment and establish God's kingdom. They wanted to win people for the gospel, for faith in the one true God and in his Savior, "in the whole world" (*en panti tō kosmō* [Col 1:6]). Their concepts for the practical implementation of Jesus' missionary commission presumably were influenced by their conviction that Jesus' return might be imminent: certainly they did not understand "world mission" as the task of reaching every single individual "privately" with the gospel. After twenty-five years of missionary work Paul wrote that he had "fully proclaimed" the gospel in a wide semicircle from Jerusalem to Illyricum (Rom 15:19), announcing his plan to go to Spain and begin missionary work there. This means that Paul either was convinced that had preached the gospel in Arabia, Syria, Cilicia, Cyprus, Galatia, Macedonia, Achaia and in province of Asia in such a manner as the nations needed to hear it before the parousia (Mk 13:10), or he assumed that other missionaries and evangelists of the local congregations would carry the gospel to cities and the thousands of villages that he had not visited.

We have also seen that the "eschatological factor" was not the central, and evidently not the most important, motivation of the early Christian missionary movement. Again Paul's missionary theology and practice served as an example: he repeatedly visited the churches that he had established in Galatia, Macedonia and Achaia; he stayed for several years in Corinth and in Ephesus; he took the time to write letters, to train new workers whom he sent to the existing churches with various tasks. Paul's main concern evidently was not to reach as many people as quickly as possible with the gospel. He spared no effort, time and energy in safeguarding the consolidation of his missionary "successes." This important priority was the reason why he ignored the warnings of Christian prophets in the spring of A.D. 57 and visited Jerusalem, as he wanted to maintain the unity between the church in Jerusalem and his "missionary churches," which included many uncircumcised Gentile Christians, through bringing the collection of these "integrated churches" to the Jewish Christians in the capital.

The early Christian missionaries were not just "teachers in transit": as the example of Peter demonstrates, they were at the same time "shepherds" and "fellow elders" in the churches (1 Pet 5:1). Converted pagans did not "lose" their sexual laxness, superstitious notions and magical practices immediately or irrevocably, and converted Jews had to get used to having fellowship with converted Gentiles. And instruction in the eschatological-messianic interpretation of the Scriptures and in the Jesus tradition could not be passed along overnight.

Paul, Peter and John, and presumably all early Christian missionaries, regarded the behavior of the followers of Jesus in the contexts of the growing churches and of daily life in their families and at their workplace as important for missionary outreach. Paul expected that the dynamic realization of the new life granted by Jesus Christ and empowered by God's Holy Spirit would make the Jews "jealous" (Rom 11:11-15). And Peter was convinced that if Christian believers live like the "chosen race," the "royal priesthood," the "holy nation, God's own people" that they are, then they will shine for the Gentiles as a "marvelous light" that will illuminate for them, through the proclamation of the mighty acts of God in Jesus Christ, the path from darkness to the light of God's salvation (1 Pet 2:9).

33

THE PRAXIS OF THE
EARLY CHRISTIAN MISSIONARIES

The New Testament documents portray the apostles as messengers who proclaim the good news of Jesus Christ, heal the sick and help the members of the new communities of believers in Jesus to grow and support each other in love, faith and hope, as they implement Jesus' example and commission to preach the gospel and heal the sick (Mt 10:7-8), make all nations into disciples (Mt 28:19-20) and witness to his life, death and resurrection unto the ends of the earth (Acts 1:3, 8). The goal of the universal and international mission to the nations—Jews and Gentiles alike—was to be reached "by word and deed" (λόγῳ καὶ ἔργῳ, *logō kai ergō* [Rom 15:18]).

33.1 The Spoken and the Written Word

The "fishing" campaign of the disciples whom Jesus had called and trained as "fishers of people" was implemented mainly in terms of the proclamation of the good news of God's redemptive revelation in Jesus Christ. The oral proclamation of the gospel was the central activity of the apostles, a basic characteristic of their mission. The apostles "proclaimed the good news" (εὐαγγελίζεσθαι, *euangelizesthai*) of Jesus the Messiah and Savior. They "proclaimed" (κηρύσσειν, *kēryssein*) the exclusive significance of the life, death and resurrection of Jesus for all people, both Jews and Gentiles. They preached and taught the "word of God" (λόγος τοῦ θεοῦ, *logos tou theou*).[1] This *logos* of the early Christian mission is the word that the missionaries proclaim to everyone who is willing to listen. The proclamation of the message of Jesus, the crucified and risen Messiah, Son of God, Lord and Savior, is the central process and task of missionary work not only for Paul but also for the Jerusalem apostles. The Twelve had no doubts about what their priorities should be: they were more than willing to delegate

---

[1]Acts 4:31; 6:7; 8:14, 11:1; 12:24; 13:5, 7, 46; 17:13; 18:11; Rom 9:6; 15:18; 1 Cor 14:36; 2 Cor 2:17; 4:2; Eph 6:17; Col 1:25; 1 Thess 1:8; 2:13; 2 Tim 2:9, 15; Tit 1:3; 2:5; Heb 4:12; 6:5; 11:3; 13:7; 1 Pet 1:23; 1 Jn 2:14; Rev 6:7.

practical ministries to other leaders in the church in order to have time for preaching the word of God (Acts 6:2, 4).

The oral proclamation of the gospel is, of course, not an end in itself. Paul was not content to confront Jews and Gentiles with the message of Jesus Christ in his preaching and teaching activities: he wants to save people (1 Thess 2:16; 1 Cor 9:19-22; 10:33), he wants to lead them to the obedience of faith (Rom 1:5; 15:18), he wants people to move from hearing to understanding and to obedience (Rom 10:14-21), and he wants to establish churches and lead believers to spiritual maturity and moral integrity.[2] The "action" that the term *euangelizesthai* implies is, however, primarily the active, oral proclamation of the gospel. Faith in the one true God and in Jesus the Messiah and Savior "comes from what is heard" (ἡ πίστις ἐξ ἀκοῆς, *he pistis ex akoēs*), from the message that the missionaries proclaim, a message in which the "word of Christ" becomes manifest (ἡ δὲ ἀκοὴ διὰ ῥήματος Χριστοῦ, *hē de akoē dia rhēmatos Christou* [Rom 10:17]). This means that Jesus Christ himself speaks and acts in the missionaries' words that proclaim God's redemptive salvation in the crucified and risen Jesus, the Messiah and Savior.[3]

The oral proclamation by the apostles was grounded in the person, life and words of Jesus. At the same time it was fundamentally linked with the sacred Scriptures of Moses, David and the prophets. The conviction that God's promises in Scripture were fulfilled in Jesus' mission was a basic characteristic of the apostolic preaching. Peter and Paul emphasized this connection particularly in their missionary preaching in the synagogues. Paul's letters to the churches in which a majority of the members came from Gentile backgrounds demonstrates that the apostles interpreted and quoted the sacred Scriptures as God's authoritative promise and revelation not only for Jewish Christians but also for Gentile believers.

The written word assumed an eminent authority in the early church, in contrast to the pagan religions of the Greco-Roman world.[4] In the first three centuries written texts did not constitute a major factor in the missionary expansion of the Christian faith, mainly due to the cost involved in writing and producing texts for non-Christians. However, outsiders quickly came to realize that the Christians relied on written texts, in the first century mostly on the documents of the Hebrew Bible, the sacred Scriptures of the Jewish people. In the synagogues the importance of written texts had been a matter of course for centuries. We need to realize, however, that in a pagan context the emphasis on the written word was extraordinary. The Greco-Roman tradition acknowledged the value of written texts and even knew a certain awe with regard to the written

---

[2]See Bowers 1987. The comment that follows above is contra Cook 1982.
[3]See Käsemann, *Röm*, 285 (ET 295); Wilckens, *Röm*, 2:229.
[4]See Harris 1989, 218-21, 298-306. For reactions to Harris's study see Beard 1991.

word. However, in the diverse realities of pagan religiosity written texts such as honorary inscriptions, religious laws inscribed on stone, magic curses and oracles represented an "extra" that was never the center of religious faith or of religious practice.

This view, which has been confirmed by the work of William Harris, has been criticized. Mary Beard argues that written texts were used in cults, rituals and temples in the Greco-Roman world much more frequently than Harris allows, and she argues that written texts indeed had a central function in the description of people's relationship with a deity and in descriptions of various deities themselves.[5] Beard's main argument does not focus on texts that Harris overlooked or whose significance he may have downplayed. She indicates that her arguments rest primarily on a different view of the nature of written traditions, a view for which she appeals to Jacques Derrida, the postmodern French philosopher of literary deconstruction. Still, the ancient texts that she discusses caution us not to adopt Harris's hypothesis uncritically. The immense number of inscriptions found in temples of Asclepius in Epidauros, in Pergamon and in other cities, the over fifty bronze tablets found in the small temple of Jupiter Poeninus at the St. Bernard Pass, the nearly sixty graffiti at the fountain of Apollo in Cyrene, the wooden boards (*tituli*) that were carried along in Roman ritual processions displaying the name of the deity or the reason for the sacrifice (Suetonius, *Aug.* 59), the colonnaded halls covered with *libelli* containing vows to the gods with respect to expectations of healing for a certain illness (Juvenal, *Sat.* 12.100-101), the wax tablets affixed to cult statues with petitions and prayers (Juvenal, *Sat.* 10.54-55), and the text of the magistrate of Miletus (third century B.C.) directing citizens to no longer bring their private dedications to the new wooden hall in the temple of Apollo Delphinios but rather to the wall of plaster that serves this purpose—these thousands of religious texts that archaeologists have found and that presumably represent only a small part of the original "production" (most religious texts written on wood, wax or papyrus perished) surely had a larger significance than Harris's brief comment allows when he states that "shrines and temples accumulated written material."[6] However, whether the references to a deity and to the devotee found in these texts transforms an occasional sacrifice into a permanent relationship, as is claimed by Beard,[7] needs further discussion.

The "deeds" that accompanied the "word" of the apostles according to Rom 15:18 were not merely miracles of healing, but also the moral integrity of the behavior of the missionaries and of the followers of Jesus in the new communities, the personal interest and the genuine concern of the missionaries for the people whom they encountered, the committed mutual care among those in the Christian communities, and the patient endurance of the believers in the midst of opposition and suffering.[8]

The proclamation by the Jewish-Christian missionaries and the conduct of

---

[5]See Beard 1991, esp. 38-39; for the evidence mentioned in the comments that follow above see ibid., 39-43; also MacMullen 1981, 31-34, 157-60.
[6]Harris 1989, 219.
[7]Beard 1991, 48.
[8]See 1 Thess 2:1-12; 2 Cor 12:12; Acts 20:18-21, 31.

the new believers in Jesus Christ of the expanding and growing messianic communities caused the parting of the ways of the Christian *ekklēsiai* and the Jewish *synagōgai*. The reasons for this development cannot simply be identified with the missionary work of Paul. Rather, they are linked with the content of the preaching in Jerusalem by the Twelve, who insisted that God had raised the rejected and crucified Jesus of Nazareth from the dead, as confirmed by his appearances, and that he is the expected Messiah, who now, alone, saves from sin. Already during the first months and years of their preaching activity the followers of Jesus were faced with hostile and violent reactions and actions of the leadings priests, the Sanhedrin and the Jewish king Herod Agrippa, hostilities that culminated in the killing of the prominent Jerusalem preacher Stephen, the forced departure of the Greek-speaking Jewish Christians from Jerusalem, the killing of James the brother of Jesus, and in A.D. 48 in the forced departure of the remaining members of the Twelve from Jerusalem.[9]

The fulfillment of Jesus' missionary commission to go to all nations to the ends of the earth implied that his followers traveled, usually by foot—the use of donkeys, horses or carriages was impractical and expensive. Travelers could reach essentially every city in the Roman Empire and beyond, thanks to the *Pax Romana* and an extensive network of fortified roads—it was not until the nineteenth century that "international" travel became that easy again.[10] Paul traveled about 25,000 km (about 15,500 mi.) during the thirty-five years of his ministry, probably about 14,000 km (about 8,700 mi.) on foot, which is an astonishing achievement. We have no detailed information about the travels of other early Christian missionaries—it is not impossible that Peter traveled similar distances during the thirty-five to forty years of his missionary work, and if Thomas indeed reached India, he would have covered similar distances. Luke's account in "The Acts of the Apostles" (*praxeis apostolōn*), better called "Some Acts of Some Apostles," concentrates nearly exclusively on the ministries of Peter and of Paul, and even then is rather selective.

Experts in communication theory inform us that the successful transmission of a message depends on, among other factors, the credibility of the communicator, particularly in the initial contact. Important elements of what is called "source credibility" include competence, character and composure.[11] The early Christian missionaries as Luke describes them in the book of Acts and as Paul describes himself in his letters clearly possessed competence: they were able to present and explain their message of God's redemptive salvation in Jesus Christ to different audiences with sure knowledge, ample detail and persuasive argumentation. When the Sanhedrin forced Peter and John to give an account of the

---

[9]See Acts 4:1-21; 5:12-33; 6:8-15; 7:54-60; 8:1-3; 12:1-4.
[10]See Meeks 1983, 17.
[11]See Burgoon, Hunsaker and Dawson 1994, 39-46.

teaching that they presented in—of all places—the temple, the center of the Jewish people, the Torah experts and the polished aristocrats who listened to their explanations were "amazed" at the gripping speech of these two Galileans, unexpected for these "uneducated and ordinary men" (Acts 4:13). The fact that miracles accompanied their preaching and teaching made them even more "competent" as God's spokesmen, at least in the eyes of pagan audiences.[12] Character, the second criterion for the "source" of successful communication, includes goodness, decency and trustworthiness—again factors that can be verified for the early Christian missionaries.[13] Paul was strongly aware of the fact that his personal credibility was important both for his initial contacts with people who had never heard the gospel and for his continuing contacts with existing churches. This is why Paul defended himself when his credibility was attacked by, for example, comparisons with Sophist itinerant philosophers. The criterion of composure characterizes the early Christian missionaries as well. Since they were willing, as the examples of Stephen, James, Peter and Paul demonstrate, to die for their faith in Jesus the Messiah and Kyrios, they were able to maintain their composure in dangerous situations, which surely impressed not only Festus or King Agrippa II. However, the success of the missionary preaching and teaching of Peter and Stephen, of Barnabas and Paul and of other missionaries cannot be explained by these or other external factors such as rhetorical brilliance, as Paul emphasizes in 1 Cor 1:18—2:5.

33.2 Dialogue with the Non-Christian World

The book of Acts confirms that the early Christian missionaries interacted with the religious convictions of their audiences when they preached and taught the gospel of Jesus Christ. Paul, for example, took into account the scriptural and traditional convictions of the Jews in the synagogue of Pisidian Antiocheia (Acts 13:16-41), the popular superstition of the inhabitants of Lycaonia (Acts 14:8-20), and the natural theology of the Stoic and Epicurean philosophers in Athens (Acts 17:16-34).

The classic example of interaction with the religious convictions of listeners is Paul's speech before the council of the Areopagus in Athens (Acts 17:16-34). This is an excellent example of a "situational sermon" in which Paul provides an exposition of a particular aspect of his teaching before a particular audience. The council wanted to know whether Paul sought to introduce "foreign" gods to the Athenians, which would require at least the provision of a building site for an altar on which these gods could be worshiped. Paul emphasized that he does not want to introduce new deities: he proclaims the nature of the deity that the Athenians already honor on the altar with the inscription "To an un-

---

[12]See Eusebius *Hist. eccl.* 3.37.3, with regard to missionaries of the second century.
[13]See Acts 20:18-21; 1 Thess 2:1-12; Jas 3:17; 1 Pet 5:1; 2 Pet 1:12-21; 3:2; 1 Jn 1:1-3.

known god." Paul explained that he is not the envoy of a god who wants to be worshiped by the Athenians on an altar or in a sanctuary: the God whom he proclaims does not live in a temple because he is, as the Creator, close to every human being, a fact that their poets have already stated. Paul explained that the God whom he proclaims wants all Athenians, including the council members and the philosophers, to turn to the one true God and worship him alone, a demand that has become all the more important because God has already fixed the day of judgment for the world, determined the rules for judgment, and appointed a judge to execute judgment. Paul's "contextualized" speech prompted amazement and confusion among the audience, and some people were converted.

At the same time the early Christian missionaries refused to "contextualize" their message of the crucified and risen Jesus Christ in such a manner that the provocative, alien or scandalous elements disappear. Their conviction that God no longer grants salvation through the temple and the Torah but now does so through a human being, Jesus of Nazareth, who was executed on a cross and who is God's Son and Messiah, raised from the dead, was regarded by Jews as utterly scandalous, a blasphemy that some thought required severe punishment for those who proclaimed it. However, the early Christian missionaries never "defused" this conviction. They continued to emphasize that God has revealed himself in the *crucified* Messiah and that he now grants salvation *exclusively* through faith in Jesus as God's and Israel's Messiah. The conviction of the early missionaries that the Savior of the world is a crucified Jew from provincial Galilee who came back from the dead and will be the Judge of humankind amused, rather than incensed, the Athenian philosophers. Nevertheless, the missionaries never adapted their message to the subtle philosophical or rhetorical expectations of the Greco-Roman elite. They continued to insist that the one true God, the God of the Jews, reveals his redemptive power precisely in the *risen* man from Nazareth, the Savior of the world. Some of the miracles that happened in connection with the ministry of the apostles caused religious excitement, a prime example being the reaction of the Lycaonian population in the city of Lystra. Still, the missionaries refused to adapt their convictions or their behavior to popular piety and manipulate the seemingly favorable moment. The conviction that Jesus is the Messiah whom the Jews had expected for centuries and that he is *the* Son of God and Kyrios was dangerous in the political context of the Roman Empire and in the religious context of the imperial cult. However, the early Christian missionaries insisted on describing Jesus as Messiah and Kyrios, who will hold all human beings, without exception, accountable on the coming day of judgment.

An important aspect of the dialogue with non-Christians was the vocabulary of the New Testament texts, which suggests that the early Christian teachers and authors were unafraid of using terms that might be problematic for Christian doctrine. André Feuillet has demonstrated this fact in several areas for the Pastoral Epistles and the Epistle to the Hebrews.[14] (1) Terms for God. The adjective "blessed" (μακάριος, *makarios*) in 1 Tim 1:11; 6:15 describes God with a Hellenistic predicate for deity that highlights "God's nature, which is out of reach of all humans in its perfection and immortality."[15] The designation of Jesus Christ[16] as "great God" (μέγας θεός, *megas theos*) in Tit 2:13 adopts an epithet that was used for the gods in oriental religions and in Greco-Roman religiosity, describing "the extraordinary, the sublime, the incomparable pure and simple."[17] In the doxology of 1 Tim 1:17 the terms "immortal" (ἄφθαρτος, *aphthartos*) and "invisible" (ἀόρατος, *aoratos*) are designations of God that have Hellenistic parallels. Jürgen Roloff comments, "As the immortal and invisible one, God stands beyond all things of the material world, whose nature is visibility and transience, and therefore is removed from being grasped by the human senses."[18] Feuillet argues that the application of Hellenistic epithets for deity to Israel's God and to Jesus Christ is "l'intention missionaire."[19] (2) The "epiphany" of Jesus Christ. In the Greco-Roman world the term *epiphaneia* indicated "the appearance of the saving deity and the experience of the saving act. But it also designated the cultic presence of the godlike ruler in the Hellenistic-Roman state cult."[20] In Tit 2:11; 3:4; 2:13 the term is used for the incarnation, life, witness and return of Jesus Christ "in their universal soteriological consequence for all people."[21] Howard Marshall observes, "The language used would have aroused echoes in the Hellenistic world, but the concepts used are thoroughly Jewish, Christian, and Pauline." (3) The author of the Epistle to the Hebrews uses Hellenistic terminology in describing the contrast between temporal reality and eternal reality but places it firmly in the context of an exhortation for Christian believers who are struggling. The statement in Heb 11:3 ("By faith we understand that the worlds were prepared by the word of God, so that what is seen was made from things that are not visible") does not promote a Platonic/Hellenistic dualistic description of creation.[22] Rather, the author underscores for his readers "what they should hold on to with their faith (and the ability to comprehend given with it): to God himself and to his effective word."[23] The epistemological categories in

---

[14]Feuillet 1988, 126-28, 156-58.

[15]Roloff, *1 Tim*, 80.

[16]For the reference of Tit 2:13 to Jesus Christ see Marshall, *PastEp*, 276-82.

[17]Roloff, *1 Tim*, 201.

[18]Roloff, *1 Tim*, 98.

[19]Feuillet 1988, 127.

[20]P.-G. Müller, *EWNT* 2:111 (*EDNT* 2:44).

[21]Müller, *EWNT* 2:112 (*EDNT* 2:45). On the concept of "epiphany" in the Pastoral Epistles see Marshall, *PastEp*, 287-96; the quotation that follows above, 296.

[22]Contra Braun, *Hebr*, 341-42.

[23]Weiss, *Hebr*, 675; cf. Feuillet 1988, 156; Ellingworth, *Heb*, 569-70; for the comment that follows above see ibid., 562-63.

Heb 11 are not first Hebrew/temporal and then Greek/spatial, but rather are consistently historical and therefore temporal: the author looks ahead in the endeavor to encourage readers to persevere in their faith in Jesus Christ. (4) The statement that Jesus "came as a high priest of the good things that have come, then through the greater and perfect tent (not made with hands, that is, not of this creation)" (Heb 9:11; cf. 6:19-20; 8:1-2) may remind readers of formulations that belonged to the dualistic worldview of the Greeks. However, this statement is not an expression of denigration of the created order by the author.[24] Rather, the contrast of the earthly and the heavenly sanctuaries underlines primarily "the redemptive efficacy of the new order of salvation that is valid for all times and that is, in this sense, final."[25] The author of the Epistle to the Hebrews uses Hellenistic terminology and formulations in his description of Jesus Christ, but he has not "Platonized" the Christian faith, since he describes the significance of Jesus Christ ultimately in salvation-historical terms.[26]

33.3 Reasons for the Successes of the Early Christian Missionaries

The history of the early Christian mission in the second century is largely unknown. We hear of Christian believers in the province of Gaul only because they suffered in persecutions, because later Christian authors such as Eusebius know the names of martyrs, and because we know of Irenaeus, an eminent theologian of this period who taught in Lugdunum (Lyon). We have practically no information about the growing churches in Egypt, North Africa, Syria, Mesopotamia or in India. Does this mean that there were no great missionary figures such as Peter, Paul or Barnabas in the second century?[27] Did churches in major cities such as Antioch, Ephesus or Rome—after A.D. 70 Jerusalem cease to function as a center of the early Christian mission—concentrate only on their own affairs, failing to send out missionaries? Since the primary sources provide no answers to these questions, they must remain unanswered. There is no doubt, however, that the Christian faith continued to spread. Per Beskow attributes the growth of the church in the second century to commercial contacts that the Christians used to spread their faith, and he points to the emigration and the exchange of Christian slaves and to the movements of soldiers as further factors. He believes that neither the sending of missionaries to foreign regions nor the concept of systematic missionary work played any role in the expansion of the church during this period.[28] However, this hypothesis

---

[24]Contra Braun, *Hebr,* 265-66, 282.

[25]Weiss, *Hebr,* 466.

[26]Ellingworth, *Heb,* 76; cf. Feuillet 1988, 157-58.

[27]Thus, for example, Beskow 1970, 105.

[28]Beskow 1970, for the comment that follows above see 104.

violates his own rule that the silence of the sources should not be (mis)used as a basis for historical assumptions.

Earlier generations of scholars, including Adolf von Harnack, cited several factors that were meant to describe the "success" of Christianity (see *Praeparatio evangelica?* in §16.5). These factors are evaluated today more critically by most scholars.[29]

1. Generally favorable conditions such as the *Pax Romana,* the political stability that the Roman Empire guaranteed, allowing travelers to use the excellent network of Roman roads in relative safety and at astonishing speeds; the cultural unity of the Greco-Roman world in religion and philosophy, facilitating communication across ethnic divides; the Greek language as the lingua franca from Syria and Judea to Spain; the idea of the unity of the human race; the religious tolerance of the Roman state. These factors surely facilitated the missionary outreach of the early Christians and the growth of the church. However, we need to contrast these favorable conditions with factors that adversely influenced the expansion of the Christian faith.[30] These unfavorable factors make it difficult to recognize the auspicious conditions that were mentioned as satisfactory explanations for the successful expansion of the Christian faith in the first century. These unfavorable factors included pogroms and persecutions directed at Christians, which not only hindered and in some cases prevented missionary work (one example is Paul's initial plan for a mission to the provinces of Asia and Bithynia) but also must have been daunting to potential converts. Furthermore, the missionaries proclaimed convictions that were quite difficult for Gentiles to accept: the existence of only one God; the redemptive significance of a crucified Jew; the bodily resurrection from the dead; the claim that salvation is tied exclusively to faith in Jesus Christ. Christians convictions that were difficult to accept for Jews included the redemptive significance of a crucified Messiah; the resurrection of Jesus from the dead before the day of resurrection at the end of time; the epiphany of God in Jesus Christ; the redefinition of temple and Torah; the acceptance of uncircumcised Gentiles into the people of God. Finally, the external forms of the Christian community clashed with the traditional religious praxis of both Jews and Gentiles: the followers of Jesus had no temple(s), no altars, no image of their deity, no processions. Norbert Brox comments, "The beginnings did not suggest success. A tiny religious movement from the politically and culturally totally insignificant Jewish people at the eastern end of the Empire with its new 'superstition' clearly did not correspond to the standards of a serious religion."

2. The critique of polytheism by Platonist and Stoic philosophers. This factor cannot explain the success of the early Christian missionaries either. The philo-

---

[29]See the history of research in Praet 1992-1993.
[30]See Brox 1983, 35; for the comments that follow above see ibid.; quotation, ibid., 33.

sophical critique of polytheism never had any practical consequences for the participation of the people in pagan cults in the first or second centuries. Since pagan religiosity knew no explicit "confession of faith," no *credo,* the myths about the gods were essentially irrelevant for the cultic practices. The critique of the myths had no influence whatsoever on the rites that were practiced in the temples. And we do not know who listened to the Epicureans and Stoics.[31]

3. The disintegration of the system of the Greek *polis* discredited the gods. This hypothesis focuses too much on Greece and does not even apply to Greece as far as the first century is concerned.

4. Religious syncretism, with its tolerance and its occasional tendency to fuse several gods into a single deity or to interpret all gods as different aspects of a transcendent *dynamis.*[32] Greco-Roman syncretism did not, however, lead to monotheism; it promoted, at most, a hierarchical polytheism.[33]

5. The Hellenistic ruler cult, implying the possibility of a "god-man." This "parallel" that is attested for some traditions of pagan religiosity explains neither the incarnation of Jesus nor the crucified Messiah.

6. The decline of pagan religiosity in the third century A.D.[34] This hypothesis of a general religious crisis has either been abandoned or heavily modified: it cannot be verified with the available chronological or geographical data, it evaluates the extant information rather selectively, and it ignores clear and ample evidence for the vitality and the unbroken spirit of paganism in the third century. It was not the priests who became more silent, but the stonecutters, as Ramsay MacMullen asserts: "Religion, like many other aspects of life, rises and falls on the quantity of surviving evidence like a boat on the tide."[35]

7. Status inconsistency—that is, diverging evaluations of the social position of an individual by that individual or by others. Wayne Meeks regards this sociological category as an important factor for the conversion to the Christian faith of women, wealthy Jews in pagan cities, well-to-do freedmen stigmatized by their origin: they embraced the Christian faith and the Christian community as "substitute careers" providing new possibilities of personal development.[36] However, this explanation neither fits the available data nor reckons with the complex manner in which people think about themselves and their social "status."[37]

8. The feelings of anxiety, insecurity and helplessness and the Hellenistic "yearning for salvation" caused by material and moral insecurity, by the political

---

[31]See MacMullen 1981, 71-82, 77; Lane Fox 1986, 32, 93, 95; Praet 1992-1993, 14-15.
[32]See MacMullen 1981, 86, 187 n. 48.
[33]MacMullen 1981, 89; Lane Fox 1986, 34-35; Praet 1992-1993, 15-16.
[34]Geffcken 1929; Dodds 1965, 132-33; Hinson 1981, 23.
[35]MacMullen 1981, 127; cf. Lane Fox 1986, 52-55, 75-82, 574-75; Praet 1992-1993, 20-22.
[36]Meeks 1983, 191.
[37]See Lane Fox 1986, 319-22; Praet 1992-1993, 60-62.

alienation of people in absolutist monarchies and by the threat of slavery and similar problems.[38] This explanation likewise is unconvincing. The ample evidence for the general optimism of people and the firm belief in the pagans gods in the second and third centuries more than neutralizes the "anxieties" of some Greek or Roman intellectuals.[39]

9. The exclusiveness of the Christian faith, which rejected all compromises and syncretistic forms and practices.[40] Although an exclusivist position may be attractive for some people, in the sense of a "fundamental opposition" to the status quo, the pagans of the second and third centuries did not complain about the numerous religious options that were available. Polytheism has its advantages, as Robin Lane Fox points out.[41]

10. The anonymity and loneliness of life in the cities, which rendered the Christian communities, with their sense of belonging, attractive. This sociopsychological explanation, although of some value, seems more apropos of modern feelings. Apart from the huge cities of Rome and Alexandria, most of the cities in the Mediterranean world in Asia Minor, Greece, Gaul, Syria and Babylonia were small cities that remained closely connected with the countryside. The population of the vast majority of cities consisted of identifiable social groups in which the traditional social contacts and controls were still intact.

The three most popular explanations for the success of the early Christian missionary expansion in the time before Constantine (A.D. 307-337) are the following.

11. Miracles and exorcisms are the most important, perhaps even the only, reason for the conversions to Christianity during this time, according to Ramsay MacMullen.[42] However, as important as miracles connected with the missionary work of the early Christians might have been, this factor does not explain the continuous expansion of the Christian faith. Pagans asked for and received miracles from their gods as well, and pagan philosophers could easily offer different explanations for miracles. And the awe and excitement that people displayed when miracles happened did not necessarily lead to acceptance of the Christian faith with its exclusive claims, as the experience of Paul and Barnabas in Lycaonian Lystra demonstrates.[43]

12. The courage of the martyrs, impressing the crowds that witnessed their "inspiration" by a powerful God and by a faith that they were willing to die for.[44]

---

[38]Dodds 1965, esp. 3-4, 137.
[39]See Lane Fox 1986, 65-66.
[40]Dodds 1965, 133-34.
[41]Lane Fox 1986, 575.
[42]MacMullen 1981, 49-112; 1984, 17-42; see also Bardy 1988, 167-70; Praet 1992-1993, 24-29.
[43]See Lane Fox 1986, 329-30.
[44]See Baus 1965, 474; Dodds 1965, 132; MacMullen 1984, 30; Praet 1992-1993, 29-35; Stark 1997, 163-89.

There is no doubt that the amazing martyrdom of numerous Christians impressed many pagans, as is confirmed by Tertullian, who asserted that the blood of the martyrs is the seed of the church (*semen est sanguis Christianorum* [Tertullian, *Apol.* 50.13]). We should remember, however, that Epictetus and Marcus Aurelius offered less flattering explanations for the willingness of Christians to die for their faith: they saw theatrical affectation, foolish stubbornness and an irrational death-wish on the part of Christians.[45] Spectators who were impressed by the courageous steadfastness of the Christian martyrs would not automatically have accepted the Christian message, as they would have pondered the possibly deadly consequences of such a decision.

13. The ideal Christian love and the praxis of Christian charity.[46] The mutual love and support of the Christians indeed impressed many pagans. According to Rodney Stark, this was particularly significant in the epidemic of A.D. 165-180 (smallpox?), when perhaps a quarter to a third of the population of the empire perished, and in the epidemic of A.D. 251 (measles?), during which five thousand deaths per day are reported for the city of Rome alone.[47] However, the "heartlessness" of pagans should not be exaggerated.[48] And we should remember that some Christians displayed intolerance and even hatred for fellow Christians who held different theological views, and such sentiments did not go unnoticed in the ancient world.[49] Michael Sievernich observes that the family-like conduct of the Christians "and the generous acts of charity and the care for the poor, which was not limited to their own group, attracted considerable attention . . . the new way of life and the charity of the Christians became a model of social integration in the cities. Whereas the Greco-Roman world sought to promote social integration by the expansion of civil equality, the Christians realized a social and ethnic equality for all, linked with Christian brotherhood and anchored 'in Christ.' In this manner there arose a Christian 'radicalization of ancient democratic traditions' or, to put it differently, a fusion of the compatible elements of Christianity and ancient urban life."[50]

Occasionally four additional factors are mentioned to help explain the spread of the Christian faith and the numerous conversions in the second and third centuries.

14. The Christian belief in life after death, with the offer of resurrection and eternal bliss, which encountered a pagan religiosity in which death was the con-

---

[45]Arrian, *Diatr.* 4.7.6; Marcus Aurelius 11.3. See Praet 1992-1993, 29-30.

[46]Tertullian, *Apol.* 39.7; note the comment by Emperor Julian reported by Eusebius, *Hist. eccl.* 9.8.11-14. See Praet 1992-1993, 49-52.

[47]Stark 1991a, esp. 166-70; 1997, 73-94.

[48]See MacMullen 1981, 37, 42; Lane Fox 1986, 61-62, 591.

[49]Ammianus Marcellinus 22.5.4. For a critique of Rodney Stark see J. Sanders 1992; B. A. Pearson, *Religion* 29 (1999): 171-76.

[50]Sievernich 1990, 107, with a quotation from Theissen 1989, 271 (ET, 1982, 110).

clusion of human existence.[51] However, the very idea of a bodily resurrection remained unacceptable to many pagans.[52] And the message of a second coming of Jesus and an eternal damnation of unbelievers was difficult to accept as well.

15. The historical nature of the Christian faith, including the unique personality of its founder, Jesus of Nazareth, in contrast to the complex mythologies of pagan gods. However, pagan intellectuals such as Celsus countered this argument, advanced by the apologists of the church, by asking why the Christian Savior came so late, leaving generations of people without salvation, and by questioning what he really brought to his faithful devotees other than persecution.[53]

16. The social inclusiveness of the Christians, which transcended national and ethnical ties, social and financial barriers as well as geographical boundaries, integrating both men and women.[54] However, this inclusiveness was an attractive "improvement" only for people at the lower end of the social ladder, whereas most wealthy citizens would have seen as impudence the requirement that, for example, they submit to "elders" who were slaves but were more mature as Christians.

17. The social networks that allowed for "vertical" connections in the hierarchal social structures of Roman society, particularly attractive for converts from the lower classes.[55] Personal connections within a *familia* or a "house" that included slaves and servants surely were an important factor in the spread of the gospel. However, the example of Sergius Paullus, the Roman governor of Cyprus, and his relatives in Pisidian Antiocheia shows that social networks, though potentially useful for conversions, did not automatically lead to successful encounters, nor can they "explain" conversions. Rodney Stark's quantitative sociological analyses—for example, the idea that the larger the city and the more limited the Roman influence were, the easier the dissemination of the Christian faith became—are not very helpful. Since the sources of the first and second centuries provide no data about the number of Christians in small towns and villages, statistical operations with the population figures of urban centers remain totally hypothetical. And the degree of Romanization surely is not to be understood as a function of the geographical distance from Rome.[56]

Historians of the Roman Empire debate whether the Christian movement needed the conversion of Constantine in A.D. 312 (or slightly earlier) to be transformed from a "minority religion" to a "world religion,"[57] or whether the decisive

---

[51]See MacMullen 1981, 53-57; see also Bardy 1988, 143-55; Praet 1992-1993, 34-37.

[52]Origen, *Cels.* 5.14.

[53]Origen, *Cels.* 4.7; 8.69. See Praet 1992-1993, 38-42.

[54]See Praet 1992-1993, 45-49.

[55]See White 1991; Stark 1997, 55-57.

[56]Stark 1991b; 1997, 129-45. Stark, a sociologist, admits that he is neither a theologian nor a historian (see idem 1997, xii).

[57]Thus MacMullen 1984; Lane Fox 1986; cf. Praet 1992-1993.

period was the third century, in which the church grew rapidly and was increasingly accepted by the wider population.[58] None of the seventeen factors that have been mentioned and no combination of some of these factors can sufficiently explain the astonishing expansion of the Christian faith and the Christian churches. It may be more than "Christian bias" if a historian sees the growth of the church in the first three centuries as the work of divine providence. It is in this sense that the French patristic scholar Gustave Bardy gave this answer to the question of why the Greco-Roman world converted to the Christian faith: "A satisfactory answer to this question is not possible. The mystery of the human soul belongs to itself, and we should not forget the powerful effect of divine grace, which chooses whom it wants, leading them onto those paths that lead to Him."[59]

---

[58]Thus Frend 1974-1980; P. Brown 1996.
[59]Bardy 1988, 126-27.

34

THE MESSAGE OF THE
EARLY CHRISTIAN MISSIONARIES

The early Christian missionaries proclaimed a message with Jesus at its center—his person, his life and ministry in Galilee and in Jerusalem, his messianic dignity, his prophetic teaching, his death and resurrection, his exaltation at God's right hand as Kyrios, his gift of the Holy Spirit, his return as Judge. They called their listeners, both Jews and Gentiles, to repent, to turn to the living God and accept Jesus as Messiah and Savior. They challenged the Jews of Jerusalem to abandon their ignorance that caused the rejection, condemnation and crucifixion of Jesus, and to accept him as God's Messiah, who alone, through his atoning death, forgives sins. They challenged the Gentiles whom they encountered in the cities and towns of the Roman Empire to turn away from idols, to turn to the one true God, the God of Israel and the Jewish people, and to accept Jesus, the Son of God sent into the world, as the Kyrios and Savior, who alone can forgive sins.[1]

34.1 God's Redemptive Messianic Revelation

Peter's sermon at the Feast of Pentecost in Jerusalem in A.D. 30 (Acts 2:14-36) summarizes the basic points of the message that Peter and his fellow apostles preached to Jewish audiences. (1) The coming of Jesus of Nazareth and particularly his gift of God's Spirit signified the arrival of the last days of which the prophets spoke. The days of the Messiah have arrived, the promised new covenant has been inaugurated. This is why Jews need to repent, as being a member of God's old covenant people no longer suffices for salvation in the final judgment. The apostles argued that their Jewish contemporaries are like the Israel of the wilderness generation at the time of Israel's redemption from slavery in Egypt: a "corrupt generation" (Acts 2:40). Their rejection of Jesus as the Messiah, the arrest, condemnation and crucifixion of Jesus, have shown that Israel

---

[1]See Acts 2:36; 5:30-31; 10:34-43; 13:25-41; 17:30; 1 Cor 15:3-5; 2 Cor 5:21; Rom 4:25.

is as "corrupt" a generation as Israel in the wilderness. The impending judgment requires that they let themselves be rescued from their rebellion against God's second great act of redemption. There is still time before the arrival of the great Day of the Lord for Israel to repent and find salvation (Acts 2:38). (2) Salvation is tied to calling on the name of "the Lord Jesus Christ"—that is, to the acknowledgment of Jesus as the Messiah, to his death as the divine atonement for sins, to his resurrection from the dead, to his exaltation at God's right hand, to his position as Lord who sends the Spirit of God, a position that he occupies as the crucified, risen and exalted Messiah. (3) Salvation is tied to baptism "in the name of Jesus Christ," demonstrating repentance and coming to faith in Jesus the Messiah and exalted Lord. (4) Faith in Jesus Christ leads to the reception of the Spirit and grants membership in the messianic people of God in the new covenant. (5) The Jews who accept God's new redemptive revelation and believe in Jesus as Messiah belong to the restoration of Israel that had been promised, to the messianic people that God gathers in the last days. (6) The gathering of the new people of God in Israel includes the ingathering of the Gentiles that was expected for the last days (Acts 2:39).

The Greek-speaking Jewish Christians of Jerusalem apparently were the first to grasp the consequences of Jesus' death and resurrection for the identity of Israel as the people of God. They understood and taught that the biblical conviction that Yahweh does not live in temples made by human hands has consequences, now that the messianic days have been inaugurated, for the temple and its cult and thus for the Torah. If Jesus is the Messiah, and if his death on the cross and his resurrection on the third day constitute the eschatological revelation of God's redemption action, then the temple is no longer the place of God's redemptive presence, and the sacrifices stipulated by the Torah no longer forgive sins.

Paul's sermon in the synagogue in Pisidian Antiocheia (Acts 13:16-41) underscores essentially the same convictions but with somewhat different emphasis. (1) God has planned and ordered Israel's history with Jesus of Nazareth as its climax. He has continued to send saviors and prophets such as Samuel, Saul, David and John. The climax of God's history of salvation in Israel is the sending of Jesus the Messiah. (2) God has fulfilled his promises in the life, death and resurrection of Jesus, the Savior of Israel. The inhabitants of Jerusalem and their leading representatives rejected Jesus because they did not recognize who he was and failed to grasp the meaning of the witness of the prophets. Paul emphasizes that Jesus' rejection by the Jews of Jerusalem was part of God's plan. God raised Jesus from the dead, and he appeared to his followers during many days, which confirms that Jesus is the Servant of God, through whom God offers forgiveness of sins—forgiveness that God offers to the audience in the synagogue. (3) Since the forgiveness of sins that God now offers in Jesus the Messiah covers all sins, which the Torah could not do, applied to "everyone who believes" (Acts 13:38-39), Paul warns the listeners of the danger of disregarding God's gift and thus fulfilling the prophecy of Hab 1:5.

The early Christian preaching to Gentile audiences[2] emphasized the following fundamental truths. (1) The God of Israel is the only true God; the gods of the pagans are nothing, and worshiping them is futile. Gentiles must leave their gods and turn to the one true God. Paul was able to speak knowledgeably and with rhetorical skill about pagan religiosity and its consequences for society and for the individual (Rom 1:18-32). And he was able to elaborate with incisive logic and with philosophical acumen on true and false views of God (Acts 17:22-31). (2) The life, ministry, death and resurrection of Jesus of Nazareth are *good news:* it is through faith in Jesus that God forgives the sins of people. He now invites the Gentiles to become members of his people through faith in Jesus the Savior. God forgives sins through Jesus because he took the sinners' death sentence upon himself and atoned for their sins on the cross.[3] Jesus died on the cross in place of sinners and for the benefit of sinners who accept him as messianic savior. (3) God begins to establish his rule (*basileia*) with the coming of Jesus his Son (cf. 1 Thess 2:12; Gal 5:21). This teaching was potentially dangerous in the political context of the Roman Empire and the imperial cult. However, Paul evidently was convinced that this truth was so integral to the message of Jesus Christ that he did not downplay it in his sermons to Gentile audiences. (4) In God's coming judgment Jesus, the risen Son of God, will return and save those who believe in him. The redemption that God offers thus receives a note of urgency. (5) Paul spoke in his missionary sermons about the obedience that God demands of all people and that those who have been reconciled to God through faith in Jesus Christ fulfill gratefully, empowered by the Holy Spirit. Faith in Jesus Christ is realized in the love of God and the love of others and becomes visible in the fruit of the Holy Spirit. Repenting, turning to the living God, and believing in Jesus have as their goal true worship realized in one's entire life—a life according to the will of God, controlled by the Holy Spirit, characterized by holiness that transforms conduct in the family and at the workplace, among friends and acquaintances, in the home and away from home.

34.2 The New Identity

The early Christian missionaries called listeners to "turn" (*epistrephein*)—that is, to abandon false convictions and behavioral patterns (*metanoein*) and to accept and rely on God's revelation in Jesus Christ (*pisteuein*). Gentiles must abandon false notions about God, and Jews must do the same with false notions about the Messiah and about Jesus. Jews need to come to faith in Jesus as the crucified

---

[2] See 1 Thess 1:9-10; 4:2-7; 1 Cor 1:17-18; 2 Cor 5:20; 11:4; Rom 1:18-32; Acts 17:22-31.
[3] See Rom 1:16-17; 3:25-26; 5:9; 6:3-9; 8:3, 32; 1 Cor 1:18, 24; 5:7; 2 Cor 5:19-21; Gal 1:4; 3:13; Eph 1:7; 2:13; 5:2; Col 2:10; Phil 2:8; 3:18.

and risen Messiah and Savior. Gentiles need to accept and believe that there is only one true God, who sent Jesus his Son into the world as the Savior who forgives sin and is the only true Kyrios. The process and event of conversion is described in the New Testament with different metaphors: conversion is new birth,[4] resurrection with Jesus Christ to a new life,[5] removing old clothes and putting on new ones,[6] change of owners,[7] movement from darkness to light[8] and from death to life.[9]

Christians have a new identity as a result of their faith in Jesus Christ and as a result of their integration into the community his followers. It makes no difference in the Christian community whether one is a Jew or a Greek or a Scythian (Gal 3:28; Col 3:11), for all are "baptized into one body" by the Spirit of God (1 Cor 12:13).

Christian are "aliens without citizenship rights" (*paroikoi*) in the cities, towns and villages in which they live, "resident aliens" (*parepidēmoi*), a minority in the "dispersion" (*diaspora*) (1 Pet 1:1, 17; 2:11). Paul states in Phil 3:20 that the "citizenship" of the believers is "in heaven." Wilhelm Hadorn asserted a century ago that the Christian faith implies and constitutes "a break with nationality."[10] The distance between church and society, between Christians and culture, is a result of the new birth "into a living hope through the resurrection of Jesus Christ from the dead" (1 Pet 1:3), which the merciful God and Father grants to those "who have been chosen and destined by God the Father and sanctified by the Spirit to be obedient to Jesus Christ and to be sprinkled with his blood" (1 Pet 1:2).[11] To be a Christian means to be born again, which means that faith in Jesus Christ distances Christians from their previous life and lifestyle, which were characterized by the worship of false gods and by unholy desires (1 Pet 1:14-16). To be a Christian implies and grants a living hope, which means that the saving faith in Jesus Christ distances Christians from the futility and transience of the present world, in which people face death and judgment (1 Pet 4:17).

Miroslav Volf comments on the significance of new birth for the social identity of Christians: "Christians do not come into their social world from outside seeking either to accommodate to their new home (like second generation immigrants would), shape it in the image of the one they have left behind (like colonizers would), or establish a little haven in the strange new world reminiscent of the old (as resident aliens would). They are not outsiders who either

---

[4] Jn 1:13; 3:3-6; 1 Jn 2:29; 3:9-10; 4:7; 5:4, 18; Tit 3:5; 1 Pet 1:3, 23; 2:2; Jas 1:18.
[5] Rom 6:3-4; Col 3:1-4.
[6] Col 3:9-10; Gal 3:27.
[7] Rom 6:17-18.
[8] Acts 26:18; 2 Cor 4:6; 1 Pet 2:9; 1 Jn 2:9-11.
[9] Jn 5:24; Eph 2:1-6.
[10] Hadorn 1901, 13; cf. Belser 1912, 384.
[11] Volf 1994, 18; for the comments that follow above see ibid., 18-19.

seek to become insiders or maintain strenuously the status of outsiders. Christians are the *insiders* who have diverted from their culture by being born again. They are by definition those who are not what they used to be, those who do not live like they used to live. Christian difference is therefore not an insertion of something new into the old from outside, but a bursting out of the new *precisely within the proper space of the old.*"[12] The question is not whether Christians should adopt or reject the behavioral patterns of non-Christian society—that question is posed by outsiders. As insiders, Christians ask which values and behaviors of society they must reject because they have become different people through new birth, and which values and behaviors they can retain because they do not adversely affect life with God, and which values and behaviors they can and should transform so that they reflect the values of God's new creation more authentically.

According to Peter, two truths are important regarding the new identity of the Christians. (1) The different character of Christians that results from their new birth is not initially the private piety and lifestyle of the individual Christian; rather, it has an ecclesiological dimension: it is linked with the fact that they belong to the community of Jesus Christ. The exhortation to live as "aliens and exiles" in the world (1 Pet 2:11) is prefaced with this statement: "But you are a chosen race, a royal priesthood, a holy nation, God's own people, in order that you may proclaim the mighty acts of him who called you out of darkness into his marvelous light. Once you were not a people, but now you are God's people; once you had not received mercy, but now you have received mercy" (1 Pet 2:9-10). (2) The identity as "aliens" refers neither to ignorance of the world nor withdrawal from the world. The goal of Christian existence is the proclamation of the "mighty acts" of God (1 Pet 2:9)—not isolation from the world, but mission in the world.

In the second century the unknown author of the *Epistle to Diognetus,* who earnestly acknowledges the religion of the Christians, writes the following.

Diogn. 5: "For Christians are no different from other people in terms of their country, language, or customs. ²Nowhere do they inhabit cities of their own, or live life out of the ordinary. ³They have not discovered this teaching of theirs through reflection or through the thought of meddlesome people, nor do they set forth any human doctrine, as do some. ⁴They inhabit both Greek and barbarian cities, according the lot assigned to each. And they show forth the character of their own citizenship in a marvelous and admittedly paradoxical way by following local customs in what they wear and what they eat and in the rest of their lives. ⁵They live in their respective countries, but only as resident aliens [ὡς πάροικοι]; they participate in all things as citizens, and they endure all things as foreigners [ὡς ξένοι]. Every foreign territory is a homeland for them, every homeland foreign territory [πᾶσα ξένη πατρίς ἐστιν αὐτῶν, καὶ πᾶσα πατρὶς ξένη]. ⁶They marry like everyone else and have children, but they do not expose them once they are born. ⁷They

---

[12]Volf 1994, 18-19; for the comments that follow above see ibid., 19-20, 24-25.

share their meals but not their sexual partners. [8]They are found in the flesh but do not live according to the flesh. [9]They live on earth but participate in the life of heaven. [10]They are obedient to the laws that have been made, and by their own lives they supersede the laws. [11]They love everyone and are persecuted by all. [12]They are not understood and they are condemned. They are put to death and made alive. [13]They are impoverished and make many rich. [14]They are dishonored and they are exalted in their dishonors. They are slandered and they are acquitted. [15]They are reviled and they bless, mistreated and they bestow honor. [16]They do good and are punished as evil; when they are punished they rejoice as those who have been made alive. [17]They are attacked by Jews as foreigners and persecuted by Greeks. And those who hate them cannot explain the cause of their enmity."

34.3 The Promise of Paradise Restored

John emphasizes in the last chapter of the New Testament that the community of the followers of Jesus continues to have the task of proclaiming the gospel even in the tribulation of the last days, whether people want to hear their message or not. He describes for the churches in Asia Minor the visions that God had granted him of the members of the people of God protected by God's seal, of the innumerable multitude before the throne of God, and of the two witnesses. God the Creator and Lord of creation, the Alpha and Omega, assures the churches that his hand is with his witnesses, which does not mean that because they preach the gospel they will not suffer or die. God calls the followers of Jesus to be concerned not merely to survive, but to continue to preach the gospel of Jesus Christ to the unbelieving and godless people in the cities in which they live. The darker the hour and the stronger the attacks from evil powers, the more important it is that the churches are what they are: lampstands from which the light of Jesus Christ shines into the world.

Rev 7:9-12: "After this I looked, and there was a great multitude that no one could count [ὄχλος πολύς, ὃν ἀριθμῆσαι αὐτὸν οὐδεὶς ἐδύνατο], from every nation, from all tribes and peoples and languages [ἐκ παντὸς ἔθνους καὶ φυλῶν καὶ λαῶν καὶ γλωσσῶν], standing before the throne and before the Lamb, robed in white, with palm branches in their hands. [10]They cried out in a loud voice, saying, 'Salvation belongs to our God who is seated on the throne, and to the Lamb!' [11]And all the angels stood around the throne and around the elders and the four living creatures, and they fell on their faces before the throne and worshiped God, [12]singing, 'Amen! Blessing and glory and wisdom and thanksgiving and honor and power and might be to our God forever and ever! Amen.'"

Rev 7:13-17: "Then one of the elders addressed me, saying, 'Who are these, robed in white, and where have they come from?' [14]I said to him, 'Sir, you are the one that knows.' Then he said to me, 'These are they who have come out of the great ordeal; they have washed their robes and made them white in the blood of the Lamb. [15]For this reason they are before the throne of God, and worship him day and night within his temple, and the one who is seated on the throne will shelter them. [16]They will hunger no more, and thirst no more; the sun will not strike them, nor any scorching heat; [17]for the Lamb at the center of the throne will be their shepherd, and he will guide them to springs of the water of life, and God will wipe away every tear from their eyes.'"

Rev 11:3-12: "'And I will grant my two witnesses authority to prophesy for one thousand two hundred sixty days, wearing sackcloth.' ⁴These are the two olive trees and the two lampstands that stand before the Lord of the earth. ⁵And if anyone wants to harm them, fire pours from their mouth and consumes their foes; anyone who wants to harm them must be killed in this manner. ⁶They have authority to shut the sky, so that no rain may fall during the days of their prophesying, and they have authority over the waters to turn them into blood, and to strike the earth with every kind of plague, as often as they desire. ⁷When they have finished their testimony, the beast that comes up from the bottomless pit will make war on them and conquer them and kill them, ⁸and their dead bodies will lie in the street of the great city that is prophetically called Sodom and Egypt, where also their Lord was crucified. ⁹For three and a half days members of the peoples and tribes and languages and nations will gaze at their dead bodies and refuse to let them be placed in a tomb; ¹⁰and the inhabitants of the earth will gloat over them and celebrate and exchange presents, because these two prophets had been a torment to the inhabitants of the earth. ¹¹But after the three and a half days, the breath of life from God entered them, and they stood on their feet, and those who saw them were terrified. ¹²Then they heard a loud voice from heaven saying to them, 'Come up here!' And they went up to heaven in a cloud while their enemies watched them."

John concludes with the vision of God's new creation in which paradise is restored and the nations worship before the throne of God and of the Lamb:

Rev 22:1-5: "Then the angel showed me the river of the water of life, bright as crystal, flowing from the throne of God and of the Lamb ²through the middle of the street of the city. On either side of the river is the tree of life with its twelve kinds of fruit, producing its fruit each month; and the leaves of the tree are for the healing of the nations [καὶ τὰ φύλλα τοῦ ξύλου εἰς θεραπείαν τῶν ἐθνῶν]. ³Nothing accursed will be found there any more. But the throne of God and of the Lamb will be in it, and his servants will worship him; ⁴they will see his face, and his name will be on their foreheads. ⁵And there will be no more night; they need no light of lamp or sun, for the Lord God will be their light, and they will reign forever and ever [ὅτι κύριος ὁ θεὸς φωτίσει ἐπ᾽ αὐτούς, καὶ βασιλεύσουσιν εἰς τοὺς αἰῶνας τῶν αἰώνων]."

35

THE EARLY CHRISTIAN
MISSIONARY MOVEMENT
AND MISSIONS IN THE TWENTIETH
AND TWENTY-FIRST CENTURIES

Missiologists and experts in church growth often use sociological and anthropological models for their analyses and projections that have been developed outside of the biblical tradition. Missiologists of different persuasions and backgrounds have commented on this trend critically, demanding a return to biblical and genuinely theological foundations.[1] Based on conviction that the Bible, as sacred Scripture, is the authority not only for faith but also for practice, and not only for the private life of the individual Christian but also for the life of the church of Jesus Christ as a whole, in both its universal and local expressions, attempts to adopt "lessons" from the missions of Jesus and of the apostles are to be welcomed. Indeed, if the interpretation of New Testament texts no longer serves to authenticate missionary work,[2] then scholars have capitulated to the often controversial results and aporias of source, tradition and redaction criticism. However, one will quickly find that many attempts to learn and adopt biblical "lessons" make do without historical clarification, careful exegesis and hermeneutical reflection. It is not surprising, therefore, that "principles" of missionary work or church growth that are distilled from the New Testament sometimes are somewhat simplistic.

A good example is an essay by John Amstutz, who reads the book of Acts as a witness to the "normative experience of the Christians,"[3] which must be repeated. He claims that if churches have the same Holy Spirit as did the first-century apostles (Acts 2), who turned the world "upside down" (Acts 17:6), then they will experience the same dynamic life and growth today. He formulates the

---

[1]See Bosch 1993a; Köstenberger 1995.
[2]Balz 1992, 438.
[3]Amstutz 1985, esp. 208-9; for the comments that follow above see ibid.

following principles. (1) The church, established at Pentecost, visibly expressed the love of God that the Holy Spirit had poured into their hearts. The Christians loved each other not theoretically with words but rather with practical, concrete deeds. (2) The church of the book of Acts met in the temple for public witness and in private houses for teaching new converts, a structure that made both spiritual growth and missionary witness possible. (3) The early church transcended the limitations of a professional priesthood and mobilized all members to engage in evangelism and outreach. (4) The early church constantly increased the number of active coworkers. (5) The early church quickly practiced transcultural contextualization by appointing indigenous leaders and by granting autonomy to indigenous churches. (6) The early church developed the ability to proclaim the gospel in a culturally sensitive manner. (7) The early church concentrated its missionary endeavors on people who were open to the gospel. (8) The church of the book of Acts practiced a type of evangelism that could be endlessly expanded by multiplying disciples and churches. Amstutz presents these "principles" as a deliberate missionary strategy of the early church and calls on the church today to apply them to contemporary missionary work. The following considerations highlight the problematic aspects of this proposal.

1. It is naive to think that historical experiences are normative and can or should be repeated. Historical experiences often have a complex nexus of historical causes that cannot be reproduced. This does not mean that the history of the early Christian mission does not provide lessons for missionary outreach in later periods of church history. However, before distilling "principles" from the historical narratives of the New Testament, one needs to distinguish hermeneutically between what is descriptive and what is (possibly) prescriptive. For example, when Acts 3:1 states that the Christians in Jerusalem had fixed times of prayer, in correspondence to the contemporary Jewish practice, this does not mean that such a practice must be reproduced in every Christian congregation.

2. One always needs to ask whether *every* experience of the early Christian churches can be or should be reproduced. The abrupt deaths of Ananias and Sapphira in Acts 5:1-11 have never been transformed into a "principle" of how to deal with the sin of lying.

3. Amstutz's second principle is problematic for several exegetical reasons. We know that the Christians in Jerusalem met in a public venue, but we do not have the same information for other early Christian communities. The meetings of the church in Jerusalem in the temple did not have a more intense "missionary" character than did the meetings in their private houses. The view that these two meeting venues reflect a deliberate strategy of the church is read into the text of Acts 2—4. Of course, it still may well be advisable for a church, particularly a large church, to organize public meetings for preaching and teaching and smaller gatherings that allow Christians to grow in their faith and to maintain personal and accountable relationships among themselves. However, the evi-

dence of the book of Acts does not allow us to formulate principles of regular behavior. The fact that the institution of the Jerusalem temple, with its vast area that allowed large gatherings, did not exist in other cities of the Roman Empire—synagogues generally were small, and pagan temples hardly provided favorable conditions for Christian meetings—should warn us not to jump to generalizing conclusions. The rapid proliferation of house churches in China after 1950 demonstrates that large public meetings of Christians are not a prerequisite for successful church growth.

4. Amstutz's third principle, the "liberation of the lay people," is also problematic from an exegetical point of view. True, there were no priests in the early church, but the Twelve had left their fishing nets and were "professional" preachers and teachers, "full-time" leaders who had been specifically trained for their "office" as apostles and missionaries. The suggestion that the book of Acts allowed the "total mobilization of the body of Christ" is read into the text.

5. Amstutz's fourth principle is also untenable from an exegetical standpoint. The number of coworkers did indeed soon grow from twelve to nineteen (Acts 6:1-7), and it is true that Stephen and Philip soon took over more "responsibilities" than they were initially given. However, the claim that the Seven were responsible for the "great number" of people who were converted according to Acts 6:7 has no basis in the text and is rather unlikely in the context of Acts 6:1-6. And the assertion that the ratio of the number of coworkers and conversions is "directly proportional" is highly problematic from a theological viewpoint and clearly false from the point of view of the history of missions and evangelism.

6. The Greek-speaking Jewish Christians in Jerusalem can indeed be distinguished culturally, at least in terms of native language, from the Hebrew- and Aramaic-speaking Jewish Christians. However, the event that Luke describes in Acts 6:1-6 had neither a "contextualizing" intention nor consequences for the "nationals." Rather, the purpose of the action of the apostles was to find a practical solution for a specific problem. The missionary outreach in Samaria and Syria that the Hellenistic Jewish Christians of Jerusalem initiated was not necessarily "more Hellenistic" than the missionary outreach in Judea and Galilee, and the "Hebrew" Peter also engaged in missionary work in Samaria and in the Hellenistic cities of the coastal plain. And the fact that the churches in Syria, Asia Minor and Greece administered themselves had nothing to do with some strategy of contextualization or indigenization (Amstutz's fifth principle); rather, on the one hand this corresponded to the Jewish model of independent synagogues, and on the other hand it is entirely anachronistic to expect a different "international" organizational structure of church government in the first century. And also we should remember that Jerusalem played an important role as the "center" of missionaries and churches, even for Paul.

7. The sixth principle that Amstutz formulates is essentially correct but exegetically imprecise. The statement that the integration of more "liberal" Helle-

nists such as Stephen into the leadership of the church ameliorated the "ethno-centricity" of the Palestinian Jewish Christians goes beyond the evidence of Acts 6—7. And the claim that Paul liberated the gospel from its "Jewish religious culture" when he accepted Gentiles into the church without their having to be circumcised is both a misunderstanding of the role of circumcision (which is much more than a Jewish cultural tradition) and a serious misunderstanding of Paul's use of the Old Testament.

8. Amstutz's seventh principle is untrue. Jesus preached to Jews not because they were more "open" to his message than Gentiles would have been, but because he understood this to be his mission. The parable of the sower illustrates that Jesus regarded opposition as an unavoidable part of his mission. Peter and John certainly did not seek "pockets of responsiveness" in Jewish or Samaritan areas in which to preach; rather, they preached wherever they had the opportunity, even in Jerusalem despite hostility and growing opposition. The fact that Paul initially preached in synagogues had both theological and tactical reasons. But his turn to the Gentiles in, for example, Pisidian Antiocheia (Acts 13:46) did not arise from strategic reflections, but rather was the unavoidable consequence of the separation from the synagogue, which the synagogue officials had initiated.

9. Amstutz's eighth principle is nothing particularly new or insightful, as missionary work has always consisted of the "multiplication" of believers and churches. This is not a "strategy" or a "type of evangelism." It is the nature of the Christian mission.

Further examples of exegetically one-sided or unfounded, hermeneutically flawed transfers of early Christian missionary practices to the missionary work of the modern church often can be found in the magazines of mission societies. For example, wanting to encourage Christians to work as professionals in countries in which missionaries cannot obtain visas, authors often refer to the example of Paul, who worked as a "tentmaker." They point out that there are two types of missionary work: "leaving the nets," meaning full-time missionary work, to which Peter was called, and "tentmaking," meaning part-time missionary work, to which Paul was called. It is argued that the "tentmaking" model possesses greater credibility, guarantees a better identification with the people, and promotes a more effective modeling of Christian character. And it is argued that Paul the "tentmaker" demonstrated a biblical work ethic that was a novelty in the pagan world, and that this model led to the establishment of churches that were self-financing, self-governing and self-reproducing.[4] Virtually none of these assertions is correct, although this does not negate the reality that Christian professionals indeed carry on a valuable missionary ministry in many countries. Christians, missionaries and mission agencies should realize that they do not

---

[4]See R. E. Siemens, "Tentmaking: Earn Your Living Overseas and Make Disciples," *Impact* 49 (1992): 6-8.

need to substantiate or defend every action, program or initiative with a biblical passage.

There are a good number of missiological studies that establish a connection between the early Christian mission and missionary work in the twentieth and twenty-first centuries, based on competent hermeneutical reflection, supported by theological competence, and generally informed by solid exegetical evidence.[5]

On the other hand, there are missiological studies on the history and task of missions in which the early Christian evidence plays no role whatsoever or only a marginal role.[6] Not a few writers argue that the mission of the church cannot and should not be based on Jesus' missionary commission. They contend that the appeal to a command and to obedience provides less-than-noble motivations for missions, and that a reference to Christian identity and to Jesus' promise is preferable.[7] Some authors seem to want to avoid terms such as "mission" or "evangelism" completely, as terms such as "openness" or "attractiveness" seem more acceptable in the context of the contemporary political discourse and correctness.

A recent essay by Hubert Frankemölle, a Roman Catholic New Testament scholar who has written several studies on the early Christian missionary movement and is involved in Jewish-Christian dialogue, is a good example. He formulates "ten commandments for the church in the third millennium," which he understands as "biblical impulses from the New Testament," developed on the basis of assumed deficits of Christians churches, "whether Protestant or Catholic."[8] The first sentences of his study relate his "commandments" to the early Christians in the first century: "Renewal of the church does not mean accommodation to modern society. Rather, the experiences of the first Christians two thousand years ago are, as 'remembered future,' reliable forces for continually renewed outreach." Frankemölle's first three commandments are related to Scripture and correspond to the Protestant *sola scriptura* principle: (1) read Scripture, (2) read all of Scripture, (3) live according to Scripture. The next four commandments deal with the church in terms of the local congregation: (4) live as a local church, (5) live unity in reconciled diversity, (6) live as a church family, (7) be an open church that serves. The last three commandments relate specifically to the individual Christian: (8) have courage for personal experiences of faith, (9) find a personal language, (10) be a Christian who is on the way. The early Christian reality of mission and evangelism, of active witness for faith in

---

[5]See, for example, Hesselgrave 1980; 2000; Bosch 1991; Beyerhaus 1996.

[6]See Scherer 1987.

[7]See recently Hunsberger 1994, with reference to Gruder 1985, 32; Newbigin 1987, 16, 21; cf. Legrand 1987, 19-20 with n. 32.

[8]Hubert Frankemölle, "Zehn Gebote für die Kirche im dritten Jahrtausend: Biblische Impulse aus dem Neuen Testament," *Diakonia* 32 (2001): 205-12; quotations, 205, 210-11.

Jesus Christ, of the growth of local churches and of the expansion of the church into unreached cities and regions is hidden in the seventh commandment, of which Frankemölle writes, "The churches in the New Testament were open to outsiders. . . . They were not introverted, fixed on their members, but were attractive to the non-Christian outside world because of the manner in which they lived together." These statements are not wrong; they correctly describe central aspects of the early Christian churches, but they do not go far enough. The early Christian churches were not simply "attractive," they engaged proactively in missionary work; they were not merely "open," they vigorously invited others to come to faith in Jesus Christ; there were not merely "extroverted," they sent missionaries to distant cities to establish new churches. When less than 5 percent of the urban population attends the Sunday services of the Christian churches, as is the case in post-Christian Europe, the church cannot merely reflect on its "attractiveness" and "openness," but rather must engage in robust evangelistic outreach among the agnostic and the apathetic, among atheists and neo-pagans, seeking to win them to faith in Jesus Christ, who alone liberates from guilt and sin and grants true and lasting meaning of life.

Many missionary and church leaders describe the task of Christian missions with the term "incarnation."[9] An "incarnational" model of missionary work generally is substantiated with reference to Jn 20:21 and the description of Jesus' "mission" in the Gospel of John, and with reference to the apostle Paul and his emphasis on sacrificial service (1 Cor 9:19-22; Phil 2:7-8). John Stott defines the "principle of incarnation" as identification with the people who are reached without loss of identity.[10] As God addressed and saved human beings not from a distance, but by becoming a human being in his Son Jesus Christ, so also missionaries must overcome the distance to the people whom they want to win for faith in Jesus Christ. This is not merely and not primarily a matter of what to eat or how to dress or what gestures to use, but also and most of all a matter of how to formulate and present the message of the gospel, how to organize the life of the local congregation, and what to teach new converts about how they should behave in everyday life. As Jesus became "flesh," likewise the missionary message and its expression in new churches must be consistently "local."

These kinds of concerns were not new even before the term "incarnational" was used to characterize them. They were emphasized in, for example, the modern Protestant missionary movement led by Hudson Taylor and the China Inland Mission in the nineteenth century. I submit that the use of the term "incarnational" is not very helpful to describe the task of authentic Christian mis-

---

[9]See Stott 1975, 23-30; Warren 1976, 171; Vellanickal 1981; Shaw 1988, 14-16, 190 n. 1; Stott 1992, 358, 373.

[10]Stott 1992, 373.

sionary work.[11] The event of the coming of Jesus into the world is unique, unrepeatable and incomparable, making it preferable to use other terminology to express the attitudes and behavior that Paul describes in 1 Cor 9:19-23. The Johannine missionary commission in Jn 20:21 does not demand an "incarnation" of Jesus' disciples but rather their obedience, unconditional commitment and robust activity in the service of God and in the power of the Holy Spirit. It is precisely John who describes the mission of Jesus as unique: Jesus is the "only" Son (*monogenēs* [Jn 1:14, 18; 3:14, 18]), he is preexistent (Jn 1:1, 14), his relationship to the Father is unparalleled (Jn 1:14, 18). For John, it is not the manner of Jesus' coming into the world, the Word becoming flesh, the incarnation, that is a "model" for believers; rather, it is the nature of Jesus' relationship to the Father who sent him into the world, which is one of obedience to and dependence upon the Father. Andreas Köstenberger comments, "Jesus' followers are called to imitate Jesus' selfless devotion in seeking his sender's glory, to submit to their sender's will, and to represent their sender accurately and know him intimately."[12] In Phil 2:5-11 it is not the incarnation of Jesus that is presented as a model for Christian behavior but rather Jesus' consistent humility. The terms "contextualization" or "inculturation" certainly are more helpful.[13]

Suggestions that we apply Jesus' message of the kingdom of God to the mission of the church sometimes are helpful,[14] sometimes rather general,[15] as all subjects of Jesus' preaching and teaching in the Synoptic Gospels can be linked with the concept of the kingdom of God. It is questionable, for example, whether the "diverse messages" of Jesus in the New Testament seek to indicate "that the fulfillment of human destiny is expressed in the events surrounding Jesus Christ, the mission of mankind."[16] The early Christian missionaries indeed expressed the significance of Jesus Christ in different and diverse ways in their writings, but they did not provide some sort of general philosophical reflection about the destiny of humankind and its fulfillment. Rather, they spoke of the powerful and merciful God, who came into the world in his Son Jesus Christ, who was crucified and raised from the dead in order to reconcile the world to God and ultimately to restore God's creation.

The influential missionary theology of the South African theologian David Bosch represents a similar problem.[17] He defines "salvation" as a reality that encompasses or influences all dimensions of human life, including social, eco-

---

[11]See also Köstenberger 1998a, 212-17.

[12]Köstenberger 1998a, 217.

[13]On the entire discussion see Friedli 1989. Friedli regards the historical-critical exegesis as Western "inculturation" (see ibid., 167).

[14]See Burrows 1987.

[15]See Stevens 1979.

[16]Kohler 1988, 244.

[17]Bosch 1991. For the critique that follows above see Towner 1995, esp. 100-104.

nomic, political, personal, relational, psychological and spiritual aspects. He retains the traditional understanding of salvation in terms of transcendent redemption, of people being called to faith in the one true God through Jesus Christ, to repentance and to personal faith. But he also understands salvation in terms of political and social transformation—for example, marginalized groups attaining active participation in the public discourse, broken relationships being restored, unjust social structures becoming more just.[18] For Bosch, "mission" is participation in the constant "dialogue" between God, who offers his salvation, and the world, which needs salvation.

Bosch dismisses the "apocalyptic theology" of the apostle Paul, who reckoned with an imminent return of Jesus Christ and whose corresponding understanding of his mission carried no critique of unjust social structures (e.g., slavery), arguing that we live in a different world today.[19] This seems too simplistic. One problem with Bosch's discussion is the fact that he does not define what he means when he uses the word "world" or "*kosmos*." On the one hand he warns of too much optimism, while on the other hand his emphasis on solidarity with the world and on the salvation of the world, his correlation of world and church, and his (re)interpretation of Paul's language of the Christians' battle with the world seem to suggest that he indeed has a rather positive and optimistic view of the world. An investigation of John's understanding of the "world" (*kosmos*) shows that the world is regarded as the place of culpable darkness, of blindness, of a complete lack of orientation and of sin,[20] as the place in which the power of Satan as the "ruler of this world"[21] controls and influences all human desires, motivations and principles.[22] This biblical emphasis on the necessary confrontation with the world must be a part of any authentically biblical theology of missions. According to John, followers of Jesus are "in the world" (Jn 17:11) but they are not "of the world" (Jn 15:19; 17:14, 16). The church must not dissolve this dialectic by siding with and favoring the world out of fear of being accused of "sectarian" isolation from the world and from society.[23]

Liberation theologians speak of God's "option for the poor" and appeal to the ministry of Jesus.[24] This emphasis is exegetically and theologically biased, especially when it is linked with the attempt to describe the concept of the for-

---

[18]Bosch 1991, 398-400.

[19]Bosch 1991, 174-75. For the critique that follows above see Towner 1995, 103-4 (on Bosch 1991, 176, 382); see also König 1990. On the question of the authority of the Bible in Bosch's missionary theology see Plessis 1990.

[20]Jn 1:29; 3:19; 7:7; 8:12; 9:35-41; 1 Jn 2:2, 15-16.

[21]Jn 12:31; 14:30; 16:11.

[22]Jn 8:44; 17:15; 1 Jn 2:15-16; 5:19.

[23]Towner 1995, 116-17.

[24]See J. Nissen 1984, 6-99; Justin S. Ukpong, "Jesus' Prayer for His Followers (Jn. 17) in Mission Perspective," *AThJ* 18 (1989): 49-60; Ely E. Barreto César, "The Historical Radicality of the Reign of God: A Paradigm for Our Missionary Efforts," *TJT* 8 (1992): 148-60.

giveness of sins as a notion that is not central theologically or to dismiss it with the source-critical argument that it is uncertain whether this was a concern of Jesus.[25] No one denies that the mission of the church must integrate a robust commitment to the weak and the poor, as Jesus ministered deliberately among the poor and the outcasts of Jewish society. However, this emphasis cannot be substantiated by pointing to the Samaritans or to Luke's interest for women and tax collectors.[26] None of these groups can be described as "weak" or of "low social status" even if one operates with the definition "outside of the frame of reference of the social and religious establishment of first century Palestine." Jesus indeed primarily ministered to the rural population of Galilee and thus among poor people—the vast majority of people in Galilee, indeed in the entire Mediterranean world, were economically poor. But Jesus never attempted to attack or change the social and economic structures of Galilean or Judean society, at least not directly. He never idealized poverty. He healed the sick, thus giving poor people a new dignity and new value, helping them to live lives unencumbered by physical bonds or handicaps. But Jesus also, and primarily, forgave their sins, restoring their relationship to God by connecting them with himself and his message of the dawn of God's kingdom.[27] Thus the attempt to interpret, for example, Lk 4:16-20 in connection with the Israelite jubilee year, understanding Jesus' "evangelism" as "humanization of life in its entirety" is not particularly helpful.[28]

How do we reconcile the ecclesiology of the early Christian churches, which emphasized the contrast to contemporary pagan society, with the missionary commission to go to all nations? The answer of Gerhard Lohfink deserves to be quoted at length: "The idea of church as contrast-society does not mean contradiction of the rest of society *for the sake of contradiction.* Still less does the church as contrast-society mean despising the rest of society due to elitist thought. The only thing meant is contrast *on behalf of others* and *for the sake of others,* the contrast function that is unsurpassably expressed in the images of 'salt of the earth,' 'light of the world,' and 'city on a hill' (Mt 5:13-14). *Precisely because the church does not exist for itself, but completely and exclusively for the world, it is necessary that the church not become the world, that it retain its own countenance.* If the church loses its own contours, if it lets its light be extinguished and its salt become tasteless, then it can no longer transform the rest of society. Neither missionary activity nor social engagement, no matter how strenuous, helps anymore. . . . What makes the church the divine contrast-society

---

[25]See Abesamis 1987, esp. 457-58.
[26]Bosch 1989, 5-7; the quotation that follows above, 5, with reference to Lk 9:51-56; 10:30-37; 17:11-19 (Samaritans); 8:1-3 (women); 3:12-13; 5:27-32; 18:9-14; 19:1-10 (tax collectors).
[27]See Dumais 1984.
[28]*Pace* Kavunkal 1988, 190; similarly Yoder 1972, 64-65.

is not self-acquired holiness, not cramped efforts and moral achievements, but the saving deed of God, who justifies the godless, accepts failures and reconciles himself with the guilty. Only in this gift of reconciliation, in the miracle of life newly won against all expectation, does what is here termed contrast-society flourish."[29]

Ralph Winter argues that the church always has two structures that are legitimate and that contribute to the fulfillment of the Great Commission: the church or local congregation, which uses the model of the Jewish synagogue; and the mission society, which uses the model of Jewish and early Christian teams of missionaries. He suggests that the church can be understood, from a sociological perspective, as a "modality," a structured community in which there are no differences of gender or age, while the missionary team is a "sodality," a structured community in which membership is determined by a second "decision" and limited as a result of age, gender or marital status. He argues that theologically the function of the church is important, not its form or structures.[30] This analysis has been criticized.[31] (1) The early Christian missionary teams were not a "church." The New Testament provides very little data about these teams, which means that all evaluations of their self-understanding remain hypothetical. It should be noted, however, that they are never described as *ekklēsia*. They did not exist as "organizations" independent of the church. They were constantly on the way, literally, from one city to the next. As soon as the missionary team arrived in a certain city, and as soon the first people were converted, the missionaries and thus the "team" belonged to the local congregation—for example, to the *ekklēsia* of Antiocheia or Corinth or Rome. (2) The claim that Paul's missionary team had the entire authority of a local church and therefore can be described as a "traveling church"[32] is erroneous. The authority of Paul was, as apostolic authority, focused not on his team of missionary coworkers but on the church(es) of Jesus Christ. There is no evidence for the "authority" of a missionary team in the New Testament. It also needs to be noted that the early Christian missionary teams did not adopt the form of similar Jewish "teams" of missionaries, as there is no evidence for a missionary movement in Second Temple Judaism (see §6). (3) If a "sodality" limits, according to the definition, its members, it cannot be a "church," which is always defined as a community where every follower of Jesus is a member, whether female or male, whether slave or freeborn, whether Jew or Gentile. Since missionary teams and mission agencies as "sodalities" require a "second decision" of their potential mem-

---

[29]G. Lohfink 1982, 154-70; quotation, ibid., 169-70 (ET 122-47; quotation, 146-47), referring to Acts 15:13-17, Lk 2:29-32; Rom 11:12-15, 25-26; Eph 2:1-3; 4:13-16, and other passages.
[30]R. Winter 1974; 1990.
[31]For some of the arguments that follow above see B. Camp 1995.
[32]R. Winter 1990, 58.

bers—a certain age, certain experiences, a particular expertise—they cannot constitute a "church." (4) A mission agency is, for pragmatic reasons, the most effective means of initiating and supporting missionary work in distant regions, due to the specialized knowledge in regard to country, culture, language and politics of the particular region that the mission agency possesses. The question of the relationship between a mission agency and the church and the question of the responsibilities of a mission agency with regard to the local congregation are complex and probably will remain difficult to answer. However, such questions must not be solved by removing the church and the local congregations from their primary responsibility for the task of mission and evangelism.[33]

Some missiologists interpret Abraham's call as a "model" of the calling to be a missionary: the call to become a missionary concerns individual people, it signifies leaving one's home, it is not tied to definite geographical information, it pursues universal goals, it is linked with a particular historical context, it requires the willingness to be mobile.[34] While all that may be true for a helpful description how God calls people to missionary service, it represents not a historical interpretation of Gen 12:3 but a secondary Christian application. The explanation that Paul defended his "missionary strategy" with reference to Abraham (Gal 3:6-8, 14, 26-29; Rom 4:16-17) is only generally correct. Paul defends not the necessity of missionary outreach to Gentiles, which was uncontested in the early church, but the admission of Gentiles to the church without circumcision and the nonethnic redefinition of the messianic people of God.

The attempt to extract principles of "discipleship" or maxims for society at large from the Synoptic passages that report Jesus' calling and commissioning of the Twelve is risky as well. Jesus' demand to leave possessions, house and family behind cannot authentically be read, in terms of a valid historical interpretation, as a call to social revolution and a reorganization of society.[35] In many important respects the disciples are indeed described as models for Christian living and ministry. We must remember, however, that for the early Christian churches that read the Gospels in the first century, the Twelve were primarily pioneer missionaries who had established the existing churches.

Such "actualizing" interpretations often correspond more to the personal social and cultural context of the author than to a historical analysis of the New Testament evidence. This is true for theologians from the "Two-thirds World" as much as for theologians from the "First World." An example of the latter is Werner Bieder's misunderstanding of Paul. He states, "The missionary existence of Paul the apostle to the Gentiles is characterized by a wholesome humility that

---

[33]On this subject see Hesselgrave 2000, 413-21; Bosch 1991, 368-89.
[34]See D. Howard 1979, 17-18; C. Wright 1996; for the comments that follow above see ibid.
[35]Gittins 1994, esp. 169, 172, 178.

contradicts any obvious or hidden feeling of superiority."[36] This sentence makes no sense when it is formulated as an introduction to a description of Paul as a missionary: of course Paul was aware of the fact that he owed his apostleship entirely to the grace of God, and of course he rejected "feelings of superiority." However, if we want to begin with a psychological analysis, we have to speak more relevantly of his consistent courage, unshakable confidence and amazing willingness to risk his life (cf. Rom 1:16). Bieder formulated this sentence at an ecumenical seminar for pastors and missionaries, where it is always politically correct for representatives of the "First World" to speak about humility.

Luke, the author of a history of Jesus and a history of the early Christian missionary movement, understands "mission" literally in terms of "sending" (Lat., *missio*), as the "work of God in sending the risen Jesus to the nations through the word of his chosen witnesses."[37] He never characterizes "the church" as an institution that is "sent" to accomplish God's will. Luke reports that a local congregation "sends" leading preachers and teachers as "missionaries" to other regions (see Acts 13:1-4), but the church itself is not portrayed as being "sent." The fact that Luke uses the term "apostle" ("sent one") nearly always for the Twelve, and in a couple of places for Paul, underscores an important point: the word that the witnesses of Jesus the crucified and risen Messiah and Savior proclaim has a historical foundation that is particular, unrepeatable, unique. The Twelve are a part of a specific history; their role cannot be taken over by later witnesses. This is why the church in the second and third centuries soon began to read the "witness" of these first witnesses in their services as authoritative Scripture. Luke does not intend to transform the readers of the book of Acts into "apostles"—his readers are members of the community of believers who "devoted themselves to the apostles' teaching" (Acts 2:42) and who carried it as the word of God to other people (Acts 8:4; 11:19-21). As Christians who live in the twenty-first century, we have not seen the crucified and risen Messiah, but we have believed the teaching of the apostles, who did see him and could confirm his resurrection. It is our task to hear, understand and proclaim *their* witness. We do not proclaim our own experience if and when we engage in "mission" in the New Testament sense of the word; rather, we proclaim the word of the first witnesses.

Some missiologists, pastors and evangelists think that sluggish church growth or lack of missionary success is mainly a problem of method. David Hesselgrave is correct when he states that the main problem is not methodology but theology,[38] and it is also, I believe, the interpretation of Scripture. When even evan-

---

[36]Bieder 1964, 5; with an explanation, ibid., 29-30.
[37]Bolt 1998, 211; for the comments that follow above see ibid., 211-13.
[38]D. J. Hesselgrave, "Evangelical Mission in 2001 and Beyond—Who Will Set the Agenda?" *Trinity World Forum* (spring 2001): 2.

gelical authors demand a "revolution" of our understanding of mission[39]—away from the traditional missionary focus on winning people to faith in Jesus Christ, concentrating rather on a "holistic" understanding of Jesus' claims—they can refer to "the mission of Jesus" according to Lk 4:18-19 ("The Spirit of the Lord is upon me, because he has anointed me to bring good news to the poor. He has sent me to proclaim release to the captives and recovery of sight to the blind, to let the oppressed go free, to proclaim the year of the Lord's favor") only in a very superficial way. Jesus' understanding of his "mission" included his calling of disciples whom he trained to be "fishers of people" and sent to the ends of the earth with the goal of making people into disciples of Jesus, disciples who know what Jesus taught and obey what he commanded because they believe in him as God's Messiah and Savior. What Theodor Oehler noted a century ago is still true today: Jesus' great missionary commission, which remains the normative standard for the church after Easter for its involvement in the world, did not command the Twelve to use a particular missionary method but instead assured them of the assistance of the Holy Spirit as the continuous presence of Jesus Christ himself.[40]

This does not mean, of course, that missionaries and evangelists today have nothing to learn from the New Testament in terms of method. Jesus' conversation with the Samaritan woman in Jn 4 surely allows the conclusion that probably it is not very helpful to teach an evangelistic "method" in which memorized sentences are presented to non-Christians. What Christians cannot present "by heart," they possibly have not understood. Memorized sentences may help Christians overcome psychological inhibitions about speaking of their faith—thus focusing on predicaments of the potential "witness" rather than on the unbeliever who must hear the gospel. In order to communicate effectively, Christians must possess "linguistic competence"; that is, they must understand the gospel in such a way that they can express and explain it in their own words. In addition, they must be able to assess the linguistic competence of the dialogue partner so as not to overtax the unbeliever or insult his or her intelligence.

We have already noted that the New Testament authors show little interest in statistical data about the growth of the churches (see §22.1). Luke is the only author who provides any figures, all of which are round numbers related to the growth of the church in Jerusalem (Acts 2:41; 4:4; 19:7), despite the fact that he would have been familiar with precise statistical data that the Old Testament provides for the size of Israel at different stages of history. Luke usually is content to point to the growth of the church with general formulations.[41] The prac-

---

[39]See recently Engel and Dyrness 2000.

[40]Oehler 1901, 4-6.

[41]See Acts 5:14; 6:1, 7; 8:6, 12; 9:31, 35, 42; 11:21, 24; 13:43; 14:1, 21; 16:5; 18:8, 10; 21:20. For the comment that follows above see Taber 1986, 392.

tice of some missiologists in which they provide quantitative statistical projections for the planning of church growth in a particular region or country and formulate numerical "goals" of church growth would have been regarded by the apostles as bizarre, arrogant and presumptuous. When the Gospel writers speak about growth, they generally refer to that of the kingdom of God,[42] and when Paul speaks about growth,[43] he generally refers to believers moving toward spiritual maturity. The numerical growth of the church as a whole or of the local congregations is never explicitly discussed or alluded to, not even in connection with statements regarding bringing "fruit"[44] or "harvest."[45]

Paul's explanation of his missionary conduct in 1 Cor 9:19-23 has prompted diverse "applications." Daniel Shaw points out, correctly, that Paul argues not for cultural relativism but for cultural relevance.[46] Shaw cannot appeal to Paul, however, when he writes that communicators first need to establish relevance and prove that they "belong" before they have the right to present God's "absolutes." When Paul provides a survey of the history of Israel in his sermons to Jewish audiences in the synagogues, his intention is not to prove that he is a Jew and "belongs" to them; that he was a Jew was never a matter of dispute, as his expertise in scriptural exposition established this very quickly. And Paul's Areopagus speech in Acts 17:22-31 does not "prove" that he had done his "homework" and therefore knew that a survey of Israel's salvation history would not be relevant for pagans, which allegedly is why he gave a "philosophical speech" in order to win Gentiles. Rather, Paul explains before the very specific audience of the council of the Areopagus his teaching about God in the context of their perception that he might intend to introduce a new god into the Athenian pantheon. When he wanted to win Gentiles to faith in Jesus Christ, he did not give a philosophical speech but rather spoke about Jesus the crucified Savior, even though this was not culturally "relevant." Paul is indeed aware of the importance of his audiences and listeners and their "needs," but this hardly permits the view that "Paul understood *receptor-oriented communication* and developed his message to meet the needs of his audience; it is effective communication designed to bring people face to face with truth and force a decision based on the relevance of the message." Paul argues in 1 Cor 1—2 that the proclamation of the gospel is *always* difficult, and it is always difficult precisely *because* of the human recipient or listener! From a human standpoint, the mission-

---

[42]See Mt 13:31-32/Mk 4:30-32/Lk 13:18-19 and the other parables about growth.

[43]See 1 Cor 3:5-9; Eph 4:11-16; Col 1:6; 2:19.

[44]See Mt 3:8-10; 7:15-20; 12:33-37; 21:43; Lk 6:43-45; Jn 15:1-17; Rom 7:4; Gal 5:22-23; Phil 1:11, 22, 25; Col 1:6, 10; Tit 3:14; Heb 12:11; 13:15; 2 Pet 1:5-8; Jas 3:12.

[45]See Mt 13:3-9, 18-23/Mk 4:3-9, 14-20/Lk 8:4-8, 11-15; Mt 13:24-30, 36-43; 9:37-38; Mk 4:26-29; Jn 4:35-38; Gal 6:7-10; 2 Tim 2:6; Jas 5:7-8; Heb 6:7-8. See Taber 1986, 394-98; J. Strelan 1988.

[46]Shaw 1988, 16, referring to Nida 1954, 52; for the comment that follows above see Shaw 1988, 16-20; quotation, 17.

ary proclamation of the gospel is a communicative impossibility: the message of a crucified Savior is a stumbling block for Jews and nonsense to Gentiles. This is why it is impossible to "force" a decision or to "argue" an unbeliever into the kingdom of God, even if the rhetoric is brilliant and the arguments are theologically compelling—only the power of God can convince people of the truth of the gospel.

Some missiologists view the Areopagus speech in Acts 17:22-31 as an example of the way in which Paul interacted with pagan religiosity. Depending on the interpretation suggested, Paul's speech is presented as an apologetic missionary program or, more frequently, as an inclusive missionary program. For example, Horst Bürkle interprets the reference to the *agnostos theos,* the "unknown god," (Acts 17:23) as follows: "What they have been aware of and what they have worshiped as a result of their yearning for ultimate security becomes significant for the new message. Their previous history—this at least is the interpretation of Paul the missionary—provides the building blocks for the new content of the gospel. Paul's preaching . . . aims at participation and inclusion and thus at interaction and historical transformation. Paul encounters those who do not yet know Christ as a Palestinian. . . . He sanctifies historical traditions and conventions by removing them from their autonomous context and by placing them in the theonomic context of the revelation of Jesus Christ."[47] At least the following three points need to be made. (1) In his speech to the council of the Areopagus Paul focuses not on history per se and certainly not on the history of religions but rather on God's revelation in creation and in nature. (2) Paul deals in a focused manner with the topic that he had been asked to address: his doctrine of deity and particularly the question of whether he intends to introduce a new god into the Athenian pantheon. In the agora he preaches the gospel of Jesus and the resurrection (Acts 17:17-18), a message that cannot be explained without reference to things "Palestinian." (3) The reference to the pagan altar dedicated to the "unknown god" does not receive any hermeneutical significance in the course of the speech: there is not only acceptance of pagan religious and cultural traditions but also rejection of them. The view that Paul "sanctifies" non-Christian traditions and conventions needs clarification: in the biblical tradition only God can "sanctify" anything.

Paul refers to open and closed doors in connection with the geographical movement of his missionary initiatives. Luke's account in Acts 16:6-7 of Paul's travel route before the missionary outreach in Macedonia and Achaia in A.D. 49 indicates that the apostle refrained from crashing closed doors: the account of Paul's missionary work in Galatia and Macedonia shows that he was prepared to leave whenever the hostility in any given city mounted. Missionaries in the twentieth century arrived at different decisions: they refused to accept closed

---

[47]Bürkle 1979, 36.

doors and so exclude from their plans and activities countries that did not allow official Christian missionary work, arguing that the gospel must be preached to all people. These missionaries willingly and courageously endured the dangers that they faced when they engaged in surreptitious missionary work in communist or in Muslim countries. The testimony of these missionaries often is impressive and inspiring. Difficulties arise, however, when they depart from the country on their foreign passports or with the help of their diplomatic embassies, leaving behind the local believers or sympathizers who have no chance to leave the country and who not infrequently have been threatened with imprisonment and death—and often the threats were carried out.

Some Christians believe that the doctrine of election (or predestination) has negative effects on missionary work because it eliminates the personal motivation for proactive evangelistic initiatives. This suggestion is incorrect, as is shown by the statement in Acts 18:9-10, where the Lord says to Paul, "Do not be afraid, but speak and do not be silent; for I am with you, and no one will lay a hand on you to harm you, for there are many in this city who are my people." Thus it is precisely the knowledge that the success of missionary initiative depends not on one's own endeavors but on God's sovereignty that gives the missionary courage to persevere in difficult situations and joyfully continue to preach the good news of Jesus Christ. Paul explains in Rom 10:16, with the quotation from Is 53:1, that the word that God sends out and the message that God authorizes are not always accepted and are not accepted by all who hear, not even in Israel (see §24.3). The reason for such a lack of "success" is not the weakness of the preacher or the problematic methods of the missionary; rather, it is the refusal of people to submit to the gospel and accept Jesus Christ as the Messiah and Savior.

The existence of the early Christian churches as house churches underscores the importance of reaching individuals with the gospel, and it highlights the significance of personal relationships in the family for mission and evangelism.[48] Alfons Weiser comments, "The gospel spread only in this manner" because the "house" contributed to "a form of interpersonal relationships that were more worthy of God and of humankind." In societies such as those of the industrialized countries, in which the economic way of life has changed—singles live alone, employees do not live with the family of the employer—a return to house churches does not provide a general solution to the question of how fellow citizens should be reached with the gospel.[49] However, several elements of the ancient "house" and the early Christian house churches illustrate important factors of missionary work and church growth. (1) The house churches represented

---

[48]For the comments that follow above see Weiser 1990, 84-86; quotations, 84, 85.
[49]Note the enthusiasm of Del Birkey (1991), which has not been affected by historical knowledge.

small groups in which everyone knew one another, which made mutual sharing and care possible. A large church can reach some people more effectively when it reaches them in small groups. (2) The house churches served the "local church" as well as believers in need and traveling missionaries. Since the ancient house was essentially "open" (e.g., to relatives, new employees, servants or slaves), the early Christian house church must not be confused with an "in-group" that focuses on satisfying the personal needs of its individual members. (3) The social and cultural influences that impact "houses" and families and churches need continual assessment "in the Lord," as the New Testament household codes illustrate. Small groups help believers learn and practice the significance and practical consequences of Jesus' message and the apostles' teaching—that is, today, the sacred Scriptures of the Old and New Testaments.

The dangers that the early Christian missionaries faced should prevent us from thinking, somewhat nostalgically, that "the early church" had it easy in the ideal setting of the *Pax Romana* and of dramatic signs and wonders.[50] The danger presented by Jews who reacted with hostility to the Christian message, the danger accompanying extensive missionary travels on land and on sea, the danger incurred by unregistered weekly meetings, the danger resulting from the proclamation of a Jewish Savior of the world who had been crucified by the Roman authorities, the danger inherent in the emperor cult—all these dangers were real. In the first century Christian believers and missionaries died for their faith in Jesus Christ. The proclamation of Jesus as the crucified and risen Savior, as the Son of God and Kyrios, has never been easy, especially in a world steeped in religious pluralism. As the Western world increasingly becomes multicultural and multireligious, and as Western Christians increasingly encounter people of others faiths in their neighborhoods, they have to learn afresh what it means to preach and teach the gospel in a pluralistic context. For Christians in Africa and Asia this situation is not new; Christians in the West need to learn from their fellow believers and fellow missionaries in the East and in the South. Christians who live in a society characterized by religious pluralism recognize in a new way that the gospel is indeed a stumbling block, a scandal: it is the conviction that God grants salvation only through Jesus Christ and that piety and spirituality are "foolish" if they are not rooted in his cross and resurrection. The Christian message was not "politically correct" in the first century, and it is not politically correct today. This situation, new in many areas of the Western world, is a chance for the gospel, but it also carries a risk—the risk of discrimination against Christians as "intolerant fundamentalists" who believe that there is only one truth.

The message of the early Christian mission is "exclusive" in terms of the offer of the forgiveness of sins, salvation and justification on judgment day by faith in

---

[50]See B. Winter 2000, esp. 294; for the arguments that follow above see ibid.

Jesus the crucified and risen Messiah; it is "inclusive" in terms of people of all nations, tribes and languages being invited and called to believe in Jesus Christ. The exclusive character of the gospel of Jesus Christ that the early Christian missionaries preached in the first century was a stumbling block for Jews and foolishness for Greeks. And it continues to be provocative. The Indian theologian S. J. Anthonysamy sees in the Old Testament a development from exclusivistic convictions (exodus, conquest) to inclusivistic exhortations (the prophets) and to service-oriented humility (Isaiah's Servant of the Lord); in the New Testament he sees exclusivistic tendencies (1 Cor 8:5-6) and inclusivistic emphases (Gal 3:28), and, as the alleged climax, the Gospels, with a description of Jesus as Savior of the world in the form of a humble servant.[51] The Argentinian liberation theologian Enrique Dussel reads the Servant Songs in the book of Isaiah as communicating a "universalism without limits" (*universalismo sin límites*) in which all particularism disappears and "mission" consists of the existential realization of grace. He argues that religious communities need to be liberated both from nationalistic particularism and from a centripetal temporal universalism; that is, the traditional missionary initiatives to "make proselytes" and to convert individuals should be abandoned because the "conversion of humanity" will take place in the eschaton in a passive manner ("vencer definitivamente la pasividad de disminución").[52] Johnson Samuel reads the Areopagus speech in Acts 17:22-31 as an indication that the Christian witness needs to be positive and inclusive in a pluralistic context, emphasizing continuity, in order to be effective.[53] In the context of such positions the New Testament is only "one text among many,"[54] subordinated to one's own personal and subjective opinions and convictions.

Robert Tannehill attempts to read the book of Acts in such a manner that the Christian faith does not appear as "religious exclusivism," despite the numerous conflict stories in Luke's account. This program clearly is prejudiced. Tannehill argues that "religious exclusivism" takes God prisoner, isolates the believer from the unbeliever, promotes an imperialistic attitude among Christians and makes the solution of political controversies nearly impossible because unbelievers are relegated to the realm of hostile darkness.[55] Tannehill reads the narrative of Paul's sea journey from Caesarea to Rome in Acts 27, during which all passengers on the ship are rescued in the storm, on a "second level" in terms of a story that "anticipates salvation (in some sense) for every individual of a pluralistic community." This interpretation shows that for Tannehill, political hopes have

---

[51]Anthonysamy 1993.

[52]Dussel 1964, 457, 462-63.

[53]Samuel 1986, esp. 30-31.

[54]See R. S. Sugirtharajah, "The Text and the Texts: Use of the Bible in a Multi-Faith Context," in Lande and Ustorf 1996, 183-92.

[55]Tannehill 1990, 247, with reference to Boers 1971; for the comments that follow above see Tannehill 1990, 255-63; quotation, 261.

become the parent of exegesis. Such positions show little sign of a hermeneutically responsible analysis of the biblical evidence or a theologically responsible application of biblical truth. As desirable as peace, tolerance and harmony unquestionably are, the terrorist attacks in the United States on September 11, 2001, demonstrated once again that the pluralism called for by Western intellectuals as a political and religious program continues to be unrealistic.

Should the Christian church engage in missionary work among Jews in the twenty-first century? Should Gentile Christians preach the gospel to Jews? Is Christian missionary outreach among Jews tantamount to the claim that the Jewish faith is futile? Is such mission anti-Jewish? These questions have been vigorously debated in Germany, particularly since the declaration that the synod of the regional Protestant Church in the Rhineland accepted on January 11, 1980.[56] The declaration states in section IV.6, "We believe that Jews and Christians are God's witnesses before the world and before each other, each according to their calling; this is the reason why we are convinced that the church cannot carry out its witness with regard to the Jewish people as it carries out its mission to the nations." Heinz Kremers, who helped prepare the declaration, maintains with regard to Rom 9—11 that God himself will evangelize "all Israel" at Christ's parousia, that until that time only a few Jews come to faith in Jesus Christ, and that "we" the Gentile Christians should be "silent" and let the "witness of our lives" speak.[57] Conservative evangelicals protested,[58] arguing that such a fundamental rejection of missionary work among Jews constitutes theological confusion and that Christians should support all ministries that seek to bring the gospel, in a responsible manner, to the Jewish people.

The importance of these questions is demonstrated by the consequences that some theologians imply in their rejection of missionary work among the Jewish people. It seems only a small step from rejecting missionary work among Jews to rejecting missionary initiatives altogether as an essential part of the character of the church. For example, Günther Baumbach remarks, "Church and synagogue are both on their way to the consummation of salvation, the integration of all creation under God's rule, including the resurrection of the dead. This comprehensive hope for the entire world, this certainty that in principle there are no 'hopeless cases' after Jesus' cross and resurrection, has been granted by Jesus Christ. We therefore are not entitled 'to decree eschatological verdicts in the name of the Son of Man in the here and now' and to condemn unbelievers."[59]

---

[56]Reproduced in Kremers and Lubahn 1985, 123-26. See also the opening paragraphs of "The Question of the Salvation of the Jewish People" in §28.1 of the present work.

[57]Heinz Kremers, "Mission an Israel in heilsgeschichtlicher Sicht," in Kremers and Lubahn 1985, 65-91.

[58]The declaration entitled "Mission to Israel—Until Today" (March 1980) is reprinted in Kremers and Lubahn 1985, 126-28.

[59]Baumbach 1986, 142, with a quotation from Ulrich Luz.

Conservative theologians likewise have neutralized Jesus' great missionary commission when they allow general theological or hermeneutical positions to cloud their view of the scope of the authority of Scripture. Johann Tobias Beck, a theologian of the nineteenth century who is known for his emphasis on salvation history, provides a good example. He argued that the Christian churches of his day had lost both the ability to do missionary work as well as the divine calling to initiate missionary projects. He believed that God would bring to an end the era of grace that the Gentile-Christian church has enjoyed, which means for committed Christians that they should focus on belonging to the future remnant of the people of God rather than on new missionary efforts. He compared the missionary endeavors of his day with the missionary activity of the Jews in the first century who believed that the dawn of the kingdom of God was dependent on their own human efforts.[60]

I close by quoting, again, the commission of Jesus, the crucified and risen Messiah and Savior, as recorded by Luke in the first chapter of his history of the missionary activity of the early church: "So when they had come together, they asked him, 'Lord, is this the time when you will restore the kingdom to Israel?' He replied, 'It is not for you to know the times or periods that the Father has set by his own authority. But you will receive power when the Holy Spirit has come upon you; and you will be my witnesses in Jerusalem, in all Judea and Samaria, and to the ends of the earth.'" The book of Acts, as a history of the mission of the church, has no ending as long as Jesus' promise to return remains unfulfilled—the time and hour of which only God knows. The new song that the followers of Jesus, the Lamb of God, sing in the vision of John in Rev 5:9 thus continues to express the implicit commission to reach all nations to the ends of the earth with the good news of Jesus Christ: "They sing a new song: 'You are worthy to take the scroll and to open its seals, for you were slaughtered and by your blood you ransomed for God saints from every tribe and language and people and nation.'"

---

[60]Johann Tobias Beck, *Christliche Rede* (Vierte Sammlung; Stuttgart: Steinkopf, 1857); cf. Oehler 1902.

Maps and Figures

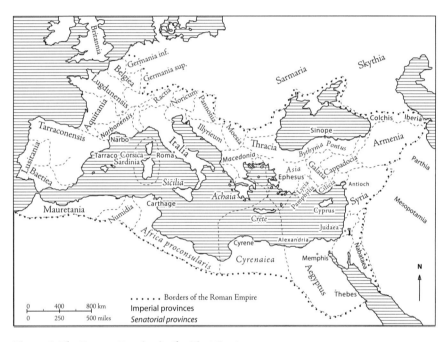

Figure 1. The Roman Empire in the First Century

Figure 2. Palestine Between 37 B.C. and A.D. 33

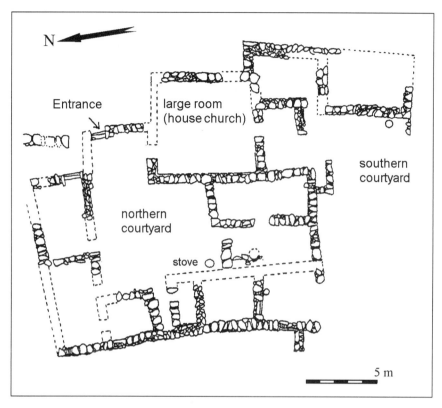

Figure 3. Peter's House in Capernaum

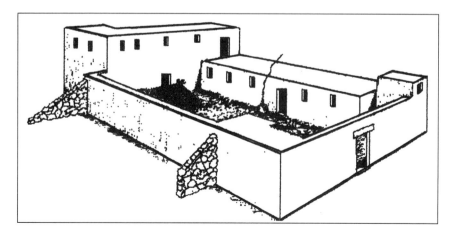

Figure 4. The Fisherman's House in Bethsaida

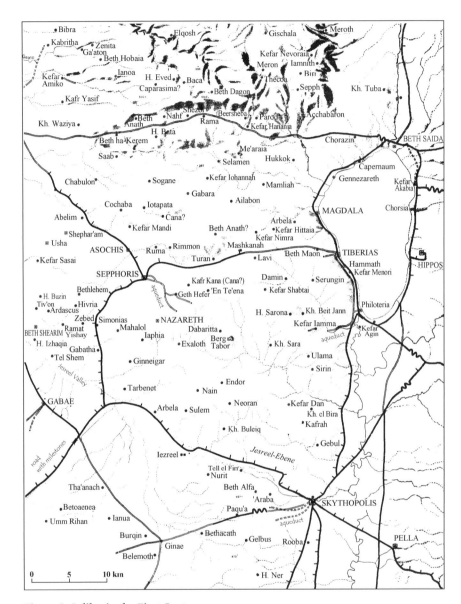

Figure 5. Galilee in the First Century

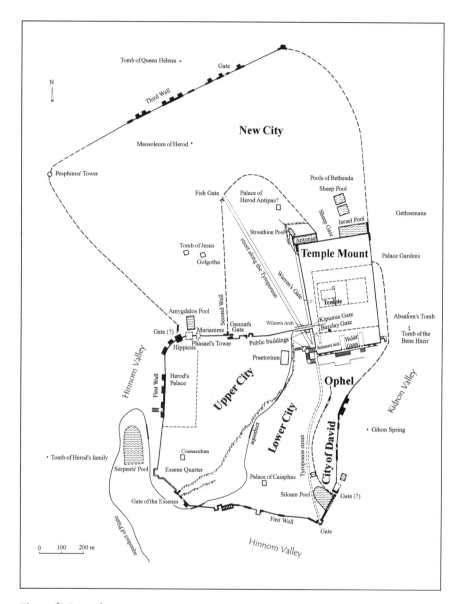

Figure 6. Jerusalem

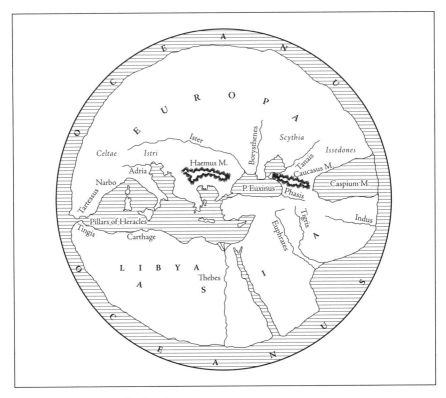

Figure 7. World Map of Hekataios

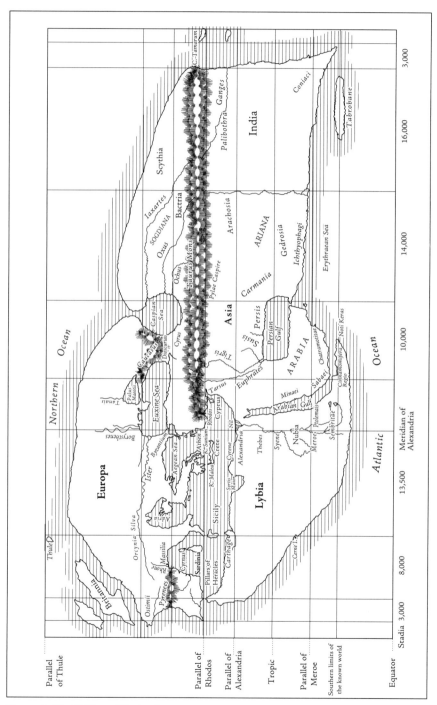

Figure 8. World Map of Eratosthenes

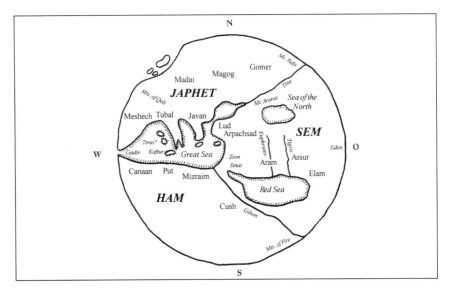

Figure 9. World Map According to *Jubilees*

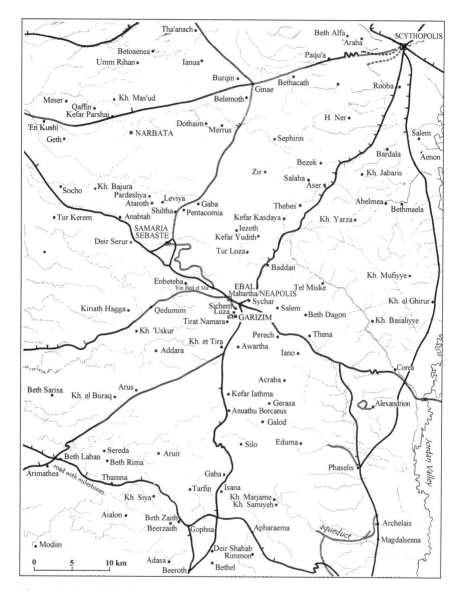

Figure 10. Samaria in the First Century

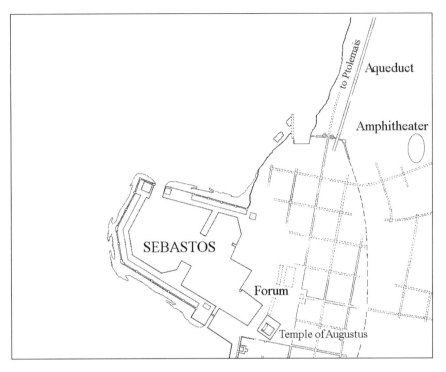

Figure 11. Caesarea

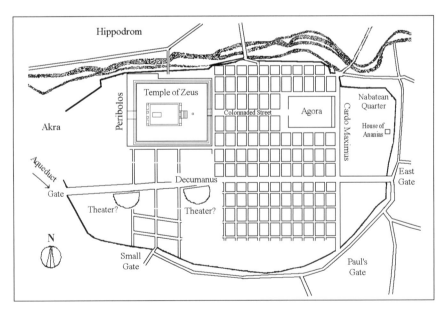

Figure 12. Damascus

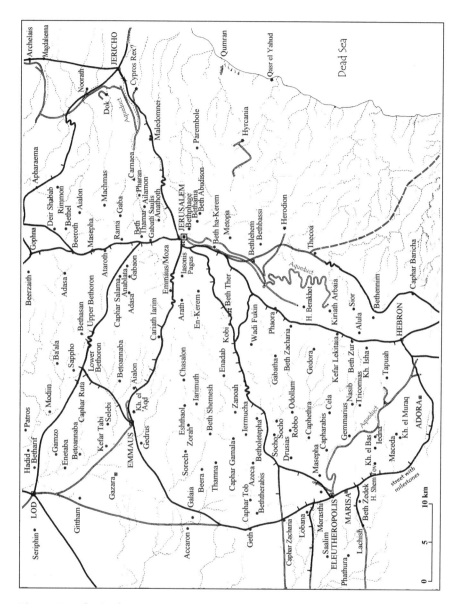

Figure 13. Judea in the First Century

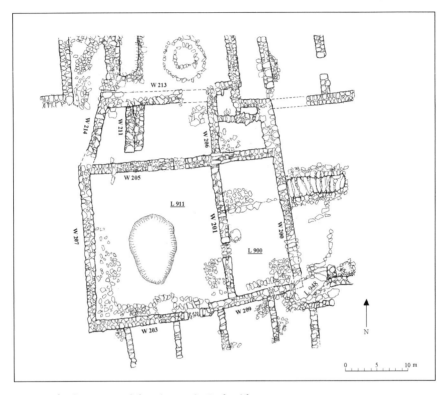

Figure 14. The House of the Vintner in Bethsaida

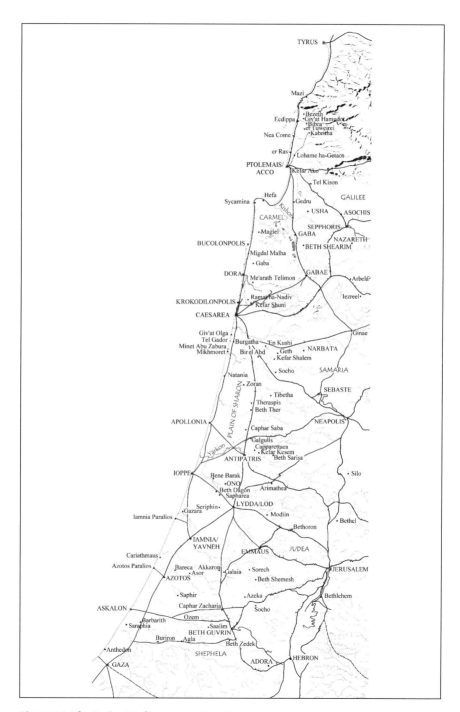

Figure 15. The Syrian Mediterranean Coast

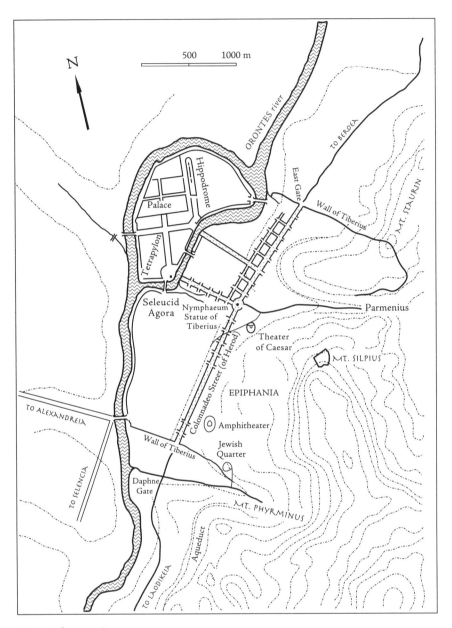

Figure 16. Antioch

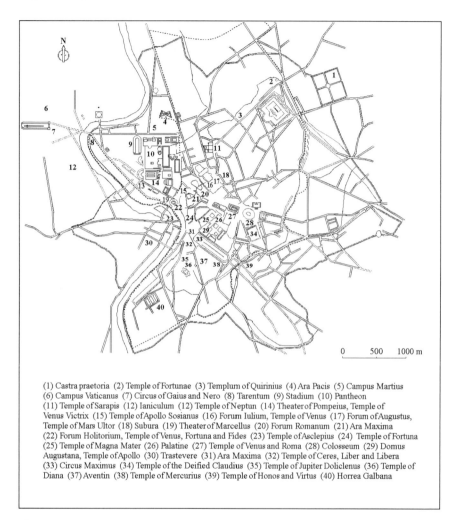

Figure 17. Rome

(1) Castra praetoria (2) Temple of Fortunae (3) Templum of Quirinius (4) Ara Pacis (5) Campus Martius (6) Campus Vaticanus (7) Circus of Gaius and Nero (8) Tarentum (9) Stadium (10) Pantheon (11) Temple of Sarapis (12) Ianiculum (12) Temple of Neptun (14) Theater of Pompeius, Temple of Venus Victrix (15) Temple of Apollo Sosianus (16) Forum Iulium, Temple of Venus (17) Forum of Augustus, Temple of Mars Ultor (18) Subura (19) Theater of Marcellus (20) Forum Romanum (21) Ara Maxima (22) Forum Holitorium, Temple of Venus, Fortuna and Fides (23) Temple of Asclepius (24) Temple of Fortuna (25) Temple of Magna Mater (26) Palatine (27) Temple of Venus and Roma (28) Colosseum (29) Domus Augustana, Temple of Apollo (30) Trastevere (31) Ara Maxima (32) Temple of Ceres, Liber and Libera (33) Circus Maximus (34) Temple of the Deified Claudius (35) Temple of Jupiter Doliclenus (36) Temple of Diana (37) Aventin (38) Temple of Mercurius (39) Temple of Honos and Virtus (40) Horrea Galbana

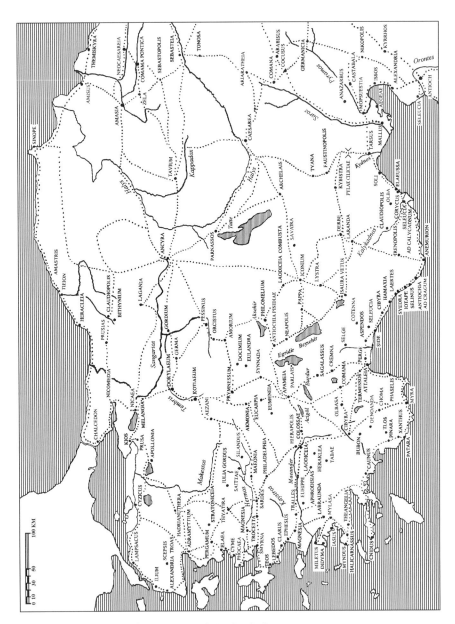

Figure 18. Asia Minor I (Provinces and Territories)

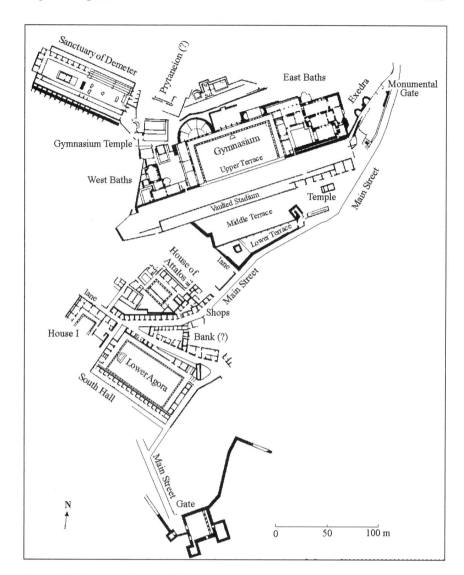

Figure 19. Pergamon (Lower City)

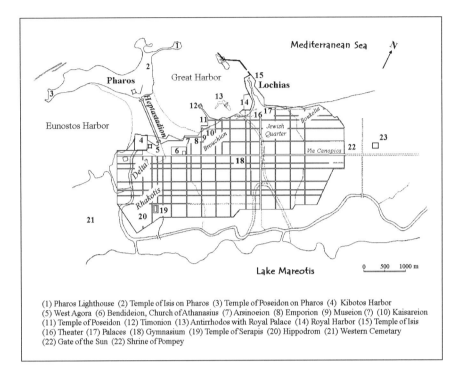

(1) Pharos Lighthouse (2) Temple of Isis on Pharos (3) Temple of Poseidon on Pharos (4) Kibotos Harbor
(5) West Agora (6) Bendideion, Church of Athanasius (7) Arsinoeion (8) Emporion (9) Museion (?) (10) Kaisareion
(11) Temple of Poseidon (12) Timonion (13) Antirrhodos with Royal Palace (14) Royal Harbor (15) Temple of Isis
(16) Theater (17) Palaces (18) Gymnasium (19) Temple of Serapis (20) Hippodrom (21) Western Cemetary
(22) Gate of the Sun (22) Shrine of Pompey

Figure 20. Alexandria

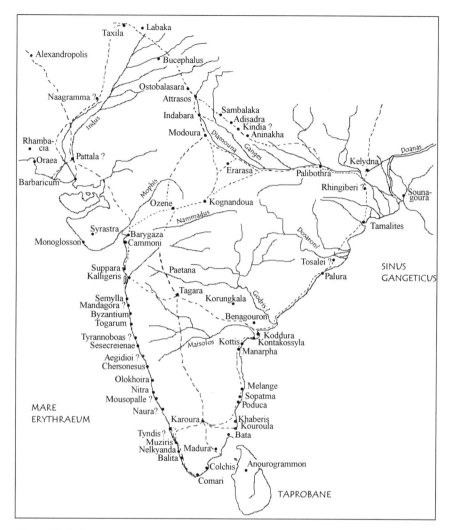

Figure 21. India

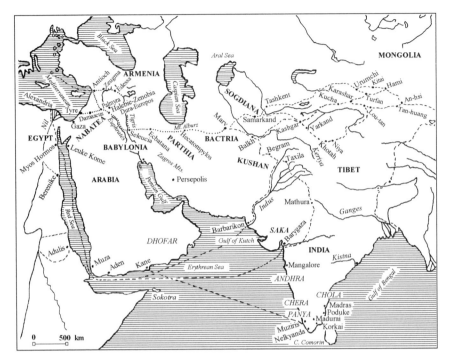

Figure 22. India: Travel Routes

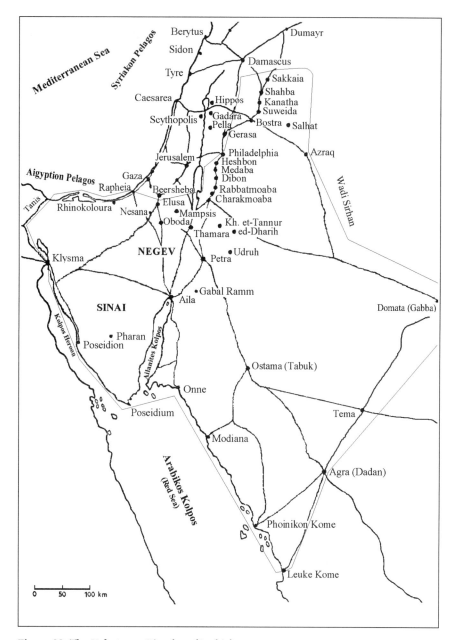

Figure 23. The Nabataean Kingdom (Arabia)

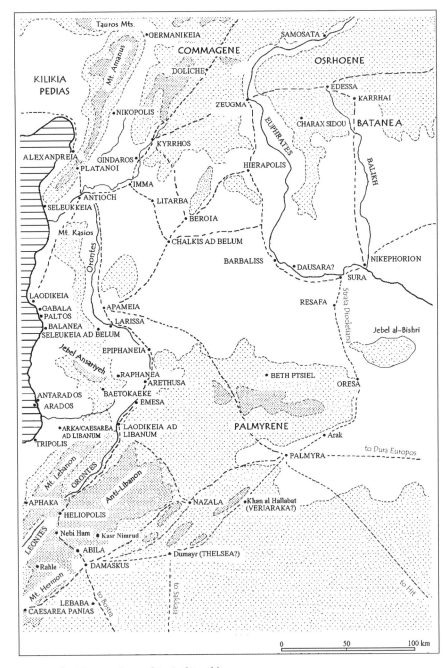

Figure 24a. The Province of Syria (North)

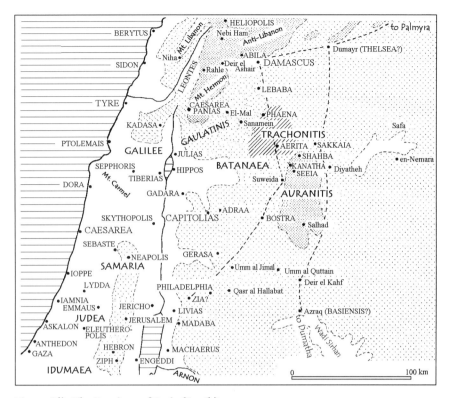

Figure 24b. The Province of Syria (South)

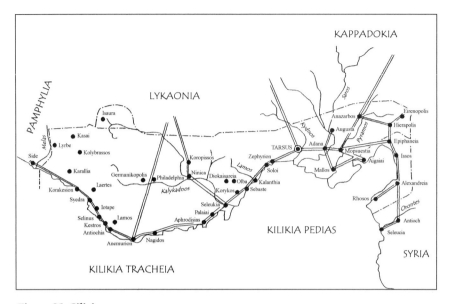

Figure 25. Cilicia

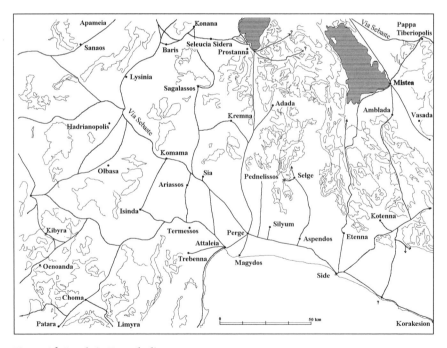

Figure 26. Roads in Pamphylia

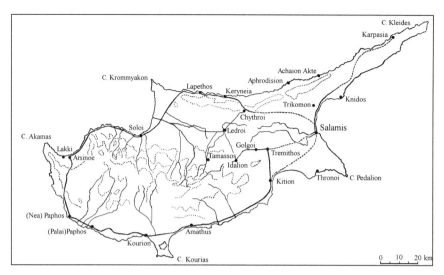

Figure 27. Cyprus

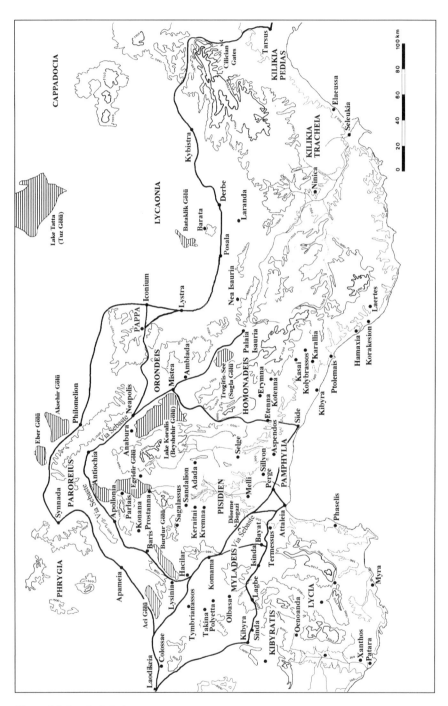

Figure 28. South Galatia

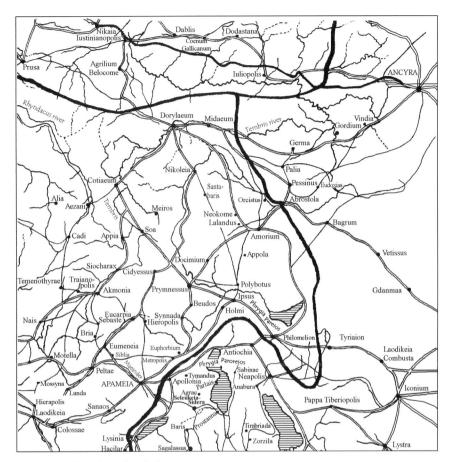

Figure 29. Phrygia and Galatia

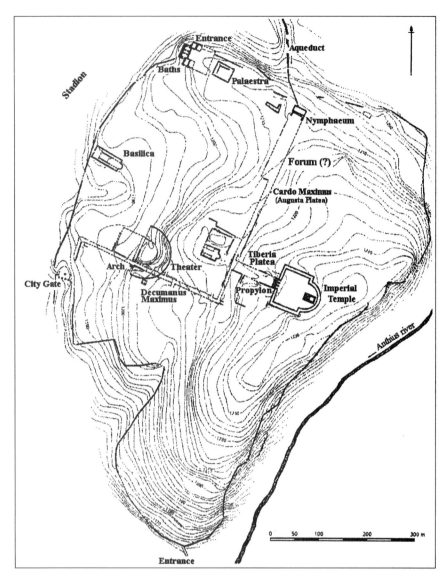

Figure 30. Antiochia

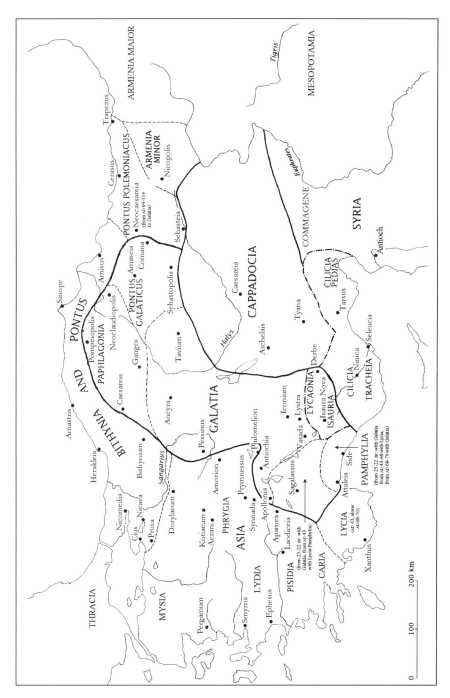

Figure 31. Asia Minor II (Cities and Roads)

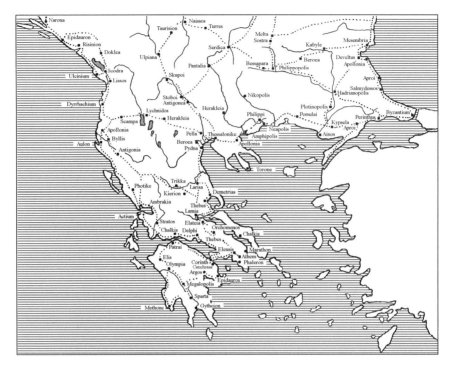

Figure 32. Greece

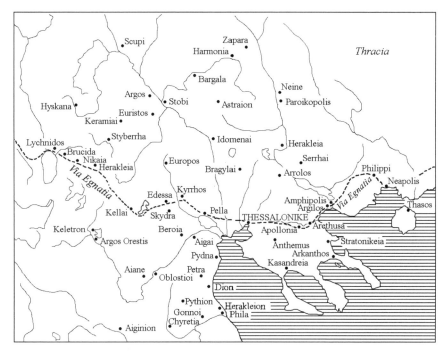

Figure 33. Macedonia

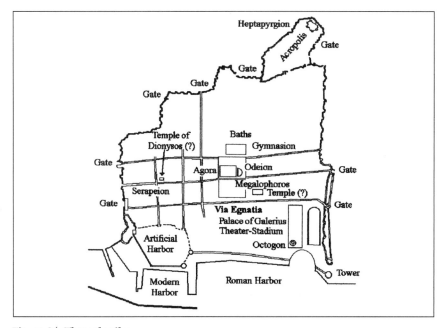

Figure 34. Thessalonike

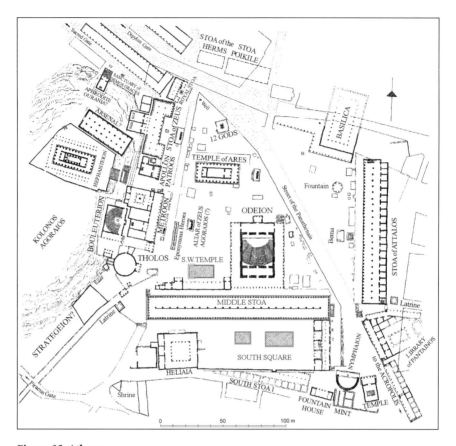

Figure 35. Athens

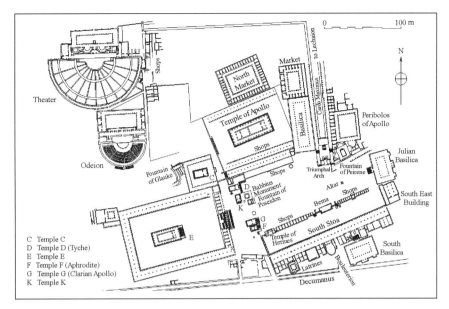

Figure 36. Corinth

C Temple C
D Temple D (Tyche)
E Temple E
F Temple F (Aphrodite)
G Temple G (Clarian Apollo)
K Temple K

Figure 37. Illyricum

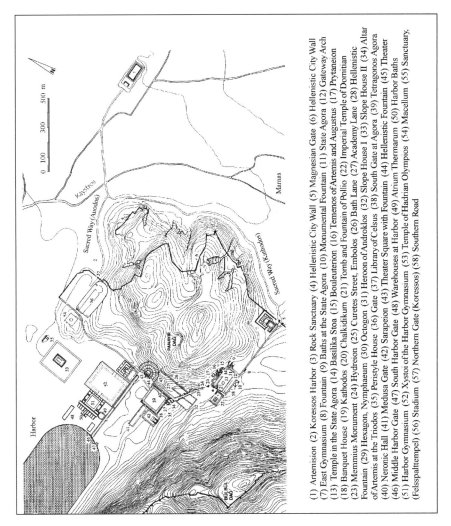

(1) Artemision (2) Koressos Harbor (3) Rock Sanctuary (4) Hellenistic City Wall (5) Magnesian Gate (6) Hellenistic City Wall (7) East Gymnasium (8) Fountain (9) Baths at the State Agora (10) Monumental Fountain (11) State Agora (12) Gateway Arch (13) Temple in the State Agora (14) Basilika Stoa (15) Bouleuterion (16) Temenos of Artemis and Augustus (17) Prytaneion (18) Banquet House (19) Kathodos (20) Chalkidikum (21) Tomb and Fountain of Pollio (22) Imperial Temple of Domitian (23) Memmius Monument (24) Hydreion (25) Curetes Street, Embolos (26) Bath Lane (27) Academy Lane (28) Hellenistic Fountain (29) Hexagon, Nymphaeum (30) Octogon (31) Heroon of Androklos (32) Slope House I (33) Slope House II (34) Altar of Artemis at the Triodos (35) Peristyle House (36) Gate (37) Library of Celsus (38) South Gate at Agora (39) Tetragonos Agora (40) Neronic Hall (41) Medusa Gate (42) Sarapeion (43) Theater Square with Fountain (44) Hellenistic Fountain (45) Theater (46) Middle Harbor Gate (47) South Harbor Gate (48) Warehouses at Harbor (49) Atrium Thermarum (50) Harbor Baths (51) Harbor Gymnasium (52) Xystoi of the Harbor Gymnasium (53) Temple of Hadrian Olympios (54) Macellum (55) Sanctuary, (Felsspalttempel) (56) Stadium (57) Northern Gate (Koressos) (58) Southern Road

Figure 38. Ephesus

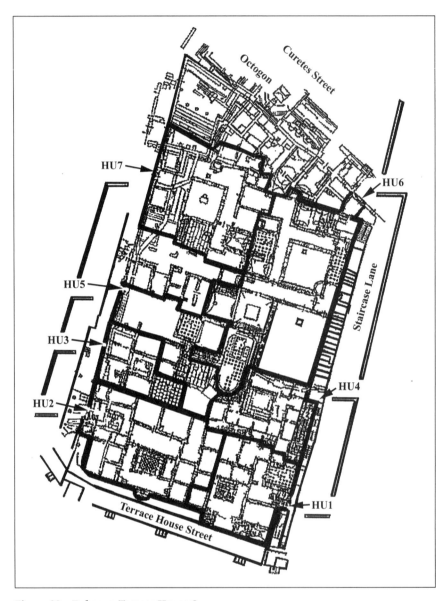

Figure 39a. Ephesus, Terrace House 2

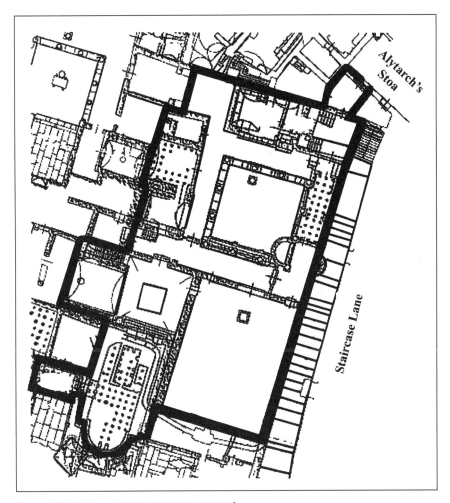

Figure 39b. Ephesus, Terrace House 2, Unit 6

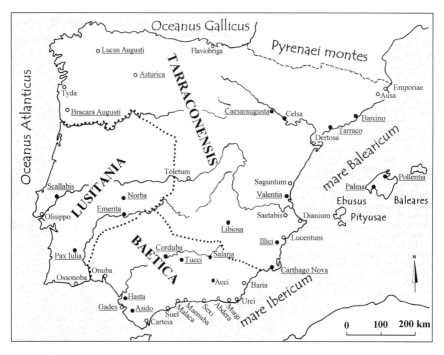

Figure 40. Spain

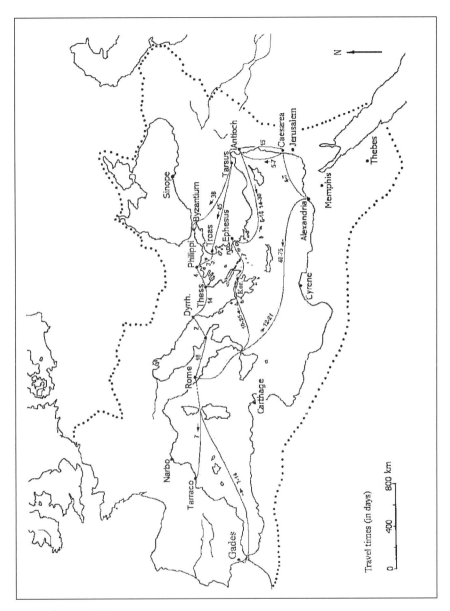

Figure 41. Travel Times

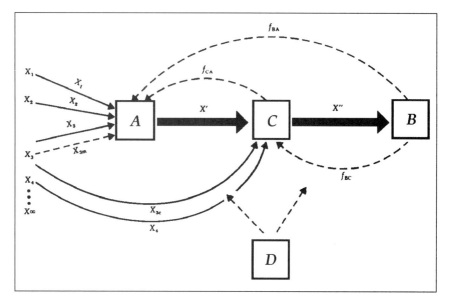

Figure 42. Communication Model (modified from Westley and MacLean)

BIBLIOGRAPHY

I. SOURCES AND RESOURCES

A. Texts, Editions, Translations, Inscriptions

1. Bible

Aland, Barbara and Kurt, et al., eds. *Novum Testamentum Graece.* 27th rev. ed. Stuttgart: Deutsche Bibelgesellschaft, 1993.

Aland, Kurt. *Synopsis Quattuor Evangeliorum.* 13th ed. Stuttgart: Deutsche Bibelgesellschaft, 1985.

Aland, Kurt, et al., eds. *The Greek New Testament.* 4th rev. ed. Stuttgart: Deutsche Bibelgesellschaft, 1993.

Die Bibel im heutigen Deutsch: Die Gute Nachricht. Standardausgabe mit Spätschriften des AT. Stuttgart: Deutsche Bibelgesellschaft, 1982.

Die Bibel: Einheitsübersetzung. Standardausgabe. Ökumenischer Text. Stuttgart: Deutsche Bibelgesellschaft and Katholisches Bibelwerk, 1991.

Elberfelder Bibel. Revidierte Fassung. Wuppertal: Brockhaus, 1987 [1985].

Elliger, K., and W. Rudolph, eds. *Biblia Hebraica Stuttgartensia.* 4th ed. of the Editio Funditus Renovata. Stuttgart: Württembergische Bibelanstalt, 1990 [1967-1977].

Lutherbibel. Textfassung 1984. Standardausgabe mit Apokryphen. Stuttgart: Deutsche Bibelgesellschaft, 1985.

Neue Jerusalemer Bibel. Einheitsübersetzung mit dem Kommentar der Jerusalemer Bibel. Edited by A. Deissler and A. Vögtle. Freiburg: Herder, 1985.

Rahlfs, Alfred. *Septuaginta; Id est Vetus Testamentum graece iuxta LXX interpres.* 2 vols. Editio Nona. Stuttgart: Württembergische Bibelanstalt, 1935.

Septuaginta: Vetus Testamentum Graecum. Auctoritate Academiae Scientiarum Gottingensis editum. 16 vols. Göttingen: Vandenhoeck & Ruprecht, 1931-.

Weber, R., ed. *Biblia Sacra iuxta vulgatam versionem.* 2 vols. Editio Altera. Stuttgart: Württembergische Bibelanstalt, 1975 [1969].

2. Second Temple Judaism

Anthologies:

Barrett, Charles K., and Claus-Jürgen Thornton. *Texte zur Umwelt des Neuen Testaments.* 2nd ed. UTB 1591. Tübingen: Mohr-Siebeck, 1991 [1959].

Charles, Robert H., ed. *The Apocrypha and Pseudepigrapha of the Old Testa-*

ment. 2 vols. Oxford: Clarendon, 1963 [1913].

Charlesworth, James H., ed. *The Old Testament Pseudepigrapha.* 2 vols. Garden City, N.Y.: Doubleday, 1983-1985.

Dupont-Sommer, André, and Marc Philonenko, eds. *La Bible: Écrits Intertestamentaires.* Paris: Gallimard, 1987.

Kautzsch, Emil, ed. *Die Apokryphen und Pseudepigraphen des Alten Testaments.* 2 vols. Repr., Hildesheim: Olms, 1994 [1900].

Kümmel, Werner Georg, and Hermann Lichtenberger, eds. *Jüdische Schriften aus hellenistisch-römischer Zeit.* Gütersloh: Gütersloher Verlagshaus; Munich: Kaiser, 1973-.

Riessler, Paul. *Altjüdisches Schrifttum außerhalb der Bibel.* 4th ed. Heidelberg: Kerle, 1982 [1928].

Aristeas, Epistle of:

Andrews, H. T. "The Letter of Aristeas." *APOT* 2:83-122.

Hadas, Moses. *Aristeas to Philocrates (Letter of Aristeas).* Jewish Apocryphal Literature. New York: Harper & Row, 1951.

Meisner, Norbert. "Aristeasbrief." *JSHRZ* 2.1 (1977): 35-87.

Pelletier, A. *Lettre d'Aristée à Philocrate.* SC 89. Paris: Cerf, 1962.

Shutt, R. J. H. "Letter of Aristeas." *OTP* 2:7-34.

Thackeray, H. St. J. "The Letter of Aristeas." H. B. Swete. *Introduction to the Old Testament in Greek.* Cambridge, 1902, Appendix.

Wendland, Paul. "Der Aristeasbrief." *APAT* 2:1-31.

Baruch, Apocalypse of:

Bogaert, Pierre-Maurice. *Apocalypse de Baruch: Introduction, Traduction du Syriaque et Commentaire.* SC 144-145. Paris: Cerf, 1969.

Klijn, Albertus F. J. "Die syrische Baruch-Apokalypse." *JSHRZ* 5.2 (1976): 103-91.

———. "2 (Syriac Apocalypse of) Baruch." *OTP* 1:615-52.

Ryssel, V. "Die Syrische Baruchapokalypse." *APAT* 1:404-46.

Violet, Bruno. *Die Apokalypsen des Esra und des Baruch in deutscher Gestalt.* GCS 32. Leipzig: Hinrichs, 1924.

Enoch, Apocalypse of:

Beer, G. "Das Buch Henoch." *APAT* 2:217-310.

Black, Matthew. *Apocalypsis Henochi Graeci.* PVTG 3. Leiden: Brill, 1970.

———. *The Book of Enoch or I Enoch: A New English Edition.* SVTP 7. Leiden: Brill, 1985.

Charles, R. H. "1 Enoch." *APOT* 2:163-281.

Isaac, E. "1 (Ethiopic Apocalypse of) Enoch." *OTP* 1:5-90.

Milik, J. T. *The Books of Enoch: Aramaic Fragments of Qumrân Cave 4.* Oxford: Clarendon, 1976.

Uhlig, Siegbert. "Äthiopisches Henochbuch." *JSHRZ* 5.6 (1985): 461-780.

Exegetes:
Walter, Nikolaus. "Jüdisch-hellenistische Exegeten: Aristobulos, Demetrios, Aristeas." JSHRZ 3.2 (1975): 257-79.

Ezra, Apocalypse of:
Box, George H. "4 Ezra." *APAT* 2:542-624.
Klijn, Albertus F. J. *Die Esra-Apokalypse (IV. Esra): Nach dem lateinischen Text unter Benutzung der anderen Versionen.* Berlin: Akademie-Verlag, 1992.
Metzger, Bruce M. "The Fourth Book of Ezra." *OTP* 1:517-60.
Schreiner, Josef. "Das 4. Buch Esra." *JSHRZ* 5.4 (1981): 289-412.
Violet, Bruno. *Die Esra-Apokalypse (IV. Esra).* Die Griechischen Schriftsteller der ersten drei Jahrhunderte 18. Leipzig: Hinrichs, 1910.
————. *Die Apokalypsen des Esra und des Baruch in deutscher Gestalt.* GCS 32. Leipzig: Hinrichs, 1924.

Joseph and Aseneth:
Burchard, Christoph. "Joseph und Aseneth." *JSHRZ* 2.4 (1983): 573-735.
————. "Joseph and Aseneth." *OTP* 2:177-247.
Philonenko, Marc. *Joseph et Aséneth.* StPB 13. Leiden: Brill, 1968.

Jubilees:
Berger, Klaus. "Das Buch der Jubiläen." *JSHRZ* 2.3 (1981): 273-575.
Charles, R. H. "The Book of Jubilees." *APOT* 2:1-82.
Wintermute, O. S. "Jubilees." *OTP* 2:35-142.

Judith:
Cowley, A. E. "The Book of Judith." *APOT* 1:242-67.
Löhr, M. "Das Buch Judith." *APAT* 1:147-64.
Zenger, Erich. "Das Buch Judith." *JSHRZ* 1.6 (1981): 427-534.

Maccabees:
Kautzsch, E. "Das erste Buch der Makkabäer." *APAT* 1:24-81.
Oesterley, W. O. E. "I Maccabees." *APOT* 1:59-124.
Schunck, Klaus-Dietrich. "1. Makkabäerbuch." *JSHRZ* 1.4 (1980): 287-373.

Psalms of Solomon:
Gray, G. Buchanan. "The Psalms of Solomon." *APOT* 2:625-52.
Holm-Nielsen, Svend. "Die Psalmen Salomos." *JSHRZ* 4.2 (1977): 49-112.
Wright, R. B. "Psalms of Solomon." *OTP* 2:639-70.

Pseudo-Phocylides:

Horst, Pieter Willem van der. "Pseudo-Phocylides." *OTP* 2:565-82.

Walter, Nikolaus. "Pseudepigraphische jüdisch-hellenistische Dichtung: Pseudo-Phokylides, Pseudo-Orpheus, Gefälschte Verse auf Namen griechischer Dichter." *JSHRZ* 4.3 (1983): 173-276.

Sibylline Oracles:

Blass, F. "Die Sibyllinischen Orakel." *APAT* II, 177-217.

Collins, John J. "Sibylline Oracles." *OTP* 1:317-472.

Geffcken, Johannes. *Die Oracula Sibyllina.* GCS 8. Amsterdam: Hakkert, 1970 [1902].

Lanchester, H. C. O. "The Sibylline Oracles." *APOT* 2:368-406.

Sirach:

Box, George H., and William O. E. Oesterley. "The Book of Jesus Sirach." *APOT* 1:268-517.

Lella, Alexander A. Di. *The Hebrew Text of Sirach: A Text-Critical and Historical Study.* The Hague: Mouton, 1966.

Ryssel, V. "Die Sprüche Jesus, des Sohnes Sirachs." *APAT* 1:230-475.

Sauer, Georg. "Jesus Sirach (Ben Sira)." *JSHRZ* 3.5 (1981): 483-644.

Smend, Rudolf. *Die Weisheit des Jesus Sirach: Hebräisch und Deutsch.* Berlin: Reimer, 1906.

Syriac Psalms:

Woude, Adam Simon van der. "Die fünf syrischen Psalmen (einschließlich Psalm 151)." *JSHRZ* 4.1 (1977): 29-47.

Testaments of the Twelve Patriarchs:

Becker, Jürgen. "Die Testamente der zwölf Patriarchen." *JSHRZ* 3.1 (1980): 15-163.

Charles, R. H. "The Testaments of the XII Patriarchs." *APOT* 2:282-367.

Jonge, Marinus de. *Testamenta XII Patriarcharum.* 2nd ed. PVTG 1.1. Leiden: Brill, 1970 [1964].

———. *The Testaments of the Twelve Patriarchs: A Critical Edition of the Greek Text.* PVTG 1.2. Leiden: Brill, 1978.

Kee, H. C. "Testament of the Twelve Patriarchs." *OTP* 1:775-828.

Wisdom of Solomon:

Georgi, Dieter. "Weisheit Salomos." *JSHRZ* 3.4 (1980): 389-478.

Holmes, Samuel. "The Wisdom of Solomon." *APOT* 1:518-68.

Siegfried, Karl G. A. "Die Weisheit Salomos." *APAT* 1:476-507.

Winston, David. *The Wisdom of Solomon: A New Translation with Introduction and Commentary.* AncB 43. Garden City, N.Y.: Doubleday, 1979.

Qumran:

Beyer, Klaus. *Die aramäischen Texte vom Toten Meer samt den Inschriften aus Palästina, dem Testament Levis aus der Kairoer Genisa, der Fastenrolle und den alten talmudischen Zitaten.* 2 vols. Göttingen: Vandenhoeck & Ruprecht, 1984-1994.

Charlesworth, James H., ed. *The Dead Sea Scrolls: Hebrew, Aramaic, and Greek Texts with English Translations [Princeton Theological Seminary Dead Sea Scrolls Project].* Tübingen: Mohr-Siebeck, 1994-.

Discoveries in the Judean Desert [of Jordan]. Oxford: Clarendon, 1955-2002.

Fitzmyer, Joseph A. *The Genesis Apocryphon of Qumran Cave I: A Commentary.* 2nd ed. Biblica et orientalia 18A. Rome: Biblical Institute Press, 1971.

García Martínez, Florentino. *The Dead Sea Scrolls Translated: The Qumran Texts in English.* Leiden: Brill, 1994 [Spanish, 1992].

García Martínez, Florentino, and Eibert J. C. Tigchelaar, eds. *The Dead Sea Scrolls Study Edition.* 2 vols. Leiden: Brill, 1997-1998.

Jongeling, B., et al. *Aramaic Texts from Qumran: With Translations and Annotations.* Semitic Study Series 4. Leiden: Brill, 1976.

Kittel. Bonnie P. *The Hymns of Qumran: Translation and Commentary.* SBLDS 50. Chico, Calif.: Scholars Press, 1981.

Lohse, Eduard. *Die Texte aus Qumran Hebräisch und Deutsch: Mit masoretischer Punktation, Übersetzung, Einführung und Anmerkungen.* 4th ed. Darmstadt: Wissenschaftliche Buchgesellschaft, 1986 [1962].

Maier, Johann. *Die Qumran-Essener: Die Texte vom Toten Meer.* 3 vols. UTB 1862, 1863, 1916. Basel and Munich: Reinhardt, 1995-1996.

———. *Die Tempelrolle vom Toten Meer: Übersetzt und erläutert.* UTB 829. Basel and Munich: Reinhardt, 1978.

Newsom, Carol. *Songs of the Sabbath Sacrifice: A Critical Edition.* Harvard Semitic Series 27. Atlanta: Scholars Press, 1985.

Vermes, Géza. *The Dead Sea Scrolls in English.* 4th ed. Sheffield: Sheffield Academic Press, 1995 [1962].

Josephus:

Aus meinem Leben (Vita). Edited and translated by F. Siegert. Tübingen: Mohr-Siebeck, 2000.

De Bello Judaico; Der jüdische Krieg. Edited by O. Michel, and O. Bauernfeind. 3 vols. Darmstadt: Wissenschaftliche Buchgesellschaft, 1959-1969 [1982].

Flavii Josephi Opera. Edited by B. Niese. 2nd ed. 7 vols. Berlin: Akademie-Verlag, 1955 [1885-1895].

Geschichte des Jüdischen Krieges. Translated by H. Clementz. Wiesbaden: Fourier, 1977 [1900].

Josephus. Edited by H. St. J. Thackeray, R. Marcus and L. H. Feldman. 10 vols. LCL.

Cambridge, Mass.: Harvard University Press; London: Heinemann, 1926-1965.
Jüdische Altertümer. Translated by H. Clementz. Wiesbaden: Fourier, 1979 [1899].

Philo:

Philo: Works; Greek Text and English Translation. Edited by F. M. Colson, G. H.
Whitaker and R. Marcus. 10 vols. LCL. London: Heinemann, 1929-1962.
Philo von Alexandrien: Die Werke in deutscher Übersetzung. Edited by L. Cohn
et al. 7 vols. 2nd ed. Berlin: de Gruyter, 1962-1964 [1919-1964].
Philonis Alexandrini opera quae supersunt. Edited by L. Cohn and P. Wendland.
Editio Major. 8 vols. Berlin: Akademie-Verlag, 1896-1930.
The Works of Philo: Complete and Unabridged. Edited by C. D. Yonge. Peabody,
Mass.: Hendrickson, 1993 [1854-1855].

3. Rabbinic Writings

Mishnah:

Albeck, Hanock, ed. *Shishah sidre mishnah.* 6 vols. Jerusalem: Bialik Institute,
1954-1959.
Beer, G., et al., eds. *Die Mischna: Text, Übersetzung und ausführliche Erk-
lärung.* Giessen: Töpelmann; Berlin: de Gruyter, 1912-.
Blackman, Philip. *Mishnayoth.* New York: Judaica, 1963.
Danby, Herbert. *The Mishnah: Translated from the Hebrew with Introduction
and Brief Explanatory Notes.* Oxford: University Press, 1980 [1933].
*Mishnajot: Die sechs Ordnungen der Mischna; Hebräischer Text mit Punktua-
tion, deutscher Übersetzung und Erklärung.* 3rd ed. Basel: Goldschmidt,
1968.
Neusner, Jacob. *The Mishnah: A New Translation.* New Haven: Yale University
Press, 1988.

Tosefta:

Lieberman, S., ed. *Tosefta.* New York: Louis Rabinowitz Research Institute in
Rabbinics, 1937-1955.
Neusner, J., and R. S. Sarason, eds. *The Tosefta Translated from the Hebrew.* New
York and Hoboken, N.J.: Ktav, 1977-1986.
Rengstorf, K. H., et al., eds. *Rabbinische Texte, Erste Reihe: Die Tosefta.* Stuttgart,
Kohlhammer: 1953.
Zuckermandel, M. S., ed. *Tosefta.* Repr. with supplement by S. Lieberman. Jeru-
salem: Bamberger and Vahrman, 1937 [1877-1882].

Talmud:

Eppstein, I., ed. *The Babylonian Talmud: Translated into English with Notes,*

Glossary and Indices. 35 vols. London: Soncino, 1961 [1935-1952].

Goldschmidt, Lazarus. *Der Babylonische Talmud*. 4th ed. 12 vols. Darmstadt: Wissenschaftliche Buchgesellschaft, 1996 [1929-1936; 2nd ed., 1967].

Hengel, M., H. P. Rüger, and P. Schäfer, eds. *Übersetzung des Talmud Yerushalmi*. Tübingen: Mohr-Siebeck, 1975-.

Neusner, Jacob. *The Talmud of the Land of Israel*. Chicago: University of Chicago Press, 1982-.

―――. *The Talmud of Babylonia: An American Translation*. BJS. Atlanta: Scholars Press, 1984-1993.

Schwab, M. *Le Talmud de Jérusalem 1-11*. 6 vols. Paris: Maisonneuve, 1969 [1871-1889].

Talmud Babli. 12 vols. Wilna: Wittwe & Romm, 1895-1908.

Talmud Yerushalmi. Repr. of the Krotoschin ed., 1866. Jerusalem, 1969.

Talmud Yerushalmi. 7 vols. Repr. of the Wilna ed., 1922. Jerusalem, 1973.

Targumim:

Chilton, Bruce D. *The Isaiah Targum: Introduction, Translation, Apparatus and Notes*. AramBib 11. Wilmington, Del.: Glazier, 1987.

Clarke, E. G., ed. *Targum Pseudo-Jonathan of the Pentateuch: Text and Concordance*. Hoboken, N.J.: Ktav, 1984.

Déaut, Robert Le. *Targum des Chroniques*. 2 vols. AnBib 51. Rome: Biblical Institute Press, 1971.

―――. *Targum du Pentateuque*. 5 vols. Paris, 1978-1981.

Drazin, Israel. *Targum Onkelos to Exodus: An English Translation of the Text with Analysis and Commentary*. Based on the A. Sperber and A. Berliner eds. Hoboken, N.J.: Ktav, 1990.

Grossfeld, Bernard. *The Targum to the Five Megilloth: Edited, with an Introduction*. New York: Hermon, 1973.

―――. *The Two Targums of Esther: Translated, with Apparatus and Notes*. AramBib 18. Collegeville, Minn.: Liturgical Press, 1991.

―――. *The Targum Onqelos to Genesis*. AramBib 6. Wilmington, Del.: Glazier, 1988.

Klein, M. L. *The Fragment-Targums of the Pentateuch According to Their Extant Sources*. 2 vols. AnBib 76. Rome: Biblical Institute Press, 1980.

Maher, Michael. *Targum Pseudo-Jonathan: Genesis*. Translated, with Introduction and Notes. AramBib 1B. Collegeville, Minn.: Liturgical Press, 1992.

McNamara, M. *Targum Neofiti I: Genesis*. Translated, with Apparatus and Notes. AramBib 1A. Collegeville, Minn.: Liturgical Press, 1992.

Sperber, A. *The Bible in Aramaic*. 4 vols. Leiden: Brill, 1959-1968.

Tal, A. *The Samaritan Targum of the Pentateuch: A Critical Edition*. 2 vols. Tel Aviv: University Press, 1981.

Midrashim and Other Texts:

Finkelstein, Louis. *Sifre on Leviticus.* 4 vols. New York: Jewish Theological Seminary of America, 1983.

———. *Sifre al Sefer Devarim: Sifre on Deuteronomy.* Berlin: Jüdischer Kulturbund, 1939 [New York: Bet ha-midrash le-rabanim ba-Amerikah, 1969].

Horovitz, H. Saul, and Israel A. Rabin. *Mechilta d'Rabbi Ishmael.* 2nd ed. Jerusalem: Wahrmann, 1970.

Lauterbach, Jacob Z. *Mekilta de-Rabbi Ishmael.* 3 vols. Philadelphia: Jewish Publication Society, 1933-1935 [new ed., 2001].

Levertoff, Paul P. *Midrash Sifre on Numbers.* London: SPCK, 1926.

Neusner, Jacob. *Mekhilta According to Rabbi Ishmael: An Analytical Translation.* Atlanta: Scholars Press, 1988.

Winter, Jacob. *Sifra: Halachischer Midrasch zu Leviticus.* Breslau: Münz, 1938.

4. Early Christian Writings

Acts of Apostles (*see also* Apocrypha, New Testament):

Acta Andreae. Edited by Jean-Marc Prieur. 2 vols. CCSA 5-6. Turnhout: Brepols, 1989.

Acta Iohannis. Edited by Eric Junod and Jean-Daniel Kaestli. CCSA 1-2. Turnhout: Brepols, 1983.

Acta Philippi. Edited by François Bovon, Bertrand Bouvier and Frédéric Amsler. 2 vols. CCSA 11-12. Turnhout: Brepols, 1999.

The Acts of Thomas: An Introduction, Text, Commentary. Edited by A. F. J. Klijn. NovTSup 5. Leiden: Brill, 1962.

Sancti Barnabae Apostoli Laudatio auctore Alexandro monacho, et Sanctorum Bartholomaei et Barnabae Vita Pro Menologio Imperiali Conscripta. Edited by Peter van Deun. CCSG 26. Turnhout: Brepols; Leuven: Leuven University Press, 1993.

Apocrypha, New Testament:

Bovon, François, and Pierre Geoltrain, eds. *Écrits apocryphes chrétiens.* Bibliothèque de la Pléiade. Paris: Gallimard, 1997.

Elliott, J. Keith. *The Apocryphal New Testament: A Collection of Apocryphal Christian Literature in an English Translation.* Oxford: Oxford University Press, 1993.

Hennecke, Edgar, and Wilhelm Schneemelcher, eds. *Neutestamentliche Apokryphen in deutscher Übersetzung.* 6th ed. 2 vols. Tübingen: Mohr-Siebeck, 1990-1997 [3rd ed., 1959-1964; 5th ed., 1987-1989; study ed., 1999]. English: *New Testament Apocrypha.* From 3rd German ed. Philadelphia: Westminster Press, 1963-1966.

James, Montague Rhodes. *The Apocryphal New Testament.* Oxford: Clarendon, 1955 [1924].

Apostolic Fathers:

Ehrman, Bart D. *The Apostolic Fathers.* LCL. Cambridge, Mass.: Harvard University Press, 2003.

Fischer, Joseph A., and Ulrich Körtner, eds. *Schriften des Urchristentums 1: Die Apostolischen Väter.* 10th ed. Darmstadt: Wissenschaftliche Buchgesellschaft, 1993 [1976].

Lightfoot, Joseph B. *The Apostolic Fathers: A Revised Text with Introduction, Notes, Dissertations, and Translations.* 5 vols. London and New York: MacMillan, 1885.

―――. *The Apostolic Fathers: Revised Greek Texts with Introductions and English Translations.* Edited by J. R. Harmer. Grand Rapids: Baker, 1987 [1891; 1984].

Lindemann, Andreas. *Die Clemensbriefe.* Die Apostolischen Väter I. HNT 17. Tübingen: Mohr-Siebeck, 1992.

Lindemann, Andreas, and Henning Paulsen, eds. *Die Apostolischen Väter: Griechisch-deutsche Parallelausgabe.* Tübingen: Mohr-Siebeck, 1992.

Lona, Horacio E. *Der erste Clemensbrief.* Kommentar zu den Apostolischen Vätern 2. Göttingen: Vandenhoeck & Ruprecht, 1998.

Church Councils, Acts of:

Gelzer, Heinrich, Heinrich Hilgenfeld, and Otto Cuntz. *Patrum nicaenorum nomina Latine, Graece, Coptice, Syriace, Arabice, Armeniace.* Bibliotheca Teubneriana. Stuttgart: Teubner, 1898 [1995].

Synaxarium Ecclesiae Constantinopolitanae e codice Sirmondiano. Edited by Hippolyte Delehaye. Brüssel: Bolland, 1902 [repr., Louvain: Anastatique, 1954].

Church Fathers:

The Ante-Nicene Fathers: Translations of the Fathers Down to A.D. 325. Edited by Alexander Roberts and James Donaldson. 10 vols. Grand Rapids: Eerdmans, 1978-1981 [1899-1900].

A Select Library of Nicene and Post-Nicene Fathers of the Christian Church. First and Second Series. Edited by Philip Schaff and Henry Wace. 14 vols. Grand Rapids: Eerdmans, 1978 [1886-1895].

Didache:

Wengst, K., ed. *Schriften des Urchristentums II: Didache (Apostellehre), Barnabasbrief, Zweiter Klemensbrief, Schrift an Diognet.* Munich: Kösel, 1984.

Didascalia Apostolorum:

The Didascalia Apostolorum: The Syriac Version Translated. Edited by Richard H. Connolly. Oxford: Clarendon, 1929.

The Didascalia Apostolorum: English and Syriac. Edited by Arthur Vööbus. 2 vols. CSCO 402, 408. Leuven: Secrétariat du Corpus Scriptorum Christianorum Orientalium, 1979.

Die syrische Didaskalia, übersetzt und erklärt. Vol. 2 of *Die ältesten Quellen des orientalischen Kirchenrechts.* Edited by Hans Achelis and Johannes Flemming. TUGAL 10.2. Leipzig: Hinrichs, 1904.

Doctrina Addai:

The Doctrine of Addai, the Apostle. Edited by G. Phillips. London: Trübner, 1876.

Histoire du roi Abgar et de Jésus: Présentation et traduction du texte syriaque intégral de La Doctrine d'Addaï. Edited by Desreumaux Alain. Apocryphes 3. Turnnhout: Brepols, 1993.

The Teaching of Addai. Edited by George Howard. SBLTT 16. Chico, California: Scholars Press, 1981.

Eusebius:

Eusebi Chronicorum libri duo. Edited by Alfred Schoene. 2 vols. Berlin: Weidmann, 1875 [repr., 1967].

Eusebii Pamphili Chronici Canones. Edited by John K. Fotheringham. London: Milford, 1923.

Eusebius: Kirchengeschichte. Edited by H. Kraft. Munich: Kösel, 1967.

Eusebius: The Ecclesiastical History. Edited by Kirsopp Lake. LCL. Cambridge, Mass.: Harvard University Press, 1953 [1926].

The Onomasticon by Eusebius of Caesarea: Palestine in the Fourth Century A.D. Edited by Joan E. Taylor. Translated by G. S. P. Freeman-Grenville. Jerusalem: Carta, 2003.

Das Onomastikon der biblischen Ortsnamen. Die griechischen christlichen Schriftsteller der ersten drei Jahrhunderte 2.1 (Eusebius 3.1). Edited by Erich Klostermann. Leipzig: Hinrich 1904 [repr., Hildesheim: Olms 1966].

Hermas, Shepherd of:

Körtner, Ulrich, and Martin Leutzsch, eds. *Papiasfragmente: Hirt des Hermas.* Schriften des Urchristentums 3. Darmstadt: Wissenschaftliche Buchgesellschaft, 1998.

Irenaeus:

Epideixis: Adversus Haereses; Darlegung der Apostolischen Verkündigung: Gegen die Häresien. Edited by Norbert Brox. 5 vols. Fontes Christiani 8.1-5. Freiburg: Herder, 1993-2001.

Justin:

Goodspeed, Edgar J., ed. *Die ältesten Apologeten: Texte mir kurzen Einleitungen.* Göttingen: Vandenhoeck & Ruprecht, 1984 [1914].

Ristow, Helmut, ed. *Die Apologeten.* Berlin: Evangelische Verlagsanstalt, 1963.

Martyrs, Acts of:

Musurillo, Harold. *The Acts of the Christian Martyrs.* Oxford: Clarendon, 1972.

Nag Hammadi:

Robinson, James M., ed. *The Nag Hammadi Library.* 3rd ed. Leiden: Brill, 1988.

Origen:

Vogt, Hermann, ed. *Origen: Der Kommentar zum Evangelium nach Mattäus.* 3 vols. BGL 18, 30, 38. Stuttgart: Hiersemann, 1983-1993.

Papias:

Körtner, Ulrich, and Martin Leutzsch, eds. *Papiasfragmente: Hirt des Hermas.* Schriften des Urchristentums 3. Darmstadt: Wissenschaftliche Buchgesellschaft, 1998.

Polycarp:

Buschmann, Gerd. *Das Martyrium des Polykarp.* Kommentar zu den Apostolischen Vätern 6. Göttingen: Vandenhoeck & Ruprecht, 1998.

Thomas, Gospel of:

Fieger, M. *Das Thomasevangelium: Einleitung, Kommentar und Systematik.* Münster: Aschendorff, 1991.

5. Greek and Roman Sources and Inscriptions[1]

Anthologies:

Barrett, Charles K., and Claus-Jürgen Thornton. *Texte zur Umwelt des Neuen Testaments.* 2nd ed. UTB 1591. Tübingen: Mohr-Siebeck, 1991 [1959].

Braund, David. *Augustus to Nero: A Sourcebook on Roman History, 31 BC—AD 68.* Totowa, N.J.: Barnes & Noble, 1985.

Ehrenberg, Victor, and A. H. M. Jones, eds. *Documents Illustrating the Reigns of Augustus and Tiberius.* 2nd. enl. ed. Oxford: Clarendon, 1979 [1955; 1949].

Die Fragmente der griechischen Historiker. Edited by Felix Jacoby. 3 vols. Berlin: Weidmann, 1923-1958 [repr., Leiden: Brill, 1954-1969].

---

[1]For epigraphical publications see G. H. R. Horsley and J. A. L. Lee, "A Preliminary Checklist of Abbreviations of Greek Epigraphic Volumes," *Epigraphica* 56 (1994): 129-69.

Geographi Graeci Minores. Edited by Carl Müller. 3 vols. Paris: Didot, 1855-1882 [repr., Hildesheim: Olms, 1965-1990].

Geographi Latini Minores. Edited by Alexander Riese. Heilbronn: Henninger, 1878 [repr., Hildesheim: Olms, 1964].

Greek and Latin Authors on Jews and Judaism. Edited by Menachem Stern. 3 vols. Jerusalem: Israel Academy of Science and Humanities, 1974-1984.

New Documents Illustrating Early Christianity. Edited by G. H. R. Horsley and S. R. Llewelyn. 9 vols. North Ryde, N.S.W.: Macquarie University, Ancient History Documentary Research Centre; Grand Rapids: Eerdmans, 1981-2002.

Thesaurus Linguae Graecae. CD ROM E. Irvine, Calif.: University of California, 2000.

Tyana: Archäologisch-historische Untersuchungen zum südwestlichen Kappadokien. Edited by Dietrich Berges and Johannes Nollé. 2 vols. IK 55. Bonn: Habelt, 2000.

The Wolfe-Expedition to Asia Minor. Edited by John R. S. Sterrett. Papers of the Americal School of Classical Studies at Athens 3. Boston: Damrell & Upham, 1888.

Coins:

Aulock, Hans von. *Münzen und Städte Lykaoniens.* Tübingen: Wasmuth, 1976.

Carson, Robert A. G. *The Principal Coins of the Romans.* 3 vols. London: British Museum, 1978-1981.

Houghton, Arthur A. *Coins of the Seleucid Empire from the Collection of Arthur Houghton.* Ancient Coins in North American Collections: American Numismatic Society 4. New York: American Numismatic Society, 1983.

Mattingly, H., and R. A. G. Carson. *Coins of the Roman Empire in the British Museum.* 8 vols. London: British Museum, 1923-1976.

Newell, Edward. *The Coinage of the Eastern Seleucid Mints, from Seleucus I to Antiochus III.* New York: American Numismatic Society, 1978 [1938].

Stumpf, Gerd R. *Numismatische Studien zur Chronologie der römischen Statthalter in Kleinasien (122 v.Chr.-163 n.Chr.).* Saarbrücker Studien zur Archäolgoie und Alten Geschichte 4. Saarbrücken: Saarbrücker Druckerei und Verlag, 1991.

Inscriptions:

Ancient Greek Inscriptions in the British Museum. Edited by E. L. Hicks et al. 4 vols. Oxford: Clarendon, 1874-1916.

The Athenian Agora. Vol. 3, *The Literary and Epigraphical Testimonia.* Edited by R. E. Wycherley. Princeton, N.J.: American School of Classical Studies at Athens, 1957 [1973].

Corinth: Results of Excavations Conducted by the American School of Classical Studies at Athens. Vol. 8.3, *The Inscriptions 1926-1950.* Edited by John H. Kent. Princeton, N.J.: American School of Classical Studies at Athens, 1966.

Corpus Cultus Iovis Sabazii. Edited by Maarten J. Vermaseren and Eugene N. Lane. 3 vols. Leiden: Brill, 1983-1989.

Corpus Inscriptionum Judaicarum. Edited by Jean-Baptiste Frey. 2 vols. Rome: Pontificio istituto di archeologia cristiana, 1936-1952. Vol. 1 republished with prolegomenon. Edited by Baruch Lifshitz. New York: Ktav, 1975.

Corpus Inscriptionum Graecarum. Edited by August Böckh. Berlin: Reimer, 1828-1877 [repr., Hildesheim: Olms, 1977].

Corpus Inscriptionum Latinarum. Berlin: Akademie der Wissenschaften, 1862-.

Corpus Inscriptorum Regni Bosporani. Edited by V. V. Struve. Moscow: Academia Scientiarum, 1965.

Corpus jüdischer Zeugnisse aus der Cyrenaika. Edited by Gertz Lüderitz. BTAVO B 53. Wiesbaden: Reichert, 1983.

Corpus Monumentorum Religionis Dei Menis. Edited by Eugene N. Lane. 4 vols. Leiden: Brill, 1971-1978.

Donateurs et fondateurs dans les synagogues juives: Répertoire des dédicaces grecques relatives à la construction et à la réfection des synagogues. Edited by Baruch Lifshitz. Cahiers de la Revue Biblique 7. Paris: Gabalda, 1967.

Greek and Latin Inscriptions in the Manisa Museum. Edited by Hasan Malay. ETAM 19. Vienna: Österreichische Akademie der Wissenschaften, 1994.

Greeks and Romans in Imperial Asia: Mixed Language Inscriptions and Linguistic Evidence for Cultural Interaction until the End of AD III. Edited by Rosalinde A. Kearsley. IK 59. Bonn: Habelt, 2001.

Guarducci, Margherita. *Epigrafia greca.* 4 vols. Rome: Istituto poligrafico dello Stato, Libreria dello Sato, 1967-1978.

Historische griechische Inschriften in Übersetzung. Edited by Kai Brodersen, W. Günther and Hatto H. Schmitt. 3 vols. Texte zur Forschung 59, 68, 71. Wissenschaftliche Buchgesellschaft: Darmstadt, 1992-1999.

Jewish Inscriptions of Graeco-Roman Egypt; With an Index of the Jewish Inscriptions of Egypt and Cyrenaica. Edited by William Horbury and David Noy. Cambridge: Cambridge University Press, 1992.

Jewish Inscriptions of Western Europe. Edited by David Noy. 2 vols. Cambridge: Cambridge University Press, 1993-1995.

Die Inschriften von Anazarbos und Umgebung. Edited by Mustafa Hamdi Sayar. IK 56. Bonn: Habelt 2000.

Die Inschriften von Assos. Edited by R. Merkelbach. IK 4. Bonn: Habelt 1976.

Die Inschriften von Ephesos. Edited by Hermann Wankel et al. 10 vols. IK 11-17.4. Bonn: Habelt, 1979-1984.

Die Inschriften von Erythrai und Klazomenaihrai. Edited by H. Engelmann and R. Merkelbach. 2 vols. IK 1.1-2. Bonn: Habelt, 1972-1973.

Die Inschriften von Kios. Edited by Thomas Corsten. IK 29. Bonn: Habelt, 1985.

Die Inschriften von Knidos. Edited by Wolfgang Blümel. IK 41. Bonn: Habelt, 1992.

Die Inschriften von Kyzikos und Umgebung. Edited by Elmar Schwertheim. 2 vols. IK 18, 26. Bonn: Habelt, 1980-1983.

Die Inschriften von Laodikeia am Lykos: Teil I, Die Inschriften. Edited by Thomas Corsten. IK 49.1. Bonn: Habelt, 1997.

Die Inschriften von Magnesia am Sipylos. Edited by T. Ihnken. IK 8. Bonn: Habelt, 1978.

Die Inschriften von Perge. Edited by Sencer Şahin. IK 54. Bonn: Habelt, 1999.

Die Inschriften von Pergamon. Edited by Max Fränkel. 2 vols. Altertümer von Pergamon 8. Berlin: Spemann, 1890-1895.

Inschriften von Priene. Edited by Hiller von Gaertringen. Berlin: de Gruyter, 1968 [1906].

Die Inschriften von Prusa ad Olympum. Edited by Thomas Corsten. 2 vols. IK 39-40. Bonn: Habelt, 1991-1993.

Die Inschriften von Smyrna. Edited by Georg Petzl. IK 23-24. 2 vols. Bonn: Habelt, 1982-1990.

Die Inschriften von Stratonikeia. Edited by Sencer Şahin. 2 vols. IK 21-22. Bonn: Habelt, 1981-1990.

Inschriften griechischer Städte aus Kleinasien. Kommission für die archäologische Erforschung Kleinasiens bei der Österreichischen Akademie der Wissenschaften und Institut für Altertumskunde der Universität Köln. Bonn: Habelt, 1972-.

Inscriptiones antiquae orae septentrionalis Pontis Euxini Graecae et Latine. Edited by Vasilii V. Latyshev. 3 vols. St. Petersburg: Russkoe arkheologicheskoe obshchestvo, 1885-1901 [repr., Hildesheim: Olms, 1965].

Inscriptiones Graecae. Edited by Otto Kern. Bonn: Marcus & Weber, 1913.

Inscriptiones Graecae ad res Romanas pertinentes. Edited by René Cagnat et al. 4 vols. Paris: Leroux, 1906-1927 [repr., 4 vols. in 3; Chicago: Ares, 1975].

Inscriptiones Graecae in Bulgaria repertae. Edited by G. Mihailov. 4 vols. Sofia: Academia Litteratum Bulgarica, 1956-1970.

Inscriptiones Graecae Urbis Romanae. Edited by Luigi Moretti. Rome: Bardi, 1968-.

Inscriptiones Judaicae Orientis. Edited by David Noy et al. 3 vols. TSAJ 99, 101, 102. Tübinger: Mohr-Siebeck, 2004.

Inscriptiones Latinae Selectae. Edited by Hermann Dessau. Berlin: Weidmann, 1892 [repr., Chicago: Ares, 1979].

Inscriptiones antiquae orae septentrionalis Ponti Euxini Graecae et Latinae per annos 1885-1900 repertae. 3 vols. Edited by Vasilii Vasil'evich Latyshev. Inscriptiones antiquae orae septentrionalis Ponti Euxini Graecae et Latinae. St. Petersburg: Impensis Societatis Archaeologicae Imperii Russici, 1885-1901.

The Inscriptions of Alexandreia Troas. Edited by Marijana Ricl. IK 53. Bonn: Habelt, 1997.

The Inscriptions of Central Pisidia. Edited by G. H. R. Horsley and S. Mitchell. IK 57. Bonn: Habelt, 2000.

Inscriptions de Cilicie. Edited by Gilbert Dagron and Denis Feissel. Travaux et Mémoires du centre de recherche d'histoire et civilisation de Byzance. Monographies 4. Paris: Boccard, 1987.

The Inscriptions of Cos. Edited by W. R. Paton and E. L. Hicks. Oxford: Clarendon, 1891.

Inscriptions de Délos. Edited by A. Plassart et al. 7 vols. Paris: Champion and Boccard, 1926-1972.

Inscriptions grecques et latines. Edited by P. Le Bas and W. H. Waddington. Paris: Didot, 1870 [repr., 2 vols; Subsidia Epigraphica 1-2; Hildesheim: Olms, 1972].

Inscriptions grecques et latines de la Syrie. Edited by L. Jalabert et al. Beirut and Paris: Geuthner, 1929-1986.

Inventaire des inscriptions de Palmyre X. Edited by J. Starcky. Beirut: Damas, 1949.

Die kaiserzeitlichen Inschriften Lykaoniens. Edited by Gertrud Laminger-Pascher. ETAM 15. Vienna: Österreichische Akademie der Wissenschaften, 1992.

Le Bohec, Yann. "Inscriptions Juives et Judaisantes de l'Afrique Romaine." *Antiquités Africaines* 17 (1981): 165-207.

Monumenta Asiae Minoris Antiqua. Edited by W. M. Calder et al. 9 vols. Manchester: Manchester University Press; London: Society for the Promotion of Roman Studies, 1928-1988.

The Moral Edicts of King Asoka, Including the Greco-Aramaic Inscription of Kandahar and Further Inscriptions of the Mauryan Period. Edited by P. H. L. Eggermont and J. Hoftijzer. Leiden: Brill, 1962.

Orientis graeci inscriptiones selectae. Edited by Wilhelm Dittenberger. 2 vols. Leipzig: Hirzel, 1903-1905 [repr., Hildesheim: Olms, 1960].

Recueil des inscriptions chrétiennes de Macédonie au IIIe au VIe siècle. BCH Supplement 8. Edited by Denis Feissel. Paris: Boccard, 1983.

Regional Epigraphic Catalogues of Asia Minor II: The Ankara District; The Inscriptions of North Galatia. Edited by Stephen Mitchell. British Archaeological Reports International Series 135. Oxford: British Institute of Archaeology, 1982.

Robert, Louis, "Les inscriptions." In *Laodicée du Lycos.* Edited by J. des Gagniers, 265-77. Québec: Les Presses de l'Université Laval; Paris: Boccard, 1969.

Supplementum epigraphicum graecum. Leiden: Sijthoff; Amsterdam: Gieben, 1923- (suspended, 1972-1975).

Sylloge inscriptionum graecarum. Edited by Wilhelm Dittenberger. 3rd ed. 4 vols. Leipzig: Hirzel, 1915-1924.

Tituli Asiae Minoris. Vol. 5.1-2, *Tituli Lydiae linguis graeca et latina conscripti.* Edited by I. Keil and P. Herrmann. 2 vols. Vienna: Österreichische Akademie der Wissenschaften, 1981-1989.

Papyri:

Catalogue of the Greek Papyri in the John Rylands Library at Manchester. Edited by A. S. Hunt et al. Manchester: University Press, 1911-1952 [1965].

Collectanea Papyrologica: Texts Published in Honor of H. C. Youtie. Edited by Ann Ellis Hanson. Papyrologische Texte und Abhandlungen 19–20. Bonn: Habelt, 1976.

Corpus Papyrorum Judaicarum. Edited by V. Tcherikover and A. Fuks. 3 vols. Jerusalem: Magnes; Cambridge, Mass.: Harvard University Press, 1957-1963.

Cowley, Arthur E. *Aramaic Papyri of the Fifth Century B.C.* Osnabrück: Zeller, 1967.

The Documents from the Bar Kokhba Period in the Cave of Letters: Greek Papyri. Edited by N. Lewis. Judean Desert Studies. Jerusalem: Israel Exploration Society, 1989.

The Greek Magical Papyri in Translation, Including the Demotic Spells. Edited by Hans Dieter Betz. 2nd ed. Chicago: University of Chicago Press, 1992 [1986].

Greek Papyri in the British Museum. Edited by F. Kenyon et al. London: British Museum, 1893-1974.

Grelot, Pierre. *Documents araméens d'Égypte.* Littératures anciennes du Proche-Orient 5. Paris: Cerf, 1972.

Kölner Papyri. Edited by B. Kramer and R. Hübner. Papyrologica Coloniensia 7-9. Opladen: Westdeutscher Verlag, 1976.

Kraeling, Emil. *The Brooklyn Museum Aramaic Papyri: New Documents of the Fifth Century B.C. from the Jewish Colony at Elephantine.* New York: Arno, 1969.

Oxyrhynchus Papyri. Edited by B. P. Grenfell et al. London: Egypt Exploration Fund, 1898-.

Papyri graecae magicae: Die griechischen Zauberpapyri. Edited by Karl Preisendanz. 2 vols. Stuttgart: Teubner, 1973 [1928].

Sachau, Eduard. *Aramäische Papyrus und Ostraka aus einer jüdischen Militärkolonie zu Elephantine: Altorientalische Sprachdenkmäler des 5. Jahrhunderts vor Chr.* Leipzig: Hinrichs, 1911.

Select Papyri. Edited by A. S. Hunt and C. C. Edgar. 3 vols. LCL. Cambridge, Mass.: Harvard University Press, 1932-1941.

Van Haelst, Joseph. *Catalogue des papyrus littéraires juifs et chrétiens.* Série papyrologie 1. Paris: Publication de la Sorbonne, 1976.

Zauzich, Karl-Theodor. *Papyri von der Insel Elephantine.* Demotische Papyri aus den Staatlichen Museen zu Berlin 1. Berlin: Akademie-Verlag, 1978.

Aelius Aristides:

Aelii Aristidis Smyrnaei quae supersunt omnia. Edited by Bruno Keil. 2 vols. Berlin: Weidmann, 1898 [repr., 1958].

Aristides. Edited by Charles A. Behr. LCL. Cambridge, Mass.: Harvard University Press, 1973.

Aristides ex recensione G. Dindorfii. Edited by Wilhelm Dindorf. 3 vols. Leipzig: Teubner, 1828 [repr., Hildesheim: Olms, 1964].

P. Aelii Aristides Opera Quae Extant Omnia. 2 vols. Edited by Charles A. Behr and Friedrich W. Lenz. Leiden: Brill, 1976-1986.

P. Aelii Aristidis Orationem ΕΙΣ ΡΩΜΗΝ. In *Die Romrede des Aelius Aristides.* Edited by Richard Klein. Texte zur Forschung 45. Darmstadt: Wissenschaftliche Buchgesellschaft, 1983.

P. Aelius Aristides: The Complete Works. 2 vols. Edited by Charles A. Behr. Leiden: Brill, 1981-1986.

Ammianus Marcellinus:

Ammiani Marcellini Rerum gestarum libri qui supersunt. Edited by Wolfgang Seyfarth. Stuttgart: Teubner, 1999.

Ammianus Marcellinus. Edited by John C. Rolfe. Revised Edition. 3 vols. LCL. Cambridge, Mass.: Harvard University Press, 1982-1986 [1935-1939].

Ammianus Marcellinus: Römische Geschichte. Lateinisch-deutsch. Edited by Wolfgang Seyfarth. 5th ed. 2 vols. Berlin: Akademie-Verlag, 1983.

Caesar:

C. Julius Caesar: Bellum Gallicum; Der Gallische Krieg. Lateinisch-deutsch. Edited by Georg Dorminger. 4th ed. Tusculum. Munich: Heimeran, 1977 [1962].

Cassius Dio:

Cassius Dio: Römische Geschichte. Edited by Otto Veh and Gerhard Wirth. 5 vols. Zürich: Artemis 1985-1987.

Dio's Roman History. Edited by Earnest Cary. 9 vols. LCL. Cambridge, Mass.: Harvard University Press, 1914-27 [1961].

Diodoros Siculus:

Diodori Bibliotheca Historica. Edited by F. Vogel and K. T. Fischer. 6 vols. Bibliotheca scriptorum Graecorum et Romanorum Teubneriana. Stuttgart: Teubner, 1964-1969 [1888-1906].

Diodoros: Griechische Weltgeschichte. Edited by Gerhard Wirth and Otto Veh. Bibliothek der griechischen Literatur. Stuttgart: Hiersemann, 1992-1998.

Diodorus Siculus: Library of History. Edited by C. H. Oldfather. 12 vols. Cambridge, Mass.: Harvard University Press, 1976-1993 [1933-1967].

Epictetus:

Epictetus: The Discourses as Reported by Arrian, the Manual, and Fragments.

Edited by W. A. Oldfather. 2 vols. LCL. Cambridge, Mass.: Harvard University Press, 1925 [1966].

Juvenal:

D. Junii Juvenalis Saturarum Libri V (mit erklärenden Anmerkungen), I-II. Edited by L. Friedländer. Hildesheim: Olms, 1967 [1895].

Martial:

M. Valerius Martialis: Epigramme. Lateinisch-deutsch. Edited by P. Barié and W. Schindler. Munich: Artemis & Winkler, 1999.
Martial: Epigrams. Edited by D. R. Shackleton Bailey. LCL. Cambridge, Mass.: Harvard University Press, 1993.

Orosius, Paulus:

Die antike Weltgeschichte in christlicher Sicht. Edited by A. Lippold and C. Andresen. 2 vols. Zürich: Artemis, 1985-1986.
Paulus Orosius: Histoire. Edited by Marie-Pierre Arnaud-Lindet. 2 vols. Paris: Les Belles Lettres, 1991-1992.
Paulus Orosius: The Seven Books of History Against the Pagans. Edited by Roy J. Deferrari. Washington, D.C.: Catholic University of America Press, 1964.

Periplus:

The Periplus Maris Erythraei: Text with Introduction, Translation, and Commentary. Edited by Lionel Casson. Princeton, N.J.: Princeton University Press, 1989.

Philostratus:

The Life of Apollonius of Tyana. Edited by F. C. Conybeare. 2 vols. LCL. Cambridge, Mass.: Harvard University Press, 1912.

Plato:

Plato. Edited by H. N. Fowler, W. R. M. Lamb et al. 12 vols. LCL. Cambridge, Mass.: Harvard University Press, 1914-1935.
Werke in acht Bänden: Griechisch und Deutsch. Sonderausgabe nach der 2./3. unveränderten Auflage. Edited by Gunther Eigler. Darmstadt: Wissenschaftliche Buchgesellschaft, 1990.

Pliny the Elder:

C. Plinius Secundus d. Ä: Naturkunde. Lateinisch-deutsch. Edited by R. König, G. Winkler and K. Brodersen. 37 vols. Tusculum. Zürich: Artemis & Winkler, 1973-1999.
Pliny: Natural History. Edited by H. Rackham. 10 vols. LCL. Cambridge, Mass.: Harvard University Press, 1938-1963.

Pliny the Younger:
Plinius Caecilius Secundus, Gaius: Briefe. Epistularum. Lateinisch-deutsch. Edited by H. Kasten. 7th ed. Tusculum. Zürich: Artemis & Winkler, 1995.
Pliny the Younger: Letters and Panegyricus. Edited by Betty Radice. 2 vols. LCL. Cambridge, Mass.: Harvard University Press, 1969.

Polybius:
Polybius: The Histories. Edited by W. R. Paton. 6 vols. LCL. Cambridge, Mass.: Harvard University Press, 1922-1927.

Pomponius Mela:
Pomponius Mela: Kreuzfahrt durch die Alte Welt. Edited by Kai Brodresen. Darmstadt: Wissenschaftliche Buchgesellschaft, 1994.
Pomponius Mela's Description of the World. Edited by Frank E. Romer. Ann Arbor: University of Michigan Press, 1998.

Seneca:
Seneca: Ad Lucilium; Epistulae Morales. Edited by Richard Gummere. 3 vols. LCL. Cambridge, Mass.: Harvard University Press, 1920–1926 [1962].
Seneca: Moral Essays. Edited by John W. Basore. 3 vols. LCL. Cambridge, Mass.: Harvard University Press, 1928-1932 [1998].

Strabo:
The Geography of Strabo. Edited by H. L. Jones. 8 vols. LCL. Cambridge, Mass.: Harvard University Press, 1917-1930.
Strabons Erdbeschreibung in siebzehn Büchern. 4 vols. Edited by Christoph G. Groskurd. Berlin: Nicolai, 1831-1934.

Suetonius:
Cäsarenleben. Edited by Max Heinemann. Stuttgart: Kröner, 1957.
Die Kaiserviten/Berühmte Männer; De vita Caesarum/De viris illustribus. Lateinisch-deutsch. Edited by Hans Martinet. Tusculum. Munich: Artemis & Winkler, 1997.
Suetonius. Edited by J. C. Rolfe. 2 vols. LCL. Cambridge, Mass.: Harvard University Press, 1997-1998 [1913-1914].

Tacitus:
Tactitus: Annalen. Edited by Walther Sontheimer. Stuttgart: Reclam, 1967.
Tacitus: Annalen. Lateinisch-deutsch. Edited by Manfred Fuhrmann. 2nd ed. Tusculum. Munich: Artemis & Winkler, 1992.
Tactitus: The Histories; The Annals. Edited by Clifford H. Moore and John Jackson. 4 vols. LCL. Cambridge, Mass.: Harvard University Press, 1969.

Thucydides:
The History of the Peloponnesian War. Translated by R. Crawley. London: Longmans, Green, 1874.

Valerius Maximus:
Facta et dicta memorabilia; Denkwürdige Tagen und Worte. Edited by Ursula Blank-Sangmeister. Stuttgart: Reclam, 1991.
Factorum et dictorum memorabilium. Edited by C. Kempf. Leipzig: Teubner, 1966 [1888].

Vegetius, Flavius:
Flavius Vegetius Renatus: Epitoma Rei Militaris. Edited by Leo V. Stelten. New York: Peter Lang, 1990.
Publius Flavius Vegetius Renatus: Epitoma rei militaris, Abriß des Militärwesens; lateinisch und deutsch mit Einleitung, Erläuterungen und Indices. Edited by Friedhelm L. Müller. Stuttgart: Steiner, 1997.
Vegetius: Epitome of Military Science; Translated with Notes and Introduction. Edited by Nicholas P. Milner. Translated Texts for Historians 16. Liverpool: Liverpool University Press, 1993 [2nd ed., 1996].
Vegetius Renatus: Epitoma rei militaris. Edited by Alf Önnerfors. Stuttgart: Teubner, 1995.

Xenophon of Ephesus:
Die Waffen des Eros oder Anthia und Habrokomas: Roman. Edited by Bernhard Kytzler. Frankfurt: Ullstein, 1968.
Xenophon: Les Éphésiaques ou le roman d'Habrocomès et d'Anthia. Edited by Georges Dalmeyda. Paris: Les Belles Lettres, 1962 [1926].
Xenophon of Ephesus: An Ephesian Tale. Translated by Graham Anderson. In *Collected Ancient Greek Novels.* Edited by Bryan P. Reardon, 125-69. Berkeley: University of California Press, 1989.

B. Resources

Alexander, T. D., and B. S. Rosner, eds. *New Dictionary of Biblical Theology.* Downers Grove, Ill.: InterVarsity Press.
Avi-Yonah, Michael, and Ephraim Stern, eds. *Encyclopedia of Archaeological Excavations in the Holy Land.* 4 vols. Englewood Cliffs, N.J.: Prentice-Hall, 1975-1978.
Balz, Horst, and Schneider Gerhard, eds. *Exegetical Dictionary of the New Testament.* 3 vols. Grand Rapids: Eerdmans, 1990-1993. Original: *Exegetisches Wörterbuch zum Neuen Testament.* 2nd ed. 3 vols. Stuttgart: Kohlhammer,

1992 [1980-1983].

Bardenhewer, O., J. Zellinger and J. Martin. *Bibliothek der Kirchenväter*. 2. Reihe. 20 vols. Munich: Kösel, 1932-1939.

Bauer, Walter. *Griechisch-deutsches Wörterbuch zu den Schriften des Neuen Testaments und der frühchristlichen Literatur*. Edited by Kurt Aland and Barbara Aland. 6th ed. Berlin and New York: de Gruyter, 1988.

Bauer, Walter, William F. Arndt, F. Wilbur Ginrich, and Frederick W. Danker. *A Greek-English Lexicon of the New Testment and Other Early Christian Literature*. 3rd ed. Chicago: University of Chicago Press, 2000.

Baumgartner, Walter, et al. *Hebräisches und Aramäisches Lexikon zum Alten Testament*. 3rd ed. 5 vols. Leiden: Brill, 1967-1995.

Bautz, Friedrich Wilhelm. *Biographisch-bibliographisches Kirchenlexikon*. Hamm: Bautz, 1970-.

Berkowitz, L., and K. A. Squitier. *Thesaurus Linguae Graecae: Canon of Greek Authors*. 3rd ed. Oxford: Oxford University Press, 1990.

Beyer, Klaus. *Semitische Syntax im Neuen Testament*. Vol. 1, *Satzlehre Teil 1*. 2nd ed. StUNT 1. Göttingen: Vandenhoeck & Ruprecht, 1968 [1962].

Blass, F., A. Debrunner and F. Rehkopf. *Grammatik des neutestamentlichen Griechisch*. 17th ed. Göttingen: Vandenhoeck & Ruprecht, 1990 [14th ed., 1976; 1896].

Botterweck, G. Johannes, and Helmer Ringgren, eds. *Theological Dictionary of the Old Testament*. 13 vols. Grand Rapids: Eerdmans, 1977-2004. Original: *Theologisches Wörterbuch zum Alten Testament*. 10 vols. Stuttgart: Kohlhammer, 1970-2000.

Bromiley, G. W. ed. *The International Standard Bible Encyclopedia*. Grand Rapids: Eerdmans, 1979-1988.

Brown, Colin, ed. *The New International Dictionary of New Testament Theology*. 4 vols. Grand Rapids: Eerdmans, 1975-1978.

Buchwald, W., et al., eds. *Tusculum-Lexikon griechischer und lateinischer Autoren des Altertums und des Mittelalters*. 3rd ed. Munich: Artemis, 1982 [1963-1948].

Cancik, Hubert, and Helmuth Schneider, eds. *Der Neue Pauly: Enzyklopädie der Antike*. 15 vols. Stuttgart and Weimer: Metzler, 1996-2002. English: *Brill's New Pauly: Encyclopaedia of the Ancient World*. 20 vols. Leiden: Brill, 2001-.

Clines, David J. A., ed. *The Dictionary of Classical Hebrew*. Sheffield: Academic Press, 1993-.

Coenen, L., and K. Haacker, eds. *Theologisches Begriffslexikon zum Neuen Testament*. Rev. ed. 2 vols. Wuppertal: Brockhaus, 1997-2000.

Davids, P. H., and R. P. Martin, eds. *Dictionary of the Later New Testament and Its Developments*. Downers Grove, Ill.: InterVarsity Press, 1997.

Encyclopaedia Judaica. 16 vols. Jerusalem: Keter, 1974 [1972].

Evans, C. A., and S. E. Porter. *Dictionary of New Testament Background*. Downers Grove, Ill.: InterVarsity Press, 2000.

Fahlbusch, Erwin, et al., eds. *Evangelisches Kirchenlexikon: Internationale theologische Enzyklopädie.* 3rd ed. 5 vols. Göttingen: Vandenhoeck & Ruprecht, 1986-1997.

Fraser, Peter M., and Edwin Matthews, eds. *A Lexicon of Greek Personal Names.* 3 vols. in 4. Oxford: Oxford University Press, 1987-2000.

Freedman, D. N., ed. *Anchor Bible Dictionary.* 6 vols. New York: Doubleday, 1992.

Görg, Manfred, and Bernhard Lang, eds. *Neues Bibel-Lexikon.* 3 vols. Zürich: Benziger, 1988-2001.

Green, J. B., S. McKnight, and I. H. Marshall, eds. *Dictionary of Jesus and the Gospels.* Downers Grove, Ill.: InterVarsity Press, 1992.

Hawthorne, G. F., R. P. Martin, and D. G. Reid, eds. *Dictionary of Paul and His Letters.* Downers Grove, Ill.: InterVarsity Press, 1993.

Hoffmann, Ernst G., and Heinrich von Siebenthal. *Griechische Grammatik zum Neuen Testament.* Riehen: Immanuel, 1985.

Hornblower, Simon, and Antony Spawforth. *Oxford Classical Dictionary.* 3rd ed. Oxford: Oxford University Press, 1996.

Douglas, J. D., ed. *The Illustrated Bible Dictionary.* Leicester: Inter-Varsity Press; Downers Grove, Ill.: InterVarsity Press, 1980.

Haase, Wolfgang, and Hildegard Temporini, eds. *Aufstieg und Niedergang der römischen Welt.* Berlin: de Gruyter, 1972-.

Jenni, Ernst, and Claus Westermann, eds. *Theological Lexicon of the Old Testament.* 3 vols. Peabody, Mass.: Hendrickson, 1997. Original: *Theologisches Handwörterbuch zum Alten Testament.* 2 vols. Munich: Kaiser, 1971-1976.

Kasper, Walter, ed. *Lexikon für Theologie und Kirche.* 3rd ed. 11 vols. Freiburg: Herder, 1993-2000.

Kittel, Gerhard, and Gerhard Friedrich, eds. *Theological Dictionary of the New Testament.* 10 vols. Grand Rapids: Eerdmans, 1964-1976. Original: *Theologische Wörterbuch zum Neuen Testament.* 10 vols. Stuttgart: Kohlhammer, 1933-1979.

Koehler, Ludwig, Walter Baumgartner, and Johann Jakob Stamm. *The Hebrew and Aramaic Lexicon of the Old Testament in English.* 4 vols. Leiden: Brill, 1994-1999.

Liddell, H. G., R. Scott, and H. S. Jones. *A Greek-English Lexicon.* 9th ed., with revised supplement, by H. S. Jones and R. McKenzie. Oxford: Oxford University Press, 1996 [1940; 1966].

Lietaert Peerbolte, Lambertus J. *Paul the Missionary.* CBET 34. Leuven: Peeters, 2003.

Lipinski, Edward, ed. *Dictionnaire de la civilisation phénicienne et punique.* Turnhout: Brepols, 1992.

Louw, Johannes P., and Eugene A. Nida. *Greek-English Lexicon of the New Testament Based on Semantic Domains.* 2nd ed. New York: United Bible Society, 1989 [1988].

Lust, J., E. Eynikel, and K. Hauspie. *A Greek-English Lexicon of the Septuagint.* 2 vols. Stuttgart: Deutsche Bibelgesellschaft, 1992-1996.

Meyers, Eric M., ed. *Oxford Encyclopedia of Archaeology in the Near East.* 5 vols. Oxford: Oxford University Press, 1997.

Metzger, Bruce M. *A Textual Commentary on the Greek New Testament.* 2nd ed. Stuttgart and New York: United Bible Societies, 1994.

Moulton, James H., and George Milligan. *The Vocabulary of the Greek Testament Illustrated from the Papyri and other Non-literary Sources.* Grand Rapids: Eerdmans, 1982 [1930].

Oxford English Dictionary. Edited by J. A. Simpson and E. S. C. Weiner. 2nd ed. (online). Oxford: Oxford University Press, 1989.

Pauly, August Friedrich von, and Georg Wissowa et al. *Paulys Realencyclopädie der classischen Altertumswissenschaft.* 49 vols. Stuttgart: Metzler, 1893-1963; *Supplement,* 1903-1978.

Reicke, B., and L. Rost., eds. *Biblisch-historisches Handwörterbuch: Landeskunde, Geschichte, Religion, Kultur.* 4 vols. Göttingen: Vandenhoeck & Ruprecht, 1962-1966.

Ronchi, Giulia. *Lexicon theonymon rerumque sacrarum et divinarum ad Aegyptum pertinentium quae in papyris ostracis titulis Graecis Latinisque in Aegypto repertis laudantur.* 5 vols. Milan: Istituto Editoriale Cisalpino, La Goliardica, 1974-1977.

Schiffman, Lawrence H., and James C. VanderKam, eds. *Encyclopedia of the Dead Sea Scrolls.* 2 vols. Oxford: Oxford University Press, 2000.

Spicq, Ceslas. *Theological Lexicon of the New Testament.* 3 vols. Peabody, Mass.: Hendrickson, 1995. Original: *Lexique théologique du Nouveau Testament.* 3 vols. Fribourg: Editions Universitaires; Paris: Cerf, 1991 [1978-1982].

Stern, Ephraim, ed. *The New Encyclopedia of Archaeological Excavations in the Holy Land.* 4 vols. Jerusalem: Israel Exploration Society; New York: Carta and Simon & Schuster, 1993.

Stillwell, Richard, ed. *The Princeton Encyclopedia of Classical Sites.* Princeton, N.J.: Princeton University Press, 1976.

Strack, Hermann L., and Paul Billerbeck. *Kommentar zum Neuen Testament aus Talmud und Midrasch.* 6 vols. Munich: Beck, 1922-1961 [10th ed., 1994].

Toorn, Karel van der, et al. *Dictionary of Deities and Demons in the Bible.* Leiden: Brill, 1995.

VanGemeren, Willem A., ed. *New International Dictionary of Old Testament Theology and Exegesis.* Grand Rapids: Zondervan, 1997.

Ziegler, Konrad, Walter Sontheimer, and Hans Gärtner, eds. *Der Kleine Pauly: Lexikon der Antike.* 5 vols. Munich: Deutscher Taschenbuchverlag, 1979 [1964-1975].

C. Maps

Avi-Yonah, Michael. *Map of Roman Palestine.* 2nd ed. London: Oxford University Press, 1940.

————. *The Holy Land from the Persian to the Arab Conquest (536 BC—AD 640).* Rev. ed. Grand Rapids: Baker, 1977.

Calder, W. M., and G. E. Bean. *A Classical Map of Asia Minor.* London: British Institute of Archaeology at Ankara, 1958.

Hammond, N. G. L., ed. *Atlas of the Greek and Roman World in Antiquity.* Park Ridge, N.J.: Noyes, 1981.

Höhne, Ernst, and Hermann Wahle. *Palästina: Historisch-archäologische Karte.* Göttingen: Vandenhoeck & Ruprecht, 1981 [Maps, 1979].

Mittmann, Siegfried, and Götz Schmitt, eds. *Tübinger Bibelatlas: Auf der Grundlage des Tübinger Atlas des Vorderen Orients* (= *Tübingen Bible Atlas: Based on the Tübingen Atlas of the Near and Middle East*). Stuttgart: Deutsche Bibelgesellschaft, 2001.

Pritchard, James B., and Othmar Keel, eds. *Herders grosser Bibel-Atlas.* Freiburg: Herder, 1989.

Talbert, Richard J. A., ed. *Atlas of Classical History.* New York: Macmillan, 1985.

————, ed. *Barrington Atlas of the Greek and Roman World.* Princeton, N.J.: Princeton University Press, 2000.

————, ed. *Barrington Atlas of the Greek and Roman World: Map-by-Map Directory.* 2 vols. Princeton, N.J.: Princeton University Press, 2000.

Tsafrir, Yoram, Leah di Segni, and Judith Green. *Iudaea-Palaestina: Eretz Israel in the Hellenistic, Roman and Byzantine Periods; Maps and Gazetteer.* Tabula Imperii Romani. Jerusalem: Israel Academy of Sciences and Humanities, 1994.

Tübinger Atlas des Vorderen Orients. Wiesbaden: Reichert, 1977-1994.

II. COMMENTARIES

Achtemeier, Paul J. *1 Peter.* Hermeneia. Minneapolis: Fortress, 1996.

Althaus, Paul. *Der Brief an die Römer.* 11th ed. NTD 6. Göttingen: Vandenhoeck & Ruprecht, 1970 [1935].

Barrett, C. K. *The Gospel According to St. John.* 2nd ed. London: SPCK, 1978 [1955].

————. *The Acts of the Apostles.* 2 vols. ICC. Edinburgh: T & T Clark, 1994-1998.

————. *A Commentary on the First Epistle to the Corinthians.* BNTC. London: Black, 1968.

Barth, Markus. *Ephesians.* 2 vols. AncB 34-34A. New York: Doubleday, 1974.

Barth, Markus, and Helmut Blanke. *Colossians.* AncB 34B. New York: Doubleday, 1994.

Beale, Gregory K. *The Book of Revelation.* NIGTC. Grand Rapids: Eerdmans; Carlisle: Paternoster, 1999.

Becker, Jürgen. *Der Brief an die Galater.* In *Die Briefe an die Galater, Epheser und Kolosser,* by Jürgen Becker und Ulrich Luz, 7-103. NTD 8.1. Göttingen: Vandenhoeck & Ruprecht, 1998.

Bengel, Johann A. *Gnomon Novi Testamenti.* Edited by P. Steudel. 8th ed. Stuttgart: Steinkopf, 1887 [1742].

Best, Ernest. *A Critical and Exegetical Commentary on Ephesians.* ICC. Edinburgh: T & T Clark, 1998.

Betz, Hans Dieter. *Galatians.* Hermeneia. Philadelphia: Fortress, 1979.

Bock, Darrell L. *Luke.* 2 vols. BECNT. Grand Rapids: Baker, 1995-1996.

Bovon, François. *Das Evangelium nach Lukas.* 3 vols. EKK 3. Zürich: Benziger; Neukirchen-Vluyn: Neukirchener Verlag, 1989-2001.

Braun, Herbert. *An die Hebräer.* HNT 14. Tübingen: Mohr-Siebeck, 1984.

Brown, Raymond E. *The Epistles of John.* AncB 30. New York: Doubleday, 1982.

Brox, Norbert. *Der erste Petrusbrief.* 3rd ed. EKK 21. Zürich: Benzinger; Neukirchen-Vluyn: Neukirchener Verlag, 1989 [1979].

Bruce, F. F. *The Book of the Acts.* Rev. ed. NICNT. Grand Rapids: Eerdmans, 1988 [1979].

————. *The Epistle to the Galatians.* NIGTC. Grand Rapids: Eerdmans, 1982.

————. *The Epistle to the Colossians.* 9th ed. NICNT. Grand Rapids: Eerdmans, 1977 [1957].

————. *1 and 2 Thessalonians.* WBC 45. Waco, Tex.: Word, 1982.

Bultmann, Rudolf. *Das Evangelium des Johannes.* 10th ed. KEK 2. Göttingen: Vandenhoeck & Ruprecht, 1978. English: *The Gospel of John: A Commentary.* Oxford: Blackwell, 1971.

————. *Der Zweite Brief an die Korinther.* Edited by E.Dinkler. 2nd ed. KEK Sonderband. Göttingen: Vandenhoeck & Ruprecht, 1976 [1988]. English: *The Second Letter to the Corinthians.* Minneapolis: Augsburg, 1985.

Burchard, Christoph. *Der Jakobusbrief.* HNT 15.1. Tübingen: Mohr-Siebeck, 2000.

Burton, Ernest De Witt. *A Critical and Exegetical Commentary on the Epistle to the Galatians.* ICC. Edinburgh: T & T Clark, 1921.

Caird, George B. *The Revelation of Saint John.* BNTC. Peabody: Hendrickson, 1971 [1966].

Carson, Donald A. *Matthew.* EBC 8. Grand Rapids: Zondervan, 1984.

————. *John.* PNTC. Grand Rapids: Eerdmans; Leicester: Inter-Varsity, 1991.

Childs, Brevard S. *The Book of Exodus*. 3rd ed. Philadelphia: Westminster Press, 1976 [1974].

———. *Isaiah*. OTL. Louisville: Westminster John Knox, 2001.

Collins, Raymond R. *First Corinthians*. Sacra Pagina 7. Collegeville, Minn.: Liturgical Press, 1999.

Conzelmann, Hans. *Die Apostelgeschichte*. 2nd ed. HNT 7. Tübingen: Mohr-Siebeck, 1972 [1963]. English: *Acts of the Apostles: A Commentary on the Acts of the Apostles*. Hermeneia. Philadelphia: Fortress, 1987.

———. *Der erste Brief an die Korinther*. 2nd ed. KEK 5. Göttingen: Vandenhoeck & Ruprecht, 1981 [1969]. English: *1 Corinthians*. Philadelphia: Fortress, 1975.

Cranfield, C. E. B. *The Gospel According to Saint Mark*. CGTC. Cambridge: Cambridge University Press, 1959.

———. *The Epistle to the Romans*. Corr. ed. 2 vols. ICC. Edinburgh: T & T Clark, 1980-1983 [1975-1979].

Davids, Peter H. *The Epistle of James*. NIGTC. Exeter: Paternoster, 1982.

———. *The First Epistle of Peter*. NICNT. Grand Rapids: Eerdmans, 1990.

Davies, William D., and Dale C. Allison. *The Gospel According to Saint Matthew*. 3 vols. ICC. Edinburgh: T & T Clark, 1988-1997.

Dibelius, Martin. *Die Pastoralbriefe*. Edited by H. Conzelmann. 4th ed. HNT 13. Tübingen: Mohr-Siebeck, 1966 [2nd ed., 1931; 1913].

———. *An die Thessalonicher I-II; An die Philipper*. 3rd ed. HNT 11. Tübingen: Mohr, 1937.

Dunn, James D. G. *Romans*. 2 vols. WBC 38A-B. Dallas: Word, 1988.

———. *The Epistle to the Galatians*. BNTC. London: Black, 1993.

———. *The Epistles to the Colossians and to Philemon*. NIGTC. Grand Rapids: Eerdmans; Carlisle: Paternoster, 1996.

———. *The Acts of the Apostles*. Epworth Commentaries. London: Epworth, 1996.

Eckey, Wilfried. *Die Apostelgeschichte: Der Weg des Evangeliums von Jerusalem nach Rom*. 2 vols. Neukirchen-Vluyn: Neukirchener Verlag, 2000.

Elliger, Karl. *Deuterojesaja*. BKAT 11.1. Neukirchen-Vluyn: Neukirchener Verlag, 1978.

———. *Das Buch der zwölf Kleinen Propheten II: Die Propheten Nahum, Habakuk, Zephanja, Haggai, Sacharja, Maleachi*. 5th ed. ATD 25. Göttingen: Vandenhoeck & Ruprecht, 1964.

Ellingworth, Paul. *The Epistle to the Hebrews*. NIGTC. Carlisle: Paternoster, 1993.

Elliott, John H. *1 Peter*. AncB 37B. New York: Doubleday 2000.

Ellis, E. Earle. *The Gospel of Luke*. NCBC. Grand Rapids: Eerdmans, 1991 [1966; 2nd ed., 1974].

Evans, Craig A. *Mark 8:27—16:20*. WBC 34B. Nashville: Nelson 2001.

Fee, Gordon D. *The First Epistle to the Corinthians*. NICNT. Grand Rapids: Eerdmans, 1987.

————. *Paul's Letter to the Philippians*. NICNT. Grand Rapids: Eerdmans, 1995.

————. *1 and 2 Timothy, Titus*. NIBC. Peabody, Mass.: Hendrickson, 1988 [San Francisco: Harper & Row, 1984].

Fitzmyer, Joseph A. *The Gospel According to Luke: Introduction, Translation, and Notes*. 2nd ed. 7th pr. 2 vols. AncB 28-28A. New York: Doubleday, 1986 [1981-1985].

————. *The Acts of the Apostles: A New Translation with Introduction and Commentary*. AncB 31. New York: Doubleday, 1998.

————. *Romans: A New Translation with Introduction and Commentary*. AncB 33. New York: Doubleday, 1993.

————. *The Letter to Philemon: A New Translation with Introduction and Commentary*. AncB 34C. New York: Doubleday, 2000.

France, R. T. *The Gospel According to Matthew*. TNTC. Leicester: Inter-Varsity Press, 1988.

————. *The Gospel of Mark*. NIGTC. Grand Rapids: Eerdmans, 2002.

Gaechter, P. *Das Matthäus-Evangelium*. Innsbruck: Tyrolia, 1963.

Giesen, Heinz. *Die Offenbarung des Johannes*. RNT. Regensburg: Pustet, 1997.

Gnilka, Joachim. *Das Matthäusevangelium*. 2nd ed. 2 vols. HThKNT 1.1-2. Freiburg: Herder, 1988 [1986].

————. *Das Evangelium nach Markus*. 2 vols. EKK 2.1-2. Zürich: Benziger; Neukirchen-Vluyn: Neukirchener Verlag, 1978-1979.

————. *Der Philipperbrief*. 4th ed. HThKNT 10.3. Freiburg: Herder, 1987 [1968].

————. *Der Kolosserbrief*. HThKNT 10.1. Freiburg: Herder, 1980.

Gooding, David. *True to the Faith: A Fresh Approach to the Acts of the Apostles*. London: Hodder & Stoughton, 1990.

Goppelt, Leonhard. *Der erste Petrusbrief*. KEK 12.1. Göttingen: Vandenhoeck & Ruprecht, 1978.

Green, Joel. *The Gospel of Luke*. NICNT. Grand Rapids: Eerdmans, 1997.

Grundmann, Walter. *Das Evangelium nach Matthäus*. 6th ed. ThHK 1. Berlin: Evangelische Verlagsanstalt, 1986 [1968].

————. *Das Evangelium nach Lukas*. 10th ed. ThHK 3. Berlin: Evangelische Verlagsanstalt, 1984 [1961].

Guelich, Robert A. *Mark 1—8:26*. WBC 34A. Dallas: Word, 1989.

Gundry, Robert H. *Mark: A Commentary on His Apology for the Cross*. Grand Rapids: Eerdmans, 1993.

Hadorn, Wilhelm. *Die Offenbarung des Johannes*. ThHNT 18. Leipzig: Deichert, 1928.

Haenchen, Ernst. *Die Apostelgeschichte*. 7th ed. KEK 3. Göttingen: Vandenhoeck & Ruprecht, 1977 [1959]. English: *The Acts of the Apostles: A Commentary*. Philadelphia: Westminster Press, 1971.

Hagner, Donald A. *Matthew*. 2 vols. WBC 33A-B. Dallas: Word, 1993-1995.

————. *Hebrews*. NIBC 14. Peabody, Mass.: Hendrickson, 1993 [1983; 1990].

Hamilton, Victor P. *The Book of Genesis*. 2 vols. NICOT. Grand Rapids: Eerdmans, 1990-1995.

Hasler, Victor. *Die Briefe an Timotheus und Titus*. ZBK 12. Zürich: Theologischer Verlag, 1978.

Hawthorne, Gerald F. *Philippians*. WBC 43. Waco, Tex.: Word, 1983.

Hays, Richard B. *First Corinthians*. Interpretation. Louisville: Knox, 1997.

Hengstenberg, Ernst Wilhelm. *Die Offenbarung des heiligen Johannes*. Berlin: Oehmigke, 1849 [1951].

Hill, David. *The Gospel of Matthew*. NCBC. Grand Rapids: Eerdmans, 1972.

Hoehner, Harold W. *Ephesians: An Exegetical Commentary*. Grand Rapids: Baker, 2002.

Holtz, Gottfried. *Die Pastoralbriefe*. 4th ed. ThHK 13. Berlin: Evangelische Verlagsanstalt, 1986 [1966].

Holtz, Traugott. *Der erste Brief an die Thessalonicher*. EKK 13. Zürich: Benziger; Neukirchen-Vluyn: Neukirchener Verlag, 1986.

Horst, Friedrich. *Die Zwölf Kleinen Propheten: Nahum bis Maleachi*. HAT 14. Tübingen: Mohr-Siebeck, 1938.

Hübner, Hans. *An Philemon; An die Kolosser; An die Epheser*. HNT 12. Tübingen: Mohr-Siebeck, 1997.

Jeremias, Joachim. *Die Briefe an Timotheus und Titus*. 12th ed. NTD 9. Göttingen: Vandenhoeck & Ruprecht, 1981 [1936].

Jervell, Jacob. *Die Apostelgeschichte*. KEK 3. Göttingen: Vandenhoeck & Ruprecht, 1998.

Johnson, Luke T. *The Acts of the Apostles*. Sacra Pagina 5. Collegeville, Minn.: Liturgical Press, 1992.

—————. *The First and Second Letters to Timothy*. AncB 35A. New York: Doubleday, 2001.

Kaiser, Otto. *Der Prophet Jesaja, Kapitel 13-39*. 3rd ed. ATD 18. Göttingen: Vandenhoeck & Ruprecht, 1983.

Käsemann, Ernst. *An die Römer*. 4th ed. HNT 8a. Tübingen: Mohr-Siebeck, 1980 [1973]. English: *Commentary on Romans*. Grand Rapids: Eerdmans, 1980.

Keener, Craig S. *A Commentary on the Gospel of Matthew*. Grand Rapids: Eerdmans, 1999.

Kelly, John N. D. *A Commentary on the Pastoral Epistles*. BNTC. London: Black, 1963 [1986].

Klauck, Hans-Josef. *1. Korintherbrief*. 3rd ed. NEB 7. Würzburg: Echter, 1993 [1984].

Klostermann, E. *Das Matthäusevangelium*. 4th ed. HNT 4. Tübingen: Mohr-Siebeck, 1971 [1909].

Knight, George W. *The Pastoral Epistles*. NIGTC. Grand Rapids: Eerdmans, 1992.

Koester, Craig R. *Hebrews*. AncB 36. New York: Doubleday, 2001.

Kraft, Heinrich. *Die Offenbarung des Johannes*. HNT 16a. Tübingen: Mohr-Siebeck, 1974.

Kraus, Hans-Joachim. *Psalmen.* 2nd ed. 2 vols. BKAT 15.1-2. Neukirchen-Vluyn: Neukirchener Verlag, 1961. English: *Psalms: A Continental Commentary.* 2 vols. Minneapolis: Fortress, 1988-1993.

Kremer, Jakob. *Der Erste Brief an die Korinther.* RNT. Regensburg: Pustet, 1997.

Lambrecht, Jan. *Second Corinthians.* Sacra Pagina 8. Collegeville, Minn.: Liturgical Press, 1999.

Lang, Friedrich. *Die Briefe an die Korinther.* NTD 7. Göttingen: Vandenhoeck & Ruprecht, 1986.

Lietzmann, Hans. *An die Korinther I.II.* Augmented by W. G. Kümmel. 5th ed. HNT 9. Tübingen: Mohr-Siebeck, 1969.

Lightfoot, J. B. *Saint Paul's Epistle to the Galatians.* London: Macmillan, 1881.

———. *Saint Paul's Epistles to the Colossians and to Philemon.* Rev. ed. London: Macmillan, 1886.

Lincoln, Andrew T. *Ephesians.* WBC 42. Dallas: Word, 1990.

Lindemann, Andreas. *Der Erste Korintherbrief.* HNT 9.1. Tübingen: Mohr-Siebeck, 2000.

Lohmeyer, Ernst. *Das Evangelium des Matthäus.* Edited by W. Schmauch. 2nd ed. KEK Sonderband. Göttingen: Vandenhoeck & Ruprecht, 1958.

———. *Die Briefe an die Philipper, an die Kolosser und an Philemon.* 15th ed. KEK 9. Göttingen: Vandenhoeck & Ruprecht, 1977 [1965].

Lohse, Eduard. *Die Briefe an die Kolosser und an Philemon.* 2nd ed. KEK 9.2. Göttingen: Vandenhoeck & Ruprecht, 1977 [1968]. English: *A Commentary on the Epistles to the Colossians and to Philemon.* Philadelphia: Fortress, 1971.

Longenecker, Richard N. *Galatians.* WBC 31. Dallas: Word, 1990.

Luz, Ulrich. *Das Evangelium nach Matthäus.* 4 vols. EKK 1. Zürich: Benzinger; Neukirchen-Vluyn: Neukirchener Verlag, 1985-2002. English: *Matthew 1—7: A Commentary.* Minneapolis: Augsburg, 1989; *Matthew 8—20: A Commentary.* Hermeneia. Minneapolis: Fortress, 2001.

———. *Der Brief an die Epheser.* In *Die Briefe an die Galater, Epheser und Kolosser,* by Jürgen Becker und Ulrich Luz, 105-80. NTD 8.1. Göttingen: Vandenhoeck & Ruprecht, 1998.

———. *Der Brief an die Kolosser.* In *Die Briefe an die Galater, Epheser und Kolosser,* by Jürgen Becker und Ulrich Luz, 181-244. NTD 8.1. Göttingen: Vandenhoeck & Ruprecht, 1998.

Malherbe, Abraham J. *The Letters to the Thessalonians.* AncB 32B. New York: Doubleday, 2000.

Manson, William. *The Epistle to the Hebrews.* London: Hodder & Stoughton, 1951.

Marcus, Joel. *Mark 1—8.* AncB 27. New York: Doubleday, 2000.

Marshall, I. Howard. *The Gospel of Luke.* NIGTC. Exeter: Paternoster, 1978.

———. *The Acts of the Apostles.* TNTC. Leicester: Inter-Varsity Press, 1980.

———. *1 and 2 Thessalonians.* NCBC. Grand Rapids: Eerdmans, 1983.

————. *The Pastoral Epistles.* ICC. Edinburgh: T & T Clark, 1999.

————. *1 Peter.* IVP New Testament Commentary Series. Leicester: Inter-Varsity Press, 1991.

————. *The Epistles of John.* NICNT. Grand Rapids: Eerdmans, 1978.

Martin, Ralph P. *2 Corinthians.* WBC 40. Waco, Tex.: Word, 1986.

Martyn. J. Louis. *Galatians.* AncB 33A. New York: Doubleday, 1997.

Merkel, Helmut. *Die Pastoralbriefe.* NTD 9.1. Göttingen: Vandenhoeck & Ruprecht, 1991.

Meyer, Heinrich A. W. *Kritisch-Exegetisches Handbuch über die Apostelgeschichte.* 4th ed. KEK 3. Göttingen: Vandenhoeck & Ruprecht, 1896 [1835].

Michel, Otto. *Der Brief an die Römer.* 5th ed. KEK 4. Göttingen: Vandenhoeck & Ruprecht, 1978.

————. *Der Brief an die Hebräer.* 7th ed. KEK 13. Göttingen: Vandenhoeck & Ruprecht, 1975.

Moo, Douglas J. *The Epistle to the Romans.* NICNT. Grand Rapids: Eerdmans, 1996.

Moore, Carey A. *Judith.* AncB 40. Garden City, N.Y.: Doubleday, 1985.

Moule, C. F. D. *The Epistles of Paul the Apostle to the Colossians and to Philemon.* CGTC. Cambridge: Cambridge University Press, 1968 [1957].

Mounce, Robert H. *The Book of Revelation.* Rev. ed. NICNT. Grand Rapids: Eerdmans, 1998.

Mounce, William D. *Pastoral Epistles.* WBC 46. Nashville: Nelson, 2000.

Müller, Ulrich B. *Die Offenbarung des Johannes.* ÖTKNT 19. Gütersloh: Mohn, 1984.

Munck, Johannes. *The Acts of the Apostles.* AncB 31. New York: Doubleday, 1967.

Mussner, Franz. *Der Galaterbrief.* 5th ed. HThKNT 9. Freiburg: Herder, 1988 [1974].

————. *Der Jakobusbrief.* 5th ed. HThKNT 13.1. Freiburg: Herder, 1987.

Neil, William. *The Acts of the Apostles.* NCBC. Grand Rapids: Eerdmans, 1987 [1973].

Nolland, John. *Luke.* 3 vols. WBC 35A-C. Dallas: Word, 1989-1993.

Oberlinner, Lorenz. *Die Pastoralbriefe.* Vol. 1, *Kommentar zum ersten Timotheusbrief.* HThKNT 9. Freiburg: Herder, 1994.

O'Brien, Peter T. *The Letter to the Ephesians.* PNTC. Grand Rapids: Eerdmans, 1999.

————. *The Epistle to the Philippians.* NIGTC. Grand Rapids: Eerdmans, 1991.

————. *Colossians, Philemon.* WBC 44. Waco, Tex.: Word, 1982.

Osborne, Grant R. *Revelation.* BECNT. Grand Rapids: Baker, 2002.

Oswalt, John N. *The Book of Isaiah.* 2 vols. NICOT. Grand Rapids: Eerdmans, 1986-1998.

Pesch, Rudolf. *Das Markusevangelium.* 5th ed. 2 vols. HThKNT 2. Freiburg: Herder, 1989-1991 [1976-1977].

————. *Die Apostelgeschichte.* 2 vols. EKK 5. Zürich: Benzinger; Neukirchen-Vluyn: Neukirchener Verlag, 1986.

Pokorný, Petr. *Der Brief des Paulus an die Kolosser.* 2nd. ed. ThHK 10.1. Berlin: Evangelische Verlagsanstalt, 1990 [1987].

Ramsay, William M. *A Historical Commentary on St. Paul's Epistle to the Galatians.* 2nd ed. London: Hodder & Stoughton, 1900 [1899].

Reicke, Bo. *The Epistles of James, Peter and Jude.* AncB. Garden City: Doubleday, 1964.

Robertson, Archibald T., and Alfred Plummer. *The First Epistle of St. Paul to the Corinthians.* ICC. Edinburgh: T & T Clark, 1914.

Roloff, Jürgen. *Die Apostelgeschichte.* 2nd ed. NTD 5. Göttingen: Vandenhoeck & Ruprecht, 1988 [1981].

————. *Der erste Brief an Timotheus.* EKK 15. Zürich: Benzinger; Neukirchen-Vluyn: Neukirchener Verlag, 1988.

Sand, Alexander. *Das Evangelium nach Matthäus.* RNT. Regensburg: Pustet, 1986.

Schille, Gottfried. *Die Apostelgeschichte des Lukas.* 3rd ed. ThHK 5. Berlin: Evangelische Verlagsanstalt, 1989 [1983].

Schlatter, Adolf. *Der Evangelist Matthäus.* 6th ed. Stuttgart: Calwer, 1963 [1948].

————. *Das Evangelium des Lukas: Aus seinen Quellen erklärt.* 3rd ed. Stuttgart: Calwer, 1975.

————. *Der Evangelist Johannes: Ein Kommentar zum vierten Evangelium.* 4th ed. Stuttgart: Calwer, 1975.

————. *Gottes Gerechtigkeit: Ein Kommentar zum Römerbrief.* 5th ed. Stuttgart: Calwer, 1975 [1935].

————. *Paulus der Bote Jesu: Eine Deutung seiner Briefe an die Korinther.* Stuttgart: Calwer, 1982 [1934].

————. *Die Kirche der Griechen im Urteil des Paulus: Eine Auslegung seiner Briefe an Timotheus und Titus.* 3rd ed. Stuttgart: Calwer, 1983 [1936].

Schlier, Heinrich. *Der Römerbrief.* 3rd ed. HThKNT 6. Freiburg: Herder, 1987 [1977].

————. *Der Brief an die Galater.* 6th ed. KEK 7. Göttingen: Vandenhoeck & Ruprecht, 1989 [1949].

Schnackenburg, Rudolf. *Das Johannesevangelium.* 6th ed. 3 vols. HThKNT IV. Freiburg: Herder, 1986-1990 [5th ed., 1965-1975]. English: *The Gospel According to St. John.* 3 vols. London: Burns & Oates, 1968-1982.

————. *Der Brief an die Epheser.* EKK 10. Neukirchen-Vluyn: Neukirchener Verlag, 1982.

Schneider, Gerhard. *Die Apostelgeschichte.* 2 vols. HThKNT 5. Freiburg: Herder, 1980-1982.

Schniewind, Julius. *Das Evangelium nach Matthäus.* 12th ed. NTD 2. Göttingen: Vandenhoeck & Ruprecht, 1968 [1936].

Schrage, Wolfgang. *Der erste Brief an die Korinther.* 4 vols. EKK 7. Zürich: Benzinger; Neukirchen-Vluyn: Neukirchener Verlag, 1991-2001.

Schürmann, Heinz. *Das Lukasevangelium.* 2 vols. HThKNT 3. Freiburg: Herder, 1990-1994 [1969].

Schweizer, Eduard. *Das Evangelium nach Matthäus.* 4th ed. NTD 2. Göttingen: Vandenhoeck & Ruprecht, 1984 [1973]. English: *The Good News According to Matthew.* Atlanta: John Knox Press, 1975.

———. *Der Brief an die Kolosser.* EKK 12. Neukirchen-Vluyn: Neukirchener Verlas, 1976.

Scott, James M. *2 Corinthians.* NIBC. Carlisle: Paternoster; Peabody, Mass.: Hendrickson, 1998.

Selwyn, Edward G. *The First Epistle of St. Peter.* 2nd ed. London: Macmillan, 1947.

Senior, Donald. *1 and 2 Peter.* New Testament Message 20. Wilmington, Del.: Glazier, 1980.

Spicq, Ceslas. *Les Épîtres pastorales.* 4th ed. 2 vols. in 1. Études Bibliques. Paris: Gabalda, 1969 [1947].

———. *L'Épître aux Hébreux.* 2 vols. Études bibliques. Paris: Gabalda, 1952-1953.

Stählin, Gustav. *Die Apostelgeschichte.* NTD 5. Göttingen: Vandenhoeck & Ruprecht, 1962.

Stuhlmacher, Peter. *Der Brief an die Römer.* NTD 6. Göttingen: Vandenhoeck & Ruprecht, 1989. English: *Paul's Letter to the Romans: A Commentary.* Louisville: Westminster John Knox, 1994.

———. *Der Brief an Philemon.* 2nd ed. EKK 18. Zürich: Benzinger; Neukirchen-Vluyn: Neukirchener Verlag, 1981 [1975].

Taylor, Vincent. *The Gospel According to St. Mark.* 2nd ed. Thornapple Commentaries. Grand Rapids: Baker, 1981 [London: Macmillan, 1966].

Thiselton, Anthony C. *The First Epistle to the Corinthians.* NIGTC. Grand Rapids: Eerdmans, 2000.

Thrall, Margaret. *II Corinthians.* 2 vols. ICC. Edinburgh: T & T Clark, 1994-2000.

Verhoef, Pieter A. *The Books of Haggai and Malachi.* NICOT. Grand Rapids: Eerdmans, 1987.

Volz, Paul. *Jesaja übersetzt und erklärt.* KAT 9. Leipzig: Deichert, 1932.

Wanamaker, Charles A. *The Epistles to the Thessalonians.* NIGTC. Exeter: Paternoster; Grand Rapids: Eerdmans, 1990.

Weiser, Alfons. *Die Apostelgeschichte.* 2nd ed. 2 vols. ÖTKNT 5.1-2 Gütersloh: Mohn; Würzburg: Echter, 1989 [1981-1985].

Weiss, Hans-Friedrich. *Der Brief an die Hebräer.* KEK 13. Göttingen: Vandenhoeck & Ruprecht, 1991.

Wenham, Gordon J. *Genesis.* 2 vols. WBC 1-2. Waco, Tex., and Dallas: Word, 1987-1994.

Westermann, Claus. *Genesis.* Vol. 1, *Genesis 1—11.* BKAT 1.1. Neukirchen-Vluyn: Neukirchener Verlag, 1974. English: *Genesis 1—11. A Commentary.* Minneapolis: Augsburg, 1984.

————. *Das Buch Jesaja Kap. 40-66.* 5th ed. ATD 19. Göttingen: Vandenhoeck & Ruprecht, 1986 [1970].

Wiefel, Wolfgang. *Das Evangelium nach Lukas.* ThHK 3. Berlin: Evangelische Verlagsanstalt, 1988.

Wilckens, Ulrich. *Das Evangelium nach Johannes.* NTD 4. Göttingen: Vandenhoeck & Ruprecht, 1998.

————. *Der Brief an die Römer.* 3 vols. EKK 6. Neukirchen-Vluyn: Neukirchener Verlag; Einsiedeln: Benzinger, 1978-1982.

Witherington, Ben. *The Gospel of Mark: A Socio-Rhetorical Commentary.* Grand Rapids: Eerdmans, 2001.

————. *The Acts of the Apostles: A Socio-Rhetorical Commentary.* Grand Rapids: Eerdmans, 1998.

Wolff, Christian. *Der erste Brief des Paulus an die Korinther II.* 3rd ed. ThHK 7.2. Berlin: Evangelische Verlagsanstalt, 1990 [1982].

————. *Der zweite Brief des Paulus an die Korinther.* ThHK 8. Berlin: Evangelische Verlagsanstalt, 1989.

Wolter, Michael. *Der Brief an die Kolosser; Der Brief an Philemon.* ÖTKNT 12. Gütersloh: Mohn; Würzburg: Echter, 1993.

Wright, N. T. *The Epistles of Paul to the Colossians and to Philemon.* TNTC 12. Leicester: Inter-Varsity Press, 1986.

Zahn, Theodor. *Das Evangelium des Matthäus.* Wuppertal: Brockhaus, 1984 [4th ed., 1922].

————. *Das Evangelium des Lucas.* Wuppertal: Brockhaus, 1988 [4th ed., 1920].

————. *Die Apostelgeschichte des Lucas.* 3rd ed. Leipzig: Deichert, 1922 [1919; 1921].

————. *Der Brief des Paulus an die Galater.* Wuppertal: Brockhaus, 1990 [3rd ed., 1922].

Zeller, Dieter. *Der Brief an die Römer.* RNT. Regensburg: Pustet, 1985.

Zmijewski, Josef. *Die Apostelgeschichte.* RNT. Regensburg: Pustet, 1994.

III. SECONDARY LITERATURE

Abesamis, Carlos H. 1987. "The Mission of Jesus and Good News to the Poor: Exegetico-Pastoral Considerations for a Church in the Third World." *AJT* 1:429-60.

Abrahamsen, Valerie A. 1995. *Women and Worship at Philippi: Diana/Artemis and Other Cults in the Early Christian Era.* Portland, Maine: Astarte Shell Press.

Adloff, Kristlieb. 1986. "Die missionarische Existenz des Apostels Paulus nach dem Zweiten Korintherbrief." *Berliner Theologische Zeitschrift* 3:11-27.

Ådna, Jostein. 1997. "Die Heilige Schrift als Zeuge der Heidenmission: Die Rezeption von Amos 9,11-12 in Apg 15,16-18." In *Evangelium, Schriftauslegung, Kirche,* FS Peter Stuhlmacher, edited by J. Ådna et al., 1-23. Göttingen: Vandenhoeck & Ruprecht.

———. 1999a. *Jerusalemer Tempel und Tempelmarkt im 1. Jahrhundert n.Chr.* Abhandlungen des Deutschen Palästina-Vereins 25. Wiesbaden: Harrassowitz.

———. 1999b. "The Encounter of Jesus with the Gerasene Demoniac." In Chilton and Evans 1999b, 279-301.

———. 2000a. *Jesu Stellung zum Tempel: Die Tempelaktion und das Tempelwort als Ausdruck seiner messianischen Sendung.* WUNT 2.119. Tübingen: Mohr-Siebeck.

———. 2000b. "James' Position at the Summit Meeting of the Apostles and the Elders in Jerusalem (Acts 15)." In Ådna and Kvalbein 2000, 125-61.

Ådna, Jostein, and Hans Kvalbein, eds. 2000. *The Mission of the Early Church to Jews and Gentiles.* WUNT 127. Tübingen: Mohr-Siebeck.

Aejmelaeus, Lars. 1987. *Die Rezeption der Paulusbriefe in der Miletrede (Apg 20,18-35).* AASF B.232. Helsinki: Suomalainen Tiedeakatemia.

Akurgal, Ekrem. 1987. *Griechische und römische Kunst in der Türkei.* Munich: Hirmer.

Aland, Kurt. 1967. *Studien zur Überlieferung des Neuen Testaments und seines Textes.* Berlin: de Gruyter.

———. 1979. "Der Schluß des Markusevangeliums." In *Neutestamentliche Entwürfe,* 246-83. TB 63. Munich: Kaiser.

Alcock, Susan E., ed. 1997. *The Early Roman Empire in the East.* Oxbow Monograph 95. Oxford: Oxbow.

Alexander, Loveday C. A. 1993a. *The Preface to Luke's Gospel: Literary Convention and Social Context in Luke 1.1-4 and Acts 1.1.* SNTSMS 78. Cambridge: Cambridge University Press.

———. 1993b. "Chronology." *DPL* 115-23.

Alexander, Philip S. 1992. "The Parting of the Ways from the Perspective of Rabbinic Judaism." In Dunn 1992, 1-26.

Alexander, Thomas C. 1990. "Paul's Final Exhortation to the Elders from Ephesus: The Rhetoric of Acts 20:17-38." Ph.D. diss., Emory University.

Alexander, T. D. 1997. "Further Observations on the Term 'Seed' in Genesis." *TynBul* 48:363-67.

Alexandrov, Georgi. 1976. *Naissus, Dyrrhachion, Scupi, Serdica, Thessalonike.* TIR K 34. Ljubljana: Slovenska akademija znanosti in umetnosti.

Alföldy, Géza. 1975. *Römische Sozialgeschichte.* Wissenschaftliche Paperbacks 8. Wiesbaden: Steiner [3rd ed., 1984]. English: *The Social History of Rome.*

London: Routledge, 1985.

———. 1986. *Die römische Gesellschaft: Ausgewählte Beiträge.* Stuttgart: Steiner.

Alkier, Stefan. 1993. *Urchristentum: Zur Geschichte und Theologie einer exegetischen Disziplin.* BHTh 83. Tübingen: Mohr-Siebeck.

Allchin, F. Raymond. 1995. *The Archaeology of Early Historic South Asia: The Emergence of Cities and States.* Cambridge: Cambridge University Press.

Allen, Roland. 1977. *Missionary Methods: St. Paul's or Ours? A Study of the Church in the Four Provinces.* 9th ed. Grand Rapids: Eerdmans [London: Scott, 1912].

Allison, Dale C. 1985. "Paul and the Missionary Discourse." *ETL* 61:369-75.

———. 1989. "Who Will Come from East and West? Observations on Matt. 8.11-12—Luke 13.28-29." *IBS* 11:158-70.

———. 1993. *The New Moses: A Matthean Typology.* Minneapolis: Fortress.

Alon, Gedalyahu. 1980-1984. *The Jews in Their Land in the Talmudic Age, 70-640 C.E.* 2 vols. Jerusalem: Magnes.

Alt, Albrecht. 1949. "Die Stätten des Wirkens Jesu in Galiläa territorialgeschichtlich betrachtet." In *Kleine Schriften zur Geschichte des Volkes Israel,* 2:441-47. 3 vols. Munich: Beck, 1953-1959.

Alter, Robert. 1981. *The Art of Biblical Narrative.* New York: Basic Books.

Altmann, Peter. 1964. *Erwählungstheologie und Universalismus im Alten Testament.* BZAW 92. Berlin: de Gruyter.

Alzinger, Wilhelm. 1974. *Augusteische Architektur in Ephesos.* Sonderschriften 16. Vienna: Österreichisches Archäologisches Institut.

Ameling, Walter. 1996. "Die jüdischen Gemeinden im antiken Kleinasien." In Jütte and Kustermann 1996, 29-55.

———. 1999. "Ein Verehrer des Θεὸς Ὕψιστος in Prusa (IK 39, 115)." *EA* 31:105-8.

Amjad-Ali, Christine M. 1988. "The Literary Evidence for Thomas in India." In Rooney 1988, 32-40.

Amsler, Frédéric. 1999. *Acta Philippi: Commentarius.* CCSA 12. Turnhout: Brepols.

Amstutz, John. 1985. "Beyond Pentecost: A Study of Some Sociological Dimensions of New Testament Church Growth from the Book of Acts." In *Essays on Apostolic Themes,* FS H. M. Ervin, edited by P. Elbert, 208-25. Peabody, Mass.: Hendrickson.

Anderson, Gerald H., ed. 1961. *The Theology of the Christian Mission.* New York: McGraw-Hill.

Andresen, Carl. 1979. "'Siegreiche Kirche' im Aufstieg des Christntums: Untersuchungen zu Eusebius von Caesarea und Dionysios von Alexandrien." *ANRW* II.23.1:387-459.

Annen, Franz. 1976. *Heil für die Heiden: Zur Bedeutung und Geschichte der Tradition vom besessenen Gerasener (Mk 5,1-20 parr.).* Freiburger theologische

Studien 20. Frankfurt: Knecht.

Anthonysamy, S. J. 1993. "Christian Mission in the Context of Many Religions Today: A Biblical Perspective." *ITS* 30:93-107.

Applebaum, Shimon. 1979. *Jews and Greeks in Ancient Cyrene.* SJLA 28. Leiden: Brill.

Applegate, Judith K. 1992. "The Co-Elect Woman of 1 Peter." *NTS* 38:587-604.

Appold, Mark. 1995a. "The Mighty Works of Bethsaida: Witness of the New Testament and Related Traditions." In Arav and Freund 1995-1999, 1:229-42.

———. 1995b. "Bethsaida and a First-Century House Church?" In Arav and Freund 1995-1999, 2:373-96.

Arav, Rami, and Richard A. Freund, eds. 1995-1999. *Bethsaida: A City by the North Shore of the Sea of Galilee.* 2 vols. Bethsaida Excavations Project Reports and Contextual Studies 1. Kirksville, Mo.: Thomas Jefferson University Press.

Arnal, William E. 2001. *Jesus and the Village Scribes: Galilean Conflicts and the Setting of Q.* Minneapolis: Fortress.

Arnold, Clinton E. 1997. "Centers of Christianity." *DLNTD* 144-52.

Ascough, Richard. 1998. "Civic Pride at Philippi," *NTS* 44:93-103.

———. 2000. "Christianity in Caesarea Maritima." In Donaldson 2000, 153-79.

———. 2002. "Greco-Roman Philosophic, Religious, and Voluntary Associations." In Longenecker 2002, 3-19.

Attridge, Harold W., and Gohei Hata, eds. 1992. *Eusebius, Christianity, and Judaism.* Detroit: Wayne State University Press.

Aujac, Germaine. 1966. *Strabon et la science de son temps.* Paris: Les Belles Lettres.

———. 1987a. "The Foundations of Theoretical Cartography in Archaic and Classical Greece." In Harley and Woodward 1987, 1:130-47.

———. 1987b. "The Growth of an Empirical Cartography in Hellenistic Greece." In Harley and Woodward 1987, 1:148-60.

———. 1987c. "Greek Cartography in the Early Roman World." In Harley and Woodward 1987, 1:161-76.

Aulock, Hans von. 1976. *Münzen und Städte Lykaoniens.* Tübingen: Wasmuth.

Aune, David E. 1983. *Prophecy in Early Christianity and the Ancient Mediterranean World.* Grand Rapids: Eerdmans.

———. 1991. "Romans as a Logos Protreptikos in the Context of Ancient Religious and Philosophical Propaganda." In Hengel and Heckel 1991, 91-121.

Aus, Roger D. 1979. "Paul's Travel Plans to Spain and the 'Full Number of the Gentiles' of Rom 11.25." *NovT* 21:232-62.

Ausbüttel, Frank M. 1998. *Die Verwaltung des römischen Kaiserreiches: Von der Herrschaft des Augustus bis zum Niedergang des Weströmischen Reiches.* Darmstadt: Wissenschaftliche Buchgesellschaft.

Austin, Norman J. E., and N. Boris Rankov. 1995. *Exploratio: Military and Polit-*

ical Intelligence in the Roman World from the Second Punic War to the Battle of Adrianople. London: Routledge.

Avemarie, Friedrich. 1994. "Esaus Hände, Jakobs Stimme: Edom als Sinnbild Roms in der frühen rabbinischen Literatur." In Feldmeier and Heckel 1994, 177-208.

———. 1996. "Bund als Gabe und Recht: Semantische Überlegungen zu bᵉrît in der rabbinischen Literatur." In Avemarie and Lichtenberger 1996, 163-216.

Avemarie, Friedrich, and Herrmann Lichtenberger, eds. 1996. *Bund und Tora: Zur theologischen Begriffsgeschichte in altestamentlicher, frühjüdischer und urchristlicher Tradition.* WUNT 92. Tübingen: Mohr-Siebeck.

Avigad, Nahman. 1983. *Discovering Jerusalem.* Nashville: Nelson.

Avramea, Anna, and Pavlina Karanastassi. 1993. *Philippi.* TIR K 35.1. Athens: Académie d'Athènes.

Axenfeld, Karl. 1904. "Die jüdische Propaganda als Vorläuferin und Wegbereiterin der urchristlichen Mission." In *Missionswissenschaftliche Studien,* FS Gustav Warneck, 1-80. Berlin: Warneck.

Badura, Bernhard. 1995. "Mathematische und soziologische Theorie der Kommunikation." In *Kommunikationstheorien,* edited by R. Burkart and W. Hömberg, 16-22. Studienbücher zur Publizistik- und Kommunikationswissenschaft 8. Vienna: Braumüller.

Bagatti, Bellarmino. 1971. *Villaggi Cristiani di Galilea.* Jerusalem: Franciscan Printing Press.

Bagnall, Roger S., and Bruce W. Frier. 1994. *The Demography of Roman Egypt.* Cambridge: Cambridge University Press.

Bailey, Donald M., ed. 1996. *Archaeological Research in Roman Egypt.* JRASup 19. Ann Arbor, Mich.: Journal of Roman Archaeology.

Bailey, James W. 1909. "Paul's Second Missionary Journey." *Biblical World* 33:414-23.

Bakirtzis, Charalambos, and Helmut Koester, eds. 1998. *Philippi at the Time of Paul and after His Death.* Harrisburg, Pa.: Trinity.

Balch, David L. 1981. *Let Wives Be Submissive: The Domestic Code in I Peter.* SBLMS 26. Chico, Calif.: Scholars Press.

———, ed. 1991. *Social History of the Matthean Community: Cross-Disciplinary Approaches.* Minneapolis: Fortress.

———. 1995. "Paul in Acts: '. . . you teach all the Jews . . . to forsake Moses, telling them not to observe the customs' (Act. 21,21)." In *Panchaia,* FS K. Thraede, edited by M. Wacht, 11-23. JAC Ergänzungsband 22. Aschendorff: Münster.

Balch, David L., et al., eds. 1990. *Greeks, Romans, and Christians.* FS A. J. Malherbe. Minneapolis: Fortress.

Baldi, Donatus. 1955. *Enchiridion Locorum Sanctorum.* Jerusalem: Franciscan Printing Press [3rd ed., 1982].

Ball, Warwick. 2000. *Rome in the East: The Transformation of an Empire*. London: Routledge [repr., 2002].

Balz, Heinrich. 1992. "Mission, Missionstheologie." *EKL* 3:425-44.

Bamberger, Bernard J. 1939. *Proselytism in the Talmudic Period*. Cincinnati: Hebrew Union College Press.

Bammel, Ernst. 1961. "Matthäus 10.23." *StTh* 15:79-92.

Banks, Robert. 1980. *Paul's Idea of Community: The Early House Churches in Their Historical Setting*. Grand Rapids: Eerdmans.

Barbi, Augusto. 1990. "La missione negli Atti degli apostoli." In Ghiberti 1990b, 127-54.

Barclay, John M. G. 1996. *Jews in the Mediterranean Diaspora: From Alexander to Trajan (323 BCE -117 CE)*. Edinburgh: T & T Clark.

Bardy, Gustave. 1948. "Les problèmes linguistiques et l'évangélisation du monde." In *La question des langues dans l'église ancienne*, 1-79. Études de théologique historique. Paris: Beauchesne.

————. 1988. *Menschen werden Christen: Das Drama der Bekehrung in den ersten Jahrhunderten*. Freiburg: Herder. French: *La Conversion au Christianisme durant les premiers siècles*. Paris: Montaigne, 1949.

Bar-Ilan, Meir. 1992. "Illiteracy in the Land of Israel in the First Centuries C.E." In *Essays in the Social Scientific Study of Judaism and Jewish Society*, vol. 2, edited by S. Fishbane et al., 46-61. Hoboken, N.J.: Ktav.

Bar-Kochva, Bezalel. 1976. *The Seleucid Army: Organization and Tactics in the Great Campaigns*. Cambridge: Cambridge University Press.

Barnard, Leslie W. 1960. "St. Stephen and Early Alexandrian Christianity." *NTS* 7:31-45.

————. 1963. "The Background of Early Egyptian Christianity II: The Egyptian Diaspora." *Church Quarterly Review* 164:428-41.

————. 1968. "The Origins and Emergence of the Church in Edessa During the First Two Centuries." *VigChr* 22:161-75.

Barnett, Paul W. 1990. *Behind the Scenes of the New Testament*. Downers Grove, Ill.: InterVarsity Press.

————. 1993. "Tentmaking." *DPL* 925-27.

————. 1999. *Jesus and the Rise of Early Christianity: A History of New Testament Times*. Downers Grove, Ill.: InterVarsity Press.

————. 2000. "Jewish Mission in the Era of the New Testament and the Apostle Paul." In Bolt and Thompson 2000, 263-83.

Baron, Salo. 1952. *A Social and Religious History of the Jews*. Vols. 1-2, *Ancient Times*. 2nd ed. Philadelphia: Jewish Publication Society [1937; repr., 4th ed., 1962].

Barrett, C. K. 1953. "Paul and the 'Pillar' Apostles." In *Studia Paulina*, FS J. de Zwaan, edited by J. N. Sevenster and W. C. van Unnik, 1-19. Haarlem: Bohn.

————. 1962. *From First Adam to Last: A Study in Pauline Theology*. New York: Scribner.

————. 1964. "Christianity at Corinth." *BJRL* 64:269-97.

————. 1969. "Titus." In Barrett 1982, 118-31.

————. 1982. *Essays on Paul.* London: SPCK.

————. 1988. "The Gentile Mission as an Eschatological Phenomenon." In *Eschatology and the New Testament,* FS G. R. Beasley-Murray, edited by W. H. Gloer, 65-75. Peabody, Mass.: Hendrickson (= Barrett 1995, 185-93).

————. 1989. "Paulus als Missionar und Theologe." *ZThK* 86:18-32 (= Barrett 1991; ET, Barrett 1995, 149-62).

————. 1991. "Paulus als Missionar und Theologe." In Hengel and Heckel 1991, 1-15.

————. 1993. *Church, Ministry, and Sacraments in the New Testament.* Carlisle: Paternoster.

————. 1994a. *Paul: An Introduction to His Thought.* Louisville: Westminster John Knox.

————. 1994b. "Imitatio Christi in Acts." In Green and Turner 1994, 251-62.

————. 1995. *Jesus and the Word and Other Essays.* PTMS 41. Allison Park, Pa.: Pickwick.

————. 1999. "The Historicity of Acts." *JTS* 50:491-514.

Bartchy, S. Scott. 2002. "Divine Power, Community Formation, and Leadership in the Acts of the Apostles." In Longenecker 2002, 89-104.

Barth, Gerhard. 1959. "Das Gesetzesverständnis des Evangelisten Matthäus." In *Überlieferung und Auslegung im Matthäusevangelium,* by G. Barth, G. Bornkamm and H. J. Held, 48-154. 7th ed. WMANT 1. Neukirchen-Vluyn: Neukirchener Verlag [1975].

Barth, Markus. 1990. "Die Juden im Johannes-Evangelium." In *Teufelskinder oder Heilsbringer: Die Juden im Johannes-Evangelium,* edited by D. Neuhaus, 39-94. Arnoldshainer Texte 64. Frankfurt: Haag & Herrchen.

Bartnicki, Roman. 1988. "Die Jünger Jesu in Mt 9,35—11,1." *Collectanea Theologica* 58:39-56.

Barton, Ian M., ed. 1996. *Roman Domestic Buildings.* Exeter Studies in History. Exeter: University of Exeter Press.

Barton, Stephen C. 1996. "'All Things to All People': Paul and the Law in the Light of 1 Corinthians 9.19-23." In Dunn 1996, 271-85.

Bartsch, Hans-Werner. 1959. "Die Passions- und Ostergeschichten bei Matthäus." In Margull and Hermelink 1959, 27-41.

Bash, Anthony. 1997. *Ambassadors for Christ: An Exploration of Ambassadorial Communication in the New Testament.* WUNT 2.92. Tübingen: Mohr-Siebeck.

Bassler, Jouette M. 1982. *Divine Impartiality: Paul and a Theological Axiom.* SBLDS 59. Chico, Calif.: Scholars Press.

————. 1985. "Luke and Paul on Impartiality." *Bib* 66:546-52.

Batey, Richard A. 1984. "Is Not This the Carpenter?" *NTS* 30:249-58.

————. 1991. *Jesus and the Forgotten City: New Light on Sepphoris and the Urban World of Jesus*. Grand Rapids: Baker.

Bauckham, Richard J. 1988. "The Apocalypse as a Christian War Scroll." In Bauckham 1993, 210-37.

————. 1990. *Jude and the Relatives of Jesus in the Early Church*. Edinburgh: T & T Clark.

————. 1992. "The Martyrdom of Peter in Early Christian Literature." *ANRW* II.26.1:539-95.

————. 1993a. *The Climax of Prophecy: Studies on the Book of Revelation*. Edinburgh: T & T Clark.

————. 1993b. "The Acts of Paul as a Sequel to Acts." In Winter and Clarke 1993, 105-52.

————, ed. 1995a. *The Book of Acts in Its Palestinian Setting*. The Book of Acts in Its First-Century Setting 4. Exeter: Paternoster.

————. 1995b. "James and the Jerusalem Church." In Bauckham 1995a, 415-80.

————. 1996a. "James and the Gentiles (Acts 15.13-21)." In Witherington 1996, 154-84.

————. 1996b. "Kerygmatic Summaries in the Speeches of Acts." In Witherington 1996, 185-217.

————, ed. 1998. *The Gospels for All Christians: Rethinking the Gospel Audiences*. Grand Rapids: Eerdmans.

————. 1999. *God Crucified: Monotheism and Christology in the New Testament*. Grand Rapids: Eerdmans [Carlisle: Paternoster, 1998].

————. 2002. *Gospel Women: Studies of the Named Women in the Gospels*. Grand Rapids: Eerdmans.

Bauer, Walter. 1934. *Rechtgläubigkeit und Ketzerei im ältesten Christentum*. Edited by von G. Strecker. BHTh 10. Tübingen: Mohr-Siebeck [2nd ed., 1964]. English: *Orthodoxy and Heresy in Earliest Christianity*. Philadelphia: Fortress, 1971 [1996].

Baugh, Steven M. 1990. "Paul and Ephesus: The Apostle among His Contemporaries." Ph.D. diss., University of California.

Baum, Armin D. 1993. *Lukas als Historiker der letzten Jesusreise*. Monographien und Studienbücher. Wuppertal: Brockhaus.

————. 1996a. "Hat Lukas Jesus und die Apostel genau zitiert? Die *oratio recta* im lukanischen Werk zwischen antiker Profan- und Kirchengeschichtsschreibung." In Maier 1996, 105-45.

————. 1996b. "Die weltweite Dimension der Mission Jesu." In Kasdorf and Walldorf 1996, 55-79.

————. 2000. "Die Authentizität der synoptischen Worte Jesu." In *Das Studium des Neuen Testaments,* edited by H. W. Neudorfer and E. J. Schnabel, 2:155-77. 2 vols. Bibelwissenschaftliche Monographien 5. Wuppertal: Brockhaus.

————. 2001. *Pseudepigraphie und literarische Fälschung im frühen Christen-*

tum. WUNT 2.138. Tübingen: Mohr-Siebeck.

Baum, Horst. 1977. *Mut zum Schwachsein—in Christi Kraft: Theologische Grundelemente einer missionarischen Spiritualität anhand von 2 Kor.* Studia Insituti Missiologici Societas Verbi Divini 17. St. Augustin: Steyler.

Baumbach, Günther. 1967. "Die Mission im Matthäus-Evangelium." *ThLZ* 92:889-93.

———. 1986. "Das Neue Testament—ein judenfeindliches Buch? Zur Frage nach der Entstehung und Verbreitung antijüdischer Tendenzen im frühen Christentum." *Zeichen der Zeit* 40:138-42.

Baumgarten, Albert I. 1992. "Literary Evidence for Jewish Christianity in the Galilee." In L. Levine 1992, 39-50.

———. 1997. *The Flourishing of Jewish Sects in the Maccabean Era: An Interpretation.* JSJSup 55. Leiden: Brill.

Baumgarten, Joseph M. 1972. "The Exclusion of the 'Netinim' and Proselytes in 4Q Florilegium." *RevQ* 8:87-96 (= *Studies in Qumran Law* [SJLA 24. Leiden: Brill, 1977] 75-87).

———. 1982. "Exclusions from the Temple: Proselytes and Agrippa I." *JJS* 33:215-25.

Baur, Ferdinand Christian. 1853. *Das Christentum und die christliche Kirche der drei ersten Jahrhunderte.* Tübingen: Fues.

———. 1866. *Paulus, der Apostel Jesu Christi: Sein Leben und Wirken, seine Briefe und seine Lehre; Ein Beitrag zu einer kritischen Geschichte des Urchristentums.* Edited by E. Zeller. 2nd ed. 2 vols. Leipzig: Deichert 1967 [1845].

Baus, Karl. 1965. *Von der Urgemeinde zur frühchristljichen Großkirche.* Handbuch der Kirchengeschichte 2.1. Freiburg: Herder.

Bavinck, Johan H. *An Introduction to the Science of Missions.* Nutley: Presbyterian & Reformed, 1977.

Bayer, Hans F. 1987. "'Machet zu Jüngern alle Völker' (Mt 28,18-20)—das Ziel der Mission nach dem Sendungsbefehl Jesu." *Evangelikale Missiologie* 10:21-29.

———. 1998. "The Preaching of Peter in Acts." In Marshall and Peterson 1998, 257-74.

Beale, Greg K. 1997. "The Eschatological Conception of New Testament Theology." In *"Let the Reader Understand": Eschatology in Bible and Theology,* edited by K. E. Brower and M. W. Elliott, 11-52. Downers Grove, Ill.: InterVarsity Press.

———. 1999. "Peace and Mercy Upon the Israel of God: The Old Testament Background of Galatians 6,16b." *Bib* 80:203-23.

Bean, George E. 1966. *Aegean Turkey: An Archaeological Guide.* New York: Praeger.

———. 1968. *Turkey's Southern Shore: An Archaeological Guide.* London: Benn.

————. 1971. *Turkey Beyond the Maeander: An Archaeological Guide*. London: Benn.

Beard, Mary. 1991. "Writing and Religion: Ancient Literacy and the Function of the Written Word in Roman Religion." In Beard et al. 1991, 35-58.

Beard, Mary, et al., eds. 1991. *Literacy in the Roman World*. JRASup 3. Ann Arbor, Mich.: Journal of Roman Archaeology.

Beard, Mary, John North, and Simon Price. 1998. *Religions of Rome*. 2 vols. Cambridge: Cambridge University Press.

Beare, Francis W. 1970. "The Mission of the Disciples and the Mission Charge: Matthew 10 and Parallels." *JBL* 89:1-13.

Beasley-Murray, George R. 1968. *Die christliche Taufe: Eine Untersuchung über ihr Verständnis in Geschichte und Gegenwart*. Kassel: Oncken.

————. 1986. *Jesus and the Kingdom of God*. Grand Rapids: Eerdmans.

————. 1991. *Gospel of Life: Theology in the Fourth Gospel*. Peabody, Mass.: Hendrickson.

————. 1992. "The Mission of the Logos-Son." In Van Segbroeck et al. 1992, 3:1855-68.

————. 1993. *Jesus and the Last Days: The Interpretation of the Olivet Discourse*. Peabody, Mass.: Hendrickson.

Beasley-Murray, Paul. 1993. "Pastor, Paul as." *DPL* 654-58.

Beatrice, Pier F. 1995. "Apollos of Alexandria and the Origins of the Jewish-Christian Baptist Encratism." *ANRW* II.26.2:1232-75.

Bechard, Dean Philip. 2000. *Paul Outside the Walls: A Study of Luke's Socio-Geographical Universalism in Acts 14:8-20*. AnBib 143. Rome: Pontificio Istituto Biblico.

Becker, Jürgen. 1987. "Paulus und seine Gemeinden." In Becker et al. 1987, 102-59.

————. 1992. *Paulus: Der Apostel der Völker*. 2nd ed. Tübingen: Mohr-Siebeck [1989]. English: *Paul: Apostle to the Gentiles*. Louisville: Westminster John Knox, 1993.

————. 1995. *Jesus von Nazareth*. Berlin: de Gruyter.

————. 1997. "Der Völkerapostel Paulus im Spiegel seiner neuesten Interpreten." *ThLZ* 122:978-90.

Becker, Jürgen, et al. 1987. *Die Anfänge des Christentums: Alte Welt und neue Hoffnung*. Stuttgart: Kohlhammer.

Beckheuer, Burkhard. 1997. *Paulus und Jerusalem: Kollekte und Mission im theologischen Denkern des Heidenapostels*. EHS 23.611. Frankfurt: Lang.

Bedell, Clifford H. 1998. "Mission in Intertestamental Judaism." In Larkin and Williams 1998, 21-29.

Begley, Vimala, ed. 1996. *The Ancient Port of Arikamedu: New Excavations and Researches 1982-1992*. Mémoires archéologiques 22. Pondicherry: École française d'Extrême-Orient.

Begley, Vimala, and Richard D. de Puma, eds. 1991. *Rome and India: The Ancient Sea Trade.* Madison: University of Wisconsin Press.

Beker, J. Christiaan. 1987. *Paul the Apostle: The Triumph of God in Life and Thought.* 2nd ed. Philadelphia: Fortress [1980]. German: *Der Sieg Gottes: Eine Untersuchung zur Struktur des paulinischen Denkens.* SBS 132. Stuttgart: Katholisches Bibelwerk, 1988.

Belke, Klaus [with Marcell Restle]. 1984. *Galatien und Lykaonien.* TIB 4. Vienna: Österreichische Akademie der Wissenschaften.

Belke, Klaus, and Norbert Mersich. 1990. *Phrygien und Pisidien.* TIB 7. Vienna: Österreichische Akademie der Wissenschaften.

———. 1996. *Paphlagonien und Honorias.* TIB 9. Vienna: Österreichische Akademie der Wissenschaften.

Bell, H. Idris. 1944. "Evidences of Christianity in Egypt During the Roman Period." *HTR* 37:185-208.

Bell, Richard H. 1994. *Provoked to Jealousy: The Origin and Purpose of the Jealousy Motif in Romans 9-11.* WUNT 2.63. Tübingen: Mohr-Siebeck.

Beloch, Julius. 1886. *Die Bevölkerung der griechisch-römischen Welt.* Repr., New York: Arno, 1979.

Belser, Johannes E. 1912. "Das Missionsverfahren im apostolischen Zeitalter." *ThQ* 94:359-411.

Ben-David, Arye. 1974. *Talmudische Ökonomie: Die Wirtschaft des jüdischen Palästina zur Zeit der Mischna und des Talmud.* Vol. 1. Hildesheim: Olms.

Bendlin, Andreas. 1997. "Peripheral Centres—Central Peripherie: Religious Communication in the Roman Empire." In Cancik and Rüpke 1997, 35-68.

Benko, Stephen. 1980. "Pagan Criticism of Christianity During the First Two Centuries A.D." *ANRW* II.23.2:1055-1118.

Bennett, Charles T. 1980. "Paul the Pragmatist: Another Look at His Missionary Methods." *Evangelical Missions Quarterly* 16:133-38.

Bérard, J. 1935. "Recherches sur les itinéraires de Saint Paul en Asie Mineure." *Revue Archéologique* 6.5:57-90.

Berger, Klaus. 1994a. *Theologiegeschichte des Urchristentums: Theologie des Neuen Testaments.* UTB für Wissenschaft. Tübingen and Basel: Francke.

———. 1994b. "Propaganda und Gegenpropaganda im frühen Christentum: Simon Magus als Gestalt des samaritanischen Christentums." In Bormann, Del Tredici and Standhartinger 1994, 313-17.

Berges, Dietrich, and Johannes Nollé. 2000. *Tyana: Archäologisch-historische Untersuchungen zum südwestlichen Kappadokien.* 2 vols. IK 55. Bonn: Habelt.

Bernand, André. 1998. *Alexandrie la grande.* Rev. ed. Paris: Hachette.

Bernecker, Annemarie. 1989. *Die Feldzüge des Tiberius und die Darstellung der unterworfenen Gebiete in der "Geographie des Ptolemäus."* Bonn: Habelt.

Bertholet, Alfred. 1896. *Die Stellung der Israeliten und der Juden zu den Frem-*

den. Freiburg and Leipzig: Mohr.

Beskow, Per. 1970. "Mission, Trade and Emigration in the Second Century." *SEÅ* 35:104-14.

Best, Ernest. 1981. *Following Jesus: Discipleship in the Gospel of Mark.* JSNTSup 4. Sheffield: JSOT Press.

———. 1984. "The Revelation to Evangelize the Gentiles." *JTS* 35:1-30.

Betz, Hans Dieter. 1967. *Nachfolge und Nachahmung Jesu Christi im Neuen Testament.* BHTh 37. Tübingen: Mohr-Siebeck.

Betz, Otto. 1961. "Donnersöhne, Menschenfischer und der davidische Messias." *RevQ* 3:41-70.

———. 1994a. "Mission III. Neues Testament." *TRE* 23:23-31.

———. 1994b. "Jesus and the Cynics: Survey and Analysis of a Hypothesis." *JR* 74:453-75.

Betz, Otto, and Werner Grimm. 1977. *Wesen und Wirklichkeit der Wunder Jesu.* ANTJ 2. Frankfurt: Lang.

Beydon, France. 1986. "Luc et 'ces ames de la haute société.' " *Études théologiques et religieuses* 61:331-41.

Beyerhaus, Peter. 1975. "Das Programm des Dialogs mit Vertretern der Religionen und Ideologien unserer Zeit." In *Reich Gottes oder Weltgemeinschaft?* edited by W. Künneth and P. Beyerhaus, 208-29. Bad Liebenzell: Verlag der Liebenzeller Mission.

———. 1996. *Er sandte sein Wort: Theologie der christlichen Mission.* Wuppertal: Brockhaus.

Bianchi, Ugo. 1976. *The Greek Mystries.* Leiden: Brill.

———. 1990. "Diffusione, proselitismo, missione: Tre esempi di fenomonelogia religiosa." In Ghiberti 1990b, 13-24.

Bickerman, Elias J. 1976. *Studies in Jewish and Christian History.* AGJU 9. Leiden: Brill.

Bieberstein, Klaus, and Hanswulf Bloedhorn. 1994. *Jerusalem: Grundzüge der Baugeschichte vom Chalkolithikum bis zur Frühzeit der osmanischen Herrschaft.* 3 vols. BTAVO 100. Wiesbaden: Reichert.

Bieder, Werner. 1950. *Grund und Kraft der Mission nach dem 1. Petrusbrief.* ThSt 29. Zürich: Evangelischer Verlag.

———. 1960. *Die Apostelgeschichte in der Historie: Ein Beitrag zur Auslegungsgeschichte des Missionsbuchs der Kirche.* ThSt 61. Zürich: Evangelischer Verlag.

———. 1961. *Die Berufung im Neuen Testament.* AThANT 38. Zürich: Zwingli.

———. 1964. *Gottes Sendung und der missionarische Auftrag der Kirche nach Matthäus, Lukas, Paulus und Johannes.* ThSt 82. Zürich: Evangelischer Verlag.

———. 1980. "Spiritus Sanctus Pro Mundi Vita." In Sundermeier 1980, 59-68.

Bieritz, Karl-Heinrich and Christoph Kähler. 1985. "Haus III." *TRE* 14:478-92.

Bietenhard, Hans. 1977. "Die syrische Dekapolis von Pompeius bis Traian." *ANRW* II.8:220-61.

Bihler, Johannes. 1963. *Die Stephanusgeschichte im Zusammenhang der Apostelgeschichte*. Münchener theologische Studien 1.16. Munich: Hüber.

Bilde, Per, et al., eds. 1992. *Ethnicity in Hellenistic Egypt*. Studies in Hellenistic Civilization 3. Aarhus: Aarhus University Press.

Billerbeck, Margarethe. 1978. *Epiktet: Vom Kynismus*. Philosophia Antiqua 34. Leiden: Brill.

———. 1979. *Der Kyniker Demetrius: Ein Beitrag zur Geschichte der frühkaiserzeitlichen Popularphilosophie*. Philosophia Antiqua 36. Leiden: Brill.

Billington, Antony. 1995. "The Paraclete and Mission in the Fourth Gospel." In Billington et al. 1995, 90-115.

Billington, Antony, et al., eds. 1995. *Mission and Meaning*. FS P. Cotterell. Carlisle: Paternoster.

Binder, Donald D. 1999. *Into the Temple Courts: The Place of Synagogues in the Second Temple Period*. SBLDS 169. Atlanta: Society of Biblical Literature.

Bin Seray, Hamad M. 1996. "Christianity in the East of the Arabian Peninsula." *Aram* 8:315-32.

Birkey, Del. 1991. "The House Church: A Missiological Model." *Missiology* 19:69-80.

Birnbaum, E. 1993. "The Place of Judaism in Philo's Thought: Israel, Jews, and Proselytes." In *SBLSP*, 54-69.

Bivar, A. D. H. 1983. "The History of Eastern Iran." *CHI* 3:181-23.

Black, Matthew. 1967. *An Aramaic Approach to the Gospels*. 3rd ed. Peabody, Mass.: Hendrickson [1998].

Black, Robert Allen. 1985. "The Conversion Stories in the Acts of the Apostles." Ph.D. diss., Emory University. [*non vidi*]

Blackburn, Barry L. 1997. "Stephen." *DLNTD* 1123-26.

Blair, Edward P. 1965. "Paul's Call to the Gentile Mission." *Biblical Research* 10:19-43.

Blanchetiere, François. 1981. *Le christianisme asiate aux IIème et IIIème siècles*. Lille: Service de reproduction des theses, Université de Lille.

Blank, Josef. 1968. *Paulus und Jesus: Eine theologische Grundlegung*. StANT 18. Munich: Kösel.

Blank, Sheldon H. 1936. "Studies in Post-Exilic Universalism." *HUCA* 11:159-91.

Blaser, Klauspeter. 1987. "Reich Gottes." In *Lexikon missionstheologischer Grundbegriffe,* edited by K. Müller and T. Sundermeier, 405-11. Berlin: Reimer.

Blasi, Anthony J., Jean Duhaime and Paul-André Turcotte, eds. 2002. *Handbook of Early Christianity: Social Science Approaches*. Walnut Creek, Calif.: AltaMira.

Blauw, Johannes. 1961. *Gottes Werk in dieser Welt: Grundzüge einer biblischen*

Theologie der Mission. Munich: Kaiser.

Bleicken, Jochen. 1978. *Verfassungs- und Sozialgeschichte der römischen Kaiserzeit.* 2 vols. UTB 838-839. Paderborn: Schöningh [3rd ed., 1989].

———. 1982. *Zum Regierungsstil des römischen Kaisers: Eine Antwort auf Fergus Millar.* Wiesbaden: Steiner.

Blenkinsopp, Joseph. 1983. *A History of Prophecy in Israel.* Philadelphia: Westminster.

———. 1988. "Second Isaiah—Prophet of Universalism." *JSOT* 41:83-103.

Blomberg, Craig. 1987. *The Historical Reliability of the Gospels.* Downers Grove, Ill.: InterVarsity Press. German: *Die historische Zuverlässigkeit der Evangelien.* Nürnberg: VTR, 1998.

———. 1998. "The Christian and the Law of Moses." In Marshall and Peterson 1998, 397-416.

Blue, Bradley B. 1994. "Acts and the House Church." In Gill and Gempf 1994, 119-222.

———. 1997. "Architecture, Early Church." *DLNTD* 91-95.

———. 1998. "The Influence of Jewish Worship on Luke's Presentation of the Early Church." In Marshall and Peterson 1998, 473-98.

Böcher, Otto. 1978. "Johannes der Täufer in der neutestamentlichen Überlieferung." In *Rechtfertigung, Realismus, Universalismus in biblischer Sicht,* FS A. Köberle, edited by G. Müller, 45-68. Darmstadt: Wissenschaftliche Buchgesellschaft.

———. 1989. "Das sogenannte Aposteldekret." In Frankemölle and Kertelge 1989, 325-36.

———. 1996. "Petrus I. Neues Testament." *TRE* 26:262-73.

Bock, Darrell L. 1987. *Proclamation from Prophecy and Pattern: Lucan Old Testament Christology.* JSNTSup 12. Sheffield: JSOT Press.

———. 1990. "The Use of the Old Testament in Luke-Acts: Christology and Mission." In *SBLSP,* 494-511.

———. 1993. "Athenians Who Have Never Heard." In Crockett and Sigountos 1993, 117-24.

———. 1998. "Scripture and the Realisation of God's Promises." In Marshall and Peterson 1998, 41-62.

Bockmuehl, Markus. 1990. *Revelation and Mystery in Ancient Judaism and Pauline Christianity.* WUNT 2.36. Tübingen: Mohr-Siebeck.

———. 2000. *Jewish Law in Gentile Churches: Halakhah and the Beginning of Christian Public Ethics.* Edinburgh: T & T Clark.

Boers, Hendrikus. 1971. *Theology Out of the Ghetto: A New Testament Exegetical Study Concerning Religious Exclusiveness.* Leiden: Brill.

Bohak, Gideon. 2000. "The Impact of Jewish Monotheism on the Greco-Roman World." *JSQ* 7:1-21.

Böhm, Martina. 1999. *Samarien und die Samaritai bei Lukas: Eine Studie zum religionsgeschichtlichen und traditionsgeschichtlichen Hintergrund der lukanischen Samarientexte und zu deren topographischer Verhaftung.* WUNT 2.111. Tübingen: Mohr-Siebeck.

Bokser, Ben-Zion. 1979. "Witness and Mission in Judaism." In *Isssues in the Jewish-Christian Dialogue: Jewish Perpectives on Covenant, Mission and Witness,* edited by H. Croner and L. Klenicki, 89-107. New York: Paulist.

Bolt, Peter G. 1998. "Mission and Witness." In Marshall and Peterson 1998, 191-214.

Bolt, Peter G., and M. Thompson, eds. 2000. *The Gospel to the Nations: Perspectives on Paul's Mission.* FS P. O'Brien. Leicester: Inter-Varsity Press.

Bolyki, János. 1998. *Jesu Tischgemeinschaften.* WUNT 2.96. Tübingen: Mohr-Siebeck.

Boomershine, Thomas E. 1981. "Mark 16:8 and the Apostolic Commission." *JBL* 100:225-39.

Borg, Marcus J. 1984. *Conflict, Holiness and Politics in the Teachings of Jesus.* New York: Mellen.

————. 1994. *Jesus in Contemporary Scholarship.* Valley Forge, Pa.: Trinity.

Borgen, Peder. 1996. *Early Christianity and Hellenistic Judaism.* Edinburgh: T & T Clark [1998].

Bormann, Lukas. 1995. *Philippi: Stadt und Christengemeinde zur Zeit des Paulus.* NovTSup 78. Leiden: Brill.

Bormann, Lukas, Kelly Del Tredici and Angela Standhartinger, eds. 1994. *Religious Propaganda and Missionary Competition in the New Testament World.* FS Dieter Georgi. NovTSup 74. Leiden: Brill.

Bornhäuser, Karl B. 1928. *Das Johannesevangelium, eine Missionsschrift für Israel.* BFChTh 2.15. Gütersloh: Bertelsmann.

Bornkamm, Günther. 1964. "Der Auferstandene und der Irdische. Mt 28,16-20." In *Zeit und Geschichte,* FS R. Bultmann, edited by E. Dinkler, 171-91. Tübingen: Mohr-Siebeck. English: "The Risen Lord and the Earthly Jesus: Mt 28,16-20." In *The Future of Our Religious Past,* FS R. Bultmann, edited by J. M. Robinson, 203-29. New York: Harper & Row, 1971.

————. 1966-1971. *Gesammelte Aufsätze.* 4 vols. Munich: Kaiser.

————. 1971. "Das missionarische Verhalten des Paulus nach 1 Kor 9,19-23 und in der Apostelgeschichte." In Bornkamm 1966-1971, 4:149-61.

————. 1993. *Paulus.* 7th ed. Stuttgart: Kohlhammer [1969]. English: *Paul.* Minneapolis: Fortress, 1995 [1971].

————. 1995. *Jesus von Nazareth.* 15th ed. Stuttgart: Kohlhammer [1956]. English: *Jesus of Nazareth.* Minneapolis: Fortress, 1995 [1960].

Borse, Udo. 1986. "Lukanische Komposition im Umfeld der ersten Missionsreise." *SNTU* 11:169-94.

Bosch, David J. 1956. "Der alttestamentliche Missionsgedanke." *Evangelisches Missionsmagazin* 100:174-88.

————. 1959. *Die Heidenmission in der Zukunftsschau Jesu: Eine Untersuchung zur Eschatologie der synoptischen Evangelien.* AThANT 36. Zürich: Zwingli.

————. 1969. "'Jesus and the Gentiles'—Review after Thirty Years." In *The Church Crossing Frontiers: Essays on the Nature of Mission,* FS Bengt Sundkler, edited by C. F. Hallencreuz and P. Beyerhaus, 3-19. Studia Missionalia Upsaliensia 11. Uppsala: Gleerup.

————. 1989. "Mission in Jesus' Way: A Perspective from Luke's Gospel." *Missionalia* 17:3-21.

————. 1991. *Transforming Mission: Paradigm Shifts in the Theology of Mission.* Maryknoll, N.Y.: Orbis [6th ed., 1993].

————. 1993a. "Reflections on Biblical Models of Missions." In *Toward the Twenty-First Century in Christian Mission,* FS G. H. Anderson, edited by J. M. Phillips and R. T. Coote, 175-92. Grand Rapids: Eerdmans.

————. 1993b. "Hermeneutical Principles in the Biblical Foundation for Mission." *EvRT* 17:437-51.

Bösen, Willibald. 1985. *Galiläa als Lebensraum und Wirkungsfeld Jesu: Eine zeitgeschichtliche und theologische Untersuchung.* Freiburg: Herder, 1985.

Bosold, Iris. 1978. *Pazifismus und prophetische Provokation: Das Grußverbot Lk 10,4b und sein historischer Kontext.* SBS 90. Stuttgart: Katholisches Bibelwerk.

Bosworth, A. Brian. 1988. *Conquest and Empire: The Reign of Alexander the Great.* Cambridge: Cambridge University Press [1995].

————. 1996. *Alexander and the East: The Tragedy of Triumph.* Oxford: Clarendon.

Botermann, Helga. 1991. "Paulus und das Urchristentum in der antiken Welt." *ThR* 56:296-305.

————. 1993. "Der Heidenapostel und sein Historiker: Zur historischen Kritik der Apostelgeschichte." *ThBeitr* 24:62-84.

————. 1996. *Das Judenedikt des Kaisers Claudius: Römischer Staat und Christiani im 1. Jahrhundert.* Hermes Einzelschriften 71. Stuttgart: Steiner.

Böttger, Paul C. 1981. *Der König der Juden, das Heil für die Völker: Die Geschichte Jesu Christi im Zeugnis des Markusevangeliums.* Neukirchener Studienbücher 13. Neukirchen-Vluyn: Neukirchener Verlag.

Bottino, Adriana. 1990. "Il discorso missionario di Paolo (At 13,16-41)." In Ghiberti 1990c, 81-97.

Boussac, Marie-Françoise, and Jean-François Salles, eds. 1995. *Athens, Aden, Arikamedu: Essays on the Interrelations between India, Arabia and the Eastern Mediterranean.* New Delhi: Manohar [1993].

Bousset, Wilhelm. 1926. *Die Religion des Judentums im späthellenistischen Zeitalter.* Edited by Hugo Gressmann. 3rd ed. HNT 21. Tübingen: Mohr-Siebeck [4th ed., 1966; 1903].

Bovati, Pietro. 1990. "La missione nella religione dell'antico Israele." In Ghiberti 1990b, 25-44.

Bovon, François, ed. 1981. *Les Actes apocryphes des apôtres: Christianisme et monde païen.* Publications de la Faculté de Théologie de l'Université de Genève 4. Genf: Labor et Fides.

———. 1982. "Pratiques missionnaires et communication de l'Évangile dans le christianisme primitif." *RTP* 114:369-81.

———. 1983. "Israel, die Kirche und die Völker im lukanischen Doppelwerk." In Bovon 1985, 120-38.

———. 1985. *Lukas in neuer Sicht: Gesammelte Aufsätze.* BThSt 8. Neukirchen-Vluyn: Neukirchener Verlag.

———. 1993. "Le discours missionnaire de Jésus: Réception patristique et narration apocryphe." *Études Théologiques et Religieuses* 68:481-97.

———. 1995. "Jesus' Missionary Speech as Interpreted in Patristic Commentaries and Apocryphal Narratives." In Fornberg and Hellholm 1996, 871-86.

Bovon, François, Bertrand Bouvier and Frédéric Amsler, eds. 1999. *Acta Philippi: Textus.* CCSA 11. Turnhout: Brepols.

Bovon, François, and Pierre Geoltrain, eds. 1997. *Écrits apocryphes chrétiens.* Bibliothèque de la Pléiade. Paris: Gallimard.

Bowen, Gillian E. 1998. "The Spread of Christianity in Egypt in Light of Recent Discoveries from Ancient Kellis." Ph.D. diss., Monash University, Melbourne.

Bowers, Paul W. 1975. "Jewish Communities in Spain in the Time of Paul the Apostle." *JTS* 26:395-402.

———. 1976. "Studies in Paul's Understanding of His Mission." Ph.D. diss., Cambridge University.

———. 1979. "Paul's Route Through Mysia: A Note on Acts XVI.8." *JTS* 30:507-11.

———. 1980. "Paul and Religious Propaganda in the First Century." *NovT* 22:316-23.

———. 1987. "Fulfilling the Gospel: The Scope of the Pauline Mission." *JETS* 30:185-98.

———. 1991. "Church and Mission in Paul." *JSNT* 44:89-111.

———. 1993. "Mission." *DPL* 608-19.

Bowersock, Glen W. 1983. *Roman Arabia.* Cambridge, Mass., and London: Harvard University Press [1996].

Bowker, John W. 1967-1968. "Speeches in Acts: A Study in Proem and Yelammedenu Form." *NTS* 14:96-111.

Boyd, Gregory A. 1995. *Cynic Sage or Son of God?* Wheaton, Ill.: Victor.

Brandenburger, Egon. 1984. *Markus 13 und die Apokalyptik.* FRLANT 134. Göttingen: Vandenhoeck & Ruprecht.

———. 1988. "Pistis und Sophia: Zum Versthenshorizont von 'Glaube' im Urchristentum." *ZThK* 85:165-98.

Brändle, Rudolf, and Ekkehard W. Stegemann. 1996. "Die Entstehung der ersten 'christlichen Gemeinde' Roms im Kontext der jüdischen Gemeinden." *NTS*

42:1-11. English: "The Formation of the First 'Christian Congregations' in Rome in the Context of the Jewish Congregations." In Donfried and Richardson 1998, 117-27.

Brandt, Hartwin. 1992. *Gesellschaft und Wirtschaft Pamphyliens und Pisidiens im Altertum.* Asia Minor Studien 7. Bonn: Habelt.

Branick, Vincent P. 1989. *The House Church in the Writings of Paul.* Zacchaeus Studies: NT. Wilmington, Del.: Glazier.

Braude, William G. 1940. *Jewish Proselytizing in the First Five Centuries of the Common Era.* Providence: Brown University Press.

Braun, Willi. 1991. "The Historical Jesus and the Mission Speech in Q 10.2-12." *Forum* 7:279-316.

Braund, David. 1985. *Augustus to Nero: A Sourcebook on Roman History, 31 BC—AD 68.* Totowa, N.J.: Barnes & Noble.

Brece, Yves-Marie. 1990. *The History of Peasant Revolts.* Ithaca, N.Y.: Cornell University Press.

Bremmer, Jan N., ed. 1995. *The Apocryphal Acts of John.* Studies on the Apocryphal Acts of the Apostles 1. Kampen: Kok Pharos.

———, ed. 1996. *The Apocryphal Acts of Paul and Thecla.* Studies on the Apocryphal Acts of the Apostles 2. Kampen: Kok Pharos.

———, ed. 1998. *The Apocryphal Acts of Peter: Magic, Miracles and Gnosticism.* Studies on the Apocryphal Acts of the Apostles 3. Leuven: Peeters.

———, ed. 2000. *The Apocryphal Acts of Andrew.* Studies on the Apocryphal Acts of the Apostles 5. Kampen: Kok Pharos.

Brenk, Beat. 1991a. "Die Christianisierung des jüdischen Stadtzentrums von Kapernaum." In *Byzantine East, Latin West: Art-Historical Studies,* FS Kurt Weitzmann, edited by C. Moss and K. Kiefer, 15-26. Princeton, N.J.: Department of Art and Archaeology, Princeton University Press.

———. 1991b. "Die Umwandlung der Synagoge von Apamea in eine Kirche: Eine mentalitätsgeschichtliche Studie." In *Tesserae,* FS Josef Engemann, 1-24. JAC Ergänzungsband 18. Münster: Aschendorff.

Breytenbach, Cilliers. 1989. *Versöhnung: Eine Studie zur paulinischen Soteriologie.* WMANT 60. Neukirchen-Vluyn: Neukirchener Verlag.

———. 1990. "Paul's Proclamation and God's 'thriambos' (Notes on 2 Corinthians 2.14-16b)." *Neot* 24:257-71.

———. 1993. "Zeus und der lebendige Gott: Anmerkungen zu Apostelgeschichte 14.11-17." *NTS* 39:396-413.

———. 1996. *Paulus und Barnabas in der Provinz Galatien: Studien zu Apostelgeschichte 13f.; 16,6; 18,23 und den Adressaten des Galaterbriefes.* AGAJU 38. Leiden: Brill.

Briggs, C. W. 1913. "The Apostle Paul in Arabia." *Biblical World* 41:255-59.

Brisson, Jean-Paul. 1958. *Autonomisme et Christianisme dans l'Afrique romaine de Septime Severe à l'invasion vandale.* Paris: Bochard.

Brixhe, Claude. 1987a. *Essai sur le Grec Anatolien au début de notre ère.* Travaux et mémoires: Études anciennes 1. Nancy: Presses Universitaires de Nancy.

———. 1987b. "La Langue comme critère d'acculturation: l'exemple du grec d'un district phrygien." In *Hethitica VIII: Acta Anatolica E. Laroche oblata,* edited by R. Lebrun, 45-80. Leuven: Peeters.

Brödner, Erika. 1989. *Wohnen in der Antike.* Darmstadt: Wissenschaftliche Buchgesellschaft.

Brock, Sebastian. 1992. "Eusebius and Syriac Christianity." In Attridge and Hata 1992, 212-34.

Brocke, Christoph vom. 2001. *Thessaloniki—Stadt der Kassander und Gemeinde des Paulus: Eine frühe christliche Gemeinde in ihrer heidnischen Umwelt.* WUNT 2.125. Tübingen: Mohr-Siebeck.

Brodersen, Kai. 1994. *Pomponius Mela: Kreuzfahrt durch die Alte Welt.* Darmstadt: Wissenschaftliche Buchgesellschaft.

———. 1995. *Terra Cognita: Studien zur römischen Raumerfassung.* Spudasmata 59. Hildesheim and New York: Olms.

Broek, Roelof van den. 1988. "Der Brief des Jakobus an Quadratus und das Problem der judenchristlichen Bischöfe von Jerusalem (Eusebius, *HE* IV,5,1-3)." In *Text and Testimony,* FS A. F. J. Klijn, edited by T. Baarda et al., 56-65. Kampen: Kok.

Broer, Ingo. 1994. "Die Konversion des Königshauses von Adiabene nach Josephus (Ant XX)." In *Nach den Anfängen Fragen,* FS G. Dautzenberg, edited by G. Mayer et al., 133-62. Giessen: Fachbereich Evangelische Theologie und Katholische Theologie.

Brooke, George J. 1985. *Exegesis at Qumran: 4QFlorilegium in Its Jewish Context.* JSOTSup 29. Sheffield: JSOT Press.

Brooks, Oscar S. 1981. "Matthew 28.16-20 and the Design of the First Gospel." *JSNT* 10:2-18.

Broshi, Magen. 1975. "La population de l'ancienne Jérusalem." *RB* 82:5-12.

———. 1980. "The Population of Western Palestine in the Roman-Byzantine Period." *BASOR* 236:1-10.

Brown, Peter. 1996. *The Rise of Western Christendom: Triumph and Diversity, AD 200-1000.* Cambridge: Blackwell.

Brown, Raymond E., ed. 1973. *Peter in the New Testament.* New York: Paulist.

———. 1993. *The Birth of the Messiah: A Commentary on the Infancy Narratives in the Gospels of Matthew and Luke.* New York: Doubleday.

Brown, Raymond E., and John P. Meier. 1983. *Antioch and Rome: New Testament Cradles of Catholic Christianity.* New York: Paulist.

Brown, Schuyler. 1977. "The Two-Fold Representation of the Mission in Matthew's Gospel." *StTh* 31:21-32.

———. 1978. "The Mission to Israel in Matthew's Central Section." *ZNW* 69:73-90.

————. 1980. "The Matthean Community and the Gentile Mission." *NovT* 22:193-221.

Brox, Norbert. 1961. *Zeuge und Märtyrer: Untersuchungen zur frühchristlichen Zeugnis-Terminologie.* StANT 5. Munich: Kösel.

————. 1982. "Zur christlichen Mission in der Spätantike." In Kertelge 1982, 190-237.

————. 1983. *Kirchengeschichte des Altertums.* Leitfaden Theologie 8. Düsseldorf: Patmos [2nd ed., 1992]. English: *A History of the Early Church.* London: SCM Press, 1994.

————, ed. 1993-2001. *Epideixis: Adversus Haereses; Darlegung der Apostolischen Verkündigung: Gegen die Häresien.* 5 vols. Fontes Christiani 8.1-5. Freiburg: Herder.

Bruce, F. F. 1969. "The Kerygma of Hebrews." *Int* 23:3-19.

————. 1974. *Jesus and Christian Origins Outside the New Testament.* London: Hodder & Stoughton.

————. 1977. *Paul: Apostle of the Free Spirit.* Exeter: Paternoster, 1977.

————. 1979. *Men and Movements in the Primitive Church: Studies in Early Non-Pauline Christianity.* Exeter: Paternoster.

————. 1985a. "The Acts of the Apostles: Historical Record or Theological Reconstruction?" *ANRW* II.25.3:2569-2603.

————. 1985b. "The Church of Jerusalem in the Acts of the Apostles." *BJRL* 67:641-61.

————. 1989. "Philip and the Ethiopian." *JSS* 34:377-86.

————. 1990. "The Significance of the Speeches for Interpreting Acts." *SwJT* 33:20-28.

————. 1992. "Travel and Communication." *ABD* 6:648-53.

————. 1993. "Paul in Acts and Letters." *DPL* 679-92.

————. 1995. *The Pauline Circle.* Carlisle: Paternoster [1985].

Bruggen, Jacob van. 2000. *Paulus: Pionier voor de Messias van Israël.* Kampen: Kok.

Brunner, Emil. 1934. *Die Unentbehrlichkeit des Alten Testaments für die missionierende Kirche.* Basel: Evangelischer Missionsverlag.

Bryan, Stephen M. 2002. *Jesus and Israel's Traditions of Judgement and Restoration.* SNTSMS 117. Cambridge: Cambridge University Press.

Buchanan, George W. 1984. *Jesus, the King and His Kingdom.* Macon, Ga.: Mercer University Press.

Büchler, Adolf. 1906. *Der galiläische 'Am-h'Ares des zweiten Jahrhunderts.* Vienna: Israelitisch-Theologische Lehranstalt [repr., Hildesheim: Olms, 1968].

Buckwalter, H. Douglas. 1998. "The Divine Saviour." In Marshall and Peterson 1998, 107-23.

Bühner, Jan Adolf. 1977. *Der Gesandte und sein Weg im 4. Evangelium: Die kultur- und religionsgeschichtliche Entwicklung.* WUNT 2.2. Tübingen: Mohr-Siebeck.

Bultmann, Christoph. 1992. *Der Fremde im antiken Juda: Eine Untersuchung zum sozialen Typenbegriff 'ger' und seinem Bedeutungswandel in der alttestamentlichen Gesetzgebung.* FRLANT 153. Göttingen: Vandenhoeck & Ruprecht.

Bultmann, Rudolf. 1910. *Der Stil der paulinischen Predigt und die kynisch-stoische Diatribe.* FRLANT 13. Göttingen: Vandenhoeck & Ruprecht.

———. 1984. *Theologie des Neuen Testaments.* Revised by Otto Merk. 9th ed. UTB 630. Tübingen: Mohr-Siebeck [1948-1953]. English: *Theology of the New Testament.* 2 vols. London: SCM Press, 1952-1955.

———. 1995. *Die Geschichte der synoptischen Tradition.* 10th ed. FRLANT 12. Göttingen: Vandenhoeck & Ruprecht [1921]. English: *The History of the Synoptic Tradition.* Oxford: Blackwell, 1968.

Bundy, David. 1990. "The *Life of Abercius*: Its Significance for Early Syriac Christianity." *The Second Century* 7:163-76.

———. 1992. "Christianity: Christianity in Syria." *ABD* 1:970-79.

Burchard, Christoph. 1970. *Der dreizehnte Zeuge: Traditions- und Kompositionsgeschichtliche Untersuchungen zu Lukas' Darstellung der Frühzeit des Paulus.* FRLANT 103. Göttingen: Vandenhoeck & Ruprecht.

———. 1978. "Formen der Vermittlung christlichen Glaubens im Neuen Testament: Beobachtungen anhand von κήρυγμα, μαρτυρία und verwandten Wörtern." *EvTh* 38:313-40.

———. 1980. "Jesus für die Welt: Über das Verhältnis von Reich Gottes und Mission." In Sundermeier 1980, 13-27.

———. 1984. "Erfahrungen multikulturellen Zusammenlebens im Neuen Testament." In *Multikulturelles Zusammenleben: Theologische Erfahrungen,* edited by J. Micksch, 24-41. Frankfurt: Limbeck, 1984.

———. 1987. "Jesus von Nazareth." In Becker et al. 1987, 12-58.

———. 1993. "Zu Matthäus 8,5-13." *ZNW* 84:278-88.

Burdick, Donald W. 1978. "With Paul in the Troad." *Near Eastern Archaeological Society* 12:31-65.

Burer, Michael H., and Daniel B. Wallace. 2001. "Was Junia Really an Apostle? A Re-examination of Rom 16.7." *NTS* 47:76-91.

Burfeind, Carsten. 2000. "Paulus *muß* nach Rom: Zur politischen Dimension der Apostelgeschichte." *NTS* 46:75-91.

Burge, Gary M. 1987. *The Anointed Community: The Holy Spirit in the Johannine Tradition.* Grand Rapids: Eerdmans.

Burgoon, Michael, Frank G. Hunsaker and Edwin J. Dawson. 1994. *Human Communication.* 3rd ed. London: Sage.

Burgoyne, Michael. 1988. *Jerusalem: Baugeschichte von den Anfängen bis in frühosmanische Zeit.* TAVO Karte B IV 7. Wiesbaden: Reichert.

Burkert, Walter. 1987. *Ancient Mystery Cults.* Cambridge, Mass.: Harvard University Press. German: *Antike Mysterien: Funktionen und Gehalt.* Munich: Beck, 1990.

————. 1996. "'Mein Gott?' Persönliche Frömmigkeit und unverfügbare Götter." In Cancik 1996, 3-14.

Burkhardt, Helmut. 1978. *Die biblische Lehre von der Bekehrung.* Giessen and Basel: Brunnen.

Burkill, T. Alec. 1966. "The Syrophoenician Woman: The Congruence of Mk 7.24-31." *ZNW* 57:23-37.

Burkitt, F. C. 1904. *Early Eastern Christianity.* London: Murray.

Bürkle, Horst. 1979. *Missionstheologie.* Theologische Wissenschaft 18. Stuttgart: Kohlhammer.

Burrows, Reg. 1987. "The Kingdom of God and Mission." *Churchman* 101:5-21.

Buss, Matthäus F.-J. 1980. *Die Missionspredigt des Apostels Paulus im Pisidischen Antiochien: Analyse von Apg 13,16-41 im Hinblick auf die literarische und thematische Einheit der Pauluspredigt.* FB 38. Stuttgart: Katholisches Bibelwerk.

Busse, Ulrich. 1989. "Nachfolge auf dem Weg Jesu: Ursprung und Verhältnis von Nachfolge und Berufung im Neuen Testament." In Frankemölle and Kertelge 1989, 68-81.

Bussmann, Claus. 1971. *Themen der paulinischen Missionspredigt auf dem Hintergrund der spätjüdisch-hellenistischen Missionsliteratur.* EHS 23.3. Bern and Frankfurt: Lang.

Bussmann, Claus, and Walter Radl, eds. 1991. *Der Treue Gottes trauen: Beiträge zum Werk des Lukas.* FS Gerhard Schneider. Freiburg: Herder.

Byatt, A. 1973. "Josephus and Population Numbers in First Century Palestine." *PEQ* 105:51-60.

Cahill, Michael. 1992. "The Neglected Parallelism in Colossians 1,24-25." *ETL* 68:142-47.

Cameron, Ron. 1994. "Alternative Beginnings—Different Ends: Eusebius, Thomas, and the Construction of Christian Origins." In Bormann, Del Tredici and Standhartinger 1994, 501-25.

Camp, Bruce K. 1995. "A Theological Examination of the Two-Structure Theory." *Missiology* 23:197-209.

Camp, John McK. 1980. *Gods and Heroes in the Athenian Agora.* Excavations of the Athenian Agora, Picture Book 19. Princeton, N.J.: American School of Classical Studies at Athens.

————. 2001. *The Archaeology of Athens.* New Haven: Yale University Press.

Campbell, Alastair. 1992. "Do the Work of an Evangelist" *EvQ* 64:117-29.

Campbell, Douglas A. 1996. "Unravelling Colossians 3.11b." *NTS* 42:120-32.

Campbell, Thomas H. 1955. "Paul's 'Missionary Journeys' as Reflected in His Letters." *JBL* 74:80-87.

Campbell, William S. 1990. "Paul's Missionary Practice and Policy in Romans." In Campbell 1991, 81-97.

————. 1991. *Paul's Gospel in an Intercultural Context: Jew and Gentile in the*

Letter to the Romans. SIHC 69. Frankfurt: Lang.

———. 1993a. "Israel." *DPL* 441-46.

———. 1993b. "Judaizers." *DPL* 512-16.

Campenhausen, Hans Freiherr von. 1963. *Kirchliches Amt und geistliche Vollmacht in den ersten drei Jahrhunderten*. BHTh 14. Tübingen: Mohr-Siebeck. English: *Ecclesiastical Authority and Spiritual Power in the Church of the First Three Centuries*. London: Black, 1969 [repr., Peabody, Mass.: Hendrickson, 1997].

———. 1974. "Das Martyrium in der Mission." In Frohnes and Knorr 1974, 71-85.

Cancik, Hubert, ed. 1996. *Geschichte, Tradition, Reflexion*. FS Martin Hengel. Vol. 2, *Griechische und Römische Religion*. Tübingen: Mohr-Siebeck.

———. 1997. "Die 'Repraesentatin' von 'Provinz' (nationes, gentes) in Rom." In Cancik and Rüpke 1997, 129-43.

Cancik, Hubert, and Jörg Rüpke, eds. 1997. *Römische Reichsreligion und Provinzialreligion*. Tübingen: Mohr-Siebeck.

Canivet, Pierre. 1989. "Le christianisme en Syrie des origines à l'avènement de l'islam." In Dentzer and Orthmann 1989, 117-48.

Capper, Brian. 1995. "The Palestinian Cultural Context of Earliest Christian Community of Goods." In Bauckham 1995a, 323-56.

———. 1998. "Reciprocity and the Ethic of Acts." In Marshall and Peterson 1998, 499-518.

Cara, Robert J. 2001. "The Ambiguous Characterization of Barnabas in Acts 15:36-41." Ph.D. diss., Westminster Theological Seminary.

Caragounis, Chrys C. 1966. *The Ephesian Mysterion: Meaning and Content*. ConBNT 8. Lund: Gleerup.

———. 1990. *Peter and the Rock*. BZNW 58. Berlin: de Gruyter.

———. 1998. "From Obscurity to Prominence: The Development of the Roman Church Between Romans and 1 Clement." In Donfried and Richardson 1998, 245-79.

Carson, Donald A. 1986. "Pauline Inconsistency: Reflections on I Corinthians 9.19-23 and Galatians 2.11-14." *Churchman* 100:6-45.

———. 1988. *Showing the Spirit: A Theological Exposition of 1 Corinthians 12-14*. Grand Rapids: Baker.

———. 2000. "Paul's Mission and Prayer." In Bolt and Thompson 2000, 175-84.

Carson, D. A., et al., eds. 2001. *Justification and Variegated Nomism: A Fresh Appraisal of Paul and Second Temple Judaism*. WUNT 2.140. Tübingen: Mohr-Siebeck.

Carson, D. A., D. J. Moo and L. Morris. 1992. *An Introduction to the New Testament*. Leicester: Inter-Varsity Press.

Carter, Warren. 1993. "The Crowds in Matthew's Gospel." *CBQ* 55:54-67.

Cartledge, Mark J. 1993. "A Model of Hermeneutical Method—An Exegetical Missiological Reflection upon Suffering in 2 Corinthians 4.7-15." *EvRT* 17:472-83.

Casalegno, Alberto. 1994. "Missâo e inter-relacionamento humano no envio dos setenta e dois e em outros textos lucanos." *Perspectiva Teológica* 26:27-45.

Caspi, Mishael M., ed. 1981. *Jewish Tradition in the Diaspora*. FS Walter J. Fischel. Berkeley, Calif.: Judah L. Magnes Memorial Museum.

Casson, Lionel. 1989. *The Periplus Maris Erythraei: Text with Introduction, Translation, and Commentary*. Princeton, N.J.: Princeton University Press.

———. 1994. *Travel in the Ancient World*. Baltimore: Johns Hopkins University Press [London: Allen & Unwin, 1974]. German: *Reisen in der alten Welt*. Munich: Beck, 1976.

———. 2001. *Libraries in the Ancient World*. New Haven: Yale University Press.

Catchpole, David R. 1991. "The Mission Charge in Q." *Semeia* 55:147-74.

———. 1992. "The Cenurion's Faith and Its Function in Q." In Van Segbroeck et al. 1992, 1:517-40.

———. 1993. *The Quest for Q*. Edinburgh: T & T Clark.

Cepas, Adela, et al. 1997. *Tabula Imperii Romani K/J 31: Pyrénées Orientales-Baleares; Tarraco, Baleares*. Madrid: Consejo Superior de Investigaciones Científicas and Ministerio de Cultura.

Cerfaux, Lucien. 1951. "Saint Paul et le 'serviteur de Dieu' d'Isaïe." In Cerfaux 1954, 439-54.

———. 1953. "Saint Pierre et sa succession." In Cerfaux 1954, 239-51.

———. 1954. *Receuil Lucien Cerfaux: Études d'exégèse et d'histoire religieuse de Monseigneur Cerfaux, réunies a l'occasion de son soixante-dixième anniversaire*. Vol. 2. BETL 7. Gembloux: Duculot, 1954.

———. 1957. *Discours de mission dans l'évangile de Saint Matthieu*. Tournai: Desclée. English: *Apostle and Apostolate According to the Gospel of St. Matthew*. New York: Desclée, 1960.

———. 1967. *The Christian in the Theology of St. Paul*. New York: Herder & Herder.

Chadwick, Henry. 1954-1955. "'All Things to All Men' (1Cor 9.22)." *NTS* 1:261-75.

Chae, Daniel J.-S. 1997. *Paul as Apostle to the Gentiles: His Apostolic Self-Awareness and Its Influence on the Soteriological Argument in Romans*. Carlisle: Paternoster.

Chakrabarti, Dilip K. 1998. *The Archaeology of Ancient Indian Cities*. Delhi: Oxford University Press.

Chappuis, Jean-Marc 1982. "Jesus and the Samaritan Woman: The Variable Geometry of Communication." *Ecumenical Review* 34:8-34.

Charette, Blaine. 1990. "A Harvest for the People? An Interpretation of Matthew 9.37f." *JSNT* 38:29-35.

Charlesworth, James H. 1995. *The Beloved Disciple: Whose Witness Validates the Gospel of John?* Valley Forge, Pa.: Trinity.

Chaumont, Marie-Louise. 1988. *La Christianisation de l'Empire Iranian des orig-*

ines aux grandes persécutions du IVe siècle. CSCO 499. Leuven: Peeters.

Cheriyan, C. V. 1973. *A History of Christianity in Kerala: From the Mission of St. Thomas to the Arrival of Vasco Da Gama, A.D. 52-1498.* Kottayam: Kerala Historical Society.

Chesnutt, Randall D. 1995. *From Death to Life: A Descriptive and Comparative Study of Conversion in Joseph and Aseneth.* JSPSup 16. Sheffield: Sheffield Academic Press.

Chester, Andrew. 1992. "The Parting of the Ways: Eschatology and Messianic Hope." In Dunn 1992, 239-313.

Childs, Brevard S. 1985. *Old Testament Theology in a Canonical Context.* London: SCM Press.

Chilton, Bruce, and Craig A. Evans, eds. 1994. *Studying the Historical Jesus: Evaluations of the State of Current Research.* NTTS 19. Leiden: Brill.

———. 1997. *Jesus in Context: Temple, Purity, and Restoration.* AGAJU 39. Leiden: Brill.

———, eds. 1999a. *Authenticating the Words of Jesus.* NTTS 28.1. Leiden: Brill.

———, eds. 1999b. *Authenticating the Activities of Jesus.* NTTS 28.2. Leiden: Brill.

———, eds. 1999c. *James the Just and Christian Origins.* NovTSup 98. Leiden: Brill.

Chilton, Bruce, and Jacob Neusner, eds. 2001. *The Brother of Jesus: James the Just and His Mission.* Louisville: Westminster John Knox.

Christ, Karl. 1992. *Geschichte der römischen Kaiserzeit: Von Augustus bis zu Konstantin.* 2nd ed. Munich: Beck [1988].

Cimino, Rosa Maria, ed. 1994. *Ancient Rome and India: Commercial and Cultural Contacts Between the Roman World and India.* New Delhi: Munshiram Manoharlal.

Cineira, David Alvarez. 1999. *Die Religionspolitik des Kaisers Claudius und die paulinische Mission.* Herders biblische Studien 19. Freiburg: Herder.

Cipriani, Settimio 1990. "'Evangelizzazione' e 'Missione' nella prima lettera di Pietro." In Ghiberti 1990c, 125-38.

Citron, B. 1954. "The Multitudes in the Synoptic Gospels." *SJT* 7:408-18.

Clark, Andrew C. 1998. "The Role of the Apostles." In Marshall and Peterson 1998, 167-90.

Clarke, Andrew D. 1993. *Secular and Christian Leadership in Corinth: A Sociohistorical and Exegetical Study of 1 Corinthians 1-6.* AGAJU 18. Leiden: Brill.

———. 1994. "Rome and Italy." In Gill and Gempf 1994, 455-81.

———. 2000. *Serve the Community of the Church: Christians as Leaders and Ministers.* Grand Rapids: Eerdmans.

Clavier, Henri. 1970. "Méthode et inspiration dans la mission de Paul." In *Verborum Veritas,* FS Gustav Stählin, edited by O. Böcher and K. Haacker, 171-87. Wuppertal: Brockhaus.

Clemen, Carl. 1929. "Die Missionstätigkeit der nichtchristlichen Religionen." *ZMR* 44:225-43.

Cohen, Getzel M. 1995. *The Hellenistic Settlements in Europe, the Islands, and Asia Minor.* Hellenistic Culture and Society 17. Berkeley: University of California Press.

Cohen, Norman J. 1992. "Judaism and Christianity: The Parting of the Ways." *Thought* 67:409-19.

Cohen, Shaye J. D. 1979. *Josephus in Galilee and Rome: His Vita and Development as a Historian.* Columbia Studies in the Classical Tradition 8. Leiden: Brill [repr., 2002].

————. 1987. "Respect for Judaism by Gentiles according to Josephus." *HTR* 80:409-30.

————. 1989. "Crossing the Boundary and Becoming a Jew." *HTR* 82:13-33.

————. 1990. "The Rabbinic Conversion Ceremony." *JJS* 41:177-203.

————. 1991. "Adolph Harnack's 'The Mission and Expansion of Judaism': Christianity Succeeds Where Judaism Fails." In Pearson 1991, 163-69.

————. 1999. "The Rabbi in Second-Century Jewish Society." *CHJ* 3:922-90.

Cole, Dan P. 1988. "Corinth and Ephesus: Why Did Paul Spend Half His Journeys in These Cities?" *BRev* 4:20-30.

Colenso, John William. 1861. *St. Paul's Epistle to the Romans: Newly Translated and Explained from a Missionary Point of View.* London: Macmillan [New York: Appleton, 1863].

Collins, John J. 1995. *The Scepter and the Star: The Messiahs of the Dead Sea Scrolls and Other Ancient Literature.* New York: Doubleday.

————. 2000. *Between Athens and Jerusalem: Jewish Identity in the Hellenistic Diaspora.* 2nd ed. Grand Rapids: Eerdmans [1983].

Collins, John N. 1990. *Diakonia: Re-interpreting the Ancient Sources.* Oxford: Oxford University Press.

Colpe, Carsten 1987. "Die älteste judenchristliche Gemeinde." In Becker et al. 1987, 59-79.

————. 1990. "Die Ausbildung des Heidenbegriffs in antikem Judentum und früher Kirche und das Zweideutigwerden des Christentums." In *Das Siegel der Propheten: Historische Beziehungen zwischen Judentum, Judenchristentum, Heidentum und frühem Islam,* 90-122. ANTZ 3. Berlin: Institut Kirche und Judentum.

Congar, Yves. 1970. "Souci du salut des païens et conscience missionnaire dans le christianisme postapostolique et préconstantinien." In *Kyriakon,* FS J. Quasten, edited by P. Granfield and J. A. Jungmann, 1:3-11. 2 vols. Münster: Aschendorff.

Conn, Harvie M. 1985. "Lucan Perspectives and the City." *Missiology* 13:409-28.

Conzelmann, Hans. 1962. *Die Mitte der Zeit: Studien zur Theologie des Lukas.* 4th ed. [= 7th ed., 1993]. BHTh 17. Tübingen: Mohr-Siebeck [1954]. English: *The*

Theology of St. Luke. London: Faber & Faber; New York: Harper, 1960 [repr., Philadelphia: Fortress, 1982].

———. 1967. *Grundriss der Theologie des Neuen Testaments.* Edited by A. Lindemann. 5th ed. Einführung in die evangelische Theologie 2. Munich: Kaiser [2nd ed., 1968]. English: *An Outline of the Theology of the New Testament.* London: SCM Press, 1969.

———. 1969. *Geschichte des Urchristentums.* GNT 5. Göttingen: Vandenhoeck & Ruprecht [6th ed., 1989]. English: *History of Primitive Christianity.* Nashville: Abingdon, 1973.

Conzelmann, Hans, and Andreas Lindemann. 1995. *Arbeitsbuch zum Neuen Testament.* 11th ed. UTB 52. Tübingen: Mohr-Siebeck [1975].

Cook, J. G. 1993. "Some Hellenistic Responses to the Gospels and Gospel Traditions." *ZAW* 84:233-54.

Cook, John M. 1973. *The Troad: An Archaeological and Topographical Study.* Oxford: Clarendon.

Cook, Richard B. 1981. "Paul, the Organizer." *Missiology* 9:485-98.

———. 1982. "St Paul—Preacher, Evangelist or Organizer?" *ExpTim* 93:171-73.

Corbo, Virgilio. 1972. *The House of St. Peter at Capharnaum: A Preliminary Report of the First Two Campaigns of Excavations, April 16-June 19, Sept. 12-Nov. 26, 1968.* 2nd ed. Publications of the Studium Biblicum Franciscanum, collectio minor 5. Jerusalem: Franciscan Printing Press [1969].

———. 1993. "The Church of the House of St. Peter." In *Ancient Churches Revealed,* edited by Y. Tsafrir, 71-76. Jerusalem: Israel Exploration Society.

Corsten, Thomas. 1997. *Die Inschriften von Laodikeia am Lykos.* IK 49.1. Bonn: Habelt.

Cothenet, Édouard. 1978a. "Un grand voyageur." *CaE* 26:26-29.

———. 1978b. "Premier voyage missionnaire." *CaE* 26:30-48.

———. 1978c. "Second voyage missionnaire." *CaE* 26:49-62.

———. 1978d. "Troisième voyage missionnaire." *CaE* 26:63-69.

Cotter, Wendy J. 1992. "The Parables of the Mustard Seed and the Leaven: Their Function in the Earliest Stratum of Q." *TJT* 8:38-51.

———. 2000. "Cornelius, the Roman Army and Religion." In Donaldson 2000, 279-301.

Cotterell, Peter, and Max Turner. 1989. *Linguistics and Biblical Interpretation.* London: SPCK.

Cousland, J. Robert C. 2002. *The Crowds in the Gospel of Matthew.* NovTSup 102. Leiden: Brill.

Crockett, William V., and James G. Sigountos, eds. 1993. *Through No Fault of Their Own? The Fate of Those Who Have Never Heard.* Grand Rapids: Baker [1991].

Crossan, John Dominic. 1991. *The Historical Jesus: The Life of a Mediterranean Jewish Peasant.* San Francisco: HarperSanFrancisco. German: *Der historische*

Jesus. Munich: Beck, 1994.

———. 1998. *The Birth of Christianity: Discovering What Happened in the Years Immediately after the Execution of Jesus.* San Francisco: HarperSanFranciso.

Crouch, James E. 1972. *The Origin and Intention of the Colossian Haustafel.* FRLANT 109. Göttingen: Vandenhoeck & Ruprecht.

Crown, Alan D., ed. 1989. *The Samaritans.* Tübingen: Mohr-Siebeck.

Cullmann, Oscar. 1936. "Der eschatologische Charakter des Missionsauftrages und des apostolischen Sendungsbewußtseins bei Paulus." In Cullmann 1966, 305-36.

———. 1941. "Eschatologie und Mission im Neuen Testament." In Cullmann 1966, 348-60.

———. 1952. *Petrus: Jünger, Apostel, Märtyrer; Das historische und das theologische Petrusproblem.* Zürich: Zwingli. English: *Peter: Disciple, Apostle, Martyr.* 2nd ed. London: SCM Press; Philadelphia: Westminster Press, 1962 [1953].

———. 1953. "Samarien und die Anfänge der christlichen Mission: Wer sind die ΆΛΛΟΙ von Joh 4,38?" In Cullmann 1966, 232-40.

———. 1966. *Vorträge und Aufsätze 1925-1962.* Edited by K. Fröhlich. Tübingen: Mohr-Siebeck.

———. 1994. *Gebet im Neuen Testament.* Tübingen: Mohr-Siebeck. English: *Prayer in the New Testament.* Minneapolis: Fortress, 1995.

Culpepper, Alan. 1994. *John, the Son of Zebedee: The Life of a Legend.* Columbia: University of South Carolina Press [Minneapolis: Fortress, 2000].

Culver, R. D. 1968. "What Is the Church's Commission?" *BSac* 125:243-53.

Cuntz, Otto, ed. 1929. *Itineraria Romana.* Vol. 1, *Itineraria Antonini Augusti et Burdigalense.* Leipzig: Teubner [repr., Stuttgart: Teubner 1990].

Czajkowski, Michal. 1988. "Die Inkulturation des Evangeliums Jesu im Neuen Testament und heute." *Collectanea Theologica* 58:29-38.

Dabelstein, Rolf. 1981. *Die Beurteilung der "Heiden" bei Paulus.* Beiträge zur biblischen Exegese und Theologie 14. Frankfurt: Lang.

Dahl, Nils A. 1977. *Studies in Paul: Theology for the Early Christian Mission.* Minneapolis: Augsburg.

Dahlheim, Werner. 1982. "Die Funktion der Stadt im römischen Herrschaftsverband." In *Stadt und Herrschaft: Römische Kaiserzeit und hohes Mittelalter,* edited by F. Vittinghoff, 13-74. Historische Zeitschrift Beiheft 7. Munich: Oldenbourg.

Dahlmann, Joseph. 1912. *Die Thomas-Legende und die ältesten historischen Beziehungen des Christentums zum fernen Osten im Lichte der indischen Altertumskunde.* Freiburg: Herder.

Dalbert, Peter. 1954. *Die Theologie der hellenistisch-jüdischen Missionsliteratur unter Ausschluss von Philo und Josephus.* Hamburg: Reich.

Dalton, William J. 1991. "Once More: Paul Among Jews and Gentiles." *Pacifica* 4:51-61.

Daniel, David. 1986. *The Orthodox Church of India: History.* 2nd ed. 2 vols. New Delhi: Rachel David [1972].

Dar, Saifur Rahman. 1988. "Gondophares and Taxila." In Rooney 1988, 16-30.

Dassmann, Ernst. 1979. *Der Stachel im Fleisch: Paulus in der frühchristlichen Literatur bis Irenäus.* Münster: Aschendorff.

———. 1989. "Archäologische Spuren frühchristlicher Paulusverehrung." *Römische Quartalschrift* 84:271-98.

———. 1991. *Kirchengeschichte.* Vol. 1, *Ausbreitung, Leben und Lehre der Kirche in den ersten drei Jahrhunderten.* Studienbücher Theologie 10. Stuttgart: Kohlhammer.

Daube, David. 1947. "κερδαίνω as a Missionary Term." In Daube 1956, 352-61.

———. 1948. "Jewish Missionary Maxims in Paul." In Daube 1956, 336-51.

———. 1956. *The New Testament and Rabbinic Judaism.* London: University of London Press [repr., Peabody, Mass.: Hendrickson, 1994].

———. 1981. "Conversion to Judaism and Early Christianity." In *Ancient Jewish Law,* 1-47. Leiden: Brill.

Dauer, Anton. 1984. *Johannes und Lukas: Untersuchungen zu den johanneisch-lukanischen Parallelperikopen Joh 4,46-54/Lk 7,1-10—Joh 12,1-8/Lk 7,36-50; 10,38-42—Joh 20,19-29/Lk 24,36-49.* FB 50. Würzburg: Echter.

———. 1996. *Paulus und die christliche Gemeinde im syrischen Antiochia: Kritische Bestandsaufnahme der modernen Forschung mit einigen weiterführenden Überlegungen.* Weinheim: Beltz Athenäum.

Dautzenberg, Gerhard. 1979. "Der Wandel der Reich-Gottes-Verkündigung in der urchristlichen Mission." In *Zur Geschichte des Urchristentums,* edited by G. Dautzenberg, H. Merklein and K. Müller, 11-32. QD 87. Freiburg: Herder.

———. 1983. "Zur Stellung der Frauen in den paulinischen Gemeinden." In *Die Frau im Urchristentum,* edited by G. Dautzenberg et al., 182-224. QD 95. Freiburg: Herder.

———. 1991. "Frühes Christentum—Gilt die Tora weiterhin? Hellenistische Mission, Paulus und das Markusevangelium." *Orientierung* 55:243-46.

Davey, Francis N. 1961. "The Gospel According to St. John and the Christian Mission." In Anderson 1961, 85-93.

Davids, P. H., and R. P. Martin, eds. 1997. *Dictionary of the Later New Testament and Its Developments.* Downers Grove, Ill.: InterVarsity Press.

Davies, Graham I. 1979. *The Way of the Wilderness: A Geographical Study of the Wilderness Itineraries in the Old Testament.* Cambridge: Cambridge University Press.

———. 1989. "The Destiny of the Nations in the Book of Isaiah." In *The Book of Isaiah/Le Livre d'Isaïe: Les oracles et leurs reflectures unité complexité de l'ouvrage,* edited by J. Vermeylen, 93-120. BETL 81. Leuven: Leuven University Press.

Davies, Philip R. 1995. "Who Can Join the 'Damascus Covenant'?" *JJS* 46:134-42.

Davies, William D. 1967. *Paul and Rabbinic Judaism: Some Rabbinic Elements in Pauline Theology.* 2nd ed. London: SPCK [1948].

———. 1974. *The Gospel and the Land: Early Christianity and Jewish Territory Doctrine.* Berkeley: University of California Press [repr., Sheffield: Sheffield Academic Press, 1994].

Davies, William D., and Dale C. Allison. 1992. "Matt 28.16-20: Texts Behind the Text." *RHPR* 72:89-98.

Davies, William D., et al., eds. 1989. *The Cambridge History of Judaism.* Vol. 2, *The Hellenistic Age.* Cambridge: Cambridge University Press.

———, et al., eds. 1999. *The Cambridge History of Judaism.* Vol. 3, *The Early Roman Period.* Cambridge: Cambridge University Press.

Day, John. 1942. *An Economic History of Athens under Roman Domination.* New York: Arno [1973].

Debord, Pierre. 1982. *Aspects sociaux et économiques de la vie religieuse dans l'anatolie gréco-romaine.* EPRO 88. Leiden: Brill.

Degenhardt, Johannes J., ed. 1991. *Die Freude an Gott—unsere Kraft.* FS O. Knoch. Stuttgart: Katholisches Bibelwerk.

Deines, Roland. 1994. "Die Abwehr der Fremden in den Texten aus Qumran: Zum Verständnis der Fremdenfeindlichkeit in der Qumrangemeinde." In Feldmeier and Heckel 1994, 59-91.

———. 1997. *Die Pharisäer.* WUNT 101. Tübingen: Mohr-Siebeck.

Deissmann, Adolf. 1923. *Licht vom Osten: Das Neue Testament und die neuentdeckten Texte der hellenistisch-römischen Welt.* 4th ed. Tübingen: Mohr-Siebeck. English: *Light from the Ancient East: The New Testament Illustrated by Recently Discovered Texts of the Graeco-Roman World.* 4th ed. London: Hodder & Stoughton, 1927 [repr., Grand Rapids: Eerdmans, 1980].

———. 1925. *Paulus: Eine Kultur- und Religionsgeschichtliche Skizze.* 2nd ed. Tübingen: Mohr. English: *Paul: A Study in Social and Religious History.* London: Hodder & Stoughton, 1926.

Deissmann, Marieluise. 1990. *Daten zur antiken Chronologie und Geschichte.* Stuttgart: Reclam.

Delbrück, Hans. 1964-1966. *Geschichte der Kriegskunst im Rahmen der politischen Geschichte: Erster Teil, Das Altertum; Zweiter Teil, Die Germanen.* 2 vols. Berlin: de Gruyter [= 3rd ed., 1920-1921; 1900-1909]. English: *History of the Art of War within the Framework of Political History.* Vol. 1, *Antiquity;* vol. 2, *Germans.* Contributions in Military History 9, 20. Westport, Conn.: Greenwood, 1975-1980.

Delling, Gerhard. 1965a. "Josephus und die heidnischen Religionen." In Delling 1970, 45-52.

———. 1965b. "Zur Taufe von 'Häusern' im Urchristentum." In Delling 1970, 288-310.

———. 1970. *Studien zum Neuen Testament und zum hellenistischen Juden-*

tum: Gesammelte Aufsätze 1950-1968. Edited by F. Hahn et al. Göttingen: Vandenhoeck & Ruprecht.

———. 1986. "Die Begegnung zwischen Hellenismus und Judentum." *ANRW* II.20.1:3-39.

———. 1987. *Die Bewältigung der Diasporasituation durch das hellenistische Judentum.* Göttingen: Vandenhoeck & Ruprecht.

Delville, Jean-Pierre. 1995. "L'Épître aux Hébreux à la lumière du prosélytisme juif." *Revista Catalana de Teologia* 10.2:323-68.

Denis, Albert-Marie. 1957. "L'apôtre Paul, prophète 'messianique' des Gentils: Étude thématique de 1 Thess. II, 1-6." *ETL* 23:245-318.

———. 1970. *Introduction aux pseudépigraphes grecs d'Ancien Testament.* SVTP 1. Leiden: Brill.

Dentzer, Jean-Marie, and Winfried Orthmann, eds. 1989. *Archéologie et histoire de la Syrie II: La Syrie de l'époque achéménide à l'avènement de l'Islam.* Schriften zur vorderasiatischen Archäologie 1. Saarbrücken: Saarbrücker Druckerei und Verlag.

Derrett, J. D. M. 1984. "The Lucan Christ and Jerusalem: τελειοῦμαι (Lk 13.32)." *ZNW* 75:36-43.

———. 1997. "Paul as Master-builder." *EvQ* 69:129-37.

Derwacter, F. M. 1930. *Preparing the Way for Paul: The Proselyte Movement in Later Judaism.* New York: Macmillan.

deSilva, David A. 2002. *Introducing the Apocrypha: Message, Context, and Significance.* Grand Rapids: Baker.

Desreumaux, Alain. 1993. *Histoire du roi Abgar et de Jésus: Présentation et traduction du texte syriaque intégral de La Doctrine d'Addaï.* Apocryphes 3. Turnhout: Brepols.

Dewey, Arthur J. 1994. "ΕΙΣ ΤΗΝ ΣΠΑΝΙΑΝ: The Future and Paul." In Bormann, Del Tredici and Standhartinger 1994, 321-49.

Dexinger, Ferdinand. 1988. "Judentum," *TRE* 17:331-77.

Dexinger, Ferdinand, and Reinhard Pummer. 1992. *Die Samaritaner.* WF 604. Darmstadt: Wissenschaftliche Buchgesellschaft.

Dibelius, Martin. 1939. "Paulus auf dem Areopag." In Dibelius 1968, 29-70. English: in Dibelius 1956, 26-77.

———. 1947a. "Das Apostelkonzil." In Dibelius 1968, 84-90. English: in Dibelius 1956, 92-101.

———. 1947b. "Die Bekehrung des Cornelius." In Dibelius 1968, 96-107. English: in Dibelius 1956, 109-22.

———. 1949. "Die Reden der Apostelgeschichte und die antike Geschichtsschreibung." In Dibelius 1968, 120-62 [ET, 138-91].

———. 1956. *Studies in the Acts of the Apostles.* London: SCM Press; New York: Scribner.

———. 1968. *Aufsätze zur Apostelgeschichte.* Edited by H. Greeven. 5th ed.

FRLANT 60. Göttingen: Vandenhoeck & Ruprecht [1951]. English: *Studies in the Acts of the Apostles.* London: SCM Press; New York: Scribner.

Di Berardino, Angelo. 1999. "Christianity on the Road." *Augustinianum* 39:231-44.

Dickey, Samuel. 1979. "Die Bedeutung wirtschaftlicher und sozialer Faktoren für die Ausbreitung des Christentums in Kleinasien." In *Zur Soziologie des Urchristentums,* edited by W. A. Meeks, 49-66. TB 62. Munich: Kaiser 1979.

Dickson, John P. 2003. *Mission-Commitment in Ancient Judaism and in the Pauline Communities: The Shape, Extent and Background of Early Christian Mission.* WUNT 159. Tübingen: Mohr-Siebeck.

Dieckmann, Hermann. 1920. *Antiochien, ein Mittelpunkt urchristlicher Missionstätigkeit.* Abhandlungen aus Missionskunde und Missionsgeschichte 17. Aachen: Xaverius-Verlag. [*non vidi*]

Dietzfelbinger, Chistian. 1985. *Die Berufung des Paulus als Ursprung seiner Theologie.* WMANT 58. Neukirchen-Vluyn: Neukirchener Verlag [2nd ed., 1989].

Dihle, Albrecht. 1962. "Zur Hellenistischen Ethnographie." In Dihle 1984, 21-46.

———. 1963. "Neues zur Thomas-Tradition." In Dihle 1984, 61-77.

———. 1964. "The Conception of India in Hellenistic and Roman Literature." In Dihle 1984, 89-97.

———. 1974. "Der Seeweg nach Indien." In Dihle 1984, 109-17.

———. 1978. "Die entdeckungsgeschichtlichen Voraussetzungen des Indienhandels der römischen Kaiserzeit." In Dihle 1984, 118-52.

———. 1980. "Plinius und die geographische Wissenschaft in der römischen Kaiserzeit." In Dihle 1984, 174-90.

———. 1983. "Serer und Chinesen." In Dihle 1984, 201-15.

———. 1984. *Antike und Orient: Gesammelte Aufsätze.* Edited by V. Pöschl and H. Petersmann. Supplemente zu den Sitzungsberichten der Heidelberger Akademie der Wissenschaften, Philosophisch-historische Klasse 2. Heidelberg: Winter.

———. 1994. *Die Griechen und das Fremde.* Munich: Beck.

Dilke, Oswald A. E. 1987a. "Itineraries and Geographical Maps in the Early and Late Roman Empires." In Harley and Woodward 1987, 1:234-57.

———. 1987b. "Maps in the Service of the State: Roman Cartography to the End of the Augustan Era." In Harley and Woodward 1987, 1:201-11.

———. 1998. *Greek and Roman Maps.* Baltimore: Johns Hopkins University Press [Ithaca, N.Y.: Cornell University Press, 1985].

Diller, Aubrey. 1986. *The Tradition of the Minor Greek Geographers.* Philological Monographs 14. Amsterdam: Hakkert [New York: American Philological Association, 1952].

Dinzelbacher, Peter, ed. 1993. *Europäische Mentalitätsgeschichte: Hauptthemen in Einzeldarstellunten.* Stuttgart: Kröner.

Dion, P.-É. 1970. "L'universalisme religieux dans les différentes couches rédactionelles d'Isaïe 40-55." *Bib* 51:161-82.

di Segni, Leah. 1999. "Epigraphic Documentation on Building in the Provinces of *Palaestina* and *Arabia*. 4th-7th c." In Humphrey 1995-1999, 2:150-78.

Dobbeler, Axel von. 1987. *Glaube als Teilhabe: Historische und semantische Grundlagen der paulinischen Theologie und Ekklesiologie des Glaubens*. WUNT 22. Tübingen: Mohr-Siebeck.

―――. 2000a. *Der Evangelist Philippus in der Geschichte des Urchristentums: Eine prosopographische Skizze*. TANZ 30. Tübingen and Basel: Francke.

―――. 2000b. "Die Restitution Israels und die Bekehrung der Heiden: Das Verhältnis von Mt 10,5b.6 und Mt 28,18-20 unter dem Aspekt der Komplementarität; Erwägungen zum Standort des Matthäusevangeliums." *ZNW* 91:18-44.

Dobesch, Gerhard, and Georg Rehrenböck, eds. 1993. *Die epigraphische und altertumskundliche Erforschung Kleinasiens*. ETAM 14. Vienna: Österreichische Akademie der Wissenschaften.

Dockx, Stanislas. 1989. "The First Missionary Voyage of Paul: Historical Reality or Literary Creation of Luke?" In *Chronos, Kairos, Christos: Nativity and Chronological Studies,* FS Jack Finegan, edited by J. Vardaman and E. M. Yamauchi, 209-21. Winona Lake, Ind.: Eisenbrauns.

Dodd, C. H. 1953. *The Interpretation of the Fourth Gospel*. Cambridge: Cambridge University Press.

―――. 1963. *Historical Tradition in the Fourth Gospel*. Cambridge: Cambridge University Press.

―――. 1975. *Der Mann, nach dem wir Christen heißen*. Limburg: Lahn-Verlag.

Dodds, Eric R. 1965. *Pagan and Christian in an Age of Anxiety: Some Aspects of Religious Experience from Marcus Aurelius to Constantine*. Cambridge: Cambridge University Press.

Doer, Bruno. 1969. "Civis Romanus sum: Der Apostel Paulus als römischer Bürger." *Helikon* 8:49-69.

Dollar, Harold E. 1993. *A Biblical-Missiological Exploration of the Cross-Cultural Dimensions in Luke-Acts*. San Francisco: Mellen Research University Press.

Dommershausen, Werner. 1987. *Die Umwelt Jesu: Politik und Kultur in neutestamentlicher Zeit*. 4th ed. Theologisches Seminar. Freiburg: Herder [1977].

Donaldson, Terence L. 1985. *Jesus on the Mountain: A Study in Matthean Theology*. JSNTSup 8. Sheffield: JSOT Press.

―――. 1990. "Proselytes or 'Righteous Gentiles'? The Status of Gentiles in Eschatological Pilgrimage Patterns of Thought." *JSP* 7:3-27.

―――. 1993. "'Riches for the Gentiles' (Rom 11:12): Israel's Rejection and Paul's Gentile Mission." *JBL* 112:81-98.

―――. 1994. "'The Gospel That I Proclaim Among the Gentiles' (Gal 2.2): Universalistic or Israel-Centered?" In Jervis and Richardson 1994, 166-93.

―――. 1997a. *Paul and the Gentiles: Remapping the Apostle's Convictional World*. Minneapolis: Fortress.

―――. 1997b. "Israelite, Convert, Apostle to the Gentiles: The Origin of Paul's

Gentile Mission." In Longenecker 1997, 62-84.

————, ed. 2000. *Religious Rivalries and the Struggle for Success in Caesarea Maritima*. Studies in Christianity and Judaism 8. Waterloo, Ont.: Wilfrid Laurier University Press.

Donfried, Karl P., ed. 1991a. *The Romans Debate*. Rev. and exp. ed. Peabody, Mass.: Hendrickson, 1977.

————. 1991b. "War Timotheus in Athen? Exegetische Überlegungen zu 1 Thess 3,1-3." In Degenhardt 1991, 189-96. English: in Donfried 2002, 209-19.

————. 2002. *Paul, Thessalonica, and Early Christianity*. Grand Rapids: Eerdmans.

Donfried, Karl P., and Peter Richardson, eds. 1998. *Judaism and Christianity in First-Century Rome*. Grand Rapids: Eerdmans.

Dorsey, David. 1991. *The Roads and Highways of Ancient Israel*. Baltimore: Johns Hopkins University Press.

Downey, Glanville. 1961. *A History of Antioch in Syria: From Seleucus to the Arab Conquest*. Princeton, N.J.: Princeton University Press.

————. 1963. *Ancient Antioch*. Princeton: Princeton University Press.

Downing, F. Gerald. 1982. "Common Ground with Paganism in Luke and in Josephus." *NTS* 28:546-59.

————. 1988. *Christ and the Cynics: Jesus and Other Radical Preachers in First-Century Tradition*. JSOT Manuals 4. Sheffield: JSOT Press.

————. 1992. *Cynics and Christian Origins*. Edinburgh: T & T Clark.

————. 1996. "A Cynic Preparation for Paul's Gospel for Jew and Greek, Slave and Free, Male and Female." *NTS* 42:454-62.

————. 1998. *Cynics, Paul and the Pauline Churches*. New York: Routledge.

Dräger, Michael. 1993. *Die Städte der Provinz Asia in der Flavierzeit: Studien zur kleinasiatischen Stadt- und Regionalgeschichte*. EHS 3.576. Frankfurt: Lang.

Drane, John W. 1994. "Patterns of Evangelization in Paul and Jesus: A Way Forward in the Jesus-Paul Debate?" In Green and Turner 1994, 281-96.

Dressel, Gert. 1996. *Historische Anthropologie: Eine Einführung*. Cologne: Böhlau.

Drew-Bear, Thomas, and Christian Naour. 1990. "Divinités de Phrygie." *ANRW* II.18.3:1907-2044.

Drew-Bear, Thomas, et al., eds. 1999. *First International Congress on Pisidian Antioch*. Izmir: Kocaeli.

Drexhage, Raphaela. 1988. *Untersuchungen zum römischen Osthandel*. Bonn: Habelt.

Drijvers, Han J. W. 1970. "Edessa und das jüdische Christentum." *VigChr* 24:4-33.

Dschulnigg, Peter. 1989. "Gestalt und Funktion des Petrus im Matthäusevangelium." *SNTU* 14:161-83.

————. 1994. "Aspekte und Hintergrund der Theologie des 1. Petrusbriefes." *ThGl* 84:318-29.

————. 1996. *Petrus im Neuen Testament.* Stuttgart: Katholisches Bibelwerk.

DuBose, Francis M. 1983. *God Who Sends: A Fresh Quest for Biblical Mission.* Nashville: Broadman.

Dudley, Donald R. 1937. *A History of Cynicism from Diogenes to the 6th Century A.D.* London: Methuen [2nd ed., Bristol: Bristol Classical Press, 1998].

Dueck, Daniela. 2000. *Strabo of Amasia: A Greek Man of Letters in Augustan Rome.* London and New York: Routledge.

Dumais, Marcel. 1976. *Le langage de l'Évangelisation: L'annonce missionaire en milieu juif (Actes 13,16-41).* Recherches 16. Tournai-Montreal: Desclée.

————. 1981. "La rencontre de la foi et des cultures." *Lumière et vie* 30:72-86.

————. 1984. "L'évangelisation des pauvres." *Science et Esprit* 26:297-321.

————. 1990. "La vie de la communauté chrétienne et sa portée missionnaire dans l'Eglise des temps apostoliques." *Neue Zeitschrift für Missionswissenschaft* 46:49-61.

————. 1993. "Le salut universel par le Christ selon les Actes des Apôtres." *SNTU* 18:113-31.

Duncan, George S. 1930. *St. Paul's Ephesian Ministry.* New York: Scribner.

Duncan-Jones, Richard D. 1982. *The Economy of the Roman Empire: Quantitataive Studies.* 2nd ed. Cambridge: Cambridge University Press [1974].

Dunn, James D. G. 1970. *Baptism in the Holy Spirit: A Re-examination of the New Testament Teaching on the Gift of the Spirit in Relation to Pentecostalism Today.* London: SCM Press [4th pr., 1977].

————. 1982. "The Relationship between Paul and Jerusalem According to Galatians 1 and 2." *NTS* 28:461-78.

————. 1985. *The Evidence for Jesus.* Philadelphia: Westminster.

————. 1987. "'A Light to the Gentiles': The Significance of the Damascus Road Christophany for Paul." In Hurst and Wright 1987, 251-66.'"

————. 1988. "Matthew 12:28/Luke 11:20—A Word of Jesus?" In *Eschatology and the New Testament,* edited by W. H. Gloer, 29-49. Peabody, Mass.: Hendrickson.

————. 1990. *Jesus, Paul and the Law: Studies in Mark and Galatians.* Louisville: Westminster John Knox.

————. 1991. *The Partings of the Ways: Between Christianity and Judaism and Their Significance for the Character of Christianity.* London: SCM Press; Philadelphia: Trinity [repr., 1996].

————, ed. 1992. *Jews and Christians: The Parting of the Ways A.D. 70 to 135.* WUNT 66. Tübingen: Mohr-Siebeck [with new English translations, Grand Rapids: Eerdmans, 1999].

————. 1993. *The Theology of Paul's Letter to the Galatians.* New Testament Theology. Cambridge: Cambridge University Press.

————. 1994. "How New Was Paul's Gospel? The Problem of Continuity and Discontinuity." In Jervis and Richardson 1994, 367-88.

————, ed. 1996. *Paul and the Mosaic Law.* WUNT 89. Tübingen: Mohr-Siebeck.

————. 1998. *The Theology of Paul the Apostle.* Grand Rapids: Eerdmans.

Dupont, Jacques. 1960. "Repentir et conversion d'après les Actes des Apôtres." In Dupont 1967a, 421-51.

————. 1966. *Paulus an die Seelsorger: Das Vermächtnis von Milet (Apg 20,18-36).* Düsseldorf: Patmos.

————. 1967a. *Études sur les Actes des Apôtres.* LD 45. Paris: Cerf.

————. 1967b. "La mission de Paul 'à Jérusalem' (Acts 12.25)." In Dupont 1967a, 217-41.

————. 1967c. "Le salut des gentils et la signification théologique du livre des Actes." In Dupont 1967a, 393-419.

Dussel, Enrique. 1964. "Universalismo y misión en los poemas del Siervo de Iehvah." *Ciencia y Fe* 20:419-63.

Eckert, Jost. 1992. "Zur Erstverkündigung des Paulus." In *Theologie im Werden: Studien zu den theologischen Konzeptionen im Neuen Testament,* edited by J. Hainz, 279-99. Paderborn: Schöningh.

Eddy, Paul R. 1996. "Jesus as Diogenes? Reflections on the Cynic Jesus." *JBL* 115:449-69.

Edmundson, George. 1913. *The Church in Rome in the First Century: An Examination of Various Controverted Questions Relating to Its History, Chronology, Literature and Traditions.* London: Longmans, Green.

Edwards, Douglas R. 1992. "The Socio-Economic and Cultural Ethos of the Lower Galilee in the First Century: Implications for the Nascent Jesus Movement." In L. Levine 1992, 53-91.

Edwards, Douglas R., and Thomas C. McCollough, eds. 1997. *Archaeology and the Galilee: Texts and Contexts in the Graeco-Roman and Byzantine Periods.* SFSHJ 143. Atlanta: Scholars Press.

Egelkraut, Helmuth L. 1976. *Jesus' Mission to Jerusalem: A Redaction-Critical Study of the Travel Narrative in the Gospel of Luke, Lk 9:51-19:48.* EHS 23.80. Frankfurt: Lang.

Egger, Rita. 1986. *Josephus Flavius und die Samaritaner: Eine terminologische Untersuchung zur Identitätsklärung der Samaritaner.* NTOA 4. Fribourg: Editions Universitaires; Göttingen: Vandenhoeck & Ruprecht.

Ego, Beate. 1994. "'Denn die Heiden sind der Umkehr nahe': Rabbinische Interpretationen zur Buße der Leute von Ninive." In Feldmeier and Heckel 1994, 158-76.

Ehrenberg, Victor, A. H. M. Jones and D. L. Stockton, eds. 1979. *Documents Illustrating the Reigns of Augustus and Tiberius.* 2nd enl. ed. Oxford: Clarendon [1955; 1949].

Eichholz, Georg. 1959. "Paulus im Umgang mit jungen Kirchen: Exegetische Beobachtungen zu 1.Kor 1,18-25." In Margull amd Hermelink 1959, 49-59.

————. 1961. "Der ökumenische und missionarische Horizont der Kirche: Eine exegetische Studie zu Röm 1,8-15." *EvTh* 21:15-27.

———. 1972. *Die Theologie des Paulus im Umriss*. Neukirchen-Vluyn: Neukirchener Verlag [7th ed., 1991].

Eisen, Ute E. 1996. *Amtsträgerinnen im frühen Christentum*. FKDG 61. Göttingen: Vandenhoeck & Ruprecht.

Eissfeldt, Otto. 1954. "Partikularismus und Universalismus in der israelitisch-jüdischen Religionsgeschichte." *ThLZ* 79:283-84.

———. 1964. *Einleitung in das Alte Testament*. 3rd ed. Tübingen: Mohr-Siebeck. English: *The Old Testament*. London: Blackwell, 1965.

Elderen, Bastiaan van. 1970. "Some Archaeological Observations on Paul's First Missionary Journey." In Gasque and Martin 1970, 151-61.

Ellenberger, John 1993. "Is Hell a Proper Motivation for Missions?" In Crockett and Sigountos 1993, 217-27.

Elliger, Winfried. 1987. *Paulus in Griechenland: Philippi, Thessaloniki, Athen, Korinth*. 2nd ed. SBS 92-93. Stuttgart: Katholisches Bibelwerk [1978].

———. 1992. *Ephesos: Geschichte einer antiken Weltstadt*. 2nd ed. Stuttgart: Kohlhammer [1985].

Elliott, John H. 1966. *The Elect and the Holy: An Exegetical Examination of 1 Peter 2.4-10 and the Phrase βασίλειον ἱεράτευμα*. NovTSup 12. Leiden: Brill.

———. 1980. "Peter, Silvanus and Mark in I Peter and Acts." In *Wort in der Zeit: Neutestamentliche Studien*, FS K. H. Rengstorf, edited by W. Haubeck and M. Bachmann, 250-67. Leiden: Brill.

———. 1981. *A Home for the Homeless: A Sociological Exegesis of 1 Peter, Its Situation and Strategy*. Philadelphia: Fortress [2nd ed., 1990].

———. 1991. "Household and Meals vs. Temple Purity: Replication Patterns in Luke-Acts." *BTB* 21:102-8.

Elliott, J. Keith. 1993. *The Apocryphal New Testament: A Collection of Apocryphal Christian Literature in an English Translation*. Oxford: Oxford University Press.

Elliott, Mark Adam. 2000. *The Survivors of Israel: A Reconsideration of the Theology of Pre-Christian Judaism*. Grand Rapids: Eerdmans.

Ellis, Earl E. 1968. "The Circumcision Party and the Early Christian Mission." In Ellis 1978, 116-28.

———. 1971. "Paul and His Co-Workers." In Ellis 1978, 3-22.

———. 1978. *Prophecy and Hermeneutic in Early Christianity: New Testament Essays*. WUNT 18. Tübingen: Mohr-Siebeck [4th ed., 1993].

———. 1989. *Pauline Theology: Ministry and Society*. Exeter: Paternoster.

———. 1991. "'Das Ende der Welt' (Apg 1,8)." In Bussmann and Radl 1991, 277-87. English: "'The End of the Earth' (Acts 1:8)." *BBR* 1 (1991): 123-32.

———. 1993. "Coworkers, Paul and His." *DPL* 183-89.

———. 1999. *The Making of the New Testament Documents*. Biblical Interpretation Series 39. Leiden: Brill.

Eltester, Walter, ed. 1972. *Jesus in Nazareth*. BZNW 40. Berlin: de Gruyter.

Engel, James F., and William A. Dyrness. 2000. *Changing the Mind of Missions: Where Have We Gone Wrong?* Downers Grove, Ill.: InterVarsity Press.

Engelmann, Helmut, and Dieter Knibbe, eds. 1989. *Das Zollgesetz der Provinz Asia: Eine neue Inschrift aus Ephesos*. Epigraphica Anatolica 14. Bonn: Habelt.

Engels, Donald W. 1978. *Alexander the Great and the Logistics of the Macedonian Army*. Berkeley: University of California Press.

———. 1990. *Roman Corinth: An Alternative Model for the Classical City*. Chicago: University of Chicago Press.

Engen, Charles Van. 1993. "The Effect of Universalism on Mission Effort." In Crockett and Sigountos 1993, 183-94.

Engen, Charles Van, et al., eds. 1993. *The Good News of the Kingdom: Mission Theology for the Third Millennium*. FS A. F. Glasser. Maryknoll, N.Y.: Orbis.

Enslin, Morton S. 1980. "The Samaritan Ministry and Mission." *HUCA* 51:29-38.

Ensor, Peter W. 1996. *Jesus and His "Works": The Johannine Sayings in Historical Perspective*. WUNT 2.85. Tübingen: Mohr-Siebeck.

Epp, Eldon J. 1993. "The Significance of the Papyri for Determining the Nature of the New Testament Text in the Second Century." In *Studies in the Theory and Method of New Testament Textual Criticism,* edited by E. J. Epp and G. D. Fee, 274-97. Studies and Documents 45. Grand Rapids: Eerdmans.

Epstein, Lawrence J. 1992. *The Theory and Practice of Welcoming Converts to Judaism: Jewish Universalism*. Lewiston, N.Y.: Mellen.

Erdmann, Martin. 1998. "Mission in John's Gospel and Letters." In Larkin and Williams 1998, 207-26.

Errington, Robert. 1986. *History of Macedonia*. Berkeley: University of California Press. German: *Geschichte Makedoniens: Von den Anfängen bis zum Untergang des Königreiches*. Munich: Beck 1986.

Escobar, Samuel. 1993. "A Pauline Paradigm of Mission: A Latin American Reading." In Engen et al. 1993, 56-66.

Esler, Philip F. 1992. "Glossolalia and the Admission of Gentiles into the Early Christian Community." *BTB* 22:136-42.

Etienne, Robert. 1974. *Pompeji: Das Leben in einer antiken Stadt*. Stuttgart: Reclam.

Evans, Craig A. 1989. *Life of Jesus Research: An Annotated Bibliography*. NTTS 13. Leiden: Brill.

———. 1995. *Jesus and His Contemporaries: Comparative Studies*. AGAJU 25. Leiden: Brill.

———. 1997. "Christianity and Judaism: Partings of the Ways." *DLNTD* 159-70.

———. 2000. "Mark's Incipit and the Priene Calendar Inscription: From Jewish Gospel to Greco-Roman Gospel." *JGRChJ* 1:67-81.

Everts, Janet M. 1993a. "Financial Support." *DPL* 295-300.

————. 1993b. "Conversion and Call of Paul." *DPL* 156-63.

Fansa, Mamoun, et al., eds. 2000. *Damaskus-Aleppo: 5000 Jahre Stadtentwicklung in Syrien.* Beiheft der Archäologischen Mitteilungen aus Nordwestdeutschland 28. Mainz: Zabern.

Farmer, William R. 1976. *The Synoptic Problem: A Critical Analysis.* 2nd ed. Dillsboro: Western North Carolina Press [1964].

————, ed. 1983. *New Synoptic Studies: The Cambridge Gospel Conference and Beyond.* Macon, Ga.: Mercer University Press.

Farrer, Austin. 1955. "On Dispensing with Q." In *Studies in the Gospels,* FS R. H. Lightfoot, edited by D. E. Nineham, 55-88. Oxford: Blackwell.

Farquhar, John N. 1926. "The Apostle Thomas in North India." *BRJL* 10:80-111.

————. 1927. "The Apostle Thomas in South India." *BRJL* 11:20-50.

Fatás Cabeza, Guillermo, et al. 1993. *Tabula Imperii Romani K 30: Madrid; Caesaraugusta-Clunia.* Madrid: Consejo Superior de Investigaciones Científicas and Ministerio de Cultura.

Fear, Andrew T. 1996. *Rome and Baetica: Urbanization in Southern Spain c. 50 BC-AD 150.* Oxford: Clarendon.

Fee, Gordon D. 1994. *God's Empowering Presence: The Holy Spirit in the Letters of Paul.* Peabody, Mass.: Hendrickson.

Feichtinger, Barbara. 1993. "Individuum/Familie/Gesellschaft." In Dinzelbacher 1993, 1-17.

Feldman, Louis H. 1950 "Jewish 'Sympathizers' in Classical Literature and Inscriptions." *TAPA* 81:200-208.

————. 1986. "The Omnipresence of the God-Fearers." *BAR* 12:58-69.

————. 1989. "Proselytes and 'Sympathizers' in the Light of the New Inscriptions from Aphrodisias." *REJ* 148:265-305.

————. 1992. "Jewish Proselytism." In Attridge and Hata 1992, 372-408.

————. 1993a. *Jew and Gentile in the Ancient World: Attitudes and Interactions from Alexander to Justinian.* Princeton, N.J.: Princeton University Press.

————. 1993b. "Proselytism by Jews in the Third, Fourth, and Fifth Centuries." *JSJ* 24:1-58.

Feldman, Louis H., and Meyer Reinhold, eds. 1996. *Jewish Life and Thought among Greeks and Romans: Primary Readings.* Minneapolis: Fortress.

Feldmeier, Reinhard. 1994a. "Die Syrophönizierin (Mk 7,24-30)—Jesu 'verlorenes' Streitgespräch?" In Feldmeier and Heckel 1994, 211-27.

————. 1994b. "Weise hinter 'eisernen Mauern': Tora und jüdisches Selbstverständnis zwischen Akkulturation und Absonderung im Aristeasbrief." In Hengel and Schwemer 1994, 20-37.

Feldmeier, Reinhard, and Ulrich Heckel, eds. 1994. *Die Heiden: Juden, Christen und das Problem des Fremden.* WUNT 70. Tübingen: Mohr-Siebeck.

Feldtkeller, Andreas. 1993. *Identitätssuche des syrischen Urchristentums: Mission, Inkulturation und Pluralität im ältesten Heidenchristentum.* NTOA 25.

Göttingen: Vandenhoeck & Ruprecht.

———. 1994. *Im Reich der syrischen Göttin: Eine religiös plurale Kultur als Umwelt des frühen Christentums*. Studien zum Verständnis fremder Religionen 8. Gütersloh: Mohn.

Fellows, R. G. 2001. "Was Titus Timothy?" *JSNT* 81:33-58.

Fentress, Elizabeth, ed. 2000. *Romanization and the City: Creation, Transformations, and Failures*. JRASup 38. Portsmouth, R.I.: Journal of Roman Archaeology.

Ferguson, Everett. 1973. "Some Factors in the Growth of the Early Church." *RestQ* 16:32-52.

Ferrando, M. A. 1990. "La misión de los discípulos de Jesús." *Teología y Vida* 31:121-31.

Ferrill, Arthur. 1991. *Roman Imperial Grand Strategy*. Lanham, Md.: University Press of America.

Feuillet, André. 1961. "Les origens et la signification de Mt 10.23b." *CBQ* 23: 182-98.

———. 1988. "Le dialogue avec le monde non-chrétien dans les épîtres pastorales et l'épître aux Hébreux." *Esprit et Vie* 98:125-28, 152-59.

Fieger, Michael. 1998. *Im Schatten der Artemis: Glaube und Ungehorsam in Ephesus*. Bern and Frankfurt: Lang.

Fiey, Jean Maurice. 1965-1968. *Assyrie chretienne contribution a l'etude de l'histoire et de la geographie ecclesiastiques et monastiques du nord de l'Iraq*. 3 vols. Beirut: Impr. catholique.

———. 1970. *Jalons pour une histoire de l'Église en Iraq*. CSCO 310. Louvain: Secrétariat du CorpusSCO.

———. 1977. *Nisibe, métropole syriaque orientale et ses suffragants des origines à nos jours*. CSCO 388. Louvain: Secrétariat du CorpusSCO.

Fiensy, David. 1991. *The Social History of Palestine in the Herodian Period*. Lewiston, N.Y.: Mellen.

———. 1995. "The Composition of the Jerusalem Church." In Bauckham 1995a, 213-36.

Figueras, Paul. 1990. "Epigraphic Evidence for Proselytism in Ancient Judaism." In *The New Testament and Christian-Jewish Dialogue*, FS David Flusser, edited by M. Lowe, 194-206. Immanuel 24-25. Jerusalem: Ecumenical Theological Research Fraternity in Israel.

Filson, Floyd V. 1939. "The Significance of the Early House Churches." *JBL* 58:105-12.

Finley, Moses I. 1977. *The Ancient Economy*. 2nd ed. London: Chatto & Windus. German: *Die antike Wirtschaft*. Munich: Deutscher Taschenbuch Verlag, 1977.

Finn, Thomas M. 1985. "The God-Fearers Reconsidered." *CBQ* 47:75-84.

Fiorenza, Elisabeth Schüssler. 1983. *In Memory of Her: A Feminist Theological*

Reconstruction of Christian Origins. London: SCM Press.

Firth, Cyril Bruce. 1976. *An Introduction to Indian Church History.* 3rd ed. The Christian Student's Library 23. Madras: Christian Literature Society [1961].

Fischer, Irmtraud. 1995. *Tora für Israel, Tora für die Völker: Das Konzept des Jesajabuches.* SBS 164. Stuttgart: Katholisches Bibelwerk.

———. 1996. "Schwerter oder Pflugscharen? Versuch einer kanonischen Lektüre von Jes 2, Joel 4 und Micha 4." *Bibel und Liturgie* 69:208-16.

Fischer, Moshe, et al. 1996. *Roman Roads in Judaea II: The Jaffa-Jerusalem Roads.* British Archaeological Reports International Series 628. Oxford: Tempus Reparatum.

Fishwick, Duncan. 1993. *The Imperial Cult in the Latin West.* 2 vols. EPRO 108. Leiden: Brill [1987-1992].

Fittschen, Klaus, and Gideon Foerster, eds. 1996. *Judaea and the Greco-Roman World in the Time of Herod in the Light of Archaeological Evidence.* AAWG-PHK 215. Göttingen: Vandenhoeck & Ruprecht.

Fitzmyer, Joseph A. 1979. *A Wandering Aramean: Collected Aramaic Essays.* SBLMS 25. Missoula, Mont.: Scholars Press.

———. 1989a. *Luke the Theologian: Aspects of His Teaching.* New York: Paulist.

———. 1989b. *Paul and His Theology: A Brief Sketch.* 2nd ed. Englewood Cliffs, N.J.: Prentice Hall.

Fleischer, Robert. 1973. *Artemis von Ephesos und verwandte Kultstatuen aus Anatolien und Syrien.* EPRO 35. Leiden: Brill.

———. 1978. "Artemis von Ephesos und verwandte Kultstatuen aus Anatolien und Syrien." In Şahin et al. 1978, 324-58.

Fleming, Kenneth C. 1993. "Missionary Service in the Life of Paul." *Emmaus Journal* 2:65-77.

Flesher, Paul V. M. 1995. "Palestinian Synagogues before 70 C.E." In Urman and Flesher 1995, 1:27-39.

Flusser, David. 1994. "Noachitische Gebote. I. Judentum." *TRE* 24:582-85.

Flusser, David, and Shmuel Safrai. 1986. "Das Aposteldekret und die Noachitischen Gebote." In *"Wer Tora vermehrt, vermehrt Leben,"* FS H. Kremers, edited by E. Broche and H. Barkenings, 173-92. Neukirchen-Vluyn: Neukirchener Verlag.

Foakes-Jackson, Frederik J. 1927. *Peter: Prince of Apostles; A Study in the History and Tradition of Christianity.* New York: Doran.

Foakes-Jackson, Frederik J., and Kirsopp Lake, eds. 1920-1933. *The Beginnings of Christianity: Part I. The Acts of the Apostles.* 5 vols. London: Macmillan.

Forbes, Christopher B. 1995. *Prophecy and Inspired Speech in Early Christianity and Its Hellenistic Environment.* WUNT 2.75. Tübingen: Mohr-Siebeck.

Ford, J. Massyngbaerde. 1988. "The Holy Spirit and Mission in the New Testament." *Missiology* 16:439-53.

Fornberg, Tord, and David Hellholm, eds. 1996. *Texts and Contexts: Biblical*

Texts in their Textual and Situational Contexts. FS Lars Hartmann. Oslo, Copenhagen and Stockholm: Scandinavian University Press.

Forrester, Duncan B. 1980. *Caste and Christianity: Attitudes and Policies on Caste of Anglo-Saxon Protestant Missions in India.* London Studies on South Asia 1. London: Curzon.

Fossey, John M. 1988. *Topography and Population of Ancient Boiotia.* Chicago: Ares.

Foster, John. 1948-1949. "Was Sergius Paulus Converted? Acts 13.12." *ExpTim* 60:354-55.

Fournier, Marianne. 1997. *The Episode at Lystra: A Rhetorical and Semiotic Analysis of Acts 14:7-20a.* American University Studies Series 7, Theology and Religion 197. New York: Lang.

Fraenkel, Jona. 1993. "Das Verhältnis von Juden und Heiden im Talmud." In *Lernen in Jerusalem, Lernen mit Israel: Anstöße zur Erneuerung in Theologie und Kirche,* edited by M. Stöhr, 59-69. Veröffentlichungen aus dem Institut Kirche und Judentum 20. Berlin: Institut Kirche und Judentum.

France, R. T. 1971. *Jesus and the Old Testament: His Application of Old Testament Passages to Himself and His Mission.* London: Tyndale.

———. 1993. "Conversion in the Bible." *EvQ* 65:291-310.

France, R. T., et al., eds. 1980-1986. *Gospel Perspectives.* 6 vols. Sheffield: JSOT Press.

Franke, Chris. 1999. "Is DI 'PC'? Does Israel Have Most Favored Nation Status? Another Look at 'The Nations' in Deutero-Isaiah." In *SBLSP,* 272-91.

Frankemölle, Hubert. 1982. "Zur Theologie der Mission im Matthäusevangelium." In Kertelge 1982, 93-129.

———. 1984a. "Juden und Christen nach Paulus: Israel als Volk Gottes und das Selbstverständnis der christlichen Kirche." *ThGl* 74:59-80.

———. 1984b. *Jahwebund und Kirche Christi: Studien zur Form- und Traditionsgeschichte des "Evangeliums" nach Matthäus.* NTA Neue Folge 10. 2nd ed. Münster: Aschendorff [1974].

———. 1989. "Jesus als deuterojesajanischer Freudenbote? Zur Rezeption von Jes 52,7 und 61,1 im Neuen Testament, durch Jesus und in den Targumim." In Frankemölle and Kertelge 1989, 34-67.

Frankemölle, Hubert, and Karl Kertelge, eds. 1989. *Vom Urchristentum zu Jesus.* FS J. Gnilka. Freiburg: Herder.

Frankfurter, David. 1998. *Religion in Roman Egypt: Assimilation and Resistance.* Princeton, N.J.: Princeton University Press.

Franklin, Eric. 1975. *Christ the Lord: A Study in the Purpose and Theology of Luke-Acts.* London: SPCK.

Fraser, Peter M. 1972. *Ptolemaic Alexandria.* 3 vols. Oxford: Oxford University Press.

———. 1996. *Cities of Alexander the Great.* Oxford: Clarendon.

Frateantonio, Christa. 1997. "Autonomie der antiken Stadt und Zentralisierung religiöser Administration in der Kaiserzeit und Spätantike." In Cancik and Rüpke 1997, 85-97.

Fredouille, Jean-Claude. 1986. "Heiden." *RAC* 13:1113-49.

Fredriksen, Paula. 1991. "Judaism, the Circumcision of Gentiles, and Apocalyptic Hope: Another Look at Galatians 1 and 2." *JTS* 42:532-64.

Freeman-Grenville, G. S. P. 2003. *The Onomasticon by Eusebius of Caesarea: Palestine in the Fourth Century A.D.* Edited by Joan E. Taylor. Jerusalem: Carta.

Frei, Hans W. 1974. *The Eclipse of Biblical Narrative.* New Haven: Yale University Press.

Freitag, Anton. 1912. "Die Missionsmethode des Weltapostels Paulus auf seinen Reisen." *Zeitschrift für Mission* 2:114-25.

————. 1917. "Die missionarische Predigt im apostolischen und nachapostolischen Zeitalter." *ThGl* 9:124-45.

French, David H. 1980. "The Roman Road-System of Asia Minor." *ANRW* II.7.2:698-729.

————. 1981-1988. *Roman Roads and Milestones of Asia Minor.* 2 vols. British Institute of Archaeology International Series 392. Oxford: British Institute of Archaeology at Ankara.

————. 1992. "Roads in Pisidia." In Schwertheim 1992, 167-75.

————. 1994a. *Studies in the History and Topography of Lycia and Pisidia.* London: British Institute of Archaeology at Ankara.

————. 1994b. "Acts and the Roman Roads of Asia Minor." In Gill and Gempf 1994, 49-58.

Frend, William H. C. 1974. "Der Verlauf der Mission in der Alten Kirche bis zum 7. Jahrhundert." In Frohnes and Knorr 1974, 32-50.

————. 1980. "Bekehrung I. Alte Kirche und Mittelalter." *TRE* 5:443-57.

Frey, Jörg. 1994. "Heiden, Griechen, Gotteskinder: Zu Gestalt und Funktion der Rede von den Heiden im 4. Evangelium." In Feldmeier and Heckel 1994, 228-68.

Freyne, Seán. 1980. *Galilee from Alexander the Great to Hadrian, 323 B.C.E. to 135 C.E.: A Study of Second Temple Judaism.* Wilmington, Del.: Glazier.

————. 1988. *Galilee, Jesus and the Gospels: Literary Approaches and Historical Investigations.* Philadelphia: Fortress.

————. 1992a. "Galilee (Hellenistic/Roman)." *ABD* 2:895-99.

————. 1992b. "Urban-Rural Relations in First-Century Galilee: Some Suggestions from the Literary Sources." In L. Levine 1992, 75-91.

————. 1994. "The Geography, Politics, and Economics of Galilee and the Quest for the Historical Jesus." In *Studying the Historical Jesus: Evaluations of the State of Current Research,* edited by B. Chilton and C. A. Evans, 75-122. NTTS 19. Leiden: Brill.

————. 1996. "Jesus and the Urban Culture of Galilee." In Freyne 2000, 183-207.

————. 1997a. "Town and Country Once More: The Case of Roman Galilee." In Freyne 2000, 59-72.

————. 1997b. "Christianity in Sepphoris and in Galilee." In Freyne 2000, 299-307.

————. 2000. *Galilee and Gospel: Collected Essays.* WUNT 125. Tübingen: Mohr-Siebeck.

Friedli, Richard. 1989. "Die Ortskirche als Ort evangelisierenden Handelns: Sinn, Notwendigkeit und Grenzen von Inkulturation." *Freiburger Zeitschrift für Philosophie und Theologie* 36:159-72.

Friesen, Steven. 1993. *Twice Neokoros: Ephesus, Asia and the Cult of the Flavian Imperial Family.* Leiden: Brill.

Frizzi, Giuseppe. 1984. "La 'missione' in Luca-Atti: Semantica, critica e apologia lucana." *RivB* 32:395-423.

Froehlich, Karlfried. 1996. "Petrus II. Alte Kirche." *TRE* 26:273-78.

Frohnes, Heinzgünter, and Uwe W. Knorr, eds. 1974. *Kirchengeschichte als Missionsgeschichte.* Vol. 1, *Die Alte Kirche.* Munich: Kaiser.

Fuchs, Albert. 1992. "Die synoptische Aussendungsrede in quellenkritischer und traditionsgeschichtlicher Sicht." *SNTU* 17:77-168.

————. 1994. "Die Sehnsucht nach der Vergangenheit." *SNTU* 19:69-111.

Fuhrmann, Manfred. 1984. *Die antike Rhetorik.* Munich and Zürich: Artemis & Winkler [3rd ed., 1990].

Funk, Robert W. 1967. "The Apostolic *Parousia:* Form and Significance." In *Christian History and Interpretation,* FS John Knox, edited by W. R. Farmer et al., 249-69. Cambridge: Cambridge University Press.

Fusco, Vittorio. 1990. "Dalla missione di Galilea alla missione universale: La tradizione del discorso missionario (Mt 9,35—10,42; Mc 6,7-13; Lc 9,1-6; 10,1-16)." In Ghiberti 1990b, 101-25.

Gabba, Emilio. 1999. "The Social, Economic and Political History of Palestine 63 BCE-CE 70." *CHJ* 3:94-167.

Gaca, Kathy L. 1999. "Paul's Uncommon Declaration in Romans 1:18-32 and Its Problematic Legacy for Pagan and Christian Relations." *HTR* 92:165-98.

Gager, John G. 1986. "Jews, Gentiles, and Synagogues in the Book of Acts." *HTR* 79:91-99.

Gagnon, Robert A. J. 1994. "Luke's Motives for Redaction in the Account of the Double Delegation in Luke 7:1-10." *NovT* 36:122-45.

Gallagher, Eugene V. 1993. "Conversion and Community in Late Antiquity." *JR* 73:1-15.

Garbe, Richard. 1914. *Indien und das Christentum.* Tübingen: Mohr-Siebeck.

García Martínez, Florentino. 1993. "Messianische Erwartungen in den Qumranschriften." *JBTh* 8:171-208.

Garlington, Don B. 1991. *The Obedience of Faith: A Pauline Phrase in Historical*

Context. WUNT 2.38. Tübingen: Mohr-Siebeck.

Garnsey, Peter. 1970. *Social Status and Legal Privilege in the Roman Empire.* Oxford: Clarendon.

Garnsey, Peter, and Richard Saller. 1987. *The Roman Empire: Economy, Society and Culture.* London: Duckworth. German: *Das römische Kaiserreich: Wirtschaft, Gesellschaft, Kultur.* Reinbek: Rowohlt, 1989.

Gasque, W. Ward. 1989a. *A History of the Interpretation of the Acts of the Apostles.* 2nd ed. Peabody, Mass.: Hendrickson [1975].

———. 1989b. "The Historical Value of Acts." *TynBul* 40:136-57.

Gasque, W. Ward, and Ralph P. Martin, eds. 1970. *Apostolic History and the Gospel.* FS F. F. Bruce. Exeter: Paternoster.

Gates, Marie-Henriette. 1995. "Archaeology in Turkey." *AJA* 99:207-55.

Gaventa, Beverly R. 1982. "'You Will Be My Witnesses': Aspects of Mission in the Acts of the Apostles." *Missiology* 10:413-25.

Gawlikowski, Michael. 1989. "Les temples dans la Syrie à l'époque hellénistique et romaine." In Dentzer and Orthmann 1989, 323-46.

Geagan, Daniel J. 1979. "Roman Athens: Some Aspects of Life and Culture I. 86 BC-AD 267." *ANRW* II.7.1:371-437.

Gebauer, Roland. 1998. "Mission und Zeugnis: Zum Verhältnis von missionarischer Wirksamkeit und Zeugenschaft in der Apostelgeschichte." *NovT* 40:54-72.

Geffcken, Johannes. 1929. *Der Ausgang des griechisch-römischen Heidentums.* Religionswissenschaftliche Bibliothek 6. Heidelberg: Winter [repr., Darmstadt: Wissenschaftliche Buchgesellschaft, 1963].

Gehring, Roger W. 2000. *Hausgemeinde und Mission: Die Bedeutung antiker Häuser und Hausgemeinden—von Jesus bis Paulus.* Bibelwissenschaftliche Monographien 9. Giessen: Brunnen. English: *House Church and Mission: The Importance of Household Structures in Early Christianity.* Peabody, Mass.: Hendrickson, 2004.

Gelston, A. 1992. "Universalism in Second Isaiah." *JTS* 43:379-98.

Gelzer, Heinrich, Heinrich Hilgenfeld and Ottos Cuntz. 1898. *Patrum nicaenorum nomina Latine, Graece, Coptice, Syriace, Arabice, Armeniace.* Bibliotheca Teubneriana. Stuttgart: Teubner [1995].

Gempf, Conrad. 1988. "Historical and Literary Appropriateness in the Mission Speeches of Paul in Acts." Ph.D. diss., University of Aberdeen. [*non vidi*]

———. 1993. "Athens, Paul at." *DPL* 51-55.

———. 1993b. "Public Speaking and Published Accounts." In Winter and Clarke 1993, 259-303.

———. 1995. "Mission and Misunderstanding—Paul and Barnabas in Lystra (Acts 14.8-20)." In Billington et al. 1995, 56-69.

Gensichen, Hans-Werner. 1971. *Glaube für die Welt: Theologische Aspekte der Mission.* Gütersloh: Mohn.

————. 1980. "Bekehrung V. Religionsgeschichtlich." *TRE* 5:483-86.

————. 1985. "Heidentum I: Biblisch/Kirchen-/missionsgeschichtlich." *TRE* 14:2011-13.

Georgi, Dieter. 1964. *Die Gegner des Paulus im 2. Korintherbrief: Studien zur religiösen Propaganda in der Spätantike.* WMANT 11. Neukirchen-Vluyn: Neukirchener Verlag. English: *The Opponents of Paul in Second Corinthians.* Philadelphia: Fortress, 1986.

————. 1965. *Die Geschichte der Kollekte des Paulus für Jerusalem.* ThF 38. Hamburg: Reich. English: *Remembering the Poor: The History of Paul's Collection for Jerusalem.* Nashville: Abingdon, 1992.

————. 2001. "Synkretismus IV. Judentum." *TRE* 32:534-38.

Gerhardsson, Birger. 1961. *Memory and Manuscript: Oral Tradition and Written Transmission in Rabbinic Judaism and Early Christianity.* ASNU 22. Uppsala: Gleerup [2nd ed., 1964].

————. 1979. *The Origins of the Gospel Tradition.* Philadelphia: Fortress; London: SCM Press.

Gerlitz, Peter. 1990. "Konversion I. Religionsgeschichtlich." *TRE* 19:559-63.

Gesemann, Björn. 1996. *Die Straßen der antiken Stadt Pompeji: Entwicklung und Gestaltung.* EHS 38.56. Frankfurt: Lang.

Ghiberti, Guiseppe. 1990a. "Missione di Gesù e dei discepoli nel quarto Vangelo." In Ghiberti 1990b, 185-200.

————, ed. 1990b. *La missione nel mondo antico e nella Bibbia: XXX Settimana Biblica Nazionale (Roma, 12-16 settembre 1988).* Ricerche Storico Bibliche 2.1. Bologna: Dehoniane.

————, ed. 1990c. *La Bibbia, libro sacro, e la sua interpretazione: Simposio per il XL dell ABI (Milano, 2-4 giugno 1988).* Ricerche Storico Bibliche 2.2. Bologna: Dehoniane.

Gibson, Elsa. 1978. *The "Christians for Christians" Inscriptions of Phrygia: Greek Texts, Translation and Commentary.* HTS 32. Missoula, Mont.: Scholars Press.

Gibson, Richard J. 2000. "Paul and the Evangelization of the Stoics." In Bolt and Thompson 2000, 309-26.

Gielen, Malies. 1990. *Tradition und Theologie neutestamentlicher Haustafelethik: Ein Beitrag zur Frage einer christlichen Auseinandersetzung mit gesellschaftlichen Normen.* BBB 75. Frankfurt: Hain.

Gilbert, Gary. 1991. "The Making of a Jew: 'God-Fearer' or Convert in the Story of Izates." *USQR* 44:299-313.

Gill, David W. J. 1990. "The Importance of Roman Portraiture for Head Coverings in 1 Corinthians 11.2-16." *TynBul* 41:245-60.

————. 1991. "Behind the Classical Façade: Local Religions of the Roman Empire." In *One God, One Lord in a World of Religious Pluralism,* edited by B. W. Winter and A. D. Clarke, 72-87. Cambridge: Tyndale House.

————. 1993. "Corinth: A Roman Colony in Achea." *BZ* 37:259-64.

————. 1994a. "Acts and Roman Religion A. Religion in a Local Setting." In Gill and Gempf 1994, 79-92.

————. 1994b. "Acts and the Urban Élites." In Gill and Gempf 1994, 105-18.

————. 1994c. "Macedonia." In Gill and Gempf 1994, 397-417.

————. 1994d. "Achaia." In Gill and Gempf 1994, 433-53.

————. 1995a. "Acts and Roman Policy in Judaea." In Bauckham 1995a, 15-26.

————. 1995b. "Paul's Travels Through Cyprus (Acts 13:4-12)." *TynBul* 46:219-28.

Gill, David W. J., and Conrad Gempf, eds. 1994. *The Book of Acts in Its Graeco-Roman Setting.* The Book of Acts in Its First-Century Setting 2. Exeter: Paternoster, 1994.

Gilliland, Dean S. 1983. *Pauline Theology and Mission Practice.* Grand Rapids: Baker.

Gillman, John. 1990. "Paul's ΔΙΣΟΔΟΣ: The Proclaimed and the Proclaimer (1Thes 2,8)." In *The Thessalonian Correspondence,* edited by R. F. Collins, 62-70. BETL 87. Leuven: Leuven University Press.

Gittins, Anthony J. 1994. "Beyond Hospitality? The Missionary Status and Role Revisited." *CurTM* 21:164-82.

Gniesmer, Dirk F. 2000. *In den Prozeß verwickelt: Erzähltextanalytische und textpragmatische Erwägungen zur Erzählung vom Prozeß Jesu vor Pilatus (Joh 18,28-19,16a.b).* EHS 23.688. Frankfurt: Lang.

Gnilka, Joachim. 1990. *Jesus von Nazareth: Botschaft und Geschichte.* HThKNTSup 3. Freiburg: Herder [6th ed., 2000].

————. 1994. *Theologie des Neuen Testaments.* HThKNTSup 5. Freiburg: Herder.

————. 1996. *Paulus von Tarsus: Apostel und Zeuge.* HThKNTSup 6. Freiburg: Herder.

————. 2002. *Petrus und Rom: Das Petrusbild in den ersten zwei Jahrhunderten.* Freiburg: Herder.

Goddard, A. J., and S. A. Cummins. 1993. "Ill or Ill-Treated? Conflict and Persecution as the Content of Paul's Original Ministry in Galatia (Galatians 4.12-20)." *JETS* 52:93-126.

Goerner, H. Cornell. 1981. "Jesus and the Gentiles." In *Perspectives on the World Christian Movement: A Reader,* edited by R. Winter and S. C. Hawthorne, A.96-103. Rev. ed. Pasadena, Calif.: William Carey Library; Carlisle: Paternoster [2nd ed., 1992].

Goldenberg, R. 1979. "The Jewish Sabbath in the Roman World Up to the Time of Constantine the Great." *ANRW* II.19.1:414-47.

Goldhill, Simon, ed. 2001. *Being Greek under Rome: Cultural Identity, the Second Sophistic and the Development of Empire.* Cambridge: Cambridge University Press.

Goodacre, Mark. 2002. *The Case Against Q: Studies in Markan Priority and the*

Synoptic Problem. Harrisburg, Pa.: Trinity.

Goodman, Felicitas D. 1972. *Speaking in Tongues: Cross-Cultural Study of Glossolalia.* Chicago: Chicago University Press.

Goodman, Martin. 1983. *State and Society in Roman Galilee, A.D. 132-212.* Totowa, N.J.: Rowman & Allanheld.

———. 1987. *The Ruling Class of Judaea: The Origins of the Jewish Revolt Against Rome, A.D. 66-70.* Cambridge: Cambridge University Press.

———. 1989a. "Proselytising in Rabbinic Judaism." *JJS* 40:175-85.

———. 1989b. "Nerva, the Fiscus Judaicus and Jewish Identity." *JRS* 79:40-44.

———. 1992a. "Jewish Proselytizing in the First Century A.D." In Rajak et al. 1992, 53-78.

———. 1992b. "Diaspora Reactions to the Destruction of the Temple." In Dunn 1992, 27-38.

———. 1994. *Mission and Conversion: Proselytizing in the Religious History of the Roman Empire.* Oxford: Clarendon [2nd pr., 1995].

———. 1996. "The Function of Minim in Early Rabbinic Judaism." In Schäfer 1996, 501-10.

———, ed. 1998. *Jews in a Graeco-Roman World.* Oxford: Clarendon.

Goppelt, Leonhard. 1954. *Christentum und Judentum im 1. und 2. Jahrhundert: Ein Aufriß der Urgeschichte der Kirche.* BFChTh 2.55. Gütersloh: Bertelsmann. Cf. in English: *Jesus, Paul and Judaism: An Introduction to New Testament Theology.* London and New York: Nelson, 1964.

———. 1959. "Der Missionar des Gesetzes." In *Christologie und Ethik: Aufsätze zum Neuen Testament,* 137-46. Göttingen: Vandenhoeck & Ruprecht, 1968.

———. 1962. *Die apostolische und nachapostolische Zeit.* Die Kirche in ihrer Geschichte 1/A. Göttingen: Vandenhoeck & Ruprecht [2nd ed., 1966].

———. 1975-1976. *Theologie des Neuen Testaments.* Göttingen: Vandenhoeck & Ruprecht, 1991 [3rd ed., 1985].

Gottlieb, Gunther. *Christentum und Kirche in den ersten drei Jahrhunderten.* Heidelberger Studienhefte zur Altertumswissenschaft. Heidelberg: Winter, 1991.

Goulder, Michael D. 1989. *Luke: A New Paradigm.* JSNTSup 20. Sheffield: JSOT Press.

———. 1991. "Nicodemus." *SJT* 44:153-68.

———. 1992. "Silas in Thessalonica." *JSNT* 48:87-106.

———. 1994. *A Tale of Two Missions.* London: SCM Press.

———. 1996a. "Differences of Mission in the New Testament." In Lande and Ustorf 1996, 175-82.

———. 1996b. "The Jewish-Christian Mission, 30-130." *ANRW* II.26.3:1979-2037.

———. 2001. *Paul and the Competing Mission in Corinth.* Peabody, Mass.: Hendrickson.

Grafe, Hugald. 1981. "Das Zeitalter der Thomaschristen." In *Evangelische Kirche in Indien: Auskunft und Einblicke,* edited by H. Grafe., 65-71. Erlangen: Verlag der Evangelisch-Lutherischen Mission.

Grainger, John D. 1990. *The Cities of Seleukid Syria.* Oxford: Oxford University Press.

———. 1991. *Hellenistic Phoenicia.* Oxford: Clarendon.

Grant, Robert M. 1986. *Gods and the One God.* Library of Early Christianity. Philadelphia: Westminster Press.

Grappe, Christian. 1992. *D'un Temple à l'autre: Pierre et l'Eglise primitive de Jérusalem.* Études d'histoire et de philosophie religieuses 17. Paris: Presses Universitaires de France.

———. 1995. *Images de Pierre aux deux premiers siècles.* Etudes d'Histoire et de philosophie religieuses 75. Paris: Presses Universitaires de France.

Grassi, Joseph A. 1965. *A World to Win: The Missionary Methods of Paul the Apostle.* Maryknoll, N.Y.: Orbis.

Graus, František. 1987. "Mentalität—Versuch einer Begriffsbestimmung und Methoden der Untersuchung." In *Mentatlitäten im Mittelalter: Methodische und inhaltliche Probleme,* edited by F. Graus, 9-48. Vorträge und Forschungen 35. Sigmaringen: Thorbecke.

Gray, Sherman W. 1989. *The Least of My Brothers: Matthew 25:31-46; A History of Interpretation.* SBLDS 114. Atlanta: Scholars Press.

Green, Henry A. 1986. "The Socio-Economic Background of Christianity in Egypt." In Pearson and Goehring 1986, 100-113.

Green, Joel B. 1994a. "The Demise of the Temple as 'Culture Center' in Luke-Acts: An Exploration of the Rending of the Temple Veil (Luke 23.44-49)." *RB* 101:495-515.

———. 1994b. "Good News to Whom? Jesus and the 'Poor' in the Gospel of Luke." In Green and Turner 1994, 59-74.

———. 1997. "Cornelius." *DLNTD* 243-45.

———. 1998. "Salvation to the End of the Earth: God as the Saviour in the Acts of the Apostles." In Marshall and Peterson 1998, 83-106.

Green, J. B., S. McKnight and I. H. Marshall, eds. 1992. *Dictionary of Jesus and the Gospels.* Downers Grove, Ill.: InterVarsity Press.

Green, Joel B., and Max Turner, eds. 1994. *Jesus of Nazareth: Lord and Christ.* FS I. H. Marshall. Grand Rapids: Eerdmans; Carlisle: Paternoster.

Green, Michael. 1970. *Evangelism in the Early Church.* London: Hodder & Stoughton [2nd ed., 1978]. German: *Evangelisation zur Zeit der ersten Christen: Motivation, Methodik und Strategie.* TELOS-Wissenschaftliche Reihe 4014. Neuhausen-Stuttgart: Hänssler, 1977.

Greeven, Heinrich. 1958. "Die missionierende Gemeinde nach den apostolischen Briefen." In *Sammlung und Sendung: Vom Auftrag der Kirche in der Welt,* edited by J. Heubach and H.- H. Ulrich, 59-71. Berlin: Christlicher Zeitschriftenverlag.

Grégoire, H. 1955-1957. "Bardesane et S. Abercius." *Byzantion* 25-27:363-68.

Gregory, Timothy E., ed. 1993. *The Corinthia in the Roman Period.* JRASup 8. Ann Arbor, Mich.: Journal of Roman Archaeology.

Griffin, Miriam T. 2000. *Nero: The End of a Dynasty.* London: Batsford [1984].

Griggs, C. Wilfred. 1991. *Early Egyptian Christianity: From Its Origins to 451 c.e.* Coptic Studies 2. Leiden: Brill [3rd ed., 1993 = 2001].

Grilli, Massimo. 1992. *Comunità e missione: Le direttive di Matteo; Indagine esegetica su Mt 9.35-11.1.* EHS 21.458. Frankfurt: Lang.

Groh, Dennis E. 1995. "The Stratigraphic Chronology of the Galilean Synagogue from the Early Roman Period Through the Early Byzantine Period." In Urman and Flesher 1995, 1:51-69.

———. 1997. "The Clash Between Literary and Archaeological Models of Provincial Palestine." In Edwards and McCollough 1997, 29-37.

Gross, Walter. 1989. "ᴊʜᴡʜ und die Religionen der Nicht-Israeliten." *ThQ* 169:34-44.

———. 1993. "Israel und die Völker: Die Krise des ᴊʜᴡʜ-Volk-Konzepts im Jesajabuch." In *Der Neue Bund im Alten,* edited by E. Zenger, 149-67. QD 146. Freiburg: Herder.

Grossmann, Peter. 2002. *Christliche Architektur in Ägypten.* Handbuch der Orientalistik 62. Leiden: Brill.

Gruder, Darrel L. 1985. *Be My Witnesses.* Grand Rapids: Eerdmans.

Gruenler, Royce G. 1998. "The Mission-Lifestyle Setting of 1 Tim 2:8-15." *JETS* 41:215-38.

Gundry, Robert H. 1987. "The New Jerusalem: People as Place, Not Place for People." *NovT* 29:254-64.

Gundry Volf, Judith M. 1990. *Paul and Perseverance: Staying in and Falling Away.* WUNT 2.37. Tübingen: Mohr-Siebeck.

Gunther, John J. 1982. "The Association of Mark and Barnabas with Egyptian Christianity." *EvQ* 54:219-32.

Günther, Matthias. 1995. *Die Frühgeschichte des Christentums in Ephesus.* ARGU 1. Frankfurt: Lang.

Guralnick, Eleanor, ed. 1987. *Sardis: Twenty-Seven Years of Discovery.* Chicago: Chicago Society of the Archaeological Institute of America.

Guthrie, Donald. 1975. *The Apostles.* Grand Rapids: Zondervan.

Güttgemanns, Erhardt. 1966. *Der leidende Apostel und sein Herr: Studien zur paulinischen Christologie.* FRLANT 90. Göttingen: Vandenhoeck & Ruprecht.

Haacker, Klaus. 1972. "Die Gallio-Episode und die paulinische Chronologie." *BZ* 16:252-55.

———. 1980. "Dibelius und Cornelius: Ein Beispiel formgeschichtlicher Überlieferungskritik." *BZ* 24:234-51.

———. 1984. "Glaube II. Altes und Neues Testament." *TRE* 13:277-305.

———. 1988a. "Urchristliche Mission und kulturelle Identität: Beobachtungen zu Strategie und Homiletik des Apostels Paulus." *ThBeitr* 19:61-72.

———. 1988b. "Verwendung und Vermeidung des Apostelbegriffs im lukanischen Werk." *NovT* 30:9-38.

———. 1995a. "Die Stellung des Stephanus in der Geschichte des Urchristentums." *ANRW* II.26.2:1515-53.

———. 1995b. "Zum Werdegang des Apostels Paulus: Biographische Daten und ihre theologische Relevanz." *ANRW* II.26.2:815-938, 1924-33.

Haag, H. 1985. *Der Gottesknecht bei Deuterojesaja.* EdF 233. Darmstadt: Wissenschaftliche Buchgesellschaft.

Haas, Odo. 1971. *Paulus der Missionar: Ziel, Grundsätze und Methode in der Missionstätigkeit des Apostels Paulus nach seinen eigenen Aussagen.* Münsterschwarzacher Studien 11. Münsterschwarzach: Vier-Türme-Verlag [Lizentiatsarbeit 1959-1960].

Habbe, Joachim. 1996. *Palästina zur Zeit Jesu: Die Landwirtschaft in Palästina als Hintergrund der synoptischen Evangelien.* Neukirchener Theologische Dissertationen und Habilitationen 6. Neukirchen-Vluyn: Neukirchener Verlag.

Habicht, Christian 1994. *Athen in hellenistischer Zeit: Gesammelte Aufsätze.* Munich: Beck. English: *Athens from Alexander to Antony.* Cambridge, Mass.: Harvard University Press, 1999.

———. 1995. *Athen: Die Geschichte der Stadt in hellenistischer Zeit.* Munich: Beck.

Hadas-Lebel, Moses. 1979. "Le paganisme à travers les sources rabbiniques des IIe et IIIe siècles." *ANRW* II.19.2:397-485.

Hadorn, Wilhelm. 1901. *Mission und Nationalität im Blick auf die Mission der ältesten Christenheit.* Basler Missionsstudien 6. Basel: Missionsbuchhandlung.

Hafemann, Scott J. 1990. *Suffering and Ministry in the Spirit: Paul's Defense of His Ministry in II Cor 2:14-3:3.* Grand Rapids: Eerdmans [rev. ed. of WUNT 2.19; Tübingen: Mohr-Siebeck, 1986].

———. 2000. "The Role of Suffering in the Mission of Paul." In Ådna and Kvalbein 2000, 165-84.

Hagner, Donald A. 1997. "Jewish Christianity." *DLNTD* 579-87.

Hahn, Ferdinand. 1963. *Das Verständnis der Mission im Neuen Testament.* WMANT 13. Neukirchen-Vluyn: Neukirchener Verlag. English: *Mission in the New Testament.* London: SCM Press, 1981 [1965].

———. 1971a. "Mission im Neuen Testament und in der frühen Kirche." In Hahn 1999, 55-66.

———. 1971b. "Genesis 15,6 im Neuen Testament." In *Probleme biblischer Theologie,* FS G. von Rad, edited by H. W. Wolff, 90-107. Munich: Kaiser, 1971.

———. 1972. "Mission und Bekenntnis im Neuen Testament." In *Probleme japanischer und deutscher Missionstheologie in Japan,* edited by F. Hahn, 95-

111. Heidelberg: Ostasienmission.

———. 1980. "Der Sendungsauftrag des Auferstandenen. Matthäus 28,16-20." In Hahn 1999, 11-26.

———. 1984. "Biblische Begründung der Mission." In Hahn 1999, 43-53.

———. 1999. *Mission in neutestamentlicher Sicht: Aufsätze, Vorträge und Predigten.* Missionswissenschaftliche Forschungen 8. Erlangen: Erlanger Verlag für Mission.

Hainz, Josef. 1981. "Gemeinschaft (κοινωνία) zwischen Paulus und Jerusalem (Gal 2,9f): Zum paulinischen Verständnis von der Einheit der Kirche." In *Kontinuität und Einheit,* FS F. Mussner, edited by W. Stenger and P.- G. Müller, 30-42. Freiburg: Herder.

———. 1982. *Koinonia: "Kirche" als Gemeinschaft bei Paulus.* BU 16. Regensburg: Pustet.

———. 1994. "ΚΟΙΝΩΝΙΑ bei Paulus." In Bormann, Del Tredici and Standhartinger 1994, 375-91.

Halfmann, Helmut. 1979. *Die Senatoren aus dem östlichen Teil des Imperium Romanum bis zum Ende des 2. Jahrhunderts n.Chr.* Hypomnemata 58. Göttingen: Vandenhoeck & Ruprecht.

Hamm, Dennis. 1990. "Paul's Blindness and Its Healing: Clues to Symbolic Intent (Acts 9; 22 and 26)." *Bib* 71:53-72.

Hammond, N. G. L. 1967. *Epirus: The Geography, the Ancient Remains, the History and the Topography of Epirus and Adjacent Areas.* Oxford: Clarendon.

———. 1972-1988. *A History of Macedonia.* 3 vols. Oxford: Clarendon.

Hammond, Philip C. 1973. *The Nabateans: Their History, Culture and Archaeology.* Studies in Mediterranean Archaeology 7. Göteburg: Aströms.

Hampel, Volker. 1989. "'Ihr werdet mit den Städten Israels nicht zu Ende kommen': Eine exegetische Studie über Matthäus 10,23." *ThZ* 45:1-31.

Hanfmann, George M. A., ed. 1983. *Sardis from Prehistoric to Roman Times: Results of the Archaeological Exploration of Sardis 1958-1975.* Cambridge, Mass.: Harvard University Press.

Hansen, G. Walter. 1989. "Paul's Three-Dimensional Application of Genesis 15:6 in Galatians." *TJ* 1:59-77.

———. 1994. "Galatia." In Gill and Gempf 1994, 377-95.

———. 1998. "The Preaching and Defence of Paul." In Marshall and Peterson 1998, 295-324.

Hansen, Mogens H. 1991. *The Athenian Democracy in the Age of Demosthenes.* Oxford: Oxford University Press.

Hanson, Richard P. C. 1985. "The Christian Attitude to Pagan Religions." In *Studies in Christian Antiquity,* 144-229. Edinburgh: T & T Clark.

Haraguchi, Takaaki. 1993. "Das Unterhaltsrecht des frühchristlichen Verkündigers: Eine Untersuchung zur Bezeichnung ἐργάτης im Neuen Testament." *ZNW* 84:178-95.

Hare, Douglas R. A., and Daniel J. Harrington. 1975. "'Make Disciples of All Gentiles' (Mt 28.19)." *CBQ* 37:359-69.

Harley, J. Brian, and David Woodward, eds. 1987. *The History of Cartography.* Vol. 1, *Cartography in Prehistoric, Ancient, and Medieval Europe and the Mediterranean.* Chicago and London: University of Chicago Press.

Harman, A. M. 1969. "Missions in the Thought of Jesus." *EvQ* 41:131-42.

Harnack, Adolf von. 1893-1904. *Geschichte der altchristlichen Literatur bis Eusebius: I. Die Überlieferung und der Bestand; II. Die Chronologie.* 4 vols. 2nd ed. Leipzig: Hinrichs [1958].

—————. 1906-1911. *Beiträge zur Einleitung in das Neue Testament.* 4 vols. Leipzig: Deichert.

—————. 1910. "Das Problem des zweiten Thessalonicherbriefes." In *Sitzungsberichte der königlichen preussischen Akademie der Wissenschaften,* 560-78. Philosophisch-historische Klasse 31. Berlin: Sitzungsbericht der Preussischen Akademie der Wissenschaften.

—————. 1924. *Die Mission und Ausbreitung des Christentums in den ersten drei Jahrhunderten.* 4th impr. and enl. ed. 2 vols. Leipzig: Hinrichs [1902; 2nd ed., 1905; 3rd ed., 1915; repr., 1965]. English: *The Mission and Expansion of Christianity in the First Three Centuries.* 2nd enl. and rev. ed. 2 vols. Theological Translation Library 19-20. London: Williams & Norgate; New York: Putnam, 1908 [1904-1905; repr., Eugene, Ore.: Wipf & Stock, 1998].

Harris, William V. 1989. *Ancient Literacy.* Cambridge, Mass.: Harvard University Press.

Hartin, Patrick J. 1993. "The Religious Nature of First-Century Galilee as a Setting for Early Christanity." *Neot* 27:331-50.

Harvey, Anthony E. 1987. "Christ as Agent." In Hurst and Wright 1987, 239-50.

Harvey, John D. 1998a. "Mission in Jesus' Teaching." In Larkin and Williams 1998, 30-49.

—————. 1998b. "Mission in Matthew." In Larkin and Williams 1998, 119-36.

Haspels, C. H. Emilie. 1971. *The Highlands of Phrygia: Sites and Monuments.* 2 vols. Princeton, N.J.: Princeton University Press.

Hassoun, Jacques, ed. 1981. *Histoire des Juifs du Nil.* Paris: Minerve [2nd ed., 1990].

Haubeck, Wilfrid, and Heinrich von Siebenthal. 1994-1997. *Neuer sprachlicher Schlüssel zum griechischen Neuen Testament.* 2 vols. Giessen: Brunnen.

Haufe, Günter. 1985. "Reich Gottes bei Paulus und in der Jesustradition." *NTS* 31:467-72.

Hawthorne, G. F., R. P. Martin and D. G. Reid, eds. 1993. *Dictionary of Paul and His Letters.* Downers Grove, Ill.: InterVarsity Press.

Hayes, Alan L. 2002. "Christian Ministry in Three Cities of the Western Empire (160–258 C.E.)." In Longenecker 2002, 129-56.

Hays, Richard B. 1989. *Echoes of Scripture in the Letters of Paul.* New Haven: Yale University Press.

———. 1996. *The Moral Vision of the New Testament: A Contemporary Introductioni to New Testament Ethics.* San Francisco: HarperCollins.

———. 1999. "The Conversion of the Imagination: Scripture and Eschatology in 1 Corinthians." *NTS* 45:391-412.

Hayward, Robert. 1998. "Abraham as Proselytizer at Beer-Sheba in the Targums of the Pentateuch." *JJS* 49:24-37.

Head, Peter. 1993. "Acts and the Problem of Its Texts." In Winter and Clarke 1993, 415-44.

Heckel, Theo K. 1999. *Vom Evangelium des Markus zum viergestaltigen Evangelium.* WUNT 120. Tübingen: Mohr-Siebeck.

Heckel, Ulrich. 1994. "Das Bild der Heiden und die Identität der Christen bei Paulus." In Feldmeier and Heckel 1994, 269-96.

Hegermann, Harald. 1966. "Das hellenistische Judentum." In Leipoldt and Grundmann 1990, 292-345.

Heiligenthal, Roman. 1994. "Noachitische Gebote. II. Neues Testament." *TRE* 24:585-87.

Heinen, Heinz. 2001. "Greeks, Iranians and Romans on the Northern Shore." In Tsetskhladze 2001, 1-23 (Cf. "Griechische Geschichte und Kultur am Nordufer des Schwarzen Meeres." In *Academiae Analecta,* 57.1:61-78. Brussels: Koninklijke Academie voor Wetenschappen, Letteren en Schone Kunsten).

Heinisch, Paul. 1916. *Die Idee der Heidenbekehrung im Alten Testament.* Biblische Zeitfragen 8.1-2. Münster: Aschendorff.

Hellenkemper, Hansgerd, and Friedrich Hild. 1986. *Neue Forschungen in Kilikien.* Veröffentlichungen der Kommission für die Tabula Imperii Byzantini 4. Vienna: Österreichische Akademie der Wissenschaften.

Hemer, Colin J. 1986. *The Letters to the Seven Churches of Asia in Their Local Setting.* JSNTSup 11. Sheffield: JSOT Press [1989].

———. 1989. *The Book of Acts in the Setting of Hellenistic History.* Edited by C. Gempf. WUNT 49. Tübingen: Mohr-Siebeck [repr., Winona Lake, Ind.: Eisenbrauns, 1990].

Hempel, Johannes. 1954. "Die Wurzel des Missionswillens im Glauben des Alten Testaments." *ZAW* 66:244-72.

Hengel, Martin. 1963. "Maria Magdalena und die Frauen als Zeugen." In *Abraham unser Vater,* FS Otto Michel, edited by O. Betz et al., 243-56. AGSU 5. Leiden: Brill.

———. 1968. *Nachfolge und Charisma: Eine exegetisch-religionsgeschichtliche Studie zu Mt 8,21f und Jesu Ruf in die Nachfolge.* BZNW 34. Berlin: de Gruyter. English: *The Charismatic Leader and His Followers.* New York: Crossroad, 1981.

———. 1969. *Judentum und Hellenismus: Studien zur ihrer Begegnung unter besonderer Berücksichtigung Palästinas bis zur Mitte des 2. Jh.s v.Chr.* WUNT 10. Tübingen: Mohr-Siebeck [3rd ed., 1988]. English: *Judaism and Hellenism:*

Studies in Their Encounter in Palestine during the Early Hellenistic Period. 2 vols. Philadelphia: Fortress, 1974.

———. 1971. "Proseuche und Synagoge: Jüdische Gemeinde, Gotteshaus und Gottesdienst in der Diaspora und in Palästina." In *Tradition und Glaube,* FS K. G. Kuhn, edited by G. Jeremias et al., 157-84. Göttingen: Vandenhoeck & Ruprecht, 1971.

———. 1971-1972. "Die Ursprünge der christlichen Mission." *NTS* 18:15-38. English: Hengel 1983a, 48-64.

———. 1975. "Zwischen Jesus und Paulus: Die 'Hellenisten,' die 'Sieben' und Stephanus (Apg 6,1-15; 7,54-8,3)." *ZThK* 72:151-206. English: Hengel 1983a, 1-29.

———. 1976a. *Die Zeloten: Untersuchungen zur jüdischen Freiheitsbewegung in der Zeit von Herodes I bis 70 n. Chr.* Rev. ed. AGJU 1. Leiden: Brill [1961].

———. 1976b. *Juden, Griechen und Barbaren.* Stuttgart: Calwer.

———. 1979. *Zur urchristlichen Geschichtsschreibung.* Stuttgart: Calwer [2nd rev. and enl. ed., 1984].

———. 1983a. *Between Jesus and Paul: Studies in the Earliest History of Christianity.* London: SCM Press.

———. 1983b. "Der Historiker Lukas und die Geographie Palästinas in der Apostelgeschichte." *ZDPV* 99:147-183. English: In Hengel 1983a, 97-128.

———. 1985. "Jakobus der Herrenbruder—der erste Papst?" In *Glaube und Eschatologie,* FS W. G. Kümmel, edited by E. Gräßer and O. Merk, 71-104. Göttingen: Vandenhoeck & Ruprecht.

———. 1990. "Der vorchristliche Paulus." *ThBeitr* 21 (1990): 174-95.

———. 1991. "Der vorchristliche Paulus." In Hengel and Heckel 1991, 177-293.

———. 1992. "Christological Titles in Early Christianity." In *The Messiah: Developments in Earliest Judaism and Christianity,* edited by J. H. Charlesworth, 425-48. Minneapolis: Fortress.

———. 1993. *Die johanneische Frage: Ein Lösungsversuch.* WUNT 67. Tübingen: Mohr-Siebeck. English: *The Johannine Question.* London: SCM Press; Philadelphia: Trinity, 1989.

———. 1994a. "Einleitung." In Feldmeier and Heckel 1994, ix-xviii.

——— [with Roland Deines]. 1994b. "Die Septuaginta als 'christliche Schriftensammlung,' ihre Vorgeschichte und das Problem ihres Kanons." In Hengel and Schwemer 1994, 182-284.

———. 1995. "The Geography of Palestine in Acts." In Bauckham 1995a, 27-78.

———. 1996. "Die Stellung des Apostels Paulus zum Gesetz in den unbekannten Jahren zwischen Damaskus und Antiochien." In Dunn 1996, 25-51.

———. 2000. "Paulus in Arabien." In *Antike Randgesellschaften und Randgruppen im östlichen Mittelmeerraum,* edited by H.-P. Müller and F. Siegert, 137-57. Münsteraner judaistische Studien 5. Münster: Harrassowitz, 2000. English: "Paul in Arabia." *BBR* 12 (2002): 47-66.

Hengel, Martin, and Roland Deines. 1995. "E. P. Sanders' 'Common Judaism,' Jesus, and the Pharisees." *JTS* 46:1-70.

Hengel, Martin, and Ulrich Heckel, eds. 1991. *Paulus und das antike Judentum.* WUNT 58. Tübingen: Mohr-Siebeck.

Hengel, Martin, and Anna Maria Schwemer, eds. 1991. *Königsherrschaft Gottes und himmlischer Kult im Judentum, Urchristentum und in der hellenistischen Welt.* WUNT 55. Tübingen: Mohr-Siebeck.

———, eds. 1994. *Die Septuaginta zwischen Judentum und Christentum.* WUNT 72. Tübingen: Mohr-Siebeck.

———. 1998. *Paulus zwischen Damaskus und Antiochien: Die unbekannten Jahre des Apostels.* WUNT 108. Tübingen: Mohr-Siebeck [2nd pr., 2000]. English: *Paul Between Damascus and Antioch: The Unknown Years.* London: SCM Press, 1997.

Hennecke, Edgar, and Wilhelm Schneemelcher, eds. 1990-1997. *Neutestamentliche Apokryphen in deutscher Übersetzung.* 6th ed. 2 vols. Tübingen: Mohr-Siebeck [3rd ed., 1959-1964; 5th ed. 1987-1989; study ed., 1999]. English: *New Testament Apocrypha.* From 3rd German ed. Philadelphia: Westminster Press, 1963-1966.

Henneken, Bartholomäus. 1969. *Verkündigung und Prophetie im Ersten Thessalonicherbrief: Ein Beitrag zur Theologie des Wortes Gottes.* SBS 29. Stuttgart: Katholisches Bibelwerk.

Hermisson, Hans-Jürgen. 1982. "Israel und der Gottesknecht bei Deuterojesaja." *ZThK* 79:1-24.

———. 1996a. "Das vierte Gottesknechtslied im deuterojesajanischen Kontext." In *Der leidende Gottesknecht: Jesaja 53 und seine Wirkungsgeschichte,* edited by B. Janowski and P. Stuhlmacher, 1-25. Forschungen zum Alten Testament 14. Tübingen: Mohr-Siebeck.

———. 1996b. "Gottesknecht und Gottes Knechte: Zur ältesten Deutung eines deutero-jesajanischen Themas." In Schäfer 1996, 43-68.

Herrenbrück, Fritz. 1990. *Jesus und die Zöllner: Historische und neutestamentlich-exegetische Untersuchungen.* WUNT 2.41. Tübingen: Mohr-Siebeck.

Herscher, Ellen. 1995. "Archaeology of Cyprus." *AJA* 99:257-94.

Hertig, Paul A. 1997. "Galilean Christianity." *DLNTD* 385-88.

Hertling, L. von. 1934. "Die Zahl der Christen zu Beginn des vierten Jahrhunderts." *ZKTh* 58:245-64.

Herweg, Dirk, and Rachel M. Herweg. 1995. "Über Land und Meer für einen Proselyten? Übertritt in Antike und talmudischer Zeit." In Homolka and Seidel 1995, 44-55.

Herzer, Jens. 1998. *Petrus oder Paulus? Studien über das Verhältnis des Ersten Petrusbriefes zur paulinischen Tradition.* WUNT 103. Tübingen: Mohr-Siebeck.

Hesberg, Henner. 1996. "The Significance of the Cities in the Kingdom of

Herod." In Fittschen and Foerster 1996, 9-25.

Hesselgrave, David J. 1980. *Communicating Christ Cross-Culturally: An Introduction to Missionary Communication.* 4th ed. Grand Rapids: Zondervan.

———. 2000. *Planting Churches Cross-Culturally.* 2nd ed. Grand Rapids: Baker.

Hezser, Catherine. 2001. *Jewish Literacy in Roman Palestine.* TSAJ 81. Tübingen: Mohr-Siebeck.

Hild, Friedrich, and Hansgerd Hellenkemper. 1990. *Kilikien und Isaurien.* 2 vols. TIB 5. Vienna: Österreichische Akademie der Wissenschaften.

Hild, Friedrich, and M. Restle. 1981. *Kappadokien.* TIB 2. Vienna: Österreichische Akademie der Wissenschaften.

Hill, Craig C. 1992. *Hellenists and Hebrews: Reappraising Division within the Earliest Church.* Minneapolis: Fortress.

———. 1996. "Division or Diversity in Acts 6.1-8.4." In Witherington 1996, 129-53.

———. 1997. "Hellenists, Hellenistic and Hellenistic-Jewish Christianity." *DLNTD* 462-69.

Hillard, T., A. Nobbs and B. W. Winter. 1993. "Acts and the Pauline Corpus I: Ancient Literary Parallels." In Winter and Clarke 1993, 183-213.

Hinson, E. Glenn. 1981. *The Evangelization of the Roman Empire: Identity and Adaptability.* Macon, Ga.: Mercer University Press.

Hirschfeld, Yizhar. 1997. "Jewish Rural Settlement in Judaea in the Early Roman Period." In Alcock 1997, 72-88.

Hirshman, Marc. 2000. "Rabbinic Universalism in the Second and Third Centuries." *HTR* 93:101-15.

Hoehner, Harold W. 1972. *Herod Antipas.* SNTSMS 17. Cambridge: Cambridge University Press.

Hoekema, Anthony. 1972. *Holy Spirit Baptism.* Grand Rapids: Eerdmans.

Hoepfner, Wolfram, ed. 2002. *Antike Bibliotheken.* Mainz: Zabern.

Hoffmann, Paul. 1972. *Studien zur Theologie der Logienquelle.* NTA 8. Münster: Aschendorff.

Hofius, Otfried. 1994. "Glaube und Taufe nach dem Zeugnis des Neuen Testaments." *ZThK* 91:134-56.

Hofmann, Johannes. 2000. "Christliche Frauen im Dienst kleinasiatischer Gemeinden des ersten und zweiten Jahrhunderts: Eine propographische Studie." *VigChr* 54:283-308.

Hofrichter, Peter. 1992. "Von der zweifachen Speisung des Markus zur zweifachen Aussendung des Lukas: Die Auseinandersetzung um die Heidenmission in der Redaktionsgeschichte der Evangelien." In *Theologie im Werden,* edited by J. Hainz, 143-55. Paderborn: Schöningh.

———. 1993. "Paulus und die Anfänge der Kirche in Syrien." In *Syrien: Von den Aposteln zu den Kalifen,* edited by E. M. Ruprechtsberger, 13-31. Linzer Archäologische Forschungen 21. Linz: Stadtmuseum Nordico.

Hölbl, Günther. 2001. *A History of the Ptolemaic Empire*. London: Routledge. German: *Geschichte des Ptolemäerreiches*. Wiesbaden: Wissenschaftliche Buchgesellschaft, 1994.

Holl, Karl. 1912. "Die Missionsmethode der alten und die der mittelalterlichen Kirche." In Frohnes and Knorr 1974, 3-17.

Holladay, Carl R. 1992. "Jewish Responses to Hellenistic Culture." In Bilde et al. 1992, 139-63.

Holladay, John S. 1992. "House, Israelite." *ABD* 3:308-18.

Hollander, Harm W. 1994. "The Testing by Fire of the Builders' Works: 1 Corinthians 3.10-15." *NTS* 40:89-104.

Hollander, Harm W., and Marinus de Jonge. 1985. *The Testaments of the Twelve Patriarchs: A Commentary*. SVTP 8. Leiden: Brill.

Holmberg, Bengt. 1978. *Paul and Power: The Structure of Authority in the Primitive Church as Reflected in the Pauline Epistles*. ConBNT 11. Lund: Gleerup.

Holtheide, Bernard. 1983. *Römische Bürgerrechtspolitik und römische Neubürger in der Provinz Asia*. Hochschulsammlung Philosophie: Geschichte 5. Freiburg: Hochschulverlag.

Holtz, Traugott. 1986. "Der antiochenische Zwischenfall (Galater 2.11-14)." *NTS* 32:344-61.

Holum, Kenneth G., et al. 1988. *King Herod's Dream: Caesarea on the Sea*. New York: Norton.

Homolka, Walter, and Esther Seidel, eds. 1995. *Nicht durch Geburt allein: Übertritt zum Judentum*. Darmstadt: Wissenschaftliche Buchgesellschaft.

Hong, John Sungchul. 1994. "On the Great Commission." *EvJ* 12:67-74.

Honig, Anton G. 1951. *Bijdrage tot het onderzoek naar de fundering van de zendingsmethode der comprehensive approach in het Nieuwe Testament*. Kampen: Kok.

Hooker, Morna D. 1996. "1 Thessalonians 1.9-10: A Nutshell—but What Kind of Nut?" In Lichtenberger 1996c, 435-48.

———. 1997. *The Signs of a Prophet: The Prophetic Actions of Jesus*. Harrisburg, Pa.: Trinity.

Hopfe, Lewis M. 1990. "Caesarea Palestinae as a Religious Center." *ANRW* II.18.4:2380-2411.

Horbury, William. 1998. *Jews and Christians in Contact and Controversy*. Edinburgh: T & T Clark.

Horn, Friedrich W. 1983. *Glaube und Handeln in der Theologie des Lukas*. GThA 26. Göttingen: Vandenhoeck & Ruprecht.

———. 1996. "Der Verzicht auf die Beschneidung im frühen Christentum." *NTS* 42:479-505.

———, ed. 2001. *Das Ende des Paulus: Historische, theologische und literaturgeschichtliche Aspekte*. BZNW 106. Berlin: de Gruyter.

Hornschuh, Manfred. 1959. "Die Anfänge des Christentums in Ägypten." Diss.,

Friedrich-Wilhelms-Universität, Bonn. [*non vidi*]

———. 1965. *Studien zur Epistula Apostolorum.* PTS 5. Berlin: de Gruyter.

Horsley, Richard A. 1987. *Jesus and the Spiral of Violence: Popular Jewish Resistance in Roman Palestine.* San Francisco: Harper & Row [repr., Minneapolis: Fortress, 1993].

———. 1989. *Sociology and the Jesus Movement.* New York: Crossroad [2nd ed., 1994].

———. 1994. "The Historical Jesus and Archaeology of the Galilee: Questions from Historical Jesus Research to Archaeologists." In *SBLSP,* 91-135.

———. 1995. *Galilee: History, Politics, People.* Valley Forge, Pa.: Trinity.

Horsley, Richard A., and John S. Hanson. 1999. *Bandits, Prophets, and Messiahs: Popular Movements at the Time of Jesus.* Harrisburg, Pa.: Trinity [New Voices in Biblical Studies; Minneapolis: Winston, 1985].

Horst, Pieter W. van der. 1988. "The Jews of Ancient Crete." In Horst 1990, 148-65.

———. 1989a. "The Altar of the 'Unknown God' in Athens (Acts 17:23) and the Cult of 'Unknown Gods' in the Graeco-Roman World." In Horst 1989, 187-220.

———. 1989b. "Jews and Christians in Aphrodisias in the Light of Their Relations in Other Cities of Asia Minor." In Horst 1990, 166-81.

———. 1990. *Essays on the Jewish World of Early Christianity.* NTOA 14. Fribourg: Universitätsverlag; Göttingen: Vandenhoeck & Ruprecht.

———. 1992. "A New Altar of a Godfearer?" In Horst 1998, 65-71

———. 1994. "The Birkat ha-minim in Recent Research." In Horst 1998, 113-25.

———. 1998. *Hellenism, Judaism, Christianity: Essays in Their Interaction.* 2nd ed. CBET 8. Leuven: Peeters.

Hough, James. 1839-1860. *The History of Christianity in India from the Commencement of the Christian Era.* 5 vols. London: Seeley & Burnside.

Houten, Christiana van. 1991. *The Alien in Israelite Law.* JSOTSup 107. Sheffield: JSOT Press.

Howard, David. 1979. *Student Power in World Missions.* Downers Grove, Ill.: InterVarsity Press.

Howard, George. 1990. *Paul: Crisis in Galatia; A Study in Early Christian Theology.* 2nd ed. SNTSMS 35. Cambridge: Cambridge University Press [1979].

Howego, Christopher. 1992. "The Supply and Use of Money in the Roman World 200 B.C. to A.D. 300." *JRS* 82:1-31.

Howell, Don N. 1996. "Confidence in the Spirit as the Governing Ethos of the Pauline Mission." *TJ* 17:203-21.

———. 1998a. "Mission in Paul's Epistles: Genesis, Pattern, and Dynamics." In Larkin and Williams 1998, 63-91.

———. 1998b. "Mission in Paul's Epistles: Theological Bearings." In Larkin and Williams 1998, 92-116.

Hre Kio, Stephen. 1990. "Understanding and Translating 'Nations' in Mt 28.19." *The Bible Translator* 41:230-38.

Hubbard, Benjamin J. 1974. *The Matthean Redaction of a Primitive Apostolic Commissioning: An Exegesis of Matthew 28:16-20.* SBLDS 19. Missoula, Mont.: Scholars Press.

―――. 1978. "The Role of Commissioning Accounts in Acts." In *Perspectives on Luke-Acts,* Edited by C. H. Talbert, 187-98. Edinburgh: T & T Clark.

Huber, Friedrich. 1976. *Jahwe, Juda und die anderen Völker beim Propheten Jesaja.* BZAW 137. Berlin: de Gruyter.

Hübner, Hans. 1978. *Das Gesetz bei Paulus: Ein Beitrag zum Werden der paulinischen Theologie.* FRLANT 119. Göttingen: Vandenhoeck & Ruprecht [3rd ed., 1982].

―――. 1984. *Gottes Ich und Israel: Zum Schriftgebrauch des Paulus in Römer 9-11.* FRLANT 136. Göttingen: Vandenhoeck & Ruprecht.

―――. 1990-1995. *Biblische Theologie des Neuen Testaments.* 3 vols. Göttingen: Vandenhoeck & Ruprecht.

―――. 1996. "Paulus, Apostel I. Neues Testament." *TRE* 26:133-53.

Huffard, Everett W. 1991. "Eschatology and the Mission of the Church." *RestQ* 33:1-11.

Hultgren, Arland J. 1985. *Paul's Gospel and Mission: The Outlook from His Letter to the Romans.* Philadelphia: Fortress.

Hummel, Reinhart. 1966. *Die Auseinandersetzung zwischen Kirche und Judentum im Matthäusevangelium.* 2nd rev. ed. BEvTh 33. Munich: Kaiser [1963].

Humphrey, John H., ed. 1995-2002. *The Roman and Byzantine Near East: Some Recent Archaeological Research.* 3 vols. JRASup 14, 31, 49. Ann Arbor, Mich.; Portsmouth, R.I.: Journal of Roman Archaeology.

Hunger, Herbert, ed. 1976-. *Tabula Imperii Byzantini.* Vienna: Österreichische Akademie der Wissenschaften.

Hunsberger, George R. 1994. "Is There Biblical Warrant for Evangelism?" *Int* 48:131-44.

Hunter, Archibald M. 1976. "Apollos the Alexandrian." In *Biblical Studies,* FS W. Barclay, edited by J. R. McKay and J. F. Miller, 147-56. Philadelphia: Westminster.

Huppenbauer, Hans Walter. 1977. "Missionarische Dimensionen des Gottesvolkes im Alten Testament." *Zeitschrift für Mission* 3:37-47.

Hurst, L. D., and N. T. Wright, eds. 1987. *The Glory of Christ in the New Testament: Studies in Christology.* FS G. B. Caird. Oxford: Clarendon.

Hurtado, Larry W. 2003. *Lord Jesus Christ: Devotion to Jesus in Earliest Christianity.* Grand Rapids: Eerdmans.

Hüttenmeister, Frowald G. 1977. *Die antiken Synagogen in Israel.* Vol. 1, *Die jüdischen Synagogen, Lehrhäuser und Gerichtshöfe.* BTAVO B 12.1. Wiesbaden: Reichert.

Hvalvik, Reidar. 1996. *The Struggle for Scripture and Covenant: The Purpose of the Epistle of Barnabas and Jewish-Christian Competition in the Second Century.* WUNT 2.82. Tübingen: Mohr-Siebeck.

Hyldahl, Niels. 1997. *The History of Early Christianity.* SRHEC 3. Frankfurt: Lang.

Iovino, Paolo. 1990. "Paolo: Esperienza e teoria della missione." In Ghiberti 1990b, 155-83.

Isaac, Benjamin. 1993. *The Limits of Empire: The Roman Army in the East.* Oxford: Clarendon [1990].

———. 1996. "Eusebius and the Geography of Roman Pr ovinces." In D. Kennedy 1996, 153-67.

Jacobson, Arland D. 1992. *The First Gospel: An Introduction to Q.* Sonoma, Calif.: Polebridge.

Jacobson, David M. 2001. "Three Roman Client Kings: Herod of Judaea, Archelaus of Cappadocia and Juba of Mauretania." *PEQ* 133:22-38.

Jantsch, Johanna. 1990. *Die Entstehung des Christentums bei Adolf von Harnack und Eduard Meyer.* Habelts Dissertationsdrucke, Reihe Alte Geschichte 28. Bonn: Habelt.

Jáuregui, José Antonio. 1981. "Fundamentación bíblica de la misión cristiana universal." *Estudios ecclesiásticos* 56:1451-1532.

Jellicoe, Sidney. 1960. "St. Luke and the Seventy[-two]." *NTS* 6:319-21.

Jeremias, Joachim. 1952. "The Gentile World in the Thought of Jesus." *SNTS Bulletin* 3:18-28.

———. 1954. "Die missionarische Aufgabe in der Mischehe (1.Kor 7,16)." In Jeremias 1966, 292-98.

———. 1956. *Jesu Verheißung für die Völker.* Franz Delitzsch-Vorlesungen 1953. Stuttgart: Kohlhammer [2nd ed., 1959]. English: *Jesus' Promise to the Nations.* London: SCM Press, 1958 [Philadelphia: Fortress, 1982].

———. 1959. "Paarweise Sendung im Neuen Testament." In Jeremias 1966, 132-39.

———. 1963. *Jerusalem zur Zeit Jesu: Eine kulturgeschichtliche Untersuchung zur neutestamentlichen Zeitgeschichte.* 3rd ed. Göttingen: Vandenhoeck & Ruprecht. English: *Jerusalem in the Time of Jesus: An Investigation into Economic and Social Conditions During the New Testament Period.* London: SCM Press; Philadelphia: Fortress, 1969.

———. 1966. *Abba: Studien zur neutestamentlichen Theologie und Zeitgeschichte.* Göttingen: Vandenhoeck & Ruprecht.

———. 1984. *Die Gleichnisse Jesu.* 10th ed. Göttingen: Vandenhoeck & Ruprecht [1947].

———. 1988. *Neutestamentliche Theologie, Erster Teil: Die Verkündigung Jesu.* 3rd ed. Gütersloh: Mohn [1971]. English: *New Testament Theology.* New York: Scribner, 1971.

Jervell, Jacob. 1965. "Das gespaltene Israel und die Heidenvölker: Zur Motivierung der Heidenmission in der Apostelgeschichte." *StTh* 19:68-96.

———. 1972. *Luke and the People of God.* Minneapolis: Fortress.

————. 1983. "The Acts of the Apostles and the History of Early Christianity." *StTh* 37:17-32.

————. 1984. *The Unknown Paul: Essays on Luke-Acts and Early Christian History.* Minneapolis: Augsburg.

————. 1991. "Gottes Treue zum untreuen Volk." In Bussmann and Radl 1991, 15-27.

————. 1996. *The Theology of the Acts of the Apostles.* New Testament Theology. Cambridge: Cambridge University Press.

Jervis, L. Ann, and Peter Richardson, eds. 1994. *The Gospel in Paul.* FS R. N. Longenecker. Sheffield: JSOT Press.

Jewett, Robert. 1971. "The Agitators and the Galatian Congregation." *NTS* 17:198-212.

————. 1979. *A Chronology of Paul's Life.* Philadelphia: Fortress. German: *Paulus-Chronologie.* Munich: Kaiser 1982.

————. 1988. "Paul, Phoebe, and the Spanish Mission." In *The Social World of Formative Christianity and Judaism,* FS H. C. Kee, edited by P. Borgen et al., 142-61. Philadelphia: Fortress.

————. 1992. "Ecumenical Theology for the Sake of Mission: Romans 1:1-17 + 15:14-16:24." In *SBLSP,* 598-612.

————. 1994. "Tenement Churches and Pauline Love Feasts." *Quarterly Review* 14:43-58.

————. 1997. "Mapping the Route of Paul's 'Second Missionary Journey' from Dorylaeum to Troas." *TynBul* 48:1-22.

Johnson, Sherman E. 1987. *Paul the Apostle and His Cities.* Good New Studies 21. Wilmington, Del.: Glazier.

Jones, A. Hugh Martin. 1937. *The Cities of the Eastern Roman Provinces.* Oxford: Clarendon [rev. ed., New York: Oxford University Press, 1998].

Joubert, Stephan. 2000. *Paul as Benefactor: Reciprocity, Strategy and Theological Reflection in Paul's Collection.* WUNT 2.124. Tübingen: Mohr-Siebeck.

Judge, Edwin A. 1994. "Judaism and the Rise of Christianity: A Roman Perspective." *TynBul* 45:355-68.

Judge, Edwin A., and Stuart R. Pickering. 1977. "Papyrus Documentation of Church and Community in Egypt to the Mid-Fourth Century." *RAC* 20:47-71.

Judge, Edwin A., and G. S. R. Thomas. 1966. "The Origin of the Church at Rome: A New Solution?" *Reformed Theological Review* 25:81-93.

Jülicher, Adolf. 1906. *Einleitung in das Neue Testament.* 6th ed. Tübingen: Mohr.

Junod, Eric. 1981. "Origène, Eusèbe et la tradition sur la répartition des champs de mission des apôtres (Eusèbe, Histoire ecclésiastique, III, 1,1-3)." In Bovon 1981, 233-48.

————. 1983. "Créations romanesques et traditions ecclésiastiques dans les Actes apocryphes des apôtres." *Augustinianum* 23:271-85.

Junod, Eric, and Jean-Daniel Kaestli. 1983. *Acta Iohannis.* 2 vols. CCSA 1-2.

Turnhout: Brepols.

Juster, Jean. 1914. *Les juifs dans l'empire Romain: Leur condition juridique, économique et sociale.* 2 vols. Paris: Geuthner [repr., 1965].

Jütte, Robert, and Abraham P. Kustermann, eds. 1996. *Jüdische Gemeinden und Organisationsformen von der Antike bis zur Gegenwart.* Aschkenas Beiheft 3. Vienna: Böhlau.

Kaestli, Jean-Daniel. 1981. "Les scènes d'atrtribution des champs des mission et de départ de l'apôtre dans les Actes Apocryphes." In Bovon 1981, 249-64.

Kaiser, Walter C. 1981. "Israel's Missionary Call." In *Perspectives on the World Christian Movement.* Edited by R. P. Winter and S. C. Hawthorne. Pasadena, Calif.: Carey.

———. 2000. *Mission in the Old Testament: Israel as a Light to the Nations.* Grand Rapids: Baker.

Kalu, Ogbu. 1986. "Luke and the Gentile Mission: A Study on Acts 15." *African Journal of Biblical Studies* 1:59-65.

Kant, L. H. 2001. "Earliest Christian Inscription." *BRev* 17:10-19.

Karrer, Martin. 1989. "Petrus im paulinischen Gemeindekreis." *ZNW* 80:210-31.

———. 1991. *Der Gesalbte: Die Grundlagen des Christustitels.* FRLANT 151. Göttingen: Vandenhoeck & Ruprecht.

Karris, Robert J. 1979. "Missionary Communities: A New Paradigm for the Study of Luke-Acts." *CBQ* 41:80-97.

Karwiese, Stefan. 1995. *Groß ist die Artemis von Ephesos: Die Geschichte einer der großen Städte der Antike.* Vienna: Phoibos.

Kasdorf, Hans, and Friedemann Walldorf, eds. 1996. *Werdet meine Zeugen: Weltmission im Horizont von Theologie und Geschichte.* Neuhausen-Stuttgart: Hänssler.

Käsemann, Ernst. 1952. "Die Johannesjünger in Ephesus." In Käsemann 1970, 1:158-68. English: Käsemann 1964, 136-48.

———. 1959. "Eine paulinische Variation des 'amor fati.'" In Käsemann 1970, 2:223-39. English: in Käsemann 1969b, 217-35.

———. 1960. "Die Anfänge christlicher Theologie." In Käsemann 1970, 2:82-104. English: in Käsemann 1969b, 82-107.

———. 1963. "Paulus und der Frühkatholizismus." In Käsemann 1970, 2:239-52. English: Käsemann 1969b, 236-51.

———. 1964. *Essays on New Testament Themes.* SBT 41. London: SCM Press.

———. 1969a. *Paulinische Perspektiven.* Tübingen: Mohr-Siebeck [3rd ed., 1993]. English: *Perspectives on Paul.* London: SCM Press, 1971.

———. 1969b. *New Testament Questions of Today.* New Testament Library. London: SCM Press.

———. 1970. *Exegetische Versuche und Besinnungen.* 3rd ed. 2 vols. in 1. Göttingen: Vandenhoeck & Ruprecht [1960-1964]. English: Käsemann 1964; Käsemann 1969b.

Kasher, Aryeh. 1985. *Jews in Hellenistic and Roman Egypt: The Struggle for Equal Rights.* TSAJ 7. Tübingen: Mohr-Siebeck.

―――. 1988. *Jews, Idumaeans, and Ancient Arabs: Relations of the Jews in Eretz-Israel with the Nations of the Frontier and the Desert during the Hellenistic and Roman Era (332 BCE-70 CE).* TSAJ 18. Tübingen: Mohr-Siebeck.

―――. 1990. *Jews and Hellenistic Cities in Eretz-Israel: Relations of the Jews in Eretz-Israel with the Hellenistic Cities during the Second Temple Period (332 BCE-70 CE).* TSAJ 21. Tübingen: Mohr-Siebeck.

―――. 1995. "Synagogues as 'Houses of Prayer' and 'Holy Places' in the Jewish Communities of Hellenistic and Roman Egypt." In Urman and Flesher 1995, 1:205-20.

Kasser, Rodolphe. 1962. "Les origines du Christianisme Egyptien." *RTP* 12:11-28.

Kasting, Heinrich. 1969. *Die Anfänge der urchristlichen Mission.* BEvTh 55. Munich: Kaiser.

Kato, Zenji. 1986. *Die Völkermission im Markusevangelium: Eine redaktionsgeschichtliche Untersuchung.* EHS 23.252. Frankfurt and Bern: Lang.

Kaufmann, Carl Maria. 1917. *Handbuch der altchristlichen Epigraphik.* Freiburg: Herdersche Verlagsbuchhandlung.

Kautzsch, Emil. 1911. *Biblische Theologie des Alten Testaments.* Tübingen: Mohr.

Kavunkal, Jacob. 1988. "Jubilee the Framework of Evangelization." *Vidyajyoti* 52:181-90.

Kawerau, Peter. 1983. *Ostkirchengeschichte.* Vol. 1, *Das Christentum in Asien und Afrika bis zum Auftreten der Portugiesen im indischen Ozean.* CSCO 451. Leuven: Peeters.

Kearsley, Rosalinde A. 1994. "The Asiarchs." In Gill and Gempf 1994, 363-76.

―――. 1999. "Women in Public Life in the Roman East: Iunia Theodora, Claudia Metrodora and Phoebe, Benefactress of Paul." *TynBul* 50:189-211.

Keathley, Naymond H. 1999. *The Church's Mission to the Gentiles: Acts of the Apostles, Epistles of Paul.* Macon, Ga.: Smyth & Helwys.

Keay, Frank E. 1960. *A History of the Syrian Church in India.* 3rd ed. Delhi: SPCK [1938].

Kee, Howard C. 1990a. *Good News to the Ends of the Earth: The Theology of Acts.* London: SCM Press.

―――. 1990b. "The Transformation of the Synagogue after 70 C.E.: Its Import for Early Christianity." *NTS* 36:1-24.

―――. 1995. "Defining the First-Century CE Synagogue: Problems and Progress." *NTS* 41, 481-500.

Keener, Craig S. 1992. *Paul, Women and Wives: Marriage and Women's Ministry in the Letters of Paul.* Peabody, Mass.: Hendrickson.

Keith, Graham. 1992. "Justin Martyr and Religious Exclusivism." *TynBul* 43:57-80.

Kelhoffer, James A. 2000. *Miracle and Mission: The Authentication of Mission-*

aries and their Message in the Longer Ending of Mark. WUNT 2.112. Tübingen: Mohr-Siebeck.

Keller, Winfrid. 1998. *Gottes Treue, Israels Heil: Röm 11,25-27—Die These vom "Sonderweg" in der Diskussion.* SBB 40. Stuttgart: Katholisches Bibelwerk 1998.

Kennedy, David, ed. 1996. *The Roman Army in the East.* JRASup 18. Ann Arbor, Mich.: Journal of Roman Archaeology.

Kennedy, George A. 1972. *The Art of Rhetoric in the Roman World, 300 B.C.—A.D. 300.* Princeton, N.J.: Princeton University Press.

Ker, Donald P. 1986. "Missionary Motivation in Paul: The Jewish Environment." *IBS* 8:162-78.

———. 1988. "Jesus and Mission to the Gentiles." *IBS* 10:89-101.

Kern-Ulmer, Brigitte. 1994. "Die Bewertung er Proselyten im rabbinischen Schrifttum." *Judaica* 50:1-17.

Kertelge, Karl. 1970. *Die Wunder Jesu im Markusevangelium.* StANT 23. Munich: Kösel.

———, ed. 1982. *Mission im Neuen Testament.* QD 93. Freiburg: Herder.

Kienast, Dietmar. 1982. *Augustus: Prinzeps und Monarch.* Darmstadt: Wissenschaftliche Buchgesellschaft.

———. 1990. *Römische Kaisertabelle: Grundzüge einer römischen Kaiserchronologie.* Darmstadt: Wissenschaftliche Buchgesellschaft [2nd ed., 1996].

Kiley, Mark. 1986. *Colossians as Pseudepigraphy.* The Biblical Seminar 4. Sheffield: JSOT.

Kilgallen, John J. 1976. *The Stephen Speech: A Literary and Redactional Study of Acts 7,2-53.* AnBib 67. Rome: Biblical Institute Press.

Kilpatrick, G. D. 1955. "The Gentile Mission in Mark and Mark 13:9-11." In *Studies in the Gospels,* FS R. H. Lightfoot, 145-58. Oxford: Oxford University Press.

Kim, Myungsoo. 1990. *Die Trägergruppe von Q: Sozialgeschichtliche Forschung zur Q-Überlieferung in den synoptischen Evangelen.* WBEH 1.1. Ammersbek: Lottbek-Jensen.

Kim, Seyoon. 1981. *The Origin of Paul's Gospel.* WUNT 2.4. Tübingen: Mohr-Siebeck [2nd ed., 1984].

———. 1997. "The 'Mystery' of Rom 11.25-26 Once More." *NTS* 43:412-29.

Kim, Tae Hun. 1998. "The Anarthrous υἰὸς θεοῦ in Mark 15,39 and the Roman Imperial Cult." *Bib* 79:221-41.

Kimelman, Reuven. 1981. "Birkat Ha-Minim and the Lack of Evidence for an Anti-Christian Jewish Prayer in Late Antiquity." In E. Sanders et al. 1981, 226-44.

Kirkland, Alastair. 1995. "The Beginnings of Christianity in the Lycus Valley: An Exercise in Historical Reconstruction." *Neot* 29:109-24.

Kittel, Gisela. 1990. *Der Name über alle Namen: Biblische Theologie.* Vol. 2. BThS 3. Göttingen: Vandenhoeck & Ruprecht.

Kitzberger, Ingrid. 1986. *Bau der Gemeinde: Das paulinische Wortfeld οἰκοδομή/*

(ἐπ)οικοδομεῖν. FB 53. Würzburg: Echter.

Klassen, William. 1996. *Judas: Betrayer or Friend of Jesus?* Minneapolis: Fortress.

Klauck, Hans-Josef. 1981. *Hausgemeinde und Hauskirche im frühen Christentum*. SBS 103. Stuttgart: Katholisches Bibelwerk.

———. 1985. "Gemeinde ohne Amt? Erfahrungen mit der Kirche in den johanneischen Schriften." *BZ* 29:193-220.

———. 1986. *Herrenmahl und hellenistischer Kult: Eine religionsgeschichtliche Untersuchung zum ersten Korintherbrief*. 2nd ed. NTA 15. Münster: Aschendorff [1981].

———. 1987. *Judas—ein Jünger des Herrn*. QD 111. Freiburg: Herder.

———. 1989. *Gemeinde, Amt, Sakrament: Neutestamentliche Perspektiven*. Würzburg: Echter.

———. 1992a. *Gemeinde zwischen Haus und Stadt: Kirche bei Paulus*. Freiburg: Herder.

———. 1992b. "Judas der 'Verräter'? Eine exegetische und wirkungsgeschichtliche Studie." *ANRW* II.26.1:717-40.

———. 1995-1996. *Die religiöse Umwelt des Urchristentums*. 2 vols. Studienbücher Theologie 9.1-2. Stuttgart: Kohlhammer. English: *The Religious Context of Early Christianity: A Guide to Graeco-Roman Religions*. Studies of the New Testament and Its World. Edinburgh: T & T Clark, 2000.

———. 1996. *Magie und Heidentum in der Apostelgeschichte des Lukas*. SBS 167. Stuttgart: Katholisches Bibelwerk. English: *Magic and Paganism in Early Christianity: The World of the Acts of the Apostles*. Edinburgh: T & T Clark, 2000.

———. 1997. "Gottesfürchtige im Magnificat?" *NTS* 43:134-39.

Klausner, Joseph. 1950. *Von Jesus zu Paulus*. Jerusalem: Jewish Publishing House [Hebrew original, 1939; repr. of German ed., 1980].

Klein, Gottlieb. 1909. *Der älteste christliche Katechismus und die jüdische Propaganda-Literatur*. Berlin: Reimer.

Klein, Günter. 1961. *Die zwölf Apostel: Ursprung und Gehalt einer Idee*. FRLANT 77. Göttingen: Vandenhoeck & Ruprecht.

Klein, Richard. 1981. *Die Romrede des Aelius Aristides: Einführung*. Darmstadt: Wissenschaftliche Buchgesellschaft.

Kliesch, Klaus. 1975. *Das heilsgeschichtliche Credo in den Reden der Apostelgeschichte*. BBB 44. Bonn: Hanstein.

Klijn, Albertus F. J. 1965. *Edesa: Die Stadt des Apostels Thomas; Das älteste Christentum in Syrien*. Neukirchen-Vluyn: Neukirchener Verlag.

———. 1986. "Jewish Christianity in Egypt." In Pearson and Goehring 1986, 161-75.

Klijn, Albertus F. J., and Gerrit J. Reinink. 1973. *Patristic Evidence for Jewish Christian Sects*. NovTSup 36. Leiden: Brill.

Klinghardt, Matthias. 1988. *Gesetz und Volk Gottes: Das lukanische Verständnis des Gesetzes nach Herkunft, Funktion und seinem Ort in der Geschichte des Urchristentums.* WUNT 2.32. Tübingen: Mohr-Siebeck.

Kloppenborg, John S., ed. 1996. *Jesus' Followers in Galilee.* Philadelphia: Trinity.

Kloppenborg Verbin, John S. 2000. *Excavating Q: The History and Setting of the Sayings Gospel.* Minneapolis: Fortress.

Kneppe, Alfred. 1994. *Metus temporum: Zur Bedeutung von Angst in Politik und Gesellschaft der römischen Kaiserzeit des 1. und 2. Jahrhunderts n.Chr.* Stuttgart: Steiner.

Knights, C. H. 1990. "Jethro Merited That His Descendants Should Sit in the Chamber of Hewn Stone." *JJS* 41:247-53.

Knoch, Otto B. 1991. "Gab es eine Petrusschule in Rom? Überlegungen zu einer bedeutsamen Frage." *SNTU* 16:105-26.

Knorr, Uwe W. 1974. "Bibliographie zu Mission und Ausbreitung des Christentums in der alten Welt." In Frohnes and Knorr 1974, 421-46.

Knox, John. 1950. *Chapters in a Life of Paul.* New York: Abingdon.

———. 1964. "Romans 15:14-33 and Paul's Conception of His Apostolic Mission." *JBL* 83:1-11.

Koch, Dietrich-Alex. 1999. "Kollektenbericht, 'Wir'-Bericht und Itinerar: Neue (?) Überlegungen zu einem alten Problem." *NTS* 45:367-90.

Koch, Michael. 1977. "Zur frühen jüdischen Diaspora auf der Iberischen Halbinsel." In *Homenaje a Garcia Bellido,* FS Antonio García y Bellido, 3:225-54. 4 vols. Madrid: Universidad Complutense de Madrid, 1976-1979.

Koder, Johannes, and Friedrich Hild. 1976. *Hellas und Thessalia.* TIB 1. Vienna: Österreichische Akademie der Wissenschaften.

Koenen, Klaus. 1990. "Völkervernichtung und Völkermission: Die theologische Bedeutung der Textgeschichte erörtert am Beispiel von Ps 9.21." *BNot* 54-55:22-28.

Koester, Craig R. 1989. "Hearing, Seeing, and Believing in the Gospel of John." *Bib* 70:327-48.

Koester, Helmut. 1982. *Introduction to the New Testament.* 2 vols. Hermeneia: Foundations and Facets. New York: de Gruyter. German: *Einführung in das Neue Testament.* Berlin: de Gruyter, 1980.

———. 1994. "Archäologie und Paulus in Thessalonike." In Bormann, Del Tredici and Standhartinger 1994, 393-404.

———, ed. 1995a. *Ephesos: Metropolis of Asia; An Interdisciplinary Approach to Its Archaeology, Religion, and Culture.* HTS 41. Valley Forge, Pa.: Trinity.

———. 1995b. "Ephesos in Early Christian Literature." In H. Koester 1995a, 119-40.

———, ed. 1998. *Pergamon, Citadel of the Gods: Archaeological Record, Literary Description, and Religious Development.* Harrisburg, Pa.: Trinity.

Koet, Bart J. 1996. "'As Close to the Synagogue as Can Be'—Paul in Corinth According to Acts 18.1-18." In *The Corinthian Correspondence,* edited by R. Bieringer, 397-415. BETL 125. Leuven: Leuven University Press.

Kofsky, Aryeh. 2002. *Eusebius of Caesarea Against Paganism*. Leiden: Brill.

Köhler, Jens. 1996. *Pompai: Untersuchungen zur hellenistischen Festkultur*. EHS 38.61. Frankfurt: Lang.

Kohler, Werner. 1988. *Umkehr und Umdenken: Grundzüge einer Theologie der Mission*. Edited by Jörg Salaquarda. Studien zur interkulturellen Geschichte des Christentums 56. Frankfurt: Lang.

Kokkinos, Nikos. 1997. *The Herodian Dynasty: Origins, Role in Society and Eclipse*. JSPSup 26. Sheffield: Sheffield Academic Press.

Kolb, Frank. 1984. *Die Stadt im Altertum*. Munich: Beck.

———. 1995. *Rom: Die Geschichte der Stadt in der Antike*. Munich: Beck.

———. 1996. "Antiochia in der früheren Kaiserzeit." In Cancik 1996, 97-118.

Kolb, Frank, and Barbara Kupke. 1992. *Lykien: Geschichte Lykiens im Altertum*. Mainz: Zabern.

Kollmann, Bernd. 1998. *Joseph Barnabas: Leben und Wirkungsgeschichte*. SBS 175. Stuttgart: Katholisches Bibelwerk.

———. 2000. "Philippus der Evangelist und die Anfänge der Heidenmission." *Bib* 81:551-65.

Kondoleon, Christine. 2000. *Antioch the Lost Ancient City*. Princeton, N.J.: Princeton University Press.

König, Adrio. 1990. "Apocalyptic, Theology, Missiology." *Missionalia* 18:20-33.

Korn, Manfred. 1993. *Die Geschichte Jesu in veränderter Zeit: Studien zur bleibenden Bedeutung Jesu im lukanischen Doppelwerk*. WUNT 2.51. Tübingen: Mohr-Siebeck.

Körtner, Ulrich. 1998. *Papiasfragmente*. Schriften des Urchristentums 3. Darmstadt: Wissenschaftliche Buchgesellschaft.

Köstenberger, Andreas J. 1995. "The Challenge of a Systematized Biblical Theology of Mission: Missiological Insights from the Gospel of John." *Missiology* 23:445-64.

———. 1998a. *The Missions of Jesus and the Disciples according to the Fourth Gospel*. Grand Rapids: Eerdmans.

———. 1998b. "Mission in the General Epistles." In Larkin and Williams 1998, 189-206.

———. 2000a. "Women in the Pauline Mission." In Bolt and Thompson 2000, 221-47.

———. 2000b. "Mission." *NDBT* 663-68.

———. 2002. "Jesus the Good Shepherd Who Will Also Bring Other Sheep (John 10:16)." *BBR* 12:67-96.

Köstenberger, Andreas J., and Peter T. O'Brien. 2001. *Salvation to the Ends of the Earth: A Biblical Theology of Mission*. NSBT 11. Downers Grove, Ill.: InterVarsity Press.

Kraabel, A. Thomas. 1969. "Hypsistos and the Synagogue at Sardis." *GRBS* 10:91-93.

———. 1979. "The Diaspora Synagogue: Archaeological and Epigraphic Evidence since Sukenik." *ANRW* II.19.1:477-510 (also in Urman and Flesher 1995, 1:95-126).

———. 1982. "The Roman Diaspora: Six Questionable Assumptions." *JJS* 33:445-64.

———. 1983. "The Synagogue and the Jewish Community." In Hanfmann 1983, 178-90.

———. 1991. "The God-Fearers Meet the Beloved Disciple." In Pearson 1991, 276-84.

———. 1994. "Immigrants, Exiles, Expatriates, and Missionaries." In Bormann, Del Tredici and Standhartinger 1994, 71-88.

Kraeling, Carl H. 1957. *The Excavations at Dura-Europos, Final Report VIII, Part 1: The Synagogue.* New Haven: Yale University Press.

Kraft, Heinrich. 1981. *Die Entstehung des Christentums.* Darmstadt: Wissenschaftliche Buchgesellschaft.

Kraus, Wolfgang. 1996. *Das Volk Gottes: Zur Grundlegung der Ekklesiologie bei Paulus.* WUNT 85. Tübingen: Mohr-Siebeck.

———. 1999. *Zwischen Jerusalem und Antiochia: Die "Hellenisten," Paulus und die Aufnahme der Heiden in das endzeitliche Gottesvolk.* SBS 179. Stuttgart: Katholisches Bibelwerk.

Kremer, Jacob. 1982. "Weltweites Zeugnis für Christus in der Kraft des Geistes: Zur lukanischen Sicht der Mission." In Kertelge 1982, 145-63.

Kremers, Heinz, and Erich Lubahn, eds. 1985. *Mission an Israel in heilsgeschichtlicher Sicht.* Neukirchen-Vluyn: Neukirchener Verlag.

Krentz, Edgar. 1995. "Caesarea and Early Christianity." In Humphrey 1995-1999, 1:261-67.

Krüger, Julian. 1990. *Oxyrhynchos in der Kaiserzeit: Studien zur Topographie und Literaturrezeption.* EHS 3.441. Frankfurt: Lang.

Kruijf, T. de. 1993. "Go Therefore and Make Disciples of All Nations: Mt 28.19." *Bijdragen* 54:19-29.

Kruse, Colin G. 1992. "The Price Paid for a Ministry Among Gentiles: Paul's Persecution at the Hands of the Jews." In *Worship, Theology and Ministry in the Early Church,* FS R. P. Martin, edited by M. Wilkins and T. Paige, 260-72. JSNTSup 87. Sheffield: JSOT Press.

Kuck, David W. 1992. *Judgment and Community Conflict: Paul's Use of Apocalyptic Judgement Language in 1 Cor 3:5—4:5.* NovTSup 66. Leiden: Brill.

Kügler, Joachim. 1988. *Der Jünger den Jesus liebte: Literarische, theologische und historische Untersuchungen zu einer Schlüsselgestalt johanneischer Theologie und Geschichte.* SBB 16. Stuttgart: Katholisches Bibelwerk.

Kuhl, Josef. 1967. *Die Sendung Jesu und der Kirche nach dem Johannes-Evangelium.* Studia Instituti Missiologici Societatis Verbi Divini 11. St. Augustin: Steyler Verlag.

Kuhn, Heinz-Wolfgang. 1995. "Bethsaida in the Gospels: The Feeding Story in Luke 9 and the Q Saying in Luke 10." In Arav and Freund 1995-1999, 1:243-56.

Kuhn, Karl Georg. 1939. "Ursprung und Wesen der talmudischen Einstellung zum Nichtjuden." *Forschungen zur Judenfrage* 3:199-234.

———. 1950. *Achtzehngebet und Vaterunser und der Reim.* Tübingen: Mohr.

———. 1954. "Das Problem der Mission in der Urchristenheit." *EMZ* 11:161-68.

———. 1959. "προσήλυτος." *ThWNT* 6:727-45. English: *TDNT* 6:727-44.

Kuhn, Karl Georg, and Hartmut Stegemann. 1962. "Proselyten." PWSup 9:1248-83.

Kümmel, Werner Georg. 1987. "Das Urchristentum, II. Arbeiten zu Spezialproblemen. (e) Mission und Stellung zum Staat." *ThR* 52:268-85.

Kurichianil, John. 1994. "The Holy Spirit, the Main Agent in the Mission of the Church." *ITS* 31:348-67.

Kurz, William S. 1993. *Reading Luke-Acts: Dynamics of Biblical Narrative.* Louisville: Westminster John Knox.

Küster, Volker. 1996. *Jesus und das Volk im Markusevangelium: Ein Beitrag zum interkulturellen Gespräch in der Exegese.* BThSt 28. Neukirchen-Vluyn: Neukirchener Verlag.

Kvalbein, Hans. 2000. "Has Matthew Abandoned the Jews?" In Ådna and Kvalbein 2000, 45-62. German: "Hat Matthäus die Juden aufgegeben? Bemerkungen zu Ulrich Luz' Matthäus-Deutung." *ThBeitr* 29 (1998): 301-14.

Labahn, Michael. 1999. *Jesus als Lebensspender: Untersuchungen zu einer Geschichte der johanneischen Tradition anhand ihrer Wundergeschichten.* BZAW 98. Berlin: de Gruyter.

Ladd, George Eldon. 1993. *A Theology of the New Testament.* Edited by D. A. Hagner. Rev. ed. Grand Rapids: Eerdmans [1974].

LaGrand, James. 1995. *The Earliest Christian Mission to "All Nations": In the Light of Matthew's Gospel.* University of South Florida International Studies in Formative Christianity and Judaism 1. Atlanta: Scholars Press [repr., Grand Rapids: Eerdmans, 1999].

Lalleman, Pieter J. 1998. *The Acts of John: A Two-Stage Initiation into Johannine Gnosticism.* Studies on the Apocryphal Acts of the Apostles 4. Leuven: Peeters.

Laminger-Pascher, Gertrud. 1984. *Beiträge zu den griechischen Inschriften Lykaoniens.* ETAM 11. Vienna: Österreichische Akademie der Wissenschaften.

———. 1989. *Lykaonien und die Phrygier.* Vienna: Österreichische Akademie der Wissenschaften.

———. 1992. *Die kaiserzeitlichen Inschriften Lykaoniens: Faszikel I, Der Süden.* ETAM 15. Vienna: Österreichische Akademie der Wissenschaften.

Lampe, Peter. 1987. *Die stadtrömischen Christen in den ersten beiden Jahrhunderten: Untersuchungen zur Sozialgeschichte.* WUNT 2.18. Tübingen: Mohr-Siebeck [2nd ed., 1988].

———. 1992. "Acta 19 im Spiegel der ephesischen Inschriften." *BZ* 36:59-76.

———. 2001. "Urchristliche Missionswege nach Rom: Haushalte paganer Herrschaft als jüdisch-christliche Keimzellen." *ZNW* 92:123-27.

———. 2003. *From Paul to Valentinus: Christians at Rome in the First Two Centuries.* Minneapolis: Fortress.

Lampe, Peter, and Ulrich Luz. 1987. "Nachpaulinisches Christentum und pagane Gesellschaft." In Becker et al. 1987, 185-216.

Lande, Aasulv, and Werner Ustorf, eds. 1996. *Mission in a Pluralist World.* SIHC 97. Frankfurt: Lang.

Landmesser, Christof. 2001. *Jüngerberufung und Zuwendung zu Gott: Ein exegetischer Beitrag zum Konzept der matthäischen Soteriologie im Anschluß an Mt 9,9-13.* WUNT 133. Tübingen: Mohr-Siebeck.

Lane, Thomas J. 1996. *Luke and the Gentile Mission: Gospel Anticipates Acts.* EHS 23.571. Frankfurt: Lang.

Lane, William L. 1962. "Times of Refreshment: A Study of Eschatological Periodization in Judaism and Christanity." Th.D. diss., Harvard Divinity School. [*non vidi*]

Lane Fox, Robin. 1986. *Pagans and Christians.* New York: Knopf [repr., London: Penguin, 1988].

Lang, Friedrich. 1978. "'Über Sidon mitten ins Gebiet der Dekapolis': Geographie und Theologie in Markus 7,31." *ZDPV* 94:145-60.

———. 1996. "Paulus und seine Gegner in Korinth und in Galatien." In Lichtenberger 1996c, 417-34.

Lange, Joachim. 1973. *Das Erscheinen des Auferstandenen im Evangelium nach Matthäus: Eine traditions- und redaktionsgeschichtliche Untersuchung zu Mt 28,16-20.* FB 11. Würzburg: Echter.

Lange, Nicholas R. M. de, and Clemens Thoma. 1978. "Antisemitismus II. Die jüdische Reaktion auf den antiken Antisemitismus." *TRE* 3:113-22.

Lapide, Pinchas. 1995. "Hat das Judentum einen Missionsauftrag?" In Homolka and Seidel 1995, 10-21.

Larkin, William J. 1996. "Mission." In *Evangelical Dictionary of Biblical Theology,* edited by W. A. Elwell, 534-38. Grand Rapids: Baker.

———. 1998a. "Mission in Luke." In Larkin and Williams 1998, 152-69.

———. 1998b. "Mission in Acts." In Larkin and Williams 1998, 170-86.

Larkin, William J., and Joel F. Williams, eds. 1998. *Mission in the New Testament: An Evangelical Approach.* American Society of Missiology Series 27. New York: Orbis.

Larsen, J. A. O. 1938. *Roman Greece: An Economic Survey of Ancient Rome.* Vol. 4. Edited by Tenney Frank et al. Baltimore: Johns Hopkins Press.

Larsson, Edvin. 1962. *Christus als Vorbild: Eine Untersuchung zu den paulinischen Tauf- und Eikontexten.* ASNU 23. Uppsala: Gleerup.

———. 1987. "Die Hellenisten und die Urgemeinde." *NTS* 33:205-25.

Laurence, Ray, and Joanne Berry, eds. 1998. *Cultural Identity in the Roman Empire.* London: Routledge.

Lassus, Jean. 1978. "La ville d'Antioche à l'époque romaine d'après l'archéologie." *ANRW* II.8:54-102.

Latte, Kurt. 1992. *Römische Religionsgeschichte.* 2nd ed. Handbuch der Altertumswissenschaft 5.4. Munich: Beck [1967].

Lauffer, Siegfried, ed. 1989. *Griechenland: Lexikon der historischen Stätten von den Anfängen bis zur Gegenwart.* Munich: Beck.

Lauha, Aarre. 1977. "'Der Bund des Volkes': Ein Aspekt der deuterojesajanischen Missionstheologie." In *Beiträge zur Alttestamentlichen Theologie,* FS W. Zimmerli, edited by H. Donner et al., 257-61. Göttingen: Vandenhoeck & Ruprecht.

Lausberg, Heinrich. 1960. *Handbuch der literarischen Rhetorik: Eine Grundlegung der Literaturwissenschaft.* Stuttgart: Steiner [3rd ed., 1990].

LaVerdiere, Eugene. 1990. "Jesus Among the Gentiles." *Emmanuel* 96:338-45.

Légasse, Simon. 1991. *Paul Apôtre: Essai de biographie critique.* Paris: Cerf.

———. 1992. *Stephanos: Histoire et discours d'Étienne dans les actes des Apôtres.* LD 147. Paris: Cerf.

———. 1995. "Paul's Pre-Christian Career According to Acts." In Bauckham 1995a, 365-90.

Legrand, Lucien. 1987. "The Missionary Command of the Risen Lord Mt 28:16-20." *ITS* 24:5-28.

———. 1988. *Le Dieu qui vient: La mission dans la Bible.* Paris: Desclée.

———. 1989. "Alcuni aspetti missionari di 2 Corinti." In *The Diakonía of the Spirit (2 Co 4.7-7.4),* edited by L. de Lorenzi, 305-25. Monographic Series of "Benedictina." Biblical-Ecumenical Section 10. Rome: St. Paul's Abbey.

———. 1990. *Unity and Plurality: Mission in the Bible.* Maryknoll, N.Y.: Orbis.

———. 1995. "Gal 2:9 and the Missionary Strategy of the Early Church." In *Bible, Hermeneutics, Mission: A Contribution to the Contextual Study of Holy Scripture,* edited by T. Fornberg, 21-83. Missio 10. Uppsala: Swedish Institute for Missionary Research.

Leipoldt, Johannes, and Walter Grundmann, eds. 1990. *Umwelt der Urchristentums.* Vol. 1., *Darstellung des neutestamentlichen Zeitalters.* 8th ed. Berlin: Evangelische Verlagsanstalt [1966].

LeMoyne, Jean. 1972. *Les Sadducéens.* Paris: Gabalda.

Lentz, John C. 1993. *Luke's Portrait of Paul.* SNTSMS 77. Cambridge: Cambridge University Press.

Leon, Harry J. 1960. *The Jews of Ancient Rome.* Rev. ed. Peabody, Mass.: Hendrickson, 1995.

Lerle, Ernst. 1960. *Proselytenwerbung und Urchristentum.* Berlin: Evangelische Verlagsanstalt.

Lerner, Jeffrey D. 1999. *The Impact of Seleucid Decline on the Eastern Iranian*

Plateau: The Foundations of Arsacid Parthia and Graeco-Baktria. Historia: Einzelschriften 123. Stuttgart: Steiner.

Levick, Barbara. 1967. *Roman Colonies in Southern Asia Minor.* Oxford: Oxford University Press.

———. 1990. *Claudius.* New Haven: Yale University Press.

———. 1999a. *Tiberius the Politician.* New York: Routledge [1976].

———. 1999b. *Vespasian.* New York: Routledge.

Levieils, Xavier. 2001. "Juifs et Grecs dans la communauté johannique." *Bib* 82:51-78.

Levine, Amy-Jill. 1988. *The Social and Ethnic Dimensions of Matthean Social History: "Go Nowhere among the Gentiles . . ." (Matt. 10:5b).* SBEC 14. Lewiston, N.Y.: Mellen.

Levine, Lee I. 1975. *Caesarea under Roman Rule.* Leiden: Brill.

———, ed. 1992. *The Galilee in Late Antiquity.* New York and Jerusalem: Jewish Theological Seminary of America.

———. 2000. *The Ancient Synagogue: The First Thousand Years.* New Haven: Yale University Press.

———. 2001. "Synagoge," *TRE* 32:499-508.

Levine, Lee I., and Zeev Weiss, eds. 2000. *From Dura to Sepphoris: Studies in Jewish Art and Society in Late Antiquity.* JRASup 40. Portsmouth, R.I.: Journal of Roman Archaeology.

Levinskaya, Irina. 1996. *The Book of Acts in Its Diaspora Setting.* The Book of Acts in Its First-Century Setting 5. Carlisle: Paternoster.

Levy, Udi. 1996. *Die Nabatäer: Versunkene Kultur am Rande des Heiligen Landes.* Stuttgart: Urachhaus.

Liagre-Böhl, Franz M. N. Th. de. 1950. "Missions- und Erwählungsgedanke in Alt-Israel." In *Festschrift, Alfred Bertholet,* edited by W. Baumgartner et al., 77-96. Tübingen: Mohr.

Lichtenberger, Hermann. 1987. "Täufergemeinden und frühchristliche Täuferpolemik im letzten Drittel des 1. Jahrhunderts." *ZThK* 84:36-57.

———. 1990. "Daß du nicht vergißt (Devarim-Dtn 4,9): Von der Lebenskraft der Tora." *ThBeitr* 21:196-204.

———. 1994. "'Im Lande Israel zu wohnen wiegt alle Gebote der Tora auf': Die Heiligkeit des Landes und die Heiligung des Lebens." In Feldmeier and Heckel 1994, 92-107.

———. 1996a. "Jews and Christians in Rome in the Time of Nero: Josephus and Paul in Rome." *ANRW* II.26.3:2142-76.

———. 1996b. "Organisationsformen und Ämter im antiken Griechenland und Italien." In Jütte and Kustermann 11-27.

———, ed. 1996c. *Geschichte, Tradition, Reflexion.* FS Martin Hengel. Vol. 3, *Frühes Christentum.* Tübingen: Mohr-Siebeck.

Liebenam, Wilhelm. 1890. *Zur Geschichte und Organisation des römischen*

Vereinswesens. Repr., Aalen: Scientia, 1964.

Liechtenhan, Rudolf. 1946. *Die urchristliche Mission: Voraussetzungen, Motive und Methoden.* AThANT 9. Basel: Zwingli.

———. 1947. "Paulus als Judenmissionar." *Judaica* 2:56-70.

Liefeld, Walter L. 1967. "The Wandering Preacher as a Social Figure in the Roman Empire." Ph.D. diss., Columbia University.

———. 1987. "Women and Evangelism in the Early Church." *Missiology* 15:291-98.

Lietzmann, Hans. 1935. "Die Anfänge des Christentums in Syrien und in seinem Hinterland." In Lietzmann 1958b, 2:94-96.

———. 1958a. "Zwei Notizen zu Paulus." In Lietzmann 1958b, 2:284-91.

———. 1958b. *Kleine Schriften I-II.* 2 vols. TUGAL 67-68. Berlin: Akademie-Verlag.

Lightfoot, J. B. 1890. *The Apostolic Fathers: Revised Greek Texts with Introductions and English Translations.* Edited by J. R. Harmer. London: Macmillan; 2nd ed. Grand Rapids: Baker [1992].

———. 1893. *Biblical Essays.* London: MacMillan [1904].

Lightfoot, R. H. 1935. *History and Interpretation in the Gospels.* London: Hodder & Stoughton.

Lim, David S. 1997. "Evangelism in the Early Church." *DLNTD* 353-59.

Limbeck, Meinrad. 1989. "Die Religionen im Neuen Testament." *ThQ* 169:44-56.

Linday, Mary Gee. 1993. "Lydia: A Cultural and Social History." D.Phil. diss., Oxford University.

Lincoln, Andrew T. 2000. *Truth on Trial: The Lawsuit Motif in John's Gospel.* Peabody, Mass.: Hendrickson.

Lindemann, Andreas. 1979. *Paulus im ältesten Christentum: Das Bild des Apostels und die Rezeption der paulinischen Theologie in der frühchristlichen Literatur bis Marcion.* BHTh 58. Tübingen: Mohr-Siebeck.

———. 1993. "Samaria und Samaritaner im Neuen Testament." *Wort und Dienst* 22:51-76.

———. 1995. "Die Christuspredigt des Paulus in Athen (Act 17,16-33)." In Lindemann 1999, 241-51.

———. 1998. "Paulus als Zeuge der Auferstehung Jesu Christi." In Lindemann 1999, 27-36.

———. 1999. *Paulus, Apostel und Lehrer der Kirche: Studien zu Paulus und zum frühen Paulusverständnis.* Tübingen: Mohr-Siebeck.

Lips, Hermann von. 1979. *Glaube, Gemeinde, Amt: Zum Verständnis der Ordination in den Pastoralbriefen.* FRLANT 122. Göttingen: Vandenhoeck & Ruprecht.

Lipsius, Richard A. 1883-1890. *Die apokryphen Apostelgeschichten und Apostellegenden: Ein Beitrag zur altchristlichen Literaturgeschichte und zu einer zusammenfassenden Darstellung der neutestamentlichen Apokryphen.* 2 vols. Braunschweig: Schwetschke [repr., Amsterdam: Philo Press, 1976].

———. 1897. "Pauli Missionsverfahren." In *Glauben und Wissen: Ausgewählte*

Vorträge und Aufsätze, 182-96. Berlin: Schwetschke.

Llewelyn, Stephen R. 2001. "The Use of Sunday for Meetings of Believers in the New Testament." *NovT* 43:205-23.

Lohfink, Gerhard. 1969. "Christologie und Geschichtsbild in Apg 3,19-21." *BZ* 13:223-41.

———. 1975. *Die Sammlung Israels: Eine Untersuchung zur lukanischen Ekklesiologie.* StANT 39. Munich: Kösel.

———. 1982. *Wie hat Jesus Gemeinde gewollt? Zur gesellschaftlichen Dimension des christlichen Glaubens.* Freiburg: Herder [9th ed., 1991]. English: *Jesus and Community: The Social Dimension of Christian Faith.* London: SPCK, 1985.

Lohfink, Norbert. 1991. "Der neue Bund und die Völker." *Kirche und Israel* 6:115-33.

Lohmeyer, Ernst. 1936. *Galiläa und Jerusalem.* FRLANT 34. Göttingen: Vandenhoeck & Ruprecht.

———. 1951. "'Mir ist gegeben alle Gewalt!' Eine Exegese von Matt. 28,16-20." In *In Memoriam Ernst Lohmeyer,* edited by W. Schmauch, 22-49. Stuttgart: Evangelisches Verlagswerk.

Lohmeyer, Monika. 1995. *Der Apostelbegriff im Neuen Testament: Eine Untersuchung auf dem Hintergrund der synoptischen Aussendungsreden.* SBB 29. Stuttgart: Katholisches Bibelwerk.

Löhr, Hermut. 2001. "Zur Paulus-Notiz in 1 Clem 5,5-7." In Horn 2001, 197-213.

Löhr, Max. 1896. *Der Missionsgedanke im Alten Testament: Ein Beitrag zur alttestamentlichen Religionsgeschichte.* Freiburg and Leipzig: Mohr.

Lohse, Eduard. 1954. "Missionarisches Handeln Jesu nach dem Evangelium des Lukas." *ThZ* 10:1-13.

———. 1960. "Mission II. Jüdische Mission." *RGG* 4:971-73.

———. 1989. *Grundriß der neutestamentlichen Theologie.* 4th ed. Theologische Wissenschaft 5.1. Stuttgart: Kohlhammer [1974].

———. 1991. "Weitergabe des Glaubens." In Degenhardt 1991, 170-175.

———. 1994. *Umwelt des Neuen Testaments.* 9th ed. GNT 1. Göttingen: Vandenhoeck & Ruprecht [1971]. English: *The New Testament Environment.* London: SCM Press, 1976.

———. 1996. *Paulus: Eine Biographie.* Munich: Beck.

Lomas, Kathryn. 1997. "The Idea of a City: Élite Ideology and the Evolution of Urban Forms in Italy, 200 BC-AD 100." In *Roman Urbanism,* edited by H. M. Parkins, 21-41. London: Routledge.

Long, Anthony A., and David N. Sedley. 1987. *The Hellenistic Philosophers.* 2 vols. Cambridge, Mass.: Harvard University Press.

Longenecker, Richard N. 1971. *The Ministry and Message of Paul.* Grand Rapids: Eerdmans.

———, ed. 1997. *The Road from Damascus: The Impact of Paul's Conversion on His Life, Thought, and Ministry.* Grand Rapids: Eerdmans.

————, ed. 2002. *Community Formation in the Early Church and in the Church Today*. Peabody, Mass.: Hendrickson.

Löning, Karl. 1973. *Die Saulustradition in der Apostelgeschichte*. NTA 9. Münster: Aschendorff.

————. 1985. "Das Evangelium und die Kulturen: Heilsgeschichtliche und kulturelle Aspekte kirchlicher Realität in der Apostelgeschichte." *ANRW* II.25.3:2604-46.

————. 1987. "Der Stephanuskreis und seine Mission." In Becker et al. 1987, 80-101.

Lorenz, Thuri. 1987. *Römische Städte*. Darmstadt: Wissenschaftliche Buchgesellschaft.

Lövestam, Evald. 1983. "Der Rettungsappell in Ag 2,40." *Annual of the Swedish Theological Institute* 12:84-92.

Lübbe, John. 1996. "The Exclusion of the *Ger* from the Future Temple," in *Mogilany 1993*, FS H. Burgmann, edited by Z. J. Kapera, 175-82. Qumranica Mogilanesia 13. Krakow: Enigma.

Lübking, Hans-Martin. 1986. *Paulus und Israel im Römerbrief: Eine Untersuchung zu Römer 9-11*. EHS 23.260. Frankfurt and Bern: Lang.

Lüdemann, Gerd. 1980. *Paulus, der Heidenapostel*. Vol. 1, *Studien zur Chronologie*. FRLANT 123. Göttingen: Vandenhoeck & Ruprecht. English: *Paul, Apostle to the Gentiles: Studies in Chronology*. Philadelphia: Fortress, 1984.

————. 1983. *Paulus, der Heidenapostel*. Vol. 2, *Antipaulinismus im frühen Christentum*. FRLANT 130. Göttingen: Vandenhoeck & Ruprecht. English: *Opposition to Paul in Jewish Christianity*. Minneapolis: Fortress, 1989.

————. 1987. *Das frühe Christentum nach den Traditionen der Apostelgeschichte: Ein Kommentar*. Göttingen: Vandenhoeck & Ruprecht. English: *Early Christianity According to the Traditions in Acts: A Commentary*. Minneapolis: Fortress, 1989.

————. 1994. *Die Auferstehung Jesu*. Göttingen: Vandenhoeck & Ruprecht. English: *The Resurrection of Jesus: History, Experience, Theology*. Minneapolis: Fortress, 1995.

Lüderitz, Gert. 1983. *Corpus jüdischer Zeugnisse aus der Cyrenaika*. BTAVO B 53. Wiesbaden: Reichert.

Lührmann, Dieter. 1976. *Glaube im frühen Christentum*. Gütersloh: Gütersloher Verlagshaus.

————. 1990. "The Beginnings of the Church at Thessalonica." In *Greeks, Romans, and Christians*, FS A. J. Malherbe, edited by E. Ferguson et al., 237-49. Minneapolis: Fortress.

————. 1994. "Neutestamentliche Wundergeschichten und antike Medizin." In Bormann, Del Tredici and Standhartinger 1994, 195-204.

Lukasz, C. 1993. *Evangelizzazione e conflitto: Indagine sulla coerenza letteraria e tematica della pericope di Cornelio (Atti 10.1-11.18)*. EHS 23.484. Frankfurt: Lang.

Lütgert, Wilhelm. 1919. *Gesetz und Geist: Eine Untersuchung zur Vorgeschichte des Galaterbriefes.* BFChTh 22.6. Gütersloh: Bertelsmann.

Luttikhuizen, Gerard P. 1985. *The Revelation of Elchasai: Investigations into the Evidence for a Mesopotamian Jewish Apocalypse of the Second Century and Its Reception by Judeo-Christian Propagandists.* TSAJ 8. Tübingen: Mohr-Siebeck.

Luttwak, Edward N. 1976. *The Grand Strategy of the Roman Empire from the First Century A.D. to the Third.* Baltimore: Johns Hopkins University Press.

Lutz, Hans-Martin. 1968. *Jahwe, Jerusalem und die Völker: Zur Vorgeschichte von Sach 12,1-8 und 14,1-5.* WMANT 27. Neukirchen: Neukirchener Verlag.

Luz, Ulrich. 1992. "Matthew's Anti-Judaism: Its Origin and Contemporary Significance." *CurTM* 19:405-15.

———. 1993. *Die Jesusgeschichte des Matthäus.* Neukirchen-Vluyn: Neukirchener Verlag.

———. 2000. "Has Matthew Abandoned the Jews?" In Ådna and Kvalbein 2000, 63-68.

MacAdam, Henry I. 1986. *Studies in the History of the Roman Province of Arabia: The Northern Sector.* British Archaeological Reports 295. Oxford: British Institute of Archaeology.

MacDonald, Dennis. 1992. "Legends of the Apostles." In Attridge and Hata 1992, 166-80.

MacDonald, Margaret Y. 1993. "The Ideal of the Christian Couple: Ign. Pol. 5.1-2 Looking Back to Paul." *NTS* 40:105-25.

MacDonald, William L. 1982. *The Architecture of the Roman Empire I: An Introductory Study.* Revised ed. Yale Publications in the History of Art 17. New Haven: Yale University Press [1965].

Mack, Burton L. 1988. *The Myth of Innocence: Mark and Christian Origins.* Philadelphia: Fortress.

———. 1993. *The Lost Gospel: The Book of Q and Christian Origins.* New York: HarperCollins.

MacLennan, R. S., and A. T. Kraabel. 1986. "The God-Fearers—A Literary and Theological Invention." *BAR* 12:46-53, 64.

MacMullen, Ramsay. 1974. *Roman Social Relations 50 B.C. to A.D. 284.* New Haven: Yale University Press.

———. 1981. *Paganism in the Roman Empire.* New Haven: Yale University Press [2nd pr., 1983].

———. 1984. *Christianizing the Roman Empire (A.D. 100-400).* New Haven: Yale University Press.

———. 2000. *Romanization in the Time of Augustus.* New Haven: Yale University Press.

Macro, Anthony D. 1980. "The Cities of Asia Minor under the Roman Imperium." *ANRW* II.7.2:659-97.

Maddox, Robert. 1980. *Witnesses to the Ends of the Earth: The Pattern of Mission in the Book of Acts.* Melbourne: Joint Board of Christian Education.

———. 1982. *The Purpose of Luke-Acts.* FRLANT 126. Göttingen: Vandenhoeck & Ruprecht [repr., Edinburgh: T & T Clark, 1985].

Magie, David. 1950. *Roman Rule in Asia Minor to the End of the Third Century after Christ.* 2 vols. Princeton: Princeton University Press [repr., Salem, N.H.: Ayer 1988].

Maiburg, Ursula. 1983. "Und bis an die Grenzen der Erde . . . Die Ausbreitung des Christentums in den Länderlisten und deren Verwendung in Antike und Christentum." *JAC* 26:38-53.

Maier, Friedrich Wilhelm. 1929. *Israel in der Heilsgeschichte nach Röm 9-11.* Biblische Zeitfragen 12:11-12. Münster: Aschendorff.

Maier, Gerhard, ed. 1996. *Israel in Geschichte und Gegenwart.* Wuppertal: Brockhaus.

Maier, Johann. 1978. *Jesus von Nazareth in der talmudischen Überlieferung.* EdF 82. Darmstadt: Wissenschaftliche Buchgesellschaft.

———. 1982. *Jüdische Auseinandersetzung mit dem Christentum in der Antike.* EdF 177. Darmstadt: Wissenschaftliche Buchgesellschaft.

Maier, Johann, and K. Schubert. 1973. *Die Qumran-Essener: Texte der Schriftrollen und Lebensbild der Gemeinde.* UTB 224. Munich and Basel: Reinhardt.

Mainville, Odette. 1991. *L'esprit dans l'œuvre de Luc.* Héritage et projet 45. Montreal: Fides.

Malay, Hasan. 1999. *Researches in Lydia, Mysia and Aiolis.* ETAM 23. Vienna: Österreichische Akademie der Wissenschaften.

Malchow, Bruce V. 1990. "Causes of Tolerance and Intolerance Toward Gentiles in the First Testament." *BTB* 20:3-9.

Maletzke, Gerhard. 1988. *Massenkommunikationstheorien.* Medien in Forschung und Unterricht B7. Tübingen: Niemeyer.

Malherbe, Abraham J. 1987. *Paul and the Thessalonians: The Philosophic Tradition of Pastoral Care.* Philadelphia: Fortress.

Malina, Bruce J. 1970. "The Literary Structure and Form of Matthew 28.16-20." *NTS* 17:87-103.

Malina, Bruce J., and Jerome H. Neyrey. 1996. *Portraits of Paul: An Archaeology of Ancient Personality.* Louisville: Westminster John Knox.

Malitz, Jürgen. 1996. "Mommsen, Caesar und die Juden." In Cancik 1996, 371-87.

Malkin, Irad. 1987. *Religion and Colonization in Ancient Greece.* Studies in Greek and Roman Religion 3. Leiden: Brill.

———. 1990. "Missionaries païens dans la Gaule grecque." In *La France et la Méditerranée: Vingt-sept siècles d'interdépendance,* edited by I. Malkin, 42-52. Leiden: Brill.

Malony, H. N., and A. A. Lovekin. 1985. *Glossolalia: Behavioural Science Perspectives on Speaking in Tongues.* Oxford: Oxford University Press.

Mánek, Jindřich. 1958. "Fishers of Men." *NovT* 2:138-41.

Maness, Stephen. 1998. "The Pauline Congregations, Paul, and His Co-workers: Determinative Trajectories for the Ministries of Paul's Partners in the Gospel." Ph.D. diss., Southwestern Baptist Theological Seminary.

Mann, John C. 1974. "The Frontiers of the Principate." *ANRW* II.1:508-33.

―――. 1979. "Power, Force and the Frontiers of the Empire." *JRS* 69:175-83.

Mann, Thomas W. 1991. "'All the Families of the Earth': The Theological Unity of Genesis." *Int* 45:341-53.

Manns, Frédéric, and Eugenio Alliata, eds. 1993. *Early Christianity in Context: Monuments and Documents.* FS E. Testa. Studium Biblicum Franciscanum, collectio maior 38. Jerusalem: Franciscan Printing Press.

Manson, T. W. 1949. *The Sayings of Jesus.* London: SCM Press [repr., 1975].

―――. 1964. *Only to the House of Israel? Jesus and the Non-Jews.* Philadelphia: Fortress [1st ed., *Jesus and the Non-Jews.* London: Athlone, 1955].

―――. 1967. *The Teaching of Jesus: Studies of Its Form and Context.* Cambridge: Cambridge University Press.

Manson, William. 1951. *The Epistle to the Hebrews: An Historical and Theological Reconsideration.* London: Hodder & Stoughton.

Marco, Angelico-Savatore di. 1992. "Πέμπω: Per una ricerca del 'campo semantico' nel NT." *RivB* 40:385-419.

Margull, Hans Jochen. 1960. "Mission III: Christliche Mission." *RGG* 4:973-80.

Margull, H. J., and J. Hermelink, eds. 1959. *Basileia.* FS W. Freytag. Stuttgart: Evangelischer Missionsverlag.

Marinkoví, Peter. 1994. "'Geh in Frieden' (2 Kön 5,19): Sonderformen legitimer JHWHverehrung durch 'Heiden' in 'heidnischer' Mitwelt." In Feldmeier and Heckel 1994, 3-21.

Markschies, Christoph. 1997. "Stadt und Land: Beobachtungen zu Ausbreitung und Inkulturaiton des Christentums in Palästina." In Cancik and Rüpke 1997, 265-98.

Marshall, I. Howard. 1970. *Luke: Historian and Theologian.* Exeter: Paternoster [3rd ed., 1988].

―――. 1979. "Culture and the New Testament." In *Gospel and Culture,* edited by J. Coote and J. Stott, 21-46. Pasadena, Calif.: William Carey Library.

―――. 1989. "Inter-faith Dialogue in the New Testament." *EvRT* 13:196-15.

―――. 1990. "Luke's View of Paul." *SwJT* 33:41-51.

―――. 1992a. *The Acts of the Apostles.* New Testament Guides. Sheffield: JSOT Press.

―――. 1992b. "Dialogue with Non-Christians in the New Testament." *EvRT* 16:28-47.

―――. 1993. "Acts and the 'Former Treatise.'" In Winter and Clarke 1993, 163-82.

―――. 2000a. "Who Were the Evangelists?" In Ådna and Kvalbein 2000, 251-63.

————. 2000b. "Luke's Portrait of the Pauline Mission." In Bolt and Thompson 2000, 99-113.

Marshall, I. Howard, and David Peterson, eds. 1998. *Witness to the Gospel: The Theology of Acts*. Grand Rapids: Eerdmans.

Marshall, Peter. 1987. *Enmity in Corinth: Social Conventions in Paul's Relations with the Corinthians*. WUNT 2.23. Tübingen: Mohr-Siebeck.

Martin, Josef. 1974. *Antike Rhetorik: Technik und Methode*. Handbuch des Altertums 3.3. Munich: Beck.

Martin, Luther H. 1995. "Gods or Ambassadors of God? Barnabas and Paul in Lystra." *NTS* 41:152-56.

Martin, Ralph P. 1981. *Reconciliation: A Study of Paul's Theology*. Atlanta: John Knox Press.

————. 1993. "Center of Paul's Theology." *DPL* 92-95.

Martin, Raymond A. 1993. *Studies in the Life and Ministry of the Early Paul and Related Issues*. Lewiston, N.Y.: Mellen Biblical Press.

Martin, Troy. 1996. "Pagan and Judeo-Christian Time-Keeping Schemes in Gal 4.10 and Col 2.16." *NTS* 42:105-19.

Martin, V. 1995. *A House Divided: The Parting of the Ways Between Synagogue and Church*. New York: Paulist.

Martin-Achard, Robert. 1959. *Israël et les nations: La perspective missionnaire de l'Ancien Testament*. Cahiers Théologique 42. Neuchâtel and Paris: Delachaux & Niestlé. English: *A Light to the Nations: A Study of the Old Testament Conception of Israel's Mission to the World*. Edinburgh: Oliver & Boyd, 1962.

Martyn. J. Louis. 1985. "A Law-Observant Mission to Gentiles: The Background of Galatians." *SJT* 38:307-24.

————. 1996. "The Question of a Gentile Mission That Replaced an Earlier Jewish Mission." In *Exploring the Gospel of John*, FS D. Moody Smith, edited by R. A. Culpepper and C. C. Black, 124-44. Louisville: Westminster John Knox.

Marxsen, Willi. 1959. *Der Evangelist Markus: Studien zur Redaktionsgeschichte des Evangeliums*. 2nd ed. FRLANT 67. Göttingen: Vandenhoeck & Ruprecht [1956].

Maser, Peter. 1993. "Synagoge und Ekklesia." In *Begegnungen zwischen Christentum und Judentum in Antike und Mittelalter*, FS Heinz Schreckenberg, edited by D.-A. Koch and H. Lichtenberger, 270-92. Schriften des Institutum Judaicum Delitzschianum 1. Göttingen: Vandenhoeck & Ruprecht.

Mason, Steven. 1990. *Flavius Josephus on the Pharisees*. StPB 39. Leiden: Brill.

Mathewson, Dave. 2002. "The Destiny of the Nations in Revelation 21:1—22:5." *TynBul* 53:121-42.

Matson, David Lertis. 1996. *Household Conversion Narratives in Acts: Pattern and Interpretation*. JSNTSup 123. Sheffield: Sheffield Academic Press.

Matthews, Christopher R. 2002. *Philip, Apostle and Evangelist: Configurations of a Tradition*. NovTSup 105. Leiden: Brill.

May, Elmer C., et al. 1984. *Ancient and Medieval Warfare*. Wayne, N.J.: Avery.

Mazur, Belle D. 1935. *Studies on Jewry in Greece*. Athens: Hestia.

McDaniel, Ferris L. 1998. "Mission in the Old Testament." In Larkin and Williams 1998, 11-20.

McDonagh, Bernard. 2001. *Turkey: The Aegean and Mediterranean Coasts*. Blue Guide. London: Black; New York: Norton [1995].

McDonald, Lee M. 1992. "Christianity: Christianity in Greece." *ABD* 1:960-65.

McEleney, Neil J. 1974. "Conversion, Circumcision and the Law." *NTS* 20:328-33.

McIlraith, Donal A. 1989. *The Reciprocal Love Between Christ and the Church in the Apocalypse*. Rome: Columban Fathers.

McKnight, Scot. 1986. "New Shepherds for Israel: An Historical and Critical Study of Matthew 9:35-11:1." Ph.D. diss., University of Nottingham.

———. 1991. *A Light Among the Gentiles: Jewish Missionary Activity in the Second Temple Period*. Minneapolis: Fortress.

———. 1992. "Gentiles." *DJG* 259-65.

———. 1993. "Collection for the Saints." *DPL* 143-47.

———. 1997. "Gentiles, Gentile Mission." *DLNTD* 388-94.

———. 2001. "Jesus and the Twelve." *BBR* 11:203-31.

———. 2002. *Turning to Jesus: The Sociology of Conversion in the Gospels*. Louisville: Westminister John Knox.

McLaren, James S. 2001. "Ananus, James, and Earliest Christianity: Josephus' Account of the Death of James." *JTS* 52:1-25.

McLean, Bradley H. 1991. "Galatians 2.7-9 and the Recognition of Paul's Apostolic Status at the Jerusalem Conference: A Critique of G. Luedemann's Solution." *NTS* 37:67-76.

McNicol, Allan J., et al. 1996. *Beyond the Q Impasse: Luke's Use of Matthew; A Demonstration by the Research Team of the International Institute for Gospel Studies*. Valley Forge, Pa.: Trinity.

McPolin, J. 1969. "Mission in the Fourth Gospel." *ITQ* 26:113-22.

McRay, John R. 1991. *Archaeology and the New Testament*. Grand Rapids: Baker.

Meagher, P. 1992. "Paul and Mission." *Vidyajyoti* 56:250-59.

Medlycott, Adolphus E. 1905. *India and the Apostle Thomas*. London: Nutt.

Meeks, Wayne A. 1983. *The First Urban Christians: The Social World of the Apostle Paul*. New Haven and London: SCM Press. German: *Christentum und Stadtkultur: Die soziale Welt der paulinischen Gemeinden*. Gütersloh: Kaiser and Gütersloher Verlagshaus, 1993.

Meeks, Wayne, and Robert Wilken. 1978. *Jews and Christians in Antioch in the First Four Centuries of the Common Era*. SBLSBS 13. Missoula, Mont.: Scholars Press.

Meier, John P. 1977. "Nations or Gentiles in Matthew 28:19?" *CBQ* 39:94-102.

———. 1991-2001. *A Marginal Jew: Rethinking the Historical Jesus*. 3 vols. AncBRL. New York: Doubleday.

———. 1997. "The Circle of the Twelve: Did It Exist During Jesus' Public Ministry?" *JBL* 116:635-72.

Meijer, Fik, and Onno van Nijf. 1992. *Trade, Transport and Society in the Ancient World: A Source-Book.* New York: Routledge.

Meinardus, Otto F. A. 1981. *Die Reisen des Apostels Paulus: Nachvollzogen im 20. Jahrhundert.* Hamburg: Agentur des Rauhen Hauses; Regensburg: Pustet.

Meinertz, Max. 1908. *Jesus und die Heidenmission.* NTA 1.1-2. Münster: Aschendorff [2nd ed., 1925].

———. 1911. "Jesus als Begründer der Heidenmission." *Zeitschrift für Missionswissenschaft* 1:21-41.

———. 1959. "Zum Ursprung der Heidenmission." *Bib* 40:762-77.

Meiser, Martin. 1998. *Die Reaktion des Volkes auf Jesus.* BZNW 96. Berlin: de Gruyter.

Mélèze-Modrzejewski, Joseph. 1981. "Splendeurs grecques et misères romaines: Les Juifs d'Égypte dans l'Antiquité." In Hassoun 1981, 15-49.

———. 1991. *Les Juifs d'Égypte: De Ramsès II à Hadrien.* Quadrige 247. Paris: Presses universitaires de France.

Mell, Ulrich. 1994. *Die "anderen" Winzer: Eine exegetische Studie zur Vollmacht Jesu Christi nach Markus 11,27-12,34.* WUNT 77. Tübingen: Mohr-Siebeck.

Mellink, Machteld J. 1993. "Archaeology in Anatolia." *AJA* 97:105-33.

Mendels, Doron. 1992. *The Rise and Fall of Jewish Nationalism: The History of Jewish and Christian Ethnicity in Palestine Within the Greco-Roman Period (200 B.C.E.-135 C.E.).* New York: Doubleday.

———. 1996. "Pagan or Jewish? The Presentation of Paul's Mission in the Book of Acts." In Schäfer 1996, 431-52.

Menzies, Robert P. 1991. *The Development of Early Christian Pneumatology with Special Reference to Luke-Acts.* JSNTSup 54. Sheffield: JSOT Press.

Merkelbach Reinhold. 1997a. *Philologica: Ausgewählte Kleine Schriften.* Edited by W. Blümel et al. Stuttgart and Leipzig: Teubner.

———. 1997b. "Grabepigramm und Vita des Bischofs Aberkios von Hierapolis." In Merkelbach 1997a, 381-99.

Merklein, Helmut. 1987. *Studien zu Jesus und Paulus.* WUNT 43. Tübingen: Mohr-Siebeck.

Metzger, Bruce M. 1958-1959. "Seventy or Seventy-two Disciples?" *NTS* 5: 299-306.

———. 1968a. *Historical and Literary Studies: Pagan, Jewish, and Christian.* NTTS 8. Grand Rapids: Eerdmans.

———. 1968b. "The Christianization of Nubia and the Old Nubian Version of the New Testament." In Metzger 1968a, 111-22.

Metzger, Wolfgang. 1976. *Die letzte Reise des Apostels Paulus: Beobachtungen und Erwägungen zu seinem Itinerar nach den Pastoralbriefen.* AzTh 59. Stuttgart: Calwer.

Meyer, Ben F. 1986. *The Early Christians: Their World Mission and Self-Discovery.* GNS 16. Wilmington, Del.: Glazier.

———. 1987. "The World Mission and the Emergent Realization of Christian Identity." In *Jesus, the Gospels, and the Church,* FS W. R. Farmer, edited by E. P. Sanders, 243-63. Macon, Ga.: Mercer University Press.

———. 1992. "'Phases' in Jesus' Mission." *Gregorianum* 73:5-17.

Meyer, Eduard. 1921-1923. *Ursprung und Anfänge des Christentums.* 3 vols. Stuttgart: Cotta [repr., Darmstadt: Wissenschaftliche Buchgesellschaft, 1962].

Meyer, Paul D. 1970. "The Gentile Mission in Q." *JBL* 89:405-17.

Meyer, Regina P. 1977. *Kirche und Mission im Epheserbrief.* SBS 86. Stuttgart: Katholisches Bibelwerk.

Meyers, Eric M. 1976. "Galilean Regionalism as a Factor in Historical Reconstruction." *BASOR* 221:93-102.

———. 1979. "The Cultural Setting of Galilee: The Case of Regionalism and Early Judaism." *ANRW* II.19.1:686-702.

———. 1985. "Galilean Regionalism: A Reappraisal." In *Approaches to Ancient Judaism,* edited by W. S. Green, 115-31. BJS 32. Atlanta: Scholars Press.

———. 1997. "Jesus and His Galilean Context." In Edwards and McCollough 1997, 57-66.

Meyers, Eric M., and James F. Strange. 1981. *Archaeology, the Rabbis and Early Christianity.* Nashville: Abingdon.

Meyers, Eric M., et al. 1992. *Sepphoris.* Winona Lake, Ind.: Eisenbrauns.

Meynet, Roland. 1992. "Le cantique de Moïse et le cantique de l'Agneau (Ap 15 et Ex 15)." *Gregorianum* 73:19-55.

Michaels, J. Ramsay. 1999. "The Itinerant Jesus and His Hometown." In Chilton and Evans 1999b, 177-93.

Michel, Hans-Joachim. 1973. *Die Abschiedsrede des Paulus an die Kirche Apg 20,17-38: Motivgeschichte und theologische Bedeutung.* StANT 35. Munich: Kösel.

Michel, Otto. 1941. "Menschensohn und Völkerwelt." *EMZ* 2:257-67.

Milgrom, Jacob. 1993. "The Concept of Impurity in *Jubilees* and the *Temple Scroll.*" *RevQ* 16:277-84.

Millar, Fergus. 1992. *The Emperor in the Roman World (31 BC-AD 337).* London: Duckworth [1977].

———. 1993. *The Roman Near East, 31 BC-AD 337.* Cambridge, Mass.: Harvard University Press.

———. 1996. *The Roman Empire and Its Neighbours.* London: Duckworth [1967; 2nd ed., 1981].

Millard, Alan R. 1987. "Carthography in the Ancient Near East." In Harley and Woodward 1987, 1:107-29.

Miller, Johnny V. 1998. "Mission in Revelation." In Larkin and Williams 1998, 227-38.

Minear, Paul S. 1959. "Gratitude and Mission in the Epistle to the Romans." In Margull and Hermelink 1959, 42-48.

———. 1974. "The Disciples and the Crowds in the Gospel of Matthew." *AThRSup* 3:28-44.

Minnerath, Roland. 1994. *De Jérusalem à Rome: Pierre et l'unité de l'église apostolique.* Théologie Historique 101. Paris: Beauchesne.

Misset-van de Weg, Magda. 1998. "'For the Lord Always Takes Care of His Own': The Purpose of the Wondrous Works and Deeds in the *Acts of Peter.*" In Bremmer 1998, 97-110.

Mitchell, Christopher W. 1987. *The Meaning of BRK "To Bless" in the Old Testament.* SBLDS 95. Atlanta: Scholars Press.

Mitchell, Margaret M. 1992. "New Testament Envoys in the Context of Greco-Roman Diplomatic and Epistolary Conventions: The Example of Timothy and Titus." *JBL* 111:641-62.

Mitchell, Stephen. 1980. "Population and the Land in Roman Galatia." *ANRW* II.7.2:1053-81.

———. 1986. "Galatia under Tiberius." *Chiron* 16:17-33.

———. 1995a. *Anatolia: Land, Men, and Gods in Asia Minor.* 2 vols. Oxford: Oxford University Press [1993].

———. 1995b. *Cremna in Pisidia: An Ancient City in Peace and War.* London: Duckworth.

———. 1998. "Wer waren die Gottesfürchtigen?" *Chiron* 28:55-64.

———. 1999. "The Cult of Theos Hypsistos between Pagans, Jews, and Christians." In *Pagan Monotheism in Late Antiquity,* edited by P. Athanassiadi and M. Frede, 81-148. Oxford: Clarendon.

Mitchell, Stephen, and Marc Waelkens. 1998. *Pisidian Antioch: The Site and its Monuments.* London: Duckworth.

Mitford, Terence. 1980. "Roman Rough Cilicia." *ANRW* II.7.2:1230-61.

Mlakuzhyil, George. 1993. "Mission in the Gospel of John." *Vidyajyoti* 57:257-68.

Moberly, Robert B. 1993. "When Was Acts Planned and Shaped?" *EvQ* 65: 5-26.

Moessner, David P. 1989. *Lord of the Banquet: The Literary and Theological Significance of the Lukan Travel Narrative.* Minneapolis: Fortress.

Moffett, Samuel H. 1992. *A History of Christianity in Asia.* Vol. 1, *Beginnings to 1500.* San Francisco: HarperCollins [1998].

Mohrmann, Christine. 1954. "Das Sprachenproblem in der frühchristlichen Mission." *Zeitschrift für Missionskunde und Religionswissenschaft* 38:103-11.

Molinari, Andrea Lorenzo. 2000. *The Acts of Peter and the Twelve Apostels (NHC 6.1): Allegory, Ascent, and Ministry in the Wake of the Decian Persecution.* SBLDS. Atlanta: Society of Biblical Literature.

Molland, Einar. 1962. "Besaß die Alte Kirche ein Missionsprogramm und bewußte Missionsmethoden?" In Frohnes and Knorr 1974, 51-67.

Molthagen, Joachim. 1991. "Die ersten Konflikte der Christen in der griechisch-römischen Welt." *Historia* 40:42-76.

Momigliano, Arnaldo. 1981. *Claudius: The Emperor and His Achievement.* Repr. of 2nd ed., Westport, Conn.: Greenwood Press [1961; 1st ed., 1934].

Moo, Douglas. 1993. "Romans 2: Saved Apart from the Gospel?" In Crockett and Sigountos 1993, 137-45.

Moore, George F. 1927. *Judaism in the First Centuries of the Christian Era: The Age of the Tannaim.* Cambridge, Mass.: Harvard University Press [11th ed., 1970].

Moore, Thomas S. 1997. "'To the End of the Earth': The Geographical and Ethnic Universalism of Acts 1:8 in Light of Isaianic Influence on Luke." *JETS* 40:389-99.

Moors, Steven Menno. 1992. De Decapolis: Steden en dorpen in de Romeinse provincies Syria en Arabia. Diss., Rijksuniversiteit Leiden.

Morosco, R. E. 1984. "Matthew's Formation of a Commissioning Type-Scene Out of the Story of Jesus' Commissioning of the Twelve." *JBL* 103:539-56.

Mosley, Derek J. 1973. *Envoys and Diplomacy in Ancient Greece.* Historia Einzelschriften 22. Wiesbaden: Steiner.

Motyer, Stephen. 1993. "John 8:31-59 and the Rhetoric of Persuasion in the Fourth Gospel." Ph.D. diss. University of London. [*non vidi*]

Moule, C. F. D. 1962. *The Birth of the New Testament.* London: Black.

Mowery, Robert L. 2002. "Son of God in Roman Imperial Titles and Matthew." *Bib* 83:100-110.

Mugambi, Jesse N. Kanyua. 1991. *The Biblical Basis for Evangelization: Theological Reflections Based on an African Experience.* Oxford: Oxford University Press.

Mulder, Martin J., ed. 1988. *Mikra: Text, Translation, Reading, and Interpretation of the Hebrew Bible in Ancient Judaism and Early Christianity.* CRINT 2.1. Assen: Van Gorcum [repr., 1990].

Mullen, Roderic L. 2001. "The Spread of Christianity in Egypt: Some New Papyrological Evidence Since Judge and Pickering (1978)." Paper presented at the annual meeting of the Society of Biblical Literature, Denver, Colorado [cf. *SBL Abstracts 2001,* 130-31].

Müller, Carl Werner, Kurt Sier and Jürgen Werner, eds. 1992. *Zum Umgang mit Fremdsprachlichkeit in der griechisch-römischen Antike.* Palingenesia 36. Stuttgart: Steiner.

Müller, Karl. 1956. *Das universale Heilsdenken des Völkerapostels nach dem Galater- und Römerbrief.* Studia Missionalia 69. Rome: Pontificia Università Gregoriana.

———. 1985. *Missionstheologie: Eine Einführung.* Berlin: Reimer.

Müller, Peter. 1988. *Anfänge der Paulusschule: Dargestellt am zweiten Thessalonicherbrief und am Kolosserbrief.* AThANT 74. Zürich: Theologischer Verlag.

Müller, Peter. 1989. "Grundlinien paulinischer Theologie (Röm 15,14-33)." *KD* 35:212-35.

———. 1994. "Der Glaube aus dem Hören: Über das gesprochene und das geschriebene Wort bei Paulus." In Bormann, Del Tredici and Standhartinger 1994, 405-42.

Müller, Ulrich B. 1976. *Zur frühgeschichtlichen Theologiegeschichte.* Gütersloh: Mohn.

Mullins, T. Y. 1976. "Commissioning Stories in Luke-Acts: A Study of their Antecedents, Form and Content." *JBL* 95:603-14.

Munck, Johannes. 1954. *Paulus und die Heilsgeschichte.* Acta Jutlandica 26.1. Aarhus: Universitetsforlaget.

———. 1956. *Christus und Israel: Eine Auslegung von Römer 9-11.* Acta Jutlandica 28.3. Aarhus: Universitetsforlaget. English: *Christ and Israel: An Interpretation of Romans 9-11.* Philadelphia: Fortress, 1967.

———. 1959. *Paul and the Salvation of Mankind.* Atlanta: John Knox Press [repr., 1977].

———. 1962-1963. "1Thess 1.9-10 and the Missionary Preaching of Paul." *NTS* 9:95-110.

Mundadan, A. Mathias. 1984. *History of Christianity in India.* Vol. 1, *From the Beginning up to the Middle of the Sixteenth Century (up to 1542).* Bangalore: Church History Association of India, Theological Publications.

Murphy, James J. 1993. "Early Christianity as a 'Persuasive Campaign': Evidence from the Acts of the Apostles and the Letters of Paul." In *Rhetoric and the New Testament,* edited by S. E. Porter and T. H. Olbricht, 90-99. JSNTSup 90. Sheffield: JSOT Press.

Murphy-O'Connor, Jerome. 1970. "An Essene Missionary Document? CD II,14-VI,1," *RB* 77:201-32.

———. 1982. "Pauline Missions before the Jerusalem Conference." *RB* 89:71-91.

———. 1983. *St. Paul's Corinth: Texts and Archaeology.* Wilmington, Del.: Glazier.

———. 1992a. "A First-Century Jewish Mission to Gentiles?" *Pacifica* 5:32-42.

———. 1992b. "Prisca and Aquila: Travelling Tentmakers and Church Builders." *BRev* 8:40-51.

———. 1992c. "Lots of God-Fearers? *Theosebeis* in the Aphrodisias Inscription." *RB* 99:418-24.

———. 1993. "Paul in Arabia." *CBQ* 55:732-37.

———. 1994. "What Was Paul Doing in 'Arabia'?" *BRev* 10:46-47.

———. 1996. *Paul: A Critical Life.* Oxford: Oxford University Press.

Murray, Michele. 2000. "Jews and Judaism in Caesarea Maritima." In Donaldson 2000, 127-52.

Mussner, Franz. 1973. "Gab es eine 'galiläische Krise'?" In *Orientierung an Jesus: Zur Theologie der Synoptiker,* edited by P. Hoffmann et al., 238-52. Freiburg: Herder.

———. 1991. "Die Erzählintention des Lukas in der Apostelgeschichte." In Bussmann and Radl 1991, 29-42.

Musurillo, Harold. 1972. *The Acts of the Christian Martyrs*. Oxford: Clarendon.

Muth, Robert. 1988. *Einführung in die griechische und römische Religion*. Darmstadt: Wissenschaftliche Buchgesellschaft.

Myers, Ched. 1988. *Binding the Strong Man: A Political Reading of Mark's Story of Jesus*. Maryknoll, N.Y.: Orbis.

Nägele, Sabine. 1995. *Laubhütte Davids und Wolkensohn: Eine auslegungsgeschichtliche Studie zu Amos 9,11 in der jüdischen und christlichen Exegese*. AGAJU 24. Leiden: Brill.

Nagy, Rebecca Martin, ed. 1996. *Sepphoris in Galilee: Crosscurrents of Culture*. Winona Lake, Ind.: Eisenbrauns.

Naldini, Mario. 1998. *Il cristianesimo in Egitto: Lettere private nei papiri dei secoli II-IV*. Rev. ed. Biblioteca patristica 32. Fiesole: Nardini [Studi e testi di papirologia 3; Florence: Le Monnier, 1968].

Narain, A. K. 1957. *The Indo-Greeks*. Oxford: Clarendon [Delhi: Oxford University Press, 1980].

Ndyabahika, Odomaro. 1993. "Paul's Evangelization Approach to Gentile Religion: An Exegetical-theological Examination Based on the Evidence of Rom 1,18-32." Diss., University of Würzburg. [*non vidi*]

Negev, Avraham. 1978. "The Nabataeans and the Provincia Arabia." *ANRW* II.8:520-686.

————. 1986. *Nabatean Archaeology Today*. New York: New York University Press.

Neill, Stephen C. 1984. *A History of Christianity in India: The Beginnings to A.D. 1707*. Cambridge: Cambridge University Press.

Nellessen, Ernst. 1976. *Zeugnis für Jesus und das Wort: Exegetische Untersuchungen zum lukanischen Zeugnisbegriff*. BBB 43. Cologne: Hanstein.

Nelson, Edwin S. 1982. "Paul's First Missionary Journey as Paradigm: A Literary-Critical Assessment of Acts 13-14." Ph.D. diss., Boston University.

Nepper-Christensen, Poul. 1995. "Matth 10,23—et crux interpretum?" *Dansk Teologisk Tidsskrift* 58:161-75.

Neudorfer, Heinz-Werner. 1983. *Der Stephanuskreis in der Forschungsgeschichte seit F. C. Baur*. Giessen and Basel: Brunnen.

————. 1998. "The Speech of Stephen." In Marshall and Peterson 1998, 275-94.

Neufeld, Alfred. 1994. *Die alttestamentlichen Grundlagen der Missionstheologie*. Missiologica Evangelica 5. Bonn: Verlag für Kultur und Wissenschaft.

Neumann, Günter, and Jürgen Untermann, eds. 1980. *Die Sprachen im Römischen Reich der Kaiserzeit: Kolloquium vom 8. bis 10. April 1974*. Beihefte der Bonner Jahrbücher 40. Cologne: Rheinland-Verlag; Bonn: Habelt.

Newbigin, Lesslie. 1987. *Mission in Christ's Way*. Genf: WCC Publications.

Neyrey, Jerome H., ed. 1991. *The Social Word of Luke-Acts: Models for Interpretation*. Peabody, Mass.: Hendrickson [1993].

Nickelsburg, George W. E. 1981. *Jewish Literature between the Bible and the*

Mishnah: A Historical and Literary Introduction. London: SCM Press.

———. 1984. "Stories of Biblical and Early Post-Biblical Times." In Stone 1984, 33-87.

Nida, Eugene A. 1954. *Customs and Cultures: Anthropology for Christian Missions.* Pasadena, Calif.: William Carey Library [1979].

Niebuhr, Karl-Wilhelm. 1987. *Gesetz und Paränese: Katechismusartige Weisungsreihen in der frühjüdischen Literatur.* WUNT 2.28. Tübingen: Mohr-Siebeck.

———. 1992. *Heidenapostel aus Israel: Die jüdische Identität des Paulus nach ihrer Darstellung in seinen Briefen.* WUNT 62. Tübingen: Mohr-Siebeck.

Nielsen, Helge Kjaer. 1987. *Heilung und Verkündigung: Das Verständnis der Heilung und ihres Verhältnisses zur Verkündigung bei Jesus und in der ältesten Kirche.* Acta Theologica Danica 22. Leiden: Brill.

Nigdelis, Pantelis M. 1994. "Synagoge(n) und Gemeinde der Juden in Thessaloniki: Fragen aufgrund einer neuen jüdischen Grabinschrift der Kaiserzeit." *ZPE* 102:297-306.

Nilsson, Martin P. 1925. *A History of Greek Religion.* Oxford: Clarendon [2nd ed., 1949 = 1980].

———. 1941-1950. *Geschichte der griechischen Religion.* 2 vols. Handbuch der Altertumswissenschaft 5.1-2. Munich: Beck [3rd ed., 1967-1974; repr., 1992].

Nissen, Andreas. 1974. *Gott und der Nächste im antiken Judentum: Untersuchungen zum Doppelgebot der Liebe.* WUNT 15. Tübingen: Mohr-Siebeck.

Nissen, Johannes. 1984. *Poverty and Mission: New Testament Perspectives on a Contemporary Theme.* IIMO Research Pamphlet 10. Leiden and Utrecht: Interuniversitair Instituut voor Missiologie.

———. 1999. *New Testament and Mission: Historical and Hermeneutical Perspectives.* Frankfurt: Lang.

Noack, Christian. 2000. *Gottesbewußtsein: Exegetische Studien zur Soteriologie und Mystik bei Philo von Alexandrien.* WUNT 2.116. Tübingen: Mohr-Siebeck.

Nobbs, Alanna. 1994. "Cyprus." In Gill and Gempf 1994, 279-89.

Nock, Arthur D. 1933. *Conversion: The Old and the New in Religion from Alexander the Great to Augustine of Hippo.* Oxford: Clarendon [repr., Lanham, Md.: University Press of America, 1988].

Noethlichs, Karl-Leo. 1971. "Die gesetzgeberischen Maßnahmen der christlichen Kaiser des vierten Jahrhunderts gegen Häretiker, Heiden und Juden." Diss., University of Cologne. [*non vidi*]

———. 1996. *Das Judentum und der römische Staat: Minderheitenpolitik im antiken Rom.* Darmstadt: Wissenschaftliche Buchgesellschaft.

Nolland, John. 1979. "Proselytism or Politics in Horace *Satires* 1,4,138-43?" *VigChr* 33:347-55.

———. 1981. "Uncircumcised Proselytes?" *JSJ* 12:173-94.

———. 1998. "Salvation-History and Eschatology." In Marshall and Peterson 1998, 63-81.

Nollé, Johannes. 1992. "Zur Geschichte der Stadt Etenna in Pisidien." In Schwertheim 1992, 61-141.

———. 1993. "Die feindlichen Schwestern—Betrachtungen zur Rivalität der pamphylischen Städte." In Dobesch and Rehrenböck 1993, 297-317.

Noordegraaf, Albert. 1983. *Creatura Verbi: De groei van de gemeente volgens de Handelingen der Apostelen.* s'-Gravenhage: Boekencentrum [2nd ed., 1984].

Norden, Eduard. 1913. *Agnostos Theos: Untersuchungen zur Formengeschichte religöser Rede.* Darmstadt: Wissenschaftliche Buchgesellschaft [2nd ed., 1923; repr., 1956].

Nordheim, Eckhard von. 1994. "Das Buch Jona und die Anfänge der hellenistisch-jüdischen Mission." In *Nach den Anfängen fragen,* FS G. Dautzenberg, edited by C. Mayer et al. Giessen: Fachbereich Evangelische Theologie und Katholische Theologie.

Norris, F. W. 1978. "Antiochien I. Neutestamentlich." *TRE* 3:99-103.

———. 1990. "Antioch on-the-Orontes as a Religious Center I: Paganism before Constantine." *ANRW* II.18.4:2322-79.

North, Robert. 1979. *A History of Biblical Map Making.* BTAVO B 32. Wiesbaden: Reichert.

Northedge, Alastair, ed. 1992. *Studies on Roman and Islamic Amman.* Vol. 1, *History, Site and Architecture.* British Academy Monographs in Archaeology 3. Oxford: Oxford University Press.

Novak, David. 1983. *The Image of the Non-Jew in Judaism: An Historical and Constructive Study of the Noachide Laws.* Toronto Studies in Theology 14. New York: Mellen.

Nun, Mendel. 1993. "Cast Your Net upon the Waters: Fish and Fishermen in Jesus' Time." *BAR* 19:46-65, 70.

———. 1996. *The Land of the Gadarenes.* Ein Gev: Sea of Galilee Fishing Museum.

———. 1999. "Ports of Galilee." *BAR* 25:18-31.

———. 2001. *Der See Genezareth und die Evangelien: Archäologische Forschungen eines jüdischen Fischers.* Giessen: Brunnen.

Núñez Regodón, J. 1984. "El universalismo de los Cantos del Siervo." In *Palabra y vida,* FS J. A. Díaz, edited by A. Vargas-Machucu, 67-76. Madrid: Universidad Pontificia Comillas de Madrid.

Oakman, Douglas E. 1986. *Jesus and the Economic Questions of His Day.* SBEC 8. Lewiston, N.Y.: Mellen.

———. 1991. "The Countryside in Luke-Acts." In Neyrey 1991, 151-79.

O'Brien, Peter T. 1992. "Paul's Missionary Calling within the Purposes of God." In *In the Fullness of Time,* FS Donald Robinson, edited by D. Peterson and J. Pryor, 131-48. Homebush West, N.S.W.: Lancer.

———. 1995. *Gospel and Mission in the Writings of Paul: An Exegetical and Theological Analysis.* Exeter: Paternoster; Grand Rapids: Baker [1993].

Oehler, Theodor. 1901. *Enthält das Neue Testament bindende missionsmethodische Vorschriften?* Basler Missionsstudien 3. Basel: Missionsbuchhandlung.

———. 1902. *Die Mission und die Zukunft des Reiches Gottes.* Basler Missionsstudien 10. Basel: Missionsbuchhandlung.

Oehler, Wilhelm. 1936. *Das Johannesevangelium eine Missionsschrift für die Welt.* Gütersloh: Mohn.

———. 1941. *Zum Missionscharakter des Johannesevangeliums.* BFChTh 1.42. Gütersloh: Mohn.

Oepke, Albrecht. 1920. *Die Missionspredigt des Apostels Paulus: Eine biblisch-theologische und religionsgeschichtliche Untersuchung.* Missionswissenschaftliche Forschungen 2. Leipzig: Hinrichs.

———. 1941. "Das missionarische Christuszeugnis des Johannesvangeliums." *EMZ* 2:4-21.

Öhler, Markus. 2003. *Barnabas: Die historische Person und ihre Rezeption in der Apostelgeschichte.* WUNT 156. Tübingen: Mohr-Siebeck.

Ohm, Thomas. 1962. *Macht zu Jüngern alle Völker: Theorie der Mission.* Freiburg: Wewel.

Okure, Teresa. 1988. *The Johannine Approach to Mission: A Contextual Study of John 4.1-42.* WUNT 2.31. Tübingen: Mohr-Siebeck.

Ollrog, Wolf-Henning. 1979. *Paulus und seine Mitarbeiter.* WMANT 50. Neukirchen-Vluyn: Neukirchener Verlag.

Olshausen. Eckart. 1991. *Einführung in die Historische Geographie der Alten Welt.* Darmstadt: Wissenschaftliche Buchgesellschaft.

Olsson, Birger. 1986-1987. "Mission According to Luke, John, and Peter" [Swedish]. *SEÅ* 51-52:180-91.

Oppenheimer, Aharon. 1977. *The Am Ha-aretz: A Study in the Social History of the Jewish People in the Hellenistic-Roman Period.* ALGHJ 8. Leiden: Brill.

———. 1983. *Babylonia Judaica in the Talmudic Period.* BTAVO B 47. Wiesbaden: Reichert.

Osborne, Grant R. 1989. "Women in Jesus' Ministry." *WTJ* 51:259-91.

Osborne, R. E. 1968. "Where Did Peter Go?" *CJT* 14:274-77.

Osei-Bonsu, Joseph. 1990. "The Contextualization of Christianity: Some New Testament Antecedents." *IBS* 12:129-48.

Oss, Douglas A. 1992. *Paul's Use of Isaiah and Its Place in His Theology, with Special Reference to Romans 9-11.* Ph.D. diss., Westminster Theological Seminary.

Oster, Richard E. 1974. "A Historical Commentary on the Missionary Success Stories in Acts 19:11-40." Ph.D. diss., Princeton Theological Seminary. [*non vidi*]

———. 1990. "Ephesus as a Religious Center under the Principate, I. Paganism before Constantine." *ANRW* II.18.3:1661-1728.

———. 1992a. "Christianity: Christianity in Asia Minor." *ABD* 1:938-54.

———. 1992b. "Ephesus." *ABD* 2:542-49.

Oswalt, John N. 1993. "The Mission of Israel to the Nations." In Crockett and Sigountos 1993, 85-95.

Otzen, Benedikt. 1990. *Judaism in Antiquity: Political Development and Religious Currents from Alexander to Hadrian*. Biblical Seminar 7. Sheffield: JSOT Press.

Overman, J. Andrew. 1990. *Matthew's Gospel and Formative Judaism: The Social World of the Matthean Community*. Minneapolis: Fortress.

———. 1993. "Recent Advances in the Archaeology of the Galilee in the Roman Period." *Currents in Research* 1:35-57.

———. 1996. *Matthean Community in Crisis: The Gospel According to Matthew*. Valley Forge, Pa.: Trinity.

———. 1997. "Jesus of Galilee and the Historical Peasant." In Edwards and McCollough 1997, 67-73.

Packer, James I. 1961. *Evangelism and the Sovereignty of God*. Leicester: Inter-Varsity Press [1976].

———. 1979. "The Gospel: Its Content and Communication; A Theological Perspective." In *Gospel and Culture*, edited by J. Coote and R. T. Stott, 135-53. Pasadena, Calif.: William Carey Library.

Padberg, Lutz von. 1991. "Mediävistik und evangelikale Kirchengeschichtsschreibung." *JETh* 5:100-121.

———. 1995. *Mission und Christianisierung: Formen und Folgen bei Angelsachsen und Franken im 7. und 8. Jahrhundert*. Stuttgart: Steiner.

Padgett, Alan. 1987. "The Pauline Rationale for Submission: Biblical Feminism and the *hina* Clauses of Titus 2.1-10." *EvQ* 59:39-52.

Paget, J. Carleton. 1994. *The Epistle of Barnabas: Outlook and Background*. WUNT 2.64. Tübingen: Mohr-Siebeck.

———. 1999. "Jewish Christianity." *CHJ* 3:731-75.

Painter, John. 1997. *Just James: The Brother of Jesus in History and Tradition*. Studies on Personalities in the New Testament. Columbia: University of South Carolina Press [Minneapolis: Fortress, 1999].

Pak, James Y. S. 1991. *Paul as Missionary: A Comparative Study of Missionary Discourse in Paul's Epistles and Selected Contemporary Jewish Texts*. EHS 23.410. Frankfurt: Lang.

Pallas, Demetrios I. 1977. *Les monuments paléochrétiens de Grèce découverts de 1959 à 1973*. Vatican: Pontificio Istituto di archeologia cristiana.

Palmer, Darryl W. 1974. "The Resurrection of Jesus and the Mission of the Church." In *Reconciliation and Hope: New Testament Essays on Atonement and Eschatology*, FS L. L. Morris, edited by R. J. Banks, 205-23. Exeter: Paternoster.

———. 1993. "Acts and the Ancient Historical Monograph." In Winter and Clarke 1993, 1-29.

Palmer, G. 1966. Trance and Dissociation: A Cross-Cultural Study in Psychophysiology." Master's thesis, University of Minnesota. [*non vidi*]

Pao, David W. 2000. *Acts and the Isaianic New Exodus*. WUNT 2.130. Tübingen: Mohr-Siebeck.

Papazoglou, Fanoula. 1979. "Quelques aspects de l'histoire de la province de Macédonie." *ANRW* II.7.1:302-69.

————. 1988. *Les villes de Macédonie à l'époque romaine*. Bulletin de correspondance hellénique supplément 16. Athens: École française d'Athènes; Paris: Boccard.

Park, Eung Chun. 1995. *The Mission Discourse in Matthew's Interpretation*. WUNT 2.81. Tübingen: Mohr-Siebeck.

Parker, David C. 1992. *Codex Bezae: An Early Christian Manuscript and Its Text*. Cambridge: Cambridge University Press.

Pawlikowski, John T. 1988. "Judentum und Christentum." *TRE* 17:386-403.

Peace, Richard V. 1999. *Conversion in the New Testament: Paul and the Twelve*. Grand Rapids: Eerdmans.

Pearson, Birger A. 1986. "Earliest Christianity in Egypt: Some Observations." In Pearson and Goehring 1986, 132-59.

————, ed. 1991. *The Future of Early Christianity*. FS H. Koester. Minneapolis: Fortress.

————. 1992. "Christianity: Christianity in Egypt." *ABD* 1:954-60.

Pearson, Birger A., and J. A. Goehring, eds. 1986. *The Roots of Egyptian Christianity*. Philadelphia: Fortress.

Pekáry, Thomas. 1980. "Kleinasien unter römischer Herrschaft." *ANRW* II.7.2:596-657.

————. 1985. *Das römische Kaiserbildnis in Staat, Kultur und Gesellschaft*. Berlin: Mann.

Penna, Romano. 1982. "Les Juifs à Rome au temps de l'apôtre Paul." *NTS* 28:321-47.

Penney, John M. 1997. *The Missionary Emphasis of Lukan Pneumatology*. JPTSS 12. Sheffield: Sheffield Academic Press.

Pereira, Francis. 1983. *Ephesus: Climax of Universalism in Luke-Acts: A Redaction-Critical Study of Paul's Ephesian Ministry (Acts 18:23-20:1)*. Jesuit Theological Forum Studies 1. Anand, India: Gujarat Sahitya Prakash.

Perelmuter, Hayim G. 1994. "Mission II. Judentum." *TRE* 23:20-23.

Pericoli-Ridolfini, Francesco. 1962. "Le origini della Chiesa d'Alessandria d'Egitto e la Cronologia dei Vescovi Alessandrini dei secoli I e II." *Rendiconti morali: Accademia Nazzionale dei Lincei,* Series 8, 17:317-43.

Perkins, Pheme. 1986. "Christianity and World Religions: New Testament Questions." *Int* 40:367-78.

————. 1994. *Peter: Apostle for the Whole Church*. Studies on Personalities of the New Testament. Columbia: University of South Carolina Press [repr., Minneapolis: Fortress, 2000].

Perriman, Andrew. 1989. "Between Troas and Macedonia: 2 Cor 2.13-14." *Exp-Tim* 101:39-41.

Pervo, Richard I. 1987. *Profit with Delight: The Literary Genre of the Acts of the Apostles.* Philadelphia: Fortress.

Pesce, Mauro. 1994. *Le due fasi della predicazione di Paolo: Dall'evangelizzazione alla guida delle communità.* Studi biblici 22. Bologna: Dehoniane.

Pesch, Rudolf. 1969. "Berufung und Sendung, Nachfolge und Mission: Eine Studie zu Mk 1,16-20." *ZKTh* 91:1-31.

————. 1980. *Simon-Petrus: Geschichte und geschichtliche Bedeutung des ersten Jüngers Jesu Christi.* Päpste und Papsttum 15. Stuttgart: Hiersemann.

————. 1982. "Voraussetzungen und Anfänge der urchristlichen Mission." In Kertelge 1982, 11-70.

————. 1989. "La rédaction lucanienne du logion des pêcheurs d'hommes (Lc., V, 10c)." In *L'Évangile de Luc/The Gospel of Luke.* Edited by F. Neirynck. 2nd ed. BETL 32. Leuven: Leuven University Press and Peeters, 135-54.

Peterlin, Davorin. 1995. *Paul's Letter to the Philippians in the Light of Disunity in the Church.* NovTSup 79. Leiden: Brill.

Peterman, Gerald W. 1997. *Paul's Gift from Philippi: Conventions of Gift-Exchange and Christian Giving.* SNTSMS 92. Cambridge: Cambridge University Press.

Peters, George W. 1972. *A Biblical Theology of Missions.* Chicago: Moody [3rd ed., 1975]. German: *Missionarisches Handeln und biblischer Auftrag: Eine biblisch-evangelische Missionstheologie.* 2nd ed. Bad Liebenzell: Liebenzeller Verlag, 1985 [1977].

————. 1984. "Die Theologie des Paulus im Rahmen seines Missionsauftrages." In *Epochen der Heilsgeschichte: Beiträge zur Förderung heilsgeschichtlicher Theologie,* edited by H. Stadelmann, 67-75. Wuppertal: Brockhaus.

Petersen, William L. 1992. "Christianity: North African Christianity." *ABD* 1: 965-68.

Peterson, Peter M. 1958. *Andrew, Brother of Simon Peter: His History and Legends.* NovTSup 1. Leiden: Brill [repr., 1963].

Petzl, Georg. 1994. *Die Beichtinschriften Westkleinasiens.* Epigraphica Anatolica 22. Bonn: Habelt.

————. 1995. "Ländliche Religiosität in Lydien." In Schwertheim 1995, 27-48.

Pfitzner, Victor C. 1967. *Paul and the Agon Motif: Traditional Athletic Imagery in the Pauline Literature.* NovTSup 16. Leiden: Brill.

Piattelli, Daniela. 1990. "'Missione' e 'proselitismo' in Israele: Effetti della insurrezione maccabaica nel pensiero di Qumran e nella letteratura rabbinica." In Ghiberti 1990b, 87-100.

Pichler, Josef. 1997. *Paulusrezeption in der Apostelgeschichte: Untersuchungen zur Rede im pisidischen Antiochien.* IThS 50. Innsbruck: Tyrolia.

Pieper, Karl. 1921. "Zur religiösen Physiognomie des urchristlichen Missionsgebietes." *Zeitschrift für Mission* 11:1-14.

―――. 1929. *Paulus—seine missionarische Persönlichkeit und Wirksamkeit.* Münster: Aschendorff [1926].

Pilhofer, Peter. 1995-2000. *Philippi.* 2 vols. WUNT 87, 119. Tübingen: Mohr-Siebeck.

―――. 1999. "Luke's Knowledge of Pisidian Antioch." In Drew-Bear et al. 1999, 69-76.

Pillai, C. A. Joachim. 1979. *Early Missionary Preaching: A Study of Luke's Report in Acts 13.* Hicksville, N.Y.: Exposition Press.

Pinnock, Clark H. 1993. "Acts 4.12—No Other Name under Heaven." In Crockett and Sigountos 1993, 107-15.

Pixner, Bargil. 1994. *Wege des Messias und Stätten der Urkirche: Jesus und das Judenchristentum im Licht neuer archäologischer Erkenntnisse.* 2nd ed. Giessen: Brunnen [1991].

Platner, Samuel B., and Ashby Thomas. 1965. *Topographical Dictionary of Ancient Rome.* Rome: Bretschneider.

Plessis, J. G. Du. 1990. "For Reasons of the Heart: A Critical Appraisal of David J. Bosch's Use of Scripture in the Foundation of Christian Mission." *Missionalia* 18:75-85.

Plümacher, Eckhard. 1972. *Lukas als hellenistischer Schriftsteller: Studien zur Apostelgeschichte.* StUNT 9. Göttingen: Vandenhoeck & Ruprecht.

―――. 1978a. "Apostelgeschichte." *TRE* 3:483-528.

―――. 1978b. "Apokryphe Apostelakten." PWSup 15:11-70.

―――. 1993. "Die Missionsreden der Apostelgeschichte und Dionys von Halikarnass." *NTS* 39:161-77.

Plumley, Jack A. 1957. "Early Christianity in Egypt." *PEQ* 89:70-89.

Plummer, Robert L. 2001. "The Church's Missionary Nature: The Apostle Paul and His Churches." Ph.D. diss., Southern Baptist Theological Seminary.

Pokorný, Petr. 1998. *Theologie der lukanischen Schriften.* FRLANT 174. Göttingen: Vandenhoeck & Ruprecht.

Polag, Athanasius. 1977. *Die Christologie der Logienquelle.* WMANT 45. Neukirchen-Vluyn: Neukirchener Verlag.

Polhill, John B. 1981. "Paul: Theology Born of Mission." *RevExp* 78:233-47.

Pollard, Nigel. 2000. *Soldiers, Cities and Civilians in Roman Syria.* Ann Arbor: University of Michigan Press.

Pollet, Gilbert, ed. 1987. *India and the Ancient World History: Trade and Culture before A.D. 650.* Leiden: Department Oriëntalistiek.

Polomé, Edgar C. 1983. "The Linguistic Situation in the Western Provinces of the Roman Empire." *ANRW* II.29.2:509-53.

Popkes, Wiard. 1978. "Zum Verständnis der Mission bei Johannes." *Zeitschrift für Mission* 4:63-69.

Portefaix, L. 1989. "Women and Mission in the New Testament: Some Remarks on the Perspective of Audience." *StTh* 43:141-52.

Porter, Stanley E. 1990. "Thucydides 1.22.1 and Speeches in Acts: Is There a Thucydidean View?" *NovT* 32:121-42.

———. 1994a. "The 'We' Passages." In Gill and Gempf 1994, 545-74.

———. 1994b. "Jesus and the Use of Greek in Galilee." In Chilton and Evans 1994, 123-54.

———. 1999. *The Paul of Acts: Essays in Literary Criticism, Rhetoric and Theology.* WUNT 115. Tübingen: Mohr-Siebeck.

———. 2000. *The Criteria for Authenticity in Historical-Jesus Research: Previous Discussion and New Proposals.* JSNTSup 191. Sheffield: Sheffield Academic Press.

Porton, Gary G. 1985. "Forbiden Transactions: Prohibited Commerce with Gentiles in Earliest Rabbinism." In *"To See Ourselves As Others See Us": Christians, Jews, "Others" in Late Antiquity,* edited by J. Neusner and E. S. Frerichs, 317-55. Scholars Press Studies in the Humanities. Chico, Calif.: Scholars Press.

———. 1988. *Goyim: Gentiles and Israelites in Mishnah-Tosefta.* BJS 155. Atlanta: Scholars Press.

———. 1993. "Gentiles in Israelites in Mishnah-Tosefta: A Study in Ethnicity." In *Bits of Honey,* FS S. H. Levey, edited by S. F. Chyet and D. H. Ellenson, 93-111. SFSHJ 74. Atlanta: Scholars Press.

———. 1994. *The Stranger Within Your Gates: Converts and Conversion in Rabbinic Literature.* Chicago: University of Chicago Press.

Posch, Walter. 1995. *Baktrien zwischen Griechen und Kuschan.* Wiesbaden: Harrassowitz.

Poupon, Gérard. 1989. "Les 'Actes des Pierre' et leur remaniement." *ANRW* II.25.6:4363-83.

Praet, Danny. 1992-1993. "Explaining the Christianization of the Roman Empire: Older Theories and Recent Developments." *Sacris Erudiri* 33:5-119.

Prast, Franz. 1979. *Presbyter und Evangelium in nachapostolischer Zeit: Die Abschiedsrede des Paulus in Milet (Apg 20.17-38).* FB 29. Stuttgart: Katholisches Bibelwerk.

Pratscher, Wilhelm. 1979. "Der Verzicht des Paulus auf finanziellen Unterhalt durch seine Gemeinden: Ein Aspekt seiner Missionsweise." *NTS* 25:284-98.

———. 1987. *Der Herrenbruder Jakobus und die Jakobustradition.* FRLANT 139. Göttingen: Vandenhoeck & Ruprecht.

Preuss, Horst Dietrich. 1971. *Verspottung fremder Religionen im Alten Testament.* BWANT 92. Stuttgart: Kohlhammer.

———. 1991-1992. *Theologie des Alten Testaments.* 2 vols. Stuttgart: Kohlhammer.

Price, Simon R. F. 1984. *Rituals and Power: The Roman Imperial Cult in Asia Minor.* Cambridge: Cambridge University Press.

Prieur, Jean-Marc. 1989. *Acta Andreae.* 2 vols. CCSA 5-6. Turnhout: Brepols.

Prior, Michael. 1989. *Paul the Letter-Writer and the Second Letter to Timothy.*

JSNTSup 23. Sheffield: JSOT Press.

Priotto, Michelangelo. 1990. "Giuditta e Sapienza: due aspetti dell'atteggiamento dei popoli di fronte a Israele." In Ghiberti 1990b, 45-70.

Pritz, Ray A. 1988. *Nazarene Jewish Christianity: From the End of the New Testament Period until Its Disappearance in the Fourth Century.* StPB 37. Jerusalem: Magnes; Leiden: Brill.

Prümm, Karl. 1962. "Zum Vorgang der Heidenmission nach paulinischer Sicht: Eine fundamental- und missionstheologische Studie." *ZKTh* 84:427-70.

Puthiakunnel, Thomas. 1970. "Jewish Colonies of India Paved the Way for St. Thomas." In *The Malabar Church,* FS P. J. Podipara, edited by Jacob Vellian, 187-91. Orientalia Christiana Analecta 186. Rome: Pont. Institutum Orientalium Studiorum.

Pyke, J. H. 1958. "An Inquiry into the New Testament Basis of the Missionary Obligation and Method." Ph.D. diss., Drew University.

Quesnell, Quentin. 1983. "The Women at Luke's Supper." In *Political Issues in Luke-Acts,* edited by R. J. Cassidy and P. Scharper, 59-79. Maryknoll, N.Y.: Orbis.

Raban, Avner, and Kenneth G. Holum, eds. 1996. *Caesarea Maritima: Retrospective after Two Millennia.* Documenta et monumenta orientis antiqui 21. Leiden: Brill.

Rabello, Alfredo Mordechai. 1980. "The Legal Condition of the Jews in the Roman Empire." *ANRW* II.13:662-762.

Rad, Gerhard von. 1960. *Theologie des Alten Testaments.* 2 vols. Munich: Kaiser [5th ed., 1968; 6th ed., 1969; 9th ed. 1987]. English: *Old Testament Theology.* 2 vols. Edinburgh: Oliver & Boyd; New York: Harper & Row, 1962 [repr., Louisville: Westminster John Knox, 2001].

Radke, Gerhard. 1973. "Viae Publicae Romanae." PWSup 13:1417-1686.

Radl, Walter. 1991. "Rettung in Israel." In Bussmann and Radl 1991, 43-60.

Radt, Wolfgang. 1988. *Pergamon: Geschichte und Bauten, Funde und Erforschung einer antiken Metropole.* Cologne: DuMont.

———. 1999. *Pergamon: Geschichte und Bauten einer antiken Metropole.* Darmstadt: Primus and Wissenschaftliche Buchgesellschaft.

Raguin, Yves. 1947. *Théologie missionnaire de l'Ancien Testament.* Paris: Seuil.

Rainer, Thom S. 1990. "Church Growth and Evangelism in the Book of Acts." *Criswell Theological Review* 5:57-68.

Räisänen, Heikki. 1983. *Paul and the Law.* WUNT 29. Tübingen: Mohr-Siebeck.

———. 1995a. "Die 'Hellenisten' der Urgemeinde." *ANRW* II.26.2:1468-1514.

———. 1995b. "The Nicolaitans: Apoc. 2; Acta 6." *ANRW* II.26.2:1602-44.

———. 1995c. "The Clash between Christian Styles of Life in the Book of Revelation." In *Mighty Minorities? Minorities in Early Christianity—Positions and Strategies,* FS J. Jervell, edited by D. Hellholm et al., 151-66. Oslo and Kopenhagen: Scandinavian University Press, 1995.

Rajak, Tessa. 1984. "Was There a Roman Charter for the Jews?" *JRS* 74:107-23.

———. 1994. "A Missionary Faith?" *Times Literary Supplement,* May 6, p. 24.

———. 1996. "Benefactors in the Greco-Jewish Diaspora." In Schäfer 1996, 305-19.

Rajak, Tessa, and David Noy. 1993. "*Archisynagogoi:* Office, Title and Social Status in the Greco-Jewish Synagogue." *JRS* 83:75-93.

Rajak, Tessa, et al., eds. 1992. *The Jews Among Pagans and Christians in the Roman Empire.* London: Routledge.

Ramsay, William Mitchell. 1890. *The Historical Geography of Asia Minor.* London: Murray [repr., Amsterdam: Hakkert, 1962].

———. 1893. *The Church in the Roman Empire Before A.D. 170.* London: Hodder & Stoughton [5th ed., 1897].

———. 1895-1897. *The Cities and Bishoprics of Phrygia, Being an Essay of the Local History of Phrygia from the Earliest Times to the Turkish Conquest.* 2 vols. Oxford: Clarendon [repr., New York: Arno, 1975].

———. 1896. *St. Paul the Traveller and the Roman Citizen.* London: Hodder & Stoughton [6th ed. 1902; repr., Grand Rapids: Baker, 1979].

———. 1904. *The Letters to the Seven Churches.* Rev. ed. Edited by M. W. Wilson. Peabody, Mass.: Hendrickson, 1994.

———. 1907. *The Cities of St. Paul, Their Influences on His Life and Thought: The Cities of East Asia Minor.* London: Hodder & Stoughton [repr., Grand Rapids: Baker, 1960].

Rankin, H. David. 1987. "The Galatians." In *Celts and the Classical World.* London: Croom Helm, 188-207.

Rappaport, Uriel. 1965. "Jewish Religious Propaganda and Proselytism in the Period of the Second Commonwealth." Diss., Hebrew University, Jerusalem. [*non vidi*]

Rapske, Brian. 1992. "The Lukan Defense of the Missionary Prisoner Paul." Ph.D. diss., University of Aberdeen.

———. 1994a. *The Book of Acts and Paul in Roman Custody.* The Book of Acts in Its First-Century Setting 3. Exeter: Paternoster.

———. 1994b. "Acts, Travel and Shipwreck." In Gill and Gempf 1994, 1-47.

———. 1997. "Rome and Roman Christianity." *DLNTD* 1063-68.

———. 1998. "Opposition to the Plan of God and Persecution." In Marshall and Peterson 1998, 235-56.

Raschke, M. 1978. "New Studies in Roman Commerce with the East." *ANRW* II.9.2:604-1361.

Rathbone, Dominic W. 1990. "Villages, Land and Population in Graeco-Roman Egypt." *PCPS* 36:103-42.

Rau, Eckhard. 1994. *Von Jesus zu Paulus: Entwicklung und Rezeption der antiochenischen Theologie im Urchristentum.* Stuttgart: Kohlhammer.

Ravens, David A. S. 1996. *Luke and the Restoration of Israel.* JSNTSup 119. Sheffield: Sheffield Academic Press.

Reader, William W. 1996. *The Severed Hand and the Upright Corpse: The Declamations of Marcus Antonius Polemo.* SBLTT 42. Atlanta: Scholars Press.

Reasoner, Mark. 1999. "The Theme of Acts: Institutional History of Divine Necessity in History?" *JBL* 118:635-59.

Rebell, Walter. 1988. "Gemeinde als Missionsfaktor im Urchristentum: 1 Kor 14.24f als Schlüsselsituation." *ThZ* 44:117-34.

Reck, Reinhold. 1991. *Kommunikation und Gemeindeaufbau: Eine Studie zu Entstehung, Leben und Wachstum paulinischen Gemeinden in den Kommunikationsstrukturen der Antike.* SBS 22. Stuttgart: Katholisches Bibelwerk.

Reed, Jonathan L. 1994. "Population Numbers, Urbanization, and Economics: Galilean Archaeology and the Historical Jesus." In *SBLSP,* 203-19.

————. 2000. *Archaeology and the Galilean Jesus: A Re-Examination of the Evidence.* Harrisburg, Pa.: Trinity.

Refoulé, François. 1984. *". . . et ainsi tout Israël sera sauvé": Romains 11.25-32.* LD 117. Paris: Cerf.

————. 1993. "Le discours de Pierreà l'assemblée de Jérusalem." *RB* 100, 239-251.

Reichardt, Michael. 1999. *Psychologische Erklärung der paulinischen Damaskusvision?* SBB 42. Stuttgart: Katholisches Bibelwerk.

Reicke, Bo. 1982. *Neutestamentliche Zeitgeschichte: Die biblische Welt von 500 v.Chr. bis 100 n.Chr.* 3rd ed. Berlin: de Gruyter [1965].

————. 1984. "Die Entstehungsverhältnisse der synoptischen Evangelien." *ANRW* II.25.2:1758-91.

Reinach, Salomon. 1924. "La première allusion au christianisme dans l'histoire." *RHR* 89:108-22.

Reinbold, Wolfgang. 2000. *Propaganda und Mission im ältesten Christentum: Eine Untersuchung zu den Modalitäten der Ausbreitung der frühen Kirche.* FRLANT 188. Göttingen: Vandenhoeck & Ruprecht.

Reinhardt, Wolfgang 1995a. *Das Wachstum des Volkes Gottes: Untersuchung zum Gemeindewachstum im lukanischen Doppelwerk auf dem Hintergrund des Alten Testaments.* Göttingen: Vandenhoeck & Ruprecht.

————. 1995b. "The Population Size of Jerusalem and the Numerical Growth of the Jerusalem Church." In Bauckham 1995a, 237-65.

Reiser, Marius. 1995. "Hat Paulus Heiden bekehrt?" *BZ* 39:76-91.

————. 2001. "Von Caesarea nach Malta: Literarischer Charakter und historische Glaubwürdigkeit von Act 27." In Horn 2001, 49-74.

Rémy, Bernard. 1986. *L'évolution administrative de l'Anatolie aux trois premiers siècles de notre ère.* Collection du Centre d'Études Romaines et Gallo-Romaines n.s. 5. Lyon: Boccard.

————. 1988. *Les fastes sénatoriaux des provinces romaines d'Anatolie au Haut-Empire (31 av. J.-C.– 284 ap. J.-C.).* Paris: Editions Recherche sur les Civilisations.

Rendtorff, Rolf. 1994. "Israel, die Völker und die Kirche." *Kirche und Israel* 9:126-37.

Rengstorf, Karl H. 1962. "The Election of Matthias." In *Current Issues in New Testament Interpretation,* FS O. A. Piper, edited by W. Klassen and G. F. Snyder, 178-92. New York: Harper.

Rétif, André. 1953. *Foi au Christ et mission, d'après les Acts des Apôtres.* Paris: Cerf.

Reumann, John. 1993. "Contributions of the Philippian Community to Paul and to Earliest Christanity." *NTS* 39:438-57.

Reventlow, Henning Graf. 1977. "'Internationalismus' in den Patriarchenüberlieferungen." In *Beiträge zur alttestamentlichen Theologie,* FS W. Zimmerli, edited by Herbert Donner et al., 354-70. Göttingen: Vandenhoeck & Ruprecht.

Rey-Coquais, Jean-Paul. 1989. "La Syrie, de Pompée à Dioclétien: Histoire politique et administrative." In Dentzer and Orthmann 1989, 45-62.

Reymond, Robert L. 2000. *Paul, Missionary Theologian: A Survey of his Missionary Labours and Theology.* Fearn, Scotland: Christian Focus Pulbications.

Reynolds, Joyce, and Robert Tannenbaum. 1987. *Jews and God-fearers at Aphrodisias: Greek Inscriptions with Commentary.* Proceedings of the Cambridge Philological Association Supplement 12. Cambridge: Cambridge Philological Society.

Rhoads, David M. 1995a. "Network for Missions: The Social System of the Jesus Movement as Depicted in the Narrative of the Gospel of Mark." *ANRW* II.26.2:1692-1729.

———. 1995b. "Mission in the Gospel of Mark." *CurTM* 22:340-55.

Richards, E. Randolph. 1991. *The Secretary in the Letters of Paul.* WUNT 2.42. Tübingen: Mohr-Siebeck.

Richardson, John S. 1996. *The Romans in Spain.* Oxford: Blackwell.

Richardson, Peter. 1979-1980. "Pauline Inconsistency: I Corinthians 9.19-23 and Galatians 2.11-14." *NTS* 26:347-62.

———. 1999. *Herod: King of the Jews and Friend of the Romans.* Minneapolis: Fortress.

Riches, John. 1980. *Jesus and the Transformation of Judaism.* London: Darton, Longman & Todd.

Richter, Julius. 1924. *Indische Missionsgeschichte.* 2nd ed. Allgemeine evangelische Missionsgeschichte Band 1. Gütersloh: Bertelsmann [1906].

———. 1929. *Die Briefe des Paulus als missionarische Sendschreiben.* Allgemeine Missions-Studien 7. Gütersloh: Bertelsmann.

Ricl, Marijana. 1995. "The Appeal to Divine Justice in the Lydian Confession-Inscriptions." In Schwertheim 1995, 67-76.

———, ed. 1997. *The Inscriptions of Alexandreia Troas.* IK 53. Bonn: Habelt.

Ridderbos, Herman. 1975. *Paul: An Outline of His Theology.* Grand Rapids: Eerdmans. German: *Paulus: Ein Entwurf seiner Theologie.* Wuppertal: Brockhaus, 1970.

Riddle, Donald Wayne. 1938. "Early Christian Hospitality: A Factor in the Gospel Transmission." *JBL* 57:141-54.

Ridgway, John K. 1999. *"Let Your Peace Come upon It": Healing and Peace in Matthew 10:1-15.* StBL 2. New York: Lang.

Riehm, E. 1880. "Der Missionsgedanke im Alten Testament." *Allgemeine Missions-Zeitschrift* 7:453-65.

Riepl, Wolfgang. 1913. *Das Nachrichtenwesen des Altertums mit besonderer Rücksicht auf die Römer.* Leipzig: Teubner [repr., Hildesheim: Olms, 1972].

Riesenfeld, Harald. 1969. "Translating the Gospel in New Testament Times." In *The Church Crossing Frontiers,* FS Bengt Sundkler, edited by C. F. Hallencreuz and P. Beyerhaus, 20-26. Uppsala: Gleerup.

Riesner, Rainer. 1978. "Der Aufbau der Reden im Matthäus-Evangelium." *ThBeitr* 9:172-82.

———. 1987. "Bethany Beyond the Jordan (John 1.28): Topography, Theology and History in the Fourth Gospel." *TynBul* 38:29-63.

———. 1988. *Jesus als Lehrer: Eine Untersuchung zum Ursprung der Evangelien-Überlieferung.* 3rd ed. WUNT 2.7. Tübingen: Mohr-Siebeck [1981].

———. 1994. *Die Frühzeit des Apostels Paulus: Studien zur Chronologie, Missionsstrategie und Theologie.* WUNT 71. Tübingen: Mohr-Siebeck. English: *Paul's Early Period: Chronology, Mission Strategy, Theology.* Grand Rapids: Eerdmans, 1998.

———. 1995a. "Das Jerusalemer Essenerviertel und die Urgemeinde." *ANRW* II.26.2:1775-1922.

———. 1995b. "Synagogues in Jerusalem." In Bauckham 1995a, 179-211.

———. 1997. "Lukas (1. Jh. n.Chr.)." In *Hauptwerke der Geschichtsschreibung,* edited by V. Reinhardt, 391-94. Stuttgart: Kröner.

———. 2000. "A Pre-Christian Jewish Mission?" In Ådna and Kvalbein 2000, 211-50.

———. 2002. *Bethanien jenseits des Jordan: Topographie und Theologie im Johannes-Evangelium.* Giessen: Brunnen.

Rissi, Mathias. 1965. *Was ist und was geschehen soll danach: Die Zeit- und Geschichtsauffassung der Offenbarung des Johannes.* AThANT 46. Zürich: Zwingli.

———. 1966. *Die Zukunft der Welt: Eine exegetische Studie über die Johannesoffenbarung 19,11 bis 22,15.* Basel: Reinhardt. English: *The Future of the World: An Exegetical Study of Rev. 19:11-22:15.* SBT 2.23. London: SCM Press, 1972.

———. 1995. *Die Hure Babylon und die Verführung der Heiligen: Eine Studie zur Apokalypse des Johannes.* BWANT 137. Stuttgart: Kohlhammer.

Ritt, Hubert. 1989. "Die Frau als Glaubensbotin: Zum Verständnis der Samaritanerin von Joh 4,1-42." In Frankemölle and Kertelge 1989, 307-24.

Robert, Louis. 1962. *Villes d'Asie Mineure: Études de geographie ancienne.* 2nd ed. Paris: Boccard [1935].

―――. 1964. *Nouvelles inscriptions de Sardes.* Archaeological Exploration of Sardis 1. Paris: Maisonneuve.

―――. 1969-1990. *Opera minora selecta: Épigraphie et antiquités grecques.* 7 vols. Amsterdam: Hakkert.

―――. 1980. *À travers l'Asie Mineure.* Bibliothèque des écoles françaises d'Athènes et de Rome 239. Athens and Paris: École française d'Athènes and Boccard.

Roberts, Charles W. 1993. "The Role of Barnabas in the Acts of the Apostles." Th.M. thesis, Columbia Theological Seminary.

Roberts, Colin H. 1949. "The Christian Book and the Greek Papyri." *JTS* 50:155-68.

―――. 1970. "Books in the Graeco-Roman World and in the New Testament." In *The Cambridge History of the Bible,* vol. 1, *From the Beginnings to Jerome,* edited by P. R. Ackroyd and C. F. Evans, 48-66. Cambridge: Cambridge University Press.

―――. 1979. *Manuscript, Society, and Belief in Early Christian Egypt.* Oxford: Oxford University Press.

Roberts, Colin H., and Theodore C. Skeat. 1983. *The Birth of the Codex.* Oxford: Oxford University Press.

Robinson, Bernard P. 1988. "The Two Persecuted Prophet-Witnesses of Rev 11." *Scripture Bulletin* 19:14-19.

Robinson, John A. T. 1957. *Jesus and His Coming.* London: SCM Press.

―――. 1976. *Redating the New Testament.* London: SCM Press. German: *Wann entstand das Neue Testament?* Paderborn: Bonifatius; Wuppertal: Brockhaus, 1986.

―――. 1985. *The Priority of John.* London: SPCK [repr., 1987].

Robinson, Phil J. 1989. "Some Missiological Perspectives from I Peter 2:4-10." *Missionalia* 17:176-87.

Robinson, Thomas A. 1988. *The Bauer Thesis Examined: The Geography of Heresy in the Early Christian Church.* SBEC 11. Lewiston, N.Y.: Mellen.

Roels, E. D. 1962. *God's Mission: The Epistle to the Ephesians in Missions Perspective.* Franeker: Wever.

Rokéah, David. 1970. "On the Attitude of the Sages toward Gentiles and Proselytes." [Hebrew]. *Mahalachim* 5:68-74.

―――. 1996. "Ancient Jewish Proselytism in Theory and in Practice." *ThZ* 52:206-23.

Roloff, Jürgen. 1965. *Apostolat, Verkündigung, Kirche: Ursprung, Inhalt und Funktion des kirchlichen Apostelamtes nach Paulus, Lukas und den Pastoralbriefen.* Gütersloh: Mohn.

―――. 1978. "Apostel/Apostolat/Apostolizität. I. Neues Testament." *TRE* 3:430-45.

―――. 1991. "Konflikte und Konfliktlösungen in der Apostelgeschichte." In Bussmann and Radl 1991, 111-26.

————. 1993. *Die Kirche im Neuen Testament*. Grundrisse zum Neuen Testament 10. Göttingen: Vandenhoeck & Ruprecht.

Romano, David G. 2000. "A Tale of Two Cities: Roman Colonies at Corinth." In Fentress 2000, 83-104.

Romaniuk, Casmir. 1964. "Die 'Gottesfürchtigen' im Neuen Testament: Beitrag zur neutestamentlichen Theologie der Gottesfurcht." *Aegyptus* 44:66-91.

Romer, Frank E. 1998. *Pomponius Mela's Description of the World*. Ann Arbor: University of Michigan Press.

Romm, James S. 1992. *The Edges of the Earth in Ancient Thought: Geography, Exploration, and Fiction*. Princeton, N.J.: Princeton University Press.

Roncaglia, Martiniano P. 1966. *Histoire de l'Église Copte*. Vol. I, *Les origines du christianisme en Égypte: Du judéo-christianisme au christianisme hellénistique (Ier-IIe siècles)*. Histoire de l'Église en Orient. Beirut: Dar Al-Kalima [2nd ed., 1985].

Rooney, John. 1984. *Shadows in the Dark*. Pakistan Christian History Monograph 1. Rawalpindi: Christian Study Centre Publication.

————, ed. 1988. *St. Thomas and Taxila: A Symposium on Saint Thomas*. Pakistan Christian History: Studies Series 1. Rawalpindi: Christian Study Centre Publication.

Rorem, Paul. 1990. "Mission and Ministry in the Early Church: Bishop, Presbyters and Deacons, but . . ." *CurTM* 17:15-22.

Rosen, Georg, Friedrich Rosen and Georg Bertram. 1929. *Juden und Phönizier: Das antike Judentum als Missionsreligion und die Entstehung der jüdischen Diaspora*. 2nd ed. Tübingen: Mohr.

Rosen, Haiim B. 1980. "Die Sprachsituation im römischen Palästina." In Neumann and Untermann 1980, 215-39.

Rosenbaum, Elisabeth, Gerhard Huber and Somay Onurkan. 1967. *A Survey of Coastal Cities in Western Cilicia: Preliminary Report*. Türk Tarih Kurumu Yayinlarindan 6.8. Ankara: Türk Tarih Kurumu Basimevi.

Rosenkranz, Gerhard. 1980. "Heidentum—Was ist das?" In Sundermeier 1980, 69-79.

Rosner, Brian S. 1994. *Paul, Scripture and Ethics: A Study of 1 Corinthians 5-7*. AGAJU 22. Leiden: Brill [Grand Rapids: Baker, 1999].

————. 1998. "The Progress of the Word." In Marshall and Peterson 1998, 215-33.

Ross, Steven K. 2001. *Roman Edessa: Politics and Culture on the Eastern Fringes of the Roman Empire. 114-242 CE*. New York: Routledge.

Rostovtzeff, Michael. 1929. *Gesellschaft und Wirtschaft im römischen Kaiserreich*. 2 vols. Leipzig: Quelle & Meyer. English: *The Social and Economic History of the Roman Empire*. 2 vols. Oxford: Clarendon, 1926 [rev. ed., 1957].

Rossano, Pietro. 1990. "La missione nella Bibbia e nelle religioni." In Ghiberti 1990b, 9-11.

Rowley, Harold H. 1955. *The Missionary Message of the Old Testament.* London: Carey [1944].

Ruiz, Rodriguez M. 1987. *Der Missionsgedanke des Johannesevangeliums: Ein Beitrag zur johanneischen Soteriologie und Ekklesiologie.* FB 55. Würzburg: Echter.

Runesson, Anders. 1999. "Particularistic Judaism and Universalistic Christianity? Some Critical Remarks on Terminology and Theology." *StTh* 53:55-75.

———. 2001. *The Origins of the Synagogue: A Socio-Historical Study.* ConBNT 37. Stockholm: Almqvist & Wiksell.

Rusche, Helga. 1958. *Gastfreundschaft in der Verkündigung des Neuen Testaments und ihr Verhältnis zur Mission.* Veröffentlichungen des Instituts für Missionswissenschaft der Westfälischen Wilhelms-Universität Münster 7. Münster: Aschendorff.

Russell, Donald A. 1983. *Greek Declamation.* Cambridge: Cambridge University Press.

Rutgers, Leonard V. 1989. "Roman Policy toward the Jews: Expulsions from the City of Rome during the First Century C.E." In Donfried and Richardson 1998, 93-116.

———. 1992. "Archaeological Evidence for the Interaction of Jews and Non-Jews in Late Antiquity." *AJA* 96:101-18.

———. 1995. *The Jews in Late Ancient Rome: Evidence of Cultural Interaction in the Roman Diaspora.* Religions in the Graeco-Roman World 126. Leiden: Brill.

Sacchi, Alessandro. 1990. "La missione davanti alla parola di Dio." In Ghiberti 1990b, 201-11.

Sack, Dorothee. 1989. *Damaskus: Entwicklung und Struktur einer orientalisch-islamischen Stadt.* Damaszener Forschungen 1. Mainz: Zabern.

Saddington, Dennis B. 1996. "Roman Military and Administrative Personnel in the New Testament." *ANRW* II.26.3:2409-35.

Safrai, Shmuel. 1981. *Die Wallfahrt im Zeitalter des Zweiten Tempels.* Neukirchen-Vluyn: Neukirchener Verlag.

———. 1987. *The Literature of the Sages, Part 1: Oral Tora, Halakha, Mishna, Tosefta, Talmud, External Tractates.* CRINT 2.1. Assen: Van Gorcum.

Safrai, Shmuel, and Menachem Stern, eds. 1987. *The Jewish People in the First Century: Historical Geography, Political History, Social, Cultural and Religious Life and Institutions.* 2nd ed. CRINT 1.2. Assen: Van Gorcum [1976].

Safrai, Ze'ev. 1994. *The Economy of Roman Palestine.* London: Routledge.

Şahin, Sencer, et al., eds. 1978. *Studien zur Religion und Kultur Kleinasiens.* FS F. K. Dörner. EPRO 66. Leiden: Brill.

Sakellariou, M. V. 1989. *The Polis-State Definition and Origin.* Meletemata 4. Athens: Research Centre for Greek and Roman Antiquity; Paris: Boccard.

Saldarini, Anthony J. 1988. *Pharisees, Scribes and Sadducees in Palestinian Society.* Edinburgh: T & T Clark.

————. 1992. "The Gospel of Matthew and Jewish-Christian Conflict in the Galilee." In L. Levine 1992, 23-38.

————. 1994. *Matthew's Christian-Jewish Community.* CSHJ. Chicago: University of Chicago Press.

Samarin, William J. 1972. *Tongues of Men and Angels: The Religious Language of Pentecostalism.* London: Macmillan.

Samuel, S. Johnson. 1986. "Paul on the Areopagus: A Misson Perspective." *Bangalore Theological Forum* 18:17-32.

Sanders, E. P. 1977. *Paul and Palestinian Judaism: A Comparison of Patterns of Religion.* London: SCM Press. German: *Paulus und das palästinische Judentum: Ein Vergleich zweier Religionsstrukturen.* StUNT 17. Göttingen: Vandenhoeck & Ruprecht, 1985.

————. 1983. *Paul, the Law, and the Jewish People.* Philadelphia: Fortress.

————. 1985. *Jesus and Judaism.* Philadelphia: Fortress [3rd pr., 1987; 3rd ed., 1991].

————. 1991. *Paul.* Oxford: Oxford University Press. German: *Paulus: Eine Einführung.* Stuttgart: Reclam, 1995.

————. 1992. *Judaism: Practice and Belief 63 BCE-66 CE.* London: SCM Press.

————. 1993. *The Historical Figure of Jesus.* London: Allen Lane and Penguin. German: *Sohn Gottes: Eine historische Biographie Jesu.* Stuttgart: Klett-Cotta, 1996.

Sanders, E. P., and Margaret Davies. 1989. *Studying the Synoptic Gospels.* London: SCM; Philadelphia: Trinity.

Sanders, E. P., et al., eds. 1981. *Jewish and Christian Self-Definition.* Vol. 2, *Aspects of Judaism in the Graeco-Roman Period.* Philadelphia: Fortress.

Sanders, Jack T. 1987. *The Jews in Luke-Acts.* Philadelphia: Fortress.

————. 1992. "Christians and Jews in the Roman Empire: A Conversation with Rodney Stark." *Sociological Analysis* 53:433-45.

————. 1996. "The First Decades of Jewish-Christian Relations: The Evidence of the New Testament (Gospels and Acts)." *ANRW* II.26.3:1937-78.

Sandnes, Karl Olav. 1991. *Paul—One of the Prophets? A Contribution to the Apostle's Self-Understanding.* WUNT 2.43. Tübingen: Mohr-Siebeck.

Sandt, Huub van de. 1990. "The Fate of the Gentiles in Joel and Acts 2." *ETL* 66:56-77.

————. 1994. "Acts 28,28: No Salvation for the People of Israel? An Answer in the Perspective of the LXX." *ETL* 70:341-58.

Sänger, Dieter. 1980. *Antikes Judentum und die Mysterien: Religionsgeschichtliche Untersuchungen zu Joseph und Aseneth.* WUNT 2.5. Tübingen: Mohr-Siebeck.

————. 1994. *Die Verkündigung des Gekreuzigten und Israel: Studien zum Verhältnis von Kirche und Israel bei Paulus und im frühen Christentum.* WUNT 75. Tübingen: Mohr-Siebeck.

————. 1995. "Schriftauslegung im Horizont der Gottesherrschaft: Die Antithesen der Bergpredigt (Mt 5,21-48) und die Verkündigung Jesu." In *Christlicher Glaube und religiöse Bildung*, FS F. Kriechbaum, edited by H. Deuser and G. Schmalenberg, 75-109. Giessener Schriften zur Theologie und Religionspädagogik 10. Giessen: Fachbereich Evangelische Theologie und Katholische Theologie.

Sass, Gerhard. 1995. *Leben aus den Verheißungen: Traditionsgeschichtliche und biblisch-theologische Untersuchungen zur Rede von Gottes Verheißungen im Frühjudentum und beim Apostel Paulus*. FRLANT 164. Göttingen: Vandenhoeck & Ruprecht.

Satake, Akira. 1966. *Die Gemeindeordnung in der Johannesapokalypse*. WMANT 21. Neukirchen-Vluyn: Neukirchener Verlag.

Sato, Migaku. 1988. *Q und Prophetie: Studien zur Gattungs- und Traditionsgeschichte der Quelle Q*. WUNT 2.29. Tübingen: Mohr-Siebeck.

Sautter, Gerhard. 1985. *Heilsgeschichte und Mission: Zum Verständnis der Heilsgeschichte in der Missionstheologie*. Monographien und Studienbücher 321. Giessen and Basel: Brunnen.

Sawicki, Marianne. 2000. *Crossing Galilee: Architectures of Contact in the Occupied Land of Jesus*. Harrisburg, Pa.: Trinity.

Sayar, Mustafa H. 1993. "Epigraphische Forschungen in Ostkilikien 1990." In Dobesch and Rehrenböck 1993, 319-27.

Scaer, David P. 1991. "The Relation of Matthew 28.16-20 to the Rest of the Gospel." *CTQ* 55:245-66.

Schade, Hans-Heinrich. 1984. *Apokalyptische Christologie bei Paulus: Studien zum Zusammenhang von Christologie und Eschatologie in den Paulusbriefen*. GThA 18. 2nd ed. Göttingen: Vandenhoeck & Ruprecht [1981].

Schäfer, Peter. 1978. *Studien zur Geschichte und Theologie des rabbinischen Judentums*. AGSU 15. Leiden: Brill.

————, ed. 1996. *Geschichte, Tradition, Reflexion*. FS Martin Hengel. Vol. 1, *Judentum*. Tübingen: Mohr-Siebeck.

————. 1997. *Judeophobia: Attitudes Toward the Jews in the Ancient World*. Cambridge, Mass.: Harvard University Press.

Schäferdiek, Knut. 1991. "Christian Mission and Expansion." In *Early Christianity: Origins and Evolution to AD 600*, FS W. H. C. Frend, edited by I. Hazlett, 65-77. London: SPCK.

Schaper, Joachim. 1995. *Eschatology in the Greek Psalter*. WUNT 2.76. Tübingen: Mohr-Siebeck.

Scharlemann, Martin H. 1968. *Stephen: A Singular Saint*. AnBib 34. Rome: Biblical Institute Press.

Scheidel, Walter. 1996. *Measuring Sex, Age and Death in the Roman Empire: Explorations in Ancient Demography*. JRASup 21. Ann Arbor, Mich.: Journal of Roman Archaeology.

Schelkle, Karl-Heinz, ed. 1981. *Paulus: Leben, Briefe, Theologie.* WF 152. Darmstadt: Wissenschaftliche Buchgesellschaft.

Schenke, Ludger. 1990. *Die Urgemeinde: Geschichtliche und theologische Entwicklung.* Stuttgart: Kohlhammer.

Scherer, James A. 1987. *Gospel, Church and Kingdom: Comparative Studies in World Mission Theology.* Minneapolis: Augsburg.

Schermann, Theodor. 1907. *Propheten- und Apostellegenden, nebst Jüngerkatalogen des Dorotheus und verwandter Texte.* TUGAL 31.3. Leipzig: Hinrichs.

Scherrer, Peter, ed. 1995. *Ephesos: Der neue Führer; 100 Jahre Österreichische Ausgrabungen 1895-1995.* Vienna: Österreichisches Archäologisches Institut.

Scheurer, Erich. 1996. *Altes Testament und Mission: Zur Begründung des Missionsauftrags.* Giessen: Brunnen.

Schick Edwin A. 1989. "Priestly Pilgrims: Mission Outside the Camp in Hebrews." *CurTM* 16:372-76.

Schiffman, Lawrence H. 1982. "Proselytism in the Writings of Josephus." In *Josephus Flavius: Historian of Eretz-Israel in the Hellenistic-Roman Period,* edited by U. Rappaport, 247-65. Jerusalem: Yad Izhak Ben-Zvi.

———. 1982-1984. "Legislation Concerning Relations with Non-Jews in the *Zadokite Fragments* and in Tannaitic Literature." *RevQ* 11:379-89.

———. 1985. *Who Was a Jew? Rabbinic and Halakhic Perspectives on the Jewish-Christian Schism.* Hoboken, N.J.: Ktav.

———. 1987. "The Conversion of the Royal House of Adiabene in Josephus and Rabbinic Sources." In *Josephus, Judaism, and Christianity,* edited by L. H. Feldman and G. Hata, 293-312. Detroit: Wayne State University Press.

Schille, Gottfried. 1961. "Missionstheologie im Neuen Testament: Zwei verschiedene Maßstäbe der ältesten Missionsmethode in der Apostelgeschichte." *Monatsschrift für Praktische Theologie* 50:201-12.

———. 1966. *Anfänge der Kirche: Erwägungen zur apostolischen Frühgeschichte.* BEvTh 43. Munich: Kaiser.

———. 1967. *Die urchristliche Kollegialmission.* AThANT48. Zürich: Zwingli.

———. 1969. "Anfänge der christlichen Mission." *KD* 15:320-39.

———. 1992. "Christianity: Early Jewish Christianity." *ABD* 1:935-38.

———. 1994. "Die Jesusbewegung und die Entstehung der Kirche." *ThLZ* 119:100-112.

Schlatter, Adolf. 1922. *Die Theologie der Apostel.* Stuttgart: Calwer [4th ed., 1984].

Schlier, Heinrich. 1942. "Die Entscheidung für die Heidenmission in der Urchristenheit." in *Die Zeit der Kirche: Exegetische Aufsätze und Vorträge,* 90-107. Freiburg: Herder [4th ed., 1966].

———. 1978. *Grundzüge einer paulinischen Theologie.* Freiburg: Herder.

Schlueter, Carol J. 1995. *Filling up the Measure: Polemical Hyperbole in 1 Thessalonians 2.14-16.* JSNTSup 98. Sheffield: Sheffield Academic Press.

Schlunck, Martin. 1937. *Paulus als Missionar.* Gütersloh: Mohn.

Schmeller, Thomas. 1994. "Jesus im Umland Galiläas: Zu den markinischen Berichten vom Aufenthalt Jesu in den Gebieten von Tyros, Caesarea Philippi und der Dekapolis." *BZ* 38:44-66.

———. 1997. "Kollege Paulus: Die Jesusüberlieferung und das Selbstverständnis des Völkerapostels." *ZNW* 88:260-83.

Schmidt, A. 1992. "Das Missionsdekret in Galater 2,7-8 als Vereinbarung vom ersten Besuch Pauli in Jerusalem." *NTS* 38:149-52.

Schmidt, Frederick W. 1993. "Jesus and the Salvation of the Gentiles." In Crockett and Sigountos 1993, 97-105.

Schmidt, Helmut. 1968. *Israel, Zion und die Völker: Eine motivgeschichtliche Untersuchung zum Verständnis des Universalismus im Alten Testament.* Marburg: Elwert.

Schmidt, Karl Ludwig. 1935. "ἔθνος." *ThWNT* 2:366-70.

———. 1945. "Israels Stellung zu den Fremdlingen und Beisassen und Israels Wissen um seine Fremdling- und Beisassenschaft." *Judaica* 1:269-96.

Schmidt, Thomas E. 1994. "Cry of Dereliction or Cry of Judgment? Mark 15.34 in Context." *BBR* 4:145-53.

Schmithals, Walter. 1961. *Das kirchliche Apostelamt.* FRLANT 81. Göttingen: Vandenhoeck & Ruprecht. English: *The Office of Apostle in the Early Church.* Nashville: Abingdon, 1969.

———. 1963. *Paulus und Jakobus.* FRLANT 85. Göttingen: Vandenhoeck & Ruprecht. English: *Paul and James.* London: SCM Press; Naperville, Ill.: Allenson, 1965.

———. 1965. "Die Häretiker in Galatien." In *Paulus und die Gnostiker,* 9-46. ThF 35. Hamburg: Reich.

———. 1969. *Die Gnosis in Korinth: Eine Untersuchung zu den Korintherbriefen.* FRLANT 66. Göttingen: Vandenhoeck & Ruprecht. English: *Gnosticism in Corinth: An Investigation of the Letters to the Corinthians.* Nashville: Abingdon, 1971.

———. 1989. "Paulus als Heidenmissionar und das Problem seiner theologischen Entwicklung." In *Jesu Rede von Gott und ihre Nachgeschichte im frühen Christentum: Beiträge zur Verkündigung Jesu und zum Kerygma der Kirche,* FS W. Marxsen, edited by D.-A. Koch, 235-51. Gütersloh: Mohn.

———. 1994. *Theologiegeschichte des Urchristentums: Eine problemgeschichtliche Darstellung.* Stuttgart: Kohlhammer. English: *The Theology of the First Christians.* Louisville: Westminster John Knox, 1997.

Schmitt, Götz. 1995. *Siedlungen Palästinas in griechisch-römischer Zeit: Ostjordanland, Negeb und (in Auswahl) Westjordanland.* BTAVO B 93. Wiesbaden: Reichert.

Schmitt, Joseph. 1981. "Les discours missionnaires des Actes et l'histoire des traditions prépauliniennes." *RSR* 69:165-80.

Schmitt, Rüdiger. 1980. "Die Ostgrenze von Armenien über Mesopotamien, Syrien bis Arabien." In Neumann and Untermann 1980, 187-214.

———. 1983. "Die Sprachverhältnisse in den östlichen Provinzen des Römischen Reiches." *ANRW* II.29.2:554-86.

Schmitt-Korte, Karl. 1976. *Die Nabatäer: Spuren einer arabischen Kultur der Antike.* Hannover: Veröffentlichungen der Deutsch-Jordanischen Gesellschaft.

Schmökel, H. 1934. *Jahwe und die Fremdvölker.* Breslau: Maruschke & Berendt.

Schnabel, Eckhard J. 1985. *Law and Wisdom from Ben Sira to Paul: A Tradition Historical Enquiry into the Relation of Law, Wisdom, and Ethics.* WUNT 2.16. Tübingen: Mohr-Siebeck.

———. 1991. "Glaube als unbedingtes Vertrauen im Neuen Testament." *JETh* 5:63-86.

———. 1993. *Das Reich Gottes als Wirklichkeit und Hoffnung: Neuere Entwicklungen in der evangelikalen Theologie.* Wuppertal: Brockhaus.

———. 1994. "Jesus and the Beginnings of the Mission to the Gentiles." In Green and Turner 1994, 37-58.

———. 1996a. "Die Gemeinde des Neuen Bundes in Kontinuität und Diskontinuität zur Gemeinde des Alten Bundes." In Maier 1996, 147-213.

———. 1996b. "Die urchristliche Heidenmission als endzeitliches Phänomen." In Kasdorf and Walldorf 1996, 81-104.

———. 1997. "Mission, Early Non-Pauline." *DLNTD* 752-75.

———. 1998. "Die Nationen in der Johannesoffenbarung." In *Die Mission der Theologie,* FS Hans Kasdorf, edited by S. Holthaus and K. W. Müller, 59-76. Bonn: Verlag für Kultur und Wissenschaft.

———. 1999. "Die ersten Christen in Ephesus: Neuerscheinungen zur frühchristlichen Missionsgeschichte." *NovT* 41:349-82.

———. 2002a. "Evangelisation im Neuen Testament." In *Evangelisation mit Gegenwind: Zur Theologie und Praxis der Glaubensverkündigung in der säkularen Gesellschaft,* edited by H. H. Klement, 11-45. Giessen: Brunnen-Verlag.

———. 2002b. "Die Zentralität des Kreuzes in der urchristlichen Verkündigung." In *Evangelisation mit Gegenwind: Zur Theologie und Praxis der Glaubensverkündigung in der säkularen Gesellschaft,* edited by H. H. Klement, 46-64. Giessen: Brunnen-Verlag.

———. 2002c. "Israel, the People of God, and the Nations." *JETS* 45:35-57.

———. 2002d. "John and the Future of the Nations." *BBR* 12:243-71.

———. 2003. "Divine Tyranny and Public Humiliation: A Suggestion for the Interpretation of the Lydian and Phrygian Confession Inscriptions." *NovT* 45:160-88.

Schnackenburg, Rudolf, et al., eds. 1978. *Die Kirche des Anfangs.* FS H. Schürmann. Freiburg: Herder.

———. 1984. "Der Missionsgedanke des Johannesevangeliums im heutigen

Horizont." In *Das Johannesevangelium*, 58-72. HThKNT 4.4. Freiburg: Herder [4th ed., 1990].

———. 1986-1988. *Die sittliche Botschaft des Neuen Testaments*. 2 vols. HThKNTSup 1-2. Freiburg: Herder.

———. 1991. "Ephesus: Entwicklung einer Gemeinde von Paulus zu Johannes." *BZ* 35:41-64.

———. 1993. *Die Person Jesu Christi im Spiegel der vier Evangelien*. HThKNTSup 4. Freiburg: Herder.

Schneider, Gerhard. 1969. "Urchristliche Gottesverkündigung in hellenistischer Umwelt." In Schneider 1985b, 280-96.

———. 1970. "Die zwölf Apostel als 'Zeugen': Wesen, Ursprung und Funktion einr lukanischen Konzeption." In Schneider 1985b, 61-85.

———. 1981. "Anknüpfung, Kontinuität und Widersprpuch in der Areopagrede Apg 17,22-31." In Schneider 1985b, 297-302.

———. 1982. "Der Missionsauftrag Jesu in der Darstellung der Evangelien." In Schneider 1985b, 184-205.

———. 1985a. "Die Petrusrede vor Kornelius: Das Verhältnis von Tradition und Komposition in Apg 10,34-43." In Schneider 1985b, 253-79.

———. 1985b. *Lukas, Theologe der Heilsgeschichte: Aufsätze zum lukanischen Doppelwerk*. BBB 59. Königstein: Hanstein.

Schnelle, Udo. 1983. *Gerechtigkeit und Christusgegenwart: Vorpaulinische und paulinische Tauftheologie*. GThA 24. Göttingen: Vandenhoeck & Ruprecht [2nd ed., 1986].

———. 1987. *Antidoketische Christologie im Johannesevangelium: Eine Untersuchung zur Stellung des vierten Evangeliums in der johanneischen Schule*. FRLANT 144. Göttingen: Vandenhoeck & Ruprecht.

———. 1991. "Johanneische Ekklesiologie." *NTS* 37:37-50.

———. 1994. *Einleitung in das Neue Testament*. UTB 1830. Göttingen: Vandenhoeck & Ruprecht.

———. 2003. *Paulus: Leben und Denken*. Berlin: de Gruyter.

Schoeps, Hans-Joachim. 1949. *Theologie und Geschichte des Judenchristentums*. Tübingen: Mohr-Siebeck.

———. 1959. *Paulus: Die Theologie des Apostels im Lichte der jüdischen Religionsgeschichte*. Tübingen: Mohr-Siebeck [repr., 1972]. English: *Paul: The Theology of the Apostle in the Light of Jewish Religious History*. Philadelphia: Westminster Press, 1961.

Schottroff, Luise. 1970. *Der Glaubende und die feindliche Welt*. WMANT 37. Neukirchen-Vluyn: Neukirchener Verlag.

Schramm, Tim. 1971. *Der Markus-Stoff bei Lukas: Eine literarkritische und redaktionsgeschichtliche Untersuchung*. SNTSMS 14. Cambridge: Cambridge University Press.

Schreiner, Thomas R. 2001. *Paul, Apostle of God's Glory in Christ: A Pauline The-*

ology. Downers Grove, Ill.: InterVarsity Press.

Schrenk, Gottlob. 1954. "Der Römerbrief als Missionsdokument." In *Studien zu Paulus,* 81-106. AThANT 26. Zürich: Theologischer Verlag.

Schröter, Jens. 1993. *Der versöhnte Versöhner: Paulus als unentbehrlicher Mittler im Heilsvorgang zwischen Gott und Gemeinde nach 2Kor 2,14-7,4.* TANZ 10. Tübingen: Francke.

—————. 2000. "Jerusalem und Galiläa: Überlegungen zur Verhältnisbestimmung von Pluralität und Kohärenz für die Konstruktion einer Geschichte des frühen Christentums." *NovT* 42:127-59.

Schuler, Christof. 1998. *Ländliche Siedlungen und Gemeinden im hellenistischen und römischen Kleinasien.* Vestigia 50. Munich: Beck.

Schult, H. 1975. "Naemans Übertritt zum Yahwismus (2. Könige 5,1-19a) und die biblischen Bekehrungsgeschichten." *Dielheimer Blätter zum Alten Testament* 9:2-20.

Schultz, Richard. 1996. "Und sie verkünden meine Herrlichkeit unter den Nationen." In Kasdorf and Walldorf 1996, 33-53.

Schulz, Anselm. 1962. *Nachfolgen und Nachahmen: Studien über das Verhältnis der neutestamentlichen Jüngerschaft zur urchristlichen Vorbildethik.* StANT 6. Munich: Kösel.

Schulz, Hans-Joachim. 1995. *Die apostolische Herkunft der Evangelien.* 2nd ed. QD 145. Herder: Freiburg [1993].

Schulz, Siegfried. 1972. *Q: Die Spruchquelle der Evangelisten.* Zürich: Theologischer Verlag.

—————. 1985. "Der frühe und der späte Paulus: Überlegungen zur Entwicklung seiner Theologie und Ethik." *ThZ* 41:228-36.

Schumacher, Rudolf. 1916. *Der Alexandriner Apollos: Eine exegetische Studie.* Kempten: Kösel.

Schürer, Emil. 1894. *Die ältesten Christengemeinden im römischen Reiche.* Rede zum Antritt des Rektorates der Christian-Albrechts-Universität in Kiel. Kiel: Universitätsbuchhandlung.

—————. 1897. "Die Juden im bosporanischen Reich und die Genossenschaften der σεβόμενοι θεὸν ὕψιστον daselbst." *Sitzungsberichte der preussischen Akademie zu Berlin,* 200-25. Berlin: Preussische Akademie.

—————. 1973-1987. *The History of the Jewish People in the Age of Jesus Christ (175 B.C.-A.D. 135).* 3 vols. Revised and edited by Géza Vermès, Fergus Millar and Matthew Black. Edinburgh: T & T Clark.

Schürmann, Heinz. 1962. "Das Testament des Paulus für die Kirche (Apg 20,18-35)." In Schürmann 1968, 18-35.

—————. 1968. *Traditionsgeschichtliche Untersuchungen zu den synoptischen Evangelien.* Düsseldorf: Patmos.

Schwartz, Daniël R. 1986. "The End of the GE (Acts 1.8): Beginning or End of the Christian Vision?" *JBL* 105:669-76.

————. 1990. *Agrippa I: The Last King of Judaea.* TSAJ 23. Tübingen: Mohr-Siebeck.

————. 1992a. *Studies in the Jewish Background of Christianity.* WUNT 60. Tübingen: Mohr-Siebeck.

————. 1992b. "On Sacrifice by Gentiles in the Temple of Jerusalem." In Schwartz 1992a, 102-16.

————. 1996. "God, Gentiles, and Jewish Law: On Acts 15 and Josephus' Adiabene Narrative." In Schäfer 1996, 263-82.

Schwartz, Joshua J. 1995. "Peter and Ben Stada in Lydda." In Bauckham 1995a, 391-414.

Schwarz, Eberhard. 1982. *Identität durch Abgrenzung: Abgrenzungsprozesse in Israel im 2. vorchristlichen Jahrhundert und ihre traditionsgeschichtlichen Voraussetzungen.* EHS 23.162. Frankfurt and Bern: Lang.

Schwarz, Günther. 1988. *Jesus und Judas: Aramaistische Untersuchungen zur Jesus-Judas-Überlieferung der Evangelien und der Apostelgeschichte.* BWANT 123. Stuttgart: Kohlhammer.

————. 1991. "Τῆς τροφῆς αὐτοῦ oder τῆς μισθοῦ αὐτοῦ?" *BNot* 56:25.

Schwemer, Anna Maria. 1996. "Zum Verhältnis von Diatheke und Nomos in den Schriften der jüdischen Diaspora Ägyptens in hellenistisch-römischer Zeit." In Avemarie and Lichtenberger 1996, 67-109.

————. 1998. "Paulus in Antiochien." *BZ* 42:161-80.

Schwertheim, Elmar, ed. 1990. *Mysische Studien.* AMSt 1. Bonn: Habelt.

————, ed. 1992. *Forschungen in Pisidien.* AMSt 6. Bonn: Habelt.

————, ed. 1995. *Forschungen in Lydien.* AMSt 17. Bonn: Habelt.

————, ed. 1999. *Die Troas: Neue Forschungen III.* AMSt 33. Bonn: Habelt.

Schwertheim, Elmar, and Hans Wiegartz, eds. 1994. *Neue Forschungen zu Neandria und Alexandria Troas.* AMSt 11. Bonn: Habelt.

————, eds. 1996. *Die Troas: Neue Forschungen zu Neandria und Alexandria Troas II.* AMSt 22. Bonn: Habelt.

Schwier, Helmut. 1989. *Tempel und Tempelzerstörung: Untersuchungen zu den theologischen und ideologischen Faktoren im ersten jüdisch-römischen Krieg (66-74 n.Chr.).* NTOA 11. Fribourg, Universitätsverlag; Göttingen: Vandenhoeck & Ruprecht.

Scobie, Charles H. H. 1984. "Jesus or Paul? The Origin of the Universal Mission of the Christian Church." In *Jesus to Paul,* FS F. W. Beare, edited by P. Richardson and J. C. Hurd, 47-60. Waterloo, Ont.: Wilfrid Laurier University Press.

————. 1992. "Israel and the Nations: An Essay in Biblical Theology." *TynBul* 43:283-305.

Scott, James M. 1993. "Restoration of Israel." *DPL* 796-805.

————. 1994. "Luke's Geographical Horizon." In Gill and Gempf 1994, 483-544.

————. 1995. *Paul and the Nations: The Old Testament and Early Jewish Background of Paul's Mission to the Nations with Special Reference to the Destina-*

tion of Galatians. WUNT 84. Tübingen: Mohr-Siebeck.

———. 2000. "Acts 2:9-11 as an Anticipation of the Mission to the Nations." In Ådna and Kvalbein 2000, 87-123.

———. 2002. *Geography in Early Judaism and Christianity: The Book of Jubilees.* SNTSMS 113. Cambridge: Cambridge University Press.

Scott, J. Julius. 1978. "Stephen's Defense and the World Mission of the People of God." *JETS* 21:131-41.

———. 1990. "Gentiles and the Ministry of Jesus: Further Observations on Matt 10:5-6; 15:21-28." *JETS* 33:16-169.

Seager, A. R., and A. T. Kraabel. 1983. "The Synagogue and the Jewish Community." In Hanfmann 1983, 168-90.

Seccombe, David. 1998. "The New People of God." In Marshall and Peterson 1998, 349-72.

———. 2000. "The Story of Jesus and the Missionary Strategy of Paul." In Bolt and Thompson 2000, 115-29.

Sedlar, J. D. 1980. *India and the Greek World: A Study in the Transmission of Culture.* Totowa, N.J.: Rowan & Littlefield.

Seeley, David. 1996. "Jesus and the Cynics: A Response to Hans Dieter Betz." *JHC* 3:284-90.

———. 1997. "Jesus and the Cynics Revisited." *JBL* 116:222-34.

Segal, Alan F. 1988. "The Costs of Proselytism and Conversion." In *SBLSP,* 336-49.

———. 1990. *Paul the Convert: The Apostolate and Apostasy of Saul the Pharisee.* New Haven: Yale University Press.

———. 1992a. "Conversion and Messianism: Outline for a New Approach." In *The Messiah: Developments in Earliest Judaism and Christianity,* edited by J. H. Charlesworth, 296-340. Minneapolis: Fortress.

———. 1992b. "Jewish Christianity." In Attridge and Hata 1992, 326-51.

Segal, Arthur. 1988. *Town Planning and Architecture in Provincia Arabia.* Oxford: Oxford University Press.

Segal, J. B. 1970. *Edessa, the Blessed City.* Oxford: Clarendon.

———. 1980. "When Did Christianity Come to Edessa?" In *Middle Eastern Studies and Libraries,* FS J. D. Pearson, edited by B. C. Bloomfield, 179-91. London: Mansell.

Segalla, Giuseppe. 1983. *La pregliera di Gesú al Padre (Giov. 17): Un addio missionario.* Brescia: Paideia.

Seibert, Jakob. 1985. *Die Eroberung des Perserreiches durch Alexander d. Gr. auf kartographischer Grundlage.* BTAVO B 68. Wiesbaden: Reichert.

Seidel, Esther. 1995. "Gruppenübertritte zum Judemtum." In Homolka and Seidel 1995, 56-65.

Seifrid, Mark A. 1989. "Messiah and Mission in Acts: A Brief Response to J. B. Tyson." *JSNT* 36:47-50.

Selinger, Reinhard. 1997. "Die Demetriosunruhen (Apg 19,23-40): Eine Fallstudie aus rechtshistorischer Perspektive." *ZNW* 88:242-59.

Sellin, Ernst. 1925. "Der Missionsgedanke im Alten Testament." *NAMZ* 42:33-45, 66-72.

Sellin, Gerhard. 1986. *Der Streit um die Auferstehung der Toten: Eine religionsgeschichtliche und exegetische Untersuchung von 1 Korinther 15.* FRLANT 138. Göttingen: Vandenhoeck & Ruprecht.

Sellin, Volker. 1985. "Mentalität und Mentalitätsgeschichte." *Historische Zeitschrift* 241:555-98.

Seneviratna, Anuradha, ed. 1994. *King Aśoka and Buddhism: Historical and Literary Studies.* Kandy, Sri Lanka: Buddhist Publication Society.

Senior, Donald. 1982. "The Eucharist in Mark: Mission, Reconciliation, Hope." *BTB* 12:67-72.

———. 1983. "The Mission Perspective of Luke/Acts." In Senior and Stuhlmueller, 1983, 255-79.

———. 1984. "The Struggle to Be Universal: Mission as Vantage Point for New Testament Investigation." *CBQ* 46:63-81.

Senior, Donald, and Carroll Stuhlmueller. 1983. *The Biblical Foundations for Mission.* Maryknoll, N.Y.: Orbis.

Setzer, Claudia J. 1994. *Jewish Responses to Early Christians: History and Polemics, 30-150 C.E.* Minneapolis: Fortress.

Shanor, J. 1988. "Paul as Master Builder: Construction Terms in First Corinthians." *NTS* 34:461-71.

Shaw, R. Daniel. 1988. *Transculuration: The Cultural Factor in Translation and Other Communication Tasks.* Pasadena, Calif.: William Carey Library.

Shear, J. Leslie. 1981. "Athens: From City-State to Provincial Town." *Hesperia* 50:356-77.

Shelton, James B. 1991. *Mighty in Word and Deed: The Role of the Holy Spirit in Luke-Acts.* Peabody, Mass.: Hendrickson.

Sherk, Robert K. 1974. "Roman Geographical Exploration and Military Maps." *ANRW* II.1:534-62.

———. 1980. "Roman Galatia: The Governors from 25 B.C. to A.D. 114." *ANRW* II.7.2:955-1052.

Sherwin-White, Adrian Nicolas. 1963. *Roman Society and Roman Law in the New Testament.* The Sarum Lectures 1960-1961 [repr., Grand Rapids: Baker 1992].

Sherwin-White, Susan, and Amélie Kuhrt. 1993. *From Samarkhand to Sardis: A New Approach to the Seleucid Empire.* Berkeley: University of California Press.

Shillington, George. 1991. "Paul's Success in the Conversion of Gentiles: Dynamic Center in Cultural Diversity." *Direction* 20:125-34.

Sidebotham, Steven E. 1986. *Roman Economic Policy in the Erythra Thalassa 30*

B.C.-A.D. 217. Mnemosyne Supplements 91. Leiden: Brill.

Siegert, Folker. 1974. "Gottesfürchtige und Sympathisanten." *JSJ* 4:109-64.

———. 1980-1992. *Drei hellenistisch-jüdische Predigten.* 2 vols. WUNT 20, 61. Tübingen: Mohr-Siebeck.

———. 1993. "Mass Communication and Prose Rhythm in Luke-Acts." In *Rhetoric and the New Testament,* edited by S. E. Porter and T. H. Olbricht, 42-58. JSNTSup 90. Sheffield: JSOT Press.

———. 1994a. "Die Heiden in der pseudo-philonischen Predigt *De Jona.*" In Feldmeier and Heckel 1994, 52-58.

———. 1994b. "Communication de masse et rythmes de prose dans Luc/Actes." *RHPR* 74:113-27.

Siegfried, Carl. 1890. "Prophetische Missionsgedanken und jüdische Missionsbestrebungen." *Jahrbücher für protestantische Theologie* 1890:435-53.

Sievernich, Michael. 1990. "Urbanität und Christentum: Konturen einer Theologie der Stadt." *Pastoraltheologie* 79:95-115.

Sievers, Joseph. 1985. "Heidentum II. Judentum." *TRE* 14:601-5.

Signer, Michael A. 1990. "Konversion II. Judentum." *TRE* 19:563-66.

Siker, Jeffrey S. 1992. "'First to the Gentiles:' A Literary Analysis of Luke 4.16-30." *JBL* 111:73-90.

Silva, Moises. 1996. *Explorations in Exegetical Method: Galatians as a Test Case.* Grand Rapids: Baker.

Sim, David C. 1995. "The Gospel of Matthew and the Gentiles." *JSNT* 57:10-48.

———. 1998. *The Gospel of Matthew and Christian Judaism.* Edinburgh: T & T Clark.

Simon, Marcel. 1948. *Verus Israel: Étude sur les relations entre chrétiens et juifs dans l'Empire romain.* Bibliothèque des Écoles françaises d'Athènes et de Rome 166. Paris: Boccard [2nd ed., 1964].

Singh, Ajoy Kumar. 1988. *Indo-Roman Trade: An Archaeological Perspective.* New Delhi: Commonwealth Publishers.

Skarsaune, Oskar. 1976. "The Conversion of Justin Martyr." *StTh* 30:53-73.

———. 2000. "The Mission to the Jew—A Closed Chapter?" In Ådna and Kvalbein 2000, 69-83.

Slingerland, H. Dixon. 1991. "Acts 18.1-18, the Gallio Inscription, and Absolute Pauline Chronology." *JBL* 110:439-49.

———. 1992. "Suetonius Claudius 25,4, Acts 18, and Paulus Orosius' Historiarum adversum Paganos Libri VII: Dating the Claudian Expulsions(s) of Roman Jews." *JQR* 83:127-44.

———. 1997. *Claudian Policymaking and the Early Imperial Repression of Judaism at Rome.* SFSHJ 160. Atlanta: Scholars Press.

Sloan, Robert. 1991. "'Signs and Wonders': A Rhetorical Clue to the Pentecost Discourse." *EvQ* 63:225-40.

Sly, Dorothy I. 1996. *Philo's Alexandria.* London: Routledge.

Smalley, Stephen S. 1978. *John: Evangelist and Interpreter.* Exeter: Paternoster [2nd ed., 1998].

Smallwood, E. Mary. 1976. *The Jews under Roman Rule: From Pompey to Diocletian; A Study in Political Relations.* SJLA 20. Leiden: Brill [2nd ed., 1981; repr., 2001].

———. 1999. "The Diaspora in the Roman Period before CE 70." *CHJ* 3:168-91.

Smick, Elmer. 1989. "Old Testament Cross-Culturalism: Paradigmatic or Enigmatic?" *JETS* 32:3-16.

Smillie, Gene R. 2002. "'Even the Dogs': Gentiles in the Gospel of Matthew." *JETS* 45:73-97.

Smith, Charles W. F. 1959. "Fishers of Men." *HTR* 52:187-203.

Smith, Christopher R. 1990. "The Portrayal of the Church as the New Israel in the Names and Order of the Tribes in Revelation 7:5-8." *JSNT* 39:111-18.

Smith, R. Morton. 1984. "Jewish Religious Life in the Persian Period." *CHJ* 1:279-307.

———. 1997. *Kings and Coins in India: Greek and Śaka Self-Advertisement.* New Delhi: Harman.

———. 1999. "The Gentiles in Judaism 125 BCE-CE 66." *CHJ* 3:192-249.

Smith, R. R. R. 1990. "Myth and Allegory in the Sebasteion." In *Aphrodisias Papers (1): Recent Work on Architecture and Sculpture,* edited by Charlotte Roueché and Kenan T. Erim, 89-100. JRASup 1. Ann Arbor: University of Michigan Press.

Smith, Vincent. 1924. *The Early History of India: From 600 B.C. to the Muhammadan Conquest.* Oxford: Clarendon [4th ed., 1962].

Snodgrass, Klyne R. 1983. *The Parable of the Wicked Tenants: An Inquiry into Parable Interpretation.* WUNT 27. Tübingen: Mohr-Siebeck.

Snyder, Graydon F. 1992. "Christianity: Christianity in Rome." *ABD* 1:968-70.

Soden, Hans von. 1924. "Die christliche Mission in Altertum und Gegenwart." In Frohnes and Knorr 1974, 18-31.

Söder, Rosa. 1932. *Die apokryphen Apostelgeschichten und die romanhafte Literatur der Antike.* Würzburger Studien zur Altertumswissenschaft 3. Stuttgart: Kohlhammer [repr., Darmstadt: Wissenschaftliche Buchgesellschaft 1968].

Söding, Thomas. 1985. *Glaube bei Markus: Glaube an das Evangelium, Gebetsglaube und Wunderglaube im Kontext der markinischen Basileiatheologie und Christologie.* SBB 12. Stuttgart: Katholisches Bibelwerk [2nd ed., 1987].

———. 1990a "Eucharistie und Mysterien: Urchristliche Herrenmahlstheologie und antike Mysterienreligiosität im Spiegel von 1Kor 10." *Bibel und Kirche* 45:140-45.

———. 1990b. "Widerspruch und Leidensnachfolge: Neutestamentliche Gemeinde im Konflikt mit der paganen Gesellschaft." *Münchener theologische Zeitschrift* 41:137-56.

———. 1992. "Kreuzestheologie und Rechtfertigungslehre: Zur Verbindung von

Christologie und Soteriologie im Ersten Korintherbrief und im Galaterbrief." *Catholica* 46:31-60.

———. 2000. "Der Skopos der paulinischen Rechtfertigungslehre." *ZThK* 97:404-33.

Solin, Heikki. 1983. "Juden und Syrer im westlichen Teil der römischen Welt: Eine ethnisch-demographische Studie mit besonderer Berücksichtigung der sprachlichen Zustände." *ANRW* II.29.2:587-798 (index, 1222-49).

Sordi, Marta. 1986. *The Christians and the Roman Empire*. Norman: University of Oklahoma Press.

Soustal, Peter. 1981. *Nikopolis und Kephallenia*. TIB 3. Vienna: Österreichische Akademie der Wissenschaften.

———. 1991. *Thrakien (Thrakē, Rodopē und Haimimontos)*. TIB 6. Vienna: Österreichische Akademie der Wissenschaften.

Southern, Pat. 1998. *Augustus*. New York: Routledge.

Sown, S., and S. K. Stowers. 1980. "The Matthean Community and the Gentile Mission." *NovT* 22:193-221.

Spanos, N. P., and E. C. Hewitt. 1979. "Glossolalia: Test of the Trance and Psychopathology Hypotheses." *Journal of Abnormal Psychology* 88:427-34.

Spencer, Aída Besançon. 1993. "Romans 1: Finding God in Creation." In Crockett and Sigountos 1993, 125-35.

Spencer, F. Scott. 1992. *The Portrait of Philip in Acts: A Study of Roles and Relations*. JSNTSup 67. Sheffield: JSOT Press.

———. 1997a. *Acts*. Readings. Sheffield: Sheffield Academic Press.

———. 1997b. "Philip the Evangelist." *DLNTD* 929-31.

Sperber, Daniel. 1978. *Roman Palestine, 200-400, the Land: Crisis and Change in Agrarian Society as Reflected in Rabbinic Sources*. Ramat-Gan: Bar-Ilan University.

Speyer, Wolfgang. 1970. *Bücherfunde in der Glaubenswerbung der Antike mit einem Ausblick auf Mittelalter und Neuzeit*. Hypomnemata 24. Göttingen: Vandenhoeck & Ruprecht.

Spindler, Marc R. 1981. *Bible and Mission: A Partly Annotated Bibliography 1960-1980*. Leiden: Brill.

Spitta, Friedrich. 1909. *Jesus und die Heidenmission*. Giessen: Töpelmann.

Staab, Karl. 1933. *Pauluskommentare aus der griechischen Kirche: Aus Katenenhandschriften gesammelt und herausgegeben*. Münster: Aschendorff [1984].

Stähelin, Felix. 1907. *Geschichte der kleinasiatischen Galater*. Osnabrück: Zeller [2nd ed., 1973].

Stählin, Gustav. 1934. "Κατὰ τὸ θέλημα τοῦ θεοῦ: Von der Dynamik der urchristlichen Mission." In *Wort und Geist,* FS Karl Heim, 99-119. Berlin: Furche-Verlag.

———. 1940. "Urchristliche Missionspraxis." In *Grundzüge christlicher Missionsarbeit in zwei Jahrtausenden I. Sendende Gemeinde* 60:2-15. Berlin.

————. 1950. "Die Endschau Jesu und die Mission." *EMZ* 7:97-105, 134-47.

————. 1951-1952. "Kirche, Mission, Eschatologie in der Sicht des Neuen Testaments." *Lutherisches Missions-Jahrbuch:* 21-39.

Stambaugh, John E. 1988. *The Ancient Roman City.* Baltimore: Johns Hopkins University Press.

Stambaugh, John E., and David L. Balch. 1986. *The New Testament in Its Social Environment.* Library of Early Christianity, Philadelphia: Westminster. German: *Das soziale Umfeld des Neuen Testaments.* GNT 9. Göttingen: Vandenhoeck & Ruprecht, 1992.

Stange, Erich. 1918. *Paulinische Reisepläne.* BFChTh 2.5. Gütersloh: Mohn.

Stanton, Graham N. 1974. *Jesus of Nazareth in New Testament Preaching.* SNTSMS 27. Cambridge: Cambridge University Press.

————. 1994. "Revisiting Matthew's Communities." In *SBLSP,* 9-23.

Stark, Rodney. 1991a. "Epidemics, Networks, and the Rise of Christianity." *Semeia* 56:159-75.

————. 1991b. "Christianizing the Urban Empire: An Analysis Based on 22 Greco-Roman Cities." *Sociological Analysis* 52:77-88.

————. 1997. *The Rise of Christianity: How the Obscure, Marginal Jesus Movement Became the Dominant Religious Force in the Western World in a Few Centuries.* San Francisco: HarperSanFrancisco [Princeton, N.J.: Princeton University Press, 1996]. German: *Der Aufstieg des Christentums: Neue Erkenntnisse aus soziologischer Sicht.* Weinheim: Beltz Athenäum, 1997.

Stärk, W. 1925. "Ursprung und Grenzen der Missionskraft der alttestamentlichen Religion." *Theologische Blätter* 4:25-37.

Stavroulakis, Nicholas P., and Timothy J. DeVinney. 1992. *Jewish Sites and Synagogues of Greece.* Athens: Talos.

Steck, Odil Hannes. 1971. "Genesis 12,1-3 und die Urgeschichte des Jahwisten." In *Probleme biblischer Theologie,* FS G. von Rad, edited by H. W. Wolf, 525-54. Munich: Kaiser.

Stegemann, Ekkehard W., ed. 1993. *Messias-Vorstellungen bei Juden und Christen.* Stuttgart: Kohlhammer.

Stegemann, Ekkehard W., and Wolfgang Stegemann. 1995. *Urchristliche Sozialgeschichte: Die Anfänge im Judentum und die Christusgemeinden in der mediterranen Welt.* Stuttgart: Kohlhammer. English: *The Jesus Movement: A Social History of Its First Century.* Minneapolis: Fortress, 1999.

Stegemann, Hartmut. 1993. *Die Essener, Qumran, Johannes der Täufer und Jesus.* Herder Spektrum 4128. Freiburg: Herder.

Stegemann, Wolfgang. 1991. "'Licht der Völker' bei Lukas." In Bussmann and Radl 1991, 81-97.

Stein, Robert H. 1993. "Jerusalem." *DPL* 463-74.

Stemberger, Günther. 1977. "Die sogenannte 'Synagoge von Jabne' und das frühe Christentum." *Kairos* 19:14-21.

————. 1991. *Pharisäer, Sadduzäer, Essener.* SBS 144. Stuttgart: Katholisches Bibelwerk.

Stendahl, Krister. 1976. *Paul among Jews and Gentiles and Other Essays.* Philadelphia: Fortress.

Stenger, Werner. 1988. *"Gebt dem Kaiser, was des Kaisers ist . . . !" Eine sozialgeschichtliche Untersuchung zur Besteuerung Palästinas in neutestamentlicher Zeit.* BBB 68. Frankfurt: Athenäum.

Stenschke, Christoph W. 1998. "The Need for Salvation." In Marshall and Peterson 1998, 125-44.

————. 1999a. *Luke's Portrait of Gentiles Prior to Their Coming to Faith.* WUNT 2.108. Tübingen: Mohr-Siebeck.

————. 1999b. "Hinweise zu einem wiederentdeckten Gebiet der Actaforschung." *Communio Viatorum* 41:65-91.

Stephan, Eckhard. 2002. *Honoratioren, Griechen, Polisbürger: Kollektive Identitäten innerhalb der Oberschicht des kaiserzeitlichen Kleinasien.* Hypomnemata 143. Göttingen: Vandenhoeck & Ruprecht.

Stern, Ephraim, ed. 1993. *The New Encyclopedia of Archaeological Excavations in the Holy Land.* 4 vols. New York: Simon & Schuster.

Stern, Menachem, ed. 1974-1984. *Greek and Latin Authors on Jews and Judaism.* 3 vols. Jerusalem: Israel Academy of Science and Humanities.

————. 1987. "The Jewish Diaspora." In Safrai and Stern 1987, 117-83.

Stern, Sacha. 1994. *Jewish Identity in Early Rabbinic Writings.* AGAJU 23. Leiden: Brill.

Stettler, Hanna. 2000. "An Interpretation of Colossians 1:24 in the Framework of Paul's Mission Theology." In Ådna and Kvalbein 2000, 185-208.

Steuernagel, Valdir R. 1986. "An Exiled Community as a Missionary Community: A Study Based on 1 Peter 2:9,10." *EvRT* 10:8-18.

Stevens, Bruce. 1979. "The Kingdom of God the Motive for Missions." *Southeast Asia Journal of Theology* 20:39-47.

Stock, Klemens. 1982. "Theologie der Mission bei Markus." In Kertelge 1982, 130-44.

Stoevesandt, Helene. 1943. "Jesus und die Heidenmission." Diss., University of Göttingen.

Stoldt, Hans-Herbert. 1977. *Geschichte und Kritik der Markushypothese.* Göttingen: Vandenhoeck & Ruprecht [2nd enl. ed., Giessen: Brunnen, 1986].

Stolle, Volker. 1973. *Der Zeuge als Angeklagter: Untersuchungen zum Paulusbild des Lukas.* BZAW 102. Stuttgart: Kohlhammer.

Stolz, F. 1970. *Strukturen und Figuren im Kult von Jerusalem.* BZAW 118. Berlin: de Gruyter.

Stone, Michael E., ed. 1984. *Jewish Writings of the Second Temple Period.* CRINT 2.2. Assen: Van Gorcum.

Stoops, Robert F. 1994. "Departing to Another Place: The *Acts of Peter* and the

Canonical Acts of the Apostles." In *SBLSP,* 390-404.

Storm, Hans Martin. 1995. *Die Paulusberufung nach Lukas und das Erbe der Propheten: Berufen zu Gottes Dienst.* ANTJ 10. Frankfurt: Lang.

Stott, John R. W. 1975. *Christian Mission in the Modern World.* Downers Grove, Ill.: InterVarsity Press.

———. 1992. *The Contemporary Christian: Applying God's Word to Today's World.* Leicester: Inter-Varsity Press.

Stott, John R., and Robert T. Coote, eds. 1979. *Gospel & Culture.* The Papers of a Consultation on the Gospel and Culture, Convened by the Lausanne Committee's Theology and Education Group. Pasadena: William Carey.

Stowasser, Martin. 2001. "Am 5,25-27; 9,11f. in der Qumranüberlieferung und in der Apostelgeschichte." *ZNW* 92:47-63.

Stowers, Stanley K. 1981. *The Diatribe and Paul's Letter to the Romans.* SBLDS 57. Chico, Calif.: Scholars Press.

———. 1984. "Social Status, Public Speaking and Private Teaching: The Circumstances of Paul's Preaching Activity." *NovT* 26:59-82.

Strack, Hermann L., and Günther Stemberger. 1982. *Einleitung in Talmud und Midrasch.* Munich: Beck [8th ed., 1993]. English: *Introduction to the Talmud and Midrash.* Minneapolis: Fortress, 1992.

Strange, James F. 1992. "Six Campaigns at Sepphoris." In L. Levine 1992, 339-56.

———. 1994. "First-Century Galilee from Archaeology and from the Texts." In *SBLSP,* 81-90.

———. 1997. "First-Century Galilee from Archaeology and from the Texts." In Edwards and McCollough 1997, 39-48.

Strange, W. A. 1992. *The Problem of the Text of Acts.* SNTSMS 71. Cambridge: Cambridge University Press.

———. 2000. "The Jesus-Tradition in Acts." *NTS* 46:59-74.

Strecker, Georg. 1960. "Noachische Gebote." *RGG* 4:1500-1501.

———. 1971. *Der Weg der Gerechtigkeit: Untersuchungen zur Theologie des Matthäus.* 3rd ed. FRLANT 82. Göttingen: Vandenhoeck & Ruprecht [1962].

———. 1972. "Literarkritische Überlegungen zum εὐαγγέλιον-Begriff im Markusevangelium." In *Neues Testament und Geschichte: Historisches Geschehen und Deutung im Neuen Testament,* FS O. Cullmann, edited by H. Baltensweiler et al., 91-104. Tübingen: Mohr.

———. 1988. "Judenchristentum." *TRE* 17:310-25.

Strelan, John G. 1988. "'For Thine Are The Statistics?' Sermon Study on Mark 4:26-29." *LThJ* 22:32-36.

Strelan, Richard E. 1996. *Paul, Artemis and Jews in Ephesus.* BZNW 80. Berlin: de Gruyter.

Strickert, Fred. 1995. "Coins of Philip." In Arav and Freund 1995-1999, 1:165-89.

Strobach, Anika. 1997. *Plutarch und die Sprachen: Ein Beitrag zur Fremdsprachenproblematik in der Antike.* Palingenesia 64. Stuttgart: Steiner.

Strobel, Karl. 1996. *Die Galater: Geschichte und Eigenart der keltischen Staaten-bildung auf dem Boden des hellenistischen Kleinasien.* Untersuchungen zur Geschichte und historischen Geographie des hellenistischen und römischen Kleinasien 1. Berlin: Akademie-Verlag.

Ström, Åke V. 1994. "Mission I. Religionsgeschichte." *TRE* 23:18-20.

Stroumsa, Guy G. 1996. "Philosophy of the Barbarians: On Early Christian Ethnological Representations." In Cancik 1996, 339-68.

Stuhlmacher, Peter. 1965. *Gerechtigkeit Gottes bei Paulus.* FRLANT 87. Göttingen: Vandenhoeck & Ruprecht [2nd ed., 1966].

————. 1968. *Das paulinische Evangelium: I. Vorgeschichte.* FRLANT 95. Göttingen: Vandenhoeck & Ruprecht.

————. 1981. "Weg, Stil und Konsequenzen urchristlicher Mission." *ThBeitr* 12:107-35.

————. 1989. "Die Stellung Jesu und des Paulus zu Jerusalem: Versuch einer Erinnerung." *ZThK* 86:140-56.

————. 1992-1999. *Biblische Theologie des Neuen Testaments.* 2 vols. Göttingen: Vandenhoeck & Ruprecht.

————. 1999. "Zur missionsgeschichtlichen Bedeutung von Mt 28,16-20." *EvTh* 59:108-29. English: "Matt 28:16-20 and the Course of Mission in the Apostolic and Postapostolic Age." In Ådna and Kvalbein 2000, 17-43.

Stumpf, Gerd R. 1991. *Numismatische Studien zur Chronologie der römischen Statthalter in Kleinasien (122 v.Chr.-163 n.Chr.).* Saarbrücker Studien zur Archäologie und Alten Geschichte 4. Saarbrücken: Saarbrücker Druckerei und Verlag.

Suhl, Alfred. 1975. *Paulus und seine Briefe: Ein Beitrag zur paulinischen Chronologie.* StNT 11. Gütersloh: Mohn.

————. 1992. "Der Beginn der selbständigen Mission des Paulus: Ein Beitrag zur Geschichte des Urchristentums." *NTS* 38:430-47.

Sullivan, Richard D. 1977. "The Dynasty of Judaea in the First Century." *ANRW* II.8:296-354.

Sundermeier, Theo, ed. 1980. *Fides pro mundi vita.* FS H.-W. Gensichen. Missionswissenschaftliche Forschungen 14. Gütersloh: Mohn.

————. 1990. "'Mission nach der Weise Abrahams': Eine Predigt über Gen 12,1-9." In *Die hebräische Bibel und ihre zweifache Nachgeschichte,* FS Rolf Rendtorf, edited by E. Blum, 575-80. Neukirchen-Vluyn: Neukirchener Verlag.

Sundkler, Bengt. 1936. "Jésus et les païens." *RHPR* 16:462-99 (= in *Contributions à l'étude de la pensée missionaire dans le Nouveau Testament,* edited by B. Sundkler and A. Fridrichsen, 24-40. ASNU 6. Uppsala: Neutestamentliches Seminar zu Uppsala 1937.

————. 1954. *The World of Missions.* Grand Rapids: Eerdmans; London: SCM Press.

Svartik, Jesper. 2000. *Mark and Mission: Mk 7:1-23 in Its Narrative and Historical Contexts.* ConBNT 32. Stockholm: Almqvist & Wiksell.

Swain, Simon. 1998. *Hellenism and Empire: Language, Classicism, and Power in the Greek World, AD 50-250.* Oxford: Oxford University Press [1996].

Swigchem, Douwe van. 1955. *Het Missionair karakter van de Christlijke gemeente volgens de brieven van Paulus en Petrus.* Kampen: Kok.

Syme, Ronald. 1979-1991. *Roman Papers.* Edited by E. Badian and Anthony R. Birley. 7 vols. Oxford: Clarendon.

———. 1995. *Anatolica: Studies in Strabo.* Edited by A. Birley. Oxford: Clarendon.

Taber, Charles R. 1986. "The New Testament Language of Quantity and Growth in Relation to the Church." *Missiology* 14:387-99.

Taeger, Jens-W. 1982. *Der Mensch und sein Heil: Studien zum Bild des Menschen und zur Sicht der Bekehrung bei Lukas.* StNT 14. Gütersloh: Mohn.

Tajra, Harry W. 1989. *The Trial of St. Paul: A Juridical Exegesis of the Second Half of the Acts of the Apostles.* WUNT 2.35. Tübingen: Mohr-Siebeck.

Talbert, Charles H. 1974. *Literary Patterns, Theological Themes and the Genre of Luke-Acts.* SBLMS 20. Missoula, Mont.: Scholars Press.

———. 1991. "Once Again: The Gentile Mission in Luke-Acts." In Bussmann and Radl 1991, 99-109.

———. 1992. "The Place of the Resurrection in the Theology of Luke." *Int* 46:19-30.

Tannehill, Robert C. 1986-1990. *The Narrative Unity of Luke-Acts: A Literary Interpretation.* 2 vols. Minneapolis: Fortress.

———. 1990. "Paul Outside the Christian Ghetto: Stories of Incultural Conflict and Cooperation in Acts." In *Text and Logos: The Humanistic Interpretation of the New Testament,* edited by T. W. Jennings, 247-63. Scholars Press Homage Series. Atlanta: Scholars Press.

———. 1991. "The Function of Peter's Mission Speeches in the Narrative of Acts." *NTS* 37:400-414.

———. 1992. "The Narrator's Strategy in the Scenes of Paul's Defense: Acts 21:27-26:32." *Forum* 8:255-69.

Tarn, William W. 1984. *The Greeks in Bactria and India.* 3rd ed. Chicago: Ares [1938].

Taşlıalan, Mehmet. 1997. *Yalvaç: Pisidia Antiocheia.* Yalvaç: Göltaş Kültür Dizisi.

———. 2001a. *Pisidian Antioch: The Journeys of St. Paul to Antioch.* 3rd rev. ed. Yalvaç: Yalvaç Museum [1991].

———. 2001b. *First International Congress on Antioch in Pisidia, July 2-4 1997.* Yalvaç: Yalvaç Museum.

Tassin, Claude. 1992. "Finances et mission selon saint Paul." *Spiritus* 33:452-67.

Taylor, Joan E. 1990. "The Phenomenon of Early Jewish-Christianity: Reality of Scholarly Invention?" *VigChr* 44:313-34.

Taylor, Justin. 1994. "Why Were the Disciples First Called 'Christians' at Antioch? (Acts 11,26)." *RB* 101:75-94.

──────. 1995. "St Paul and the Roman Empire: Acts of the Apostles 13-14." *ANRW* II.26.2:1189-1231.

Taylor, Nicholas. 1992. *Paul, Antioch and Jerusalem: A Study in Relationships and Authority in Earliest Christianity.* JSNTSup 66. Sheffield: JSOT Press.

Tcherikover, V. 1956. "Jewish Apologetic Literature Reconsidered." *Eos* 48:169-93.

Teixidor, Javier. 1977. *The Pagan God: Popular Religion in the Greco-Roman Near East.* Princeton, N.J.: Princeton University Press.

Teja, Ramon. 1980. "Die römische Provinz Kappadokien in der Prinzipatszeit." *ANRW* II.7.2:1083-1124.

Thapar, Romila. 1961. *Aśoka and the Decline of the Mauryas.* London: Oxford University Press [rev. ed., 1998].

──────. 1994. "Aśoka and Buddhism as Reflected in the Aśokan Edicts." In Seneviratna 1994, 11-25.

Theissen, Gerd. 1973. "Wanderradikalismus: Literatursoziologische Aspekte der Überlieferung von Worten Jesu im Urchristentum." In Theissen 1989, 79-105. English: "The Wandering Radicals: Light Shed by the Sociology of Literature on the Early Transmission of Jesus' Sayings." In Theissen 1992b, 33-59.

──────. 1974a. *Urchristliche Wundergeschichten: Ein Beitrag zur formgeschichtlichen Erforschung der synoptischen Evangelien.* SNT 8. Gütersloh: Mohn. English: *The Miracle Stories of the Early Christian Tradition.* Edinburgh: T & T Clark, 1983.

──────. 1974b. "Soziale Schichtung in der korinthischen Gemeinde." In Theissen 1989, 231-71. English: "Social Stratification in the Corinthian Community: A Contribution to the Sociology of Early Hellenistic Christianity." In Theissen 1982, 69-119.

──────. 1974-1975. "Legitimation und Lebensunterhalt: Ein Beitrag zur Soziologie urchristlicher Missionare." In Theissen 1989, 201-30. English: "Legitimation and Subsistence: An Essay on the Sociology of Early Christian Missionaries." In Theissen 1982, 27-67.

──────. 1977. "'Wir haben alles verlassen' (Mc X,28)." In Theissen 1989, 106-41. English: "'We Have Left Everything . . . ' (Mark 10:28)." In Theissen 1992a, 60-93.

──────. 1982. *The Social Setting of Pauline Christianity: Essays on Corinth.* Philadelphia: Fortress [repr., 1988].

──────. 1983. *Psychologische Aspekte paulinischer Theologie.* FRLANT 131. Göttingen: Vandenhoeck & Ruprecht [2nd ed., 1993]. English: *Psychological Aspects of Pauline Theology.* Philadelphia: Fortress, 1987.

──────. 1989. *Studien zur Soziologie des Urchristentums.* 3rd ed. WUNT 19. Tübingen: Mohr-Siebeck [1979].

————. 1991. "Judentum und Christentum bei Paulus: Sozialgeschichtliche Überlegungen zu einem beginnenden Schisma." In Hengel and Heckel 1991, 331-59.

————. 1992a. *Lokalkolorit und Zeitgeschichte in den Evangelien: Ein Beitrag zur Geschichte der synoptischen Tradition.* 2nd ed. Fribourg: Universitätsverlag; Göttingen: Vandenhoeck & Ruprecht [1989]. English: *The Gospels in Context: Social and Political History in the Synoptic Tradition.* Minneapolis: Fortress, 1991.

————. 1992b. *Social Reality and the Early Christians: Theology, Ethics, and the World of the New Testament.* Minneapolis: Fortress.

————. 1996. "Hellenisten und Hebräer (Apg 6,1ff): Gab es eine Spaltung der Urgemeinde?" In Lichtenberger 1996c, 323-43.

Theissen, Gerd, and Annette Merz. 1996. *Der historische Jesus: Ein Lehrbuch.* Göttingen: Vandenhoeck & Ruprecht [3rd ed., 2001]. English: *The Historical Jesus: A Comprehensive Guide.* Minneapolis: Fortress, 1998.

Theissen, Gerd, and Dagmar Winter. 1997. *Die Kriterienfrage in der Jesusforschung.* NTOA 34. Freiburg: Universitätsverlag; Göttingen: Vandenhoeck & Ruprecht. English: *The Quest for the Plausible Jesus: The Question of Criteria.* Louisville: Westminster John Knox, 2002.

Thiede, Carsten-Peter. 1987. *Das Petrusbild in der neueren Forschung.* Wuppertal: Brockhaus.

Thiessen, Werner. 1995. *Christen in Ephesus: Die historische und theologische Situation in vorpaulinischer und paulinischer Zeit und zur Zeit der Apostelgeschichte und der Pastoralbriefe.* TANZ 12. Tübingen and Basel: Francke.

Thoma, P. 1924. "The South Indian Tradition of the Apostle Thomas." In *Centenary Supplement to the Journal of the Royal Asiatic Society of Great Britain and Ireland,* 213-23. London: Royal Asiatic Society of Great Britain and Ireland.

Thompson, James W. 1971. "The Gentile Mission as an Eschatological Necessity." *RestQ* 14:18-27.

Thompson, Michael B. 1998. "The Holy Internet: Communication Between Churches in the First Christian Generation." In Bauckham 1998, 49-70.

Thornton, Claus-Jürgen. 1991. *Der Zeuge des Zeugen: Lukas als Historiker der Paulusreisen.* WUNT 56. Tübingen: Mohr-Siebeck.

Thornton, T. C. G. 1977-1978. "To the End of the Earth: Acts 1.8." *ExpTim* 89:374-75.

Tidball, Derek J. 1993. "Social Setting of Mission Churches." *DPL* 883-92.

Tiede, David L. 1984. "Religious Propaganda and the Gospel Literature of the Early Christian Mission." *ANRW* II.25.2:1705-29.

Tiénou, Tite. 1993. "Eternity in Their Hearts?" In Crockett and Sigountos 1993, 209-15.

Tiessen, Terrance L. 1993. *Irenaeus on the Salvation of the Unevangelized.* ATLA Monograph Series 31. Metuchen, N.J.; London: Scarecrow Press.

Tilborg, Sief Van. 1972. *The Jewish Leaders in Matthew.* Leiden: Brill.

Tisera, Guido. 1993. *Universalism According to the Gospel of Matthew.* EHS 23.490. Frankfurt: Lang.

Touratsoglou, Ioannis. 1997. *Makedonien: Geschichte, Monumente, Museen.* Athens: Ekdotike Athenon. English: *Macedonia: History, Monuments, Museums.* Athens: Ekdotike Athenon, 2000.

Towner, Philip H. 1989. *The Goal of Our Instruction: The Structure of Theology and Ethics in the Pastoral Epistles.* JSNTSup 34. Sheffield: JSOT Press.

———. 1995. "Paradigms Lost: Mission to the *Kosmos* in John and in David Bosch's Biblical Models of Mission." *EvQ* 67:99-119.

———. 1998. "Mission Practice and Theology under Construction (Acts 18-20)." In Marshall and Peterson 1998, 417-36.

Townsend, John T. 1986. "Missionary Journeys in Acts and European Missionary Societies." *AThR* 68:99-104.

Tracey, Robyn. 1994. "Syria." In Gill and Gempf 1994, 223-78.

Trautmann, Maria. 1980. *Zeichenhafte Handlungen Jesu: Ein Beitrag zur Frage nach dem historischen Jesus.* FB 37. Würzburg: Echter.

Trebilco, Paul. 1989. "Paul and Silas—'Servants of the Most High God' (Acts 16.16-18)." *JSNT* 36:51-73.

———. 1991. *Jewish Communities in Asia Minor.* SNTSMS 69. Cambridge: Cambridge University Press.

———. 1993. "Itineraries, Travel Plans, Journeys, Apostolic Parousia." *DPL* 446-56.

———. 1994. "Asia." In Gill and Gempf 1994, 291-362.

———. 2002. "What Shall We Call Each Other? Part One: The Issue of Self-Designation in the Pastoral Epistles." *TynBul* 53:238-58.

Trilling, Wolfgang. 1964. *Das wahre Israel: Studien zur Theologie des Matthäusevangeliums.* 3rd rev. ed. StANT 10. Munich: Kösel.

———. 1978. "Die Entwicklung des Zwölferkreises: Eine geschichtskritische Überlegung." In Schnackenburg et al. 1978, 201-22.

Trites, Allison A. 1977. *The New Testament Concept of Witness.* SNTSMS 31. Cambridge: Cambridge University Press.

———. 1988. "Church Growth in the Book of Acts." *BSac* 145:162-73.

Trocmé, Etienne. 1992. "L'apôtre Paul et Rome: Réflexions sur une fascination." *RHPR* 72:41-51.

Troiani, Lucio. 1990. "La missione nel mondo greco-romano." In Ghiberti 1990b, 71-85.

Tsetskhladze, Gocha R., ed. 1998. *The Greek Colonisation of the Black Sea Area: Historical Interpretation of Archaeology.* Historia Einzelschriften 121. Stuttgart: Steiner.

———, ed. 2001. *Pontic Archaeology: Recent Discoveries and Studies.* Colloquia pontica 6. Leiden: Brill.

Tubach, Jürgen. 1986. *Im Schatten des Sonnengottes: Der Sonnenkult in Edessa, Ḥarrān und Ḥaṭrā Vorabend der christlichen Mission.* Wiesbaden: Harrassowitz.

Tuckett, Christopher M. 1984. "Paul and the Synoptic Mission Discourse?" *ETL* 60:376-81.

———. 1996. *Q and the History of Early Christianity: Studies on Q.* Peabody, Mass.; Hendrickson; Edinburgh: T & T Clark.

Turner, Max. 1994. "Empowerment for Mission." *VE* 24:103-22.

———. 1995. "Mission and Meaning in Terms of 'Unity' in Ephesians." In Billington et al. 1995, 138-66.

———. 1996a. *Power from on High: The Spirit in Israel's Restoration and Witness in Luke-Acts.* JPTSS 9. Sheffield: Sheffield Academic Press.

———. 1996b. *The Holy Spirit and Spiritual Gifts Then and Now.* Carlisle: Paternoster.

———. 1997. "The Spirit in Luke-Acts." *VE* 27:75-101.

———. 1998. "The 'Spirit of Prophecy' as the Power of Israel's Restoration and Witness." In Marshall and Peterson 1998, 327-48.

Twelftree, Graham H. 1993. *Jesus the Exorcist: A Contribution to the Study of the Historical Jesus.* WUNT 2.54. Tübingen: Mohr-Siebeck.

———. 1999. *Jesus the Miracle Worker: A Historical and Theological Study.* Downers Grove, Ill.: InterVarsity Press.

Tyson, Joseph B. 1987. "The Gentile Mission and the Authority of Scripture in Acts." *NTS* 33:619-31.

———, ed. 1988. *Luke-Acts and the Jewish People: Eight Critical Perspectives.* Minneapolis: Augsburg.

———. 1992. *Images of Judaism in Luke-Acts.* Columbia: University of South Carolina Press.

———. 1995. "Jews and Judaism in Luke-Acts: Reading as a Godfearer." *NTS* 41:19-38.

Ukpong, Justin S. 1995. "The Problem of the Gentile Mission in Matthew's Gospel." *Vidyajyoti* 51:388-408.

Ulrichsen, Karl Henning. 1991. *Die Grundschrift der Testamente der Zwölf Patriarchen: Eine Untersuchung zu Umfang, Inhalt und Eigenart der ursprünglichen Schrift.* Acta Universitatis Upsaliensis, Historia religionum 10. Uppsala: Almqvist & Wiksell.

Umemoto, Naoto. "Juden, 'Heiden' und das Menschengeschlecht in der Sicht Philos von Alexandria." In Feldmeier and Heckel 1994, 22-51.

Unnik, Willem C. van. 1952. "Tarsus or Jerusalem: The City of Paul's Youth." In Unnik 1973-1980, 1:259-320.

———. 1960. "The 'Book of Acts'—Confirmation of the Gospel." In Unnik 1973-1980, 1:340-73.

———. 1960b. "Die Rücksicht auf die Reaktion der Nicht-Christen als Motiv in der altchristlichen Paränese." In Unnik 1973-1980, 1:307-22.

———. 1964. "Die Anklage gegen die Apostel in Philippi (Apostelgeschichte 16,20f)." In Unnik 1973-1980, 1:374-85.

———. 1966. "Der Ausdruck ΕΩΣ ΕΣΧΑΤΟΥ ΤΗΣ ΓΗΣ (Apostelgeschichte 1,8) und sein alttestamentlicher Hintergrund." In Unnik 1973-1980, 1:386-401.

———. 1973-1980. *Sparsa Collecta I-II.* 2 vols. NovTSup 29-30. Leiden: Brill.

Urbach, Ephraim E. 1975. *The Sages: Their Concepts and Beliefs.* Jerusalem: Magnes [2nd enl. ed., 1979].

———. 1981. "Self-Isolation and Self-Affirmation in Judaism in the First Three Centuries: Theory and Practice." In E. Sanders et al. 1981, 269-98.

Urman, Dan. 1995. "Public Structures and Jewish Communities in the Golan Heights." In Urman and Flesher 1995, 2:373-617.

Urman Dan, and Paul V. M. Flesher, eds. 1995. *Ancient Synagogues: Historical Analysis and Archaeological Discovery.* 2 vols. StPB 47. Leiden: Brill.

Uro, Risto. 1987. *Sheep Among the Wolves: A Study on the Mission Instructions of Q.* AASFDHL 47. Helsinki: Suomalainen Tiedeakatemia.

Utzschneider, Helmut. 1989. *Künder oder Schreiber? Eine These zum Problem der "Schriftprophetie" auf Grund von Mal 1,6—2,9.* Frankfurt: Lang.

Vaage, Leif E. 1994. *Galilean Upstarts: Jesus' First Followers According to Q.* Valley Forge, Pa.: Trinity.

Vadakkekara, Benedict. 1995. *Origin of India's St. Thomas Christians: A Historiographical Critique.* Delhi: Media House.

Vanhoye, Albert, ed. 1986. *L'Apôtre Paul: Personnalité, Style et Conception du Ministère.* BETL 73. Leuven: Leuven University Press.

———. 1990. "Le origini della missione apostolica nel Nuovo Testamento." *Civiltà Cattolica* 141:544-58.

Vann, Robert L., et al., eds. 1992-1999. *Caesarea Papers.* 2 vols. JRASup 5, 35. Ann Arbor, Mich., and Portsmouth, R.I.: Journal of Roman Archaeology.

Van Segbroeck, Frans, et al., eds. 1992. *The Four Gospels 1992.* FS Frans Neirynck. BETL 100. Leuven: Leuven University Press.

Van Winkle, D. W. 1985. "The Relationship of the Nations to Yahweh and to Israel in Isaiah xl-lv." *VT* 35:446-58.

Väth, Alfons. 1925. *Der heilige Thomas, der Apostel Indiens: Eine Untersuchung über den historischen Gehalt der Thomas-Legende.* Aachen: Xaverius-Verlag.

Vellanickal, Matthew. 1981. "Church and Its Mission According to the Gospels." *Biblebhashyam* 7:82-98.

Venetz, H.-J. 1994. "Amt und Besoldung: Impressionen aus der Urkirche." *Theologisch-Praktische Quartalschrift* 142:113-22.

Vermes, Géza. 1983. *Jesus the Jew: A Historian's Reading of the Gospels.* 2nd ed. London: SCM Press [London: Collins, 1973]. German: *Jesus der Jude: Ein Historiker liest die Evangelien.* Neukirchen-Vluyn: Neukirchener Verlag, 1993.

———. 1984. *Jesus and the World of Judaism.* Minneapolis: Fortress.

————. 1993. *The Religion of Jesus the Jew.* Minneapolis: Fortress; London, SCM Press.

Verseput, Don J. 1993. "Paul's Gentile Mission and the Jewish Christian Community: A Study of the Narrative in Galatians 1 and 2." *NTS* 39:36-58.

Viberg, Åke. 1994. "Wakening a Sleeping Metaphor: A New Interpretation of Malachi 1.11." *TynBul* 45:297-319.

Vidal Manzanares, César. 1995. *El judea-cristianismo palestino en el siglo I: De Pentecostés a Jamnia.* Paradigmas 5. Madrid: Trotta.

Vielhauer, Philipp. 1950. "Zum Paulinismus der Apostelgeschichte." In Vielhauer 1965, 9-27.

————. 1965. *Aufsätze zum Neuen Testament.* TB 31. Munich: Kaiser.

————. 1981. *Geschichte der urchristlichen Literatur: Einleitung in das Neue Testament, die Apokryphen und die Apostolischen Väter.* 3rd ed. Berlin and New York: de Gruyter [1975].

Vittinghoff, Friedrich. 1952. *Römische Kolonisation und Bürgerrechtspolitik unter Caesar und Augustus.* Wiesbaden: Steiner.

————, ed. 1990. *Europäische Wirtschafts- und Sozialgeschichte in der römischen Kaiserzeit.* Handbuch der europäischen Wirtschafts- und Sozialgeschichte 1. Stuttgart: Klett-Cotta.

Viviano, Benedict T. 1979. "Where Was the Gospel according to St. Matthew Written?" *CBQ* 41:533-46.

————. 1984. "The Missionary Program of John's Gospel." *Bible Today* 22:387-93.

Vogler, Werner. 1982. "Die Bedeutung der urchristlichen Hausgemeinden für die Ausbreitung des Evangeliums." *ThLZ* 107:785-94.

————. 1983. *Judas Iskarioth: Untersuchungen zu Tradition und Redaktion von Texten des Neuen Testaments und ausserkannonischer Schriften.* Theologische Arbeiten 42. Berlin: Evangelische Verlagsanstalt.

Vögtle, Anton. 1964. "Das christologische und ekklesiologische Anliegen von Mt 28,18-20." *SE* 2:266-94 [= in *Das Evangelium und die Evangelien: Beiträge zur Evangelienforschung,* 253-72. Düsseldorf: Patmos, 1971].

————. 1996. *Gott und seine Gäste: Das Schicksal des Gleichnisses Jesu vom großen Gastmahl (Lukas 14,16b-24; Matthäus 22,2-14).* BThSt 29. Neukirchen-Vluyn: Neukirchener Verlag.

Volf, Miroslav. 1994. "Soft Difference: Theological Reflections on the Relation Between Church and Culture in 1 Peter." *Ex Auditu* 10:15-30.

Vouga, François. 1994. *Geschichte des frühen Christentums.* UTB 1733. Tübingen and Basel: Francke.

Vouga, François, and A. Riggert. 1993. "Die Geschichte des frühen Christentums als Evolution eines deterministischen Chaos." *Wort und Dienst* 22:77-85.

Wagner, Harald, ed. 1985. *Judas Iskariot: Menschliches oder heilsgeschichtliches Drama?* Frankfurt: Knecht.

Wagner, J. Ross. 2002. *Heralds of the Good News: Isaiah and Paul "In Concert" in the Letter to the Romans.* NovTSup 101. Leiden: Brill.

Waldmann, Helmut. 1996. *Das Christentum in Indien und der Königsweg der Apostel in Edessa, Indien und Rom.* Tübinger Gesellschaft, Wissenschaftliche Reihe 5. Tübingen: Tübinger Gesellschaft.

Waldstein, Michael. 1990. "Die Sendung Jesu und der Jünger im Johannesevangelium." *Internationale katholische Zeitschrift* 19:203-21.

Walker, Rolf. 1967. *Die Heilsgeschichte im ersten Evangelium.* FRLANT 91. Göttingen: Vandenhoeck & Ruprecht.

Wall, Robert W. 1987. "Peter, 'Son' of Jonah: The Conversion of Cornelius in the Context of Canon." *JSNT* 29:79-90.

Walls, Andrew F. 1970. "The First Chapter of the Epistle to the Romans and the Modern Missionary Movement." In Gasque and Martin 1970, 346-57.

Walter, Nikolaus. 1995. "Zur theologischen Problematik des christologischen 'Schriftbeweises' im Neuen Testament." *NTS* 41:338-57.

Walton, Steve. 2000. *Leadership and Lifestyle: The Portrait of Paul in the Miletus Speech and 1 Thessalonians.* SNTSMS 108. Cambridge: Cambridge University Press.

Waltzing, Jean-Pierre. 1895-1900. *Étude historique sur les corporations professionelles chez les Romains.* 4 vols. Repr., Hildesheim: Olms, 1970.

Wanamaker, Charles A. 1990. "Paul's Mission at Thessalonica." In *The Epistles to the Thessalonians,* 6-16. NIGTC. Exeter: Paternoster; Grand Rapids: Eerdmans.

Wander, Bernd. 1994. *Trennungsprozesse zwischen Frühem Christentum und Judentum im 1. Jh. n.Chr.* TANZ 16. Tübingen and Basel: Francke [2nd ed., 1997].

———. 1998. *Gottesfürchtige und Sympathisanten: Studien zum heidnischen Umfeld von Diasporasynagogen.* WUNT 104. Tübingen: Mohr-Siebeck.

———. 2001. "Warum wollte Paulus nach Spanien? Ein forschungs- und motivgeschichtlicher Überblick." In Horn 2001, 175-95.

Ward, Roy B. 1992. "James of Jerusalem in the First Two Centuries." *ANRW* II.26.1:779-812.

Ware, James P. 1992. "The Thessalonians as a Missionary Congregation: 1 Thessalonians 1,5-8." *ZNW* 83:125-31.

———. 1996. "'Holding Forth the Word of Life': Paul and the Mission of the Church in the Letter to the Philippians in the Context of Second Temple Judaism." Ph.D. diss., Yale University.

Warmington, Eric H. 1928. *The Commerce Between the Roman Empire and India.* London: Curzon [2nd ed., 1974].

Warneck, Johannes. 1913. *Paulus im Lichte der heutigen Heidenmission.* Berlin: M. Warneck [2nd ed., 1914].

Warren, Max. 1976. *I Believe in the Great Commission.* London: Hodder & Stoughton [repr., 1979].

Wasserberg, Günter. 1998. *Aus Israels Mitte—Heil für die Welt: Eine narrativ-exegetische Studie zur Theologie des Lukas.* BZNW 92. Berlin: de Gruyter.

Watson, Duane F. 1989. "A Rhetorical Analysis of 3 John: A Study in Epistolary Rhetoric." *CBQ* 51:479-501.

Watson, Francis. 1986. *Paul, Judaism, and the Gentiles: A Sociological Approach.* SNTSMS 56. Cambridge: Cambridge University Press.

Weaver, Dorothy J. 1990. *Matthew's Missionary Discourse: A Literary Critical Analysis.* JSNTSup 38. Sheffield: JSOT Press.

Weber, Emil. 1905. *Die Beziehungen von Röm. 1-3 zur Missionspraxis des Paulus.* BFChTh 9.4. Gütersloh: Bertelsmann.

Weber, Valentine. 1920. *Des Paulus Reiserouten bei der zweimaligen Durchquerung Kleinasiens: Neues Licht für die Paulusforschung.* Würzburg: Becker.

Wechsler, Andreas. 1991. *Geschichtsbild und Apostelstreit: Eine forschungsgeschichtliche und exegetische Studie über den antiochenischen Zwischenfall (Gal 2,11-14).* BZNW 62. Berlin: de Gruyter.

Wedderburn, Alexander J. M. 1989. "Paul and Jesus: The Problem of Continuity." In *Paul and Jesus: Collected Essays,* edited by A. J. M. Wedderburn, 99-115. JSNTSup 37. Sheffield: JSOT Press.

———. 1994. "Traditions and Redactions in Acts 2.1-13." *JSNT* 55:27-54.

———. 2002. "Paul's Collection: Chronology and History." *NTS* 48:95-110.

Weder, Hans. 1978. *Die Gleichnisse Jesu als Metaphern: Traditions- und redaktionsgeschichtliche Analysen und Interpretationen.* FRLANT 120. Göttingen: Vandenhoeck & Ruprecht [3rd ed., 1984].

Wegner, Uwe. 1985. *Der Hauptmann von Kafarnaum (Mt 7,28a; 8,5-10,13 par Lk 7,1-10): Ein Beitrag zur Q-Forschung.* WUNT 2.14. Tübingen: Mohr-Siebeck.

Wehnert, Jürgen. 1997. *Die Reinheit des "christlichen Gottesvolkes" aus Juden und Heiden: Studien zum historischen und theologischen Hintergrund des sogenannten Aposteldekrets.* FRLANT 173. Göttingen: Vandenhoeck & Ruprecht.

Wehr, Lothar. 1996. *Petrus und Paulus—Kontrahenten und Partner: Die beiden Apostel im Spiegel des Neuen Testaments, der Apostolischen Väter und früher Zeugnisse ihrer Verehrung.* NTA 30. Münster: Aschendorff.

Weidmann, Frederick W. 1999. *Polycarp and John: The Harris Fragments and Their Challenge to the Literary Traditions.* Christianity and Judaism in Antiquity 12. Notre Dame, Ind.: University of Notre Dame Press.

Weinrich, William C. 1981. "Evangelism in the Early Church." *CTQ* 45:61-75.

Weiser, Alfons. 1983. "Die Rolle der Frau in der urchristlichen Mission." In *Die Frau im Urchristentum,* edited by G. Dautzenberg et al., 158-81. QD 95. Freiburg: Herder.

———. 1990. "Evangelisierung im 'Haus.'" *BZ* 34:63-86.

Weiss, Peter. 1995. "Götter, Städte und Gelehrte: Lydiaka und 'Patria' um Sardes und den Tmolos." In Schwertheim 1995, 85-86.

Welles, C. Bradford. 1962. "Hellenistic Tarsus." *Mélanges de l'Université Saint-Joseph* 38:43-75.

Wellhausen, Julius. 1907. *Noten zur Apostelgeschichte.* Nachrichten von der Gesellschaft der Wissenschaften zu Göttingen, philologisch-historische Klasse 1, 1-21. Berlin and Göttingen: Gesellschaft der Wissenschaften zu Göttingen.

Wendel, Ulrich. 1998. *Gemeinde in Kraft: Das Gemeindeverständnis in den Summmarien der Apostelgeschichte.* NTDH 20. Neukirchen-Vluyn: Neukirchener Verlag.

Wengst, Klaus. 1984. *Didache (Apostellehre), Barnabasbrief, Zweiter Klemensbrief, Schrift an Diognet.* Schriften des Urchristentums 2. Munich: Kösel.

———. 1990. "Die Darstellung 'der Juden' im Johannes-Evangelium as Reflex jüdisch-judenchristlicher Kontroverse." In *Teufelskinder oder Heilsbringer: Die Juden im Johannes-Evangelium,* edited by D. Neuhaus, 22-38. Arnoldshainer Texte 64. Frankfurt: Haag and Herrchen.

———. 1992. *Bedrängte Gemeinde und verherrlichter Christus: Ein Versuch über das Johannesevangelium.* 4th ed. Kaiser Taschenbücher 114. Munich: Kaiser [1981].

Wenham, David. 1993. "Acts and the Pauline Corpus II: The Evidence of Parallels." In Winter and Clarke 1993, 215-58.

———. 1995. *Paul: Follower of Jesus or Founder of Christianity?* Grand Rapids: Eerdmans.

———. 2000. "From Jesus to Paul—via Luke." In Bolt and Thompson 2000, 83-97.

Wenham, John W. 1972. "Did Peter Go to Rome in A.D. 42?" *TynBul* 23:94-102.

———. 1975. "The Relatives of Jesus." *EvQ* 47:6-15.

———. 1991a. *Redating Matthew, Mark and Luke.* London: Hodder & Stoughton.

———. 1991b. "The Identification of Luke." *EvQ* 63:3-44.

Wenning, Robert. 1987. *Die Nabatäer: Denkmäler und Geschichte; Eine Bestandsaufnahme der archäologischen Befundes.* NTOA 3. Freiburg: Universitätsverlag.

Wernle, Paul. 1909. *Paulus als Heidenmissionar.* 2nd ed. Sammlung Gemeinverständlicher Vorträge 14. Tübingen: Mohr [1899].

Westenholz, Joan G., ed. 1995. *The Jewish Presence in Ancient Rome.* Jerusalem: Bible Lands Museum.

Westermann, Claus. 1978. *Theologie des Alten Testaments in Grundzügen.* ATD Ergänzungsband 6. Göttingen: Vandenhoeck & Ruprecht [2nd ed., 1985]. English: *Elements of Old Testament Theology.* Atlanta: John Knox Press, 1982.

———. 1987. *Prophetische Heilsworte im Alten Testament.* FRLANT 145. Göttingen: Vandenhoeck & Ruprecht.

White, L. Michael. 1985-1986. "Adolf Harnack and the 'Expansion' of Early Christianity: A Reappraisal of Social History." *Second Century* 5:97-127.

————. 1991. "Finding the Ties That Bind: Issues from Social Description." *Semeia* 56:3-22.

————. 1992. "Christianity: Early Social Life and Organization." *ABD* 1:927-35.

————. 1995. "Urban Development and Social Change in Imperial Ephesos." In H. Koester 1995a, 27-79.

————. 1996-1997. *The Social Origins of Christian Architecture.* 2 vols. HTS 42-43. Valley Forge, Pa.: Trinity.

Whittaker, Charles R. 1994. *Frontiers of the Roman Empire: A Social and Economic Study.* Baltimore: Johns Hopkins University Press.

Whittaker, Molly. 1984. *Jews and Christians: Graeco-Roman Views.* Cambridge: Cambridge University Press.

Wiarda, Timothy. 2000. *Peter in the Gospels: Pattern, Personality and Relationship.* WUNT 2.127. Tübingen: Mohr-Siebeck.

Wickert, Ulrich. 1990. "Kleinasien." *TRE* 19:244-65.

Widbin, R. Bryan. 1993. "Salvation for People Outside Israel's Covenant?" In Crockett and Sigountos 1993, 73-83.

Wiefel, Wolfgang. 1991. "The Jewish Community in Ancient Rome and the Origins of Roman Christianity." In Donfried 1991a, 85-101.

Wikenhauser, Alfred. 1921. *Die Apostelgeschichte und ihr Geschichtswert.* NTA 8. Münster: Aschendorff.

Wilckens, Ulrich. 1974. *Die Missionsreden der Apostelgeschichte: Form- und traditionsgeschichtliche Untersuchungen.* 3rd ed. WMANT 5. Neukirchen-Vluyn: Neukirchener Verlag [1961].

————. 1982. "Zur Entwicklung des paulinischen Gesetzesverständnisse," *NTS* 28:154-90.

————. 2002. *Theologie des Neuen Testaments.* Vol. 1, *Geschichte der urchristlichen Theologie: I. Geschichte des Wirkens Jesu in Galiläa; II. Jesu Tod und Auferstehung und die Entstehung der Kirche aus Juden und Heiden.* Neukirchen-Vluyn: Neukirchener Verlag.

Wilcox, Max. 1981. "The 'God-Fearers' in Acts—A Reconsideration." *JSNT* 13:102-12.

Wildhaber, Bruno. 1987. *Paganisme populaire et prédication apostolique: D'après l'exégèse de quelques séquences des Acts; Eléments pour une théologie lucanienne de la mission.* Geneva: Labor et Fides.

Wilhelm, F. 1915. "Die Oeconomica der Neupythagoreer Bryson, Kallikratidas, Periktione, Phyntis." *Rheinisches Museum für Philologie* 70:161-223.

Wilk, Florian. 2002. *Jesus und die Völker in der Sicht der Synoptiker.* BZNW 109. Berlin and New York: de Gruyter.

Wilkes, John J. 1992. *The Illyrians.* Oxford: Blackwell.

Will, Édouard, and Claude Orrieux. 1992. *Prosélytisme juif? Histoire d'une erreur.* Paris: Les Belles Lettres.

Will, Ernest. 1989. "Les villes de la Syrie à l'époque hellénistique et romaine." In

Dentzer and Orthmann 1989, 232-50.

Williams, Charles K. 1993. "Roman Corinth as a Commercial Center." In Gregory 1993:31-46.

Williams, Joel F. 1995. *Other Followers of Jesus: Minor Characters as Major Figures in Mark's Gospel*. JSNTSup 102. Sheffield: Sheffield Academic Press.

———. 1998. "Mission in Mark." In Larkin and Williams 1998, 137-51.

Williams, Margaret H. 1997. "The Meaning and Function of *Ioudaios* in Graeco-Roman Inscriptions." *ZPE* 116:249-62.

———. 1998. "The Structure of the Jewish Community in Rome." In *Jews in a Graeco-Roman World*, 215-28. Oxford: Clarendon.

Williamson, Hugh G. M. 1998. *Variations on a Theme: King, Messiah and Servant in the Book of Isaiah*. Carlisle: Paternoster.

Williamson, Paul R. 2000. *Abraham, Israel and the Nations: The Patriarchal Promise and Its Covenantal Development in Genesis*. JSOTSup 315. Sheffield: Sheffield Academic Press.

Wilson, Andrew. 1986. *The Nations in Deutero-Isaiah: A Study on Composition and Structure*. Ancient Near Eastern Texts and Studies 1. Lewiston, N.Y.: Mellen.

Wilson, Stephen G. 1973. *The Gentiles and the Gentile Mission in Luke-Acts*. SNTSMS 23. Cambridge: Cambridge University Press.

———. 1983. *Luke and the Law*. SNTSMS 50. Cambridge: Cambridge University Press.

———. 1995. *Related Strangers: Jews and Christians, 70-170 C.E.* Minneapolis: Fortress.

Wilson, Walter T. 2001. "Urban Legends: Acts 10:1-11:18 and the Strategies of Greco-Roman Foundation Narratives." *JBL* 120:77-99.

Winkelmann, Friedhelm. 1996. *Geschichte des frühen Christentums*. Beck'sche Reihe 2041. Munich: Beck.

Winter, Bruce W. 1990. "Theological and Ethical Responses to Religious Pluralism—1 Corinthians 8-10." *TynBul* 41:209-26.

———. 1991. "In Public and in Private: Early Christian Interactions with Religious Pluralism." In *One God, One Lord in a World of Religious Pluralism,* edited by B. W. Winter and A. D. Clarke, 112-34. Cambridge: Tyndale House.

———. 1994. "Acts and Roman Religion. B. The Imperial Cult." In Gill and Gempf 1994, 93-103.

———. 1996. "On Introducing Gods to Athens: An Alternative Reading of Acts 17.18-20." *TynBul* 47:71-90.

———. 1997. *Philo and Paul among the Sophists*. SNTSMS 96. Cambridge: Cambridge University Press.

———. 2000. "Dangers and Difficulties for the Pauline Missions." In Bolt and Thompson 2000, 285-95.

———. 2001. *After Paul Left Corinth: The Influence of Secular Ethics and Social*

Change. Grand Rapids: Eerdmans.

Winter, Bruce W., and Andrew D. Clarke, eds. 1993. *The Book of Acts in Its Ancient Literary Setting.* The Book of Acts in Its First-Century Setting 1. Exeter: Paternoster.

Winter Ralph. 1974. "The Two Structures of God's Redemptive Mission." *Missiology* 2:121-39.

———. 1990. "Momentum Building in Global Missions." *International Journal of Frontier Missions* 7:49-59.

Wiplinger, Gilbert, and Gudrun Wlach. 1995. *Ephesos: 100 Jahre Österreichische Forschungen.* Vienna: Böhlau [2nd ed., 1996].

Wischmeyer, Oda. 1995. *Die Kultur der Buches Jesus Sirach.* BZNW 77. Berlin: de Gruyter.

Wischmeyer, Wolfgang. 1980. "Die Aberkiosinschrift als Grabepigramm." *JAC* 22:22-47.

Wisdom, Jeffrey R. 2001. *Blessing for the Nations and the Curse of the Law: Paul's Citation of Genesis and Deuteronomy in Galatians 3.8-10.* WUNT 2.133. Tübingen: Mohr-Siebeck.

Wiseman, James. 1979. "Corinth and Rome I: 228 B.C.-A.D. 267." *ANRW* II.7.1:438-548.

Witherington, Ben. 1979. "On the Road with Mary Magdalene, Joanna, Susanna, and other Disciples—Lk 8:1-3." *ZNW* 70:243-48.

———. 1994a. *Jesus the Sage: The Pilgrimage of Wisdom.* Edinburgh: T & T Clark.

———. 1994b. *Paul's Narrative Thought World: The Tapestry of Tragedy and Triumph.* Louisville: Westminster John Knox.

———. 1995. *The Jesus Quest: The Third Search for the Jew of Nazareth.* Downers Grove, Ill.: InterVarsity Press.

———, ed. 1996. *History, Literature, and Society in the Book of Acts.* Cambridge: Cambridge University Press.

———. 1998a. *The Paul Quest: The Renewed Search for the Jew of Tarsus.* Downers Grove, Ill.: InterVarsity Press.

———. 1998b. "Salvation and Health in Christian Antiquity: The Soteriology of Luke-Acts in Its First Century Setting." In Marshall and Peterson 1998, 145-66.

———. 2001. *New Testament History: A Narrative Account.* Grand Rapids: Baker.

Witulski, Thomas. 2000. *Die Adressaten des Galaterbriefes: Untersuchungen zur Gemeinde von Antiochia ad Pisidiam.* FRLANT 193. Göttingen: Vandenhoeck & Ruprecht.

Wlosok, Antonie, ed. 1978. *Römischer Kaiserkult.* WF 372. Darmstadt: Wissenschaftliche Buchgesellschaft.

Wodecki, Bernard. 1981. "Heilsuniversalismus im Buch des Propheten Jesaja." In *Dein Wort beachten: Alttestamentliche Aufsätze,* edited by J. Reindl and G. Hentschel, 76-101. Leipzig: St. Benno.

————. 1982. "Der Heilsuniversalismus bei Trito-Jesaja." *VT* 32:248-52.

Wohlers-Scharf, Traute. 1995. *Die Forschungsgeschichte von Ephesos: Entdeckungen, Grabungen und Persönlichkeiten.* EHS 38.54. Lang: Frankfurt [2nd ed., 1996].

Wolff, Hans Walter. 1951. "Israel und die Völker bei Deuterojesaja." *EMZ* 8:1-14.

————. 1960. "Das Geschichtsverständnis der alttestamentlichen Propheten." *EvTh* 20:218-35.

Wolff, Katherine Elena. 1989. *"Geh in das Land, das ich Dir zeigen werde"* . . . *Das Land Israel in der frühen rabbinischen Tradition und im Neuen Testament.* EHS 23.340. Frankfurt: Lang.

Wolter, Michael. 1980. "Bekehrung I. Alte Kirche und Mittelalter: 1. Die altkirchliche Umwelt." *TRE* 5, 440-443.

————. 1987. "Apollos und die ephesinischen Johannes-Jünger (Act 18,24-19,7)." *ZNW* 78:49-73.

Wong, Kun-Chun. 1992. *Interkulturelle Theologie und multikulturelle Gemeinde im Matthäusevangelium: Zum Verhältnis von Juden- und Heidenchristen im ersten Evangelium.* NTOA 22. Fribourg: Universitätsverlag; Göttingen: Vandenhoeck & Ruprecht.

Wright, Christopher. 1996. "The Old Testament and Christian Mission." *Evangel* 14:37-43.

Wright, G. Ernest. 1961. "The Old Testament Basis for the Christian Mission." In Anderson 1961, 17-30.

Wright, N. T. 1991. *The Climax of the Covenant: Christ and the Law in Pauline Theology.* Edinburgh: T & T Clark.

————. 1992. *The New Testament and the People of God.* Christian Origins and the Question of God 1. London: SPCK; Minneapolis: Fortress [2nd pr., 1993].

————. 1996. *Jesus and the Victory of God.* Christian Origins and the Question of God 2. London: SPCK; Minneapolis: Fortress.

————. 1997. *What Saint Paul Really Said: Was Paul of Tarsus the Real Founder of Christianity?* Grand Rapids: Eerdmans.

————. 2003. *The Resurrection of the Son of God.* Christian Origins and the Question of God 3. London: SPCK; Minneapolis: Fortress.

Wuellner, William. 1967. *The Meaning of "Fishers of Men."* Philadelphia: Westminster.

Würz, Friedrich. 1922. *Die Mission der ersten Christen.* Stuttgart: Evangelischer Missionsverlag.

Yarbro Collins, Adela. 1998. "Pergamon in Early Christian Literature." In H. Koester 1998, 163-84.

Yarshater, Ehsan, ed. 1983. *Cambridge History of Iran.* Vol. 3, *The Seleucid, Parthian, and Sasanian Periods.* Cambridge: Cambridge University Press.

Yavetz, Zvi. 1993. "Judeophobia in Classical Antiquity: A Different Approach." *JJS* 44:1-22.

Yegül, Fikret K. 2000. "Memory, Metaphor, and Meaning in the Cities of Asia Minor." In Fentress 2000, 133-53.

Yeung, Maureen W. 2002. *Faith in Jesus and Paul.* WUNT 2.147. Tübingen: Mohr-Siebeck.

Yoder, John Howard. 1972. *The Politics of Jesus: Vicit Agnus Noster.* Grand Rapids: Eerdmans [2nd ed., 1994]. German: *Die Politik Jesu—der Weg des Kreuzes.* Maxdorf: Agape Verlag, 1981.

Young, Frances. 1989. "Mission in the Corinthian Correspondence." *Epworth Review* 16:76-84.

Zahn, Theodor. 1877. "Weltverkehr und Kirche während der drei ersten Jahrhunderte." In *Skizzen aus dem Leben der Alten Kirche,* 156-95, 302-9. Erlangen and Leipzig: Deichert [2nd ed., 1898].

———. 1880. *Acta Joannis unter Benutzung von C. v. Tischendorf's Nachlass bearbeitet.* Erlangen: Deichert [repr., Hildesheim: Olms 1975].

———. 1886. "Missionsmethoden im Zeitalter der Apostel." In *Skizzen aus dem Leben der Alten Kirche,* 106-55, 296-301. Erlangen and Leipzig: Deichert [2nd ed., 1898].

———. 1900. *Forschungen zur Geschichte des neutestamentlichen Kanons und der altkirchlichen Literatur.* Vol. 6, *Teil I: Apostel und Apostelschüler in der Provinz Asien; Teil II: Brüder und Vettern Jesu.* Leipzig: Deichert.

———. 1924. *Einleitung in das Neue Testament.* 3rd ed. 2 vols. Sammlung theologischer Lehrbücher. Leipzig: Deichert [repr., Wuppertal: Brockhaus, 1994]. English: *Introduction to the New Testament.* 3 vols. Edinburgh: T & T Clark, 1909.

Zangenberg, Jürgen. 1998. *Frühes Christentum in Samarien: Topographische und traditionsgeschichtliche Studien zu den Samarientexten im Johannesevangelium.* TANZ 27. Tübingen and Basel: Francke.

Zanker, Paul. 2000. "The City as Symbol: Rome and the Creation of an Urban Image." In Fentress 2000, 25-41.

Zapff, Burkhard. 1999. "The Perspective of the Nations in the Book of Micah as a 'Systematization' of the Nations' Role in Joel, Jonah and Nahum?" In *SBLSP,* 596-616.

Zeller, Dieter. 1976. *Juden und Heiden in der Mission des Paulus.* FB 8. Stuttgart: Katholisches Bibelwerk.

———. 1977. *Die weisheitlichen Mahnsprüche bei den Synoptikern.* FB 17. Würzburg: Echter.

———. 1982a. "Theologie der Mission bei Paulus." In Kertelge 1982, 164-89.

———. 1982b. "Redaktionsprozesse und wechselnder 'Sitz im Leben' beim Q-Material." In *Logia: Les paroles de Jésus; The Sayings of Jesus,* FS J. Coppens, edited by J. Delobel, 395-409. BETL 59. Leuven: University Press.

———. 1991. "Heidenmission." *NBL* 2:84-85.

Zenger, Erich. 1989. "Der Gott Abrahams und die Völker: Beobachtungen zu

Psalm 47." In *Die Väter Israels,* FS J. Scharbert, edited by M. Görg, 413-30. Stuttgart: Katholisches Bibelwerk.

——. 1991. "Israel und Kirche im gemeinsamen Gottesbund: Beobachtungen zum theologischen Programm des 4. Psalmenbuchs (Ps 90-106)." In *Israel und Kirche heute,* FS E. L. Ehrlich, edited by M. Marcus et al., 236-54. Freiburg: Herder.

Zettner, Christoph. 1991. *Amt, Gemeinde und kirchliche Einheit in der Apostelgeschichte des Lukas.* EHS 23.423. Frankfurt: Lang.

Zgusta, Ladislav. 1980. "Die Rolle des Griechischen im römischen Kaiserreich." In Neumann and Untermann 1980, 121-45.

Ziegler, Ruprecht. 1985. *Städtisches Prestige und kaiserliche Politik: Studien zum Festwesen in Ostkilikien im 2. und 3. Jahrhundert n.Chr.* Kultur und Erkenntnis 2. Düsseldorf: Schwann.

——. 1993. *Kaiser, Heer und städtisches Geld: Untersuchungen zur Münzprägung von Anazarbos und anderer ostkilikischer Städte.* ETAM 16. Vienna: Österreichische Akademie der Wissenschaften.

Zimmerli, Walther. 1972. *Grundriss der alttestamentlichen Theologie.* Stuttgart: Kohlhammer [6th ed., 1989]. English: *Old Testament Theology in Outline.* Atlanta: John Knox Press, 1978.

Zimmermann, Alfred F. 1984. *Die urchristlichen Lehrer: Studien zum Tradentenkreis der* διδάσκαλοι *im frühen Urchristentum.* WUNT 2.12. Tübingen: Mohr-Siebeck [2nd ed., 1988].

Zimmerman, Johannes. 1998. *Messianische Texte aus Qumran: Königliche, priesterliche und prophetische Messiasvorstellungen in den Schriftenfunden von Qumran.* WUNT 2.104. Tübingen: Mohr-Siebeck.

Zimmermann, Martin. 1992. *Untersuchungen zur historischen Landeskunde Zentrallykiens.* Antiquitas 1.42. Bonn: Habelt.

Zingg, Paul. 1974. *Das Wachsen der Kirche: Beiträge zur Frage der lukanischen Redaktion und Theologie.* OBO 3. Fribourg: Universitätsverlag.

Zmijewski, Josef. 1995. "Die Aufnahme der ersten Heiden in die Kirche nach Apg 10,1–11,18: Eine Interpretationsstudie." *ANRW* II.26.2:1554-1601.

PERMISSIONS

Excerpts from Eusebius, *Ecclesiastical History*, are reprinted by permission of the publishers and the Trustees of the Loeb Classical Library from *Eusebius: Volume I*, Loeb Classical Library Volume 153, translated by Kirsopp Lake, Cambridge, Mass.: Harvard University Press, 1926, and *Volume II*, Loeb Classical Library Vol 265, translated by J. E. L. Oulton, Cambridge, Mass.: Harvard University Press, 1932. The Loeb Classical Library® is a registered trademark of the President and Fellows of Harvard College.

Excerpts from Pliny the Elder, *Natural History*, are reprinted by permission of the publishers and the Trustees of the Loeb Classical Library from *Pliny: Volume II*, Loeb Classical Library Volume 352, translated by H. Rackham, Cambridge, Mass.: Harvard University Press, 1938-1962. The Loeb Classical Library® is a registered trademark of the President and Fellows of Harvard College.

Excerpts from Strabo, *Geography*, are reprinted by permission of the publishers and the Trustees of the Loeb Classical Library from *Strabo: Volumes VI-VII*, Loeb Classical Library Volumes 223 and 241, translated by Horace L. Jones, Cambridge, Mass.: Harvard University Press, 1917-1932. The Loeb Classical Library® is a registered trademark of the President and Fellows of Harvard College.

Excerpts from Philo, *De vita Mosis*, *De specialibus legibus*, *De virtutibus*, *In Flaccum* and *Legatio ad Gaium* are reprinted by permission of the publishers and the Trustees of the Loeb Classical Library from *Philo: Volumes VI, VII, VIII, IX, X*, Loeb Classical Library Volumes 289, 320, 341, 363, 379, translated by F. H. Colson, Cambridge, Mass.: Harvard University Press, 1929-1962. The Loeb Classical Library® is a registered trademark of the President and Fellows of Harvard College.

Excerpts from *1 Enoch, Testaments of the Twelve Patriarchs, Psalms of Solomon, 2 Baruch*, 4 Ezra and *Sibylline Oracles* are from *The Old Testament Pseudepigrapha* Volumes I and II by James H. Charlesworth, ed., copyright © 1985 by James H. Charlesworth. Used by permission of Doubleday, a division of Random House, Inc.

3. SECOND TEMPLE LITERATURE

Apocalypse of Abraham

Aristeas, Letter of
(EpArist)

Assumptio Mosis

2 Baruch (Syriac)